# A CONCORDANCE TO BRONTË'S *WUTHERING HEIGHTS*

GARLAND REFERENCE LIBRARY
OF THE HUMANITIES
(VOL. 428)

# A CONCORDANCE TO
# BRONTË'S *WUTHERING HEIGHTS*

C. Ruth Sabol
Todd K. Bender

GARLAND PUBLISHING, INC. • NEW YORK & LONDON
1984

**Library of Congress Cataloging in Publication Data**

Sabol, C. Ruth.
   A concordance to Brontë's Wuthering Heights.

   (Garland reference library of the humanities ;
v. 428)
   Includes bibliographical references and index.
   1. Brontë, Emily, 1818–1848. Wuthering Heights—
Concordances.   I. Bender, Todd K.   II. Brontë, Emily,
1818–1848. Wuthering Heights.   III. Title.   IV. Series.
PR4172.W73S25   1984      823′.8      83-48260
ISBN 0-8240-9088-8 (alk. paper)

Printed on acid-free, 250-year-life paper
Manufactured in the United States of America

# CONTENTS

# PREFACE

*A Concordance to Brontë's "Wuthering Heights"* (based on *Wuthering Heights: A Novel* by Ellis Bell, London: Thomas Cautley Newby, 1847) is the second in a series of concordances to the complete works of all the Brontës. The concordances provide data for our research on style in the writings of the Brontës and are intended, not as editions of any of the texts, but as research tools to make accessible to scholars replications of the original texts with some additional information—a list of every occurrence of each word in the text (no words are stopped or omitted), immediate access to the context of each word (in the Field of Reference), and a quick count of the number of occurrences of each word (in the Word Frequency Table).

Several issues for research become obvious as we examine the data presented in the concordances: can we know to what extent typeset print diverges from authorial intention when no holograph or other primary source is extant? In the 1847 edition of *Wuthering Heights*, for example, aberrant or variant spellings abound: *al, annihiliate, beguilnig, cheeking, comninations, dept, dont, en-jyomnets, exelaimed, expences, fulfil, Gimmerden, girnning, guaged, had'nt, handherchief, heen, her's, hypocricy, journies, modlld, mutsn't, Peniston, Pennistow, shant, shodld, strengh, surpressed, tak, therto, villanous, was'nt, wern't, wont,* to list several. In some few instances, type face seems not to have been properly inked—*ffin* where *coffin* seems to be called for—an issue which might properly be addressed by scholars interested in the evolution of the technology of printing.

Analysis and interpretation of data on any given text must certainly lie with linguists, literary scholars, and critics. Concordances can, however, display words of complete texts (or the complete works of any writer) unchained from the syntagmatic structures into which they were originally fixed by authors. This display becomes another source of data amenable to interpretation. For example, the occurrences of the attributive relative *that* (57 in Ford Madox Ford's *The Good Soldier* and 26 in Joseph Conrad's *Lord Jim* in a 10,000 word spread sample taken from each text) would hardly arrest the spontaneous critical attention of even the most diligent reader, and it would be dull work indeed to pore through 224,000 words in order to strain out 83 occurrences of one specific type of *that*, should anyone be able to conjure a reason for so doing.[1] With *A Concordance to Ford Madox Ford's "The Good Soldier"*[2] and *A Concordance to Conrad's "Lord Jim,"*[3] however, what would certainly be overlooked by even the most scrupulous reading of the texts by the most diligent of scholars becomes immediately evident by comparing the information displayed in the Word Frequency Tables of the two concordances—*The Good Soldier*, a relatively short text, contains nearly twice the number of occurrences of *that* as does the significantly longer *Lord Jim*. Careful analy-

sis of the occurrences of the various types of *that* can provide extensive information for interpretation of style and meaning in a text[4].

The work of M.A.K. Halliday has long since dispelled the naive notion that function words such as articles and conjunctions exert no substantial influence on the interpretation of a text. Halliday makes it eminently clear that in Yeats's "Leda and the Swan" the word *the*, which normally functions cataphorically as a defining term, functions anaphorically so that *the* in "the dark webs" does not identify the webs by their being dark, but rather identifies them by anaphoric reference to the title of the poem.[5]

In short, we consider it important to our work that we produce concordances that reflect as exactly as possible the actual condition of the printed original—corresponding page and line numbers, replication of any irregular or variant orthography, duplication of mechanical conventions, and listing of each occurrence (token) of every word (type). Therefore, the user of this concordance should be aware of the following errata.

(1) Line 32.01a should be included in the Field of Reference preceding line 32.01:

> 32.01a "That you may settle with your host. I

(2) Correspondingly, word counts in the frequency table should be corrected to read:

| | | | | | |
|---:|---|---:|---|---:|---|
| 10 | *host* (p. 204) | 30 | *settle* (p. 211) | 804 | *with* (p. 216) |
| 3535 | *I* (p. 204) | 1196 | *that* (p. 214) | 1740 | *you* (p. 216) |
| 106 | *may* (p. 206) | | | 407 | *your* (p. 216) |

(3) Finally, each word should be included appropriately in the index:

> *host* (p. 78), *I* (p. 80), *may* (p. 103), *settle* (p. 139), *that* (p. 152), *with* (p. 185), *you* (p. 189), and *your* (p. 192).

A word is defined as any string of characters between two spaces. *Wuthering Heights* (1847) contains 116,758 words in the running text with 9,714 distinct vocabulary items. Words and numerals bracketed in the Word Frequency Table are not concorded as part of the text; they merely designate books, chapters, chapter numbers, and book endings. For emphasis, the Brontës used frequent underlinings which are indicated as italics in the 1847 print text; these italics are designated in the Field of Reference by (\ #), used to enclose italicized words (e.g., \you#). The virgule (/) marks the open parenthesis, while the double virgule (//) is used to indicate a closed parenthesis.

We are grateful to the Research Tools Division of the National Endowment for the Humanities. They support the Wisconsin Old Spanish Dictionary Project whose computer programs were used to produce this concordance. We are particularly grateful to Professor John Nitti, Professor Lloyd Kasten, and Mrs. Jean Anderson for their generous help in preparing the publication.

C R S
Athens, Georgia
June 12, 1983

# NOTES

1. C. Ruth Sabol, "Focus and Attribution in Ford and Conrad: The Attributive Relative *That* in *The Good Soldier* and *Lord Jim*," in Richard W. Bailey, ed., *Computing in the Humanities: Papers from the Fifth International Conference on Computing in the Humanities* (Amsterdam: North-Holland, 1982), p. 47.

2. C. Ruth Sabol and Todd K. Bender, *A Concordance to Ford Madox Ford's "The Good Soldier"* (New York: Garland, 1981).

3. James W. Parins et al., *A Concordance to Conrad's "Lord Jim"* (New York: Garland, 1976).

4. C. Ruth Sabol, "Lexical Selection in Ford Madox Ford's *The Good Soldier*: Structure, Style, and Motif," Diss. Univ. of Wisconsin-Madison, 1980.

5. Michael A.K. Halliday, "Descriptive Linguistics in Literary Studies" (1962), rpt. in Angus MacIntosh and Michael A.K. Halliday, *Patterns of Language* (Bloomington: Indiana Univ. Press, 1967), p. 58.

# VERBAL INDEX

| | | | | | |
|---|---|---|---|---|---|
| 'bacca | 013.06 | 041.06 | 071.10 | 107.13 | 137.05 |
|  476.07 | 013.08 | 041.08 | 071.17 | 107.14 | 137.09 |
| 'baht | 013.09 | 041.12 | 071.19 | 108.03 | 137.15 |
|  456.18 | 014.03 | 041.12 | 071.21 | 108.05 | 137.22 |
|  720.12 | 014.08 | 041.15 | 072.03 | 108.08 | 138.05 |
| 'bide | 014.08 | 041.16 | 072.15 | 108.10 | 139.02 |
|  699.12 | 015.01 | 042.01 | 073.20 | 109.10 | 139.05 |
| 'but | 015.05 | 042.03 | 073.22 | 109.21 | 139.10 |
|  567.17 | 015.08 | 042.17 | 074.04 | 110.01 | 140.01 |
| 'cahnt | 015.10 | 043.07 | 074.06 | 110.02 | 140.13 |
|  457.21 | 016.03 | 043.11 | 074.13 | 110.18 | 140.14 |
| 'em | 016.18 | 043.14 | 074.17 | 111.01 | 140.21 |
|  043.03 | 016.19 | 044.06 | 075.03 | 111.02 | 141.06 |
|  043.20 | 017.01 | 044.08 | 075.08 | 111.03 | 141.06 |
|  043.21 | 017.01 | 044.09 | 075.09 | 111.05 | 141.22 |
|  193.16 | 017.02 | 044.13 | 076.03 | 111.06 | 142.14 |
|  232.16 | 017.07 | 044.14 | 076.12 | 111.07 | 142.18 |
|  232.18 | 017.12 | 045.07 | 076.13 | 111.09 | 143.06 |
|  298.08 | 018.01 | 045.19 | 076.16 | 111.13 | 143.06 |
|  472.05 | 018.09 | 046.01 | 076.17 | 111.15 | 143.13 |
|  696.17 | 018.18 | 046.09 | 076.19 | 112.06 | 143.13 |
|  713.07 | 018.20 | 046.18 | 076.22 | 112.07 | 144.09 |
|  721.05 | 019.07 | 046.21 | 077.12 | 112.12 | 144.16 |
|  760.18 | 019.18 | 047.01 | 077.20 | 113.09 | 144.18 |
|  761.10 | 019.21 | 047.02 | 078.02 | 114.01 | 144.18 |
| 'em's | 019.22 | 047.03 | 078.02 | 114.01 | 145.07 |
|  028.21 | 020.06 | 047.13 | 078.18 | 114.03 | 146.01 |
|  232.10 | 020.08 | 047.14 | 078.21 | 114.03 | 146.03 |
| 'feard | 020.14 | 047.19 | 079.13 | 114.08 | 146.09 |
|  565.16 | 020.16 | 048.03 | 079.14 | 114.10 | 146.12 |
| 'munn't | 020.18 | 048.05 | 079.20 | 114.19 | 147.06 |
|  456.18 | 021.01 | 048.07 | 080.12 | 115.05 | 147.10 |
| 'quest | 021.07 | 049.02 | 080.15 | 115.16 | 147.11 |
|  232.10 | 021.09 | 049.18 | 081.01 | 115.17 | 147.17 |
| 'sizes | 022.02 | 050.08 | 081.03 | 115.18 | 148.13 |
|  232.14 | 022.04 | 050.17 | 081.06 | 116.02 | 148.20 |
| 'ud | 022.07 | 051.02 | 081.07 | 116.03 | 149.02 |
|  187.20 | 022.08 | 051.17 | 081.17 | 116.11 | 149.20 |
| 'ull | 022.22 | 052.02 | 082.01 | 116.15 | 150.02 |
|  187.11 | 023.02 | 052.05 | 082.02 | 116.19 | 150.05 |
|  696.15 | 023.19 | 052.14 | 082.07 | 117.07 | 152.06 |
|  713.06 | 024.12 | 053.04 | 082.11 | 119.15 | 152.16 |
| 1500 | 024.14 | 053.07 | 082.18 | 119.22 | 153.01 |
|  005.02 | 024.16 | 053.13 | 082.22 | 119.22 | 153.08 |
| 1778 | 025.01 | 053.15 | 083.15 | 120.01 | 153.15 |
|  136.11 | 025.07 | 053.18 | 085.19 | 120.21 | 154.04 |
| 1801 | 025.16 | 053.19 | 087.06 | 121.04 | 154.12 |
|  001.03 | 025.17 | 054.02 | 087.12 | 121.16 | 154.13 |
| 1802 | 025.17 | 054.02 | 088.04 | 122.01 | 154.15 |
|  688.02 | 026.05 | 054.07 | 088.08 | 122.04 | 154.19 |
| a | 026.07 | 054.17 | 088.11 | 122.05 | 155.04 |
|  001.03 | 026.18 | 054.21 | 088.14 | 123.02 | 155.11 |
|  001.05 | 026.07 | 055.06 | 088.19 | 123.09 | 156.03 |
|  001.07 | 027.12 | 055.11 | 089.13 | 123.12 | 156.09 |
|  001.09 | 027.14 | 055.16 | 089.16 | 123.16 | 156.16 |
|  001.10 | 027.15 | 056.05 | 090.01 | 123.18 | 156.17 |
|  001.11 | 027.17 | 056.06 | 090.02 | 124.01 | 156.19 |
|  002.03 | 027.22 | 056.20 | 090.07 | 124.03 | 156.21 |
|  002.07 | 028.03 | 057.01 | 090.09 | 124.06 | 157.17 |
|  003.03 | 028.06 | 057.17 | 090.11 | 124.08 | 158.04 |
|  004.04 | 028.12 | 059.05 | 090.15 | 124.09 | 158.07 |
|  004.11 | 028.14 | 059.07 | 091.15 | 124.22 | 158.08 |
|  004.12 | 028.18 | 059.14 | 092.21 | 125.08 | 158.14 |
|  004.20 | 028.22 | 059.16 | 093.02 | 125.08 | 159.07 |
|  004.22 | 029.04 | 060.08 | 093.10 | 125.09 | 159.13 |
|  005.03 | 029.15 | 060.16 | 093.13 | 125.10 | 160.02 |
|  005.04 | 029.17 | 061.06 | 093.17 | 125.15 | 160.03 |
|  005.16 | 029.17 | 061.09 | 094.03 | 126.03 | 160.03 |
|  005.17 | 029.20 | 061.11 | 094.22 | 126.07 | 160.08 |
|  006.03 | 030.03 | 061.12 | 095.03 | 126.14 | 160.13 |
|  006.06 | 030.09 | 061.17 | 096.03 | 127.04 | 162.05 |
|  006.10 | 030.14 | 061.18 | 096.04 | 127.08 | 162.07 |
|  006.16 | 031.02 | 061.20 | 097.16 | 127.18 | 163.03 |
|  006.17 | 031.02 | 062.02 | 098.04 | 127.22 | 163.17 |
|  006.21 | 031.06 | 062.04 | 098.17 | 128.05 | 164.07 |
|  006.22 | 031.13 | 062.09 | 098.18 | 128.05 | 164.09 |
|  007.07 | 031.16 | 062.11 | 099.04 | 128.09 | 164.11 |
|  007.09 | 032.02 | 062.12 | 099.10 | 128.13 | 154.12 |
|  007.10 | 032.06 | 062.15 | 099.11 | 129.01 | 164.17 |
|  007.11 | 032.08 | 062.17 | 100.07 | 129.17 | 164.19 |
|  007.11 | 032.10 | 062.17 | 100.08 | 130.08 | 165.07 |
|  007.15 | 032.10 | 063.02 | 100.13 | 130.13 | 165.14 |
|  007.16 | 033.09 | 063.09 | 100.20 | 130.21 | 165.17 |
|  007.22 | 033.18 | 063.11 | 100.22 | 131.01 | 165.20 |
|  008.05 | 034.02 | 063.16 | 101.05 | 131.03 | 166.03 |
|  008.08 | 034.12 | 063.21 | 101.05 | 131.11 | 166.03 |
|  008.11 | 035.06 | 064.06 | 101.10 | 131.11 | 166.06 |
|  008.13 | 036.03 | 064.15 | 101.18 | 131.12 | 167.15 |
|  008.13 | 036.11 | 064.20 | 101.19 | 131.15 | 167.16 |
|  008.18 | 037.04 | 064.22 | 101.21 | 132.06 | 167.17 |
|  008.21 | 037.09 | 065.08 | 102.02 | 132.22 | 168.03 |
|  009.08 | 038.02 | 065.09 | 102.18 | 133.08 | 168.05 |
|  009.14 | 038.02 | 066.01 | 102.18 | 133.09 | 168.18 |
|  009.15 | 038.03 | 066.06 | 103.05 | 134.07 | 168.21 |
|  009.18 | 038.07 | 066.10 | 103.17 | 135.02 | 169.05 |
|  009.19 | 038.10 | 066.13 | 103.18 | 135.05 | 169.13 |
|  009.21 | 038.11 | 066.22 | 104.02 | 135.06 | 169.16 |
|  010.05 | 038.12 | 067.06 | 104.04 | 135.22 | 170.07 |
|  010.07 | 038.12 | 068.02 | 104.05 | 136.01 | 170.07 |
|  011.10 | 038.18 | 069.05 | 104.13 | 136.05 | 170.08 |
|  011.12 | 038.22 | 069.07 | 104.18 | 136.05 | 170.16 |
|  011.15 | 039.08 | 070.01 | 105.01 | 136.05 | 170.18 |
|  011.16 | 039.18 | 070.04 | 105.10 | 136.11 | 170.21 |
|  011.19 | 039.19 | 070.11 | 105.22 | 136.12 | 171.05 |
|  012.02 | 039.21 | 070.11 | 106.15 | 136.13 | 171.08 |
|  012.03 | 039.21 | 070.15 | 106.18 | 136.14 | 171.20 |
|  012.08 | 040.05 | 070.15 | 106.20 | 136.14 | 172.06 |
|  012.13 | 040.06 | 070.20 | 106.21 | 136.17 | 173.06 |
|  012.15 | 040.10 | 071.02 | 107.03 | 136.19 | 173.18 |
|  012.22 | 040.12 | 071.05 | 107.12 | 137.04 | 174.07 |
|  013.05 | 040.21 | | | | |

| | | | | | |
|---|---|---|---|---|---|
| 174.20 | 213.02 | 247.17 | 284.10 | 317.03 | 350.14 |
| 175.21 | 213.03 | 248.03 | 284.11 | 317.04 | 350.15 |
| 175.21 | 213.19 | 248.10 | 284.11 | 317.18 | 351.01 |
| 176.12 | 214.04 | 248.14 | 284.22 | 317.18 | 351.03 |
| 178.01 | 214.10 | 248.17 | 285.02 | 318.13 | 351.04 |
| 178.02 | 214.10 | 248.18 | 287.17 | 318.19 | 351.14 |
| 178.05 | 214.17 | 248.21 | 288.05 | 319.12 | 352.06 |
| 178.17 | 214.21 | 249.11 | 288.11 | 319.14 | 352.17 |
| 179.13 | 215.01 | 249.12 | 289.01 | 319.16 | 353.03 |
| 179.16 | 215.04 | 249.18 | 289.11 | 319.21 | 353.08 |
| 181.13 | 215.10 | 249.19 | 289.12 | 320.09 | 353.08 |
| 181.18 | 215.15 | 250.01 | 289.16 | 320.16 | 353.15 |
| 182.04 | 215.22 | 251.04 | 289.20 | 320.17 | 354.09 |
| 152.13 | 216.04 | 251.20 | 290.09 | 320.21 | 354.09 |
| 183.01 | 216.13 | 251.20 | 290.10 | 321.01 | 354.10 |
| 183.01 | 216.19 | 252.02 | 290.16 | 321.02 | 354.22 |
| 183.06 | 216.20 | 252.06 | 290.17 | 321.03 | 355.03 |
| 183.08 | 217.07 | 252.21 | 291.01 | 321.03 | 355.04 |
| 183.09 | 217.08 | 253.02 | 291.05 | 321.07 | 355.07 |
| 183.19 | 217.18 | 253.03 | 291.15 | 321.10 | 355.17 |
| 184.05 | 217.19 | 253.08 | 291.17 | 321.12 | 356.09 |
| 184.22 | 217.20 | 253.09 | 291.17 | 321.14 | 356.16 |
| 185.04 | 217.21 | 253.14 | 291.21 | 321.19 | 356.17 |
| 185.09 | 218.03 | 254.22 | 292.03 | 322.04 | 358.03 |
| 185.15 | 218.09 | 255.13 | 292.11 | 322.10 | 358.03 |
| 185.19 | 218.15 | 256.04 | 292.12 | 323.01 | 358.05 |
| 186.18 | 218.16 | 256.09 | 292.19 | 323.01 | 358.08 |
| 186.19 | 218.17 | 256.20 | 292.20 | 323.02 | 358.09 |
| 186.21 | 219.09 | 257.08 | 292.21 | 323.03 | 358.11 |
| 187.21 | 219.11 | 257.14 | 293.03 | 323.16 | 358.18 |
| 188.04 | 219.11 | 258.11 | 293.17 | 323.20 | 359.09 |
| 188.11 | 219.12 | 258.16 | 294.01 | 324.04 | 359.17 |
| 188.13 | 219.17 | 258.20 | 294.06 | 325.09 | 360.11 |
| 188.20 | 221.05 | 259.03 | 294.08 | 326.01 | 360.12 |
| 189.01 | 222.03 | 259.04 | 294.09 | 326.01 | 360.12 |
| 189.02 | 222.04 | 259.06 | 294.22 | 326.12 | 360.16 |
| 189.03 | 222.07 | 259.06 | 295.07 | 326.14 | 361.21 |
| 189.04 | 222.16 | 259.17 | 295.09 | 327.07 | 362.06 |
| 189.05 | 222.16 | 259.20 | 295.16 | 327.08 | 362.08 |
| 189.08 | 222.20 | 259.20 | 295.19 | 327.13 | 362.13 |
| 189.17 | 223.16 | 259.21 | 295.21 | 327.15 | 362.13 |
| 189.19 | 224.06 | 260.05 | 296.05 | 328.04 | 364.08 |
| 190.22 | 224.08 | 260.12 | 297.04 | 328.05 | 364.14 |
| 191.15 | 224.19 | 260.18 | 298.03 | 328.07 | 364.18 |
| 192.04 | 225.02 | 260.18 | 298.10 | 329.08 | 364.20 |
| 193.17 | 225.03 | 260.21 | 298.10 | 329.18 | 366.07 |
| 193.19 | 225.06 | 261.06 | 298.11 | 330.04 | 367.05 |
| 193.22 | 225.08 | 261.15 | 298.17 | 330.08 | 367.05 |
| 194.02 | 225.10 | 262.03 | 298.19 | 330.16 | 367.12 |
| 194.17 | 225.14 | 262.13 | 298.20 | 330.19 | 368.10 |
| 194.22 | 225.16 | 263.03 | 299.12 | 331.01 | 369.04 |
| 194.22 | 226.12 | 263.05 | 299.17 | 331.02 | 369.09 |
| 195.14 | 226.20 | 263.05 | 300.01 | 331.03 | 369.11 |
| 195.18 | 226.22 | 263.17 | 301.05 | 331.07 | 370.07 |
| 196.03 | 228.16 | 264.19 | 301.09 | 331.09 | 370.14 |
| 196.11 | 229.08 | 265.14 | 302.04 | 331.15 | 370.22 |
| 196.14 | 229.16 | 265.16 | 302.16 | 331.20 | 371.03 |
| 197.02 | 229.21 | 266.03 | 303.01 | 331.20 | 371.06 |
| 197.12 | 229.22 | 266.04 | 303.09 | 332.22 | 371.10 |
| 197.13 | 229.22 | 266.18 | 304.02 | 333.11 | 371.14 |
| 197.15 | 230.01 | 268.02 | 304.04 | 333.15 | 371.21 |
| 197.16 | 230.01 | 269.06 | 304.06 | 333.20 | 372.03 |
| 197.17 | 230.06 | 269.09 | 304.09 | 334.07 | 372.07 |
| 198.05 | 230.07 | 270.11 | 305.07 | 334.14 | 372.10 |
| 199.03 | 230.08 | 270.13 | 305.08 | 334.16 | 373.13 |
| 199.16 | 230.11 | 270.17 | 305.11 | 335.02 | 373.17 |
| 199.17 | 231.12 | 270.18 | 305.21 | 335.07 | 373.18 |
| 200.04 | 231.13 | 270.19 | 305.21 | 335.13 | 374.01 |
| 201.02 | 231.16 | 271.07 | 305.22 | 335.13 | 374.12 |
| 201.02 | 232.02 | 271.16 | 307.10 | 335.14 | 374.21 |
| 201.10 | 232.07 | 272.03 | 307.11 | 336.01 | 375.01 |
| 201.11 | 232.09 | 272.08 | 308.13 | 336.01 | 375.01 |
| 202.02 | 232.12 | 272.11 | 308.14 | 336.05 | 375.05 |
| 202.04 | 232.19 | 272.16 | 308.16 | 336.06 | 375.09 |
| 202.05 | 232.20 | 273.08 | 309.02 | 336.09 | 375.13 |
| 203.10 | 232.20 | 273.19 | 309.05 | 336.15 | 375.17 |
| 203.10 | 233.16 | 274.22 | 309.06 | 337.13 | 375.19 |
| 203.13 | 234.03 | 275.07 | 309.09 | 338.04 | 375.20 |
| 203.15 | 234.11 | 275.08 | 309.11 | 338.07 | 375.21 |
| 204.18 | 234.18 | 275.08 | 309.16 | 338.10 | 376.09 |
| 205.01 | 234.19 | 275.12 | 309.19 | 338.12 | 376.11 |
| 205.03 | 235.02 | 275.13 | 310.01 | 338.13 | 376.15 |
| 205.04 | 235.03 | 275.13 | 310.02 | 338.16 | 376.16 |
| 205.05 | 235.22 | 275.20 | 310.04 | 338.17 | 377.11 |
| 205.07 | 236.18 | 275.22 | 310.20 | 339.03 | 377.11 |
| 205.08 | 237.11 | 276.09 | 311.01 | 339.07 | 377.16 |
| 206.05 | 237.12 | 277.06 | 311.05 | 339.09 | 377.21 |
| 206.06 | 238.04 | 277.15 | 311.05 | 339.19 | 378.06 |
| 206.13 | 238.21 | 277.22 | 311.10 | 339.20 | 378.06 |
| 206.16 | 238.22 | 278.04 | 311.19 | 340.02 | 378.09 |
| 206.18 | 239.07 | 278.12 | 312.02 | 340.21 | 378.12 |
| 207.04 | 239.17 | 278.21 | 312.06 | 341.05 | 378.14 |
| 207.15 | 241.03 | 279.08 | 312.15 | 341.16 | 378.16 |
| 207.16 | 242.03 | 279.17 | 312.17 | 341.17 | 379.03 |
| 207.21 | 242.06 | 279.18 | 312.19 | 341.17 | 379.04 |
| 208.04 | 243.01 | 280.02 | 312.19 | 341.18 | 379.06 |
| 208.17 | 243.03 | 280.12 | 312.22 | 341.21 | 379.08 |
| 209.06 | 243.05 | 280.20 | 314.04 | 342.11 | 379.21 |
| 209.09 | 243.07 | 281.17 | 314.07 | 342.13 | 379.22 |
| 209.13 | 243.09 | 281.21 | 314.07 | 343.05 | 380.04 |
| 210.01 | 243.13 | 281.21 | 314.09 | 343.10 | 380.05 |
| 210.03 | 243.15 | 282.03 | 314.15 | 345.09 | 381.03 |
| 210.22 | 243.17 | 282.10 | 315.14 | 345.15 | 382.03 |
| 211.01 | 244.02 | 282.12 | 315.15 | 345.20 | 382.04 |
| 211.16 | 244.04 | 282.14 | 315.16 | 346.04 | 382.11 |
| 211.19 | 244.07 | 282.20 | 315.16 | 346.18 | 382.16 |
| 211.22 | 244.11 | 283.01 | 315.21 | 347.06 | 382.22 |
| 212.06 | 245.05 | 283.02 | 316.05 | 348.08 | 383.07 |
| 212.07 | 245.11 | 283.08 | 316.10 | 348.10 | 383.07 |
| 212.10 | 245.14 | 283.15 | 317.01 | 349.07 | 383.14 |
| 212.15 | 245.17 | 283.22 | 317.02 | 349.08 | 383.18 |

| | | | | | |
|---|---|---|---|---|---|
| 383.20 | 420.19 | 452.21 | 492.21 | 531.16 | 577.02 |
| 383.21 | 421.02 | 453.04 | 493.02 | 531.18 | 577.16 |
| 384.16 | 421.20 | 453.08 | 493.05 | 532.03 | 578.02 |
| 384.22 | 421.21 | 453.15 | 493.11 | 532.12 | 578.03 |
| 386.08 | 422.21 | 453.18 | 493.13 | 532.18 | 578.07 |
| 386.09 | 423.02 | 453.22 | 493.17 | 532.20 | 578.20 |
| 386.20 | 424.09 | 454.02 | 493.21 | 534.03 | 579.09 |
| 387.01 | 424.11 | 454.04 | 494.01 | 534.09 | 579.15 |
| 388.05 | 425.01 | 454.06 | 494.08 | 534.09 | 580.02 |
| 388.18 | 425.01 | 454.22 | 495.01 | 534.10 | 581.01 |
| 388.21 | 425.05 | 455.01 | 495.08 | 534.11 | 581.05 |
| 389.14 | 425.10 | 455.06 | 495.22 | 534.12 | 582.10 |
| 390.02 | 425.10 | 455.08 | 496.10 | 534.16 | 582.21 |
| 390.09 | 425.15 | 456.19 | 497.09 | 534.17 | 583.02 |
| 390.13 | 425.16 | 457.18 | 497.16 | 534.20 | 583.02 |
| 390.16 | 425.18 | 458.05 | 497.18 | 537.04 | 583.03 |
| 390.16 | 425.21 | 460.13 | 497.18 | 537.05 | 583.06 |
| 390.20 | 425.21 | 460.16 | 497.20 | 538.08 | 583.08 |
| 391.07 | 426.02 | 461.16 | 498.05 | 538.10 | 583.09 |
| 391.10 | 426.05 | 462.04 | 499.06 | 538.19 | 583.11 |
| 391.14 | 426.11 | 462.21 | 500.12 | 539.05 | 583.22 |
| 392.04 | 426.17 | 463.03 | 500.19 | 539.10 | 583.22 |
| 393.03 | 427.14 | 463.05 | 501.04 | 539.12 | 585.06 |
| 394.11 | 427.17 | 463.06 | 502.06 | 540.21 | 585.07 |
| 394.16 | 428.03 | 463.13 | 502.16 | 541.05 | 585.10 |
| 394.21 | 428.15 | 463.17 | 503.02 | 541.06 | 585.11 |
| 395.01 | 429.05 | 463.19 | 503.13 | 541.08 | 586.03 |
| 395.06 | 429.07 | 463.19 | 503.22 | 541.11 | 586.12 |
| 395.18 | 429.11 | 463.21 | 504.02 | 542.07 | 586.12 |
| 396.06 | 429.15 | 464.14 | 504.15 | 542.10 | 586.16 |
| 396.12 | 430.03 | 464.18 | 504.16 | 542.10 | 586.20 |
| 396.13 | 430.12 | 464.19 | 504.17 | 542.21 | 588.18 |
| 396.14 | 430.18 | 464.19 | 504.20 | 543.17 | 588.19 |
| 396.17 | 430.21 | 465.02 | 505.15 | 544.04 | 589.01 |
| 396.18 | 430.22 | 465.02 | 505.20 | 544.05 | 589.05 |
| 397.05 | 431.04 | 465.05 | 505.21 | 544.06 | 589.09 |
| 397.12 | 431.17 | 465.06 | 506.07 | 544.07 | 590.02 |
| 397.14 | 431.18 | 465.09 | 506.12 | 544.20 | 592.04 |
| 397.18 | 431.18 | 466.09 | 507.01 | 545.09 | 592.16 |
| 398.07 | 431.21 | 466.18 | 507.04 | 545.11 | 594.10 |
| 398.11 | 431.22 | 466.20 | 507.04 | 545.16 | 594.18 |
| 398.12 | 432.02 | 467.02 | 507.13 | 545.17 | 595.01 |
| 398.14 | 432.13 | 467.03 | 507.22 | 546.01 | 597.04 |
| 398.17 | 432.13 | 467.03 | 508.08 | 546.09 | 597.11 |
| 399.17 | 432.14 | 467.16 | 508.13 | 546.15 | 597.15 |
| 399.21 | 432.18 | 467.20 | 508.14 | 546.19 | 598.04 |
| 401.11 | 433.04 | 468.12 | 508.18 | 547.12 | 598.17 |
| 401.13 | 433.06 | 468.16 | 509.01 | 547.19 | 598.20 |
| 401.14 | 433.07 | 468.19 | 509.20 | 547.22 | 600.06 |
| 401.16 | 433.09 | 468.22 | 510.01 | 548.06 | 600.10 |
| 402.08 | 433.09 | 470.09 | 511.01 | 548.11 | 601.06 |
| 402.12 | 433.19 | 470.11 | 511.05 | 548.14 | 602.04 |
| 402.16 | 433.22 | 470.11 | 511.21 | 549.01 | 602.05 |
| 402.21 | 434.04 | 470.15 | 512.12 | 549.02 | 602.20 |
| 403.20 | 434.11 | 470.19 | 512.15 | 549.03 | 603.01 |
| 403.21 | 434.13 | 471.02 | 512.16 | 549.05 | 603.10 |
| 404.12 | 434.14 | 471.04 | 513.03 | 551.21 | 603.14 |
| 404.20 | 434.17 | 471.12 | 514.01 | 552.02 | 603.15 |
| 404.21 | 435.07 | 471.15 | 514.02 | 552.12 | 604.13 |
| 405.04 | 435.18 | 473.02 | 514.06 | 552.16 | 604.14 |
| 405.12 | 436.05 | 473.05 | 514.10 | 552.20 | 605.03 |
| 405.17 | 436.15 | 473.05 | 515.04 | 552.22 | 605.05 |
| 405.17 | 437.08 | 473.11 | 515.10 | 553.18 | 607.02 |
| 405.18 | 437.14 | 475.10 | 516.08 | 553.20 | 607.12 |
| 406.03 | 438.05 | 475.19 | 516.15 | 554.02 | 607.16 |
| 406.06 | 438.08 | 476.01 | 517.01 | 554.09 | 608.01 |
| 406.14 | 438.15 | 476.04 | 517.02 | 555.01 | 608.08 |
| 407.01 | 438.16 | 476.05 | 517.03 | 555.11 | 608.11 |
| 408.07 | 439.13 | 476.06 | 517.06 | 556.10 | 609.05 |
| 409.02 | 440.09 | 476.18 | 517.12 | 556.10 | 609.21 |
| 409.08 | 440.15 | 477.09 | 517.14 | 556.11 | 610.01 |
| 409.15 | 440.17 | 477.09 | 517.16 | 557.06 | 610.07 |
| 409.19 | 441.14 | 477.12 | 517.17 | 557.07 | 610.14 |
| 409.21 | 441.17 | 478.14 | 518.15 | 557.13 | 610.17 |
| 410.05 | 441.21 | 478.17 | 518.17 | 557.14 | 611.02 |
| 410.06 | 442.02 | 478.19 | 518.20 | 557.19 | 611.10 |
| 410.07 | 442.08 | 479.01 | 518.22 | 558.03 | 611.12 |
| 410.13 | 442.10 | 479.04 | 519.11 | 558.15 | 611.12 |
| 410.17 | 442.13 | 479.12 | 519.11 | 558.20 | 611.13 |
| 410.19 | 442.22 | 479.19 | 519.11 | 560.07 | 611.17 |
| 410.20 | 443.02 | 479.20 | 519.18 | 560.13 | 611.17 |
| 410.22 | 443.03 | 479.21 | 520.11 | 560.17 | 612.02 |
| 411.01 | 443.06 | 480.03 | 520.15 | 561.05 | 614.05 |
| 411.05 | 443.07 | 480.05 | 521.06 | 561.09 | 614.08 |
| 411.09 | 444.05 | 480.05 | 521.07 | 561.10 | 614.09 |
| 411.09 | 444.17 | 480.15 | 521.15 | 561.19 | 614.11 |
| 412.14 | 445.17 | 480.17 | 522.03 | 562.17 | 614.15 |
| 413.04 | 446.03 | 480.20 | 522.15 | 563.03 | 615.12 |
| 413.07 | 446.06 | 482.14 | 522.20 | 563.16 | 616.04 |
| 413.16 | 446.07 | 482.15 | 523.14 | 563.22 | 616.06 |
| 413.22 | 446.14 | 482.18 | 523.15 | 564.09 | 616.17 |
| 414.04 | 446.16 | 483.09 | 523.20 | 564.11 | 616.18 |
| 414.04 | 447.04 | 484.10 | 524.02 | 564.15 | 617.02 |
| 414.09 | 448.02 | 486.15 | 524.18 | 565.20 | 618.16 |
| 414.10 | 448.05 | 487.09 | 524.22 | 566.04 | 618.22 |
| 414.11 | 449.11 | 488.16 | 525.10 | 566.19 | 620.06 |
| 414.15 | 449.12 | 488.21 | 525.12 | 567.18 | 620.15 |
| 415.08 | 449.15 | 489.02 | 525.13 | 568.15 | 620.16 |
| 415.20 | 450.02 | 489.20 | 526.01 | 568.17 | 621.10 |
| 416.09 | 450.06 | 489.21 | 526.05 | 568.20 | 621.16 |
| 416.11 | 450.07 | 490.05 | 527.05 | 569.06 | 621.18 |
| 416.16 | 450.15 | 490.16 | 527.07 | 569.18 | 621.19 |
| 417.05 | 450.16 | 490.16 | 527.13 | 570.06 | 621.21 |
| 417.08 | 450.18 | 490.21 | 528.11 | 572.18 | 622.02 |
| 417.15 | 450.20 | 491.01 | 528.15 | 574.02 | 622.10 |
| 418.05 | 450.20 | 491.19 | 530.02 | 575.03 | 622.21 |
| 418.21 | 450.21 | 491.21 | 531.01 | 575.05 | 623.05 |
| 419.21 | 451.02 | 492.02 | 531.02 | 575.07 | 623.08 |
| 420.17 | 451.17 | 492.06 | 531.02 | 576.20 | 624.04 |
| 420.19 | 452.17 | 492.08 | 531.14 | 577.02 | 624.10 |
| | | 492.19 | | | |

| | | | | | |
|---|---|---|---|---|---|
| 624.12 | 667.21 | 701.12 | 748.17 | about | 556.02 |
| 625.03 | 668.01 | 701.16 | 749.14 | 004.21 | 557.09 |
| 625.04 | 668.06 | 701.18 | 749.18 | 005.19 | 561.09 |
| 626.02 | 668.09 | 701.19 | 750.13 | 022.03 | 562.21 |
| 626.06 | 668.17 | 701.21 | 750.17 | 024.16 | 563.17 |
| 626.06 | 669.04 | 702.18 | 750.18 | 033.01 | 566.07 |
| 626.09 | 669.04 | 703.02 | 750.22 | 037.05 | 569.12 |
| 627.06 | 669.06 | 704.03 | 751.13 | 049.11 | 572.02 |
| 627.15 | 669.07 | 704.13 | 751.16 | 057.12 | 576.01 |
| 628.07 | 669.08 | 704.20 | 751.19 | 060.02 | 576.16 |
| 629.04 | 669.11 | 704.22 | 751.21 | 067.17 | 583.03 |
| 629.07 | 670.18 | 704.22 | 752.06 | 070.12 | 590.01 |
| 630.14 | 671.22 | 705.21 | 752.12 | 074.06 | 590.13 |
| 630.17 | 672.12 | 707.19 | 752.18 | 075.19 | 594.20 |
| 631.08 | 673.04 | 707.22 | 752.20 | 077.10 | 604.07 |
| 631.13 | 673.12 | 708.02 | 753.01 | 089.20 | 622.01 |
| 631.17 | 674.10 | 708.03 | 753.07 | 089.21 | 626.09 |
| 632.20 | 675.02 | 708.05 | 754.01 | 097.03 | 627.11 |
| 632.22 | 675.07 | 708.11 | 754.02 | 099.01 | 628.20 |
| 633.19 | 675.10 | 708.13 | 754.10 | 099.07 | 635.04 |
| 633.19 | 675.15 | 709.01 | 755.14 | 102.09 | 641.01 |
| 634.07 | 675.18 | 709.08 | 755.21 | 102.13 | 646.19 |
| 634.21 | 676.06 | 710.02 | 756.02 | 112.09 | 652.07 |
| 635.21 | 676.11 | 710.03 | 758.14 | 122.05 | 659.10 |
| 636.11 | 676.19 | 711.01 | 758.18 | 141.04 | 660.07 |
| 636.22 | 676.19 | 713.18 | 758.21 | 141.21 | 665.02 |
| 637.09 | 676.19 | 714.06 | 759.06 | 143.15 | 677.06 |
| 637.11 | 677.16 | 715.12 | 759.13 | 152.21 | 685.09 |
| 637.18 | 677.17 | 716.05 | 760.07 | 153.14 | 695.14 |
| 638.06 | 677.21 | 716.08 | 760.20 | 160.10 | 697.04 |
| 638.07 | 678.06 | 716.13 | 760.21 | 170.13 | 698.06 |
| 639.01 | 678.09 | 718.01 | 761.01 | 175.18 | 698.17 |
| 639.03 | 678.13 | 718.17 | 761.02 | 177.20 | 700.04 |
| 639.11 | 679.08 | 719.07 | 761.08 | 184.03 | 702.02 |
| 640.05 | 679.09 | 720.02 | 762.08 | 188.21 | 704.01 |
| 643.08 | 679.10 | 720.12 | 763.02 | 195.03 | 715.04 |
| 644.04 | 679.22 | 720.17 | 763.05 | 199.19 | 719.06 |
| 644.14 | 680.04 | 720.19 | 763.11 | 201.11 | 721.13 |
| 644.19 | 680.19 | 721.13 | 763.12 | 205.03 | 722.08 |
| 644.22 | 680.20 | 721.18 | 763.14 | 206.21 | 729.04 |
| 645.08 | 681.01 | 722.02 | 763.17 | 210.01 | 730.11 |
| 645.15 | 681.15 | 722.10 | a-most | 212.19 | 739.02 |
| 645.19 | 681.16 | 724.02 | 232.11 | 216.01 | 746.09 |
| 645.19 | 681.19 | 724.06 | 472.07 | 219.01 | 747.08 |
| 646.01 | 682.02 | 724.09 | a-day | 235.17 | 750.11 |
| 646.05 | 682.05 | 724.16 | 664.06 | 238.20 | 751.17 |
| 646.16 | 683.04 | 725.09 | a-night | 243.02 | 760.20 |
| 646.18 | 684.05 | 725.11 | 654.20 | 263.13 | above |
| 647.09 | 685.05 | 726.04 | abaht | 267.04 | 004.22 |
| 647.17 | 685.15 | 726.08 | 184.15 | 269.02 | 006.08 |
| 647.20 | 685.16 | 726.10 | 691.10 | 270.01 | 053.07 |
| 647.22 | 685.20 | 726.19 | abancon | 270.10 | 081.16 |
| 648.01 | 686.07 | 726.21 | 578.21 | 271.05 | 101.08 |
| 648.12 | 686.11 | 727.03 | abandoned | 272.17 | 119.16 |
| 649.04 | 686.13 | 727.13 | 338.08 | 274.10 | 166.08 |
| 649.05 | 686.20 | 727.16 | 338.12 | 276.09 | 209.14 |
| 649.10 | 686.21 | 727.18 | 415.04 | 283.14 | 217.11 |
| 649.11 | 688.03 | 728.09 | 443.21 | 285.07 | 294.12 |
| 650.09 | 688.06 | 728.09 | abandonment | 289.18 | 313.17 |
| 650.10 | 688.07 | 729.06 | 516.05 | 293.03 | 317.18 |
| 651.03 | 688.08 | 729.07 | abashed | 298.09 | 361.09 |
| 651.05 | 689.05 | 729.13 | 166.18 | 298.19 | 371.07 |
| 651.11 | 689.07 | 729.21 | abduction | 299.18 | 380.05 |
| 651.12 | 689.11 | 730.04 | 029.15 | 309.07 | 389.15 |
| 651.14 | 689.14 | 730.09 | abetted | 321.18 | 429.05 |
| 651.17 | 689.21 | 731.03 | 399.06 | 338.05 | 470.16 |
| 652.04 | 690.05 | 731.04 | abhorred | 339.19 | 512.07 |
| 652.09 | 690.14 | 731.05 | 412.20 | 350.03 | 518.02 |
| 653.01 | 690.16 | 731.20 | 718.06 | 353.06 | 520.15 |
| 653.22 | 691.17 | 731.21 | abhorrence | 355.02 | 542.14 |
| 654.03 | 691.18 | 732.09 | 327.05 | 367.06 | 557.16 |
| 654.18 | 691.18 | 732.15 | abhors | 369.02 | 560.17 |
| 654.20 | 691.19 | 732.20 | 232.02 | 377.13 | 593.07 |
| 655.03 | 692.04 | 733.01 | abide | 379.02 | 644.04 |
| 655.04 | 692.12 | 733.13 | 410.15 | 385.11 | 652.10 |
| 655.06 | 692.15 | 733.13 | 639.10 | 391.08 | 690.03 |
| 655.13 | 692.17 | 733.13 | abject | 403.12 | 733.17 |
| 655.14 | 692.18 | 733.18 | 340.12 | 412.03 | abroad |
| 655.18 | 693.01 | 733.22 | 600.21 | 412.08 | 337.20 |
| 656.05 | 693.08 | 734.04 | abjured | 420.05 | 413.12 |
| 656.18 | 693.12 | 734.15 | 224.01 | 428.16 | abrupt |
| 658.02 | 693.12 | 735.03 | able | 433.09 | 427.07 |
| 659.04 | 694.01 | 737.09 | 103.22 | 437.08 | abruptly |
| 659.05 | 694.04 | 737.19 | 125.18 | 438.12 | 122.06 |
| 659.10 | 694.04 | 738.01 | 143.12 | 439.02 | 160.06 |
| 659.11 | 694.11 | 738.06 | 215.16 | 451.19 | 255.15 |
| 659.20 | 694.13 | 738.19 | 253.01 | 461.08 | 360.07 |
| 660.02 | 694.15 | 739.10 | 346.22 | 465.02 | 649.09 |
| 660.03 | 694.15 | 739.10 | 383.22 | 469.06 | absence |
| 660.07 | 694.18 | 739.15 | 386.11 | 477.12 | 021.11 |
| 660.17 | 694.19 | 739.15 | 389.20 | 485.07 | 077.01 |
| 661.20 | 695.10 | 739.22 | 493.19 | 490.16 | 098.11 |
| 662.03 | 695.14 | 740.02 | 550.02 | 494.09 | 115.13 |
| 662.04 | 696.02 | 740.05 | 582.04 | 497.08 | 132.02 |
| 662.10 | 696.10 | 741.15 | 610.09 | 499.09 | 148.08 |
| 662.11 | 696.14 | 741.17 | 616.05 | 500.10 | 151.01 |
| 663.01 | 696.16 | 741.17 | 619.19 | 503.11 | 192.19 |
| 663.05 | 696.22 | 742.18 | 628.07 | 504.19 | 234.06 |
| 663.10 | 697.02 | 743.09 | abode | 507.02 | 269.11 |
| 664.05 | 697.03 | 744.07 | 007.08 | 509.16 | 289.21 |
| 664.16 | 698.02 | 744.10 | 241.05 | 514.08 | 308.03 |
| 665.04 | 699.05 | 744.17 | 322.13 | 519.05 | 346.21 |
| 665.13 | 699.09 | 744.19 | 397.16 | 521.11 | 418.08 |
| 665.19 | 699.14 | 745.13 | 411.08 | 523.12 | 430.07 |
| 666.01 | 699.14 | 745.13 | 466.01 | 528.17 | 462.14 |
| 666.11 | 699.18 | 745.21 | 688.04 | 541.21 | 498.19 |
| 666.22 | 699.20 | 747.04 | abominable | 543.09 | 535.15 |
| 667.06 | 700.04 | 747.15 | 106.13 | 550.03 | 547.16 |
| 667.11 | 700.09 | 747.21 | 163.19 | 551.01 | 648.22 |
| 667.17 | 700.11 | 748.17 | 409.09 | 552.15 | 664.15 |
| 667.20 | 700.17 | | | | |

absences
725.07
absent
185.09
215.19
240.12
301.02
353.04
530.11
736.07
absented
100.06
absolute
011.07
109.17
absolutely
239.04
265.08
361.16
686.10
absolve
599.19
absolved
050.02
absorbed
063.13
215.08
234.19
295.14
407.04
490.12
528.12
594.15
749.19
absorbing
655.15
abstain
021.12
759.20
abstaining
400.05
abstinence
749.12
abstract
239.20
abstracted
287.01
676.20
abstracting
509.07
706.14
abstraction
313.04
absurd
047.01
213.01
729.08
745.16
absurdities
511.12
absurdity
258.07
340.09
abundant
516.20
abuse
195.15
238.21
262.03
494.18
621.17
725.14
abused
370.02
abusing
572.12
abyss
282.14
377.05
accede
482.21
accent
181.05
560.11
accents
054.11
360.13
696.05
accept
003.02
036.09
222.13
620.06
accepted
119.08
172.10
172.12
668.11
711.18
accepting
608.06
access
058.16
258.18
295.22
accident
081.08
102.04
166.02
704.19
737.12

accidental
036.06
accommodate
747.05
accommodated
697.11
accommodation
219.16
accommodations
032.06
448.05
accompanied
060.21
411.02
503.14
510.14
674.09
accompany
065.18
198.21
261.11
292.01
310.08
418.17
445.22
517.02
581.21
607.02
705.08
754.16
accompanying
477.17
accomplice
642.11
accomplished
394.08
561.20
562.10
613.12
716.05
accord
105.20
269.08
299.16
341.11
618.19
according
021.17
120.14
275.05
503.14
664.05
732.18
accordingly
693.18
accosted
731.06
account
091.03
096.12
164.02
205.02
233.14
263.18
266.19
286.18
291.22
292.21
402.14
415.21
456.22
477.04
482.21
500.12
501.10
528.19
595.03
598.02
604.02
649.02
667.09
671.21
682.07
734.13
accumulations
679.02
accursed
151.14
386.06
653.12
723.15
accusations
104.20
227.01
679.04
accuse
339.20
accused
327.10
accusing
443.09
accustomed
009.19
134.22
220.21
337.22
718.05
ached
100.16
281.11

aches
045.05
475.22
achieved
339.10
616.16
aching
200.09
361.04
383.02
acknowledge
573.17
acknowledged
425.14
486.22
acknowledgment
119.04
674.19
acquaintance
008.05
018.08
099.05
146.17
150.07
221.21
256.19
481.13
501.08
505.08
675.15
677.03
acquaintances
236.09
acquainted
064.20
135.16
231.18
292.17
317.09
444.13
577.11
acquainting
472.20
acquiesce
583.02
acquiesced
256.19
659.03
acquire
136.04
425.17
acquired
150.02
acquirements
680.10
acquisition
109.20
acquisitions
147.04
across
047.04
065.18
123.15
139.08
189.04
215.12
249.02
251.01
410.09
549.04
553.04
act
091.04
143.11
147.11
156.14
162.03
308.15
318.07
365.21
418.09
521.15
617.04
657.01
660.09
664.14
698.10
734.01
752.07
acted
195.18
272.03
377.16
727.03
acting
338.18
484.16
action
054.15
245.07
325.04
609.10
actions
137.18
174.04
283.20
active
087.03
136.01
296.17
491.03

548.06
591.02
activity
728.16
acts
108.12
502.18
actual
594.20
635.11
actually
209.20
272.18
339.08
524.21
583.18
731.11
actuate
008.06
add
057.09
383.18
405.07
534.10
636.06
added
059.08
107.13
124.06
152.17
185.14
212.10
315.07
351.22
360.20
469.18
474.07
476.02
503.07
525.17
537.17
603.09
607.21
624.15
656.04
696.16
711.07
721.15
727.05
730.18
738.01
756.05
adding
268.02
334.06
addition
369.11
482.05
607.08
address
048.07
214.11
addressed
029.05
390.22
440.04
655.16
710.03
addressing
212.21
255.17
360.21
396.21
438.20
446.07
451.13
485.17
490.21
701.10
adhere
236.06
adieu
378.18
429.19
686.12
adieux
066.22
adjective
004.05
327.01
adjourned
066.02
adjuration
322.18
administer
402.20
administered
128.13
610.06
admirable
019.09
admiration
111.17
147.03
228.22
235.19
340.06
492.22
admire
004.20

083.06
141.12
253.02
admired
119.13
727.10
admission
257.01
admit
101.16
286.11
325.04
335.17
355.16
638.14
admittance
015.14
047.02
433.22
690.10
695.22
756.19
admitted
607.03
admonition
739.11
ado
757.11
adopt
147.06
adoration
239.01
adored
141.16
adrift
336.20
adroitly
675.11
advance
028.03
668.09
advanced
009.09
455.10
563.19
579.12
605.04
645.05
683.11
697.05
advances
267.21
473.02
534.02
advancing
158.10
706.14
advantage
007.01
314.16
326.13
423.02
655.21
advantages
013.09
114.12
674.03
advent
004.02
044.07
241.03
adventure
112.04
445.13
adventures
431.01
adversary
399.19
advice
031.04
288.17
582.04
606.10
619.11
753.18
advise
195.04
240.05
661.04
advised
088.17
220.12
403.06
418.18
451.06
adviser
148.21
advising
456.09
afeard
436.12
affair
248.06
420.15
affairs
070.12
449.01
640.19
698.09
affect
350.09

affectation
164.13
affectations
600.01
600.03
affected
058.05
160.12
185.08
508.13
517.04
712.08
affecting
738.13
affection
099.08
150.15
198.10
204.09
220.13
224.07
229.21
306.21
333.09
336.08
469.15
521.06
576.13
631.14
affectionate
509.10
592.12
affections
082.03
145.13
413.21
425.06
affirm
525.18
590.05
affirmation
530.12
affirmations
118.18
affirmed
082.21
164.01
185.14
218.12
444.17
471.04
536.15
552.07
566.19
630.12
affirming
058.06
128.17
142.21
319.21
347.10
368.01
397.08
418.19
474.06
affirms
222.02
392.10
581.09
760.17
afflict
405.05
affliction
504.06
afford
021.20
220.01
223.13
afore
029.03
233.12
afraid
017.16
029.12
097.18
108.08
159.02
163.22
194.21
212.17
266.12
274.01
277.19
330.02
399.04
490.01
554.13
564.09
602.12
606.04
608.09
608.17
613.18
617.06
617.08
617.09
634.09
702.14
733.10
733.12
762.19

| | | | | | |
|---|---|---|---|---|---|
| afresh | 487.12 | 620.14 | 632.01 | 417.10 | 305.03 |
| 057.11 | 495.14 | 646.01 | 634.19 | 426.08 | 384.11 |
| 123.19 | 500.03 | 662.16 | 638.01 | 428.19 | 386.07 |
| 453.06 | 508.17 | 663.14 | 638.20 | 454.06 | 434.04 |
| after | 521.18 | 699.16 | 640.01 | 482.06 | 450.03 |
| 002.10 | 521.22 | 717.22 | 646.04 | 486.03 | 486.14 |
| 006.03 | 532.12 | 725.04 | 649.16 | 493.06 | 500.05 |
| 007.07 | 538.22 | again | 652.01 | 508.06 | 605.13 |
| 011.16 | 544.12 | 008.01 | 661.07 | 577.13 | 621.05 |
| 011.20 | 545.13 | 009.22 | 661.20 | 618.21 | 631.16 |
| 015.05 | 545.19 | 018.09 | 663.13 | 635.11 | 689.03 |
| 016.21 | 546.14 | 026.17 | 668.03 | 746.10 | 698.12 |
| 033.07 | 547.01 | 038.15 | 669.12 | agean | aha |
| 049.18 | 548.18 | 039.03 | 672.05 | 232.18 | 435.06 |
| 062.08 | 548.21 | 040.21 | 681.10 | 319.10 | 499.03 |
| 067.21 | 555.02 | 048.19 | 684.12 | 713.07 | ahr |
| 069.06 | 558.10 | 051.07 | 689.13 | aged | 232.10 |
| 070.08 | 559.19 | 053.09 | 694.06 | 029.06 | 720.14 |
| 076.03 | 564.10 | 056.16 | 697.13 | 276.12 | aht |
| 077.04 | 566.10 | 062.13 | 702.04 | agent | 187.15 |
| 081.21 | 569.05 | 064.07 | 705.04 | 290.19 | 191.01 |
| 090.01 | 572.02 | 072.13 | 707.14 | ages | 191.04 |
| 090.17 | 581.14 | 078.06 | 710.10 | 010.19 | 193.21 |
| 092.05 | 591.05 | 084.08 | 711.16 | 024.14 | 319.13 |
| 093.05 | 597.14 | 093.19 | 718.11 | aggravate | 458.10 |
| 100.04 | 612.14 | 100.18 | 721.05 | 005.08 | 712.19 |
| 100.12 | 613.16 | 110.13 | 722.21 | 261.19 | aid |
| 105.02 | 615.06 | 114.14 | 726.13 | aggravating | 003.22 |
| 107.17 | 631.13 | 117.13 | 730.16 | 198.08 | 019.21 |
| 109.01 | 632.12 | 122.20 | 743.06 | aggravation | 034.02 |
| 118.13 | 636.19 | 127.14 | 744.21 | 732.10 | 063.11 |
| 120.03 | 640.20 | 130.14 | 746.04 | aggressor | 181.21 |
| 130.01 | 641.20 | 132.18 | 755.14 | 402.17 | 290.14 |
| 131.17 | 643.02 | 141.11 | 763.04 | aghast | 325.07 |
| 145.08 | 646.22 | 159.04 | against | 538.14 | 334.04 |
| 158.21 | 651.09 | 160.07 | 032.16 | 712.04 | 343.15 |
| 160.08 | 655.18 | 167.10 | 035.17 | aght | 415.22 |
| 172.05 | 658.04 | 176.13 | 038.16 | 028.22 | 576.18 |
| 176.17 | 659.03 | 178.15 | 039.04 | agility | 658.12 |
| 176.21 | 661.06 | 183.11 | 050.15 | 518.03 | 667.05 |
| 184.07 | 664.01 | 210.08 | 051.04 | agitated | aided |
| 193.12 | 668.05 | 212.19 | 053.05 | 244.11 | 399.06 |
| 194.01 | 672.16 | 215.13 | 062.16 | agitation | aiding |
| 195.04 | 676.06 | 216.11 | 090.03 | 035.05 | 458.05 |
| 198.16 | 677.01 | 221.19 | 093.07 | 055.01 | 680.07 |
| 209.10 | 683.19 | 234.13 | 124.07 | 153.20 | ail |
| 209.21 | 688.11 | 236.19 | 128.07 | 188.11 | 472.03 |
| 212.10 | 697.16 | 247.04 | 137.04 | 297.18 | ailing |
| 217.18 | 701.11 | 261.21 | 157.10 | 359.12 | 091.13 |
| 234.03 | 707.13 | 267.14 | 162.10 | 366.21 | 411.12 |
| 238.14 | 709.06 | 271.02 | 198.20 | 538.01 | 453.12 |
| 239.17 | 717.11 | 279.10 | 207.06 | 567.10 | ails |
| 250.01 | 726.15 | 282.20 | 209.07 | 589.10 | 192.03 |
| 250.19 | 727.09 | 283.04 | 223.04 | 683.10 | 297.13 |
| 255.19 | 736.02 | 288.08 | 231.10 | 728.19 | 472.01 |
| 258.04 | 736.10 | 293.22 | 244.19 | ago | 546.19 |
| 262.09 | 737.08 | 294.13 | 250.14 | 138.11 | aim |
| 262.17 | 741.10 | 303.15 | 252.18 | 201.11 | 352.14 |
| 264.14 | 744.01 | 306.13 | 257.09 | 232.07 | 749.17 |
| 267.14 | 750.09 | 313.06 | 259.04 | 284.02 | aimed |
| 271.07 | after-thought | 332.23 | 261.06 | 357.14 | 050.12 |
| 275.22 | 692.07 | 335.18 | 265.18 | 461.10 | 719.11 |
| 280.14 | afternoon | 339.14 | 267.08 | 575.03 | air |
| 281.21 | 014.02 | 359.20 | 272.09 | 654.05 | 015.10 |
| 290.21 | 135.10 | 360.02 | 277.05 | 659.11 | 039.09 |
| 293.21 | 148.22 | 364.01 | 281.07 | 698.15 | 065.13 |
| 294.16 | 151.03 | 365.10 | 285.05 | 731.03 | 130.07 |
| 298.08 | 152.05 | 366.09 | 290.02 | 760.20 | 174.02 |
| 298.13 | 172.04 | 375.21 | 313.20 | agony | 206.14 |
| 302.07 | 186.15 | 385.17 | 316.02 | 061.03 | 283.14 |
| 306.15 | 224.05 | 386.06 | 325.12 | 223.09 | 287.17 |
| 310.09 | 243.03 | 386.15 | 334.16 | 281.01 | 303.10 |
| 311.05 | 328.12 | 390.01 | 344.16 | 356.03 | 372.20 |
| 326.05 | 364.11 | 391.05 | 364.05 | 375.06 | 457.20 |
| 332.02 | 365.02 | 397.02 | 373.14 | 405.18 | 462.19 |
| 335.21 | 419.16 | 410.16 | 377.09 | 407.10 | 463.10 |
| 338.01 | 498.16 | 427.04 | 400.02 | 540.05 | 476.05 |
| 350.13 | 516.14 | 435.04 | 402.02 | 601.02 | 486.08 |
| 355.07 | 516.15 | 449.19 | 403.15 | 615.20 | 559.14 |
| 357.02 | 555.18 | 468.15 | 419.18 | 653.03 | 569.13 |
| 359.01 | 577.16 | 469.03 | 434.15 | 730.11 | 649.18 |
| 360.12 | 598.03 | 475.01 | 443.04 | agreeable | 693.08 |
| 360.21 | 598.04 | 479.12 | 488.21 | 019.14 | 693.10 |
| 367.17 | 626.02 | 480.19 | 490.09 | 146.12 | 731.16 |
| 369.05 | 665.04 | 485.09 | 499.02 | 204.06 | 743.15 |
| 369.10 | 705.12 | 490.22 | 529.05 | 229.01 | ajar |
| 372.01 | 743.07 | 494.20 | 538.09 | 317.14 | 044.09 |
| 372.19 | 755.12 | 501.13 | 573.21 | 667.08 | 095.12 |
| 375.10 | afternoons | 504.10 | 590.20 | agreed | 191.21 |
| 376.01 | 504.18 | 506.08 | 605.05 | 088.19 | 279.17 |
| 378.12 | 544.02 | 510.19 | 611.02 | 558.08 | akin |
| 382.22 | afterward | 512.16 | 630.21 | 588.02 | 056.18 |
| 384.15 | 682.09 | 522.05 | 634.01 | 643.07 | 469.09 |
| 391.02 | afterwards | 540.13 | 636.04 | 685.01 | al |
| 403.08 | 021.14 | 543.08 | 641.08 | agreement | 299.04 |
| 404.03 | 080.12 | 547.04 | 650.17 | 184.10 | alacrity |
| 407.18 | 085.07 | 555.14 | 655.20 | 346.17 | 336.21 |
| 412.12 | 111.08 | 559.06 | 663.02 | ague | alarm |
| 424.08 | 169.11 | 563.11 | 676.18 | 467.01 | 186.21 |
| 427.15 | 191.15 | 565.12 | 692.05 | ah | 265.03 |
| 429.06 | 216.06 | 571.16 | 722.18 | 018.15 | 274.18 |
| 433.06 | 254.15 | 580.03 | 726.10 | 025.21 | 293.09 |
| 435.15 | 293.01 | 590.08 | 743.11 | 070.17 | 416.04 |
| 442.06 | 370.08 | 604.18 | 748.01 | 104.02 | 434.08 |
| 447.03 | 477.19 | 605.11 | agait | 160.03 | 587.02 |
| 450.19 | 498.05 | 609.16 | 035.19 | 230.21 | 615.02 |
| 454.04 | 506.14 | 611.13 | age | 246.20 | 642.07 |
| 454.18 | 528.08 | 615.02 | 089.04 | 249.17 | alarmed |
| 462.21 | 556.14 | 616.02 | 115.17 | 275.09 | 234.09 |
| 466.20 | 576.20 | 619.21 | 149.03 | 287.07 | 365.19 |
| 477.21 | 584.02 | 624.02 | 383.13 | 290.05 | 383.03 |

573.16
601.18
732.16

alas
046.07
202.03
528.18

ale
007.04
119.16
531.02
699.05

alert
290.04
473.04
728.14

alienation
296.10

alighted
598.16

alike
219.15

alive
025.05
034.18
164.05
198.17
223.14
362.02
396.09
402.20
558.04
635.17
636.18
734.03

all
001.06
004.08
004.13
008.19
010.07
020.13
020.21
023.06
028.06
028.21
030.05
031.20
038.22
040.02
041.04
046.10
047.15
048.22
050.05
061.01
066.13
069.03
074.06
074.11
076.22
077.13
078.16
081.13
083.12
085.07
085.18
088.02
090.08
090.17
091.17
092.05
093.01
094.03
095.21
098.03
099.12
100.12
102.13
106.08
106.19
107.17
110.01
113.11
115.03
117.18
118.17
119.17
119.21
121.12
124.07
125.02
126.06
128.20
131.08
131.14
134.09
140.07
145.14
148.05
154.01
157.06
158.19
165.01
167.14
171.12
173.19
173.22
174.03
174.04
176.01

178.09
180.22
181.14
182.19
182.21
184.09
187.14
188.06
190.01
190.06
191.03
191.03
192.08
193.16
195.05
196.18
197.14
199.15
199.19
199.21
201.07
203.03
203.15
207.13
219.08
219.18
220.02
221.07
224.21
226.07
231.09
231.10
232.04
239.03
242.04
243.13
245.08
262.11
262.21
263.04
268.04
271.09
273.19
274.06
274.13
281.16
282.09
282.09
284.01
285.20
288.11
292.19
293.04
296.13
299.22
301.08
303.07
311.10
312.15
316.04
317.03
318.20
319.10
321.15
322.06
322.12
324.03
326.11
329.15
332.16
335.04
335.19
336.03
339.15
340.12
344.22
345.16
347.09
349.04
353.12
358.20
360.21
361.10
366.17
367.06
367.10
367.19
371.07
373.02
373.08
374.05
378.07
383.02
385.08
386.10
393.13
397.10
399.05
403.17
407.18
413.07
415.15
415.21
424.07
430.22
437.07
440.19
447.04
453.01
461.12
463.10

463.18
468.10
469.09
472.11
475.15
475.20
483.21
488.01
490.06
493.05
493.15
496.11
499.16
501.17
503.05
503.05
512.11
512.21
521.01
523.08
525.22
528.16
534.07
536.06
538.13
540.02
543.18
547.01
552.08
555.10
558.01
558.02
563.08
572.10
572.22
574.01
581.15
582.08
602.01
603.15
611.09
611.20
613.02
614.10
614.19
615.06
620.17
621.04
623.11
624.14
627.08
630.11
632.02
632.14
632.19
632.19
636.04
639.14
641.02
644.04
645.01
646.11
647.03
651.16
652.05
659.20
660.21
666.01
667.01
667.04
670.11
678.11
680.16
683.04
691.06
692.09
692.22
696.12
698.17
710.20
710.20
714.03
716.09
719.13
720.16
721.20
722.08
722.11
724.17
728.13
739.02
742.08
746.06
746.21
754.03
759.09
762.21

all's
697.09

atlas
322.07
326.11
565.14
688.11

allayed
384.01

alleviation
223.11

alley
657.03

alliance
198.12
225.13

allies
711.21

allow
002.16
135.12
135.15
226.18
240.18
252.20
257.22
405.09
412.22
419.02
420.04
547.06
581.04
582.18
607.17
712.09
749.21

allowed
042.15
063.01
077.09
198.06
365.14
443.20
521.08
622.16
643.10
649.04
667.05

allowing
155.17

allus
187.14

allusion
740.09

ally
083.04
313.19
582.21

almanack
152.22

almost
008.07
019.20
021.08
024.04
046.12
052.21
058.14
068.02
075.03
075.14
077.21
136.11
146.06
150.04
165.07
193.06
204.08
269.03
303.02
312.11
313.22
370.17
370.18
380.03
403.15
404.08
475.07
483.14
494.05
508.01
514.05
545.11
564.01
567.03
571.02
583.13
602.21
603.03
631.15
653.17
691.14
704.17
733.20
738.09
738.10
745.17
752.16

alms
004.14

alone
009.07
009.16
030.15
072.02
094.15
102.02
118.17
127.08
134.03
135.17
152.20
169.22
184.13

198.13
219.01
223.09
230.03
230.05
239.08
250.12
265.10
269.12
277.20
281.20
285.09
307.02
314.01
339.13
344.13
352.22
363.16
363.16
403.18
418.19
431.10
478.09
487.18
510.18
531.02
541.02
552.02
560.09
597.14
605.11
608.02
614.07
622.03
629.12
631.07
651.20
663.03
666.06
684.11
689.19
701.13
732.09
739.20
748.22
755.20
757.01
761.15

along
006.12
014.09
132.15
227.17
282.01
518.01
552.16
601.03
620.07
650.08
692.16
693.02

aloof
198.04

aloud
011.02
053.19
079.16
155.12
266.19
375.19
407.15
483.01
493.12
525.17
540.08
573.11
611.16
654.22
675.13
703.21

already
028.01
041.19
063.08
127.19
261.04
330.08
395.15
452.08
483.15
543.02
585.02
615.11
636.07
682.13
689.02

also
017.21
050.02
051.12
063.19
066.10
073.04
108.16
117.21
138.02
165.11
189.14
197.13
200.09
214.20

224.15
241.05
302.11
323.11
340.17
358.07
409.03
413.22
418.16
457.14
470.11
478.07
507.01
521.22
523.16
538.19
570.03
573.19
581.13
595.06
607.19
635.02
637.13
664.18
682.17
696.01
701.06
729.05
750.19

alter
540.18
540.20

alteration
205.13
588.16
596.03

alterations
070.21

altered
098.10
177.02
208.15
225.18
244.21
272.07
330.22
351.10
361.08
392.10
636.15
645.06
700.02
728.20
738.20

altering
353.20

alternately
293.02

altogether
005.15
040.04
174.04
202.01
334.03
464.05
489.03
499.17
570.20
625.02
682.01
754.22

always
059.04
059.04
075.14
090.03
090.12
090.13
091.10
093.13
093.17
124.20
147.19
153.12
156.15
163.05
175.05
175.06
183.07
183.08
183.09
218.14
222.13
228.15
269.03
269.03
277.05
285.04
351.16
353.07
361.02
377.03
391.05
414.10
425.19
427.20
446.11
476.08
476.09
500.10
520.03

| | | | | | |
|---|---|---|---|---|---|
| 535.17 | amazed | amused | 149.05 | 416.05 | 734.20 |
| 571.02 | 096.03 | 040.13 | 149.16 | 417.06 | 736.05 |
| 571.22 | 213.17 | 523.07 | 150.04 | 419.02 | 738.16 |
| 575.08 | 227.10 | amusement | 151.11 | 426.04 | 738.17 |
| 579.11 | 502.21 | 013.02 | 152.01 | 426.05 | 741.10 |
| 592.15 | amazement | 252.20 | 152.03 | 426.13 | 743.11 |
| 632.12 | 200.02 | 352.13 | 157.15 | 430.15 | 743.21 |
| 654.21 | 208.01 | 426.04 | 167.02 | 431.14 | 746.08 |
| 661.05 | 252.11 | 478.13 | 168.22 | 432.07 | 748.02 |
| 665.21 | ambassadress | 493.01 | 171.19 | 435.02 | 748.08 |
| 666.04 | 710.05 | 497.12 | 172.16 | 438.09 | 760.19 |
| 678.03 | amber | 524.16 | 177.21 | 441.11 | an' |
| 701.11 | 693.01 | 548.10 | 181.05 | 445.18 | 466.21 |
| 716.20 | ambition | 608.13 | 182.14 | 452.10 | 720.01 |
| 732.09 | 147.06 | 618.16 | 185.16 | 456.16 | anatomy |
| am | 562.09 | 618.21 | 193.13 | 456.19 | 006.05 |
| 012.17 | amends | 700.13 | 195.11 | 457.19 | ancestors |
| 016.13 | 619.09 | 705.16 | 198.12 | 461.15 | 056.16 |
| 021.17 | 740.06 | amusements | 202.08 | 461.17 | 583.10 |
| 031.21 | america | 100.10 | 205.13 | 467.01 | ancient |
| 032.12 | 203.11 | 503.10 | 207.11 | 475.13 | 034.07 |
| 059.15 | american | amuses | 209.03 | 479.21 | 139.03 |
| 068.01 | 109.22 | 236.10 | 211.11 | 481.12 | 222.04 |
| 075.05 | amiable | 738.12 | 213.05 | 492.20 | 308.22 |
| 134.19 | 018.12 | amusing | 214.22 | 497.01 | 417.13 |
| 137.07 | 024.01 | 430.17 | 217.11 | 501.08 | 444.19 |
| 137.08 | 024.03 | 575.05 | 218.20 | 504.05 | 502.11 |
| 138.07 | 024.05 | an | 219.02 | 505.07 | 759.03 |
| 154.18 | 126.19 | 003.16 | 222.06 | 505.12 | and |
| 177.21 | 146.03 | 003.16 | 223.18 | 513.10 | 001.09 |
| 179.11 | 620.04 | 003.18 | 225.13 | 515.02 | 001.10 |
| 183.07 | 674.21 | 006.05 | 228.19 | 516.09 | 002.02 |
| 183.09 | amid | 006.16 | 229.01 | 516.14 | 002.20 |
| 202.08 | 118.08 | 007.02 | 229.12 | 518.06 | 003.01 |
| 203.18 | 442.10 | 007.13 | 229.13 | 521.15 | 003.07 |
| 214.18 | 576.16 | 007.19 | 231.13 | 523.13 | 003.09 |
| 227.09 | amiss | 009.10 | 233.13 | 523.22 | 003.14 |
| 245.06 | 007.12 | 011.07 | 234.21 | 531.21 | 003.17 |
| 253.06 | 087.12 | 011.09 | 236.15 | 535.14 | 004.01 |
| 262.06 | among | 015.02 | 241.06 | 539.11 | 004.12 |
| 263.04 | 004.22 | 016.11 | 241.08 | 541.10 | 004.17 |
| 264.12 | 007.06 | 017.05 | 244.07 | 548.03 | 004.21 |
| 274.07 | 018.15 | 017.09 | 244.17 | 551.01 | 005.01 |
| 276.16 | 022.08 | 018.16 | 245.20 | 553.13 | 005.02 |
| 278.18 | 029.22 | 019.09 | 252.04 | 553.14 | 005.04 |
| 282.22 | 067.05 | 020.05 | 257.06 | 554.07 | 005.07 |
| 287.21 | 088.05 | 021.20 | 257.21 | 558.01 | 005.13 |
| 307.19 | 099.05 | 021.22 | 258.10 | 558.11 | 005.17 |
| 317.03 | 137.17 | 023.07 | 260.07 | 565.04 | 005.18 |
| 327.14 | 146.19 | 023.10 | 267.04 | 568.20 | 005.21 |
| 329.01 | 269.04 | 024.04 | 267.18 | 571.04 | 005.22 |
| 345.13 | 271.21 | 029.07 | 276.12 | 580.07 | 006.02 |
| 345.15 | 272.05 | 032.14 | 278.11 | 581.08 | 006.07 |
| 346.06 | 275.13 | 032.15 | 282.12 | 582.18 | 006.08 |
| 349.02 | 283.03 | 037.04 | 292.09 | 587.04 | 006.10 |
| 357.03 | 284.15 | 039.13 | 297.04 | 588.01 | 006.10 |
| 357.12 | 287.15 | 040.11 | 298.02 | 588.15 | 006.18 |
| 357.18 | 318.08 | 040.11 | 299.11 | 589.03 | 006.20 |
| 363.12 | 345.18 | 040.14 | 301.06 | 590.07 | 007.01 |
| 371.11 | 365.07 | 040.16 | 304.07 | 591.14 | 007.02 |
| 376.22 | 373.02 | 040.19 | 305.09 | 595.03 | 007.08 |
| 428.02 | 385.16 | 042.17 | 305.14 | 599.21 | 007.10 |
| 428.20 | 392.02 | 047.13 | 305.15 | 600.21 | 007.14 |
| 429.10 | 408.03 | 048.06 | 308.04 | 601.01 | 007.14 |
| 436.20 | 433.14 | 051.05 | 308.21 | 608.12 | 007.21 |
| 449.08 | 442.06 | 051.21 | 309.19 | 612.08 | 007.21 |
| 449.17 | 492.05 | 053.08 | 316.07 | 613.11 | 008.09 |
| 461.10 | 507.16 | 054.08 | 321.20 | 617.19 | 008.17 |
| 464.12 | 515.07 | 054.20 | 322.20 | 618.07 | 008.18 |
| 464.12 | 519.12 | 058.09 | 323.09 | 620.10 | 008.19 |
| 484.10 | 557.09 | 058.16 | 325.07 | 627.02 | 008.22 |
| 485.06 | 558.20 | 060.11 | 327.06 | 629.13 | 009.02 |
| 486.20 | 578.09 | 063.03 | 333.21 | 631.12 | 009.10 |
| 490.01 | 583.16 | 063.04 | 334.06 | 635.09 | 009.12 |
| 494.05 | 602.20 | 064.01 | 338.02 | 639.12 | 009.14 |
| 520.02 | 651.12 | 064.05 | 340.06 | 642.07 | 010.05 |
| 520.10 | 659.07 | 065.13 | 340.12 | 643.12 | 010.12 |
| 531.16 | 671.14 | 067.10 | 344.04 | 645.10 | 010.13 |
| 534.17 | 673.10 | 070.14 | 346.04 | 661.20 | 010.15 |
| 543.14 | 686.06 | 071.06 | 346.17 | 665.22 | 010.16 |
| 545.14 | 690.05 | 073.09 | 347.12 | 667.11 | 010.19 |
| 548.02 | 748.18 | 074.09 | 352.11 | 670.17 | 010.20 |
| 570.17 | 764.07 | 074.16 | 353.18 | 672.03 | 010.21 |
| 570.20 | amongst | 082.01 | 354.19 | 675.02 | 011.04 |
| 571.01 | 032.20 | 083.14 | 361.04 | 676.20 | 011.08 |
| 580.19 | 078.17 | 084.10 | 361.19 | 677.02 | 011.11 |
| 581.10 | 693.10 | 088.03 | 361.22 | 679.03 | 011.13 |
| 593.17 | amongst' | 094.13 | 369.12 | 681.19 | 011.13 |
| 599.18 | 314.02 | 107.14 | 370.05 | 684.18 | 011.15 |
| 600.06 | amount | 109.01 | 371.15 | 684.19 | 012.06 |
| 606.06 | 679.06 | 109.21 | 373.14 | 687.02 | 012.17 |
| 607.21 | amounted | 118.11 | 375.07 | 689.10 | 012.20 |
| 610.14 | 444.09 | 119.04 | 383.03 | 690.15 | 013.07 |
| 617.09 | amounting | 121.05 | 384.21 | 692.07 | 013.07 |
| 623.12 | 730.10 | 121.09 | 386.19 | 693.07 | 013.10 |
| 634.12 | ample | 123.02 | 386.21 | 696.09 | 013.13 |
| 639.21 | 323.04 | 125.17 | 387.04 | 703.22 | 014.02 |
| 646.06 | amuse | 129.19 | 387.20 | 704.18 | 014.04 |
| 647.08 | 118.17 | 130.07 | 388.14 | 705.15 | 014.07 |
| 672.09 | 153.16 | 130.09 | 392.10 | 707.18 | 014.12 |
| 677.02 | 203.22 | 130.20 | 393.21 | 709.07 | 015.02 |
| 702.13 | 252.21 | 135.11 | 394.13 | 712.09 | 015.02 |
| 730.03 | 307.20 | 139.07 | 396.11 | 716.02 | 015.05 |
| 731.18 | 348.04 | 145.01 | 399.06 | 717.21 | 015.10 |
| 734.09 | 452.11 | 145.05 | 399.21 | 719.20 | 015.12 |
| 742.20 | 476.14 | 145.11 | 401.02 | 719.21 | 015.15 |
| amang | 555.09 | 145.15 | 404.16 | 722.12 | 016.01 |
| 194.01 | 589.15 | 146.08 | 405.16 | 724.15 | 016.10 |
| 232.22 | 589.19 | 147.14 | 405.17 | 729.08 | 016.19 |
| 696.18 | 670.13 | 148.04 | 411.12 | 730.18 | 016.21 |
| | | 148.21 | 412.21 | 732.10 | 017.01 |

| | | | | | |
|---|---|---|---|---|---|
| 017.02 | 040.03 | 059.10 | 077.10 | 091.08 | 103.04 |
| 017.06 | 040.06 | 059.12 | 077.11 | 091.11 | 103.05 |
| 017.07 | 040.17 | 059.13 | 077.12 | 091.11 | 103.08 |
| 017.11 | 041.01 | 059.14 | 077.13 | 091.13 | 103.18 |
| 017.13 | 041.06 | 059.20 | 077.16 | 091.18 | 103.21 |
| 017.13 | 041.07 | 060.01 | 078.01 | 091.19 | 104.01 |
| 018.02 | 041.10 | 060.03 | 078.03 | 091.20 | 104.02 |
| 018.05 | 041.12 | 060.07 | 078.06 | 092.03 | 104.03 |
| 018.05 | 041.13 | 060.10 | 078.06 | 092.10 | 104.04 |
| 018.21 | 041.13 | 060.18 | 078.08 | 092.11 | 104.04 |
| 019.04 | 041.17 | 060.19 | 078.12 | 092.13 | 104.07 |
| 019.08 | 042.06 | 060.22 | 078.13 | 092.14 | 104.08 |
| 019.09 | 042.09 | 061.01 | 078.16 | 092.16 | 104.09 |
| 019.10 | 042.10 | 061.06 | 078.18 | 092.21 | 104.12 |
| 019.14 | 042.11 | 061.10 | 078.19 | 092.22 | 104.18 |
| 019.18 | 042.12 | 061.14 | 078.20 | 093.01 | 104.19 |
| 020.05 | 042.16 | 061.16 | 078.22 | 093.03 | 105.02 |
| 020.13 | 042.19 | 061.22 | 078.22 | 093.06 | 105.08 |
| 020.13 | 042.20 | 062.06 | 079.06 | 093.08 | 105.08 |
| 020.15 | 043.01 | 062.07 | 079.07 | 093.12 | 105.13 |
| 020.19 | 043.03 | 062.08 | 079.07 | 093.15 | 105.20 |
| 021.02 | 043.10 | 062.09 | 079.09 | 093.15 | 105.22 |
| 021.03 | 044.02 | 062.11 | 079.10 | 093.16 | 106.04 |
| 021.05 | 044.03 | 062.20 | 079.16 | 093.20 | 106.06 |
| 021.06 | 044.06 | 063.01 | 079.18 | 093.22 | 106.07 |
| 021.09 | 044.08 | 063.03 | 080.01 | 094.02 | 106.10 |
| 021.13 | 044.09 | 063.10 | 080.05 | 094.04 | 106.18 |
| 021.19 | 044.10 | 063.13 | 080.08 | 094.05 | 106.19 |
| 022.06 | 044.12 | 063.13 | 080.09 | 094.06 | 107.04 |
| 022.09 | 044.13 | 063.16 | 080.16 | 094.07 | 107.09 |
| 023.05 | 044.15 | 063.22 | 080.17 | 094.08 | 107.13 |
| 023.11 | 045.05 | 064.01 | 080.18 | 094.09 | 108.06 |
| 023.12 | 045.07 | 064.03 | 080.19 | 094.12 | 108.13 |
| 023.16 | 045.09 | 064.05 | 080.20 | 094.14 | 108.15 |
| 023.18 | 045.09 | 064.09 | 080.20 | 094.22 | 108.22 |
| 023.22 | 045.10 | 064.15 | 080.22 | 095.01 | 109.06 |
| 024.02 | 045.14 | 064.19 | 081.06 | 095.04 | 109.10 |
| 024.09 | 045.20 | 065.01 | 081.07 | 095.05 | 109.11 |
| 024.16 | 046.03 | 065.03 | 081.08 | 095.07 | 110.02 |
| 025.02 | 046.06 | 065.07 | 081.15 | 095.08 | 110.07 |
| 026.04 | 046.07 | 065.12 | 081.15 | 095.14 | 110.11 |
| 026.06 | 046.14 | 065.14 | 081.16 | 095.19 | 110.15 |
| 026.15 | 046.16 | 065.14 | 081.19 | 095.20 | 110.22 |
| 026.21 | 046.20 | 065.17 | 082.02 | 096.02 | 111.01 |
| 027.09 | 047.07 | 065.20 | 082.03 | 096.03 | 111.02 |
| 027.11 | 047.09 | 065.21 | 082.03 | 096.04 | 111.04 |
| 027.13 | 047.09 | 066.01 | 082.06 | 096.06 | 111.05 |
| 027.18 | 047.18 | 066.08 | 082.07 | 097.02 | 111.05 |
| 027.18 | 048.03 | 066.10 | 082.09 | 097.04 | 111.07 |
| 027.19 | 048.04 | 066.13 | 082.12 | 097.08 | 111.08 |
| 028.02 | 048.05 | 066.14 | 082.16 | 097.09 | 111.09 |
| 028.06 | 048.07 | 066.19 | 082.17 | 097.10 | 111.10 |
| 028.10 | 048.10 | 066.22 | 082.21 | 097.11 | 111.10 |
| 028.12 | 048.17 | 067.05 | 082.22 | 097.15 | 111.12 |
| 028.18 | 048.17 | 067.10 | 083.02 | 097.15 | 111.13 |
| 028.22 | 048.18 | 067.13 | 083.03 | 097.15 | 111.22 |
| 029.05 | 048.18 | 067.16 | 083.05 | 097.16 | 112.01 |
| 029.21 | 048.19 | 067.20 | 083.11 | 097.20 | 112.04 |
| 030.05 | 048.19 | 067.22 | 083.12 | 097.21 | 112.06 |
| 030.05 | 048.19 | 067.22 | 083.16 | 098.04 | 112.12 |
| 030.10 | 049.03 | 068.03 | 083.17 | 098.06 | 113.04 |
| 030.11 | 049.08 | 069.04 | 083.20 | 098.12 | 113.06 |
| 030.14 | 049.08 | 069.08 | 084.01 | 098.12 | 113.08 |
| 031.03 | 049.10 | 069.09 | 084.03 | 098.12 | 113.10 |
| 031.18 | 049.13 | 070.02 | 084.07 | 098.13 | 114.03 |
| 032.15 | 049.15 | 070.12 | 084.11 | 098.14 | 114.13 |
| 032.18 | 050.08 | 070.15 | 084.12 | 098.16 | 114.18 |
| 033.07 | 050.10 | 070.22 | 084.14 | 098.17 | 114.20 |
| 033.17 | 050.14 | 071.03 | 084.18 | 098.19 | 114.20 |
| 034.03 | 050.16 | 071.09 | 084.19 | 098.21 | 115.04 |
| 034.12 | 050.21 | 071.10 | 084.19 | 098.21 | 115.05 |
| 034.13 | 051.04 | 071.15 | 084.21 | 098.21 | 115.06 |
| 034.14 | 051.06 | 071.18 | 085.04 | 099.03 | 115.12 |
| 034.17 | 051.06 | 072.05 | 085.05 | 099.05 | 115.16 |
| 034.17 | 051.10 | 072.12 | 085.06 | 099.06 | 115.17 |
| 034.19 | 051.11 | 072.20 | 085.08 | 099.06 | 115.18 |
| 034.21 | 051.12 | 073.03 | 085.10 | 099.07 | 115.20 |
| 035.06 | 051.15 | 073.10 | 085.13 | 099.09 | 115.21 |
| 035.07 | 051.15 | 073.16 | 085.17 | 099.15 | 115.22 |
| 035.10 | 051.20 | 073.18 | 085.18 | 099.20 | 116.06 |
| 035.15 | 052.05 | 073.22 | 085.18 | 100.02 | 116.07 |
| 036.01 | 052.16 | 074.03 | 087.03 | 100.05 | 116.10 |
| 036.04 | 052.18 | 074.07 | 087.04 | 100.07 | 116.13 |
| 036.08 | 052.19 | 074.08 | 087.06 | 100.08 | 116.18 |
| 036.08 | 052.19 | 074.16 | 088.02 | 100.11 | 116.18 |
| 036.09 | 052.20 | 074.18 | 088.06 | 100.12 | 116.20 |
| 036.11 | 053.05 | 074.20 | 088.08 | 100.15 | 116.21 |
| 036.13 | 053.16 | 074.22 | 088.12 | 100.19 | 116.21 |
| 037.03 | 053.19 | 075.02 | 088.16 | 100.21 | 116.22 |
| 037.05 | 054.02 | 075.04 | 088.16 | 101.06 | 117.04 |
| 037.09 | 054.04 | 075.07 | 088.18 | 101.08 | 117.05 |
| 038.01 | 054.06 | 075.09 | 088.21 | 101.09 | 117.12 |
| 038.03 | 054.11 | 075.17 | 089.04 | 101.09 | 117.18 |
| 038.07 | 054.13 | 075.18 | 089.05 | 101.10 | 117.21 |
| 038.11 | 054.17 | 075.18 | 089.10 | 101.11 | 118.04 |
| 038.15 | 054.18 | 076.03 | 089.11 | 101.13 | 118.05 |
| 038.16 | 055.01 | 076.05 | 089.14 | 101.14 | 118.06 |
| 038.20 | 055.13 | 076.05 | 089.15 | 101.19 | 118.09 |
| 039.01 | 055.15 | 076.06 | 089.17 | 101.21 | 118.09 |
| 039.02 | 055.20 | 076.11 | 089.21 | 102.06 | 118.14 |
| 039.02 | 056.03 | 076.13 | 090.01 | 102.12 | 118.14 |
| 039.05 | 056.08 | 076.15 | 090.03 | 102.14 | 118.15 |
| 039.10 | 056.08 | 076.20 | 090.07 | 102.15 | 118.17 |
| 039.13 | 056.18 | 076.20 | 090.08 | 102.17 | 119.01 |
| 039.15 | 058.01 | 076.21 | 090.14 | 102.18 | 119.01 |
| 039.16 | 058.06 | 077.01 | 090.16 | 102.20 | 119.07 |
| 039.17 | 058.15 | 077.04 | 090.17 | 102.22 | 119.13 |
| 039.18 | 058.20 | 077.06 | 090.17 | 103.01 | 119.16 |
| 039.21 | 059.04 | | 090.21 | 103.01 | 119.18 |
| 040.01 | 059.06 | | 091.05 | 103.01 | 119.20 |
| 040.01 | | | 091.07 | 103.02 | |

| | | | | | |
|---|---|---|---|---|---|
| 119.21 | 133.10 | 153.02 | 174.04 | 190.18 | 207.01 |
| 119.22 | 133.12 | 153.08 | 174.06 | 191.04 | 207.03 |
| 120.01 | 133.13 | 153.12 | 174.09 | 191.05 | 207.05 |
| 120.03 | 134.03 | 154.02 | 174.13 | 191.07 | 207.06 |
| 120.04 | 134.07 | 154.05 | 174.13 | 191.10 | 207.12 |
| 120.06 | 134.08 | 154.10 | 174.13 | 191.11 | 207.17 |
| 120.10 | 134.12 | 154.13 | 174.14 | 191.11 | 207.18 |
| 120.14 | 134.14 | 154.14 | 174.16 | 191.17 | 207.21 |
| 120.17 | 134.18 | 154.16 | 174.19 | 192.01 | 208.10 |
| 120.18 | 135.17 | 154.17 | 175.01 | 192.02 | 208.14 |
| 120.19 | 136.02 | 154.20 | 175.05 | 192.05 | 208.18 |
| 120.21 | 136.06 | 155.06 | 175.06 | 192.08 | 208.20 |
| 121.01 | 136.09 | 155.07 | 175.06 | 192.12 | 208.21 |
| 121.05 | 136.10 | 155.09 | 175.08 | 192.12 | 209.05 |
| 121.09 | 136.12 | 155.21 | 175.14 | 192.21 | 209.07 |
| 121.09 | 136.16 | 156.02 | 175.17 | 192.22 | 209.08 |
| 121.11 | 136.20 | 156.05 | 175.19 | 193.01 | 209.17 |
| 121.12 | 137.17 | 156.06 | 175.22 | 193.05 | 209.17 |
| 121.14 | 137.18 | 156.08 | 176.01 | 193.16 | 209.20 |
| 121.14 | 137.20 | 156.10 | 176.01 | 193.18 | 210.02 |
| 121.19 | 138.01 | 156.14 | 176.03 | 193.20 | 210.06 |
| 121.20 | 138.03 | 156.20 | 176.04 | 194.05 | 211.03 |
| 121.22 | 138.03 | 157.03 | 176.06 | 194.05 | 211.08 |
| 122.03 | 138.04 | 157.08 | 176.14 | 194.13 | 211.09 |
| 122.05 | 138.08 | 157.10 | 176.14 | 194.17 | 211.15 |
| 122.22 | 139.03 | 157.12 | 176.19 | 195.04 | 212.05 |
| 123.02 | 139.08 | 157.14 | 176.20 | 195.09 | 212.12 |
| 123.06 | 140.02 | 157.16 | 176.22 | 195.12 | 212.13 |
| 123.07 | 140.03 | 157.20 | 177.01 | 195.15 | 212.17 |
| 123.08 | 140.06 | 158.04 | 177.01 | 195.17 | 212.22 |
| 123.10 | 140.06 | 158.07 | 177.02 | 195.20 | 213.04 |
| 123.13 | 140.06 | 158.11 | 177.07 | 196.04 | 213.07 |
| 123.13 | 140.10 | 158.14 | 177.08 | 196.05 | 213.08 |
| 123.14 | 140.12 | 158.19 | 177.11 | 196.05 | 213.12 |
| 123.19 | 140.19 | 159.02 | 177.14 | 196.07 | 213.13 |
| 124.01 | 140.20 | 159.05 | 177.16 | 196.10 | 213.14 |
| 124.02 | 141.02 | 159.07 | 177.20 | 196.12 | 213.16 |
| 124.02 | 141.03 | 159.11 | 177.21 | 196.12 | 213.21 |
| 124.03 | 141.04 | 159.14 | 178.01 | 196.13 | 214.02 |
| 124.05 | 141.07 | 160.05 | 178.16 | 196.13 | 214.03 |
| 124.06 | 141.10 | 160.06 | 178.20 | 196.17 | 214.05 |
| 124.07 | 141.15 | 160.08 | 178.21 | 196.17 | 214.06 |
| 124.10 | 141.16 | 160.14 | 179.05 | 196.17 | 214.12 |
| 124.12 | 141.16 | 160.15 | 179.09 | 196.18 | 214.17 |
| 124.13 | 141.19 | 160.18 | 179.12 | 196.22 | 214.20 |
| 124.17 | 142.01 | 160.20 | 179.13 | 197.01 | 215.05 |
| 124.18 | 142.08 | 161.02 | 179.17 | 197.04 | 215.12 |
| 124.20 | 142.12 | 162.03 | 179.18 | 197.04 | 215.13 |
| 124.20 | 142.14 | 162.08 | 179.20 | 197.06 | 215.17 |
| 125.02 | 142.19 | 162.09 | 180.03 | 197.14 | 215.17 |
| 125.05 | 143.01 | 162.10 | 180.07 | 197.15 | 215.18 |
| 125.06 | 143.07 | 163.03 | 180.12 | 197.16 | 215.19 |
| 125.10 | 143.08 | 163.10 | 180.14 | 197.16 | 215.20 |
| 125.11 | 143.09 | 163.10 | 180.18 | 197.21 | 216.02 |
| 125.12 | 143.16 | 163.16 | 180.21 | 198.02 | 216.05 |
| 125.13 | 143.19 | 163.18 | 180.22 | 198.03 | 216.06 |
| 125.17 | 144.02 | 163.20 | 181.01 | 198.04 | 216.14 |
| 125.19 | 144.02 | 164.01 | 181.15 | 198.04 | 216.18 |
| 125.20 | 144.02 | 164.06 | 181.19 | 198.07 | 216.21 |
| 125.21 | 144.05 | 164.11 | 181.21 | 198.12 | 217.01 |
| 126.01 | 144.05 | 164.13 | 182.03 | 198.16 | 217.08 |
| 126.02 | 144.07 | 164.22 | 182.09 | 198.17 | 217.16 |
| 126.04 | 144.08 | 165.01 | 182.11 | 198.21 | 217.19 |
| 126.05 | 144.11 | 165.03 | 182.12 | 199.02 | 218.04 |
| 126.08 | 144.12 | 165.04 | 182.17 | 199.05 | 218.07 |
| 126.09 | 144.15 | 165.13 | 182.18 | 199.07 | 218.12 |
| 126.11 | 144.16 | 165.16 | 182.20 | 199.11 | 218.12 |
| 126.11 | 144.18 | 165.21 | 182.21 | 199.13 | 218.13 |
| 126.14 | 144.22 | 166.04 | 182.21 | 199.13 | 218.16 |
| 126.15 | 144.23 | 166.14 | 183.12 | 199.17 | 218.18 |
| 126.18 | 145.02 | 166.18 | 183.13 | 199.18 | 218.21 |
| 126.19 | 145.07 | 167.05 | 184.04 | 199.20 | 219.07 |
| 127.01 | 145.09 | 167.11 | 184.05 | 199.21 | 219.08 |
| 127.02 | 145.14 | 167.16 | 184.07 | 200.02 | 219.11 |
| 127.04 | 145.19 | 167.19 | 184.09 | 200.06 | 219.12 |
| 127.07 | 145.22 | 167.20 | 184.20 | 200.07 | 219.13 |
| 127.10 | 146.03 | 167.21 | 185.01 | 200.10 | 219.15 |
| 128.07 | 146.06 | 168.04 | 185.05 | 201.03 | 219.17 |
| 128.08 | 146.19 | 168.17 | 185.14 | 201.04 | 220.05 |
| 128.10 | 146.20 | 169.05 | 185.16 | 201.05 | 220.07 |
| 128.12 | 147.02 | 169.08 | 185.20 | 201.05 | 220.10 |
| 128.15 | 147.03 | 169.14 | 185.21 | 201.06 | 220.16 |
| 128.16 | 147.04 | 169.15 | 186.01 | 201.07 | 220.18 |
| 128.17 | 147.06 | 169.17 | 186.02 | 202.02 | 220.20 |
| 128.19 | 147.10 | 169.20 | 186.08 | 202.05 | 220.22 |
| 129.01 | 147.14 | 170.02 | 186.08 | 202.06 | 221.11 |
| 129.02 | 147.18 | 170.05 | 186.10 | 202.07 | 221.12 |
| 129.06 | 147.19 | 170.06 | 187.04 | 202.13 | 221.13 |
| 129.09 | 147.22 | 171.06 | 187.08 | 202.14 | 221.14 |
| 130.01 | 148.04 | 171.06 | 187.11 | 203.04 | 221.17 |
| 130.04 | 148.08 | 171.09 | 188.05 | 203.10 | 222.06 |
| 130.05 | 148.09 | 171.16 | 188.10 | 203.12 | 222.07 |
| 130.06 | 148.14 | 171.16 | 188.12 | 204.01 | 222.12 |
| 130.14 | 148.19 | 171.19 | 188.15 | 204.05 | 222.22 |
| 130.16 | 149.01 | 172.10 | 188.16 | 204.05 | 223.01 |
| 130.19 | 149.03 | 172.14 | 188.18 | 204.08 | 223.02 |
| 131.06 | 149.06 | 172.17 | 188.18 | 204.14 | 223.12 |
| 131.09 | 149.10 | 172.20 | 189.02 | 204.15 | 223.16 |
| 131.12 | 149.12 | 173.09 | 189.04 | 204.15 | 223.20 |
| 131.14 | 149.17 | 173.12 | 189.06 | 205.04 | 224.06 |
| 131.15 | 149.19 | 173.12 | 189.09 | 205.08 | 224.07 |
| 131.18 | 150.02 | 173.14 | 189.11 | 205.11 | 224.09 |
| 131.19 | 150.05 | 173.16 | 189.11 | 205.11 | 224.17 |
| 131.21 | 150.09 | 173.16 | 189.15 | 205.19 | 224.20 |
| 132.05 | 150.12 | 173.17 | 189.21 | 205.22 | 225.02 |
| 132.07 | 150.20 | 173.19 | 190.03 | 206.02 | 225.06 |
| 132.11 | 151.01 | 174.01 | 190.04 | 206.08 | 225.10 |
| 132.16 | 151.21 | 174.02 | 190.05 | 206.12 | 225.14 |
| 132.20 | 151.22 | 174.03 | 190.06 | 206.13 | 225.19 |
| 133.09 | 152.04 | 174.04 | 190.08 | 206.15 | 225.20 |
| 133.10 | 152.07 | 174.04 | 190.14 | 206.18 | 226.03 |

| | | | | | |
|---|---|---|---|---|---|
| 226.08 | 247.22 | 271.01 | 288.19 | 308.08 | 326.15 |
| 226.09 | 248.01 | 271.02 | 288.20 | 308.09 | 326.16 |
| 226.10 | 248.03 | 271.12 | 289.07 | 308.12 | 326.18 |
| 226.14 | 248.07 | 272.06 | 289.12 | 308.17 | 327.02 |
| 226.19 | 248.16 | 272.16 | 289.21 | 308.19 | 327.04 |
| 226.21 | 249.02 | 272.21 | 290.08 | 309.01 | 327.10 |
| 227.02 | 249.03 | 273.09 | 290.13 | 309.06 | 328.03 |
| 227.06 | 249.08 | 273.14 | 291.03 | 309.07 | 328.04 |
| 227.14 | 250.01 | 273.17 | 291.06 | 309.10 | 328.06 |
| 227.20 | 250.01 | 273.18 | 291.07 | 309.13 | 329.01 |
| 228.09 | 250.05 | 273.22 | 291.09 | 309.17 | 329.05 |
| 228.15 | 250.13 | 274.02 | 291.11 | 309.19 | 329.08 |
| 228.17 | 250.18 | 274.05 | 291.22 | 310.07 | 329.15 |
| 229.06 | 251.04 | 274.11 | 292.03 | 310.08 | 329.17 |
| 229.09 | 251.13 | 274.16 | 292.12 | 310.09 | 330.01 |
| 229.14 | 251.19 | 274.18 | 292.14 | 310.10 | 330.07 |
| 229.18 | 252.01 | 274.19 | 292.18 | 310.18 | 330.11 |
| 229.21 | 252.03 | 274.20 | 292.22 | 310.19 | 330.12 |
| 230.06 | 252.04 | 275.01 | 293.02 | 310.20 | 330.18 |
| 230.09 | 252.08 | 275.04 | 293.02 | 311.01 | 330.21 |
| 230.10 | 252.12 | 275.08 | 293.05 | 311.06 | 331.02 |
| 230.12 | 252.17 | 275.08 | 293.12 | 311.09 | 331.02 |
| 230.14 | 252.21 | 275.12 | 294.01 | 311.16 | 331.04 |
| 231.04 | 253.02 | 275.12 | 294.09 | 311.21 | 331.08 |
| 231.06 | 253.12 | 275.17 | 294.10 | 312.01 | 331.12 |
| 231.08 | 253.13 | 275.21 | 294.12 | 312.06 | 331.21 |
| 231.13 | 253.15 | 276.01 | 294.13 | 312.07 | 331.22 |
| 231.17 | 253.20 | 276.05 | 294.20 | 312.11 | 332.02 |
| 231.19 | 254.02 | 276.08 | 295.02 | 312.13 | 332.06 |
| 232.03 | 254.09 | 276.10 | 295.02 | 312.13 | 332.09 |
| 232.05 | 254.11 | 276.13 | 295.04 | 312.15 | 332.12 |
| 232.06 | 254.12 | 276.14 | 295.12 | 312.17 | 332.16 |
| 232.06 | 254.13 | 276.21 | 295.12 | 312.20 | 332.17 |
| 232.18 | 255.01 | 276.22 | 295.15 | 312.22 | 332.22 |
| 233.10 | 255.05 | 276.22 | 295.18 | 313.02 | 333.02 |
| 233.14 | 255.10 | 277.08 | 295.18 | 313.03 | 333.07 |
| 234.05 | 255.13 | 277.09 | 296.02 | 313.04 | 333.11 |
| 234.07 | 256.01 | 277.13 | 296.07 | 313.09 | 333.15 |
| 234.09 | 256.06 | 277.15 | 296.13 | 313.12 | 333.17 |
| 234.13 | 256.18 | 277.17 | 296.15 | 313.16 | 333.17 |
| 234.17 | 256.22 | 277.21 | 296.17 | 314.03 | 334.02 |
| 234.20 | 257.01 | 278.01 | 296.19 | 314.04 | 334.05 |
| 235.04 | 257.04 | 278.06 | 296.20 | 314.05 | 334.12 |
| 235.11 | 257.05 | 278.09 | 297.06 | 314.05 | 334.14 |
| 235.17 | 257.13 | 278.17 | 297.19 | 314.06 | 334.21 |
| 235.19 | 257.16 | 278.18 | 298.01 | 314.07 | 335.03 |
| 235.19 | 257.18 | 278.19 | 298.04 | 314.10 | 335.07 |
| 236.01 | 258.05 | 279.04 | 298.09 | 314.11 | 335.08 |
| 236.04 | 258.08 | 279.09 | 298.10 | 314.12 | 335.18 |
| 236.06 | 258.08 | 279.13 | 298.13 | 314.15 | 335.21 |
| 236.09 | 258.13 | 279.19 | 298.15 | 314.18 | 336.06 |
| 236.10 | 258.16 | 280.05 | 298.21 | 315.03 | 336.13 |
| 236.13 | 258.19 | 280.11 | 299.01 | 315.07 | 336.16 |
| 236.15 | 258.20 | 280.15 | 299.02 | 315.08 | 337.05 |
| 237.03 | 259.10 | 280.16 | 299.06 | 315.18 | 337.19 |
| 237.04 | 259.13 | 280.18 | 299.11 | 316.08 | 338.01 |
| 237.10 | 259.16 | 280.22 | 299.14 | 316.12 | 338.01 |
| 237.16 | 259.19 | 281.02 | 299.22 | 316.15 | 338.05 |
| 237.16 | 259.21 | 281.03 | 301.04 | 317.02 | 338.09 |
| 237.19 | 260.01 | 281.04 | 301.07 | 317.05 | 338.09 |
| 237.21 | 260.05 | 281.05 | 301.08 | 317.06 | 338.14 |
| 238.01 | 260.19 | 281.06 | 301.09 | 317.06 | 338.18 |
| 238.05 | 260.21 | 281.08 | 301.10 | 317.12 | 338.21 |
| 238.06 | 261.03 | 281.11 | 302.03 | 317.15 | 338.22 |
| 238.20 | 261.08 | 281.13 | 302.05 | 317.16 | 339.02 |
| 238.20 | 261.13 | 281.14 | 302.07 | 317.18 | 339.06 |
| 239.05 | 261.18 | 281.17 | 302.09 | 317.21 | 339.14 |
| 239.06 | 261.20 | 281.19 | 302.11 | 318.01 | 339.19 |
| 239.11 | 262.01 | 281.20 | 302.18 | 318.04 | 340.01 |
| 240.04 | 262.03 | 282.02 | 302.22 | 318.05 | 340.14 |
| 240.07 | 262.04 | 282.08 | 302.22 | 318.10 | 340.16 |
| 240.10 | 262.10 | 282.08 | 303.02 | 319.01 | 340.18 |
| 240.16 | 263.01 | 282.10 | 303.04 | 319.03 | 340.21 |
| 240.16 | 263.09 | 282.11 | 303.06 | 319.16 | 341.05 |
| 240.17 | 263.12 | 282.12 | 303.06 | 319.18 | 341.06 |
| 240.20 | 263.21 | 282.18 | 303.07 | 319.18 | 341.18 |
| 241.01 | 264.01 | 282.20 | 303.13 | 319.20 | 341.19 |
| 241.04 | 264.21 | 282.21 | 303.14 | 320.03 | 342.05 |
| 241.08 | 265.03 | 282.21 | 303.16 | 320.04 | 342.07 |
| 241.09 | 265.07 | 283.11 | 303.16 | 320.06 | 342.13 |
| 241.10 | 265.08 | 283.13 | 303.19 | 320.17 | 342.16 |
| 242.03 | 265.18 | 283.16 | 303.21 | 320.19 | 343.01 |
| 242.07 | 266.01 | 283.20 | 304.01 | 320.21 | 343.02 |
| 242.08 | 266.03 | 283.21 | 304.03 | 321.08 | 343.05 |
| 243.04 | 266.05 | 284.02 | 304.07 | 321.19 | 343.16 |
| 243.04 | 266.07 | 284.06 | 304.09 | 322.11 | 343.20 |
| 243.08 | 266.16 | 284.07 | 304.09 | 322.12 | 343.21 |
| 243.10 | 266.19 | 284.11 | 304.10 | 322.17 | 344.02 |
| 243.10 | 267.01 | 284.12 | 304.16 | 322.19 | 344.02 |
| 243.12 | 267.04 | 284.14 | 304.19 | 322.21 | 344.03 |
| 243.14 | 267.14 | 284.15 | 304.22 | 323.05 | 344.06 |
| 243.17 | 267.14 | 284.19 | 305.04 | 323.08 | 344.11 |
| 243.18 | 267.14 | 284.22 | 305.08 | 323.12 | 344.12 |
| 243.20 | 267.17 | 285.11 | 305.13 | 323.15 | 344.13 |
| 244.01 | 267.18 | 285.12 | 305.15 | 323.19 | 344.17 |
| 244.06 | 267.22 | 285.14 | 305.16 | 323.21 | 344.18 |
| 244.14 | 268.05 | 285.18 | 305.18 | 324.06 | 344.22 |
| 245.04 | 269.02 | 285.19 | 305.20 | 324.07 | 345.03 |
| 245.12 | 269.03 | 285.21 | 306.06 | 324.09 | 345.04 |
| 245.16 | 269.04 | 286.06 | 306.07 | 324.22 | 345.10 |
| 245.21 | 269.08 | 286.09 | 306.08 | 325.01 | 345.13 |
| 246.01 | 269.09 | 286.10 | 306.11 | 325.05 | 345.20 |
| 246.03 | 269.12 | 286.12 | 306.15 | 325.06 | 346.01 |
| 246.07 | 270.03 | 286.19 | 306.16 | 325.10 | 346.03 |
| 246.09 | 270.11 | 286.20 | 306.18 | 325.13 | 346.03 |
| 246.13 | 270.16 | 287.05 | 307.11 | 325.15 | 346.05 |
| 246.20 | 270.17 | 287.10 | 307.15 | 325.20 | 346.08 |
| 247.10 | 270.18 | 287.17 | 307.16 | 326.01 | 346.09 |
| 247.11 | 270.21 | 288.04 | 308.02 | 326.03 | 346.11 |
| 247.16 | 270.22 | 288.14 | 308.04 | 326.07 | 346.15 |
| 247.20 | 271.01 | 288.15 | 308.07 | 326.14 | 346.16 |

| | | | | | |
|---|---|---|---|---|---|
| 346.19 | 364.18 | 383.21 | 398.17 | 416.12 | 434.19 |
| 346.21 | 365.01 | 383.22 | 399.08 | 417.01 | 434.21 |
| 347.01 | 365.07 | 384.04 | 399.09 | 417.08 | 435.07 |
| 347.06 | 365.20 | 384.05 | 399.12 | 417.15 | 435.08 |
| 347.07 | 366.09 | 384.06 | 399.13 | 418.01 | 435.11 |
| 347.09 | 366.18 | 384.11 | 399.16 | 418.04 | 435.14 |
| 347.15 | 366.19 | 384.14 | 399.19 | 418.05 | 435.17 |
| 347.19 | 366.19 | 384.16 | 399.20 | 418.08 | 435.18 |
| 347.21 | 367.02 | 384.18 | 400.01 | 418.09 | 436.05 |
| 348.01 | 367.05 | 384.21 | 400.02 | 418.10 | 436.08 |
| 348.02 | 367.08 | 385.01 | 400.07 | 418.11 | 436.14 |
| 348.06 | 367.15 | 385.07 | 400.11 | 418.14 | 437.02 |
| 348.10 | 367.16 | 385.12 | 400.12 | 418.17 | 437.06 |
| 349.02 | 367.17 | 385.14 | 401.01 | 418.18 | 437.06 |
| 349.03 | 367.19 | 385.15 | 401.03 | 419.01 | 437.08 |
| 349.08 | 367.20 | 385.15 | 401.05 | 419.08 | 437.10 |
| 350.04 | 367.22 | 385.20 | 401.07 | 419.11 | 437.13 |
| 350.05 | 368.02 | 385.21 | 401.10 | 419.16 | 437.14 |
| 350.12 | 368.06 | 386.05 | 401.14 | 419.18 | 437.14 |
| 350.15 | 368.11 | 386.14 | 401.16 | 419.21 | 437.17 |
| 350.18 | 369.04 | 386.15 | 402.01 | 419.22 | 437.17 |
| 350.19 | 370.01 | 386.16 | 402.04 | 420.01 | 437.18 |
| 350.22 | 370.06 | 386.17 | 402.06 | 420.03 | 438.03 |
| 351.01 | 370.11 | 387.01 | 402.08 | 420.03 | 438.09 |
| 351.02 | 370.13 | 387.02 | 402.21 | 420.04 | 438.12 |
| 351.07 | 370.13 | 387.04 | 403.01 | 421.03 | 438.13 |
| 351.09 | 370.16 | 387.07 | 403.05 | 421.05 | 438.18 |
| 351.14 | 370.16 | 387.08 | 403.08 | 421.06 | 438.22 |
| 351.17 | 370.18 | 387.09 | 403.15 | 421.11 | 439.02 |
| 351.20 | 370.19 | 387.12 | 403.17 | 421.12 | 439.15 |
| 352.01 | 371.01 | 387.12 | 403.20 | 422.07 | 440.02 |
| 352.02 | 371.07 | 387.13 | 403.21 | 422.13 | 440.07 |
| 352.04 | 371.15 | 388.01 | 404.01 | 422.17 | 440.16 |
| 352.06 | 371.16 | 388.05 | 404.05 | 423.01 | 440.19 |
| 352.11 | 371.18 | 388.08 | 404.07 | 423.03 | 440.22 |
| 352.14 | 371.19 | 388.10 | 404.08 | 423.04 | 441.03 |
| 352.16 | 372.02 | 388.17 | 404.11 | 424.07 | 441.05 |
| 352.17 | 372.18 | 389.01 | 404.13 | 424.09 | 441.09 |
| 352.18 | 372.19 | 389.02 | 404.15 | 424.09 | 441.15 |
| 352.20 | 373.07 | 389.02 | 404.19 | 425.03 | 441.18 |
| 352.21 | 373.07 | 389.03 | 405.07 | 425.04 | 441.21 |
| 353.02 | 373.08 | 389.04 | 405.13 | 425.05 | 442.04 |
| 353.09 | 373.11 | 389.06 | 405.20 | 425.06 | 442.04 |
| 354.02 | 373.15 | 389.07 | 406.01 | 425.10 | 442.06 |
| 354.03 | 373.16 | 389.09 | 406.02 | 425.10 | 442.07 |
| 354.09 | 373.19 | 389.19 | 406.03 | 425.11 | 442.14 |
| 354.10 | 373.20 | 390.01 | 406.10 | 425.13 | 443.04 |
| 354.11 | 374.02 | 390.06 | 406.15 | 425.16 | 443.07 |
| 354.12 | 374.02 | 390.09 | 406.15 | 425.20 | 443.09 |
| 354.16 | 374.09 | 390.10 | 406.20 | 426.04 | 443.10 |
| 354.16 | 374.12 | 390.17 | 406.20 | 426.05 | 443.12 |
| 354.20 | 374.13 | 390.22 | 406.22 | 426.06 | 444.03 |
| 355.02 | 374.14 | 390.22 | 407.12 | 426.07 | 444.06 |
| 355.06 | 374.16 | 391.03 | 408.04 | 426.16 | 444.07 |
| 355.11 | 374.18 | 391.04 | 408.06 | 426.17 | 444.10 |
| 355.17 | 375.04 | 391.07 | 408.09 | 427.05 | 444.11 |
| 355.18 | 375.14 | 391.13 | 408.12 | 427.09 | 444.17 |
| 356.02 | 375.20 | 391.14 | 408.17 | 427.10 | 444.20 |
| 356.11 | 375.21 | 391.17 | 408.21 | 427.15 | 445.03 |
| 356.16 | 376.01 | 391.18 | 408.22 | 427.19 | 445.06 |
| 356.18 | 376.02 | 391.20 | 408.22 | 427.21 | 445.07 |
| 356.19 | 376.03 | 392.01 | 409.06 | 428.07 | 445.08 |
| 356.22 | 376.03 | 392.04 | 409.10 | 428.09 | 445.08 |
| 357.06 | 376.09 | 392.05 | 409.12 | 428.10 | 445.13 |
| 357.14 | 376.15 | 392.06 | 409.13 | 428.17 | 445.20 |
| 357.17 | 376.19 | 392.09 | 409.15 | 428.19 | 445.20 |
| 358.01 | 377.10 | 392.09 | 409.16 | 429.07 | 446.02 |
| 358.04 | 377.12 | 392.11 | 409.18 | 429.12 | 446.07 |
| 358.09 | 377.14 | 392.18 | 410.01 | 429.16 | 446.12 |
| 358.09 | 377.14 | 392.19 | 410.06 | 429.18 | 446.12 |
| 358.10 | 377.21 | 393.04 | 410.08 | 429.19 | 446.12 |
| 358.14 | 378.02 | 393.07 | 410.10 | 430.16 | 446.15 |
| 359.01 | 378.03 | 393.08 | 410.12 | 430.16 | 446.19 |
| 359.03 | 378.04 | 393.11 | 410.17 | 430.17 | 447.02 |
| 359.11 | 378.06 | 393.12 | 410.18 | 430.21 | 447.03 |
| 359.17 | 378.06 | 393.19 | 410.19 | 431.01 | 448.04 |
| 359.19 | 378.12 | 394.02 | 410.20 | 431.03 | 448.05 |
| 359.20 | 378.15 | 394.07 | 410.22 | 431.06 | 448.05 |
| 360.04 | 378.20 | 394.09 | 411.01 | 431.09 | 448.08 |
| 360.12 | 379.03 | 394.11 | 411.07 | 431.14 | 449.01 |
| 360.19 | 379.07 | 394.13 | 411.11 | 431.16 | 449.09 |
| 360.20 | 379.09 | 394.16 | 411.21 | 431.17 | 449.13 |
| 361.02 | 379.13 | 394.21 | 412.04 | 431.18 | 449.15 |
| 361.03 | 379.15 | 395.01 | 412.05 | 431.20 | 449.17 |
| 361.05 | 380.01 | 395.02 | 412.17 | 431.22 | 449.19 |
| 361.05 | 380.02 | 395.06 | 412.22 | 432.01 | 449.19 |
| 361.06 | 380.04 | 395.07 | 413.03 | 432.02 | 449.21 |
| 361.09 | 380.05 | 395.09 | 413.07 | 432.04 | 449.22 |
| 361.14 | 381.05 | 395.13 | 413.08 | 432.07 | 450.09 |
| 361.17 | 381.05 | 395.16 | 413.10 | 432.09 | 450.12 |
| 361.20 | 381.06 | 395.20 | 413.16 | 432.10 | 450.15 |
| 361.21 | 381.09 | 395.22 | 413.18 | 432.11 | 451.05 |
| 361.22 | 381.11 | 396.03 | 413.21 | 432.18 | 451.07 |
| 362.04 | 381.12 | 396.04 | 413.21 | 432.20 | 451.10 |
| 362.06 | 381.12 | 396.07 | 414.03 | 433.05 | 451.16 |
| 362.07 | 381.12 | 396.07 | 414.11 | 433.09 | 451.18 |
| 362.11 | 382.03 | 396.10 | 414.12 | 433.10 | 451.19 |
| 362.15 | 382.05 | 396.14 | 414.16 | 433.13 | 452.01 |
| 362.19 | 382.05 | 397.02 | 414.16 | 433.14 | 452.03 |
| 363.01 | 382.08 | 397.04 | 414.19 | 433.16 | 452.08 |
| 363.01 | 382.09 | 397.09 | 414.20 | 433.20 | 452.10 |
| 363.02 | 382.12 | 397.11 | 415.02 | 433.21 | 452.11 |
| 363.06 | 382.17 | 397.11 | 415.04 | 434.01 | 452.14 |
| 363.06 | 382.20 | 397.14 | 415.06 | 434.08 | 452.22 |
| 363.07 | 383.05 | 397.18 | 415.08 | 434.09 | 453.01 |
| 363.10 | 383.06 | 397.21 | 415.09 | 434.10 | 453.03 |
| 363.21 | 383.12 | 397.22 | 415.10 | 434.11 | 453.04 |
| 363.22 | 383.15 | 398.01 | 415.11 | 434.12 | 453.09 |
| 364.01 | 383.16 | 398.02 | 415.16 | 434.15 | 453.14 |
| 364.06 | 383.17 | 398.07 | 416.06 | 434.16 | 453.15 |
| 364.12 | 383.21 | 398.11 | 416.11 | 434.16 | 453.20 |

| | | | | | |
|---|---|---|---|---|---|
| 453.20 | 470.14 | 487.15 | 506.19 | 523.23 | 544.03 |
| 453.21 | 470.16 | 487.17 | 507.02 | 524.03 | 544.11 |
| 454.01 | 470.20 | 487.19 | 507.04 | 524.03 | 544.13 |
| 454.07 | 471.02 | 488.02 | 507.06 | 524.04 | 544.14 |
| 454.10 | 471.04 | 488.13 | 507.09 | 524.07 | 544.16 |
| 454.11 | 471.12 | 489.01 | 507.12 | 524.13 | 544.22 |
| 454.13 | 471.20 | 489.10 | 507.14 | 524.14 | 545.06 |
| 454.14 | 472.13 | 489.11 | 507.15 | 524.16 | 545.10 |
| 454.18 | 472.18 | 489.14 | 507.18 | 525.01 | 545.10 |
| 454.21 | 473.05 | 489.19 | 508.04 | 525.02 | 545.11 |
| 455.01 | 473.09 | 490.03 | 508.07 | 525.03 | 545.14 |
| 455.03 | 473.11 | 490.13 | 508.11 | 525.19 | 545.15 |
| 455.07 | 473.11 | 490.18 | 508.12 | 525.22 | 546.04 |
| 455.11 | 474.04 | 491.02 | 508.18 | 526.03 | 546.06 |
| 455.14 | 474.04 | 491.04 | 508.21 | 526.06 | 546.08 |
| 455.14 | 474.08 | 491.06 | 509.01 | 526.09 | 546.15 |
| 455.15 | 474.11 | 491.07 | 509.03 | 526.10 | 546.21 |
| 456.02 | 475.08 | 491.09 | 509.04 | 526.12 | 547.02 |
| 456.08 | 475.10 | 491.12 | 509.06 | 526.12 | 547.05 |
| 456.12 | 475.12 | 491.20 | 509.08 | 526.16 | 547.11 |
| 456.15 | 475.14 | 492.01 | 509.10 | 526.20 | 547.15 |
| 457.01 | 475.18 | 492.08 | 509.12 | 527.01 | 547.18 |
| 457.01 | 475.21 | 492.10 | 509.13 | 527.04 | 547.21 |
| 457.01 | 475.21 | 492.11 | 509.13 | 527.04 | 548.01 |
| 457.04 | 475.22 | 492.12 | 509.19 | 527.07 | 548.04 |
| 457.13 | 476.01 | 492.13 | 510.04 | 527.09 | 548.12 |
| 457.16 | 476.05 | 492.14 | 510.05 | 527.10 | 548.12 |
| 457.19 | 476.07 | 492.20 | 510.10 | 527.10 | 548.17 |
| 458.02 | 476.07 | 493.02 | 510.14 | 527.13 | 548.21 |
| 458.04 | 476.08 | 493.14 | 510.19 | 527.14 | 549.02 |
| 458.06 | 476.08 | 493.18 | 511.07 | 527.17 | 550.03 |
| 459.04 | 476.10 | 493.20 | 511.11 | 528.07 | 550.03 |
| 459.09 | 476.12 | 493.21 | 511.22 | 528.08 | 550.08 |
| 459.11 | 476.12 | 494.03 | 512.04 | 528.09 | 550.12 |
| 460.01 | 476.13 | 494.07 | 512.07 | 528.11 | 551.10 |
| 460.04 | 476.16 | 494.11 | 512.10 | 528.16 | 551.11 |
| 460.19 | 476.19 | 494.14 | 512.12 | 529.02 | 551.13 |
| 460.20 | 477.01 | 495.11 | 513.09 | 529.04 | 551.14 |
| 460.21 | 477.06 | 495.16 | 513.10 | 529.10 | 551.14 |
| 461.02 | 477.07 | 495.17 | 513.13 | 529.10 | 551.15 |
| 461.05 | 477.09 | 495.21 | 513.16 | 529.22 | 551.17 |
| 461.07 | 477.13 | 496.13 | 513.18 | 530.03 | 551.20 |
| 461.09 | 477.14 | 496.17 | 513.21 | 530.06 | 551.22 |
| 462.03 | 477.17 | 497.15 | 513.22 | 531.04 | 552.01 |
| 462.11 | 477.21 | 497.21 | 514.01 | 531.10 | 552.03 |
| 462.15 | 478.09 | 498.02 | 514.02 | 531.18 | 552.04 |
| 462.16 | 478.15 | 498.09 | 514.08 | 531.20 | 552.04 |
| 462.17 | 478.17 | 498.09 | 514.08 | 531.21 | 552.06 |
| 462.19 | 478.18 | 498.10 | 514.13 | 532.01 | 552.10 |
| 462.20 | 478.20 | 498.11 | 515.02 | 532.16 | 552.13 |
| 463.01 | 479.09 | 498.14 | 515.04 | 532.18 | 553.01 |
| 463.01 | 479.11 | 498.18 | 515.06 | 532.21 | 553.02 |
| 463.06 | 479.12 | 499.10 | 515.09 | 532.21 | 553.03 |
| 463.09 | 479.13 | 499.12 | 515.10 | 533.10 | 553.07 |
| 463.10 | 479.14 | 499.16 | 516.04 | 533.13 | 553.10 |
| 463.11 | 479.15 | 499.18 | 516.05 | 533.13 | 553.12 |
| 463.12 | 479.15 | 499.22 | 516.06 | 533.19 | 553.14 |
| 463.14 | 479.16 | 500.07 | 516.12 | 534.10 | 553.19 |
| 463.17 | 479.17 | 500.08 | 516.16 | 534.12 | 554.03 |
| 463.18 | 479.18 | 500.09 | 516.17 | 534.13 | 554.11 |
| 463.19 | 479.19 | 500.10 | 516.19 | 534.14 | 554.15 |
| 463.20 | 479.21 | 500.13 | 516.22 | 534.15 | 554.19 |
| 463.20 | 480.07 | 500.13 | 517.01 | 534.19 | 555.01 |
| 464.01 | 480.10 | 500.16 | 517.04 | 534.21 | 555.02 |
| 464.02 | 480.11 | 501.04 | 517.07 | 535.01 | 555.03 |
| 464.04 | 480.12 | 501.05 | 517.08 | 535.07 | 555.04 |
| 464.04 | 480.12 | 501.10 | 517.12 | 535.09 | 555.07 |
| 464.04 | 480.16 | 501.11 | 517.14 | 535.14 | 555.08 |
| 464.05 | 480.18 | 501.14 | 517.18 | 535.17 | 555.10 |
| 464.06 | 480.20 | 501.18 | 517.21 | 536.03 | 555.16 |
| 464.08 | 481.04 | 501.21 | 518.01 | 536.06 | 555.19 |
| 464.08 | 481.10 | 501.22 | 518.03 | 536.09 | 555.20 |
| 464.11 | 481.14 | 502.03 | 518.04 | 536.11 | 555.21 |
| 464.16 | 481.15 | 502.03 | 518.11 | 536.11 | 556.01 |
| 464.16 | 481.19 | 502.07 | 518.21 | 536.12 | 556.03 |
| 464.22 | 481.21 | 502.11 | 519.01 | 536.15 | 556.06 |
| 465.05 | 482.05 | 502.15 | 519.05 | 537.01 | 556.09 |
| 465.10 | 482.06 | 502.19 | 519.07 | 537.06 | 556.10 |
| 465.18 | 482.13 | 502.20 | 519.09 | 537.17 | 556.11 |
| 465.19 | 482.13 | 502.20 | 519.13 | 537.19 | 556.12 |
| 465.20 | 482.15 | 502.22 | 519.13 | 537.21 | 556.16 |
| 466.04 | 482.17 | 503.01 | 519.16 | 538.09 | 556.17 |
| 466.07 | 482.18 | 503.03 | 520.01 | 538.17 | 556.18 |
| 466.09 | 483.02 | 503.05 | 520.01 | 538.19 | 556.18 |
| 466.13 | 483.18 | 503.09 | 520.02 | 539.03 | 556.20 |
| 466.16 | 483.20 | 503.10 | 520.05 | 539.04 | 556.20 |
| 466.17 | 483.21 | 503.11 | 520.08 | 539.09 | 556.21 |
| 467.05 | 484.01 | 503.12 | 520.10 | 539.10 | 557.01 |
| 467.07 | 484.05 | 503.15 | 520.10 | 539.13 | 557.09 |
| 467.09 | 484.10 | 503.17 | 520.12 | 539.18 | 557.10 |
| 467.10 | 484.15 | 504.03 | 520.14 | 540.05 | 557.11 |
| 467.15 | 484.18 | 504.03 | 520.20 | 540.07 | 557.11 |
| 467.16 | 484.21 | 504.06 | 521.02 | 540.13 | 557.15 |
| 467.17 | 485.06 | 504.10 | 521.03 | 541.04 | 557.16 |
| 467.20 | 485.08 | 504.11 | 521.05 | 541.07 | 557.16 |
| 467.21 | 485.12 | 504.11 | 521.06 | 541.09 | 557.17 |
| 468.04 | 485.17 | 504.19 | 521.08 | 541.12 | 557.17 |
| 468.05 | 485.18 | 504.22 | 521.13 | 541.14 | 557.18 |
| 468.07 | 486.01 | 505.02 | 521.16 | 541.17 | 557.21 |
| 468.11 | 486.05 | 505.06 | 521.22 | 541.17 | 557.21 |
| 468.18 | 486.05 | 505.09 | 522.04 | 541.17 | 557.22 |
| 468.21 | 486.08 | 505.17 | 522.05 | 541.21 | 557.22 |
| 469.01 | 486.12 | 505.19 | 522.13 | 542.02 | 558.02 |
| 469.04 | 486.22 | 505.21 | 522.15 | 542.07 | 558.05 |
| 469.04 | 487.01 | 506.04 | 522.18 | 542.09 | 558.06 |
| 469.09 | 487.05 | 506.07 | 522.18 | 542.20 | 558.07 |
| 469.15 | 487.06 | 506.09 | 522.19 | 543.05 | 558.09 |
| 469.20 | 487.07 | 506.11 | 522.22 | 543.08 | 558.10 |
| 469.22 | 487.07 | 506.14 | 523.08 | 543.17 | 558.12 |
| 470.05 | 487.08 | 506.17 | 523.10 | 543.19 | 558.14 |
| 470.07 | 487.10 | 506.18 | 523.15 | 544.01 | 558.15 |

| | | | | | |
|---|---|---|---|---|---|
| 558.21 | 571.05 | 587.14 | 609.13 | 628.07 | 644.21 |
| 558.21 | 571.06 | 587.16 | 609.16 | 628.15 | 645.03 |
| 558.21 | 571.07 | 587.19 | 609.19 | 628.18 | 645.08 |
| 558.22 | 571.07 | 588.03 | 610.03 | 628.22 | 645.09 |
| 559.02 | 571.08 | 588.05 | 610.05 | 629.04 | 645.14 |
| 559.04 | 571.10 | 588.08 | 610.15 | 629.07 | 645.15 |
| 559.05 | 571.10 | 588.10 | 610.15 | 630.02 | 645.22 |
| 559.06 | 571.11 | 588.13 | 610.16 | 630.03 | 646.01 |
| 559.06 | 571.12 | 588.16 | 610.17 | 630.05 | 646.02 |
| 559.09 | 571.12 | 588.20 | 610.21 | 630.06 | 646.04 |
| 559.10 | 571.14 | 588.21 | 611.02 | 630.13 | 646.06 |
| 559.11 | 571.15 | 589.02 | 611.08 | 630.13 | 646.07 |
| 559.13 | 571.21 | 589.06 | 611.10 | 630.14 | 646.08 |
| 559.14 | 572.03 | 589.09 | 611.14 | 630.15 | 646.09 |
| 559.14 | 572.05 | 589.14 | 611.15 | 630.17 | 646.14 |
| 559.17 | 572.06 | 589.16 | 611.21 | 630.18 | 646.19 |
| 559.18 | 572.06 | 589.16 | 612.01 | 630.20 | 646.22 |
| 559.20 | 572.16 | 589.20 | 612.02 | 631.01 | 647.01 |
| 560.01 | 572.17 | 589.22 | 612.03 | 631.06 | 647.01 |
| 560.03 | 572.18 | 590.01 | 612.04 | 631.07 | 647.04 |
| 560.05 | 572.22 | 590.08 | 612.14 | 631.10 | 647.06 |
| 560.07 | 573.09 | 590.09 | 612.18 | 631.13 | 647.07 |
| 560.07 | 573.10 | 590.11 | 612.20 | 631.13 | 647.08 |
| 560.12 | 573.13 | 590.11 | 613.05 | 631.14 | 647.15 |
| 560.15 | 573.14 | 590.12 | 613.12 | 631.16 | 647.19 |
| 560.17 | 573.16 | 590.14 | 613.16 | 631.20 | 648.02 |
| 560.18 | 573.19 | 590.15 | 613.18 | 631.22 | 648.03 |
| 561.01 | 573.21 | 591.02 | 613.19 | 632.02 | 648.04 |
| 561.04 | 573.22 | 591.05 | 613.20 | 632.12 | 648.08 |
| 561.10 | 574.02 | 591.07 | 613.22 | 632.16 | 648.15 |
| 561.15 | 574.07 | 591.10 | 614.03 | 632.16 | 648.19 |
| 561.18 | 575.09 | 591.13 | 614.11 | 632.18 | 649.03 |
| 562.01 | 575.10 | 591.16 | 614.13 | 632.19 | 649.05 |
| 562.10 | 576.01 | 591.19 | 614.16 | 632.20 | 649.09 |
| 562.13 | 576.01 | 592.10 | 614.17 | 632.21 | 649.14 |
| 562.13 | 576.03 | 592.12 | 614.17 | 633.01 | 649.19 |
| 562.17 | 576.08 | 593.01 | 614.22 | 633.03 | 649.19 |
| 562.18 | 576.09 | 593.10 | 615.04 | 633.05 | 649.21 |
| 563.02 | 576.14 | 593.18 | 615.06 | 633.06 | 650.01 |
| 563.03 | 576.16 | 593.19 | 615.08 | 633.07 | 650.02 |
| 563.05 | 577.04 | 594.01 | 615.18 | 633.07 | 650.08 |
| 563.08 | 577.06 | 594.06 | 616.02 | 633.10 | 650.09 |
| 563.08 | 577.09 | 594.09 | 616.04 | 633.11 | 650.12 |
| 563.09 | 577.11 | 594.14 | 616.08 | 633.12 | 650.14 |
| 563.10 | 577.13 | 594.19 | 616.16 | 633.13 | 650.17 |
| 563.13 | 577.14 | 594.21 | 616.21 | 633.13 | 650.18 |
| 563.13 | 577.17 | 595.07 | 616.22 | 633.15 | 650.21 |
| 563.14 | 577.18 | 596.09 | 617.05 | 633.22 | 651.09 |
| 563.17 | 577.21 | 597.02 | 617.10 | 634.02 | 651.12 |
| 563.20 | 577.22 | 597.05 | 617.14 | 634.03 | 651.18 |
| 564.01 | 578.05 | 597.09 | 617.14 | 634.04 | 651.20 |
| 564.02 | 578.07 | 597.10 | 617.20 | 634.04 | 652.03 |
| 564.05 | 578.12 | 597.12 | 618.16 | 634.05 | 652.04 |
| 564.07 | 578.18 | 597.20 | 618.20 | 634.06 | 652.10 |
| 564.09 | 578.21 | 598.09 | 618.21 | 634.08 | 652.13 |
| 564.10 | 579.02 | 598.11 | 618.22 | 634.09 | 652.17 |
| 564.12 | 579.03 | 598.11 | 619.04 | 634.10 | 653.03 |
| 564.13 | 579.06 | 598.16 | 619.09 | 634.18 | 653.06 |
| 565.01 | 579.08 | 598.18 | 619.11 | 634.19 | 653.08 |
| 565.03 | 579.10 | 599.04 | 619.13 | 634.21 | 653.11 |
| 565.06 | 579.16 | 599.12 | 619.14 | 635.02 | 653.12 |
| 565.17 | 579.17 | 599.13 | 619.16 | 635.03 | 653.14 |
| 565.21 | 579.20 | 599.17 | 619.19 | 635.05 | 653.15 |
| 566.01 | 579.21 | 599.21 | 620.02 | 635.09 | 653.17 |
| 566.04 | 580.04 | 599.22 | 620.07 | 635.15 | 653.22 |
| 566.09 | 580.10 | 600.08 | 620.10 | 635.17 | 654.01 |
| 566.10 | 580.11 | 600.11 | 620.16 | 635.17 | 654.12 |
| 566.12 | 580.12 | 600.16 | 620.18 | 635.21 | 654.18 |
| 566.13 | 580.14 | 600.18 | 620.21 | 636.01 | 654.19 |
| 566.15 | 580.20 | 600.21 | 620.21 | 636.13 | 654.19 |
| 566.16 | 580.21 | 601.01 | 621.07 | 636.19 | 655.08 |
| 566.21 | 580.22 | 601.06 | 621.08 | 637.01 | 655.14 |
| 566.21 | 581.03 | 601.07 | 621.14 | 637.07 | 655.16 |
| 566.21 | 581.06 | 601.09 | 621.15 | 637.08 | 655.19 |
| 567.02 | 581.10 | 601.09 | 622.03 | 637.14 | 655.21 |
| 567.03 | 581.13 | 601.11 | 622.10 | 637.19 | 656.06 |
| 567.05 | 581.15 | 601.12 | 622.16 | 637.22 | 656.11 |
| 567.05 | 581.17 | 601.17 | 622.18 | 638.03 | 656.17 |
| 567.06 | 581.18 | 601.17 | 622.21 | 638.06 | 657.02 |
| 567.08 | 582.03 | 601.20 | 623.01 | 638.10 | 658.05 |
| 567.08 | 582.04 | 601.21 | 623.04 | 638.12 | 658.06 |
| 567.09 | 582.07 | 601.22 | 623.08 | 638.13 | 658.09 |
| 567.12 | 582.09 | 601.22 | 623.09 | 639.01 | 658.10 |
| 567.15 | 582.11 | 602.08 | 623.14 | 639.02 | 659.02 |
| 567.15 | 582.13 | 602.15 | 623.16 | 639.04 | 659.03 |
| 567.20 | 582.16 | 602.18 | 623.18 | 639.12 | 659.06 |
| 568.02 | 582.17 | 602.21 | 623.21 | 639.16 | 659.12 |
| 568.04 | 582.21 | 603.05 | 624.05 | 639.21 | 659.17 |
| 568.05 | 583.04 | 604.01 | 624.06 | 639.22 | 659.18 |
| 568.09 | 583.06 | 604.04 | 624.08 | 640.02 | 659.19 |
| 568.10 | 583.10 | 604.04 | 624.18 | 640.09 | 659.20 |
| 568.12 | 583.15 | 605.02 | 624.21 | 640.11 | 660.02 |
| 568.14 | 583.18 | 605.04 | 624.22 | 640.17 | 660.05 |
| 568.21 | 583.19 | 605.07 | 624.22 | 641.01 | 660.07 |
| 569.03 | 583.20 | 606.10 | 625.01 | 641.07 | 660.10 |
| 569.05 | 584.01 | 606.17 | 625.01 | 641.17 | 660.11 |
| 569.08 | 584.05 | 606.20 | 625.03 | 641.22 | 660.13 |
| 569.11 | 585.04 | 607.01 | 625.04 | 642.01 | 660.17 |
| 569.12 | 585.04 | 607.08 | 625.04 | 642.03 | 660.18 |
| 569.17 | 585.07 | 607.11 | 626.03 | 642.08 | 660.18 |
| 570.08 | 585.08 | 607.16 | 626.04 | 642.08 | 660.20 |
| 570.09 | 586.02 | 607.17 | 626.06 | 642.10 | 660.21 |
| 570.11 | 586.06 | 607.19 | 626.11 | 643.03 | 661.02 |
| 570.13 | 586.11 | 607.22 | 626.12 | 643.11 | 661.05 |
| 570.15 | 586.13 | 608.01 | 627.01 | 644.01 | 661.07 |
| 570.18 | 586.14 | 608.02 | 627.02 | 644.01 | 661.08 |
| 570.21 | 586.16 | 608.10 | 627.12 | 644.03 | 661.14 |
| 570.22 | 586.17 | 608.14 | 627.16 | 644.03 | 661.18 |
| 571.01 | 586.22 | 608.21 | 627.19 | 644.06 | 661.21 |
| 571.02 | 587.01 | 609.06 | 627.20 | 644.12 | 662.02 |
| 571.02 | 587.07 | 609.08 | 628.03 | 644.16 | 662.06 |

| | | | | | |
|---|---|---|---|---|---|
| 662.07 | 677.06 | 695.13 | 710.18 | 730.10 | 749.09 |
| 662.10 | 677.06 | 695.14 | 710.19 | 730.11 | 749.16 |
| 662.11 | 677.09 | 695.19 | 710.20 | 730.15 | 749.20 |
| 662.15 | 677.10 | 695.20 | 711.02 | 730.20 | 749.22 |
| 662.21 | 678.01 | 696.01 | 711.07 | 730.21 | 750.02 |
| 663.03 | 678.04 | 696.02 | 711.10 | 731.13 | 750.05 |
| 663.05 | 678.09 | 696.04 | 711.11 | 731.16 | 750.08 |
| 663.06 | 678.10 | 696.22 | 711.13 | 731.19 | 750.09 |
| 663.07 | 678.11 | 697.01 | 711.20 | 732.01 | 750.11 |
| 663.08 | 678.11 | 697.05 | 712.01 | 732.06 | 750.11 |
| 663.15 | 678.12 | 697.13 | 712.01 | 732.11 | 750.12 |
| 663.16 | 678.20 | 697.15 | 712.07 | 732.12 | 750.16 |
| 663.20 | 678.20 | 697.16 | 712.12 | 732.19 | 750.21 |
| 663.20 | 679.03 | 697.20 | 712.19 | 732.19 | 751.01 |
| 663.22 | 679.10 | 698.05 | 713.03 | 732.21 | 751.01 |
| 664.02 | 679.12 | 698.10 | 713.10 | 733.15 | 751.05 |
| 664.02 | 679.12 | 698.16 | 713.18 | 733.15 | 751.06 |
| 664.03 | 679.15 | 698.17 | 713.19 | 733.16 | 751.09 |
| 664.06 | 679.17 | 699.08 | 713.21 | 733.18 | 751.16 |
| 664.09 | 679.21 | 699.10 | 713.21 | 733.21 | 751.16 |
| 664.12 | 679.22 | 699.12 | 713.22 | 734.02 | 751.19 |
| 664.17 | 680.05 | 699.16 | 715.04 | 734.05 | 751.21 |
| 664.18 | 680.05 | 699.21 | 715.08 | 734.05 | 752.07 |
| 664.20 | 680.06 | 700.01 | 715.10 | 734.07 | 752.08 |
| 665.01 | 680.08 | 700.06 | 716.01 | 734.08 | 752.16 |
| 665.07 | 680.11 | 700.07 | 716.01 | 735.05 | 752.19 |
| 665.08 | 680.12 | 700.11 | 716.07 | 735.08 | 753.01 |
| 665.08 | 680.13 | 700.12 | 716.11 | 736.05 | 753.02 |
| 665.11 | 680.15 | 700.13 | 716.15 | 736.07 | 753.10 |
| 665.15 | 680.15 | 700.18 | 716.22 | 736.11 | 753.12 |
| 665.17 | 680.21 | 700.19 | 717.02 | 737.01 | 753.13 |
| 665.22 | 681.01 | 701.01 | 717.05 | 737.04 | 754.02 |
| 666.03 | 681.05 | 701.07 | 717.08 | 737.05 | 754.04 |
| 666.06 | 681.12 | 701.09 | 717.12 | 737.05 | 754.08 |
| 666.08 | 681.15 | 701.10 | 717.15 | 737.09 | 754.09 |
| 666.09 | 681.17 | 701.11 | 717.17 | 737.11 | 754.15 |
| 666.10 | 681.18 | 701.12 | 717.17 | 737.12 | 754.16 |
| 666.12 | 682.01 | 701.14 | 717.20 | 737.16 | 754.21 |
| 666.15 | 682.05 | 701.17 | 717.22 | 737.20 | 754.22 |
| 666.16 | 682.07 | 701.20 | 718.05 | 738.01 | 755.01 |
| 666.21 | 682.09 | 702.01 | 718.10 | 738.09 | 755.02 |
| 667.01 | 682.14 | 702.16 | 718.15 | 738.10 | 755.02 |
| 667.02 | 682.14 | 702.17 | 718.17 | 738.11 | 755.07 |
| 667.04 | 682.16 | 703.05 | 718.18 | 738.14 | 755.11 |
| 667.06 | 682.18 | 703.08 | 718.20 | 738.19 | 755.13 |
| 667.11 | 682.20 | 703.10 | 719.02 | 739.06 | 755.14 |
| 667.12 | 683.01 | 703.11 | 719.05 | 739.19 | 755.15 |
| 667.14 | 683.01 | 703.13 | 719.08 | 739.20 | 755.18 |
| 667.15 | 683.06 | 703.21 | 719.10 | 739.21 | 755.18 |
| 667.17 | 683.10 | 704.01 | 719.21 | 740.05 | 756.04 |
| 667.20 | 683.14 | 704.03 | 720.05 | 740.10 | 756.11 |
| 667.20 | 683.17 | 704.05 | 720.18 | 740.12 | 756.14 |
| 668.01 | 683.18 | 704.11 | 720.20 | 740.12 | 756.15 |
| 668.07 | 683.19 | 704.11 | 720.21 | 740.16 | 756.17 |
| 668.11 | 684.04 | 704.12 | 721.06 | 740.17 | 756.17 |
| 668.13 | 684.07 | 704.13 | 721.12 | 740.18 | 756.19 |
| 668.13 | 684.21 | 704.14 | 721.14 | 740.19 | 756.20 |
| 668.18 | 685.11 | 704.16 | 722.01 | 741.04 | 756.21 |
| 669.02 | 685.16 | 704.22 | 722.02 | 741.06 | 757.01 |
| 669.02 | 685.21 | 705.03 | 722.04 | 741.10 | 757.04 |
| 669.05 | 686.02 | 705.07 | 722.06 | 741.14 | 757.06 |
| 669.16 | 686.06 | 705.11 | 722.07 | 741.15 | 757.11 |
| 669.18 | 686.09 | 705.14 | 722.08 | 741.20 | 757.17 |
| 669.20 | 686.10 | 705.17 | 722.11 | 742.03 | 757.17 |
| 670.04 | 686.12 | 705.18 | 723.02 | 742.07 | 757.20 |
| 670.05 | 686.14 | 705.18 | 723.05 | 742.08 | 757.21 |
| 670.08 | 686.16 | 705.20 | 723.07 | 742.22 | 757.22 |
| 670.20 | 687.01 | 706.07 | 724.01 | 743.04 | 758.02 |
| 671.05 | 687.03 | 706.14 | 724.04 | 743.07 | 758.04 |
| 671.07 | 688.04 | 706.17 | 724.07 | 743.09 | 758.10 |
| 671.09 | 688.09 | 706.18 | 724.11 | 743.16 | 758.11 |
| 671.11 | 689.02 | 706.20 | 724.12 | 743.18 | 758.13 |
| 671.14 | 689.05 | 707.02 | 724.16 | 743.22 | 758.17 |
| 671.15 | 689.08 | 707.04 | 724.16 | 744.09 | 758.19 |
| 671.16 | 689.12 | 707.09 | 724.19 | 744.10 | 759.01 |
| 671.18 | 689.15 | 707.10 | 725.03 | 744.11 | 759.01 |
| 671.19 | 689.18 | 707.11 | 725.14 | 744.16 | 759.02 |
| 672.01 | 689.20 | 707.13 | 725.20 | 744.18 | 759.04 |
| 672.01 | 690.03 | 707.16 | 725.22 | 744.20 | 759.10 |
| 672.04 | 690.08 | 707.17 | 726.05 | 744.22 | 759.12 |
| 672.05 | 690.09 | 708.04 | 726.06 | 745.04 | 759.19 |
| 672.10 | 690.13 | 708.10 | 726.08 | 745.09 | 760.03 |
| 672.12 | 690.15 | 708.13 | 726.13 | 745.15 | 760.03 |
| 672.15 | 691.11 | 708.14 | 726.15 | 745.16 | 760.08 |
| 673.02 | 691.12 | 708.14 | 726.16 | 745.17 | 760.09 |
| 673.05 | 691.13 | 708.15 | 726.17 | 745.18 | 760.10 |
| 673.10 | 691.17 | 708.15 | 726.20 | 746.01 | 760.14 |
| 673.11 | 691.19 | 708.18 | 727.01 | 746.03 | 760.15 |
| 674.06 | 691.20 | 708.19 | 727.02 | 746.06 | 760.16 |
| 674.07 | 691.20 | 708.20 | 727.05 | 746.08 | 760.19 |
| 674.09 | 692.02 | 708.22 | 727.05 | 746.09 | 760.22 |
| 674.14 | 692.16 | 709.01 | 727.10 | 746.10 | 761.02 |
| 674.16 | 692.17 | 709.02 | 727.11 | 746.14 | 761.03 |
| 674.18 | 692.19 | 709.03 | 727.13 | 746.17 | 761.04 |
| 675.06 | 692.20 | 709.05 | 727.17 | 746.20 | 761.08 |
| 675.08 | 693.03 | 709.08 | 727.19 | 747.01 | 761.16 |
| 675.11 | 693.07 | 709.10 | 727.22 | 747.04 | 761.18 |
| 675.14 | 693.09 | 709.12 | 728.01 | 747.07 | 761.20 |
| 675.17 | 693.11 | 709.13 | 728.07 | 747.10 | 762.04 |
| 676.01 | 693.11 | 709.15 | 728.09 | 747.11 | 762.06 |
| 676.04 | 693.18 | 709.20 | 728.15 | 747.14 | 762.08 |
| 676.05 | 693.21 | 710.02 | 728.22 | 747.16 | 762.09 |
| 676.06 | 693.22 | 710.03 | 729.04 | 747.17 | 762.21 |
| 676.08 | 693.22 | 710.05 | 729.09 | 747.18 | 763.01 |
| 676.10 | 694.02 | 710.07 | 729.10 | 747.19 | 763.05 |
| 676.12 | 694.09 | 710.08 | 729.12 | 748.01 | 763.06 |
| 676.13 | 694.14 | 710.08 | 729.12 | 748.04 | 763.08 |
| 676.18 | 694.16 | 710.09 | 729.17 | 748.11 | 763.18 |
| 676.19 | 695.03 | 710.11 | 730.03 | 748.19 | 763.19 |
| 676.19 | 695.05 | 710.16 | 730.07 | 749.02 | 763.22 |
| 677.04 | 695.10 | | | 749.04 | 764.02 |

| | | | | | |
|---|---|---|---|---|---|
| 764.04 | animation | 401.02 | 118.03 | 629.21 | 083.08 |
| 764.08 | 070.02 | 404.17 | 133.15 | 631.18 | 087.09 |
| 764.09 | 287.08 | 408.10 | 146.14 | 633.18 | 091.03 |
| anecdote | 498.08 | 409.19 | 151.06 | 634.12 | 099.17 |
| 680.01 | 599.01 | 410.21 | 155.01 | 646.19 | 106.17 |
| anecdotes | 599.01 | 417.16 | 155.12 | 651.01 | 128.01 |
| 498.10 | ankle | 421.08 | 163.14 | 660.01 | 129.13 |
| anew | 106.12 | 477.21 | 168.10 | 662.21 | 136.12 |
| 441.22 | 113.03 | 539.07 | 172.19 | 667.18 | 143.05 |
| 513.18 | 318.11 | 542.14 | 173.01 | 670.04 | 148.11 |
| 724.07 | annie's | 544.11 | 176.19 | 670.17 | 149.11 |
| angel | 697.02 | 544.12 | 178.09 | 674.15 | 149.12 |
| 024.09 | annihilate | 551.08 | 180.05 | 675.16 | 151.15 |
| 223.18 | 106.17 | 559.21 | 192.07 | 679.11 | 155.05 |
| 370.22 | 645.19 | 575.04 | 194.16 | 681.11 | 159.19 |
| 446.12 | annihilated | 589.12 | 195.07 | 683.09 | 161.01 |
| 479.21 | 182.22 | 591.05 | 210.06 | 689.06 | 164.02 |
| 548.03 | 311.11 | 604.18 | 211.21 | 690.20 | 168.09 |
| 638.19 | 605.02 | 611.19 | 214.20 | 692.11 | 169.04 |
| 675.02 | 755.09 | 613.04 | 217.13 | 694.08 | 171.01 |
| angel's | annihilate | 613.05 | 218.20 | 697.12 | 172.08 |
| 239.15 | 752.10 | 624.08 | 220.14 | 698.06 | 175.03 |
| angels | anniversary | 624.22 | 228.11 | 707.12 | 177.04 |
| 124.19 | 478.05 | 625.01 | 236.12 | 708.14 | 183.09 |
| 178.21 | 478.07 | 628.15 | 238.13 | 711.10 | 183.16 |
| 316.04 | announce | 648.19 | 247.04 | 713.01 | 184.12 |
| 390.14 | 150.17 | 652.14 | 249.16 | 716.17 | 188.19 |
| anger | 295.20 | 669.17 | 250.16 | 717.10 | 197.11 |
| 261.19 | 355.03 | 672.16 | 254.07 | 720.08 | 198.01 |
| 264.10 | 416.02 | 672.17 | 266.16 | 733.09 | 203.17 |
| 286.01 | announced | 693.08 | 272.20 | 738.05 | 204.21 |
| 359.22 | 002.04 | 694.08 | 279.09 | 739.05 | 211.07 |
| 382.10 | 027.03 | 696.14 | 283.07 | 741.03 | 220.17 |
| 425.11 | 323.16 | 698.01 | 288.17 | 751.12 | 228.10 |
| 529.04 | 339.07 | 700.21 | 292.16 | 762.03 | 231.19 |
| 576.15 | 364.16 | 702.18 | 293.16 | answering | 237.09 |
| 590.17 | 448.02 | 706.18 | 298.07 | 127.09 | 256.13 |
| 600.08 | 456.08 | 708.01 | 299.16 | 132.06 | 261.18 |
| 615.16 | 674.06 | 712.20 | 310.18 | 205.17 | 264.10 |
| 683.18 | announcement | 731.02 | 314.21 | 372.12 | 265.04 |
| angered | 594.08 | 744.01 | 320.15 | 497.07 | 270.05 |
| 245.20 | 635.06 | 744.16 | 329.10 | answers | 276.02 |
| angle | announcing | 745.10 | 338.13 | 508.02 | 284.01 |
| 513.10 | 305.12 | 750.06 | 341.12 | anticipate | 286.01 |
| angrily | 644.11 | 757.13 | 353.20 | 220.02 | 288.01 |
| 127.04 | 656.01 | 758.12 | 363.22 | 520.07 | 299.13 |
| 167.01 | annoy | another's | 365.13 | anticipated | 300.02 |
| 230.19 | 443.02 | 289.04 | 368.05 | 143.17 | 302.17 |
| 250.04 | 591.13 | anguish | 374.15 | 225.05 | 306.02 |
| 321.11 | 686.14 | 682.11 | 375.19 | 682.15 | 307.06 |
| 352.21 | 717.08 | answer | 382.16 | 718.22 | 327.16 |
| 472.10 | 739.20 | 002.07 | 387.07 | anticipating | 336.14 |
| 624.06 | annoyance | 022.20 | 394.06 | 213.05 | 343.18 |
| angry | 215.10 | 029.10 | 396.20 | 456.16 | 345.05 |
| 061.01 | 571.04 | 041.09 | 398.10 | 594.15 | 345.19 |
| 110.06 | 659.05 | 047.15 | 406.17 | anticipation | 350.06 |
| 150.12 | 705.18 | 054.08 | 412.08 | 578.03 | 352.02 |
| 178.22 | annoyances | 088.15 | 428.04 | 734.10 | 352.11 |
| 212.08 | 264.02 | 103.06 | 434.02 | anticipations | 365.06 |
| 223.03 | 301.08 | 121.07 | 440.04 | 314.11 | 377.04 |
| 255.08 | annoyed | 141.07 | 451.22 | 448.09 | 385.05 |
| 257.20 | 051.13 | 170.14 | 452.13 | antipathy | 386.22 |
| 287.08 | 134.06 | 171.19 | 453.10 | 148.09 | 397.07 |
| 306.09 | 675.16 | 173.22 | 455.20 | 181.15 | 411.15 |
| 329.01 | annoying | 184.20 | 457.11 | 442.02 | 412.07 |
| 435.02 | 387.16 | 204.21 | 458.01 | 475.14 | 419.15 |
| 447.01 | annum | 236.18 | 461.05 | 726.05 | 422.10 |
| 497.20 | 047.18 | 246.12 | 464.14 | antique | 432.09 |
| 499.07 | anon | 249.07 | 471.18 | 039.12 | 435.19 |
| 554.13 | 063.22 | 251.12 | 472.04 | anxiety | 440.20 |
| 554.14 | 519.13 | 257.19 | 479.04 | 296.21 | 443.01 |
| 581.03 | another | 265.01 | 482.11 | 302.02 | 445.03 |
| 590.16 | 005.16 | 265.02 | 484.03 | 367.20 | 450.17 |
| 600.05 | 013.14 | 267.15 | 484.21 | 397.07 | 457.06 |
| 605.07 | 016.18 | 306.09 | 486.13 | 521.03 | 462.10 |
| 621.03 | 023.17 | 313.01 | 488.05 | anxious | 464.09 |
| 708.12 | 032.19 | 353.18 | 489.10 | 010.09 | 470.18 |
| 722.02 | 033.18 | 354.21 | 490.14 | 101.14 | 478.06 |
| 741.03 | 040.01 | 363.04 | 496.01 | 170.05 | 481.06 |
| 753.18 | 040.01 | 376.04 | 500.22 | 261.13 | 481.06 |
| 754.12 | 045.01 | 402.15 | 504.08 | 263.13 | 482.21 |
| anguish | 046.10 | 427.03 | 513.17 | 345.20 | 483.12 |
| 060.20 | 056.01 | 429.03 | 514.10 | 375.15 | 488.06 |
| 166.09 | 077.14 | 430.05 | 521.12 | 457.01 | 492.09 |
| 258.19 | 134.16 | 444.02 | 523.04 | 459.11 | 494.14 |
| 282.03 | 138.04 | 480.06 | 524.01 | 587.04 | 497.15 |
| 286.20 | 170.17 | 539.21 | 528.21 | 684.05 | 503.21 |
| 356.14 | 177.13 | 564.06 | 535.12 | 738.14 | 510.01 |
| 370.19 | 178.04 | 580.07 | 537.02 | 756.16 | 510.22 |
| 407.05 | 185.17 | 591.04 | 538.05 | anxiously | 520.09 |
| 601.15 | 200.08 | 623.06 | 543.11 | 115.07 | 521.03 |
| 613.08 | 213.10 | 627.07 | 544.19 | 277.16 | 524.14 |
| 641.14 | 216.10 | 641.18 | 546.14 | 523.19 | 527.19 |
| 653.18 | 225.03 | 677.15 | 551.13 | 623.04 | 533.03 |
| 732.06 | 237.21 | 684.18 | 560.11 | 710.12 | 563.14 |
| anguished | 246.04 | 696.09 | 561.06 | 750.06 | 570.13 |
| 510.04 | 249.07 | 702.19 | 569.07 | any | 573.15 |
| 749.05 | 254.10 | 706.08 | 570.16 | 002.16 | 583.13 |
| animal | 290.19 | 742.19 | 579.05 | 005.11 | 588.11 |
| 018.09 | 304.17 | 748.13 | 580.01 | 005.20 | 593.01 |
| 068.01 | 305.06 | answered | 586.09 | 007.05 | 602.03 |
| 237.12 | 311.02 | 020.08 | 591.19 | 017.21 | 602.19 |
| 291.07 | 320.08 | 031.01 | 592.15 | 019.22 | 607.08 |
| 682.18 | 324.04 | 033.19 | 593.16 | 022.18 | 619.18 |
| animals | 334.02 | 037.08 | 604.10 | 032.11 | 624.19 |
| 012.01 | 346.12 | 064.14 | 606.05 | 045.08 | 631.06 |
| animated | 347.05 | 093.16 | 612.21 | 054.09 | 636.19 |
| 146.15 | 347.22 | 097.17 | 618.17 | 061.16 | 641.08 |
| 727.20 | 349.02 | 102.05 | 620.05 | 065.03 | 651.02 |
| 741.22 | 368.08 | 105.19 | 623.18 | 067.08 | 664.19 |
| 742.02 | 385.16 | 111.21 | 624.07 | 076.15 | 665.06 |

670.07
670.09
671.17
685.02
685.07
691.05
705.06
705.08
708.06
721.22
723.04
729.02
732.14
739.14
741.07
741.21
746.18
751.19
754.07
758.08
764.10

**anybody**
037.06
075.20
390.19
511.19
535.08
536.08
600.13
614.07
617.02
621.04
745.09

**anyone**
147.08

**anything**
041.08
064.16
074.05
075.19
077.19
092.03
153.15
153.16
214.18
214.21
223.13
271.05
271.10
279.05
286.10
293.08
331.13
343.21
391.16
399.07
407.05
420.18
512.09
512.21
533.08
569.12
608.09
665.02
673.07
707.06
720.07
734.03
743.02
749.13
751.16
754.20

**anywhere**
136.21
151.04
166.21
386.06
413.02
490.16
581.06
671.01

**apart**
119.10

**apartment**
006.20
017.04
210.10
240.12
304.16
312.16
322.20
456.13
475.19
498.18
514.03
552.09
568.16
634.14
635.21
645.01
704.18
751.04

**apartments**
320.22

**apathetic**
271.14
629.08

**apathy**
263.11
588.18

**ape**
494.08

**apology**
218.07
257.22
305.15

**appal**
279.07

**appalled**
225.12
377.18

**appalling**
316.20
339.07

**apparent**
060.09
584.03

**apparently**
019.09
150.06
178.04
221.05
249.06
255.11
313.02
368.12
400.08
415.01
426.17
443.19
539.12
599.11
674.02
724.06
749.03

**apparition**
244.15
319.02
691.15

**appeal**
236.15
361.16
531.19

**appealing**
022.18
228.07
438.11

**appear**
253.14
277.06
439.21
588.09
728.10

**appearance**
026.04
040.07
128.03
148.02
150.01
286.06
333.05
351.09
432.05
487.03
496.06
639.16
655.14
665.11
730.09
730.10
741.12

**appeared**
005.06
016.20
033.01
054.05
097.02
144.19
188.05
213.11
243.21
247.21
305.13
325.07
330.17
351.16
362.09
371.01
403.16
419.08
442.21
503.03
508.16
528.14
534.12
548.09
556.17
560.07
569.14
603.21
640.14
652.15
663.20
677.10
726.19
740.13
744.09

**appears**
125.01
619.10

**appellation**
058.07
347.12

**appetite**
129.19
136.15
323.18

**applause**
119.19

**apple**
716.06
737.06

**apple-sauce**
128.06

**apples**
076.19
206.07

**applied**
062.05
157.16
523.09
609.20
676.05

**applying**
290.04

**appointed**
131.06
378.01
483.16

**apppeared**
719.01

**appreciate**
009.07
067.08
686.07

**approach**
374.02
485.08
532.04
568.13
577.21
586.15
594.16
652.18
701.08
756.04
762.20

**approached**
027.15
038.06
053.22
170.02
259.16
309.13
355.04
426.14
437.10
606.20
616.20
626.03
664.22
675.10
723.02

**approaching**
165.10
188.06
207.02
362.04
441.07
519.16
523.13
674.13
730.04
752.01

**approbation**
251.19

**appropriate**
044.12
680.10

**approval**
682.20

**approve**
251.13
251.15

**approved**
559.18

**april**
414.03
737.03

**apron**
020.05
064.01
416.12
507.18
639.03

**apt**
426.06

**arabian**
431.14

**arc**
323.09

**arch**
006.16
042.15
728.10

**arched**
124.13

**archer**
140.17

**architect**
004.14

**ardent**
328.06
413.17

**ardently**
223.11

**ardour**
508.11

**are**
001.10
003.15
004.16
012.10
012.14
012.16
016.05
018.12
018.15
020.11
022.15
025.21
029.12
030.03
031.19
031.20
035.19
041.02
044.18
052.08
056.08
056.09
059.22
064.07
069.02
070.18
072.02
072.21
073.08
085.08
097.11
103.07
111.22
114.08
117.16
117.19
121.03
123.13
123.14
124.08
124.21
125.01
127.16
127.16
127.19
135.16
136.21
137.04
142.05
151.03
151.04
152.10
152.20
153.03
155.01
155.08
155.10
158.09
169.22
172.18
174.07
174.21
175.03
175.18
178.08
179.12
179.12
180.18
183.18
183.19
190.10
190.11
192.05
194.17
204.01
206.01
208.06
208.07
208.15
216.16
219.14
219.15
220.05
227.11
228.16
228.19
230.19
233.17
235.03
235.04
236.09
238.09
239.15
239.21
239.23
249.11
249.12
250.11
250.13
251.21
252.02
252.04
252.19
252.22
255.22
257.10
259.02
259.02
261.16
262.06
264.09
264.20
264.20
272.17
273.05
276.01
276.02
276.14
276.16
276.18
277.01
277.04
277.18
284.20
285.03
287.07
287.07
287.09
287.09
287.10
292.17
299.13
302.20
303.06
303.07
306.17
311.13
316.16
317.02
322.16
329.04
336.13
339.12
341.06
341.09
341.10
342.11
343.13
345.16
347.20
357.01
357.16
358.18
358.20
359.06
361.05
361.07
365.11
366.12
366.17
372.09
387.19
388.19
391.17
394.19
394.20
395.03
395.06
406.14
421.06
427.05
427.15
427.17
427.18
427.19
428.05
428.07
434.04
434.10
435.18
437.08
450.03
450.04
451.16
464.10
468.17
476.10
479.02
480.01
481.21
482.09
486.20
487.19
488.07
492.06
494.12
494.14
495.15
497.01
499.04
502.01
502.03
505.01
511.03
519.06
519.15
520.03
520.05
520.08
523.04
524.02
526.13
531.16
533.02
534.07
534.14
537.06
539.19
540.09
541.22
542.01
545.03
545.03
545.10
551.03
560.21
570.16
571.06
579.11
581.03
586.06
586.19
587.14
588.05
588.05
590.05
590.15
593.08
593.11
593.14
599.21
600.03
602.04
603.08
606.03
606.15
606.18
608.01
608.10
613.02
613.19
613.20
614.06
616.07
617.06
618.15
627.21
632.15
634.17
638.20
647.09
648.07
648.08
665.21
669.10
670.17
677.02
678.14
685.04
685.19
691.01
691.04
697.13
706.20
707.05
707.08
712.22
718.07
722.08
723.01
728.06
728.07
730.08
731.15
733.10
734.05
742.13
742.17
748.11
748.14
752.15
752.21
753.21
755.09
760.13
762.01
762.04
762.14
762.19

**area**
017.01

**argue**
255.03
285.05
421.19

**argued**
346.15

**argument**
231.07
682.05

**arguments**
304.15

**arid**
229.14

**arising**
351.21
387.20

**arm**
044.03
051.21
052.04
059.07
084.01
094.13
100.16

| | | | | | |
|---|---|---|---|---|---|
| 156.04 | arrival | 064.04 | 150.13 | 229.15 | 332.11 |
| 237.21 | 002.10 | 064.05 | 152.06 | 229.16 | 332.15 |
| 249.05 | 131.10 | 064.05 | 153.07 | 231.09 | 333.03 |
| 265.18 | 160.17 | 065.02 | 154.10 | 231.20 | 333.04 |
| 275.01 | 441.07 | 065.14 | 154.14 | 232.20 | 334.18 |
| 305.02 | 448.11 | 066.09 | 154.14 | 234.16 | 334.19 |
| 358.13 | 507.03 | 067.02 | 154.16 | 235.21 | 335.11 |
| 361.15 | 508.22 | 067.09 | 159.15 | 236.12 | 335.11 |
| 395.22 | 639.04 | 068.02 | 159.15 | 237.11 | 336.04 |
| 399.03 | 640.21 | 071.05 | 159.19 | 237.20 | 336.05 |
| 406.05 | 659.15 | 071.19 | 159.19 | 237.20 | 336.06 |
| 458.06 | arrive | 071.19 | 160.02 | 240.04 | 336.06 |
| 483.13 | 622.06 | 073.11 | 160.02 | 241.02 | 336.07 |
| 519.16 | arrived | 073.22 | 163.10 | 243.09 | 336.08 |
| 526.19 | 015.06 | 073.22 | 164.07 | 243.20 | 336.13 |
| 532.09 | 017.03 | 074.18 | 164.19 | 243.20 | 336.14 |
| 538.10 | 165.19 | 074.18 | 164.20 | 245.09 | 338.11 |
| 563.20 | 295.19 | 075.05 | 164.20 | 246.02 | 339.07 |
| 570.05 | 328.04 | 077.20 | 165.06 | 247.09 | 340.13 |
| 594.07 | 412.12 | 077.21 | 167.11 | 248.01 | 341.10 |
| 605.17 | 445.13 | 077.21 | 168.01 | 248.01 | 344.13 |
| 626.07 | 637.07 | 078.19 | 169.09 | 248.03 | 344.13 |
| 634.19 | 692.22 | 078.19 | 169.11 | 248.03 | 345.11 |
| 645.12 | arriving | 079.04 | 169.12 | 248.20 | 345.18 |
| 657.01 | 585.10 | 080.07 | 170.06 | 248.20 | 345.19 |
| 704.22 | arrogance | 081.07 | 170.22 | 250.06 | 346.04 |
| 724.04 | 145.10 | 081.12 | 173.21 | 251.18 | 346.05 |
| arm's | arrows | 082.01 | 177.13 | 251.19 | 346.10 |
| 245.04 | 105.21 | 082.02 | 177.14 | 252.22 | 346.22 |
| arm-chair | art | 082.18 | 179.03 | 252.22 | 347.21 |
| 007.03 | 029.19 | 082.18 | 179.03 | 253.08 | 348.01 |
| 556.18 | 049.18 | 083.14 | 179.13 | 253.08 | 349.05 |
| 667.12 | 112.15 | 084.14 | 179.13 | 254.13 | 350.02 |
| arms | 249.19 | 084.14 | 180.18 | 254.13 | 350.02 |
| 011.11 | 468.02 | 085.15 | 180.18 | 259.03 | 350.08 |
| 062.06 | artery | 085.15 | 180.20 | 259.04 | 350.19 |
| 077.18 | 399.21 | 086.04 | 180.20 | 260.15 | 351.05 |
| 094.17 | artful | 086.05 | 181.07 | 261.09 | 351.10 |
| 143.14 | 148.03 | 088.22 | 181.07 | 262.19 | 352.05 |
| 157.20 | article | 090.01 | 181.13 | 264.01 | 353.10 |
| 165.01 | 384.05 | 090.06 | 181.14 | 265.04 | 354.22 |
| 211.14 | 385.15 | 091.17 | 182.03 | 265.04 | 355.01 |
| 254.01 | articles | 092.05 | 183.04 | 266.03 | 356.05 |
| 267.01 | 321.09 | 092.05 | 183.08 | 267.09 | 356.20 |
| 286.19 | 692.03 | 093.19 | 183.10 | 268.03 | 357.21 |
| 290.12 | 700.12 | 093.19 | 185.02 | 270.10 | 357.21 |
| 355.19 | artillery | 094.03 | 186.05 | 270.13 | 358.12 |
| 365.09 | 035.16 | 094.03 | 186.05 | 270.19 | 359.04 |
| 367.01 | artist's | 094.11 | 187.18 | 272.13 | 359.04 |
| 367.11 | 492.20 | 095.19 | 187.22 | 272.13 | 360.04 |
| 441.03 | as | 097.19 | 187.22 | 277.05 | 362.08 |
| 450.13 | 002.02 | 097.19 | 189.01 | 280.17 | 362.15 |
| 468.05 | 002.04 | 097.21 | 189.01 | 280.17 | 364.08 |
| 554.12 | 002.09 | 098.01 | 189.11 | 281.07 | 365.03 |
| 576.09 | 002.09 | 099.17 | 190.04 | 282.09 | 365.03 |
| 615.03 | 003.08 | 099.17 | 190.04 | 282.15 | 365.14 |
| 652.01 | 004.13 | 099.22 | 190.07 | 283.15 | 365.14 |
| 710.16 | 006.21 | 099.22 | 191.04 | 283.15 | 369.12 |
| 747.16 | 007.10 | 100.14 | 191.12 | 286.13 | 370.09 |
| arms-length | 007.11 | 100.14 | 191.13 | 290.03 | 370.09 |
| 753.08 | 008.14 | 104.15 | 192.04 | 291.22 | 370.17 |
| army | 008.14 | 108.12 | 192.04 | 295.14 | 370.17 |
| 213.22 | 010.22 | 108.12 | 192.19 | 296.09 | 370.18 |
| 259.04 | 011.01 | 110.15 | 192.19 | 296.15 | 372.13 |
| arn | 012.02 | 111.11 | 193.05 | 297.21 | 374.07 |
| 720.01 | 013.14 | 111.11 | 193.12 | 299.01 | 374.07 |
| arose | 014.08 | 111.13 | 193.20 | 299.02 | 375.14 |
| 089.04 | 015.03 | 116.04 | 194.14 | 299.03 | 375.19 |
| 281.18 | 019.22 | 118.05 | 194.21 | 302.18 | 376.04 |
| around | 020.21 | 118.05 | 194.22 | 304.10 | 376.12 |
| 188.17 | 023.20 | 118.19 | 196.02 | 305.04 | 376.21 |
| 296.07 | 024.01 | 119.04 | 196.02 | 307.19 | 376.22 |
| 307.07 | 025.11 | 120.01 | 196.13 | 307.21 | 383.04 |
| 321.09 | 025.16 | 121.22 | 196.14 | 308.05 | 383.04 |
| 351.16 | 026.17 | 122.11 | 197.10 | 308.09 | 387.05 |
| 407.06 | 028.15 | 123.08 | 197.15 | 308.10 | 390.08 |
| 737.16 | 029.15 | 123.14 | 198.12 | 308.21 | 390.09 |
| arrange | 030.12 | 124.02 | 198.13 | 310.21 | 390.18 |
| 123.11 | 031.04 | 124.03 | 198.15 | 310.22 | 391.08 |
| 150.18 | 031.04 | 124.03 | 199.11 | 313.12 | 391.10 |
| 254.10 | 032.05 | 125.02 | 199.14 | 314.20 | 392.03 |
| 304.16 | 032.18 | 125.03 | 202.09 | 315.08 | 392.12 |
| 354.10 | 033.03 | 126.20 | 202.12 | 316.02 | 393.09 |
| 448.05 | 033.03 | 127.11 | 202.12 | 316.03 | 393.13 |
| 542.17 | 038.12 | 127.12 | 205.09 | 316.03 | 394.13 |
| 672.07 | 039.09 | 128.05 | 205.09 | 317.13 | 394.19 |
| 689.11 | 039.09 | 130.22 | 205.15 | 319.09 | 394.19 |
| 737.12 | 042.07 | 131.04 | 207.07 | 319.09 | 395.10 |
| arranged | 042.14 | 132.21 | 207.13 | 320.03 | 395.11 |
| 470.14 | 042.14 | 133.01 | 207.13 | 320.03 | 395.15 |
| 697.11 | 044.05 | 133.04 | 207.21 | 320.03 | 396.12 |
| arrangement | 044.05 | 136.18 | 209.11 | 320.07 | 397.16 |
| 314.01 | 046.16 | 136.21 | 211.19 | 322.04 | 398.05 |
| 643.12 | 047.17 | 137.07 | 212.06 | 325.09 | 398.13 |
| 700.10 | 047.21 | 138.04 | 213.03 | 325.22 | 398.13 |
| arrangements | 049.04 | 138.05 | 214.11 | 326.11 | 399.04 |
| 392.07 | 051.03 | 139.09 | 215.02 | 328.02 | 399.16 |
| 419.12 | 052.14 | 140.12 | 217.11 | 328.02 | 400.13 |
| arrest | 053.16 | 141.11 | 218.20 | 328.07 | 400.13 |
| 480.21 | 054.18 | 141.12 | 218.22 | 328.08 | 400.18 |
| 731.11 | 054.18 | 141.19 | 220.01 | 329.02 | 401.19 |
| arrested | 057.14 | 143.07 | 220.02 | 329.12 | 401.19 |
| 165.21 | 057.14 | 143.07 | 220.06 | 329.12 | 402.14 |
| 212.20 | 058.13 | 143.17 | 220.06 | 329.22 | 403.15 |
| 295.08 | 059.06 | 143.20 | 220.22 | 330.01 | 403.21 |
| 315.07 | 060.05 | 143.20 | 221.09 | 330.04 | 404.09 |
| 523.13 | 060.11 | 144.19 | 221.09 | 331.02 | 404.09 |
| arresting | 062.09 | 146.19 | 223.11 | 331.03 | 404.19 |
| 235.14 | 062.10 | 148.07 | 223.11 | 331.13 | 405.19 |
| 645.12 | 062.20 | 148.10 | 223.16 | 332.04 | 406.04 |
| | 062.21 | | 224.07 | 332.11 | 406.04 |

| | | | | | |
|---|---|---|---|---|---|
| 406.05 | 511.18 | 587.07 | 678.16 | ascertained | 246.16 |
| 406.06 | 511.18 | 589.03 | 679.14 | 379.05 | 247.03 |
| 410.07 | 511.20 | 589.04 | 680.18 | ascertaining | 256.04 |
| 414.02 | 512.10 | 589.04 | 681.04 | 368.11 | 277.03 |
| 414.02 | 512.11 | 590.15 | 682.12 | ascribed | 280.04 |
| 414.07 | 514.13 | 592.04 | 683.05 | 051.13 | 296.19 |
| 415.14 | 516.08 | 592.17 | 687.02 | 205.13 | 298.04 |
| 415.14 | 516.09 | 593.15 | 689.09 | ash | 310.03 |
| 417.05 | 519.05 | 597.16 | 689.10 | 373.14 | 311.18 |
| 417.15 | 519.06 | 598.16 | 692.19 | ashamed | 316.19 |
| 418.06 | 520.21 | 600.05 | 693.12 | 042.13 | 329.09 |
| 418.06 | 520.22 | 600.05 | 694.02 | 123.04 | 330.18 |
| 418.09 | 520.22 | 600.12 | 694.04 | 146.21 | 374.20 |
| 421.07 | 522.03 | 603.21 | 694.04 | 159.02 | 376.04 |
| 421.07 | 522.13 | 605.11 | 695.02 | 223.06 | 379.16 |
| 423.02 | 523.12 | 605.19 | 697.12 | 396.09 | 389.12 |
| 425.10 | 523.12 | 606.20 | 697.12 | 503.21 | 406.03 |
| 429.03 | 524.13 | 608.12 | 699.18 | 511.05 | 412.03 |
| 429.21 | 524.19 | 610.21 | 700.21 | 562.12 | 416.09 |
| 430.04 | 524.19 | 611.05 | 701.11 | 599.14 | 418.17 |
| 431.22 | 525.18 | 611.07 | 701.11 | 650.05 | 427.06 |
| 431.22 | 527.06 | 611.17 | 702.06 | 711.09 | 438.07 |
| 433.06 | 527.06 | 611.17 | 702.11 | ashes | 439.08 |
| 436.18 | 527.20 | 612.15 | 704.02 | 061.10 | 445.20 |
| 438.16 | 528.03 | 613.09 | 704.03 | 390.22 | 461.02 |
| 438.21 | 528.11 | 613.09 | 704.07 | 408.04 | 464.01 |
| 439.03 | 528.12 | 613.21 | 704.13 | 513.22 | 468.09 |
| 439.18 | 528.17 | 616.17 | 705.13 | 531.17 | 472.01 |
| 441.09 | 536.03 | 618.08 | 708.09 | 532.20 | 478.17 |
| 443.07 | 536.03 | 619.05 | 708.09 | 743.14 | 483.01 |
| 443.09 | 536.13 | 619.07 | 711.13 | aside | 486.09 |
| 445.11 | 536.13 | 619.07 | 711.13 | 134.12 | 489.07 |
| 446.07 | 537.08 | 621.14 | 712.11 | 158.11 | 490.20 |
| 449.08 | 538.13 | 623.02 | 713.10 | 225.13 | 496.11 |
| 449.14 | 539.01 | 629.03 | 715.06 | 235.21 | 500.16 |
| 450.13 | 541.05 | 630.07 | 717.07 | 252.09 | 504.21 |
| 450.13 | 541.12 | 630.07 | 717.19 | 281.22 | 512.13 |
| 450.15 | 541.12 | 630.09 | 720.09 | 455.20 | 519.16 |
| 450.15 | 541.21 | 631.05 | 722.14 | 482.12 | 528.07 |
| 450.21 | 542.04 | 632.13 | 723.06 | 508.19 | 531.07 |
| 451.14 | 542.04 | 635.22 | 723.06 | 553.11 | 534.01 |
| 451.16 | 542.09 | 635.22 | 724.12 | 583.06 | 534.14 |
| 452.12 | 542.19 | 636.03 | 725.01 | 686.02 | 540.15 |
| 452.21 | 543.14 | 636.03 | 725.01 | 747.11 | 542.17 |
| 452.22 | 543.14 | 636.09 | 725.15 | 757.15 | 544.17 |
| 453.19 | 544.02 | 636.09 | 726.13 | ask | 550.05 |
| 455.11 | 544.18 | 638.21 | 726.13 | 020.12 | 558.14 |
| 456.16 | 544.21 | 639.15 | 727.03 | 029.15 | 563.16 |
| 458.08 | 545.15 | 639.15 | 728.19 | 031.12 | 566.16 |
| 459.05 | 546.02 | 643.05 | 729.20 | 077.02 | 576.02 |
| 460.21 | 546.17 | 643.11 | 732.19 | 092.10 | 590.12 |
| 461.03 | 546.17 | 644.19 | 733.03 | 102.07 | 593.01 |
| 463.03 | 546.17 | 646.05 | 733.03 | 121.20 | 601.19 |
| 463.04 | 546.17 | 646.05 | 734.19 | 123.05 | 603.17 |
| 464.02 | 546.20 | 646.15 | 735.07 | 180.12 | 624.06 |
| 464.02 | 547.16 | 647.12 | 737.04 | 184.11 | 627.10 |
| 464.03 | 547.17 | 647.12 | 737.04 | 209.04 | 628.16 |
| 470.07 | 552.22 | 647.14 | 738.04 | 223.16 | 633.09 |
| 470.08 | 555.15 | 647.14 | 738.04 | 267.10 | 633.16 |
| 470.08 | 556.11 | 647.18 | 738.14 | 269.08 | 634.14 |
| 473.04 | 556.14 | 647.18 | 738.14 | 284.15 | 658.12 |
| 475.08 | 558.08 | 651.16 | 739.07 | 307.02 | 659.20 |
| 475.08 | 558.09 | 652.18 | 739.22 | 343.21 | 665.02 |
| 478.09 | 559.13 | 652.18 | 739.22 | 345.12 | 670.21 |
| 478.10 | 559.13 | 653.21 | 740.06 | 395.08 | 670.22 |
| 479.18 | 559.20 | 654.18 | 741.16 | 439.18 | 674.04 |
| 479.19 | 560.08 | 656.10 | 741.17 | 455.05 | 675.13 |
| 480.14 | 560.15 | 659.07 | 744.05 | 475.06 | 677.11 |
| 481.07 | 561.10 | 659.08 | 745.08 | 477.14 | 683.15 |
| 482.06 | 561.20 | 660.21 | 745.22 | 491.13 | 692.13 |
| 482.07 | 561.20 | 664.03 | 746.09 | 523.23 | 721.01 |
| 483.21 | 562.06 | 664.03 | 746.17 | 569.16 | 733.08 |
| 484.01 | 562.06 | 665.09 | 746.17 | 580.18 | 738.03 |
| 484.13 | 562.09 | 665.10 | 746.22 | 658.04 | 744.03 |
| 484.13 | 562.10 | 665.13 | 747.17 | 669.19 | 753.20 |
| 484.19 | 562.17 | 665.13 | 748.08 | 669.22 | 760.12 |
| 485.09 | 562.17 | 666.05 | 748.15 | 702.07 | 761.07 |
| 485.14 | 562.18 | 666.13 | 750.22 | 702.08 | asking |
| 487.05 | 563.12 | 667.02 | 752.02 | 739.04 | 073.13 |
| 490.02 | 564.07 | 667.03 | 753.06 | 740.19 | 078.09 |
| 491.11 | 564.17 | 667.10 | 753.06 | 741.19 | 097.11 |
| 492.14 | 564.18 | 667.10 | 753.07 | askance | 552.04 |
| 492.15 | 566.02 | 667.11 | 753.11 | 159.22 | 597.21 |
| 493.08 | 566.02 | 667.11 | 755.10 | asked | 699.08 |
| 494.03 | 566.17 | 667.18 | 755.10 | 011.18 | 725.19 |
| 494.05 | 566.17 | 667.18 | 757.04 | 020.04 | 749.21 |
| 494.05 | 569.18 | 668.12 | 759.14 | 020.10 | asleep |
| 494.10 | 570.02 | 669.06 | 760.02 | 022.18 | 046.06 |
| 494.10 | 570.08 | 669.06 | 760.09 | 037.07 | 057.18 |
| 495.17 | 570.08 | 669.14 | 760.10 | 052.08 | 107.17 |
| 496.11 | 570.21 | 669.14 | 760.11 | 056.07 | 191.17 |
| 497.03 | 570.21 | 670.19 | 761.15 | 071.08 | 365.11 |
| 498.04 | 571.05 | 671.13 | 762.03 | 076.13 | 372.18 |
| 498.04 | 571.06 | 671.13 | 762.03 | 095.02 | 393.11 |
| 498.20 | 571.06 | 671.18 | 762.11 | 097.16 | 450.19 |
| 501.14 | 571.06 | 671.18 | 763.01 | 140.09 | 454.19 |
| 503.16 | 571.06 | 672.02 | 763.08 | 141.20 | 528.06 |
| 504.06 | 571.07 | 672.03 | ascended | 151.04 | 540.05 |
| 504.14 | 571.07 | 673.03 | 566.10 | 158.22 | 558.06 |
| 504.14 | 572.03 | 673.09 | ascending | 165.09 | 570.05 |
| 505.01 | 572.07 | 673.12 | 010.03 | 170.21 | 591.16 |
| 505.01 | 572.08 | 673.12 | 295.05 | 171.18 | 591.18 |
| 506.07 | 577.02 | 674.10 | ascent | 172.05 | 630.09 |
| 507.03 | 578.08 | 674.18 | 320.20 | 180.04 | aspect |
| 507.08 | 579.05 | 675.01 | ascertain | 182.02 | 007.09 |
| 507.14 | 580.06 | 675.06 | 189.16 | 184.01 | 149.07 |
| 507.14 | 583.13 | 675.06 | 362.05 | 210.05 | 154.15 |
| 508.06 | 583.13 | 675.11 | 530.10 | 212.04 | 177.22 |
| 508.10 | 584.01 | 676.09 | 738.14 | 217.11 | 216.10 |
| 508.17 | 584.01 | 676.09 | 746.18 | 228.07 | 266.07 |
| 508.17 | 585.11 | 678.13 | | 239.17 | 299.11 |

| | | | | | |
|---|---|---|---|---|---|
| 313.05 | 238.18 | 074.08 | 189.03 | 290.16 | 403.21 |
| 351.19 | 327.07 | 075.14 | 190.16 | 291.06 | 407.15 |
| 420.22 | 339.10 | 077.06 | 190.20 | 291.14 | 408.06 |
| 444.19 | 619.21 | 077.16 | 190.21 | 291.18 | 408.14 |
| 451.03 | 753.05 | 078.02 | 192.14 | 292.10 | 409.15 |
| 487.06 | assured | 079.02 | 193.20 | 292.21 | 411.03 |
| 514.09 | 110.10 | 079.19 | 193.21 | 293.15 | 413.11 |
| 655.12 | 510.10 | 081.19 | 194.18 | 293.19 | 415.15 |
| 676.20 | 554.17 | 082.08 | 199.22 | 294.11 | 415.20 |
| 727.06 | 639.08 | 082.09 | 202.05 | 297.11 | 416.07 |
| 732.03 | assuredly | 083.15 | 203.11 | 298.05 | 418.15 |
| 738.21 | 026.16 | 084.05 | 204.22 | 298.11 | 418.16 |
| aspirations | assuring | 088.14 | 205.06 | 302.13 | 419.09 |
| 293.20 | 320.02 | 090.12 | 208.06 | 302.20 | 419.14 |
| aspiring | astir | 091.17 | 209.03 | 303.08 | 420.19 |
| 413.18 | 063.08 | 092.06 | 210.14 | 304.21 | 421.09 |
| ass | astonished | 092.13 | 212.08 | 305.13 | 421.21 |
| 187.16 | 072.15 | 092.17 | 213.11 | 306.15 | 422.08 |
| assailant | 157.16 | 093.03 | 214.10 | 306.20 | 429.12 |
| 050.10 | 316.09 | 094.09 | 214.13 | 308.01 | 430.05 |
| assassin | 460.04 | 097.15 | 214.15 | 309.11 | 431.13 |
| 394.14 | 698.14 | 098.19 | 218.14 | 309.18 | 432.06 |
| assault | astonishing | 098.20 | 219.06 | 310.16 | 432.11 |
| 010.21 | 013.18 | 099.04 | 219.07 | 311.02 | 432.13 |
| 026.05 | astonishment | 099.08 | 219.10 | 313.07 | 432.17 |
| assembly | 286.08 | 099.19 | 220.03 | 313.18 | 432.22 |
| 050.06 | 367.08 | 100.13 | 221.16 | 313.21 | 433.16 |
| assent | 382.10 | 100.18 | 222.05 | 314.08 | 434.02 |
| 061.18 | 434.19 | 101.10 | 222.11 | 314.11 | 434.07 |
| 585.03 | 439.17 | 102.05 | 224.12 | 316.09 | 434.16 |
| assert | 586.22 | 102.18 | 224.13 | 317.11 | 434.18 |
| 205.18 | 635.01 | 104.14 | 225.07 | 318.16 | 435.11 |
| 345.09 | 691.07 | 105.04 | 225.12 | 320.01 | 435.12 |
| asserted | asunder | 105.11 | 226.10 | 320.06 | 438.16 |
| 284.04 | 170.06 | 106.08 | 226.10 | 321.01 | 438.18 |
| 372.06 | 262.21 | 106.21 | 227.10 | 321.20 | 438.22 |
| 536.21 | 361.20 | 107.14 | 231.04 | 322.01 | 440.16 |
| 735.02 | 582.16 | 107.18 | 232.01 | 322.05 | 441.05 |
| asserting | 718.21 | 108.11 | 232.08 | 325.10 | 441.13 |
| 305.17 | asylum | 109.03 | 232.10 | 327.06 | 442.01 |
| assertion | 401.02 | 110.01 | 232.20 | 327.16 | 443.14 |
| 137.04 | at | 110.14 | 233.01 | 328.04 | 444.03 |
| 227.11 | 004.08 | 111.07 | 233.03 | 328.11 | 444.15 |
| 298.02 | 004.11 | 113.02 | 234.04 | 330.07 | 446.13 |
| 339.12 | 005.06 | 115.11 | 234.09 | 330.16 | 446.19 |
| 441.11 | 005.14 | 117.10 | 234.13 | 331.18 | 448.07 |
| 491.14 | 005.16 | 117.11 | 235.06 | 331.20 | 450.08 |
| 590.06 | 007.06 | 117.14 | 235.09 | 335.13 | 450.09 |
| assertions | 008.11 | 117.16 | 236.21 | 338.19 | 451.14 |
| 528.17 | 008.18 | 117.20 | 237.09 | 338.22 | 451.21 |
| 567.07 | 008.21 | 117.21 | 237.10 | 339.05 | 452.10 |
| asses | 009.02 | 119.07 | 237.11 | 340.18 | 453.17 |
| 164.15 | 009.08 | 121.09 | 239.21 | 342.13 | 454.12 |
| asseverated | 010.13 | 124.05 | 241.05 | 346.07 | 455.03 |
| 044.04 | 013.02 | 124.07 | 242.04 | 349.04 | 456.12 |
| assiduity | 014.11 | 126.06 | 242.11 | 351.06 | 456.14 |
| 021.09 | 015.06 | 127.01 | 243.06 | 351.15 | 457.03 |
| assiduously | 015.20 | 129.20 | 243.13 | 352.08 | 457.16 |
| 155.21 | 017.03 | 131.21 | 243.16 | 352.18 | 458.02 |
| assist | 017.12 | 132.03 | 244.08 | 352.19 | 460.04 |
| 019.23 | 017.21 | 133.06 | 245.08 | 353.07 | 462.05 |
| 418.01 | 018.06 | 133.18 | 246.15 | 353.11 | 462.17 |
| 527.14 | 022.07 | 134.07 | 246.19 | 354.05 | 463.13 |
| assistance | 022.09 | 135.11 | 246.20 | 354.16 | 464.06 |
| 011.02 | 024.17 | 136.02 | 248.09 | 355.18 | 469.04 |
| 385.22 | 024.22 | 137.02 | 249.08 | 356.11 | 474.11 |
| 462.12 | 027.02 | 140.16 | 249.13 | 357.17 | 475.15 |
| 522.20 | 030.08 | 140.17 | 251.09 | 359.06 | 476.13 |
| 660.22 | 031.19 | 141.19 | 251.21 | 359.08 | 477.09 |
| 668.11 | 032.14 | 142.17 | 253.11 | 360.06 | 478.03 |
| assistant | 033.01 | 143.01 | 253.13 | 361.15 | 478.09 |
| 325.19 | 033.13 | 144.20 | 255.08 | 361.18 | 479.13 |
| assistants | 034.11 | 145.03 | 256.03 | 362.06 | 480.02 |
| 260.06 | 035.06 | 145.05 | 256.08 | 363.21 | 480.11 |
| assisting | 035.09 | 146.02 | 256.09 | 364.07 | 481.02 |
| 150.18 | 035.12 | 147.12 | 259.03 | 366.20 | 481.12 |
| associate | 035.21 | 147.14 | 260.09 | 367.10 | 483.05 |
| 459.09 | 039.15 | 147.20 | 260.16 | 367.22 | 483.14 |
| associated | 040.06 | 148.05 | 261.19 | 369.03 | 483.15 |
| 734.03 | 040.11 | 148.13 | 265.08 | 369.08 | 484.19 |
| associates | 046.10 | 150.10 | 265.21 | 371.08 | 486.19 |
| 470.17 | 049.01 | 152.05 | 266.06 | 372.03 | 487.02 |
| association | 049.07 | 152.16 | 267.03 | 373.03 | 487.21 |
| 057.04 | 049.14 | 152.22 | 267.13 | 373.13 | 487.22 |
| 282.08 | 050.12 | 154.01 | 269.10 | 374.01 | 488.22 |
| associations | 050.19 | 154.07 | 270.01 | 375.08 | 490.13 |
| 275.06 | 053.01 | 154.19 | 270.14 | 376.01 | 492.11 |
| 304.13 | 054.03 | 154.20 | 271.09 | 378.08 | 492.21 |
| 417.13 | 054.07 | 157.02 | 272.08 | 380.06 | 493.06 |
| 680.14 | 055.10 | 157.09 | 272.15 | 386.03 | 494.20 |
| 730.20 | 056.02 | 163.01 | 279.01 | 388.09 | 495.01 |
| assume | 056.13 | 165.13 | 279.03 | 389.13 | 495.15 |
| 430.01 | 057.07 | 165.20 | 280.07 | 390.04 | 496.17 |
| assumed | 058.20 | 166.09 | 281.10 | 390.06 | 496.19 |
| 266.07 | 059.03 | 167.09 | 281.16 | 390.07 | 500.14 |
| 316.10 | 059.04 | 167.19 | 282.06 | 390.17 | 501.17 |
| 409.06 | 059.05 | 171.03 | 282.09 | 391.16 | 502.02 |
| 495.14 | 060.11 | 173.22 | 282.10 | 392.04 | 502.21 |
| 603.04 | 060.15 | 176.11 | 282.21 | 393.03 | 503.04 |
| 724.07 | 061.01 | 177.04 | 283.02 | 393.09 | 504.16 |
| assuming | 061.02 | 177.08 | 284.02 | 393.15 | 505.15 |
| 021.18 | 061.20 | 180.08 | 285.15 | 394.02 | 505.17 |
| 254.16 | 063.03 | 180.10 | 285.17 | 395.03 | 505.20 |
| 457.19 | 064.07 | 181.15 | 285.20 | 395.14 | 506.04 |
| assurance | 065.12 | 186.04 | 286.20 | 397.06 | 507.13 |
| 335.17 | 065.22 | 186.06 | 286.21 | 397.08 | 507.14 |
| 371.15 | 066.05 | 186.08 | 288.06 | 398.13 | 507.19 |
| assurances | 066.20 | 186.14 | 289.10 | 400.15 | 509.16 |
| 462.14 | 067.08 | 188.12 | 289.21 | 400.19 | 509.19 |
| assure | 069.05 | 188.17 | 290.04 | 401.19 | 512.06 |
| 056.05 | 073.07 | 188.19 | | 401.20 | 512.12 |

| | | | | | |
|---|---|---|---|---|---|
| 512.21 | 636.01 | 720.12 | 422.02 | attribute | avoids |
| 513.15 | 636.16 | 725.17 | 541.15 | 026.18 | 572.09 |
| 514.07 | 637.07 | 727.08 | 547.03 | attributes | aw |
| 515.07 | 637.19 | 727.15 | 562.14 | 008.02 | 028.20 |
| 518.05 | 638.05 | 728.13 | 625.05 | atween | 187.19 |
| 518.22 | 638.08 | 728.20 | 680.02 | 696.15 | 187.20 |
| 519.02 | 639.10 | 729.01 | 706.16 | audacity | 191.01 |
| 519.10 | 640.14 | 730.05 | 726.02 | 355.12 | 193.15 |
| 524.20 | 640.15 | 731.02 | attempted | audible | 194.04 |
| 526.12 | 641.12 | 731.16 | 019.22 | 027.07 | 194.05 |
| 528.14 | 641.14 | 732.16 | 024.12 | 603.03 | 310.13 |
| 528.22 | 641.16 | 735.06 | 087.10 | audibly | 310.17 |
| 531.21 | 643.09 | 736.03 | 158.11 | 189.17 | 318.12 |
| 533.10 | 643.09 | 736.11 | 167.07 | 314.12 | 318.13 |
| 533.13 | 647.14 | 737.10 | 257.16 | 359.11 | 318.14 |
| 534.04 | 649.01 | 738.07 | 278.10 | audience | 318.15 |
| 534.06 | 649.05 | 738.18 | 283.16 | 430.22 | 318.16 |
| 538.14 | 649.07 | 739.14 | 357.05 | aught | 319.10 |
| 539.16 | 652.10 | 743.08 | 462.08 | 627.18 | 322.06 |
| 541.02 | 652.13 | 743.21 | 525.02 | august | 324.20 |
| 541.14 | 652.15 | 746.05 | 629.20 | 598.04 | 324.21 |
| 541.19 | 653.03 | 746.07 | 633.09 | 690.04 | 326.10 |
| 543.14 | 654.03 | 746.20 | 723.19 | aunt | 401.11 |
| 546.11 | 654.11 | 747.17 | attempting | 157.11 | 420.09 |
| 547.12 | 655.20 | 748.19 | 009.11 | 449.11 | 420.10 |
| 547.19 | 656.06 | 748.21 | 127.16 | 501.22 | 455.19 |
| 548.09 | 656.16 | 749.01 | 309.13 | 520.17 | 456.17 |
| 550.02 | 657.01 | 749.04 | 374.21 | 520.20 | 457.22 |
| 551.15 | 659.05 | 751.14 | attempts | 536.17 | 472.05 |
| 552.08 | 659.15 | 752.15 | 133.11 | 537.08 | 564.15 |
| 552.22 | 659.19 | 752.20 | 147.20 | aunt's | 564.18 |
| 553.19 | 661.13 | 755.04 | 623.02 | 449.03 | 691.03 |
| 555.06 | 662.15 | 755.13 | 664.08 | austere | 696.10 |
| 555.11 | 663.11 | 756.04 | 758.10 | 023.07 | 713.05 |
| 556.11 | 663.21 | 756.13 | attend | author | 719.10 |
| 557.18 | 664.08 | 758.10 | 234.05 | 166.01 | 719.10 |
| 558.08 | 664.19 | 758.19 | 379.12 | authoritative | 719.11 |
| 558.11 | 665.21 | 760.09 | 413.06 | 457.19 | 719.12 |
| 558.15 | 666.08 | 761.01 | 628.08 | authoritatively | 719.16 |
| 558.19 | 666.15 | 762.14 | attendance | 310.03 | 719.17 |
| 561.08 | 667.13 | 762.17 | 017.17 | authority | 719.19 |
| 562.08 | 667.21 | 763.02 | 143.05 | 087.07 | 719.20 |
| 562.14 | 668.06 | 763.03 | 288.15 | 294.09 | 720.08 |
| 563.01 | 668.18 | 763.07 | 408.18 | 641.03 | 758.18 |
| 564.05 | 669.04 | 763.13 | 600.01 | automatons | 761.09 |
| 565.16 | 670.07 | ate | 760.04 | 704.05 | aw'd |
| 565.19 | 670.21 | 070.01 | attendant | autumn | 193.15 |
| 566.11 | 671.12 | 111.13 | 495.19 | 515.02 | 319.10 |
| 567.11 | 671.18 | 233.07 | 532.05 | 644.21 | 420.08 |
| 568.06 | 671.21 | 321.03 | attended | 763.21 | 696.06 |
| 568.08 | 672.04 | 471.11 | 198.05 | auxiliary | 719.11 |
| 568.10 | 673.09 | 471.14 | 445.15 | 013.07 | 719.12 |
| 568.19 | 674.04 | 472.05 | 616.18 | avail | 720.01 |
| 569.09 | 674.05 | 716.20 | attending | 341.09 | aw'll |
| 571.21 | 674.08 | athletic | 021.10 | 378.19 | 016.15 |
| 571.21 | 675.16 | 213.19 | 079.17 | availed | aw'm |
| 572.10 | 675.17 | 442.03 | 143.02 | 644.12 | 194.03 |
| 574.05 | 675.20 | atlantic | 346.02 | avarice | 194.04 |
| 575.04 | 676.02 | 313.13 | 418.13 | 230.10 | 324.17 |
| 578.08 | 677.10 | atmosphere | 547.22 | avaricious | 696.17 |
| 580.09 | 678.01 | 027.09 | attention | 584.04 | aw's |
| 581.07 | 679.20 | 285.18 | 119.02 | averred | 190.21 |
| 582.03 | 679.21 | 687.04 | 256.11 | 205.04 | 471.16 |
| 582.21 | 680.02 | atmospheric | 270.07 | aversion | 712.17 |
| 583.01 | 682.20 | 004.06 | 287.04 | 007.19 | await |
| 583.09 | 688.06 | atom | 314.17 | 145.11 | 044.07 |
| 585.09 | 690.21 | 136.19 | 352.12 | 150.06 | 643.08 |
| 586.07 | 692.09 | atoms | 408.02 | 218.20 | awaited |
| 588.01 | 692.15 | 049.16 | 487.14 | 237.14 | 396.15 |
| 589.12 | 694.14 | atrocious | 492.22 | 388.02 | 553.07 |
| 589.14 | 695.01 | 041.01 | 524.08 | 412.01 | awaiting |
| 590.06 | 695.05 | 403.06 | 629.05 | 413.01 | 586.15 |
| 591.04 | 695.07 | attached | 668.21 | 471.04 | awake |
| 591.15 | 695.11 | 315.15 | 706.01 | 488.18 | 051.18 |
| 594.07 | 696.01 | 414.20 | 732.14 | 498.06 | 540.02 |
| 598.14 | 697.09 | 725.22 | 749.19 | 536.16 | 557.22 |
| 599.09 | 698.04 | attachment | attentive | 621.14 | 669.03 |
| 599.13 | 698.20 | 222.06 | 048.03 | 736.05 | awakened |
| 600.14 | 699.05 | 226.02 | 204.10 | avert | 057.07 |
| 602.01 | 699.10 | 336.02 | 533.21 | 258.18 | 226.03 |
| 603.08 | 700.10 | 414.12 | 534.03 | averted | 314.15 |
| 603.19 | 700.13 | 542.03 | 534.04 | 249.05 | awakens |
| 605.17 | 700.17 | 687.02 | attenuated | 492.18 | 730.20 |
| 609.05 | 701.03 | attachments | 602.08 | 519.14 | aware |
| 609.08 | 701.08 | 145.12 | attire | averting | 183.04 |
| 609.21 | 701.14 | 338.08 | 384.17 | 739.05 | 203.19 |
| 610.10 | 702.03 | 425.07 | attired | avoid | 226.02 |
| 611.08 | 702.15 | attack | 442.04 | 127.09 | 234.05 |
| 612.10 | 703.17 | 035.15 | 449.01 | 185.12 | 251.21 |
| 613.06 | 704.03 | 257.21 | attitude | 190.18 | 262.06 |
| 614.10 | 704.19 | 292.05 | 005.06 | 261.06 | 286.13 |
| 618.21 | 705.05 | 488.10 | attorney | 273.18 | 314.13 |
| 619.04 | 705.13 | attacked | 422.14 | 325.22 | 336.22 |
| 620.21 | 705.21 | 445.16 | 637.01 | 332.17 | 373.06 |
| 621.01 | 706.17 | attain | 638.16 | 391.09 | 403.03 |
| 621.22 | 708.14 | 734.06 | attract | 432.03 | 422.10 |
| 622.14 | 708.19 | attained | 312.18 | 503.09 | 437.20 |
| 623.16 | 711.01 | 754.21 | 749.18 | 521.03 | 494.14 |
| 624.09 | 712.04 | attaining | attracted | 527.18 | 525.14 |
| 625.05 | 712.07 | 652.08 | 080.04 | 603.05 | 574.06 |
| 626.09 | 712.14 | attainments | 161.01 | 724.09 | 582.05 |
| 627.22 | 716.04 | 679.08 | 285.14 | avoided | 623.13 |
| 628.06 | 716.16 | attempt | 427.08 | 147.21 | 677.02 |
| 629.01 | 716.22 | 052.16 | 669.03 | 198.07 | 753.21 |
| 629.03 | 717.09 | 234.21 | attraction | 334.04 | away |
| 631.16 | 718.01 | 239.06 | 136.07 | 340.20 | 025.06 |
| 632.11 | 718.09 | 317.02 | 225.06 | 413.06 | 029.13 |
| 633.20 | 718.15 | 341.20 | attractions | 457.05 | 060.03 |
| 635.05 | 718.17 | 389.13 | 174.17 | avoiding | 062.06 |
| 635.13 | 719.01 | 394.21 | attractive | 563.14 | 063.16 |
| 635.19 | | 399.07 | 025.13 | 726.05 | 064.09 |

064.13
085.15
100.11
118.04
124.17
133.11
137.12
139.05
149.15
152.18
155.12
159.11
162.04
167.20
183.14
185.11
189.22
202.20
202.20
209.20
217.22
222.15
228.05
249.04
260.04
276.05
294.13
308.18
312.11
347.09
347.21
352.20
354.02
358.07
364.11
374.05
385.02
388.06
395.22
399.15
401.06
411.04
430.11
438.09
471.19
488.07
495.14
498.17
533.17
535.10
538.17
542.04
561.15
565.18
572.19
596.02
612.03
613.01
619.07
621.01
624.08
633.11
634.18
634.18
640.11
645.13
649.22
669.09
678.01
683.18
684.20
692.12
692.15
695.06
710.18
723.01
729.03
737.02
742.09
749.10
757.02

a.e
441.21
594.04

awful
040.19
211.11
273.13
391.19
613.11
759.04

awfully
388.14

awhile
082.05

awkward
436.17
482.06

awkwardly
286.15

awkwardness
560.18
744.14

awn
712.18
719.16

awoke
326.17

ay
531.11
531.12

a ye
246.22
247.04
454.09
564.17

b
563.03

babies
042.11

baby
141.20
153.15
245.16
385.02
387.09
436.06
453.22
465.02
606.17

baby-work
276.04

babyish
512.03

back
009.13
010.16
015.05
017.13
020.13
034.04
038.14
039.21
040.20
043.17
046.05
052.04
058.12
062.19
063.20
076.11
080.12
095.08
116.19
121.21
127.03
133.17
157.19
163.02
169.01
178.21
180.01
190.08
193.01
203.10
206.15
208.02
209.07
210.08
211.15
215.05
219.10
247.07
257.17
258.20
259.22
264.06
271.01
274.05
278.12
283.13
292.02
294.11
294.21
298.20
299.14
302.10
303.16
311.18
316.12
317.05
321.02
330.01
333.16
340.17
355.02
356.16
360.03
360.08
366.05
376.10
385.17
389.03
399.14
407.12
409.12
410.06
421.13
432.04
435.03
448.08
456.18
462.03
468.04
474.07
478.20
482.10
494.19
500.11
510.01
513.17
523.19
531.13
537.21
541.16
555.05
560.04
569.07
591.17
605.03
607.01
610.17
616.05
621.01
621.15
635.21
637.12
654.16
656.18
665.12
668.18
671.17
676.18
686.13
690.11
692.08
699.01
709.10
718.09
733.22
745.01
757.16

back-kitchen
044.04
061.06
098.15

bad
023.01
046.07
046.07
081.18
103.09
118.12
125.10
129.01
144.15
144.15
149.04
159.19
168.19
171.11
173.11
173.13
186.14
231.16
242.08
248.09
253.08
258.06
289.03
416.05
437.08
440.22
443.01
445.03
459.07
484.11
492.09
497.15
502.17
515.10
562.15
567.17
571.01
571.02
647.22
678.16
679.20
726.08
739.15

bad-natured
476.15

bad-tempered
204.15

bade
127.04
168.17
180.03
247.16

badly
092.05
295.19
587.19

bahn
566.17

baht
322.06

bairn
139.10
141.10

bairnies
169.17

bairns
078.12

bait
704.04

baiting
091.20

baking
005.19

balance
302.11

balancing
682.06

ball
558.19

ballad
544.05
544.07
681.19

ban
197.13

band
131.10

bane
745.22

bang
319.12
319.12

banged
397.17

banish
231.15

banished
101.04
334.18
599.22
685.03
704.17

banishment
080.13
742.12

bank
449.22
480.07
517.18
557.07

bank-notes
712.13

banks
410.10
480.10

banning
233.04

bannister
165.03
325.16
638.13

baptists'
665.18

bare
006.05
011.11
028.02
140.16
243.03
295.09
321.10
427.12
440.16
627.09
764.05

barefoot
103.15

barely
281.01
417.09

bargain
166.05

bargin
758.17

bark
355.02
377.14

barn
016.04
028.05
169.10
184.19
246.06
320.02
566.04

barred
015.20
280.17

barrel
315.16

barren
066.08

barrier
003.06
651.21

bars
106.06
244.19

barthens
720.01

base
397.10
562.19

basely
222.01

basement
104.01

baseness
255.22

bashfully
438.04

bashfulness
666.01

basilisk
404.12

basin
025.02
075.09
111.04
270.18
320.17
471.02
747.15

basins
319.15

basked
041.07

basket
075.09
206.06
431.21
626.07

bass
131.12

bassoons
131.12

bathed
279.20

bathos
493.19

battle
445.17

battledoors
558.21

bay
260.09

be
001.05
007.05
007.22
008.05
009.19
012.07
012.21
013.08
014.10
018.04
019.19
020.08
021.19
023.13
025.03
027.05
027.11
028.01
028.05
029.19
029.22
030.03
030.07
030.13
031.12
032.02
032.10
033.14
037.11
037.12
038.07
041.20
042.13
043.01
044.17
046.08
046.13
046.22
047.09
050.02
059.09
059.13
059.16
064.22
067.19
071.05
072.01
074.13
074.15
076.04
076.10
077.02
077.09
077.16
080.03
082.16
083.12
085.05
087.09
087.12
088.18
089.02
090.11
090.21
091.12
092.16
093.13
093.17
095.02
095.06
098.01
102.09
108.08
108.10
109.11
110.06
110.11
111.11
114.10
114.11
116.12
117.10
117.18
118.05
118.06
118.06
119.09
119.15
120.08
122.07
123.04
123.14
124.04
127.06
129.02
129.02
129.12
130.11
131.04
132.22
138.02
138.09
140.03
140.07
141.04
142.04
142.10
143.12
144.13
145.05
146.21
147.13
147.22
148.18
150.14
150.20
151.10
153.12
153.15
155.13
155.15
157.18
158.18
158.19
159.20
159.20
160.04
163.15
163.16
164.05
164.10
167.02
170.21
172.02
172.04
172.06
172.10
172.18
172.19
173.10
173.16
173.16
173.18
174.18
175.03
175.06
175.07
175.16
175.19
177.08
177.16
178.06
178.09
178.19
179.05
180.14
180.19
181.01
181.12
181.13
181.20
182.13
182.21
184.15
186.13
187.14
187.20
188.02
188.07
188.09
189.13
189.20
190.14
190.17
191.02
192.10
193.09
194.13
194.20
196.14
196.16
197.18
198.16
201.09
202.15
204.15
205.07
205.21
207.08
208.07

210.08
210.19
211.07
211.20
212.01
212.18
212.22
214.21
215.16
215.19
218.14
219.22
220.19
222.21
223.06
224.18
226.18
228.06
228.12
228.15
228.18
229.08
230.03
230.05
230.09
231.06
233.15
235.12
235.21
236.07
236.18
237.09
239.10
239.18
240.01
240.03
240.12
240.17
242.11
244.08
244.10
244.20
245.19
248.13
250.06
251.06
251.21
252.03
253.12
254.14
255.14
257.22
259.05
260.20
260.21
262.21
263.01
263.03
263.05
264.12
264.19
265.04
265.07
265.10
271.08
272.12
272.15
274.01
274.21
277.14
277.21
280.13
281.04
281.14
283.03
285.03
288.07
288.16
289.04
289.06
289.13
293.06
293.22
294.16
294.17
295.09
297.18
297.20
302.11
303.12
304.04
304.18
305.08
307.20
308.07
309.17
310.02
312.22
313.07
313.12
313.19
315.07
316.07
316.21
317.04
317.07
317.12
318.02
318.11
318.14
319.08

320.01
320.05
322.16
322.22
324.14
327.02
327.12
329.03
329.12
332.21
333.08
334.04
334.05
334.06
334.08
335.18
335.22
336.07
336.08
336.11
336.14
338.01
338.06
339.10
341.03
342.15
342.18
343.22
344.09
344.15
345.02
345.22
346.10
346.22
347.01
347.13
348.08
350.06
350.20
351.01
356.21
357.11
357.18
358.05
358.21
359.08
359.16
359.22
361.02
361.08
361.08
361.09
361.10
361.12
362.01
363.13
364.17
365.06
365.18
366.16
367.05
367.12
368.07
368.08
369.09
370.10
370.22
371.10
372.01
373.06
373.11
375.15
377.03
383.03
383.03
385.17
388.07
388.11
388.16
388.19
391.05
392.08
393.14
395.01
395.09
395.12
395.13
396.03
396.09
397.13
398.10
401.18
405.09
406.01
407.18
410.13
411.12
411.17
413.13
418.19
418.20
419.04
419.14
422.04
422.20
425.09
425.14
425.15
425.18
426.21
429.20

434.05
436.10
436.13
437.01
437.03
437.21
439.06
439.13
439.18
440.06
440.21
441.10
442.11
444.02
444.13
446.13
446.20
447.01
449.11
449.16
450.02
450.05
451.20
452.09
453.19
454.15
455.07
456.09
457.05
459.11
460.03
460.05
460.19
461.14
462.01
462.15
464.07
464.09
466.02
468.22
469.02
469.05
469.07
469.12
469.14
470.08
473.04
475.09
476.20
477.18
479.04
479.22
480.02
480.11
482.08
482.15
483.09
483.21
484.05
484.18
485.01
485.12
488.14
489.04
489.17
491.02
492.05
492.11
492.14
493.19
494.04
496.11
499.18
502.01
502.02
503.21
504.06
504.10
505.07
505.08
511.04
511.06
511.07
513.04
515.09
519.18
519.22
520.04
520.05
520.13
520.15
521.07
521.18
521.19
522.14
523.22
525.04
525.22
527.07
527.09
527.11
528.21
534.02
535.02
535.18
536.13
537.07
540.04
540.10
540.11

541.11
541.14
542.06
542.22
543.19
544.16
546.08
547.07
547.10
551.04
554.07
554.08
554.14
554.19
555.12
558.04
558.05
558.13
559.02
561.20
562.09
562.16
562.19
564.18
565.15
566.17
566.19
567.08
570.07
570.17
571.05
571.06
571.20
571.21
573.01
573.05
575.05
575.07
576.05
576.17
577.08
578.02
578.04
578.20
578.22
581.17
583.18
586.02
588.17
588.20
589.13
590.08
590.15
590.18
591.16
591.19
592.20
593.12
594.11
597.11
597.13
597.22
599.07
600.07
601.08
601.22
602.17
603.03
603.14
604.04
604.12
604.14
605.19
607.16
611.08
612.19
613.15
613.19
615.11
615.12
616.05
616.09
617.10
617.19
618.03
619.07
619.13
619.18
619.19
621.10
621.19
622.12
624.03
627.08
628.06
630.01
630.06
630.16
631.09
632.11
635.17
636.15
637.10
637.11
638.01
638.20
639.05
639.10
641.05
643.08
644.01

645.15
646.16
646.20
648.11
648.17
648.17
649.03
650.08
652.02
652.03
652.20
654.11
654.20
656.02
659.21
661.03
664.01
666.13
667.03
670.03
670.06
671.12
671.23
672.10
673.12
674.05
675.18
676.15
676.16
677.06
678.02
679.08
679.20
683.20
685.05
685.18
691.16
695.15
696.15
696.20
697.11
700.20
703.01
706.05
707.02
707.20
708.05
709.17
709.20
710.05
711.07
711.09
711.12
713.06
713.17
713.22
714.04
714.06
715.05
716.09
717.08
725.11
726.02
726.21
727.17
729.11
729.15
732.09
734.08
738.16
739.02
741.06
742.09
744.15
746.21
752.12
752.13
752.15
754.06
754.10
754.14
754.14
754.20
755.19
756.21
757.01
757.08
757.10
759.14
761.04
761.20
762.04
762.10
763.20
beacon
410.12
beaded
237.17
beamless
693.01
bear
017.16
026.19
043.09
091.07
117.11
141.17
144.04
156.10
180.22
181.01

197.19
223.08
224.14
237.15
242.10
274.08
345.01
345.10
356.03
356.08
376.06
387.11
387.12
396.12
398.12
447.02
502.09
529.08
533.08
541.03
568.09
597.05
601.05
611.11
620.19
631.20
665.06
673.04
684.02
723.17
739.18
756.11
beard
108.05
bearing
021.08
034.11
421.01
471.02
681.06
685.20
699.14
735.03
bearishly
021.06
beast
085.10
106.20
241.08
377.11
385.09
420.02
560.07
beasts
034.16
120.14
431.17
616.01
675.08
689.16
beat
188.19
291.14
359.11
559.05
604.03
675.21
733.21
beaten
077.19
103.14
235.18
257.22
654.13
729.15
beating
261.16
beautiful
001.06
018.09
030.10
104.02
111.08
154.13
371.01
449.12
461.16
478.14
559.19
614.04
737.16
beautifully
095.18
463.10
beauty
114.08
140.14
235.12
311.10
351.11
425.02
467.03
675.02
695.08
beaver
114.03
became
088.08
089.18
099.10
144.22

148.16
179.15
283.19
502.08
668.21
701.13
704.20

because
007.13
030.19
055.11
064.13
075.15
079.03
088.02
099.20
103.14
105.02
106.05
110.15
116.22
122.12
135.09
140.07
142.08
144.12
173.09
173.12
173.14
174.12
178.08
179.10
179.10
181.02
194.13
205.09
218.09
220.16
228.05
230.03
230.05
238.21
246.18
255.21
279.03
283.06
293.18
299.20
299.20
313.22
346.11
350.04
353.18
363.06
366.14
374.13
385.04
387.09
389.13
407.01
414.08
423.04
427.17
431.08
443.08
464.06
471.09
478.06
493.09
495.02
499.15
500.21
501.03
501.04
501.20
516.21
519.17
521.18
530.11
534.19
543.12
550.05
555.20
557.02
559.01
559.16
561.21
562.19
572.01
580.19
581.20
592.15
603.19
604.02
617.09
620.05
630.16
631.03
636.12
649.07
679.17
697.22
702.16
728.14
734.08

beck
209.13
353.02
743.17

becks
303.07

beclouded
115.22

become
180.20
433.03
597.05
730.17
740.14

becomes
660.08

becoming
699.15

bed
032.07
036.15
038.01
046.06
054.03
058.13
060.10
074.15
077.08
079.22
090.10
094.07
101.13
123.01
134.08
135.01
178.14
190.13
191.12
193.09
276.13
279.11
281.10
283.11
285.21
291.09
296.12
299.09
304.17
314.19
321.20
326.06
382.17
393.11
403.07
452.13
455.21
457.13
460.04
462.12
475.20
505.14
550.07
569.11
604.12
616.04
616.09
639.12
642.02
661.06
663.13
703.08
716.08
736.10
739.13
745.03
745.07
750.10
757.08
758.22

bed-clothes
052.20
757.20

bed-room
312.22
321.13
454.22
691.19

bed-rume
321.14

bed-rumes
321.15

bed-side
218.04
548.09

beds
398.13
673.11

bedside
202.05
503.19
599.18
662.13

bedtime
120.21

beef
006.08

been
006.04
006.21
012.11
019.14
019.15
033.21
035.09
035.14
040.04
041.04
045.12
047.17
049.11
053.13
056.20
056.22
059.02
072.13
073.12
074.09
074.12
079.14
087.03
091.10
093.06
097.09
102.10
104.10
106.15
115.13
119.08
130.21
131.17
137.10
139.12
140.22
144.08
145.20
163.14
166.11
171.22
181.14
182.17
184.13
187.17
191.13
192.07
197.05
198.15
199.17
202.14
206.07
207.13
208.16
213.22
220.20
221.13
221.14
223.10
226.02
226.15
227.12
231.22
232.05
234.22
238.19
241.02
249.14
255.19
256.03
256.14
262.15
263.07
273.14
273.14
281.16
282.05
282.07
282.10
282.13
284.02
285.14
286.09
288.13
288.21
292.10
293.13
295.07
297.04
306.07
307.18
315.21
318.20
319.15
327.15
329.20
330.06
337.01
338.02
341.18
343.21
346.10
351.06
351.13
352.13
358.11
362.18
373.17
378.13
379.01
379.05
381.08
384.15
385.21
386.11
390.04
390.13
394.01
401.09
404.09
404.17
406.06
407.17
407.17
414.19
415.18
417.02
418.16
422.11
423.05
426.09
428.01
428.03
429.21
433.15
434.02
434.14
435.09
438.13
443.09
446.20
448.12
450.21
450.22
453.11
460.02
465.01
477.10
477.16
481.01
485.21
490.04
490.07
491.10
502.13
502.14
508.02
510.11
510.21
516.04
517.05
534.18
535.01
539.17
547.08
547.14
553.18
553.21
554.06
554.21
562.15
572.03
574.06
578.05
578.08
580.05
582.07
585.09
587.12
590.14
594.01
604.05
605.13
608.10
610.09
613.10
616.03
617.03
622.04
626.12
627.05
627.21
641.19
644.09
644.19
649.21
650.18
651.07
654.01
663.06
664.07
664.12
666.04
667.17
671.13
680.03
681.14
682.17
686.21
695.04
703.04
711.19
713.12
716.05
726.20
727.02
729.20
731.06
739.03
740.03
748.02

bees
557.08

befall
169.07

befallen
130.02

befitting
118.16
383.13
442.05

before
004.19
007.04
012.06
013.13
019.06
020.19
026.03
028.06
031.03
041.08
046.12
051.08
058.08
075.12
085.21
090.07
093.10
094.18
103.02
108.11
115.12
120.19
126.16
130.08
133.19
135.04
135.18
140.03
153.18
165.18
167.11
171.19
172.19
181.10
185.16
186.01
189.19
190.08
194.11
198.15
203.17
205.16
217.01
226.14
237.03
243.15
258.02
260.13
281.03
283.11
284.07
287.14
288.08
292.07
296.13
311.15
312.11
315.20
317.08
322.20
333.19
335.01
339.16
341.19
350.11
352.06
353.13
356.01
365.10
371.06
374.05
384.14
384.22
392.21
395.16
398.10
400.14
403.13
407.21
409.01
412.11
413.11
424.10
426.21
427.20
435.10
439.06
445.21
446.17
449.20
451.12
461.01
465.15
466.04
471.03
475.01
479.11
480.18
482.02
482.13
488.04
490.17
498.17
505.21
511.09
520.07
520.09
523.08
525.04
528.04
533.04
547.13
555.02
562.12
563.11
569.13
572.13
579.04
590.01
594.13
598.15
604.05
606.17
607.20
620.03
620.19
623.02
637.11
641.21
642.05
644.19
645.22
659.11
674.18
684.07
690.09
692.22
693.21
694.15
699.07
705.01
706.16
707.13
713.13
715.08
719.06
725.05
734.22
745.08
747.15
749.15
751.18
754.11
758.08
761.02

before-named
150.15

beforehand
263.19
520.16

befriend
033.02

beg
020.03
053.11
073.13
092.16
164.04
250.12
408.16
648.22
660.22
708.20
742.08

began
016.17
020.22
023.15
027.07
040.17
045.17
046.12
053.15
079.11
087.02
093.21
097.13
126.05
128.18
140.19
141.10
159.05
169.16
184.08
188.16
191.06
199.02
218.17
237.22
264.08
270.12
274.18
281.04
289.03
296.18
317.20
323.22
332.09
389.09
401.16
433.11
453.05
456.15
462.21
480.11
495.06
498.13
527.16
534.08
540.07
553.16

558.07
567.16
570.06
583.17
591.09
610.12
619.02
624.17
632.01
644.02
648.22
651.08
652.04
660.11
662.03
666.16
667.22
670.15
675.08
694.13
702.15
704.13
708.11
719.09
734.17
746.01
751.06

**beggar**
317.04
418.21
724.16

**beggarly**
085.06

**beggars**
181.20

**begged**
077.09
119.09
131.04
191.09
195.20
559.10
642.02

**begging**
589.11

**begin**
037.10
105.02
253.12
262.03
273.15
292.15
439.13
469.15
505.13
544.07
577.22
706.03
725.15

**beginner**
681.16

**beginning**
012.20
075.21
081.18
099.08
182.18
195.08
309.11
351.07
370.09
493.17
511.13
516.14
543.05
701.07

**begins**
306.04
338.20

**begone**
053.10
127.15
158.07
238.06
408.12
439.15
469.17
564.04
648.19
722.05
738.04

**beguile**
655.05

**beguiled**
737.11

**beguiling**
705.14

**beguilnig**
445.21

**begun**
149.10
154.19

**behalf**
026.08
081.01
185.14

**behave**
492.08
497.16
562.08
640.16

702.09

**behaved**
100.02
124.02
204.06
221.02
385.04
443.18
548.03
572.15

**behaving**
092.05

**behaviour**
032.20
097.06
110.11
144.09
170.10
194.01
254.08
409.09
541.14
599.16
666.02
701.12

**beheld**
001.13
243.21
248.20
319.05
356.05
434.12
480.20
486.14
529.06
564.12
568.17
624.13
727.07
758.09

**behest**
533.14

**behind**
016.20
054.19
058.14
085.11
105.18
116.01
130.05
155.06
160.07
206.16
277.16
308.05
364.22
375.10
397.17
437.15
479.17
538.02
566.04
665.12
668.12
683.21
685.14
692.17
694.22
706.17
729.04
756.04

**behold**
040.13
126.10
130.06
213.17

**beholding**
019.11
116.01
166.07

**being**
004.04
015.11
022.04
024.18
025.05
027.13
029.12
030.20
031.05
060.17
079.01
083.02
092.13
100.01
103.04
124.03
146.21
149.04
152.08
162.08
162.09
180.16
182.05
183.10
212.12
212.14
213.01
220.06
226.20
237.06

250.13
254.11
261.21
266.12
271.14
272.21
277.19
280.14
280.15
295.19
297.02
302.03
305.18
318.01
321.18
323.20
330.02
336.04
337.18
340.03
341.18
342.16
345.22
360.22
369.11
387.15
388.18
388.21
389.20
396.05
400.15
414.13
420.12
430.16
432.06
440.05
440.20
441.08
441.14
446.02
452.04
459.02
469.21
471.13
497.10
496.01
501.09
509.15
512.10
532.19
533.13
543.17
554.13
563.04
569.07
577.13
578.15
580.07
582.05
582.12
582.16
606.21
608.02
621.06
623.05
627.12
636.06
643.10
650.21
651.20
659.04
661.10
664.16
665.06
685.03
694.01
710.17
715.03
717.16
730.01
731.04
734.05
739.13
746.07
753.17
761.17
761.18

**beings**
534.07

**belie**
237.07

**belied**
060.09

**belief**
244.05

**believe**
001.07
005.11
044.16
067.04
090.18
104.13
143.10
205.18
215.16
220.10
228.21
230.21
263.17
276.20
305.20

334.22
352.08
372.09
377.00
411.08
426.01
442.15
476.17
496.09
501.01
525.10
543.07
571.05
571.08
581.08
583.14
602.04
630.19
663.09
675.01
685.02
726.09
734.19
755.21
762.14

**believed**
198.17
270.18
270.20
339.05
655.01

**believing**
081.13

**bell**
217.02
265.14
387.01
662.04
662.05
694.05

**bellows**
063.09
751.20

**bells**
353.01

**belonged**
078.22
197.09

**belonging**
006.21
340.03

**beloved**
644.04

**below**
101.08
132.01
165.07
166.15
211.04
216.03
254.04
393.03
400.18
552.07
623.01
628.18
690.03
705.08
747.07

**bemoaned**
369.12
759.12

**bench**
062.19
169.13
179.18
232.15
712.05

**benches**
061.12

**bend**
083.13
209.13
506.18
719.19
744.11

**bending**
204.11
317.17
527.01
540.16
597.07
652.11
733.21

**beneath**
040.20
114.19
149.22
169.18
183.05
229.21
252.19
283.21
324.22
355.01
390.15
409.15
410.15
578.13
750.10
763.15

**benefactor**
083.09

**beneficent**
026.01

**benefit**
149.09
542.02
602.19
617.21
647.11
732.10

**benefiting**
242.09

**benevolence**
229.21

**benevolent**
035.10

**benign**
764.06

**bent**
034.16
190.10
237.17
244.01
276.13
283.13
314.06
323.09
355.06
360.06
374.14
442.21
456.06
684.04
695.02
711.17

**benumbed**
067.20

**bequeath**
576.18

**bequeathed**
664.11

**bereavement**
369.08

**beseech**
307.12

**beseeching**
189.09

**besetting**
230.11

**beside**
123.12
213.19
215.14
302.07
313.18
370.18
402.05
404.06
449.22
531.02
538.08
587.20
641.05
676.08
710.18
715.06

**besides**
013.01
131.13
141.05
144.07
156.07
164.13
231.19
262.02
298.17
344.17
379.14
385.20
418.06
427.11
469.21
483.03
545.10
599.12
603.04
646.20
651.05
680.16
689.10
695.07
708.21

**besought**
368.01

**bespeak**
600.13

**bespoke**
635.06

**best**
021.12
054.10
123.07
134.03
147.20
182.07
322.22
331.18
434.17
463.14
494.15

514.06
527.08
590.11
602.06
634.20
643.07
674.02
691.22
704.09

**bestir**
490.10

**bestirring**
325.06

**bestow**
008.02
229.16
752.06

**bestowed**
116.16
226.03
355.21
411.01
706.01

**bestowing**
061.22
248.18
378.16

**betook**
191.11

**betray**
362.20
378.21

**betrayal**
347.11
573.18

**betrayed**
213.09

**betrayer**
602.05

**better**
009.16
025.07
033.14
074.02
079.01
084.05
095.16
106.06
122.04
138.08
140.16
141.05
146.15
151.18
159.20
168.09
188.06
196.12
204.01
204.07
217.22
231.18
259.17
280.01
304.01
326.02
330.21
337.18
344.09
347.20
352.15
361.05
367.04
367.04
368.02
396.16
396.20
413.19
416.19
420.09
442.09
454.01
456.02
459.10
482.15
484.04
488.20
521.16
521.20
535.08
536.05
536.08
539.04
546.21
551.04
552.03
556.07
566.19
570.17
577.01
581.14
587.06
587.06
592.03
592.10
592.13
592.18
595.01
598.17
615.14
636.15

648.02
649.10
650.10
651.04
655.20
664.03
665.22
683.08
686.07
743.01
757.01
between
001.11
003.14
010.17
014.07
019.17
020.22
024.14
047.13
061.21
063.12
082.15
104.21
106.18
111.02
111.12
124.11
154.10
163.04
163.21
189.20
196.09
219.02
222.22
235.04
241.09
268.05
272.14
281.19
331.16
334.02
334.13
399.18
406.09
409.13
411.06
414.15
415.19
444.07
454.13
467.20
475.17
487.15
509.06
548.10
548.16
583.01
651.21
720.05
726.08
752.03
bevy
637.18
bewail
356.20
beware
025.08
102.14
216.09
238.10
293.11
327.15
348.06
411.16
bewildered
278.19
367.19
467.09
592.22
611.03
bewilderment
274.11
bewilders
208.13
bewitched
341.09
beyond
061.04
182.14
209.07
236.10
312.05
315.02
351.17
351.17
361.09
371.06
377.22
426.09
433.09
460.17
478.11
506.20
539.16
577.08
684.22
763.19
bible
089.13
093.04

405.04
696.22
712.12
754.02
760.13
bibles
041.09
bid
017.11
067.19
077.13
094.16
102.14
115.16
195.15
212.21
236.08
261.11
277.21
316.21
331.19
410.03
418.14
429.18
441.18
448.04
467.09
485.12
511.01
522.14
534.10
548.22
550.10
560.05
567.05
568.01
586.05
622.17
628.06
649.03
660.14
663.13
667.14
675.03
686.12
691.16
715.11
729.05
741.06
753.07
755.15
756.16
756.21
761.12
bidding
092.02
110.11
255.05
410.18
467.16
716.16
bide
246.18
293.12
324.19
665.21
690.21
711.11
712.17
big
078.03
319.09
bigger
464.05
bilberries
591.10
bilberry
380.01
billowy
065.20
bind
142.16
422.06
binding
384.18
birches
450.08
bird
160.03
231.16
275.14
275.18
510.01
669.06
birds
480.09
518.11
522.10
632.16
675.08
birth
126.01
305.09
478.05
birthday
579.19
bit
088.17
127.18
217.19
260.18

320.03
320.03
324.04
339.20
434.11
476.04
505.20
509.20
519.11
546.01
566.20
586.03
668.17
695.05
710.03
718.17
739.10
bitch
006.17
010.05
bite
720.01
biter
012.12
biting
722.02
bits
507.11
634.03
666.06
719.14
bitten
012.10
109.06
437.06
bitter
027.19
082.03
095.01
201.04
203.05
216.13
223.05
223.06
314.07
348.06
489.22
502.15
570.22
572.21
647.14
708.19
720.20
759.09
bitterly
195.08
279.12
357.08
385.05
457.03
470.20
618.12
bitterness
636.06
663.01
black
001.13
006.15
015.10
020.05
029.19
084.02
088.08
097.15
114.01
116.20
124.14
125.10
187.22
207.17
214.06
239.11
250.17
277.01
277.03
379.08
391.01
397.19
408.21
427.22
438.16
448.02
449.02
464.03
464.11
531.04
606.20
626.06
665.11
716.06
723.21
733.18
741.13
744.08
758.05
763.18
black-haired
078.02
blackberry
522.19

blackbirds
557.17
blackened
381.11
513.20
709.01
blacker
317.07
blackguard
116.11
255.20
blackhorse
163.09
626.11
blackness
280.18
407.07
502.22
blacksmith's
298.11
298.13
blade
316.08
blame
081.09
086.01
090.05
197.08
226.05
254.20
484.02
569.03
670.16
721.10
blameable
262.07
blamed
289.04
332.15
502.01
blaming
045.12
blanched
266.07
367.07
519.11
blank
040.08
281.15
299.10
505.20
701.21
blanker
166.06
blasphemer
168.15
blast
051.03
279.18
398.14
blaze
020.11
063.11
156.16
blazing
696.10
bleak
015.09
154.12
201.04
285.18
651.16
bled
196.04
bleed
386.15
bleeding
035.06
383.20
433.20
bleeds
109.07
blended
594.19
blending
695.01
bless
245.01
324.01
697.07
blessed
371.22
324.01
696.11
blessing
140.21
185.12
366.07
397.13
397.14
470.19
578.19
603.15
blest
410.06
blew
274.15
649.18
651.16
blight
363.02

blighted
231.10
blightingly
397.19
blind
194.03
258.07
375.16
567.03
753.02
blind-man's
558.16
blinds
370.12
bliss
253.09
753.14
blissfully
639.19
blisters
202.07
block
243.16
380.06
542.10
blood
052.19
105.15
167.05
203.12
264.19
266.14
283.01
317.06
334.21
377.13
389.07
399.21
401.14
417.15
444.02
468.22
565.21
634.02
652.17
653.18
705.01
756.11
758.01
blood-shot
753.01
blood-vessel
610.18
bloodless
358.09
519.06
741.14
bloody
107.05
bloom
479.18
557.09
737.07
bloomed
522.07
blooming
416.17
blossom
518.22
blossomed
424.10
blotted
066.02
388.16
blow
079.20
085.20
156.22
259.20
260.10
397.18
417.12
751.18
blowing
004.10
060.19
392.18
557.14
blown
517.21
blows
050.12
081.05
084.08
303.10
blubbered
079.15
761.09
blubbering
567.09
bludgeon
260.21
blue
111.14
125.05
239.11
303.06
358.17
463.07
468.07
516.17

557.11
587.08
690.12
737.16
blue-bells
518.19
bluff
558.16
690.08
blunder
024.12
blunders
679.13
695.10
blush
524.09
blushed
057.07
679.01
709.13
blushing
128.19
438.04
blustered
092.21
board
321.02
boards
050.18
132.08
boast
406.09
boasted
084.13
389.18
boastful
647.09
boastfully
046.20
boath
194.05
326.09
bodily
029.13
223.01
244.04
302.08
406.10
boding
516.19
body
024.10
050.08
129.13
137.16
173.21
182.13
270.04
279.21
310.12
358.06
400.08
419.13
548.06
652.19
663.15
707.13
720.12
741.08
753.14
bog
031.06
103.16
bog-hoile
190.22
bog-water
628.03
boil
317.21
boiled
472.13
boiling
005.19
264.21
bold
026.18
091.18
690.08
720.14
boldly
124.15
661.13
757.11
boldness
609.05
bolt
101.11
189.08
194.07
315.09
506.09
bolts
250.14
394.07
bonds
268.04
bones
267.03
433.15
bonnet
140.10

| | | | | | |
|---|---|---|---|---|---|
| 242.04 | 096.06 | 168.03 | brains | 266.02 | 312.17 |
| 245.12 | 139.04 | 534.11 | 085.09 | 279.16 | 348.08 |
| 331.08 | 180.20 | bottom | 329.16 | 327.16 | brim |
| 343.09 | 331.02 | 065.17 | bran | 382.08 | 303.07 |
| 410.19 | 369.02 | 217.21 | 559.03 | 386.15 | brim-ful |
| 479.09 | 411.09 | 243.18 | branch | 400.07 | 510.02 |
| 626.06 | 417.11 | 305.14 | 051.02 | 408.04 | brindled |
| bonnetless | 488.05 | 451.14 | 052.01 | 476.05 | 061.09 |
| 190.03 | 493.13 | 517.02 | branches | 519.21 | bring |
| bonniest | 608.10 | 554.01 | 243.06 | 532.11 | 003.10 |
| 090.16 | 696.13 | bough | 373.16 | 541.18 | 023.05 |
| 125.10 | borne | 189.04 | 518.02 | 566.06 | 076.09 |
| bonny | 071.20 | bought | 522.08 | 598.05 | 076.19 |
| 076.08 | 341.07 | 083.15 | 527.17 | 608.14 | 078.10 |
| 093.11 | 409.09 | 119.03 | branching | 610.15 | 145.10 |
| 125.08 | 499.19 | bound | 692.21 | 652.16 | 147.15 |
| 139.03 | 513.05 | 123.14 | branded | 653.14 | 148.19 |
| 193.22 | borrowed | 287.14 | 358.21 | 722.22 | 188.07 |
| 232.18 | 110.21 | 400.11 | branderham | breathe | 198.11 |
| 275.14 | 486.07 | 667.03 | 046.02 | 098.02 | 210.08 |
| 324.19 | 508.08 | bounded | 046.04 | 558.07 | 211.06 |
| 421.06 | 549.03 | 410.07 | 047.06 | 733.20 | 289.16 |
| 436.11 | borrowing | 479.11 | 049.04 | breathed | 307.16 |
| 525.21 | 232.05 | bounding | 050.16 | 139.11 | 354.21 |
| 560.07 | both | 114.22 | 056.17 | 365.02 | 356.13 |
| 697.02 | 005.22 | 517.11 | brandy | 726.09 | 362.15 |
| 727.19 | 021.02 | boundless | 036.11 | 739.22 | 385.22 |
| bony | 044.03 | 371.18 | 168.04 | 755.12 | 386.05 |
| 564.13 | 061.15 | bounds | 233.02 | breathing | 440.01 |
| book | 078.03 | 431.08 | 390.10 | 058.15 | 453.09 |
| 029.17 | 079.01 | 700.21 | 401.08 | 747.20 | 463.18 |
| 031.03 | 079.11 | bountiful | brass | 752.03 | 469.16 |
| 039.20 | 080.17 | 103.20 | 233.07 | 764.09 | 485.07 |
| 043.12 | 094.22 | bow | brat | breathless | 486.01 |
| 044.08 | 099.22 | 066.22 | 078.11 | 084.19 | 488.14 |
| 057.05 | 103.22 | 674.18 | brat's | 113.11 | 532.17 |
| 063.11 | 105.02 | bowed | 164.21 | 128.15 | 634.21 |
| 064.15 | 114.05 | 012.20 | brave | 211.09 | 651.19 |
| 137.22 | 141.16 | 017.11 | 762.21 | 434.08 | 666.22 |
| 234.19 | 156.22 | bowl | braved | 638.21 | 685.18 |
| 352.06 | 197.01 | 317.19 | 284.13 | breathlessly | 703.20 |
| 463.19 | 204.10 | 317.22 | bravely | 355.07 | 713.03 |
| 506.19 | 209.17 | 319.10 | 140.11 | breaths | 744.16 |
| 512.16 | 213.12 | box | brazened | 206.14 | bringing |
| 528.11 | 219.17 | 027.06 | 232.17 | bred | 028.11 |
| 668.19 | 220.04 | 120.01 | bread | 081.18 | 075.08 |
| 677.16 | 224.09 | 449.15 | 025.02 | 331.02 | 292.14 |
| 694.15 | 235.05 | 612.15 | 064.08 | 727.02 | 299.14 |
| 696.11 | 240.22 | boxes | 646.21 | breead | 332.15 |
| 703.02 | 256.06 | 042.19 | 724.14 | 472.08 | 614.09 |
| 704.01 | 274.17 | boy | 748.01 | breed | 737.09 |
| 710.02 | 298.15 | 042.06 | 749.15 | 123.03 | brings |
| 711.18 | 299.01 | 079.13 | breaath | 479.05 | 455.18 |
| 713.03 | 356.20 | 083.07 | 257.05 | breeding | brink |
| 728.22 | 357.08 | 092.02 | 728.09 | 562.15 | 272.06 |
| 754.04 | 364.07 | 099.13 | break | breeze | brisk |
| book-larning | 377.15 | 108.08 | 045.11 | 557.21 | 552.22 |
| 497.02 | 394.13 | 110.01 | 085.04 | breeze-rocked | briskly |
| books | 395.03 | 115.16 | 164.20 | 518.08 | 065.01 |
| 038.19 | 405.06 | 117.09 | 263.02 | brethren | 318.19 |
| 043.02 | 410.01 | 119.10 | 293.08 | 050.03 | 490.10 |
| 053.04 | 411.21 | 151.14 | 353.19 | bribed | bristling |
| 053.16 | 414.19 | 168.08 | 371.15 | 649.22 | 531.03 |
| 149.13 | 414.19 | 190.14 | 511.16 | bride | broad |
| 269.05 | 414.21 | 244.18 | 553.18 | 306.01 | 123.15 |
| 271.21 | 420.03 | 293.17 | 563.10 | bridegroom | 233.11 |
| 272.05 | 429.08 | 311.22 | 615.11 | 578.02 | brocken |
| 274.05 | 434.09 | 421.13 | 642.05 | bridle | 324.13 |
| 274.07 | 477.17 | 443.07 | 703.06 | 290.17 | broke |
| 288.10 | 482.14 | 450.22 | 726.01 | 416.11 | 010.14 |
| 392.16 | 487.05 | 452.14 | breakfast | 560.05 | 064.03 |
| 504.22 | 488.18 | 453.08 | 065.12 | bridles | 178.20 |
| 505.01 | 511.22 | 459.04 | 226.16 | 299.01 | 265.14 |
| 512.17 | 517.07 | 465.13 | 267.09 | brief | 381.04 |
| 550.09 | 524.03 | 469.08 | 431.06 | 031.04 | 389.22 |
| 555.03 | 524.11 | 490.14 | 466.06 | 239.17 | 419.20 |
| 556.04 | 544.10 | 495.13 | 469.16 | 280.09 | 497.09 |
| 563.15 | 547.13 | 498.07 | 624.04 | 316.10 | 633.07 |
| 568.18 | 558.08 | 509.01 | 659.19 | 473.12 | 683.17 |
| 630.13 | 564.04 | 514.14 | 663.19 | 597.04 | 750.17 |
| 632.15 | 571.17 | 532.04 | 715.11 | 700.17 | broken |
| 668.02 | 599.12 | 537.10 | 718.18 | 716.05 | 052.18 |
| 677.18 | 610.07 | 581.19 | 722.03 | briefly | 103.17 |
| 678.01 | 620.08 | 600.11 | 737.08 | 378.20 | 117.12 |
| 678.06 | 622.15 | 602.08 | 739.01 | bright | 133.05 |
| 680.13 | 630.20 | 615.16 | 746.22 | 098.01 | 160.13 |
| 682.09 | 637.03 | 631.17 | 748.18 | 116.02 | 185.18 |
| 700.12 | 646.15 | 761.02 | breakfasts | 243.03 | 267.03 |
| 702.17 | 652.13 | boy's | 139.07 | 370.11 | 356.19 |
| 713.05 | 667.21 | 468.04 | breaking | 427.15 | 363.09 |
| 719.13 | 680.13 | boyhood | 195.02 | 462.19 | 363.10 |
| boor | 693.11 | 224.20 | 235.10 | 479.18 | 363.11 |
| 025.06 | 693.21 | boys | 263.02 | 519.12 | 393.15 |
| 497.20 | 711.19 | 005.01 | 363.10 | 552.12 | 433.15 |
| border | 713.19 | 031.19 | 431.08 | 557.11 | 557.19 |
| 737.19 | 717.09 | brace | 524.20 | 557.15 | 706.17 |
| bordered | 726.05 | 201.12 | breaks | 579.17 | 758.02 |
| 015.13 | 726.18 | 260.05 | 752.04 | 673.02 | brooad |
| 104.05 | 749.03 | brach | breast | 738.09 | 043.19 |
| bordering | 752.21 | 340.10 | 003.05 | brightened | brood |
| 025.11 | 753.06 | bracing | 084.17 | 123.18 | 012.03 |
| borders | bother | 004.07 | 094.01 | 727.05 | 502.22 |
| 432.14 | 417.20 | brain | 176.05 | brightening | brooded |
| bore | 660.11 | 046.04 | 314.06 | 692.19 | 596.09 |
| 033.06 | bothered | 075.04 | 361.18 | 727.04 | 729.07 |
| 039.19 | 663.10 | 279.04 | 395.20 | brighter | brooding |
| 099.19 | bothom | 280.22 | 591.07 | 486.05 | 082.04 |
| 569.18 | 190.22 | 301.05 | breath | brightness | 254.01 |
| 597.18 | 319.13 | 322.14 | 081.07 | 219.06 | 640.10 |
| born | bottle | 678.19 | 170.07 | brilliant | brooks |
| 074.07 | 012.06 | 750.13 | 259.21 | 154.07 | 303.07 |

530.04
brother
041.17
048.11
082.17
092.10
109.13
121.08
129.12
147.04
175.18
194.17
198.06
199.08
213.03
219.13
221.16
225.11
235.13
269.04
296.19
305.11
306.08
327.11
336.17
336.18
342.01
375.14
394.20
408.17
411.17
418.05
429.14
451.01
536.02
brother's
151.01
181.22
185.02
222.12
239.16
brother-in-law
418.11
brothers
536.11
brought
005.10
035.05
046.18
069.12
095.08
096.04
111.03
122.04
125.21
126.15
128.09
139.06
140.18
179.06
266.03
270.21
274.19
304.09
311.16
319.17
331.10
338.02
350.12
381.05
394.09
410.19
413.15
425.01
433.07
466.14
471.21
501.09
534.10
542.14
548.05
556.16
562.15
563.15
599.11
614.16
624.11
630.13
637.13
645.21
678.12
684.17
692.07
745.01
brow
124.12
356.17
370.20
428.12
483.15
533.02
brown
021.04
114.02
462.04
519.13
695.01
760.08
brown-eyed
244.18

brows
002.02
152.02
207.18
214.05
290.10
655.11
741.13
bruised
383.21
406.15
bruises
086.01
brush
117.18
brushes
015.02
brushing
517.14
brusts
720.15
brutal
026.07
400.11
636.05
brutality
340.05
brutally
238.13
621.09
brute
129.16
147.11
252.14
385.09
442.22
534.05
563.04
683.04
brutishness
494.01
bud
028.22
029.02
043.21
187.13
187.20
190.21
319.09
324.03
324.17
457.22
472.05
518.18
696.11
719.16
719.17
720.11
budding
373.16
bugbear
525.19
build
004.15
382.06
building
189.03
206.11
373.20
426.14
463.12
bulk
482.05
bull
257.08
bull-dog
106.10
310.01
312.02
bundle
028.14
085.19
511.05
513.18
523.05
bundled
077.18
buoyant
578.22
burden
028.17
206.11
367.05
430.01
443.14
499.18
burial
097.04
buried
025.05
028.01
042.20
124.14
281.17
419.14
463.08
641.05
651.14
760.01
764.02

buries
380.03
burn
385.14
512.09
512.14
614.20
615.11
burned
356.13
702.17
burning
028.14
103.02
260.11
274.13
282.19
394.12
611.15
727.18
burnished
114.20
burnt
497.21
burst
116.19
195.12
282.02
441.22
539.07
563.18
572.18
610.17
704.21
bursting
060.11
554.11
bursts
705.17
bury
284.18
755.03
bushes
015.14
465.19
716.01
721.03
business
027.13
102.10
111.20
179.04
195.03
220.02
295.13
311.12
392.14
426.01
455.18
461.04
572.16
606.14
637.09
645.18
651.19
659.02
697.22
698.03
705.08
747.08
business-visits
475.05
bustled
074.22
691.11
bustling
129.16
busy
093.03
139.05
151.03
373.20
430.16
448.12
576.09
705.12
716.02
726.13
but
005.05
005.14
007.07
010.03
010.10
026.05
030.07
031.04
034.19
038.22
039.07
041.08
044.11
047.17
051.13
051.18
052.04
053.18
056.09
057.08
058.04
058.08

060.03
060.17
062.13
064.06
064.16
066.12
071.17
072.15
073.13
074.19
075.05
076.14
077.08
077.20
078.15
079.13
080.19
082.05
083.17
084.18
089.09
090.15
091.07
092.17
093.19
094.08
095.02
095.14
097.17
097.20
098.05
098.18
100.10
102.06
107.07
108.08
109.17
112.10
114.13
115.15
116.21
117.13
117.19
121.07
121.19
122.15
123.04
123.20
124.15
125.16
126.20
128.02
131.20
132.03
133.04
133.10
134.05
134.13
136.19
137.19
139.11
140.09
141.09
142.16
143.10
145.19
146.02
146.14
147.12
148.16
149.18
150.10
151.10
151.17
152.07
152.14
154.03
163.06
163.13
163.21
166.13
168.01
169.02
170.07
170.21
172.15
174.21
176.10
176.12
177.03
178.03
178.11
179.10
180.02
181.18
182.12
183.06
183.10
183.14
183.20
184.20
189.21
193.02
193.17
194.03
194.18
195.10
196.21
198.10
199.04
199.13

199.18
202.03
203.16
203.21
204.12
204.20
208.05
208.15
208.20
209.15
212.19
213.10
214.06
215.05
216.09
219.04
219.14
220.14
222.02
222.21
223.15
224.03
226.14
228.18
228.20
231.11
232.06
233.13
234.08
235.20
236.12
238.14
239.01
240.02
243.13
244.07
245.11
246.17
247.21
248.15
249.01
250.04
251.10
256.12
256.17
257.15
259.12
260.08
261.04
262.09
263.04
263.17
264.05
264.10
264.13
264.20
267.03
267.21
270.03
272.02
273.15
278.12
278.20
279.05
279.11
280.10
282.06
283.17
284.16
284.20
286.02
286.14
287.12
287.17
288.07
288.14
289.07
291.15
292.17
293.03
294.08
294.13
294.17
295.01
295.08
295.17
296.17
297.02
298.19
299.04
299.20
303.12
303.20
305.13
307.12
307.16
310.21
311.20
312.12
314.01
315.06
315.10
318.16
318.21
322.08
323.01
323.06
327.03
329.01
330.01
330.08

330.17
331.07
332.01
332.21
333.14
333.16
334.21
335.16
337.10
337.16
338.19
339.17
340.05
340.17
341.07
341.20
344.09
346.16
347.19
348.04
350.17
351.10
353.12
354.04
355.16
356.01
356.13
357.05
357.15
360.04
361.04
361.21
363.18
364.03
365.10
367.18
368.05
370.09
370.18
371.11
372.05
372.16
373.12
375.03
377.11
377.19
378.07
379.13
382.17
385.08
386.10
387.10
389.09
390.15
391.17
392.13
393.06
394.14
395.02
395.09
398.14
399.05
400.06
401.15
403.06
405.10
405.22
406.04
406.17
407.09
408.16
409.04
409.17
411.05
412.09
413.13
414.06
414.22
415.13
417.03
418.02
418.14
419.11
420.02
420.07
421.11
421.20
422.04
425.03
426.12
428.09
428.18
429.12
430.14
432.07
433.08
434.06
436.13
437.08
437.11
439.03
439.16
442.04
444.01
444.08
444.18
446.02
446.20
450.01
450.17
451.02

| | | | | | |
|---|---|---|---|---|---|
| 451.10 | 565.18 | 662.22 | 009.05 | 217.02 | 400.16 |
| 452.01 | 566.11 | 663.12 | 009.10 | 218.02 | 402.21 |
| 452.11 | 566.20 | 664.07 | 013.04 | 218.04 | 403.14 |
| 452.21 | 568.03 | 665.01 | 014.03 | 218.06 | 404.13 |
| 453.05 | 568.18 | 665.20 | 015.01 | 224.02 | 407.19 |
| 453.17 | 569.07 | 666.21 | 016.06 | 235.10 | 409.22 |
| 456.22 | 569.11 | 668.03 | 023.22 | 236.17 | 411.02 |
| 457.08 | 570.03 | 669.03 | 024.18 | 238.15 | 413.09 |
| 460.06 | 571.17 | 669.22 | 029.09 | 247.18 | 416.11 |
| 460.18 | 572.06 | 670.12 | 029.21 | 248.10 | 425.05 |
| 461.01 | 572.16 | 670.20 | 030.14 | 248.22 | 425.20 |
| 463.09 | 574.04 | 671.09 | 030.21 | 252.03 | 426.10 |
| 464.03 | 575.11 | 672.02 | 034.02 | 253.20 | 428.19 |
| 465.09 | 576.06 | 673.08 | 042.07 | 254.08 | 429.01 |
| 466.01 | 577.05 | 674.01 | 042.12 | 254.16 | 430.15 |
| 467.06 | 577.16 | 674.05 | 043.10 | 255.06 | 430.18 |
| 467.14 | 578.08 | 675.02 | 044.02 | 255.11 | 431.18 |
| 470.06 | 578.19 | 675.13 | 044.03 | 255.20 | 432.01 |
| 471.13 | 580.09 | 675.21 | 046.01 | 257.09 | 433.18 |
| 473.03 | 580.19 | 677.15 | 046.01 | 259.22 | 436.07 |
| 474.10 | 581.14 | 678.19 | 051.03 | 260.11 | 440.05 |
| 476.21 | 582.10 | 679.07 | 051.18 | 260.20 | 441.08 |
| 480.10 | 585.07 | 680.04 | 057.20 | 262.12 | 441.14 |
| 481.09 | 586.11 | 681.06 | 058.15 | 263.02 | 443.03 |
| 482.04 | 587.12 | 681.21 | 059.06 | 263.06 | 443.06 |
| 482.12 | 588.05 | 683.12 | 062.22 | 263.19 | 443.13 |
| 483.05 | 589.13 | 683.22 | 063.04 | 267.08 | 445.15 |
| 483.14 | 590.19 | 685.04 | 063.11 | 273.21 | 446.06 |
| 485.05 | 591.04 | 686.14 | 063.20 | 274.03 | 446.08 |
| 485.16 | 591.20 | 690.01 | 064.06 | 276.07 | 446.14 |
| 486.13 | 592.07 | 690.10 | 064.22 | 278.12 | 449.04 |
| 487.09 | 592.18 | 692.03 | 065.09 | 278.18 | 451.20 |
| 488.12 | 594.03 | 692.14 | 070.03 | 279.14 | 452.04 |
| 488.19 | 594.07 | 693.02 | 077.03 | 283.19 | 452.09 |
| 489.06 | 596.08 | 693.15 | 079.18 | 284.12 | 453.04 |
| 489.14 | 598.10 | 694.09 | 080.03 | 284.18 | 453.12 |
| 489.20 | 598.18 | 695.10 | 080.04 | 285.09 | 454.07 |
| 490.08 | 599.14 | 696.21 | 081.08 | 285.14 | 454.21 |
| 492.03 | 600.07 | 697.17 | 082.10 | 287.04 | 458.06 |
| 493.14 | 601.07 | 698.16 | 083.03 | 288.05 | 460.07 |
| 494.05 | 602.05 | 699.04 | 083.08 | 290.19 | 466.08 |
| 494.14 | 602.07 | 699.13 | 084.21 | 291.04 | 467.21 |
| 496.04 | 603.03 | 701.04 | 085.12 | 294.15 | 472.20 |
| 496.21 | 603.15 | 702.02 | 088.15 | 299.09 | 474.06 |
| 497.09 | 604.15 | 702.03 | 089.03 | 302.01 | 476.12 |
| 498.05 | 605.01 | 702.10 | 089.15 | 303.19 | 480.07 |
| 498.12 | 606.12 | 702.21 | 090.04 | 304.04 | 482.05 |
| 498.17 | 606.16 | 703.10 | 092.20 | 304.08 | 483.17 |
| 499.01 | 606.21 | 703.17 | 094.07 | 304.11 | 487.14 |
| 499.08 | 607.07 | 704.02 | 094.13 | 304.14 | 491.11 |
| 499.19 | 608.06 | 706.02 | 100.15 | 305.09 | 492.04 |
| 500.07 | 609.10 | 708.19 | 101.22 | 308.06 | 495.15 |
| 501.03 | 610.04 | 711.16 | 102.01 | 308.13 | 499.19 |
| 501.16 | 612.09 | 713.19 | 103.04 | 309.05 | 503.19 |
| 503.16 | 614.15 | 714.02 | 103.22 | 311.05 | 504.03 |
| 504.20 | 614.21 | 716.18 | 104.05 | 311.17 | 506.12 |
| 505.11 | 615.01 | 717.01 | 105.07 | 311.21 | 506.16 |
| 505.18 | 615.13 | 721.04 | 105.09 | 312.02 | 508.03 |
| 506.13 | 617.04 | 723.10 | 106.07 | 312.20 | 509.04 |
| 507.21 | 619.15 | 725.01 | 107.21 | 313.22 | 510.05 |
| 508.16 | 620.15 | 725.17 | 113.03 | 315.03 | 514.10 |
| 509.07 | 620.20 | 728.19 | 113.07 | 316.01 | 516.18 |
| 510.22 | 621.17 | 729.05 | 118.17 | 317.20 | 517.07 |
| 511.10 | 622.06 | 729.17 | 119.02 | 323.02 | 519.21 |
| 512.06 | 622.11 | 730.12 | 123.09 | 323.18 | 520.02 |
| 513.03 | 623.13 | 730.21 | 125.20 | 325.11 | 521.02 |
| 514.05 | 624.01 | 731.14 | 126.07 | 325.12 | 521.17 |
| 514.07 | 625.02 | 732.06 | 128.19 | 326.01 | 526.19 |
| 515.03 | 626.10 | 732.15 | 130.20 | 326.15 | 529.07 |
| 517.07 | 627.04 | 733.02 | 130.22 | 328.08 | 529.12 |
| 518.06 | 627.07 | 734.12 | 131.10 | 332.12 | 530.09 |
| 519.03 | 628.04 | 735.03 | 132.14 | 332.16 | 532.14 |
| 520.17 | 629.01 | 738.05 | 133.03 | 333.09 | 535.03 |
| 521.05 | 630.05 | 739.04 | 133.08 | 333.10 | 538.10 |
| 521.21 | 631.11 | 739.18 | 135.06 | 335.01 | 539.17 |
| 522.10 | 632.01 | 741.03 | 136.17 | 335.05 | 540.20 |
| 522.17 | 632.18 | 741.17 | 142.05 | 336.09 | 541.08 |
| 524.21 | 633.09 | 742.16 | 143.02 | 337.20 | 541.18 |
| 525.16 | 633.21 | 743.12 | 145.10 | 341.14 | 542.03 |
| 526.09 | 634.07 | 743.17 | 147.02 | 345.18 | 542.05 |
| 526.15 | 634.13 | 744.10 | 149.08 | 347.05 | 542.20 |
| 527.09 | 635.06 | 745.01 | 149.14 | 347.10 | 543.16 |
| 527.21 | 637.10 | 745.07 | 150.22 | 351.13 | 545.07 |
| 528.22 | 638.11 | 745.20 | 156.20 | 352.16 | 551.17 |
| 529.06 | 638.22 | 747.01 | 159.13 | 353.14 | 553.03 |
| 532.20 | 639.06 | 747.10 | 163.02 | 354.20 | 553.06 |
| 533.15 | 640.01 | 751.04 | 163.03 | 355.03 | 553.17 |
| 534.18 | 640.10 | 753.07 | 164.19 | 359.09 | 553.20 |
| 535.03 | 641.02 | 753.14 | 165.20 | 364.06 | 555.07 |
| 535.12 | 641.05 | 755.12 | 166.12 | 364.13 | 557.20 |
| 536.05 | 645.01 | 756.16 | 169.13 | 365.21 | 560.05 |
| 536.10 | 645.19 | 757.10 | 171.09 | 367.10 | 561.01 |
| 536.15 | 647.10 | 757.19 | 173.08 | 378.15 | 561.14 |
| 539.16 | 648.01 | 758.14 | 176.13 | 378.21 | 561.17 |
| 540.04 | 649.02 | 758.22 | 180.01 | 379.08 | 563.09 |
| 541.05 | 649.08 | 759.06 | 190.19 | 379.20 | 563.20 |
| 543.16 | 649.17 | 760.11 | 191.19 | 383.18 | 564.11 |
| 544.04 | 651.03 | 761.11 | 194.12 | 388.07 | 565.20 |
| 547.18 | 652.18 | 762.15 | 198.04 | 390.09 | 567.07 |
| 548.06 | 652.21 | buy | 198.12 | 390.10 | 572.17 |
| 548.17 | 653.07 | 125.18 | 199.12 | 392.12 | 573.02 |
| 552.17 | 653.20 | 385.16 | 203.12 | 393.16 | 573.07 |
| 555.15 | 655.05 | 511.21 | 205.01 | 393.20 | 575.09 |
| 556.05 | 655.11 | by | 205.13 | 396.04 | 576.07 |
| 557.16 | 655.13 | 002.11 | 205.14 | 396.21 | 578.09 |
| 557.19 | 658.02 | 003.13 | 205.17 | 397.05 | 582.04 |
| 558.18 | 659.01 | 004.10 | 206.12 | 397.18 | 582.08 |
| 559.03 | 660.02 | 004.12 | 210.18 | 398.02 | 583.11 |
| 559.19 | 660.04 | 006.10 | 211.10 | 398.09 | 584.06 |
| 562.04 | 660.22 | 006.17 | 213.16 | 399.09 | 585.09 |
| 563.02 | 662.03 | 007.18 | 216.07 | 399.15 | 589.15 |

| | | | | | |
|---|---|---|---|---|---|
| 591.05 | by-road | calling | 506.12 | 428.02 | 669.11 |
| 596.03 |    692.20 |    002.09 | 506.17 | 440.18 | 702.02 |
| 596.05 | bye |    003.08 | 514.14 | 454.05 | 706.20 |
| 597.08 |    076.21 |    034.03 | 528.05 | 454.09 | 707.03 |
| 597.15 |    199.13 |    139.08 | 546.18 | 455.09 | 729.19 |
| 602.19 |    199.17 |    145.02 | 551.01 | 463.09 | canary |
| 604.19 |    570.11 |    152.05 | 558.09 | 463.18 |    229.15 |
| 605.13 |    594.12 |    188.17 | 559.03 | 466.15 | candid |
| 606.19 | c |    236.03 | 561.05 | 470.04 |    599.07 |
| 607.21 |    558.22 |    278.11 | 561.16 | 472.11 | candle |
| 608.04 |    559.01 |    293.20 | 569.16 | 474.08 |    031.02 |
| 608.16 |    563.03 |    397.09 | 578.01 | 486.10 |    037.03 |
| 609.06 | cabinet |    446.08 | 586.16 | 492.15 |    038.18 |
| 616.12 |    507.05 |    486.01 | 590.02 | 493.15 |    039.12 |
| 621.10 | cahnt |    491.07 | 597.01 | 494.11 |    054.17 |
| 621.18 |    233.07 |    580.09 | 612.18 | 496.03 |    055.11 |
| 621.19 | cake | calls | 623.16 | 496.15 |    059.20 |
| 622.21 |    115.04 |    045.07 | 627.13 | 505.11 |    061.08 |
| 623.04 |    121.04 |    398.05 | 628.05 | 509.02 |    094.09 |
| 629.11 |    121.11 |    430.05 | 630.14 | 518.14 |    102.16 |
| 631.19 |    531.04 |    490.03 | 637.12 | 520.06 |    145.22 |
| 636.20 | cakes |    493.08 | 651.14 | 525.06 |    284.06 |
| 642.10 |    111.06 |    537.04 | 659.01 | 525.08 |    284.07 |
| 642.11 |    118.14 |    570.21 | 659.11 | 525.11 |    308.14 |
| 645.12 | calamity |    627.13 | 660.20 | 526.09 |    325.01 |
| 645.20 |    211.12 |    646.08 | 661.13 | 526.14 |    393.10 |
| 646.08 |    295.15 | calm | 662.10 | 533.03 |    395.21 |
| 647.08 |    520.15 |    079.06 | 667.07 | 533.08 |    401.07 |
| 650.02 |    547.22 |    333.13 | 668.08 | 541.12 |    454.22 |
| 650.16 | calculate |    344.15 | 678.09 | 543.04 |    506.05 |
| 652.18 |    182.03 |    351.11 | 688.05 | 544.04 |    552.10 |
| 653.16 |    430.09 |    371.02 | 695.12 | 545.06 |    644.22 |
| 655.04 |    490.10 |    601.22 | 698.22 | 545.08 |    662.11 |
| 655.05 | calculated |    673.02 | 712.03 | 560.19 |    669.04 |
| 658.11 |    057.18 | calmer | 726.15 | 577.05 |    743.09 |
| 660.19 |    256.05 |    095.14 | 727.12 | 578.13 |    744.11 |
| 661.14 | calf |    741.11 | 744.02 | 581.17 |    744.15 |
| 662.04 |    469.17 | calmly | 746.12 | 588.07 |    751.13 |
| 662.13 | calf-skin |    457.11 | 747.02 | 606.05 | candle-light |
| 663.07 |    039.14 |    639.16 | 750.07 | 608.03 |    213.16 |
| 663.17 | call |    752.07 | 755.14 | 611.11 | candles |
| 666.12 |    005.12 | calmness | 756.19 | 617.10 |    209.04 |
| 666.14 |    023.02 |    724.08 | camels | 619.07 |    210.01 |
| 666.19 |    101.06 | cambric |    431.18 | 619.16 |    277.01 |
| 667.09 |    115.16 |    129.07 | can | 620.08 | canine |
| 667.15 |    119.21 | came |    009.07 | 621.11 |    009.11 |
| 668.15 |    130.17 |    031.01 |    020.02 | 628.01 |    445.15 |
| 668.21 |    133.02 |    047.11 |    021.20 | 628.05 | canisters |
| 670.13 |    184.18 |    052.03 |    022.06 | 634.10 |    006.11 |
| 674.19 |    201.11 |    062.10 |    022.08 | 646.16 |    019.05 |
| 675.07 |    210.18 |    070.07 |    023.17 | 651.12 |    019.20 |
| 675.13 |    219.11 |    075.12 |    028.20 | 652.11 | cannibal |
| 680.14 |    255.01 |    076.02 |    029.21 | 658.11 |    398.02 |
| 686.13 |    257.17 |    077.22 |    031.04 | 672.04 | cannot |
| 688.09 |    297.01 |    090.09 |    032.08 | 683.05 |    016.13 |
| 690.07 |    307.14 |    092.06 |    046.10 | 684.02 |    030.19 |
| 690.11 |    307.15 |    092.17 |    053.01 | 685.17 |    031.09 |
| 691.14 |    312.21 |    096.02 |    057.20 | 708.20 |    044.17 |
| 693.03 |    320.09 |    103.20 |    060.02 | 711.04 |    045.05 |
| 693.08 |    328.11 |    106.20 |    064.13 | 724.14 |    048.09 |
| 694.01 |    439.03 |    108.21 |    067.07 | 732.13 |    092.09 |
| 694.19 |    462.11 |    112.03 |    120.20 | 739.18 |    093.17 |
| 695.17 |    527.12 |    114.21 |    133.18 | 746.06 |    134.06 |
| 696.03 |    531.16 |    121.18 |    136.17 | 751.19 |    168.21 |
| 696.06 |    532.12 |    122.10 |    138.05 | 752.06 |    172.14 |
| 700.11 |    555.14 |    128.20 |    145.21 | 752.07 |    176.08 |
| 704.21 |    557.03 |    132.19 |    158.21 | 753.07 |    182.12 |
| 705.16 |    558.14 |    139.07 |    163.17 | can'le |    196.11 |
| 707.18 |    576.22 |    141.01 |    172.01 |    233.02 |    212.10 |
| 708.12 |    631.21 |    145.03 |    172.19 | can't |    218.06 |
| 709.04 |    631.21 |    147.22 |    173.01 |    045.06 |    234.02 |
| 709.11 |    649.11 |    150.16 |    181.21 |    129.03 |    243.12 |
| 710.12 |    665.17 |    154.10 |    183.16 |    141.04 |    246.18 |
| 711.04 |    707.06 |    184.10 |    186.13 |    171.07 |    262.22 |
| 712.10 |    725.02 |    188.22 |    187.21 |    176.11 |    264.19 |
| 717.01 | called |    190.06 |    202.11 |    222.21 |    272.11 |
| 719.02 |    018.05 |    194.12 |    204.15 |    231.18 |    273.03 |
| 719.18 |    055.03 |    202.17 |    207.08 |    238.08 |    282.04 |
| 720.19 |    056.20 |    205.10 |    219.22 |    287.13 |    285.20 |
| 725.14 |    081.12 |    217.02 |    223.13 |    292.08 |    297.18 |
| 725.18 |    094.07 |    221.12 |    227.09 |    306.17 |    297.20 |
| 725.22 |    132.05 |    232.04 |    228.22 |    398.21 |    307.06 |
| 726.01 |    159.18 |    243.05 |    229.01 |    406.17 |    315.17 |
| 727.13 |    184.20 |    248.12 |    232.20 |    417.06 |    338.07 |
| 731.17 |    193.03 |    291.22 |    252.03 |    453.08 |    339.20 |
| 731.17 |    214.11 |    297.05 |    256.01 |    462.06 |    367.09 |
| 732.15 |    217.14 |    306.05 |    265.04 |    464.12 |    375.16 |
| 733.22 |    217.16 |    311.20 |    265.12 |    483.02 |    377.05 |
| 734.01 |    221.09 |    326.05 |    307.13 |    496.03 |    377.06 |
| 734.02 |    234.06 |    329.22 |    310.13 |    497.15 |    377.07 |
| 735.01 |    240.17 |    331.04 |    329.02 |    499.08 |    382.17 |
| 737.14 |    247.17 |    344.12 |    333.18 |    520.02 |    390.15 |
| 741.05 |    342.11 |    353.03 |    336.12 |    523.03 |    398.06 |
| 742.10 |    403.04 |    354.12 |    336.14 |    540.01 |    398.12 |
| 744.07 |    414.06 |    379.13 |    338.15 |    540.18 |    406.01 |
| 745.21 |    414.07 |    382.19 |    339.11 |    541.02 |    459.08 |
| 748.11 |    418.16 |    394.09 |    342.08 |    541.22 |    471.11 |
| 750.06 |    475.19 |    403.12 |    346.06 |    542.12 |    496.02 |
| 750.17 |    525.07 |    407.21 |    356.08 |    572.13 |    504.21 |
| 754.22 |    534.20 |    416.02 |    364.04 |    573.01 |    527.11 |
| 755.02 |    566.02 |    420.02 |    371.15 |    591.15 |    543.03 |
| 756.09 |    593.02 |    420.15 |    383.04 |    600.01 |    561.06 |
| 759.04 |    599.18 |    431.13 |    388.09 |    600.07 |    565.16 |
| 759.08 |    622.11 |    445.07 |    388.10 |    606.02 |    571.10 |
| 760.17 |    635.12 |    448.11 |    395.09 |    621.06 |    578.21 |
| 761.19 |    640.15 |    454.10 |    399.02 |    631.18 |    589.15 |
| 763.03 |    646.03 |    477.15 |    399.03 |    631.19 |    593.04 |
| 763.12 |    658.04 |    477.21 |    405.15 |    634.06 |    599.08 |
| 763.14 |    662.06 |    478.16 |    405.22 |    634.13 |    601.05 |
| 764.03 |    704.08 |    480.18 |    415.14 |    660.16 |    618.17 |
| | |    499.16 |    426.21 |    665.18 |    647.06 |

| | | | | | |
|---|---|---|---|---|---|
| 652.20 | 619.15 | carrying | 039.20 | 303.07 | 573.18 |
| 660.04 | 656.13 | 347.09 | 040.17 | 306.06 | 574.05 |
| 664.20 | 660.08 | 515.08 | 044.20 | 306.16 | 575.10 |
| 678.16 | 671.12 | cart | 052.10 | 309.07 | 576.10 |
| 678.20 | 699.04 | 688.08 | 056.19 | 313.17 | 577.07 |
| 686.07 | 720.07 | cart-horse | 058.07 | 332.10 | 579.09 |
| 709.19 | 729.18 | 701.19 | 060.15 | 333.03 | 581.12 |
| 711.11 | 758.18 | cartwheels | 072.10 | 333.04 | 581.21 |
| 719.19 | 762.07 | 180.06 | 072.14 | 333.17 | 585.04 |
| 720.10 | cared | carve | 072.16 | 333.18 | 586.22 |
| 731.14 | 027.04 | 675.08 | 090.03 | 334.10 | 589.04 |
| 733.19 | 198.14 | carved | 091.11 | 336.06 | 589.21 |
| 740.02 | 370.07 | 073.08 | 094.17 | 336.13 | 590.11 |
| 744.06 | 376.19 | 130.03 | 099.06 | 342.02 | 590.20 |
| 752.09 | careful | 379.19 | 100.08 | 343.16 | 592.02 |
| 753.04 | 289.13 | 465.17 | 100.15 | 345.10 | 593.03 |
| 757.08 | 476.03 | carving | 102.03 | 346.09 | 596.07 |
| 761.19 | 619.13 | 004.20 | 103.13 | 348.07 | 599.07 |
| cannut | 619.14 | 163.07 | 105.06 | 350.09 | 600.04 |
| 322.07 | 709.19 | 163.13 | 105.17 | 353.10 | 600.10 |
| 472.05 | carefully | 716.22 | 109.15 | 355.13 | 601.05 |
| 696.10 | 119.09 | case | 110.16 | 356.15 | 601.06 |
| canst | 449.14 | 038.03 | 112.11 | 357.13 | 601.08 |
| 093.13 | 470.08 | 296.04 | 114.14 | 358.04 | 601.11 |
| cant | careless | 337.09 | 116.13 | 359.03 | 602.10 |
| 103.11 | 115.12 | 345.06 | 118.10 | 359.08 | 602.18 |
| 119.22 | 165.15 | 392.03 | 121.08 | 361.21 | 604.01 |
| 627.16 | 187.12 | 404.19 | 122.10 | 363.17 | 605.12 |
| canter | 283.13 | 454.20 | 122.14 | 364.19 | 605.14 |
| 462.20 | 420.17 | 623.12 | 126.13 | 366.06 | 606.01 |
| canty | 489.04 | 632.22 | 128.10 | 368.01 | 607.10 |
| 520.11 | 526.04 | 633.07 | 129.10 | 369.03 | 608.17 |
| cap | 738.13 | 693.12 | 130.06 | 372.15 | 609.12 |
| 453.03 | carelessly | 730.01 | 131.20 | 376.21 | 610.01 |
| 468.04 | 210.11 | casement | 144.16 | 385.03 | 610.19 |
| 485.22 | 330.12 | 051.16 | 146.07 | 388.14 | 612.17 |
| 495.12 | carelessness | 279.17 | 146.11 | 389.08 | 613.02 |
| capable | 100.06 | 397.17 | 146.17 | 391.08 | 613.05 |
| 046.11 | 109.13 | casement-window | 148.02 | 396.08 | 614.08 |
| 202.16 | 256.06 | 553.06 | 149.17 | 398.20 | 614.18 |
| 220.06 | cares | casements | 150.09 | 406.09 | 615.05 |
| 230.09 | 082.07 | 744.01 | 152.01 | 407.20 | 615.17 |
| 385.17 | 171.06 | cash | 152.15 | 408.17 | 616.22 |
| 607.09 | 271.05 | 422.17 | 153.08 | 409.05 | 618.12 |
| 729.11 | 346.07 | 664.20 | 154.09 | 412.13 | 619.01 |
| capacity | 598.13 | cast | 155.01 | 414.06 | 620.12 |
| 338.07 | caress | 061.20 | 155.20 | 414.08 | 622.05 |
| 425.07 | 009.11 | 074.09 | 157.01 | 428.18 | 623.03 |
| caper | 009.15 | 270.01 | 157.01 | 430.06 | 624.06 |
| 758.21 | caressed | 358.06 | 158.09 | 431.13 | 628.21 |
| capering | 588.17 | 379.07 | 159.01 | 433.08 | 629.09 |
| 437.12 | caresses | 403.21 | 160.18 | 439.08 | 630.01 |
| capital | 150.13 | 498.05 | 172.01 | 443.10 | 632.12 |
| 001.11 | 303.18 | 500.14 | 174.11 | 445.19 | 635.13 |
| 023.02 | 362.17 | 590.15 | 176.03 | 451.22 | 635.16 |
| caprice | 450.18 | 603.01 | 177.05 | 475.08 | 637.13 |
| 060.16 | 488.11 | 666.08 | 177.21 | 478.12 | 640.06 |
| caprices | caricature | castaway | 178.14 | 481.21 | 641.10 |
| 198.09 | 040.14 | 030.03 | 179.19 | 482.20 | 642.05 |
| 356.18 | caring | 109.22 | 181.03 | 485.01 | 643.08 |
| caps | 676.21 | casting | 182.02 | 487.04 | 645.10 |
| 292.18 | carn | 154.19 | 184.05 | 488.09 | 646.13 |
| captain | 233.07 | 491.01 | 184.21 | 489.07 | 647.03 |
| 415.04 | carols | 656.18 | 186.10 | 489.19 | 647.22 |
| captured | 118.17 | castle | 187.17 | 490.02 | 648.12 |
| 609.15 | 131.17 | 308.22 | 188.09 | 491.18 | 655.21 |
| caravan | carpet | cat | 191.20 | 492.21 | 658.10 |
| 431.16 | 282.02 | 061.10 | 193.02 | 496.03 | 659.05 |
| carcass | 323.01 | 061.22 | 194.10 | 497.04 | 662.17 |
| 758.17 | carpeted | 062.21 | 195.08 | 499.22 | 662.20 |
| cards | 098.17 | 064.22 | 196.18 | 501.17 | 663.11 |
| 221.16 | 104.03 | 135.17 | 204.04 | 503.12 | 664.19 |
| care | 568.16 | 160.02 | 205.10 | 504.02 | 667.07 |
| 015.21 | carriage | 193.18 | 210.16 | 505.07 | 672.01 |
| 026.08 | 126.11 | 739.22 | 211.09 | 506.03 | 674.11 |
| 055.21 | 213.21 | catastrophe | 212.22 | 511.03 | 676.03 |
| 083.01 | 383.06 | 178.02 | 215.01 | 512.19 | 676.10 |
| 119.17 | 384.08 | 374.11 | 216.16 | 517.22 | 678.04 |
| 133.17 | 411.02 | catch | 224.15 | 519.15 | 679.11 |
| 140.06 | 450.10 | 102.08 | 226.10 | 523.07 | 682.19 |
| 147.11 | 452.03 | 105.05 | 227.21 | 524.02 | 683.05 |
| 168.08 | 552.21 | 127.14 | 228.13 | 525.20 | 685.18 |
| 177.03 | carried | 190.04 | 229.09 | 527.03 | 685.20 |
| 196.05 | 029.12 | 230.13 | 231.01 | 531.06 | 686.14 |
| 227.22 | 107.08 | 373.04 | 233.09 | 533.01 | 700.06 |
| 262.18 | 122.01 | 465.16 | 234.07 | 534.01 | 700.16 |
| 272.18 | 165.02 | 558.16 | 236.03 | 535.05 | 704.11 |
| 275.11 | 267.11 | 611.12 | 237.19 | 535.19 | 705.05 |
| 302.01 | 350.05 | 739.15 | 239.14 | 537.05 | 707.16 |
| 306.20 | 419.07 | 750.19 | 240.07 | 537.15 | 709.04 |
| 316.14 | 453.15 | catching | 250.04 | 538.06 | 710.01 |
| 337.19 | 566.21 | 116.15 | 250.21 | 538.18 | 710.15 |
| 339.17 | 578.04 | 180.05 | 251.19 | 540.15 | 711.07 |
| 341.12 | 641.03 | 193.13 | 253.07 | 542.14 | 712.04 |
| 352.21 | 665.05 | 244.14 | 254.04 | 544.09 | 712.21 |
| 357.09 | 710.11 | 513.01 | 255.02 | 544.16 | 717.01 |
| 357.09 | 728.12 | 629.11 | 256.18 | 546.09 | 718.04 |
| 385.03 | 754.14 | 683.06 | 260.04 | 548.08 | 721.08 |
| 387.02 | carrion | catechised | 264.09 | 550.05 | 723.05 |
| 387.08 | 420.03 | 103.04 | 265.11 | 552.06 | 723.22 |
| 396.22 | carry | catechism | 269.07 | 553.16 | 724.07 |
| 457.02 | 184.08 | 173.03 | 272.10 | 554.05 | 724.22 |
| 501.01 | 208.18 | catgut | 274.02 | 559.02 | 725.17 |
| 507.07 | 346.18 | 654.04 | 280.01 | 560.19 | 728.07 |
| 521.13 | 628.07 | catharine | 286.03 | 562.03 | 728.08 |
| 542.05 | 637.17 | 448.07 | 286.04 | 563.07 | 729.02 |
| 545.05 | 646.04 | catherine | 287.20 | 567.16 | 731.09 |
| 578.14 | 743.09 | 039.01 | 290.03 | 569.06 | 737.08 |
| 578.17 | 751.19 | 039.02 | 292.01 | 570.15 | 741.01 |
| 590.17 | 760.03 | 039.03 | 292.12 | 571.04 | 747.02 |
| 618.09 | | 039.06 | 295.21 | 573.08 | 750.20 |

756.03
catherine's
040.02
057.05
078.04
115.12
170.19
199.04
217.05
224.03
227.07
240.15
249.13
258.13
302.06
311.10
327.10
347.07
362.13
367.01
371.22
379.06
379.17
385.02
410.22
413.14
441.09
452.14
459.04
495.08
527.22
532.13
580.16
594.07
594.17
598.08
606.09
630.11
636.16
639.14
656.21
662.09
681.08
699.21
727.03
catherines
039.10
cathy
060.13
073.11
076.05
076.14
077.01
079.09
079.16
080.18
081.16
082.17
089.09
092.08
093.06
093.14
099.20
102.10
104.14
106.07
107.06
108.21
110.08
113.02
114.08
116.15
117.13
120.19
121.16
128.19
131.03
145.04
150.18
151.03
152.11
153.20
157.11
169.19
173.06
190.01
192.03
194.16
216.02
228.17
238.16
257.07
259.09
324.11
324.11
356.08
362.20
365.08
414.10
427.03
432.08
435.13
437.02
437.20
439.11
440.09
440.19
445.05
447.02
450.12
451.09

452.06
453.15
462.15
474.02
478.04
480.02
481.01
482.08
485.10
486.10
486.18
490.21
491.13
495.18
496.12
498.17
501.02
502.17
506.14
508.15
511.15
516.03
518.22
521.04
525.09
526.19
528.05
534.08
535.06
536.15
538.08
539.06
542.01
543.04
547.08
553.05
578.06
578.14
582.21
587.19
589.13
590.18
591.09
592.19
593.21
595.05
611.14
620.02
652.21
664.05
708.08
713.09
719.05
736.05
cathy's
043.16
078.01
463.16
509.10
522.11
523.14
612.11
cats
018.17
235.17
619.18
cattle
003.15
607.22
705.11
caught
074.19
107.12
162.03
226.20
249.18
284.04
291.13
302.18
361.21
386.08
409.21
450.13
481.01
515.10
518.05
539.12
676.10
723.13
731.17
cause
025.08
051.13
186.20
216.12
256.21
282.06
289.01
292.09
305.05
326.20
334.06
339.11
343.18
405.13
405.14
524.08
609.18
640.17
759.22

caused
023.09
075.04
085.02
206.02
227.05
409.03
430.14
436.07
538.09
566.08
604.19
causes
221.22
351.22
387.21
730.10
causeway
003.08
015.13
329.22
683.14
causing
206.09
323.10
327.11
cautions
527.09
cautious
027.11
288.16
432.03
522.15
cautiously
061.05
224.13
378.20
378.20
706.13
cave
276.14
428.14
446.01
cawlf
232.12
cease
132.10
ceased
046.12
150.11
197.11
253.19
334.20
393.03
410.17
413.06
434.22
468.07
ceiling
104.05
cellar
010.03
011.05
106.17
699.11
cemented
522.18
centipede
237.12
centre
010.20
104.07
centred
287.04
668.22
century
039.21
ceremony
419.15
044.11
certain
107.07
140.15
188.07
226.12
231.03
240.08
245.19
251.12
262.04
273.05
280.19
298.16
352.22
388.03
403.20
406.11
416.13
429.10
467.13
469.21
476.19
509.01
511.14
516.21
528.18
545.12
593.13
622.13
654.12
668.14

728.09
certainly
001.05
025.21
074.17
090.06
137.15
204.11
331.01
383.09
384.06
384.09
496.18
572.14
652.18
652.20
717.08
738.19
certainty
596.10
chafing
172.16
639.02
chagrin
499.16
chain
015.12
108.04
633.13
chains
104.06
726.01
chair
017.13
020.14
023.05
031.02
032.08
038.02
055.11
064.16
077.12
092.19
130.05
135.09
159.13
178.17
235.02
237.08
258.20
259.16
326.15
330.19
360.03
361.15
384.21
392.04
394.10
410.06
410.22
434.13
453.04
453.08
466.08
476.12
532.09
537.21
538.08
556.19
559.06
570.05
607.12
621.15
623.08
639.01
646.01
667.20
737.09
751.19
chairs
006.13
104.04
217.03
323.11
cham'er
233.04
324.04
chamber
037.05
054.01
060.05
080.06
097.08
119.01
121.15
128.12
160.19
195.19
218.03
267.07
279.02
285.18
290.15
297.07
302.13
315.04
320.16
326.03
355.14
368.11
371.12

390.18
507.20
550.03
597.05
622.18
654.13
661.14
663.15
745.06
756.13
757.14
760.18
chamber-door
639.11
chambers
392.02
642.07
champion
647.09
chance
022.07
029.21
071.21
080.04
124.03
135.07
162.08
169.06
194.12
283.08
317.03
378.16
404.21
419.02
546.09
616.12
622.14
650.10
695.06
chanced
101.03
200.01
248.13
425.19
475.04
chandelier
108.13
change
022.07
124.03
130.10
183.03
289.02
296.02
304.04
337.08
351.12
384.18
392.13
487.02
490.18
510.05
529.03
547.17
597.11
649.18
651.02
730.04
732.15
754.10
changed
063.06
070.18
082.08
107.01
120.06
143.15
176.22
283.01
309.04
333.06
420.02
520.04
551.10
577.01
587.01
635.08
701.12
changeling
614.01
changes
183.04
274.18
changling
056.21
channel
225.03
chap
188.01
472.05
chapel
046.02
047.11
050.14
198.18
209.11
353.01
364.15
379.19
426.14
641.06

665.15
665.19
chapel-roof
287.16
chaplain
043.15
chapter
040.05
094.05
chapters
100.14
191.07
character
048.13
073.21
134.19
147.07
229.18
252.10
256.16
333.06
338.18
358.07
417.04
581.09
597.19
620.01
728.21
763.12
characters
038.22
498.21
charge
144.07
166.15
230.08
309.04
399.13
430.12
453.13
498.21
527.15
549.04
553.04
598.20
715.06
charged
435.16
435.21
charitable
074.13
202.04
388.19
charity
064.09
253.03
346.03
389.01
606.18
charlie
433.18
437.07
445.07
charm
228.10
712.02
charmed
559.08
charming
201.02
225.08
467.03
chart
066.02
chase
388.04
437.14
679.14
chased
492.03
chastened
148.18
chastise
611.04
chastisement
219.18
chat
074.16
chatter
005.17
120.21
589.16
chattered
126.04
193.05
449.08
chattering
134.07
434.16
498.07
cheap
498.15
cheat
180.13
cheated
074.12
244.04
473.04
499.05
cheating
133.06

| | | | | | |
|---|---|---|---|---|---|
| check | chided | 636.19 | 310.11 | clasp | 119.14 |
| 248.08 | 091.03 | 646.19 | 697.01 | 362.14 | 134.21 |
| 682.02 | chief | 726.19 | christmas | clasped | 278.06 |
| 725.08 | 100.10 | 727.21 | 113.03 | 176.15 | 314.04 |
| checked | 202.12 | children's | 115.04 | 615.02 | 395.17 |
| 029.09 | 206.04 | 095.12 | 118.16 | clasping | 544.14 |
| 409.22 | 372.22 | chill | 120.01 | 097.10 | cloes |
| 435.21 | 576.13 | 075.02 | 131.15 | 602.08 | 321.06 |
| 534.02 | 619.08 | 381.12 | chubby | class | cloised |
| 567.15 | child | 515.09 | 177.14 | 137.08 | 233.02 |
| checking | 078.03 | 517.11 | 309.14 | 686.07 | close |
| 009.17 | 081.03 | 667.10 | chuck | clatter | 210.07 |
| 285.16 | 081.12 | 741.16 | 756.06 | 005.17 | 254.19 |
| 374.15 | 082.14 | chillness | chucked | 189.06 | 268.01 |
| cheek | 085.17 | 264.21 | 675.14 | 194.09 | 296.11 |
| 116.17 | 090.07 | chills | chuckled | clause | 317.20 |
| 143.08 | 092.10 | 652.03 | 495.01 | 485.04 | 397.20 |
| 156.21 | 109.10 | chimbley | church | claws | 429.01 |
| 170.19 | 130.09 | 187.22 | 041.05 | 619.19 | 429.13 |
| 223.15 | 143.17 | chimed | 100.04 | clay | 451.06 |
| 358.09 | 157.13 | 067.09 | 109.03 | 030.05 | 456.12 |
| 362.15 | 159.19 | chimney | 122.03 | clean | 488.01 |
| 421.11 | 163.04 | 006.09 | 126.13 | 079.07 | 527.01 |
| 453.21 | 164.16 | 019.04 | 284.19 | 127.02 | 550.02 |
| 479.18 | 165.04 | 063.09 | 350.13 | 455.16 | 557.20 |
| 517.15 | 167.07 | 092.22 | 390.08 | 556.10 | 585.06 |
| 579.16 | 188.19 | 200.02 | 413.06 | cleaner | 602.22 |
| 611.15 | 192.06 | 403.16 | 578.10 | 079.21 | 608.20 |
| 617.01 | 229.18 | 436.09 | 689.19 | cleaning | 642.11 |
| 634.01 | 244.05 | 513.11 | 760.14 | 155.09 | 652.10 |
| 639.20 | 280.02 | 690.13 | churchyard | clear | 652.15 |
| 650.17 | 281.17 | 693.13 | 579.16 | 021.11 | 667.15 |
| 694.19 | 301.06 | 705.14 | 651.15 | 029.20 | 711.13 |
| 709.08 | 309.05 | chimney-corner | 689.20 | 065.14 | 744.03 |
| cheeking | 342.22 | 087.05 | 754.15 | 100.03 | 744.13 |
| 352.17 | 369.04 | chimney-piece | churl | 167.20 | 758.06 |
| cheeks | 375.21 | 028.15 | 074.04 | 251.08 | close-handed |
| 011.11 | 382.04 | 713.03 | churlish | 254.20 | 071.17 |
| 021.06 | 386.20 | chimney-stack | 015.19 | 388.05 | closed |
| 130.14 | 411.22 | 189.05 | churstmas | 496.19 | 002.19 |
| 207.16 | 418.07 | chin | 324.16 | 638.15 | 039.07 |
| 213.09 | 421.04 | 133.13 | cinders | 715.12 | 052.01 |
| 266.06 | 434.14 | 467.22 | 015.04 | 741.11 | 053.07 |
| 303.22 | 452.17 | china | 532.18 | 747.08 | 062.13 |
| 374.16 | 454.06 | 125.16 | 692.12 | cleared | 103.22 |
| 491.12 | 456.21 | chinks | 751.07 | 544.21 | 237.21 |
| 519.06 | 461.08 | 191.19 | cipher | 559.20 | 238.14 |
| 549.01 | 467.09 | chipping | 469.04 | 748.17 | 262.20 |
| 752.21 | 468.02 | 013.06 | circle | clearing | 273.13 |
| cheer | 470.02 | chirping | 027.08 | 466.06 | 279.19 |
| 259.05 | 471.07 | 510.02 | 061.12 | clearly | 358.10 |
| 303.19 | 503.20 | chit | 117.12 | 122.16 | 370.21 |
| 387.08 | 525.07 | 484.17 | circuit | 286.18 | 376.11 |
| 417.04 | 525.19 | 622.11 | 007.05 | 317.10 | 399.14 |
| 521.02 | 541.11 | chivalrous | circumstance | cleaved | 456.05 |
| 548.04 | 562.18 | 338.15 | 003.01 | 240.14 | 458.06 |
| 644.02 | 584.01 | choice | 051.17 | clefts | 473.04 |
| cheerful | 588.20 | 018.18 | 097.02 | 427.13 | 518.12 |
| 017.03 | 639.21 | 025.09 | 291.17 | clenched | 527.13 |
| 021.18 | 654.18 | 180.19 | 378.07 | 026.04 | 609.16 |
| 068.03 | 669.04 | 199.13 | circumstances | 564.07 | 654.14 |
| 118.15 | child's | 306.11 | 119.11 | 702.11 | 654.20 |
| 127.02 | 020.16 | 550.10 | 206.02 | 709.02 | closer |
| 141.22 | 052.14 | 716.07 | 225.02 | 749.15 | 018.21 |
| 173.12 | 088.07 | choke | 330.22 | clenching | 160.13 |
| 174.13 | 243.13 | 269.11 | 414.18 | 271.02 | 193.05 |
| 330.05 | 659.05 | choked | 442.15 | clergy | 364.19 |
| 370.11 | childer | 259.22 | 562.16 | 617.21 | 491.04 |
| 452.10 | 043.02 | 565.20 | 594.20 | clergyman | closet |
| 521.03 | childhood | choking | civil | 047.20 | 038.11 |
| 581.17 | 080.16 | 035.22 | 032.19 | clergyman's | 051.10 |
| 605.13 | 732.20 | 325.05 | 311.03 | 047.17 | closing |
| 738.09 | childhood's | 540.03 | 440.05 | clever | 064.15 |
| cheerfully | 149.13 | choose | 563.04 | 560.21 | 630.08 |
| 202.16 | childish | 076.10 | civilities | 679.08 | cloth |
| 536.04 | 040.11 | 141.06 | 062.20 | cleverly | 114.03 |
| cheerfulness | 059.10 | 235.05 | civility | 108.02 | 130.16 |
| 588.01 | 220.15 | 265.09 | 147.20 | click | 156.02 |
| cheerless | 275.02 | 272.14 | 248.19 | 211.08 | clothes |
| 313.08 | 385.14 | 571.03 | 667.13 | 393.09 | 022.01 |
| 686.11 | 438.17 | 634.10 | civilized | climax | 067.22 |
| cheese | 518.04 | 762.10 | 713.17 | 215.11 | 102.12 |
| 121.12 | 545.14 | chooses | claim | climb | 113.08 |
| cherish | 617.04 | 251.04 | 197.18 | 427.18 | 115.19 |
| 024.17 | children | chord | 340.21 | 480.06 | 190.05 |
| 164.14 | 075.17 | 007.17 | 389.01 | 480.11 | 207.05 |
| cherished | 076.20 | chose | 418.05 | 518.01 | 278.09 |
| 236.14 | 077.06 | 076.16 | claimant | 693.05 | 383.07 |
| 305.06 | 079.08 | 118.19 | 457.07 | climbed | 384.05 |
| 338.19 | 082.05 | 155.05 | claimed | 011.04 | 398.01 |
| 521.06 | 089.21 | 162.11 | 664.17 | 380.02 | 666.09 |
| cherishing | 091.10 | 214.13 | 695.10 | 522.05 | clothes-press |
| 614.07 | 094.12 | 320.01 | clamber | 598.21 | 038.03 |
| cheritably | 097.09 | 415.10 | 518.20 | 692.20 | cloud |
| 003.21 | 103.08 | 419.12 | clambered | climbing | 023.09 |
| cherub | 104.12 | 747.14 | 132.12 | 676.16 | 070.15 |
| 140.18 | 108.16 | chosen | clambering | clinging | 223.06 |
| chest | 110.04 | 348.04 | 433.14 | 104.01 | 404.12 |
| 406.15 | 115.17 | chosing | clamorously | cloak | 463.06 |
| 610.14 | 126.14 | 736.06 | 189.19 | 044.13 | 709.02 |
| 680.19 | 129.15 | chozzen | clamour | 095.04 | 731.15 |
| chevy | 219.15 | 191.04 | 618.01 | 110.20 | clouded |
| 679.14 | 357.16 | christendom | clamourous | 217.20 | 356.17 |
| chewing | 414.20 | 106.17 | 297.11 | 298.19 | 408.07 |
| 539.07 | 424.07 | christened | clane | 450.21 | 518.19 |
| 707.17 | 425.17 | 080.14 | 321.04 | 476.11 | 527.22 |
| 719.08 | 443.11 | 411.11 | clapped | 517.01 | cloudless |
| chicken | 454.18 | christian | 456.15 | cloaks | 479.20 |
| 468.03 | 461.12 | 049.05 | clarionets | 126.11 | cloudlessly |
| chide | 470.02 | 080.17 | 131.12 | clock | 557.12 |
| 063.15 | 611.04 | 221.05 | | 067.09 | |

clouds
188.05
275.16
516.18
557.15
588.05
706.20
727.01
cloudy
204.22
743.15
clown
024.22
174.20
440.17
495.22
clowns
686.06
clubs
050.12
clump
450.07
clung
052.05
365.21
383.16
467.14
594.06
607.01
655.09
clusters
006.07
clutch
107.14
237.19
clutched
278.09
coach
038.04
coachman
260.18
261.03
384.15
coal
017.06
154.12
693.12
coal-hole
720.06
coal-scuttles
015.02
coal-shed
017.02
coals
385.16
393.08
514.01
532.17
751.18
coarseness
493.19
coat
016.19
022.16
077.17
079.15
120.13
400.11
coat-laps
010.21
coax
132.17
coaxed
664.14
coaxing
462.12
545.16
cobweb
645.19
cockatrice
620.03
coffee
068.04
747.15
coffin
378.03
421.01
649.14
649.19
652.06
coffins
754.19
cogitating
602.17
cogitations
465.14
coincide
148.07
528.18
cold
014.02
039.16
065.14
074.19
093.01
134.08
135.11
184.10
192.08
216.16
226.20

264.18
273.22
279.18
280.10
283.07
294.01
305.13
323.18
366.10
372.04
383.19
398.02
403.17
420.03
515.10
516.17
519.18
532.17
546.19
549.03
652.02
665.07
670.13
739.15
740.08
colder
008.22
044.17
coldly
455.17
coldness
329.14
414.02
colds
475.21
cole
390.17
collar
044.02
collect
303.21
724.06
collected
109.01
collecting
276.10
325.14
collection
731.21
college
088.18
203.11
colony
259.05
479.01
colossal
063.09
496.10
colour
098.12
126.16
177.02
468.21
549.01
639.03
coloured
438.08
666.08
colourless
358.17
colours
069.09
239.10
colt
085.03
colt's
127.22
colts
083.15
column
103.05
comb
665.13
combat
065.01
375.05
combatants
010.22
combed
111.08
152.18
351.08
758.05
combine
394.18
combing
125.12
come
010.09
012.14
012.14
019.03
021.17
036.01
044.16
050.03
052.12
060.03
060.13
060.13

060.14
072.08
095.09
097.08
106.01
108.03
111.20
116.09
116.13
119.21
121.03
124.09
132.19
140.04
142.07
152.07
154.18
159.03
160.09
164.08
165.13
167.16
167.17
170.22
177.07
177.08
178.21
180.07
186.16
190.12
190.12
192.01
203.04
203.10
208.01
211.15
212.02
216.17
221.19
235.01
245.06
251.01
254.11
262.02
264.12
269.08
270.10
275.21
276.17
277.08
284.09
284.15
285.01
285.12
285.21
287.07
287.19
289.20
307.16
310.14
311.18
314.20
326.18
332.04
339.14
343.14
345.12
346.21
356.20
359.20
360.01
361.13
373.06
375.01
385.21
390.01
397.02
401.03
401.05
419.07
422.05
429.17
432.04
434.04
436.03
436.03
439.01
439.14
449.11
449.18
451.10
452.17
452.17
454.20
457.12
458.09
464.21
466.12
467.16
470.11
472.16
473.10
474.07
483.08
489.05
489.15
489.16
489.19
501.19
504.12
504.21

510.13
520.09
526.19
531.17
533.04
533.05
533.19
534.19
535.09
540.12
542.04
543.08
543.10
543.11
543.12
552.04
555.21
559.11
563.09
566.08
570.09
574.03
580.06
580.21
588.16
590.10
592.07
599.06
599.20
606.18
615.05
616.03
616.03
616.11
631.03
633.22
639.22
645.14
646.10
656.08
656.11
656.15
663.19
667.14
669.12
672.01
672.06
677.04
697.16
703.11
707.07
710.07
712.21
715.11
722.20
723.12
742.01
745.20
747.22
751.10
751.10
751.16
754.19
755.15
756.06
comed
184.14
comer
118.13
comes
042.17
120.19
123.06
193.18
279.14
316.03
337.09
427.20
435.03
476.14
511.21
564.03
733.05
comfort
090.22
099.03
204.11
248.17
313.16
362.21
387.14
404.02
444.19
472.17
526.05
574.01
582.04
597.12
693.13
700.15
comfortable
008.08
041.08
120.17
589.14
650.09
comfortably
540.04
542.11
737.15

comforted
044.06
415.09
726.17
comforting
095.16
comfortless
175.21
comforts
027.10
307.22
338.09
coming
014.06
027.17
059.09
077.05
080.12
101.18
121.03
129.12
151.08
173.15
191.18
194.05
206.06
217.19
249.18
253.12
260.03
260.17
264.05
266.18
275.17
305.22
314.02
339.22
344.10
350.20
385.18
393.20
411.16
450.04
483.06
485.11
489.02
500.11
507.01
548.04
572.11
577.21
594.06
619.03
633.06
635.16
640.11
644.07
654.10
665.03
679.06
683.13
685.05
685.09
691.08
700.05
724.02
737.20
741.01
763.21
command
033.13
168.18
185.19
280.22
377.21
397.06
605.07
723.03
commanded
041.11
commanding
091.05
commands
576.11
commence
130.07
155.09
621.16
651.04
740.13
commenced
018.09
040.19
050.09
055.10
062.01
070.05
075.12
113.06
128.09
157.09
202.19
245.10
287.20
292.19
319.18
403.18
437.12
453.20
510.16
513.09

535.14
545.02
554.20
567.09
614.22
652.07
713.15
743.22
commencement
196.01
302.14
422.08
429.12
680.05
704.19
commencing
508.11
681.19
commendation
218.15
commendations
083.02
457.02
727.03
commending
430.06
comment
019.01
527.19
commentary
040.06
173.11
commenting
701.14
comments
005.04
comminations
444.11
commissioned
459.03
commit
398.06
committed
047.08
157.03
387.01
502.21
598.20
719.03
committing
225.22
common
010.20
021.07
169.07
307.04
333.10
333.15
413.16
424.06
444.21
674.17
746.16
752.03
commonest
344.21
commonly
383.13
communicated
441.07
749.03
communication
157.21
197.11
329.11
378.10
communion
132.07
compactly
061.07
companion
044.11
046.17
062.21
066.15
109.18
126.18
154.03
179.22
189.18
234.13
239.19
293.11
308.07
314.05
333.08
350.20
358.12
393.22
399.01
417.06
462.01
464.16
483.16
492.18
495.04
497.08
504.15
521.12
523.19
541.16

| | | | | | |
|---|---|---|---|---|---|
| 546.11 | complain | comprehension | 695.15 | conflict | consented |
| 586.09 | 639.09 | 061.04 | 705.03 | 058.19 | 221.20 |
| 622.19 | 661.05 | 496.19 | condensed | confluence | 550.08 |
| 708.02 | 670.12 | compressing | 349.07 | 050.11 | 558.19 |
| 708.03 | complained | 375.04 | condescend | confound | consequence |
| 729.03 | 086.03 | compulsion | 671.10 | 055.09 | 017.17 |
| 755.20 | 185.02 | 733.22 | condescendingly | 490.11 | 025.04 |
| 760.10 | 346.15 | 734.02 | 117.07 | confounded | 033.09 |
| companion's | 532.19 | compulsory | condition | 066.11 | 137.06 |
| 365.09 | 551.21 | 635.22 | 021.11 | 128.19 | 148.12 |
| companionable | 701.01 | compunction | 085.01 | 194.17 | 220.04 |
| 075.11 | complaining | 266.01 | 091.13 | 235.15 | 350.10 |
| companions | 152.13 | 541.19 | 105.10 | 272.05 | 497.02 |
| 091.06 | 152.20 | conceal | 119.08 | 391.01 | 693.22 |
| 144.15 | 226.16 | 130.17 | 160.12 | 568.21 | 705.02 |
| 150.09 | 248.16 | 156.15 | 272.02 | 611.20 | 759.21 |
| 198.03 | 286.10 | 192.19 | 337.08 | 712.07 | consequences |
| 391.18 | 466.02 | 375.15 | 358.15 | 722.10 | 222.18 |
| 404.01 | complainings | 475.13 | 386.17 | confused | 256.22 |
| 603.01 | 262.03 | 569.21 | 401.18 | 279.04 | 293.12 |
| 761.17 | complaint | 588.15 | 405.15 | 290.03 | 399.10 |
| companionship | 548.07 | 663.01 | 418.03 | confusion | 500.13 |
| 445.02 | complaints | 707.18 | 542.02 | 009.02 | 509.08 |
| 516.07 | 157.10 | concealed | 583.16 | 053.21 | 647.15 |
| company | 582.09 | 006.08 | 720.21 | 295.13 | consequently |
| 008.12 | 726.05 | 058.14 | 733.19 | 415.06 | 390.07 |
| 059.17 | 737.14 | 204.19 | condoled | 467.02 | 477.07 |
| 059.19 | compelled | 378.07 | 036.12 | 666.16 | 481.14 |
| 090.20 | 116.12 | 500.17 | condolences | congratulating | consider |
| 099.14 | complete | 620.08 | 270.05 | 611.18 | 080.13 |
| 146.20 | 005.07 | 657.03 | conduct | congratulation | 120.05 |
| 153.19 | 023.20 | 678.15 | 021.13 | 587.02 | 137.07 |
| 154.01 | 228.14 | 759.17 | 030.13 | congregation | 185.06 |
| 155.08 | 413.04 | concealing | 041.01 | 041.06 | 229.01 |
| 218.08 | 422.21 | 435.01 | 103.10 | 048.03 | 337.22 |
| 227.22 | 510.03 | concealment | 144.05 | conjecture | 355.04 |
| 255.01 | completely | 116.16 | 170.20 | 429.10 | considerable |
| 293.18 | 001.08 | 316.13 | 185.02 | 504.18 | 070.04 |
| 320.13 | 057.05 | conceals | 233.14 | 592.20 | 259.13 |
| 326.12 | 067.15 | 229.20 | 269.07 | conjectured | 434.19 |
| 362.08 | 086.05 | conceit | 327.04 | 003.21 | 450.15 |
| 390.19 | 103.14 | 164.14 | 403.06 | 067.16 | 455.06 |
| 439.12 | 149.19 | 614.14 | 414.17 | 185.11 | 552.20 |
| 440.21 | 199.19 | conceited | 502.06 | 317.22 | considerably |
| 454.05 | 258.19 | 025.10 | 552.01 | 322.22 | 098.10 |
| 551.21 | 335.04 | 320.05 | 562.04 | 546.03 | 489.08 |
| 580.16 | 400.06 | conceive | 572.12 | 735.04 | 516.04 |
| 589.06 | 492.17 | 141.16 | 600.20 | conjectures | 685.10 |
| 608.03 | 551.16 | 593.04 | 636.05 | 026.10 | consideration |
| 666.12 | 599.22 | 740.02 | 709.06 | 643.05 | 197.18 |
| 671.11 | 736.06 | conceived | 725.09 | conjuring | 206.04 |
| 717.19 | complexion | 689.09 | conducted | 177.06 | 234.12 |
| 735.08 | 156.16 | concentrate | 312.22 | 319.01 | 470.03 |
| 741.07 | 464.15 | 136.15 | 607.12 | connect | 470.06 |
| 756.09 | 486.05 | concentrated | conducting | 681.12 | considerations |
| 762.08 | complexioned | 322.12 | 698.03 | connected | 013.04 |
| comparatively | 097.21 | concern | cones | 248.05 | considered |
| 317.14 | compliance | 051.04 | 051.04 | 332.13 | 047.01 |
| compare | 310.04 | 646.11 | confess | 731.09 | 054.10 |
| 046.10 | 347.05 | 661.04 | 008.20 | 731.12 | 118.18 |
| 333.18 | 749.13 | 670.12 | 054.10 | connection | 172.18 |
| 504.05 | complied | concernedly | 080.08 | 222.03 | 180.22 |
| compared | 582.07 | 117.20 | 148.12 | 414.11 | 305.22 |
| 013.18 | compliment | concerning | 160.15 | 499.21 | 518.04 |
| 114.11 | 259.09 | 069.10 | 330.05 | conned | 548.20 |
| 465.07 | comply | 221.10 | 417.12 | 563.03 | 569.18 |
| comparison | 244.09 | 236.14 | 601.22 | conquered | 583.10 |
| 414.15 | 563.17 | 267.17 | confessed | 301.04 | 634.20 |
| 521.13 | complying | 332.09 | 726.06 | conscience | considering |
| compassion | 430.03 | 441.12 | confession | 031.06 | 172.02 |
| 060.21 | 624.13 | 462.22 | 517.06 | 180.14 | 221.22 |
| 377.17 | composed | 466.08 | 718.16 | 195.01 | 285.01 |
| 602.11 | 277.21 | 524.07 | confessions | 242.05 | 498.11 |
| 625.06 | 295.20 | 593.10 | 734.12 | 344.14 | consisted |
| compassionate | 379.15 | 606.10 | confidant | 397.11 | 038.02 |
| 498.13 | 639.14 | 676.11 | 124.19 | 404.02 | consolation |
| compel | 645.08 | 726.06 | confide | 655.01 | 231.11 |
| 343.15 | 691.16 | 747.09 | 146.20 | 703.14 | 288.11 |
| 402.11 | composing | 754.18 | confidence | 734.19 | 413.21 |
| 584.03 | 758.22 | concerns | 294.04 | conscious | 444.04 |
| 647.02 | composition | 089.21 | 431.12 | 083.11 | 520.19 |
| 705.07 | 509.11 | 171.02 | 573.19 | 150.13 | 574.09 |
| compelled | composure | 418.11 | confident | 276.22 | 589.01 |
| 031.21 | 271.11 | concessions | 441.09 | 352.14 | 619.11 |
| 036.09 | 613.07 | 204.14 | confidently | 378.11 | console |
| 043.05 | compound | concluded | 215.06 | 498.01 | 095.15 |
| 069.08 | 003.13 | 027.13 | 404.09 | 594.14 | 329.18 |
| 082.13 | compounded | 035.08 | confiding | 651.20 | 377.22 |
| 137.10 | 017.06 | 149.10 | 692.04 | 673.06 | 472.19 |
| 210.02 | compounds | 402.05 | confine | 733.06 | 578.17 |
| 282.18 | 508.11 | 500.15 | 724.12 | consciously | consoled |
| 318.21 | comprehend | 740.18 | confined | 046.03 | 130.01 |
| 325.04 | 014.10 | concluding | 087.05 | consciousness | 252.03 |
| 333.07 | 118.10 | 050.06 | 132.04 | 057.08 | 653.03 |
| 378.14 | 225.17 | 391.02 | 444.10 | 369.06 | 653.04 |
| 386.01 | 277.14 | 508.12 | 515.11 | 403.01 | conspire |
| 389.13 | 309.16 | conclusion | 700.20 | consecrated | 402.02 |
| 471.08 | 335.20 | 079.05 | confinement | 680.14 | constable |
| 480.16 | 446.15 | 152.05 | 304.02 | consent | 391.07 |
| 567.12 | 467.11 | 395.11 | 548.05 | 171.20 | constancy |
| 592.05 | comprehended | 429.15 | confirmed | 181.10 | 145.12 |
| 638.22 | 245.15 | 509.17 | 242.08 | 333.21 | constant |
| compelling | 725.20 | 729.06 | 295.06 | 346.19 | 046.17 |
| 099.16 | 760.04 | conclusions | 420.06 | 384.17 | 150.09 |
| 443.12 | comprehending | 238.08 | 589.01 | 418.02 | 258.04 |
| compensation | 208.16 | 306.19 | 763.09 | 512.14 | 296.07 |
| 466.02 | 434.20 | concourse | confirming | 535.20 | 302.02 |
| competent | 639.07 | 364.14 | 299.07 | 581.20 | 386.20 |
| 029.19 | comprehends | condemned | conflagration | 601.12 | 428.21 |
| complacently | 182.10 | 048.22 | 683.07 | 601.19 | 449.04 |
| 253.02 | | 410.13 | | 736.04 | 502.14 |

| | | | | | |
|---|---|---|---|---|---|
| 551.18 | 226.10 | 694.04 | 180.14 | 597.21 | 157.17 |
| 732.10 | 232.04 | 694.08 | 270.02 | correction | 166.06 |
| constantly | 271.21 | contrast | 283.19 | 611.19 | 166.08 |
| 082.10 | 392.19 | 007.08 | 341.05 | correctly | 181.10 |
| 356.18 | 480.06 | 154.11 | 402.19 | 066.17 | 186.05 |
| 429.03 | 551.07 | contribute | 407.13 | 419.13 | 190.05 |
| 475.21 | 634.08 | 472.17 | 453.12 | 694.11 | 192.19 |
| 533.17 | 718.09 | 588.13 | 480.22 | 763.03 | 196.14 |
| 559.05 | 747.11 | contributed | 484.10 | correspond | 202.03 |
| 582.14 | continue | 443.05 | 501.17 | 146.09 | 202.09 |
| consternation | 121.13 | contributes | 709.18 | correspondence | 205.05 |
| 157.19 | 136.02 | 732.11 | 734.08 | 411.06 | 209.01 |
| 285.10 | 182.20 | contributing | convulsed | 508.01 | 217.06 |
| constitution | 203.07 | 261.12 | 277.22 | corresponding | 222.09 |
| 008.07 | 264.14 | contributions | 601.03 | 065.21 | 228.10 |
| 169.02 | 294.05 | 131.14 | convulsions | corroborating | 231.14 |
| 205.14 | 349.06 | contrite | 055.16 | 025.15 | 237.21 |
| 429.07 | 537.16 | 532.14 | 167.12 | corroboration | 240.17 |
| 472.18 | 582.02 | contrivances | convulsively | 481.08 | 242.10 |
| 733.14 | 643.09 | 642.13 | 361.19 | corrugated | 245.11 |
| constrained | 646.13 | contrive | cooked | 020.14 | 247.06 |
| 011.01 | 733.19 | 307.04 | 184.07 | 533.02 | 248.01 |
| constructed | continued | 527.09 | cookery | costly | 251.18 |
| 315.14 | 018.16 | 622.19 | 319.05 | 711.22 | 253.22 |
| consulting | 028.08 | 677.19 | cooks | cotch | 254.14 |
| 746.09 | 029.16 | contrived | 136.17 | 324.20 | 258.17 |
| consumed | 039.05 | 089.16 | cool | cote | 262.09 |
| 513.14 | 055.14 | 100.19 | 018.01 | 017.02 | 263.11 |
| 682.12 | 058.19 | 149.05 | 128.14 | cottage | 263.17 |
| consuming | 066.07 | 388.04 | 143.08 | 136.06 | 266.12 |
| 429.13 | 072.17 | 431.05 | 192.22 | 196.09 | 267.21 |
| consumption | 102.16 | 713.22 | 358.03 | 196.10 | 272.02 |
| 140.01 | 121.03 | contrives | 557.19 | 671.22 | 273.18 |
| 143.06 | 125.09 | 218.14 | coolly | couch | 274.08 |
| contact | 153.02 | control | 085.16 | 038.08 | 277.13 |
| 010.09 | 159.03 | 058.11 | 214.13 | 063.01 | 281.12 |
| 118.02 | 167.13 | 253.22 | 685.13 | 370.13 | 281.14 |
| 344.10 | 207.12 | 263.20 | coolness | cough | 283.11 |
| 501.09 | 228.16 | 577.08 | 389.16 | 532.21 | 285.06 |
| contained | 235.14 | 622.15 | coom | 538.11 | 285.08 |
| 182.16 | 246.14 | convalescence | 043.16 | 540.03 | 286.07 |
| 336.07 | 272.08 | 352.04 | 188.01 | 614.16 | 289.01 |
| 668.15 | 276.11 | 579.16 | 531.13 | 629.04 | 291.10 |
| containing | 286.09 | convalescent | coorting | coughed | 294.14 |
| 017.01 | 310.18 | 196.18 | 193.22 | 098.04 | 295.09 |
| 313.11 | 318.06 | convenience | copestone | 559.06 | 295.11 |
| contaminate | 320.06 | 031.13 | 034.14 | coughing | 296.06 |
| 256.21 | 334.05 | convenient | copious | 143.13 | 298.17 |
| contemplate | 354.01 | 465.10 | 035.06 | 565.20 | 301.05 |
| 655.20 | 357.07 | conveniently | 508.05 | coughs | 301.10 |
| contemplated | 359.14 | 038.08 | copper | 475.21 | 304.15 |
| 404.08 | 382.22 | conversant | 005.20 | could | 304.18 |
| contemplating | 385.13 | 502.17 | coquette | 001.07 | 305.17 |
| 287.03 | 390.20 | conversation | 148.03 | 002.17 | 308.10 |
| 759.12 | 405.10 | 027.14 | cord | 011.01 | 310.22 |
| contemplation | 409.04 | 066.19 | 741.17 | 011.19 | 312.12 |
| 235.11 | 424.02 | 126.06 | cordial | 011.22 | 313.14 |
| contempt | 436.20 | 184.04 | 214.17 | 014.09 | 313.19 |
| 148.06 | 438.10 | 228.08 | 219.13 | 018.14 | 319.21 |
| 256.06 | 456.01 | 228.11 | 464.08 | 022.10 | 320.04 |
| 310.22 | 461.21 | 253.19 | 501.16 | 022.11 | 322.10 |
| 489.22 | 475.10 | 262.14 | cordiality | 023.11 | 327.08 |
| 561.13 | 483.19 | 290.04 | 147.02 | 023.18 | 327.13 |
| 600.09 | 488.19 | 309.18 | corn | 027.22 | 332.04 |
| c00.13 | 491.19 | 342.01 | 041.13 | 028.02 | 335.17 |
| 618.19 | 493.11 | 412.17 | 187.09 | 032.17 | 336.05 |
| 659.06 | 519.09 | 493.03 | 321.04 | 037.10 | 336.07 |
| contemptible | 532.12 | 498.03 | 472.07 | 041.05 | 339.05 |
| 409.06 | 545.05 | 588.11 | 511.22 | 043.09 | 340.11 |
| 614.13 | 547.10 | 695.13 | corner | 046.08 | 340.16 |
| contemptuously | 576.12 | conversations | 020.20 | 046.19 | 343.22 |
| 129.10 | 590.08 | 573.14 | 038.19 | 053.18 | 344.11 |
| 739.06 | 603.19 | converse | 055.02 | 055.02 | 345.10 |
| content | 613.15 | 132.09 | 064.01 | 056.11 | 345.22 |
| 102.09 | 631.04 | conversing | 110.15 | 059.01 | 347.16 |
| 138.09 | 640.01 | 747.07 | 184.05 | 066.21 | 349.05 |
| 171.07 | 649.09 | converted | 189.03 | 070.13 | 349.09 |
| 285.03 | 662.22 | 123.09 | 310.02 | 071.20 | 350.08 |
| 405.11 | 665.20 | 282.10 | 321.04 | 076.15 | 355.17 |
| 479.22 | 668.20 | 542.20 | 379.22 | 078.07 | 356.03 |
| 543.01 | 669.16 | converting | 392.04 | 078.10 | 357.07 |
| 682.17 | 674.16 | 382.03 | 404.05 | 078.17 | 359.03 |
| 746.11 | 677.14 | convey | 416.12 | 085.15 | 363.07 |
| contented | 681.18 | 149.05 | 430.12 | 088.13 | 364.08 |
| 079.09 | 691.01 | 167.19 | 450.20 | 091.01 | 364.13 |
| 143.20 | 698.13 | 710.05 | 495.15 | 094.18 | 366.16 |
| 426.18 | 702.05 | conveyed | 611.17 | 095.02 | 370.22 |
| 575.08 | 706.10 | 128.12 | 631.01 | 095.06 | 375.04 |
| 668.17 | 722.01 | 295.04 | 691.18 | 095.17 | 376.06 |
| 700.17 | 735.07 | 641.19 | 705.14 | 095.20 | 378.12 |
| contentedly | contort | conveying | 737.14 | 101.07 | 381.07 |
| 338.10 | 049.21 | 196.19 | corners | 111.11 | 387.11 |
| contents | contracted | 566.09 | 004.17 | 117.15 | 387.12 |
| 057.15 | 655.11 | conviction | 042.02 | 118.10 | 388.11 |
| 276.07 | contradict | 223.19 | 102.22 | 123.15 | 388.16 |
| 317.20 | 170.15 | 290.21 | 206.10 | 123.17 | 391.17 |
| 324.07 | 198.02 | 356.04 | 506.16 | 127.09 | 405.01 |
| 379.08 | 231.18 | 651.12 | corpse | 130.11 | 405.11 |
| 507.10 | 537.11 | convince | 372.05 | 132.17 | 412.18 |
| 507.18 | 601.21 | 183.17 | 641.12 | 133.10 | 414.03 |
| 609.16 | contradiction | 229.11 | 759.09 | 134.09 | 414.20 |
| 699.15 | 186.07 | 233.20 | corpse's | 136.11 | 417.18 |
| 754.04 | contrariety | 252.05 | 379.02 | 137.22 | 422.10 |
| continent | 503.22 | 429.22 | corpses | 144.04 | 424.09 |
| 203.09 | contrary | 499.13 | 047.16 | 145.01 | 425.09 |
| continual | 136.01 | 529.02 | correct | 146.07 | 427.18 |
| 149.09 | 168.13 | 581.08 | 024.13 | 146.10 | 433.08 |
| 241.03 | 252.06 | convinced | 258.01 | 147.22 | 433.12 |
| 269.06 | 415.07 | 072.15 | 443.17 | 148.07 | 438.05 |
| continually | 618.20 | 141.01 | correcting | 150.14 | 442.01 |
| 092.14 | 683.03 | 176.07 | 057.15 | 156.01 | 442.07 |

| COULD (cont.) | couldn't | | cousin | cracked | cried |
|---|---|---|---|---|---|
| 445.10 | 083.04 | 071.05 | 496.09 | 028.19 | 031.14 |
| 445.18 | 141.16 | 108.10 | 496.22 | **cracking** | 032.03 |
| 446.05 | 180.10 | 109.09 | 501.08 | 652.07 | 035.18 |
| 453.17 | 192.13 | 124.06 | 526.18 | **crackling** | 049.18 |
| 471.05 | 203.16 | 154.12 | 532.06 | 393.08 | 084.09 |
| 475.09 | 230.08 | 201.05 | 538.13 | **cracky** | 100.20 |
| 475.14 | 237.15 | 203.13 | 539.11 | 564.11 | 102.03 |
| 479.22 | 250.03 | 217.19 | 543.18 | **cradle** | 109.08 |
| 485.15 | 275.10 | 220.19 | 547.06 | 518.09 | 116.09 |
| 494.04 | 280.19 | 272.17 | 555.19 | **craft** | 122.19 |
| 494.17 | 286.12 | 329.07 | 559.15 | 692.03 | 122.21 |
| 496.09 | 322.05 | 333.01 | 562.06 | **crag** | 124.05 |
| 498.16 | 336.04 | 426.19 | 564.21 | 151.20 | 127.14 |
| 500.18 | 345.01 | 435.15 | 573.14 | 276.14 | 129.16 |
| 501.07 | 383.01 | 463.10 | 580.12 | 276.22 | 134.15 |
| 502.08 | 394.14 | 760.11 | 585.05 | **craggs** | 152.15 |
| 502.22 | 404.20 | **country-side** | 587.13 | 427.07 | 156.13 |
| 507.21 | 447.02 | 145.06 | 590.19 | 428.21 | 159.09 |
| 509.15 | 450.01 | **couple** | 593.09 | 433.02 | 163.01 |
| 511.18 | 529.08 | 006.10 | 607.01 | 433.09 | 165.03 |
| 516.10 | 536.19 | 083.15 | 611.16 | 483.06 | 167.01 |
| 517.13 | 539.17 | 124.13 | 622.04 | **crags** | 171.03 |
| 522.10 | 555.20 | 378.14 | 659.21 | 445.13 | 177.05 |
| 522.19 | 566.20 | 431.19 | 666.03 | 727.09 | 178.18 |
| 523.13 | 568.09 | 480.21 | 668.05 | **crähnr's** | 186.18 |
| 523.18 | 571.10 | 492.16 | 676.06 | 232.09 | 192.09 |
| 525.18 | 590.05 | 503.13 | 679.01 | **cram** | 194.10 |
| 535.20 | 603.05 | **coupled** | 705.19 | 106.19 | 207.20 |
| 539.18 | 607.04 | 750.20 | 706.06 | **crammed** | 210.16 |
| 544.09 | 632.04 | **courage** | 707.08 | 163.08 | 211.17 |
| 552.06 | 639.10 | 122.06 | 707.20 | **cramming** | 215.16 |
| 558.06 | 654.14 | 126.02 | 710.19 | 127.07 | 227.10 |
| 561.21 | 663.01 | 147.16 | 715.09 | **cranky** | 231.05 |
| 566.02 | 665.06 | 200.09 | 717.06 | 321.02 | 236.17 |
| 575.10 | 665.13 | 257.21 | 719.05 | **crash** | 245.01 |
| 576.18 | 669.01 | 415.08 | 721.17 | 265.19 | 250.09 |
| 577.17 | 669.02 | 568.08 | 725.08 | **crater** | 253.07 |
| 578.16 | 679.18 | 602.15 | 732.13 | 497.20 | 260.04 |
| 580.15 | **counsel** | 617.06 | 741.02 | **craters** | 272.05 |
| 581.19 | 026.21 | 668.06 | **cousin's** | 187.13 | 278.15 |
| 581.20 | 050.01 | 710.21 | 509.12 | **craving** | 284.05 |
| 583.22 | 294.07 | 751.03 | 599.14 | 004.14 | 285.16 |
| 588.14 | 403.08 | **course** | 612.16 | **creak** | 288.03 |
| 589.18 | 432.03 | 025.04 | 632.07 | 054.19 | 289.07 |
| 597.05 | **counselled** | 087.02 | 682.04 | **create** | 297.10 |
| 602.03 | 594.22 | 169.07 | **cousins** | 347.06 | 310.15 |
| 602.15 | 639.07 | 173.01 | 440.19 | **created** | 322.04 |
| 603.21 | 678.17 | 214.17 | 484.15 | 312.20 | 324.09 |
| 604.02 | 724.22 | 233.09 | **cover** | **creating** | 336.14 |
| 607.05 | **counsellor** | 240.09 | 007.21 | 419.03 | 358.01 |
| 608.18 | 579.08 | 260.06 | 114.03 | **creation** | 366.04 |
| 618.04 | **count** | 273.01 | 502.22 | 182.15 | 366.19 |
| 620.19 | 383.01 | 295.18 | 685.14 | 388.17 | 376.13 |
| 622.11 | **counted** | 372.15 | 743.20 | **creature** | 382.12 |
| 623.06 | 520.14 | 379.11 | **covered** | 008.13 | 385.05 |
| 624.19 | **countenanance** | 421.17 | 028.05 | 052.17 | 395.07 |
| 629.10 | 465.16 | 442.18 | 038.20 | 145.08 | 396.05 |
| 631.09 | **countenance** | 488.16 | 207.17 | 156.12 | 409.02 |
| 636.06 | 006.22 | 554.19 | 258.21 | 180.19 | 428.01 |
| 636.20 | 012.13 | 582.11 | 277.15 | 181.08 | 435.06 |
| 640.03 | 019.08 | 596.03 | 404.17 | 218.07 | 437.19 |
| 643.08 | 023.14 | 745.18 | 505.17 | 223.05 | 439.16 |
| 647.05 | 070.16 | 748.13 | 532.20 | 229.12 | 440.09 |
| 653.08 | 117.05 | 748.13 | 552.13 | 238.15 | 460.12 |
| 653.17 | 146.16 | **coursed** | 649.20 | 291.02 | 462.05 |
| 653.17 | 152.16 | 295.02 | 760.06 | 338.16 | 466.11 |
| 660.19 | 166.06 | **court** | **covering** | 346.02 | 478.21 |
| 664.16 | 176.13 | 003.08 | 040.07 | 362.09 | 483.13 |
| 667.19 | 214.01 | 120.10 | 063.15 | 411.12 | 486.18 |
| 669.15 | 244.19 | 126.08 | 111.21 | 439.19 | 487.19 |
| 669.21 | 258.16 | 159.16 | 362.16 | 476.02 | 491.13 |
| 670.15 | 263.12 | 206.09 | 710.17 | 479.20 | 496.03 |
| 672.05 | 271.12 | 211.03 | **covet** | 490.09 | 499.03 |
| 676.09 | 278.20 | 248.14 | 228.22 | 632.06 | 511.18 |
| 684.15 | 295.20 | 254.12 | 239.22 | 664.13 | 512.19 |
| 686.17 | 310.20 | 261.05 | 490.06 | **creatures** | 513.01 |
| 689.11 | 342.13 | 342.11 | **coveting** | 101.02 | 523.20 |
| 693.02 | 358.08 | 544.15 | 390.19 | 374.08 | 531.14 |
| 693.20 | 387.19 | 569.21 | 504.07 | 532.16 | 534.04 |
| 695.03 | 397.19 | 632.09 | **covetousness** | **credit** | 537.03 |
| 695.05 | 407.04 | 644.07 | 222.12 | 147.15 | 537.12 |
| 697.08 | 435.02 | 690.14 | 316.11 | 308.15 | 541.17 |
| 699.07 | 452.21 | 692.08 | **cow** | 337.15 | 547.01 |
| 701.15 | 492.17 | 704.12 | 029.20 | **creditor's** | 554.05 |
| 701.16 | 505.12 | **courtesy** | 106.16 | 419.04 | 561.04 |
| 703.19 | 510.06 | 146.22 | 719.07 | **credulity** | 565.13 |
| 705.01 | 517.09 | 308.14 | **coward** | 529.05 | 571.17 |
| 705.21 | 529.10 | **courting** | 259.09 | **creep** | 576.04 |
| 706.16 | 597.08 | 289.20 | 278.16 | 340.16 | 594.11 |
| 710.21 | 655.13 | **cousin** | 602.04 | 382.01 | 599.07 |
| 719.17 | 682.10 | 073.02 | 602.11 | 568.11 | 600.10 |
| 723.17 | 684.06 | 073.03 | **coward's** | **creeping** | 606.08 |
| 726.01 | 717.20 | 440.07 | 615.16 | 552.16 | 612.12 |
| 727.06 | 738.02 | 440.09 | **cowardice** | 711.13 | 617.17 |
| 727.14 | 749.06 | 440.14 | 055.05 | 764.04 | 621.09 |
| 729.17 | **countenances** | 440.14 | 080.08 | **crept** | 624.18 |
| 729.17 | 711.17 | 441.01 | 758.12 | 061.10 | 632.20 |
| 730.15 | **counter-rappings** | 446.09 | **cowardly** | 080.05 | 634.15 |
| 737.05 | 050.14 | 448.10 | 108.15 | 103.16 | 638.19 |
| 738.04 | **counteract** | 451.15 | 567.10 | 108.16 | 660.06 |
| 741.07 | 528.19 | 452.06 | 600.06 | 132.14 | 665.05 |
| 743.19 | **counterpart** | 452.21 | 602.05 | 621.14 | 669.11 |
| 746.10 | 116.03 | 453.19 | **cowards** | 750.06 | 683.05 |
| 746.18 | **counting** | 463.17 | 394.18 | **crescents** | 691.07 |
| 750.08 | 019.23 | 474.03 | **cowed** | 238.02 | 704.14 |
| 750.19 | 057.18 | 486.16 | 255.11 | **crest-fallen** | 706.19 |
| 752.09 | **country** | 487.13 | **cows** | 489.08 | 708.03 |
| 754.05 | 001.06 | 489.05 | 034.01 | **crew** | 721.10 |
| 757.19 | 007.11 | 489.18 | 566.03 | 415.04 | 723.01 |
| 758.03 | 059.16 | 490.15 | **coxcomb** | | 723.11 |
| 764.10 | | 491.15 | 127.16 | | |

741.01
748.07
753.16
758.12
758.16
cries
510.04
565.20
631.19
crimson
026.04
104.03
323.04
679.01
crimson-covered
104.04
cringing
340.17
crisis
049.02
347.07
692.15
critical
028.18
165.20
croaked
193.12
croaker
140.20
croaking
565.12
croaks
042.19
crocuses
302.16
381.09
crooked
421.07
465.19
crooked-legged
441.17
cropped
164.10
cropping
689.21
crops
442.14
cross
031.12
116.20
218.15
226.09
260.13
425.18
431.15
436.01
487.21
506.08
530.06
559.05
570.22
706.06
725.17
cross-examination
332.12
cross-roads
419.14
585.09
crossed
050.12
097.01
274.21
283.12
530.04
640.20
669.18
682.19
683.13
crosser
091.13
crosses
153.03
crossest
592.02
crossing
197.20
332.23
crossly
155.06
211.17
631.18
crouched
075.01
crowded
078.01
crown
714.03
cruel
052.16
215.18
218.12
230.04
362.18
362.19
444.17
513.12
527.08
539.02
582.15
615.09
620.15
726.02
cruelly
280.15
572.12
cruelty
344.18
648.06
crumbling
005.01
crush
049.15
230.06
252.18
260.12
343.04
578.22
crushed
079.14
633.14
crushing
055.14
crust
722.03
cry
020.16
045.04
053.09
090.19
092.13
094.22
105.02
105.22
122.22
129.10
143.20
159.11
159.11
195.16
218.17
245.20
363.01
375.17
385.06
389.09
391.16
453.06
473.05
519.17
562.21
610.12
611.08
630.06
crying
120.07
142.15
157.09
188.18
188.20
297.07
318.02
435.14
452.09
468.07
476.17
503.18
504.08
519.15
543.16
566.18
600.18
620.20
634.08
661.08
697.06
699.09
761.03
cub
164.08
cuckoo's
074.06
cuckoos
557.17
cud
719.08
cudgel
046.21
cuffed
084.03
culinary
005.17
cullenders
005.21
culpable
109.13
culpably
443.18
culprit
128.11
cultivate
137.11
cultivation
229.13
cunning
435.18
641.22
cunningly
185.10
cup
020.08
023.16
217.06
384.22
453.15
612.02
613.03
636.07
cupboard
162.04
558.20
cups
612.01
cur
125.01
curate
088.14
088.14
099.15
100.05
100.13
109.16
145.02
199.12
246.06
246.07
247.10
247.12
curbed
605.06
cure
036.01
303.11
543.11
cured
059.15
113.04
718.12
curiosity
149.11
237.13
285.14
426.04
507.12
694.02
742.16
742.18
curious
009.05
021.13
037.11
037.12
048.13
157.22
348.08
592.04
curiousity
434.19
466.17
curiously
315.14
391.01
482.01
curl
152.19
379.03
669.06
671.16
curled
009.13
065.07
146.04
513.11
curling
425.04
690.12
curls
021.04
114.16
453.20
468.05
665.12
669.01
currant
716.01
716.06
720.18
currently
047.22
curs
012.22
curse
026.07
364.18
407.21
cursed
144.01
619.03
619.05
662.09
curses
062.15
089.14
091.20
106.16
169.01
177.11
245.14
247.08
567.20
cursing
033.20
110.06
247.08
312.12
400.12
679.17
curtain
142.02
193.09
246.07
277.10
509.21
curtainless
321.19
curtains
103.21
110.14
210.07
323.05
cushion
018.16
049.19
542.07
543.01
custody
342.17
391.07
custom
023.17
120.15
503.21
747.01
customary
444.14
cut
038.01
056.12
232.11
243.08
253.05
283.14
323.03
383.19
386.14
396.10
406.15
432.18
567.18
581.15
634.01
656.18
704.22
720.04
758.21
cutting
130.07
163.14
cynic
320.01
dacent
233.05
dad
247.07
daddy
246.12
246.13
246.18
246.21
247.08
dahn
016.06
043.02
043.03
187.08
233.11
324.05
daht
318.16
daily
100.21
144.22
442.05
497.08
508.01
525.03
597.04
611.12
646.16
682.18
730.06
dainties
127.11
431.20
476.08
daintiness
667.02
dainty
219.07
472.04
608.11
dairy
044.13
110.20
319.17
509.01
dam'n
164.18
damaged
323.11
683.06
dame
011.10
109.09
140.17
196.21
233.09
520.11
690.19
damn
142.02
193.09
246.07
363.03
366.04
374.05
395.13
467.06
488.05
605.08
649.20
756.10
damnable
064.12
496.01
722.17
damnably
494.15
617.07
damnation
168.16
317.04
damned
085.05
163.16
439.06
439.10
707.11
708.11
756.21
damp
192.05
392.02
515.10
743.15
damper
044.17
damsel
116.02
dance
131.03
264.22
308.02
390.09
523.14
558.03
600.01
697.03
dancing
523.07
danger
222.20
257.08
261.21
296.09
302.06
316.17
334.05
397.07
459.02
476.22
615.13
732.17
dangerous
720.21
dangerously
082.09
196.03
dappled
585.07
dare
045.13
057.22
089.10
114.22
122.11
148.09
166.11
177.12
275.21
284.16
295.12
309.03
329.20
339.15
341.21
356.01
382.13
385.19
406.18
439.17
468.14
494.20
519.08
535.09
537.06
543.08
601.07
602.09
611.18
617.17
619.03
642.06
661.01
669.09
722.17
739.15
744.20
dared
204.07
207.14
250.06
254.13
284.14
392.20
444.07
565.19
717.14
717.14
dares
671.18
daring
035.15
100.22
258.09
dark
007.09
027.17
029.17
032.17
039.09
066.10
077.08
077.21
127.14
131.22
151.20
166.11
188.04
207.05
207.05
243.22
308.10
325.02
378.12
398.03
425.03
437.01
463.12
516.18
552.05
621.21
645.07
652.19
732.21
745.21
760.22
761.18
darkened
205.02
491.22
darkness
283.22
287.04
312.05
528.01
680.02
744.12
darling
042.07
060.15
164.16
211.14
219.12
245.01
303.03
366.06
446.12
451.13
503.08
526.02
545.16
559.15
579.03
615.05
639.21
654.17
darlings
119.09
darnut
761.09
darr
043.01
458.10
dart
212.19
404.21
darting
513.13
dash
064.06
645.10
dashed
118.07
128.07
162.10
247.13
262.11
297.06
377.09
400.02
406.21
dashing
059.07
265.17
389.10

302.18
497.11
518.01
580.10
delightedly
114.07
delightful
059.19
313.11
433.17
449.10
690.02
delightfully
017.05
258.03
delighting
501.05
delights
560.01
delirious
283.17
283.19
deliriously
403.05
delirium
196.01
287.02
deliver
030.02
034.21
157.15
429.19
deliverance
196.20
391.10
delivered
046.01
142.11
165.15
245.15
263.16
368.12
402.14
409.18
595.05
662.09
dells
557.19
delude
596.08
deluded
164.09
596.07
deluge
238.21
delusion
024.18
338.12
700.16
delusive
462.14
delve
652.05
demand
005.06
011.02
198.07
265.11
298.01
524.08
637.02
demanded
020.04
022.15
116.05
153.13
158.09
181.13
184.16
271.15
311.12
326.18
421.16
445.06
461.18
481.15
547.16
554.03
624.02
629.09
690.18
718.14
721.13
demolish
042.04
729.10
demolished
386.11
demon
262.13
demons
745.14
demonstrations
009.17
224.21
367.10
demurely
709.11
den
056.06
189.16

324.22
651.18
755.11
denial
171.21
607.03
679.03
denied
495.07
536.14
denominated
046.22
301.05
denomination
754.07
denounce
049.03
dens
010.19
deny
256.22
500.18
618.18
denying
567.06
depart
049.11
160.01
343.13
368.01
567.12
589.07
634.20
697.13
729.04
departed
062.09
122.03
187.03
217.12
223.19
344.14
351.02
386.05
403.10
414.01
469.18
640.03
644.05
686.12
703.10
733.02
743.05
760.05
departure
005.07
180.02
257.03
305.01
438.19
474.05
541.05
594.15
612.07
depended
305.05
dependence
422.21
deplorable
229.17
deportment
420.17
deposited
028.17
047.16
depreciated
336.17
depreciation
148.10
depressed
214.05
329.14
392.09
depression
205.15
depressions
065.21
deprive
678.20
deprived
099.14
423.02
763.18
dept
751.01
depth
035.03
340.08
depths
010.02
229.20
deranged
272.21
derangement
282.05
derelictions
623.10
deriding
528.16
derision
257.06

408.11
derived
341.03
derives
693.14
desarve
324.15
descend
126.10
267.09
descended
049.02
061.05
166.17
213.04
255.05
348.02
400.18
411.02
450.14
508.20
514.03
750.12
descendent
470.01
descending
041.18
304.19
518.07
602.22
665.09
descent
165.21
427.07
describe
141.11
327.03
636.04
730.19
described
395.19
describing
097.13
description
446.03
descriptive
004.05
desert
125.02
431.15
deserted
181.02
181.04
304.07
692.14
710.21
desertion
647.15
deserve
015.18
103.08
215.19
362.21
437.09
581.02
671.15
deserved
332.15
524.11
571.09
633.20
deserves
055.22
164.05
470.18
design
378.11
484.11
484.13
designed
038.08
designing
226.06
616.18
designs
345.03
633.16
753.06
desirable
516.13
desire
005.08
064.22
202.20
228.17
288.17
305.05
310.22
328.06
343.18
345.11
388.06
428.15
429.22
457.06
485.06
523.11
562.09
580.04
583.08
599.20

618.21
675.10
730.12
754.14
desired
069.11
112.03
221.14
270.17
274.13
298.19
319.20
334.19
341.01
420.14
457.15
687.03
710.04
751.04
desires
208.10
220.02
desiring
233.15
247.05
354.14
417.16
485.20
561.15
713.21
713.22
desirous
055.04
249.04
506.19
679.05
desisted
400.07
desisting
063.14
desolate
636.01
desolation
001.11
684.15
despair
282.03
313.18
356.10
407.12
510.03
639.15
despaired
415.10
despairing
371.13
despairingly
542.18
643.04
despatched
237.05
432.10
585.11
636.22
desperate
143.21
280.16
315.16
361.17
396.05
641.18
678.02
desperately
290.11
652.14
desperation
019.18
342.03
despise
105.05
362.19
470.05
535.04
535.06
600.05
670.08
707.07
despised
273.17
535.01
562.19
708.14
despond
524.18
despondency
264.11
304.03
462.21
despot's
414.04
destination
506.12
destined
710.06
destiny
459.07
643.07
destitute
664.19
destroy
241.10

620.16
678.05
730.03
destroyed
389.04
destroying
344.18
destruction
043.19
730.02
detached
040.09
details
376.05
detain
594.07
620.08
624.19
detainer's
238.02
detect
314.09
392.12
433.08
442.08
517.13
534.16
552.16
593.19
detected
005.02
019.19
051.05
506.19
525.15
552.22
694.20
719.04
detention
636.01
deterioration
150.01
443.05
determination
343.16
determine
047.20
752.09
determined
003.01
069.03
079.03
101.16
240.13
270.10
507.13
541.11
569.09
602.18
604.03
636.17
671.22
707.05
detest
501.10
621.12
723.05
detestable
040.21
391.17
532.16
detestably
164.01
239.12
detestation
409.10
502.11
detested
250.17
341.16
detests
387.15
630.20
deuce
002.21
devastate
688.02
devastation
716.04
devil
011.18
011.21
059.11
077.22
106.12
246.12
246.20
307.11
315.22
316.02
345.22
358.18
401.03
467.07
490.04
497.06
497.13
565.10
565.10
605.18

611.13
618.01
621.11
638.01
644.06
648.08
653.22
684.01
707.01
721.12
725.13
756.08
devil's
029.13
124.16
133.01
devilish
164.14
388.12
devoid
021.02
404.15
585.06
devotedly
301.06
devotion
235.18
338.15
647.16
devour
239.05
325.13
devoured
734.09
devouring
034.18
dew
373.15
dewy
483.02
diabolical
024.04
144.20
342.07
366.16
404.11
501.05
610.10
612.14
diamond
229.22
diamonds
098.01
diary
040.10
dice
233.02
dictating
746.08
dictionary
679.16
did
003.06
008.20
024.20
037.08
041.21
045.03
049.21
052.11
055.22
058.03
065.19
070.05
072.08
072.11
073.18
076.17
077.01
078.09
080.13
080.20
082.11
088.05
089.06
091.06
091.09
095.14
095.19
098.01
100.02
105.04
106.02
106.13
106.16
109.18
110.03
115.15
117.14
122.17
129.03
130.17
132.19
141.07
145.07
145.08
146.07
148.07
148.19
156.05
159.10

161.04
166.07
170.15
178.03
178.19
181.18
186.13
194.22
196.06
199.06
203.09
203.10
210.06
210.16
215.03
217.10
219.22
226.17
234.16
237.02
238.15
240.06
251.01
254.20
256.12
258.11
260.06
261.11
262.18
262.19
263.21
266.11
267.06
267.17
270.06
271.10
276.01
280.22
281.16
292.15
296.11
296.11
300.01
305.20
307.04
308.14
309.16
309.20
310.11
314.03
315.11
318.15
326.13
330.18
337.03
339.04
343.10
350.10
355.04
355.14
356.10
356.14
362.08
362.19
362.20
363.09
366.17
367.21
373.12
374.20
374.21
375.02
375.08
376.03
378.19
382.01
384.17
391.06
401.03
404.07
406.18
408.10
415.22
417.20
419.10
425.09
426.01
426.07
426.16
430.09
431.07
436.18
439.21
443.02
446.14
460.09
460.21
467.10
473.10
475.01
475.03
478.01
480.15
480.15
481.17
483.16
489.07
493.07
496.18
499.14
499.15

506.07
509.09
510.01
511.19
528.01
532.21
536.15
537.09
537.12
537.20
537.20
538.06
538.06
538.06
538.07
543.22
548.21
550.09
552.16
560.12
562.10
569.01
569.06
575.04
579.19
581.16
586.16
588.09
589.04
590.12
591.04
591.11
592.01
597.07
601.10
604.06
614.15
619.04
627.03
631.03
631.21
636.04
636.11
644.01
649.12
654.18
659.14
661.10
669.03
673.05
679.14
690.01
690.13
699.13
700.03
700.16
701.04
702.21
703.06
704.02
709.21
710.14
711.18
714.03
716.19
718.15
726.17
732.01
734.19
735.04
736.12
738.03
739.04
743.06
744.15
745.06
745.20
750.07
750.08
755.07
759.20

**didn't**
029.20
097.17
129.05
129.09
129.09
141.09
156.12
159.09
184.09
192.20
203.17
211.21
227.22
231.12
276.01
289.08
289.09
294.17
336.23
350.05
411.22
413.14
461.02
461.07
481.08
501.18
506.13
511.15
511.15
511.16

522.21
524.17
533.04
537.10
539.06
543.18
554.02
559.04
562.01
568.01
568.02
599.18
603.01
622.12
651.17
655.17
661.11
663.13
668.10
708.17
725.13
739.09
748.04

**didst**
049.20

**die**
029.20
097.19
133.18
140.15
244.11
271.04
271.08
273.02
275.10
342.06
342.08
356.07
366.03
366.03
374.21
375.08
398.17
469.20
520.06
525.12
532.03
571.13
579.02
601.12
630.04
636.21
648.10
660.05
754.11

**died**
070.08
080.16
084.14
092.18
197.01
335.01
369.05
412.11
417.04
418.22
429.11
484.21
539.04
620.19
639.19
639.19
651.09
664.15
755.02
759.17

**dies**
620.07

**differ**
592.19

**difference**
082.15
154.09
494.06
645.09

**different**
048.11
179.13
275.05
333.03
333.05
349.04
438.08
465.06
544.20
626.03
738.05

**differently**
098.13
730.14

**differing**
321.17

**difficult**
145.15
420.20
719.08

**difficulty**
132.17
254.18
367.17
588.10

599.05

**dig**
062.18
233.05
737.12

**digest**
003.22

**digging**
649.13

**dignified**
114.01
214.07

**dignity**
027.02
126.02
236.04

**dilapidation**
040.03

**dilating**
062.19
639.18

**dilatory**
201.05

**dim**
045.17
111.15
475.02
492.02
689.02

**diminishing**
655.12

**dimly**
281.08
361.02
388.10
577.17

**dimmed**
408.09

**din**
094.14
566.21

**dine**
014.07
403.16
514.07
740.20

**dingy**
043.10
309.02

**dinner**
003.22
007.07
014.06
100.08
123.10
127.06
129.03
133.05
151.11
267.13
409.15
518.07
544.15
665.06
685.16
686.01
724.21
740.04
742.04

**dinner-time**
547.13
640.14
674.05

**dins**
016.11

**dip**
308.13

**dips**
209.16

**direct**
314.20
410.09
545.15
563.19
629.18

**directed**
062.16
267.06
644.15
689.14

**directing**
194.06
300.02
499.18

**direction**
025.16
155.04
353.21
432.09
705.19
763.15

**directions**
212.16
292.06
384.13
641.09
686.04
747.09
754.18

**directly**
059.21

084.15
094.19
110.12
128.11
140.04
167.09
185.22
210.08
247.22
273.12
298.15
326.05
331.09
355.15
362.03
402.07
433.01
451.19
477.03
570.04
605.09
615.01
697.05
725.03
739.04
745.05

**directs**
318.06

**dirtily**
319.22

**dirty**
066.13
078.02
115.16
117.19
118.05
118.06
118.06
309.06
712.13

**dis-relish**
551.09

**disadvantage**
088.04

**disadvantages**
013.10

**disagreeable**
018.02
440.21
477.06
530.07
671.02

**disagreebly**
051.07

**disagreement**
158.01
726.12

**disagreements**
089.05

**disappearance**
197.08

**disappeared**
522.10
522.15
750.05

**disappoint**
246.03
327.17

**disappointed**
399.09
470.20
500.10
504.10
594.02
630.16
654.21
677.07

**disappointment**
187.04
204.06
360.14
526.13
588.15
703.12

**disapproved**
465.21
607.04

**disapprovingly**
682.01

**disarm**
485.19

**disarmed**
728.17

**disarrange**
114.16

**disarrangement**
379.01

**discarded**
644.05

**discerned**
052.14
145.22
598.14
652.20

**discerning**
281.08
339.01
607.07

**discharge**
394.19

**discharged**
293.19

**discipline**
137.20

**disclosure**
234.10

**discomfited**
562.01

**discomfiture**
116.10

**discontent**
089.04
743.21

**discord**
335.08

**discourse**
013.09
046.01
049.09
194.06
237.10
502.09

**discoursing**
089.16

**discover**
101.07
115.11
166.01
206.21
281.13
291.04
339.04
490.03
497.11
507.22
521.09
552.06
739.03

**discovered**
031.05
039.11
053.21
081.11
083.18
094.19
130.22
226.05
287.05
378.22
394.15
411.20
645.18
668.01
716.10
727.08
763.22

**discoverer**
510.11

**discovering**
255.15
312.05

**discovery**
322.04

**discreet**
263.07

**discretion**
717.03

**discussed**
023.08
747.09

**discussing**
048.07
172.13
412.18
498.08

**discussion**
255.08
436.16

**disdainfully**
455.20

**disdaining**
236.04

**disease**
089.04

**disenchanted**
728.03

**disengage**
052.09
290.11

**disengaged**
594.08

**disgrace**
337.19
446.03

**disgraceful**
254.22
600.20

**disgraces**
340.13

**disguise**
125.15
160.15
356.10
521.04

**disguised**
617.07

**disguising**
708.08

**disgust**
032.15
148.08

409.10
441.13
669.11

**disgusted**
310.16
340.05
613.06

**dish**
136.14

**dishcloth**
128.15

**dishes**
006.01
098.20
312.18

**disinclined**
704.17

**dislike**
099.11
475.12
498.13
581.04
709.05

**disliked**
153.19
500.21
501.03

**dislikes**
501.04

**dismal**
027.08
177.06
192.04
242.10
281.21
314.11
330.04
381.12
392.17
424.03
623.14
743.22
756.01

**dismally**
115.22

**dismiss**
240.04
240.06
263.11

**dismissal**
112.12

**dismissed**
456.09
597.10

**dismisses**
130.10

**dismount**
126.12
586.14

**dismounted**
308.11
466.04
553.02

**dismounting**
416.10

**disobedience**
502.18
645.16

**disobey**
661.01
661.01

**disorder**
272.03
386.13
759.17

**disordered**
752.15

**disorderly**
175.21

**disown**
299.20

**disowned**
299.20

**disparagement**
725.12

**disparity**
024.14

**dispatch**
011.10

**dispel**
023.10
039.11

**displaced**
012.06

**displacing**
652.16

**display**
511.09

**displayed**
209.07
415.07

**displaying**
116.06

**displays**
007.19

**displeasure**
003.19
205.01
262.17
505.18
594.17

**disposal**
636.17

**disposed**
006.11
200.05

**disposition**
009.05
150.03
158.08
225.17
502.05
541.13
574.07
684.22

**dispositions**
292.18

**disputant**
538.02

**dispute**
065.04
155.19
219.10
254.14
439.14
610.04

**disputed**
657.01

**disputes**
485.05

**disputing**
593.10
641.16

**disquietude**
347.10

**disregard**
674.17
704.09

**disregarded**
250.22

**disregarding**
436.21
564.22
763.06

**disrespect**
027.01

**dissented**
598.19

**dissimilar**
008.03

**dissipation**
144.03

**dissolve**
268.04

**dissolved**
650.18

**dissolving**
650.21

**distance**
054.21
064.20
067.03
111.07
196.09
222.05
259.18
291.14
457.14
460.16
465.05
470.12
478.20
479.04
557.19
667.21
689.17
749.02

**distant**
313.10
353.12

**distasteful**
148.02
342.18

**distinct**
019.07
358.16
651.06
730.09

**distinction**
111.02
189.19
334.12
414.10

**distinctly**
051.10
176.11
398.19

**distinguish**
028.02
364.13
577.17

**distinguishable**
711.15
743.17

**distinguished**
005.16
101.18
191.16
207.04
689.20
750.15

**distorted**
245.16
387.19
571.19

**distract**
601.22

**distracted**
261.14

**distraction**
369.08
752.01

**distraught**
615.17

**distress**
030.16
335.08
359.17
359.18
419.09
441.15
539.11
599.12
604.10

**distressed**
262.01
306.09
573.16
615.11

**distresses**
148.17
582.14

**distressing**
541.19

**district**
693.12

**disturb**
465.12
540.12
573.04
640.20
650.05
662.02
664.20

**disturbance**
118.09
261.12
343.18
718.22

**disturbed**
055.07
096.11
170.05
208.08
650.07
650.11
650.12

**disturber**
051.06

**disturbing**
313.06
597.22

**diurnal**
516.11

**dived**
010.04
130.16
480.17

**diversion**
275.03
528.14
619.08
763.14

**diversions**
589.18

**divert**
134.06
352.10
509.15
751.04

**diverted**
225.02
262.10

**diverting**
028.13
517.16

**divested**
214.07

**divide**
001.11

**divided**
048.05
105.09
329.05
548.10
548.16
580.13
633.07

**dividing**
111.11
340.22
487.14

**divil**
029.02

**divil's**
232.21
758.16

**divine**
003.22
371.04
690.07
739.07

**divined**
421.11
477.04
527.21
596.09
636.08
709.04

**division**
399.18

**dizzily**
610.16

**dizzy**
036.08

**do**
001.06
002.08
006.20
012.07
018.10
022.03
028.08
030.20
032.01
032.07
035.21
056.07
060.14
060.14
064.08
064.10
064.12
064.16
074.04
078.13
082.13
084.05
088.03
088.13
090.14
092.02
094.17
099.17
103.03
103.03
106.14
123.08
124.11
125.06
125.14
133.18
133.19
134.15
136.08
136.16
152.08
153.05
153.10
153.14
153.14
153.16
154.16
161.03
163.12
166.09
168.07
168.09
171.17
172.15
172.21
173.01
173.06
173.07
175.08
175.12
176.11
176.16
176.20
179.02
186.16
186.16
187.11
190.11
195.09
196.08
199.14
203.06
207.14
208.13
208.19
219.22
220.14
221.03
226.17
231.03
237.11
238.10
246.13
247.09
251.10
251.18
252.01
254.09
260.10
262.05
274.07
279.08
279.14
279.15
284.17
288.01
290.07
292.10
299.15
309.15
309.15
310.18
315.19
321.21
327.14
333.16
333.22
335.11
339.22
342.10
343.08
343.22
344.11
346.11
357.02
357.11
358.20
360.02
361.13
363.12
365.06
367.09
372.09
373.12
374.08
377.01
377.04
386.11
387.11
394.06
395.08
396.06
400.20
400.21
400.22
402.01
402.02
406.17
412.06
416.07
439.18
450.07
452.01
452.11
452.20
454.03
456.12
461.03
465.07
468.09
469.01
470.17
475.15
483.08
484.11
490.05
497.16
497.17
504.13
510.19
510.22
511.08
512.09
513.02
513.02
520.01
521.01
521.15
523.10
526.01
533.03
534.05
535.04
535.15
538.21
539.01
540.16
542.12
542.22
543.18
544.02
545.15
546.17
556.05
556.14
557.01
560.12
564.18
566.05
566.16
566.20
570.10
571.04
573.06
575.11
578.19
579.11
580.18
580.21
586.21
590.19
592.03
600.17
603.16
606.12
613.20
614.04
617.15
617.15
618.14
619.05
621.01
627.10
647.18
651.01
651.12
656.05
660.04
660.09
660.09
662.17
662.20
667.02
669.15
669.20
677.18
683.16
691.22
699.06
701.21
702.01
702.15
703.19
705.21
706.09
707.04
707.10
707.22
708.21
711.03
718.14
719.17
721.11
722.19
723.06
729.17
730.15
732.15
734.01
740.10
751.16
751.17
752.19
753.06
755.06

**doctor**
082.21
095.05
095.08
139.12
142.02
142.03
195.21
197.19
203.01
227.04
296.04
348.02
416.16
583.14
604.13
606.10
628.14
632.10
659.21
757.01

**doctor's**
274.20
294.02
672.09

**documents**
508.02

**does**
074.11
123.13
136.05
142.16
143.05
151.13
167.03
180.16
210.05
210.12
218.09
219.04
232.06
232.21
246.16
247.10
265.03
271.08
272.07
273.01
277.06
283.01
292.12
294.01
316.17
322.01
322.02
337.19
366.13
384.12
392.06
421.16

460.14
463.21
496.08
496.14
519.04
537.01
554.08
577.06
608.07
631.05
633.19
658.10
671.15
672.06
674.02
674.21
677.12
701.19
708.04
708.10
722.15
731.13
753.14
754.07
doesn't
221.21
284.08
690.21
719.21
dog
009.16
034.08
063.16
065.01
084.09
104.19
107.02
111.12
163.03
164.11
228.16
236.18
294.21
336.10
340.01
354.22
362.06
398.17
432.07
440.02
594.10
633.19
701.18
dog's
325.21
dog-kennel
043.11
098.21
dogged
709.06
doggedly
142.20
322.19
dogs
006.18
010.06
012.07
012.17
015.15
028.12
059.22
114.21
445.07
556.13
568.13
642.06
doing
041.08
056.08
091.21
104.13
116.07
150.17
155.02
169.02
216.07
221.13
248.08
271.14
326.19
352.22
414.09
518.09
554.06
569.18
583.11
590.15
616.03
667.04
669.20
695.07
704.08
740.03
doleful
053.09
314.04
393.15
dolefully
540.15
doll
123.12

382.04
domestic
248.10
domestic's
021.09
domestics
003.12
domineer
087.10
domineering
206.01
289.07
don't
011.05
015.21
020.01
027.21
032.05
035.07
046.09
056.10
073.18
083.20
098.07
103.06
103.08
103.11
107.21
108.08
110.06
123.16
124.22
125.13
127.21
129.10
129.11
133.17
134.04
141.03
152.11
155.09
163.13
164.09
168.06
175.13
177.05
183.10
187.02
193.09
203.03
211.05
211.18
215.19
228.11
229.20
231.21
235.09
236.20
239.02
250.22
251.12
252.02
252.18
253.01
260.14
265.11
273.16
277.11
279.05
283.05
288.08
293.09
307.15
313.16
315.09
316.14
327.17
334.22
334.22
338.20
339.17
341.16
343.18
345.01
345.11
349.08
357.21
364.01
366.01
366.01
371.10
374.05
383.03
385.02
386.12
396.22
399.05
399.05
401.04
406.12
412.07
422.03
426.01
428.09
434.05
436.10
437.09
439.13
440.12
444.13
451.18

451.19
452.09
455.08
461.10
465.11
468.20
472.09
473.06
479.05
483.07
486.15
487.22
491.01
491.17
492.09
492.10
494.03
508.15
510.19
512.19
522.01
523.21
524.06
525.16
526.06
527.08
527.11
529.02
532.10
535.03
535.08
539.19
544.03
545.20
562.04
565.08
565.09
570.08
579.09
589.21
590.13
590.14
590.20
599.09
600.04
600.21
600.22
603.18
604.16
605.07
613.01
614.11
618.01
619.06
620.04
621.01
621.03
634.07
647.02
647.10
647.15
656.11
680.09
684.14
698.01
699.01
699.04
702.09
707.07
716.14
717.05
718.10
726.09
729.18
730.12
739.12
739.20
742.06
748.07
751.15
761.17
761.18
done
030.07
041.19
048.21
076.04
093.06
094.04
115.04
125.12
134.16
135.05
172.15
203.15
231.06
234.22
260.03
287.20
295.09
305.18
312.08
315.19
316.18
319.12
324.11
324.11
363.17
364.02
366.18
382.13

397.03
404.03
417.08
422.10
435.13
435.20
438.14
488.02
500.06
505.10
513.22
538.14
539.20
540.18
547.19
581.02
605.11
612.15
616.04
637.10
647.05
659.08
670.15
675.06
682.03
695.09
703.16
709.14
712.22
720.16
722.04
723.09
726.16
753.12
donned
455.12
517.01
626.05
665.11
donning
121.05
dont
707.06
748.10
doomed
160.05
352.05
415.11
581.15
door
004.22
005.06
016.08
029.08
034.10
038.01
054.01
063.03
073.08
080.05
095.12
105.21
110.12
118.19
126.09
126.21
132.01
141.19
157.21
158.10
160.07
169.01
180.08
180.10
188.11
190.18
191.21
193.21
206.12
209.05
213.11
234.20
238.14
247.22
250.02
250.22
256.03
257.18
260.01
261.08
267.07
270.16
278.11
280.17
295.01
297.21
306.20
311.02
311.21
312.14
315.05
315.18
320.21
326.04
355.17
368.11
382.07
394.01
395.15
396.02
396.20

398.09
409.18
416.11
433.21
441.16
451.06
455.03
458.07
466.05
466.16
473.04
485.13
487.14
491.02
495.20
505.17
508.22
513.19
522.03
522.13
523.08
523.18
527.13
532.15
541.07
552.08
553.09
555.18
560.15
563.18
565.06
566.15
586.12
607.18
612.09
614.20
616.15
623.18
629.01
635.06
638.08
641.17
642.01
644.08
644.17
653.11
658.04
661.07
665.01
673.08
686.16
695.13
696.01
719.01
736.12
738.18
751.08
756.20
door-handle
285.10
door-latch
077.10
door-stones
035.20
483.14
525.20
683.13
763.01
door-way
127.20
498.07
681.03
doors
015.20
078.09
084.14
099.16
101.11
107.17
116.08
195.09
201.09
207.01
226.20
282.19
350.16
368.04
370.12
373.08
419.17
456.05
476.20
593.05
597.03
642.06
671.01
684.12
693.11
739.13
747.04
doorstones
638.01
doorway
325.21
410.06
dose
056.06
170.16
281.21
402.21
593.04

662.03
dosed
051.06
dot
066.13
dote
083.04
doted
141.15
388.12
dotes
235.07
dots
153.04
dotted
305.14
double
117.04
147.06
157.02
305.04
315.15
525.17
527.22
doubt
009.01
020.22
057.02
092.11
103.08
184.19
194.16
199.19
263.15
331.14
338.07
345.17
372.04
441.06
546.04
562.13
570.19
570.20
576.06
580.05
620.09
655.01
711.19
735.02
758.03
doubted
372.01
413.19
doubtfully
280.13
486.11
doubting
124.20
242.10
603.06
doubtingly
051.05
doubtless
128.13
154.09
222.12
341.08
doubts
292.04
454.16
561.14
594.20
dour
121.15
dove
425.10
dove's
239.15
down
010.04
018.03
020.20
027.18
034.12
036.04
041.07
042.18
048.19
049.15
052.19
056.08
058.13
059.10
061.17
069.12
076.02
077.07
084.18
085.19
090.09
094.12
095.13
101.14
106.08
106.20
118.16
123.16
123.20
127.14
130.14
133.08

| | | | | | |
|---|---|---|---|---|---|
| 136.14 | 652.11 | 619.19 | 384.10 | drop | 561.07 |
| 140.09 | 655.19 | dread | 513.02 | 170.18 | 679.10 |
| 140.18 | 656.21 | 059.14 | dressed | 203.01 | 694.06 |
| 145.10 | 663.19 | 120.03 | 076.02 | 289.21 | dungeon |
| 152.01 | 665.03 | 177.22 | 098.13 | 332.03 | 136.05 |
| 158.17 | 669.15 | 279.06 | 124.02 | 630.09 | dunnock |
| 159.13 | 670.13 | 444.09 | 207.04 | dropped | 074.10 |
| 169.08 | 674.08 | 602.09 | 383.12 | 093.22 | dunnot |
| 171.09 | 676.07 | 602.09 | 478.16 | 099.03 | 669.21 |
| 178.16 | 676.15 | 607.06 | 694.14 | 106.04 | dunnut |
| 185.20 | 685.16 | 651.02 | 750.11 | 145.02 | 320.12 |
| 186.10 | 686.19 | 744.17 | dresser | 159.13 | 320.14 |
| 188.06 | 689.18 | dreaded | 006.03 | 214.12 | 565.15 |
| 189.04 | 691.11 | 225.20 | 006.16 | 248.16 | duration |
| 190.06 | 698.16 | 376.04 | 042.15 | 278.13 | 371.18 |
| 191.18 | 698.21 | 568.04 | 154.21 | 299.11 | during |
| 196.06 | 715.08 | dreadful | 168.04 | 385.15 | 021.20 |
| 209.16 | 718.10 | 162.02 | 534.09 | 499.12 | 065.09 |
| 212.16 | 722.14 | 274.01 | 668.02 | 505.08 | 076.04 |
| 214.15 | 731.14 | 278.07 | dressing | 524.17 | 135.13 |
| 237.21 | 736.11 | 540.10 | 097.09 | 524.17 | 170.17 |
| 243.17 | 737.18 | 565.20 | 462.11 | 561.17 | 226.07 |
| 247.13 | 740.04 | 596.09 | drew | 611.06 | 267.19 |
| 248.01 | 743.17 | 731.21 | 018.21 | 675.12 | 292.20 |
| 250.10 | 747.03 | dreadfully | 023.06 | 702.17 | 316.10 |
| 252.17 | 747.18 | 039.19 | 060.22 | dropping | 350.16 |
| 253.20 | 750.02 | 159.18 | 075.10 | 323.03 | 355.21 |
| 257.11 | 750.04 | 435.12 | 079.14 | 510.17 | 370.07 |
| 270.19 | 757.04 | 533.06 | 157.11 | 513.10 | 377.16 |
| 275.12 | 760.06 | dreading | 157.19 | drops | 393.05 |
| 276.07 | 761.13 | 263.07 | 170.07 | 188.16 | 400.12 |
| 276.09 | downright | dream | 249.01 | 546.05 | 436.16 |
| 279.15 | 356.03 | 024.19 | 318.18 | dropt | 453.11 |
| 284.19 | 621.16 | 045.03 | 330.01 | 191.17 | 468.06 |
| 295.02 | downs | 046.12 | 354.02 | drove | 547.21 |
| 303.03 | 074.03 | 048.03 | 375.20 | 015.04 | 591.06 |
| 303.22 | doze | 134.07 | 408.04 | 099.13 | 636.18 |
| 304.09 | 093.11 | 176.16 | 458.09 | 160.17 | 643.10 |
| 313.02 | dozed | 215.15 | 500.16 | 641.18 | 664.14 |
| 315.03 | 745.22 | 229.19 | 506.09 | drowned | 713.13 |
| 318.09 | dozen | 293.03 | 515.02 | 192.05 | 718.22 |
| 322.19 | 028.04 | 308.04 | 527.15 | 353.05 | 725.07 |
| 326.01 | 429.05 | 340.10 | 608.14 | 408.10 | 747.20 |
| 330.12 | dozing | 376.11 | 629.05 | drowsily | 754.03 |
| 343.12 | 701.17 | 621.11 | 676.04 | 045.17 | durst |
| 344.06 | drag | 702.01 | 685.12 | 591.07 | 666.14 |
| 347.19 | 049.15 | dreamily | 700.21 | drowsiness | dusk |
| 354.04 | 723.01 | 276.12 | 712.11 | 372.21 | 069.07 |
| 357.06 | dragged | 557.09 | 724.05 | drowsy | 206.08 |
| 359.20 | 067.21 | dreaming | 727.11 | 192.02 | 478.09 |
| 365.05 | 110.08 | 177.09 | 747.15 | drunk | 515.09 |
| 367.02 | 400.08 | 518.13 | 751.07 | 160.10 | 727.10 |
| 367.15 | dragging | 545.03 | 756.04 | 390.07 | 756.13 |
| 384.11 | 276.05 | 702.05 | dried | 417.05 | dusky |
| 385.01 | 467.20 | 746.01 | 111.08 | 558.05 | 117.20 |
| 390.09 | 566.06 | dreams | 454.01 | 721.01 | 557.19 |
| 391.05 | 600.15 | 058.06 | drifts | dry | dust |
| 391.14 | drank | 176.16 | 062.18 | 051.04 | 015.03 |
| 395.21 | 168.17 | 176.21 | 381.10 | 067.22 | 115.21 |
| 399.04 | 215.07 | 177.20 | drink | 130.06 | 312.20 |
| 399.18 | 271.01 | 178.13 | 168.22 | 164.17 | 323.02 |
| 402.01 | 298.20 | 279.06 | 217.07 | 243.04 | 390.22 |
| 403.12 | 334.21 | 335.19 | 232.07 | 270.22 | 424.11 |
| 406.19 | drapery | 527.10 | 266.04 | 305.13 | 450.04 |
| 408.03 | 323.10 | 593.03 | 386.15 | 384.06 | duster |
| 410.08 | 379.02 | dreamt | 410.17 | 401.15 | 330.08 |
| 417.14 | draughts | 051.07 | 443.13 | 486.01 | dusters |
| 430.17 | 202.06 | 176.20 | 533.16 | 691.09 | 155.07 |
| 432.10 | draw | 178.11 | 609.01 | 691.20 | dusting |
| 438.03 | 052.04 | 335.20 | 613.03 | dry-eyed | 691.20 |
| 449.05 | 081.07 | 390.19 | 639.02 | 640.08 | duties |
| 453.15 | 203.05 | 559.14 | 699.05 | dryer | 047.21 |
| 454.21 | 206.13 | 650.15 | 730.07 | 463.11 | 183.18 |
| 456.02 | 238.09 | 650.19 | 748.01 | drying | 270.02 |
| 458.02 | 250.14 | 698.21 | drinking | 325.15 | 418.01 |
| 458.04 | 256.10 | dreamy | 025.01 | 374.16 | 547.22 |
| 466.07 | 306.19 | 351.14 | 103.01 | 490.12 | dutiful |
| 466.13 | 315.08 | 689.03 | 319.18 | 708.18 | 645.15 |
| 467.10 | 394.07 | dreary | 393.03 | duck | duty |
| 469.02 | 414.15 | 030.14 | 419.19 | 064.05 | 023.10 |
| 478.16 | 417.03 | 177.09 | dripped | due | 242.06 |
| 503.12 | 647.17 | 273.21 | 757.21 | 112.14 | 289.11 |
| 507.01 | 648.15 | 304.13 | 304.13 | 119.19 | 333.11 |
| 514.06 | drawer | 330.14 | dripping | 216.19 | 333.15 |
| 522.14 | 507.04 | 348.01 | 054.17 | 374.18 | 333.17 |
| 527.02 | 507.08 | 381.12 | 383.11 | 374.20 | 346.03 |
| 528.09 | 508.19 | 520.04 | 399.16 | 645.21 | 371.13 |
| 533.19 | 509.18 | 572.05 | drive | 685.07 | 397.03 |
| 538.18 | 703.08 | 648.12 | 016.17 | dug | 516.08 |
| 541.16 | drawers | 686.18 | 028.04 | 379.21 | 569.18 |
| 551.04 | 154.20 | 690.06 | 074.20 | 760.07 | 579.11 |
| 554.17 | drawing | 701.21 | 187.15 | dull | 623.10 |
| 564.08 | 103.19 | dree | 216.10 | 043.07 | dwarf |
| 570.15 | 106.05 | 348.01 | 318.21 | 590.01 | 737.05 |
| 578.01 | 116.18 | dree‘ | 377.04 | 677.21 | dwell |
| 587.19 | 203.12 | 347.21 | 527.16 | duller | 307.21 |
| 588.07 | 404.04 | drench | driven | 516.04 | dwelling |
| 590.15 | 513.14 | 757.07 | 262.21 | duly | 004.04 |
| 593.19 | 597.12 | drenched | 290.17 | 595.05 | 222.17 |
| 607.17 | 705.15 | 190.02 | 389.12 | dumb | 410.14 |
| 609.13 | 709.10 | dress | 411.04 | 078.19 | 692.21 |
| 611.15 | drawing-room | 007.10 | 554.07 | 121.14 | 732.21 |
| 614.21 | 378.05 | 021.01 | 670.12 | 133.13 | dwelt |
| 623.03 | 553.06 | 117.21 | driving | 153.15 | 369.09 |
| 628.12 | drawled | 120.18 | 051.11 | 395.09 | dwindling |
| 628.17 | 246.22 | 123.10 | 382.06 | 621.17 | 226.13 |
| 633.13 | 561.01 | 150.19 | 757.07 | 625.04 | dying |
| 634.04 | drawling | 310.20 | drizzle | 662.19 | 097.18 |
| 638.05 | 681.16 | 330.14 | 530.03 | 686.10 | 270.19 |
| 639.01 | drawn | 351.03 | droll | dunce | 272.06 |
| 645.21 | 189.20 | 383.13 | 212.07 | 496.10 | 274.07 |

358.20
363.17
389.07
524.20
526.11
584.01
598.06
603.13
613.18
632.10
661.16
698.22
732.18

e
720.16

e'en
077.20

each
032.20
044.06
048.06
048.07
065.04
076.12
083.16
094.13
095.16
105.02
121.04
125.17
126.14
136.19
182.18
197.02
206.03
215.05
218.21
258.04
260.20
262.19
273.17
284.14
296.16
336.13
364.06
364.06
380.04
394.16
487.03
496.13
501.18
545.19
558.10
588.03
597.06
610.08
647.07
660.13
680.04
680.05
704.06
727.22
752.02
763.03

eager
065.02
127.02
450.15
474.03
491.02
591.20
727.20
747.20

eagerly
141.12
184.01
271.01
284.05
302.19
331.04
426.06
624.13
635.20
653.11
676.10
740.15

eagerness
354.17
355.13
361.14
584.03

ear
135.20
157.17
353.03
353.14
383.19
409.16
410.20
433.20
491.21
520.03
531.19
544.22
591.15
652.15
671.03

ear-shot
387.17

earlier
234.06

393.17
454.17
482.18
508.03
572.11

earliest
302.20
367.22
713.13

early
059.10
121.22
135.01
149.09
243.21
282.08
297.05
328.08
337.15
376.11
381.11
413.11
416.04
432.04
448.12
459.04
461.16
507.01
508.21
515.02
548.17
686.12

earn
064.08
203.12
258.06

earned
083.03

earnest
090.19
112.09
136.09
159.14
186.07
236.15
272.12
339.01
361.16
524.19
583.20
751.01
759.09

earnestly
030.17
198.11
277.12
356.11
365.16
513.05
723.12
730.12

earnestness
563.01
699.15

earning
079.19

earnshaw
005.03
026.20
031.17
032.16
035.18
039.01
039.06
039.20
052.11
056.19
062.14
072.20
072.21
073.08
075.16
076.01
077.02
078.08
079.06
081.10
083.14
085.04
087.02
088.18
089.17
091.09
098.10
101.22
109.05
109.08
109.09
110.10
112.04
112.13
115.06
117.06
119.01
119.20
128.11
130.03
131.18
135.14
139.04
140.21

142.11
143.19
146.07
146.11
149.15
160.09
166.07
189.15
192.14
198.03
207.09
217.14
217.16
217.17
232.03
312.22
314.14
315.10
316.22
318.06
333.04
357.14
376.21
379.11
386.09
390.03
392.05
394.08
396.18
397.08
402.19
403.13
407.03
414.16
415.17
416.22
422.15
434.03
443.10
463.16
492.17
496.22
556.12
560.04
561.03
563.17
566.07
570.03
627.13
653.12
659.19
665.08
667.13
669.17
670.15
673.10
675.03
679.01
704.18
705.13
708.11
710.04
712.06
713.17
715.02
716.18
723.15
724.13
725.21
728.07
740.19
760.02

earnshaw's
080.05
081.19
090.04
092.18
147.18
210.14
292.17
325.19
399.11
400.10
404.05
409.12
418.16
476.18
695.16
720.20

earnshaws
088.16
126.12

earnshaws'
425.02

ears
008.17
027.06
042.19
053.05
084.04
156.14
160.11
164.14
228.03
270.20
355.01
426.13
611.01
612.15
665.12
724.12

earshot
034.01

earth
015.09
056.22
092.18
111.18
178.21
181.09
244.02
313.12
357.12
371.07
371.14
377.03
427.13
521.11
579.04
650.18
651.21
652.13
652.22
721.19
752.10
764.11

earthenware
325.15

earthly
413.21
734.20

earthy
519.01

ease
039.15
107.18
340.18
388.09
432.07
482.18
528.22
540.11
571.21
571.21
611.08
631.16
650.08
748.20

easily
085.22
130.01
344.11
403.11
559.07
642.09
689.11

east
189.05
243.08

easter
705.10

easy
176.02
202.08
384.21
522.17
680.21
714.01
715.10

easy-chair
304.08

eat
045.08
129.03
133.10
217.07
271.01
293.01
471.05
471.18
472.11
609.01
624.11
698.18
725.03
730.07
742.03
745.04
748.01
753.04

eatable
318.02

eaten
160.01
273.08
390.16

eating
025.02
027.13
076.06
103.01
286.10
359.01
403.19
736.07
740.13

eats
701.20

eaves-droppers
525.14

eavesdropper
194.10

eccentric
707.18

ech
043.20
324.10
324.10
564.18
564.19
564.19
564.19
564.20
564.20
758.18

echo
169.01

echoed
320.11
371.05

ecstacy
558.01

ecstasy
639.18

edgar
104.09
104.17
105.11
108.20
109.01
111.07
116.22
123.12
125.04
129.04
129.18
145.04
147.16
151.01
152.04
155.14
156.01
157.14
158.17
159.15
171.18
172.21
174.12
175.04
175.22
176.01
179.04
181.14
182.11
194.11
198.15
204.18
210.10
211.13
211.13
211.14
212.19
215.10
217.07
218.08
223.17
226.19
229.06
236.22
253.10
253.15
254.18
256.04
256.12
258.07
258.15
260.09
261.20
262.13
263.01
265.12
269.11
274.02
280.15
280.19
282.17
287.07
288.09
301.07
303.01
306.12
307.17
313.17
336.02
336.13
338.06
342.03
344.04
356.19
360.02
367.07
367.20
369.07
370.15
382.17
385.18
385.20
387.08
391.06
422.08
429.02

429.07
451.03
454.22
456.19
462.15
472.19
474.05
477.11
503.06
517.05
577.14
581.19
585.03
596.04
603.10
628.10
641.04
764.02

edgar's
128.16
182.09
235.13
270.20
305.01
309.08
327.12
329.14
347.08
410.22
552.08
635.05

edge
004.10
478.18
479.05
652.10

edged
315.15
448.02

edges
506.20

edition
348.10

education
149.09
203.09
426.03
430.01

ee
692.11

eea
691.03
692.11

eedle
184.16

een
720.14

effect
054.14
097.14
240.22
258.12
528.19

effects
046.07
075.06
273.10
325.06
369.10
635.19
682.07

effectually
010.22
388.08
703.16

effeminate
450.22

efficient
253.17

efficiently
499.19

effort
023.10
339.03
588.01
730.18

efforts
352.15
584.03
605.01
609.18

eft's
621.08

egg
230.07

eggs
481.11

egotism
231.08

egress
062.22

eh
016.13
033.08
524.11
626.08
627.13

eht
564.15

eight
059.03

| | | | | | |
|---|---|---|---|---|---|
| 570.18 | enters | 509.08 | 087.09 | 735.01 | 248.01 |
| 570.18 | 477.01 | epistles | 214.20 | 747.12 | 280.17 |
| 580.16 | entertain | 512.06 | 262.19 | 749.09 | 287.09 |
| 600.07 | 133.11 | 582.09 | 329.02 | 756.11 | 290.21 |
| 603.14 | 256.13 | epithet | 402.18 | 760.15 | 303.14 |
| 624.14 | 430.18 | 064.05 | 427.08 | 763.17 | 317.08 |
| 644.09 | 492.14 | equal | 524.12 | evening | 327.02 |
| 647.10 | entertained | 048.06 | espionage | 017.08 | 335.20 |
| 660.12 | 064.22 | 220.04 | 553.11 | 019.02 | 343.10 |
| 670.06 | 619.11 | 327.09 | essay | 077.04 | 355.22 |
| 671.07 | entertainer | 372.07 | 016.18 | 092.19 | 366.17 |
| 700.08 | 035.11 | 588.13 | 309.18 | 094.15 | 376.03 |
| 712.02 | entertaining | 726.21 | essayed | 101.03 | 390.01 |
| 714.01 | 228.03 | equality | 551.08 | 131.03 | 406.01 |
| 745.09 | 732.21 | 149.16 | essence | 188.04 | 417.08 |
| 753.13 | entertainment | equalled | 322.12 | 192.11 | 422.11 |
| enquired | 105.07 | 214.09 | establish | 197.06 | 424.12 |
| 071.13 | 479.13 | equally | 309.11 | 206.05 | 426.01 |
| 141.07 | 588.14 | 007.21 | 392.03 | 217.11 | 435.09 |
| 271.10 | entertains | 145.16 | established | 221.19 | 442.09 |
| 277.11 | 237.01 | 347.01 | 224.17 | 223.02 | 465.01 |
| 432.15 | entice | 378.09 | 411.06 | 240.09 | 469.10 |
| 692.09 | 352.12 | 462.16 | 725.06 | 273.09 | 475.12 |
| 738.08 | 518.11 | 468.11 | establishment | 280.05 | 476.09 |
| enraged | enticed | equanimity | 003.11 | 286.11 | 477.15 |
| 029.06 | 061.21 | 129.20 | 069.11 | 288.14 | 482.07 |
| 297.10 | entire | 155.18 | estate | 304.14 | 484.01 |
| 537.15 | 006.05 | equipping | 071.12 | 330.14 | 493.07 |
| ensconcing | 066.01 | 438.18 | 370.03 | 350.01 | 502.12 |
| 031.02 | 136.15 | erase | 636.10 | 350.01 | 511.19 |
| ensued | entirely | 239.20 | estates | 381.03 | 519.13 |
| 070.11 | 008.03 | ere | 470.01 | 413.11 | 536.14 |
| 245.13 | 021.02 | 061.15 | esteem | 427.16 | 546.01 |
| ensure | 079.22 | 065.16 | 007.22 | 448.11 | 548.13 |
| 112.12 | 100.01 | 179.15 | 137.15 | 451.21 | 562.18 |
| 344.06 | 104.09 | 211.08 | 150.07 | 455.17 | 613.09 |
| entangled | 136.07 | 312.12 | 388.15 | 476.04 | 664.22 |
| 271.15 | 174.04 | 347.16 | 713.21 | 503.16 | 671.13 |
| enter | 182.15 | 355.16 | esteemed | 515.09 | 682.14 |
| 116.02 | 279.21 | 364.01 | 062.03 | 548.19 | 702.01 |
| 207.14 | 302.11 | 394.08 | 131.15 | 550.05 | 705.07 |
| 213.06 | 333.01 | 414.03 | 197.15 | 555.04 | 713.12 |
| 229.19 | 426.03 | 433.12 | 481.19 | 557.07 | 723.18 |
| 274.01 | 465.21 | 450.16 | 512.11 | 559.11 | 726.09 |
| 310.06 | 468.02 | 610.04 | 516.08 | 559.21 | 743.05 |
| 378.11 | 482.22 | 683.12 | 713.22 | 568.01 | 764.10 |
| 387.18 | 505.08 | 727.14 | estimating | 572.04 | every |
| 396.19 | 571.18 | 747.02 | 224.14 | 630.16 | 008.21 |
| 467.10 | 597.13 | erect | eternal | 643.02 | 015.11 |
| 484.09 | 640.04 | 007.13 | 183.05 | 645.21 | 023.11 |
| 523.22 | 752.16 | 204.14 | 236.01 | 651.15 | 023.14 |
| 566.14 | entrails | 253.01 | 391.13 | 656.05 | 026.04 |
| 648.14 | 343.05 | 259.19 | eternally | 697.18 | 038.09 |
| 746.13 | entrance | erected | 064.11 | 699.03 | 038.17 |
| 756.16 | 005.07 | 066.08 | 329.04 | 701.17 | 040.07 |
| entered | 021.14 | erecting | 359.01 | 725.05 | 048.11 |
| 003.08 | 032.04 | 020.19 | 651.09 | 736.02 | 050.15 |
| 011.16 | 054.16 | errand | 701.20 | 743.15 | 062.16 |
| 062.11 | 066.20 | 042.18 | 731.01 | 750.07 | 067.11 |
| 064.04 | 107.11 | 209.20 | eternity | 754.15 | 071.15 |
| 067.09 | 184.03 | 297.05 | 371.17 | 757.03 | 096.12 |
| 085.21 | 206.15 | 364.12 | evaporated | 760.21 | 097.02 |
| 154.06 | 249.15 | 531.21 | 591.21 | 760.22 | 119.19 |
| 162.02 | 260.02 | errands | evasive | evening's | 124.05 |
| 170.02 | 312.10 | 075.18 | 267.22 | 033.10 | 131.15 |
| 191.22 | 355.14 | erred | eve | 264.14 | 134.19 |
| 192.04 | 393.19 | 754.09 | 118.16 | 608.12 | 142.21 |
| 208.20 | 560.06 | error | even | evenings | 146.15 |
| 247.20 | 653.13 | 066.21 | 002.21 | 022.06 | 153.05 |
| 254.05 | 683.11 | 526.07 | 024.10 | 041.20 | 173.21 |
| 261.05 | 757.12 | 532.06 | 060.18 | 102.21 | 174.03 |
| 265.15 | entreated | 597.21 | 080.01 | 153.03 | 181.08 |
| 285.11 | 168.06 | escape | 100.03 | 431.06 | 182.12 |
| 297.19 | 283.16 | 015.07 | 115.15 | 475.19 | 191.13 |
| 309.02 | 429.16 | 175.20 | 125.05 | 578.11 | 221.05 |
| 326.03 | 526.06 | 203.11 | 128.05 | 704.09 | 239.12 |
| 330.03 | 541.17 | 234.21 | 145.13 | event | 244.15 |
| 371.17 | 559.10 | 261.09 | 161.01 | 223.01 | 250.18 |
| 382.08 | 673.04 | 281.02 | 171.11 | 290.13 | 269.10 |
| 426.15 | entreaties | 361.01 | 186.22 | 334.06 | 282.08 |
| 434.12 | 131.05 | 387.03 | 204.09 | 375.02 | 283.21 |
| 453.01 | 199.06 | 388.05 | 214.07 | 416.02 | 289.21 |
| 530.09 | 410.20 | 411.10 | 219.09 | 618.07 | 296.02 |
| 532.02 | 512.08 | 545.06 | 236.06 | 759.04 | 296.02 |
| 543.14 | 585.04 | 642.12 | 248.09 | events | 296.17 |
| 547.17 | 623.06 | 724.19 | 263.20 | 110.01 | 313.17 |
| 553.05 | 749.13 | 763.04 | 315.20 | 264.14 | 315.18 |
| 563.04 | entreating | escaped | 329.18 | ever | 320.03 |
| 613.09 | 723.20 | 040.06 | 340.13 | 019.11 | 320.03 |
| 618.18 | entreaty | 102.17 | 352.20 | 045.04 | 327.17 |
| 626.04 | 305.15 | 170.07 | 371.21 | 048.20 | 335.12 |
| 644.16 | 615.19 | 295.03 | 388.11 | 063.22 | 338.03 |
| 656.01 | entrust | 317.16 | 399.07 | 080.16 | 340.03 |
| 659.20 | 456.02 | 403.11 | 410.14 | 082.14 | 344.02 |
| 663.08 | envied | 410.07 | 413.06 | 089.13 | 344.03 |
| 673.11 | 122.11 | 555.16 | 425.20 | 092.12 | 360.11 |
| 674.11 | envious | 684.10 | 430.09 | 095.18 | 384.05 |
| 691.12 | 219.05 | escaping | 454.16 | 122.10 | 393.07 |
| 693.22 | 648.09 | 065.13 | 490.16 | 139.11 | 405.17 |
| 717.07 | 679.07 | 084.06 | 538.12 | 176.21 | 406.05 |
| entering | envy | 129.05 | 574.08 | 180.20 | 407.16 |
| 126.08 | 218.17 | escort | 598.12 | 194.22 | 422.16 |
| 323.15 | 678.17 | 031.09 | 612.11 | 197.04 | 445.09 |
| 344.04 | 694.02 | 430.09 | 631.06 | 199.20 | 470.15 |
| 385.04 | 714.05 | 483.17 | 635.08 | 204.20 | 488.13 |
| 488.12 | envying | escorted | 645.01 | 213.17 | 489.20 |
| 572.17 | 122.14 | 606.19 | 654.17 | 229.05 | 500.01 |
| 628.20 | epistle | 686.16 | 659.16 | 236.01 | 518.05 |
| 654.16 | 328.02 | especially | 668.13 | 237.03 | 521.17 |
| 727.12 | | 004.21 | 670.11 | 238.13 | 528.03 |
| | | 047.21 | 677.16 | | 555.04 |

| | | | | | |
|---|---|---|---|---|---|
| 557.18 | 493.17 | **excessive** | **exclaiming** | 066.14 | 728.02 |
| 567.05 | 530.06 | 004.11 | 027.22 | 182.14 | **experiments** |
| 570.10 | 616.17 | 399.20 | 067.14 | 226.05 | 340.15 |
| 582.11 | 749.01 | **exchange** | 114.06 | 260.15 | **expire** |
| 596.02 | **exaggerate** | 083.19 | 116.19 | 305.05 | 366.07 |
| 598.04 | 603.11 | 105.10 | 186.11 | 334.07 | **expiring** |
| 614.03 | **exaggerated** | 581.01 | 492.04 | 335.21 | 036.06 |
| 625.03 | 150.04 | **exchanged** | 522.22 | 359.04 | **explain** |
| 625.05 | 271.13 | 066.19 | 681.08 | 370.07 | 078.15 |
| 631.15 | 747.12 | 450.18 | **exclamation** | 372.02 | 095.11 |
| 653.02 | **exaggeratedly** | **exchanging** | 285.16 | 388.13 | 176.11 |
| 684.01 | 003.03 | 062.20 | 436.07 | 395.12 | 179.03 |
| 693.02 | **exalting** | 085.18 | 553.14 | 411.21 | 280.19 |
| 693.03 | 050.07 | 154.12 | **exclude** | 496.09 | 307.13 |
| 699.03 | **examination** | 296.15 | 053.05 | 718.11 | 414.17 |
| 711.09 | 268.01 | 487.12 | 736.04 | 734.09 | 501.13 |
| 731.15 | 379.05 | **excite** | **excluded** | 746.04 | 566.06 |
| 731.16 | 468.06 | 605.19 | 503.04 | **exit** | 619.22 |
| 731.17 | **examine** | **excited** | **excommunicated** | 032.18 | 700.03 |
| 733.03 | 027.15 | 075.02 | 047.09 | 612.08 | 754.08 |
| 738.16 | 085.14 | 211.10 | **excursion** | 616.17 | **explained** |
| 759.11 | 237.13 | 261.10 | 110.21 | 692.16 | 221.08 |
| 760.19 | 285.14 | 401.17 | 500.12 | **exotic** | 419.06 |
| **everybody** | 290.20 | 568.04 | 586.10 | 071.06 | 427.12 |
| 067.15 | 384.02 | 738.10 | 598.03 | **expanded** | 446.18 |
| 090.14 | 507.19 | 747.11 | 692.07 | 508.05 | 633.10 |
| 111.18 | 566.08 | **excitement** | 745.11 | **expanding** | 665.17 |
| 273.17 | **examined** | 131.08 | **excursions** | 481.07 | **explaining** |
| 446.13 | 040.02 | 160.22 | 559.18 | **expansive** | 241.06 |
| 570.22 | 108.21 | **exciting** | **excuse** | 319.19 | 574.04 |
| 641.01 | 642.08 | 150.06 | 030.18 | **expect** | 745.02 |
| 708.19 | 668.12 | 253.14 | 056.11 | 138.05 | **explanation** |
| **everyone** | 719.06 | **exclaim** | 137.03 | 152.07 | 058.04 |
| 374.17 | **examining** | 041.18 | 155.14 | 201.09 | 383.04 |
| **everything** | 296.04 | 227.05 | 209.03 | 204.07 | 441.11 |
| 100.17 | **example** | **exclaimed** | 249.20 | 210.12 | 523.22 |
| 174.02 | 144.16 | 021.18 | 379.13 | 235.08 | 547.16 |
| 419.07 | 332.17 | 033.05 | 382.16 | 306.18 | 599.21 |
| 494.02 | 681.05 | 049.06 | 472.22 | 327.17 | **explanations** |
| 536.19 | **exasperate** | 072.14 | 498.14 | 331.20 | 286.15 |
| 632.14 | 343.19 | 109.14 | 716.11 | 346.05 | 679.18 |
| 641.01 | 389.20 | 122.06 | 738.17 | 451.18 | **explode** |
| 729.12 | **exasperating** | 153.20 | **excused** | 574.05 | 205.10 |
| **everywhere** | 263.15 | 155.16 | 144.08 | 647.16 | **exploded** |
| 157.07 | **exceeded** | 158.12 | 226.12 | 699.01 | 399.13 |
| **evidence** | 214.09 | 168.15 | 581.12 | 703.01 | **explosion** |
| 137.04 | **exceeding** | 172.16 | **execrated** | **expectation** | 347.05 |
| 442.13 | 456.20 | 181.05 | 144.02 | 269.06 | 716.13 |
| **evident** | **exceedingly** | 190.07 | **execrations** | 312.05 | **exposed** |
| 728.18 | 012.16 | 208.12 | 107.08 | **expectations** | 004.07 |
| **evidently** | 018.01 | 211.04 | 312.07 | 230.10 | 047.09 |
| 013.16 | 036.08 | 228.20 | **execute** | 484.17 | 339.17 |
| 062.03 | 091.04 | 235.01 | 050.04 | 493.12 | 517.19 |
| 075.11 | 146.01 | 238.04 | 312.12 | **expected** | **exposing** |
| 148.04 | 174.08 | 244.03 | 396.05 | 033.12 | 055.04 |
| 213.05 | 197.08 | 252.11 | 723.03 | 077.03 | 675.17 |
| 290.19 | 329.14 | 254.21 | **executed** | 116.04 | **expostulated** |
| 313.04 | 510.21 | 259.01 | 420.20 | 224.18 | 128.22 |
| 323.06 | 548.05 | 261.14 | **execution** | 304.11 | 319.20 |
| 491.02 | 556.17 | 265.10 | 216.07 | 331.05 | 528.15 |
| 506.19 | 568.03 | 271.04 | 238.10 | 415.18 | **expostulating** |
| 528.02 | 746.07 | 280.08 | 614.22 | 448.11 | 110.22 |
| 544.20 | **excellencies** | 290.05 | **exclaimed** | 454.17 | **expostulations** |
| 588.10 | 448.10 | 297.17 | 302.21 | 467.06 | 188.15 |
| 590.07 | **excellent** | 314.17 | **exercise** | 495.03 | 270.06 |
| 657.02 | 040.14 | 321.11 | 131.09 | 504.09 | 763.06 |
| 679.19 | **excellently** | 324.10 | 516.06 | 555.12 | **express** |
| **evil** | 221.02 | 345.07 | **exerted** | 651.02 | 002.10 |
| 030.02 | **except** | 365.04 | 400.05 | 751.08 | 150.11 |
| 144.05 | 006.06 | 384.03 | **exerting** | 752.14 | 154.04 |
| 193.14 | 061.09 | 394.03 | 263.19 | **expecting** | 182.12 |
| 241.08 | 064.17 | 396.17 | 609.17 | 054.08 | 510.03 |
| 253.06 | 074.07 | 399.01 | **exertions** | 338.14 | 518.14 |
| 254.02 | 097.03 | 401.10 | 729.09 | 507.03 | 526.22 |
| 258.10 | 218.11 | 416.14 | **exhausted** | 607.12 | 744.06 |
| 262.12 | 239.07 | 435.01 | 304.14 | **expects** | **expressed** |
| 332.19 | 248.06 | 440.01 | 323.19 | 505.09 | 002.20 |
| 374.19 | 300.02 | 450.03 | 370.19 | **expedient** | 098.18 |
| 403.14 | 308.01 | 467.04 | 538.16 | 347.04 | 099.04 |
| 414.22 | 340.04 | 488.09 | **exhausting** | 402.11 | 148.06 |
| 502.05 | 379.01 | 495.13 | 226.11 | 521.10 | 166.08 |
| 520.08 | 382.22 | 500.03 | **exhaustion** | **expedition** | 223.09 |
| **evince** | 426.15 | 503.20 | 279.21 | 727.09 | 353.13 |
| 236.20 | 445.11 | 511.03 | 591.08 | **expeditions** | 419.09 |
| 495.06 | 502.18 | 518.15 | **exhibit** | 704.10 | 420.19 |
| **evinced** | 518.09 | 533.16 | 219.08 | **expeditiously** | 490.21 |
| 019.17 | 521.11 | 537.15 | 513.16 | 611.21 | 699.18 |
| 148.08 | 522.11 | 545.21 | 729.21 | **expences** | **expressing** |
| 397.11 | 555.02 | 560.20 | **exhibited** | 079.03 | 328.05 |
| 498.12 | 569.04 | 563.01 | 496.07 | **expense** | 481.13 |
| 659.05 | 573.02 | 566.13 | 613.08 | 013.02 | 492.21 |
| 717.20 | 581.07 | 586.18 | **exhibiting** | 056.02 | 580.03 |
| 728.02 | 591.08 | 590.17 | 266.18 | 143.02 | 701.15 |
| **evincing** | 665.01 | 607.14 | **exhibition** | 513.15 | **expression** |
| 099.11 | 677.08 | 608.17 | 118.11 | **expensive** | 019.15 |
| 225.06 | 713.13 | 614.02 | 172.02 | 323.05 | 032.15 |
| **exact** | 728.09 | 618.12 | 457.06 | **experience** | 124.22 |
| 333.20 | **excepting** | 626.08 | **exile** | 025.12 | 146.03 |
| 640.04 | 066.12 | 629.17 | 023.20 | 165.17 | 170.04 |
| **exacting** | 137.05 | 650.05 | 282.12 | 259.13 | 212.07 |
| 685.07 | 190.01 | 677.18 | 358.05 | 424.06 | 214.01 |
| **exactly** | **exception** | 685.10 | **exist** | 497.01 | 236.11 |
| 067.10 | 145.05 | 698.14 | 329.13 | **experienced** | 245.17 |
| 108.18 | 340.04 | 702.13 | 426.16 | 067.07 | 316.09 |
| 137.16 | 573.13 | 707.01 | 651.12 | 146.22 | 341.14 |
| 147.07 | 670.17 | 716.10 | 732.01 | 225.01 | 351.20 |
| 253.16 | **excess** | 718.08 | **existed** | 323.06 | 370.21 |
| 348.03 | 150.04 | 722.04 | 025.07 | 389.20 | 387.20 |
| 394.14 | 359.11 | 741.20 | **existence** | 403.20 | 393.21 |
| 408.20 | 425.06 | 747.22 | 017.09 | 508.08 | 404.16 |
| 485.15 | | | 023.19 | 548.01 | 425.11 |

EXPRESSION (continued)
456.19
565.04
587.11
601.01
684.06
722.12
747.12
749.05
expressions
224.16
274.17
726.05
expressive
296.03
exquisite
019.10
601.04
749.04
extended
495.12
708.23
extent
226.12
427.10
exterior
225.18
229.21
465.21
external
136.10
271.11
307.22
681.03
extinct
740.14
extinguish
758.07
extinguished
015.03
149.11
193.06
284.02
388.08
552.10
extinguisher
506.06
extinguishing
034.12
111.22
extorted
332.12
extra
040.12
292.09
693.15
extra-animal
494.02
extract
136.18
348.04
extraordinary
006.21
extreme
018.07
055.01
extremely
156.07
178.07
311.07
418.02
435.13
487.08
499.07
505.02
543.13
577.09
590.14
679.15
extremes
334.09
749.04
extremities
112.02
extremity
263.04
extricate
365.09
exuberance
224.03
exultation
420.21
758.08
exulting
397.21
eye
006.06
027.04
045.18
090.16
118.04
165.14
244.04
257.06
302.17
353.14
358.10
405.16
405.17
466.18
485.17
486.05

509.21
517.13
603.21
693.14
716.07
718.03
eye-sight
387.17
eyed
212.07
eyeing
011.19
722.11
eyes
002.01
008.14
017.21
019.14
020.20
030.10
039.07
048.19
059.07
063.13
081.07
097.21
103.02
111.14
114.21
124.12
125.05
127.22
130.06
146.05
156.22
159.05
164.17
171.10
198.01
206.14
207.18
207.19
214.05
226.14
238.11
239.11
239.15
256.08
266.06
266.21
276.08
278.10
281.08
287.03
296.11
299.10
309.07
311.09
341.13
348.08
351.13
353.21
356.13
361.17
362.02
363.22
364.02
369.11
370.16
374.02
377.10
392.20
394.11
401.10
404.12
408.03
408.20
425.03
438.06
439.22
452.15
454.01
464.04
464.11
464.17
464.17
468.08
479.19
502.15
514.08
526.21
529.10
550.06
551.18
561.10
565.03
567.02
579.17
587.08
593.15
608.20
611.13
620.22
629.08
634.19
639.17
654.15
655.10
660.20
666.09
674.15

676.06
683.07
684.04
694.17
708.18
709.22
718.10
719.02
723.21
724.05
728.04
728.06
738.20
742.21
744.08
747.19
749.08
753.01
757.16
758.07
f'r
692.11
fabulous
338.18
face
003.21
019.10
024.04
030.19
041.17
052.15
054.18
063.18
078.04
093.15
108.09
111.16
115.22
117.18
123.18
125.09
128.08
140.19
143.15
146.01
154.07
170.04
171.10
174.10
181.09
183.13
190.07
207.05
211.11
216.04
232.18
237.08
238.07
239.09
244.05
249.05
251.08
258.21
266.04
271.16
274.17
277.06
277.11
279.20
298.19
306.13
308.16
316.10
324.08
330.10
351.19
352.20
356.04
360.05
365.22
374.10
376.09
379.02
383.20
386.04
386.14
404.18
425.02
450.13
455.14
467.17
471.12
492.11
497.21
519.14
537.19
564.01
565.03
598.08
601.01
610.02
613.06
620.22
634.04
634.18
639.02
644.08
645.07
649.16
660.19
662.15

669.01
676.03
683.22
695.03
695.04
706.21
709.20
710.19
724.05
738.21
743.12
752.10
757.19
759.11
760.07
faces
010.12
126.17
137.18
193.16
273.22
299.02
364.05
466.18
670.11
718.04
727.20
731.19
facial
025.18
facing
321.11
fact
038.11
225.14
302.02
362.02
401.19
410.11
446.21
470.14
481.01
529.13
735.04
759.18
facts
332.13
faculties
137.11
728.15
734.05
faculty
730.02
faded
040.18
149.15
fading
226.14
378.17
692.19
fagots
696.21
fahl
185.13
194.02
fail
087.03
685.15
failed
142.19
155.18
613.12
failing
583.13
failings
238.22
failure
561.08
fain
375.08
429.22
436.12
451.09
498.20
596.07
660.22
663.09
faint
036.08
259.15
270.13
393.08
454.02
529.11
534.16
569.06
605.11
639.03
faint-hearted
476.01
fainted
362.05
367.03
fair
019.12
035.22
043.19
083.16
099.22
124.02
232.17

257.19
349.08
370.16
417.19
425.03
699.11
705.11
720.15
fairies
121.13
fairishes
439.03
fairly
003.05
140.17
235.18
365.07
389.22
470.01
fairy
026.01
026.12
276.14
428.14
431.22
446.01
686.21
697.01
faishion
028.20
faith
220.09
240.19
341.16
435.19
530.11
651.11
faithful
289.11
289.12
398.17
415.08
500.12
faithfully
512.15
fall
066.10
220.03
230.15
292.12
333.15
354.02
433.12
484.15
522.15
526.07
538.09
558.06
564.10
597.16
610.09
613.03
636.20
651.14
fallen
028.15
170.16
189.08
271.16
367.01
399.19
404.20
528.06
falling
114.02
falls
065.20
383.02
false
338.19
362.19
536.21
583.18
falsehood
157.03
569.02
639.08
falsehoods
231.11
525.09
537.02
570.13
familiar
022.05
206.21
304.12
382.16
492.19
744.13
familiarity
561.12
family
005.10
023.22
027.08
038.10
071.02
073.09
080.12
089.05
112.08

122.02
126.10
167.15
198.11
219.08
295.12
329.11
332.18
350.13
429.06
443.08
466.05
503.09
546.05
575.06
582.06
641.06
648.14
690.10
736.10
755.11
famous
047.05
fancied
059.06
089.03
246.02
254.14
397.22
508.14
550.08
675.11
682.12
682.16
749.07
fancies
497.01
733.01
fanciful
431.07
521.06
fancy
136.11
137.21
146.10
168.01
219.15
233.22
238.08
252.04
265.19
273.15
282.14
325.11
336.01
363.05
384.01
421.20
464.12
477.13
575.09
583.17
619.10
646.06
660.17
668.14
727.06
fancying
292.08
549.03
568.11
fangs
010.10
fanny
291.05
411.03
fantastic
225.12
far
013.14
029.18
033.03
060.05
065.08
081.16
120.12
134.14
139.05
143.20
154.20
159.15
169.11
169.11
174.11
202.12
224.14
256.14
284.01
326.17
351.17
360.04
364.22
367.04
410.12
414.13
433.08
442.11
456.14
460.18
478.10
479.14

| | | | | | |
|---|---|---|---|---|---|
| 489.17 | 319.03 | 637.22 | 285.14 | feebly | 656.08 |
| 494.10 | 493.20 | 641.21 | 314.03 | 586.17 | 663.07 |
| 511.04 | fastidiousness | 656.14 | 318.08 | feed | 668.03 |
| 533.07 | 212.08 | 664.13 | 327.07 | 078.12 | 697.06 |
| 543.06 | fasting | 683.22 | 334.11 | 140.05 | 742.22 |
| 592.21 | 122.03 | 725.10 | 347.03 | 518.11 | 763.13 |
| 619.07 | 740.07 | 725.20 | 372.16 | feeding | feigned |
| 689.03 | fat | father's | 406.11 | 120.14 | 235.15 |
| 693.20 | 387.12 | 073.05 | 408.10 | 248.13 | feigning |
| 696.04 | fate | 079.11 | 431.08 | feeing | 258.01 |
| 730.01 | 160.05 | 093.07 | 433.11 | 733.07 | fell |
| 754.09 | 181.07 | 165.01 | 468.13 | feel | 046.06 |
| 756.14 | 322.14 | 198.19 | 469.12 | 013.18 | 050.13 |
| far-off | 396.15 | 233.10 | 471.13 | 027.07 | 058.12 |
| 043.07 | fated | 298.18 | 495.08 | 074.15 | 082.06 |
| farm | 356.07 | 423.01 | 522.02 | 075.04 | 083.17 |
| 031.19 | father | 438.01 | 577.22 | 080.22 | 084.18 |
| 075.19 | 040.20 | 441.10 | 579.09 | 123.16 | 093.10 |
| 099.18 | 045.12 | 450.13 | 582.18 | 134.04 | 097.16 |
| 242.05 | 075.16 | 467.11 | 592.06 | 176.12 | 106.08 |
| 442.06 | 079.20 | 472.16 | 599.03 | 202.09 | 143.18 |
| 492.08 | 082.01 | 536.16 | 604.19 | 206.03 | 165.16 |
| farm-house | 083.21 | 538.04 | 616.12 | 219.05 | 189.04 |
| 433.18 | 085.06 | 576.11 | 651.17 | 235.08 | 197.13 |
| 465.15 | 088.10 | 581.09 | 661.09 | 279.14 | 207.16 |
| 483.05 | 091.12 | 594.16 | 684.18 | 303.11 | 221.12 |
| 530.09 | 091.21 | 604.19 | 733.13 | 343.10 | 280.18 |
| farmer | 093.18 | 636.05 | feard | 359.18 | 298.20 |
| 006.22 | 094.16 | 639.15 | 232.14 | 362.08 | 319.04 |
| 126.03 | 096.10 | 641.12 | feared | 363.22 | 373.16 |
| farmhouse | 102.22 | father-in-law | 054.11 | 371.15 | 410.01 |
| 308.11 | 125.16 | 648.18 | 070.12 | 388.01 | 462.03 |
| 445.14 | 164.09 | 662.14 | 118.01 | 388.03 | 473.09 |
| farming | 167.09 | 721.13 | 184.12 | 389.03 | 497.19 |
| 088.16 | 177.11 | father-in-law's | 215.02 | 389.05 | 522.12 |
| 747.08 | 245.06 | 725.09 | 281.06 | 439.21 | 555.02 |
| farther | 247.17 | fatherless | 321.05 | 504.04 | 565.21 |
| 008.22 | 281.17 | 081.12 | 373.10 | 525.11 | 591.06 |
| 104.15 | 299.04 | fathers' | 466.12 | 528.22 | 605.03 |
| 132.03 | 325.11 | 470.02 | fearful | 538.21 | 631.01 |
| 151.19 | 391.01 | fathur's | 075.05 | 570.22 | 652.06 |
| 179.21 | 418.22 | 233.11 | 178.02 | 587.17 | 751.05 |
| 267.08 | 429.21 | fatigue | 358.04 | 652.15 | 759.01 |
| 668.18 | 442.09 | 078.16 | 540.07 | 662.18 | fellies |
| 728.12 | 446.17 | 304.19 | 675.17 | 662.20 | 699.10 |
| farthing | 448.08 | 315.03 | fearfully | 662.22 | fellow |
| 660.02 | 451.10 | 378.13 | 207.01 | 663.03 | 001.12 |
| 660.03 | 452.22 | 383.22 | 399.09 | 663.03 | 013.01 |
| fascinating | 454.13 | 495.09 | 589.10 | 684.21 | 023.02 |
| 008.13 | 460.01 | 689.16 | 731.09 | 728.01 | 049.14 |
| fascination | 460.08 | fatigued | fearing | feeling | 073.20 |
| 348.07 | 460.12 | 451.08 | 759.19 | 007.20 | 127.05 |
| fashion | 460.13 | fault | fearless | 081.19 | 184.07 |
| 078.10 | 462.09 | 031.08 | 442.17 | 176.12 | 245.14 |
| 138.08 | 464.01 | 157.02 | fears | 204.01 | 259.16 |
| 148.21 | 467.14 | 166.19 | 245.02 | 213.11 | 320.19 |
| 189.17 | 468.20 | 529.01 | 294.19 | 215.11 | 347.01 |
| 203.22 | 474.12 | 567.06 | 457.01 | 225.01 | 416.17 |
| 239.07 | 477.17 | 721.02 | 613.14 | 248.03 | 442.02 |
| 320.04 | 478.08 | 752.17 | feast | 313.07 | 456.04 |
| 681.20 | 478.15 | 753.04 | 129.21 | 374.09 | 560.04 |
| fast | 484.08 | faults | feather | 438.08 | 635.01 |
| 008.01 | 489.21 | 092.16 | 275.17 | 441.09 | 673.12 |
| 085.15 | 490.14 | 425.15 | feathered | 508.12 | fellow-servant |
| 100.08 | 493.21 | 443.15 | 114.03 | 601.15 | 132.21 |
| 106.22 | 495.10 | 498.09 | feathers | 608.08 | 308.12 |
| 106.22 | 498.14 | 581.11 | 275.03 | 651.07 | fellow-servant's |
| 133.05 | 503.12 | favour | 275.09 | 695.19 | 763.10 |
| 191.13 | 509.18 | 029.16 | feathery | feelings | fellows |
| 237.20 | 512.04 | favourable | 015.07 | 154.04 | 637.16 |
| 278.19 | 516.05 | 296.06 | feature | 181.16 | fellowship |
| 299.02 | 521.02 | 347.06 | 214.02 | 182.11 | 221.06 |
| 364.11 | 524.15 | 392.13 | features | 225.10 | felony |
| 365.21 | 526.02 | 442.14 | 019.12 | 234.10 | 617.21 |
| 366.09 | 526.06 | 643.12 | 108.12 | 240.20 | felt |
| 386.12 | 533.21 | favoured | 149.04 | 306.16 | 003.02 |
| 393.11 | 535.03 | 026.01 | 207.16 | 333.18 | 010.20 |
| 414.02 | 536.04 | 446.03 | 245.17 | 334.13 | 013.01 |
| 415.18 | 537.14 | favourite | 296.03 | 444.10 | 023.01 |
| 523.12 | 546.06 | 081.17 | 311.07 | 446.06 | 038.15 |
| 583.13 | 548.15 | 087.11 | 370.17 | 465.21 | 075.01 |
| 587.18 | 559.18 | 243.15 | 404.08 | 493.15 | 082.11 |
| 738.04 | 565.14 | 446.06 | 407.08 | 501.02 | 097.18 |
| 739.22 | 572.01 | 492.05 | 425.04 | 546.13 | 106.06 |
| 755.02 | 573.22 | 528.14 | 442.03 | 676.07 | 134.13 |
| fasted | 577.06 | 680.17 | 456.20 | 682.05 | 141.01 |
| 237.03 | 578.21 | favourite's | 475.02 | 736.06 | 157.16 |
| 269.09 | 580.05 | 712.07 | 486.04 | feels | 171.01 |
| fasten | 580.20 | favourites | 526.21 | 272.13 | 182.18 |
| 108.04 | 582.10 | 018.15 | 528.01 | 274.06 | 189.13 |
| 283.04 | 583.22 | 018.18 | 639.17 | 345.19 | 200.05 |
| 401.03 | 590.12 | 550.12 | 651.06 | feet | 223.10 |
| 644.08 | 592.06 | favours | 694.16 | 055.01 | 240.08 |
| fastened | 593.06 | 149.14 | 727.05 | 078.05 | 241.06 |
| 037.12 | 597.03 | fawn | 731.14 | 085.13 | 244.07 |
| 042.16 | 599.05 | 115.01 | 731.20 | 111.04 | 256.17 |
| 298.11 | 599.17 | fawning | 744.05 | 154.05 | 262.20 |
| 379.04 | 600.08 | 621.11 | february | 166.01 | 275.17 |
| 393.19 | 602.07 | fear | 577.16 | 172.09 | 280.20 |
| 419.17 | 605.10 | 021.19 | fed | 174.01 | 282.04 |
| 565.06 | 605.15 | 027.05 | 390.14 | 270.01 | 286.15 |
| 612.09 | 606.08 | 052.22 | feeble | 284.19 | 290.12 |
| 623.02 | 611.09 | 094.02 | 053.15 | 291.14 | 298.16 |
| 653.11 | 611.09 | 100.22 | 068.02 | 373.20 | 363.05 |
| 673.09 | 612.14 | 107.07 | 089.18 | 380.06 | 373.10 |
| fastening | 615.07 | 192.16 | 370.01 | 383.17 | 376.01 |
| 315.12 | 618.03 | 204.19 | 468.11 | 490.13 | 377.18 |
| 555.17 | 619.01 | 222.17 | 578.20 | 504.22 | 393.22 |
| faster | 630.19 | 259.15 | 615.03 | 518.02 | 394.13 |
| 011.06 | 631.21 | 266.01 | feebleness | 530.05 | 404.01 |
| 199.16 | 633.19 | 273.01 | 654.05 | 605.16 | 432.22 |

| | | | | | |
|---|---|---|---|---|---|
| 453.12 | 251.20 | figuratively | 463.19 | 205.10 | 172.20 |
| 468.05 | 266.04 | 524.21 | 511.05 | 212.15 | 186.06 |
| 480.22 | 273.19 | figure | 619.20 | 213.16 | 218.02 |
| 493.15 | 279.18 | 007.14 | 630.21 | 214.06 | 220.18 |
| 502.10 | 283.02 | 019.08 | 656.05 | 226.21 | 224.13 |
| 539.01 | 295.07 | 146.06 | 666.20 | 235.02 | 244.17 |
| 562.07 | 321.03 | 166.07 | 693.13 | 253.20 | 248.21 |
| 571.14 | 329.18 | 487.05 | 704.09 | 258.15 | 254.19 |
| 571.14 | 351.01 | 552.16 | 716.13 | 304.06 | 255.13 |
| 579.17 | 371.06 | 612.11 | 729.21 | 309.05 | 264.08 |
| 581.19 | 373.13 | figures | finer | 312.15 | 270.14 |
| 610.17 | 383.07 | 561.04 | 071.17 | 317.17 | 281.20 |
| 613.06 | 411.10 | 675.08 | finest | 326.15 | 286.21 |
| 615.15 | 413.22 | filial | 139.11 | 382.20 | 294.16 |
| 630.17 | 484.04 | 468.17 | 428.08 | 384.12 | 297.03 |
| 631.09 | 515.04 | 606.09 | finger | 390.10 | 302.13 |
| 636.15 | 531.16 | fill | 167.09 | 392.05 | 306.06 |
| 652.20 | 548.07 | 167.09 | 232.11 | 392.12 | 307.03 |
| 653.16 | 576.20 | 295.12 | 237.20 | 397.05 | 308.15 |
| 656.10 | 578.03 | filled | 259.03 | 403.14 | 321.18 |
| 668.10 | 581.01 | 009.10 | 385.12 | 404.04 | 338.22 |
| 726.16 | 586.16 | 065.22 | 668.17 | 476.06 | 339.21 |
| 731.05 | 597.18 | 119.16 | finger-ends | 476.12 | 340.02 |
| 739.09 | 611.10 | 156.22 | 375.12 | 491.05 | 342.06 |
| 759.04 | 635.09 | 193.01 | fingers | 513.02 | 356.02 |
| 763.04 | 662.10 | 217.06 | 002.02 | 513.13 | 356.09 |
| female | 676.11 | 293.04 | 042.08 | 531.02 | 367.13 |
| 444.20 | 679.09 | 294.19 | 052.01 | 532.17 | 370.07 |
| females | 721.18 | 314.10 | 052.02 | 538.20 | 374.10 |
| 063.07 | ffin | 509.02 | 053.03 | 549.05 | 381.05 |
| fence | 760.04 | 534.09 | 054.18 | 556.10 | 384.01 |
| 432.13 | fickleness | 628.22 | 093.22 | 564.12 | 388.06 |
| 552.17 | 524.21 | 668.07 | 116.06 | 570.06 | 405.19 |
| fend | fiddle | 743.14 | 117.20 | 616.21 | 405.20 |
| 078.12 | 076.13 | filling | 127.07 | 649.09 | 411.11 |
| fender | 079.14 | 582.09 | 156.13 | 655.11 | 414.08 |
| 741.09 | fidgetting | 607.06 | 203.05 | 667.15 | 422.20 |
| ferocious | 155.13 | 634.02 | 207.06 | 682.10 | 424.08 |
| 022.16 | 155.15 | 731.16 | 213.14 | 693.13 | 430.11 |
| 050.10 | fie | final | 233.05 | 701.17 | 433.17 |
| 375.07 | 405.03 | 378.17 | 237.18 | 704.06 | 441.10 |
| 404.15 | 405.03 | finally | 238.12 | 706.17 | 453.17 |
| ferociously | 503.20 | 008.22 | 278.09 | 743.13 | 455.05 |
| 707.02 | field | 048.22 | 358.10 | 744.20 | 463.13 |
| ferocity | 139.06 | 058.13 | 365.10 | 744.22 | 464.06 |
| 144.23 | 151.10 | 069.08 | 452.15 | 751.06 | 479.13 |
| 214.04 | 184.15 | 132.07 | 468.06 | 751.14 | 486.12 |
| 489.01 | fields | 148.19 | 513.15 | 751.16 | 487.21 |
| 605.06 | 099.21 | 221.14 | 549.02 | 760.17 | 496.06 |
| ferret | 485.22 | 283.16 | 602.08 | fire-flushed | 505.17 |
| 187.02 | 515.04 | 400.07 | 609.10 | 011.11 | 546.18 |
| fertile | fiend | 445.21 | 610.02 | fire-place | 550.04 |
| 154.13 | 056.13 | 462.13 | 621.08 | 005.20 | 555.11 |
| fervently | 106.17 | 480.17 | 710.13 | 098.20 | 572.04 |
| 487.01 | 144.18 | 541.06 | 724.03 | 191.21 | 585.05 |
| fervour | 231.12 | 551.15 | 749.15 | 323.02 | 586.04 |
| 653.19 | 312.08 | 567.06 | 758.03 | 360.08 | 604.15 |
| festoons | 341.17 | 579.11 | finish | fire-side | 612.07 |
| 323.08 | 367.13 | 669.17 | 056.09 | 092.20 | 621.18 |
| fetch | 408.08 | 750.11 | 134.18 | 705.03 | 633.20 |
| 044.05 | 620.16 | find | 141.03 | firelight | 635.19 |
| 074.17 | 655.02 | 059.17 | 202.11 | 727.18 | 637.05 |
| 257.13 | 718.08 | 064.10 | 203.09 | fireplace | 639.04 |
| 266.01 | 755.21 | 075.11 | 513.21 | 145.18 | 649.03 |
| 320.18 | fiend's | 105.07 | 697.22 | 576.03 | 657.02 |
| 440.14 | 395.12 | 130.20 | finished | fires | 658.12 |
| 466.13 | fiendish | 182.02 | 023.03 | 118.15 | 659.14 |
| 523.01 | 389.18 | 185.21 | 085.12 | 691.20 | 665.02 |
| 637.01 | 495.01 | 191.08 | 094.05 | firing | 668.08 |
| 638.06 | fiends | 202.16 | 184.04 | 161.04 | 671.21 |
| 645.14 | 010.18 | 249.19 | 270.16 | firm | 674.15 |
| 699.07 | 124.14 | 275.02 | 312.12 | 237.18 | 676.02 |
| 756.17 | 124.19 | 285.02 | 384.21 | 422.13 | 680.01 |
| fetched | fierce | 315.19 | 454.18 | firmer | 682.21 |
| 441.15 | 164.12 | 344.03 | 466.06 | 066.12 | 694.11 |
| 532.18 | 164.13 | 373.10 | 506.11 | firmly | 700.01 |
| fetches | 230.01 | 377.05 | 718.20 | 365.14 | 700.17 |
| 298.03 | 289.08 | 394.14 | finishing | firs | 706.20 |
| fetching | 425.12 | 446.20 | 063.21 | 004.11 | 711.01 |
| 641.20 | 757.17 | 470.19 | 129.06 | 279.13 | 731.08 |
| feud | fiercely | 597.07 | 263.03 | 465.19 | 751.18 |
| 020.22 | 361.18 | 647.20 | 400.06 | first | 753.09 |
| fever | 683.09 | 684.01 | fir | 015.07 | first-rate |
| 143.07 | fiercer | 705.08 | 577.18 | 030.05 | 131.16 |
| 196.03 | 009.17 | 713.07 | 642.11 | 033.01 | 494.11 |
| 197.01 | 164.11 | 729.13 | 737.10 | 040.13 | firstly |
| 264.19 | fiercest | finding | fir-tree | 042.04 | 348.06 |
| 301.05 | 433.19 | 052.16 | 051.02 | 043.18 | fist |
| 429.11 | fiery | 099.04 | firbough | 045.20 | 026.04 |
| 540.21 | 198.08 | 117.09 | 051.12 | 045.20 | 070.15 |
| 739.15 | 280.01 | 132.13 | fire | 047.08 | 124.07 |
| 740.08 | fifteen | 167.08 | 014.04 | 047.09 | 259.12 |
| feverish | 131.11 | 221.17 | 017.06 | 049.01 | 309.14 |
| 274.11 | 145.05 | 313.18 | 028.13 | 050.03 | 564.07 |
| 532.21 | 688.05 | 498.08 | 041.08 | 054.19 | 702.11 |
| fevers | fifth | 609.19 | 043.07 | 057.10 | fists |
| 292.14 | 626.02 | 721.02 | 061.07 | 065.12 | 065.06 |
| few | fifty | finds | 063.20 | 074.08 | 129.18 |
| 004.11 | 090.08 | 166.04 | 068.03 | 080.11 | 456.14 |
| 005.04 | 276.18 | fine | 075.01 | 092.13 | 709.02 |
| 038.19 | 346.16 | 008.11 | 103.03 | 094.16 | fit |
| 047.16 | 402.09 | 075.21 | 111.10 | 098.09 | 043.18 |
| 071.21 | fight | 113.08 | 126.16 | 099.19 | 125.15 |
| 080.12 | 220.07 | 139.02 | 133.09 | 112.11 | 128.14 |
| 099.10 | 316.02 | 185.04 | 151.22 | 115.11 | 143.13 |
| 137.05 | 346.08 | 193.19 | 162.09 | 128.06 | 178.08 |
| 150.07 | 494.19 | 232.22 | 168.01 | 139.02 | 188.20 |
| 171.06 | 734.15 | 246.05 | 169.14 | 146.08 | 194.09 |
| 197.02 | fighting | 310.21 | 174.10 | 147.05 | 198.05 |
| 206.13 | 406.06 | 381.02 | 179.14 | 149.08 | 234.11 |
| 218.15 | | 441.17 | 189.07 | 167.09 | 245.20 |
| | | 449.14 | | | |

266.18
280.20
292.21
342.15
390.08
402.03
407.21
412.17
476.20
484.05
497.10
507.17
511.15
538.16
565.20
574.08
586.19
671.08
708.04
740.02
746.02
758.12

fits
087.08
165.04
263.18

fitted
304.20

five
007.05
014.11
021.13
039.07
113.02
121.07
146.18
166.04
166.05
199.02
355.21
365.11
376.01
394.03
460.04
543.03
568.10
625.01
695.11
731.03

fix
030.06
222.16
236.01
338.10

fixed
001.07
027.04
136.12
215.02
287.02
370.18
439.16
509.22
553.15
585.09
597.15
603.20
628.04
639.17
655.10
656.21
709.03
716.07
749.07

fixing
618.05

fixture
014.08
067.13
704.20

flagged
015.13

flags
003.14
154.05
170.19
400.03
731.15

flakes
015.08
022.01
063.08
382.06

flame
061.20
063.09
506.06
513.11

flames
015.03
513.21

flaming
696.20

flapping
757.22

flash
351.13

flashed
024.22
047.04
215.05

361.18
408.07
723.22
744.05

flashing
266.21
608.20

flatly
346.16

flatness
508.11

flatter
090.04
219.12
252.01
443.07

flattered
147.05
235.08
597.11
667.06
700.14

flattering
302.09
492.07

flattery
113.08

flaxen
019.12
449.13
468.05

flaying
164.05
419.22

flaysome
016.11
043.20
194.02
324.17
696.12
720.13

flee
106.06
409.05

fleecy
463.06

flees
233.12

flesh
167.05
351.20
399.16
416.18
621.14
652.17
756.11

flew
034.11
116.16
211.09
292.22
374.01
410.08
430.05
532.07

flies
160.05

flight
297.03
389.12
410.03

flighted
077.16

flights
256.13

flighty
142.12
628.04

flinched
242.09

fling
078.09
089.14
319.10
722.19

flinging
055.20
105.13
140.09
211.13
321.01
324.16
441.03

flings
222.15

flint
245.05

flinty
420.19

flippant
498.06

flit
071.18
628.02

flitting
274.17
318.14
373.07
557.15
598.09

floating
706.21

flock
047.22

flog
258.09

flogged
129.02
129.03

flogging
100.08
112.10
258.11
524.12

flooding
041.04

floor
006.12
017.16
055.20
093.08
098.19
119.18
130.16
157.08
186.11
260.14
275.11
280.19
304.21
312.16
323.11
379.03
385.13
397.18
457.19
558.12
611.07
676.08
731.14
750.16

floundered
046.16

flour
115.03

flourishing
011.12
034.18
046.20

flow
353.02
399.20
640.08

flowed
243.14
653.01

flower
518.18
716.08

flower-plot
103.18

flower-pot
346.04

flowers
302.20
303.20
378.04
693.09
721.09

flown
383.01

flows
384.11

fluent
434.21

flung
010.15
020.13
162.09
169.12
178.22
185.04
258.14
324.06
326.14
362.03
389.03
399.11
401.14
409.15
674.08
676.08
703.05

flurried
012.14
185.07

flurry
416.09

flushed
130.14
213.09
253.20
579.17

fluttered
352.07

fluttering
764.09

flutterings
510.04

fly
078.09

518.12

fly-leaf
039.19

flying
266.21
276.09
479.17
488.10
510.01
559.13

foamed
362.06

foe
407.04

foes
124.22
230.19
576.17

foil
425.15

fold
028.06
186.05
241.09

folded
062.06
254.01
507.11
662.13

folds
183.13

foliage
183.02
353.05
519.13

folk
035.20
438.12
688.11

folks
232.10
665.21
760.12

follow
016.21
063.02
138.07
267.06
291.08
306.17
332.17
374.19
397.21
480.17
516.12
606.10
618.08
624.01
628.08
659.01
715.03

followed
036.05
107.08
131.22
157.07
170.17
213.06
255.06
257.16
285.04
310.07
331.07
360.10
415.18
466.17
474.05
541.07
564.07
662.12
681.05
691.12
704.10
724.19
745.17

followers
445.16

following
066.17
118.04
173.03
302.14
353.08
378.02
421.03
424.03
508.20
551.19
559.11
700.22
757.03

follows
031.21
209.13

folly
013.05
060.22
183.15
210.02
223.12
541.15

600.15

fond
090.23
160.21
204.08
243.19
336.13
336.18
414.19
432.07
452.08
494.15
506.16
536.13
556.02

fonder
464.09
735.07

fondest
303.19
548.13

fondling
092.06
227.10

fondness
120.02
150.11
162.06
219.08
487.12
588.18

food
111.12
273.08
471.20
472.11
624.14
701.20
740.10
749.12
752.19

fooil
233.03

fooit
324.17

fool
107.22
172.07
252.02
294.08
323.15
327.15
336.01
366.04
493.13
493.14
522.21
537.04
561.09
651.17
702.18
721.01

fool's
419.13

fool's-craving
262.12

foolish
012.21
042.12
153.07
190.14
219.11
238.07
245.02
345.09
374.12
485.18
508.06
520.15
521.06
600.11
669.14
744.17

foolishly
256.19
385.04
577.09

foolishness
075.03

fools
614.03

foot
009.18
028.03
090.17
107.03
109.07
156.19
259.13
264.17
376.14
391.14
401.20
430.21
633.14
764.04

foot-stool
453.15

footing
254.10

footmarks
746.18

footmen
346.09

footstep
062.11
624.10

footsteps
053.22
449.20
516.12

for
008.04
009.14
009.19
012.22
015.14
015.19
016.05
017.07
019.16
020.02
020.20
021.19
024.18
024.19
027.05
027.21
028.12
029.04
030.18
031.13
032.06
035.21
037.04
038.01
038.09
040.05
040.16
041.09
041.15
042.17
044.11
045.01
045.13
046.07
046.15
047.01
048.08
050.11
052.12
053.11
053.13
054.11
056.05
056.10
057.01
059.11
059.12
062.04
062.12
062.14
062.17
063.15
064.10
065.16
065.19
067.02
067.11
067.18
068.05
070.09
070.14
071.07
073.13
075.19
076.03
076.05
076.11
076.17
077.13
077.15
078.12
078.21
079.12
079.19
080.08
080.13
080.17
080.21
081.14
081.17
082.11
083.01
084.10
085.01
088.04
088.19
089.09
090.18
091.01
092.15
093.04
094.02
094.03
094.06
095.05
097.04
098.16
098.18
100.14

| | | | | | |
|---|---|---|---|---|---|
| 100.22 | 196.20 | 285.08 | 389.05 | 476.14 | 589.18 |
| 101.04 | 197.10 | 286.01 | 389.07 | 477.18 | 590.02 |
| 103.09 | 198.01 | 286.18 | 390.05 | 478.13 | 590.10 |
| 103.15 | 198.14 | 288.11 | 390.08 | 478.16 | 590.17 |
| 105.10 | 200.08 | 289.04 | 390.09 | 480.16 | 590.21 |
| 105.11 | 202.14 | 289.14 | 390.16 | 482.15 | 591.09 |
| 107.15 | 203.17 | 292.09 | 391.07 | 482.18 | 591.12 |
| 107.20 | 205.08 | 292.12 | 391.08 | 483.09 | 592.06 |
| 109.12 | 205.21 | 292.21 | 393.13 | 484.19 | 592.09 |
| 110.02 | 207.01 | 295.01 | 394.06 | 485.22 | 593.14 |
| 110.21 | 207.07 | 295.16 | 395.07 | 488.03 | 593.22 |
| 115.06 | 208.17 | 295.17 | 397.07 | 489.17 | 594.05 |
| 115.09 | 209.10 | 296.04 | 397.10 | 491.07 | 595.01 |
| 115.12 | 211.04 | 296.20 | 397.13 | 493.01 | 595.07 |
| 117.04 | 211.18 | 296.21 | 397.15 | 493.16 | 597.02 |
| 117.16 | 212.01 | 298.02 | 398.15 | 494.01 | 597.03 |
| 119.03 | 212.06 | 298.06 | 399.07 | 494.18 | 597.18 |
| 119.16 | 212.12 | 298.18 | 399.10 | 495.08 | 598.12 |
| 120.02 | 212.13 | 299.06 | 402.03 | 498.01 | 599.10 |
| 121.04 | 214.08 | 299.13 | 402.07 | 498.15 | 599.12 |
| 121.12 | 214.10 | 301.02 | 404.14 | 499.10 | 600.04 |
| 121.17 | 215.20 | 303.14 | 405.02 | 499.20 | 600.07 |
| 122.03 | 216.11 | 304.17 | 405.16 | 500.01 | 600.08 |
| 122.05 | 216.14 | 305.05 | 405.17 | 501.01 | 600.18 |
| 123.03 | 216.15 | 305.15 | 406.11 | 501.11 | 602.04 |
| 124.05 | 218.12 | 306.02 | 407.13 | 501.22 | 603.02 |
| 124.08 | 218.16 | 306.06 | 407.17 | 502.05 | 603.14 |
| 125.03 | 219.09 | 306.16 | 408.03 | 502.09 | 603.15 |
| 125.04 | 219.16 | 307.01 | 408.18 | 502.14 | 605.02 |
| 125.15 | 220.12 | 307.12 | 410.14 | 503.01 | 612.11 |
| 128.14 | 220.15 | 308.02 | 410.20 | 503.13 | 612.18 |
| 128.18 | 220.20 | 308.20 | 411.22 | 504.02 | 613.07 |
| 128.20 | 222.01 | 310.04 | 412.18 | 504.06 | 614.08 |
| 130.18 | 222.03 | 313.16 | 413.14 | 504.08 | 614.09 |
| 132.06 | 222.11 | 315.19 | 413.22 | 504.09 | 614.12 |
| 133.20 | 222.16 | 316.02 | 414.22 | 504.11 | 615.02 |
| 133.20 | 222.19 | 316.15 | 415.06 | 504.15 | 616.07 |
| 134.08 | 222.21 | 318.01 | 416.01 | 504.17 | 616.16 |
| 135.02 | 223.08 | 318.08 | 416.15 | 507.06 | 618.04 |
| 135.11 | 223.10 | 322.16 | 417.02 | 509.05 | 618.06 |
| 136.11 | 223.16 | 323.14 | 417.15 | 511.11 | 618.09 |
| 137.11 | 224.08 | 328.05 | 418.03 | 512.11 | 618.16 |
| 137.12 | 224.19 | 329.20 | 418.13 | 512.16 | 619.03 |
| 140.14 | 225.03 | 331.13 | 419.02 | 513.07 | 619.09 |
| 141.13 | 226.04 | 331.22 | 419.12 | 514.06 | 619.16 |
| 141.14 | 227.04 | 331.22 | 419.20 | 516.10 | 623.02 |
| 143.21 | 228.03 | 332.15 | 420.01 | 517.16 | 623.05 |
| 144.16 | 228.09 | 332.18 | 420.15 | 517.20 | 627.07 |
| 144.23 | 228.10 | 332.23 | 422.16 | 518.07 | 628.18 |
| 146.08 | 229.08 | 335.11 | 422.17 | 521.01 | 628.20 |
| 147.05 | 230.18 | 336.01 | 424.08 | 521.07 | 631.05 |
| 148.05 | 230.18 | 337.08 | 425.07 | 521.13 | 631.15 |
| 149.12 | 231.05 | 337.18 | 425.09 | 523.22 | 632.03 |
| 150.11 | 231.08 | 338.07 | 426.16 | 524.12 | 632.11 |
| 152.03 | 231.16 | 339.06 | 429.17 | 524.20 | 633.21 |
| 152.09 | 236.01 | 339.13 | 430.13 | 525.01 | 634.07 |
| 152.11 | 236.16 | 340.01 | 431.04 | 525.12 | 634.08 |
| 153.03 | 236.22 | 340.05 | 431.17 | 526.20 | 634.21 |
| 153.04 | 237.01 | 340.09 | 433.02 | 527.06 | 635.14 |
| 153.15 | 237.12 | 340.22 | 433.06 | 527.16 | 636.18 |
| 153.16 | 238.06 | 341.06 | 433.22 | 528.10 | 636.19 |
| 154.04 | 238.19 | 342.10 | 436.05 | 530.07 | 637.08 |
| 154.13 | 238.22 | 344.19 | 437.16 | 531.19 | 637.16 |
| 155.20 | 240.16 | 345.16 | 438.19 | 532.05 | 640.14 |
| 157.18 | 240.20 | 346.12 | 439.14 | 533.12 | 642.04 |
| 157.22 | 247.05 | 350.21 | 440.20 | 534.08 | 642.12 |
| 158.20 | 247.08 | 351.01 | 441.03 | 539.10 | 644.01 |
| 162.07 | 248.15 | 352.09 | 441.06 | 539.12 | 646.18 |
| 163.08 | 249.20 | 352.22 | 441.14 | 540.08 | 646.21 |
| 163.21 | 251.08 | 353.04 | 441.19 | 540.20 | 647.16 |
| 164.06 | 252.07 | 353.15 | 443.01 | 542.05 | 647.20 |
| 164.06 | 252.20 | 354.14 | 444.02 | 543.07 | 648.03 |
| 165.11 | 253.03 | 355.09 | 444.16 | 543.09 | 648.10 |
| 166.04 | 254.16 | 355.20 | 445.09 | 544.15 | 648.22 |
| 168.08 | 254.22 | 356.03 | 447.03 | 544.21 | 649.03 |
| 168.09 | 256.18 | 356.18 | 448.04 | 546.06 | 649.10 |
| 170.20 | 256.21 | 357.09 | 448.06 | 546.09 | 654.14 |
| 171.08 | 258.04 | 359.05 | 449.11 | 547.02 | 656.07 |
| 173.04 | 258.06 | 359.19 | 450.17 | 547.22 | 659.21 |
| 174.15 | 258.09 | 361.03 | 451.01 | 548.07 | 661.03 |
| 175.13 | 258.14 | 361.07 | 451.07 | 551.09 | 661.09 |
| 175.17 | 258.17 | 361.08 | 452.19 | 552.15 | 662.05 |
| 178.11 | 259.15 | 363.05 | 452.20 | 555.13 | 665.22 |
| 178.16 | 259.21 | 363.05 | 453.22 | 559.02 | 666.20 |
| 179.02 | 262.15 | 363.11 | 454.07 | 559.02 | 667.02 |
| 181.08 | 262.18 | 363.18 | 454.22 | 561.15 | 667.20 |
| 182.05 | 262.21 | 364.10 | 456.12 | 562.09 | 668.09 |
| 182.09 | 262.22 | 365.04 | 456.17 | 563.16 | 668.20 |
| 182.10 | 263.05 | 365.16 | 457.01 | 564.09 | 670.10 |
| 183.02 | 263.16 | 365.17 | 459.10 | 565.03 | 670.22 |
| 183.05 | 264.02 | 366.18 | 460.01 | 566.02 | 671.05 |
| 184.12 | 264.16 | 367.21 | 460.05 | 566.07 | 671.15 |
| 184.17 | 264.17 | 370.02 | 462.11 | 570.02 | 672.15 |
| 185.05 | 265.07 | 373.18 | 463.11 | 571.18 | 672.17 |
| 185.13 | 266.02 | 374.03 | 464.09 | 572.12 | 673.06 |
| 186.03 | 266.20 | 374.07 | 465.12 | 576.13 | 674.08 |
| 186.18 | 267.02 | 374.09 | 465.14 | 577.01 | 674.10 |
| 187.18 | 267.04 | 375.10 | 466.10 | 577.21 | 674.13 |
| 187.19 | 267.20 | 376.19 | 467.12 | 578.12 | 677.16 |
| 187.21 | 269.11 | 377.21 | 468.17 | 578.13 | 678.07 |
| 188.04 | 270.11 | 379.01 | 469.01 | 578.15 | 678.14 |
| 190.02 | 270.18 | 379.03 | 470.03 | 578.16 | 679.20 |
| 190.16 | 270.20 | 381.03 | 470.05 | 578.17 | 679.21 |
| 191.01 | 272.19 | 382.11 | 470.10 | 580.16 | 683.12 |
| 191.03 | 274.04 | 384.17 | 471.13 | 581.13 | 683.22 |
| 191.03 | 275.16 | 385.03 | 472.22 | 581.19 | 684.20 |
| 193.20 | 276.06 | 385.08 | 475.07 | 583.05 | 685.05 |
| 195.06 | 277.22 | 385.22 | 475.20 | 583.07 | 687.01 |
| 195.16 | 281.06 | 386.21 | 476.09 | 583.17 | 690.01 |
| 195.20 | 281.20 | 387.09 | | 586.20 | 690.10 |
| 196.07 | 282.06 | 388.01 | | 587.16 | 691.16 |

691.18
692.02
692.04
693.17
694.05
694.10
697.12
698.10
699.01
699.04
699.04
699.21
700.04
700.18
700.21
703.13
703.14
704.20
708.02
708.06
709.06
709.19
713.10
716.11
717.20
719.06
720.07
720.16
721.10
721.19
723.18
727.21
728.21
729.18
730.03
731.12
734.13
736.02
736.09
737.19
738.15
740.06
742.08
742.12
744.04
744.20
745.09
746.03
746.08
746.22
747.03
748.08
748.10
748.22
752.03
752.04
754.06
754.10
754.13
756.10
757.14
758.13
758.18
759.18
762.11
763.11
764.11
forbearance
412.01
forbearing
256.14
forbid
250.16
579.07
580.21
forbidden
345.15
606.02
700.19
forbidding
116.11
forbids
580.20
force
112.15
112.15
255.01
283.16
399.15
606.16
612.08
617.15
617.17
forced
005.15
034.20
049.12
082.16
314.08
346.17
569.20
586.13
636.02
671.10
700.22
forces
375.17
forcibly
183.14
forcing
333.13

526.20
forebodingly
225.21
forebodings
583.17
659.12
forego
516.21
forehead
020.14
054.05
058.02
125.05
176.04
366.11
377.14
404.10
544.21
655.08
728.09
758.06
foreign
206.18
foreigners
098.08
foremost
118.07
172.20
foresee
178.02
foresight
004.15
forged
726.01
forget
042.03
054.14
076.17
134.05
146.08
195.17
273.07
285.21
342.07
357.11
359.04
389.18
520.02
522.01
656.11
forgetful
749.16
forgetfulness
598.13
forgets
236.08
forgetten
720.16
forgetting
165.08
245.01
313.03
667.07
forgie
324.01
forgive
133.22
216.14
260.07
328.11
359.19
363.19
363.19
363.21
364.02
385.07
405.16
406.01
489.12
501.22
571.15
571.16
648.02
708.20
711.03
forgiven
049.08
092.16
forgiveness
328.08
328.10
forgot
100.17
367.21
401.22
586.04
forgotten
051.18
117.01
170.09
186.13
199.19
335.07
335.09
630.11
716.17
754.04
fork
130.15
740.12

forks
685.21
forlorn
263.05
form
019.10
040.10
367.11
370.18
377.04
487.08
form's
299.06
formal
517.03
formally
736.04
formed
038.11
144.16
146.03
396.04
414.10
445.18
463.06
507.10
522.01
569.14
700.13
former
028.17
075.10
079.13
149.22
174.17
189.11
199.08
214.04
234.11
256.09
274.20
302.12
310.20
338.10
372.07
441.08
478.03
487.17
534.15
542.09
572.07
630.08
667.08
676.13
709.10
759.05
formerly
017.04
330.04
352.13
391.15
434.01
592.02
forming
302.01
338.17
forms
007.07
674.17
730.19
forrard
720.14
forsake
160.15
181.10
forsaken
241.07
forth
035.12
050.17
114.19
186.09
238.21
431.10
434.22
441.22
445.15
473.10
513.14
624.19
751.07
forthwith
040.17
fortnight
305.21
664.05
699.20
fortunate
361.06
fortunately
019.15
034.16
291.20
412.11
426.04
640.19
763.11
fortune
203.13
230.10
583.07

636.16
fortune-teller
108.18
fortunes
024.09
forty
024.16
068.01
forty-five
520.10
forward
023.05
053.16
065.01
067.01
094.07
116.09
140.20
165.06
165.11
213.12
217.03
244.01
331.04
355.06
382.19
486.22
551.01
554.11
607.14
748.19
forwarded
506.11
508.03
forwardly
063.17
forwards
436.12
483.10
foster
144.08
203.13
289.08
418.05
fostered
444.07
fought
216.12
509.05
foul
751.05
foul-mouthed
107.19
found
013.12
055.11
066.15
079.04
080.06
080.14
112.16
120.12
145.15
149.21
152.02
163.01
187.16
199.06
213.04
230.07
248.17
265.04
283.17
287.09
308.03
326.06
354.13
355.16
409.11
418.20
427.21
435.09
465.09
479.13
481.06
484.09
500.07
503.18
507.16
523.10
556.21
558.19
583.05
586.13
626.12
635.08
706.04
715.05
725.18
737.01
747.06
756.20
founded
529.13
four
015.06
048.05
049.07
049.08
049.13
059.05

067.04
174.17
201.03
313.10
313.13
319.15
358.16
429.15
433.10
477.19
489.18
512.02
577.12
625.01
637.01
637.12
751.12
759.18
four-footed
010.18
fourteen
079.13
689.05
fourth
350.11
fowks
233.05
fowling
160.20
fox
435.18
fractions
655.05
fragile
606.21
fragments
110.18
513.14
fragrance
693.09
fragrant
129.21
frail
468.11
frame
006.06
089.07
094.13
125.22
160.11
278.01
278.14
309.20
371.01
383.21
464.16
554.09
601.02
645.08
741.15
framed
153.01
738.17
framing
260.17
frances
042.07
042.09
114.11
142.04
frangrance
737.16
frank
464.08
601.22
frankly
124.18
708.22
frantic
211.20
362.17
473.05
512.08
565.04
607.02
fraternal
340.18
free
021.08
065.13
151.13
157.16
238.05
249.22
282.21
304.12
358.01
366.16
390.01
395.18
440.03
628.19
662.21
695.09
freeing
240.22
freely
091.05
671.07
freer
755.12

french
131.12
136.17
138.03
frenzied
371.13
frenzy
053.19
263.11
266.18
296.01
732.07
frequent
347.11
551.02
623.06
frequently
066.15
145.09
223.09
293.15
463.21
478.11
515.06
535.13
548.21
570.21
677.21
701.01
750.16
fresh
097.21
192.22
243.20
294.19
300.04
318.11
441.02
516.15
549.01
fresher
463.11
fret
088.05
141.04
521.11
fretful
248.16
430.16
453.12
fretfully
533.16
frets
588.20
fretted
226.08
521.09
551.14
660.17
700.20
fretting
286.09
friday
280.06
378.02
381.02
friend
040.14
082.01
116.15
137.04
146.08
180.21
185.06
213.11
220.19
222.19
230.12
230.20
236.08
249.16
255.01
259.09
263.01
265.07
333.04
346.10
367.21
416.22
494.21
576.04
579.08
582.16
602.06
688.03
696.01
711.07
711.12
friendless
370.09
418.03
friendlessness
423.04
friendly
330.18
473.02
534.02
664.07
friends
115.10
121.17

```
124.21          029.14          198.10          346.03          522.11          735.03
148.05          029.17          203.05          346.18          525.07          737.12
152.12          030.02          203.08          346.21          525.20          738.06
154.10          032.04          203.12          348.05          525.22          740.05
171.06          034.13          203.20          349.05          526.06          742.01
212.02          039.09          204.20          351.21          527.07          742.09
309.17          042.18          205.18          354.07          530.04          743.03
338.09          043.06          206.06          356.05          531.15          745.20
502.02          044.01          208.03          361.22          532.09          749.12
504.07          044.08          208.05          364.12          532.13          749.19
543.19          045.18          208.10          365.09          534.11          751.01
558.10          047.06          209.12          365.11          539.13          751.04
571.20          048.02          209.19          366.11          540.19          752.10
664.20          048.07          210.03          368.02          541.09          753.22
678.12          054.04          215.07          373.07          541.13          754.09
707.20          054.21          218.02          373.20          541.18          756.09
709.17          057.06          220.21          376.08          541.19          758.02
722.08          059.07          221.10          378.07          549.03          758.06
725.06          061.10          222.05          378.13          551.20          759.11
friendship      061.22          222.20          379.06          557.06          759.13
160.15          063.14          224.09          380.02          561.18          761.14
717.04          066.02          225.04          381.04          565.21          front
fright          067.03          225.21          382.21          566.04          004.21
053.20          067.11          231.01          383.20          567.14          073.08
185.04          072.08          231.15          385.12          569.05          141.19
384.01          075.06          236.04          387.03          573.01          260.02
frighten        077.22          237.04          387.21          573.12          365.06
165.04          079.20          237.12          388.02          578.16          394.09
262.02          081.18          239.21          388.06          581.15          451.15
264.01          089.05          240.06          389.06          582.16          465.17
525.02          090.09          240.07          389.10          586.12          560.06
629.10          091.02          240.12          390.13          589.09          569.20
647.08          091.10          242.09          391.10          591.02          638.08
743.02          093.02          245.07          392.21          592.22          673.08
frightened      093.22          245.13          393.14          593.15          692.18
078.08          096.09          245.21          393.17          597.12          727.13
312.01          097.06          246.01          394.13          597.21          736.11
391.15          099.11          246.13          395.20          598.05          748.18
434.05          099.13          252.22          397.18          599.18          froo
466.18          100.08          253.11          399.12          599.19          324.15
516.03          101.04          258.13          399.21          600.16          froo'
538.12          101.22          260.01          400.06          609.07          191.04
567.07          102.17          261.01          401.17          610.01          232.12
600.19          103.12          261.08          402.11          615.09          frost
661.14          103.20          262.10          403.19          620.16          015.10
755.18          104.06          267.04          406.13          620.22          179.14
frightening     104.20          267.07          409.15          622.09          427.20
703.15          107.07          267.20          410.06          623.01          530.03
frightens       107.07          269.12          410.07          623.10          671.09
633.06          107.10          271.16          411.11          628.07          frosty
frightful       109.14          274.15          413.02          631.02          243.03
055.07          109.15          275.03          414.11          632.20          283.14
106.03          111.15          275.18          414.12          633.03          673.02
108.16          114.01          278.13          414.13          634.22          frothing
272.12          114.02          278.20          417.18          646.09          007.04
346.01          114.06          281.02          421.01          648.07          frough
376.14          117.12          281.18          424.05          648.15          184.14
497.04          118.02          281.20          426.19          651.09          531.13
565.03          119.10          282.07          428.11          652.04          688.10
758.07          120.01          282.13          431.05          652.09          696.07
fringes         120.06          283.11          432.02          653.01          719.18
509.21          126.10          284.01          433.11          653.18          frown
frittering      126.12          285.12          436.08          653.19          126.05
137.12          126.21          286.07          438.05          654.10          205.01
frivolous       127.20          287.03          440.14          656.20          492.03
136.10          128.04          287.13          441.02          663.08          frowned
227.01          129.05          288.05          441.04          665.09          286.16
fro             132.22          288.17          441.13          667.21          670.04
052.19          134.13          290.12          441.17          668.16          707.16
067.22          134.14          291.21          442.01          669.04          717.17
188.11          136.18          293.19          443.04          671.06          frowning
314.06          137.17          294.08          444.16          671.21          172.17
373.07          137.18          299.02          445.10          673.04          593.07
382.05          138.04          301.11          450.14          673.10          frozen
523.08          143.05          304.12          452.14          675.06          650.17
533.13          147.05          305.01          455.08          675.15          fruit
623.09          147.18          305.08          457.09          676.04          127.06
740.17          148.15          305.11          460.04          677.08          246.15
751.21          148.22          305.22          460.10          677.16          522.09
757.22          150.10          307.16          460.16          681.01          693.10
frock           150.13          310.01          465.09          681.17          fryingpan
020.05          151.13          313.06          470.12          682.15          011.12
114.19          152.18          314.01          475.09          683.01          fugitives
151.07          156.02          315.13          477.04          683.05          301.02
383.14          156.08          316.08          483.06          684.14          fulfil
383.16          163.18          318.10          485.19          685.04          261.02
449.02          165.15          318.18          486.07          685.07          350.19
544.18          166.21          319.17          488.12          685.12          428.15
600.17          167.03          319.18          488.17          685.17          686.17
668.07          167.21          321.18          490.08          689.03          fulfilled
from            168.04          322.11          491.07          690.02          044.20
001.03          168.12          322.20          492.18          690.12          085.14
001.08          169.13          323.08          493.19          693.10          223.20
005.05          169.20          325.14          494.17          693.14          459.03
006.01          170.18          325.16          495.05          693.20          610.08
007.19          174.11          329.15          499.06          694.17          618.10
010.19          175.02          331.20          500.18          695.09          fulfilling
011.02          175.21          332.12          502.19          695.13          343.15
014.06          178.01          333.03          503.05          696.03          384.13
015.18          179.14          333.05          506.12          696.05          fulfilment
016.03          179.14          333.20          508.02          697.18          734.10
019.04          179.18          334.11          508.08          697.20          full
019.06          180.01          334.18          513.10          706.15          018.16
020.20          182.18          338.15          516.03          712.13          031.06
021.12          188.11          340.08          516.11          712.15          048.03
021.15          191.22          340.14          516.19          716.01          084.21
022.01          193.02          341.03          517.06          716.03          094.03
022.17          193.13          343.01          517.07          724.03          111.16
023.20          197.10          343.20          517.13          728.22          128.07
025.06          198.03          345.05          518.07          730.01          132.02
028.15          198.10          346.02          518.18          732.20          147.06
```

187.07
188.22
214.06
243.18
257.06
259.19
264.20
266.03
275.19
303.07
306.15
341.14
353.02
361.06
408.06
414.07
431.03
483.16
487.04
514.01
532.19
598.05
647.11
711.22
727.13
737.06
fully
048.06
213.16
465.13
512.10
fulness
371.19
fun
030.14
318.20
494.19
funeral
096.02
378.01
390.04
416.01
419.12
420.12
628.09
641.10
643.02
664.01
746.06
fungus
519.12
funny
116.21
679.15
fur
187.15
194.07
233.06
326.09
420.08
471.16
471.16
472.07
696.17
712.19
719.12
719.15
720.09
fur-lined
450.20
furious
081.10
112.04
392.09
409.21
425.12
564.02
719.02
furiously
142.20
265.11
610.11
furnace-heat
063.13
furnish
108.03
furnished
470.09
699.16
furniture
006.20
038.02
322.21
437.15
furred
476.11
furs
126.11
further
002.04
013.01
054.12
055.05
057.08
065.05
075.13
143.02
154.04
165.13
188.08
225.02

239.02
244.19
248.07
288.17
300.01
359.13
373.13
403.06
460.05
480.05
480.05
497.09
504.19
512.08
519.20
520.19
586.03
591.12
613.13
645.16
671.12
681.21
683.10
695.09
711.15
718.22
fury
010.15
088.11
157.11
189.01
290.10
386.08
565.05
furze
229.14
future
224.12
302.02
312.04
332.18
335.21
488.13
643.06
648.14
g
243.08
gable
105.13
gadding
533.17
gaily
235.02
435.06
gain
047.02
327.05
454.08
477.11
gained
009.06
089.19
118.01
147.03
203.18
248.02
482.04
578.18
gaining
069.10
gait
043.20
150.02
246.18
707.14
gaiters
007.02
gall
334.15
647.14
gallon
319.16
gallop
373.04
547.12
galloped
432.20
555.08
567.20
galloping
291.14
432.04
gallops
233.11
galloway
432.19
gallows
107.20
401.21
game
107.02
442.07
479.02
558.15
604.06
gaming
422.17
gang
107.17
324.02
586.03

712.17
ganging
310.02
gangs
233.04
gap
399.02
433.04
gaping
111.07
285.09
466.17
gapingly
049.20
gaps
763.18
garb
309.06
garden
015.06
065.17
110.09
193.02
206.06
209.08
247.18
250.01
269.03
290.16
291.08
294.21
344.01
354.20
368.05
465.15
490.17
509.04
552.15
560.03
621.22
656.21
673.10
675.11
700.19
704.13
715.09
716.12
719.18
720.18
737.13
740.18
746.17
750.04
762.17
garden-wall
031.10
gardeners
260.19
261.03
gardens
308.09
garment
020.18
garments
055.21
115.02
384.19
442.04
455.13
garret
041.06
061.19
127.06
132.04
132.15
284.08
321.17
532.03
622.21
623.01
719.13
garrets
320.21
gasp
291.06
gasped
030.01
278.06
297.16
510.12
593.06
602.07
628.10
gasping
365.21
400.18
gate
002.21
015.07
067.03
077.07
101.20
186.02
188.11
242.12
244.17
247.19
284.10
294.22
308.21
365.01

445.14
449.21
465.15
485.10
621.22
673.09
693.05
737.18
750.05
762.17
gates
431.08
gather
221.10
247.06
289.14
323.14
446.05
475.09
522.07
gathered
085.17
262.14
278.09
302.19
354.14
362.07
373.16
400.16
495.16
563.18
579.12
634.03
641.17
675.20
678.12
682.09
gathering
206.07
276.15
441.02
561.10
gathers
678.13
gaudily
006.11
gaumless
493.08
gaunt
004.12
311.06
403.15
gauze
432.01
gave
010.03
060.17
067.10
083.16
099.07
102.02
111.09
119.19
131.19
144.02
165.14
197.17
218.15
253.11
256.09
259.16
266.19
278.21
286.21
291.16
314.15
327.01
339.02
351.15
355.22
389.01
401.21
433.17
443.18
485.14
500.12
502.06
526.10
538.08
544.20
555.03
567.18
568.13
622.15
633.08
641.02
650.08
663.05
703.02
721.12
747.08
gay
119.02
142.19
431.22
763.10
gaze
022.17
215.02
278.02
287.01

312.18
351.17
356.12
360.13
374.14
438.05
468.12
590.09
593.19
640.01
709.03
748.19
758.08
gazed
117.20
209.18
243.16
354.16
355.13
370.01
371.03
404.08
487.02
517.16
683.19
724.04
749.01
gazing
152.15
180.04
277.12
482.01
520.18
676.13
general
098.07
146.16
405.09
735.03
generality
137.09
generally
005.13
064.06
081.15
093.04
198.07
350.15
391.03
429.09
431.09
517.03
548.17
555.07
604.08
665.15
685.17
703.22
747.14
generosity
405.22
generous
205.22
527.09
759.14
generously
484.16
695.12
genial
304.10
486.08
genius
024.01
403.14
gentle
093.12
193.16
196.11
376.11
425.10
462.20
464.06
709.08
gentleman
007.10
007.11
147.02
175.19
203.10
220.19
298.10
331.02
422.20
470.16
492.09
497.17
gentleman's
440.15
gentlemanly
681.01
gentleness
082.19
358.14
gently
115.03
154.06
353.16
553.09
582.17
595.05
669.06

gentry
212.13
genuine
022.22
158.08
340.09
get
015.21
020.02
022.08
022.20
027.21
030.22
030.23
033.17
041.06
046.19
056.01
084.08
100.15
102.12
105.03
123.10
124.22
127.17
132.11
137.01
140.15
143.12
153.14
159.11
164.12
180.11
203.10
220.21
227.02
256.01
258.03
260.04
260.16
261.19
265.01
272.02
275.15
327.13
333.20
346.22
351.01
366.15
373.12
384.16
388.05
393.20
397.02
399.02
403.07
408.12
409.22
412.18
417.16
437.22
438.20
439.04
448.04
460.19
467.10
469.02
472.10
474.08
482.17
483.10
484.16
495.13
505.14
506.03
525.08
535.20
540.13
545.08
546.20
556.03
563.22
565.16
569.21
571.03
577.11
600.15
604.15
604.15
605.08
608.03
614.21
616.04
619.02
620.21
622.20
629.21
632.17
633.03
634.10
640.01
647.01
647.11
648.19
650.11
652.11
661.13
663.17
664.02
669.09
672.01

683.05
686.01
686.13
699.10
700.14
706.11
719.21
722.04
724.15
724.22
729.09
739.20
742.05
745.09
747.02
749.14
gets
125.01
187.06
385.17
525.03
650.02
671.19
686.18
getten
232.11
310.17
318.12
564.16
getting
071.21
102.18
121.07
130.20
190.10
249.04
377.11
390.06
400.07
475.21
569.12
605.07
609.09
672.11
705.12
751.19
ghastly
271.12
403.15
744.09
ghost
033.16
646.05
732.03
ghostly
072.16
311.10
ghosts
056.03
177.07
284.14
377.02
651.11
762.11
ghoul
745.13
ghoulish
239.07
gibberish
078.07
giddiness
382.14
giddy
497.10
gie
246.07
719.16
gies
247.07
gift
077.20
gifts
324.16
425.15
giggled
496.06
gimmerden
046.02
gimmerton
095.05
131.10
169.05
190.14
190.20
198.18
208.10
209.09
210.03
217.12
222.10
232.08
243.01
284.12
297.05
298.12
299.05
353.01
364.15
373.05
383.06
384.07

426.12
434.02
475.06
478.10
533.18
577.15
626.09
665.19
688.05
688.10
689.01
697.18
705.10
743.17
gin
390.10
gingerbread
556.16
gipsy
078.10
085.03
109.10
194.02
210.15
girl
071.03
107.12
139.06
140.12
143.17
173.04
183.20
191.09
197.15
229.05
235.15
282.20
297.04
297.16
312.19
435.05
438.11
447.04
461.19
498.10
579.09
614.15
690.15
691.12
girlhood
019.09
girlish
150.13
383.12
512.11
girls
024.19
girn
232.20
girned
398.05
girnning
758.19
girt
184.16
give
031.04
031.16
036.10
041.15
044.09
045.06
079.07
082.19
108.04
115.05
126.02
129.13
129.19
149.01
176.12
180.11
203.16
212.16
214.17
257.02
265.05
265.06
276.04
283.06
283.08
288.20
306.12
331.09
331.14
344.06
350.07
372.10
375.01
378.16
383.04
385.10
386.16
391.07
407.09
411.19
431.16
488.07
501.06
510.18
524.14

548.15
551.13
574.02
582.03
590.10
592.07
604.06
605.14
608.05
608.22
612.20
613.03
614.15
628.21
631.20
632.15
632.19
666.11
667.05
684.21
703.06
732.13
740.11
753.20
given
067.15
084.01
155.04
171.19
182.05
325.10
416.07
442.19
478.19
620.20
670.10
682.02
697.10
gives
476.21
giving
250.03
253.03
299.11
340.20
403.08
437.13
457.18
499.20
521.03
556.06
629.11
glad
020.08
208.07
212.22
218.09
271.08
288.10
366.21
395.01
434.06
437.21
460.19
488.14
521.08
523.21
533.03
534.14
542.06
546.08
572.19
592.10
622.11
622.12
632.11
633.20
648.01
684.12
706.05
714.03
724.18
738.11
738.16
761.20
gladdened
305.08
gladly
234.22
313.22
326.13
597.10
675.20
gladness
211.10
glance
008.21
200.01
215.04
249.08
286.07
286.21
354.04
360.10
368.10
404.07
441.21
451.09
463.05
489.21
603.01

604.20
609.06
609.21
649.04
727.15
glanced
038.01
062.18
257.12
481.12
496.17
589.10
599.13
609.21
717.17
729.01
glances
495.10
705.18
glancing
208.03
593.07
glare
039.08
722.02
glared
267.03
glaring
311.19
glaringly
525.06
525.18
glass
012.08
036.11
051.20
110.17
124.09
168.12
266.03
278.02
278.16
406.03
449.15
752.20
763.18
glass-drops
104.06
gleam
061.06
065.12
302.17
354.09
gleamed
284.01
394.12
398.03
glee
474.03
gleefully
428.02
glees
131.18
glen
209.14
578.02
glens
690.07
glided
553.07
596.02
gliding
218.02
glimmered
054.02
101.19
glimpse
102.19
116.15
158.08
216.04
249.18
282.14
409.21
653.20
678.06
686.13
glimpses
731.17
glinting
124.16
glisten
159.05
glitter
005.20
738.20
glittering
208.10
747.19
gloom
117.04
131.08
177.21
205.11
559.20
743.13
gloomy
253.20
445.02
643.06

glories
696.12
glorious
361.01
558.03
glory
692.18
glossy
120.13
gloves
116.06
glow
278.21
370.14
491.11
692.17
glowed
017.05
213.10
694.16
710.19
727.19
glowered
320.06
glowing
027.10
098.20
gnarl
009.15
gnash
748.05
gnashed
362.06
gnasher
034.08
go
002.20
007.06
013.17
030.07
031.10
033.03
033.05
033.11
036.01
041.05
042.07
053.02
059.08
059.20
063.05
074.15
092.10
102.20
107.20
110.08
123.06
128.18
131.13
134.22
138.08
139.12
151.18
158.12
159.10
161.04
167.11
168.18
169.05
178.08
178.14
184.12
186.02
193.09
195.09
195.15
199.05
200.09
208.09
208.18
223.17
226.21
242.04
260.08
274.02
284.13
285.21
287.18
290.08
294.13
297.19
299.17
314.19
320.15
337.17
341.01
341.08
342.18
347.19
358.16
365.08
365.13
366.01
368.04
377.21
384.06
387.05
392.17
407.10
416.06
417.22

418.15
421.13
422.03
428.02
428.20
436.14
443.20
450.06
452.13
453.09
457.14
458.04
460.20
461.18
462.05
476.03
476.22
479.01
482.10
483.03
485.05
492.07
494.10
494.11
498.05
508.22
512.22
520.09
523.06
525.22
526.14
539.20
540.15
540.16
541.01
545.01
557.01
559.10
560.05
563.11
564.21
566.12
566.12
567.19
568.02
573.10
576.10
579.10
579.22
580.20
600.17
601.11
604.04
606.02
607.20
609.17
611.07
612.21
615.06
615.18
617.12
620.14
622.17
628.02
628.06
629.03
629.16
630.05
634.17
634.18
636.02
639.04
645.14
658.08
664.02
665.15
669.12
671.01
671.04
691.16
707.01
707.12
708.14
710.09
712.23
716.15
722.23
723.15
724.11
732.13
736.11
738.11
740.19
743.01
744.20
750.02
751.15
756.17
757.11
761.12
goa
016.06
029.02
043.20
456.18
531.12
719.11
goaded
377.12
goal
445.12

692.06
goan
028.22
043.22
420.08
720.17
goas
232.22
goblin
164.07
248.04
386.07
439.01
744.10
goblins
056.04
god
048.04
055.09
058.01
077.21
133.21
134.01
144.02
164.19
223.02
241.06
245.01
250.16
250.18
257.09
262.04
272.07
274.04
324.16
363.07
363.13
371.09
375.16
377.06
390.22
396.05
405.05
407.09
415.09
415.09
467.03
579.03
579.05
617.18
638.19
720.10
734.15
756.09
god's
092.11
238.06
594.05
748.08
748.10
goddess
008.13
godless
755.04
goes
168.02
174.14
183.17
193.22
535.12
603.09
697.02
going
022.15
035.20
041.02
047.04
056.15
076.08
090.13
100.04
122.07
123.01
132.10
142.06
151.04
156.10
158.09
170.03
177.03
178.19
194.05
195.20
209.20
221.03
232.13
242.12
259.15
260.10
267.08
274.05
280.20
295.01
315.06
315.17
318.07
329.04
334.08
343.13
350.04
357.18
366.12
373.05
385.08
390.06
401.06
404.04
413.02
415.22
430.10
431.15
437.07
445.20
455.21
457.09
460.07
465.08
468.01
478.16
483.12
512.03
526.08
547.03
552.03
555.01
556.01
569.11
573.01
573.04
592.07
600.12
612.05
639.21
646.21
654.08
660.22
663.20
665.07
668.17
674.07
684.19
694.06
703.08
717.10
721.04
740.12
745.03
750.09
753.02
760.21
762.01
goings
037.10
498.10
gold
019.23
104.05
317.05
385.11
494.06
632.22
golden
019.13
302.16
427.05
479.17
598.04
gone
024.10
080.03
084.20
085.10
097.12
121.19
132.21
135.04
142.15
143.07
148.22
151.12
176.22
190.14
195.04
195.11
202.12
217.18
277.18
288.11
297.15
297.15
298.08
303.02
303.03
311.22
323.19
350.13
357.03
372.21
374.16
390.17
396.08
413.20
440.13
459.08
479.07
514.05
531.21
550.07
571.22
607.22
629.14
633.22
638.05
642.02
647.01
661.06
665.20
686.03
698.04
gong
620.20
good
013.05
026.12
043.02
043.11
048.04
055.16
062.12
070.20
071.02
071.13
071.20
074.16
076.21
078.19
082.11
089.03
090.19
093.13
093.17
103.08
104.12
122.08
125.08
133.09
137.03
152.09
153.14
155.11
172.12
184.22
188.20
194.22
199.16
202.05
204.04
219.12
223.18
231.05
262.06
271.07
273.10
279.08
294.09
309.11
315.08
323.01
332.04
332.18
342.13
348.01
352.23
374.19
387.21
413.13
414.22
425.18
431.20
442.03
442.10
445.03
452.17
455.17
459.07
465.12
469.01
479.04
483.20
500.01
501.11
511.07
521.21
533.03
543.05
545.05
545.17
548.22
556.10
559.07
570.11
571.06
576.04
579.09
594.12
597.22
601.11
602.19
614.12
628.12
630.18
666.05
667.06
670.06
671.13
671.18
674.19
683.04
687.02
691.20
699.06
704.22
708.01
708.06
726.04
739.08
741.21
742.01
745.21
good-bye
571.03
656.09
good-evening
659.16
good-hearted
030.20
164.09
good-humoured
589.02
good-night
094.16
505.16
568.01
goodnatured
556.17
goodness
383.05
goods
239.22
239.23
gouge
408.21
gown
011.11
183.14
grace
185.18
214.08
487.09
graceful
116.02
146.06
graceless
720.13
gracious
147.22
graden
329.22
gradual
302.08
gradually
058.12
126.04
224.17
278.20
508.04
596.10
763.20
grain
321.08
grand
114.19
123.09
139.10
193.21
321.05
564.16
grandest
720.18
grange
002.13
002.15
022.09
033.18
067.03
071.09
071.19
102.05
102.11
102.19
105.12
113.02
125.19
196.20
204.05
222.06
224.13
233.01
241.01
243.10
248.09
270.02
282.11
292.10
293.15
298.05
306.14
308.05
325.10
327.16
329.15
339.22
344.01
353.06
373.03
387.09
391.06
402.07
407.16
410.12
415.20
421.14
433.11
438.22
446.13
510.16
522.15
524.14
528.11
551.01
555.18
559.05
563.06
567.12
569.04
574.01
619.14
621.15
627.02
628.03
642.09
649.12
652.04
662.01
667.11
667.20
715.08
726.18
744.07
749.20
460.17
463.04
469.04
478.03
480.03
481.16
487.22
489.16
535.02
545.09
555.21
574.03
580.09
581.07
583.05
586.06
588.07
603.08
615.05
620.14
622.09
628.06
632.12
634.22
637.11
641.12
643.09
646.18
665.08
675.16
678.01
684.22
689.08
690.09
692.14
697.09
697.20
700.13
716.03
760.21
761.21
762.01
grant
581.20
granted
642.03
grappling
050.09
grasp
165.16
236.05
258.13
399.12
724.03
grasped
016.01
355.18
565.05
grasping
158.16
358.11
grasps
222.14
grass
003.14
295.02
355.01
519.11
553.05
557.20
693.03
737.04
764.09
grassy
449.21
grat
169.17
grate
531.19
705.20
743.22
grated
028.19
grateful
196.21
grates
692.01
gratification
150.14
341.02
420.19
589.05
gratified
116.11
214.18
404.19
668.10
gratitude
083.08
302.05
630.21
grave
091.11
167.03
169.05
272.06
301.11
357.13
360.16
363.15
379.12

| | | | | | |
|---|---|---|---|---|---|
| 392.20 | 739.19 | grievance | 604.16 | guardianship | guns |
| 398.17 | greatly | 446.17 | 642.10 | 010.07 | 006.09 |
| 406.13 | 040.13 | 720.04 | 684.04 | 457.16 | 666.05 |
| 413.10 | 070.18 | grieve | 709.03 | 473.12 | gurgling |
| 466.20 | 157.02 | 159.21 | 715.12 | 583.04 | 530.04 |
| 494.17 | 244.21 | 186.16 | 733.17 | guarding | 743.18 |
| 511.01 | 304.14 | 205.07 | grounds | 683.01 | gush |
| 521.08 | 333.06 | 452.09 | 115.09 | guards | 060.20 |
| 526.08 | 334.11 | 554.08 | 413.09 | 024.09 | 243.13 |
| 578.12 | 453.11 | grieved | 430.21 | guess | gushed |
| 649.13 | 677.07 | 122.10 | 432.15 | 004.09 | 130.15 |
| 652.10 | 734.21 | 122.17 | 449.05 | 046.04 | 399.21 |
| 653.06 | greedy | 210.20 | 503.15 | 074.11 | 565.21 |
| 760.06 | 072.01 | 245.19 | 552.21 | 082.12 | 593.15 |
| gravely | 222.14 | 314.13 | 579.14 | 095.06 | gusto |
| 133.15 | 362.07 | 391.08 | group | 104.12 | 421.05 |
| 536.09 | greek | 435.12 | 364.20 | 140.11 | gusty |
| graver | 138.03 | 457.03 | grouse | 210.21 | 051.10 |
| 176.14 | 678.11 | 489.10 | 201.12 | 281.01 | guttural |
| graves | green | 567.16 | 481.03 | 298.08 | 009.15 |
| 284.15 | 006.14 | 700.01 | grovel | 337.10 | gypsy |
| 380.06 | 209.08 | 740.20 | 604.16 | 337.12 | 007.09 |
| 689.22 | 379.21 | grieving | grovelled | 345.18 | h |
| gravestones | 463.19 | 122.15 | 282.15 | 350.09 | 041.01 |
| 577.19 | 557.14 | 632.02 | grow | 416.10 | 045.13 |
| gravity | 578.11 | grievous | 099.22 | 432.22 | 559.01 |
| 561.15 | 637.06 | 541.12 | 109.17 | 469.03 | 559.02 |
| 717.21 | 637.09 | grievously | 114.14 | 472.05 | 559.04 |
| graze | 638.09 | 087.05 | 140.13 | 483.05 | ha´ |
| 586.14 | 638.10 | griffins | 204.21 | 500.04 | 670.15 |
| grazed | 640.22 | 005.01 | 250.19 | 613.10 | 691.09 |
| 757.22 | 688.08 | grim | 387.12 | 658.11 | habit |
| great | 737.04 | 010.06 | 421.07 | 660.19 | 114.04 |
| 024.14 | 752.04 | 023.11 | 558.07 | guessed | 114.18 |
| 077.17 | 753.11 | 116.21 | 587.18 | 008.17 | 248.18 |
| 079.15 | 760.08 | 150.05 | 745.16 | 058.14 | 318.05 |
| 082.22 | greet | 467.13 | growing | 062.22 | 414.09 |
| 089.16 | 331.04 | 655.12 | 100.21 | 269.06 | 443.01 |
| 110.17 | greeting | 686.09 | 153.13 | 326.01 | 443.09 |
| 118.15 | 154.14 | 746.05 | 205.19 | 331.11 | 508.20 |
| 125.05 | 599.08 | 761.19 | 230.11 | 408.14 | 524.10 |
| 137.09 | 684.13 | grimace | 253.21 | 517.07 | 540.09 |
| 168.13 | grew | 488.17 | 319.06 | 554.19 | 726.02 |
| 182.16 | 026.03 | grimaces | 467.15 | 597.15 | habits |
| 182.19 | 048.16 | 338.21 | 621.21 | 666.12 | 242.08 |
| 186.20 | 077.07 | grimalkin | 707.19 | 682.16 | 317.10 |
| 188.16 | 082.03 | 061.14 | growled | 739.07 | habitual |
| 202.02 | 087.05 | grimly | 009.16 | guesses | 036.07 |
| 212.18 | 099.09 | 311.13 | 026.20 | 190.15 | 327.04 |
| 219.04 | 100.13 | 412.05 | 251.03 | 190.17 | 735.01 |
| 224.19 | 143.21 | 611.05 | 312.04 | guessing | habituated |
| 248.17 | 176.14 | grin | 439.07 | 245.07 | 137.07 |
| 281.11 | 215.10 | 012.13 | 497.07 | 354.18 | 255.22 |
| 291.03 | 226.09 | 240.10 | 706.11 | guest | had |
| 307.08 | 237.15 | 561.09 | growling | 055.03 | 002.13 |
| 310.20 | 244.14 | grind | 188.15 | 155.17 | 002.14 |
| 312.15 | 258.17 | 343.06 | grown | 212.17 | 004.01 |
| 315.16 | 281.15 | grinding | 098.11 | 217.10 | 004.15 |
| 320.19 | 364.10 | 055.15 | 213.19 | 225.07 | 005.08 |
| 353.08 | 391.03 | 265.18 | 312.17 | 236.12 | 006.04 |
| 362.12 | 424.09 | 358.02 | 465.06 | 254.17 | 009.12 |
| 364.09 | 438.16 | grinds | 486.03 | 317.08 | 011.22 |
| 367.16 | 501.14 | 252.17 | 531.09 | 367.07 | 012.11 |
| 369.11 | 506.15 | grinned | 560.21 | 394.08 | 014.03 |
| 372.10 | 524.16 | 758.20 | 589.16 | 422.12 | 017.09 |
| 378.05 | 537.19 | grinning | 591.01 | 644.19 | 017.18 |
| 394.16 | 541.18 | 079.18 | 689.02 | 685.16 | 019.07 |
| 402.16 | 597.09 | gripe | 706.06 | guests | 019.11 |
| 410.19 | 601.17 | 052.21 | grows | 012.16 | 019.14 |
| 427.17 | 666.16 | 128.07 | 003.14 | guffaw | 020.17 |
| 434.18 | 694.02 | 305.09 | 577.02 | 034.13 | 023.09 |
| 437.19 | 700.17 | 607.08 | 671.20 | guidance | 028.15 |
| 440.13 | 704.16 | groan | growth | 213.06 | 028.17 |
| 465.05 | 713.15 | 059.05 | 442.12 | guide | 033.21 |
| 468.07 | 717.20 | 064.02 | grudge | 022.08 | 035.08 |
| 477.12 | 722.11 | 314.07 | 721.18 | 027.22 | 035.14 |
| 480.03 | 749.20 | 696.16 | grudged | 031.16 | 037.04 |
| 505.18 | grey | 750.18 | 597.06 | 046.15 | 037.08 |
| 532.09 | 061.09 | groaned | gruel | 248.02 | 037.09 |
| 539.10 | 110.20 | 364.18 | 074.20 | 286.01 | 038.18 |
| 557.20 | 243.11 | 389.06 | 134.08 | 323.16 | 039.07 |
| 558.11 | 276.12 | 407.11 | 196.05 | 446.05 | 040.02 |
| 570.05 | 281.09 | 654.22 | 270.18 | 576.18 | 040.06 |
| 580.04 | 312.17 | groaning | gruff | guide-post | 040.08 |
| 588.10 | 380.05 | 041.13 | 154.17 | 243.09 | 041.04 |
| 590.02 | 516.18 | 077.13 | gruffly | guide-stone | 041.17 |
| 592.16 | 689.19 | 271.03 | 018.03 | 585.09 | 042.15 |
| 650.09 | 764.02 | 376.15 | gruffness | guided | 046.14 |
| 659.08 | greyer | 756.15 | 706.12 | 112.08 | 046.18 |
| 660.17 | 689.19 | grooms | grumbled | 761.05 | 047.08 |
| 668.09 | greyhound | 552.19 | 079.06 | guides | 048.03 |
| 678.08 | 479.12 | groped | 090.02 | 066.09 | 048.09 |
| 689.16 | grief | 103.17 | 762.19 | guilp | 050.21 |
| 700.11 | 060.20 | 325.14 | grumbling | 319.11 | 051.01 |
| 703.12 | 195.12 | grotesque | 107.08 | guiltily | 052.11 |
| 707.22 | 281.11 | 004.20 | 186.09 | 506.01 | 055.05 |
| greater | 295.16 | ground | grumblings | guiltless | 056.13 |
| 319.01 | 332.01 | 065.22 | 320.19 | 202.01 | 056.22 |
| 343.06 | 404.18 | 105.09 | guaged | guilty | 057.05 |
| 359.15 | 413.03 | 174.01 | 541.13 | 623.15 | 058.07 |
| 382.10 | 441.02 | 179.22 | guard | gullet | 058.10 |
| 417.12 | 477.09 | 243.03 | 032.13 | 260.11 | 059.02 |
| 463.01 | 526.12 | 324.07 | 248.02 | gun | 061.21 |
| 543.06 | 586.22 | 374.14 | 316.15 | 107.21 | 065.04 |
| 598.22 | 622.15 | 406.21 | guarded | 161.05 | 066.05 |
| 648.07 | 640.07 | 452.04 | 443.03 | 671.05 | 066.14 |
| greatest | 683.18 | 483.02 | guardian | 704.21 | 067.15 |
| 091.01 | 759.13 | 518.13 | 342.15 | gunpowder | 069.02 |
| 173.17 | griefs | 552.13 | 378.06 | 205.09 | 069.05 |
| 424.04 | 503.21 | 565.22 | 418.09 | 666.10 | 071.18 |
| 604.09 | 648.15 | 601.03 | 492.03 | | 072.03 |

| | | | | | |
|---|---|---|---|---|---|
| 072.04 | 185.18 | 319.15 | 432.15 | 566.13 | 687.01 |
| 074.03 | 185.21 | 323.06 | 434.02 | 567.12 | 689.02 |
| 075.15 | 188.06 | 325.09 | 434.14 | 569.02 | 690.03 |
| 076.03 | 189.08 | 326.02 | 435.15 | 569.14 | 690.10 |
| 076.17 | 191.13 | 326.06 | 438.13 | 571.19 | 691.14 |
| 077.08 | 192.01 | 326.18 | 442.15 | 572.14 | 692.08 |
| 078.02 | 196.03 | 326.21 | 442.18 | 574.06 | 692.13 |
| 078.11 | 196.07 | 328.02 | 443.09 | 577.07 | 693.05 |
| 079.12 | 196.22 | 328.04 | 444.05 | 580.04 | 693.19 |
| 079.14 | 197.05 | 329.20 | 444.06 | 582.07 | 695.06 |
| 079.17 | 197.07 | 330.06 | 444.19 | 583.06 | 698.18 |
| 080.01 | 197.07 | 330.14 | 445.11 | 583.08 | 699.18 |
| 080.14 | 197.19 | 330.22 | 445.17 | 583.12 | 700.02 |
| 081.08 | 199.02 | 331.10 | 446.05 | 583.13 | 700.12 |
| 081.21 | 199.13 | 334.09 | 446.10 | 584.02 | 702.10 |
| 082.06 | 202.02 | 334.13 | 446.15 | 585.08 | 703.04 |
| 083.11 | 202.12 | 335.14 | 446.20 | 586.13 | 703.16 |
| 083.11 | 202.13 | 339.08 | 448.12 | 588.10 | 704.17 |
| 084.19 | 204.18 | 339.15 | 450.16 | 588.16 | 706.06 |
| 085.02 | 205.11 | 340.03 | 450.21 | 588.18 | 709.09 |
| 085.10 | 206.07 | 347.16 | 451.04 | 593.01 | 710.21 |
| 086.02 | 206.07 | 350.07 | 451.08 | 596.05 | 711.19 |
| 087.03 | 207.02 | 351.06 | 453.11 | 596.12 | 712.01 |
| 088.14 | 213.18 | 351.10 | 453.18 | 597.05 | 713.12 |
| 090.06 | 214.11 | 351.13 | 454.17 | 597.15 | 715.09 |
| 090.10 | 217.07 | 352.08 | 454.20 | 598.01 | 715.11 |
| 090.16 | 217.21 | 352.13 | 455.10 | 598.15 | 716.05 |
| 091.10 | 217.22 | 353.12 | 456.01 | 598.17 | 716.07 |
| 091.12 | 218.20 | 354.13 | 456.11 | 601.02 | 717.04 |
| 092.01 | 221.13 | 355.18 | 460.13 | 604.18 | 717.11 |
| 093.06 | 221.14 | 356.02 | 461.04 | 607.06 | 718.12 |
| 094.15 | 223.03 | 356.04 | 462.11 | 607.11 | 718.20 |
| 095.13 | 223.09 | 357.04 | 464.19 | 608.09 | 721.21 |
| 096.07 | 224.01 | 358.08 | 466.01 | 609.03 | 723.13 |
| 098.06 | 225.16 | 358.11 | 466.05 | 610.04 | 723.19 |
| 098.11 | 226.01 | 358.13 | 474.02 | 610.09 | 724.20 |
| 100.18 | 226.07 | 362.05 | 475.02 | 611.06 | 724.22 |
| 102.07 | 226.15 | 363.04 | 475.13 | 611.16 | 726.07 |
| 103.20 | 226.20 | 364.12 | 477.05 | 611.19 | 726.16 |
| 104.09 | 228.10 | 367.01 | 477.10 | 613.08 | 726.19 |
| 104.21 | 230.13 | 370.15 | 477.16 | 613.10 | 727.02 |
| 106.06 | 234.02 | 371.05 | 478.15 | 613.13 | 727.07 |
| 106.06 | 234.10 | 372.02 | 478.17 | 620.18 | 727.13 |
| 106.12 | 234.22 | 373.01 | 478.19 | 622.01 | 727.22 |
| 106.15 | 235.16 | 373.06 | 480.14 | 622.02 | 729.08 |
| 110.16 | 238.14 | 373.16 | 481.01 | 622.04 | 729.20 |
| 110.21 | 240.11 | 373.17 | 482.04 | 622.14 | 732.20 |
| 115.09 | 240.19 | 374.11 | 483.14 | 623.17 | 733.01 |
| 115.13 | 241.02 | 378.13 | 485.21 | 627.17 | 734.20 |
| 115.20 | 241.07 | 379.01 | 486.03 | 632.06 | 734.22 |
| 117.03 | 244.15 | 379.07 | 487.03 | 632.18 | 735.02 |
| 118.01 | 247.14 | 381.08 | 487.04 | 633.11 | 736.05 |
| 118.21 | 248.03 | 383.02 | 490.04 | 636.15 | 737.11 |
| 119.06 | 248.14 | 384.02 | 490.07 | 636.19 | 737.17 |
| 119.07 | 248.15 | 384.15 | 491.10 | 637.07 | 738.19 |
| 120.04 | 248.18 | 386.02 | 492.02 | 637.09 | 739.03 |
| 122.22 | 249.06 | 386.08 | 492.17 | 638.05 | 740.20 |
| 123.01 | 249.09 | 386.11 | 494.11 | 640.06 | 743.14 |
| 124.01 | 249.14 | 387.02 | 495.07 | 640.16 | 745.11 |
| 124.03 | 254.18 | 388.12 | 496.07 | 641.12 | 745.11 |
| 130.02 | 255.07 | 388.14 | 498.18 | 641.14 | 745.14 |
| 130.21 | 255.10 | 389.14 | 499.01 | 641.19 | 745.15 |
| 131.03 | 256.08 | 393.03 | 500.15 | 641.22 | 746.10 |
| 131.05 | 257.13 | 393.04 | 500.17 | 643.07 | 747.11 |
| 131.17 | 261.04 | 393.13 | 501.21 | 644.09 | 751.03 |
| 132.14 | 262.13 | 393.17 | 502.12 | 644.10 | 754.02 |
| 132.21 | 262.17 | 394.01 | 502.14 | 644.18 | 755.19 |
| 133.04 | 266.02 | 398.19 | 503.16 | 644.22 | 757.22 |
| 138.08 | 266.17 | 399.19 | 503.21 | 645.06 | 760.02 |
| 141.14 | 267.18 | 400.13 | 504.01 | 645.10 | 760.05 |
| 143.17 | 267.18 | 402.08 | 504.17 | 646.02 | 760.17 |
| 144.06 | 270.03 | 402.12 | 507.04 | 649.17 | 761.16 |
| 144.08 | 271.05 | 403.11 | 509.20 | 650.18 | 763.16 |
| 144.13 | 272.01 | 404.03 | 510.02 | 651.05 | 763.16 |
| 145.02 | 272.16 | 404.09 | 510.10 | 651.19 | had'nt |
| 145.06 | 274.08 | 404.17 | 516.04 | 653.20 | 082.12 |
| 145.12 | 275.04 | 405.04 | 516.07 | 654.04 | hadn't |
| 146.17 | 275.06 | 406.06 | 517.05 | 659.08 | 154.03 |
| 146.19 | 278.13 | 407.17 | 517.21 | 659.10 | 520.22 |
| 146.21 | 279.21 | 408.20 | 520.20 | 660.12 | 528.19 |
| 147.12 | 280.14 | 409.05 | 522.09 | 660.13 | 551.03 |
| 147.17 | 280.17 | 410.19 | 523.09 | 660.18 | 566.06 |
| 148.04 | 280.21 | 411.09 | 528.03 | 661.06 | hae |
| 148.13 | 281.16 | 411.18 | 528.04 | 663.06 | 016.15 |
| 148.22 | 281.18 | 412.16 | 528.06 | 663.19 | 232.09 |
| 149.02 | 282.07 | 412.20 | 528.20 | 664.11 | 319.12 |
| 149.08 | 282.13 | 413.21 | 530.02 | 664.12 | hag |
| 149.10 | 284.01 | 414.07 | 531.09 | 665.05 | 276.21 |
| 150.11 | 285.11 | 414.09 | 531.19 | 665.20 | haggard |
| 150.19 | 285.13 | 414.19 | 532.20 | 666.04 | 192.02 |
| 154.08 | 288.11 | 417.07 | 533.12 | 666.05 | 351.19 |
| 154.15 | 291.08 | 417.19 | 535.01 | 668.11 | 587.10 |
| 154.19 | 291.11 | 417.19 | 538.14 | 671.09 | haggardness |
| 155.04 | 292.06 | 418.05 | 539.18 | 674.14 | 286.05 |
| 155.17 | 295.03 | 418.16 | 540.03 | 675.06 | hagh |
| 156.15 | 295.06 | 419.07 | 540.11 | 678.03 | 028.20 |
| 157.03 | 295.22 | 420.02 | 541.08 | 678.06 | hah |
| 158.04 | 297.04 | 421.02 | 545.13 | 679.22 | 184.14 |
| 160.09 | 298.10 | 422.11 | 547.14 | 680.03 | 233.09 |
| 160.12 | 298.14 | 422.15 | 547.19 | 680.04 | 310.13 |
| 160.13 | 298.19 | 424.06 | 548.08 | 680.06 | 324.14 |
| 161.02 | 299.08 | 425.10 | 548.14 | 681.14 | hahse |
| 165.08 | 299.17 | 425.14 | 552.07 | 682.03 | 324.05 |
| 166.11 | 300.03 | 426.08 | 552.22 | 682.06 | 326.10 |
| 169.19 | 302.15 | 426.14 | 555.14 | 682.13 | 713.06 |
| 170.15 | 304.16 | 429.02 | 562.05 | 682.15 | hahsiver |
| 177.21 | 305.17 | 429.16 | 562.11 | 682.17 | 324.12 |
| 179.06 | 305.18 | 429.17 | 562.15 | 683.03 | 696.08 |
| 179.19 | 312.08 | 429.21 | 563.15 | 683.12 | hahsomdiver |
| 184.13 | 312.16 | 429.22 | 566.07 | 684.06 | 187.10 |
| 184.22 | 313.21 | 431.10 | 566.08 | 686.05 | |

| | | | | |
|---|---|---|---|---|
| hailed | 676.19 | 334.16 | 401.16 | 620.17 | 639.12 |
| 016.21 | 716.05 | 347.18 | 422.06 | 732.06 | 651.07 |
| hailing | 733.06 | 353.16 | 429.19 | 753.16 | 658.08 |
| 603.03 | 737.19 | 354.02 | 436.17 | happy | 663.21 |
| hair | 746.01 | 358.13 | 444.03 | 073.17 | 674.15 |
| 042.07 | 747.21 | 362.14 | 451.06 | 091.17 | 684.02 |
| 042.09 | 756.05 | 377.14 | 452.07 | 104.10 | 717.15 |
| 093.11 | 764.02 | 382.20 | 481.07 | 167.15 | 727.06 |
| 105.01 | half-a-day | 393.02 | 492.13 | 169.06 | 730.06 |
| 111.09 | 339.13 | 400.03 | 519.07 | 303.16 | 742.22 |
| 115.21 | half-a-dozen | 405.12 | 564.13 | 329.03 | 754.02 |
| 117.18 | 010.18 | 421.21 | 565.17 | 357.11 | hardness |
| 124.01 | 134.10 | 441.18 | 601.09 | 371.11 | 082.19 |
| 146.04 | 239.19 | 455.15 | 602.14 | 372.09 | 167.19 |
| 152.19 | 260.05 | 467.20 | 604.13 | 407.20 | hardy |
| 190.05 | 681.06 | 495.11 | 610.20 | 407.20 | 282.21 |
| 207.05 | half-an-hour | 505.21 | 636.18 | 449.17 | hare-bells |
| 218.04 | 308.08 | 506.07 | 652.06 | 479.20 | 764.08 |
| 219.06 | 364.17 | 513.13 | 662.13 | 510.06 | hareton |
| 266.20 | 403.13 | 517.14 | 666.09 | 520.22 | 005.03 |
| 276.13 | half-bred | 519.14 | 681.07 | 555.11 | 026.20 |
| 311.08 | 310.01 | 561.18 | 709.15 | 559.21 | 028.04 |
| 330.11 | half-civilized | 587.07 | 740.05 | 571.07 | 032.07 |
| 335.02 | 214.04 | 605.14 | 754.03 | 578.06 | 033.13 |
| 351.06 | half-hour | 609.03 | 759.01 | 578.08 | 034.13 |
| 357.06 | 094.03 | 609.16 | handsome | 597.11 | 062.14 |
| 373.15 | 589.12 | 610.05 | 007.14 | 639.05 | 072.20 |
| 379.04 | half-open | 616.06 | 073.16 | 651.01 | 073.10 |
| 383.11 | 368.10 | 617.01 | 114.01 | 711.04 | 074.09 |
| 397.22 | half-past | 624.16 | 123.21 | 753.13 | 143.18 |
| 425.04 | 190.12 | 629.02 | 125.14 | 753.13 | 157.07 |
| 449.12 | 466.05 | 635.15 | 173.09 | 753.16 | 157.20 |
| 464.04 | 555.07 | 638.07 | 174.13 | harass | 160.19 |
| 464.11 | 555.07 | 658.04 | 174.21 | 288.19 | 162.04 |
| 491.12 | half-way | 668.08 | 175.06 | 451.19 | 164.04 |
| 512.17 | 505.18 | 669.05 | 179.10 | harassed | 164.18 |
| 535.20 | half-whisper | 686.10 | 323.04 | 082.17 | 164.22 |
| 567.01 | 054.07 | 693.06 | 425.02 | 500.01 | 165.14 |
| 655.09 | hall | 694.18 | 464.02 | harassing | 169.15 |
| 694.07 | 255.02 | 703.05 | 470.10 | 541.12 | 177.09 |
| 723.19 | 355.08 | 706.14 | 491.19 | 750.13 | 180.11 |
| 733.18 | 454.22 | 708.23 | 673.12 | harboured | 184.06 |
| 758.06 | 455.12 | 712.06 | 694.15 | 745.21 | 185.04 |
| hair-breadths | 638.07 | 723.19 | 710.02 | hard | 188.19 |
| 655.05 | hallo | 724.05 | 720.11 | 015.09 | 191.12 |
| hairy | 466.11 | 728.22 | handsomer | 017.18 | 199.01 |
| 034.10 | 604.05 | 729.19 | 164.10 | 063.01 | 199.11 |
| haks | hallooed | 745.02 | 174.22 | 073.22 | 199.16 |
| 194.08 | 016.09 | 748.01 | handsomest | 099.17 | 244.20 |
| hale | 065.16 | 748.17 | 083.17 | 115.11 | 244.20 |
| 003.17 | 107.10 | 749.14 | handywork | 149.10 | 245.02 |
| half | halt | 758.01 | 042.19 | 171.05 | 245.06 |
| 014.03 | 248.02 | 759.10 | hang | 188.02 | 309.17 |
| 020.11 | 322.21 | 763.05 | 108.11 | 237.10 | 317.04 |
| 021.20 | 480.12 | handed | 145.18 | 243.04 | 319.07 |
| 021.22 | 561.05 | 217.03 | 339.22 | 248.01 | 319.17 |
| 046.03 | halted | 406.02 | 576.02 | 286.01 | 326.05 |
| 061.01 | 066.20 | 612.02 | hanged | 292.13 | 391.17 |
| 078.16 | 308.07 | handful | 567.09 | 363.21 | 393.10 |
| 097.06 | 314.14 | 302.16 | hanging | 420.17 | 396.07 |
| 103.21 | 386.03 | handfuls | 019.13 | 436.10 | 410.05 |
| 107.03 | 451.14 | 276.07 | 104.06 | 444.18 | 418.07 |
| 121.05 | 465.15 | 319.03 | 107.03 | 446.15 | 418.20 |
| 134.16 | 763.02 | handkerchief | 153.01 | 526.12 | 421.03 |
| 135.06 | halting | 291.05 | 272.09 | 578.22 | 422.03 |
| 135.07 | 322.20 | 374.04 | 330.12 | 582.05 | 422.19 |
| 145.01 | ham | 386.13 | 340.03 | 590.21 | 434.17 |
| 148.07 | 006.08 | 508.18 | 410.05 | 633.20 | 436.13 |
| 160.03 | hammer | 513.09 | 445.08 | 649.17 | 436.16 |
| 160.03 | 720.02 | handkerchir | happen | 679.17 | 437.17 |
| 170.06 | hammers | 321.06 | 188.02 | 719.16 | 438.02 |
| 200.03 | 261.16 | handle | 240.21 | 733.14 | 438.16 |
| 205.08 | hand | 016.18 | 293.09 | hardened | 439.21 |
| 207.17 | 003.06 | 158.16 | 666.19 | 081.03 | 440.06 |
| 212.08 | 008.04 | 189.15 | 666.21 | 092.14 | 441.13 |
| 212.08 | 035.09 | 565.05 | 689.05 | hardihood | 445.14 |
| 282.20 | 040.11 | hands | happened | 375.09 | 445.19 |
| 293.03 | 050.15 | 021.06 | 081.20 | hardly | 454.14 |
| 401.08 | 052.02 | 025.03 | 090.20 | 012.18 | 463.16 |
| 407.01 | 052.05 | 035.15 | 419.15 | 029.21 | 466.09 |
| 416.19 | 054.02 | 091.05 | 445.14 | 055.02 | 466.16 |
| 433.09 | 063.12 | 097.10 | 575.02 | 070.13 | 469.16 |
| 450.06 | 064.19 | 108.15 | 627.15 | 076.14 | 470.14 |
| 450.07 | 066.12 | 114.05 | 661.07 | 114.22 | 471.14 |
| 476.21 | 093.20 | 115.22 | 760.20 | 142.14 | 476.14 |
| 493.14 | 106.07 | 117.06 | happening | 152.07 | 476.14 |
| 513.14 | 110.10 | 117.16 | 515.09 | 182.04 | 482.03 |
| 516.18 | 118.05 | 129.06 | happier | 217.05 | 483.09 |
| 517.19 | 120.01 | 133.13 | 518.13 | 262.18 | 490.05 |
| 518.12 | 126.14 | 143.15 | 570.16 | 291.16 | 490.06 |
| 518.13 | 127.13 | 143.18 | 714.06 | 293.22 | 491.08 |
| 526.20 | 156.02 | 152.18 | 753.19 | 337.15 | 491.09 |
| 530.03 | 163.20 | 157.14 | happiest | 338.15 | 491.22 |
| 530.03 | 168.12 | 165.08 | 198.17 | 356.03 | 492.05 |
| 536.01 | 176.04 | 172.17 | 424.03 | 361.20 | 494.15 |
| 542.19 | 199.12 | 176.15 | 619.02 | 377.17 | 495.21 |
| 558.04 | 214.12 | 190.08 | happily | 381.07 | 496.18 |
| 560.14 | 221.06 | 208.01 | 004.14 | 383.21 | 497.07 |
| 563.05 | 222.15 | 213.12 | 011.09 | 392.20 | 504.15 |
| 567.21 | 238.05 | 215.13 | 498.17 | 402.18 | 524.22 |
| 570.05 | 243.06 | 271.02 | 546.02 | 408.15 | 527.04 |
| 577.20 | 244.01 | 279.13 | 638.03 | 427.13 | 531.20 |
| 591.14 | 245.12 | 288.08 | 704.06 | 488.17 | 534.05 |
| 599.13 | 247.16 | 309.09 | happiness | 496.15 | 539.02 |
| 599.14 | 249.05 | 313.02 | 023.19 | 512.01 | 544.14 |
| 609.08 | 277.21 | 324.09 | 205.20 | 520.10 | 556.12 |
| 635.20 | 281.22 | 352.20 | 218.08 | 572.10 | 561.02 |
| 655.16 | 298.18 | 363.22 | 233.20 | 575.03 | 562.05 |
| 667.07 | 316.08 | 366.19 | 318.22 | 592.07 | 565.15 |
| 669.17 | 317.21 | 390.01 | 331.22 | 595.07 | 568.07 |
| 676.19 | 331.05 | 401.10 | 557.13 | 608.05 | 569.03 |

| | | | | | |
|---|---|---|---|---|---|
| 573.15 | 205.09 | 335.11 | 547.17 | **hathecliff's** | 096.11 |
| 607.21 | 727.17 | 336.06 | 628.18 | 188.01 | 097.09 |
| 622.04 | **harmlessly** | 336.12 | 638.13 | **hatless** | 098.17 |
| 624.13 | 500.19 | 336.15 | 654.10 | 034.21 | 100.04 |
| 625.03 | **harmonized** | 338.02 | 699.07 | 113.09 | 102.06 |
| 627.14 | 764.03 | 338.07 | **hastening** | **hatred** | 102.18 |
| 634.16 | **harped** | 338.17 | 286.03 | 025.17 | 103.15 |
| 642.03 | 582.15 | 340.06 | 343.09 | 099.13 | 104.10 |
| 646.02 | **harried** | 341.07 | 526.13 | 316.20 | 104.11 |
| 646.07 | 758.16 | 342.04 | **hastily** | 334.15 | 105.06 |
| 654.07 | **harsh** | 343.21 | 130.16 | 387.20 | 105.12 |
| 663.06 | 227.09 | 366.15 | 177.19 | 591.03 | 105.17 |
| 663.10 | 227.12 | 385.06 | 297.10 | **hauding** | 106.10 |
| 666.01 | 347.12 | 385.20 | 428.05 | 232.11 | 106.14 |
| 666.21 | 360.01 | 385.21 | 594.08 | **haughtier** | 108.02 |
| 667.05 | 426.02 | 388.08 | 644.06 | 197.04 | 110.04 |
| 669.14 | 527.06 | 389.01 | 683.11 | **haughty** | 112.01 |
| 670.01 | 623.09 | 389.04 | 742.06 | 021.08 | 112.16 |
| 670.05 | 696.03 | 389.12 | **hasty** | 145.07 | 114.09 |
| 671.04 | **harshness** | 390.12 | 053.22 | 658.10 | 115.04 |
| 672.03 | 227.07 | 390.15 | 066.22 | 728.11 | 115.18 |
| 675.13 | 227.20 | 390.17 | 255.13 | **hault** | 117.01 |
| 675.21 | 710.20 | 390.20 | 400.17 | 696.06 | 117.12 |
| 676.17 | **harvest** | 392.11 | 502.06 | **haunt** | 118.03 |
| 678.09 | 076.01 | 396.18 | **hat** | 033.16 | 118.11 |
| 679.05 | 515.03 | 407.14 | 015.05 | 344.03 | 120.21 |
| 686.10 | 638.15 | 408.20 | 049.10 | 377.01 | 122.04 |
| 686.15 | 688.11 | 415.02 | 114.17 | 377.22 | 122.09 |
| 695.16 | **has** | 417.08 | 158.04 | 413.15 | 123.10 |
| 701.05 | 007.13 | 419.18 | 186.08 | **haunted** | 126.20 |
| 702.01 | 024.08 | 421.17 | 318.05 | 006.19 | 127.11 |
| 702.08 | 025.05 | 423.05 | 373.15 | 056.02 | 127.13 |
| 702.12 | 025.17 | 428.03 | 432.01 | 273.15 | 128.21 |
| 703.01 | 045.12 | 451.16 | 434.15 | 277.19 | 130.11 |
| 703.21 | 047.16 | 456.17 | 435.11 | 335.15 | 134.01 |
| 706.04 | 059.11 | 460.01 | 436.08 | **haunts** | 134.09 |
| 706.08 | 068.04 | 464.03 | 437.10 | 262.13 | 134.19 |
| 706.09 | 071.14 | 464.22 | 455.14 | **hause** | 137.06 |
| 706.09 | 073.07 | 472.21 | 522.12 | 691.03 | 137.08 |
| 706.09 | 074.09 | 484.17 | 553.10 | **have** | 137.10 |
| 707.08 | 074.12 | 488.21 | 570.15 | 001.03 | 137.19 |
| 707.21 | 080.16 | 493.12 | 698.17 | 001.07 | 137.21 |
| 709.18 | 085.07 | 494.08 | **hate** | 002.11 | 138.01 |
| 710.04 | 107.12 | 494.21 | 007.21 | 003.11 | 141.05 |
| 710.12 | 109.06 | 504.14 | 128.05 | 003.22 | 150.21 |
| 711.03 | 114.12 | 519.18 | 129.02 | 004.08 | 151.07 |
| 712.05 | 129.13 | 521.10 | 155.15 | 005.03 | 153.03 |
| 712.15 | 129.17 | 524.22 | 167.14 | 006.20 | 156.09 |
| 713.02 | 135.05 | 543.02 | 174.19 | 007.16 | 158.08 |
| 713.10 | 137.20 | 546.20 | 194.21 | 008.03 | 158.21 |
| 716.14 | 140.02 | 547.08 | 218.21 | 008.08 | 163.11 |
| 717.02 | 140.21 | 562.20 | 230.05 | 008.16 | 166.12 |
| 718.01 | 142.15 | 568.20 | 327.14 | 008.17 | 166.20 |
| 718.13 | 145.19 | 571.08 | 339.09 | 009.05 | 166.21 |
| 718.15 | 163.14 | 581.12 | 339.12 | 011.22 | 167.15 |
| 721.02 | 166.03 | 586.04 | 394.12 | 012.11 | 168.07 |
| 721.15 | 166.05 | 591.01 | 412.06 | 018.14 | 168.11 |
| 722.07 | 171.12 | 591.21 | 444.07 | 019.03 | 168.13 |
| 722.13 | 171.18 | 604.05 | 470.05 | 019.11 | 171.21 |
| 722.15 | 180.15 | 604.09 | 484.09 | 019.15 | 172.13 |
| 722.22 | 180.15 | 606.02 | 524.03 | 020.08 | 172.15 |
| 723.19 | 180.15 | 612.15 | 524.06 | 022.18 | 175.08 |
| 724.13 | 181.14 | 616.03 | 527.11 | 024.13 | 175.11 |
| 725.08 | 187.08 | 632.14 | 534.06 | 026.11 | 175.14 |
| 726.08 | 192.12 | 634.05 | 534.06 | 026.14 | 176.21 |
| 728.12 | 199.17 | 645.20 | 536.10 | 030.04 | 179.05 |
| 731.03 | 199.19 | 647.22 | 537.18 | 030.22 | 179.07 |
| 736.04 | 201.10 | 650.12 | 554.15 | 030.23 | 180.22 |
| 737.11 | 207.09 | 658.07 | 570.22 | 031.18 | 182.13 |
| 738.03 | 207.13 | 664.17 | 600.08 | 032.01 | 182.17 |
| 742.08 | 216.08 | 665.16 | 608.16 | 035.08 | 185.08 |
| 747.01 | 221.01 | 671.14 | 621.03 | 035.19 | 185.17 |
| 754.16 | 222.01 | 680.10 | 646.15 | 040.04 | 187.16 |
| 755.13 | 223.02 | 680.16 | 647.07 | 042.03 | 187.17 |
| 756.16 | 231.10 | 698.09 | 680.15 | 044.10 | 194.14 |
| 759.07 | 231.13 | 723.16 | 681.12 | 044.13 | 195.05 |
| 760.07 | 231.22 | 726.09 | 705.06 | 047.11 | 195.10 |
| **hareton's** | 231.22 | 728.08 | 708.07 | 048.21 | 197.20 |
| 075.16 | 232.05 | 729.14 | 708.08 | 049.07 | 198.15 |
| 166.13 | 236.22 | 734.09 | 708.09 | 049.10 | 200.07 |
| 324.03 | 237.03 | 740.03 | 722.12 | 049.12 | 202.10 |
| 326.07 | 238.19 | 746.20 | **hated** | 049.14 | 202.21 |
| 443.15 | 243.02 | 748.02 | 008.01 | 050.05 | 203.15 |
| 444.02 | 246.05 | **hasn't** | 043.11 | 056.04 | 207.11 |
| 498.09 | 249.17 | 293.13 | 080.19 | 056.14 | 208.09 |
| 680.19 | 255.19 | 452.01 | 088.02 | 056.20 | 208.16 |
| 722.06 | 260.20 | 504.15 | 091.21 | 057.13 | 209.04 |
| 732.03 | 262.01 | **hasped** | 249.21 | 059.01 | 209.11 |
| **hark** | 263.07 | 758.05 | 273.17 | 059.03 | 211.11 |
| 167.20 | 266.14 | **haste** | 304.13 | 061.01 | 212.15 |
| **harken** | 271.16 | 032.17 | 334.14 | 067.07 | 214.16 |
| 178.13 | 271.22 | 120.16 | 367.21 | 070.04 | 214.21 |
| **harm** | 272.21 | 120.18 | 407.19 | 070.22 | 215.17 |
| 090.18 | 274.06 | 260.08 | 525.18 | 071.20 | 215.22 |
| 130.02 | 281.05 | 439.04 | 536.14 | 072.13 | 216.04 |
| 223.01 | 288.13 | 461.15 | 537.14 | 073.12 | 216.16 |
| 230.04 | 288.21 | 478.21 | 631.04 | 074.03 | 216.20 |
| 254.11 | 289.20 | 523.22 | **hateful** | 074.20 | 217.22 |
| 343.18 | 290.05 | 647.01 | 647.05 | 077.08 | 219.09 |
| 406.10 | 292.10 | **hasten** | 647.13 | 077.14 | 220.20 |
| 484.07 | 296.19 | 126.18 | **hates** | 079.22 | 221.22 |
| 484.08 | 297.18 | **hastened** | 125.02 | 082.10 | 222.08 |
| 539.20 | 299.20 | 010.16 | 155.12 | 084.07 | 222.09 |
| 601.10 | 306.07 | 020.03 | 167.14 | 084.20 | 222.17 |
| 606.03 | 311.16 | 057.09 | 501.06 | 088.01 | 223.10 |
| **harmed** | 312.03 | 160.06 | 630.03 | 089.01 | 226.01 |
| 359.21 | 316.18 | 325.13 | 708.04 | 089.06 | 227.12 |
| **harming** | 316.19 | 366.20 | **hathecliff** | 089.08 | 228.02 |
| 194.21 | 329.06 | 402.20 | 324.19 | 094.04 | 228.10 |
| **harmless** | 335.06 | 451.11 | 456.17 | 095.17 | 229.02 |
| 064.05 | 335.09 | 485.13 | 457.20 | 096.09 | |

| | | | | | |
|---|---|---|---|---|---|
| 229.04 | 363.08 | 488.06 | 627.01 | 752.07 | hazel-nut |
| 230.14 | 363.09 | 489.15 | 627.05 | 754.01 | 260.13 |
| 231.06 | 363.10 | 490.07 | 627.08 | 754.03 | hazels |
| 233.19 | 363.10 | 490.15 | 627.21 | 754.05 | 517.18 |
| 233.22 | 364.02 | 494.09 | 628.04 | 754.09 | hazy |
| 234.22 | 365.20 | 494.13 | 630.04 | 754.20 | 585.07 |
| 235.20 | 370.06 | 494.13 | 630.05 | 755.07 | he . |
| 235.21 | 371.17 | 494.18 | 630.10 | 763.09 | 001.12 |
| 240.22 | 372.01 | 498.20 | 631.06 | haven | 002.15 |
| 242.09 | 372.16 | 499.05 | 631.08 | 372.03 | 002.21 |
| 246.10 | 373.03 | 500.06 | 631.15 | haven't | 003.05 |
| 247.05 | 374.08 | 502.13 | 632.21 | 467.04 | 003.06 |
| 247.12 | 375.09 | 504.07 | 635.12 | 511.09 | 003.18 |
| 249.19 | 375.13 | 504.14 | 640.03 | having | 003.21 |
| 250.22 | 377.03 | 505.02 | 640.09 | 036.13 | 007.09 |
| 251.03 | 378.22 | 508.01 | 641.03 | 038.06 | 007.13 |
| 251.05 | 379.05 | 510.08 | 642.02 | 038.10 | 008.05 |
| 251.20 | 380.02 | 510.16 | 647.04 | 050.08 | 009.21 |
| 251.22 | 380.04 | 510.20 | 647.05 | 056.12 | 011.18 |
| 252.14 | 382.13 | 510.21 | 648.04 | 061.02 | 012.05 |
| 254.05 | 382.21 | 511.12 | 648.05 | 064.11 | 012.14 |
| 255.04 | 383.05 | 511.13 | 648.13 | 064.22 | 013.04 |
| 255.18 | 384.04 | 512.01 | 649.07 | 070.14 | 013.08 |
| 256.03 | 385.11 | 512.17 | 649.15 | 075.09 | 013.16 |
| 256.14 | 386.03 | 513.12 | 650.01 | 094.05 | 016.05 |
| 257.21 | 386.10 | 513.16 | 650.10 | 121.16 | 016.20 |
| 259.18 | 386.14 | 517.12 | 650.19 | 122.05 | 021.01 |
| 259.20 | 387.14 | 520.14 | 651.07 | 149.04 | 021.09 |
| 262.10 | 387.17 | 521.08 | 651.11 | 154.05 | 021.22 |
| 262.15 | 387.21 | 521.14 | 651.11 | 166.09 | 022.09 |
| 265.04 | 388.13 | 523.01 | 652.01 | 170.09 | 022.16 |
| 267.11 | 389.05 | 523.04 | 653.18 | 173.18 | 022.18 |
| 272.01 | 390.04 | 523.22 | 653.20 | 179.16 | 023.03 |
| 273.08 | 390.14 | 524.08 | 654.05 | 190.18 | 024.03 |
| 273.19 | 394.16 | 525.01 | 658.02 | 191.09 | 025.15 |
| 273.20 | 395.10 | 526.01 | 658.02 | 209.21 | 025.16 |
| 276.12 | 395.21 | 527.03 | 662.05 | 213.22 | 025.17 |
| 279.15 | 396.12 | 527.05 | 662.08 | 217.03 | 026.05 |
| 282.05 | 399.06 | 533.05 | 663.01 | 227.03 | 027.03 |
| 282.16 | 401.02 | 533.07 | 664.07 | 253.01 | 027.04 |
| 282.17 | 404.17 | 534.18 | 669.07 | 270.16 | 028.17 |
| 287.11 | 405.12 | 537.08 | 670.07 | 280.20 | 030.07 |
| 287.20 | 406.14 | 539.17 | 670.09 | 287.02 | 030.12 |
| 288.07 | 407.17 | 543.06 | 670.10 | 293.04 | 032.10 |
| 288.14 | 409.08 | 543.10 | 671.02 | 293.17 | 033.03 |
| 289.12 | 409.09 | 543.12 | 675.20 | 295.15 | 033.06 |
| 290.21 | 409.11 | 543.13 | 677.15 | 296.05 | 034.01 |
| 291.10 | 412.09 | 544.07 | 678.06 | 298.19 | 036.10 |
| 294.08 | 414.21 | 544.11 | 680.04 | 312.10 | 041.14 |
| 295.03 | 415.17 | 545.06 | 680.15 | 315.14 | 041.18 |
| 295.08 | 416.15 | 546.08 | 681.11 | 321.19 | 042.18 |
| 297.08 | 417.10 | 548.07 | 686.12 | 351.19 | 043.05 |
| 298.10 | 420.01 | 548.14 | 686.21 | 369.05 | 043.08 |
| 301.06 | 420.13 | 552.14 | 690.04 | 397.05 | 044.16 |
| 303.08 | 421.20 | 553.18 | 692.13 | 400.16 | 045.09 |
| 303.15 | 422.10 | 553.21 | 693.17 | 403.17 | 045.09 |
| 307.08 | 425.21 | 554.06 | 695.04 | 441.06 | 045.12 |
| 307.13 | 427.21 | 558.15 | 695.06 | 441.15 | 045.13 |
| 307.18 | 428.01 | 559.01 | 695.14 | 451.05 | 045.14 |
| 311.22 | 428.17 | 559.21 | 697.10 | 467.01 | 048.04 |
| 312.08 | 432.18 | 562.07 | 697.18 | 468.09 | 048.06 |
| 314.21 | 433.01 | 562.12 | 698.12 | 472.22 | 048.09 |
| 315.21 | 433.13 | 563.08 | 698.18 | 486.11 | 048.20 |
| 317.05 | 435.07 | 567.03 | 698.18 | 493.15 | 048.22 |
| 317.05 | 435.09 | 570.12 | 698.20 | 498.03 | 054.07 |
| 317.06 | 435.20 | 571.22 | 699.03 | 507.17 | 054.11 |
| 318.20 | 436.04 | 572.03 | 699.05 | 534.12 | 055.01 |
| 319.21 | 436.12 | 572.10 | 699.09 | 546.09 | 055.11 |
| 320.08 | 438.14 | 572.22 | 701.06 | 550.07 | 055.14 |
| 320.09 | 439.11 | 573.22 | 701.21 | 552.01 | 058.01 |
| 327.15 | 440.19 | 574.08 | 704.08 | 563.18 | 058.04 |
| 328.10 | 442.19 | 576.02 | 705.05 | 583.02 | 058.16 |
| 329.02 | 442.21 | 577.10 | 707.10 | 631.14 | 059.08 |
| 330.07 | 444.07 | 580.06 | 708.02 | 633.16 | 060.10 |
| 331.01 | 447.01 | 581.02 | 708.12 | 636.22 | 060.11 |
| 331.13 | 449.11 | 581.04 | 709.04 | 640.14 | 060.13 |
| 331.14 | 449.14 | 581.11 | 709.14 | 649.05 | 061.20 |
| 331.15 | 450.22 | 582.08 | 716.11 | 653.10 | 062.05 |
| 331.17 | 451.09 | 587.12 | 716.13 | 661.19 | 062.09 |
| 332.01 | 452.11 | 589.16 | 716.15 | 667.22 | 062.10 |
| 332.22 | 453.19 | 589.17 | 717.03 | 689.14 | 062.16 |
| 333.14 | 455.08 | 592.09 | 719.05 | 694.15 | 062.17 |
| 334.16 | 455.22 | 594.01 | 721.06 | 695.05 | 062.18 |
| 334.18 | 456.21 | 596.07 | 721.19 | 698.01 | 063.02 |
| 334.20 | 457.07 | 599.11 | 723.09 | 710.03 | 063.20 |
| 335.01 | 458.03 | 600.14 | 728.05 | 729.07 | 064.03 |
| 335.03 | 459.06 | 601.09 | 729.14 | 743.04 | 065.19 |
| 336.06 | 461.01 | 605.13 | 730.01 | 746.07 | 066.19 |
| 337.01 | 463.15 | 607.05 | 730.08 | 750.03 | 071.12 |
| 337.02 | 465.01 | 607.16 | 731.06 | 757.12 | 071.14 |
| 337.02 | 465.01 | 607.20 | 731.06 | 759.18 | 071.18 |
| 338.04 | 466.12 | 608.03 | 732.01 | 760.14 | 071.19 |
| 338.08 | 466.14 | 608.05 | 733.01 | havoc | 071.20 |
| 339.11 | 468.22 | 608.06 | 733.07 | 596.04 | 072.03 |
| 339.17 | 469.09 | 608.08 | 733.07 | hay | 072.04 |
| 340.20 | 470.09 | 608.22 | 733.09 | 075.18 | 072.04 |
| 342.19 | 476.06 | 610.08 | 733.12 | 084.11 | 073.01 |
| 343.03 | 476.08 | 611.09 | 733.19 | 085.19 | 074.03 |
| 343.03 | 477.13 | 611.10 | 734.04 | 139.05 | 074.07 |
| 346.10 | 478.17 | 611.12 | 734.06 | hay-field | 074.08 |
| 346.20 | 479.03 | 614.08 | 734.12 | 466.10 | 074.12 |
| 348.03 | 480.08 | 614.22 | 735.04 | hay-loft | 076.03 |
| 349.03 | 481.18 | 615.04 | 739.01 | 187.01 | 076.04 |
| 351.17 | 482.12 | 616.01 | 739.16 | hazard | 076.06 |
| 356.19 | 482.13 | 616.03 | 740.02 | 160.22 | 076.13 |
| 356.22 | 483.04 | 616.08 | 741.20 | 408.10 | 076.17 |
| 359.01 | 484.01 | 617.03 | 742.10 | hazarding | 076.17 |
| 359.02 | 484.10 | 618.05 | 742.21 | 257.14 | 076.18 |
| 359.16 | 486.14 | 620.10 | 748.05 | hazel | 076.19 |
| 362.21 | 486.15 | 621.04 | 749.21 | 432.18 | 076.20 |
| 362.22 | 488.02 | 622.10 | 751.14 | | 077.02 |

| | | | | | |
|---|---|---|---|---|---|
| 077.12 | 107.13 | 157.19 | 198.10 | 232.09 | 293.12 |
| 077.13 | 108.11 | 158.04 | 198.14 | 232.17 | 293.13 |
| 077.14 | 108.13 | 158.11 | 198.18 | 232.17 | 293.21 |
| 077.17 | 108.19 | 158.14 | 199.09 | 232.17 | 294.06 |
| 077.18 | 109.05 | 159.03 | 199.10 | 232.19 | 294.12 |
| 078.10 | 109.16 | 159.07 | 199.14 | 232.21 | 294.17 |
| 078.12 | 109.19 | 159.16 | 199.17 | 232.22 | 295.14 |
| 078.13 | 110.08 | 160.01 | 199.19 | 233.07 | 296.01 |
| 078.16 | 111.13 | 160.06 | 199.20 | 233.09 | 296.08 |
| 078.20 | 112.02 | 160.21 | 201.11 | 233.12 | 297.01 |
| 078.22 | 112.08 | 161.03 | 202.01 | 237.10 | 297.21 |
| 079.01 | 112.08 | 161.04 | 203.09 | 238.13 | 297.21 |
| 079.03 | 112.10 | 162.02 | 203.10 | 239.07 | 298.04 |
| 079.04 | 112.11 | 162.07 | 203.15 | 239.16 | 298.06 |
| 079.04 | 115.12 | 163.05 | 203.18 | 240.16 | 298.07 |
| 079.12 | 115.13 | 163.16 | 203.19 | 244.10 | 298.08 |
| 079.14 | 116.01 | 163.20 | 204.19 | 245.04 | 298.09 |
| 079.15 | 116.04 | 164.03 | 204.20 | 245.10 | 299.09 |
| 080.05 | 116.12 | 164.05 | 204.22 | 245.15 | 299.22 |
| 080.18 | 117.12 | 165.02 | 205.03 | 246.01 | 299.22 |
| 081.03 | 118.03 | 165.04 | 205.05 | 246.02 | 301.07 |
| 081.04 | 118.07 | 165.08 | 207.05 | 246.08 | 301.11 |
| 081.07 | 118.18 | 165.09 | 207.11 | 246.15 | 302.04 |
| 081.11 | 118.21 | 165.14 | 208.03 | 246.16 | 302.07 |
| 081.12 | 120.03 | 165.21 | 208.18 | 246.17 | 304.09 |
| 081.12 | 120.12 | 166.04 | 208.20 | 246.22 | 307.10 |
| 081.13 | 121.01 | 166.06 | 210.05 | 247.03 | 307.11 |
| 081.14 | 121.13 | 166.11 | 210.15 | 247.04 | 308.10 |
| 081.18 | 121.19 | 166.19 | 210.21 | 247.07 | 308.14 |
| 082.03 | 121.22 | 166.21 | 211.03 | 247.07 | 308.19 |
| 082.09 | 122.05 | 167.07 | 211.04 | 247.07 | 309.16 |
| 082.10 | 122.16 | 167.10 | 211.15 | 247.08 | 310.03 |
| 082.11 | 122.17 | 167.11 | 211.18 | 247.13 | 310.18 |
| 082.12 | 122.21 | 167.14 | 212.03 | 247.20 | 310.22 |
| 082.14 | 123.13 | 168.03 | 212.05 | 248.20 | 311.12 |
| 082.18 | 123.19 | 168.10 | 212.21 | 249.01 | 311.16 |
| 082.21 | 124.03 | 168.17 | 213.06 | 249.04 | 311.18 |
| 083.08 | 125.06 | 168.21 | 213.18 | 249.06 | 311.21 |
| 083.09 | 126.08 | 169.03 | 214.10 | 249.17 | 312.06 |
| 083.11 | 126.19 | 169.11 | 214.11 | 249.18 | 312.08 |
| 083.11 | 126.20 | 169.12 | 214.13 | 249.19 | 312.12 |
| 083.18 | 127.10 | 170.15 | 214.15 | 249.20 | 312.13 |
| 083.18 | 127.11 | 170.15 | 215.01 | 249.21 | 313.01 |
| 084.05 | 127.13 | 171.01 | 215.02 | 250.16 | 314.02 |
| 084.12 | 128.01 | 172.05 | 215.03 | 251.03 | 314.03 |
| 084.14 | 128.04 | 172.05 | 215.07 | 251.17 | 314.21 |
| 084.15 | 128.05 | 173.09 | 215.10 | 253.11 | 315.05 |
| 084.18 | 128.13 | 173.12 | 216.01 | 253.22 | 315.06 |
| 084.20 | 128.14 | 173.14 | 216.20 | 254.05 | 315.13 |
| 085.04 | 128.22 | 173.16 | 217.11 | 254.19 | 316.09 |
| 085.07 | 131.04 | 174.02 | 217.12 | 254.21 | 316.11 |
| 085.11 | 132.05 | 174.03 | 217.13 | 255.05 | 316.14 |
| 085.15 | 133.08 | 174.13 | 217.16 | 255.13 | 316.19 |
| 085.21 | 133.10 | 174.17 | 217.18 | 256.12 | 316.22 |
| 086.01 | 133.12 | 174.19 | 217.18 | 256.15 | 317.10 |
| 086.02 | 133.15 | 175.01 | 217.22 | 257.08 | 317.11 |
| 086.02 | 133.18 | 175.05 | 216.10 | 257.13 | 317.15 |
| 086.03 | 134.02 | 175.08 | 218.12 | 258.12 | 317.21 |
| 087.03 | 136.15 | 177.10 | 218.13 | 258.17 | 318.09 |
| 087.04 | 136.17 | 177.13 | 218.14 | 258.20 | 319.07 |
| 087.05 | 139.12 | 179.08 | 218.16 | 259.14 | 319.20 |
| 087.11 | 140.21 | 179.19 | 220.10 | 259.14 | 320.07 |
| 088.02 | 141.09 | 179.19 | 220.14 | 259.22 | 320.11 |
| 088.11 | 141.14 | 179.20 | 220.20 | 260.06 | 320.21 |
| 088.13 | 141.15 | 180.08 | 220.21 | 260.11 | 321.01 |
| 088.17 | 141.17 | 180.10 | 220.22 | 260.17 | 321.14 |
| 088.19 | 141.19 | 180.15 | 221.02 | 261.07 | 321.17 |
| 088.22 | 141.21 | 180.16 | 221.04 | 261.22 | 322.02 |
| 089.05 | 142.03 | 180.16 | 221.08 | 262.02 | 322.04 |
| 089.11 | 142.15 | 180.17 | 221.09 | 262.14 | 322.07 |
| 089.16 | 143.02 | 180.21 | 221.09 | 262.16 | 322.18 |
| 089.19 | 143.03 | 181.03 | 221.13 | 263.07 | 324.20 |
| 089.20 | 143.09 | 181.14 | 221.18 | 264.08 | 324.21 |
| 089.22 | 143.14 | 181.16 | 221.18 | 264.09 | 324.22 |
| 090.01 | 143.19 | 181.16 | 221.19 | 266.01 | 326.03 |
| 091.10 | 143.21 | 182.20 | 221.21 | 266.14 | 326.18 |
| 091.14 | 144.01 | 182.21 | 221.22 | 267.18 | 326.21 |
| 091.22 | 144.01 | 184.11 | 222.01 | 267.19 | 327.01 |
| 092.18 | 144.13 | 184.13 | 222.09 | 267.21 | 327.04 |
| 093.10 | 144.20 | 184.15 | 222.10 | 269.05 | 327.09 |
| 094.06 | 145.17 | 184.21 | 222.13 | 270.08 | 327.10 |
| 094.07 | 146.09 | 185.10 | 222.14 | 271.08 | 327.12 |
| 094.08 | 146.14 | 185.14 | 222.15 | 271.09 | 328.07 |
| 094.09 | 146.15 | 185.14 | 222.21 | 271.16 | 329.10 |
| 094.11 | 146.16 | 185.19 | 222.22 | 271.17 | 329.17 |
| 094.15 | 147.17 | 186.03 | 223.10 | 271.21 | 330.17 |
| 095.04 | 147.19 | 186.03 | 224.03 | 271.22 | 330.20 |
| 095.09 | 147.22 | 186.08 | 224.13 | 272.07 | 330.21 |
| 096.04 | 147.22 | 186.12 | 224.17 | 272.10 | 331.01 |
| 096.06 | 149.02 | 186.12 | 224.19 | 272.13 | 331.21 |
| 096.08 | 149.05 | 186.14 | 225.16 | 272.16 | 332.01 |
| 098.11 | 149.08 | 186.17 | 225.20 | 272.18 | 332.12 |
| 098.14 | 149.11 | 187.06 | 225.21 | 273.01 | 332.16 |
| 098.17 | 149.15 | 187.13 | 226.01 | 274.06 | 334.04 |
| 099.02 | 149.18 | 187.19 | 226.01 | 276.01 | 334.06 |
| 099.13 | 149.21 | 189.12 | 226.04 | 276.01 | 334.13 |
| 099.15 | 149.21 | 189.16 | 226.05 | 280.21 | 335.10 |
| 099.19 | 150.02 | 189.17 | 229.06 | 280.22 | 336.03 |
| 100.03 | 150.05 | 190.15 | 229.20 | 284.09 | 336.04 |
| 100.14 | 150.09 | 190.17 | 230.07 | 284.09 | 336.09 |
| 102.05 | 150.11 | 191.06 | 230.08 | 285.11 | 336.12 |
| 102.13 | 150.16 | 192.03 | 230.13 | 286.03 | 336.19 |
| 102.15 | 151.08 | 192.15 | 231.12 | 286.05 | 336.20 |
| 102.16 | 151.22 | 194.22 | 231.14 | 286.07 | 336.22 |
| 103.11 | 152.11 | 196.02 | 231.21 | 286.17 | 338.13 |
| 105.19 | 153.01 | 196.04 | 231.22 | 286.19 | 341.17 |
| 106.10 | 154.03 | 196.04 | 231.22 | 287.01 | 342.02 |
| 107.01 | 154.08 | 196.07 | 232.01 | 289.17 | 342.02 |
| 107.01 | 154.15 | 196.07 | 232.02 | 292.03 | 342.03 |
| 107.07 | 154.18 | 197.13 | 232.03 | 292.03 | 342.04 |
| 107.12 | 155.12 | 198.08 | | 292.08 | 342.05 |

| | | | | | |
|---|---|---|---|---|---|
| 342.06 | 390.16 | 421.03 | 463.21 | 495.17 | 546.21 |
| 343.01 | 390.20 | 421.10 | 464.01 | 496.01 | 547.05 |
| 343.12 | 390.21 | 421.15 | 464.02 | 496.07 | 547.15 |
| 346.04 | 391.03 | 421.16 | 464.03 | 496.08 | 552.20 |
| 346.05 | 391.04 | 421.17 | 464.04 | 496.08 | 552.22 |
| 346.17 | 391.17 | 422.02 | 464.21 | 496.11 | 555.20 |
| 346.21 | 392.03 | 422.10 | 464.22 | 496.11 | 556.02 |
| 346.22 | 392.06 | 422.11 | 464.22 | 496.12 | 556.03 |
| 350.22 | 392.07 | 422.13 | 465.01 | 496.14 | 556.04 |
| 351.02 | 392.08 | 422.16 | 465.17 | 496.14 | 557.05 |
| 352.11 | 392.11 | 422.17 | 466.01 | 496.22 | 558.01 |
| 352.21 | 393.03 | 423.05 | 466.04 | 497.08 | 558.05 |
| 352.22 | 394.03 | 425.20 | 466.12 | 498.01 | 558.06 |
| 354.18 | 394.09 | 426.01 | 466.16 | 498.04 | 558.06 |
| 355.10 | 394.13 | 426.03 | 467.04 | 499.19 | 558.17 |
| 355.14 | 394.14 | 426.12 | 467.10 | 500.14 | 558.18 |
| 355.16 | 394.14 | 428.17 | 467.13 | 500.15 | 558.18 |
| 355.20 | 394.16 | 429.21 | 467.14 | 500.17 | 559.05 |
| 355.21 | 395.14 | 430.04 | 467.17 | 501.02 | 559.07 |
| 355.22 | 395.15 | 430.05 | 468.04 | 501.06 | 559.08 |
| 356.02 | 395.19 | 430.09 | 468.15 | 501.10 | 559.10 |
| 356.05 | 396.20 | 430.11 | 469.13 | 501.18 | 560.06 |
| 356.09 | 397.15 | 432.15 | 469.18 | 501.19 | 560.08 |
| 356.11 | 398.05 | 432.17 | 470.06 | 502.01 | 560.11 |
| 357.05 | 398.09 | 434.07 | 470.13 | 502.08 | 560.15 |
| 358.01 | 399.01 | 434.07 | 470.17 | 502.10 | 560.15 |
| 358.13 | 399.08 | 434.09 | 471.01 | 502.10 | 560.16 |
| 358.18 | 399.11 | 436.14 | 471.03 | 503.07 | 561.01 |
| 360.06 | 399.17 | 436.18 | 471.05 | 504.09 | 561.05 |
| 360.07 | 400.05 | 436.18 | 471.07 | 504.13 | 561.06 |
| 360.08 | 400.07 | 438.03 | 471.11 | 504.15 | 561.11 |
| 360.15 | 400.10 | 438.05 | 471.14 | 505.02 | 561.17 |
| 361.10 | 400.13 | 438.08 | 472.01 | 505.06 | 561.19 |
| 361.11 | 400.18 | 438.11 | 472.03 | 509.09 | 561.21 |
| 361.16 | 401.01 | 438.13 | 472.05 | 510.09 | 562.10 |
| 361.21 | 401.16 | 438.13 | 472.11 | 510.10 | 562.13 |
| 362.03 | 402.04 | 438.14 | 472.17 | 511.13 | 562.17 |
| 362.05 | 402.07 | 438.14 | 473.03 | 520.13 | 562.18 |
| 362.10 | 402.08 | 439.10 | 474.07 | 521.10 | 563.02 |
| 362.15 | 402.09 | 439.17 | 474.17 | 521.19 | 563.07 |
| 362.16 | 402.10 | 439.18 | 475.07 | 521.22 | 563.13 |
| 363.22 | 402.17 | 440.09 | 475.09 | 524.06 | 563.16 |
| 364.22 | 402.20 | 441.16 | 475.12 | 524.18 | 563.19 |
| 365.04 | 402.20 | 441.19 | 475.13 | 525.03 | 563.22 |
| 365.07 | 403.03 | 442.20 | 475.20 | 525.17 | 564.05 |
| 365.16 | 403.05 | 442.22 | 476.03 | 526.04 | 564.07 |
| 365.20 | 403.07 | 443.08 | 476.06 | 527.01 | 564.10 |
| 366.04 | 405.12 | 443.09 | 476.07 | 527.06 | 564.17 |
| 366.07 | 405.13 | 443.13 | 476.19 | 527.10 | 564.17 |
| 367.08 | 405.19 | 443.14 | 476.19 | 528.06 | 564.19 |
| 367.12 | 406.03 | 443.17 | 476.20 | 528.06 | 565.01 |
| 367.15 | 406.04 | 443.18 | 476.21 | 528.20 | 565.02 |
| 368.02 | 406.17 | 443.20 | 476.22 | 531.11 | 565.05 |
| 368.04 | 406.18 | 443.20 | 477.01 | 531.19 | 565.09 |
| 368.10 | 406.20 | 444.01 | 477.02 | 532.06 | 565.13 |
| 371.21 | 407.06 | 444.06 | 477.02 | 532.08 | 565.16 |
| 373.01 | 407.14 | 444.10 | 477.06 | 532.10 | 565.18 |
| 373.02 | 407.21 | 445.03 | 477.10 | 532.12 | 565.21 |
| 373.04 | 408.04 | 446.01 | 477.12 | 532.20 | 566.08 |
| 373.05 | 408.14 | 446.10 | 477.14 | 533.04 | 566.09 |
| 373.06 | 409.02 | 446.18 | 477.15 | 533.16 | 566.11 |
| 373.13 | 409.14 | 446.19 | 477.16 | 534.03 | 566.13 |
| 373.17 | 411.10 | 446.22 | 477.18 | 534.04 | 566.19 |
| 374.02 | 411.15 | 448.04 | 477.21 | 534.10 | 566.20 |
| 374.03 | 411.17 | 450.14 | 478.10 | 534.18 | 567.08 |
| 374.11 | 411.19 | 450.19 | 481.04 | 534.20 | 567.09 |
| 374.13 | 411.22 | 451.16 | 481.20 | 535.01 | 567.13 |
| 375.02 | 412.03 | 452.01 | 482.02 | 535.02 | 567.16 |
| 375.05 | 412.03 | 452.06 | 482.06 | 535.10 | 567.19 |
| 375.08 | 412.09 | 452.15 | 483.03 | 535.10 | 567.19 |
| 375.10 | 412.17 | 453.05 | 483.05 | 535.12 | 568.18 |
| 375.17 | 412.20 | 453.05 | 483.14 | 536.04 | 568.20 |
| 376.03 | 413.01 | 453.11 | 483.17 | 536.13 | 569.01 |
| 376.04 | 413.02 | 453.22 | 484.03 | 537.03 | 569.05 |
| 376.05 | 413.05 | 454.01 | 484.09 | 537.07 | 569.06 |
| 376.13 | 413.13 | 454.19 | 484.14 | 537.07 | 569.17 |
| 377.09 | 413.14 | 455.05 | 485.03 | 537.17 | 570.03 |
| 377.19 | 413.17 | 455.12 | 485.16 | 538.05 | 570.13 |
| 377.20 | 413.19 | 455.15 | 485.21 | 538.10 | 570.16 |
| 377.22 | 413.21 | 455.20 | 486.01 | 538.17 | 570.21 |
| 378.11 | 413.22 | 455.22 | 486.03 | 539.01 | 571.14 |
| 378.19 | 414.06 | 456.06 | 486.13 | 539.03 | 571.15 |
| 379.01 | 414.07 | 456.09 | 488.05 | 539.09 | 572.13 |
| 379.13 | 415.09 | 456.12 | 488.19 | 539.12 | 572.14 |
| 379.13 | 416.03 | 456.21 | 489.09 | 539.13 | 572.18 |
| 382.15 | 416.10 | 457.02 | 489.16 | 540.01 | 572.19 |
| 385.16 | 416.17 | 457.09 | 490.02 | 540.07 | 572.21 |
| 385.17 | 416.18 | 457.11 | 490.07 | 540.18 | 573.17 |
| 385.21 | 417.04 | 457.13 | 491.04 | 541.02 | 574.02 |
| 386.02 | 417.07 | 458.06 | 491.15 | 541.05 | 574.03 |
| 386.07 | 417.19 | 458.08 | 491.16 | 541.17 | 574.04 |
| 386.08 | 417.22 | 459.05 | 491.19 | 541.21 | 574.04 |
| 387.10 | 418.04 | 459.08 | 491.19 | 541.21 | 574.06 |
| 387.11 | 418.09 | 460.01 | 491.22 | 542.04 | 574.07 |
| 387.15 | 418.09 | 460.05 | 492.01 | 542.04 | 576.14 |
| 388.03 | 418.13 | 460.07 | 492.16 | 542.08 | 576.15 |
| 388.08 | 418.14 | 460.09 | 492.18 | 542.12 | 576.18 |
| 388.12 | 418.17 | 460.10 | 493.11 | 542.19 | 576.20 |
| 388.16 | 418.22 | 460.12 | 493.12 | 543.06 | 577.01 |
| 388.20 | 419.04 | 460.14 | 493.13 | 543.07 | 577.02 |
| 389.01 | 419.10 | 460.16 | 493.16 | 543.11 | 577.06 |
| 389.02 | 419.13 | 460.21 | 493.18 | 543.22 | 577.08 |
| 389.04 | 419.17 | 461.02 | 494.01 | 545.12 | 577.12 |
| 389.06 | 419.18 | 461.04 | 494.04 | 545.13 | 577.20 |
| 389.17 | 419.21 | 461.18 | 494.13 | 545.18 | 578.16 |
| 389.18 | 420.02 | 461.21 | 494.20 | 546.05 | 579.07 |
| 390.02 | 420.03 | 462.05 | 494.21 | 546.07 | 579.13 |
| 390.04 | 420.10 | 462.10 | 495.02 | 546.15 | 579.19 |
| 390.07 | 420.14 | 462.21 | 495.07 | 546.16 | 580.01 |
| 390.09 | 420.17 | 463.04 | 495.13 | 546.16 | 580.03 |
| 390.15 | 421.02 | | | 546.18 | 580.07 |

| | | | | | |
|---|---|---|---|---|---|
| 580.10 | 615.10 | 656.04 | 704.22 | 742.02 | 167.02 |
| 580.12 | 615.15 | 656.17 | 705.01 | 742.06 | 169.04 |
| 580.15 | 616.01 | 657.02 | 705.02 | 742.18 | 180.19 |
| 580.18 | 616.15 | 658.05 | 705.04 | 743.06 | 181.01 |
| 581.09 | 617.04 | 660.17 | 706.11 | 743.11 | 181.13 |
| 581.19 | 617.11 | 661.17 | 706.16 | 744.04 | 187.11 |
| 581.20 | 617.12 | 662.08 | 706.17 | 744.13 | 187.13 |
| 582.01 | 617.20 | 662.09 | 707.01 | 745.01 | 188.02 |
| 582.02 | 618.15 | 662.16 | 707.12 | 745.04 | 190.14 |
| 582.04 | 619.03 | 662.17 | 708.03 | 745.06 | 190.15 |
| 582.07 | 619.05 | 662.20 | 709.01 | 745.10 | 238.08 |
| 582.15 | 619.05 | 663.11 | 709.15 | 745.11 | 260.04 |
| 582.18 | 619.10 | 663.14 | 709.15 | 745.13 | 284.10 |
| 582.19 | 619.12 | 663.18 | 709.19 | 745.20 | 293.08 |
| 583.06 | 619.13 | 663.22 | 709.21 | 746.09 | 293.22 |
| 583.07 | 620.05 | 664.11 | 709.21 | 746.20 | 345.03 |
| 583.10 | 620.18 | 664.16 | 710.09 | 747.03 | 395.12 |
| 583.12 | 621.13 | 666.05 | 710.14 | 747.07 | 395.13 |
| 583.18 | 622.01 | 666.08 | 710.19 | 747.08 | 435.21 |
| 583.19 | 622.03 | 666.11 | 710.21 | 747.10 | 454.03 |
| 586.05 | 622.05 | 666.12 | 711.06 | 747.13 | 454.08 |
| 586.13 | 622.06 | 666.15 | 711.10 | 747.14 | 457.22 |
| 586.15 | 622.16 | 666.16 | 712.03 | 747.15 | 464.05 |
| 586.17 | 622.17 | 667.08 | 712.11 | 747.20 | 464.09 |
| 587.04 | 623.16 | 667.15 | 712.11 | 748.04 | 476.11 |
| 587.06 | 623.21 | 668.07 | 712.15 | 748.04 | 489.02 |
| 587.07 | 624.01 | 668.10 | 712.16 | 748.10 | 489.11 |
| 587.15 | 624.03 | 668.15 | 717.14 | 748.17 | 493.05 |
| 587.19 | 624.07 | 668.17 | 717.14 | 748.21 | 493.18 |
| 588.10 | 624.15 | 669.01 | 717.16 | 749.01 | 504.10 |
| 589.05 | 624.18 | 669.03 | 718.06 | 749.12 | 504.11 |
| 589.10 | 625.03 | 669.04 | 718.07 | 749.14 | 525.03 |
| 589.20 | 627.07 | 669.05 | 719.05 | 749.20 | 542.06 |
| 590.09 | 627.07 | 669.07 | 719.09 | 750.03 | 545.15 |
| 590.12 | 627.17 | 669.15 | 720.19 | 750.08 | 546.03 |
| 590.21 | 627.17 | 669.15 | 721.15 | 750.16 | 546.04 |
| 590.22 | 627.19 | 670.21 | 722.04 | 750.18 | 571.20 |
| 591.01 | 628.14 | 671.07 | 722.11 | 751.08 | 571.21 |
| 591.07 | 629.13 | 672.03 | 723.01 | 751.15 | 590.15 |
| 591.19 | 629.15 | 672.15 | 723.02 | 751.21 | 601.12 |
| 592.01 | 629.21 | 672.15 | 723.12 | 752.05 | 606.03 |
| 592.05 | 629.21 | 673.11 | 723.15 | 753.05 | 615.10 |
| 592.08 | 630.03 | 674.02 | 723.19 | 753.20 | 618.13 |
| 592.13 | 630.08 | 674.05 | 723.22 | 754.13 | 618.15 |
| 592.15 | 630.09 | 674.05 | 724.03 | 755.06 | 619.17 |
| 592.17 | 630.20 | 674.08 | 724.05 | 755.10 | 650.03 |
| 592.17 | 631.01 | 675.21 | 724.14 | 755.11 | 660.05 |
| 593.06 | 631.18 | 676.09 | 725.01 | 755.13 | 679.08 |
| 593.15 | 631.22 | 678.05 | 725.02 | 755.15 | 710.07 |
| 594.06 | 632.01 | 679.07 | 725.02 | 755.21 | 717.08 |
| 594.15 | 632.09 | 679.10 | 725.04 | 756.04 | 723.04 |
| 597.04 | 633.10 | 679.13 | 725.11 | 756.12 | 723.05 |
| 597.11 | 633.12 | 679.20 | 725.11 | 756.13 | 746.21 |
| 597.15 | 633.12 | 680.03 | 725.12 | 756.17 | he's |
| 597.16 | 633.18 | 680.10 | 725.13 | 756.19 | 034.06 |
| 597.17 | 633.19 | 680.16 | 725.17 | 756.21 | 035.22 |
| 598.01 | 634.12 | 680.20 | 727.11 | 757.08 | 043.22 |
| 598.15 | 634.15 | 681.05 | 727.21 | 757.09 | 058.01 |
| 599.04 | 634.18 | 681.07 | 728.18 | 757.17 | 071.16 |
| 600.03 | 635.09 | 682.06 | 728.19 | 757.21 | 071.17 |
| 600.11 | 635.11 | 682.09 | 728.22 | 758.03 | 094.21 |
| 601.03 | 635.13 | 682.13 | 729.05 | 758.16 | 094.21 |
| 601.05 | 635.14 | 682.15 | 729.06 | 758.17 | 108.18 |
| 602.13 | 635.20 | 682.17 | 729.07 | 758.19 | 160.05 |
| 602.22 | 635.22 | 683.08 | 730.14 | 758.21 | 167.01 |
| 603.04 | 636.08 | 683.11 | 730.18 | 758.22 | 169.02 |
| 603.06 | 636.11 | 683.12 | 730.20 | 759.08 | 177.09 |
| 603.09 | 636.13 | 683.17 | 732.12 | 759.10 | 179.10 |
| 603.16 | 636.15 | 683.20 | 732.17 | 759.20 | 179.11 |
| 603.16 | 636.17 | 684.02 | 732.19 | 760.02 | 183.07 |
| 603.19 | 637.06 | 684.04 | 732.20 | 760.13 | 184.18 |
| 603.21 | 637.07 | 684.07 | 733.01 | 760.17 | 187.01 |
| 604.07 | 637.07 | 684.13 | 733.05 | 761.03 | 187.07 |
| 604.09 | 637.09 | 685.04 | 733.09 | 761.09 | 187.12 |
| 604.12 | 637.10 | 685.13 | 733.12 | 761.12 | 190.20 |
| 604.14 | 638.19 | 686.03 | 734.17 | 761.14 | 190.21 |
| 604.16 | 639.16 | 688.09 | 734.19 | 761.15 | 193.21 |
| 605.01 | 639.19 | 689.06 | 734.22 | 761.16 | 195.04 |
| 605.02 | 639.19 | 694.13 | 735.02 | 763.11 | 195.11 |
| 605.06 | 639.20 | 695.03 | 735.06 | he'd | 229.22 |
| 605.10 | 640.16 | 695.04 | 736.03 | 186.16 | 230.01 |
| 605.20 | 641.02 | 695.12 | 736.05 | 190.18 | 231.16 |
| 606.05 | 641.03 | 696.16 | 737.01 | 223.06 | 232.14 |
| 606.20 | 641.22 | 699.11 | 738.01 | 230.06 | 232.19 |
| 606.21 | 642.01 | 699.17 | 738.03 | 230.09 | 271.19 |
| 607.07 | 642.02 | 700.05 | 738.04 | 259.17 | 284.09 |
| 607.19 | 643.10 | 700.05 | 738.05 | 260.07 | 285.01 |
| 607.21 | 644.08 | 700.06 | 738.08 | 271.08 | 293.19 |
| 608.14 | 644.10 | 700.08 | 738.18 | 275.22 | 315.05 |
| 609.04 | 644.12 | 701.10 | 738.19 | 285.01 | 315.19 |
| 609.11 | 644.16 | 701.15 | 738.19 | 327.03 | 317.01 |
| 609.12 | 644.18 | 701.16 | 739.03 | 385.17 | 341.17 |
| 610.02 | 645.12 | 701.16 | 739.05 | 388.07 | 354.19 |
| 610.05 | 645.20 | 701.18 | 739.07 | 420.08 | 360.19 |
| 611.05 | 646.06 | 701.19 | 739.18 | 546.08 | 388.18 |
| 612.01 | 646.07 | 701.21 | 739.21 | 564.15 | 388.21 |
| 612.03 | 646.18 | 702.03 | 740.03 | 586.02 | 392.10 |
| 612.15 | 647.18 | 702.06 | 740.04 | 62.12 | 392.10 |
| 612.21 | 647.18 | 702.10 | 740.06 | 649.21 | 399.01 |
| 613.07 | 647.22 | 702.14 | 740.08 | 670.02 | 407.01 |
| 613.08 | 648.02 | 702.15 | 740.12 | 670.03 | 416.18 |
| 613.09 | 649.02 | 702.17 | 740.14 | 725.14 | 417.02 |
| 613.10 | 649.03 | 702.18 | 740.19 | 740.19 | 417.09 |
| 613.12 | 649.06 | 703.05 | 740.20 | he'll | 436.01 |
| 613.13 | 649.08 | 703.06 | 741.01 | 007.21 | 437.06 |
| 613.15 | 649.17 | 703.10 | 741.03 | 018.04 | 438.15 |
| 613.17 | 649.18 | 703.10 | 741.04 | 085.09 | 440.07 |
| 613.21 | 650.07 | 704.02 | 741.06 | 127.06 | 441.01 |
| 614.03 | 651.01 | 704.04 | 741.06 | 127.10 | 441.01 |
| 614.16 | 655.16 | 704.07 | 741.10 | 129.02 | 458.09 |
| 615.02 | 655.18 | 704.19 | | 151.21 | 464.03 |

| | | | | | |
|---|---|---|---|---|---|
| 466.21 | 499.02 | 218.22 | 621.21 | 598.12 | 002.06 |
| 469.09 | 509.13 | 239.08 | 624.10 | 602.01 | 007.07 |
| 469.22 | 512.07 | 250.08 | 627.17 | 646.17 | 008.03 |
| 470.07 | 532.09 | 252.01 | 633.06 | 650.16 | 009.17 |
| 476.15 | 538.01 | 262.12 | 635.03 | 653.02 | 011.04 |
| 483.04 | 538.17 | 264.18 | 641.16 | 656.18 | 017.16 |
| 484.04 | 542.07 | 270.08 | 647.16 | 678.20 | 018.13 |
| 484.05 | 552.14 | 270.09 | 652.09 | 695.16 | 021.04 |
| 486.20 | 557.10 | 281.04 | 663.08 | 713.11 | 021.14 |
| 490.08 | 567.02 | 289.18 | 665.10 | 714.02 | 022.19 |
| 490.12 | 591.06 | 294.17 | 679.15 | 719.18 | 023.02 |
| 493.14 | 604.01 | 307.18 | 679.16 | 720.15 | 023.21 |
| 499.09 | 610.08 | 310.12 | 682.01 | 726.04 | 024.06 |
| 524.20 | 626.06 | 324.13 | 698.12 | 733.21 | 025.03 |
| 526.08 | 628.03 | 324.14 | 699.08 | 734.20 | 025.14 |
| 527.05 | 645.02 | 336.16 | 706.02 | 759.14 | 025.15 |
| 543.04 | 654.17 | 343.20 | 710.16 | heart's | 026.17 |
| 543.05 | 676.18 | 354.15 | 725.08 | 060.14 | 028.07 |
| 545.16 | 678.05 | 368.02 | 736.11 | heart-breaking | 028.13 |
| 545.17 | 709.12 | 376.06 | 741.21 | 094.22 | 029.09 |
| 546.14 | 710.15 | 384.04 | 745.05 | 425.21 | 030.17 |
| 546.17 | 716.13 | 391.12 | 755.10 | heart-broken | 031.16 |
| 564.15 | 724.04 | 391.19 | 756.15 | 210.20 | 033.11 |
| 564.16 | 733.18 | 413.03 | 761.16 | hearth | 033.17 |
| 577.04 | 739.06 | 415.13 | hearing | 011.07 | 034.13 |
| 591.16 | 747.11 | 437.09 | 080.04 | 019.01 | 035.06 |
| 592.10 | 762.14 | 439.02 | 165.09 | 044.02 | 036.05 |
| 592.11 | head-ache | 456.01 | 167.21 | 061.13 | 038.16 |
| 592.18 | 127.21 | 469.03 | 185.12 | 063.10 | 039.02 |
| 594.06 | 551.21 | 480.15 | 186.03 | 065.03 | 039.06 |
| 613.18 | head-downmost | 495.05 | 188.02 | 093.02 | 041.01 |
| 628.13 | 163.09 | 500.07 | 254.18 | 104.17 | 041.09 |
| 632.09 | head-stone | 511.20 | 386.21 | 120.20 | 043.13 |
| 645.18 | 287.17 | 533.20 | 412.04 | 134.13 | 045.06 |
| 646.10 | head-stones | 534.17 | 432.22 | 170.02 | 054.16 |
| 647.14 | 764.01 | 554.09 | 546.11 | 192.02 | 055.22 |
| 648.01 | headache | 560.21 | 569.12 | 234.17 | 056.07 |
| 662.01 | 218.16 | 563.02 | 602.20 | 254.01 | 057.21 |
| 662.21 | heads | 568.04 | 671.21 | 313.09 | 058.12 |
| 696.16 | 049.09 | 603.09 | 726.10 | 330.07 | 059.19 |
| 698.04 | 275.14 | 608.18 | hearken | 384.22 | 063.10 |
| 701.18 | 445.08 | 655.17 | 033.20 | 410.02 | 063.19 |
| 702.05 | 586.08 | 660.07 | 033.20 | 434.13 | 064.19 |
| 720.15 | 727.14 | 669.21 | 101.15 | 485.21 | 065.05 |
| 721.02 | 727.19 | 679.11 | 696.08 | 495.17 | 065.07 |
| 741.03 | headstone | 681.09 | hearsay | 531.06 | 071.09 |
| head | 380.05 | 690.13 | 444.16 | 629.05 | 072.05 |
| 008.17 | 746.14 | 693.21 | heart | 645.05 | 072.11 |
| 016.03 | headstrong | 698.22 | 001.12 | 708.22 | 072.21 |
| 016.16 | 145.07 | 706.10 | 019.16 | 728.18 | 073.05 |
| 039.04 | 196.14 | 722.19 | 024.02 | 743.04 | 073.15 |
| 045.04 | 289.06 | 723.08 | 067.20 | hearth-brush | 080.15 |
| 075.01 | health | 736.12 | 076.18 | 692.01 | 081.13 |
| 078.02 | 012.19 | 743.02 | 083.11 | hearth-stone | 082.02 |
| 088.01 | 142.21 | 753.17 | 100.15 | 403.09 | 082.08 |
| 093.09 | 226.13 | heard | 123.02 | 600.16 | 083.05 |
| 093.22 | 227.06 | 002.13 | 125.08 | hearthstone | 083.16 |
| 101.15 | 302.03 | 032.19 | 141.14 | 009.08 | 085.10 |
| 101.21 | 302.08 | 042.08 | 142.19 | 332.08 | 088.02 |
| 110.22 | 349.03 | 051.10 | 144.07 | 541.09 | 090.03 |
| 118.07 | 361.06 | 051.11 | 147.04 | 556.19 | 090.23 |
| 121.02 | 429.08 | 058.07 | 166.16 | 706.01 | 092.01 |
| 132.03 | 457.17 | 058.18 | 176.06 | hearthstun | 093.08 |
| 140.14 | 461.05 | 071.19 | 178.20 | 719.16 | 094.21 |
| 150.20 | 475.10 | 105.20 | 203.03 | heartily | 099.11 |
| 152.17 | 487.07 | 106.13 | 217.21 | 042.09 | 100.07 |
| 157.12 | 542.02 | 108.22 | 229.17 | 089.01 | 100.16 |
| 169.20 | 574.07 | 110.05 | 231.19 | 123.08 | 102.01 |
| 174.02 | 581.14 | 132.13 | 235.10 | 227.03 | 105.17 |
| 179.17 | 590.03 | 140.01 | 240.14 | 403.19 | 106.09 |
| 186.08 | 592.11 | 143.20 | 243.14 | 561.07 | 112.01 |
| 192.21 | 592.13 | 147.09 | 266.13 | heartiness | 112.10 |
| 200.10 | 593.11 | 154.05 | 272.16 | 495.14 | 115.06 |
| 208.14 | healthier | 169.18 | 281.11 | heartless | 115.11 |
| 222.20 | 463.11 | 179.19 | 284.11 | 288.21 | 116.05 |
| 229.19 | healthy | 184.22 | 293.08 | 573.06 | 116.09 |
| 243.11 | 087.03 | 191.15 | 295.15 | 631.17 | 117.06 |
| 244.01 | 143.19 | 194.08 | 305.07 | heartlessness | 117.15 |
| 255.10 | 442.04 | 197.05 | 306.13 | 009.06 | 120.02 |
| 261.17 | 571.08 | 202.14 | 329.16 | hearts | 120.16 |
| 265.17 | 614.05 | 204.20 | 334.20 | 263.02 | 122.07 |
| 274.09 | 732.19 | 206.16 | 336.06 | 389.04 | 124.08 |
| 281.07 | heap | 211.08 | 340.18 | hearty | 126.04 |
| 282.15 | 018.20 | 216.01 | 348.09 | 168.16 | 130.21 |
| 294.07 | 105.01 | 216.13 | 356.19 | 292.11 | 132.04 |
| 297.19 | 558.20 | 232.07 | 359.10 | 460.19 | 132.19 |
| 314.06 | heaped | 266.20 | 361.04 | 603.04 | 133.20 |
| 330.13 | 740.05 | 271.07 | 362.20 | 614.05 | 144.17 |
| 331.06 | heaping | 285.10 | 363.09 | heat | 145.13 |
| 335.02 | 090.05 | 306.06 | 374.12 | 005.22 | 147.09 |
| 358.01 | heaps | 325.18 | 375.14 | 068.01 | 148.05 |
| 367.02 | 015.04 | 349.03 | 376.02 | 304.10 | 148.09 |
| 370.15 | 519.13 | 366.09 | 389.02 | 589.22 | 149.01 |
| 377.09 | hear | 373.03 | 392.11 | 690.01 | 151.04 |
| 383.15 | 017.18 | 382.15 | 397.11 | 693.15 | 151.10 |
| 385.20 | 031.05 | 393.19 | 414.05 | heath | 152.21 |
| 389.17 | 047.05 | 419.20 | 417.14 | 014.04 | 153.11 |
| 393.01 | 048.22 | 443.05 | 419.04 | 179.01 | 153.20 |
| 396.08 | 060.15 | 461.01 | 425.06 | 275.18 | 155.19 |
| 400.02 | 064.12 | 468.14 | 429.02 | 288.02 | 165.12 |
| 409.16 | 073.14 | 473.05 | 446.11 | 380.01 | 165.19 |
| 415.02 | 086.06 | 495.18 | 457.04 | 424.10 | 167.20 |
| 418.18 | 131.16 | 522.21 | 471.08 | 482.16 | 168.22 |
| 428.15 | 134.10 | 528.03 | 502.12 | 557.07 | 169.09 |
| 433.20 | 162.03 | 544.14 | 511.16 | 586.15 | 170.11 |
| 436.08 | 175.18 | 556.14 | 518.04 | 598.21 | 179.06 |
| 443.08 | 177.18 | 564.11 | 524.20 | 690.08 | 179.08 |
| 456.15 | 177.18 | 566.03 | 527.22 | 764.02 | 180.07 |
| 465.20 | 179.21 | 572.11 | 548.14 | 764.08 | 180.14 |
| 467.21 | 200.04 | 572.22 | 576.14 | heathcliff | 181.10 |
| 495.21 | 210.20 | 593.06 | 596.12 | 001.10 | |

| | | | | | |
|---|---|---|---|---|---|
| 181.19 | 360.03 | 609.21 | 315.04 | heedless | 761.01 |
| 181.21 | 360.18 | 611.20 | 322.03 | 188.14 | heir |
| 183.05 | 361.12 | 616.20 | 329.11 | heels | 239.16 |
| 183.07 | 361.13 | 617.12 | 332.06 | 010.20 | 305.09 |
| 184.17 | 364.08 | 618.17 | 348.07 | 456.12 | 369.12 |
| 185.21 | 364.18 | 620.15 | 416.16 | heen | 419.02 |
| 186.21 | 365.08 | 621.09 | 421.10 | 334.13 | 485.02 |
| 187.16 | 366.03 | 622.09 | 433.10 | heifers | 583.12 |
| 194.03 | 366.04 | 623.14 | 442.20 | 276.15 | heirs |
| 194.19 | 369.06 | 630.10 | 446.07 | height | 225.15 |
| 195.07 | 373.01 | 631.12 | 455.02 | 257.05 | held |
| 197.05 | 374.21 | 632.05 | 467.15 | 292.22 | 063.12 |
| 201.10 | 378.07 | 634.21 | 472.02 | 487.04 | 077.18 |
| 203.07 | 379.07 | 636.02 | 472.20 | heights | 117.21 |
| 208.03 | 383.09 | 636.20 | 481.04 | 004.03 | 163.20 |
| 208.15 | 390.12 | 637.14 | 491.21 | 005.14 | 165.16 |
| 210.13 | 391.22 | 639.06 | 528.17 | 014.05 | 178.16 |
| 212.13 | 393.16 | 640.17 | 572.17 | 024.10 | 207.06 |
| 213.04 | 395.08 | 641.11 | 578.15 | 067.12 | 230.14 |
| 213.18 | 397.13 | 644.07 | 615.15 | 073.07 | 236.05 |
| 214.12 | 397.15 | 645.05 | 624.10 | 073.13 | 243.15 |
| 214.20 | 398.15 | 647.10 | 641.17 | 075.15 | 255.20 |
| 215.18 | 399.15 | 648.03 | 665.10 | 103.12 | 269.12 |
| 216.19 | 400.22 | 650.04 | 692.21 | 119.07 | 278.19 |
| 218.16 | 401.12 | 655.08 | 698.12 | 125.19 | 279.17 |
| 218.19 | 402.11 | 656.03 | 699.17 | 141.18 | 287.06 |
| 218.21 | 403.03 | 656.21 | 714.02 | 146.02 | 298.21 |
| 220.17 | 404.07 | 659.01 | 750.15 | 147.17 | 331.05 |
| 221.01 | 405.11 | 660.01 | 764.04 | 179.01 | 361.19 |
| 221.16 | 407.18 | 660.14 | heathen | 188.22 | 362.11 |
| 222.02 | 407.22 | 661.16 | 167.04 | 198.21 | 362.15 |
| 224.11 | 409.07 | 662.12 | heathenism | 209.14 | 375.05 |
| 224.11 | 411.13 | 663.16 | 109.17 | 217.13 | 378.10 |
| 227.19 | 413.03 | 663.22 | heather | 221.04 | 422.13 |
| 228.22 | 414.08 | 664.10 | 283.03 | 222.11 | 446.10 |
| 229.12 | 416.14 | 664.17 | heather-scented | 224.05 | 512.07 |
| 231.12 | 418.18 | 670.18 | 462.19 | 232.01 | 517.19 |
| 232.19 | 419.10 | 670.22 | heating | 241.01 | 538.16 |
| 234.05 | 420.13 | 672.02 | 119.12 | 241.05 | 582.16 |
| 234.16 | 422.18 | 674.04 | heave | 243.10 | 589.05 |
| 235.06 | 426.16 | 676.02 | 064.01 | 244.08 | 658.03 |
| 235.17 | 429.05 | 677.01 | heaved | 279.03 | 662.14 |
| 236.07 | 441.08 | 678.04 | 124.06 | 282.08 | 668.07 |
| 236.20 | 442.15 | 678.18 | 361.19 | 284.03 | 716.21 |
| 237.07 | 443.10 | 680.04 | 680.19 | 302.21 | hell |
| 238.09 | 444.01 | 683.13 | heaven | 306.05 | 033.05 |
| 239.04 | 444.17 | 683.19 | 001.09 | 307.20 | 163.03 |
| 240.02 | 457.11 | 686.02 | 095.03 | 313.21 | 208.19 |
| 241.01 | 460.08 | 686.09 | 095.18 | 328.04 | 260.12 |
| 247.02 | 465.08 | 687.01 | 104.11 | 328.12 | 283.01 |
| 247.03 | 466.11 | 697.15 | 163.03 | 345.08 | 317.06 |
| 247.14 | 467.01 | 698.07 | 178.06 | 350.02 | 324.02 |
| 247.21 | 467.19 | 698.14 | 178.10 | 353.07 | 335.21 |
| 248.12 | 468.09 | 700.03 | 178.19 | 353.10 | 335.22 |
| 248.18 | 469.08 | 704.16 | 179.05 | 369.03 | 345.17 |
| 250.02 | 471.09 | 708.10 | 239.20 | 382.22 | 359.07 |
| 250.10 | 475.11 | 716.20 | 250.19 | 387.03 | 371.15 |
| 251.11 | 477.05 | 717.08 | 316.04 | 410.16 | 407.11 |
| 251.18 | 480.22 | 718.03 | 358.05 | 417.22 | 408.07 |
| 252.16 | 481.12 | 718.17 | 370.22 | 419.06 | 608.16 |
| 253.15 | 482.12 | 720.03 | 371.08 | 422.13 | 671.04 |
| 255.09 | 483.19 | 721.01 | 374.17 | 426.16 | 707.12 |
| 256.08 | 485.12 | 721.22 | 376.17 | 427.10 | 722.16 |
| 257.05 | 486.09 | 722.17 | 558.04 | 429.02 | 734.20 |
| 258.09 | 487.13 | 723.13 | 742.21 | 433.07 | 742.20 |
| 259.03 | 489.10 | 724.20 | 754.10 | 444.08 | hellish |
| 260.08 | 491.06 | 725.16 | 754.21 | 444.15 | 312.03 |
| 261.05 | 493.04 | 726.06 | heaven's | 446.19 | 395.14 |
| 262.17 | 495.01 | 728.05 | 056.10 | 454.13 | helmet |
| 262.22 | 498.03 | 728.18 | 322.16 | 457.13 | 043.17 |
| 265.06 | 500.21 | 732.16 | 365.05 | 459.12 | help |
| 275.20 | 501.03 | 736.02 | 557.13 | 463.03 | 003.18 |
| 281.19 | 501.04 | 737.20 | 600.04 | 475.05 | 020.01 |
| 282.09 | 501.16 | 738.18 | heavens | 480.20 | 027.22 |
| 284.16 | 502.15 | 741.22 | 258.22 | 481.04 | 030.20 |
| 289.10 | 508.02 | 742.14 | heavier | 499.22 | 095.20 |
| 289.19 | 514.11 | 744.10 | 645.09 | 502.08 | 114.14 |
| 293.14 | 524.01 | 745.03 | heaviest | 529.07 | 125.06 |
| 293.15 | 524.06 | 746.12 | 090.05 | 547.04 | 125.08 |
| 294.10 | 526.11 | 747.06 | heaving | 547.19 | 163.06 |
| 298.16 | 527.20 | 748.07 | 011.15 | 554.21 | 170.23 |
| 298.21 | 530.10 | 752.11 | 062.08 | 555.06 | 173.01 |
| 305.13 | 534.01 | 753.21 | 402.13 | 559.14 | 229.10 |
| 307.10 | 535.09 | 756.21 | heavy | 568.02 | 266.12 |
| 309.01 | 536.20 | 757.15 | 006.15 | 573.02 | 292.08 |
| 310.06 | 538.03 | 761.08 | 088.19 | 574.06 | 305.18 |
| 311.16 | 538.21 | heathcliff's | 206.06 | 580.22 | 312.02 |
| 312.06 | 543.01 | 004.04 | 404.12 | 583.14 | 366.15 |
| 313.20 | 544.17 | 012.13 | 529.10 | 586.02 | 367.13 |
| 315.12 | 546.02 | 015.06 | 551.17 | 589.11 | 417.06 |
| 316.18 | 559.03 | 032.04 | 589.22 | 602.22 | 503.17 |
| 322.01 | 562.06 | 043.18 | 660.20 | 606.02 | 535.18 |
| 326.17 | 562.20 | 054.11 | 752.01 | 613.10 | 558.15 |
| 330.15 | 570.12 | 057.04 | heavy-headed | 631.03 | 571.10 |
| 331.11 | 572.09 | 080.11 | 046.21 | 636.01 | 612.04 |
| 333.12 | 578.18 | 123.18 | hector | 637.19 | 621.06 |
| 333.23 | 580.08 | 128.02 | 144.11 | 640.15 | 636.06 |
| 336.19 | 580.15 | 134.09 | hed | 649.01 | 653.09 |
| 337.13 | 583.15 | 179.16 | 719.11 | 653.10 | 660.05 |
| 337.22 | 584.02 | 182.17 | hedge | 654.12 | 663.14 |
| 341.04 | 586.19 | 192.18 | 103.17 | 656.07 | 666.15 |
| 342.11 | 590.22 | 211.15 | 432.19 | 658.02 | 668.06 |
| 345.07 | 592.08 | 215.13 | hedge-cutters | 659.15 | 761.20 |
| 350.03 | 594.04 | 225.17 | 003.15 | 672.13 | helped |
| 351.10 | 598.22 | 226.06 | heead | 673.03 | 075.18 |
| 354.08 | 602.21 | 228.02 | 187.15 | 690.22 | 141.04 |
| 355.09 | 604.15 | 233.14 | 318.14 | 692.06 | 282.16 |
| 356.19 | 605.04 | 254.08 | heed | 692.09 | helping |
| 357.04 | 606.15 | 262.08 | 565.15 | 693.16 | 384.18 |
| 357.20 | 607.13 | 267.21 | heeding | 699.19 | helpless |
| 359.16 | 609.03 | 297.15 | 476.09 | 727.09 | 283.10 |

| | | | | | |
|---|---|---|---|---|---|
| 604.19 | 093.09 | 142.18 | 197.01 | 240.20 | 292.04 |
| hemmed | 093.11 | 142.19 | 197.09 | 248.14 | 292.21 |
| 018.05 | 093.12 | 142.19 | 197.14 | 248.16 | 293.03 |
| 018.21 | 093.15 | 142.21 | 197.17 | 248.20 | 293.04 |
| hence | 094.01 | 143.03 | 197.17 | 249.02 | 294.04 |
| 276.18 | 094.17 | 143.07 | 197.20 | 249.05 | 294.07 |
| 357.13 | 094.18 | 143.08 | 198.01 | 249.05 | 294.12 |
| henceforth | 094.19 | 143.13 | 198.02 | 249.10 | 294.15 |
| 596.03 | 096.08 | 143.14 | 198.06 | 249.15 | 295.08 |
| hend | 096.12 | 143.15 | 198.06 | 249.21 | 295.21 |
| 016.15 | 097.02 | 145.08 | 198.08 | 251.04 | 296.01 |
| 318.17 | 097.03 | 145.08 | 198.09 | 251.10 | 296.02 |
| her | 097.06 | 145.09 | 198.11 | 251.10 | 296.07 |
| 009.01 | 097.07 | 145.10 | 198.18 | 253.21 | 296.18 |
| 009.02 | 097.08 | 145.13 | 199.01 | 254.16 | 296.20 |
| 009.03 | 097.10 | 146.08 | 199.06 | 255.04 | 296.21 |
| 009.12 | 097.14 | 146.17 | 199.07 | 255.11 | 297.02 |
| 009.13 | 097.19 | 146.18 | 199.21 | 255.17 | 297.03 |
| 009.14 | 097.21 | 146.20 | 200.06 | 256.05 | 297.11 |
| 010.07 | 098.02 | 147.02 | 200.07 | 257.19 | 297.16 |
| 010.16 | 098.03 | 147.04 | 202.11 | 259.09 | 297.20 |
| 011.13 | 098.07 | 147.05 | 202.13 | 261.11 | 298.01 |
| 011.16 | 099.03 | 147.06 | 204.10 | 261.13 | 298.18 |
| 015.01 | 099.05 | 147.15 | 204.19 | 261.18 | 298.19 |
| 016.13 | 099.06 | 148.04 | 204.20 | 263.18 | 298.21 |
| 017.13 | 099.07 | 148.11 | 205.13 | 263.19 | 299.04 |
| 017.20 | 099.07 | 148.12 | 205.14 | 264.01 | 299.14 |
| 017.21 | 099.08 | 148.13 | 205.14 | 264.03 | 299.16 |
| 018.07 | 099.11 | 148.17 | 208.09 | 264.17 | 299.18 |
| 019.06 | 103.15 | 149.17 | 208.11 | 265.17 | 299.20 |
| 019.07 | 104.17 | 150.11 | 208.14 | 265.18 | 300.02 |
| 019.13 | 106.07 | 150.13 | 208.14 | 265.21 | 300.04 |
| 019.20 | 106.12 | 150.18 | 210.22 | 266.04 | 301.07 |
| 019.21 | 107.08 | 151.01 | 211.10 | 266.06 | 302.07 |
| 020.05 | 108.14 | 152.17 | 211.14 | 266.06 | 302.10 |
| 020.14 | 108.14 | 154.03 | 211.16 | 266.14 | 302.12 |
| 020.14 | 108.15 | 154.10 | 211.17 | 266.20 | 302.13 |
| 020.15 | 109.02 | 155.17 | 211.22 | 266.21 | 302.15 |
| 024.08 | 109.07 | 155.18 | 212.20 | 267.01 | 302.16 |
| 024.10 | 109.07 | 156.01 | 213.11 | 267.04 | 303.04 |
| 025.03 | 109.13 | 156.05 | 214.19 | 267.07 | 303.18 |
| 025.08 | 109.17 | 156.06 | 215.02 | 267.20 | 303.19 |
| 025.08 | 110.18 | 156.13 | 215.04 | 267.22 | 303.21 |
| 025.16 | 110.22 | 156.14 | 217.01 | 269.04 | 303.22 |
| 026.12 | 110.22 | 156.15 | 219.07 | 269.07 | 304.09 |
| 029.09 | 111.02 | 156.16 | 219.07 | 269.08 | 304.11 |
| 030.10 | 111.04 | 156.18 | 219.09 | 269.11 | 304.13 |
| 030.13 | 111.06 | 156.19 | 219.11 | 270.01 | 304.15 |
| 030.15 | 111.08 | 156.21 | 219.12 | 270.09 | 304.17 |
| 031.03 | 111.09 | 157.11 | 219.13 | 270.15 | 305.05 |
| 035.16 | 111.10 | 157.14 | 220.12 | 270.16 | 305.10 |
| 035.16 | 111.11 | 158.08 | 223.20 | 270.21 | 305.11 |
| 037.04 | 111.11 | 159.05 | 224.04 | 271.02 | 305.12 |
| 039.20 | 111.15 | 159.05 | 224.05 | 271.02 | 305.16 |
| 040.18 | 112.13 | 159.09 | 224.16 | 271.07 | 306.08 |
| 042.10 | 113.03 | 159.13 | 225.11 | 271.12 | 314.20 |
| 044.20 | 113.04 | 160.19 | 225.11 | 271.16 | 328.05 |
| 057.01 | 113.05 | 167.03 | 226.02 | 272.02 | 328.06 |
| 063.12 | 113.06 | 169.20 | 226.11 | 272.03 | 328.07 |
| 063.13 | 113.07 | 169.20 | 226.12 | 272.08 | 328.11 |
| 063.14 | 114.06 | 170.04 | 226.16 | 274.09 | 329.02 |
| 063.15 | 114.06 | 170.05 | 226.18 | 274.11 | 329.04 |
| 063.17 | 114.11 | 170.10 | 226.19 | 274.12 | 329.06 |
| 063.22 | 114.12 | 170.20 | 226.22 | 274.17 | 329.08 |
| 064.01 | 114.15 | 170.23 | 227.03 | 274.18 | 329.21 |
| 064.15 | 114.20 | 171.02 | 227.05 | 274.20 | 330.01 |
| 065.07 | 114.22 | 171.10 | 227.06 | 275.02 | 330.10 |
| 065.08 | 115.01 | 172.09 | 227.08 | 275.05 | 330.10 |
| 067.13 | 116.06 | 172.17 | 227.15 | 277.10 | 330.11 |
| 070.03 | 116.15 | 173.03 | 228.13 | 277.14 | 330.13 |
| 070.08 | 117.21 | 174.09 | 229.11 | 277.14 | 330.14 |
| 070.12 | 117.21 | 176.04 | 229.11 | 277.21 | 331.09 |
| 070.16 | 118.04 | 176.05 | 229.11 | 277.21 | 331.11 |
| 071.04 | 118.10 | 176.13 | 230.16 | 278.01 | 331.14 |
| 072.10 | 119.03 | 176.14 | 231.08 | 278.01 | 332.07 |
| 072.11 | 119.09 | 177.22 | 231.14 | 278.09 | 332.07 |
| 073.03 | 121.08 | 179.20 | 231.18 | 278.10 | 332.12 |
| 073.03 | 121.17 | 180.03 | 233.10 | 278.11 | 332.15 |
| 075.10 | 121.19 | 183.13 | 234.09 | 278.20 | 332.21 |
| 075.13 | 122.12 | 183.15 | 234.10 | 279.12 | 332.23 |
| 078.17 | 122.16 | 184.05 | 234.12 | 279.17 | 332.23 |
| 079.17 | 122.19 | 185.02 | 234.13 | 279.20 | 333.05 |
| 079.18 | 123.07 | 185.05 | 234.15 | 280.01 | 333.06 |
| 079.19 | 123.09 | 185.07 | 234.18 | 283.12 | 333.08 |
| 079.20 | 123.09 | 188.17 | 234.19 | 283.14 | 333.21 |
| 079.21 | 130.05 | 190.02 | 235.09 | 283.17 | 333.22 |
| 082.17 | 130.08 | 190.05 | 235.10 | 283.17 | 334.03 |
| 090.06 | 130.10 | 190.07 | 236.03 | 283.19 | 334.07 |
| 090.12 | 130.11 | 190.08 | 236.05 | 285.05 | 334.18 |
| 090.13 | 130.13 | 190.09 | 236.10 | 285.07 | 334.19 |
| 090.22 | 130.14 | 191.10 | 236.16 | 285.09 | 335.04 |
| 091.01 | 130.15 | 191.11 | 237.05 | 285.20 | 335.06 |
| 091.02 | 130.17 | 192.13 | 237.07 | 285.21 | 335.07 |
| 091.05 | 130.17 | 192.16 | 237.17 | 286.02 | 335.16 |
| 091.06 | 131.05 | 192.21 | 237.18 | 286.07 | 335.22 |
| 091.08 | 132.08 | 193.05 | 237.21 | 286.12 | 336.08 |
| 091.12 | 132.12 | 193.07 | 238.01 | 286.20 | 336.10 |
| 091.12 | 132.13 | 194.16 | 238.05 | 287.01 | 336.10 |
| 091.15 | 132.13 | 195.13 | 238.05 | 287.03 | 336.10 |
| 091.17 | 132.17 | 195.14 | 238.12 | 287.04 | 337.08 |
| 091.18 | 132.20 | 195.15 | 238.14 | 287.06 | 337.09 |
| 091.19 | 134.12 | 195.15 | 239.01 | 288.12 | 337.12 |
| 091.21 | 140.03 | 195.17 | 239.03 | 288.14 | 338.04 |
| 091.22 | 140.14 | 195.18 | 239.03 | 288.16 | 338.05 |
| 092.02 | 140.15 | 196.02 | 239.05 | 288.20 | 338.05 |
| 092.13 | 141.01 | 196.03 | 239.06 | 289.08 | 338.10 |
| 092.14 | 141.03 | 196.04 | 239.16 | 289.09 | 338.16 |
| 092.15 | 142.06 | 196.04 | 239.20 | 290.03 | 339.02 |
| 092.16 | 142.07 | 196.19 | 240.07 | 290.08 | 339.02 |
| 093.07 | 142.08 | 196.22 | 240.19 | 290.09 | 339.04 |
| 093.07 | 142.09 | | | 290.10 | 339.06 |

| | | | | | |
|---|---|---|---|---|---|
| 339.09 | 376.08 | 440.11 | 503.17 | 551.18 | 616.05 |
| 339.16 | 376.09 | 441.05 | 503.18 | 552.01 | 616.05 |
| 339.19 | 376.10 | 441.10 | 503.18 | 552.04 | 617.01 |
| 340.01 | 376.11 | 441.12 | 504.21 | 552.08 | 617.01 |
| 340.04 | 378.02 | 441.15 | 505.16 | 552.09 | 617.05 |
| 340.06 | 378.03 | 441.16 | 505.17 | 552.14 | 619.13 |
| 340.07 | 379.14 | 441.18 | 505.17 | 553.08 | 619.14 |
| 340.11 | 379.20 | 441.18 | 505.21 | 553.09 | 620.07 |
| 340.20 | 380.03 | 441.20 | 505.21 | 553.10 | 620.09 |
| 341.02 | 382.20 | 445.06 | 506.08 | 553.12 | 620.09 |
| 341.03 | 382.20 | 445.12 | 506.09 | 553.13 | 621.10 |
| 341.12 | 383.11 | 445.16 | 506.15 | 553.17 | 623.04 |
| 341.15 | 383.11 | 445.21 | 506.17 | 554.12 | 623.22 |
| 342.12 | 383.13 | 445.22 | 507.13 | 554.18 | 626.05 |
| 343.01 | 383.14 | 446.05 | 508.03 | 554.18 | 626.06 |
| 343.22 | 383.17 | 446.08 | 508.20 | 555.05 | 626.07 |
| 344.21 | 383.17 | 446.10 | 508.22 | 564.02 | 628.01 |
| 345.11 | 384.02 | 446.11 | 509.12 | 566.05 | 628.03 |
| 345.12 | 384.13 | 446.17 | 509.17 | 566.06 | 628.04 |
| 345.12 | 384.14 | 447.03 | 509.18 | 573.12 | 628.05 |
| 345.14 | 384.17 | 448.08 | 509.22 | 573.14 | 628.06 |
| 345.17 | 384.18 | 448.10 | 510.05 | 573.14 | 628.07 |
| 345.18 | 384.22 | 449.01 | 510.06 | 573.18 | 629.16 |
| 345.21 | 385.12 | 449.02 | 510.10 | 573.19 | 629.17 |
| 346.01 | 387.03 | 449.02 | 510.14 | 573.22 | 629.18 |
| 346.02 | 389.10 | 449.03 | 510.14 | 574.01 | 630.12 |
| 346.06 | 398.17 | 449.05 | 510.17 | 575.11 | 630.21 |
| 349.06 | 398.22 | 450.09 | 511.02 | 576.01 | 631.07 |
| 349.09 | 406.12 | 450.12 | 511.16 | 576.02 | 631.15 |
| 350.11 | 408.17 | 450.13 | 512.06 | 576.05 | 631.18 |
| 350.12 | 408.18 | 451.10 | 512.20 | 576.11 | 631.22 |
| 351.04 | 408.19 | 451.10 | 512.20 | 576.13 | 632.13 |
| 351.05 | 408.20 | 452.09 | 513.06 | 576.14 | 632.15 |
| 351.07 | 408.22 | 452.18 | 513.13 | 576.19 | 632.16 |
| 351.09 | 409.10 | 452.22 | 513.15 | 577.08 | 632.16 |
| 351.09 | 410.19 | 453.15 | 513.20 | 577.12 | 632.18 |
| 351.13 | 410.21 | 453.18 | 514.03 | 578.11 | 632.20 |
| 351.16 | 411.04 | 453.21 | 514.06 | 578.14 | 632.22 |
| 351.19 | 411.06 | 457.01 | 516.03 | 578.16 | 633.03 |
| 351.21 | 411.08 | 457.02 | 516.05 | 578.17 | 633.06 |
| 352.03 | 411.10 | 459.10 | 516.06 | 578.21 | 633.08 |
| 352.04 | 411.17 | 459.12 | 516.12 | 578.22 | 633.11 |
| 352.06 | 411.18 | 461.06 | 516.21 | 579.01 | 633.13 |
| 352.12 | 411.21 | 464.19 | 517.02 | 579.02 | 633.15 |
| 352.13 | 411.22 | 472.08 | 517.07 | 579.03 | 634.01 |
| 352.14 | 412.20 | 473.11 | 517.12 | 579.04 | 634.02 |
| 352.20 | 413.17 | 474.03 | 517.13 | 579.05 | 634.02 |
| 352.20 | 414.12 | 474.06 | 517.14 | 579.08 | 634.04 |
| 352.22 | 414.13 | 474.10 | 517.16 | 579.14 | 634.09 |
| 353.17 | 415.05 | 474.12 | 518.03 | 579.19 | 635.14 |
| 353.21 | 424.10 | 475.02 | 518.04 | 580.19 | 636.17 |
| 354.02 | 425.04 | 475.09 | 518.05 | 580.20 | 636.18 |
| 354.03 | 425.08 | 478.01 | 518.08 | 580.21 | 636.19 |
| 354.04 | 425.09 | 478.05 | 519.14 | 580.22 | 636.19 |
| 354.10 | 425.11 | 478.08 | 519.14 | 581.13 | 637.03 |
| 354.15 | 425.12 | 478.12 | 519.17 | 583.10 | 637.14 |
| 354.19 | 425.15 | 478.15 | 519.20 | 583.10 | 637.15 |
| 355.14 | 425.19 | 478.19 | 519.21 | 585.05 | 637.22 |
| 355.18 | 425.20 | 479.16 | 520.21 | 587.02 | 637.22 |
| 355.18 | 426.02 | 479.17 | 522.12 | 587.07 | 639.01 |
| 356.04 | 426.03 | 479.17 | 522.14 | 587.09 | 639.02 |
| 356.06 | 426.05 | 479.19 | 522.21 | 587.20 | 639.02 |
| 356.11 | 426.10 | 480.06 | 525.20 | 588.13 | 639.04 |
| 356.17 | 426.12 | 480.12 | 526.14 | 588.15 | 639.05 |
| 357.05 | 426.13 | 480.14 | 526.17 | 590.09 | 639.07 |
| 357.14 | 426.15 | 480.18 | 526.17 | 590.19 | 639.15 |
| 357.15 | 426.17 | 480.20 | 526.20 | 591.05 | 639.17 |
| 357.18 | 426.19 | 480.21 | 528.01 | 591.10 | 639.20 |
| 358.06 | 427.08 | 481.07 | 528.07 | 594.07 | 639.21 |
| 358.06 | 428.15 | 483.09 | 528.13 | 594.10 | 640.06 |
| 358.07 | 428.19 | 483.16 | 528.14 | 594.22 | 640.11 |
| 358.07 | 428.22 | 483.17 | 528.15 | 596.08 | 640.13 |
| 358.10 | 429.06 | 484.03 | 529.05 | 596.08 | 641.12 |
| 358.12 | 429.06 | 484.06 | 529.09 | 596.12 | 641.14 |
| 358.13 | 429.09 | 484.08 | 529.09 | 597.02 | 641.16 |
| 358.15 | 429.14 | 484.09 | 534.02 | 597.02 | 641.18 |
| 359.10 | 429.17 | 484.11 | 534.10 | 597.03 | 642.09 |
| 360.03 | 429.20 | 485.15 | 534.15 | 597.06 | 642.11 |
| 360.04 | 429.21 | 485.17 | 536.16 | 597.07 | 643.11 |
| 360.12 | 430.04 | 485.18 | 536.17 | 597.08 | 645.03 |
| 361.14 | 430.10 | 485.19 | 536.18 | 597.10 | 645.12 |
| 361.16 | 430.17 | 485.20 | 536.21 | 598.11 | 646.14 |
| 361.18 | 430.20 | 487.04 | 537.19 | 599.08 | 646.20 |
| 361.22 | 430.20 | 487.04 | 538.13 | 599.13 | 646.21 |
| 362.07 | 430.22 | 487.06 | 538.18 | 601.16 | 646.22 |
| 362.14 | 431.01 | 488.10 | 539.07 | 602.13 | 648.13 |
| 362.15 | 431.07 | 489.11 | 539.13 | 602.14 | 648.14 |
| 362.16 | 431.08 | 489.17 | 540.19 | 605.16 | 648.15 |
| 362.16 | 431.16 | 490.03 | 541.19 | 605.17 | 648.18 |
| 365.14 | 432.01 | 490.08 | 542.19 | 607.02 | 648.22 |
| 365.20 | 432.05 | 490.13 | 542.20 | 607.05 | 649.01 |
| 365.22 | 432.12 | 490.17 | 544.18 | 607.12 | 649.14 |
| 366.12 | 432.17 | 492.08 | 546.13 | 608.20 | 649.16 |
| 366.14 | 432.18 | 492.14 | 547.11 | 609.05 | 650.11 |
| 367.02 | 432.19 | 492.22 | 548.09 | 609.06 | 650.21 |
| 367.06 | 433.03 | 495.18 | 548.11 | 609.10 | 651.06 |
| 367.13 | 433.15 | 499.01 | 548.12 | 609.18 | 651.10 |
| 367.18 | 434.14 | 499.13 | 548.12 | 609.19 | 651.10 |
| 367.21 | 434.14 | 499.13 | 548.14 | 609.20 | 651.17 |
| 367.21 | 434.19 | 500.02 | 548.16 | 610.05 | 652.01 |
| 370.20 | 434.22 | 500.12 | 548.19 | 610.06 | 653.04 |
| 370.20 | 436.07 | 500.16 | 549.01 | 610.20 | 653.07 |
| 370.21 | 436.08 | 500.18 | 549.02 | 610.20 | 653.09 |
| 371.08 | 436.11 | 500.19 | 550.09 | 611.01 | 653.16 |
| 372.05 | 436.14 | 502.05 | 550.10 | 611.15 | 653.17 |
| 372.17 | 437.10 | 502.18 | 550.12 | 611.16 | 654.08 |
| 372.17 | 437.12 | 503.05 | 551.09 | 613.06 | 654.09 |
| 374.07 | 438.05 | 503.05 | 551.09 | 614.01 | 654.13 |
| 374.18 | 438.18 | 503.12 | 551.15 | 615.01 | 654.17 |
| 376.02 | 438.21 | 503.13 | 551.16 | 615.03 | 655.03 |
| 376.07 | 439.22 | 503.17 | 551.17 | 615.19 | |

| | | | | | |
|---|---|---|---|---|---|
| 656.02 | 692.03 | 732.02 | 492.07 | 261.15 | high |
| 656.04 | 692.04 | 737.13 | 499.07 | 263.20 | 011.16 |
| 656.10 | 692.15 | 738.15 | 508.07 | 266.05 | 092.21 |
| 656.14 | 694.22 | 741.02 | 512.02 | 268.05 | 122.09 |
| 656.17 | 695.03 | 762.14 | 512.22 | 274.13 | 125.22 |
| 657.03 | 695.04 | 763.03 | 518.17 | 275.07 | 206.08 |
| 658.03 | 697.06 | 763.06 | 533.19 | 285.08 | 256.13 |
| 658.05 | 698.09 | her's | 544.17 | 290.11 | 425.05 |
| 658.11 | 698.10 | 145.19 | 576.08 | 292.07 | 427.19 |
| 658.11 | 699.10 | 370.20 | 580.19 | 293.01 | 433.05 |
| 658.12 | 700.01 | 660.13 | 586.06 | 332.16 | 474.03 |
| 659.01 | 700.08 | herbs | 587.16 | 339.03 | 517.18 |
| 659.02 | 700.09 | 348.06 | 589.14 | 340.05 | 542.13 |
| 659.07 | 700.13 | hercules | 590.08 | 341.08 | 542.15 |
| 659.08 | 700.20 | 339.10 | 592.22 | 343.20 | 557.10 |
| 659.15 | 700.22 | 729.11 | 594.11 | 352.10 | 599.02 |
| 659.21 | 701.03 | herd | 599.11 | 361.11 | 667.11 |
| 660.15 | 701.12 | 011.22 | 609.01 | 361.15 | 668.04 |
| 660.19 | 701.15 | herd-boy | 613.20 | 366.15 | high-backed |
| 661.08 | 703.06 | 585.11 | 614.10 | 375.20 | 006.13 |
| 661.10 | 703.11 | here | 616.09 | 426.10 | high-water |
| 662.13 | 703.12 | 003.11 | 620.08 | 428.10 | 090.12 |
| 662.13 | 703.14 | 005.12 | 620.21 | 429.22 | higher |
| 662.14 | 703.14 | 012.15 | 623.21 | 430.19 | 246.15 |
| 662.16 | 703.17 | 025.04 | 627.01 | 431.17 | 427.17 |
| 663.05 | 704.03 | 029.16 | 628.02 | 434.13 | 682.21 |
| 663.18 | 704.07 | 032.05 | 635.17 | 441.03 | highest |
| 664.01 | 704.12 | 039.01 | 646.13 | 449.21 | 105.13 |
| 664.02 | 704.15 | 042.03 | 656.15 | 450.15 | highly |
| 664.06 | 705.06 | 044.18 | 660.08 | 475.08 | 310.16 |
| 664.07 | 705.06 | 049.06 | 670.13 | 493.02 | 481.19 |
| 664.10 | 705.16 | 054.09 | 672.17 | 506.16 | highway |
| 664.12 | 705.19 | 056.09 | 677.19 | 509.16 | 243.05 |
| 664.14 | 705.21 | 057.11 | 678.12 | 518.10 | 522.09 |
| 665.01 | 706.02 | 059.02 | 684.17 | 522.06 | highways |
| 665.02 | 706.02 | 066.13 | 690.21 | 523.07 | 203.14 |
| 665.03 | 706.14 | 070.04 | 691.06 | 531.06 | higs |
| 665.05 | 706.18 | 072.12 | 697.14 | 538.08 | 233.06 |
| 665.07 | 707.17 | 075.12 | 700.05 | 548.21 | hilarity |
| 665.09 | 707.22 | 077.18 | 703.07 | 550.10 | 027.06 |
| 665.11 | 708.02 | 098.08 | 720.18 | 594.09 | hill |
| 665.12 | 708.04 | 105.11 | 742.04 | 607.06 | 015.09 |
| 665.12 | 708.06 | 106.01 | 751.10 | 614.05 | hill-back |
| 666.11 | 708.09 | 107.13 | 762.06 | 653.21 | 065.19 |
| 666.19 | 708.18 | 108.08 | 763.19 | 659.03 | hillock |
| 666.22 | 708.23 | 114.14 | here's | 659.17 | 480.07 |
| 667.01 | 709.10 | 116.05 | 168.15 | 663.17 | hillocks |
| 667.02 | 709.10 | 136.11 | 321.01 | 667.20 | 480.10 |
| 667.02 | 710.05 | 136.21 | hereafter | 671.14 | hills |
| 667.05 | 710.15 | 151.08 | 223.13 | 674.12 | 007.06 |
| 667.07 | 710.19 | 154.17 | 257.01 | 710.01 | 027.18 |
| 667.12 | 711.01 | 159.03 | 265.06 | 710.18 | 032.03 |
| 667.13 | 711.02 | 176.03 | 288.15 | hesitate | 047.13 |
| 667.14 | 712.06 | 176.03 | 299.18 | 054.05 | 137.17 |
| 668.03 | 712.08 | 180.05 | 333.09 | 228.14 | 283.04 |
| 668.05 | 713.13 | 182.16 | 371.16 | 344.05 | 303.10 |
| 668.05 | 715.09 | 193.10 | 459.09 | hesitated | 427.01 |
| 668.07 | 716.07 | 195.11 | 489.05 | 246.01 | 427.04 |
| 668.07 | 716.16 | 199.01 | 503.08 | 430.03 | 436.15 |
| 668.18 | 717.03 | 203.04 | 619.08 | 629.03 | 460.17 |
| 668.22 | 717.04 | 207.11 | heretofore | hesitating | 463.22 |
| 669.01 | 717.14 | 208.08 | 715.06 | 376.04 | 569.19 |
| 669.07 | 717.22 | 212.03 | hermit | hesitation | 598.05 |
| 669.16 | 718.04 | 212.11 | 311.18 | 193.13 | 604.12 |
| 669.19 | 719.05 | 235.03 | 413.04 | heterodox | 676.13 |
| 669.21 | 720.12 | 250.13 | hermit's | 372.13 | 689.05 |
| 670.21 | 720.14 | 255.19 | 201.02 | hev | 690.07 |
| 671.08 | 720.14 | 260.03 | hero | 191.01 | 704.21 |
| 671.09 | 721.08 | 266.21 | 202.13 | 318.13 | hilltop |
| 671.16 | 721.13 | 273.20 | 338.13 | 326.11 | 288.07 |
| 671.19 | 721.15 | 275.12 | 606.18 | 457.22 | hilly |
| 673.05 | 722.03 | 276.01 | heroine | 719.10 | 154.12 |
| 673.05 | 722.11 | 276.10 | 202.14 | 719.14 | him |
| 673.07 | 722.18 | 278.03 | herrings | 758.17 | 001.13 |
| 674.15 | 722.19 | 280.04 | 163.15 | hev'em | 007.04 |
| 674.15 | 722.20 | 286.09 | hers | 696.06 | 007.15 |
| 674.16 | 722.20 | 292.11 | 093.22 | hey | 008.03 |
| 675.03 | 722.23 | 298.04 | 204.22 | 034.08 | 010.04 |
| 675.03 | 723.01 | 303.03 | 215.07 | 034.08 | 013.12 |
| 675.06 | 723.14 | 307.06 | 446.08 | 034.08 | 013.19 |
| 675.09 | 723.17 | 311.12 | 528.02 | 309.22 | 016.07 |
| 675.10 | 723.19 | 311.17 | 631.11 | hid | 016.21 |
| 675.12 | 723.21 | 315.13 | 632.13 | 183.13 | 019.23 |
| 675.17 | 724.03 | 323.17 | 633.12 | 324.08 | 026.19 |
| 675.21 | 724.04 | 332.03 | 649.17 | 364.05 | 029.07 |
| 676.03 | 724.04 | 343.14 | 650.17 | 467.17 | 032.16 |
| 676.04 | 724.11 | 346.08 | 653.15 | hidden | 033.03 |
| 676.05 | 724.12 | 347.19 | 702.07 | 010.19 | 033.05 |
| 676.06 | 724.16 | 359.20 | 713.10 | 290.06 | 033.14 |
| 676.09 | 724.19 | 360.01 | 724.22 | 381.09 | 034.09 |
| 676.12 | 725.01 | 360.22 | herself | 516.18 | 034.09 |
| 676.18 | 725.02 | 364.17 | 025.05 | hide | 042.08 |
| 676.22 | 725.08 | 365.04 | 028.13 | 037.03 | 045.07 |
| 677.08 | 725.09 | 382.14 | 031.02 | 148.15 | 045.08 |
| 677.14 | 725.18 | 386.02 | 042.10 | 160.19 | 045.10 |
| 677.15 | 725.18 | 389.09 | 079.06 | 231.21 | 045.14 |
| 679.04 | 725.20 | 395.15 | 130.20 | 238.06 | 048.01 |
| 681.17 | 726.07 | 427.16 | 134.11 | 352.20 | 049.15 |
| 682.02 | 726.10 | 434.06 | 141.12 | 492.11 | 049.15 |
| 682.03 | 727.09 | 435.09 | 148.19 | 506.19 | 049.16 |
| 682.04 | 728.09 | 450.05 | 150.21 | 554.16 | 049.17 |
| 682.20 | 728.10 | 455.18 | 176.13 | 567.10 | 050.04 |
| 682.20 | 729.03 | 460.18 | 185.06 | 595.07 | 054.19 |
| 683.06 | 729.04 | 473.07 | 196.06 | 633.09 | 054.20 |
| 684.01 | 730.11 | 473.08 | 197.12 | hideous | 055.04 |
| 687.02 | 730.13 | 481.10 | 215.14 | 164.03 | 058.18 |
| 691.11 | 731.09 | 483.03 | 234.01 | 316.05 | 062.07 |
| 691.13 | 731.13 | 489.02 | 235.21 | 745.14 | 063.02 |
| 691.14 | 731.13 | 489.16 | 240.18 | hieroglyphics | 074.01 |
| 691.16 | 731.14 | 489.19 | 249.22 | 040.18 | 074.04 |
| 691.22 | 731.18 | 490.20 | | | |

| | | | | | |
|---|---|---|---|---|---|
| 077.03 | 157.15 | 229.05 | 342.09 | 429.18 | 487.13 |
| 079.02 | 157.21 | 229.07 | 344.05 | 429.21 | 487.20 |
| 080.14 | 159.17 | 229.17 | 344.06 | 432.15 | 489.02 |
| 080.16 | 160.04 | 230.02 | 346.16 | 439.14 | 489.14 |
| 080.19 | 160.08 | 230.11 | 346.18 | 439.18 | 490.04 |
| 080.21 | 162.12 | 231.15 | 346.20 | 441.21 | 490.09 |
| 081.02 | 165.02 | 231.20 | 347.20 | 442.16 | 491.17 |
| 081.06 | 165.03 | 232.08 | 350.03 | 442.22 | 492.21 |
| 081.12 | 165.05 | 236.14 | 352.17 | 443.07 | 493.11 |
| 081.15 | 165.16 | 238.08 | 352.21 | 443.07 | 493.20 |
| 082.12 | 166.01 | 240.09 | 355.16 | 443.12 | 494.02 |
| 082.15 | 166.20 | 242.06 | 356.02 | 443.17 | 494.05 |
| 082.19 | 166.21 | 242.09 | 356.05 | 443.19 | 494.19 |
| 084.01 | 167.04 | 244.21 | 357.06 | 444.05 | 496.13 |
| 084.03 | 167.10 | 245.22 | 360.06 | 444.07 | 496.15 |
| 084.09 | 167.13 | 246.03 | 360.10 | 444.10 | 498.04 |
| 084.17 | 167.20 | 246.19 | 360.19 | 445.20 | 498.15 |
| 085.01 | 168.09 | 247.05 | 362.07 | 445.21 | 499.11 |
| 085.05 | 169.03 | 247.16 | 362.11 | 446.07 | 499.19 |
| 085.07 | 169.07 | 247.18 | 365.14 | 446.08 | 500.16 |
| 085.13 | 171.19 | 250.17 | 368.01 | 449.11 | 501.06 |
| 085.22 | 171.19 | 250.18 | 370.18 | 451.07 | 501.09 |
| 086.04 | 172.05 | 250.19 | 373.10 | 451.08 | 501.21 |
| 087.04 | 172.10 | 252.18 | 373.17 | 451.18 | 501.22 |
| 087.06 | 172.12 | 254.22 | 373.20 | 451.20 | 502.14 |
| 087.08 | 173.06 | 256.11 | 374.07 | 451.20 | 503.15 |
| 087.12 | 173.20 | 256.13 | 375.10 | 452.01 | 504.09 |
| 088.03 | 174.04 | 257.21 | 375.17 | 452.18 | 504.15 |
| 088.12 | 174.15 | 258.19 | 377.19 | 452.21 | 504.20 |
| 089.10 | 174.19 | 259.12 | 378.10 | 453.04 | 505.01 |
| 089.20 | 174.19 | 259.13 | 378.16 | 453.19 | 505.03 |
| 089.22 | 175.14 | 259.19 | 385.09 | 453.21 | 511.09 |
| 091.02 | 177.12 | 260.14 | 385.22 | 453.22 | 511.17 |
| 091.16 | 179.09 | 260.14 | 386.10 | 454.05 | 512.17 |
| 093.11 | 179.17 | 260.16 | 387.16 | 454.07 | 515.11 |
| 093.19 | 179.20 | 261.21 | 388.01 | 454.09 | 521.02 |
| 093.21 | 180.07 | 262.02 | 388.07 | 454.20 | 521.02 |
| 094.02 | 181.15 | 262.08 | 388.10 | 455.05 | 521.03 |
| 094.07 | 181.17 | 262.10 | 388.11 | 455.09 | 521.05 |
| 094.10 | 181.22 | 262.18 | 388.15 | 456.18 | 521.08 |
| 096.05 | 182.02 | 263.09 | 388.15 | 457.02 | 521.09 |
| 098.16 | 182.09 | 266.11 | 389.02 | 457.04 | 521.15 |
| 099.12 | 184.11 | 266.17 | 389.05 | 457.06 | 521.16 |
| 099.13 | 184.18 | 268.05 | 389.21 | 457.08 | 521.18 |
| 099.14 | 185.01 | 269.12 | 390.12 | 457.09 | 521.20 |
| 099.17 | 185.03 | 271.20 | 390.14 | 457.15 | 524.03 |
| 099.20 | 185.08 | 272.12 | 391.07 | 457.15 | 524.07 |
| 099.21 | 185.19 | 272.18 | 392.08 | 457.23 | 524.22 |
| 100.03 | 185.21 | 273.03 | 393.20 | 458.04 | 525.02 |
| 100.07 | 186.01 | 273.04 | 394.03 | 458.06 | 525.05 |
| 102.02 | 186.16 | 273.11 | 394.05 | 458.10 | 526.06 |
| 102.14 | 187.02 | 275.21 | 394.15 | 459.09 | 526.09 |
| 108.11 | 187.15 | 281.02 | 395.13 | 460.01 | 527.10 |
| 108.17 | 187.18 | 282.18 | 396.02 | 460.09 | 527.11 |
| 111.21 | 188.07 | 285.02 | 396.15 | 460.20 | 529.02 |
| 112.09 | 190.16 | 285.18 | 397.07 | 460.21 | 531.03 |
| 115.15 | 191.10 | 286.06 | 397.13 | 461.01 | 532.07 |
| 115.16 | 191.14 | 286.21 | 397.14 | 461.04 | 534.06 |
| 115.16 | 194.13 | 287.05 | 399.03 | 461.08 | 536.06 |
| 116.16 | 194.14 | 292.01 | 400.01 | 461.09 | 537.04 |
| 117.05 | 194.21 | 293.09 | 400.06 | 461.11 | 537.08 |
| 117.13 | 194.21 | 293.11 | 401.02 | 461.14 | 537.10 |
| 120.04 | 195.03 | 293.17 | 401.06 | 461.15 | 538.09 |
| 120.11 | 195.09 | 294.02 | 401.09 | 462.08 | 538.16 |
| 120.12 | 195.10 | 294.14 | 401.13 | 462.12 | 540.16 |
| 121.08 | 198.13 | 294.15 | 401.15 | 462.16 | 541.15 |
| 121.20 | 198.16 | 295.20 | 402.02 | 464.08 | 541.20 |
| 122.04 | 199.03 | 296.05 | 402.19 | 464.12 | 541.22 |
| 122.15 | 199.12 | 298.17 | 403.04 | 464.12 | 542.02 |
| 123.16 | 199.21 | 305.17 | 403.07 | 465.03 | 542.08 |
| 123.20 | 202.03 | 306.10 | 404.06 | 465.11 | 545.13 |
| 123.21 | 205.18 | 306.16 | 405.14 | 465.12 | 545.15 |
| 127.01 | 207.21 | 309.01 | 405.16 | 467.12 | 545.18 |
| 127.03 | 210.06 | 309.10 | 405.18 | 467.16 | 545.20 |
| 127.05 | 210.14 | 310.15 | 405.20 | 467.20 | 545.21 |
| 127.14 | 210.18 | 312.09 | 406.02 | 469.09 | 546.06 |
| 128.12 | 211.21 | 313.06 | 406.03 | 469.12 | 546.09 |
| 128.17 | 212.02 | 314.01 | 406.03 | 469.14 | 546.19 |
| 128.21 | 212.06 | 316.02 | 407.06 | 469.20 | 555.06 |
| 129.02 | 212.07 | 316.04 | 407.10 | 470.05 | 555.15 |
| 129.04 | 212.21 | 316.14 | 407.19 | 470.05 | 555.19 |
| 129.09 | 213.07 | 316.15 | 408.06 | 470.10 | 555.20 |
| 131.01 | 213.13 | 316.15 | 409.13 | 470.13 | 556.02 |
| 132.05 | 214.12 | 316.21 | 409.21 | 470.14 | 556.04 |
| 132.07 | 214.13 | 317.02 | 411.12 | 470.16 | 556.06 |
| 132.20 | 215.02 | 317.12 | 411.17 | 470.19 | 556.07 |
| 133.01 | 217.16 | 321.11 | 412.18 | 471.10 | 559.05 |
| 133.08 | 218.10 | 325.01 | 412.19 | 472.10 | 560.08 |
| 133.09 | 218.18 | 325.22 | 413.04 | 472.19 | 560.09 |
| 133.11 | 218.20 | 326.06 | 413.15 | 472.20 | 560.10 |
| 136.16 | 218.22 | 326.11 | 414.10 | 473.10 | 561.15 |
| 140.02 | 219.01 | 326.20 | 414.15 | 474.08 | 561.16 |
| 140.17 | 220.10 | 327.06 | 415.09 | 475.01 | 562.09 |
| 141.09 | 220.12 | 327.13 | 416.15 | 475.03 | 562.12 |
| 142.17 | 220.22 | 327.14 | 416.18 | 475.12 | 562.20 |
| 142.22 | 220.22 | 328.03 | 417.07 | 475.16 | 563.12 |
| 143.02 | 221.02 | 328.06 | 417.17 | 476.14 | 563.14 |
| 143.10 | 221.13 | 331.20 | 418.07 | 476.18 | 563.16 |
| 143.19 | 221.15 | 332.11 | 418.17 | 476.20 | 563.20 |
| 143.20 | 221.17 | 334.14 | 419.02 | 477.03 | 564.06 |
| 143.21 | 221.17 | 334.16 | 419.05 | 477.07 | 564.17 |
| 147.12 | 222.09 | 334.18 | 419.16 | 477.12 | 565.18 |
| 147.19 | 222.13 | 336.09 | 419.20 | 477.14 | 566.10 |
| 147.21 | 222.20 | 336.11 | 420.01 | 482.13 | 566.17 |
| 149.14 | 223.01 | 336.12 | 420.05 | 485.14 | 567.11 |
| 149.20 | 223.08 | 336.23 | 420.10 | 485.16 | 567.18 |
| 150.15 | 224.06 | 337.01 | 421.18 | 485.19 | 569.10 |
| 151.02 | 224.17 | 340.17 | 422.05 | 486.01 | 569.13 |
| 151.20 | 225.21 | 341.10 | 426.11 | 486.14 | 571.15 |
| 152.16 | 228.15 | 341.19 | 428.07 | 487.01 | 571.16 |
| 157.13 | 229.01 | 342.05 | 429.17 | 487.11 | 572.10 |

| | | | | | |
|---|---|---|---|---|---|
| 572.11 | 660.10 | 762.08 | 679.12 | 494.03 | 062.15 |
| 572.18 | 661.02 | him's | 683.03 | 494.16 | 062.19 |
| 574.03 | 661.18 | 471.16 | 686.16 | hindley's | 062.22 |
| 576.13 | 662.15 | himself | 701.07 | 081.05 | 063.04 |
| 577.01 | 662.16 | 018.13 | 702.16 | 088.09 | 063.20 |
| 577.08 | 663.13 | 020.19 | 703.15 | 105.14 | 064.04 |
| 577.11 | 666.02 | 026.06 | 704.21 | 141.13 | 064.19 |
| 578.21 | 666.15 | 027.03 | 724.16 | 160.17 | 065.06 |
| 580.04 | 667.05 | 031.17 | 724.20 | 444.21 | 065.06 |
| 580.06 | 667.06 | 038.10 | 725.15 | hinges | 070.09 |
| 580.10 | 668.10 | 054.06 | 725.22 | 321.02 | 072.06 |
| 580.11 | 669.02 | 059.18 | 734.18 | 633.07 | 073.21 |
| 582.02 | 671.05 | 062.01 | 735.02 | hint | 074.05 |
| 582.03 | 671.19 | 077.12 | 736.07 | 227.21 | 074.07 |
| 582.11 | 674.01 | 081.08 | 750.10 | 257.15 | 074.08 |
| 582.19 | 674.08 | 085.17 | 756.15 | 288.20 | 076.07 |
| 583.05 | 679.12 | 088.17 | 758.22 | 331.07 | 076.20 |
| 584.02 | 683.01 | 089.14 | 760.09 | 422.06 | 077.01 |
| 586.09 | 683.02 | 102.01 | hinder | hips | 077.05 |
| 586.11 | 683.12 | 112.06 | 002.17 | 522.07 | 077.17 |
| 586.22 | 683.14 | 115.16 | 094.18 | hired | 077.18 |
| 589.09 | 683.19 | 116.04 | 117.15 | 440.07 | 078.18 |
| 590.04 | 683.21 | 116.12 | 163.17 | hiring | 078.22 |
| 590.10 | 684.03 | 141.15 | 175.01 | 470.02 | 080.04 |
| 590.13 | 684.09 | 143.21 | 283.11 | his | 080.06 |
| 590.20 | 689.18 | 144.03 | 417.18 | 001.13 | 081.01 |
| 591.12 | 694.15 | 144.21 | 488.11 | 002.02 | 081.07 |
| 591.18 | 694.19 | 147.21 | 607.04 | 002.04 | 081.11 |
| 592.03 | 701.10 | 149.01 | 615.13 | 003.06 | 082.01 |
| 592.06 | 701.13 | 157.09 | 641.07 | 003.22 | 082.02 |
| 592.20 | 701.14 | 165.15 | 665.09 | 004.01 | 082.03 |
| 594.14 | 702.03 | 166.09 | 690.02 | 005.05 | 082.10 |
| 597.17 | 702.07 | 167.08 | 729.17 | 005.08 | 083.01 |
| 597.18 | 702.15 | 168.21 | hindered | 007.03 | 083.04 |
| 600.12 | 703.01 | 169.12 | 267.07 | 007.03 | 083.07 |
| 600.20 | 703.15 | 182.19 | 403.19 | 007.08 | 083.09 |
| 601.15 | 705.05 | 189.21 | hindering | 007.13 | 083.11 |
| 602.09 | 708.12 | 198.17 | 344.15 | 007.18 | 083.13 |
| 602.09 | 709.16 | 207.07 | hindley | 008.04 | 084.03 |
| 602.19 | 709.17 | 221.22 | 040.21 | 009.18 | 085.01 |
| 603.15 | 710.07 | 222.04 | 041.07 | 010.04 | 085.11 |
| 604.05 | 710.08 | 240.10 | 043.15 | 011.04 | 085.12 |
| 604.06 | 710.10 | 249.08 | 044.01 | 013.02 | 085.14 |
| 604.10 | 710.21 | 251.17 | 045.03 | 013.07 | 085.18 |
| 604.20 | 712.08 | 269.04 | 045.07 | 016.03 | 086.01 |
| 605.04 | 715.12 | 270.01 | 075.16 | 019.23 | 087.03 |
| 605.20 | 716.19 | 296.04 | 076.05 | 020.18 | 087.07 |
| 605.21 | 717.11 | 310.09 | 076.13 | 020.20 | 087.11 |
| 606.09 | 717.21 | 311.04 | 079.09 | 021.01 | 088.01 |
| 607.02 | 718.17 | 333.13 | 080.19 | 021.04 | 088.06 |
| 607.05 | 720.16 | 341.15 | 083.04 | 021.05 | 088.10 |
| 607.06 | 720.17 | 358.12 | 083.18 | 021.06 | 088.12 |
| 607.09 | 721.11 | 362.03 | 084.03 | 021.06 | 088.16 |
| 608.04 | 722.08 | 365.01 | 084.09 | 021.08 | 089.03 |
| 609.10 | 722.16 | 365.09 | 084.17 | 021.11 | 089.05 |
| 610.10 | 722.18 | 375.11 | 085.12 | 021.13 | 089.07 |
| 611.19 | 723.09 | 377.19 | 088.20 | 022.01 | 089.14 |
| 613.05 | 723.10 | 378.19 | 089.22 | 022.16 | 089.15 |
| 614.15 | 723.20 | 388.07 | 096.02 | 024.04 | 089.20 |
| 615.09 | 724.13 | 390.04 | 099.10 | 025.01 | 089.21 |
| 615.19 | 724.14 | 390.18 | 101.10 | 025.02 | 091.03 |
| 617.11 | 724.15 | 392.06 | 112.01 | 025.20 | 091.10 |
| 617.14 | 725.12 | 399.11 | 114.06 | 026.04 | 091.13 |
| 617.17 | 725.14 | 403.09 | 116.10 | 027.04 | 091.14 |
| 618.16 | 725.19 | 411.18 | 126.22 | 027.06 | 091.15 |
| 619.06 | 726.08 | 415.02 | 127.15 | 028.17 | 092.01 |
| 620.06 | 727.15 | 419.19 | 129.16 | 033.06 | 092.03 |
| 620.13 | 730.16 | 423.04 | 133.06 | 033.16 | 092.03 |
| 620.18 | 731.05 | 426.03 | 133.16 | 036.06 | 092.19 |
| 622.01 | 731.07 | 452.22 | 140.02 | 036.07 | 093.03 |
| 624.20 | 731.09 | 453.14 | 144.21 | 036.10 | 093.09 |
| 627.18 | 735.05 | 455.12 | 148.22 | 036.13 | 093.15 |
| 628.15 | 736.09 | 456.13 | 151.13 | 041.07 | 093.20 |
| 629.10 | 736.11 | 468.10 | 155.03 | 041.15 | 093.22 |
| 629.11 | 736.12 | 470.05 | 163.01 | 041.21 | 093.22 |
| 630.21 | 738.07 | 474.06 | 163.14 | 042.07 | 094.01 |
| 631.21 | 738.12 | 480.22 | 165.06 | 042.08 | 094.05 |
| 632.12 | 740.17 | 487.01 | 166.17 | 042.09 | 094.08 |
| 635.08 | 740.20 | 491.11 | 166.06 | 043.13 | 094.17 |
| 635.12 | 741.05 | 495.07 | 184.09 | 043.18 | 096.09 |
| 637.09 | 741.05 | 504.19 | 190.17 | 044.01 | 098.11 |
| 638.14 | 743.10 | 526.06 | 192.01 | 044.07 | 098.12 |
| 639.16 | 744.04 | 526.16 | 193.07 | 044.16 | 098.14 |
| 640.20 | 744.19 | 529.11 | 194.12 | 045.11 | 098.18 |
| 644.16 | 745.05 | 540.08 | 195.14 | 045.14 | 099.12 |
| 644.17 | 745.16 | 542.19 | 216.06 | 046.05 | 099.19 |
| 645.11 | 745.16 | 561.20 | 221.12 | 047.22 | 100.06 |
| 645.17 | 745.17 | 567.09 | 221.20 | 048.09 | 100.16 |
| 645.19 | 746.03 | 571.21 | 222.21 | 049.19 | 104.09 |
| 645.21 | 747.15 | 583.13 | 232.05 | 050.05 | 106.13 |
| 645.22 | 748.05 | 597.11 | 243.14 | 050.11 | 106.18 |
| 646.01 | 748.15 | 605.18 | 244.03 | 050.15 | 106.20 |
| 646.04 | 748.22 | 608.15 | 247.21 | 050.17 | 107.01 |
| 646.09 | 749.11 | 611.06 | 281.18 | 054.16 | 107.03 |
| 646.12 | 749.21 | 611.18 | 325.11 | 054.18 | 107.04 |
| 647.05 | 751.04 | 611.21 | 330.15 | 054.18 | 107.04 |
| 647.06 | 751.07 | 613.08 | 335.19 | 054.21 | 108.05 |
| 647.07 | 752.06 | 619.16 | 386.11 | 055.01 | 108.09 |
| 647.11 | 755.16 | 621.13 | 391.18 | 055.05 | 108.11 |
| 647.13 | 755.17 | 623.14 | 393.01 | 055.14 | 109.06 |
| 647.17 | 756.15 | 627.20 | 395.07 | 055.14 | 109.20 |
| 648.03 | 756.16 | 636.10 | 398.07 | 055.15 | 110.03 |
| 648.09 | 756.18 | 640.16 | 398.10 | 058.02 | 112.08 |
| 649.21 | 757.09 | 640.22 | 403.09 | 058.15 | 114.13 |
| 653.14 | 757.19 | 644.12 | 406.02 | 059.06 | 115.17 |
| 655.17 | 758.15 | 649.04 | 408.19 | 059.07 | 115.19 |
| 656.17 | 759.12 | 662.10 | 408.20 | 060.09 | 115.21 |
| 660.03 | 760.01 | 667.08 | 414.16 | 061.19 | 115.22 |
| 660.08 | 760.14 | 668.17 | 415.01 | 062.03 | 116.10 |
| 660.08 | 761.03 | 671.06 | 416.22 | 062.05 | 116.16 |
| 660.10 | 761.12 | 671.18 | 416.22 | 062.06 | 116.17 |

| | | | | | |
|---|---|---|---|---|---|
| 117.05 | 169.02 | 245.10 | 326.03 | 390.01 | 443.11 |
| 117.09 | 169.04 | 245.12 | 326.18 | 390.15 | 443.16 |
| 118.02 | 170.13 | 245.16 | 326.21 | 390.18 | 443.21 |
| 118.05 | 172.03 | 246.04 | 327.03 | 390.19 | 444.03 |
| 118.21 | 174.01 | 246.12 | 327.04 | 391.01 | 444.06 |
| 120.02 | 174.02 | 246.17 | 328.03 | 391.04 | 444.08 |
| 120.03 | 174.03 | 247.05 | 329.12 | 391.04 | 444.10 |
| 120.09 | 174.04 | 247.12 | 329.18 | 391.19 | 444.18 |
| 121.01 | 177.10 | 247.13 | 330.16 | 391.20 | 446.06 |
| 121.02 | 177.11 | 247.16 | 331.02 | 392.11 | 446.22 |
| 121.11 | 177.12 | 247.17 | 331.19 | 393.01 | 448.04 |
| 121.15 | 179.12 | 248.20 | 331.21 | 393.01 | 448.06 |
| 122.01 | 180.02 | 249.05 | 331.21 | 393.17 | 449.12 |
| 122.06 | 180.06 | 251.13 | 331.22 | 394.08 | 451.03 |
| 124.07 | 180.19 | 251.18 | 332.02 | 394.10 | 451.14 |
| 126.05 | 181.14 | 252.10 | 332.08 | 394.13 | 451.17 |
| 126.19 | 181.15 | 252.17 | 332.18 | 395.20 | 452.04 |
| 127.03 | 182.11 | 253.09 | 333.09 | 395.22 | 452.15 |
| 127.07 | 184.12 | 253.16 | 333.17 | 396.14 | 452.15 |
| 127.11 | 185.12 | 254.02 | 333.19 | 397.15 | 452.21 |
| 127.13 | 185.18 | 254.10 | 334.11 | 397.19 | 453.10 |
| 127.21 | 186.08 | 254.19 | 334.14 | 397.21 | 453.12 |
| 127.22 | 186.08 | 254.20 | 334.19 | 397.22 | 453.16 |
| 128.07 | 187.15 | 255.01 | 334.20 | 398.01 | 453.20 |
| 128.12 | 189.09 | 255.10 | 334.21 | 399.07 | 453.21 |
| 128.18 | 189.15 | 255.16 | 335.02 | 399.12 | 454.01 |
| 129.07 | 189.21 | 255.21 | 336.04 | 399.17 | 454.06 |
| 133.05 | 191.16 | 255.22 | 340.18 | 399.19 | 454.13 |
| 133.06 | 193.14 | 256.06 | 342.01 | 400.02 | 455.12 |
| 133.12 | 194.06 | 256.08 | 342.07 | 401.10 | 455.13 |
| 133.12 | 195.02 | 258.16 | 344.06 | 401.13 | 455.14 |
| 133.13 | 195.03 | 258.17 | 344.07 | 401.16 | 455.15 |
| 133.15 | 197.08 | 258.21 | 344.18 | 402.06 | 455.16 |
| 135.06 | 197.14 | 259.04 | 344.19 | 402.10 | 456.04 |
| 136.15 | 198.03 | 259.18 | 345.04 | 402.15 | 456.14 |
| 136.19 | 198.19 | 259.21 | 346.06 | 402.21 | 456.15 |
| 140.19 | 199.03 | 260.12 | 346.09 | 403.06 | 456.17 |
| 141.14 | 203.09 | 260.15 | 350.05 | 403.14 | 456.20 |
| 141.15 | 203.12 | 261.02 | 352.05 | 404.08 | 456.21 |
| 142.22 | 203.18 | 261.08 | 352.15 | 404.10 | 457.02 |
| 143.09 | 203.19 | 264.02 | 355.11 | 404.12 | 457.04 |
| 143.11 | 204.09 | 264.10 | 355.18 | 404.15 | 457.10 |
| 143.14 | 205.01 | 265.08 | 355.20 | 404.18 | 457.12 |
| 143.15 | 205.02 | 266.18 | 355.22 | 404.21 | 457.17 |
| 143.22 | 205.06 | 267.16 | 356.10 | 405.08 | 457.19 |
| 144.04 | 207.06 | 267.16 | 356.12 | 405.13 | 457.22 |
| 144.08 | 207.10 | 267.17 | 356.13 | 406.22 | 459.07 |
| 144.09 | 207.16 | 270.08 | 356.16 | 406.22 | 459.10 |
| 144.12 | 210.21 | 271.20 | 357.05 | 407.05 | 460.01 |
| 144.17 | 211.14 | 271.21 | 358.01 | 407.07 | 460.04 |
| 145.13 | 212.08 | 272.05 | 358.02 | 407.08 | 460.08 |
| 145.14 | 213.12 | 274.05 | 358.14 | 407.13 | 460.11 |
| 145.17 | 213.15 | 274.05 | 360.05 | 408.02 | 462.03 |
| 145.19 | 213.21 | 281.02 | 360.08 | 408.03 | 462.09 |
| 146.10 | 213.22 | 285.17 | 361.17 | 408.04 | 462.14 |
| 146.15 | 214.01 | 286.19 | 361.18 | 408.15 | 462.21 |
| 148.01 | 214.06 | 286.19 | 362.15 | 409.20 | 462.22 |
| 148.06 | 214.12 | 291.21 | 362.15 | 409.22 | 464.07 |
| 148.07 | 215.04 | 292.04 | 364.12 | 410.01 | 464.10 |
| 148.10 | 215.11 | 292.06 | 365.09 | 410.04 | 464.17 |
| 149.07 | 216.18 | 293.08 | 366.05 | 412.01 | 464.17 |
| 149.09 | 217.08 | 293.18 | 366.20 | 412.19 | 465.13 |
| 149.13 | 217.10 | 294.07 | 367.07 | 412.21 | 465.16 |
| 149.22 | 218.10 | 294.13 | 367.11 | 413.01 | 465.16 |
| 150.03 | 220.12 | 295.14 | 367.20 | 413.05 | 465.20 |
| 150.07 | 220.19 | 298.01 | 368.13 | 413.08 | 465.20 |
| 150.10 | 221.03 | 299.09 | 369.08 | 413.10 | 466.01 |
| 150.11 | 221.07 | 299.10 | 369.11 | 414.05 | 466.08 |
| 150.17 | 221.21 | 302.01 | 370.03 | 414.12 | 466.22 |
| 150.19 | 222.02 | 302.03 | 370.03 | 414.14 | 467.01 |
| 150.20 | 222.03 | 302.09 | 370.04 | 415.03 | 467.11 |
| 151.13 | 222.17 | 305.08 | 370.15 | 415.04 | 467.14 |
| 154.04 | 222.19 | 306.13 | 370.16 | 415.18 | 467.17 |
| 154.06 | 223.12 | 308.15 | 370.16 | 415.21 | 467.20 |
| 154.13 | 224.01 | 308.15 | 370.19 | 416.11 | 467.21 |
| 154.14 | 224.02 | 308.16 | 373.14 | 416.19 | 468.05 |
| 154.16 | 224.14 | 308.17 | 373.15 | 417.04 | 468.05 |
| 155.13 | 224.17 | 309.07 | 373.21 | 418.06 | 468.06 |
| 157.03 | 224.20 | 309.07 | 374.02 | 418.07 | 468.07 |
| 157.11 | 225.04 | 309.13 | 374.10 | 418.11 | 469.15 |
| 157.12 | 225.15 | 310.10 | 374.12 | 418.14 | 469.21 |
| 157.17 | 225.18 | 310.16 | 374.13 | 418.15 | 470.09 |
| 158.04 | 225.19 | 310.18 | 374.14 | 418.18 | 470.17 |
| 159.15 | 229.18 | 310.19 | 375.04 | 418.22 | 471.07 |
| 160.05 | 230.12 | 311.07 | 375.05 | 420.16 | 471.08 |
| 160.11 | 230.15 | 311.09 | 375.09 | 420.22 | 471.09 |
| 160.18 | 231.19 | 311.09 | 375.11 | 421.11 | 471.12 |
| 160.22 | 232.06 | 312.03 | 376.05 | 422.14 | 472.06 |
| 161.02 | 232.11 | 313.02 | 376.14 | 422.17 | 472.09 |
| 162.04 | 232.17 | 313.02 | 377.09 | 423.01 | 472.11 |
| 162.06 | 232.22 | 313.04 | 377.10 | 423.02 | 472.16 |
| 162.07 | 233.04 | 313.04 | 377.14 | 423.04 | 472.17 |
| 163.18 | 233.07 | 314.06 | 378.05 | 423.04 | 472.18 |
| 163.20 | 233.08 | 314.06 | 378.08 | 426.07 | 474.05 |
| 163.22 | 233.10 | 314.14 | 378.11 | 429.19 | 475.02 |
| 165.01 | 233.14 | 314.16 | 378.15 | 429.21 | 475.14 |
| 165.01 | 234.06 | 315.13 | 378.17 | 430.01 | 475.15 |
| 165.02 | 236.13 | 315.18 | 378.21 | 430.07 | 475.18 |
| 165.08 | 237.08 | 316.08 | 379.09 | 431.15 | 475.18 |
| 165.21 | 239.19 | 316.15 | 379.12 | 436.17 | 476.11 |
| 166.01 | 240.13 | 316.16 | 382.01 | 436.17 | 476.12 |
| 166.10 | 241.03 | 317.05 | 385.11 | 438.06 | 476.19 |
| 166.14 | 241.03 | 317.06 | 385.20 | 438.10 | 477.09 |
| 167.02 | 241.05 | 317.06 | 385.22 | 441.13 | 477.17 |
| 167.08 | 241.09 | 317.15 | 386.09 | 442.05 | 478.11 |
| 167.09 | 242.07 | 317.21 | 387.18 | 442.08 | 481.13 |
| 167.18 | 242.08 | 318.04 | 387.19 | 442.09 | 481.14 |
| 168.12 | 243.22 | 318.10 | 387.21 | 442.16 | 482.06 |
| 168.18 | 244.01 | 319.21 | 389.07 | 442.21 | 483.04 |
| 169.02 | 244.18 | 324.22 | 389.14 | 443.02 | 484.17 |
| | 245.08 | 325.20 | 389.15 | 443.05 | 484.21 |

| | | | | | |
|---|---|---|---|---|---|
| 485.04 | 542.05 | 597.08 | 655.18 | 718.03 | 760.19 |
| 485.17 | 542.07 | 597.14 | 657.01 | 718.15 | 761.16 |
| 485.22 | 543.18 | 597.16 | 658.04 | 718.18 | 762.21 |
| 486.03 | 544.15 | 597.19 | 659.02 | 718.18 | 763.09 |
| 486.04 | 544.21 | 597.22 | 660.02 | 719.02 | 763.10 |
| 486.05 | 544.22 | 599.14 | 661.16 | 719.03 | 763.13 |
| 487.08 | 546.05 | 599.18 | 663.14 | 719.07 | **hisseln** |
| 487.09 | 546.06 | 601.02 | 663.15 | 719.08 | 232.12 |
| 487.13 | 546.12 | 601.14 | 664.12 | 720.20 | 322.08 |
| 487.14 | 553.04 | 602.08 | 664.13 | 721.17 | 420.08 |
| 488.17 | 556.13 | 602.13 | 664.15 | 722.02 | 458.09 |
| 489.09 | 557.12 | 603.10 | 664.18 | 722.06 | 476.03 |
| 489.11 | 558.04 | 603.11 | 664.18 | 722.22 | 476.21 |
| 489.21 | 558.06 | 603.20 | 664.20 | 723.03 | 660.18 |
| 490.03 | 559.03 | 604.01 | 666.01 | 723.19 | **history** |
| 490.06 | 559.06 | 604.02 | 666.02 | 723.21 | 005.04 |
| 490.12 | 559.07 | 604.04 | 666.05 | 724.02 | 071.04 |
| 491.04 | 560.11 | 604.11 | 666.08 | 724.03 | 074.05 |
| 491.11 | 561.08 | 604.19 | 666.09 | 724.05 | 134.09 |
| 491.12 | 561.10 | 605.01 | 666.11 | 724.05 | 203.07 |
| 492.02 | 561.10 | 605.15 | 666.12 | 724.14 | 347.20 |
| 492.03 | 561.14 | 606.08 | 666.15 | 725.07 | 349.04 |
| 492.17 | 561.18 | 607.01 | 668.11 | 725.08 | 375.01 |
| 492.18 | 561.21 | 608.14 | 668.14 | 725.10 | 699.17 |
| 493.04 | 562.12 | 608.18 | 668.16 | 725.12 | **hit** |
| 493.06 | 562.14 | 609.03 | 668.21 | 726.22 | 095.17 |
| 493.15 | 562.16 | 609.09 | 669.05 | 727.04 | 161.02 |
| 493.19 | 563.03 | 609.15 | 671.05 | 727.04 | 253.16 |
| 493.21 | 564.01 | 609.16 | 671.06 | 727.05 | 355.15 |
| 494.01 | 564.07 | 610.02 | 674.02 | 728.14 | 399.03 |
| 494.04 | 564.13 | 610.02 | 674.03 | 728.15 | 430.18 |
| 494.11 | 565.03 | 610.06 | 674.09 | 728.22 | 618.05 |
| 494.17 | 565.12 | 610.09 | 676.01 | 731.08 | **hither** |
| 494.18 | 565.19 | 612.07 | 676.07 | 732.09 | 043.16 |
| 495.10 | 565.21 | 614.16 | 678.05 | 732.12 | 164.08 |
| 495.12 | 567.06 | 615.02 | 678.08 | 732.16 | 193.18 |
| 495.16 | 567.10 | 615.03 | 679.01 | 732.17 | 467.17 |
| 495.21 | 567.20 | 615.16 | 679.02 | 732.20 | **hitherto** |
| 496.08 | 569.01 | 615.20 | 679.05 | 733.02 | 047.17 |
| 496.09 | 571.20 | 616.16 | 679.06 | 733.03 | 341.07 |
| 496.17 | 571.22 | 616.16 | 680.01 | 734.20 | 346.10 |
| 497.04 | 572.01 | 617.01 | 680.10 | 735.01 | **hitting** |
| 497.07 | 572.05 | 618.19 | 680.12 | 735.03 | 084.17 |
| 497.11 | 572.06 | 619.01 | 680.16 | 736.06 | **hive** |
| 497.21 | 572.12 | 619.10 | 681.02 | 737.12 | 010.18 |
| 498.10 | 572.21 | 619.12 | 681.07 | 738.06 | **hives** |
| 498.11 | 573.12 | 619.13 | 681.21 | 738.20 | 495.15 |
| 498.14 | 574.06 | 619.15 | 682.10 | 738.21 | **hivin** |
| 498.18 | 576.16 | 619.20 | 682.17 | 739.06 | 191.02 |
| 499.20 | 576.17 | 620.01 | 682.19 | 739.08 | **ho** |
| 501.19 | 577.06 | 620.04 | 682.21 | 740.12 | 523.20 |
| 502.05 | 577.13 | 621.13 | 683.02 | 741.09 | **hoard** |
| 502.06 | 578.16 | 621.14 | 683.10 | 741.13 | 510.11 |
| 502.08 | 578.18 | 621.15 | 683.15 | 741.14 | **hoarse** |
| 502.11 | 578.20 | 622.01 | 683.18 | 741.15 | 262.18 |
| 502.12 | 579.07 | 625.05 | 683.22 | 743.07 | 391.03 |
| 502.14 | 579.13 | 627.11 | 683.22 | 743.09 | **hoary** |
| 502.15 | 579.14 | 630.08 | 684.04 | 743.12 | 169.06 |
| 503.09 | 579.16 | 630.09 | 684.06 | 744.02 | **hob** |
| 505.01 | 579.17 | 631.02 | 684.09 | 744.05 | 075.10 |
| 509.02 | 579.18 | 632.07 | 685.17 | 744.13 | 476.13 |
| 509.03 | 580.03 | 633.14 | 686.04 | 745.02 | **hoile** |
| 509.06 | 580.05 | 633.16 | 688.04 | 745.06 | 324.05 |
| 510.10 | 580.08 | 634.18 | 694.15 | 745.18 | **hoile's** |
| 515.06 | 580.09 | 634.19 | 694.16 | 745.21 | 712.18 |
| 515.11 | 580.11 | 634.19 | 694.18 | 746.04 | **hold** |
| 516.07 | 580.12 | 635.10 | 695.01 | 746.05 | 036.02 |
| 516.13 | 580.14 | 635.11 | 695.02 | 746.08 | 054.21 |
| 517.06 | 580.15 | 635.14 | 695.17 | 746.10 | 055.12 |
| 517.08 | 581.10 | 636.05 | 695.19 | 746.14 | 069.03 |
| 517.09 | 581.20 | 636.07 | 698.22 | 746.15 | 083.10 |
| 521.08 | 582.05 | 636.08 | 700.04 | 746.19 | 105.01 |
| 524.20 | 582.06 | 636.10 | 701.08 | 747.10 | 107.18 |
| 525.03 | 582.09 | 636.11 | 701.14 | 747.14 | 114.04 |
| 526.08 | 582.10 | 636.13 | 701.20 | 747.16 | 127.17 |
| 526.13 | 582.13 | 636.15 | 701.20 | 748.01 | 132.07 |
| 526.22 | 582.15 | 636.22 | 702.04 | 748.05 | 142.08 |
| 527.01 | 582.16 | 637.07 | 702.06 | 748.17 | 145.13 |
| 527.07 | 583.07 | 637.08 | 702.10 | 748.19 | 157.14 |
| 528.05 | 583.12 | 638.01 | 702.11 | 749.05 | 197.11 |
| 528.17 | 583.16 | 639.17 | 702.17 | 749.08 | 246.02 |
| 528.19 | 583.21 | 640.02 | 703.05 | 749.11 | 285.06 |
| 529.12 | 584.03 | 640.02 | 703.13 | 749.14 | 295.17 |
| 530.11 | 584.04 | 640.04 | 704.08 | 749.15 | 297.09 |
| 531.04 | 585.03 | 640.15 | 704.10 | 749.19 | 327.13 |
| 531.05 | 586.05 | 640.18 | 704.18 | 749.22 | 355.20 |
| 531.12 | 586.12 | 640.21 | 704.21 | 749.22 | 357.07 |
| 531.21 | 587.08 | 641.03 | 704.22 | 751.02 | 395.16 |
| 532.05 | 587.12 | 641.05 | 706.15 | 751.05 | 396.01 |
| 532.06 | 588.12 | 641.06 | 709.02 | 752.01 | 471.10 |
| 532.06 | 588.13 | 641.21 | 709.03 | 755.04 | 483.08 |
| 532.09 | 588.16 | 642.03 | 709.08 | 755.11 | 499.08 |
| 532.22 | 589.09 | 642.12 | 709.20 | 755.17 | 519.07 |
| 533.02 | 590.06 | 642.13 | 709.22 | 755.19 | 538.05 |
| 533.14 | 590.17 | 644.08 | 710.13 | 756.01 | 565.17 |
| 535.15 | 591.05 | 644.11 | 710.13 | 756.04 | 567.15 |
| 535.19 | 591.06 | 645.06 | 710.19 | 756.13 | 598.18 |
| 536.16 | 591.07 | 645.07 | 710.20 | 757.16 | 616.10 |
| 537.21 | 592.02 | 645.08 | 710.20 | 757.16 | 683.08 |
| 538.01 | 592.03 | 645.18 | 712.06 | 757.19 | 683.15 |
| 538.11 | 592.06 | 645.20 | 712.07 | 758.05 | 723.13 |
| 538.13 | 592.16 | 645.21 | 712.10 | 758.06 | 725.18 |
| 538.17 | 592.22 | 646.05 | 712.11 | 758.07 | 732.05 |
| 539.03 | 593.02 | 647.13 | 712.13 | 758.10 | 744.15 |
| 539.04 | 593.09 | 647.19 | 712.15 | 758.16 | **holding** |
| 539.11 | 593.19 | 647.20 | 713.09 | 758.17 | 365.13 |
| 539.14 | 594.16 | 655.08 | 715.03 | 759.01 | 382.20 |
| 541.09 | 595.04 | 655.09 | 717.12 | 759.01 | 400.03 |
| 541.13 | 595.06 | 655.10 | 717.19 | 759.18 | 409.04 |
| 541.14 | 597.05 | 655.13 | 717.19 | 759.21 | 455.14 |
| 542.02 | 597.07 | | | 760.18 | 467.21 |

498.15
527.14
544.18
616.15
688.07
**holds**
106.11
**hole**
053.04
243.17
309.02
627.03
**holes**
276.06
**holiday**
122.01
149.02
391.11
**holier**
371.03
**holld**
034.09
034.09
**hollow**
047.13
047.13
427.22
463.19
480.18
578.05
753.01
**hollowness**
587.09
**hollows**
449.09
**holly**
119.14
**home**
008.09
013.13
024.02
027.21
030.21
046.14
052.13
077.02
079.02
096.02
112.14
122.11
124.07
128.19
140.04
141.12
147.12
148.22
159.20
160.09
175.21
178.20
188.07
208.06
253.03
279.01
281.10
284.09
287.13
300.04
307.19
313.11
337.17
338.10
346.21
371.08
387.10
390.17
426.15
430.05
434.07
434.16
435.11
445.09
459.04
460.20
462.22
469.02
480.20
482.17
498.20
509.09
523.12
525.22
527.21
539.20
547.13
555.08
559.13
566.12
567.21
569.09
576.08
580.20
582.21
586.10
589.14
594.17
600.15
605.20
607.20
613.21
615.18

617.12
619.21
628.04
630.06
644.03
645.14
649.07
653.06
654.10
665.21
674.04
676.13
698.21
705.01
712.03
725.21
746.20
763.14
**homely**
006.22
471.03
693.10
**homeward**
347.14
**homily**
041.15
**honest**
231.21
484.13
726.22
**honey**
711.13
**honeymoon**
306.01
**honeysuckles**
204.12
204.12
**honour**
002.09
050.05
198.11
220.18
294.15
426.07
471.10
**honourable**
231.13
240.16
**honoured**
201.10
**honours**
203.12
**hook**
051.16
290.17
291.12
416.11
**hoops**
558.21
**hope**
002.10
008.06
032.02
033.16
033.17
085.09
102.04
133.18
135.12
151.08
222.07
229.02
263.05
277.17
279.09
305.06
337.21
342.06
374.17
405.15
409.19
415.06
429.20
454.11
469.07
520.08
520.19
529.11
532.03
541.22
578.08
581.15
597.13
620.02
635.18
644.01
645.15
655.06
682.20
733.13
760.10
**hoped**
089.01
415.10
580.10
644.01
**hopeful**
413.18
572.03
**hopefully**
296.05

**hopeless**
242.08
**hopelessly**
172.06
**hopes**
085.14
302.09
311.03
335.04
456.22
474.09
**hoping**
041.13
070.01
080.03
115.09
332.16
500.10
**hor**
193.22
233.09
**horizontal**
517.22
**horizontally**
744.15
**horns**
106.15
131.12
**horrible**
335.17
756.01
**horrid**
056.10
168.19
567.20
**horrified**
286.07
366.11
**horror**
030.11
052.03
108.15
165.18
267.20
278.20
316.11
401.11
441.21
502.11
605.19
745.19
**horse**
003.09
003.20
076.15
086.01
114.06
160.18
187.19
187.21
194.08
294.13
336.11
419.21
431.17
438.20
439.04
466.09
490.19
523.14
523.15
527.01
560.09
586.13
633.19
665.10
686.15
**horse's**
003.05
154.04
298.11
**horse-pistols**
006.10
**horse-steps**
690.16
**horse-trough**
336.08
**horseback**
477.16
598.18
672.12
**horses**
033.07
033.10
083.19
126.12
308.19
612.06
688.07
**horses'**
291.14
586.08
**hospitable**
056.16
607.16
**host**
026.11
032.22
055.10
059.05
312.04

410.01
621.22
674.10
686.16
**hostess**
018.13
**hostile**
234.08
529.06
**hostilities**
065.05
**hostility**
717.04
**hostler**
688.06
**hot**
075.01
104.16
128.06
502.19
549.05
557.06
587.16
692.12
748.02
**hottest**
258.14
**hound**
401.04
431.18
432.06
**hour**
021.20
021.22
042.12
053.08
067.11
074.16
077.04
077.05
090.09
090.10
092.17
134.16
139.07
151.11
190.16
200.08
202.05
207.11
214.22
217.11
285.15
296.14
302.07
302.07
352.11
365.16
386.21
410.21
434.10
455.07
478.20
522.02
535.15
539.11
551.01
553.19
558.11
568.20
578.01
591.14
620.13
624.08
639.12
646.08
661.20
669.17
705.15
716.05
741.10
748.03
**hour's**
121.05
185.16
267.19
461.17
**hours**
041.17
135.01
192.17
273.19
280.12
294.12
295.07
306.14
344.01
350.16
369.04
370.07
371.06
378.14
393.05
482.09
503.13
507.06
511.06
512.02
516.11
596.06
618.07

624.09
637.08
646.03
689.17
736.08
750.06
**house**
004.12
005.12
012.16
014.09
021.10
029.20
035.21
045.10
046.20
047.19
055.17
060.01
063.07
067.10
071.17
073.07
078.11
080.10
081.19
083.12
085.21
092.21
093.05
096.12
098.16
101.08
110.03
113.10
116.03
118.15
126.15
132.01
140.19
145.01
150.16
155.08
160.07
163.18
168.01
191.21
199.10
206.12
209.15
222.06
224.08
226.19
232.02
242.10
244.13
247.21
249.08
257.01
274.05
279.12
284.01
291.21
294.11
295.01
296.14
300.03
310.15
314.10
316.21
322.02
322.10
330.05
333.19
337.18
344.17
345.04
345.16
350.15
355.08
368.13
390.13
391.14
392.05
393.06
419.18
421.01
423.02
425.01
437.12
437.21
438.12
444.18
463.13
477.02
482.17
484.10
485.09
501.19
503.09
507.16
509.14
545.02
550.03
566.22
568.12
570.01
583.09
603.08
606.05
607.15

615.12
618.18
628.20
631.08
632.13
637.07
654.07
656.16
659.20
661.21
665.03
672.04
686.19
693.15
698.04
700.22
701.07
715.05
725.07
737.10
743.06
750.04
755.15
757.05
760.15
761.19
762.07
**house-door**
044.12
763.08
**house-front**
105.14
248.22
**house-keeper**
070.09
**house-keeper's**
667.09
**household**
011.03
101.13
213.01
270.02
332.02
332.03
446.19
499.22
746.22
**housekeeper**
014.08
134.11
146.13
349.05
446.08
472.14
475.04
477.14
477.20
531.20
556.09
566.18
576.12
643.11
673.03
675.16
677.05
691.01
**housekeeper's**
199.22
491.14
**houseless**
078.19
**houses**
131.14
729.10
**housewife**
035.12
**hovel**
253.02
**hovered**
019.17
**hovering**
561.09
**how**
001.12
009.07
012.18
013.18
023.17
025.08
027.11
028.08
029.18
030.22
030.23
031.09
045.03
045.12
048.10
048.16
048.17
053.01
057.22
057.22
067.17
073.14
073.18
074.08
074.12
078.10
080.07
084.13

| | | | | | |
|---|---|---|---|---|---|
| 085.16 | 436.20 | 287.02 | **humoured** | 560.12 | 008.15 |
| 091.22 | 439.17 | 295.11 | 088.06 | 562.18 | 008.17 |
| 092.02 | 445.10 | 306.20 | 255.04 | 570.09 | 008.20 |
| 100.02 | 446.18 | 322.15 | **humouring** | 602.03 | 008.20 |
| 105.17 | 446.19 | 329.04 | 088.07 | 633.05 | 009.05 |
| 109.06 | 449.10 | 337.17 | 198.09 | 647.07 | 009.07 |
| 109.07 | 450.03 | 342.17 | 541.15 | 647.11 | 009.08 |
| 116.20 | 452.19 | 367.09 | **humours** | 671.19 | 010.10 |
| 116.21 | 457.04 | 395.22 | 506.10 | 682.04 | 010.11 |
| 116.21 | 461.10 | 402.19 | 592.02 | 723.21 | 010.15 |
| 118.10 | 464.21 | 408.09 | **hundred** | 756.06 | 010.20 |
| 119.20 | 475.06 | 425.14 | 048.05 | **hurtful** | 011.01 |
| 130.10 | 476.10 | 443.18 | 049.13 | 754.06 | 011.01 |
| 133.16 | 498.02 | 445.04 | 049.13 | **husband** | 011.05 |
| 133.17 | 500.07 | 446.05 | 226.22 | 025.03 | 011.19 |
| 134.06 | 504.04 | 454.12 | 315.21 | 073.03 | 011.21 |
| 141.17 | 504.18 | 457.09 | 465.04 | 142.19 | 012.11 |
| 141.20 | 505.03 | 470.17 | 504.16 | 173.18 | 012.11 |
| 146.07 | 505.11 | 474.08 | 567.13 | 197.01 | 012.17 |
| 146.09 | 520.04 | 508.04 | 630.18 | 199.07 | 012.17 |
| 158.01 | 520.04 | 540.12 | 654.20 | 205.13 | 012.20 |
| 163.05 | 525.06 | 543.18 | 708.13 | 211.17 | 013.01 |
| 167.03 | 525.08 | 544.20 | 750.13 | 233.16 | 013.12 |
| 172.01 | 525.17 | 557.04 | **hundreds** | 251.05 | 013.13 |
| 173.19 | 526.03 | 560.14 | 071.21 | 256.05 | 013.13 |
| 176.12 | 528.06 | 568.13 | **hung** | 264.01 | 013.17 |
| 177.10 | 529.12 | 572.15 | 042.16 | 278.12 | 013.18 |
| 177.11 | 531.15 | 577.10 | 075.19 | 295.21 | 014.02 |
| 179.09 | 538.21 | 585.10 | 122.05 | 303.04 | 014.07 |
| 180.22 | 540.06 | 607.04 | 255.10 | 332.08 | 014.10 |
| 181.01 | 542.17 | 622.22 | 296.01 | 345.17 | 014.12 |
| 185.01 | 555.19 | 636.15 | 311.08 | 379.14 | 015.05 |
| 185.07 | 555.21 | 639.14 | 323.03 | 380.03 | 015.12 |
| 192.20 | 558.13 | 641.07 | 323.07 | 412.20 | 015.17 |
| 202.03 | 562.07 | 648.04 | 367.02 | 429.06 | 015.20 |
| 203.18 | 572.13 | 664.17 | 379.06 | 546.09 | 015.21 |
| 208.12 | 575.07 | 671.11 | 434.15 | 614.09 | 015.21 |
| 214.10 | 578.14 | 695.11 | **hunger** | 645.03 | 016.01 |
| 221.01 | 581.17 | 731.10 | 273.02 | 651.17 | 016.09 |
| 221.14 | 586.20 | 752.16 | 742.02 | **husband's** | 016.13 |
| 223.06 | 593.04 | **howl** | 753.02 | 042.10 | 016.17 |
| 224.14 | 600.20 | 106.02 | **hungry** | 182.01 | 017.04 |
| 227.09 | 603.08 | 290.10 | 129.21 | 257.20 | 017.08 |
| 231.13 | 603.16 | **howled** | 136.14 | **husbands** | 017.09 |
| 231.22 | 607.05 | 015.16 | 311.19 | 414.19 | 017.11 |
| 231.22 | 608.07 | 377.10 | 318.01 | **hush** | 017.15 |
| 238.07 | 611.04 | **hubbub** | 739.02 | 094.01 | 017.18 |
| 242.04 | 617.10 | 043.14 | 739.05 | 105.16 | 017.20 |
| 242.06 | 619.06 | 169.20 | **hunter** | 105.16 | 018.05 |
| 252.13 | 621.11 | **hue** | 439.02 | 164.15 | 018.09 |
| 252.14 | 627.02 | 549.03 | **hunting** | 164.16 | 018.15 |
| 255.17 | 635.08 | 741.14 | 481.02 | 180.03 | 018.20 |
| 262.21 | 636.12 | **hug** | **hurl** | 210.18 | 019.07 |
| 266.17 | 640.16 | 115.05 | 245.10 | 250.21 | 019.11 |
| 272.07 | 645.17 | **huge** | **hurled** | 288.02 | 019.21 |
| 272.13 | 660.04 | 005.19 | 043.10 | 288.03 | 020.01 |
| 273.16 | 660.16 | 006.16 | 044.03 | 366.05 | 020.01 |
| 273.21 | 662.17 | 098.20 | 682.10 | 366.06 | 020.03 |
| 280.03 | 662.20 | 107.03 | **hurried** | 366.06 | 020.03 |
| 280.19 | 669.09 | 189.03 | 030.11 | 370.19 | 020.06 |
| 285.06 | 670.16 | 312.16 | 044.01 | 388.18 | 020.08 |
| 288.16 | 677.18 | **hugged** | 141.12 | 388.18 | 020.11 |
| 288.20 | 684.01 | 621.10 | 185.19 | 440.18 | 020.22 |
| 291.10 | 686.18 | **human** | 400.17 | 440.18 | 021.12 |
| 292.15 | 689.03 | 050.01 | 567.10 | 538.03 | 021.17 |
| 296.18 | 697.07 | 067.13 | 621.22 | 594.05 | 021.18 |
| 297.18 | 697.13 | 201.07 | 641.10 | 594.06 | 021.19 |
| 298.09 | 698.15 | 218.22 | 657.02 | 616.10 | 021.19 |
| 298.13 | 698.22 | 307.05 | 744.17 | **hypocricy** | 022.01 |
| 299.14 | 701.15 | 341.18 | **hurriedly** | 670.08 | 022.06 |
| 307.04 | 701.16 | 388.18 | 053.04 | **hypocrisy** | 022.08 |
| 307.18 | 725.19 | 388.21 | 102.03 | 397.06 | 022.11 |
| 309.14 | 726.18 | 503.04 | 362.05 | 421.02 | 022.12 |
| 314.13 | 732.12 | 731.04 | 587.15 | **hypocrite** | 022.21 |
| 316.06 | 734.21 | **humanity** | **hurry** | 029.11 | 023.01 |
| 320.04 | 738.08 | 223.02 | 290.20 | 217.19 | 023.09 |
| 329.16 | 741.07 | 302.04 | 365.05 | 249.12 | 023.09 |
| 329.17 | 745.15 | 333.10 | 482.14 | **hysterical** | 023.15 |
| 330.18 | 752.08 | 333.15 | 523.12 | 097.13 | 024.06 |
| 336.12 | 752.21 | 333.17 | 527.19 | **i** | 024.12 |
| 343.20 | 754.08 | 346.03 | 635.05 | 001.03 | 024.13 |
| 345.22 | 754.09 | **humiliation** | 685.15 | 001.04 | 025.07 |
| 347.20 | 755.05 | 034.14 | 698.02 | 001.06 | 025.08 |
| 350.09 | 764.10 | 055.04 | **hurrying** | 001.07 | 025.12 |
| 356.08 | **however** | 258.19 | 128.10 | 001.10 | 025.13 |
| 357.01 | 014.06 | 375.18 | 433.18 | 001.13 | 025.21 |
| 357.02 | 023.12 | 604.21 | 566.04 | 002.02 | 026.01 |
| 360.17 | 026.08 | **humility** | 653.15 | 002.04 | 026.08 |
| 361.20 | 029.09 | 148.18 | **hurt** | 002.06 | 026.13 |
| 362.18 | 038.21 | **humming** | 030.04 | 002.08 | 027.04 |
| 364.03 | 048.02 | 169.16 | 081.08 | 002.10 | 027.05 |
| 368.03 | 056.19 | 557.08 | 089.02 | 002.13 | 027.07 |
| 369.10 | 058.14 | 707.18 | 129.14 | 002.16 | 027.11 |
| 371.20 | 070.14 | **humour** | 156.07 | 002.17 | 027.12 |
| 373.12 | 077.05 | 013.02 | 219.06 | 003.01 | 027.15 |
| 375.02 | 082.13 | 079.18 | 259.06 | 003.02 | 027.17 |
| 375.08 | 095.07 | 126.19 | 276.15 | 003.12 | 027.21 |
| 382.13 | 099.09 | 186.14 | 290.08 | 003.21 | 027.22 |
| 384.11 | 107.01 | 195.06 | 296.20 | 004.19 | 028.02 |
| 388.09 | 120.07 | 204.19 | 366.02 | 005.01 | 028.06 |
| 392.05 | 138.07 | 219.17 | 406.11 | 005.03 | 028.08 |
| 398.21 | 167.10 | 219.21 | 446.06 | 005.07 | 028.11 |
| 401.03 | 174.14 | 289.09 | 446.08 | 005.14 | 029.04 |
| 406.03 | 177.15 | 356.17 | 468.01 | 005.16 | 029.14 |
| 407.20 | 186.07 | 472.21 | 489.11 | 005.18 | 029.19 |
| 407.20 | 188.09 | 530.06 | 510.09 | 007.16 | 030.06 |
| 414.21 | 220.03 | 559.08 | 539.15 | 007.18 | 030.13 |
| 418.10 | 223.11 | 667.06 | 539.17 | 008.01 | 030.15 |
| 426.21 | 262.20 | 734.14 | 540.02 | 008.08 | 030.17 |
| 432.22 | 268.02 | 739.08 | 543.10 | 008.09 | 030.18 |
| 435.16 | 283.09 | | 543.12 | 008.12 | 030.21 |

| | | | | | |
|---|---|---|---|---|---|
| 030.22 | 053.08 | 077.19 | 118.16 | 140.17 | 171.14 |
| 031.04 | 053.10 | 078.02 | 118.19 | 141.01 | 171.16 |
| 031.09 | 053.18 | 078.08 | 119.11 | 141.02 | 171.17 |
| 031.12 | 053.21 | 078.17 | 119.12 | 141.07 | 171.17 |
| 031.14 | 054.03 | 080.01 | 119.19 | 141.09 | 171.20 |
| 031.14 | 054.10 | 080.02 | 119.20 | 141.09 | 172.01 |
| 031.18 | 054.11 | 080.07 | 120.01 | 141.10 | 172.02 |
| 031.21 | 054.12 | 080.13 | 120.06 | 141.11 | 172.04 |
| 032.02 | 054.13 | 080.14 | 120.10 | 141.13 | 172.08 |
| 032.05 | 054.14 | 080.20 | 120.12 | 141.16 | 172.09 |
| 032.08 | 055.03 | 080.21 | 120.16 | 141.19 | 172.11 |
| 032.08 | 055.05 | 082.05 | 121.03 | 141.20 | 172.15 |
| 032.12 | 055.07 | 082.06 | 121.07 | 142.01 | 172.20 |
| 032.15 | 055.09 | 082.08 | 121.09 | 142.07 | 173.01 |
| 032.17 | 055.19 | 082.11 | 122.09 | 142.11 | 173.03 |
| 032.18 | 055.21 | 082.11 | 122.11 | 142.13 | 173.07 |
| 032.19 | 056.01 | 082.12 | 122.19 | 142.15 | 173.16 |
| 032.22 | 056.05 | 082.13 | 122.21 | 142.16 | 173.18 |
| 033.12 | 056.15 | 083.01 | 122.22 | 143.03 | 174.01 |
| 033.16 | 057.03 | 083.03 | 123.03 | 144.05 | 174.03 |
| 033.17 | 057.07 | 083.04 | 123.10 | 144.06 | 174.12 |
| 033.21 | 057.09 | 083.05 | 123.20 | 144.08 | 174.18 |
| 034.02 | 057.10 | 083.14 | 124.01 | 145.01 | 175.08 |
| 034.03 | 057.11 | 083.19 | 124.01 | 145.08 | 175.09 |
| 034.19 | 057.11 | 083.20 | 124.05 | 145.08 | 175.13 |
| 034.22 | 057.15 | 084.07 | 125.04 | 145.09 | 175.13 |
| 035.07 | 058.03 | 084.19 | 125.06 | 145.22 | 175.20 |
| 035.07 | 058.05 | 085.04 | 125.09 | 146.06 | 176.08 |
| 035.18 | 058.07 | 085.09 | 125.14 | 146.09 | 176.11 |
| 035.21 | 058.10 | 085.16 | 125.22 | 146.12 | 176.12 |
| 036.08 | 058.13 | 085.22 | 125.22 | 148.01 | 176.19 |
| 036.14 | 058.14 | 086.04 | 126.01 | 149.03 | 176.20 |
| 037.03 | 058.18 | 086.05 | 126.04 | 150.18 | 177.05 |
| 037.07 | 058.19 | 089.01 | 126.09 | 151.08 | 177.12 |
| 037.12 | 059.01 | 089.03 | 126.18 | 151.09 | 177.15 |
| 038.06 | 059.06 | 089.10 | 127.09 | 151.11 | 177.18 |
| 038.14 | 059.12 | 090.06 | 127.10 | 152.06 | 177.18 |
| 038.18 | 059.15 | 090.18 | 127.13 | 153.07 | 177.18 |
| 039.04 | 059.21 | 091.07 | 127.17 | 153.10 | 177.20 |
| 039.11 | 060.05 | 091.08 | 127.18 | 153.12 | 178.01 |
| 039.15 | 060.07 | 092.08 | 127.21 | 153.14 | 178.06 |
| 040.01 | 060.22 | 092.11 | 128.15 | 153.18 | 178.06 |
| 040.02 | 061.05 | 092.11 | 129.02 | 154.18 | 178.08 |
| 040.13 | 061.14 | 092.15 | 129.03 | 154.19 | 178.11 |
| 040.17 | 061.19 | 093.02 | 129.05 | 155.03 | 178.12 |
| 040.20 | 061.21 | 093.10 | 129.08 | 155.12 | 178.13 |
| 041.02 | 062.07 | 094.01 | 129.08 | 155.15 | 178.13 |
| 042.05 | 062.12 | 094.11 | 129.09 | 155.21 | 178.14 |
| 042.07 | 062.22 | 094.16 | 130.05 | 156.05 | 178.16 |
| 042.15 | 063.05 | 095.01 | 130.09 | 156.07 | 178.18 |
| 043.09 | 063.05 | 095.05 | 130.11 | 156.12 | 178.20 |
| 043.09 | 063.19 | 095.07 | 130.17 | 156.17 | 179.02 |
| 043.11 | 064.04 | 095.11 | 130.18 | 157.19 | 179.05 |
| 044.08 | 064.14 | 095.12 | 130.22 | 157.22 | 179.07 |
| 044.10 | 064.17 | 095.17 | 131.06 | 158.06 | 179.09 |
| 044.20 | 065.01 | 095.20 | 131.22 | 158.14 | 179.15 |
| 045.03 | 065.11 | 095.20 | 132.09 | 158.18 | 179.17 |
| 045.05 | 065.16 | 097.06 | 132.10 | 158.19 | 180.02 |
| 045.06 | 066.05 | 097.09 | 132.12 | 158.21 | 180.05 |
| 045.09 | 066.16 | 097.16 | 132.13 | 159.09 | 180.13 |
| 045.15 | 066.17 | 097.19 | 132.17 | 159.10 | 180.17 |
| 045.18 | 066.21 | 098.01 | 132.20 | 159.16 | 180.18 |
| 046.03 | 067.01 | 098.05 | 133.03 | 159.18 | 181.07 |
| 046.05 | 067.04 | 100.21 | 133.03 | 160.04 | 181.10 |
| 046.09 | 067.04 | 101.01 | 133.06 | 160.08 | 181.11 |
| 046.10 | 067.09 | 101.06 | 133.08 | 160.12 | 181.12 |
| 046.11 | 067.16 | 101.06 | 133.16 | 160.19 | 181.12 |
| 046.12 | 067.19 | 101.13 | 133.17 | 161.02 | 181.17 |
| 046.12 | 067.20 | 101.18 | 133.17 | 162.11 | 181.19 |
| 046.13 | 068.01 | 101.21 | 133.17 | 163.04 | 181.20 |
| 046.14 | 069.02 | 102.03 | 133.18 | 163.06 | 181.21 |
| 046.18 | 069.05 | 102.04 | 133.19 | 163.10 | 182.02 |
| 046.19 | 069.06 | 102.06 | 133.20 | 163.11 | 182.04 |
| 046.21 | 069.11 | 102.08 | 134.01 | 163.12 | 182.15 |
| 047.01 | 070.01 | 102.14 | 134.02 | 163.13 | 182.15 |
| 047.01 | 070.05 | 102.15 | 134.02 | 163.14 | 182.17 |
| 047.04 | 070.07 | 102.17 | 134.04 | 163.22 | 182.20 |
| 047.08 | 070.12 | 103.07 | 134.05 | 163.22 | 183.01 |
| 047.11 | 070.20 | 104.13 | 134.06 | 164.01 | 183.07 |
| 048.08 | 070.21 | 105.12 | 134.08 | 164.03 | 183.09 |
| 048.14 | 070.22 | 105.16 | 134.13 | 164.04 | 183.14 |
| 048.16 | 071.02 | 105.19 | 134.14 | 164.07 | 183.14 |
| 048.16 | 071.03 | 106.06 | 134.15 | 164.11 | 183.16 |
| 048.18 | 071.08 | 106.12 | 134.17 | 164.19 | 183.17 |
| 048.22 | 071.13 | 106.16 | 134.18 | 165.03 | 184.02 |
| 049.03 | 072.10 | 106.16 | 135.09 | 165.06 | 184.06 |
| 049.06 | 072.11 | 106.18 | 135.10 | 165.11 | 184.08 |
| 049.07 | 072.14 | 107.08 | 135.12 | 165.12 | 184.18 |
| 049.10 | 072.17 | 109.19 | 135.22 | 166.11 | 184.20 |
| 049.21 | 073.07 | 110.06 | 136.03 | 166.14 | 184.21 |
| 050.08 | 073.11 | 110.08 | 136.12 | 167.01 | 184.22 |
| 051.05 | 073.13 | 110.15 | 137.03 | 167.02 | 185.01 |
| 051.09 | 073.13 | 110.16 | 137.07 | 167.13 | 186.01 |
| 051.09 | 073.16 | 111.01 | 137.08 | 167.17 | 186.01 |
| 051.10 | 073.18 | 111.10 | 137.15 | 167.21 | 186.02 |
| 051.11 | 074.06 | 111.16 | 137.19 | 168.01 | 186.04 |
| 051.14 | 074.14 | 111.21 | 137.21 | 168.06 | 186.05 |
| 051.15 | 074.15 | 112.03 | 138.01 | 168.09 | 186.11 |
| 051.15 | 074.15 | 114.08 | 138.04 | 168.11 | 186.12 |
| 051.19 | 074.19 | 114.18 | 138.07 | 168.13 | 186.13 |
| 051.19 | 074.22 | 115.03 | 138.08 | 168.13 | 186.16 |
| 052.04 | 075.02 | 115.15 | 138.09 | 169.08 | 186.16 |
| 052.08 | 075.05 | 117.09 | 140.01 | 169.09 | 186.18 |
| 052.11 | 075.12 | 117.10 | 140.06 | 169.15 | 187.02 |
| 052.11 | 075.14 | 117.11 | 140.07 | 170.01 | 187.03 |
| 052.14 | 075.17 | 117.14 | 140.09 | 170.02 | 187.18 |
| 052.17 | 075.17 | 117.15 | 140.11 | 170.09 | 188.05 |
| 053.01 | 076.01 | 118.05 | 140.14 | 170.18 | 189.13 |
| 053.01 | 076.05 | 118.05 | 140.15 | 170.20 | 189.15 |
| 053.03 | 076.09 | 118.06 | 140.15 | 170.22 | 189.16 |
| 053.07 | 076.11 | 118.06 | | 171.05 | |

| | | | | | |
|---|---|---|---|---|---|
| 190.09 | 218.06 | 246.16 | 267.10 | 284.09 | 309.16 |
| 191.09 | 218.07 | 246.18 | 269.05 | 284.16 | 309.17 |
| 191.15 | 218.12 | 246.21 | 270.01 | 284.20 | 309.20 |
| 191.16 | 218.15 | 247.03 | 270.05 | 284.20 | 310.04 |
| 191.17 | 218.17 | 247.06 | 270.06 | 285.06 | 310.07 |
| 191.18 | 218.20 | 247.06 | 270.10 | 285.06 | 310.14 |
| 192.04 | 219.05 | 247.08 | 270.12 | 285.08 | 310.14 |
| 192.09 | 219.11 | 247.09 | 270.13 | 285.10 | 310.15 |
| 192.13 | 219.11 | 247.11 | 270.19 | 285.16 | 311.01 |
| 192.19 | 219.17 | 247.12 | 270.20 | 285.20 | 311.02 |
| 192.20 | 219.17 | 247.16 | 270.21 | 286.09 | 311.14 |
| 192.22 | 219.20 | 247.22 | 271.04 | 286.15 | 311.17 |
| 193.08 | 219.21 | 248.01 | 271.05 | 286.15 | 311.20 |
| 193.09 | 220.09 | 248.02 | 271.05 | 287.11 | 311.21 |
| 194.13 | 220.09 | 248.03 | 271.07 | 287.12 | 312.10 |
| 194.14 | 220.10 | 248.09 | 271.10 | 287.21 | 312.12 |
| 194.21 | 220.10 | 248.19 | 271.18 | 288.04 | 312.19 |
| 195.02 | 220.12 | 248.22 | 271.19 | 288.08 | 312.21 |
| 195.05 | 220.14 | 249.01 | 272.01 | 288.12 | 312.21 |
| 195.07 | 220.17 | 249.11 | 272.01 | 288.17 | 313.05 |
| 195.16 | 221.04 | 249.14 | 272.02 | 289.03 | 313.11 |
| 195.17 | 221.08 | 249.16 | 272.06 | 289.06 | 313.14 |
| 195.19 | 222.08 | 249.18 | 272.13 | 289.07 | 313.15 |
| 195.20 | 222.09 | 250.03 | 272.20 | 289.07 | 313.15 |
| 196.11 | 222.17 | 250.06 | 273.03 | 289.09 | 313.21 |
| 196.11 | 222.22 | 250.11 | 273.05 | 289.09 | 313.22 |
| 197.07 | 223.03 | 250.12 | 273.07 | 289.10 | 314.04 |
| 198.20 | 223.09 | 250.17 | 273.11 | 289.12 | 314.09 |
| 199.02 | 223.09 | 250.19 | 273.15 | 289.18 | 314.13 |
| 199.05 | 223.11 | 251.03 | 273.16 | 289.19 | 314.13 |
| 199.13 | 223.12 | 251.14 | 274.07 | 290.12 | 314.17 |
| 199.14 | 224.11 | 251.18 | 274.08 | 290.14 | 314.18 |
| 199.14 | 227.09 | 251.19 | 274.13 | 290.18 | 315.01 |
| 199.16 | 227.12 | 251.21 | 274.16 | 290.20 | 315.01 |
| 200.05 | 227.18 | 251.21 | 275.10 | 290.21 | 315.06 |
| 200.07 | 228.01 | 252.02 | 275.11 | 291.07 | 315.10 |
| 200.08 | 228.05 | 252.03 | 275.12 | 291.08 | 315.11 |
| 201.08 | 228.11 | 252.08 | 275.21 | 291.13 | 315.17 |
| 202.02 | 228.12 | 252.14 | 276.04 | 291.16 | 315.19 |
| 202.03 | 228.15 | 252.15 | 276.10 | 291.22 | 315.19 |
| 202.08 | 229.02 | 253.03 | 276.11 | 292.08 | 315.20 |
| 202.09 | 229.02 | 253.06 | 276.16 | 292.16 | 316.05 |
| 202.09 | 229.05 | 253.07 | 276.18 | 292.19 | 316.06 |
| 202.11 | 229.08 | 253.12 | 276.19 | 293.09 | 316.07 |
| 202.13 | 230.02 | 254.02 | 276.21 | 293.11 | 316.14 |
| 202.20 | 230.04 | 254.05 | 276.21 | 293.16 | 316.16 |
| 202.20 | 230.05 | 254.07 | 277.03 | 293.22 | 316.18 |
| 203.16 | 230.08 | 254.09 | 277.06 | 294.04 | 317.03 |
| 203.17 | 230.13 | 254.12 | 277.09 | 294.08 | 317.05 |
| 203.17 | 231.01 | 254.13 | 277.10 | 294.19 | 317.12 |
| 203.18 | 231.04 | 254.14 | 277.13 | 294.22 | 317.16 |
| 204.04 | 231.06 | 255.04 | 277.13 | 295.03 | 317.22 |
| 204.07 | 231.08 | 255.20 | 277.15 | 295.07 | 318.01 |
| 204.18 | 231.15 | 256.01 | 277.17 | 295.11 | 318.03 |
| 205.07 | 231.17 | 256.14 | 277.21 | 295.12 | 318.06 |
| 205.18 | 231.19 | 256.15 | 278.03 | 295.17 | 318.07 |
| 205.18 | 232.07 | 256.17 | 278.10 | 295.19 | 318.08 |
| 206.05 | 232.08 | 256.19 | 278.12 | 296.11 | 318.18 |
| 206.07 | 234.02 | 256.22 | 278.15 | 297.01 | 319.14 |
| 206.11 | 234.17 | 257.02 | 278.18 | 297.02 | 319.20 |
| 206.16 | 234.18 | 257.15 | 279.01 | 297.10 | 319.21 |
| 206.21 | 235.08 | 257.16 | 279.01 | 298.03 | 320.03 |
| 207.02 | 235.17 | 258.06 | 279.02 | 298.05 | 320.04 |
| 207.04 | 235.19 | 258.08 | 279.02 | 298.06 | 320.08 |
| 207.08 | 235.20 | 258.08 | 279.04 | 298.08 | 320.09 |
| 207.11 | 236.09 | 259.08 | 279.06 | 298.08 | 320.15 |
| 207.12 | 236.18 | 259.09 | 279.09 | 298.09 | 320.15 |
| 207.14 | 237.04 | 259.12 | 279.09 | 299.06 | 320.17 |
| 207.19 | 237.07 | 260.13 | 279.11 | 299.07 | 321.11 |
| 207.20 | 238.18 | 260.13 | 279.17 | 299.14 | 321.12 |
| 207.21 | 238.18 | 260.14 | 279.18 | 299.20 | 321.21 |
| 208.08 | 238.21 | 260.17 | 280.03 | 300.04 | 321.21 |
| 208.12 | 239.02 | 261.13 | 280.05 | 303.04 | 322.01 |
| 208.20 | 239.03 | 261.19 | 280.11 | 303.08 | 322.10 |
| 208.21 | 239.06 | 261.22 | 280.13 | 303.09 | 322.12 |
| 209.01 | 239.08 | 262.01 | 280.17 | 303.11 | 322.14 |
| 209.03 | 239.18 | 262.04 | 280.18 | 303.12 | 322.22 |
| 209.05 | 240.08 | 262.06 | 280.19 | 303.14 | 323.14 |
| 209.19 | 240.09 | 262.09 | 280.20 | 304.16 | 323.19 |
| 210.06 | 240.13 | 262.17 | 280.21 | 305.03 | 324.06 |
| 210.06 | 240.15 | 262.18 | 281.03 | 305.10 | 324.06 |
| 210.13 | 240.19 | 262.18 | 281.05 | 305.20 | 325.01 |
| 210.19 | 240.21 | 262.19 | 281.06 | 305.21 | 325.08 |
| 210.21 | 241.04 | 262.22 | 281.06 | 305.22 | 325.11 |
| 211.03 | 241.06 | 263.04 | 281.07 | 306.02 | 325.14 |
| 211.08 | 242.10 | 263.11 | 281.09 | 306.05 | 325.18 |
| 211.21 | 242.12 | 263.14 | 281.12 | 306.07 | 325.20 |
| 212.02 | 243.05 | 263.17 | 281.12 | 306.08 | 325.22 |
| 212.10 | 243.12 | 263.21 | 281.15 | 306.10 | 326.02 |
| 212.15 | 243.14 | 264.04 | 281.16 | 306.10 | 326.06 |
| 213.04 | 243.16 | 264.04 | 281.19 | 306.15 | 326.13 |
| 213.07 | 243.21 | 264.05 | 281.21 | 306.16 | 326.14 |
| 213.17 | 244.03 | 264.11 | 282.01 | 307.02 | 326.15 |
| 214.17 | 244.04 | 264.12 | 282.04 | 307.06 | 326.19 |
| 214.20 | 244.07 | 264.13 | 282.04 | 307.08 | 326.20 |
| 214.21 | 244.10 | 265.03 | 282.07 | 307.11 | 327.05 |
| 214.22 | 244.13 | 265.08 | 282.15 | 307.12 | 327.07 |
| 215.15 | 244.14 | 265.10 | 282.19 | 307.13 | 327.11 |
| 215.16 | 244.14 | 265.11 | 282.19 | 307.18 | 327.14 |
| 215.16 | 244.21 | 265.12 | 282.20 | 307.19 | 327.14 |
| 216.01 | 245.01 | 265.15 | 282.20 | 307.21 | 327.14 |
| 216.03 | 245.06 | 266.03 | 282.22 | 308.01 | 327.16 |
| 216.13 | 245.06 | 266.04 | 283.02 | 308.02 | 328.02 |
| 216.14 | 245.10 | 266.11 | 283.03 | 308.06 | 328.02 |
| 217.03 | 245.20 | 266.11 | 283.06 | 309.01 | 328.10 |
| 217.11 | 246.02 | 266.12 | 283.07 | 309.02 | 329.01 |
| 217.14 | 246.04 | 266.16 | 283.11 | 309.08 | 329.02 |
| 217.17 | 246.06 | 266.16 | 283.16 | 309.09 | 329.09 |
| 217.20 | 246.10 | 266.19 | 283.17 | 309.10 | 329.15 |
| 217.20 | 246.13 | 267.02 | 283.19 | 309.13 | 329.17 |
| 218.01 | 246.15 | 267.06 | | | |

| | | | | | |
|---|---|---|---|---|---|
| 329.20 | 345.18 | 365.15 | 389.08 | 412.02 | 444.15 |
| 329.21 | 346.08 | 365.18 | 389.13 | 412.07 | 444.16 |
| 329.22 | 346.11 | 366.03 | 389.14 | 412.08 | 445.10 |
| 330.01 | 346.15 | 366.03 | 389.19 | 412.09 | 445.11 |
| 330.03 | 346.18 | 366.09 | 389.22 | 412.16 | 446.03 |
| 330.05 | 346.19 | 366.11 | 390.01 | 412.18 | 446.05 |
| 330.06 | 346.22 | 366.13 | 390.12 | 412.19 | 446.15 |
| 330.07 | 347.03 | 366.19 | 390.15 | 413.22 | 446.18 |
| 330.17 | 347.04 | 366.21 | 391.06 | 414.15 | 446.20 |
| 330.18 | 347.04 | 367.03 | 391.08 | 414.20 | 447.01 |
| 330.21 | 347.06 | 367.09 | 391.12 | 414.22 | 449.07 |
| 331.06 | 347.08 | 367.21 | 391.16 | 415.14 | 449.14 |
| 331.08 | 347.09 | 367.22 | 392.03 | 415.21 | 449.17 |
| 331.10 | 347.16 | 368.04 | 392.15 | 416.09 | 450.04 |
| 331.17 | 347.16 | 368.05 | 392.20 | 416.14 | 450.09 |
| 332.11 | 348.01 | 368.07 | 393.09 | 416.20 | 450.18 |
| 332.11 | 348.03 | 368.08 | 393.12 | 417.03 | 451.11 |
| 332.15 | 348.08 | 368.12 | 393.12 | 417.12 | 452.01 |
| 332.20 | 348.09 | 369.12 | 393.18 | 417.14 | 452.17 |
| 333.16 | 349.02 | 369.12 | 393.20 | 417.18 | 452.20 |
| 333.19 | 349.03 | 370.01 | 393.21 | 417.20 | 453.03 |
| 333.22 | 349.08 | 371.01 | 394.06 | 417.21 | 453.08 |
| 333.23 | 349.09 | 371.03 | 394.16 | 418.03 | 453.12 |
| 333.23 | 350.02 | 371.04 | 394.22 | 418.04 | 454.09 |
| 334.08 | 350.03 | 371.10 | 395.11 | 418.06 | 454.11 |
| 334.08 | 350.04 | 371.11 | 395.19 | 418.16 | 454.17 |
| 334.09 | 350.04 | 371.14 | 395.21 | 419.06 | 454.17 |
| 334.14 | 350.07 | 371.15 | 396.01 | 419.06 | 454.20 |
| 334.14 | 350.08 | 371.19 | 396.10 | 419.07 | 455.05 |
| 334.15 | 350.12 | 372.12 | 396.12 | 419.11 | 455.05 |
| 334.17 | 350.18 | 372.16 | 396.17 | 419.11 | 455.08 |
| 334.20 | 350.19 | 372.18 | 396.22 | 419.12 | 455.11 |
| 335.01 | 350.20 | 373.10 | 397.01 | 419.15 | 455.17 |
| 335.01 | 351.02 | 373.10 | 397.01 | 420.01 | 456.01 |
| 335.03 | 351.10 | 373.11 | 397.04 | 420.12 | 456.06 |
| 335.11 | 352.02 | 373.12 | 397.09 | 420.13 | 456.07 |
| 335.14 | 352.03 | 373.18 | 397.10 | 420.21 | 458.03 |
| 335.20 | 352.08 | 374.07 | 397.11 | 421.11 | 460.06 |
| 336.01 | 353.12 | 374.10 | 397.16 | 421.18 | 460.13 |
| 336.05 | 353.15 | 374.10 | 397.21 | 421.20 | 460.17 |
| 336.06 | 353.18 | 374.15 | 398.06 | 422.01 | 461.01 |
| 336.16 | 353.22 | 374.17 | 398.06 | 422.03 | 461.05 |
| 336.22 | 354.01 | 375.13 | 398.10 | 422.07 | 461.09 |
| 336.23 | 354.02 | 375.19 | 398.16 | 425.19 | 461.10 |
| 337.03 | 354.05 | 376.01 | 398.21 | 426.01 | 461.10 |
| 337.03 | 354.07 | 376.08 | 399.02 | 426.21 | 461.12 |
| 337.08 | 354.13 | 376.19 | 399.03 | 427.01 | 461.19 |
| 337.10 | 354.18 | 376.20 | 399.06 | 427.03 | 461.20 |
| 337.11 | 354.21 | 376.22 | 399.08 | 427.12 | 462.01 |
| 337.12 | 354.22 | 376.22 | 399.08 | 427.18 | 462.01 |
| 337.21 | 354.22 | 377.02 | 400.15 | 427.21 | 462.05 |
| 337.21 | 355.10 | 377.02 | 401.18 | 428.02 | 462.06 |
| 338.15 | 355.16 | 377.05 | 401.19 | 428.02 | 462.08 |
| 338.20 | 356.01 | 377.06 | 401.22 | 428.04 | 462.11 |
| 338.20 | 356.02 | 377.07 | 402.14 | 428.09 | 462.17 |
| 339.01 | 356.08 | 377.13 | 403.10 | 428.09 | 463.08 |
| 339.02 | 356.12 | 377.15 | 403.10 | 428.10 | 464.03 |
| 339.04 | 356.21 | 377.18 | 403.12 | 428.20 | 464.11 |
| 339.04 | 356.22 | 377.21 | 403.18 | 429.05 | 464.12 |
| 339.08 | 357.01 | 378.10 | 403.20 | 429.10 | 464.13 |
| 339.10 | 357.02 | 378.10 | 403.21 | 429.10 | 464.14 |
| 339.11 | 357.07 | 378.14 | 404.03 | 430.17 | 464.14 |
| 339.11 | 357.07 | 378.22 | 404.03 | 430.20 | 465.01 |
| 339.13 | 357.08 | 379.05 | 404.07 | 431.07 | 465.02 |
| 339.14 | 357.09 | 379.09 | 404.10 | 431.09 | 465.04 |
| 339.15 | 357.10 | 382.02 | 404.11 | 431.16 | 465.16 |
| 339.17 | 357.12 | 382.03 | 404.17 | 431.20 | 466.04 |
| 339.19 | 357.14 | 382.11 | 404.19 | 432.09 | 466.12 |
| 340.02 | 357.17 | 382.12 | 404.20 | 432.15 | 466.12 |
| 340.02 | 357.18 | 382.17 | 405.01 | 432.17 | 467.06 |
| 340.06 | 357.18 | 382.17 | 405.03 | 432.22 | 467.07 |
| 340.10 | 357.19 | 382.21 | 405.11 | 433.03 | 467.09 |
| 340.12 | 358.16 | 383.01 | 405.13 | 433.06 | 468.14 |
| 340.19 | 359.02 | 383.04 | 405.14 | 433.08 | 469.03 |
| 340.19 | 359.03 | 384.02 | 405.14 | 433.11 | 469.07 |
| 341.04 | 359.06 | 384.03 | 405.15 | 433.12 | 469.07 |
| 341.19 | 359.08 | 384.09 | 405.16 | 433.14 | 469.20 |
| 341.20 | 359.16 | 384.17 | 405.21 | 433.21 | 469.20 |
| 342.06 | 359.16 | 385.02 | 405.22 | 434.01 | 469.22 |
| 342.06 | 359.18 | 385.03 | 406.01 | 434.07 | 470.04 |
| 342.08 | 360.18 | 385.04 | 406.02 | 434.10 | 470.09 |
| 342.16 | 361.06 | 385.07 | 406.04 | 434.12 | 470.17 |
| 342.19 | 361.08 | 385.08 | 406.06 | 435.01 | 470.18 |
| 342.20 | 361.09 | 385.11 | 406.17 | 435.07 | 471.06 |
| 343.03 | 361.10 | 385.18 | 406.18 | 435.12 | 471.18 |
| 343.03 | 361.11 | 385.21 | 406.21 | 435.20 | 472.13 |
| 343.04 | 361.20 | 385.22 | 407.15 | 436.03 | 472.16 |
| 343.05 | 362.01 | 386.02 | 407.19 | 436.14 | 472.22 |
| 343.09 | 362.08 | 386.05 | 408.03 | 436.20 | 473.04 |
| 343.14 | 362.08 | 386.10 | 408.06 | 436.20 | 473.04 |
| 343.17 | 362.10 | 386.12 | 408.10 | 437.02 | 473.10 |
| 343.17 | 362.11 | 386.13 | 408.14 | 437.07 | 474.08 |
| 343.18 | 362.21 | 386.21 | 408.16 | 437.10 | 475.04 |
| 343.19 | 363.09 | 387.01 | 408.16 | 437.19 | 475.06 |
| 343.22 | 363.12 | 387.02 | 408.16 | 438.12 | 475.09 |
| 344.01 | 363.12 | 387.07 | 408.18 | 438.17 | 476.01 |
| 344.03 | 363.18 | 387.07 | 409.01 | 439.01 | 476.03 |
| 344.05 | 363.19 | 387.10 | 409.04 | 439.04 | 476.17 |
| 344.07 | 364.02 | 387.14 | 409.17 | 439.06 | 477.04 |
| 344.08 | 364.03 | 387.17 | 409.18 | 439.12 | 477.08 |
| 344.12 | 364.04 | 387.18 | 409.19 | 439.18 | 477.12 |
| 344.14 | 364.07 | 387.21 | 409.21 | 439.19 | 477.20 |
| 344.16 | 364.10 | 388.04 | 410.03 | 440.07 | 477.21 |
| 344.17 | 364.11 | 388.05 | 410.04 | 440.18 | 478.21 |
| 344.22 | 364.12 | 388.09 | 410.07 | 441.05 | 479.01 |
| 345.02 | 364.16 | 388.09 | 410.13 | 442.01 | 479.02 |
| 345.11 | 364.20 | 388.10 | 410.19 | 442.07 | 479.04 |
| 345.12 | 365.04 | 388.18 | 411.08 | 442.07 | 479.09 |
| 345.13 | 365.08 | 389.01 | 411.14 | 442.15 | 479.13 |
| 345.15 | 365.10 | 389.05 | 411.19 | 443.04 | 480.01 |
| 345.15 | 365.11 | 389.06 | 411.19 | 444.13 | 480.08 |

| | | | | | |
|---|---|---|---|---|---|
| 480.11 | 506.07 | 526.01 | 548.17 | 567.20 | 593.06 |
| 480.14 | 506.08 | 526.07 | 548.20 | 568.01 | 593.10 |
| 480.16 | 506.13 | 526.10 | 549.01 | 568.02 | 593.17 |
| 480.18 | 506.17 | 526.11 | 549.04 | 568.03 | 594.01 |
| 480.20 | 506.19 | 526.15 | 550.02 | 568.03 | 594.01 |
| 480.21 | 507.08 | 526.16 | 550.05 | 568.08 | 594.03 |
| 481.07 | 507.12 | 526.19 | 550.08 | 568.08 | 594.21 |
| 481.08 | 507.15 | 527.03 | 550.09 | 568.10 | 594.22 |
| 481.10 | 507.17 | 527.13 | 551.06 | 568.11 | 595.06 |
| 481.17 | 507.21 | 527.15 | 551.13 | 568.17 | 595.07 |
| 482.08 | 507.21 | 527.21 | 552.01 | 569.02 | 597.01 |
| 482.12 | 508.08 | 528.11 | 552.02 | 569.04 | 597.15 |
| 482.14 | 508.15 | 528.15 | 552.06 | 569.07 | 597.20 |
| 482.20 | 508.17 | 528.15 | 552.08 | 569.09 | 598.17 |
| 483.02 | 508.18 | 528.17 | 552.09 | 569.17 | 598.19 |
| 483.03 | 508.21 | 528.18 | 552.13 | 569.20 | 598.19 |
| 483.04 | 509.04 | 528.22 | 552.15 | 570.03 | 599.06 |
| 483.05 | 509.07 | 528.22 | 552.18 | 570.06 | 599.18 |
| 483.05 | 509.09 | 529.01 | 553.07 | 570.09 | 599.20 |
| 483.08 | 509.13 | 529.01 | 553.12 | 570.10 | 599.20 |
| 483.13 | 509.19 | 529.02 | 553.16 | 570.17 | 599.22 |
| 483.19 | 510.14 | 529.08 | 554.02 | 570.19 | 600.06 |
| 484.01 | 510.22 | 529.10 | 554.03 | 570.20 | 600.06 |
| 484.03 | 511.01 | 530.05 | 554.05 | 570.20 | 600.12 |
| 484.09 | 511.03 | 530.11 | 554.15 | 570.22 | 600.15 |
| 484.10 | 511.08 | 531.07 | 554.17 | 570.22 | 600.18 |
| 484.11 | 511.09 | 531.09 | 554.18 | 571.01 | 601.05 |
| 484.21 | 511.10 | 531.16 | 554.19 | 571.05 | 601.06 |
| 485.06 | 511.15 | 532.03 | 555.03 | 571.06 | 601.07 |
| 485.09 | 511.15 | 532.18 | 555.06 | 571.09 | 601.21 |
| 485.18 | 511.16 | 532.21 | 555.09 | 571.10 | 602.08 |
| 486.06 | 511.18 | 533.03 | 555.09 | 571.11 | 602.09 |
| 486.20 | 511.18 | 533.08 | 555.10 | 571.12 | 602.09 |
| 487.20 | 511.20 | 533.09 | 555.11 | 571.14 | 602.17 |
| 487.20 | 512.06 | 533.12 | 555.13 | 571.14 | 602.21 |
| 488.04 | 512.08 | 533.14 | 555.16 | 571.16 | 603.05 |
| 488.13 | 512.11 | 533.16 | 555.18 | 571.18 | 603.13 |
| 488.20 | 512.12 | 534.01 | 556.01 | 571.19 | 603.18 |
| 489.10 | 512.14 | 534.06 | 556.04 | 571.22 | 603.18 |
| 489.14 | 512.16 | 534.06 | 556.05 | 572.02 | 604.06 |
| 490.01 | 512.21 | 534.17 | 556.06 | 572.09 | 604.10 |
| 490.01 | 512.22 | 534.18 | 556.14 | 572.11 | 604.10 |
| 490.06 | 513.01 | 535.04 | 556.19 | 572.13 | 604.20 |
| 490.08 | 513.03 | 535.07 | 556.21 | 572.16 | 605.10 |
| 491.01 | 513.05 | 535.08 | 557.02 | 572.19 | 605.11 |
| 491.22 | 513.09 | 535.09 | 558.02 | 572.22 | 605.13 |
| 493.07 | 513.12 | 535.16 | 558.04 | 573.08 | 605.13 |
| 493.09 | 513.16 | 535.16 | 558.05 | 573.11 | 605.18 |
| 493.13 | 513.17 | 535.20 | 558.05 | 575.04 | 605.20 |
| 493.14 | 513.22 | 536.02 | 558.11 | 575.05 | 606.01 |
| 493.16 | 514.03 | 536.08 | 558.14 | 575.09 | 606.05 |
| 494.05 | 514.05 | 536.18 | 559.01 | 576.01 | 606.06 |
| 494.09 | 514.10 | 536.19 | 559.05 | 576.04 | 606.12 |
| 494.13 | 516.08 | 537.18 | 559.09 | 576.05 | 606.12 |
| 494.14 | 516.10 | 538.03 | 559.11 | 576.06 | 606.15 |
| 494.18 | 516.20 | 538.04 | 559.13 | 576.09 | 607.04 |
| 495.02 | 516.21 | 538.16 | 559.14 | 576.21 | 607.04 |
| 495.02 | 516.22 | 538.22 | 559.16 | 577.04 | 607.11 |
| 495.18 | 517.13 | 539.01 | 559.17 | 577.05 | 607.16 |
| 496.02 | 517.16 | 539.01 | 559.20 | 577.22 | 607.19 |
| 496.03 | 518.03 | 539.03 | 559.21 | 577.22 | 607.21 |
| 496.04 | 518.05 | 539.06 | 559.21 | 578.01 | 608.03 |
| 496.14 | 518.15 | 539.15 | 560.03 | 578.03 | 608.04 |
| 496.15 | 519.05 | 539.16 | 560.08 | 578.13 | 608.05 |
| 497.19 | 519.08 | 539.18 | 560.14 | 578.13 | 608.06 |
| 498.04 | 519.08 | 540.01 | 560.19 | 578.14 | 608.07 |
| 498.12 | 519.15 | 540.02 | 560.20 | 578.21 | 608.08 |
| 498.16 | 520.01 | 540.06 | 561.04 | 579.01 | 608.09 |
| 498.20 | 520.02 | 540.10 | 561.06 | 579.01 | 608.11 |
| 499.02 | 520.02 | 540.15 | 561.07 | 579.02 | 608.16 |
| 499.04 | 520.07 | 541.01 | 561.14 | 579.05 | 608.22 |
| 499.08 | 520.10 | 541.02 | 561.16 | 579.09 | 609.01 |
| 499.12 | 520.21 | 541.07 | 561.17 | 579.20 | 609.01 |
| 499.17 | 521.11 | 541.13 | 561.20 | 580.17 | 609.13 |
| 499.17 | 521.12 | 541.20 | 562.01 | 580.19 | 610.10 |
| 500.04 | 521.14 | 541.20 | 562.03 | 581.07 | 610.12 |
| 500.06 | 521.15 | 541.22 | 562.04 | 581.10 | 610.14 |
| 500.07 | 521.16 | 542.12 | 562.04 | 581.11 | 610.16 |
| 500.09 | 521.17 | 542.17 | 562.12 | 581.14 | 611.04 |
| 501.01 | 521.17 | 542.22 | 563.04 | 581.17 | 611.07 |
| 501.03 | 521.18 | 543.06 | 563.09 | 583.14 | 611.08 |
| 501.07 | 521.20 | 543.07 | 563.12 | 583.17 | 611.12 |
| 501.10 | 521.21 | 543.08 | 563.12 | 583.22 | 611.18 |
| 501.12 | 522.14 | 543.09 | 563.13 | 584.02 | 612.05 |
| 501.13 | 522.20 | 543.10 | 563.15 | 585.04 | 612.12 |
| 501.14 | 522.21 | 543.13 | 563.17 | 586.05 | 612.18 |
| 501.19 | 523.02 | 543.14 | 564.07 | 586.18 | 613.01 |
| 501.20 | 523.03 | 543.15 | 564.08 | 587.13 | 613.03 |
| 501.20 | 523.04 | 543.18 | 564.09 | 587.17 | 613.06 |
| 502.03 | 523.04 | 543.22 | 564.11 | 587.17 | 613.10 |
| 503.08 | 523.05 | 543.22 | 564.21 | 589.04 | 614.02 |
| 503.17 | 523.08 | 544.19 | 565.17 | 589.13 | 614.15 |
| 503.18 | 523.09 | 545.02 | 565.19 | 589.14 | 615.08 |
| 503.20 | 523.12 | 545.05 | 566.01 | 589.15 | 615.14 |
| 504.03 | 523.12 | 545.08 | 566.02 | 589.17 | 616.21 |
| 504.11 | 523.17 | 545.14 | 566.06 | 589.18 | 617.09 |
| 504.13 | 523.18 | 545.15 | 566.07 | 590.01 | 617.10 |
| 504.20 | 523.22 | 545.21 | 566.10 | 590.04 | 617.11 |
| 504.21 | 524.01 | 546.03 | 566.12 | 590.17 | 617.12 |
| 504.22 | 524.06 | 546.14 | 566.12 | 590.19 | 617.14 |
| 505.03 | 524.07 | 546.17 | 566.13 | 591.01 | 617.17 |
| 505.03 | 524.07 | 547.01 | 566.13 | 591.15 | 618.01 |
| 505.05 | 524.15 | 547.05 | 566.15 | 591.18 | 618.02 |
| 505.09 | 524.19 | 547.10 | 566.17 | 592.03 | 618.04 |
| 505.13 | 525.01 | 547.17 | 566.18 | 592.03 | 619.03 |
| 505.16 | 525.07 | 547.17 | 567.01 | 592.13 | 619.04 |
| 505.17 | 525.14 | 547.20 | 567.02 | 592.20 | 619.06 |
| 505.19 | 525.16 | 547.21 | 567.07 | 592.20 | 619.07 |
| 506.04 | 525.16 | 548.02 | 567.11 | 593.04 | 619.07 |
| 506.05 | 525.18 | 548.08 | 567.12 | 593.06 | 619.21 |
| 506.06 | 525.22 | 548.16 | 567.18 | | 619.22 |

| | | | | | |
|---|---|---|---|---|---|
| 620.02 | 640.13 | 660.02 | 682.16 | 703.19 | 733.14 |
| 620.04 | 641.16 | 660.04 | 682.16 | 704.13 | 733.16 |
| 620.08 | 641.20 | 660.11 | 683.11 | 705.12 | 733.18 |
| 620.13 | 643.03 | 660.16 | 683.20 | 705.21 | 733.19 |
| 620.18 | 643.11 | 660.17 | 683.21 | 706.01 | 733.22 |
| 620.19 | 644.01 | 660.22 | 683.22 | 706.02 | 734.02 |
| 620.19 | 645.14 | 661.01 | 684.01 | 706.04 | 734.04 |
| 621.02 | 645.16 | 661.02 | 684.02 | 706.05 | 734.09 |
| 621.12 | 645.17 | 661.05 | 684.06 | 706.20 | 734.14 |
| 621.15 | 645.21 | 661.10 | 684.11 | 707.03 | 734.15 |
| 621.17 | 646.01 | 661.11 | 684.14 | 707.03 | 734.18 |
| 621.19 | 646.03 | 661.20 | 684.15 | 707.05 | 734.20 |
| 621.20 | 646.06 | 662.01 | 684.18 | 707.06 | 735.02 |
| 622.04 | 646.06 | 662.02 | 684.20 | 707.07 | 735.06 |
| 622.05 | 646.11 | 662.02 | 684.21 | 707.10 | 736.10 |
| 622.05 | 646.13 | 662.09 | 684.21 | 707.13 | 736.12 |
| 622.11 | 646.19 | 662.12 | 685.01 | 707.21 | 737.01 |
| 622.18 | 647.03 | 662.22 | 685.02 | 708.07 | 737.15 |
| 623.06 | 647.04 | 663.03 | 685.02 | 708.12 | 738.04 |
| 623.08 | 647.07 | 663.03 | 685.06 | 708.17 | 738.06 |
| 623.12 | 647.08 | 663.05 | 685.10 | 708.18 | 738.12 |
| 623.14 | 647.08 | 663.09 | 685.11 | 708.19 | 738.17 |
| 623.15 | 647.10 | 663.21 | 686.11 | 708.19 | 739.01 |
| 624.01 | 647.12 | 663.22 | 686.12 | 708.20 | 739.03 |
| 624.02 | 647.16 | 664.18 | 686.17 | 709.09 | 739.04 |
| 624.05 | 647.18 | 665.01 | 686.19 | 709.12 | 739.07 |
| 624.06 | 647.22 | 665.05 | 687.01 | 709.14 | 739.09 |
| 624.07 | 648.02 | 665.07 | 688.02 | 709.16 | 739.09 |
| 624.09 | 648.03 | 665.08 | 688.04 | 709.17 | 739.12 |
| 624.10 | 648.10 | 665.15 | 689.01 | 709.18 | 739.13 |
| 624.13 | 648.22 | 665.18 | 689.03 | 710.11 | 739.15 |
| 624.17 | 649.06 | 665.20 | 689.08 | 710.13 | 739.18 |
| 624.19 | 649.07 | 666.02 | 689.09 | 710.14 | 739.21 |
| 624.21 | 649.10 | 666.11 | 689.10 | 711.11 | 739.21 |
| 625.02 | 649.12 | 666.12 | 689.14 | 711.15 | 740.01 |
| 626.10 | 649.12 | 666.13 | 689.18 | 711.16 | 740.02 |
| 627.06 | 649.14 | 666.14 | 689.20 | 711.18 | 741.04 |
| 627.12 | 649.15 | 666.21 | 690.03 | 712.21 | 741.07 |
| 627.13 | 649.15 | 666.22 | 690.09 | 713.11 | 741.09 |
| 627.15 | 649.16 | 667.03 | 690.11 | 714.04 | 741.19 |
| 627.17 | 649.19 | 669.11 | 690.14 | 715.05 | 741.19 |
| 627.18 | 649.21 | 669.20 | 690.18 | 715.10 | 741.20 |
| 628.04 | 649.21 | 669.20 | 691.01 | 715.11 | 742.03 |
| 628.10 | 650.05 | 669.21 | 691.05 | 716.04 | 742.04 |
| 628.15 | 650.07 | 670.02 | 691.06 | 716.10 | 742.06 |
| 628.17 | 650.08 | 670.06 | 691.12 | 716.14 | 742.09 |
| 628.20 | 650.08 | 670.08 | 691.14 | 716.19 | 742.10 |
| 629.03 | 650.11 | 670.09 | 691.16 | 716.21 | 742.13 |
| 629.09 | 650.14 | 670.12 | 691.16 | 716.22 | 742.19 |
| 629.10 | 650.15 | 670.15 | 692.03 | 717.02 | 742.20 |
| 629.14 | 650.15 | 670.16 | 692.08 | 717.17 | 742.21 |
| 629.17 | 650.20 | 670.18 | 692.09 | 718.11 | 743.05 |
| 630.10 | 651.02 | 670.20 | 692.13 | 718.12 | 743.08 |
| 631.04 | 651.02 | 670.22 | 692.15 | 718.21 | 743.21 |
| 631.11 | 651.05 | 671.11 | 692.19 | 720.07 | 744.01 |
| 631.18 | 651.05 | 671.22 | 692.22 | 721.11 | 744.03 |
| 631.19 | 651.08 | 672.04 | 693.02 | 722.07 | 744.03 |
| 631.20 | 651.11 | 672.09 | 693.05 | 722.08 | 744.05 |
| 631.21 | 651.11 | 672.11 | 693.07 | 723.06 | 744.06 |
| 632.03 | 651.15 | 672.14 | 693.08 | 723.08 | 744.07 |
| 632.03 | 651.17 | 672.17 | 693.20 | 723.17 | 744.11 |
| 632.05 | 651.21 | 673.02 | 693.21 | 724.01 | 744.17 |
| 632.11 | 652.04 | 673.03 | 694.02 | 724.10 | 744.20 |
| 632.17 | 652.06 | 673.05 | 694.07 | 724.13 | 745.08 |
| 632.18 | 652.07 | 673.09 | 695.05 | 724.18 | 745.13 |
| 632.21 | 652.09 | 673.11 | 695.05 | 724.22 | 745.14 |
| 633.02 | 652.11 | 674.01 | 695.06 | 725.07 | 745.15 |
| 633.05 | 652.12 | 674.04 | 695.13 | 726.09 | 745.15 |
| 633.10 | 652.13 | 674.06 | 695.15 | 726.15 | 745.22 |
| 633.11 | 652.15 | 674.14 | 695.15 | 726.16 | 746.01 |
| 633.16 | 652.17 | 674.21 | 695.18 | 726.16 | 746.04 |
| 633.18 | 652.20 | 675.10 | 695.20 | 726.17 | 746.06 |
| 633.18 | 653.02 | 675.11 | 696.21 | 726.19 | 746.16 |
| 633.20 | 653.05 | 675.16 | 697.05 | 726.20 | 746.17 |
| 634.06 | 653.07 | 676.15 | 697.12 | 727.06 | 746.20 |
| 634.07 | 653.07 | 676.16 | 697.12 | 727.07 | 746.22 |
| 634.11 | 653.08 | 677.01 | 697.12 | 727.08 | 747.04 |
| 634.12 | 653.08 | 677.02 | 697.20 | 727.10 | 747.06 |
| 634.13 | 653.10 | 677.03 | 697.21 | 727.16 | 747.14 |
| 634.14 | 653.11 | 677.07 | 698.01 | 728.17 | 747.17 |
| 634.15 | 653.13 | 677.13 | 698.06 | 728.20 | 747.22 |
| 634.20 | 653.15 | 677.15 | 698.10 | 729.04 | 748.07 |
| 635.06 | 653.16 | 677.15 | 698.11 | 729.09 | 748.15 |
| 635.08 | 653.16 | 677.17 | 698.13 | 729.13 | 748.15 |
| 635.14 | 653.17 | 677.18 | 698.14 | 729.16 | 748.21 |
| 635.16 | 653.17 | 677.19 | 698.20 | 729.18 | 748.22 |
| 635.18 | 653.20 | 678.01 | 698.20 | 729.18 | 749.11 |
| 635.19 | 654.07 | 678.03 | 698.21 | 729.20 | 749.18 |
| 635.22 | 654.08 | 678.03 | 699.03 | 730.01 | 749.21 |
| 636.02 | 654.09 | 678.06 | 699.07 | 730.03 | 750.01 |
| 636.03 | 654.09 | 678.07 | 699.08 | 730.05 | 750.01 |
| 636.04 | 654.10 | 678.09 | 699.15 | 730.06 | 750.07 |
| 636.06 | 654.10 | 678.12 | 699.19 | 730.11 | 750.08 |
| 636.22 | 654.12 | 679.06 | 699.21 | 730.12 | 750.08 |
| 637.16 | 654.12 | 679.11 | 700.06 | 730.12 | 750.10 |
| 637.17 | 654.13 | 679.13 | 700.11 | 730.15 | 750.15 |
| 637.22 | 654.13 | 679.15 | 700.22 | 730.19 | 750.19 |
| 638.03 | 654.14 | 679.15 | 701.04 | 730.21 | 751.03 |
| 638.05 | 654.18 | 679.22 | 702.09 | 731.04 | 751.04 |
| 638.09 | 654.19 | 680.03 | 702.12 | 731.14 | 751.07 |
| 638.10 | 655.16 | 680.09 | 702.13 | 731.17 | 751.12 |
| 638.13 | 655.17 | 680.15 | 702.14 | 732.01 | 751.15 |
| 638.19 | 656.14 | 680.17 | 702.16 | 732.11 | 751.18 |
| 638.22 | 656.15 | 681.01 | 702.19 | 732.13 | 751.19 |
| 639.03 | 656.20 | 681.04 | 702.21 | 732.16 | 751.19 |
| 639.04 | 658.02 | 681.09 | 702.21 | 733.05 | 752.05 |
| 639.07 | 658.02 | 681.11 | 703.01 | 733.08 | 752.06 |
| 639.10 | 658.04 | 681.12 | 703.07 | 733.09 | 752.07 |
| 639.11 | 658.08 | 682.01 | 703.11 | 733.10 | 752.07 |
| 639.21 | 658.11 | 682.10 | 703.12 | 733.12 | 752.09 |
| 640.10 | 659.10 | 682.12 | 703.18 | | 752.09 |

| | | | | | |
|---|---|---|---|---|---|
| 752.09 | 533.07 | 396.06 | 133.15 | 562.18 | 396.04 |
| 752.11 | 535.20 | 398.04 | 134.04 | 563.07 | 397.03 |
| 752.11 | 536.07 | 401.02 | 134.06 | 567.16 | 416.17 |
| 752.14 | 544.07 | 405.09 | 134.22 | 576.09 | 435.15 |
| 753.04 | 545.17 | 412.09 | 140.15 | 587.14 | 449.15 |
| 753.05 | 554.08 | 422.04 | 152.12 | 589.21 | 470.10 |
| 753.06 | 578.14 | 435.03 | 154.18 | 590.02 | 470.13 |
| 753.09 | 578.17 | 436.03 | 155.14 | 592.07 | 470.14 |
| 753.12 | 579.03 | 439.06 | 155.20 | 592.10 | 479.07 |
| 753.16 | 589.19 | 468.18 | 156.10 | 592.11 | 481.06 |
| 753.18 | 604.04 | 469.01 | 164.20 | 593.12 | 482.02 |
| 753.21 | 608.02 | 469.12 | 171.03 | 600.07 | 493.04 |
| 754.14 | 617.20 | 472.19 | 174.11 | 601.06 | 493.11 |
| 754.20 | 619.06 | 473.07 | 175.15 | 602.11 | 493.20 |
| 754.20 | 621.10 | 473.07 | 176.07 | 602.12 | 494.02 |
| 755.04 | 660.12 | 484.13 | 176.07 | 605.06 | 494.16 |
| 755.11 | 708.05 | 488.12 | 177.03 | 605.12 | 496.13 |
| 755.17 | 716.17 | 489.14 | 180.08 | 608.02 | 510.21 |
| 755.18 | 730.16 | 489.15 | 182.04 | 608.17 | 524.13 |
| 755.21 | 748.05 | 490.08 | 183.03 | 612.05 | 539.20 |
| 756.16 | i'll | 491.13 | 192.08 | 612.20 | 554.20 |
| 756.19 | 023.21 | 499.10 | 193.04 | 618.11 | 555.01 |
| 756.20 | 029.15 | 510.19 | 207.15 | 620.20 | 572.07 |
| 757.04 | 029.18 | 519.03 | 208.19 | 621.03 | 572.20 |
| 757.05 | 030.04 | 521.04 | 212.17 | 621.06 | 577.20 |
| 757.08 | 030.04 | 521.14 | 216.21 | 622.13 | 578.05 |
| 757.13 | 030.06 | 523.06 | 218.09 | 630.01 | 578.08 |
| 757.15 | 033.03 | 524.15 | 219.05 | 632.11 | 580.05 |
| 757.17 | 036.01 | 525.09 | 221.02 | 634.09 | 590.13 |
| 757.19 | 041.09 | 527.03 | 223.18 | 645.14 | 605.11 |
| 758.02 | 042.04 | 527.05 | 230.12 | 646.18 | 614.11 |
| 758.03 | 053.10 | 537.13 | 231.03 | 646.21 | 620.20 |
| 758.05 | 059.12 | 545.05 | 235.06 | 648.01 | 624.11 |
| 758.05 | 059.13 | 545.06 | 237.01 | 649.22 | 648.01 |
| 758.06 | 060.03 | 547.03 | 251.05 | 651.04 | 654.01 |
| 758.12 | 064.13 | 563.10 | 251.07 | 655.03 | 654.21 |
| 758.21 | 064.16 | 565.08 | 251.08 | 661.11 | 655.03 |
| 759.04 | 071.01 | 565.09 | 251.12 | 661.16 | 661.07 |
| 759.17 | 074.17 | 565.10 | 257.10 | 662.21 | 661.09 |
| 759.20 | 074.18 | 565.11 | 258.03 | 667.04 | 667.17 |
| 760.03 | 084.13 | 573.07 | 260.10 | 669.20 | 671.13 |
| 760.10 | 102.12 | 573.09 | 261.14 | 670.12 | 678.19 |
| 760.16 | 108.03 | 579.07 | 261.21 | 676.17 | 684.16 |
| 760.21 | 123.11 | 580.02 | 262.04 | 676.17 | 697.11 |
| 761.01 | 123.14 | 590.04 | 272.07 | 677.21 | 706.03 |
| 761.03 | 124.10 | 594.02 | 273.20 | 684.12 | 712.22 |
| 761.06 | 125.14 | 594.11 | 276.19 | 685.09 | 721.03 |
| 761.11 | 134.03 | 602.04 | 276.22 | 685.15 | 740.08 |
| 761.12 | 135.15 | 606.10 | 277.19 | 690.04 | 753.11 |
| 761.17 | 142.06 | 612.15 | 279.03 | 691.04 | 756.07 |
| 761.18 | 151.14 | 612.21 | 282.19 | 694.06 | ice |
| 761.19 | 151.15 | 614.20 | 283.02 | 703.08 | 065.15 |
| 761.20 | 152.14 | 614.21 | 283.09 | 706.05 | 235.04 |
| 762.01 | 159.03 | 615.11 | 287.14 | 714.02 | 656.11 |
| 762.12 | 159.11 | 616.11 | 288.09 | 717.10 | ice-cold |
| 762.14 | 159.11 | 616.13 | 288.10 | 721.04 | 052.02 |
| 762.19 | 164.08 | 617.15 | 294.04 | 721.10 | ice-water |
| 763.03 | 164.20 | 618.09 | 310.21 | 730.05 | 264.20 |
| 763.07 | 176.11 | 620.12 | 311.15 | 733.06 | icicle |
| 763.16 | 176.12 | 620.13 | 314.17 | 734.07 | 667.11 |
| 763.22 | 178.14 | 620.21 | 318.07 | 739.05 | icily |
| 764.06 | 183.21 | 620.22 | 329.01 | 740.10 | 008.21 |
| i' | 184.02 | 621.09 | 345.01 | 742.02 | icy |
| 016.06 | 184.18 | 624.03 | 357.21 | 742.15 | 036.04 |
| 028.21 | 187.01 | 629.19 | 359.14 | 753.12 | idea |
| 042.21 | 195.09 | 631.19 | 360.17 | 753.13 | 030.22 |
| 193.16 | 202.15 | 631.21 | 360.22 | 754.12 | 041.16 |
| 193.20 | 203.21 | 649.11 | 360.22 | i've | 047.03 |
| 233.05 | 210.08 | 650.01 | 363.17 | 027.01 | 091.12 |
| 233.09 | 212.16 | 652.02 | 383.02 | 029.18 | 146.10 |
| 321.04 | 223.12 | 652.22 | 388.09 | 053.13 | 213.22 |
| 324.05 | 223.17 | 656.15 | 391.22 | 055.16 | 225.21 |
| 324.17 | 228.08 | 667.03 | 392.12 | 057.02 | 237.06 |
| 324.20 | 228.21 | 669.12 | 394.22 | 100.20 | 244.17 |
| 326.10 | 233.18 | 671.01 | 395.10 | 109.15 | 269.10 |
| 326.12 | 252.04 | 685.11 | 399.04 | 148.13 | 272.21 |
| 696.07 | 252.05 | 698.17 | 401.05 | 153.05 | 297.19 |
| 720.18 | 252.08 | 703.02 | 407.21 | 156.05 | 335.18 |
| i'd | 258.02 | 707.12 | 416.12 | 163.01 | 398.19 |
| 026.21 | 260.12 | 708.15 | 417.05 | 163.08 | 417.20 |
| 052.13 | 263.02 | 710.07 | 422.09 | 171.19 | 441.04 |
| 105.09 | 271.08 | 710.09 | 434.06 | 175.03 | 448.07 |
| 163.15 | 272.14 | 713.02 | 435.12 | 176.20 | 495.02 |
| 195.04 | 281.04 | 713.03 | 455.22 | 177.16 | 539.18 |
| 223.15 | 283.10 | 716.18 | 469.14 | 179.04 | 557.12 |
| 223.15 | 284.17 | 720.04 | 470.20 | 184.19 | 583.12 |
| 229.14 | 284.17 | 722.16 | 476.19 | 186.13 | 597.15 |
| 236.05 | 290.08 | 722.20 | 483.01 | 186.15 | 681.01 |
| 238.12 | 290.09 | 723.17 | 484.16 | 192.07 | 734.04 |
| 253.05 | 306.01 | 724.14 | 485.08 | 199.18 | 749.06 |
| 259.12 | 317.05 | 742.07 | 496.15 | 216.12 | ideal |
| 260.08 | 318.03 | 742.19 | 499.07 | 223.04 | 053.22 |
| 263.05 | 327.03 | 752.04 | 499.07 | 242.03 | ideas |
| 273.12 | 333.02 | 753.06 | 501.14 | 242.05 | 023.18 |
| 285.01 | 337.19 | 753.10 | 504.08 | 242.07 | 082.08 |
| 306.12 | 342.05 | 756.06 | 510.13 | 252.11 | 176.22 |
| 344.11 | 344.02 | 757.10 | 511.14 | 273.13 | 216.08 |
| 366.07 | 344.03 | 757.11 | 512.03 | 273.14 | 293.05 |
| 372.10 | 345.06 | i'm | 523.21 | 273.14 | 354.11 |
| 386.03 | 347.19 | 008.01 | 533.19 | 340.14 | 376.10 |
| 386.10 | 348.04 | 017.15 | 539.15 | 341.18 | 503.05 |
| 388.07 | 349.06 | 030.08 | 540.05 | 341.19 | 730.20 |
| 391.18 | 365.10 | 030.19 | 545.10 | 345.17 | idiocy |
| 395.01 | 366.06 | 052.12 | 545.11 | 357.15 | 228.21 |
| 398.16 | 384.03 | 055.07 | 545.11 | 363.17 | 340.09 |
| 405.12 | 385.13 | 056.15 | 545.13 | 374.03 | 525.03 |
| 407.10 | 385.14 | 076.08 | 546.08 | 383.01 | 607.09 |
| 460.14 | 394.03 | 107.07 | 546.18 | 383.02 | idiot |
| 488.20 | 395.08 | 110.04 | 551.06 | 384.10 | 008.16 |
| 490.07 | 396.01 | 116.22 | 551.12 | 385.04 | 167.02 |
| 497.18 | 396.05 | 122.07 | 554.13 | 388.06 | 252.04 |

| | | | | | |
|---|---|---|---|---|---|
| 409.01 | 170.06 | 342.11 | 526.01 | 695.18 | 498.12 |
| 497.01 | 172.08 | 343.21 | 526.04 | 700.08 | ill-natured |
| 629.17 | 174.19 | 344.04 | 526.14 | 702.01 | 148.15 |
| 720.03 | 175.03 | 344.07 | 528.17 | 702.09 | 174.08 |
| idiotic | 175.11 | 345.12 | 531.07 | 702.11 | 204.15 |
| 150.04 | 175.16 | 345.15 | 532.15 | 703.01 | ill-temper |
| idiots | 176.10 | 346.13 | 535.01 | 703.05 | 253.11 |
| 104.22 | 178.06 | 347.12 | 535.20 | 706.06 | 280.11 |
| idle | 179.05 | 348.09 | 536.06 | 708.05 | ill-tempered |
| 050.17 | 180.18 | 350.03 | 536.11 | 710.07 | 023.12 |
| 064.07 | 181.19 | 353.11 | 540.03 | 710.09 | ill-treatment |
| 150.20 | 181.20 | 355.01 | 542.09 | 713.07 | 081.04 |
| 223.07 | 182.15 | 356.20 | 543.07 | 716.14 | 442.20 |
| 495.13 | 182.19 | 359.21 | 543.10 | 722.13 | ill-turn |
| 684.18 | 182.21 | 362.05 | 544.04 | 722.15 | 088.03 |
| 684.19 | 183.16 | 362.08 | 545.12 | 722.20 | illness |
| 705.15 | 184.11 | 363.17 | 545.18 | 724.13 | 197.17 |
| 730.03 | 187.02 | 365.10 | 547.03 | 725.12 | 202.02 |
| 742.16 | 189.16 | 366.07 | 552.22 | 729.20 | 205.15 |
| 742.18 | 191.13 | 371.10 | 556.04 | 730.15 | 274.20 |
| 750.14 | 193.15 | 373.01 | 558.13 | 730.18 | 295.07 |
| 760.15 | 195.09 | 373.05 | 560.08 | 739.07 | 327.10 |
| idleness | 197.15 | 374.18 | 560.12 | 740.06 | 332.12 |
| 028.21 | 202.09 | 376.04 | 561.11 | 743.02 | 347.07 |
| 646.22 | 203.22 | 378.11 | 562.05 | 746.13 | 351.07 |
| 701.15 | 204.20 | 382.15 | 563.02 | 746.18 | 429.10 |
| idol | 207.07 | 385.17 | 563.03 | 748.08 | 521.12 |
| 157.03 | 209.04 | 386.02 | 564.03 | 748.15 | 603.11 |
| 378.17 | 211.07 | 386.08 | 565.08 | 749.12 | 733.07 |
| 733.02 | 212.16 | 388.11 | 565.08 | 749.13 | 740.02 |
| idols | 214.21 | 388.12 | 569.16 | 753.17 | 759.22 |
| 141.15 | 215.02 | 390.01 | 571.02 | 754.16 | illnesses |
| if | 217.12 | 390.18 | 571.05 | 755.06 | 424.05 |
| 002.17 | 219.09 | 392.08 | 571.09 | 755.08 | illumined |
| 004.14 | 219.22 | 393.13 | 573.03 | 758.07 | 693.13 |
| 007.06 | 222.09 | 394.17 | 573.06 | 760.12 | illusion |
| 008.15 | 223.05 | 395.15 | 577.06 | ignoble | 302.10 |
| 012.11 | 225.10 | 396.19 | 578.16 | 150.02 | illusions |
| 016.07 | 229.06 | 397.02 | 579.06 | 404.19 | 293.05 |
| 019.22 | 230.07 | 398.16 | 587.07 | ignominious | image |
| 020.21 | 231.06 | 399.02 | 588.07 | 257.04 | 236.01 |
| 021.20 | 233.14 | 401.11 | 589.18 | ignorance | 371.04 |
| 023.09 | 234.01 | 404.09 | 590.11 | 025.06 | 378.17 |
| 026.17 | 234.13 | 405.05 | 592.04 | 203.20 | 635.09 |
| 028.02 | 235.20 | 405.13 | 593.01 | 229.17 | 731.18 |
| 028.05 | 238.12 | 405.16 | 593.12 | 261.13 | imaginable |
| 031.05 | 239.08 | 406.06 | 600.12 | 423.05 | 008.19 |
| 032.07 | 240.01 | 407.09 | 600.18 | 459.10 | 434.17 |
| 033.14 | 242.10 | 408.20 | 601.10 | 468.19 | imaginary |
| 041.21 | 245.07 | 409.05 | 602.03 | 493.20 | 431.01 |
| 043.03 | 246.02 | 411.17 | 603.21 | 562.12 | 593.18 |
| 044.15 | 247.03 | 418.19 | 605.07 | 679.20 | imagination |
| 045.10 | 247.13 | 419.12 | 605.20 | 727.01 | 058.10 |
| 048.20 | 248.03 | 420.18 | 606.20 | ignorant | 291.01 |
| 051.07 | 250.06 | 421.07 | 608.03 | 060.06 | 623.13 |
| 051.14 | 251.04 | 422.02 | 609.01 | 183.18 | 731.11 |
| 053.02 | 251.09 | 425.18 | 610.21 | 256.15 | imagine |
| 053.11 | 252.01 | 425.20 | 611.12 | 286.18 | 023.18 |
| 053.16 | 252.03 | 429.17 | 612.19 | 403.03 | 229.20 |
| 054.12 | 252.04 | 431.10 | 613.11 | 498.19 | 256.01 |
| 055.22 | 253.03 | 432.15 | 613.18 | 636.12 | 307.19 |
| 056.13 | 253.15 | 433.06 | 613.20 | ill | 333.16 |
| 063.05 | 257.20 | 433.13 | 615.13 | 011.19 | 342.08 |
| 064.14 | 260.06 | 436.18 | 617.10 | 029.01 | 346.05 |
| 065.02 | 260.13 | 437.20 | 617.20 | 039.15 | 381.07 |
| 071.18 | 261.20 | 438.15 | 619.05 | 043.02 | 388.10 |
| 074.15 | 262.22 | 440.21 | 619.18 | 082.06 | 398.21 |
| 077.21 | 263.01 | 443.17 | 620.09 | 126.20 | 485.18 |
| 081.07 | 268.02 | 446.21 | 620.13 | 140.09 | 504.13 |
| 083.20 | 271.18 | 450.21 | 620.17 | 185.13 | 511.10 |
| 084.07 | 272.01 | 454.05 | 620.18 | 193.07 | 526.02 |
| 087.09 | 272.12 | 454.09 | 621.14 | 196.03 | 605.18 |
| 092.15 | 273.11 | 456.16 | 623.16 | 226.13 | 614.04 |
| 103.06 | 279.11 | 458.10 | 627.20 | 239.06 | 764.10 |
| 104.15 | 280.21 | 461.14 | 628.06 | 260.08 | imagined |
| 105.12 | 284.16 | 465.01 | 629.20 | 261.22 | 001.12 |
| 106.15 | 284.17 | 469.01 | 630.09 | 285.19 | 029.04 |
| 110.16 | 295.10 | 469.02 | 631.22 | 286.03 | 048.14 |
| 112.02 | 296.06 | 470.18 | 632.17 | 292.12 | 066.17 |
| 115.11 | 296.19 | 474.08 | 634.10 | 306.07 | 097.19 |
| 117.17 | 299.17 | 476.03 | 636.06 | 326.12 | 130.11 |
| 122.11 | 305.16 | 476.13 | 636.19 | 343.21 | 240.15 |
| 123.04 | 306.03 | 476.18 | 638.01 | 406.04 | 253.04 |
| 123.08 | 307.10 | 476.20 | 644.09 | 442.16 | 417.08 |
| 123.20 | 307.11 | 477.06 | 647.18 | 532.21 | 561.19 |
| 124.06 | 307.13 | 477.20 | 648.18 | 543.14 | 675.18 |
| 125.09 | 308.02 | 478.19 | 649.18 | 543.16 | imagines |
| 127.08 | 308.21 | 484.09 | 650.18 | 554.09 | 272.10 |
| 127.13 | 309.20 | 484.21 | 652.01 | 555.02 | imagining |
| 127.18 | 315.19 | 485.14 | 652.03 | 563.07 | 010.10 |
| 133.17 | 316.14 | 488.06 | 652.11 | 563.13 | 150.20 |
| 135.17 | 318.11 | 489.01 | 653.06 | 567.16 | 550.09 |
| 138.07 | 318.13 | 489.05 | 654.03 | 586.20 | 590.18 |
| 140.12 | 319.10 | 490.04 | 659.08 | 599.05 | 746.02 |
| 140.14 | 320.12 | 493.13 | 659.21 | 599.17 | imbecile |
| 142.07 | 320.14 | 494.04 | 660.05 | 637.14 | 614.13 |
| 144.19 | 321.05 | 494.17 | 660.09 | 637.14 | immeasurably |
| 147.22 | 322.04 | 497.18 | 660.09 | 659.22 | 111.17 |
| 148.10 | 324.18 | 500.16 | 660.21 | 663.21 | immediate |
| 150.13 | 328.12 | 501.06 | 666.15 | 720.09 | 040.16 |
| 152.08 | 330.01 | 502.14 | 669.06 | 725.19 | 613.13 |
| 153.07 | 330.06 | 503.20 | 669.12 | ill-bred | immediately |
| 159.10 | 331.12 | 506.04 | 672.15 | 317.13 | 015.05 |
| 161.04 | 332.22 | 506.17 | 674.04 | ill-founded | 084.18 |
| 163.15 | 334.17 | 507.03 | 677.07 | 462.01 | 195.15 |
| 164.05 | 334.21 | 509.09 | 677.19 | ill-humour | 244.07 |
| 164.07 | 336.03 | 512.14 | 680.18 | 122.01 | 292.02 |
| 164.19 | 339.10 | 517.04 | 683.20 | ill-meaning | 353.17 |
| 167.01 | 339.13 | 521.05 | 685.04 | 481.12 | 365.18 |
| 167.11 | 340.02 | 523.06 | 685.14 | ill-nature | 389.09 |
| 168.08 | 341.01 | 524.14 | 695.16 | 346.14 | 498.05 |

| | | | | | |
|---|---|---|---|---|---|
| 510.17 | 112.16 | 022.22 | 082.22 | 138.01 | 192.14 |
| 538.10 | 148.17 | 023.15 | 083.06 | 138.07 | 193.14 |
| 586.18 | 228.21 | 023.19 | 084.06 | 139.05 | 193.20 |
| 607.13 | 265.07 | 024.12 | 087.02 | 140.01 | 196.08 |
| 623.18 | 391.09 | 025.16 | 088.08 | 140.16 | 197.12 |
| 629.18 | 405.22 | 026.07 | 089.07 | 140.18 | 197.21 |
| 670.02 | 450.01 | 026.10 | 089.20 | 141.14 | 198.09 |
| 674.08 | 525.12 | 027.08 | 090.09 | 141.19 | 199.10 |
| 684.10 | 692.14 | 027.19 | 090.11 | 142.12 | 199.12 |
| 745.01 | 731.06 | 028.03 | 090.17 | 142.20 | 200.02 |
| 751.08 | impracticable | 028.05 | 090.19 | 143.06 | 200.04 |
| immense | 069.06 | 028.12 | 091.04 | 143.11 | 200.09 |
| 006.01 | 183.11 | 028.19 | 091.13 | 143.14 | 202.01 |
| 017.06 | 715.05 | 029.18 | 091.14 | 146.03 | 203.15 |
| 444.03 | imprecations | 030.05 | 091.15 | 146.16 | 203.21 |
| 712.10 | 168.19 | 030.19 | 092.03 | 146.20 | 205.14 |
| imminent | impressed | 031.02 | 092.19 | 147.09 | 205.19 |
| 226.11 | 162.05 | 031.06 | 092.22 | 148.06 | 205.22 |
| imminently | 291.01 | 032.08 | 093.05 | 148.07 | 206.04 |
| 584.04 | 398.19 | 032.17 | 095.03 | 148.20 | 206.05 |
| immolation | 449.03 | 035.03 | 095.03 | 149.05 | 206.10 |
| 513.21 | 503.03 | 036.01 | 095.09 | 149.08 | 206.13 |
| immortal | 553.17 | 037.05 | 095.18 | 149.12 | 206.18 |
| 732.04 | 709.08 | 038.11 | 095.19 | 149.17 | 206.19 |
| immovable | impression | 038.14 | 098.03 | 149.20 | 207.03 |
| 551.08 | 058.09 | 038.19 | 098.07 | 150.06 | 207.05 |
| immoveable | 089.17 | 038.22 | 098.10 | 150.12 | 208.01 |
| 117.05 | 145.16 | 039.04 | 098.15 | 150.14 | 208.19 |
| imp | 149.05 | 039.18 | 099.01 | 151.10 | 209.06 |
| 085.08 | 351.15 | 040.10 | 099.12 | 153.08 | 211.07 |
| impalpable | 609.19 | 041.06 | 099.21 | 153.20 | 212.11 |
| 065.14 | 651.06 | 041.12 | 100.11 | 154.10 | 213.22 |
| imparted | impressions | 042.15 | 101.10 | 154.12 | 214.01 |
| 682.14 | 338.19 | 042.17 | 101.12 | 154.20 | 214.05 |
| imparting | 358.16 | 044.16 | 101.16 | 155.05 | 214.21 |
| 655.13 | 465.16 | 044.17 | 101.18 | 155.08 | 215.08 |
| impassable | imprisoned | 046.02 | 102.10 | 155.09 | 216.03 |
| 201.05 | 612.13 | 046.06 | 102.22 | 155.13 | 217.08 |
| impatience | improper | 046.16 | 103.14 | 155.15 | 217.21 |
| 005.08 | 562.07 | 047.12 | 103.16 | 156.16 | 218.06 |
| 705.19 | improve | 047.12 | 103.22 | 157.15 | 220.09 |
| impatient | 219.18 | 048.02 | 104.06 | 157.17 | 220.19 |
| 044.12 | 349.09 | 050.08 | 104.11 | 157.19 | 221.05 |
| 296.20 | improved | 050.09 | 104.18 | 157.20 | 221.15 |
| 354.20 | 113.05 | 050.11 | 104.21 | 158.14 | 221.19 |
| 372.02 | 142.21 | 050.17 | 105.08 | 158.18 | 222.05 |
| 407.11 | improvement | 051.01 | 106.02 | 159.14 | 222.09 |
| 430.15 | 577.02 | 051.09 | 106.17 | 159.15 | 222.17 |
| 551.19 | 693.07 | 052.07 | 107.08 | 160.08 | 223.03 |
| 741.05 | improving | 052.07 | 108.03 | 160.11 | 223.19 |
| impatiently | 703.15 | 052.20 | 108.05 | 160.22 | 224.05 |
| 168.17 | imps | 053.02 | 108.09 | 162.03 | 224.07 |
| 208.19 | 406.07 | 053.04 | 108.12 | 162.04 | 224.11 |
| 416.21 | impudence | 053.10 | 108.15 | 162.07 | 224.16 |
| 543.22 | 062.04 | 053.19 | 108.17 | 162.09 | 225.09 |
| 653.16 | 249.09 | 054.07 | 109.11 | 163.09 | 225.15 |
| 694.17 | impulse | 054.16 | 109.13 | 163.17 | 226.18 |
| impelled | 098.06 | 055.06 | 109.17 | 163.20 | 227.17 |
| 156.20 | 165.21' | 056.04 | 109.20 | 164.22 | 228.17 |
| 763.04 | 244.09 | 056.06 | 111.14 | 165.08 | 228.20 |
| imperceptibly | 645.10 | 056.13 | 112.09 | 166.05 | 233.20 |
| 640.02 | 689.07 | 057.05 | 112.14 | 167.05 | 234.01 |
| imperfect | in | 057.05 | 113.06 | 168.14 | 234.07 |
| 562.14 | 001.06 | 057.16 | 114.05 | 169.17 | 234.11 |
| imperious | 002.04 | 057.20 | 115.08 | 169.20 | 234.19 |
| 204.22 | 002.12 | 059.04 | 115.10 | 170.07 | 235.01 |
| imperiously | 002.18 | 059.09 | 115.18 | 170.13 | 235.03 |
| 155.16 | 002.19 | 059.13 | 115.20 | 171.12 | 235.12 |
| impertinence | 003.03 | 059.16 | 116.08 | 172.03 | 235.18 |
| 007.22 | 003.18 | 059.18 | 116.15 | 172.16 | 236.07 |
| 128.04 | 003.20 | 060.04 | 117.07 | 174.22 | 236.17 |
| impertinent | 004.07 | 060.13 | 117.21 | 176.05 | 236.18 |
| 228.19 | 004.16 | 060.13 | 118.14 | 176.06 | 237.13 |
| 437.18 | 006.03 | 060.20 | 118.21 | 176.06 | 237.16 |
| implements | 006.15 | 061.06 | 119.14 | 176.20 | 238.15 |
| 395.19 | 006.16 | 061.12 | 119.21 | 177.10 | 238.22 |
| implore | 007.02 | 061.18 | 120.08 | 177.12 | 239.07 |
| 405.20 | 007.03 | 062.01 | 120.13 | 177.22 | 240.04 |
| implored | 007.05 | 062.03 | 121.22 | 178.05 | 240.08 |
| 390.21 | 007.09 | 062.15 | 123.06 | 178.06 | 240.14 |
| 573.22 | 007.09 | 063.14 | 123.16 | 178.10 | 240.19 |
| 607.01 | 008.14 | 064.11 | 124.13 | 179.05 | 242.03 |
| imploring | 009.17 | 065.06 | 125.04 | 179.06 | 242.03 |
| 505.12 | 010.02 | 065.22 | 125.15 | 180.07 | 244.06 |
| 639.05 | 010.09 | 066.03 | 125.22 | 180.16 | 245.08 |
| imploringly | 010.12 | 066.10 | 126.09 | 181.02 | 247.16 |
| 329.09 | 011.03 | 067.06 | 126.11 | 182.11 | 248.13 |
| implying | 011.19 | 069.12 | 126.13 | 182.16 | 249.18 |
| 256.05 | 012.01 | 071.10 | 127.07 | 182.19 | 250.07 |
| import | 012.16 | 071.13 | 129.01 | 183.03 | 250.10 |
| 354.14 | 013.06 | 071.16 | 129.16 | 183.08 | 252.06 |
| important | 014.02 | 072.02 | 130.18 | 183.13 | 252.11 |
| 349.06 | 015.07 | 074.03 | 131.03 | 183.19 | 252.21 |
| importation | 015.21 | 074.11 | 131.08 | 184.14 | 253.03 |
| 716.02 | 015.21 | 075.10 | 131.22 | 184.18 | 253.09 |
| importunate | 016.20 | 076.15 | 133.13 | 185.04 | 254.02 |
| 051.21 | 017.03 | 077.11 | 134.10 | 185.11 | 254.07 |
| importunately | 017.05 | 077.18 | 134.18 | 185.18 | 254.11 |
| 638.12 | 017.13 | 077.19 | 134.19 | 186.07 | 254.12 |
| importuned | 018.01 | 078.19 | 135.01 | 187.01 | 254.18 |
| 331.09 | 018.04 | 079.15 | 135.16 | 187.05 | 255.06 |
| importunity | 018.07 | 079.17 | 136.04 | 188.11 | 256.04 |
| 607.03 | 019.14 | 079.22 | 136.05 | 188.22 | 257.08 |
| impose | 019.23 | 080.01 | 136.05 | 189.08 | 257.19 |
| 087.10 | 020.14 | 080.08 | 136.09 | 189.11 | 258.22 |
| 164.08 | 021.03 | 080.16 | 136.09 | 189.14 | 260.11 |
| imposed | 021.10 | 081.01 | 136.09 | 189.17 | 260.12 |
| 147.01 | 021.11 | 081.07 | 136.12 | 189.22 | 261.09 |
| impossible | 021.15 | 081.19 | 136.19 | 190.02 | 261.12 |
| 023.12 | 022.03 | 081.20 | 137.12 | 190.06 | 261.13 |
| 055.12 | 022.04 | | | 192.11 | 261.16 |

| | | | | | |
|---|---|---|---|---|---|
| 592.03 | 666.11 | 720.05 | 701.13 | 511.22 | inexpressible |
| 592.10 | 667.10 | 721.08 | incapacitated | 534.06 | 568.17 |
| 592.13 | 667.12 | 723.19 | 547.21 | 546.04 | infamous |
| 592.22 | 668.02 | 723.22 | incapacity | 572.11 | 342.01 |
| 593.03 | 668.14 | 724.04 | 588.13 | 607.05 | infancy |
| 593.05 | 668.16 | 724.09 | incarnate | 621.14 | 145.09 |
| 593.12 | 668.22 | 725.07 | 386.07 | 685.03 | 745.16 |
| 594.03 | 669.08 | 725.12 | 745.14 | 726.08 | infant |
| 594.15 | 669.11 | 726.04 | incautiously | 741.04 | 320.05 |
| 594.21 | 669.15 | 726.10 | 266.19 | 757.03 | 370.05 |
| 596.09 | 671.03 | 726.14 | incessantly | indefinite | 412.03 |
| 597.17 | 671.09 | 726.15 | 650.13 | 035.03 | infantile |
| 597.18 | 671.09 | 726.19 | inch | 588.15 | 225.08 |
| 597.22 | 672.03 | 727.02 | 406.05 | indentations | infatuated |
| 598.09 | 672.11 | 728.18 | inches | 323.12 | 198.16 |
| 600.10 | 672.12 | 729.12 | 335.01 | independent | 229.04 |
| 601.08 | 672.14 | 730.05 | 655.05 | 069.03 | infatuation |
| 603.03 | 673.07 | 730.06 | incidents | 672.03 | 339.02 |
| 603.09 | 674.05 | 731.01 | 075.06 | indian | inferior |
| 604.12 | 674.07 | 731.05 | 202.12 | 125.17 | 071.11 |
| 604.14 | 674.09 | 731.08 | incipient | indicating | inferiority |
| 604.18 | 674.12 | 731.15 | 452.15 | 065.21 | 492.02 |
| 606.09 | 675.09 | 731.16 | incitement | indications | infernal |
| 607.11 | 676.01 | 731.17 | 682.16 | 597.19 | 015.02 |
| 608.14 | 676.14 | 732.17 | inclination | indicative | 145.01 |
| 609.03 | 678.10 | 732.21 | 092.04 | 420.18 | 164.13 |
| 609.09 | 678.15 | 733.19 | 147.12 | indies | 359.05 |
| 610.19 | 678.20 | 734.10 | 198.20 | 237.12 | 410.14 |
| 611.09 | 679.08 | 735.08 | 290.12 | indifference | 469.17 |
| 611.13 | 680.02 | 736.07 | 647.19 | 148.10 | 654.02 |
| 613.07 | 680.16 | 736.10 | 740.13 | 204.17 | 695.17 |
| 613.12 | 680.19 | 737.01 | inclined | 755.04 | 718.09 |
| 613.19 | 681.03 | 737.03 | 023.01 | indifferent | infernally |
| 614.10 | 681.07 | 737.06 | 186.05 | 130.07 | 251.22 |
| 615.02 | 681.15 | 737.15 | 234.14 | 173.15 | 251.22 |
| 615.03 | 681.19 | 737.21 | 312.11 | 236.13 | 252.12 |
| 615.13 | 682.10 | 738.13 | 355.10 | 272.19 | 252.14 |
| 615.19 | 683.18 | 738.17 | 403.16 | indigenae | infinite |
| 616.04 | 683.22 | 738.20 | 419.04 | 071.06 | 371.02 |
| 616.08 | 684.05 | 739.13 | 512.10 | indignant | infinitely |
| 616.11 | 684.06 | 739.20 | 560.14 | 064.02 | 204.07 |
| 617.18 | 684.07 | 739.21 | 730.17 | 360.14 | inflexions |
| 617.19 | 684.13 | 740.09 | 734.18 | 458.05 | 539.14 |
| 618.03 | 684.15 | 740.17 | includes | 494.20 | inflict |
| 618.19 | 685.07 | 741.11 | 005.13 | 679.03 | 205.05 |
| 619.12 | 685.15 | 741.15 | including | 683.07 | 301.10 |
| 621.04 | 685.19 | 744.03 | 023.06 | indignantly | 363.07 |
| 621.17 | 686.02 | 744.10 | incoherent | 235.16 | inflicted |
| 623.02 | 686.18 | 744.12 | 035.02 | 471.20 | 551.18 |
| 623.08 | 688.03 | 744.13 | income | indignation | inflicter |
| 623.12 | 689.01 | 744.17 | 125.18 | 181.05 | 682.07 |
| 623.13 | 689.10 | 744.21 | 583.07 | 230.17 | inflicting |
| 624.04 | 689.17 | 745.02 | incomparably | 250.04 | 253.10 |
| 626.05 | 690.05 | 745.16 | 361.09 | 319.06 | 573.02 |
| 626.10 | 690.06 | 747.14 | 371.06 | 439.22 | influence |
| 627.03 | 690.07 | 748.18 | incomprehensible | indigo-coloured | 039.16 |
| 627.11 | 691.05 | 749.04 | 122.14 | 321.20 | 089.18 |
| 627.12 | 691.07 | 749.09 | inconsideration | indiscretion | 248.09 |
| 627.13 | 691.11 | 749.13 | 057.07 | 234.09 | 263.21 |
| 627.21 | 691.19 | 749.22 | inconvenience | indiscretions | 459.06 |
| 628.01 | 691.19 | 751.11 | 002.17 | 763.10 | 693.18 |
| 628.08 | 692.02 | 751.16 | inconvenienced | indispensable | 737.14 |
| 631.08 | 692.04 | 751.21 | 002.11 | 716.22 | inform |
| 632.09 | 692.18 | 752.20 | incorporeal | indisposition | 048.20 |
| 632.22 | 692.22 | 753.08 | 508.14 | 429.15 | 150.22 |
| 633.16 | 693.12 | 754.02 | increase | indistinctly | 160.09 |
| 634.14 | 693.22 | 754.14 | 048.01 | 010.02 | 272.11 |
| 635.08 | 694.08 | 754.15 | 343.07 | individual | 286.12 |
| 635.21 | 695.05 | 755.01 | increased | 007.03 | 292.16 |
| 636.02 | 695.16 | 755.03 | 131.09 | 017.09 | 306.12 |
| 636.17 | 695.17 | 755.12 | 274.10 | 146.08 | 333.02 |
| 637.09 | 695.18 | 755.15 | 482.04 | 397.18 | 345.02 |
| 638.02 | 695.21 | 756.17 | 517.08 | 482.03 | 429.14 |
| 638.07 | 696.04 | 757.07 | increases | 727.07 | 484.14 |
| 639.16 | 696.09 | 757.08 | 071.15 | individuals | 547.05 |
| 640.13 | 696.20 | 757.12 | increasing | 025.07 | 617.20 |
| 640.18 | 697.17 | 757.15 | 664.08 | indolence | 662.07 |
| 641.05 | 698.02 | 758.20 | 679.05 | 703.14 | 672.13 |
| 642.12 | 699.14 | 759.09 | 682.15 | indoors | informant |
| 643.03 | 700.14 | 761.18 | incredible | 516.01 | 294.14 |
| 644.06 | 700.17 | 761.19 | 297.20 | induced | 659.07 |
| 644.08 | 700.21 | 762.09 | incredulous | 223.08 | informant's |
| 644.13 | 701.02 | 763.09 | 334.17 | 292.01 | 644.15 |
| 645.18 | 701.03 | 763.15 | incur | 393.22 | information |
| 645.22 | 701.07 | 763.17 | 641.15 | indulge | 069.10 |
| 646.03 | 701.09 | 763.21 | incurable | 171.12 | 221.10 |
| 646.07 | 702.13 | 764.02 | 111.22 | 220.01 | 411.19 |
| 646.12 | 703.07 | 764.11 | 429.12 | indulged | 477.11 |
| 646.22 | 703.11 | in-door | indeed | 010.12 | 598.01 |
| 647.04 | 703.19 | 666.06 | 004.09 | 312.06 | 628.21 |
| 648.22 | 703.22 | inadequacy | 005.22 | 425.16 | 675.21 |
| 649.21 | 704.04 | 407.13 | 011.21 | 448.08 | informed |
| 651.11 | 704.20 | inadequate | 022.12 | 541.11 | 096.07 |
| 651.15 | 705.11 | 358.14 | 070.10 | indulgence | 110.11 |
| 652.01 | 705.12 | inanimate | 078.04 | 083.08 | 235.19 |
| 652.12 | 705.19 | 400.08 | 086.03 | 258.04 | 328.03 |
| 652.17 | 706.21 | inarticulate | 098.16 | 591.01 | 455.02 |
| 652.19 | 708.15 | 063.04 | 197.09 | indulgences | 460.05 |
| 653.22 | 710.01 | 195.13 | 211.10 | 338.14 | 663.22 |
| 654.07 | 710.02 | 553.14 | 254.09 | indulgent | 703.11 |
| 654.10 | 711.01 | 564.01 | 282.17 | 198.09 | 737.20 |
| 654.12 | 712.16 | inattention | 296.12 | 577.09 | informing |
| 658.04 | 713.23 | 694.20 | 378.22 | 601.16 | 618.07 |
| 658.07 | 714.06 | inaudible | 389.08 | indulging | infringement |
| 659.20 | 716.05 | 711.06 | 389.08 | 430.22 | 641.08 |
| 661.09 | 716.08 | incapability | 420.21 | industry | ingenious |
| 662.10 | 716.21 | 338.22 | 426.18 | 727.04 | 147.02 |
| 663.18 | 717.03 | incapable | 440.11 | inefficient | 327.04 |
| 664.18 | 717.04 | 134.13 | 467.12 | 516.09 | ingenuity |
| 665.06 | 717.12 | 277.13 | 505.05 | inexperienced | 703.17 |
| 665.11 | 720.02 | 617.03 | 505.05 | 579.14 | |

ingratitude: 258.07, 720.20
inhabit: 762.11
inhabitant: 011.09
inhabitants: 372.07, 463.01
inherited: 609.07
inhospitable: 011.20, 313.09
inhospitality: 015.19
inhumanity: 080.09
initiatory: 041.02
injudicious: 173.04
injunction: 274.20, 586.05
injunctions: 618.19
injure: 405.19, 602.02
injured: 039.17, 166.21, 167.01, 222.01
injuries: 082.04, 282.21, 720.20
injury: 340.08, 407.05, 485.20, 514.02, 703.18
injustice: 080.22, 502.18, 753.12
injustices: 752.13, 753.11
ink: 040.06, 044.08
inmate: 475.11
inmates: 015.17, 322.11, 345.04, 676.12, 693.16, 693.19
inn: 689.10
innate: 340.06
inner: 036.12, 063.03, 250.21, 261.08, 531.15, 552.16
innocent: 009.01, 065.03, 095.19, 124.19, 177.14, 629.13
innumerable: 448.09
inquire: 035.12, 142.01, 267.17, 402.09, 418.10, 528.05, 677.20, 689.15
inquired: 078.20, 122.17, 171.14, 210.10, 221.04, 246.06, 251.14, 299.14, 312.21, 387.02, 411.14, 453.06, 463.04, 474.12, 481.21, 538.22, 566.05, 581.13, 591.01, 623.16, 632.05, 742.13
inquiries: 080.06, 595.06, 752.05
inquiring: 006.05, 133.14, 495.18, 552.03
inquiry: 300.01, 307.12, 587.04
inquisitive: 109.01
inquisitively: 316.05
inroads: 596.06
insane: 160.22, 268.03, 730.16
insanity: 285.05
inscribed: 514.11
inscription: 039.20, 495.19, 560.16, 746.08
insensible: 083.10, 362.03, 403.04, 407.05
inserting: 353.16
inside: 016.08, 038.07, 444.19, 487.15, 525.07, 565.06, 634.01, 655.02
insipid: 346.02
insist: 042.05, 184.03
insisted: 099.15, 132.20, 196.19, 227.02, 250.04, 278.03, 323.19, 384.13, 420.12, 446.21, 516.05, 582.11, 640.11, 737.08
insisting: 641.04
insolence: 091.22, 108.07, 194.11, 231.07, 724.12
insolent: 083.09, 250.07, 721.21
inspect: 308.08, 468.08
inspected: 507.08
inspecting: 005.09
inspection: 466.20
inspector: 468.08
inspiration: 049.02, 750.17
install: 222.04
instance: 083.14, 237.12, 493.17
instanced: 536.16
instant: 051.05, 053.08, 152.01, 157.15, 165.13, 257.02, 267.04, 356.05, 361.19, 416.05, 455.07, 553.13, 632.01, 709.07, 717.21
instantaneously: 245.02
instantly: 128.08, 223.17, 227.06, 288.05, 295.10, 323.20, 366.16, 392.22, 435.20, 622.01, 661.17, 668.02
instead: 014.04, 052.01, 099.16, 113.09, 116.03, 124.12, 132.13, 138.08, 170.08, 220.16, 247.21, 295.01, 313.13, 370.04, 390.09, 401.15, 409.13, 415.04, 482.09, 504.07, 533.05, 549.02, 552.04, 582.12, 604.11, 611.14, 628.17, 636.16, 668.18, 680.07, 683.01, 704.03, 739.13, 750.09
instil: 454.06
instilled: 149.14, 444.05
instinct: 007.18, 389.21, 709.04
instinctively: 371.04, 527.21, 616.22
instructed: 384.15, 580.07
instructions: 099.15, 263.15, 472.14, 640.16, 717.07
instructors: 454.14
instrument: 166.10, 316.07, 609.08
instruments: 238.09
insufferable: 254.21
insult: 032.14, 128.02, 252.22, 343.19, 404.20
insulted: 158.03, 446.13, 498.02
insults: 010.11, 667.08
intellect: 149.05, 296.10, 426.05
intelligence: 160.17, 289.14, 339.08, 346.20, 374.11, 629.11, 635.19
intelligent: 013.12, 214.03, 562.17, 726.22
intelligible: 408.15
intend: 018.10, 135.09, 181.11, 264.14
intended: 110.17, 133.03, 246.02, 396.15, 467.12, 528.20, 740.06, 758.21
intending: 147.07, 207.07, 638.10
intense: 052.03, 425.07, 514.02, 601.14, 635.03
intensest: 166.09
intensity: 211.22, 327.06, 356.12, 412.21
intent: 610.02
intention: 014.12, 029.07, 054.13, 071.08, 085.18, 099.03, 128.01, 150.17, 257.13, 278.11, 312.13, 343.13, 674.07
intentions: 636.05
intently: 135.19, 724.04
intentness: 465.19
intercepted: 058.15
intercepting: 705.22
intercommunication: 332.03
intercourse: 069.04
interdict: 573.22
interest: 013.09, 030.15, 040.16, 070.13, 084.08, 206.03, 218.10, 307.08, 352.01, 419.03, 463.01, 477.07, 492.20, 588.12, 646.11, 727.21, 730.06, 747.20
interested: 003.02, 134.19, 422.08, 576.01
interesting: 202.10, 446.04, 505.03, 544.05, 608.03, 703.22
interfere: 392.06, 661.10, 720.05
interference: 332.18, 436.21
interfering: 422.09, 610.01
interim: 314.10
interior: 743.13
interloper: 085.06
intermeddling: 314.03
interment: 379.17
intermission: 516.02
internally: 027.02
interpose: 010.16
interposed: 063.12, 157.01, 260.17, 288.12, 409.13, 439.12, 752.12
interpret: 025.19
interpreter: 354.19
interpreting: 048.09
interred: 514.01
interrogatively: 293.07, 711.08
interrupt: 203.03
interrupted: 002.16, 024.03, 063.22, 065.04, 105.16, 126.07, 142.03, 178.14, 187.17, 208.18, 216.17, 264.16, 273.12, 276.04, 335.03, 343.12, 386.12, 405.03, 482.08, 505.13, 535.06, 562.03, 572.16, 587.15, 696.03, 707.21, 718.18, 720.03, 742.18
interrupting: 134.11, 170.11
interruptions: 713.16
interspersed: 006.01
interval: 009.10, 023.15, 070.14, 113.06, 202.08, 419.17, 430.15, 450.16
intervals: 066.06, 188.17, 314.08, 352.08, 393.09, 403.21, 462.18, 474.11, 519.10, 582.03, 695.01
interview: 018.06, 267.19, 333.21, 581.08, 582.18, 592.05, 700.01
intimacy: 160.13, 264.15, 547.06, 713.15
intimate: 024.07, 236.09, 421.21, 677.03
intimated: 582.17
intimately: 444.13
intimating: 063.04, 085.01, 580.07, 725.04
intimation: 010.03, 201.08, 255.16, 326.13
into: 005.10, 005.15, 008.12, 008.21, 010.15, 011.12, 012.13, 014.12, 028.04, 030.09, 032.16, 035.13, 036.05, 042.01, 043.11, 044.03, 046.19, 047.03, 047.20, 048.05, 051.17, 055.14, 058.12, 059.09, 060.11, 063.07, 063.17, 065.13, 077.12, 078.11, 079.03, 087.08, 088.01, 091.20, 093.10, 097.07, 104.16, 110.09, 110.10, 111.06, 113.10, 116.19, 119.22, 120.10, 121.18, 123.09, 125.11, 126.15, 126.16, 127.06, 129.18, 132.16, 132.21, 138.01, 143.18, 148.18, 148.21, 149.14, 150.04, 150.16, 150.20, 160.07, 162.09, 165.04, 167.11, 168.04, 169.08, 170.16, 175.21, 178.22, 181.09, 184.12, 188.10, 189.06, 192.20, 193.11, 195.12, 203.20, 212.03, 213.08, 213.14, 217.19, 218.03, 219.12

| | | | | | |
|---|---|---|---|---|---|
| 220.16 | 546.18 | 713.06 | 700.18 | 138.11 | 256.20 |
| 225.02 | 552.14 | 719.13 | 749.20 | 140.08 | 257.08 |
| 225.16 | 552.18 | 758.17 | irritated | 140.09 | 259.06 |
| 229.15 | 553.18 | inuendo's | 010.14 | 140.11 | 259.10 |
| 230.15 | 554.11 | 444.11 | 127.01 | 142.04 | 259.14 |
| 235.22 | 557.19 | invaded | 153.13 | 143.07 | 259.14 |
| 236.01 | 564.06 | 061.16 | 172.16 | 143.07 | 260.17 |
| 240.10 | 565.04 | invading | 225.11 | 145.17 | 261.18 |
| 243.14 | 566.01 | 689.13 | 536.20 | 146.13 | 262.11 |
| 244.04 | 566.22 | invalid | 685.10 | 146.15 | 265.07 |
| 244.06 | 568.11 | 303.13 | irritating | 151.06 | 266.10 |
| 245.17 | 568.15 | 532.19 | 563.14 | 151.11 | 271.14 |
| 250.01 | 569.13 | 580.04 | irritation | 151.19 | 271.17 |
| 257.01 | 572.18 | 589.01 | 028.09 | 153.09 | 271.21 |
| 258.14 | 576.07 | 607.12 | 256.07 | 154.01 | 272.09 |
| 260.01 | 588.18 | invariable | 437.19 | 155.12 | 272.12 |
| 260.20 | 589.09 | 146.22 | 678.08 | 159.18 | 272.16 |
| 264.19 | 594.18 | invariably | is | 163.05 | 275.08 |
| 271.16 | 596.10 | 240.14 | 001.05 | 163.05 | 275.08 |
| 274.09 | 600.21 | 315.20 | 002.15 | 163.10 | 275.12 |
| 280.16 | 607.09 | 352.02 | 004.03 | 164.04 | 276.09 |
| 282.10 | 611.17 | 425.17 | 004.06 | 164.14 | 276.13 |
| 283.01 | 613.03 | 478.08 | 005.15 | 164.16 | 277.03 |
| 290.17 | 619.04 | 517.04 | 007.04 | 165.09 | 277.05 |
| 291.08 | 621.19 | invent | 007.09 | 166.19 | 277.08 |
| 297.06 | 622.20 | 091.01 | 007.10 | 166.21 | 277.17 |
| 299.06 | 624.16 | 525.19 | 007.17 | 170.20 | 277.19 |
| 308.20 | 628.03 | 570.13 | 008.07 | 171.14 | 278.06 |
| 310.14 | 629.10 | invented | 011.18 | 172.12 | 278.15 |
| 317.16 | 639.03 | 462.17 | 013.17 | 173.09 | 278.16 |
| 317.18 | 641.20 | invention | 016.08 | 173.12 | 278.16 |
| 317.21 | 644.18 | 340.15 | 022.07 | 174.07 | 280.03 |
| 319.04 | 648.14 | investing | 022.18 | 174.13 | 280.06 |
| 319.15 | 650.18 | 304.13 | 023.15 | 175.01 | 282.06 |
| 320.07 | 657.03 | inveterate | 023.17 | 175.08 | 284.07 |
| 320.22 | 659.17 | 423.01 | 024.05 | 176.02 | 285.19 |
| 321.17 | 660.20 | invisible | 024.10 | 177.02 | 286.14 |
| 325.21 | 661.13 | 101.09 | 024.19 | 178.11 | 286.16 |
| 326.14 | 664.14 | 209.15 | 025.01 | 178.18 | 286.16 |
| 329.16 | 665.03 | 287.01 | 025.04 | 179.13 | 287.15 |
| 337.13 | 667.06 | 531.20 | 025.14 | 180.05 | 287.15 |
| 347.17 | 669.07 | 730.13 | 026.13 | 180.12 | 288.11 |
| 350.12 | 676.20 | invitation | 026.15 | 180.16 | 290.06 |
| 356.04 | 678.05 | 003.02 | 026.20 | 181.06 | 290.17 |
| 356.13 | 679.10 | 075.13 | 031.03 | 182.07 | 297.12 |
| 361.01 | 681.07 | 119.07 | 031.07 | 182.07 | 297.17 |
| 362.04 | 687.03 | 213.05 | 031.17 | 182.10 | 297.20 |
| 366.05 | 690.11 | invited | 032.10 | 182.13 | 299.19 |
| 367.15 | 690.14 | 023.04 | 033.07 | 182.19 | 303.01 |
| 374.10 | 692.01 | 119.06 | 033.09 | 183.02 | 303.02 |
| 382.03 | 698.04 | 217.14 | 033.18 | 183.11 | 303.03 |
| 385.22 | 701.17 | 217.16 | 040.21 | 184.15 | 303.06 |
| 387.20 | 704.12 | 379.11 | 041.01 | 186.02 | 306.02 |
| 390.01 | 705.20 | 688.02 | 042.01 | 186.03 | 306.07 |
| 391.07 | 715.08 | invoked | 044.12 | 186.12 | 306.08 |
| 399.14 | 720.06 | 673.10 | 047.14 | 187.13 | 306.11 |
| 399.17 | 722.19 | invokes | 047.18 | 190.12 | 306.15 |
| 402.09 | 722.21 | 730.13 | 047.21 | 191.04 | 307.01 |
| 413.04 | 744.22 | involuntarily | 049.14 | 192.09 | 307.03 |
| 415.05 | 745.07 | 060.07 | 050.01 | 200.07 | 307.09 |
| 416.03 | 745.22 | 244.03 | 050.03 | 202.01 | 307.09 |
| 416.06 | 746.17 | 387.19 | 054.09 | 202.08 | 307.10 |
| 420.03 | 750.10 | 748.15 | 055.03 | 206.17 | 307.11 |
| 425.01 | 751.03 | involuntary | 056.03 | 208.02 | 307.14 |
| 426.05 | 755.14 | 257.04 | 057.10 | 208.02 | 307.20 |
| 427.21 | 756.13 | involving | 067.02 | 208.06 | 309.03 |
| 429.19 | 756.14 | 335.07 | 067.03 | 208.08 | 309.08 |
| 439.12 | 760.06 | inward | 071.05 | 211.15 | 309.10 |
| 439.22 | 763.05 | 119.19 | 071.12 | 211.19 | 311.18 |
| 441.03 | intolerable | 149.06 | 072.01 | 212.17 | 314.19 |
| 441.18 | 654.02 | 375.05 | 072.04 | 217.18 | 315.17 |
| 444.05 | intolerance | 526.23 | 072.05 | 218.09 | 315.22 |
| 454.02 | 696.04 | irefully | 072.09 | 218.19 | 317.04 |
| 454.07 | intoxicated | 341.13 | 072.20 | 220.02 | 317.10 |
| 456.13 | 403.05 | irks | 073.01 | 220.15 | 321.12 |
| 462.03 | intractable | 360.21 | 073.10 | 221.04 | 321.16 |
| 463.05 | 253.21 | irksome | 073.11 | 221.20 | 322.15 |
| 467.01 | introduce | 750.12 | 073.14 | 222.04 | 323.17 |
| 476.22 | 131.01 | iron | 073.20 | 222.22 | 327.04 |
| 477.15 | 376.05 | 084.01 | 074.10 | 228.07 | 329.03 |
| 480.17 | 417.16 | 323.09 | 076.12 | 228.21 | 329.10 |
| 482.17 | introduced | 609.18 | 084.02 | 229.12 | 332.20 |
| 486.19 | 013.08 | ironed | 089.11 | 229.17 | 332.22 |
| 490.17 | introducing | 703.18 | 102.03 | 230.10 | 333.03 |
| 490.18 | 136.16 | ironing | 104.13 | 231.10 | 333.05 |
| 491.06 | introduction | 712.22 | 105.18 | 231.12 | 333.06 |
| 497.09 | 080.11 | irrational | 106.08 | 231.18 | 333.07 |
| 499.01 | 201.02 | 676.12 | 109.11 | 231.21 | 333.12 |
| 499.05 | 445.18 | irrationality | 109.11 | 232.01 | 336.09 |
| 501.09 | introductory | 393.03 | 109.18 | 232.03 | 336.11 |
| 503.15 | 005.11 | irregular | 109.19 | 233.01 | 336.18 |
| 505.14 | intruded | 058.15 | 111.17 | 233.13 | 336.22 |
| 507.11 | 743.07 | irregularly | 111.18 | 233.20 | 337.07 |
| 507.18 | intruder | 290.18 | 114.10 | 235.10 | 337.14 |
| 508.05 | 054.05 | irrepressible | 114.11 | 236.10 | 337.22 |
| 509.02 | 365.19 | 314.12 | 116.05 | 236.22 | 339.06 |
| 509.14 | 383.09 | 393.21 | 117.08 | 239.16 | 340.13 |
| 513.13 | intrusion | irresistible | 120.17 | 240.03 | 341.04 |
| 513.18 | 013.16 | 019.15 | 120.17 | 248.05 | 341.05 |
| 513.20 | 059.14 | 225.06 | 122.12 | 249.13 | 342.08 |
| 522.05 | 152.03 | 244.07 | 127.06 | 249.18 | 342.08 |
| 524.18 | 224.15 | irresistibly | 129.12 | 251.03 | 342.21 |
| 526.07 | 436.18 | 156.20 | 133.20 | 252.10 | 343.05 |
| 531.18 | intrusions | 129.12 | 134.17 | 253.06 | 343.20 |
| 533.10 | 345.05 | 763.04 | 134.21 | 253.06 | 345.09 |
| 537.21 | intuh | irresolutely | 135.01 | 253.08 | 345.19 |
| 538.20 | 043.18 | 495.11 | 136.02 | 253.10 | 345.20 |
| 539.14 | 187.10 | irrevocably | 136.07 | 254.21 | 346.12 |
| 540.20 | 194.07 | 620.17 | 136.19 | 254.22 | 347.19 |
| 542.21 | 233.10 | irritable | 136.07 | 255.17 | 347.21 |
| 546.02 | 696.13 | 087.06 | 138.04 | 255.21 | 349.07 |
| | | 301.09 | | | |

| | | | | | |
|---|---|---|---|---|---|
| 353.11 | 472.11 | 612.14 | 754.14 | 014.03 | 078.20 |
| 354.07 | 476.07 | 614.02 | 754.22 | 016.02 | 078.22 |
| 357.15 | 476.15 | 617.07 | 756.08 | 017.05 | 079.01 |
| 359.04 | 477.02 | 617.19 | 760.09 | 018.20 | 079.02 |
| 360.17 | 480.03 | 618.10 | 761.06 | 021.12 | 079.04 |
| 360.18 | 481.19 | 618.20 | 762.15 | 022.20 | 079.07 |
| 360.21 | 482.02 | 622.11 | isabella | 023.09 | 079.07 |
| 363.18 | 482.11 | 626.09 | 104.13 | 023.10 | 079.08 |
| 363.21 | 482.14 | 627.06 | 108.16 | 023.12 | 079.22 |
| 364.16 | 483.02 | 627.22 | 111.06 | 023.15 | 080.02 |
| 365.04 | 484.06 | 628.02 | 114.10 | 023.17 | 080.03 |
| 365.07 | 484.08 | 628.10 | 114.12 | 024.11 | 080.05 |
| 366.02 | 484.13 | 629.09 | 116.22 | 024.15 | 080.06 |
| 366.04 | 485.01 | 629.14 | 128.09 | 024.22 | 080.07 |
| 366.16 | 485.03 | 630.21 | 129.13 | 025.10 | 080.15 |
| 369.09 | 486.09 | 631.09 | 131.05 | 026.17 | 080.16 |
| 370.10 | 486.13 | 632.05 | 147.03 | 026.22 | 082.13 |
| 371.08 | 486.19 | 632.10 | 152.04 | 027.21 | 082.21 |
| 371.17 | 487.16 | 632.14 | 212.12 | 029.20 | 083.17 |
| 371.20 | 488.02 | 634.14 | 217.02 | 031.03 | 083.18 |
| 372.16 | 490.11 | 634.15 | 219.10 | 031.07 | 084.05 |
| 376.17 | 491.15 | 634.16 | 224.04 | 031.15 | 084.12 |
| 377.06 | 491.19 | 635.16 | 225.05 | 031.21 | 084.17 |
| 380.01 | 492.10 | 635.17 | 225.22 | 032.01 | 084.20 |
| 382.17 | 492.12 | 638.09 | 227.14 | 032.02 | 085.02 |
| 384.07 | 493.17 | 638.18 | 228.09 | 032.11 | 085.11 |
| 385.10 | 494.06 | 638.19 | 229.03 | 032.17 | 085.12 |
| 386.09 | 494.07 | 646.05 | 230.07 | 034.04 | 088.04 |
| 386.16 | 494.15 | 646.22 | 231.03 | 038.07 | 088.08 |
| 387.10 | 494.15 | 647.03 | 234.07 | 038.11 | 088.13 |
| 388.02 | 496.05 | 647.12 | 234.18 | 038.12 | 089.02 |
| 388.20 | 496.11 | 647.13 | 235.13 | 038.20 | 089.06 |
| 390.02 | 496.12 | 647.19 | 236.03 | 039.15 | 089.06 |
| 390.21 | 496.22 | 649.16 | 236.21 | 039.18 | 089.06 |
| 391.22 | 497.06 | 650.03 | 240.03 | 040.01 | 090.19 |
| 392.03 | 497.13 | 652.02 | 249.22 | 040.04 | 092.03 |
| 392.07 | 500.08 | 652.03 | 250.12 | 041.09 | 092.06 |
| 392.11 | 501.04 | 656.05 | 251.09 | 043.10 | 092.22 |
| 392.13 | 502.02 | 659.13 | 253.04 | 045.05 | 093.01 |
| 396.08 | 504.18 | 660.02 | 261.17 | 046.08 | 093.11 |
| 398.18 | 505.09 | 661.16 | 262.10 | 046.10 | 095.13 |
| 398.18 | 510.08 | 661.17 | 267.18 | 046.13 | 097.14 |
| 399.01 | 512.02 | 664.02 | 273.22 | 047.01 | 099.02 |
| 400.20 | 514.11 | 665.19 | 296.17 | 047.11 | 100.10 |
| 400.20 | 518.17 | 666.14 | 305.10 | 047.12 | 101.03 |
| 401.07 | 519.18 | 673.12 | 311.14 | 047.21 | 101.15 |
| 402.03 | 520.09 | 675.02 | 327.19 | 048.10 | 102.02 |
| 405.06 | 521.01 | 675.14 | 329.19 | 050.21 | 102.08 |
| 405.16 | 521.22 | 679.05 | 331.13 | 051.13 | 102.13 |
| 405.22 | 523.17 | 679.07 | 336.14 | 051.13 | 104.02 |
| 406.05 | 524.05 | 680.11 | 339.12 | 051.14 | 104.09 |
| 407.18 | 524.07 | 684.02 | 341.12 | 051.19 | 105.03 |
| 416.20 | 525.11 | 684.19 | 342.16 | 052.05 | 105.03 |
| 419.01 | 526.11 | 685.06 | 379.16 | 052.10 | 106.15 |
| 419.02 | 529.01 | 685.17 | 389.09 | 052.14 | 106.18 |
| 421.14 | 532.08 | 686.03 | 398.04 | 052.16 | 106.19 |
| 421.15 | 533.09 | 689.03 | 410.17 | 052.18 | 108.08 |
| 427.02 | 533.15 | 690.18 | 448.03 | 052.20 | 108.10 |
| 427.04 | 533.17 | 691.10 | 449.12 | 053.05 | 109.11 |
| 427.16 | 533.21 | 693.07 | 501.22 | 054.01 | 110.05 |
| 427.20 | 536.13 | 693.12 | 502.07 | 054.10 | 112.16 |
| 428.08 | 537.05 | 693.16 | 520.17 | 055.02 | 115.04 |
| 432.20 | 542.03 | 697.01 | 520.20 | 055.03 | 115.07 |
| 433.10 | 542.04 | 698.07 | 537.08 | 055.12 | 117.11 |
| 434.07 | 542.05 | 701.18 | isabella's | 055.12 | 117.16 |
| 434.07 | 543.07 | 702.02 | 219.06 | 055.16 | 117.18 |
| 435.03 | 545.09 | 702.14 | 248.05 | 055.19 | 120.07 |
| 437.01 | 545.14 | 708.07 | 291.04 | 056.01 | 121.22 |
| 437.02 | 546.06 | 708.07 | 295.05 | 056.03 | 122.11 |
| 437.05 | 548.06 | 713.01 | 299.06 | 056.04 | 123.08 |
| 437.06 | 556.02 | 716.10 | 412.15 | 056.11 | 123.19 |
| 437.07 | 556.09 | 718.07 | 456.22 | 057.13 | 125.01 |
| 437.21 | 570.01 | 720.10 | island | 058.08 | 125.03 |
| 438.10 | 570.10 | 721.01 | 627.02 | 058.14 | 126.20 |
| 440.13 | 576.08 | 721.02 | isn't | 059.02 | 126.22 |
| 440.14 | 577.01 | 728.12 | 108.19 | 059.16 | 128.07 |
| 445.03 | 577.01 | 728.13 | 184.14 | 060.11 | 128.17 |
| 445.04 | 577.21 | 729.06 | 319.13 | 060.17 | 129.18 |
| 449.07 | 579.05 | 729.06 | 336.19 | 061.03 | 130.14 |
| 451.15 | 579.09 | 729.12 | 434.06 | 061.16 | 131.15 |
| 452.06 | 581.09 | 729.18 | 438.01 | 062.13 | 131.20 |
| 452.10 | 581.14 | 730.01 | 468.01 | 063.07 | 131.20 |
| 452.19 | 587.16 | 730.04 | 538.05 | 063.14 | 132.02 |
| 455.21 | 587.21 | 731.01 | 632.13 | 064.15 | 132.16 |
| 456.04 | 588.04 | 731.01 | 666.01 | 065.18 | 133.01 |
| 457.13 | 588.06 | 731.11 | isolation | 066.15 | 133.02 |
| 457.17 | 589.22 | 731.12 | 015.18 | 067.04 | 133.18 |
| 459.08 | 590.21 | 731.21 | 346.01 | 067.07 | 133.20 |
| 459.09 | 590.22 | 732.07 | issue | 069.05 | 134.03 |
| 461.16 | 591.14 | 732.09 | 445.15 | 070.01 | 136.02 |
| 461.18 | 592.13 | 733.17 | 695.14 | 071.15 | 136.16 |
| 461.21 | 592.17 | 733.21 | issued | 071.21 | 138.02 |
| 463.03 | 593.13 | 733.22 | 010.19 | 072.03 | 138.04 |
| 463.08 | 599.04 | 734.03 | 035.12 | 072.16 | 140.05 |
| 463.09 | 599.05 | 734.15 | 308.13 | 072.19 | 140.05 |
| 463.11 | 599.09 | 739.14 | 526.10 | 074.06 | 140.06 |
| 463.13 | 599.17 | 741.01 | 567.14 | 074.13 | 140.07 |
| 463.16 | 600.15 | 741.19 | issuing | 074.20 | 140.13 |
| 464.01 | 600.20 | 742.04 | 291.20 | 075.21 | 140.16 |
| 464.02 | 601.08 | 742.12 | it | 076.10 | 141.04 |
| 464.04 | 603.07 | 744.14 | 002.17 | 076.22 | 141.04 |
| 464.07 | 603.10 | 745.08 | 003.07 | 077.07 | 141.11 |
| 465.05 | 603.13 | 745.13 | 004.15 | 077.16 | 143.06 |
| 465.08 | 603.13 | 746.06 | 005.12 | 077.20 | 143.07 |
| 465.10 | 604.07 | 748.02 | 005.13 | 077.21 | 144.12 |
| 468.03 | 606.14 | 751.10 | 006.08 | 078.05 | 144.19 |
| 468.21 | 607.15 | 751.12 | 007.17 | 078.05 | 145.15 |
| 469.19 | 607.21 | 751.17 | 007.22 | 078.09 | 145.18 |
| 470.03 | 608.05 | 753.04 | 008.20 | 078.13 | 146.03 |
| 470.07 | 608.07 | 753.05 | 012.21 | 078.18 | 146.13 |
| 472.01 | 612.04 | 753.20 | 013.17 | | 147.14 |

| | | | | | |
|---|---|---|---|---|---|
| 148.16 | 215.03 | 278.04 | 329.12 | 392.13 | 470.19 |
| 149.02 | 215.05 | 278.18 | 329.17 | 392.17 | 471.03 |
| 150.19 | 215.15 | 279.14 | 331.14 | 393.12 | 471.05 |
| 151.06 | 218.19 | 279.14 | 331.15 | 393.13 | 471.11 |
| 151.11 | 219.04 | 279.19 | 331.18 | 394.11 | 471.18 |
| 151.20 | 219.13 | 280.03 | 332.05 | 394.19 | 471.19 |
| 152.02 | 220.15 | 280.05 | 332.16 | 395.17 | 471.21 |
| 152.06 | 220.18 | 280.12 | 333.02 | 395.21 | 475.13 |
| 154.01 | 220.20 | 280.13 | 335.15 | 396.05 | 478.06 |
| 155.20 | 221.08 | 281.01 | 336.11 | 397.13 | 481.15 |
| 156.11 | 223.07 | 281.04 | 337.12 | 398.05 | 482.08 |
| 156.15 | 223.08 | 281.14 | 337.15 | 398.18 | 482.21 |
| 157.16 | 223.16 | 281.22 | 339.03 | 399.12 | 483.08 |
| 160.06 | 224.15 | 282.01 | 339.06 | 399.15 | 484.07 |
| 161.03 | 225.02 | 282.05 | 339.10 | 399.16 | 484.08 |
| 163.01 | 225.20 | 283.05 | 339.16 | 399.16 | 485.04 |
| 163.05 | 226.03 | 283.10 | 339.19 | 401.07 | 485.07 |
| 163.14 | 227.06 | 283.13 | 340.01 | 401.15 | 488.04 |
| 164.01 | 227.21 | 284.06 | 340.08 | 402.11 | 488.06 |
| 164.02 | 228.10 | 284.07 | 341.20 | 402.16 | 488.20 |
| 164.05 | 228.21 | 284.12 | 342.05 | 404.17 | 489.04 |
| 164.11 | 229.17 | 285.05 | 343.05 | 404.19 | 489.06 |
| 164.14 | 230.03 | 285.15 | 343.10 | 405.06 | 489.12 |
| 164.16 | 232.07 | 286.13 | 344.09 | 405.09 | 489.17 |
| 164.17 | 234.01 | 286.14 | 344.11 | 405.12 | 490.04 |
| 166.08 | 234.14 | 286.16 | 345.09 | 405.16 | 490.09 |
| 166.11 | 234.20 | 286.16 | 345.11 | 405.22 | 490.10 |
| 166.19 | 234.22 | 287.05 | 345.22 | 407.17 | 490.11 |
| 168.14 | 235.12 | 287.15 | 346.05 | 407.18 | 492.06 |
| 169.10 | 237.14 | 288.21 | 346.07 | 408.02 | 493.08 |
| 169.17 | 239.02 | 289.03 | 347.03 | 409.15 | 493.10 |
| 170.07 | 239.06 | 289.13 | 347.03 | 409.16 | 493.14 |
| 171.13 | 240.06 | 289.18 | 347.06 | 409.18 | 493.17 |
| 171.14 | 240.08 | 290.21 | 347.12 | 411.15 | 494.09 |
| 171.16 | 241.09 | 291.01 | 349.06 | 412.06 | 494.10 |
| 171.16 | 242.05 | 291.07 | 350.07 | 412.08 | 494.15 |
| 171.20 | 243.01 | 291.08 | 350.10 | 412.09 | 496.02 |
| 171.21 | 243.09 | 291.10 | 350.12 | 412.10 | 496.03 |
| 172.04 | 243.15 | 291.11 | 351.08 | 412.19 | 496.04 |
| 172.12 | 243.21 | 291.12 | 352.09 | 414.04 | 496.05 |
| 173.01 | 243.12 | 291.17 | 353.03 | 414.06 | 498.02 |
| 173.04 | 244.06 | 292.15 | 353.07 | 414.07 | 499.01 |
| 174.07 | 244.11 | 292.19 | 353.17 | 414.10 | 499.08 |
| 174.07 | 244.14 | 292.22 | 353.18 | 415.18 | 499.16 |
| 174.16 | 244.16 | 294.08 | 353.22 | 415.21 | 500.18 |
| 175.11 | 245.10 | 294.10 | 353.22 | 416.13 | 500.21 |
| 176.08 | 245.21 | 294.17 | 354.01 | 416.20 | 501.02 |
| 176.11 | 246.01 | 295.01 | 354.02 | 417.09 | 501.15 |
| 176.11 | 246.04 | 295.02 | 354.03 | 417.20 | 502.10 |
| 177.03 | 246.10 | 295.04 | 354.07 | 420.04 | 502.14 |
| 177.04 | 246.15 | 295.06 | 354.07 | 420.19 | 503.06 |
| 177.18 | 248.06 | 295.17 | 354.12 | 420.22 | 504.18 |
| 177.18 | 248.17 | 297.18 | 355.04 | 421.08 | 505.07 |
| 178.11 | 249.04 | 297.20 | 355.16 | 422.03 | 505.09 |
| 179.07 | 251.03 | 297.20 | 356.09 | 422.10 | 506.04 |
| 179.07 | 251.21 | 298.09 | 357.01 | 422.15 | 506.19 |
| 179.19 | 252.02 | 298.16 | 357.15 | 425.12 | 507.07 |
| 180.12 | 252.08 | 298.20 | 359.04 | 425.14 | 508.01 |
| 181.18 | 252.13 | 299.04 | 360.07 | 425.19 | 509.11 |
| 182.07 | 253.07 | 300.04 | 361.02 | 425.21 | 510.02 |
| 182.07 | 253.08 | 300.05 | 361.03 | 426.04 | 510.22 |
| 182.12 | 253.10 | 303.11 | 361.04 | 426.21 | 511.04 |
| 183.02 | 253.22 | 304.04 | 361.05 | 427.02 | 511.09 |
| 183.03 | 254.14 | 305.05 | 361.11 | 427.03 | 511.09 |
| 183.11 | 254.15 | 305.18 | 362.09 | 427.09 | 512.03 |
| 183.14 | 254.21 | 305.19 | 363.09 | 427.15 | 512.11 |
| 183.17 | 255.21 | 306.01 | 363.10 | 427.20 | 513.22 |
| 184.07 | 255.22 | 306.02 | 363.10 | 428.16 | 514.05 |
| 184.09 | 256.01 | 306.04 | 363.13 | 429.02 | 515.02 |
| 187.20 | 256.10 | 306.15 | 363.18 | 430.14 | 516.08 |
| 188.04 | 257.04 | 306.17 | 363.18 | 432.20 | 518.05 |
| 189.13 | 257.08 | 307.09 | 363.21 | 433.01 | 518.21 |
| 190.08 | 257.18 | 307.20 | 364.08 | 433.17 | 519.03 |
| 190.12 | 257.22 | 308.06 | 366.02 | 434.06 | 519.03 |
| 192.19 | 258.03 | 308.10 | 370.05 | 435.17 | 519.04 |
| 192.20 | 258.11 | 308.14 | 370.06 | 436.21 | 519.18 |
| 193.09 | 258.14 | 309.03 | 371.10 | 437.08 | 519.22 |
| 194.13 | 259.21 | 309.03 | 372.06 | 437.11 | 520.14 |
| 195.02 | 261.22 | 309.04 | 373.12 | 437.15 | 521.10 |
| 195.19 | 262.15 | 309.10 | 373.12 | 438.01 | 521.17 |
| 196.01 | 263.06 | 310.12 | 375.04 | 440.20 | 521.22 |
| 196.15 | 264.18 | 311.05 | 376.20 | 441.18 | 522.14 |
| 197.09 | 265.03 | 315.09 | 377.06 | 442.18 | 523.06 |
| 197.21 | 265.07 | 315.17 | 377.17 | 443.18 | 523.14 |
| 199.18 | 265.11 | 315.19 | 377.18 | 444.02 | 524.06 |
| 202.18 | 265.14 | 315.22 | 379.21 | 446.15 | 524.07 |
| 202.20 | 265.15 | 316.08 | 380.02 | 447.03 | 524.13 |
| 203.20 | 266.04 | 316.10 | 380.03 | 449.10 | 524.17 |
| 203.22 | 267.08 | 316.11 | 382.03 | 449.13 | 524.18 |
| 204.11 | 268.04 | 316.13 | 382.05 | 449.14 | 525.11 |
| 204.20 | 270.11 | 316.20 | 382.11 | 449.16 | 527.14 |
| 205.10 | 270.21 | 317.02 | 383.04 | 450.21 | 528.14 |
| 205.21 | 272.12 | 317.05 | 384.07 | 452.20 | 528.15 |
| 206.02 | 272.12 | 317.07 | 384.11 | 454.08 | 528.20 |
| 206.07 | 273.11 | 317.08 | 384.12 | 456.01 | 529.01 |
| 206.18 | 274.01 | 317.18 | 385.02 | 457.04 | 531.10 |
| 206.20 | 274.03 | 318.02 | 385.12 | 459.09 | 532.11 |
| 207.08 | 275.11 | 318.20 | 385.13 | 463.08 | 532.15 |
| 208.02 | 275.13 | 318.22 | 385.14 | 463.09 | 533.06 |
| 208.02 | 275.15 | 319.11 | 386.11 | 463.13 | 534.10 |
| 208.12 | 275.17 | 322.08 | 386.20 | 464.07 | 534.20 |
| 208.14 | 275.20 | 325.09 | 386.21 | 465.08 | 538.05 |
| 208.16 | 276.10 | 325.11 | 387.01 | 465.10 | 538.12 |
| 209.16 | 277.05 | 325.12 | 388.02 | 465.12 | 538.12 |
| 209.21 | 277.06 | 326.11 | 389.02 | 466.05 | 539.10 |
| 210.11 | 277.07 | 327.02 | 389.03 | 466.14 | 540.03 |
| 211.03 | 277.14 | 327.11 | 389.13 | 466.15 | 540.04 |
| 211.07 | 277.15 | 329.03 | 391.08 | 467.05 | 540.10 |
| 214.02 | 277.17 | 329.10 | | 467.12 | 540.20 |
| 214.06 | 277.17 | | | 468.21 | 541.12 |
| 214.21 | 277.18 | | | 469.06 | 541.14 |
| | 278.03 | | | | |

542.09
542.11
542.14
542.17
543.09
543.18
545.03
546.06
547.06
547.08
548.06
549.04
551.10
552.14
552.17
554.16
554.19
555.08
557.03
558.13
558.18
559.04
559.19
560.09
560.12
560.12
560.14
561.12
561.13
562.07
562.08
562.13
562.21
563.03
564.10
565.06
565.06
567.06
569.01
569.11
569.14
569.14
569.15
569.21
570.07
570.19
571.11
571.12
571.12
572.14
572.15
573.05
573.08
573.10
573.11
576.04
576.06
577.12
577.15
577.22
578.13
578.22
579.05
579.20
580.02
580.06
581.14
585.06
587.15
588.06
589.05
589.22
591.14
592.04
594.03
596.09
597.01
598.05
598.06
598.09
599.02
599.04
599.09
599.20
600.14
600.15
601.05
601.10
602.04
603.07
603.13
603.14
606.06
606.17
606.17
607.19
608.04
608.07
608.22
609.07
609.09
609.11
610.04
612.02
612.04
612.05
612.18
612.18
614.15
616.18
618.09

618.10
618.20
619.04
619.05
619.07
621.21
622.04
622.08
623.10
623.12
623.13
623.21
624.08
624.09
624.15
626.05
627.07
627.08
630.05
630.21
631.09
631.20
632.13
632.13
633.10
633.13
633.14
633.19
634.14
634.15
634.16
634.20
635.01
635.06
636.06
636.17
636.20
637.19
638.02
638.07
638.09
638.11
638.15
639.03
640.04
640.13
641.13
641.18
642.01
644.18
647.12
647.12
647.13
648.02
649.02
649.08
649.15
649.16
649.18
649.18
649.20
649.22
650.01
651.04
651.05
651.08
651.16
652.02
652.03
652.05
652.09
652.13
652.16
652.20
653.05
653.11
654.07
654.21
655.04
655.09
655.19
655.20
655.20
656.05
659.06
661.02
661.04
662.02
663.05
665.19
667.21
668.07
669.06
669.21
670.03
672.06
672.10
673.11
674.06
675.02
675.14
675.18
675.20
676.01
676.02
676.05
676.08
676.10
677.04
678.05
679.14

679.19
679.22
680.11
680.21
681.17
682.11
683.20
685.01
685.09
685.11
686.21
689.03
689.08
689.22
690.03
690.04
692.14
692.22
693.06
693.14
694.11
695.03
697.02
698.07
698.18
698.22
699.05
699.07
699.08
699.12
699.18
700.08
700.19
701.08
702.02
702.11
702.17
703.02
703.05
703.07
703.10
703.11
703.16
703.21
704.08
704.09
705.04
705.05
705.06
706.14
706.16
706.16
707.22
708.01
708.05
708.07
708.07
709.05
709.21
710.03
710.04
710.07
710.08
710.09
710.11
710.13
710.14
711.11
712.08
712.12
713.01
713.06
713.16
713.23
714.01
715.05
716.10
716.13
716.19
717.07
718.04
718.07
718.13
719.06
719.15
719.19
720.04
720.15
721.02
721.11
723.13
723.17
723.18
724.15
725.13
726.02
727.02
727.07
727.11
727.17
728.12
728.13
728.19
728.21
729.01
729.06
729.06
729.17
730.01
730.15
731.01

731.02
731.06
732.07
732.08
732.11
733.05
733.06
733.21
733.22
734.06
734.07
734.08
734.09
734.15
734.15
734.21
735.01
735.02
737.05
739.10
739.12
739.14
741.12
742.05
742.06
742.19
742.22
743.08
743.19
744.09
744.12
744.13
745.01
745.09
745.18
746.09
747.04
747.15
748.02
748.02
748.22
749.02
749.03
749.08
749.16
750.12
751.06
751.07
751.10
751.12
752.10
753.04
753.05
753.09
753.20
754.05
754.06
754.07
754.08
754.14
755.05
755.08
756.10
756.20
757.04
758.03
758.09
759.14
759.19
759.21
760.05
760.06
760.09
761.20
761.20
762.12
762.15

it's
028.22
043.19
053.12
074.06
077.21
127.22
140.14
140.21
155.11
158.07
164.13
168.21
174.08
176.10
177.16
186.20
193.22
199.18
218.22
222.16
223.11
235.08
245.03
254.09
254.11
259.06
263.04
275.13
276.22
277.05
277.16
278.07
284.11

284.13
292.13
312.03
318.14
318.16
319.12
321.02
322.03
324.14
326.10
370.09
386.08
396.10
406.12
407.14
416.06
435.13
436.14
438.01
455.19
472.06
476.05
479.07
479.21
483.19
484.04
496.01
496.04
504.09
511.07
520.07
532.17
533.18
534.17
542.12
546.19
567.17
592.04
608.08
617.20
627.10
627.15
630.02
632.13
696.10
720.08
720.13
756.10

iteration
347.11

its
004.06
006.05
006.12
028.16
040.03
044.14
051.14
051.12
052.17
052.21
060.22
061.22
063.17
064.21
078.04
078.05
078.21
085.13
104.19
118.02
125.02
129.20
135.18
163.21
168.15
168.16
187.03
191.22
202.11
209.10
209.17
215.11
223.07
223.11
224.14
225.22
226.05
237.06
239.10
241.07
243.08
243.11
244.05
255.07
257.09
270.03
270.13
273.10
275.16
275.19
276.07
278.21
291.06
291.08
296.05
302.10
310.01
316.13
319.02
322.13

322.21
324.06
325.06
325.10
325.12
332.14
345.04
350.09
351.08
351.19
352.07
354.14
355.01
358.08
369.09
370.09
370.13
371.18
371.18
371.19
372.06
372.07
379.08
387.16
388.13
392.22
399.14
401.17
410.09
412.04
412.11
414.12
414.13
418.09
421.11
422.07
425.06
429.12
432.07
444.19
445.01
449.16
463.01
478.03
479.18
484.14
500.13
503.02
506.11
507.10
510.04
516.05
516.08
519.01
519.12
546.02
552.18
553.03
558.12
560.13
576.09
578.05
585.02
587.08
590.18
593.20
596.03
598.13
607.08
609.16
622.21
641.08
642.10
647.15
682.07
690.05
693.18
694.20
694.22
695.07
700.20
710.06
719.08
728.20
730.05
734.10
743.18
743.18
745.07
749.19
754.09
754.10
759.10
760.10
760.10
763.16
764.04

itself
058.09
308.09
314.08
383.22
457.05
490.10
538.16
579.15
598.12
731.01
753.15

itsseln
187.12

```
187.13            016.02            713.06            judicious         justice           kennel
iver              016.14            719.01             224.15            136.16             441.18
 310.11           028.11            720.08             403.08            396.07           kenneth
 322.08           029.16            734.19            jug                571.05             140.16
 401.11           030.10            744.18             320.07            625.05             142.09
 696.13           031.18            744.22             638.06            696.18             142.22
jabes             032.07            747.07             638.13            740.10             163.09
 046.02           033.21            747.13            jugs              justice-meeting     169.03
 046.04           040.14            755.13             006.02            234.03             196.02
 047.05           041.14            758.13            july              justified           198.04
 048.03           041.14            758.13             432.02            334.08             201.08
 049.03           042.17            762.07            518.20            justly              227.05
 049.18           044.04            763.09            557.06            206.01             291.20
 056.17           046.15           joseph´s           jump             jutted              293.06
jabes´            047.07            091.19            053.18            763.19              294.20
 051.01           048.20            118.18            638.08           jutting              295.19
jacket            050.10            187.04            jumped            004.17              301.10
 509.03           061.17            284.08            015.12           keen                347.19
jade              076.03            391.12            185.04            225.09             416.01
 064.12           089.10            476.07            246.15            225.10             416.20
jailer            093.03            678.08            697.06            225.10             417.16
 545.10           094.04            716.06           jumping            283.15             420.01
 615.21           095.02            716.17            113.10            757.17             628.14
 625.04           095.11            737.14            435.06           keep               632.10
 637.03           098.14           journey           june              015.20             661.03
january           100.05            076.03            139.02            032.05             756.17
 672.11           100.15            109.21            578.10            035.01             759.16
jargon            105.13            243.01            583.05            045.05            kept
 309.16           120.17            284.11            junior            053.07             009.19
jaws              121.09            284.13            025.04            059.21             017.21
 106.19           127.04            314.18            juno              071.12             047.17
 310.19           144.05            347.14            018.06            090.20             054.12
 719.07           144.11            347.15            060.01            091.02             065.08
jealous           151.17            428.17            702.06            106.21             094.03
 002.03           151.19            451.07            just              106.22             096.09
 010.07           180.05            453.11            001.03            112.13             100.03
 087.11           184.04            455.08            015.07            127.02             117.05
 251.06           185.09            460.11            042.15            127.05             119.09
 251.07           186.06            569.15            042.20            140.03             145.13
 251.08           189.09            595.01            057.01            141.01             146.17
 253.06           190.21            608.01            063.21            149.16             148.01
 263.01           191.15            638.03            074.17            171.08             166.20
 469.14           193.13            685.06            077.10            183.21             188.10
 673.08           195.20            688.04            084.20            184.01             192.16
jealously         196.12           journeying         091.21            203.04             198.04
 316.12           197.13            047.05            102.09            218.08             215.01
jealousy          221.11           journeys           126.09            222.20             228.01
 362.07           232.07            032.03            134.16            246.17             254.04
jenny             233.13           journies           140.19            250.18             259.18
 108.05           284.08            656.07            163.08            256.18             270.21
jerked            308.12           joy               165.20            261.13             281.05
 183.14           310.07            140.14            177.13            262.22             312.03
 668.16           315.04            164.17            185.02            278.01             357.06
jerking           317.17            179.02            193.15            284.17             382.01
 152.17           319.05            212.17            199.02            287.13             390.04
jest              322.10            215.09            201.10            306.02             447.03
 026.18           324.10            259.08            216.03            338.04             491.04
 157.18           326.05            302.05            218.22            340.19             500.09
 174.07           391.16            308.02            250.17            350.14             539.10
 174.08           392.10            371.19            264.13            360.16             582.10
 232.21           393.11            393.13            275.04            368.06             609.21
 524.22           398.05            398.20            281.12            394.03             664.17
jesting           400.04            403.07            281.17            394.05             670.11
 174.11           401.10            407.11            291.20            411.18             694.17
jet               402.05            411.03            294.13            435.17             709.02
 277.02           410.04            413.17            306.01            440.21            key
jewel             419.08            420.18            311.20            454.05             258.02
 619.12           434.09            435.02            318.12            454.09             258.13
jocks             443.05            448.07            322.07            457.06             326.21
 699.11           443.19            558.01            324.12            461.04             394.06
john              444.05            568.17            326.18            469.08             507.06
 108.04           455.03            587.02            332.20            484.06             523.01
 232.16           455.10            599.02            342.06            492.13             555.19
join              455.17            635.02            383.04            501.08             608.22
 059.21           457.18            639.15            390.17            511.10             609.03
 374.18           458.08            741.13            395.06            513.07             611.06
 463.21           466.07           joyful            416.17            519.08             628.02
 474.03           466.17            486.19            420.22            547.03             632.17
 561.11           466.20            738.20            427.04            555.13             634.10
 581.06           469.16           joyfully          438.06            564.03             641.21
 585.05           471.01            114.21            449.07            586.06             757.13
 619.06           471.20            699.21            450.06            599.20            keys
 630.20           472.04           jubilee           454.17            602.11             507.16
 643.10           486.01            210.22            460.17            605.13             523.05
joined            493.08            558.03            466.06            618.09             523.09
 095.01           527.05           judas             472.06            621.08            kick
 121.09           531.01            249.11            482.16            676.07             085.09
 221.16           531.14           judge             495.15            691.03             259.13
 401.16           531.17            115.08            504.17            700.08             560.10
 437.18           533.15            182.04            504.22            712.02             621.09
 701.09           556.11            399.06            511.20            724.11             653.14
joining           564.12            415.14            526.02            741.09            kicked
 065.11           565.12            696.17            528.20            762.08             043.13
joins             566.15           judged            553.02           keeper              400.01
 209.13           608.01            308.06            577.17            443.02             400.13
joint             646.03            514.05            586.01           keeping             406.20
 484.19           654.22            521.10            592.04            008.04             564.10
 518.11           658.03            690.11            598.08            163.18            kicker
joke              659.17            695.13            610.21            171.14             125.03
 236.07           663.06           judges            619.05            225.22            kicking
joked             663.09            232.15            627.19            246.04             029.07
 666.15           663.14            595.02            643.07            286.18             164.22
jokes             665.15           judging           645.22            332.04            kicks
 091.10           665.19            551.17            683.03            509.21             125.01
jonah             686.01            620.10            701.18            551.04            kidnapped
 189.14           686.14           judgment          716.07            591.05             125.20
joseph            699.08            050.04            724.01            650.10            kill
 003.09           701.02            189.13            729.08            654.02             163.11
 003.16           704.05            442.20            735.06           keeps               168.21
 010.01           705.10            623.09            744.21            294.07             220.10
 010.02           712.03            732.18            760.22            322.07             273.11
```

| | | | | | |
|---|---|---|---|---|---|
| 273.12 | 553.17 | 508.21 | 500.16 | 251.22 | 339.18 |
| 334.03 | 571.08 | 530.09 | 501.07 | 253.13 | 407.16 |
| 342.07 | 619.16 | 533.10 | 501.10 | 261.12 | 467.07 |
| 388.07 | 619.20 | 564.06 | 518.06 | 265.09 | 542.05 |
| 489.18 | 630.11 | 612.08 | 532.01 | 272.07 | 575.07 |
| 521.05 | 664.08 | 622.17 | 536.19 | 275.13 | 613.17 |
| 565.08 | 670.07 | 660.21 | 559.18 | 276.18 | 622.06 |
| 565.09 | kindred | 675.04 | 563.12 | 289.08 | knuckles |
| 565.10 | 441.12 | 684.11 | 572.13 | 289.09 | 015.15 |
| 565.11 | kinds | 686.03 | 580.15 | 298.01 | 051.20 |
| 722.20 | 038.22 | 690.12 | 595.07 | 309.03 | 257.09 |
| killed | king | 695.21 | 652.17 | 316.16 | labour |
| 077.14 | 035.04 | 696.09 | 691.08 | 334.22 | 063.22 |
| 129.11 | 259.04 | 701.03 | knife | 335.10 | 099.16 |
| 160.03 | 708.05 | 701.05 | 163.07 | 335.11 | 150.10 |
| 167.02 | kingdom | 702.13 | 163.13 | 338.20 | 339.09 |
| 356.22 | 229.08 | 704.20 | 163.20 | 352.02 | 402.01 |
| 359.02 | kingdoms | 705.13 | 205.05 | 354.20 | 490.01 |
| 362.22 | 077.15 | 708.16 | 283.15 | 359.02 | 653.03 |
| 376.22 | kinsman | 719.14 | 315.15 | 359.03 | 660.15 |
| 388.07 | 438.21 | 722.19 | 316.12 | 366.13 | 682.18 |
| 433.15 | kirk | 751.06 | 398.07 | 369.07 | laboured |
| 566.13 | 284.13 | 755.14 | 399.13 | 371.10 | 680.20 |
| 601.08 | 577.15 | 760.17 | 409.15 | 372.11 | 727.10 |
| 638.01 | 665.16 | 762.09 | 669.07 | 373.12 | labourer |
| killing | 755.04 | 763.08 | 740.12 | 377.02 | 021.07 |
| 316.01 | 763.15 | kitten | knighthood | 382.17 | 432.13 |
| 476.05 | kirkyard | 068.02 | 259.01 | 390.03 | labourers |
| 655.04 | 285.03 | 135.18 | knitted | 399.05 | 144.12 |
| kills | 379.22 | knack | 152.02 | 405.14 | labouring |
| 753.14 | 392.19 | 089.15 | knitting | 412.07 | 729.20 |
| kin | 478.10 | knave | 093.03 | 428.09 | labours |
| 071.07 | 746.13 | 233.06 | 203.06 | 428.09 | 325.18 |
| 390.15 | kiss | knaw | 690.15 | 452.20 | laced |
| 418.08 | 123.07 | 191.05 | knives | 461.11 | 043.21 |
| kind | 164.17 | 232.13 | 377.12 | 468.09 | lachrymose |
| 019.18 | 164.18 | 457.23 | 685.21 | 469.10 | 045.02 |
| 076.17 | 164.18 | 692.11 | knock | 478.01 | lack |
| 101.05 | 251.04 | knaws | 123.15 | 479.01 | 307.21 |
| 137.16 | 309.10 | 564.17 | 344.05 | 481.17 | 340.15 |
| 143.22 | 363.01 | 564.17 | 525.09 | 483.20 | 477.04 |
| 205.07 | 364.01 | knee | 564.08 | 490.05 | 493.03 |
| 236.07 | 505.16 | 039.18 | 609.13 | 491.01 | 516.08 |
| 237.02 | 532.10 | 042.10 | 638.08 | 493.16 | 541.18 |
| 240.16 | 694.09 | 070.15 | 638.11 | 496.04 | 588.12 |
| 292.21 | 709.08 | 093.08 | 693.06 | 496.08 | 649.10 |
| 305.15 | 709.18 | 169.15 | 752.18 | 499.04 | lacked |
| 321.07 | kissed | 318.11 | knocked | 503.08 | 429.08 |
| 335.15 | 076.20 | 353.17 | 015.14 | 508.15 | laconic |
| 348.03 | 093.20 | 357.04 | 123.20 | 521.17 | 013.06 |
| 352.11 | 099.06 | 382.05 | 154.06 | 528.22 | 735.08 |
| 363.12 | 115.03 | 544.02 | 189.04 | 534.05 | lad |
| 385.21 | 162.08 | 610.06 | 410.04 | 540.04 | 035.22 |
| 419.15 | 199.16 | 620.21 | 477.18 | 543.13 | 074.10 |
| 429.11 | 356.02 | 675.12 | 673.09 | 545.14 | 088.04 |
| 464.06 | 410.22 | 710.14 | 690.10 | 554.06 | 099.17 |
| 469.07 | 487.01 | knee-breeches | knocking | 554.15 | 107.13 |
| 469.12 | 503.12 | 007.02 | 051.20 | 558.17 | 124.06 |
| 469.14 | 558.10 | kneel | 085.13 | 592.17 | 125.09 |
| 482.19 | 759.10 | 359.20 | 102.01 | 603.18 | 129.17 |
| 527.07 | kisses | 620.20 | 257.11 | 606.16 | 139.11 |
| 534.13 | 116.17 | kneeling | 311.03 | 611.04 | 144.19 |
| 571.06 | 352.18 | 063.10 | 330.03 | 612.13 | 164.10 |
| 580.09 | 355.22 | 171.09 | 389.17 | 618.11 | 187.06 |
| 581.05 | 363.02 | 404.05 | 433.22 | 630.20 | 232.18 |
| 588.11 | 488.06 | knees | 644.11 | 631.06 | 298.03 |
| 601.11 | 695.11 | 010.15 | knocks | 634.17 | 309.22 |
| 605.19 | kissing | 015.01 | 395.14 | 647.22 | 417.05 |
| 619.13 | 042.11 | 133.12 | knot | 648.02 | 421.06 |
| 619.14 | 453.21 | 156.08 | 291.12 | 650.03 | 434.18 |
| 648.12 | 602.14 | 159.13 | knotted | 651.08 | 439.07 |
| 670.03 | 639.20 | 189.09 | 377.09 | 658.08 | 443.17 |
| 670.10 | kitchen | 401.13 | know | 660.01 | 456.17 |
| 675.17 | 005.13 | 467.21 | 007.18 | 661.12 | 457.22 |
| 741.15 | 005.15 | 503.18 | 012.18 | 665.16 | 469.01 |
| kinder | 011.09 | 510.17 | 022.03 | 666.02 | 469.16 |
| 088.05 | 032.04 | 662.14 | 030.21 | 689.03 | 490.07 |
| 546.07 | 036.05 | 759.01 | 035.07 | 702.12 | 491.19 |
| kindest | 118.15 | knelt | 037.08 | 708.11 | 497.18 |
| 303.18 | 119.13 | 357.04 | 049.17 | 711.11 | 564.16 |
| kingle | 120.17 | 541.16 | 058.03 | 726.18 | 565.15 |
| 751.16 | 121.18 | 542.20 | 071.04 | 732.08 | 568.15 |
| kindled | 126.21 | 611.15 | 074.04 | 733.05 | 604.03 |
| 040.16 | 132.21 | knew | 074.06 | 739.09 | 616.05 |
| 263.10 | 157.21 | 025.12 | 089.06 | knowing | 668.09 |
| 290.10 | 162.04 | 054.11 | 091.08 | 083.10 | 683.16 |
| 464.18 | 169.08 | 078.21 | 097.17 | 147.21 | 696.15 |
| kindliness | 185.01 | 098.05 | 109.03 | 293.03 | 696.16 |
| 007.20 | 189.06 | 108.01 | 123.07 | 388.15 | 712.16 |
| kindling | 192.01 | 134.02 | 125.01 | 676.21 | 720.14 |
| 111.13 | 206.12 | 194.14 | 137.01 | knowledge | 762.08 |
| 228.16 | 212.05 | 197.10 | 138.04 | 057.13 | lad's |
| 486.18 | 212.11 | 223.06 | 143.04 | 065.03 | 120.05 |
| 670.21 | 249.01 | 228.05 | 144.08 | 149.12 | 663.09 |
| kindly | 250.06 | 248.20 | 151.09 | 387.21 | ladder |
| 033.12 | 254.07 | 278.04 | 151.21 | 679.06 | 061.17 |
| 338.05 | 255.07 | 288.18 | 154.01 | known | 132.12 |
| 359.14 | 309.02 | 289.06 | 163.05 | 114.09 | 191.16 |
| 376.12 | 311.21 | 298.09 | 171.17 | 141.05 | laden |
| kindness | 317.16 | 298.14 | 172.01 | 272.01 | 006.07 |
| 092.02 | 364.21 | 300.04 | 179.09 | 293.17 | 624.13 |
| 108.10 | 386.04 | 302.05 | 180.16 | 418.20 | 737.19 |
| 115.15 | 392.01 | 304.01 | 180.17 | 517.06 | lads |
| 119.04 | 393.16 | 314.02 | 190.11 | known't | 022.09 |
| 158.07 | 398.09 | 325.11 | 192.20 | 247.06 | 083.16 |
| 196.22 | 410.03 | 350.02 | 203.18 | knows | 218.20 |
| 223.07 | 455.01 | 350.19 | 207.14 | 049.16 | lady |
| 258.04 | 455.10 | 367.20 | 211.21 | 071.15 | 014.08 |
| 396.06 | 491.06 | 434.01 | 219.21 | 125.16 | 021.10 |
| 469.15 | 507.02 | 476.01 | 225.18 | 262.05 | 022.17 |
| 527.06 | | 476.21 | 230.08 | 262.21 | 024.01 |

**LADY** (continued)
024.03
024.05
064.15
072.05
110.02
111.01
114.10
146.02
147.01
155.16
174.09
175.19
193.22
197.03
205.06
215.11
225.08
228.04
248.13
251.16
282.11
297.09
297.14
298.10
298.18
318.08
333.05
337.07
384.03
432.16
439.13
445.10
478.16
485.14
488.20
489.13
492.10
508.20
512.21
516.21
522.04
535.06
537.12
590.06
601.14
614.04
628.08
634.22
637.03
643.02
658.12
666.20
671.03
673.05
713.16
724.18
727.08
737.17

lady's
073.02
118.13
213.10
270.08
330.06
424.05
514.04
583.07

laid
017.07
095.13
136.17
157.14
158.04
167.09
226.05
249.04
281.20
352.09
370.15
382.04
405.11
419.21
443.14
453.02
509.04
547.20
549.04
568.17
578.05
612.01
627.09
650.01
710.13
740.14
757.16
760.08

laiking
043.01

lair
310.02

laith
016.07

lamb
082.18
169.09
257.07
259.06
375.19
434.12

lambs
761.02

761.04

lame
083.17
466.09

lamed
109.12

lament
128.09
144.01

lamentable
053.06

lamentation
318.18

lamentations
287.11
441.20
474.04
538.18
582.09

lamented
720.19

lamenting
199.07

land
088.17
232.06
358.05
422.16
481.04
586.06
617.18
721.20
721.21
722.06

landed
061.06

landing
080.02

landlord
001.04
009.09
060.08
065.16
444.18
672.13
689.12

landlord's
071.01

landmarks
030.21

lands
305.08
470.03
664.16

landscape
427.10
492.19
598.08
644.21

lane
139.08

lang
324.18

langs
232.17

language
008.16
025.19
058.03
110.03
255.19
327.03
342.12
446.10

languid
464.17
487.08
587.10

lankly
330.12

lantern
034.02
034.06
101.19
106.21
110.09
310.19

lap
093.09
111.07
354.03
611.16
675.09
681.08

lapse
240.10
350.11

lapsed
676.20

lapwing
275.22

lapwing's
275.13

lapwings
276.02

larch
368.07
424.09

larches
373.02

large
004.17
017.03
038.03
039.01
146.05
245.05
317.18
321.19
354.22
399.21
431.18
463.09
464.17
523.09
531.03
565.03
587.08
677.21
693.16
712.12
715.12
743.19

largely
471.06
594.19

larger
010.22

larks
303.16
381.10
479.14
557.10
557.16

lascar
109.21

lashes
237.17
303.21
389.10
404.14

lass
093.14
119.22
141.06
193.19
292.11
298.13
299.03
436.11
466.22
483.10
497.18
525.22
627.16
646.20

last
008.09
008.18
025.10
050.19
054.07
060.15
062.08
067.16
073.10
077.06
083.04
088.14
090.05
092.17
097.15
101.10
106.21
108.22
117.10
122.21
133.18
139.03
145.03
163.01
171.03
174.14
186.08
194.19
195.07
201.12
216.13
220.03
235.06
281.15
291.06
294.09
303.08
306.05
314.11
317.11
321.01
335.16
338.20
343.22
347.13
352.18
354.05
361.18
366.02
372.03
375.08
381.02
385.10
389.13

390.13
394.21
401.01
406.13
407.10
409.21
418.01
429.09
432.11
435.03
438.18
453.18
463.05
490.11
515.08
518.18
520.12
523.10
558.08
565.19
570.10
572.10
575.02
575.04
578.19
579.08
587.13
591.15
597.22
603.16
619.12
624.14
628.14
630.12
632.11
641.14
650.15
661.13
668.06
669.04
673.09
678.12
686.13
700.16
704.13
718.01
731.02
731.12
742.14
742.19
746.05
752.18
763.02

lasted
041.16
391.03
538.12

lasts
647.12

latch
016.01
207.07
208.20
211.08
317.16
393.16
473.09
560.16
561.18
624.06

late
072.09
073.01
109.20
121.16
145.17
149.10
190.16
234.21
272.13
282.02
284.08
285.15
326.21
392.16
460.11
465.10
476.04
478.07
510.06
515.03
599.04
637.04
651.18
699.04
723.13
747.03
750.08

lately
293.14
311.15

later
191.18

latest
376.10

lath
497.19

latin
138.03
678.10

latitude
240.19

latter
006.04
144.17
199.09
234.08
256.10
310.21
397.18
451.05
487.17
517.21
536.12
542.08
572.08
583.12
608.18
616.16
704.10
721.17

latter's
369.08
441.11
640.20
726.10

lattice
051.03
060.11
101.14
193.01
209.06
279.14
285.09
329.22
396.14
495.17
622.10
623.04
642.10
743.12
757.22

lattices
465.18
693.11

lauded
699.15

laugh
100.13
116.19
117.14
142.17
148.13
163.08
232.20
234.16
256.09
308.02
432.03
440.10
467.02
495.01
496.17
512.11
564.11
565.12
572.18
653.06
666.14
702.14
717.17
718.02
742.19
756.01

laughed
035.07
092.15
093.16
105.04
105.19
108.22
117.10
137.14
147.13
167.18
178.16
215.13
234.13
408.06
437.17
491.22
556.20
679.20
679.21
681.16
702.17

laughing
027.02
077.12
090.13
103.02
212.08
220.08
227.21
234.14
282.21
382.09
383.10
386.16
434.16
469.13

522.22
545.08
561.07
666.13
718.12

laughs
534.06

laughter
386.16
401.17

launched
489.21

lave
318.15

lavish
488.10

lavished
004.20
195.14
303.18

lavishing
150.14

law
121.09
129.18
163.17
216.07
340.19
342.12
617.18
696.18

lawful
759.02

laws
608.10

lawyer
418.14
418.15
637.06
640.14

lay
006.05
046.15
082.09
085.22
104.14
107.21
134.12
190.06
197.08
205.09
209.07
253.22
265.17
279.20
281.07
283.22
288.08
295.21
306.20
313.10
331.08
352.06
371.02
418.04
427.11
444.03
446.16
453.14
475.20
487.16
528.09
541.10
542.14
553.11
579.03
586.15
623.03
629.06
635.09
644.21
661.20
747.03

laying
035.14
683.14

laziness
200.09
496.21

lazy
014.12
135.22

lead
590.13
649.21
686.15
759.19

leading
037.02
126.21
452.18
553.01

leads
237.13

leaf
020.06
353.06
677.17

league
500.08

**leagued**
233.17
**lean**
039.18
544.01
605.05
**leaned**
710.15
**leaning**
017.12
028.13
049.19
143.11
305.01
356.15
394.10
537.21
712.06
743.11
**leant**
002.21
039.04
093.07
133.12
165.06
165.11
207.06
211.03
258.20
360.04
373.14
393.01
403.15
538.17
611.02
655.19
676.18
748.19
**leap**
135.13
**leaped**
054.21
410.08
**leaping**
138.09
**leapt**
010.15
432.19
**lear**
035.04
**learn**
103.05
124.17
133.21
246.13
264.13
272.13
374.04
415.22
470.13
506.13
562.11
724.09
728.01
**learning**
149.13
622.14
667.01
**learns**
181.16
**learnt**
079.16
081.21
099.20
205.07
339.06
386.02
426.06
461.09
475.18
572.07
573.18
573.19
584.02
698.09
**least**
005.16
015.20
040.07
065.22
098.03
100.18
117.16
135.11
181.16
190.16
218.14
255.08
267.03
287.10
292.21
317.12
330.07
364.07
373.13
378.08
408.14
415.15
451.21
481.02
502.02
534.04
541.02
562.08
568.08
583.09
589.12
619.04
635.13
643.09
671.16
674.03
695.11
699.05
749.04
**leave**
012.02
079.04
098.16
140.22
144.07
157.05
158.18
160.02
178.17
198.21
203.21
265.13
272.16
282.18
303.13
317.01
329.07
333.17
333.19
341.19
345.08
357.19
363.04
372.17
374.18
377.05
417.22
419.15
430.05
437.03
447.01
451.07
454.20
460.02
468.19
473.07
476.03
478.19
520.02
537.08
537.10
540.14
560.09
573.09
574.03
576.16
581.06
586.14
591.18
601.07
615.06
630.03
631.07
660.10
660.14
666.05
671.22
685.13
713.02
713.05
721.12
724.16
724.17
739.20
752.02
752.08
761.20
**leaves**
352.08
378.04
381.11
506.21
516.17
**leaving**
010.05
063.01
095.11
135.07
157.21
189.22
209.21
225.13
241.02
321.10
406.05
415.06
547.12
556.03
579.02
636.16
699.20
**lecture**
112.07
197.14
572.17
**lectures**
391.13
**led**
009.01
060.06
102.10
120.05
147.06
198.18
213.13
307.19
308.19
372.02
443.02
511.12
653.06
724.18
**ledge**
006.12
038.11
038.18
104.02
106.05
743.11
**leeches**
202.07
**lees**
607.22
**left**
009.12
028.05
040.08
066.03
066.16
087.04
096.04
105.18
111.10
121.08
127.08
142.07
187.07
191.10
196.07
199.13
203.08
217.03
218.18
226.20
231.09
234.01
243.06
244.21
254.03
262.09
281.01
302.13
306.11
306.15
311.21
350.14
358.17
359.01
363.18
369.12
376.08
396.14
398.12
403.07
412.20
418.10
420.10
429.20
457.08
477.10
477.20
495.16
507.07
510.02
532.15
548.08
551.22
555.03
564.05
594.14
597.13
620.18
632.02
641.20
658.03
663.02
681.05
689.18
697.15
701.08
704.01
730.08
744.12
750.03
757.01
761.19
**leg**
281.08
**legal**
309.08
342.16
752.05
**legally**
664.19
**legion**
406.06
**legions**
522.15
762.22
**legitimate**
040.05
**legs**
006.07
009.13
560.13
**leisure**
017.17
185.06
384.02
507.19
511.06
**leisurely**
134.17
166.17
265.15
692.16
**lend**
505.01
556.04
605.16
**length**
017.03
035.12
053.01
058.21
066.08
069.05
161.04
188.13
209.03
214.15
245.04
270.13
393.15
450.09
462.06
465.06
480.11
512.12
519.02
539.16
567.11
583.01
624.09
712.14
**lengthened**
763.14
**lengthening**
135.09
**lengths**
443.20
**leniently**
419.05
**less**
074.01
081.20
082.16
091.13
123.21
134.20
136.09
154.17
161.03
171.14
188.01
197.21
205.08
240.02
240.20
252.16
295.13
391.14
392.09
405.12
421.15
516.06
516.13
524.13
527.05
545.14
562.16
578.02
588.19
592.11
592.12
608.10
608.11
623.15
654.01
674.14
**lesson**
032.02
**lessons**
246.09
339.05
475.18
503.13
604.07
**lest**
087.12
115.01
120.03
290.21
297.01
385.19
459.11
**let**
008.06
009.16
031.10
035.01
037.06
043.20
045.07
048.01
052.07
052.07
052.20
053.01
053.02
053.10
062.07
071.09
076.10
079.07
085.22
091.08
101.11
102.12
106.10
110.18
114.16
120.18
124.10
132.09
134.03
152.19
158.07
171.16
175.17
184.11
196.04
198.13
219.01
226.21
229.07
230.02
230.04
230.14
239.04
250.12
260.15
264.18
265.10
273.01
275.10
276.03
279.14
279.15
288.14
290.08
299.03
303.20
322.17
329.06
338.04
339.13
344.12
346.07
346.20
348.06
352.22
354.02
360.04
363.16
363.16
364.01
384.14
387.11
396.02
398.04
398.09
418.19
422.03
436.04
439.14
440.02
440.12
449.18
451.20
452.13
461.15
466.14
483.03
502.14
519.07
526.14
539.19
541.02
544.01
555.13
560.20
563.08
564.07
565.08
565.09
567.19
570.11
571.20
581.01
587.16
597.16
600.17
601.12
602.03
603.09
605.10
613.17
614.07
615.04
617.12
617.17
618.11
629.16
629.17
632.18
633.04
640.07
646.13
658.05
659.02
660.07
664.01
666.02
670.22
671.15
698.17
698.22
706.13
707.02
722.20
723.10
732.08
742.08
744.11
752.12
760.05
**lethargy**
271.17
589.09
**lets**
109.16
**letter**
305.21
307.01
328.05
331.05
331.20
346.18
350.05
353.15
354.11
395.20
448.02
506.11
512.16
514.10
580.14
582.05
675.15
676.08
677.09
677.15
**letters**
039.08
199.03
243.07
496.08
508.05
524.14
533.07
597.18
619.10
**letting**
084.21
358.16
521.02
613.02
701.13
**level**
066.01
149.22
308.16
405.19
**levelled**
253.01
259.20
**leveret**
259.07
**levers**
729.09
**levity**
762.16
**liar**
233.14
376.16
537.18
708.11
**liberal**
222.10
**liberally**
008.02
045.13
**liberated**
131.04
610.05
**liberating**
641.15
**liberties**
716.12
**liberty**
102.18
224.12
236.16
264.06

| | | | | | |
|---|---|---|---|---|---|
| 311.03 | 429.13 | lighter | 495.22 | limbs | 198.15 |
| 400.15 | 435.10 | 449.13 | 497.16 | 004.13 | 204.08 |
| 404.04 | 485.01 | 626.03 | 511.20 | 007.01 | 209.01 |
| 677.20 | 512.02 | 713.11 | 522.20 | 200.10 | 210.05 |
| library | 520.04 | lightest | 525.16 | 468.10 | 211.01 |
| 040.02 | 539.03 | 090.17 | 525.16 | lime | 212.07 |
| 138.01 | 598.05 | lighting | 534.18 | 066.09 | 213.13 |
| 234.08 | 601.08 | 454.22 | 536.03 | 151.19 | 214.16 |
| 267.17 | 621.05 | 642.09 | 539.09 | limit | 216.17 |
| 285.12 | 636.18 | lightly | 540.06 | 680.09 | 218.02 |
| 430.12 | 643.10 | 130.10 | 545.20 | limited | 219.01 |
| 453.01 | 653.22 | lightning | 545.21 | 066.22 | 219.20 |
| 456.08 | 660.02 | 179.14 | 548.03 | 079.01 | 222.18 |
| 478.09 | 670.10 | lights | 559.04 | 226.11 | 223.21 |
| 507.05 | 686.18 | 102.19 | 562.04 | limits | 225.05 |
| 512.03 | 699.10 | 208.05 | 570.08 | 030.06 | 226.08 |
| 528.08 | 701.16 | 373.07 | 581.17 | 302.05 | 227.01 |
| 549.05 | 704.15 | like | 587.21 | 340.19 | 228.07 |
| 550.07 | 711.10 | 008.21 | 592.03 | 413.08 | 228.20 |
| 556.05 | 730.06 | 011.15 | 594.10 | limping | 230.08 |
| 597.03 | 754.01 | 018.17 | 598.08 | 445.07 | 230.16 |
| 643.03 | life-like | 020.16 | 599.03 | line | 231.09 |
| 644.16 | 758.08 | 021.07 | 611.02 | 066.06 | 231.17 |
| 677.21 | lifeless-looking | 025.19 | 613.01 | 209.09 | 233.13 |
| 713.09 | 367.11 | 029.02 | 614.06 | 582.11 | 236.17 |
| licking | lifetime | 042.11 | 617.13 | 763.20 | 238.04 |
| 135.18 | 181.14 | 054.20 | 622.22 | lineage | 240.03 |
| lid | lift | 057.18 | 629.13 | 444.06 | 240.11 |
| 649.14 | 259.03 | 066.10 | 634.07 | linen | 248.19 |
| 651.03 | 392.20 | 071.04 | 646.09 | 705.12 | 249.22 |
| lids | 458.05 | 073.14 | 647.10 | lines | 250.14 |
| 124.18 | 541.20 | 073.19 | 648.08 | 124.11 | 251.13 |
| 159.05 | 729.13 | 074.09 | 648.09 | 329.18 | 251.15 |
| 273.14 | lifted | 076.10 | 655.17 | ling | 252.11 |
| 370.21 | 064.19 | 083.20 | 656.11 | 602.20 | 253.19 |
| 518.12 | 114.06 | 105.21 | 658.11 | linger | 254.15 |
| 630.09 | 130.13 | 107.15 | 660.21 | 255.03 | 254.18 |
| 654.19 | 157.19 | 108.18 | 663.04 | 469.05 | 255.08 |
| lie | 165.03 | 114.10 | 663.05 | lingered | 255.17 |
| 034.20 | 208.20 | 116.14 | 669.03 | 159.16 | 257.10 |
| 056.08 | 244.05 | 118.06 | 669.20 | 206.13 | 257.15 |
| 101.14 | 281.22 | 124.16 | 669.21 | 417.14 | 259.01 |
| 135.03 | 291.07 | 127.22 | 676.15 | 487.14 | 259.17 |
| 186.22 | 354.11 | 134.18 | 676.16 | 526.20 | 259.22 |
| 194.16 | 421.04 | 145.08 | 677.12 | 541.04 | 261.04 |
| 260.18 | 452.04 | 146.13 | 684.02 | 694.03 | 261.10 |
| 275.11 | 468.07 | 147.11 | 696.22 | 729.03 | 263.06 |
| 276.07 | 519.14 | 163.03 | 701.18 | 764.06 | 265.02 |
| 284.17 | 605.04 | 163.13 | 704.05 | lingering | 265.21 |
| 304.21 | 728.04 | 173.16 | 706.05 | 039.16 | 266.09 |
| 339.19 | lifting | 175.04 | 709.01 | 346.12 | 267.16 |
| 359.02 | 171.09 | 177.01 | 709.16 | 367.05 | 269.02 |
| 433.09 | 377.10 | 177.08 | 719.07 | 472.22 | 270.15 |
| 514.06 | 401.10 | 183.02 | 725.19 | 507.02 | 271.19 |
| 518.08 | lig | 189.20 | 729.11 | linked | 272.10 |
| 525.06 | 324.05 | 189.21 | 733.21 | 322.14 | 273.07 |
| 525.18 | light | 194.14 | 739.04 | linnets | 278.04 |
| 540.02 | 005.22 | 198.13 | 753.01 | 557.17 | 278.17 |
| 542.06 | 019.07 | 211.21 | 755.05 | linton | 282.11 |
| 551.04 | 034.12 | 215.13 | 761.17 | 039.03 | 285.11 |
| 552.04 | 038.15 | 219.02 | 761.18 | 039.06 | 287.07 |
| 554.10 | 044.10 | 219.11 | like's | 052.10 | 288.03 |
| 558.01 | 054.02 | 220.22 | 232.17 | 052.11 | 288.18 |
| 578.13 | 054.20 | 230.06 | liked | 052.12 | 289.19 |
| 586.10 | 060.19 | 235.17 | 088.02 | 056.19 | 292.18 |
| 631.16 | 094.12 | 239.03 | 091.04 | 058.08 | 293.06 |
| 654.14 | 101.05 | 239.06 | 228.05 | 072.10 | 293.21 |
| 750.12 | 101.19 | 251.09 | 247.03 | 072.14 | 294.01 |
| lies | 103.19 | 251.10 | 487.20 | 072.18 | 294.18 |
| 047.12 | 111.22 | 253.09 | 499.02 | 104.08 | 296.12 |
| 135.02 | 124.01 | 257.07 | 556.15 | 107.10 | 297.13 |
| 235.12 | 140.19 | 260.12 | likely | 107.21 | 297.17 |
| 253.09 | 146.04 | 262.13 | 024.15 | 108.14 | 299.08 |
| 376.09 | 191.22 | 273.16 | 089.12 | 109.01 | 301.03 |
| 380.03 | 238.22 | 276.09 | 097.19 | 109.14 | 302.15 |
| 427.02 | 283.22 | 277.02 | 260.21 | 110.03 | 303.18 |
| 630.19 | 304.06 | 292.11 | 341.05 | 110.19 | 305.20 |
| life | 308.13 | 310.12 | 355.10 | 111.05 | 311.14 |
| 023.19 | 312.16 | 311.09 | 370.10 | 112.05 | 328.10 |
| 033.09 | 338.16 | 311.19 | 407.22 | 114.10 | 332.20 |
| 074.04 | 351.04 | 328.12 | 413.02 | 116.22 | 333.03 |
| 077.20 | 379.03 | 332.21 | 577.05 | 119.08 | 335.12 |
| 109.12 | 383.16 | 336.11 | 592.18 | 123.12 | 335.18 |
| 136.11 | 410.12 | 338.02 | 627.16 | 127.03 | 340.14 |
| 137.12 | 463.06 | 362.06 | 666.03 | 127.20 | 343.19 |
| 176.20 | 518.04 | 363.14 | likeness | 128.22 | 344.04 |
| 201.02 | 552.18 | 364.09 | 728.08 | 131.05 | 346.09 |
| 216.13 | 559.13 | 371.21 | 731.08 | 145.14 | 351.03 |
| 258.17 | 595.06 | 375.01 | liker | 148.06 | 352.08 |
| 272.19 | 662.15 | 375.20 | 671.14 | 148.08 | 353.15 |
| 281.15 | 693.01 | 377.11 | likes | 152.04 | 355.06 |
| 283.08 | 694.22 | 377.11 | 293.18 | 154.06 | 363.05 |
| 302.06 | 705.22 | 385.02 | 672.15 | 155.05 | 364.22 |
| 310.04 | 744.05 | 390.20 | likewise | 157.02 | 365.18 |
| 332.22 | 744.20 | 394.13 | 222.07 | 158.17 | 366.20 |
| 334.15 | 751.11 | 398.17 | 248.16 | 158.22 | 367.16 |
| 335.14 | 763.03 | 407.03 | liking | 160.18 | 368.08 |
| 340.12 | lighted | 419.21 | 058.18 | 171.18 | 370.02 |
| 343.11 | 040.13 | 420.21 | 247.05 | 175.12 | 370.15 |
| 356.01 | 069.05 | 424.09 | likker | 179.04 | 372.15 |
| 356.08 | 113.11 | 427.04 | 187.19 | 180.21 | 378.05 |
| 359.21 | 209.04 | 427.05 | lilac | 181.08 | 382.14 |
| 370.06 | 212.15 | 436.01 | 518.20 | 181.12 | 402.08 |
| 371.17 | 534.09 | 437.14 | lilting | 181.21 | 411.11 |
| 376.11 | 611.19 | 453.22 | 493.02 | 182.06 | 412.13 |
| 377.07 | 644.22 | 460.09 | limb | 183.02 | 415.07 |
| 398.20 | 662.11 | 464.01 | 015.11 | 193.18 | 418.02 |
| 399.07 | lightened | 464.12 | 053.19 | 194.05 | 421.16 |
| 405.05 | 454.02 | 479.12 | 244.15 | 194.12 | 422.08 |
| 413.07 | lightening | 491.17 | 309.06 | 194.18 | 422.15 |
| 424.04 | 522.04 | 492.08 | 653.02 | 196.16 | 426.10 |

| | | | | | |
|---|---|---|---|---|---|
| 428.16 | 571.19 | 500.11 | 256.03 | 434.13 | 620.19 |
| 429.19 | 572.12 | 500.17 | 479.14 | 434.20 | 672.01 |
| 429.20 | 572.14 | 502.13 | 637.16 | 435.18 | 677.19 |
| 435.16 | 572.21 | 513.07 | 661.20 | 444.16 | 685.02 |
| 449.07 | 573.16 | 532.01 | listless | 445.10 | 756.02 |
| 450.19 | 574.01 | 548.08 | 330.11 | 447.04 | 762.06 |
| 451.04 | 575.10 | 565.17 | 588.18 | 449.15 | 762.09 |
| 451.13 | 578.15 | 568.12 | listlessness | 450.06 | lived |
| 452.06 | 578.20 | 593.15 | 039.04 | 452.07 | 037.09 |
| 453.14 | 580.03 | 594.20 | lit | 453.19 | 070.04 |
| 454.19 | 582.07 | 596.04 | 751.14 | 460.16 | 222.07 |
| 455.19 | 582.17 | 597.18 | literally | 461.19 | 239.08 |
| 455.21 | 586.01 | 603.02 | 637.20 | 470.18 | 245.08 |
| 456.11 | 586.04 | 631.01 | literary | 471.15 | 308.21 |
| 456.19 | 588.09 | 638.22 | 679.02 | 474.02 | 411.14 |
| 457.15 | 589.08 | 643.10 | litter | 480.05 | 429.05 |
| 458.01 | 590.04 | 649.13 | 410.05 | 480.05 | 434.01 |
| 459.03 | 591.04 | 649.20 | little | 482.15 | 475.07 |
| 460.03 | 591.21 | 654.06 | 001.12 | 486.20 | 499.06 |
| 461.02 | 592.09 | 659.17 | 005.01 | 491.20 | 520.11 |
| 462.03 | 592.22 | 662.15 | 012.15 | 495.09 | 701.16 |
| 464.11 | 593.11 | 664.10 | 013.06 | 502.10 | 754.01 |
| 465.04 | 594.05 | 764.03 | 018.10 | 503.22 | liveliness |
| 466.18 | 598.14 | lintons | 019.10 | 505.11 | 463.02 |
| 468.01 | 599.10 | 073.12 | 030.09 | 505.14 | lively |
| 468.07 | 599.13 | 088.16 | 034.10 | 509.01 | 130.04 |
| 468.12 | 600.13 | 102.20 | 038.11 | 514.14 | 425.06 |
| 471.03 | 601.02 | 111.15 | 045.03 | 516.03 | 556.09 |
| 471.18 | 602.02 | 119.04 | 052.02 | 518.17 | 576.01 |
| 473.01 | 603.10 | 126.10 | 056.13 | 527.04 | 604.07 |
| 474.12 | 603.21 | 146.18 | 056.21 | 529.12 | 604.09 |
| 475.18 | 604.08 | 153.04 | 061.20 | 532.13 | liver-coloured |
| 477.01 | 604.15 | 198.12 | 062.20 | 534.03 | 006.17 |
| 478.19 | 604.18 | 287.16 | 066.19 | 537.18 | liverpool |
| 481.16 | 605.18 | lintons' | 074.17 | 539.17 | 076.08 |
| 483.21 | 606.01 | 379.20 | 076.10 | 545.16 | 078.20 |
| 484.03 | 607.01 | 425.03 | 077.01 | 548.03 | 109.21 |
| 484.20 | 608.04 | lip | 079.19 | 556.19 | lives |
| 484.21 | 608.07 | 009.13 | 081.14 | 563.16 | 072.21 |
| 485.21 | 609.12 | 065.07 | 082.19 | 568.18 | 105.10 |
| 486.15 | 611.07 | 158.05 | 086.02 | 571.22 | 161.01 |
| 486.18 | 611.14 | 308.17 | 088.16 | 572.08 | 176.06 |
| 486.20 | 612.12 | 319.19 | 091.05 | 578.06 | 423.01 |
| 486.21 | 612.17 | 332.06 | 093.02 | 580.02 | 460.16 |
| 487.22 | 614.08 | 358.09 | 094.14 | 585.10 | 478.01 |
| 488.07 | 615.01 | 539.07 | 095.15 | 589.17 | 483.05 |
| 488.21 | 615.14 | 683.06 | 097.19 | 595.06 | 488.22 |
| 489.14 | 616.02 | 695.05 | 104.07 | 598.12 | livid |
| 490.13 | 617.13 | 707.17 | 104.19 | 598.17 | 157.13 |
| 490.21 | 618.02 | 719.02 | 107.12 | 605.01 | 266.07 |
| 495.16 | 618.09 | lips | 109.21 | 612.11 | 360.05 |
| 496.06 | 619.08 | 062.06 | 111.12 | 613.06 | living |
| 496.17 | 619.15 | 107.04 | 113.10 | 614.06 | 007.08 |
| 497.14 | 619.16 | 130.13 | 119.03 | 618.16 | 044.06 |
| 498.14 | 623.17 | 170.05 | 121.04 | 619.17 | 048.01 |
| 499.06 | 629.06 | 234.18 | 126.03 | 629.17 | 071.10 |
| 499.15 | 636.04 | 245.13 | 129.20 | 632.20 | 088.15 |
| 501.13 | 636.21 | 266.14 | 132.14 | 635.03 | 137.17 |
| 502.02 | 641.04 | 285.17 | 133.10 | 636.03 | 140.13 |
| 504.18 | 641.11 | 366.08 | 139.03 | 637.09 | 164.20 |
| 508.02 | 641.15 | 370.21 | 153.19 | 638.16 | 182.19 |
| 510.07 | 641.18 | 374.13 | 155.18 | 641.19 | 189.17 |
| 512.01 | 645.03 | 393.22 | 157.07 | 645.06 | 218.07 |
| 514.12 | 646.14 | 402.12 | 160.19 | 655.04 | 221.14 |
| 515.06 | 646.22 | 404.15 | 164.04 | 656.09 | 231.22 |
| 520.12 | 647.03 | 561.10 | 165.18 | 659.11 | 232.22 |
| 523.20 | 649.06 | 587.02 | 169.09 | 660.19 | 306.03 |
| 524.10 | 650.02 | 631.02 | 177.09 | 663.06 | 314.01 |
| 524.18 | 658.06 | 656.10 | 183.06 | 667.04 | 363.13 |
| 525.21 | 659.14 | 758.11 | 191.12 | 673.04 | 376.22 |
| 526.03 | 660.14 | liquid | 197.15 | 682.03 | 398.18 |
| 526.11 | 662.06 | 319.22 | 199.01 | 700.07 | 407.17 |
| 527.04 | 663.12 | 613.16 | 199.16 | 705.14 | 444.14 |
| 529.01 | 687.01 | lisping | 203.15 | 706.01 | 502.13 |
| 529.11 | 713.14 | 108.16 | 211.22 | 709.09 | 535.08 |
| 532.08 | linton's | listen | 215.22 | 711.04 | 575.09 |
| 533.01 | 073.01 | 165.07 | 222.20 | 725.03 | 578.07 |
| 534.05 | 073.05 | 177.15 | 228.19 | 727.08 | 652.17 |
| 535.12 | 105.11 | 233.18 | 229.15 | 729.04 | 658.09 |
| 536.01 | 105.20 | 264.06 | 234.02 | 730.06 | 686.06 |
| 536.14 | 125.05 | 366.12 | 235.09 | 737.13 | 704.14 |
| 537.03 | 145.04 | 386.19 | 240.19 | 745.20 | 733.15 |
| 537.13 | 179.13 | 412.19 | 244.01 | 747.05 | lo |
| 537.20 | 213.13 | 500.07 | 245.14 | 761.02 | 050.01 |
| 539.15 | 214.02 | 547.02 | 252.06 | 761.06 | 505.19 |
| 539.19 | 220.09 | 563.09 | 252.21 | live | loaded |
| 540.17 | 239.13 | 681.18 | 275.20 | 064.08 | 398.07 |
| 541.08 | 248.11 | 706.19 | 294.08 | 071.16 | loading |
| 543.09 | 256.11 | 724.13 | 294.21 | 075.12 | 151.19 |
| 544.11 | 274.09 | listened | 296.21 | 136.08 | loath |
| 545.12 | 286.06 | 051.05 | 305.07 | 181.07 | 013.01 |
| 547.05 | 289.06 | 053.08 | 309.22 | 196.04 | lobbies |
| 555.08 | 290.12 | 061.01 | 311.22 | 210.14 | 060.06 |
| 556.18 | 292.01 | 095.20 | 329.08 | 280.10 | lobby |
| 558.14 | 295.07 | 169.19 | 331.03 | 357.02 | 005.11 |
| 559.04 | 305.07 | 179.19 | 340.01 | 363.12 | 285.13 |
| 560.02 | 328.05 | 314.09 | 349.07 | 363.14 | locality |
| 561.16 | 332.17 | 353.10 | 362.14 | 365.10 | 046.13 |
| 561.20 | 336.02 | 353.11 | 376.01 | 377.06 | 063.06 |
| 562.10 | 344.19 | 355.06 | 378.12 | 377.07 | 689.02 |
| 563.05 | 346.20 | 552.08 | 385.03 | 454.12 | lock |
| 563.20 | 347.17 | 572.14 | 391.19 | 460.14 | 261.08 |
| 564.05 | 360.10 | 627.19 | 409.19 | 461.03 | 284.10 |
| 565.01 | 371.21 | 693.22 | 412.14 | 488.01 | 315.08 |
| 566.07 | 378.01 | 750.11 | 414.09 | 520.22 | 379.09 |
| 566.13 | 417.13 | 764.08 | 418.20 | 521.18 | 394.07 |
| 568.05 | 424.11 | listener | 422.08 | 524.20 | 449.12 |
| 568.17 | 441.07 | 262.08 | 424.05 | 536.12 | 507.17 |
| 570.04 | 453.03 | listening | 428.12 | 546.16 | 525.10 |
| 570.08 | 471.12 | 079.10 | 430.14 | 546.17 | 526.10 |
| | 487.07 | 188.18 | 434.05 | 579.02 | 527.14 |

| | | | | | |
|---|---|---|---|---|---|
| 545.06 | 144.05 | longest | 020.19 | 743.12 | lot |
| 555.17 | 146.04 | 544.09 | 038.06 | 748.21 | 189.11 |
| 616.20 | 149.16 | 546.16 | 058.20 | 760.18 | 477.09 |
| 624.01 | 170.17 | longing | 073.15 | looks | lots |
| 660.09 | 177.16 | 303.08 | 078.04 | 008.16 | 415.11 |
| locked | 181.07 | 491.01 | 094.09 | 008.19 | lottery |
| 130.22 | 192.19 | 564.08 | 115.05 | 107.14 | 166.03 |
| 257.18 | 198.12 | 591.21 | 117.17 | 122.11 | loud |
| 292.22 | 205.22 | look | 138.01 | 140.11 | 050.18 |
| 322.08 | 209.09 | 024.20 | 146.14 | 174.03 | 095.01 |
| 361.22 | 211.08 | 025.16 | 159.22 | 416.17 | 186.05 |
| 410.01 | 216.02 | 025.17 | 166.01 | 464.04 | 566.02 |
| 431.09 | 216.20 | 029.16 | 170.04 | 485.14 | 638.12 |
| 522.13 | 220.01 | 033.07 | 206.08 | 487.07 | 641.07 |
| 566.15 | 223.10 | 035.21 | 209.18 | 490.13 | 748.10 |
| 607.19 | 243.16 | 061.20 | 212.05 | 519.03 | louder |
| 756.20 | 254.04 | 077.07 | 214.03 | 634.09 | 167.10 |
| locket | 262.22 | 091.19 | 236.13 | 735.01 | 531.10 |
| 379.06 | 280.03 | 103.22 | 266.09 | 758.19 | lounged |
| locking | 280.10 | 108.08 | 286.20 | looped | 151.22 |
| 308.21 | 284.02 | 109.06 | 316.09 | 110.14 | lounging |
| 350.16 | 296.13 | 112.09 | 330.21 | looping | 442.06 |
| 390.18 | 298.12 | 114.09 | 338.01 | 277.09 | love |
| locks | 302.17 | 116.20 | 372.18 | loose | 007.21 |
| 127.17 | 303.15 | 123.12 | 374.10 | 019.13 | 008.15 |
| 271.15 | 304.02 | 126.05 | 394.13 | 085.10 | 024.18 |
| 276.17 | 304.10 | 150.03 | 397.19 | 106.10 | 092.09 |
| 330.12 | 305.21 | 152.22 | 407.03 | 250.03 | 136.11 |
| 358.11 | 316.03 | 154.19 | 408.09 | 351.03 | 136.12 |
| 512.17 | 334.19 | 171.11 | 436.18 | 479.17 | 149.12 |
| 695.02 | 346.17 | 177.08 | 452.02 | 506.20 | 156.05 |
| 723.20 | 351.06 | 187.19 | 491.18 | 517.20 | 157.01 |
| lockwood | 354.05 | 187.21 | 496.14 | 649.19 | 164.11 |
| 002.08 | 357.14 | 191.01 | 510.07 | 651.21 | 172.21 |
| 012.15 | 364.20 | 192.04 | 532.21 | loosed | 173.06 |
| 055.09 | 373.18 | 195.05 | 538.19 | 355.20 | 173.19 |
| 059.08 | 376.22 | 207.15 | 541.06 | loosen | 174.01 |
| 098.08 | 393.10 | 235.09 | 548.22 | 237.18 | 174.03 |
| 134.05 | 398.13 | 238.09 | 551.15 | 726.03 | 174.12 |
| 137.22 | 413.14 | 257.20 | 558.11 | loosened | 174.15 |
| 203.16 | 417.02 | 263.12 | 560.16 | 527.14 | 175.22 |
| 346.15 | 426.21 | 276.03 | 564.02 | 609.09 | 179.09 |
| 415.14 | 427.15 | 284.05 | 565.02 | lord | 180.16 |
| 639.19 | 436.20 | 294.18 | 566.07 | 003.18 | 180.21 |
| 684.13 | 450.03 | 303.16 | 577.15 | 030.02 | 183.02 |
| 691.04 | 455.08 | 309.06 | 586.17 | 189.10 | 183.04 |
| 697.07 | 461.10 | 315.13 | 591.04 | 318.09 | 211.06 |
| 714.01 | 469.09 | 320.22 | 599.02 | 324.01 | 220.10 |
| 735.05 | 480.15 | 334.17 | 602.21 | 324.01 | 229.05 |
| 744.06 | 499.06 | 342.13 | 609.04 | 392.11 | 229.06 |
| 762.13 | 502.09 | 353.12 | 610.21 | 401.12 | 230.08 |
| lockwood's | 518.22 | 356.04 | 612.10 | 417.05 | 236.22 |
| 003.09 | 531.08 | 356.16 | 616.22 | 470.01 | 249.20 |
| lodge | 533.06 | 360.06 | 628.20 | 696.17 | 271.09 |
| 037.06 | 535.19 | 363.21 | 635.11 | lore | 288.01 |
| 067.02 | 538.12 | 367.12 | 635.20 | 518.10 | 310.04 |
| 216.21 | 544.05 | 394.02 | 653.16 | lose | 316.02 |
| 222.11 | 546.17 | 404.01 | 660.21 | 317.03 | 331.21 |
| 322.01 | 551.05 | 418.11 | 662.15 | 357.15 | 336.04 |
| 523.02 | 552.02 | 425.21 | 663.05 | 440.05 | 336.12 |
| 691.05 | 557.20 | 428.11 | 674.13 | 490.01 | 337.09 |
| lodged | 575.07 | 471.04 | 684.07 | 579.06 | 339.04 |
| 270.04 | 578.10 | 483.09 | 689.19 | 661.11 | 340.11 |
| 627.01 | 580.13 | 491.02 | 693.22 | loses | 360.18 |
| 627.22 | 587.03 | 492.21 | 698.11 | 180.21 | 364.03 |
| lodging | 603.16 | 493.07 | 702.03 | losing | 371.18 |
| 697.21 | 604.06 | 498.05 | 705.20 | 067.05 | 371.21 |
| lodgings | 627.02 | 500.14 | 718.15 | 100.22 | 388.08 |
| 036.09 | 632.03 | 505.15 | 718.17 | 227.12 | 398.11 |
| loike | 647.12 | 509.09 | 728.19 | 335.21 | 413.18 |
| 187.22 | 654.05 | 510.10 | 738.05 | 504.16 | 425.12 |
| 232.12 | 659.10 | 518.15 | 740.15 | 598.19 | 429.04 |
| 318.14 | 663.02 | 545.13 | 747.17 | 732.17 | 446.11 |
| 320.13 | 697.12 | 551.17 | looker-on | loss | 460.21 |
| 320.14 | 698.15 | 568.19 | 136.08 | 094.19 | 460.22 |
| 401.11 | 700.16 | 575.11 | looking | 141.17 | 461.09 |
| london | 726.20 | 586.21 | 003.20 | 214.10 | 461.10 |
| 030.23 | 734.07 | 590.14 | 007.12 | 334.11 | 461.12 |
| 411.09 | 734.15 | 600.05 | 028.11 | 398.22 | 484.15 |
| 440.14 | 758.06 | 605.17 | 030.08 | 546.05 | 490.08 |
| 672.14 | longed | 614.11 | 052.15 | 578.17 | 508.05 |
| 684.20 | 088.03 | 616.13 | 079.10 | 643.05 | 510.08 |
| 697.16 | 373.11 | 621.01 | 122.18 | 684.15 | 519.15 |
| lonelier | longer | 621.02 | 184.17 | 753.03 | 521.16 |
| 689.20 | 023.01 | 621.05 | 187.18 | losses | 521.20 |
| loneliness | 027.04 | 645.20 | 214.13 | 619.09 | 524.11 |
| 701.01 | 035.02 | 649.05 | 244.16 | lost | 524.19 |
| lonely | 058.10 | 655.14 | 265.21 | 022.04 | 525.12 |
| 382.02 | 094.04 | 656.18 | 329.21 | 052.13 | 527.07 |
| 518.22 | 127.18 | 659.03 | 337.07 | 079.17 | 535.07 |
| 578.05 | 185.10 | 668.01 | 345.20 | 083.04 | 535.08 |
| 648.08 | 190.13 | 672.15 | 351.15 | 098.12 | 536.05 |
| 689.20 | 200.04 | 676.02 | 361.16 | 126.05 | 536.08 |
| long | 217.11 | 683.22 | 436.03 | 149.08 | 563.07 |
| 008.14 | 255.03 | 702.04 | 442.03 | 166.05 | 571.09 |
| 009.15 | 351.15 | 707.13 | 450.14 | 221.17 | 571.10 |
| 029.17 | 386.22 | 709.16 | 451.05 | 253.09 | 575.10 |
| 031.03 | 407.06 | 711.02 | 484.04 | 311.08 | 576.05 |
| 065.11 | 472.22 | 717.15 | 492.11 | 329.02 | 576.06 |
| 074.18 | 475.12 | 718.05 | 526.12 | 400.15 | 582.17 |
| 076.12 | 516.07 | 720.12 | 532.14 | 416.19 | 615.14 |
| 076.22 | 543.03 | 731.14 | 533.10 | 442.10 | 616.07 |
| 090.02 | 568.09 | 738.06 | 591.09 | 451.16 | 617.14 |
| 114.03 | 574.05 | 741.22 | 600.18 | 494.12 | 619.06 |
| 120.21 | 580.02 | 752.20 | 603.19 | 618.14 | 647.04 |
| 127.19 | 598.10 | 755.15 | 614.19 | 627.12 | 648.03 |
| 130.18 | 613.07 | 757.11 | 668.18 | 696.15 | 648.04 |
| 133.17 | 665.06 | 763.02 | 669.14 | 704.22 | 666.22 |
| 135.01 | 671.06 | looked | 670.04 | 730.02 | 678.14 |
| 135.04 | 705.22 | 008.18 | 711.16 | 732.01 | 680.17 |
| 141.02 | 708.08 | 017.12 | 738.16 | | 724.15 |

| | | | | |
|---|---|---|---|---|
| 732.04 | lumber | 178.17 | 485.15 | malt |
| loved | 043.08 | 179.12 | 521.10 | 321.08 |
| 007.22 | lumber-hole | 184.06 | 545.17 | mama |
| 131.19 | 321.07 | 189.18 | 560.14 | 464.22 |
| 131.20 | lumps | 196.11 | 563.10 | 544.02 |
| 225.11 | 319.09 | 199.03 | 570.19 | mamma |
| 228.18 | lunatic | 206.20 | 573.07 | 009.03 |
| 229.05 | 396.13 | 217.07 | 583.15 | 105.22 |
| 313.12 | lungs | 219.16 | 590.01 | 105.22 |
| 336.03 | 515.11 | 222.21 | 595.01 | 106.01 |
| 336.11 | lurk | 224.08 | 606.17 | 124.05 |
| 357.14 | 124.15 | 227.07 | 609.14 | 129.08 |
| 357.15 | 206.10 | 234.10 | 619.09 | 460.13 |
| 360.17 | lurked | 237.01 | 629.19 | 461.02 |
| 363.03 | 214.05 | 254.15 | 629.20 | 461.07 |
| 388.10 | lurking | 255.13 | 647.01 | man |
| 397.09 | 006.15 | 261.08 | 647.05 | 003.03 |
| 407.19 | 187.02 | 2o7.02 | 647.06 | 003.16 |
| 408.17 | 194.01 | 275.04 | 647.13 | 011.04 |
| 490.07 | lurks | 275.21 | 648.05 | 016.19 |
| 537.17 | 348.07 | 292.03 | 667.08 | 018.03 |
| 548.14 | lustre | 322.18 | 674.02 | 020.17 |
| 601.09 | 486.07 | 341.19 | 680.11 | 024.15 |
| 621.04 | lusty | 350.07 | 697.21 | 026.15 |
| 630.12 | 011.10 | 350.15 | 700.07 | 033.01 |
| lovely | luxuriant | 358.03 | 707.04 | 043.21 |
| 365.02 | 442.14 | 361.21 | 708.01 | 044.16 |
| 467.03 | luxury | 381.02 | 711.04 | 049.18 |
| lover | 062.07 | 392.20 | 716.15 | 059.17 |
| 526.04 | 646.22 | 408.21 | 723.17 | 076.08 |
| 671.14 | lying | 426.04 | 724.15 | 088.11 |
| lovers | 051.09 | 432.05 | 725.18 | 088.18 |
| 160.16 | 093.08 | 436.11 | 737.05 | 092.08 |
| loves | 156.12 | 439.18 | 740.06 | 093.17 |
| 173.14 | 279.02 | 479.03 | 752.05 | 107.06 |
| 173.21 | 341.17 | 495.02 | 753.19 | 136.14 |
| 174.14 | 354.22 | 524.22 | 757.10 | 140.13 |
| 176.01 | 433.19 | 537.08 | maker | 144.02 |
| 648.02 | 557.06 | 541.06 | 168.15 | 157.16 |
| 648.09 | 563.05 | 543.16 | 372.17 | 163.18 |
| loving | 578.10 | 556.10 | makes | 167.18 |
| 175.02 | 704.01 | 562.11 | 164.11 | 169.04 |
| 273.18 | ma'am | 571.09 | 229.19 | 179.06 |
| 326.19 | 210.04 | 589.06 | 264.21 | 184.16 |
| 388.11 | 271.10 | 592.16 | 534.03 | 187.21 |
| 511.16 | 272.20 | 605.01 | 679.13 | 198.17 |
| 511.17 | 279.08 | 606.20 | 728.10 | 202.04 |
| 511.19 | 331.21 | 609.19 | making | 207.04 |
| 511.20 | 341.10 | 611.21 | 010.12 | 213.19 |
| 511.22 | 354.07 | 633.22 | 101.05 | 222.16 |
| 512.05 | 670.02 | 638.08 | 107.14 | 225.14 |
| 713.20 | mad | 639.01 | 115.03 | 230.02 |
| 713.21 | 058.01 | 644.10 | 118.14 | 232.02 |
| low | 078.14 | 648.13 | 174.07 | 251.14 |
| 069.07 | 106.16 | 650.02 | 209.03 | 259.20 |
| 093.21 | 140.17 | 663.14 | 248.02 | 292.03 |
| 154.15 | 195.20 | 665.11 | 249.20 | 298.15 |
| 179.07 | 240.04 | 679.02 | 277.01 | 307.10 |
| 255.03 | 280.21 | 683.12 | 277.14 | 311.06 |
| 321.19 | 307.10 | 685.18 | 307.12 | 315.17 |
| 380.01 | 341.06 | 686.11 | 322.04 | 317.01 |
| 383.14 | 357.21 | 692.16 | 339.09 | 321.11 |
| 390.08 | 362.06 | 705.04 | 409.02 | 326.07 |
| 519.08 | 365.22 | 705.06 | 420.04 | 350.14 |
| 530.06 | 377.04 | 708.05 | 433.05 | 364.11 |
| 548.05 | 390.04 | 708.12 | 442.22 | 377.11 |
| 751.01 | 401.01 | 720.16 | 445.04 | 391.21 |
| low-browed | 564.19 | 741.05 | 494.10 | 392.10 |
| 465.18 | 566.17 | 756.07 | 524.11 | 394.17 |
| low-spirited | 609.14 | 758.13 | 530.07 | 402.17 |
| 517.04 | 614.03 | 763.16 | 570.02 | 407.01 |
| lower | 644.09 | madling | 579.01 | 407.11 |
| 061.05 | 717.09 | 324.15 | 588.01 | 415.03 |
| 212.14 | madam | madman | 617.11 | 417.08 |
| 297.12 | 010.14 | 341.05 | 674.12 | 433.04 |
| 494.01 | 018.11 | madman's | 716.21 | 471.06 |
| 522.09 | maddening | 162.07 | 730.18 | 482.01 |
| 603.10 | 052.21 | madness | makking | 482.11 |
| 667.01 | 282.22 | 229.11 | 233.05 | 491.10 |
| 761.13 | 730.14 | 274.11 | 472.07 | 501.05 |
| lowering | madder | 317.11 | maks | 524.03 |
| 207.18 | 250.19 | 322.13 | 326.12 | 531.09 |
| lowest | made | magically | 457.21 | 537.05 |
| 432.20 | 005.03 | 011.14 | mal-appropriated | 553.04 |
| 695.17 | 011.09 | magisterial | 692.02 | 577.03 |
| loyal | 015.10 | 340.18 | malady | 614.02 |
| 415.08 | 019.21 | magistrate | 143.01 | 618.22 |
| luck | 042.14 | 108.05 | 292.01 | 619.01 |
| 126.20 | 046.08 | 402.08 | male | 620.15 |
| 326.02 | 052.16 | 413.05 | 225.15 | 637.01 |
| luckily | 060.22 | magnanimity | 694.13 | 645.07 |
| 642.08 | 063.01 | 602.13 | malefactors | 679.19 |
| luckless | 080.07 | 729.21 | 401.20 | 694.14 |
| 112.04 | 081.10 | magpie | malevolence | 696.22 |
| 368.13 | 082.19 | 678.13 | 233.19 | 708.01 |
| 415.06 | 088.15 | maid | 402.13 | 712.03 |
| lucky | 089.02 | 110.20 | 442.21 | 719.21 |
| 166.03 | 090.19 | 118.13 | 481.14 | 721.04 |
| 546.06 | 092.13 | 312.21 | malice | 723.04 |
| 695.03 | 093.07 | 338.04 | 620.16 | 723.07 |
| lug | 097.08 | 384.16 | 680.18 | 728.20 |
| 719.13 | 098.02 | 455.01 | malignant | 745.21 |
| lught | 106.03 | 509.02 | 034.20 | 753.08 |
| 233.03 | 109.20 | maid-servant | 564.11 | 760.17 |
| lugs | 111.02 | 314.19 | 695.20 | 761.06 |
| 043.01 | 112.04 | maiden | malignantly | man's |
| 696.07 | 130.04 | 072.10 | 308.17 | 033.09 |
| lull | 132.02 | maids | malignity | 050.15 |
| 070.03 | 159.02 | 297.04 | 030.09 | 138.05 |
| 169.08 | 166.09 | 382.11 | 245.17 | man-servant |
| 225.02 | 177.22 | 428.14 | 389.15 | 103.04 |

main
399.15
maintained
052.21
420.17
655.16
maintaining
069.07
maintains
386.20
maintenance
430.01
maister
034.06
034.06
042.20
043.15
043.16
187.10
193.15
232.13
320.14
322.03
324.12
391.19
455.19
466.21
471.14
586.12
691.07
712.16
719.19
maister's
320.13
323.17
699.11
maisters
016.06
318.13
mak
016.11
022.15
make
017.18
023.10
024.15
029.19
032.02
037.04
041.21
045.04
046.05
064.14
066.21
067.04
074.04
075.18
078.17
089.16
092.06
094.14
120.16
120.18
122.07
123.21
127.21
129.12
144.18
145.15
145.21
155.04
163.07
171.07
176.08
183.16
185.21
195.01
203.13
210.22
223.17
234.14
238.01
252.08
257.21
260.08
267.21
290.08
290.09
300.01
315.22
318.03
323.06
331.15
335.17
341.15
384.12
386.14
388.03
396.11
398.04
405.19
409.03
422.04
439.03
452.18
453.18
461.15
463.19
466.15
470.04
478.21

manage
263.20
285.20
375.04
523.06
568.11
593.04
698.09
managed
067.04
121.13
150.22
367.18
616.13
660.16
689.16
management
444.20
mane
127.22
manes
457.20
manger
228.17
236.19
manhood
577.05
mania
422.17
maniac's
290.10
manifestations
007.20
088.10
manifested
002.22
293.21
478.06
manly
404.11
manner
011.19
018.01
048.09
088.09
154.15
167.05
206.19
214.07
238.16
271.13
297.11
309.09
326.19
336.16
358.19
422.19
463.17
437.10
502.07
511.01
557.05
588.17
666.19
732.16
738.13
754.13
755.18
manners
007.10
079.21
102.07
113.04
137.07
185.13
225.09
235.20
manoeuvres
331.12
mantle
453.04
553.12
manual
682.02
manuscript
045.18
many
007.11
023.18
037.10
065.22
070.21
100.14
100.20
140.01
148.13
171.06
172.18
205.03
323.12
347.15
349.02
352.11
357.02
357.16
367.17
417.08
440.19
449.19
475.16
480.10

499.05
508.17
535.10
535.12
623.09
630.14
752.13
763.17
many-week's
304.07
march
110.12
259.04
302.14
478.14
704.19
marched
121.14
marching
016.21
marcy
319.12
mare
169.04
mark
090.13
124.11
249.15
380.06
marked
153.05
154.09
558.22
marking
596.02
marks
137.06
150.15
214.03
487.12
marred
159.19
324.02
662.03
marriage
216.01
305.12
married
024.18
026.14
070.08
073.05
181.19
202.15
307.14
311.16
329.06
337.03
342.04
484.16
556.03
613.15
613.19
762.04
marry
171.18
175.12
175.14
175.17
179.04
179.08
179.20
181.20
251.10
253.04
577.07
613.17
614.02
617.13
618.08
618.13
620.13
672.05
marrying
183.19
230.09
251.14
501.22
marsh
163.10
439.02
626.11
627.12
627.21
marshes
022.04
209.12
410.11
martyrs
049.14
marvel
146.07
marvelled
146.09
marvelling
403.10
marvellous
211.19
339.03
marvellously
514.08

562.01
752.15
mary
108.07
297.12
mass
507.22
masses
311.08
427.12
master
010.04
011.16
033.06
035.16
037.04
042.03
070.09
073.19
076.02
077.11
078.15
079.16
081.21
083.06
084.21
088.05
089.02
089.18
093.10
094.06
100.01
102.14
112.07
118.08
127.01
127.20
128.22
129.17
130.22
140.18
141.07
145.17
147.21
155.11
189.21
190.19
192.10
196.12
199.14
205.07
210.19
212.12
213.08
213.20
224.09
234.04
241.05
246.10
254.03
255.13
257.12
258.12
259.18
260.21
264.05
267.06
270.07
272.20
286.16
287.21
292.16
293.18
295.14
297.09
297.09
299.17
304.06
328.03
331.19
333.14
334.02
340.11
344.10
345.03
350.08
364.17
366.10
366.18
372.18
378.13
382.01
403.01
410.04
411.07
412.17
416.02
417.17
418.04
422.01
422.12
430.03
434.06
438.10
443.11
445.01
453.06
454.03
455.04
455.09

458.03
465.04
470.08
472.10
475.07
476.17
484.17
492.03
498.18
500.13
502.14
504.02
507.15
511.08
514.04
514.11
515.10
520.09
520.22
526.16
528.04
531.07
533.21
535.02
536.20
538.03
538.21
543.01
547.14
548.17
550.07
562.06
570.01
577.10
579.12
582.12
583.02
583.15
586.04
586.19
590.22
595.03
597.10
598.22
603.13
612.12
620.07
626.12
627.03
627.06
627.19
630.10
631.12
632.11
635.16
636.12
637.18
644.12
646.14
658.06
659.19
660.06
661.01
662.06
663.12
665.07
666.14
671.18
691.04
697.22
701.06
702.08
716.10
717.18
718.14
721.07
722.10
727.11
738.16
744.19
747.02
748.07
753.16
759.02
759.17
master's
072.09
144.15
160.20
214.09
225.01
240.14
317.10
401.01
438.07
440.06
448.03
451.01
462.11
466.08
471.07
573.11
640.18
644.13
725.21
757.06
masters
034.20
285.20
mat
455.16

match
306.18
386.09
matches
028.14
mate
026.12
231.16
646.10
material
323.05
353.14
730.09
materials
677.16
mathew
232.16
matronly
014.08
matter
011.18
078.15
081.14
097.17
121.20
134.22
172.13
234.14
240.04
262.07
266.11
278.15
288.05
297.12
397.01
439.04
453.07
460.06
479.10
496.21
497.12
510.08
522.17
572.20
633.10
662.07
739.16
741.19
747.09
754.07
761.06
matters
095.11
112.05
295.18
418.13
689.11
752.07
mattocks
729.10
mattress
276.06
mature
234.12
maturity
728.03
maw
188.01
319.09
mawkish
239.09
maxillary
055.15
may
004.09
008.03
025.03
025.10
030.02
030.21
032.22
044.16
049.16
050.02
059.08
076.10
085.04
109.11
116.09
116.13
136.15
152.07
170.22
175.05
175.06
203.15
205.18
209.11
216.20
220.03
220.22
240.03
245.19
258.09
261.22
282.14
284.10
284.18
287.18
288.07
289.14
292.19

306.18
316.03
324.21
328.11
333.02
334.04
334.17
337.10
341.08
342.02
342.06
342.18
345.12
363.01
374.17
376.12
376.13
376.21
384.01
392.06
394.05
401.12
405.16
412.10
419.04
432.22
438.22
450.05
457.14
460.18
463.21
469.02
472.17
484.15
488.13
489.05
504.20
505.03
511.04
521.18
523.06
528.21
541.21
544.04
544.05
571.03
576.05
579.07
580.18
592.08
619.10
620.13
628.14
630.04
630.06
652.12
653.06
656.05
672.15
677.19
686.01
720.06
722.14
731.10
734.13
754.05
754.16
me
002.17
003.02
003.07
003.20
007.17
008.06
008.06
008.15
008.18
010.05
011.19
012.06
013.09
015.04
015.10
016.15
016.21
017.12
017.12
017.19
018.01
019.22
020.12
020.20
021.15
021.20
022.10
022.17
023.04
024.22
025.11
027.04
027.11
027.21
029.05
029.09
029.15
030.18
031.05
031.10
031.14
031.16
032.11

| | | | | | |
|---|---|---|---|---|---|
| 033.02 | 120.07 | 220.20 | 296.08 | 360.21 | 421.13 |
| 034.11 | 120.18 | 221.10 | 297.01 | 361.07 | 421.17 |
| 034.18 | 121.02 | 223.02 | 299.18 | 361.10 | 425.08 |
| 034.21 | 122.05 | 223.08 | 299.21 | 361.13 | 428.11 |
| 035.01 | 122.07 | 223.14 | 300.02 | 362.06 | 428.13 |
| 035.01 | 124.01 | 227.13 | 302.21 | 362.13 | 430.14 |
| 035.15 | 125.06 | 227.17 | 303.13 | 362.18 | 431.13 |
| 035.21 | 125.13 | 228.05 | 303.15 | 362.19 | 432.18 |
| 036.05 | 126.02 | 228.08 | 304.06 | 363.01 | 433.01 |
| 036.11 | 129.17 | 229.06 | 306.11 | 363.03 | 433.07 |
| 036.12 | 134.03 | 229.10 | 306.18 | 363.04 | 433.17 |
| 036.15 | 135.12 | 230.21 | 307.07 | 363.05 | 435.09 |
| 037.05 | 137.03 | 231.10 | 307.14 | 363.11 | 435.16 |
| 040.16 | 137.20 | 232.08 | 307.16 | 363.16 | 435.21 |
| 042.05 | 139.08 | 233.20 | 309.19 | 363.18 | 436.01 |
| 044.10 | 142.17 | 236.06 | 310.08 | 363.20 | 437.16 |
| 045.04 | 145.11 | 236.08 | 310.14 | 364.01 | 438.11 |
| 046.08 | 148.20 | 236.10 | 310.17 | 364.01 | 439.01 |
| 046.17 | 152.11 | 236.22 | 311.15 | 364.03 | 439.08 |
| 046.19 | 152.19 | 238.13 | 311.17 | 366.07 | 439.08 |
| 047.04 | 153.05 | 241.04 | 311.21 | 367.14 | 439.17 |
| 048.20 | 153.16 | 243.12 | 312.01 | 367.16 | 448.04 |
| 049.03 | 153.18 | 244.09 | 312.05 | 368.02 | 449.04 |
| 049.12 | 154.19 | 244.16 | 312.13 | 371.10 | 451.05 |
| 050.08 | 155.04 | 245.09 | 314.15 | 371.14 | 451.06 |
| 050.13 | 155.06 | 245.20 | 314.20 | 372.13 | 452.13 |
| 050.20 | 155.12 | 246.07 | 314.20 | 372.21 | 454.04 |
| 051.14 | 155.14 | 246.18 | 315.07 | 374.05 | 454.10 |
| 051.18 | 156.03 | 247.07 | 315.22 | 374.12 | 454.19 |
| 052.04 | 156.07 | 247.08 | 316.01 | 375.01 | 455.02 |
| 052.07 | 156.10 | 248.06 | 316.06 | 376.03 | 455.20 |
| 052.07 | 156.21 | 250.05 | 317.01 | 377.01 | 456.03 |
| 052.16 | 157.07 | 250.22 | 317.09 | 377.03 | 456.11 |
| 052.20 | 157.08 | 251.06 | 318.06 | 377.04 | 456.17 |
| 052.22 | 158.18 | 251.09 | 318.18 | 377.05 | 459.03 |
| 053.01 | 158.21 | 251.22 | 318.22 | 377.18 | 460.13 |
| 053.02 | 159.02 | 252.07 | 320.02 | 377.20 | 461.07 |
| 056.14 | 162.03 | 252.19 | 320.07 | 377.21 | 462.07 |
| 056.21 | 163.02 | 252.20 | 320.16 | 378.07 | 464.22 |
| 057.18 | 164.03 | 252.21 | 320.20 | 382.16 | 465.01 |
| 057.21 | 164.06 | 253.03 | 322.17 | 383.06 | 466.12 |
| 059.11 | 164.12 | 253.04 | 325.04 | 384.14 | 467.14 |
| 059.12 | 164.17 | 253.18 | 325.12 | 385.01 | 468.09 |
| 060.15 | 164.18 | 254.18 | 326.07 | 385.10 | 468.14 |
| 060.22 | 164.19 | 255.01 | 326.17 | 385.11 | 468.17 |
| 061.07 | 166.21 | 255.01 | 327.09 | 385.17 | 470.04 |
| 061.10 | 167.08 | 255.06 | 327.10 | 385.18 | 470.07 |
| 062.21 | 170.12 | 257.13 | 327.18 | 386.01 | 472.09 |
| 063.20 | 170.15 | 257.17 | 328.04 | 386.08 | 473.07 |
| 064.10 | 171.08 | 258.10 | 328.09 | 387.11 | 477.11 |
| 064.14 | 171.09 | 259.11 | 329.06 | 387.12 | 477.14 |
| 065.16 | 171.16 | 260.07 | 329.14 | 387.15 | 478.16 |
| 065.18 | 171.18 | 260.15 | 329.21 | 387.17 | 479.11 |
| 066.15 | 171.21 | 261.11 | 330.18 | 388.03 | 480.14 |
| 067.14 | 173.14 | 261.17 | 330.19 | 388.04 | 481.09 |
| 067.15 | 174.08 | 262.01 | 331.04 | 388.12 | 481.12 |
| 067.19 | 175.15 | 262.16 | 331.07 | 389.03 | 481.17 |
| 070.02 | 176.11 | 263.08 | 331.09 | 389.12 | 482.12 |
| 070.03 | 176.13 | 263.13 | 331.19 | 391.08 | 483.11 |
| 070.09 | 176.21 | 265.01 | 332.09 | 392.21 | 484.09 |
| 070.13 | 177.01 | 265.03 | 332.12 | 394.02 | 485.05 |
| 072.16 | 177.22 | 265.06 | 333.05 | 394.06 | 485.09 |
| 074.14 | 178.16 | 265.13 | 333.21 | 395.09 | 485.12 |
| 075.02 | 178.22 | 266.01 | 334.10 | 396.08 | 488.08 |
| 075.04 | 179.08 | 266.20 | 334.12 | 396.09 | 488.10 |
| 075.11 | 180.10 | 267.06 | 334.22 | 396.14 | 488.12 |
| 075.20 | 180.11 | 267.07 | 334.22 | 396.21 | 488.22 |
| 076.05 | 180.12 | 267.08 | 335.10 | 397.08 | 489.09 |
| 076.17 | 181.14 | 270.11 | 335.13 | 397.10 | 489.17 |
| 076.19 | 181.18 | 271.05 | 335.15 | 397.12 | 489.18 |
| 079.07 | 183.17 | 271.09 | 335.17 | 397.15 | 490.02 |
| 082.07 | 183.20 | 271.09 | 336.11 | 397.17 | 493.06 |
| 082.10 | 186.15 | 272.10 | 337.14 | 398.04 | 493.21 |
| 082.16 | 193.03 | 273.16 | 337.20 | 398.09 | 494.15 |
| 082.17 | 194.06 | 273.18 | 338.13 | 398.10 | 494.18 |
| 082.22 | 194.11 | 274.19 | 338.20 | 398.19 | 496.15 |
| 083.01 | 194.18 | 275.10 | 338.22 | 399.04 | 499.05 |
| 083.19 | 194.22 | 276.03 | 339.09 | 400.03 | 499.19 |
| 084.01 | 195.19 | 278.19 | 339.12 | 400.04 | 500.09 |
| 084.14 | 196.04 | 279.06 | 339.14 | 401.03 | 500.14 |
| 085.22 | 197.08 | 279.07 | 339.20 | 402.02 | 501.04 |
| 089.02 | 197.12 | 279.14 | 339.21 | 402.04 | 504.09 |
| 091.06 | 199.07 | 279.15 | 342.04 | 402.05 | 504.11 |
| 091.20 | 199.08 | 280.16 | 342.07 | 402.13 | 505.15 |
| 095.04 | 199.09 | 280.18 | 342.14 | 403.19 | 507.19 |
| 095.09 | 201.10 | 280.21 | 343.15 | 404.02 | 508.10 |
| 095.15 | 201.11 | 281.01 | 344.05 | 405.11 | 508.16 |
| 097.08 | 202.16 | 281.19 | 344.08 | 406.05 | 510.19 |
| 098.14 | 203.03 | 282.16 | 344.12 | 406.18 | 513.21 |
| 102.02 | 204.20 | 282.18 | 345.10 | 407.03 | 517.07 |
| 102.07 | 205.03 | 283.08 | 345.15 | 407.09 | 520.02 |
| 102.12 | 206.16 | 284.18 | 346.17 | 408.08 | 520.20 |
| 105.05 | 207.14 | 284.20 | 348.04 | 409.03 | 523.13 |
| 105.17 | 208.04 | 284.20 | 348.06 | 409.13 | 524.03 |
| 106.11 | 208.14 | 285.04 | 350.15 | 409.14 | 524.14 |
| 107.14 | 210.02 | 285.20 | 352.02 | 410.18 | 525.21 |
| 108.02 | 211.18 | 286.07 | 354.16 | 411.01 | 526.12 |
| 108.13 | 211.19 | 286.18 | 355.16 | 411.13 | 528.07 |
| 108.21 | 212.22 | 287.13 | 356.05 | 412.04 | 528.09 |
| 109.15 | 214.16 | 287.19 | 356.20 | 412.06 | 528.12 |
| 110.07 | 215.21 | 288.08 | 356.22 | 416.04 | 529.06 |
| 110.09 | 216.01 | 288.11 | 357.11 | 417.02 | 531.15 |
| 110.10 | 216.09 | 288.19 | 357.17 | 417.08 | 532.10 |
| 110.12 | 216.11 | 288.20 | 357.21 | 417.12 | 532.11 |
| 114.16 | 216.11 | 289.13 | 358.19 | 417.20 | 533.03 |
| 115.03 | 216.14 | 289.16 | 359.02 | 418.14 | 533.06 |
| 115.05 | 217.14 | 290.08 | 359.20 | 418.15 | 533.10 |
| 117.02 | 218.04 | 291.13 | 359.21 | 418.17 | 533.20 |
| 118.03 | 218.05 | 292.02 | 360.13 | 419.18 | 534.06 |
| 119.22 | 218.08 | 294.19 | 360.16 | 420.14 | 534.14 |
| 120.05 | 219.14 | 295.04 | 360.19 | | 534.20 |

| | | | | | |
|---|---|---|---|---|---|
| 534.20 | 598.20 | 660.07 | 741.06 | 367.08 | meeting |
| 535.01 | 599.09 | 660.11 | 742.02 | 387.05 | 115.07 |
| 535.04 | 599.11 | 660.14 | 742.08 | 406.10 | 148.05 |
| 535.15 | 599.19 | 661.14 | 742.09 | 441.19 | 216.09 |
| 535.17 | 600.05 | 662.06 | 742.13 | 471.09 | 294.16 |
| 535.18 | 600.08 | 663.02 | 742.22 | 501.13 | 411.13 |
| 536.03 | 601.07 | 663.15 | 744.09 | 630.09 | 570.11 |
| 536.05 | 601.09 | 663.18 | 744.12 | 666.11 | 585.08 |
| 536.13 | 601.12 | 664.04 | 745.10 | meantime | 587.03 |
| 537.01 | 601.20 | 666.19 | 746.16 | 003.20 | 594.02 |
| 537.11 | 601.22 | 669.10 | 748.04 | 186.10 | 639.10 |
| 538.13 | 602.02 | 669.13 | 748.11 | 252.06 | 736.03 |
| 538.17 | 602.03 | 669.18 | 749.09 | 400.03 | meets |
| 539.03 | 602.07 | 670.22 | 751.16 | 495.04 | 008.05 |
| 539.03 | 603.03 | 672.02 | 753.17 | 582.02 | 344.05 |
| 539.20 | 604.03 | 673.04 | 754.13 | 679.11 | 686.08 |
| 539.21 | 605.10 | 674.09 | 754.16 | 691.17 | melancholy |
| 540.02 | 605.14 | 674.16 | 754.20 | 722.02 | 052.05 |
| 540.06 | 605.14 | 675.01 | 754.22 | 751.21 | 351.14 |
| 540.16 | 606.03 | 676.11 | 755.07 | meanwhile | 392.21 |
| 540.20 | 606.16 | 677.05 | 755.15 | 020.17 | 413.16 |
| 541.02 | 606.19 | 678.18 | 755.18 | 052.08 | 517.08 |
| 543.11 | 607.14 | 678.21 | 755.21 | 310.19 | 519.03 |
| 543.13 | 607.17 | 679.10 | 756.04 | 320.05 | mellow |
| 543.19 | 608.09 | 680.12 | 760.20 | 364.10 | 206.05 |
| 543.20 | 608.22 | 680.14 | 763.11 | 375.06 | 353.02 |
| 544.01 | 609.21 | 684.19 | meadow | 382.06 | 370.14 |
| 544.06 | 610.01 | 686.16 | 139.08 | measles | 588.06 |
| 545.13 | 610.14 | 689.07 | 187.10 | 082.06 | mells |
| 547.05 | 611.14 | 690.02 | meal | measure | 322.08 |
| 547.12 | 612.02 | 690.04 | 017.08 | 021.15 | melt |
| 548.04 | 612.20 | 691.05 | 023.08 | 082.22 | 181.09 |
| 548.05 | 613.01 | 691.18 | 077.04 | 115.08 | 356.14 |
| 548.15 | 613.04 | 692.08 | 121.10 | 200.03 | melted |
| 548.22 | 613.22 | 694.09 | 217.05 | 216.19 | 303.01 |
| 550.05 | 614.18 | 697.01 | 269.11 | 498.14 | 414.02 |
| 551.08 | 615.04 | 697.05 | 319.03 | 512.12 | 569.13 |
| 551.22 | 615.04 | 697.14 | 390.16 | 726.19 | melting |
| 553.20 | 615.05 | 697.15 | 674.13 | measured | 220.16 |
| 554.08 | 615.06 | 697.21 | 686.12 | 257.05 | member |
| 554.08 | 615.13 | 698.04 | 740.18 | 314.14 | 038.09 |
| 555.13 | 617.06 | 698.09 | meals | 428.18 | members |
| 555.19 | 617.12 | 698.17 | 548.11 | measures | 755.10 |
| 556.16 | 617.13 | 698.22 | 716.20 | 299.13 | memoranda |
| 558.19 | 617.15 | 699.05 | 736.03 | 345.04 | 731.21 |
| 559.11 | 618.07 | 699.16 | 749.22 | 345.06 | memories |
| 560.01 | 618.13 | 700.02 | mean | 525.02 | 470.06 |
| 560.05 | 619.11 | 700.05 | 024.06 | measuring | memory |
| 560.05 | 621.01 | 700.05 | 056.07 | 750.16 | 057.06 |
| 560.08 | 621.04 | 700.08 | 057.20 | meat | 245.08 |
| 563.03 | 621.07 | 702.02 | 117.14 | 185.16 | 282.02 |
| 563.06 | 621.12 | 702.20 | 181.12 | meddle | 358.21 |
| 563.08 | 622.10 | 703.09 | 238.15 | 012.04 | 388.17 |
| 563.09 | 623.10 | 703.21 | 256.12 | 074.01 | 413.17 |
| 563.16 | 624.14 | 704.12 | 263.01 | 167.13 | 475.02 |
| 564.03 | 626.12 | 705.07 | 271.18 | 397.01 | 485.19 |
| 564.08 | 628.07 | 705.09 | 283.09 | 661.05 | 486.15 |
| 564.10 | 629.18 | 706.07 | 357.02 | 664.16 | 578.01 |
| 565.08 | 630.03 | 706.13 | 405.07 | 758.14 | 759.05 |
| 565.09 | 630.03 | 706.19 | 406.18 | meddling | men |
| 566.03 | 630.04 | 707.02 | 462.06 | 128.18 | 024.17 |
| 566.11 | 632.16 | 707.04 | 481.09 | mediation | 174.22 |
| 566.16 | 633.04 | 707.08 | 483.20 | 456.06 | 255.02 |
| 566.21 | 633.05 | 707.09 | 600.07 | medical | 257.13 |
| 566.22 | 633.05 | 708.04 | 608.07 | 290.13 | 375.14 |
| 567.05 | 633.08 | 708.04 | 627.10 | medicine | 388.19 |
| 567.12 | 633.12 | 708.05 | 695.19 | 202.19 | 637.12 |
| 567.15 | 633.21 | 708.08 | 707.06 | 527.08 | 641.16 |
| 567.19 | 633.22 | 708.09 | 707.07 | medicines | 731.19 |
| 568.14 | 634.01 | 708.14 | 732.15 | 142.22 | 760.03 |
| 568.15 | 634.05 | 708.15 | mean-minded | 348.05 | 760.05 |
| 568.19 | 634.17 | 708.16 | 340.10 | meditate | menaced |
| 568.19 | 635.02 | 708.20 | meanest | 343.17 | 238.13 |
| 569.01 | 636.02 | 710.05 | 223.14 | meditated | 397.07 |
| 569.06 | 638.08 | 711.03 | meaning | 026.05 | 613.11 |
| 569.18 | 639.08 | 711.04 | 299.10 | 200.08 | mend |
| 570.02 | 641.02 | 711.09 | 331.11 | 216.03 | 029.01 |
| 570.08 | 641.14 | 711.11 | 421.11 | meditating | 112.05 |
| 570.12 | 646.06 | 715.06 | 467.11 | 242.02 | mended |
| 570.19 | 646.09 | 715.08 | 570.07 | 393.02 | 545.06 |
| 570.21 | 646.20 | 717.01 | 601.20 | 509.14 | mending |
| 571.04 | 646.20 | 718.09 | means | meditation | 568.15 |
| 571.09 | 647.02 | 718.11 | 032.18 | 070.15 | mensful |
| 572.09 | 647.06 | 718.13 | 042.14 | 133.14 | 691.10 |
| 572.16 | 647.06 | 719.18 | 083.03 | 546.15 | 712.18 |
| 573.17 | 647.08 | 721.19 | 133.03 | 655.18 | mental |
| 576.02 | 648.02 | 722.13 | 150.22 | meditations | 024.17 |
| 576.06 | 649.03 | 722.18 | 173.08 | 234.19 | 150.01 |
| 576.20 | 649.17 | 723.10 | 203.19 | 746.03 | 347.07 |
| 576.22 | 650.10 | 723.16 | 222.10 | meditative | 351.21 |
| 578.16 | 650.12 | 724.09 | 236.17 | 690.17 | 632.07 |
| 578.19 | 651.10 | 724.16 | 257.19 | medium | 655.15 |
| 579.04 | 652.03 | 724.17 | 323.21 | 258.11 | 728.15 |
| 580.20 | 652.21 | 725.02 | 334.01 | meek | mentally |
| 581.03 | 653.05 | 726.07 | 343.09 | 250.18 | 015.17 |
| 581.04 | 653.06 | 729.05 | 367.17 | meet | 370.01 |
| 581.05 | 653.08 | 729.15 | 517.16 | 109.04 | mention |
| 581.11 | 653.16 | 729.17 | 541.18 | 181.06 | 029.13 |
| 581.17 | 653.22 | 730.09 | 607.07 | 273.21 | 115.19 |
| 590.01 | 654.21 | 730.10 | 636.20 | 365.05 | 192.18 |
| 590.02 | 655.02 | 730.14 | 642.10 | 429.09 | 227.05 |
| 590.13 | 655.06 | 730.17 | 725.18 | 449.06 | 288.04 |
| 590.20 | 655.16 | 731.13 | 755.02 | 462.09 | 300.01 |
| 591.04 | 656.04 | 731.20 | meant | 523.21 | 305.10 |
| 591.11 | 656.10 | 732.12 | 071.18 | 580.11 | 341.21 |
| 592.01 | 656.11 | 734.12 | 078.13 | 582.02 | 345.15 |
| 592.12 | 658.05 | 738.01 | 090.18 | 590.12 | 376.03 |
| 592.17 | 658.07 | 738.04 | 170.06 | 654.08 | 472.09 |
| 592.19 | 659.13 | 739.20 | 262.11 | 654.09 | 489.01 |
| 593.14 | 659.17 | 739.20 | 270.19 | meeterly | 489.04 |
| 598.16 | 660.05 | 740.11 | 298.06 | 321.04 | 489.06 |

499.14
573.15
594.02
596.12
mentioned
134.20
345.14
353.13
461.14
583.19
597.01
745.08
mentioning
428.14
mentions
345.13
merchant
431.15
mercy
168.07
168.11
mercy's
264.16
264.17
mere
042.01
100.13
136.19
197.12
235.10
302.04
337.13
356.17
541.10
620.16
678.14
merely
051.02
160.12
228.01
354.15
383.18
459.12
436.06
493.17
5C3.07
562.11
631.13
729.02
merest
008.16
merit
494.10
merited
347.12
372.03
merrily
142.12
493.02
556.20
merriment
036.06
118.08
497.10
merry
111.11
118.19
130.04
177.08
177.17
318.20
387.12
432.02
451.16
572.03
mess
131.02
276.09
319.14
471.04
716.16
message
142.11
208.18
456.02
628.07
662.09
710.11
messenger
373.05
509.05
585.11
met
127.01
194.14
232.08
264.04
285.17
298.03
340.12
361.20
485.16
560.05
628.15
718.04
757.16
760.14
method
134.17
253.17
430.18

551.09
methodist
390.20
methodists'
665.18
mew
061.11
mice
094.03
259.05
michael
555.03
555.17
569.16
michaelmas
515.03
middle
104.18
124.13
178.22
189.08
218.01
274.14
275.15
321.10
401.14
476.06
557.08
621.18
764.02
midnight
095.14
188.21
298.13
478.11
745.10
750.09
midst
011.12
366.21
716.08
might
007.15
008.16
012.02
014.10
019.22
022.09
023.13
024.13
027.05
041.15
043.06
054.12
072.12
080.03
089.08
090.22
094.14
100.14
100.15
105.12
106.19
107.18
114.05
116.01
119.09
131.04
145.04
145.20
148.21
153.15
161.03
165.01
172.04
178.01
181.09
189.16
189.20
191.08
198.13
219.18
220.10
221.22
225.16
229.06
237.11
240.22
250.08
251.17
262.02
263.19
265.19
270.08
277.10
295.08
304.04
305.03
311.04
312.21
313.12
341.01
341.19
344.12
346.04
346.21
347.06
358.04
370.06
372.01
372.04

373.04
394.18
396.12
405.04
405.13
405.13
405.21
406.13
412.01
415.17
419.11
420.13
429.20
430.18
442.13
450.22
457.04
466.02
485.19
497.11
500.19
501.19
502.13
508.13
511.20
517.11
521.05
529.11
535.14
538.14
552.14
554.19
556.14
559.02
561.11
568.11
571.05
578.13
580.12
582.01
583.08
588.17
598.06
602.17
616.17
622.06
622.19
652.05
659.21
669.07
671.04
677.17
689.09
695.06
705.08
733.01
750.02
751.13
752.18
753.07
753.18
759.19
mightily
544.11
mighty
183.01
591.20
migrated
687.03
mild
205.22
425.10
692.18
743.15
mildewed
038.19
mildness
412.21
mile
067.11
303.10
426.11
433.06
433.06
433.09
450.06
450.07
586.12
mile'
689.05
miles
007.05
015.06
067.04
076.11
196.09
298.12
313.10
313.14
465.05
470.12
480.19
489.18
688.05
milk
140.06
298.04
319.16
320.18
325.16
467.05

472.13
476.09
476.09
509.06
milk-blood
259.08
milk-fetcher
506.12
milk-porridge
471.02
milking
034.01
566.03
miller
511.21
million
110.18
milo
181.07
mim
310.10
310.11
310.11
minching
310.12
mind
014.03
055.17
066.04
114.13
120.06
123.05
135.16
141.09
146.09
160.11
177.02
183.08
189.14
194.18
197.14
202.03
203.19
216.09
225.19
225.20
228.11
232.19
239.21
249.07
251.20
266.16
267.02
273.05
275.06
287.16
288.12
293.04
302.10
313.16
345.21
348.04
350.07
360.17
368.06
368.07
371.02
392.05
396.18
401.07
401.18
415.01
442.08
452.08
464.07
485.15
492.09
521.04
527.08
547.02
555.06
573.07
597.18
599.22
606.13
607.16
614.12
620.04
640.20
648.13
697.01
700.04
701.04
701.21
717.05
717.18
727.04
731.01
735.01
753.10
754.17
minded
086.01
443.06
minding
090.04
694.10
minds
713.20
mine
018.12

053.03
083.20
111.03
136.02
143.08
179.12
202.02
214.10
239.23
240.01
244.06
264.20
277.21
283.18
309.09
321.16
325.12
327.02
329.12
336.03
359.17
360.18
363.11
389.05
421.06
449.13
469.22
494.05
494.08
505.01
516.09
537.17
545.18
557.13
558.05
558.07
580.21
581.09
588.08
605.15
612.04
632.13
632.14
632.15
632.19
633.03
649.02
650.01
661.04
663.16
680.11
733.04
756.11
757.16
mine's
163.18
mingled
027.18
034.13
258.18
497.21
694.01
minister
665.16
754.06
754.19
ministering
024.08
minny
428.13
439.15
462.20
473.11
555.04
559.13
567.15
569.17
594.08
632.17
676.15
minny's
560.06
minor
664.16
minute
035.02
100.17
100.18
127.08
194.08
214.10
226.04
250.01
259.21
274.22
294.22
315.20
326.14
346.13
355.07
365.17
382.11
396.10
450.02
454.04
456.19
497.19
504.02
523.15
548.11
598.20

624.17
628.01
640.04
648.19
666.11
680.19
699.14
707.15
716.10
717.11
747.09
747.21
minute's
072.15
090.11
152.06
minute-hand
200.03
minutely
136.03
minutes
021.13
039.08
044.11
060.04
068.01
121.07
189.22
202.18
217.05
355.21
376.01
394.03
395.17
419.16
437.01
475.16
538.22
543.03
591.06
610.19
622.03
662.10
709.20
731.03
minutes'
176.17
257.03
minx
056.19
mire
115.20
mirror
272.09
277.12
278.17
mirth
496.06
561.12
589.03
mis-pronunciations
680.12
misanthropical
313.05
misanthropist's
001.09
misanthropists
686.06
misbehaviour
012.22
mischief
090.12
129.12
161.03
217.20
344.15
538.14
547.19
566.08
mischievous
081.16
234.18
291.11
miscreants
034.22
misdoubting
341.13
miser
019.22
166.03
miserable
158.19
158.19
178.07
178.09
256.16
335.13
521.19
533.18
569.11
617.10
617.11
618.03
648.05
648.07
708.18
miseries
182.16
182.17
308.03

misery
223.05
253.10
281.17
363.06
397.14
405.10
543.06
573.02
648.07
misery-maker
367.05
misfortune
055.06
197.07
225.05
577.07
misfortunes
623.11
misgivings
347.16
454.10
750.14
misguided
167.18
misplaced
431.12
miss
022.05
043.16
071.20
073.11
076.14
078.01
080.18
089.09
093.06
102.03
109.05
109.08
109.09
112.11
114.14
116.13
117.13
120.19
145.04
150.18
151.09
155.03
155.20
156.09
159.18
169.19
170.01
172.01
173.06
174.11
177.05
178.14
181.02
182.01
183.17
190.09
191.02
191.20
193.19
204.04
212.12
217.01
226.08
230.16
231.15
233.13
248.05
248.19
249.20
269.02
270.05
271.09
289.20
291.04
293.21
294.01
296.17
308.01
324.11
324.11
369.06
386.12
404.20
405.03
427.03
428.04
428.18
435.01
435.12
437.02
437.20
438.14
439.11
440.04
440.19
445.05
450.12
463.16
478.04
480.02
482.08
485.10
489.19

490.02
491.13
496.11
497.10
498.17
502.17
504.01
505.07
505.19
509.10
511.03
514.12
517.22
518.15
520.14
523.20
525.09
527.02
532.08
534.05
535.04
540.10
542.01
543.02
545.01
546.09
547.02
553.16
560.19
562.03
567.16
573.08
577.07
592.19
595.05
604.08
605.18
608.04
614.08
618.02
620.02
623.17
629.09
630.15
646.15
miss's
187.08
553.02
missed
555.01
622.14
670.18
missile
245.10
409.20
missing
417.06
missis
016.10
017.09
139.12
140.08
667.10
missis's
298.06
missive
347.17
675.18
missy
626.11
missy's
119.02
mist
209.09
463.06
518.20
mista'en
324.18
mistake
009.03
166.12
298.17
499.13
692.02
694.12
mistaken
157.18
219.20
276.19
483.04
662.01
mistakes
680.12
mistaking
532.04
mistress
070.07
079.05
080.22
091.05
113.05
118.09
130.04
142.01
185.18
197.16
199.11
208.09
210.12
213.08

226.18
227.10
235.02
250.09
251.07
254.06
256.04
264.17
270.06
285.19
290.01
291.08
293.17
318.13
346.19
350.21
356.01
362.01
366.18
411.04
434.05
548.03
552.18
598.15
606.13
616.21
628.12
629.04
635.04
638.16
644.04
656.10
690.20
705.14
mistress's
288.18
478.07
529.08
716.21
mistrusting
222.01
misty
014.02
283.22
530.02
577.16
misunderstood
229.02
misused
385.15
mitch
560.12
586.02
713.07
mither
169.18
mitigated
487.10
mitigating
239.01
mixed
111.05
mixture
560.17
moan
073.11
605.03
moaned
359.08
367.20
539.09
660.17
moaning
053.09
382.04
393.06
527.17
614.17
632.02
moans
591.08
mock
030.09
176.10
731.20
mockery
148.15
321.15
564.22
758.20
mocking
432.03
707.11
mode
444.14
682.06
733.15
model
625.04
666.01
749.18
moderate
224.16
modern
323.06
modlled
030.05
moist
516.17
739.14

moisture
047.14
molest
411.22
moment
029.04
047.01
055.18
097.01
123.18
156.19
165.20
180.09
288.04
306.15
308.01
334.19
336.01
360.16
377.19
398.14
408.07
411.16
430.03
440.03
464.19
496.19
531.17
548.08
564.09
571.14
578.15
597.07
604.17
610.01
654.14
669.09
704.13
722.10
724.06
738.06
762.17
momentary
244.05
744.07
moments
597.22
monday
280.05
705.10
715.02
money
071.15
074.08
078.22
096.08
182.01
203.18
221.17
232.05
420.15
630.04
631.05
722.01
722.06
monkey
132.19
228.19
614.06
monomania
733.01
monopolized
336.08
monopolizing
469.14
monotonous
057.17
monster
164.19
341.17
388.15
monsters
034.11
month
008.11
381.03
401.02
616.04
667.17
690.05
760.20
month's
115.20
575.05
months
140.01
197.11
244.22
289.01
301.02
301.03
411.10
415.19
424.08
428.19
449.07
486.04
524.09
554.09
578.04
589.17

596.04
672.14
698.16
763.17
months'
369.04
429.15
monument
379.19
746.08
mood
135.16
135.22
735.02
moodily
684.05
moods
274.18
352.15
592.04
moody
317.15
mools
169.18
moon
206.08
206.15
283.21
398.14
552.12
638.15
644.20
692.18
693.04
763.02
moonbeam
179.13
moonlight
186.21
559.19
561.17
moons
208.05
moor
052.13
065.18
227.17
243.06
275.15
279.15
380.02
410.10
479.02
479.06
613.09
659.12
689.21
760.15
764.01
moor-cock's
275.12
moor-game
480.01
moors
022.05
044.14
100.11
122.02
186.22
303.05
308.06
413.10
428.06
442.06
463.15
478.18
500.05
535.13
549.04
557.08
557.18
583.04
583.20
654.09
688.03
695.15
761.15
moped
269.02
moral
235.11
256.20
343.05
moralizing
415.13
morally
222.21
morbid
464.18
more
003.03
011.10
018.13
018.21
027.09
030.22
032.03
033.09
033.11
034.16
035.09

035.10
045.08
049.17
051.07
060.14
062.11
071.05
071.21
080.01
089.17
089.18
091.03
092.01
100.21
106.04
111.20
115.13
120.08
122.12
122.22
124.01
129.12
134.20
136.09
136.09
137.09
137.21
143.05
144.09
144.22
146.02
148.18
151.15
153.13
166.17
172.08
179.04
179.11
183.09
183.21
187.19
187.20
189.19
193.10
195.05
197.04
199.04
199.20
203.13
206.01
206.13
212.06
213.17
215.06
215.18
215.22
220.12
222.06
226.01
226.22
229.05
235.07
243.20
244.13
245.19
258.01
263.12
264.18
271.20
276.01
280.13
286.18
288.01
291.04
292.05
293.10
293.16
299.18
301.06
303.12
305.21
311.03
320.18
321.18
329.16
333.07
334.07
336.03
340.22
343.04
349.05
350.06
352.03
355.22
359.14
361.06
370.22
373.21
376.02
383.14
385.05
386.01
388.19
389.16
392.09
401.07
407.22
411.07
412.14
414.13
420.05

| | | | | | |
|---|---|---|---|---|---|
| 422.09 | 122.20 | 764.04 | **mounds** | 360.11 | 219.01 |
| 434.11 | 135.04 | **mossy** | 066.01 | 362.13 | 223.21 |
| 435.19 | 139.02 | 449.09 | 760.10 | 409.02 | 224.11 |
| 437.18 | 192.22 | **most** | 541.06 | **movements** | 227.19 |
| 449.13 | 195.04 | 008.13 | **mount** | 010.08 | 231.12 |
| 457.07 | 204.02 | 019.10 | 041.12 | 240.13 | 232.03 |
| 461.17 | 217.15 | 025.17 | 294.13 | 487.07 | 234.05 |
| 474.11 | 238.20 | 048.13 | 745.05 | 629.07 | 236.07 |
| 479.10 | 267.10 | 050.10 | **mounted** | **moves** | 241.01 |
| 493.09 | 280.06 | 052.05 | 061.14 | 606.17 | 247.03 |
| 494.14 | 291.19 | 089.11 | 132.03 | 730.14 | 251.13 |
| 497.07 | 299.05 | 091.21 | 320.20 | **moving** | 251.15 |
| 497.18 | 302.16 | 180.19 | 453.01 | 126.07 | 254.08 |
| 498.13 | 329.21 | 239.09 | 456.12 | 134.13 | 256.10 |
| 499.18 | 339.07 | 252.08 | 463.06 | 149.20 | 257.09 |
| 500.14 | 345.09 | 253.16 | 473.10 | 207.03 | 258.15 |
| 501.01 | 347.22 | 256.21 | **mounting** | 296.14 | 259.22 |
| 503.11 | 368.03 | 281.14 | 014.11 | 310.18 | 265.02 |
| 504.07 | 370.11 | 294.20 | 098.02 | 625.05 | 265.21 |
| 508.08 | 403.12 | 332.13 | 248.07 | **mr** | 267.16 |
| 509.11 | 413.11 | 335.13 | 304.19 | 001.09 | 271.18 |
| 509.12 | 416.04 | 341.05 | 366.10 | 002.06 | 274.09 |
| 510.03 | 419.20 | 355.10 | 516.19 | 002.08 | 285.11 |
| 510.22 | 431.13 | 360.21 | **mounts** | 003.09 | 288.18 |
| 514.12 | 448.12 | 366.16 | 060.01 | 004.03 | 289.10 |
| 516.06 | 461.16 | 407.22 | **mourn** | 007.07 | 289.19 |
| 520.13 | 488.13 | 424.12 | 520.15 | 008.03 | 291.20 |
| 525.01 | 489.20 | 446.21 | **mourned** | 009.17 | 293.06 |
| 534.03 | 507.02 | 448.09 | 053.12 | 011.04 | 293.14 |
| 534.13 | 509.17 | 455.13 | **mourner** | 012.15 | 294.18 |
| 535.02 | 514.10 | 501.05 | 371.13 | 021.03 | 296.12 |
| 536.04 | 530.02 | 506.09 | 408.13 | 023.21 | 297.13 |
| 542.11 | 547.20 | 530.07 | 421.02 | 031.15 | 299.08 |
| 546.07 | 557.07 | 557.12 | **mourners** | 033.17 | 302.15 |
| 551.19 | 559.15 | 678.19 | 097.05 | 035.18 | 305.07 |
| 560.01 | 573.18 | 680.17 | 379.14 | 036.05 | 307.10 |
| 567.21 | 586.20 | 731.11 | **mournful** | 055.09 | 310.06 |
| 568.10 | 587.17 | 731.18 | 354.16 | 055.22 | 311.16 |
| 569.10 | 593.05 | 759.07 | **mournfully** | 059.08 | 312.22 |
| 570.13 | 613.19 | **mostly** | 643.04 | 072.11 | 315.10 |
| 571.07 | 623.05 | 413.11 | **mourning** | 072.21 | 318.05 |
| 573.16 | 625.03 | **mother** | 109.11 | 073.05 | 322.01 |
| 575.03 | 626.02 | 008.07 | 416.06 | 075.15 | 325.11 |
| 577.13 | 637.11 | 009.11 | 448.04 | 076.01 | 326.17 |
| 581.10 | 659.18 | 029.02 | **mouse** | 079.06 | 329.14 |
| 584.04 | 663.18 | 075.15 | 160.03 | 080.05 | 330.15 |
| 588.21 | 674.19 | 092.11 | 437.14 | 083.14 | 332.17 |
| 589.13 | 703.12 | 102.22 | 611.17 | 087.02 | 333.23 |
| 598.11 | 737.01 | 109.06 | **mouth** | 088.18 | 338.06 |
| 599.03 | 745.04 | 125.17 | 017.20 | 089.17 | 341.04 |
| 606.20 | 751.10 | 167.03 | 062.12 | 091.09 | 343.19 |
| 637.01 | 756.14 | 219.11 | 107.04 | 092.17 | 346.15 |
| 645.08 | 757.05 | 301.05 | 128.17 | 096.02 | 347.08 |
| 645.13 | **morning's** | 348.11 | 163.19 | 098.08 | 350.03 |
| 650.09 | 500.03 | 369.05 | 218.11 | 101.22 | 354.07 |
| 650.21 | 740.09 | 412.11 | 309.07 | 104.08 | 364.22 |
| 652.13 | **morose** | 414.11 | 375.05 | 107.20 | 366.19 |
| 654.01 | 007.14 | 425.08 | 406.22 | 109.14 | 367.16 |
| 660.07 | 705.13 | 428.22 | 428.22 | 110.10 | 371.21 |
| 663.11 | **moroseness** | 451.17 | 497.16 | 111.05 | 373.01 |
| 664.07 | 036.07 | 457.15 | 531.05 | 112.01 | 379.11 |
| 667.17 | 150.05 | 457.21 | 565.21 | 112.05 | 382.14 |
| 670.20 | 317.13 | 460.21 | 569.01 | 115.06 | 390.03 |
| 671.11 | 588.21 | 461.13 | 621.16 | 116.10 | 392.05 |
| 671.11 | **morrow** | 468.16 | 631.01 | 117.06 | 396.18 |
| 671.19 | 034.04 | 468.18 | 634.02 | 119.01 | 398.06 |
| 671.20 | 080.03 | 472.06 | 680.16 | 128.11 | 402.07 |
| 674.14 | 112.06 | 472.09 | 695.17 | 130.03 | 402.19 |
| 684.01 | 119.06 | 485.19 | 702.04 | 133.06 | 403.13 |
| 684.16 | 223.21 | 520.11 | 706.15 | 134.05 | 407.03 |
| 685.02 | 267.14 | 537.14 | **mouthful** | 137.22 | 407.17 |
| 686.20 | 337.16 | 632.22 | 130.13 | 140.02 | 411.13 |
| 690.06 | 351.01 | **mother's** | 217.08 | 142.09 | 415.14 |
| 690.07 | 381.07 | 056.18 | **move** | 143.18 | 416.01 |
| 704.16 | 381.12 | 073.04 | 018.07 | 147.16 | 416.14 |
| 704.16 | 555.16 | 434.14 | 094.09 | | 416.20 |
| 705.07 | 559.16 | 461.05 | 099.01 | 148.22 | 418.01 |
| 708.06 | 569.08 | 464.17 | 199.06 | 149.15 | 419.10 |
| 708.10 | 715.02 | 468.02 | 283.05 | 150.22 | 420.13 |
| 711.10 | **morsel** | 491.16 | 305.01 | 155.03 | 422.15 |
| 711.11 | 040.08 | 578.11 | 333.01 | 155.14 | 426.10 |
| 713.04 | 370.07 | 633.08 | 391.13 | 160.17 | 426.16 |
| 716.15 | 464.14 | 642.09 | 490.22 | 163.13 | 428.16 |
| 717.03 | **morsels** | **moths** | 550.03 | 166.07 | 433.10 |
| 723.05 | 079.15 | 764.07 | 604.02 | 168.06 | 434.03 |
| 727.17 | **mortagaged** | **motion** | 621.08 | 169.03 | 435.16 |
| 732.14 | 419.01 | 019.21 | 700.19 | 172.21 | 440.06 |
| 735.08 | **mortal** | 059.06 | **moveable** | 174.12 | 441.08 |
| 743.05 | 020.21 | 178.17 | 664.12 | 175.12 | 442.15 |
| 747.12 | 057.01 | 255.14 | **moved** | 184.09 | 444.17 |
| 748.19 | 181.08 | 403.01 | 011.06 | 189.15 | 451.13 |
| 756.12 | 327.01 | **motioned** | 049.03 | 190.17 | 454.22 |
| 757.10 | 358.06 | 355.15 | 053.16 | 192.14 | 455.02 |
| 758.03 | 358.07 | 513.21 | 081.06 | 196.02 | 455.21 |
| 763.03 | 615.15 | **motioning** | 158.03 | 198.03 | 456.11 |
| **moreover** | 722.12 | 644.16 | 255.10 | 201.10 | 457.11 |
| 075.02 | **mortally** | **motionless** | 290.18 | 203.07 | 459.03 |
| 235.19 | 257.10 | 017.13 | 364.19 | 203.16 | 460.08 |
| 691.13 | **mortgaged** | 652.03 | 374.14 | 204.08 | 462.15 |
| **morn** | 422.16 | **motive** | 377.17 | 204.18 | 465.08 |
| 432.17 | **mortgagee** | 182.05 | 378.15 | 207.08 | 466.11 |
| 458.09 | 422.18 | 372.22 | 441.14 | 208.21 | 467.15 |
| 696.07 | **mortification** | 373.01 | 477.08 | 210.10 | 469.08 |
| **morning** | 498.01 | **motives** | 560.15 | 210.14 | 472.19 |
| 022.10 | 680.20 | 684.14 | 601.17 | 211.01 | 475.11 |
| 046.14 | **mortified** | **mould** | 661.10 | 214.02 | 477.11 |
| 062.12 | 561.19 | 023.17 | 694.01 | 215.08 | 478.18 |
| 075.21 | **mortifying** | 380.03 | **movement** | 216.19 | 480.22 |
| 095.10 | 156.06 | 760.09 | 002.22 | 217.14 | 481.16 |
| 100.11 | **moss** | **mound** | 063.02 | 217.16 | 483.19 |
| 121.22 | 519.11 | 578.11 | 179.17 | 217.17 | 486.09 |
| | | | 354.05 | | |

| | | | | | |
|---|---|---|---|---|---|
| 487.13 | 021.03 | 662.12 | 721.14 | 267.01 | 350.22 |
| 488.21 | 024.06 | 663.16 | 723.06 | 387.18 | 353.17 |
| 498.03 | 025.14 | 665.17 | 728.01 | 609.18 | 354.06 |
| 499.15 | 028.12 | 666.18 | 738.10 | muse | 357.19 |
| 500.21 | 029.09 | 670.18 | 756.10 | 519.10 | 365.08 |
| 501.03 | 030.17 | 672.08 | 759.08 | mused | 365.13 |
| 501.04 | 033.11 | 675.01 | mucky | 217.20 | 365.18 |
| 501.16 | 063.10 | 675.12 | 472.07 | 454.09 | 373.11 |
| 503.06 | 065.07 | 677.01 | 707.11 | 464.11 | 388.05 |
| 510.06 | 069.11 | 680.01 | muckying | 745.13 | 398.15 |
| 515.06 | 071.08 | 680.04 | 321.05 | music | 399.08 |
| 517.05 | 072.05 | 687.01 | mud | 131.19 | 409.10 |
| 520.12 | 073.01 | 690.18 | 014.04 | 353.05 | 411.16 |
| 524.01 | 073.15 | 692.13 | 318.15 | 557.18 | 418.10 |
| 528.16 | 073.20 | 697.04 | 322.06 | musical | 421.13 |
| 530.10 | 074.13 | 697.14 | 720.12 | 696.05 | 422.01 |
| 535.09 | 077.02 | 698.07 | mug | musing | 425.14 |
| 546.02 | 078.08 | 714.02 | 007.03 | 240.11 | 430.08 |
| 547.05 | 081.19 | 724.11 | 319.21 | 578.09 | 431.16 |
| 548.08 | 104.08 | 762.03 | mugs | 643.03 | 433.01 |
| 552.08 | 108.14 | 763.06 | 119.15 | 718.19 | 444.02 |
| 570.11 | 110.19 | much | muh | musingly | 459.07 |
| 572.09 | 112.12 | 007.11 | 191.02 | 360.20 | 460.05 |
| 572.17 | 115.06 | 041.21 | 324.20 | musn't | 460.20 |
| 573.16 | 119.01 | 049.14 | 326.11 | 439.18 | 465.01 |
| 580.08 | 119.08 | 051.14 | 531.12 | 615.06 | 469.13 |
| 582.17 | 127.03 | 068.03 | 713.07 | must | 476.06 |
| 592.07 | 131.18 | 071.11 | 719.19 | 003.22 | 476.08 |
| 594.04 | 134.15 | 083.06 | 758.17 | 004.08 | 479.04 |
| 602.21 | 135.08 | 090.23 | mule | 017.16 | 480.12 |
| 605.04 | 135.14 | 096.12 | 704.12 | 022.12 | 482.10 |
| 607.13 | 137.01 | 113.05 | mulled | 025.08 | 489.03 |
| 611.20 | 137.14 | 136.18 | 119.16 | 026.14 | 489.06 |
| 615.15 | 142.11 | 138.05 | multiply | 028.08 | 499.08 |
| 617.12 | 145.22 | 141.04 | 264.01 | 030.13 | 501.20 |
| 620.14 | 180.21 | 146.09 | multitude | 030.18 | 505.08 |
| 627.14 | 181.12 | 153.20 | 050.11 | 032.06 | 508.01 |
| 628.10 | 196.16 | 160.02 | 518.18 | 033.11 | 511.12 |
| 632.05 | 202.10 | 161.02 | multitudes | 041.05 | 521.22 |
| 634.21 | 202.17 | 163.22 | 198.15 | 045.09 | 523.02 |
| 635.05 | 208.21 | 181.13 | mumbled | 051.19 | 529.01 |
| 636.20 | 210.05 | 186.06 | 010.02 | 056.20 | 537.07 |
| 637.06 | 212.07 | 190.04 | mumbling | 059.03 | 540.15 |
| 637.09 | 214.15 | 194.22 | 401.05 | 063.05 | 541.01 |
| 638.22 | 218.02 | 197.20 | mummy | 067.17 | 542.17 |
| 639.19 | 219.20 | 198.20 | 476.18 | 074.03 | 543.11 |
| 640.17 | 222.18 | 204.03 | mumn't | 074.20 | 546.16 |
| 640.22 | 227.01 | 214.01 | 187.15 | 077.20 | 547.06 |
| 648.03 | 228.07 | 215.08 | mun | 083.19 | 547.10 |
| 650.04 | 228.20 | 218.22 | 247.08 | 092.11 | 548.13 |
| 655.08 | 231.09 | 219.14 | 297.08 | 094.06 | 563.08 |
| 659.01 | 231.17 | 221.09 | 318.13 | 098.14 | 564.21 |
| 660.14 | 236.17 | 230.12 | 455.19 | 114.13 | 566.12 |
| 661.16 | 238.04 | 248.05 | 457.22 | 123.05 | 569.17 |
| 663.22 | 240.11 | 252.22 | 712.19 | 123.06 | 571.14 |
| 664.17 | 248.11 | 261.10 | 719.10 | 125.04 | 571.16 |
| 666.20 | 249.22 | 264.11 | 719.10 | 127.11 | 572.21 |
| 669.14 | 252.11 | 283.18 | mun'n't | 134.18 | 574.04 |
| 670.01 | 253.19 | 291.10 | 036.01 | 135.12 | 576.09 |
| 670.05 | 254.15 | 296.09 | munching | 139.12 | 578.14 |
| 670.22 | 255.08 | 304.03 | 310.12 | 140.04 | 579.01 |
| 672.02 | 257.15 | 330.22 | munificent | 141.02 | 582.18 |
| 674.04 | 259.01 | 332.11 | 199.08 | 142.09 | 583.18 |
| 676.01 | 261.10 | 333.06 | murder | 142.09 | 591.18 |
| 678.04 | 270.15 | 336.05 | 035.20 | 149.21 | 593.22 |
| 678.18 | 273.07 | 337.18 | 107.18 | 158.12 | 606.12 |
| 679.05 | 278.04 | 345.18 | 163.04 | 158.14 | 612.17 |
| 683.13 | 278.17 | 347.20 | 167.22 | 171.16 | 615.07 |
| 684.13 | 282.10 | 350.21 | 197.21 | 172.06 | 615.07 |
| 686.09 | 286.05 | 363.11 | 260.14 | 173.08 | 615.08 |
| 691.04 | 288.03 | 367.04 | 398.06 | 181.14 | 615.18 |
| 692.21 | 289.06 | 371.20 | 567.19 | 185.20 | 616.10 |
| 697.07 | 292.18 | 374.07 | 724.10 | 186.01 | 620.06 |
| 697.15 | 295.07 | 384.01 | murdered | 189.13 | 621.05 |
| 700.03 | 301.03 | 395.10 | 377.01 | 203.01 | 624.07 |
| 702.08 | 328.05 | 405.15 | 407.14 | 205.21 | 627.01 |
| 704.16 | 332.06 | 407.02 | murderer | 210.18 | 637.10 |
| 707.21 | 332.20 | 428.07 | 364.03 | 212.01 | 639.04 |
| 708.09 | 337.22 | 429.18 | 502.16 | 212.15 | 646.10 |
| 710.04 | 344.19 | 441.05 | murderers | 216.14 | 649.11 |
| 714.01 | 347.17 | 443.05 | 377.02 | 220.21 | 654.11 |
| 716.14 | 348.05 | 451.20 | murderess | 231.08 | 654.18 |
| 716.20 | 351.03 | 454.01 | 317.02 | 233.19 | 663.19 |
| 717.08 | 353.15 | 460.09 | murderous | 238.10 | 677.14 |
| 718.03 | 355.06 | 461.16 | 389.19 | 244.20 | 684.21 |
| 718.17 | 360.10 | 464.14 | murmur | 250.12 | 691.17 |
| 721.01 | 372.12 | 473.03 | 271.07 | 255.18 | 698.08 |
| 724.20 | 378.01 | 475.17 | 353.04 | 263.08 | 700.06 |
| 725.15 | 383.09 | 493.14 | 743.16 | 265.02 | 701.21 |
| 728.05 | 395.08 | 504.14 | murmured | 280.13 | 706.19 |
| 728.17 | 409.07 | 516.09 | 033.11 | 282.05 | 709.04 |
| 732.15 | 417.13 | 520.22 | 216.01 | 284.12 | 709.16 |
| 735.05 | 424.02 | 536.20 | 275.07 | 288.16 | 712.21 |
| 736.02 | 424.11 | 539.19 | 428.10 | 293.12 | 719.05 |
| 737.20 | 429.05 | 543.02 | 464.22 | 306.07 | 724.09 |
| 741.21 | 436.11 | 548.15 | 489.17 | 306.10 | 739.02 |
| 742.14 | 502.12 | 556.21 | 533.01 | 307.15 | 742.03 |
| 744.06 | 525.16 | 562.06 | 540.01 | 309.09 | 744.03 |
| 744.10 | 527.08 | 570.16 | 542.15 | 309.10 | 751.18 |
| 745.03 | 575.03 | 576.06 | 594.05 | 313.15 | 753.09 |
| 747.06 | 609.14 | 592.11 | 600.03 | 314.21 | 754.03 |
| 748.07 | 612.21 | 592.12 | 635.14 | 315.01 | 755.07 |
| 750.15 | 626.08 | 594.22 | 639.20 | 330.05 | 757.09 |
| 752.11 | 627.03 | 600.05 | 676.14 | 331.19 | mustered |
| 753.10 | 641.11 | 620.04 | 711.02 | 333.20 | 147.16 |
| 753.21 | 645.03 | 630.07 | murmuring | 334.01 | mustering |
| 756.17 | 649.06 | 670.03 | 756.15 | 338.04 | 131.10 |
| 757.15 | 656.13 | 672.18 | murthering | 338.05 | mustn't |
| 762.13 | 658.05 | 700.02 | 401.09 | 342.17 | 385.03 |
| mrs | 659.14 | 708.09 | muscles | 343.14 | 396.02 |
| 017.16 | 661.02 | 717.06 | 025.18 | 345.11 | 482.20 |

| | | | | | |
|---|---|---|---|---|---|
| 519.17 | 026.02 | 072.16 | 182.18 | 277.09 | 338.15 |
| 555.05 | 026.08 | 072.17 | 183.02 | 279.02 | 338.18 |
| 563.12 | 026.11 | 074.14 | 183.04 | 279.04 | 339.02 |
| 570.13 | 026.13 | 075.01 | 183.08 | 279.06 | 340.12 |
| musty | 026.14 | 075.04 | 183.10 | 279.11 | 340.15 |
| 039.19 | 026.16 | 075.15 | 183.14 | 279.19 | 342.01 |
| mute | 026.20 | 076.06 | 184.07 | 281.01 | 342.17 |
| 017.14 | 027.01 | 076.08 | 186.14 | 281.06 | 343.09 |
| 094.03 | 027.06 | 077.20 | 187.03 | 281.07 | 343.13 |
| 159.01 | 028.10 | 079.05 | 189.14 | 281.08 | 343.16 |
| 677.02 | 030.16 | 080.08 | 189.18 | 281.11 | 344.09 |
| mutely | 030.21 | 080.13 | 195.01 | 281.15 | 344.17 |
| 514.02 | 031.13 | 080.22 | 198.20 | 281.17 | 345.03 |
| mutsn't | 031.14 | 081.06 | 202.05 | 281.22 | 345.13 |
| 543.09 | 032.14 | 082.08 | 203.03 | 282.02 | 346.08 |
| mutter | 032.17 | 083.01 | 203.17 | 282.09 | 346.10 |
| 210.02 | 034.07 | 083.05 | 203.22 | 282.13 | 346.12 |
| muttered | 034.11 | 084.01 | 204.06 | 283.01 | 346.18 |
| 011.21 | 034.14 | 085.03 | 205.04 | 284.05 | 347.01 |
| 016.16 | 035.05 | 085.06 | 206.11 | 285.08 | 347.05 |
| 026.07 | 035.11 | 093.03 | 206.14 | 285.09 | 347.08 |
| 033.21 | 036.04 | 095.01 | 206.15 | 285.19 | 347.14 |
| 051.19 | 036.13 | 095.04 | 206.20 | 286.15 | 347.15 |
| 054.06 | 038.01 | 101.14 | 207.21 | 287.13 | 347.20 |
| 059.19 | 038.15 | 101.15 | 208.18 | 287.14 | 348.09 |
| 154.02 | 038.18 | 101.21 | 209.20 | 288.07 | 349.04 |
| 280.13 | 039.04 | 102.12 | 209.21 | 289.17 | 350.02 |
| 318.09 | 039.07 | 105.10 | 210.01 | 290.06 | 350.05 |
| 420.07 | 039.11 | 106.19 | 212.01 | 290.14 | 350.07 |
| 421.05 | 039.17 | 108.01 | 212.17 | 290.20 | 350.08 |
| 438.09 | 040.14 | 108.07 | 213.06 | 291.01 | 350.19 |
| 444.11 | 040.20 | 108.19 | 213.20 | 291.03 | 350.20 |
| 490.02 | 041.17 | 109.10 | 214.09 | 291.16 | 354.14 |
| 525.15 | 042.18 | 109.20 | 216.06 | 291.22 | 355.11 |
| 539.06 | 042.19 | 110.04 | 216.09 | 293.11 | 356.01 |
| 547.08 | 043.10 | 110.10 | 217.21 | 293.13 | 356.08 |
| 554.04 | 044.11 | 110.11 | 218.02 | 294.14 | 356.19 |
| 604.14 | 045.04 | 110.15 | 218.03 | 295.05 | 357.16 |
| 617.05 | 045.18 | 112.03 | 218.03 | 295.14 | 358.21 |
| 652.12 | 046.04 | 118.14 | 218.08 | 295.17 | 359.04 |
| 671.04 | 046.13 | 119.17 | 221.16 | 296.11 | 359.19 |
| 683.21 | 046.14 | 119.22 | 222.12 | 299.09 | 360.01 |
| 686.02 | 046.17 | 120.06 | 222.19 | 299.10 | 360.18 |
| 703.05 | 047.03 | 125.09 | 223.17 | 299.19 | 360.19 |
| 711.06 | 047.12 | 126.01 | 225.01 | 306.08 | 362.01 |
| 718.13 | 048.03 | 126.18 | 230.11 | 306.13 | 362.02 |
| 723.07 | 048.18 | 127.13 | 230.14 | 306.21 | 362.04 |
| 742.06 | 049.10 | 129.03 | 231.10 | 307.11 | 362.09 |
| 745.22 | 049.13 | 129.06 | 234.04 | 307.19 | 362.11 |
| 750.18 | 050.01 | 129.12 | 235.09 | 307.22 | 363.01 |
| muttering | 050.10 | 132.21 | 235.21 | 308.03 | 364.03 |
| 168.22 | 050.19 | 133.10 | 236.01 | 308.07 | 364.16 |
| 310.09 | 051.03 | 133.14 | 236.21 | 308.16 | 366.05 |
| 343.02 | 051.20 | 137.02 | 237.09 | 309.15 | 366.08 |
| 401.04 | 052.01 | 137.03 | 239.04 | 309.18 | 366.10 |
| 734.17 | 052.04 | 138.07 | 240.13 | 309.20 | 366.11 |
| mutton | 052.13 | 139.02 | 241.04 | 310.04 | 366.19 |
| 006.08 | 053.05 | 140.10 | 242.04 | 310.20 | 366.21 |
| mutual | 053.21 | 140.10 | 242.05 | 311.14 | 369.11 |
| 007.20 | 053.22 | 141.13 | 242.11 | 312.04 | 371.02 |
| 104.20 | 054.05 | 143.18 | 243.01 | 312.18 | 372.22 |
| 204.13 | 054.10 | 144.07 | 243.02 | 313.03 | 372.22 |
| 215.08 | 054.15 | 145.17 | 243.14 | 313.07 | 374.01 |
| 407.04 | 055.06 | 146.10 | 243.21 | 313.10 | 374.16 |
| 441.06 | 055.10 | 148.15 | 244.04 | 313.19 | 374.16 |
| my | 055.21 | 152.18 | 244.17 | 314.05 | 375.06 |
| 001.04 | 056.02 | 152.18 | 244.20 | 314.18 | 376.19 |
| 001.12 | 057.06 | 153.19 | 245.02 | 316.01 | 376.20 |
| 002.04 | 057.07 | 155.03 | 245.12 | 316.09 | 377.07 |
| 002.10 | 057.13 | 155.15 | 245.21 | 318.05 | 377.07 |
| 002.11 | 057.22 | 155.20 | 246.01 | 318.13 | 377.17 |
| 002.15 | 058.04 | 155.22 | 246.05 | 319.05 | 377.22 |
| 003.05 | 058.06 | 156.02 | 248.08 | 320.08 | 378.13 |
| 003.20 | 058.10 | 156.08 | 248.12 | 320.17 | 382.01 |
| 003.20 | 058.19 | 157.09 | 249.14 | 320.20 | 382.05 |
| 004.02 | 058.20 | 157.20 | 250.04 | 321.13 | 382.10 |
| 005.06 | 059.05 | 163.06 | 250.07 | 322.13 | 382.10 |
| 008.02 | 059.09 | 163.21 | 251.01 | 322.14 | 383.07 |
| 008.06 | 059.14 | 163.21 | 251.15 | 323.15 | 384.01 |
| 008.07 | 060.08 | 164.16 | 253.01 | 323.18 | 384.03 |
| 008.14 | 060.14 | 165.14 | 253.05 | 323.18 | 384.11 |
| 008.15 | 060.19 | 166.15 | 253.08 | 323.19 | 384.13 |
| 009.09 | 060.21 | 166.15 | 257.09 | 324.06 | 384.20 |
| 009.13 | 061.02 | 167.21 | 257.12 | 324.08 | 386.04 |
| 009.15 | 061.04 | 168.01 | 258.04 | 324.08 | 386.06 |
| 010.07 | 061.08 | 169.09 | 259.12 | 325.05 | 386.21 |
| 010.13 | 062.03 | 169.15 | 259.13 | 325.05 | 387.10 |
| 010.15 | 062.12 | 170.09 | 259.18 | 325.11 | 388.06 |
| 010.20 | 062.21 | 170.13 | 260.11 | 325.16 | 388.08 |
| 012.11 | 063.01 | 171.10 | 261.12 | 325.19 | 388.09 |
| 012.17 | 063.06 | 173.11 | 261.16 | 326.16 | 388.17 |
| 013.02 | 064.09 | 175.03 | 261.19 | 326.20 | 389.01 |
| 013.10 | 064.11 | 176.06 | 262.06 | 327.05 | 389.02 |
| 013.16 | 064.13 | 176.06 | 263.01 | 327.07 | 389.21 |
| 014.03 | 065.10 | 176.10 | 263.02 | 327.11 | 392.07 |
| 014.10 | 065.16 | 176.20 | 263.09 | 329.03 | 392.14 |
| 015.05 | 066.03 | 176.22 | 265.01 | 329.10 | 392.15 |
| 015.15 | 066.03 | 177.02 | 265.07 | 329.16 | 392.18 |
| 015.20 | 066.14 | 178.17 | 266.13 | 331.06 | 392.20 |
| 018.08 | 067.01 | 178.20 | 267.02 | 331.08 | 393.09 |
| 019.01 | 067.08 | 178.20 | 270.01 | 331.18 | 393.22 |
| 019.16 | 067.13 | 179.03 | 270.04 | 333.18 | 393.22 |
| 021.15 | 067.18 | 179.17 | 270.06 | 334.01 | 394.10 |
| 022.13 | 067.20 | 179.22 | 270.07 | 334.13 | 394.11 |
| 023.10 | 068.02 | 180.13 | 271.11 | 334.15 | 395.13 |
| 024.02 | 068.05 | 181.16 | 272.07 | 335.14 | 395.20 |
| 024.05 | 069.04 | 181.22 | 272.19 | 335.15 | 396.01 |
| 025.01 | 069.09 | 182.08 | 273.13 | 335.21 | 396.04 |
| 025.11 | 069.11 | 182.11 | 274.19 | 336.17 | 396.10 |
| 025.14 | 071.01 | 182.15 | 275.01 | 337.07 | 397.03 |
| 025.15 | 072.09 | 182.16 | 276.02 | | 397.05 |

| | | | | | |
|---|---|---|---|---|---|
| 397.06 | 497.10 | 568.18 | 650.17 | 724.18 | 315.12 |
| 397.11 | 498.17 | 569.13 | 652.01 | 726.16 | 318.07 |
| 397.22 | 498.21 | 569.22 | 652.05 | 726.19 | 320.17 |
| 399.01 | 499.09 | 570.18 | 652.06 | 727.08 | 324.07 |
| 399.02 | 499.09 | 571.11 | 652.08 | 729.09 | 325.06 |
| 399.10 | 499.16 | 572.04 | 652.15 | 729.12 | 326.16 |
| 400.17 | 500.05 | 573.04 | 653.01 | 729.14 | 347.16 |
| 401.17 | 500.13 | 573.07 | 653.03 | 729.19 | 382.18 |
| 402.04 | 501.01 | 573.11 | 653.12 | 730.06 | 384.10 |
| 402.12 | 501.10 | 573.18 | 653.13 | 731.01 | 385.08 |
| 402.18 | 502.04 | 576.04 | 653.15 | 731.04 | 386.04 |
| 403.07 | 506.01 | 576.07 | 653.19 | 731.11 | 395.02 |
| 403.10 | 506.07 | 576.08 | 654.03 | 731.19 | 398.16 |
| 404.01 | 507.12 | 576.21 | 654.14 | 732.04 | 409.04 |
| 404.07 | 507.14 | 578.06 | 654.19 | 732.04 | 410.11 |
| 404.18 | 507.16 | 578.08 | 655.01 | 732.05 | 414.16 |
| 405.18 | 507.18 | 578.17 | 656.09 | 732.05 | 417.18 |
| 406.05 | 507.19 | 578.19 | 656.16 | 732.05 | 432.12 |
| 406.08 | 508.20 | 579.12 | 656.18 | 732.06 | 454.09 |
| 407.10 | 509.13 | 580.20 | 658.11 | 732.18 | 466.13 |
| 408.12 | 509.21 | 581.09 | 659.07 | 733.14 | 493.16 |
| 409.16 | 511.01 | 581.14 | 661.07 | 733.18 | 504.08 |
| 409.16 | 512.07 | 582.12 | 661.11 | 733.21 | 520.02 |
| 410.03 | 512.21 | 583.01 | 661.13 | 734.05 | 521.16 |
| 410.20 | 513.01 | 583.03 | 661.14 | 734.09 | 521.20 |
| 411.07 | 514.04 | 583.07 | 662.03 | 734.12 | 532.19 |
| 412.16 | 515.10 | 583.17 | 667.04 | 737.08 | 552.10 |
| 414.22 | 516.11 | 583.17 | 667.12 | 737.09 | 553.13 |
| 415.13 | 516.12 | 586.09 | 667.13 | 737.17 | 555.09 |
| 416.02 | 516.20 | 589.15 | 670.10 | 740.05 | 560.01 |
| 416.06 | 517.01 | 589.18 | 671.03 | 740.09 | 569.18 |
| 417.01 | 517.13 | 590.05 | 671.03 | 742.21 | 570.20 |
| 417.14 | 518.10 | 590.10 | 671.12 | 742.21 | 578.09 |
| 418.04 | 519.16 | 590.11 | 671.22 | 744.10 | 597.21 |
| 418.05 | 520.03 | 590.12 | 672.06 | 746.03 | 607.21 |
| 419.09 | 520.10 | 591.15 | 672.13 | 747.01 | 608.11 |
| 420.13 | 521.12 | 593.06 | 673.03 | 747.06 | 617.15 |
| 421.06 | 521.14 | 595.03 | 673.09 | 748.13 | 618.02 |
| 421.21 | 522.04 | 597.10 | 674.07 | 749.13 | 621.19 |
| 422.02 | 523.05 | 598.15 | 674.18 | 750.13 | 623.08 |
| 422.07 | 523.05 | 599.17 | 675.17 | 752.08 | 631.19 |
| 424.04 | 523.11 | 599.19 | 675.18 | 752.08 | 635.07 |
| 424.04 | 523.19 | 599.22 | 677.05 | 753.04 | 638.09 |
| 428.12 | 524.06 | 600.03 | 678.01 | 753.11 | 638.14 |
| 430.03 | 525.20 | 600.08 | 678.06 | 753.14 | 650.08 |
| 430.06 | 525.21 | 600.17 | 678.18 | 753.14 | 651.22 |
| 430.09 | 526.02 | 601.08 | 678.19 | 754.18 | 661.09 |
| 430.12 | 526.08 | 601.14 | 678.20 | 754.21 | 662.01 |
| 431.12 | 527.15 | 602.07 | 680.17 | 756.09 | 683.20 |
| 432.03 | 527.15 | 602.19 | 681.02 | 757.05 | 689.12 |
| 433.16 | 528.12 | 603.01 | 681.05 | 758.03 | 700.14 |
| 434.12 | 529.01 | 603.07 | 683.16 | 758.10 | 714.06 |
| 435.02 | 529.07 | 603.13 | 684.13 | 759.04 | 729.11 |
| 435.07 | 530.05 | 606.13 | 684.18 | 761.06 | 729.16 |
| 436.09 | 531.08 | 606.14 | 685.07 | 763.07 | 733.20 |
| 436.18 | 532.11 | 606.18 | 685.12 | 763.14 | 740.01 |
| 437.13 | 533.12 | 607.14 | 685.12 | **myself** | 742.11 |
| 438.17 | 535.01 | 611.15 | 686.15 | 002.09 | 744.21 |
| 438.20 | 535.06 | 613.03 | 686.16 | 003.04 | 745.15 |
| 439.04 | 536.01 | 613.18 | 686.17 | 008.10 | 746.02 |
| 440.02 | 536.02 | 615.07 | 688.04 | 008.21 | 756.07 |
| 440.09 | 536.06 | 615.08 | 688.07 | 013.18 | 761.19 |
| 440.14 | 537.03 | 616.05 | 689.01 | 020.02 | **mysteries** |
| 440.14 | 537.12 | 616.21 | 689.10 | 024.12 | 446.01 |
| 440.15 | 541.04 | 617.20 | 689.12 | 035.10 | **mysterious** |
| 441.01 | 541.15 | 618.06 | 689.14 | 037.12 | 507.13 |
| 441.03 | 543.08 | 618.18 | 691.14 | 039.10 | **mystery** |
| 445.05 | 544.12 | 619.12 | 692.05 | 041.10 | 602.17 |
| 445.10 | 545.10 | 620.12 | 692.06 | 048.18 | **n't** |
| 446.22 | 546.11 | 620.17 | 692.16 | 052.09 | 190.16 |
| 447.03 | 547.03 | 620.22 | 693.06 | 055.20 | 691.10 |
| 448.03 | 547.14 | 621.16 | 693.08 | 057.15 | **na** |
| 449.20 | 547.17 | 622.18 | 695.05 | 061.14 | 531.11 |
| 451.01 | 547.22 | 623.06 | 695.18 | 067.05 | 531.12 |
| 453.06 | 548.03 | 623.09 | 696.01 | 069.03 | **nab** |
| 456.06 | 548.04 | 623.11 | 696.07 | 071.02 | 482.16 |
| 456.12 | 548.09 | 623.13 | 697.22 | 097.19 | 593.07 |
| 457.16 | 550.03 | 624.02 | 700.01 | 100.20 | 761.09 |
| 459.08 | 550.04 | 624.16 | 700.04 | 117.15 | **nah** |
| 460.12 | 550.06 | 628.12 | 700.07 | 118.17 | 326.10 |
| 462.11 | 550.09 | 628.17 | 701.09 | 130.09 | 400.20 |
| 464.01 | 551.21 | 629.04 | 705.14 | 135.11 | 400.21 |
| 464.16 | 552.10 | 629.05 | 705.22 | 137.15 | 457.23 |
| 466.13 | 552.17 | 629.07 | 706.06 | 158.06 | 560.19 |
| 467.06 | 553.11 | 630.02 | 706.21 | 159.12 | 688.10 |
| 467.17 | 553.16 | 630.04 | 707.08 | 170.21 | 719.17 |
| 468.03 | 554.12 | 631.21 | 708.17 | 179.11 | **nails** |
| 468.18 | 555.13 | 633.16 | 709.12 | 182.11 | 055.14 |
| 469.15 | 555.19 | 633.19 | 710.12 | 183.09 | 238.01 |
| 469.19 | 556.01 | 634.21 | 710.15 | 186.19 | 609.19 |
| 470.01 | 556.06 | 635.01 | 711.07 | 191.11 | **naked** |
| 470.01 | 556.08 | 636.05 | 711.12 | 200.06 | 321.18 |
| 473.11 | 559.15 | 636.12 | 712.17 | 204.05 | **name** |
| 477.07 | 559.18 | 637.03 | 712.22 | 209.01 | 002.05 |
| 478.07 | 559.18 | 637.18 | 713.18 | 212.13 | 004.03 |
| 478.16 | 560.02 | 638.07 | 714.03 | 216.08 | 005.02 |
| 479.09 | 560.05 | 638.16 | 715.06 | 235.07 | 026.20 |
| 479.11 | 560.09 | 638.17 | 717.06 | 252.21 | 029.14 |
| 479.16 | 561.11 | 638.19 | 718.07 | 270.21 | 038.22 |
| 479.16 | 561.15 | 639.03 | 719.10 | 273.12 | 039.11 |
| 482.11 | 563.01 | 640.18 | 719.13 | 278.06 | 057.05 |
| 482.17 | 563.15 | 641.07 | 719.13 | 280.03 | 057.16 |
| 483.13 | 564.21 | 643.02 | 719.16 | 281.13 | 072.10 |
| 484.13 | 567.01 | 644.03 | 719.18 | 283.03 | 072.17 |
| 484.18 | 567.01 | 644.03 | 720.01 | 283.10 | 080.15 |
| 485.13 | 567.02 | 644.04 | 720.02 | 284.18 | 094.08 |
| 487.19 | 567.07 | 645.16 | 720.15 | 289.03 | 096.08 |
| 490.01 | 567.18 | 646.04 | 721.20 | 305.03 | 206.20 |
| 491.15 | 567.21 | 646.11 | 722.01 | 307.20 | 270.08 |
| 493.12 | 568.13 | 646.19 | 722.21 | 313.15 | 274.06 |
| 496.22 | 568.16 | 650.16 | | | 288.04 |

| | | | | | |
|---|---|---|---|---|---|
| 299.19 | 488.09 | 121.04 | needless | 598.01 | 418.08 |
| 311.14 | 505.15 | 138.11 | 329.10 | 623.03 | 448.06 |
| 340.13 | 505.16 | 141.21 | 384.07 | 634.16 | 491.16 |
| 345.13 | 510.21 | 177.14 | needn't | 676.21 | 576.21 |
| 354.16 | 537.06 | 184.10 | 118.03 | 693.05 | 581.10 |
| 375.03 | 612.04 | 199.01 | 143.02 | 702.03 | 597.16 |
| 390.12 | 634.08 | 209.10 | 163.08 | 728.01 | 636.13 |
| 412.04 | 702.19 | 210.20 | 208.07 | 732.17 | nephew's |
| 414.07 | nausea | 261.14 | 220.14 | 733.12 | 574.07 |
| 426.13 | 039.16 | 291.06 | 251.06 | 740.08 | 595.04 |
| 444.06 | nave | 303.01 | 331.15 | 743.01 | nephews |
| 468.02 | 319.09 | 335.06 | 396.07 | 755.19 | 239.19 |
| 486.19 | nay | 335.09 | 440.21 | 761.11 | nerve |
| 525.21 | 003.16 | 390.16 | 469.12 | nell | 755.19 |
| 559.03 | 060.02 | 404.13 | 511.10 | 141.21 | nerveless |
| 561.02 | 092.08 | 450.15 | 547.01 | 164.05 | 601.02 |
| 561.21 | 127.09 | 516.02 | 557.02 | 469.18 | nerves |
| 593.02 | 142.20 | 517.22 | 600.13 | nelly | 075.04 |
| 635.14 | 168.06 | 564.06 | 616.12 | 102.13 | 301.09 |
| 644.12 | 174.07 | 566.21 | 627.08 | 103.11 | 344.22 |
| 750.20 | 190.20 | 569.09 | 662.02 | 106.12 | 375.14 |
| named | 190.20 | 572.07 | 665.09 | 110.07 | 389.15 |
| 076.13 | 208.15 | 588.04 | 750.01 | 111.19 | 646.05 |
| 236.18 | 216.10 | 636.13 | needs | 122.07 | 654.03 |
| 414.06 | 235.08 | 718.20 | 041.05 | 123.20 | 752.14 |
| nameless | 246.22 | 754.21 | neeght | 140.05 | nervous |
| 225.14 | 320.12 | neat | 016.12 | 152.17 | 258.16 |
| names | 333.01 | 020.05 | 187.21 | 155.02 | nervously |
| 103.06 | 359.21 | neatly | 319.08 | 163.07 | 180.04 |
| 210.19 | 407.14 | 522.18 | 696.07 | 167.17 | nervousness |
| 397.10 | 436.10 | 710.02 | neglect | 169.22 | 718.05 |
| nap | 438.03 | necessarily | 033.10 | 171.08 | nest |
| 218.02 | 493.06 | 149.21 | 120.03 | 172.10 | 275.16 |
| narrative | 624.18 | necessary | 135.20 | 173.21 | 275.19 |
| 200.06 | 690.20 | 048.10 | 330.09 | 176.16 | 373.20 |
| 243.02 | 708.05 | 066.15 | 370.08 | 177.15 | 490.17 |
| narrator | 711.09 | 088.09 | 659.06 | 178.06 | 510.02 |
| 349.08 | 720.15 | 183.07 | 755.08 | 179.10 | nesting |
| narrow | 741.03 | 293.10 | neglected | 181.17 | 518.12 |
| 004.16 | nb | 384.16 | 226.19 | 183.07 | nests |
| 060.06 | 014.06 | 691.21 | 442.12 | 186.13 | 479.03 |
| 287.13 | near | necessities | 548.11 | 193.19 | 481.02 |
| 443.06 | 017.07 | 069.01 | 631.09 | 206.16 | neutralized |
| 612.10 | 038.04 | necessity | neglecting | 208.07 | 027.10 |
| 622.22 | 047.14 | 038.09 | 293.13 | 210.07 | never |
| 700.20 | 054.16 | 325.04 | negligence | 219.09 | 006.04 |
| narrow-minded | 071.17 | 333.08 | 007.13 | 220.08 | 008.08 |
| 659.04 | 088.11 | 386.01 | 446.22 | 223.05 | 008.15 |
| nasty | 093.04 | 472.18 | negligent | 229.10 | 017.10 |
| 156.09 | 145.03 | 518.07 | 100.01 | 232.09 | 017.20 |
| 720.09 | 153.02 | neck | 532.05 | 235.09 | 033.17 |
| native | 157.08 | 019.14 | negotiated | 245.03 | 035.21 |
| 071.05 | 188.14 | 036.04 | 556.01 | 245.03 | 037.06 |
| natural | 191.20 | 067.06 | negus | 245.07 | 046.19 |
| 114.12 | 205.10 | 085.05 | 111.05 | 247.17 | 048.14 |
| 115.18 | 243.17 | 094.17 | neighbourhood | 249.13 | 053.10 |
| 165.20 | 254.13 | 128.08 | 689.13 | 261.14 | 058.07 |
| 351.08 | 276.16 | 143.15 | neighbour | 261.20 | 077.19 |
| 370.02 | 284.01 | 163.02 | 001.04 | 262.06 | 081.01 |
| 419.02 | 317.12 | 164.21 | 025.11 | 272.12 | 083.07 |
| 508.06 | 332.09 | 195.02 | 026.02 | 273.15 | 088.21 |
| 570.19 | 342.14 | 211.14 | 050.16 | 276.02 | 090.07 |
| 583.08 | 361.10 | 267.01 | 109.20 | 276.11 | 091.16 |
| 618.20 | 404.04 | 351.09 | neighbour's | 277.19 | 095.13 |
| naturally | 411.09 | 362.15 | 132.22 | 281.04 | 096.07 |
| 120.04 | 433.08 | 379.06 | 233.08 | 282.16 | 102.09 |
| 150.03 | 444.17 | 383.16 | 239.22 | 290.05 | 121.01 |
| 464.08 | 479.08 | 384.12 | 239.23 | 290.06 | 124.15 |
| 759.13 | 479.14 | 554.12 | 349.04 | 292.08 | 132.01 |
| nature | 500.17 | 560.06 | neighbourhood | 331.14 | 133.05 |
| 023.01 | 506.17 | 632.21 | 173.17 | 335.10 | 142.19 |
| 035.13 | 531.03 | 638.17 | 335.16 | 340.11 | 143.06 |
| 108.11 | 540.06 | 669.07 | 411.05 | 342.12 | 143.20 |
| 128.02 | 557.04 | 703.06 | 422.20 | 343.14 | 145.11 |
| 147.14 | 603.02 | neckerchief | 463.14 | 360.15 | 148.03 |
| 219.01 | 603.07 | 311.06 | 500.17 | 361.05 | 151.21 |
| 258.05 | 615.17 | need | 617.01 | 368.06 | 153.18 |
| 288.19 | 616.12 | 003.22 | 695.19 | 416.03 | 156.14 |
| 289.06 | 639.12 | 047.02 | 760.02 | 466.11 | 163.22 |
| 307.05 | 646.07 | 049.05 | neighbours | 467.05 | 176.16 |
| 388.12 | 669.13 | 059.14 | 074.14 | 469.01 | 179.09 |
| 412.21 | 703.11 | 095.15 | 089.15 | 472.12 | 181.18 |
| 442.17 | 737.06 | 121.05 | 096.03 | 483.08 | 193.17 |
| 503.04 | 737.18 | 134.10 | 488.01 | 483.11 | 194.18 |
| 571.11 | 748.02 | 143.04 | neither | 490.01 | 195.07 |
| 571.20 | 760.14 | 194.20 | 026.11 | 493.06 | 195.10 |
| 647.22 | neared | 201.08 | 096.07 | 526.13 | 195.17 |
| 671.13 | 522.03 | 211.20 | 144.01 | 603.08 | 197.05 |
| 726.22 | nearer | 213.01 | 147.15 | 606.09 | 202.13 |
| naught | 075.01 | 235.03 | 192.18 | 607.16 | 205.02 |
| 088.21 | 108.16 | 258.11 | 203.18 | 627.16 | 205.15 |
| 246.17 | 207.04 | 306.18 | 204.16 | 627.22 | 211.18 |
| 298.09 | 244.13 | 354.19 | 217.06 | 650.07 | 215.20 |
| 441.19 | 349.03 | 416.13 | 253.22 | 696.02 | 217.06 |
| 476.09 | 373.06 | 521.01 | 264.12 | 698.03 | 219.05 |
| 669.20 | 418.08 | 573.04 | 271.18 | 720.06 | 230.02 |
| 683.17 | 480.19 | 649.08 | 355.20 | 720.08 | 231.20 |
| 683.17 | 690.03 | 656.06 | 371.14 | 720.09 | 233.15 |
| 707.10 | 717.02 | 673.12 | 379.18 | 724.16 | 248.14 |
| naughtiness | 747.16 | 752.20 | 393.04 | 730.04 | 260.07 |
| 462.08 | nearest | 754.19 | 394.18 | 733.09 | 262.14 |
| naughty | 034.04 | 754.19 | 403.16 | 740.08 | 262.15 |
| 091.16 | 050.10 | needed | 420.18 | 742.07 | 266.16 |
| 100.19 | 325.21 | 548.18 | 432.08 | 751.09 | 267.09 |
| 119.10 | 362.04 | 587.07 | 481.06 | 754.12 | 269.05 |
| 156.20 | 583.04 | needful | 512.15 | 762.13 | 271.09 |
| 192.09 | nearly | 152.02 | 527.12 | nelly's | 273.13 |
| 227.09 | 061.13 | 664.03 | 533.08 | 696.10 | 275.22 |
| 432.05 | 077.14 | needles | 541.05 | nephew | 277.08 |
| 435.05 | 087.07 | 104.16 | 544.19 | 073.01 | 284.03 |
| 435.05 | 104.21 | | 568.19 | 309.08 | 284.21 |

| | | | | | |
|---|---|---|---|---|---|
| 286.10 | 749.09 | 632.15 | 378.08 | 173.08 | 370.22 |
| 287.11 | 752.14 | 666.02 | 540.07 | 174.08 | 371.12 |
| 296.12 | 753.10 | nicely | 540.10 | 174.18 | 372.16 |
| 303.12 | never | 129.17 | 578.07 | 177.16 | 373.21 |
| 307.22 | 477.01 | 492.14 | 625.01 | 179.04 | 378.10 |
| 329.02 | nevertheless | 568.15 | nimbly | 179.21 | 379.13 |
| 330.03 | 051.19 | nicer | 522.15 | 180.15 | 383.10 |
| 330.21 | 135.08 | 428.07 | nine | 180.17 | 384.10 |
| 332.21 | new | 588.06 | 059.04 | 181.08 | 388.11 |
| 334.01 | 002.08 | nicest | 121.14 | 183.21 | 388.11 |
| 334.15 | 047.03 | 563.15 | 314.05 | 184.02 | 389.01 |
| 334.17 | 099.05 | nicety | 622.16 | 184.19 | 389.08 |
| 339.19 | 118.13 | 320.01 | 690.15 | 184.20 | 392.08 |
| 340.12 | 120.13 | nick | ninety | 185.10 | 393.05 |
| 345.13 | 121.17 | 044.05 | 048.06 | 186.20 | 394.05 |
| 345.14 | 225.04 | nigh | 049.08 | 188.12 | 396.04 |
| 348.04 | 252.10 | 318.16 | ninety-first | 190.13 | 400.15 |
| 352.09 | 307.19 | night | 049.13 | 194.16 | 406.08 |
| 359.16 | 319.16 | 027.17 | ninny | 196.12 | 411.19 |
| 359.21 | 322.04 | 028.06 | 490.03 | 199.10 | 412.16 |
| 360.17 | 335.07 | 031.14 | nip | 199.11 | 415.06 |
| 362.01 | 360.11 | 046.09 | 156.10 | 199.18 | 416.16 |
| 364.19 | 392.20 | 056.09 | 194.07 | 204.13 | 422.09 |
| 369.05 | 411.08 | 057.11 | 416.12 | 205.10 | 426.12 |
| 371.03 | 449.02 | 058.21 | niver | 207.09 | 427.03 |
| 376.07 | 454.06 | 067.16 | 029.01 | 207.09 | 429.22 |
| 379.13 | 462.22 | 090.01 | 190.21 | 208.05 | 433.08 |
| 392.05 | 466.01 | 090.01 | 232.21 | 208.16 | 434.09 |
| 393.14 | 503.04 | 092.07 | 318.15 | 211.20 | 434.09 |
| 397.12 | 534.17 | 101.12 | 565.15 | 212.10 | 435.13 |
| 405.04 | 656.14 | 121.12 | 720.11 | 214.03 | 436.04 |
| 411.04 | 700.04 | 122.21 | nivir | 217.13 | 441.06 |
| 414.06 | 720.01 | 135.10 | 471.14 | 220.09 | 442.17 |
| 414.07 | 725.06 | 140.06 | no | 222.17 | 449.03 |
| 415.20 | 742.12 | 143.10 | 002.22 | 223.12 | 450.05 |
| 425.11 | 762.04 | 158.19 | 003.13 | 224.04 | 453.05 |
| 425.12 | newly | 169.17 | 004.01 | 226.03 | 456.11 |
| 432.05 | 314.15 | 185.15 | 005.08 | 227.21 | 457.05 |
| 434.22 | 688.08 | 192.12 | 005.18 | 228.04 | 459.06 |
| 436.01 | news | 192.15 | 008.01 | 228.17 | 462.01 |
| 438.13 | 204.04 | 194.02 | 008.14 | 229.04 | 465.12 |
| 440.07 | 236.21 | 194.19 | 010.03 | 231.16 | 468.12 |
| 442.22 | 294.19 | 195.07 | 012.01 | 233.13 | 468.15 |
| 443.01 | 373.11 | 218.01 | 012.09 | 233.20 | 468.16 |
| 443.02 | 416.05 | 223.18 | 013.16 | 234.14 | 472.22 |
| 451.04 | 433.01 | 232.04 | 020.11 | 235.13 | 474.09 |
| 460.13 | 474.05 | 276.22 | 022.07 | 235.13 | 479.07 |
| 464.21 | 635.05 | 280.06 | 022.11 | 236.17 | 482.11 |
| 465.09 | 666.08 | 281.21 | 023.01 | 247.12 | 483.12 |
| 468.16 | 677.07 | 294.09 | 027.01 | 248.02 | 483.20 |
| 475.08 | 741.21 | 294.10 | 027.14 | 249.07 | 484.17 |
| 476.01 | 742.01 | 296.11 | 028.10 | 251.05 | 485.03 |
| 478.05 | next | 301.07 | 030.03 | 252.15 | 485.04 |
| 485.08 | 035.19 | 306.05 | 030.22 | 255.03 | 489.15 |
| 488.02 | 045.01 | 315.18 | 031.19 | 257.13 | 489.19 |
| 489.11 | 062.11 | 317.11 | 031.20 | 258.02 | 493.14 |
| 490.13 | 069.06 | 344.01 | 032.03 | 260.12 | 495.02 |
| 493.18 | 118.19 | 344.02 | 032.10 | 262.07 | 501.02 |
| 503.22 | 129.17 | 368.03 | 032.10 | 263.15 | 502.17 |
| 505.07 | 138.10 | 369.02 | 034.19 | 264.18 | 503.11 |
| 510.01 | 142.05 | 373.02 | 047.20 | 266.02 | 504.19 |
| 510.19 | 166.04 | 377.17 | 049.04 | 267.12 | 505.05 |
| 510.19 | 191.02 | 394.06 | 049.17 | 270.05 | 505.05 |
| 517.06 | 216.10 | 406.13 | 050.08 | 270.20 | 505.07 |
| 521.14 | 233.03 | 410.15 | 056.05 | 271.04 | 510.12 |
| 521.14 | 234.04 | 419.19 | 057.02 | 271.08 | 514.12 |
| 521.14 | 248.12 | 433.11 | 058.10 | 271.22 | 516.07 |
| 528.22 | 267.10 | 476.05 | 060.17 | 272.15 | 517.10 |
| 533.20 | 289.13 | 499.14 | 064.22 | 272.21 | 518.07 |
| 536.08 | 289.14 | 507.14 | 066.21 | 273.07 | 519.02 |
| 539.02 | 289.16 | 521.17 | 073.01 | 275.10 | 519.09 |
| 539.03 | 294.02 | 527.10 | 075.13 | 277.08 | 519.20 |
| 540.12 | 297.09 | 529.06 | 077.05 | 280.01 | 522.17 |
| 545.18 | 303.14 | 530.02 | 080.01 | 280.21 | 522.20 |
| 548.01 | 309.18 | 540.03 | 090.18 | 283.21 | 531.19 |
| 548.02 | 346.20 | 549.01 | 091.12 | 286.21 | 532.10 |
| 548.20 | 370.11 | 551.19 | 095.17 | 288.17 | 533.12 |
| 555.01 | 406.08 | 559.07 | 098.06 | 290.12 | 535.07 |
| 569.12 | 456.10 | 572.01 | 102.04 | 292.04 | 536.08 |
| 571.20 | 463.14 | 572.13 | 103.08 | 294.06 | 539.18 |
| 571.21 | 488.10 | 613.20 | 106.14 | 295.15 | 541.18 |
| 580.19 | 499.15 | 614.19 | 107.22 | 299.18 | 542.22 |
| 581.16 | 514.10 | 615.10 | 107.22 | 301.05 | 544.19 |
| 581.17 | 526.16 | 623.14 | 112.10 | 302.05 | 545.07 |
| 602.18 | 529.06 | 624.22 | 118.01 | 304.15 | 546.08 |
| 606.05 | 535.07 | 632.02 | 121.07 | 305.18 | 547.16 |
| 621.04 | 544.19 | 646.08 | 130.02 | 313.01 | 548.10 |
| 621.05 | 555.14 | 650.12 | 131.05 | 316.22 | 551.06 |
| 626.10 | 568.03 | 660.18 | 132.03 | 318.18 | 551.06 |
| 630.06 | 571.16 | 661.13 | 133.03 | 320.09 | 552.06 |
| 634.05 | 588.06 | 689.09 | 134.01 | 322.18 | 554.03 |
| 639.22 | 590.08 | 691.06 | 134.22 | 329.10 | 554.04 |
| 646.01 | 594.11 | 712.09 | 135.14 | 331.14 | 558.18 |
| 660.07 | 613.21 | 731.16 | 135.15 | 331.15 | 562.13 |
| 661.01 | 618.06 | 736.10 | 137.06 | 335.03 | 563.13 |
| 670.18 | 621.20 | 739.02 | 140.08 | 336.15 | 564.05 |
| 674.18 | 624.22 | 742.15 | 145.06 | 337.06 | 565.02 |
| 677.05 | 655.12 | 742.19 | 146.19 | 339.05 | 566.16 |
| 678.04 | 672.14 | 756.14 | 149.07 | 340.05 | 569.10 |
| 681.09 | 684.20 | 759.09 | 149.19 | 341.13 | 569.21 |
| 684.06 | 750.01 | 760.19 | 150.14 | 342.15 | 570.12 |
| 685.07 | 764.01 | night-walking | 151.06 | 343.03 | 574.04 |
| 695.04 | nice | 738.12 | 152.09 | 343.03 | 575.09 |
| 697.01 | 222.16 | nightmare | 154.01 | 343.17 | 579.13 |
| 698.21 | 322.10 | 052.03 | 155.01 | 345.17 | 580.01 |
| 702.12 | 337.19 | 055.07 | 156.09 | 346.12 | 580.05 |
| 710.09 | 439.12 | 061.02 | 158.16 | 351.14 | 581.04 |
| 721.21 | 463.15 | 241.04 | 160.04 | 352.23 | 583.12 |
| 727.16 | 505.01 | nights | 163.11 | 353.13 | 583.14 |
| 728.05 | 544.05 | 273.13 | 163.17 | 356.06 | 583.15 |
| 730.16 | 558.13 | 378.06 | 171.01 | 366.01 | 586.13 |

| | | | | | |
|---|---|---|---|---|---|
| 587.06 | nob´dy | 746.19 | northern | 095.20 | 180.17 |
| 589.07 | 298.16 | nonsense | 006.22 | 096.11 | 181.07 |
| 593.03 | 322.08 | 042.12 | 201.04 | 100.03 | 181.11 |
| 597.19 | 720.11 | 103.11 | nose | 100.21 | 181.11 |
| 599.12 | nobbut | 109.08 | 035.06 | 102.07 | 182.02 |
| 602.11 | 016.10 | 173.07 | 063.17 | 103.07 | 182.07 |
| 603.13 | 042.20 | 183.16 | 108.14 | 103.20 | 183.01 |
| 604.09 | 324.20 | 288.13 | 111.13 | 104.08 | 183.08 |
| 607.03 | 324.21 | 467.22 | 128.17 | 105.09 | 183.21 |
| 607.07 | nobility | 504.13 | 310.10 | 105.12 | 184.02 |
| 609.19 | 727.06 | 525.11 | 325.12 | 105.17 | 185.06 |
| 611.11 | noble | 542.05 | 472.02 | 106.13 | 185.18 |
| 613.07 | 647.16 | 600.10 | 531.12 | 107.07 | 186.04 |
| 613.13 | nobody | 704.07 | 667.13 | 108.10 | 188.09 |
| 614.19 | 016.08 | 718.01 | nostril | 111.18 | 190.10 |
| 615.13 | 071.14 | 745.18 | 728.10 | 112.15 | 192.16 |
| 618.05 | 078.07 | 761.16 | nostrils | 114.10 | 193.09 |
| 621.01 | 081.08 | nooin | 062.19 | 114.12 | 194.14 |
| 628.12 | 101.11 | 233.03 | 693.08 | 114.13 | 194.19 |
| 628.12 | 115.15 | nook | not | 115.04 | 194.20 |
| 629.15 | 145.02 | 044.07 | 001.06 | 115.19 | 196.06 |
| 632.06 | 151.08 | 392.15 | 002.11 | 116.05 | 197.19 |
| 636.06 | 207.02 | 518.16 | 002.16 | 117.09 | 198.09 |
| 640.19 | 262.21 | noon | 007.12 | 117.10 | 199.06 |
| 644.10 | 278.03 | 403.13 | 009.13 | 117.11 | 200.04 |
| 645.09 | 313.19 | 640.09 | 009.19 | 117.14 | 201.08 |
| 645.13 | 340.22 | 689.08 | 010.09 | 117.15 | 202.01 |
| 649.02 | 367.20 | 740.04 | 012.10 | 118.10 | 202.10 |
| 650.12 | 370.06 | nor | 014.09 | 120.12 | 204.01 |
| 651.19 | 376.08 | 005.20 | 014.09 | 122.02 | 204.11 |
| 652.17 | 396.09 | 045.08 | 015.20 | 123.08 | 205.05 |
| 655.01 | 435.18 | 096.08 | 018.12 | 124.21 | 205.07 |
| 656.06 | 469.13 | 144.01 | 019.03 | 127.09 | 206.03 |
| 656.13 | 506.03 | 147.15 | 021.01 | 127.10 | 207.14 |
| 661.04 | 533.14 | 204.17 | 022.11 | 128.03 | 207.14 |
| 665.16 | 540.05 | 217.07 | 023.11 | 128.21 | 207.15 |
| 667.12 | 542.05 | 232.16 | 023.18 | 129.11 | 208.07 |
| 671.06 | 572.16 | 232.16 | 024.20 | 130.11 | 209.01 |
| 671.12 | 593.08 | 253.22 | 025.11 | 130.17 | 210.06 |
| 671.14 | 594.03 | 264.12 | 025.18 | 133.18 | 210.12 |
| 672.04 | 625.02 | 270.05 | 026.08 | 134.22 | 210.16 |
| 674.05 | 629.01 | 270.06 | 026.15 | 135.05 | 210.18 |
| 677.07 | 634.16 | 296.11 | 027.22 | 135.12 | 213.01 |
| 677.15 | 648.04 | 310.17 | 029.12 | 136.07 | 215.04 |
| 677.18 | 648.09 | 327.02 | 030.06 | 137.16 | 215.09 |
| 678.14 | 648.09 | 327.03 | 031.15 | 137.22 | 215.16 |
| 680.10 | 650.07 | 335.19 | 032.11 | 138.01 | 216.02 |
| 680.21 | 660.05 | 335.19 | 032.18 | 140.15 | 216.10 |
| 681.21 | 664.22 | 355.20 | 033.13 | 142.07 | 217.10 |
| 684.21 | 665.01 | 371.14 | 035.09 | 142.08 | 218.10 |
| 685.13 | 678.16 | 379.20 | 035.15 | 142.16 | 219.04 |
| 685.13 | 698.10 | 385.22 | 037.03 | 142.17 | 219.05 |
| 686.05 | 742.10 | 393.04 | 037.08 | 143.04 | 219.22 |
| 691.19 | nod | 420.18 | 037.10 | 143.05 | 223.15 |
| 694.11 | 002.07 | 432.08 | 039.07 | 143.22 | 224.01 |
| 696.20 | 045.17 | 432.08 | 040.04 | 144.04 | 225.05 |
| 699.03 | nodded | 443.18 | 041.05 | 144.06 | 226.17 |
| 705.21 | 048.17 | 476.02 | 041.21 | 145.01 | 228.01 |
| 706.08 | 326.15 | 481.06 | 043.09 | 145.08 | 228.21 |
| 707.03 | 330.01 | 512.15 | 045.09 | 146.07 | 229.04 |
| 708.08 | nodding | 512.16 | 046.18 | 147.11 | 229.22 |
| 711.15 | 061.15 | 512.17 | 047.04 | 147.22 | 231.12 |
| 713.19 | 134.08 | 512.17 | 053.11 | 148.03 | 233.18 |
| 714.05 | 134.14 | 512.18 | 053.18 | 148.07 | 235.08 |
| 716.15 | noise | 512.21 | 053.22 | 148.09 | 236.06 |
| 717.03 | 037.04 | 527.12 | 054.08 | 148.20 | 236.09 |
| 718.22 | 041.21 | 533.08 | 054.14 | 150.19 | 237.02 |
| 720.05 | 056.11 | 541.06 | 055.21 | 151.09 | 237.22 |
| 728.08 | 098.03 | 544.19 | 056.15 | 151.13 | 238.16 |
| 732.10 | 101.05 | 568.19 | 056.17 | 151.15 | 239.16 |
| 732.13 | 165.07 | 578.16 | 058.03 | 152.14 | 240.17 |
| 733.07 | 186.18 | 583.13 | 058.18 | 154.18 | 244.21 |
| 733.09 | 297.10 | 598.02 | 059.01 | 155.17 | 245.08 |
| 733.12 | 366.20 | 599.02 | 059.14 | 156.01 | 245.11 |
| 735.02 | 378.22 | 634.16 | 064.16 | 156.05 | 245.15 |
| 738.09 | 616.11 | 636.04 | 065.11 | 156.10 | 247.10 |
| 739.05 | 662.08 | 668.15 | 065.20 | 157.17 | 248.05 |
| 741.11 | 758.14 | 676.21 | 070.05 | 158.12 | 248.18 |
| 743.07 | noiselessly | 691.09 | 070.11 | 158.17 | 251.05 |
| 745.11 | 179.18 | 693.05 | 071.07 | 158.18 | 251.07 |
| 746.10 | 553.07 | 702.04 | 071.12 | 159.03 | 252.16 |
| 751.15 | noises | 712.18 | 071.20 | 164.02 | 253.06 |
| 752.02 | 106.03 | 728.02 | 072.16 | 164.04 | 254.14 |
| 753.06 | noisily | 732.18 | 073.16 | 164.06 | 254.20 |
| 753.12 | 058.19 | 733.13 | 073.21 | 165.13 | 256.12 |
| 754.19 | noisy | 733.13 | 074.11 | 166.06 | 256.15 |
| 756.07 | 497.10 | 743.01 | 074.15 | 167.01 | 257.10 |
| 756.12 | none | 754.19 | 075.05 | 167.03 | 257.21 |
| 757.10 | 021.09 | 755.19 | 076.17 | 167.13 | 258.11 |
| 758.01 | 175.04 | 761.11 | 077.14 | 168.13 | 258.18 |
| 758.03 | 194.11 | nor-ne | 078.21 | 170.09 | 259.06 |
| 762.13 | 222.19 | 016.15 | 079.04 | 170.15 | 259.12 |
| no-where | 240.01 | north | 080.13 | 173.04 | 260.17 |
| 384.04 | 286.11 | 004.10 | 082.19 | 173.22 | 260.19 |
| noa | 314.21 | 243.08 | 083.09 | 174.18 | 261.11 |
| 016.15 | 374.06 | 461.05 | 084.15 | 175.06 | 262.18 |
| 028.22 | 374.08 | 546.18 | 084.19 | 175.14 | 263.06 |
| 320.12 | 442.18 | 652.02 | 086.05 | 175.20 | 263.21 |
| 457.18 | 467.22 | 688.03 | 088.05 | 176.10 | 264.11 |
| 457.20 | 495.03 | north-east | 088.13 | 177.03 | 265.03 |
| 457.21 | 520.06 | 427.22 | 090.11 | 177.16 | 266.03 |
| noah | 523.10 | northeast | 090.14 | 178.03 | 266.11 |
| 189.11 | 526.09 | 274.15 | 090.20 | 178.08 | 266.12 |
| noan | 552.07 | 381.04 | 091.07 | 178.11 | 267.17 |
| 188.01 | 573.04 | norther | 091.11 | 178.19 | 270.09 |
| 190.20 | 603.04 | 187.21 | 093.01 | 179.06 | 271.06 |
| 194.04 | 640.03 | 232.15 | 093.13 | 179.10 | 271.08 |
| 232.14 | 656.15 | 457.22 | 094.02 | 180.08 | 271.09 |
| 232.16 | 660.08 | 691.09 | 094.09 | 180.08 | 272.01 |
| 719.20 | 725.03 | 696.18 | 095.06 | 180.15 | 272.02 |
| 720.08 | 729.17 | 712.18 | 095.15 | 180.16 | 272.13 |

| | | | | | |
|---|---|---|---|---|---|
| 273.01 | 361.12 | 453.17 | 532.21 | 627.04 | 718.15 |
| 273.03 | 362.08 | 454.01 | 535.09 | 627.11 | 722.15 |
| 273.18 | 362.10 | 454.19 | 535.12 | 627.17 | 723.04 |
| 274.08 | 362.21 | 457.09 | 535.16 | 628.10 | 723.08 |
| 274.21 | 363.09 | 458.01 | 535.17 | 628.14 | 723.17 |
| 275.01 | 364.22 | 460.09 | 536.10 | 629.16 | 723.21 |
| 275.18 | 365.05 | 460.17 | 537.01 | 630.01 | 725.04 |
| 275.21 | 365.13 | 461.01 | 539.19 | 630.22 | 726.17 |
| 276.18 | 365.15 | 461.20 | 540.12 | 631.05 | 728.11 |
| 276.19 | 365.17 | 463.08 | 541.15 | 631.19 | 729.06 |
| 277.18 | 366.02 | 463.09 | 542.01 | 632.01 | 729.14 |
| 280.22 | 366.13 | 464.05 | 542.03 | 636.03 | 730.21 |
| 281.12 | 366.15 | 464.07 | 542.12 | 636.11 | 731.04 |
| 281.16 | 367.22 | 464.12 | 543.08 | 636.20 | 731.12 |
| 282.21 | 368.04 | 464.14 | 543.16 | 637.15 | 731.13 |
| 283.09 | 368.09 | 464.14 | 545.03 | 637.17 | 733.05 |
| 283.22 | 372.05 | 464.19 | 545.09 | 638.12 | 733.09 |
| 284.17 | 373.09 | 465.02 | 545.10 | 638.16 | 733.10 |
| 285.02 | 373.12 | 467.07 | 545.15 | 639.08 | 734.01 |
| 285.08 | 374.03 | 467.10 | 546.03 | 641.05 | 734.03 |
| 286.13 | 375.04 | 467.13 | 547.07 | 642.06 | 734.12 |
| 287.02 | 376.06 | 467.22 | 547.10 | 644.05 | 735.03 |
| 287.15 | 376.17 | 468.22 | 550.09 | 644.10 | 735.05 |
| 288.20 | 376.17 | 469.02 | 551.03 | 644.22 | 736.04 |
| 289.01 | 376.18 | 469.08 | 551.06 | 645.15 | 736.12 |
| 292.12 | 376.21 | 469.20 | 552.08 | 646.06 | 738.16 |
| 292.13 | 377.04 | 471.05 | 552.17 | 646.10 | 739.04 |
| 294.04 | 377.10 | 473.07 | 554.14 | 646.13 | 739.05 |
| 294.12 | 378.19 | 473.08 | 554.18 | 646.15 | 739.10 |
| 295.03 | 379.16 | 473.10 | 555.09 | 646.21 | 739.14 |
| 295.11 | 384.01 | 475.03 | 557.16 | 647.12 | 740.08 |
| 295.12 | 384.06 | 475.15 | 558.07 | 648.08 | 740.20 |
| 296.09 | 384.14 | 476.15 | 561.11 | 649.07 | 741.03 |
| 296.11 | 385.08 | 476.19 | 561.12 | 649.20 | 741.16 |
| 297.17 | 385.19 | 477.06 | 561.16 | 650.03 | 742.03 |
| 298.12 | 385.20 | 478.01 | 562.04 | 650.05 | 742.15 |
| 299.19 | 386.02 | 479.07 | 562.11 | 651.04 | 743.06 |
| 300.01 | 386.09 | 479.22 | 565.02 | 652.21 | 743.12 |
| 303.01 | 387.13 | 480.15 | 565.19 | 653.08 | 743.16 |
| 303.02 | 388.03 | 480.15 | 567.11 | 653.17 | 743.19 |
| 305.17 | 388.21 | 481.17 | 569.03 | 653.21 | 744.04 |
| 305.20 | 389.05 | 482.11 | 569.06 | 654.04 | 744.09 |
| 306.07 | 389.06 | 483.12 | 570.20 | 655.04 | 744.20 |
| 306.18 | 390.05 | 483.16 | 571.18 | 655.11 | 745.06 |
| 307.11 | 390.16 | 484.04 | 573.03 | 658.03 | 746.10 |
| 309.03 | 391.06 | 484.05 | 573.05 | 658.06 | 748.16 |
| 309.16 | 392.03 | 485.03 | 575.04 | 658.10 | 748.21 |
| 309.20 | 392.06 | 485.15 | 575.10 | 660.02 | 749.07 |
| 313.07 | 392.13 | 487.11 | 576.08 | 660.09 | 749.21 |
| 313.14 | 394.21 | 489.03 | 577.08 | 660.22 | 750.07 |
| 314.03 | 396.01 | 489.06 | 577.08 | 661.03 | 750.08 |
| 314.13 | 397.01 | 489.15 | 578.14 | 664.16 | 751.03 |
| 315.11 | 398.18 | 489.20 | 578.17 | 666.14 | 752.08 |
| 315.17 | 401.05 | 490.16 | 579.19 | 666.19 | 752.11 |
| 316.03 | 402.17 | 491.15 | 579.22 | 669.02 | 753.04 |
| 316.11 | 403.05 | 491.19 | 580.13 | 670.13 | 753.13 |
| 316.17 | 404.07 | 492.10 | 580.18 | 671.15 | 753.14 |
| 318.07 | 406.04 | 493.05 | 581.03 | 672.06 | 754.05 |
| 319.21 | 406.11 | 493.13 | 581.09 | 672.17 | 754.07 |
| 321.12 | 406.14 | 496.08 | 581.19 | 673.05 | 755.09 |
| 322.01 | 407.01 | 496.12 | 581.21 | 673.06 | 756.06 |
| 322.10 | 407.17 | 496.14 | 583.22 | 674.10 | 757.19 |
| 322.15 | 408.10 | 496.18 | 586.16 | 674.21 | 758.09 |
| 327.02 | 408.20 | 497.14 | 586.19 | 675.02 | 759.20 |
| 327.03 | 411.15 | 498.16 | 588.09 | 677.02 | 759.22 |
| 327.08 | 411.17 | 498.18 | 588.15 | 677.16 | 761.04 |
| 329.01 | 413.19 | 499.14 | 591.04 | 678.06 | 762.15 |
| 329.12 | 414.20 | 499.15 | 591.11 | 679.07 | 763.11 |
| 330.14 | 415.13 | 499.17 | 591.18 | 682.01 | notable |
| 330.15 | 416.04 | 500.06 | 592.17 | 685.02 | 144.23 |
| 331.19 | 416.14 | 501.03 | 593.13 | 685.15 | note |
| 333.02 | 417.18 | 501.07 | 594.03 | 686.17 | 107.01 |
| 334.01 | 419.10 | 501.12 | 594.22 | 690.02 | 305.12 |
| 335.11 | 419.22 | 501.17 | 596.12 | 690.13 | 329.08 |
| 336.11 | 420.02 | 501.20 | 597.07 | 693.20 | 337.04 |
| 336.12 | 421.19 | 501.22 | 597.13 | 694.06 | 504.20 |
| 336.22 | 422.10 | 502.03 | 599.01 | 695.03 | 505.11 |
| 337.18 | 425.05 | 502.04 | 599.05 | 695.09 | 581.05 |
| 337.19 | 425.09 | 502.08 | 599.15 | 695.16 | 673.04 |
| 339.04 | 426.09 | 502.14 | 601.07 | 698.09 | 675.12 |
| 340.08 | 426.16 | 504.08 | 601.10 | 698.12 | notebook |
| 341.09 | 427.18 | 504.16 | 602.05 | 699.13 | 685.12 |
| 341.18 | 428.05 | 504.20 | 602.09 | 700.03 | notes |
| 341.20 | 429.02 | 505.01 | 602.12 | 700.16 | 505.14 |
| 341.21 | 429.04 | 505.04 | 602.15 | 701.04 | 514.12 |
| 342.15 | 429.04 | 505.13 | 603.21 | 701.18 | nothing |
| 342.20 | 429.10 | 505.16 | 604.02 | 702.10 | 006.21 |
| 343.13 | 430.03 | 507.21 | 606.03 | 702.18 | 007.17 |
| 344.05 | 430.08 | 509.09 | 606.06 | 702.19 | 012.05 |
| 345.08 | 430.09 | 509.15 | 606.14 | 703.01 | 032.01 |
| 345.10 | 431.08 | 510.10 | 607.15 | 703.06 | 038.21 |
| 348.03 | 434.07 | 510.20 | 608.17 | 703.10 | 056.11 |
| 350.07 | 435.03 | 510.21 | 608.18 | 703.19 | 061.09 |
| 350.08 | 436.01 | 511.13 | 610.21 | 706.06 | 087.06 |
| 350.10 | 436.18 | 514.13 | 612.05 | 707.05 | 098.05 |
| 354.13 | 438.05 | 518.17 | 615.04 | 708.04 | 116.07 |
| 355.04 | 439.21 | 519.03 | 616.07 | 708.05 | 124.20 |
| 355.15 | 440.06 | 519.04 | 616.11 | 708.07 | 127.10 |
| 356.10 | 441.01 | 520.15 | 617.06 | 709.05 | 135.15 |
| 356.14 | 441.01 | 520.20 | 618.04 | 709.09 | 140.03 |
| 356.21 | 442.16 | 521.04 | 618.10 | 709.20 | 150.17 |
| 356.22 | 443.02 | 523.06 | 618.15 | 710.13 | 152.22 |
| 357.17 | 444.21 | 524.10 | 620.12 | 710.14 | 154.02 |
| 359.04 | 445.04 | 524.21 | 620.15 | 710.21 | 154.02 |
| 359.08 | 445.10 | 525.14 | 620.21 | 711.18 | 159.10 |
| 359.15 | 446.03 | 526.01 | 620.22 | 713.01 | 168.08 |
| 360.04 | 446.14 | 526.15 | 621.03 | 713.17 | 174.15 |
| 360.06 | 446.16 | 528.02 | 622.02 | 713.18 | 177.09 |
| 360.15 | 450.05 | 528.10 | 623.12 | 714.03 | 178.18 |
| 360.18 | 451.15 | 529.01 | 624.10 | 717.10 | 181.09 |
| 361.02 | 452.20 | 529.02 | 627.04 | 717.14 | 186.18 |

| | | | | | |
|---|---|---|---|---|---|
| 192.21 | 748.04 | 203.07 | 543.05 | numerous | obdurate |
| 195.16 | 754.17 | 205.11 | 543.19 | 206.10 | 709.05 |
| 197.21 | noticed | 212.02 | 546.17 | 487.12 | obedient |
| 226.18 | 063.02 | 213.16 | 551.04 | 516.11 | 576.10 |
| 228.02 | 179.16 | 215.04 | 555.10 | nur | obey |
| 229.18 | 209.11 | 220.17 | 562.19 | 187.21 | 195.17 |
| 232.06 | 234.18 | 227.14 | 563.12 | 232.15 | 275.02 |
| 236.12 | 285.13 | 233.12 | 567.05 | 232.16 | 315.06 |
| 236.22 | 298.15 | 236.19 | 569.15 | 420.10 | 470.14 |
| 255.21 | 371.19 | 237.09 | 572.05 | 457.21 | 605.01 |
| 262.11 | 407.22 | 248.20 | 572.06 | 696.07 | 615.07 |
| 264.04 | 497.03 | 251.20 | 572.22 | 696.18 | 615.08 |
| 266.10 | 640.03 | 254.11 | 577.22 | nurse | 622.19 |
| 267.22 | 693.08 | 257.02 | 580.21 | 082.14 | 721.15 |
| 280.10 | 739.21 | 260.04 | 589.18 | 140.05 | 723.04 |
| 286.14 | noticing | 260.14 | 591.14 | 196.11 | obeyed |
| 286.16 | 021.12 | 262.11 | 596.05 | 245.03 | 018.05 |
| 287.21 | 275.01 | 264.18 | 597.13 | 359.22 | 036.13 |
| 289.18 | noting | 272.18 | 600.02 | 401.06 | 060.05 |
| 295.17 | 132.01 | 274.22 | 605.06 | 482.14 | 126.20 |
| 299.04 | 487.17 | 276.18 | 605.16 | 520.21 | 255.15 |
| 306.20 | notion | 278.16 | 609.12 | 548.13 | 257.15 |
| 328.11 | 037.04 | 279.20 | 611.07 | 660.09 | 377.21 |
| 331.17 | 088.01 | 284.16 | 613.02 | 687.02 | 510.14 |
| 332.04 | 122.14 | 287.12 | 613.18 | nursed | 594.09 |
| 333.14 | 122.15 | 293.02 | 614.11 | 072.11 | 656.19 |
| 335.18 | 180.15 | 295.09 | 616.02 | 075.15 | 686.04 |
| 337.05 | 182.13 | 296.01 | 617.09 | 184.06 | 699.21 |
| 357.09 | 227.20 | 303.09 | 618.13 | 301.06 | 739.21 |
| 359.13 | 255.18 | 305.18 | 620.05 | nursery | 748.15 |
| 363.07 | 272.03 | 307.18 | 627.22 | 009.12 | obeying |
| 373.03 | 274.08 | 310.02 | 630.18 | 382.03 | 640.18 |
| 376.02 | 315.11 | 311.20 | 634.13 | 426.19 | obeys |
| 376.19 | 316.06 | 317.15 | 641.11 | 518.10 | 754.18 |
| 383.15 | 335.14 | 320.21 | 643.03 | nursing | object |
| 384.04 | 338.06 | 325.08 | 643.05 | 234.01 | 062.16 |
| 395.08 | 338.18 | 332.20 | 646.11 | 397.16 | 096.12 |
| 401.19 | 374.12 | 333.03 | 647.01 | 476.21 | 119.19 |
| 403.19 | 385.19 | 335.06 | 650.09 | 618.22 | 175.20 |
| 412.18 | 440.16 | 340.08 | 655.03 | nursling | 221.01 |
| 421.14 | 492.02 | 341.07 | 662.17 | 139.03 | 237.10 |
| 435.21 | 499.06 | 342.16 | 663.08 | nurture | 251.05 |
| 440.05 | 614.07 | 343.14 | 664.02 | 646.21 | 394.04 |
| 452.11 | 679.22 | 349.03 | 665.17 | nut | 470.20 |
| 457.08 | notions | 351.07 | 666.18 | 016.10 | 501.18 |
| 459.07 | 125.22 | 352.16 | 667.02 | 042.21 | 526.17 |
| 479.10 | 579.15 | 354.01 | 671.07 | 187.13 | 555.21 |
| 482.04 | notwithstanding | 356.11 | 681.11 | 232.16 | 583.21 |
| 490.15 | 013.17 | 356.15 | 683.08 | 324.04 | 590.18 |
| 494.09 | 089.08 | 361.12 | 683.16 | o | 610.03 |
| 494.13 | 290.20 | 362.18 | 685.11 | 124.08 | 652.08 |
| 496.21 | 347.14 | 365.04 | 694.09 | 151.17 | 731.17 |
| 500.15 | 375.09 | 371.08 | 702.05 | 156.09 | 749.07 |
| 501.11 | 442.12 | 380.04 | 703.02 | 385.09 | objected |
| 518.09 | 544.12 | 384.12 | 706.06 | 510.18 | 186.06 |
| 519.18 | 642.12 | 384.20 | 707.14 | 679.07 | 274.16 |
| 521.11 | 672.08 | 387.14 | 708.19 | 696.17 | 446.18 |
| 521.13 | nourish | 392.07 | 714.02 | 734.15 | 580.08 |
| 524.05 | 427.14 | 393.07 | 717.05 | o'clock | objection |
| 538.15 | nourishment | 394.22 | 720.03 | 014.07 | 148.04 |
| 548.18 | 088.07 | 395.09 | 720.03 | 059.01 | 224.04 |
| 581.02 | novelty | 398.18 | 722.08 | 077.10 | 384.10 |
| 590.17 | 170.21 | 404.11 | 723.15 | 121.14 | objections |
| 591.07 | 728.01 | 407.17 | 726.20 | 135.06 | 544.13 |
| 604.21 | november | 408.19 | 729.15 | 190.11 | objects |
| 608.06 | 516.15 | 416.07 | 733.06 | 291.18 | 304.11 |
| 616.07 | now | 421.06 | 739.17 | 308.07 | 351.16 |
| 621.02 | 019.07 | 421.20 | 741.14 | 369.02 | 446.04 |
| 632.18 | 023.04 | 422.12 | 742.06 | 390.06 | 487.15 |
| 661.21 | 025.21 | 422.19 | 743.01 | 431.14 | 493.01 |
| 670.09 | 027.22 | 428.19 | 747.22 | 460.04 | 730.08 |
| 677.09 | 030.14 | 430.21 | 748.21 | 548.18 | obleeged |
| 685.09 | 036.02 | 430.21 | 754.05 | 568.10 | 586.02 |
| 690.06 | 041.21 | 434.17 | 761.18 | 622.16 | obligation |
| 690.06 | 059.15 | 436.04 | now't | 623.16 | 342.18 |
| 698.18 | 062.12 | 438.20 | 194.04 | 638.05 | 582.15 |
| 698.20 | 063.16 | 439.20 | nowhere | 674.06 | oblige |
| 730.03 | 065.14 | 445.01 | 101.07 | 713.01 | 090.21 |
| 738.10 | 067.19 | 449.01 | 310.06 | 743.08 | 177.15 |
| 739.18 | 076.08 | 451.13 | nowt | o'er | 329.05 |
| 745.04 | 080.18 | 452.10 | 028.22 | 187.09 | 647.02 |
| 753.12 | 089.01 | 455.11 | 184.14 | 318.13 | obliged |
| 759.18 | 091.09 | 456.01 | 187.15 | 324.12 | 080.07 |
| 761.11 | 104.12 | 457.17 | 191.01 | 689.05 | 083.12 |
| 762.19 | 114.10 | 459.06 | 194.07 | oak | 114.04 |
| notice | 120.06 | 461.20 | 232.21 | 006.03 | 195.17 |
| 008.14 | 123.10 | 463.20 | 319.09 | 038.03 | 234.05 |
| 026.09 | 125.12 | 465.10 | 324.03 | 051.10 | 267.22 |
| 110.03 | 126.18 | 468.20 | 420.11 | 054.19 | 345.02 |
| 153.07 | 129.01 | 480.04 | 457.20 | 346.04 | 391.22 |
| 153.10 | 140.02 | 485.16 | 471.14 | oak-bedstead | 449.04 |
| 161.02 | 141.02 | 486.09 | 691.09 | 323.04 | 460.02 |
| 239.02 | 143.08 | 488.20 | 691.10 | oak-panelled | 474.06 |
| 257.02 | 151.10 | 489.19 | 696.14 | 281.10 | 533.19 |
| 318.18 | 155.11 | 490.04 | 720.09 | oaks | 559.10 |
| 377.20 | 156.06 | 493.16 | nud | 517.19 | 622.12 |
| 387.17 | 159.11 | 496.13 | 194.07 | oat | 670.03 |
| 403.06 | 163.05 | 497.17 | nudged | 531.04 | 700.09 |
| 427.08 | 164.09 | 500.06 | 048.20 | oatcakes | 701.05 |
| 568.13 | 171.19 | 503.05 | nuh | 006.07 | 746.11 |
| 591.12 | 173.19 | 503.09 | 310.17 | oath | 754.12 |
| 610.02 | 174.05 | 512.02 | nuisance | 059.02 | obliterated |
| 641.02 | 175.08 | 517.11 | 341.01 | 309.19 | 323.02 |
| 674.01 | 175.17 | 519.20 | number | 438.09 | oblivion |
| 674.16 | 176.19 | 527.22 | 280.12 | oaths | 236.02 |
| 697.10 | 179.08 | 531.17 | 291.15 | 162.02 | obscure |
| 705.21 | 181.17 | 533.08 | 383.02 | oatmeal | 018.16 |
| 707.08 | 190.15 | 537.14 | 619.18 | 317.19 | 305.14 |
| 717.05 | 194.20 | 537.18 | 668.01 | oats | obscurely |
| 726.18 | 199.10 | 538.21 | 700.11 | 688.08 | 052.14 |
| 734.02 | 200.06 | 542.03 | | | |

obscurity
312.19
observable
021.03
observation
712.09
729.02
observations
597.16
observe
017.08
367.01
426.20
433.17
487.16
observed
005.18
018.18
026.10
051.18
127.19
137.01
146.12
151.14
168.22
171.05
187.06
204.18
239.14
246.21
280.11
293.06
330.02
336.19
354.22
377.13
407.15
412.05
420.21
421.12
493.04
501.17
507.08
519.05
527.02
536.04
579.20
586.05
590.05
622.05
680.03
698.08
701.19
729.06
739.13
757.05
762.12
observing
244.17
322.11
379.03
532.06
obstacle
176.02
obstinacy
190.02
obstinate
135.11
220.06
402.10
704.02
755.01
obstinately
338.17
462.10
515.11
obtain
342.04
342.05
384.17
446.15
523.23
623.06
obtained
597.02
obtaining
757.12
obtrusive
039.11
obviate
038.09
304.19
459.02
obvious
223.21
588.14
obviously
064.20
337.10
492.02
516.13
681.14
occasion
048.12
150.16
227.16
240.11
350.17
364.09
371.20
415.22

504.05
550.04
599.01
665.02
702.14
739.08
750.01
occasioned
085.20
332.01
542.03
569.02
occasions
137.12
413.07
426.11
occupant
370.14
occupants
136.06
209.17
255.07
occupation
002.12
057.17
063.14
155.22
352.10
528.12
551.10
630.08
occupations
267.18
349.06
442.05
516.11
671.06
701.09
726.14
733.16
occupied
465.13
502.12
615.21
655.21
717.18
occupy
271.20
291.16
307.22
392.06
685.06
occurrence
344.21
occurs
214.18
ocean
065.20
october
092.19
516.14
672.16
odd
037.04
048.13
117.17
239.08
277.06
292.11
305.22
401.17
488.02
508.10
552.01
608.08
673.07
683.20
733.01
760.19
oddly
060.09
651.08
odious
391.20
534.07
odour
564.12
odour
039.14
oe'red
042.21
of
001.08
002.09
002.12
003.11
003.19
003.20
003.22
004.03
004.05
004.09
004.11
004.12
004.12
004.14
004.20
004.22
005.05
005.17
005.19

005.20
006.01
006.06
006.07
006.07
006.10
006.10
006.12
006.18
007.03
007.05
007.08
007.15
007.16
007.17
007.19
007.20
007.22
008.04
008.10
008.11
008.13
008.14
008.19
009.05
009.06
009.08
009.10
009.13
009.18
010.03
010.06
010.13
010.18
010.21
011.03
011.07
011.09
011.12
011.22
012.01
012.03
012.08
012.22
012.22
013.05
013.05
013.06
013.07
013.09
013.10
013.11
013.16
014.04
015.04
015.08
016.03
017.05
017.06
017.17
018.07
018.08
018.17
018.18
018.20
019.02
019.05
019.07
019.11
019.18
019.20
020.06
020.20
021.02
021.07
021.09
021.10
021.11
021.11
021.14
022.02
022.04
022.07
022.16
023.15
023.16
023.19
023.19
024.08
024.09
024.14
024.16
024.18
024.20
025.01
025.04
025.04
025.17
025.18
025.19
025.20
026.01
026.05
026.11
026.12
026.18
027.07
027.13
027.14
027.19

028.12
028.14
028.18
029.04
029.07
029.07
029.12
029.20
030.14
031.05
031.06
031.10
032.12
032.15
032.18
032.19
033.09
033.10
034.02
035.03
035.03
035.04
035.05
035.13
035.14
036.04
036.11
038.02
038.08
038.10
038.12
038.16
038.22
039.08
039.12
039.14
039.16
039.21
040.03
040.07
040.08
040.10
040.11
040.14
041.13
042.05
042.13
042.15
043.07
044.02
044.08
045.10
045.20
046.02
046.05
046.07
046.11
046.13
047.08
047.15
047.21
048.09
048.13
049.01
049.04
049.09
050.03
050.11
050.17
051.02
051.11
052.01
052.02
052.03
052.11
053.08
053.16
053.19
054.03
054.19
054.21
055.04
055.17
056.16
057.04
057.08
057.10
057.14
058.07
058.13
058.16
058.21
059.06
059.14
059.15
059.22
060.08
060.08
060.12
060.17
060.20
061.07
061.12
061.13
061.15
062.02
062.04
062.15
062.19
062.20

063.03
063.08
063.11
064.01
064.08
064.11
065.02
065.03
065.03
065.06
065.09
065.10
065.12
065.13
065.17
066.01
066.02
066.05
066.06
066.06
066.08
066.14
066.18
066.20
067.11
069.03
069.09
069.11
070.15
071.05
071.19
071.21
073.10
073.11
073.11
074.05
074.14
075.02
075.03
075.06
075.06
075.09
076.01
076.19
077.01
077.05
077.06
077.16
077.21
078.09
078.18
078.20
079.13
080.02
080.09
080.15
082.02
082.06
082.07
083.01
083.08
083.15
083.21
084.07
084.14
085.07
085.08
085.19
086.01
086.03
087.02
087.07
088.10
088.17
089.04
089.15
090.02
090.08
090.23
091.03
095.03
095.07
097.05
097.18
098.05
098.11
098.14
099.07
099.13
099.14
099.15
099.16
100.03
100.10
100.19
100.22
101.05
101.16
101.19
102.14
102.19
103.05
103.12
103.22
104.05
104.15
104.18
105.01
105.12
106.15
106.20

107.04
108.18
110.11
110.20
111.04
111.05
111.06
111.09
111.14
111.14
111.16
111.20
113.07
113.09
114.03
115.17
115.22
116.03
116.15
118.07
118.08
118.09
118.12
118.18
119.04
119.12
119.17
120.02
120.09
120.13
121.04
121.16
121.17
122.12
122.14
122.15
123.01
123.04
124.03
124.08
124.12
124.14
124.21
124.22
125.16
125.17
125.22
126.01
126.03
126.14
126.14
127.05
127.11
127.13
127.17
128.02
128.03
128.06
128.14
129.06
129.16
129.21
130.08
130.20
131.02
131.08
131.09
131.10
131.13
131.21
132.02
132.13
132.15
132.16
133.01
133.09
133.14
134.04
134.07
134.13
134.21
135.04
135.07
135.15
135.16
135.20
135.21
136.08
136.13
137.05
137.06
137.10
137.12
137.16
137.18
137.18
138.02
138.03
138.03
138.05
138.09
138.10
139.02
139.03
140.06
140.13
140.13
140.16
140.16
141.06
142.18

| | | | | | |
|---|---|---|---|---|---|
| 143.01 | 183.06 | 218.09 | 256.16 | 293.13 | 335.02 |
| 143.11 | 183.10 | 218.15 | 257.06 | 293.16 | 335.04 |
| 143.13 | 183.13 | 218.17 | 257.06 | 293.19 | 335.08 |
| 143.22 | 183.15 | 219.06 | 257.07 | 294.11 | 335.14 |
| 144.13 | 183.16 | 219.07 | 257.08 | 294.15 | 335.14 |
| 144.17 | 183.18 | 220.04 | 257.14 | 294.20 | 336.04 |
| 144.18 | 184.04 | 220.06 | 257.20 | 295.01 | 336.13 |
| 144.20 | 184.22 | 220.16 | 258.01 | 295.10 | 336.18 |
| 145.06 | 185.02 | 220.17 | 258.05 | 295.22 | 336.22 |
| 145.21 | 185.16 | 221.03 | 258.06 | 296.02 | 337.08 |
| 146.11 | 185.17 | 221.06 | 258.10 | 296.05 | 337.14 |
| 146.21 | 186.03 | 221.13 | 258.11 | 296.10 | 337.16 |
| 147.03 | 186.05 | 222.08 | 258.14 | 297.02 | 338.06 |
| 147.04 | 186.20 | 222.18 | 258.18 | 297.03 | 338.09 |
| 147.06 | 188.11 | 223.01 | 258.20 | 297.03 | 338.13 |
| 147.18 | 188.14 | 223.20 | 259.05 | 298.12 | 338.16 |
| 148.01 | 188.15 | 224.03 | 259.08 | 298.20 | 338.18 |
| 148.06 | 188.20 | 224.07 | 260.05 | 299.10 | 339.01 |
| 148.11 | 189.03 | 224.12 | 260.06 | 299.16 | 339.02 |
| 148.11 | 189.05 | 224.16 | 260.18 | 301.04 | 339.03 |
| 149.02 | 189.06 | 224.19 | 261.21 | 302.02 | 339.07 |
| 149.03 | 189.09 | 225.01 | 262.03 | 302.04 | 339.10 |
| 149.06 | 189.15 | 225.04 | 262.12 | 302.06 | 339.20 |
| 149.07 | 191.19 | 225.05 | 262.17 | 302.14 | 339.20 |
| 149.09 | 192.11 | 225.08 | 263.03 | 302.16 | 339.22 |
| 149.12 | 192.16 | 225.09 | 263.08 | 302.17 | 340.03 |
| 149.13 | 192.18 | 225.13 | 263.09 | 302.22 | 340.07 |
| 149.15 | 194.11 | 225.15 | 263.12 | 303.05 | 340.08 |
| 149.20 | 194.21 | 225.21 | 263.18 | 304.03 | 340.09 |
| 150.05 | 195.02 | 226.04 | 263.18 | 304.04 | 340.14 |
| 150.07 | 195.09 | 226.11 | 264.02 | 304.19 | 340.15 |
| 150.10 | 195.13 | 226.13 | 264.06 | 305.06 | 340.19 |
| 150.15 | 195.14 | 227.05 | 264.18 | 305.09 | 341.02 |
| 150.17 | 196.01 | 227.20 | 264.20 | 305.22 | 341.05 |
| 151.01 | 196.06 | 228.22 | 264.21 | 306.01 | 341.09 |
| 151.09 | 196.22 | 229.11 | 265.01 | 306.02 | 341.11 |
| 151.20 | 197.02 | 229.14 | 265.16 | 306.16 | 341.15 |
| 152.04 | 197.05 | 229.18 | 265.18 | 306.20 | 341.21 |
| 152.06 | 197.06 | 229.20 | 266.07 | 307.01 | 342.12 |
| 152.08 | 197.08 | 230.01 | 266.18 | 307.05 | 343.07 |
| 152.12 | 197.12 | 230.09 | 267.01 | 307.22 | 343.10 |
| 152.13 | 198.05 | 231.16 | 267.20 | 308.03 | 343.22 |
| 152.19 | 199.15 | 232.02 | 267.22 | 308.11 | 344.04 |
| 152.20 | 199.22 | 232.21 | 268.04 | 308.13 | 344.18 |
| 153.09 | 200.04 | 233.14 | 269.08 | 308.21 | 345.03 |
| 154.15 | 200.06 | 233.15 | 270.07 | 309.06 | 345.21 |
| 157.02 | 200.09 | 234.05 | 270.13 | 311.03 | 345.21 |
| 157.14 | 200.10 | 234.10 | 270.18 | 311.08 | 346.06 |
| 157.21 | 201.06 | 234.11 | 271.12 | 312.02 | 346.20 |
| 158.08 | 201.08 | 235.03 | 272.02 | 312.05 | 347.02 |
| 159.02 | 201.09 | 235.05 | 272.03 | 312.07 | 347.08 |
| 160.11 | 201.12 | 235.11 | 272.06 | 312.07 | 347.11 |
| 160.14 | 201.12 | 235.18 | 272.21 | 312.19 | 348.03 |
| 160.15 | 202.02 | 236.08 | 272.21 | 313.13 | 348.06 |
| 160.17 | 202.14 | 237.02 | 273.02 | 314.15 | 348.11 |
| 160.20 | 202.16 | 237.05 | 273.05 | 314.16 | 350.02 |
| 160.21 | 203.05 | 237.06 | 274.04 | 315.11 | 350.11 |
| 160.22 | 203.06 | 237.09 | 274.06 | 317.03 | 350.16 |
| 161.01 | 203.07 | 237.10 | 274.09 | 317.11 | 350.16 |
| 161.03 | 203.19 | 237.14 | 274.14 | 317.19 | 351.05 |
| 161.04 | 204.08 | 237.17 | 274.18 | 317.20 | 351.07 |
| 162.03 | 204.09 | 237.19 | 275.15 | 318.04 | 351.13 |
| 162.05 | 204.19 | 238.01 | 275.19 | 319.01 | 351.15 |
| 162.08 | 204.22 | 238.03 | 276.03 | 319.03 | 351.18 |
| 162.09 | 205.01 | 238.10 | 276.17 | 319.05 | 351.18 |
| 163.02 | 205.04 | 238.21 | 277.13 | 319.16 | 351.22 |
| 163.05 | 205.08 | 239.01 | 277.19 | 321.07 | 352.04 |
| 163.06 | 205.11 | 239.08 | 277.22 | 321.08 | 352.10 |
| 163.11 | 205.16 | 239.10 | 278.11 | 321.09 | 352.14 |
| 163.22 | 205.16 | 240.09 | 278.21 | 321.14 | 352.18 |
| 165.11 | 205.19 | 240.22 | 279.21 | 322.02 | 352.22 |
| 165.18 | 206.07 | 241.01 | 280.08 | 322.12 | 353.02 |
| 166.02 | 206.09 | 242.08 | 280.12 | 322.21 | 353.04 |
| 166.07 | 206.10 | 242.12 | 280.20 | 323.05 | 353.09 |
| 166.10 | 206.11 | 243.12 | 280.22 | 323.12 | 353.09 |
| 166.20 | 206.14 | 243.13 | 281.09 | 323.13 | 353.14 |
| 168.03 | 206.19 | 243.18 | 281.15 | 323.16 | 353.21 |
| 168.19 | 207.12 | 243.19 | 281.21 | 323.21 | 354.09 |
| 169.01 | 208.05 | 244.02 | 282.03 | 323.21 | 354.19 |
| 169.07 | 208.14 | 244.11 | 282.11 | 325.03 | 355.03 |
| 170.04 | 209.09 | 244.14 | 282.12 | 325.04 | 355.14 |
| 170.08 | 209.09 | 245.04 | 282.14 | 325.08 | 356.06 |
| 171.10 | 209.13 | 245.13 | 282.19 | 325.09 | 356.12 |
| 173.01 | 210.01 | 245.14 | 283.02 | 325.12 | 357.13 |
| 173.04 | 211.02 | 245.17 | 283.06 | 325.16 | 358.05 |
| 173.17 | 211.08 | 246.04 | 283.08 | 326.13 | 358.11 |
| 173.18 | 211.22 | 246.17 | 283.14 | 326.20 | 358.14 |
| 173.19 | 212.14 | 247.21 | 285.08 | 326.21 | 358.15 |
| 174.07 | 213.02 | 248.08 | 285.10 | 327.10 | 359.07 |
| 175.03 | 213.07 | 248.18 | 285.18 | 327.11 | 359.09 |
| 176.12 | 213.08 | 248.22 | 286.05 | 327.13 | 359.10 |
| 177.02 | 213.09 | 249.01 | 286.11 | 327.15 | 359.11 |
| 177.04 | 213.18 | 249.04 | 286.12 | 327.16 | 359.17 |
| 179.01 | 213.22 | 249.18 | 286.13 | 328.08 | 360.03 |
| 179.01 | 214.02 | 250.05 | 286.19 | 329.03 | 360.13 |
| 179.07 | 214.03 | 250.13 | 286.21 | 329.18 | 360.16 |
| 179.12 | 214.06 | 251.06 | 287.09 | 330.02 | 360.22 |
| 179.15 | 214.07 | 251.07 | 287.11 | 330.09 | 361.04 |
| 180.01 | 214.17 | 251.13 | 288.20 | 330.09 | 361.15 |
| 180.06 | 215.20 | 252.05 | 289.01 | 331.11 | 362.08 |
| 180.15 | 215.22 | 252.08 | 289.11 | 331.15 | 362.09 |
| 181.05 | 216.01 | 252.10 | 291.02 | 332.04 | 362.13 |
| 181.07 | 216.04 | 253.08 | 291.14 | 332.11 | 362.21 |
| 181.09 | 216.05 | 253.17 | 291.15 | 332.13 | 363.08 |
| 181.22 | 216.09 | 254.20 | 291.22 | 333.01 | 363.13 |
| 182.05 | 216.09 | 255.02 | 292.04 | 333.07 | 364.13 |
| 182.08 | 216.19 | 255.15 | 292.13 | 333.10 | 364.20 |
| 182.10 | 217.19 | 255.18 | 292.20 | 333.11 | 366.21 |
| 182.14 | 217.21 | 255.22 | 292.21 | 333.15 | 368.04 |
| 182.15 | 218.01 | 256.06 | 292.22 | 334.05 | 368.11 |
| 183.02 | 218.06 | 256.13 | 293.04 | 334.06 | 368.13 |

| | | | | | |
|---|---|---|---|---|---|
| 370.04 | 400.07 | 433.03 | 475.22 | 509.20 | 557.08 |
| 370.06 | 400.10 | 433.07 | 476.03 | 509.21 | 557.13 |
| 370.07 | 400.17 | 433.15 | 476.05 | 510.02 | 557.20 |
| 370.11 | 401.07 | 433.19 | 476.06 | 510.11 | 558.02 |
| 370.12 | 401.14 | 434.03 | 476.10 | 511.05 | 558.20 |
| 370.17 | 401.15 | 434.18 | 476.20 | 511.05 | 559.03 |
| 370.19 | 401.18 | 434.20 | 476.22 | 511.13 | 559.14 |
| 370.20 | 401.20 | 434.21 | 477.05 | 511.16 | 559.18 |
| 370.21 | 402.12 | 436.09 | 477.09 | 511.20 | 560.17 |
| 371.01 | 402.16 | 437.11 | 478.05 | 512.17 | 561.19 |
| 371.04 | 402.21 | 438.21 | 478.06 | 513.15 | 562.12 |
| 371.12 | 403.03 | 440.17 | 478.07 | 514.01 | 563.15 |
| 371.15 | 403.20 | 440.19 | 478.14 | 514.02 | 563.16 |
| 372.03 | 404.02 | 441.07 | 478.18 | 514.05 | 564.04 |
| 372.04 | 404.04 | 441.11 | 479.01 | 514.11 | 565.04 |
| 372.05 | 404.15 | 441.21 | 479.05 | 515.04 | 565.05 |
| 372.07 | 404.16 | 442.05 | 479.10 | 515.08 | 565.17 |
| 372.15 | 404.18 | 442.10 | 479.13 | 516.01 | 565.20 |
| 372.21 | 404.21 | 442.13 | 480.18 | 516.15 | 566.11 |
| 373.03 | 405.02 | 442.18 | 480.21 | 516.22 | 567.11 |
| 373.04 | 405.18 | 442.18 | 480.21 | 517.02 | 567.14 |
| 373.08 | 406.05 | 443.08 | 481.01 | 517.08 | 567.15 |
| 373.18 | 406.06 | 443.09 | 481.02 | 517.13 | 567.20 |
| 374.01 | 406.11 | 443.11 | 481.08 | 517.16 | 567.21 |
| 374.01 | 407.04 | 443.14 | 481.16 | 517.17 | 568.06 |
| 374.06 | 407.13 | 443.15 | 482.05 | 518.16 | 568.13 |
| 374.08 | 407.15 | 443.16 | 482.09 | 518.19 | 568.18 |
| 374.11 | 408.01 | 444.05 | 482.16 | 519.07 | 570.18 |
| 375.02 | 408.01 | 444.06 | 482.22 | 519.11 | 570.19 |
| 375.11 | 408.07 | 444.08 | 483.01 | 519.11 | 571.04 |
| 375.18 | 408.11 | 444.09 | 484.07 | 519.13 | 571.17 |
| 376.15 | 408.12 | 444.14 | 484.08 | 520.09 | 572.04 |
| 377.13 | 409.07 | 444.19 | 484.14 | 521.07 | 572.13 |
| 377.14 | 409.12 | 444.21 | 485.16 | 522.02 | 572.14 |
| 377.16 | 409.14 | 445.06 | 485.19 | 522.06 | 572.16 |
| 378.11 | 409.21 | 445.09 | 486.03 | 522.08 | 572.20 |
| 378.14 | 410.01 | 445.09 | 486.04 | 523.05 | 573.04 |
| 378.15 | 410.05 | 445.12 | 487.03 | 523.14 | 573.14 |
| 378.16 | 410.12 | 445.14 | 487.12 | 524.10 | 573.15 |
| 378.17 | 410.15 | 446.01 | 488.16 | 524.12 | 573.18 |
| 378.19 | 410.18 | 446.04 | 488.20 | 524.16 | 574.06 |
| 379.02 | 411.15 | 446.22 | 488.22 | 524.18 | 574.07 |
| 379.03 | 411.16 | 448.03 | 489.04 | 525.03 | 576.09 |
| 379.09 | 411.20 | 448.07 | 489.22 | 525.12 | 576.15 |
| 379.11 | 411.21 | 448.09 | 492.02 | 526.22 | 576.22 |
| 379.12 | 411.22 | 448.10 | 492.13 | 527.10 | 577.02 |
| 379.15 | 412.13 | 448.11 | 493.01 | 527.17 | 577.10 |
| 379.17 | 412.16 | 449.09 | 493.03 | 529.07 | 577.13 |
| 379.18 | 412.21 | 449.10 | 493.17 | 529.12 | 577.21 |
| 379.19 | 413.03 | 449.12 | 493.19 | 529.12 | 578.01 |
| 379.20 | 413.05 | 450.07 | 493.21 | 530.07 | 578.11 |
| 379.22 | 413.07 | 451.15 | 494.04 | 531.01 | 578.19 |
| 381.02 | 413.08 | 452.08 | 494.05 | 531.02 | 579.15 |
| 381.08 | 413.10 | 453.18 | 494.07 | 531.04 | 579.18 |
| 381.11 | 414.01 | 454.06 | 494.08 | 532.05 | 580.14 |
| 382.02 | 414.09 | 454.06 | 494.10 | 532.09 | 581.12 |
| 382.04 | 415.05 | 454.11 | 494.14 | 532.19 | 581.16 |
| 382.08 | 415.08 | 455.01 | 494.15 | 533.05 | 582.05 |
| 382.11 | 415.17 | 456.05 | 494.15 | 534.11 | 582.11 |
| 383.02 | 415.21 | 456.14 | 494.19 | 534.16 | 582.13 |
| 383.16 | 415.22 | 456.15 | 495.06 | 535.02 | 582.16 |
| 384.05 | 416.05 | 456.20 | 495.08 | 536.13 | 583.07 |
| 384.22 | 416.12 | 457.02 | 495.08 | 536.13 | 583.10 |
| 385.10 | 417.13 | 457.03 | 495.15 | 537.21 | 583.11 |
| 385.18 | 418.08 | 457.06 | 495.18 | 538.01 | 583.16 |
| 386.03 | 418.11 | 457.15 | 496.06 | 539.07 | 585.06 |
| 386.06 | 419.03 | 458.06 | 496.10 | 539.11 | 585.08 |
| 386.06 | 419.15 | 459.02 | 496.19 | 539.14 | 586.05 |
| 386.07 | 419.17 | 459.08 | 497.02 | 540.08 | 586.12 |
| 386.17 | 420.16 | 459.10 | 497.10 | 540.09 | 587.01 |
| 386.21 | 420.18 | 461.01 | 497.12 | 541.10 | 587.02 |
| 387.08 | 420.20 | 461.09 | 497.13 | 541.11 | 588.10 |
| 387.15 | 421.17 | 462.08 | 497.19 | 541.18 | 588.11 |
| 387.16 | 422.02 | 462.09 | 498.01 | 542.02 | 588.12 |
| 387.18 | 422.09 | 462.12 | 498.05 | 542.10 | 588.19 |
| 387.20 | 422.12 | 462.20 | 498.10 | 544.06 | 588.19 |
| 387.21 | 422.16 | 463.07 | 498.19 | 545.02 | 588.21 |
| 388.17 | 422.21 | 464.09 | 498.21 | 545.03 | 589.01 |
| 389.07 | 423.02 | 464.16 | 499.13 | 545.17 | 589.03 |
| 389.19 | 423.03 | 464.19 | 499.18 | 546.01 | 589.07 |
| 389.21 | 423.04 | 465.14 | 499.22 | 546.09 | 589.10 |
| 389.22 | 424.04 | 465.21 | 500.12 | 546.12 | 590.07 |
| 390.19 | 425.08 | 465.21 | 502.06 | 546.15 | 591.01 |
| 391.10 | 426.08 | 466.15 | 502.10 | 546.19 | 591.08 |
| 391.14 | 426.09 | 466.18 | 502.11 | 547.16 | 591.10 |
| 392.04 | 427.01 | 467.02 | 502.18 | 549.03 | 592.16 |
| 392.13 | 427.07 | 467.11 | 502.20 | 549.05 | 593.05 |
| 393.08 | 427.10 | 467.22 | 502.22 | 550.02 | 593.18 |
| 393.09 | 427.12 | 468.12 | 503.02 | 550.04 | 594.04 |
| 393.10 | 428.06 | 468.14 | 503.04 | 550.09 | 594.14 |
| 393.16 | 428.12 | 468.16 | 503.13 | 550.10 | 594.18 |
| 393.21 | 428.14 | 468.19 | 504.01 | 550.12 | 595.03 |
| 394.10 | 429.07 | 468.20 | 504.07 | 551.09 | 595.04 |
| 394.18 | 429.11 | 469.14 | 504.14 | 551.21 | 596.03 |
| 394.22 | 429.11 | 469.19 | 505.07 | 552.05 | 596.06 |
| 395.01 | 429.14 | 469.21 | 505.20 | 552.12 | 597.03 |
| 395.11 | 429.15 | 469.22 | 506.01 | 552.17 | 597.12 |
| 395.17 | 430.01 | 470.01 | 506.09 | 552.19 | 597.19 |
| 396.06 | 430.08 | 470.20 | 506.16 | 553.06 | 598.04 |
| 396.15 | 430.12 | 471.02 | 506.20 | 553.11 | 598.05 |
| 397.06 | 430.15 | 471.04 | 507.01 | 554.01 | 598.13 |
| 397.10 | 430.22 | 471.07 | 507.03 | 554.13 | 598.19 |
| 397.14 | 431.16 | 471.13 | 507.11 | 554.19 | 598.21 |
| 398.11 | 431.19 | 472.18 | 507.22 | 555.17 | 599.02 |
| 398.12 | 431.20 | 473.02 | 508.06 | 555.18 | 599.02 |
| 398.14 | 431.21 | 473.05 | 508.10 | 556.02 | 599.22 |
| 398.20 | 432.07 | 474.05 | 508.11 | 556.03 | 601.01 |
| 398.21 | 432.11 | 474.09 | 509.01 | 556.05 | 601.16 |
| 399.10 | 432.14 | 474.12 | 509.17 | 556.13 | 601.20 |
| 399.10 | 432.15 | 475.05 | 509.18 | 557.06 | 602.05 |
| 399.20 | 432.21 | 475.14 | 509.18 | 557.07 | 603.05 |

| | | | | | |
|---|---|---|---|---|---|
| 604.11 | 650.19 | 690.18 | 732.03 | 122.19 | 327.01 |
| 604.13 | 650.21 | 691.18 | 732.04 | 155.07 | offend |
| 604.19 | 651.02 | 692.03 | 732.10 | 157.20 | 202.04 |
| 605.05 | 651.06 | 692.06 | 732.17 | 167.08 | offended |
| 605.08 | 651.15 | 692.09 | 733.02 | 171.11 | 234.12 |
| 607.07 | 651.17 | 692.12 | 733.06 | 181.15 | 305.17 |
| 607.09 | 651.20 | 692.17 | 733.07 | 189.03 | 320.01 |
| 608.01 | 652.08 | 692.18 | 733.10 | 193.17 | offending |
| 608.09 | 652.10 | 692.22 | 733.13 | 194.13 | 013.05 |
| 608.12 | 652.16 | 693.01 | 733.15 | 202.13 | 147.21 |
| 608.17 | 653.01 | 693.03 | 734.10 | 203.08 | 406.12 |
| 608.18 | 653.03 | 693.08 | 734.14 | 210.21 | offer |
| 609.05 | 653.14 | 693.09 | 735.01 | 212.19 | 123.06 |
| 609.06 | 653.19 | 693.15 | 735.06 | 216.11 | 222.10 |
| 609.09 | 653.19 | 693.17 | 735.07 | 228.15 | 253.08 |
| 609.15 | 654.02 | 693.18 | 737.10 | 232.11 | 317.01 |
| 610.04 | 654.05 | 693.20 | 737.14 | 233.08 | 591.11 |
| 610.07 | 654.13 | 694.02 | 738.15 | 235.14 | 608.07 |
| 610.08 | 655.02 | 694.20 | 738.21 | 237.20 | 670.08 |
| 610.15 | 655.04 | 695.06 | 739.08 | 238.12 | 682.11 |
| 611.06 | 655.05 | 696.04 | 739.11 | 243.06 | 716.11 |
| 611.10 | 655.06 | 696.08 | 739.12 | 292.22 | 739.10 |
| 611.13 | 655.10 | 696.09 | 739.13 | 294.15 | 753.18 |
| 611.14 | 655.13 | 697.08 | 740.02 | 297.16 | offered |
| 611.17 | 655.14 | 698.01 | 741.07 | 309.20 | 065.17 |
| 613.11 | 655.14 | 698.12 | 741.13 | 312.01 | 133.09 |
| 613.16 | 656.15 | 698.21 | 741.15 | 318.05 | 199.08 |
| 613.18 | 658.07 | 699.05 | 742.20 | 318.21 | 245.21 |
| 614.17 | 658.12 | 699.10 | 742.21 | 319.11 | 267.09 |
| 615.01 | 660.06 | 699.17 | 743.11 | 344.08 | 330.18 |
| 615.12 | 660.08 | 699.20 | 743.15 | 352.21 | 436.13 |
| 615.15 | 661.04 | 700.06 | 743.16 | 362.11 | 442.17 |
| 616.18 | 661.09 | 700.12 | 743.21 | 364.12 | 457.05 |
| 617.03 | 661.14 | 700.19 | 744.17 | 372.21 | 542.08 |
| 617.06 | 661.20 | 701.01 | 745.12 | 373.15 | 556.04 |
| 617.15 | 662.04 | 701.13 | 745.14 | 374.01 | 632.15 |
| 617.21 | 663.07 | 704.03 | 745.19 | 391.05 | 666.14 |
| 618.05 | 663.09 | 704.06 | 746.06 | 400.10 | 667.12 |
| 618.15 | 663.12 | 704.14 | 746.07 | 402.07 | 670.20 |
| 618.18 | 664.11 | 704.18 | 746.15 | 432.02 | offering |
| 618.19 | 664.20 | 704.19 | 747.04 | 434.10 | 221.06 |
| 618.22 | 665.03 | 705.01 | 747.15 | 435.17 | 253.08 |
| 619.05 | 666.02 | 705.17 | 748.13 | 453.14 | 274.03 |
| 619.11 | 666.06 | 705.18 | 748.13 | 458.09 | 453.21 |
| 619.13 | 666.10 | 705.19 | 748.17 | 460.06 | 595.04 |
| 619.15 | 667.21 | 707.08 | 749.05 | 462.13 | 649.01 |
| 619.18 | 668.01 | 707.14 | 749.11 | 468.04 | 725.09 |
| 619.20 | 668.18 | 707.22 | 749.14 | 479.12 | offers |
| 620.04 | 668.22 | 708.01 | 749.16 | 480.03 | 290.01 |
| 620.10 | 669.11 | 708.16 | 749.18 | 483.17 | office |
| 621.11 | 669.20 | 710.03 | 750.09 | 492.14 | 413.05 |
| 621.17 | 669.22 | 710.17 | 750.20 | 506.16 | 674.09 |
| 621.18 | 670.05 | 711.09 | 750.21 | 517.14 | offspring |
| 621.21 | 670.09 | 711.10 | 751.02 | 522.12 | 494.19 |
| 622.02 | 670.11 | 711.18 | 751.05 | 525.10 | offspring's |
| 623.03 | 671.01 | 711.22 | 752.06 | 533.18 | 494.18 |
| 623.10 | 671.09 | 712.04 | 752.10 | 546.05 | often |
| 623.11 | 671.17 | 712.07 | 752.13 | 547.11 | 022.05 |
| 624.19 | 673.06 | 712.14 | 753.03 | 552.22 | 058.08 |
| 624.22 | 674.01 | 713.11 | 753.09 | 553.09 | 077.01 |
| 625.04 | 674.03 | 713.19 | 753.11 | 556.13 | 083.05 |
| 625.05 | 674.07 | 714.03 | 753.12 | 560.15 | 113.05 |
| 627.15 | 674.09 | 714.04 | 754.04 | 561.19 | 126.13 |
| 628.17 | 674.17 | 715.02 | 754.07 | 562.11 | 151.13 |
| 628.21 | 675.08 | 715.12 | 754.13 | 563.20 | 198.05 |
| 629.07 | 675.09 | 716.02 | 754.21 | 567.01 | 215.04 |
| 631.01 | 675.11 | 716.06 | 755.03 | 567.13 | 240.08 |
| 632.11 | 675.18 | 716.07 | 755.10 | 568.09 | 284.14 |
| 632.13 | 676.12 | 716.08 | 756.12 | 570.15 | 345.20 |
| 632.17 | 676.20 | 716.13 | 758.08 | 581.15 | 391.22 |
| 634.03 | 677.03 | 717.12 | 758.12 | 586.07 | 412.03 |
| 634.09 | 677.05 | 717.16 | 759.06 | 591.20 | 431.05 |
| 635.01 | 677.08 | 718.07 | 759.16 | 600.15 | 449.15 |
| 635.06 | 678.06 | 718.11 | 759.18 | 608.01 | 461.09 |
| 635.09 | 678.08 | 718.12 | 759.21 | 609.13 | 461.15 |
| 635.13 | 678.14 | 719.07 | 760.01 | 611.01 | 484.05 |
| 635.19 | 678.14 | 720.19 | 760.18 | 616.01 | 488.04 |
| 636.08 | 678.18 | 721.18 | 761.01 | 618.16 | 506.17 |
| 636.16 | 678.19 | 722.03 | 762.07 | 621.08 | 517.12 |
| 636.18 | 678.21 | 722.03 | 762.11 | 627.15 | 531.16 |
| 637.03 | 679.02 | 722.12 | 762.15 | 629.03 | 555.09 |
| 638.06 | 679.04 | 722.15 | 762.19 | 633.05 | 577.20 |
| 639.04 | 679.05 | 723.14 | 763.05 | 633.13 | 579.16 |
| 639.12 | 679.06 | 724.02 | 763.10 | 649.14 | 587.17 |
| 640.04 | 680.01 | 724.17 | 763.12 | 652.11 | 646.06 |
| 640.18 | 680.07 | 724.19 | 763.15 | 663.13 | 653.21 |
| 640.19 | 680.16 | 725.03 | 763.18 | 665.10 | 654.22 |
| 641.04 | 680.18 | 725.09 | 763.20 | 670.11 | 681.15 |
| 641.08 | 680.20 | 725.19 | off | 675.14 | 696.03 |
| 641.15 | 681.01 | 726.05 | 010.22 | 685.05 | 701.05 |
| 641.17 | 681.10 | 726.14 | 030.04 | 685.09 | oftener |
| 642.05 | 681.16 | 726.20 | 032.12 | 692.21 | 090.08 |
| 642.10 | 681.19 | 726.21 | 039.15 | 703.05 | oh |
| 642.11 | 682.06 | 727.01 | 043.17 | 703.15 | 022.12 |
| 643.04 | 682.20 | 727.13 | 052.17 | 704.12 | 024.07 |
| 644.02 | 683.01 | 727.21 | 059.13 | 706.11 | 030.01 |
| 644.05 | 683.15 | 728.01 | 061.01 | 710.14 | 042.06 |
| 644.11 | 684.12 | 728.03 | 065.08 | 722.18 | 048.16 |
| 644.12 | 685.03 | 728.07 | 074.22 | 727.01 | 055.09 |
| 644.15 | 685.20 | 728.09 | 076.21 | 729.13 | 060.14 |
| 645.02 | 686.07 | 728.10 | 077.04 | 741.06 | 060.14 |
| 645.03 | 686.14 | 729.11 | 077.13 | 758.16 | 071.01 |
| 647.11 | 686.20 | 729.21 | 084.09 | 763.19 | 073.18 |
| 647.17 | 687.04 | 730.02 | 102.12 | 763.21 | 074.17 |
| 648.06 | 688.03 | 730.19 | 105.13 | offald | 094.20 |
| 648.12 | 688.05 | 730.21 | 106.04 | 187.12 | 105.22 |
| 648.14 | 688.07 | 731.04 | 107.02 | offalld | 106.01 |
| 648.15 | 688.08 | 731.05 | 110.08 | 443.13 | 106.01 |
| 649.10 | 689.13 | 731.19 | 110.20 | offence | 106.01 |
| 649.19 | 690.08 | 731.21 | 114.15 | 057.09 | 106.02 |
| 650.10 | 690.15 | | 116.06 | 101.05 | 108.07 |

| | | | | | |
|---|---|---|---|---|---|
| 136.21 | 184.16 | 036.11 | 133.12 | 234.11 | 336.20 |
| 139.10 | 196.16 | 036.12 | 133.13 | 234.18 | 338.01 |
| 152.16 | 199.02 | 037.10 | 133.14 | 235.07 | 338.18 |
| 164.03 | 209.15 | 038.20 | 134.07 | 239.10 | 339.18 |
| 167.02 | 214.16 | 039.12 | 134.21 | 242.02 | 339.22 |
| 171.03 | 233.13 | 039.17 | 135.18 | 242.04 | 340.15 |
| 177.05 | 242.12 | 040.13 | 136.01 | 243.01 | 342.04 |
| 180.10 | 258.22 | 041.12 | 136.14 | 243.06 | 347.10 |
| 181.11 | 275.21 | 041.20 | 138.08 | 243.08 | 347.16 |
| 192.09 | 279.12 | 042.05 | 139.02 | 243.08 | 349.08 |
| 201.04 | 282.07 | 042.10 | 141.03 | 243.08 | 350.17 |
| 201.06 | 308.12 | 042.17 | 141.12 | 243.11 | 351.01 |
| 207.09 | 317.10 | 043.01 | 141.15 | 243.22 | 352.06 |
| 211.13 | 319.22 | 043.20 | 141.22 | 244.14 | 353.03 |
| 211.14 | 325.09 | 044.01 | 143.11 | 244.17 | 353.07 |
| 223.04 | 326.07 | 044.10 | 145.13 | 247.22 | 353.17 |
| 228.04 | 333.04 | 044.14 | 145.18 | 248.07 | 354.22 |
| 253.06 | 370.02 | 045.05 | 145.19 | 248.19 | 357.01 |
| 258.22 | 373.14 | 046.14 | 146.05 | 249.05 | 357.04 |
| 264.15 | 391.20 | 046.16 | 147.01 | 249.14 | 358.16 |
| 271.04 | 392.16 | 047.15 | 149.02 | 250.05 | 361.11 |
| 273.14 | 400.16 | 048.11 | 149.19 | 251.02 | 361.15 |
| 277.18 | 402.17 | 049.02 | 150.15 | 252.15 | 361.18 |
| 279.01 | 416.22 | 050.13 | 150.15 | 253.14 | 362.04 |
| 279.11 | 417.06 | 050.18 | 150.19 | 253.16 | 364.07 |
| 282.19 | 418.04 | 052.01 | 151.07 | 253.17 | 364.08 |
| 285.16 | 420.06 | 052.13 | 151.19 | 254.01 | 365.06 |
| 297.08 | 428.20 | 052.18 | 152.12 | 254.02 | 366.07 |
| 317.04 | 430.17 | 053.09 | 152.20 | 254.10 | 369.09 |
| 322.03 | 432.07 | 055.11 | 152.22 | 255.01 | 370.01 |
| 331.17 | 436.05 | 055.20 | 154.05 | 255.15 | 370.15 |
| 335.10 | 443.08 | 056.18 | 156.04 | 256.10 | 371.04 |
| 345.17 | 463.12 | 057.15 | 156.21 | 258.12 | 371.07 |
| 356.08 | 471.06 | 057.16 | 157.08 | 258.20 | 371.19 |
| 356.08 | 503.10 | 058.20 | 157.11 | 259.10 | 373.16 |
| 360.15 | 518.09 | 060.08 | 159.13 | 259.17 | 374.14 |
| 363.13 | 531.09 | 060.10 | 164.02 | 259.19 | 376.09 |
| 366.01 | 558.20 | 061.13 | 164.08 | 261.05 | 377.03 |
| 376.18 | 564.22 | 063.10 | 165.07 | 261.15 | 378.02 |
| 377.06 | 578.10 | 064.09 | 166.01 | 262.16 | 378.12 |
| 383.02 | 601.15 | 064.15 | 166.07 | 263.10 | 378.17 |
| 401.22 | 654.22 | 066.05 | 166.13 | 266.04 | 379.03 |
| 405.14 | 668.14 | 066.09 | 167.07 | 266.14 | 379.04 |
| 407.09 | 675.15 | 066.11 | 167.09 | 266.18 | 379.21 |
| 428.01 | 678.11 | 067.21 | 168.01 | 267.14 | 381.07 |
| 436.04 | 681.19 | 069.05 | 168.07 | 267.16 | 382.05 |
| 440.12 | 686.14 | 070.08 | 168.11 | 270.05 | 383.06 |
| 449.16 | 690.15 | 070.15 | 168.13 | 270.06 | 383.11 |
| 454.03 | 696.01 | 071.01 | 169.04 | 270.15 | 383.15 |
| 461.12 | 696.22 | 073.04 | 169.13 | 271.02 | 384.06 |
| 467.05 | 699.05 | 073.04 | 169.15 | 272.06 | 384.13 |
| 476.05 | 729.14 | 075.10 | 176.04 | 275.01 | 384.22 |
| 480.05 | 754.01 | 077.03 | 176.05 | 275.04 | 385.04 |
| 490.11 | 758.19 | 078.05 | 179.01 | 275.11 | 385.12 |
| 491.13 | 760.16 | 079.17 | 179.22 | 277.01 | 387.14 |
| 503.20 | old-fashioned | 080.02 | 181.01 | 279.12 | 388.12 |
| 510.05 | 038.08 | 080.03 | 184.20 | 280.10 | 389.01 |
| 510.16 | older | 080.06 | 185.14 | 280.18 | 389.17 |
| 513.02 | 078.04 | 080.12 | 186.08 | 283.03 | 392.16 |
| 519.22 | 214.01 | 080.20 | 186.22 | 287.05 | 393.01 |
| 521.14 | 428.18 | 081.01 | 187.07 | 288.07 | 393.02 |
| 532.03 | 501.14 | 082.07 | 187.14 | 288.08 | 393.22 |
| 537.15 | 545.13 | 083.05 | 188.13 | 290.01 | 395.02 |
| 545.05 | omen | 083.11 | 189.14 | 290.14 | 397.17 |
| 554.05 | 231.16 | 084.17 | 190.06 | 291.01 | 398.19 |
| 561.07 | ominous | 085.17 | 190.10 | 293.16 | 399.07 |
| 565.02 | 240.10 | 085.19 | 190.13 | 294.02 | 399.11 |
| 601.05 | omit | 086.01 | 191.15 | 294.16 | 399.16 |
| 602.10 | 315.09 | 089.08 | 191.16 | 295.05 | 400.01 |
| 615.05 | 378.19 | 089.14 | 192.01 | 296.04 | 401.09 |
| 617.05 | on | 089.17 | 192.13 | 297.04 | 403.09 |
| 628.10 | 001.07 | 090.05 | 193.16 | 298.03 | 403.17 |
| 634.15 | 005.21 | 091.03 | 195.14 | 299.01 | 404.03 |
| 638.09 | 007.04 | 091.11 | 196.05 | 299.09 | 405.11 |
| 670.17 | 008.01 | 092.18 | 196.19 | 299.22 | 405.15 |
| 676.17 | 008.02 | 093.08 | 197.09 | 302.15 | 406.20 |
| 680.09 | 010.15 | 093.09 | 198.18 | 303.05 | 406.21 |
| 685.03 | 011.17 | 094.01 | 200.02 | 303.18 | 409.22 |
| 696.14 | 012.12 | 095.04 | 202.05 | 303.21 | 410.01 |
| 698.07 | 013.09 | 095.17 | 203.09 | 304.21 | 410.18 |
| 744.06 | 013.12 | 096.12 | 203.14 | 305.01 | 411.01 |
| 756.10 | 014.06 | 097.07 | 205.02 | 305.04 | 412.04 |
| oho | 014.11 | 097.14 | 206.05 | 305.05 | 412.10 |
| 109.19 | 015.01 | 098.13 | 206.12 | 307.21 | 412.15 |
| old | 015.09 | 099.17 | 206.15 | 308.06 | 413.07 |
| 003.16 | 018.01 | 100.04 | 207.02 | 309.19 | 413.09 |
| 003.17 | 019.01 | 103.18 | 207.06 | 311.09 | 415.07 |
| 006.09 | 019.13 | 104.01 | 207.16 | 313.09 | 415.18 |
| 029.11 | 020.20 | 104.17 | 209.03 | 313.12 | 415.22 |
| 044.15 | 021.10 | 105.08 | 209.16 | 314.06 | 416.11 |
| 057.12 | 022.06 | 106.07 | 209.18 | 314.22 | 417.18 |
| 073.09 | 024.04 | 106.15 | 211.01 | 316.15 | 417.21 |
| 073.10 | 025.12 | 108.06 | 215.02 | 316.16 | 418.05 |
| 076.02 | 026.08 | 108.14 | 216.07 | 317.10 | 419.07 |
| 076.14 | 027.04 | 110.19 | 217.16 | 317.13 | 420.12 |
| 081.10 | 028.11 | 111.18 | 218.03 | 317.19 | 421.04 |
| 088.11 | 028.21 | 111.21 | 221.22 | 318.07 | 422.07 |
| 092.08 | 031.13 | 112.06 | 223.12 | 320.17 | 423.01 |
| 099.12 | 032.03 | 112.07 | 223.14 | 321.02 | 426.03 |
| 104.08 | 032.08 | 116.01 | 223.21 | 323.10 | 426.11 |
| 107.22 | 033.14 | 116.17 | 226.05 | 323.20 | 427.02 |
| 110.02 | 033.20 | 119.08 | 226.13 | 324.07 | 427.09 |
| 119.20 | 034.04 | 119.15 | 226.21 | 324.08 | 427.22 |
| 121.19 | 034.10 | 120.02 | 227.15 | 326.03 | 428.01 |
| 130.10 | 034.14 | 121.10 | 227.19 | 326.07 | 430.10 |
| 140.20 | 034.17 | 121.11 | 229.15 | 329.20 | 430.18 |
| 145.12 | 035.01 | 121.12 | 229.17 | 332.08 | 430.20 |
| 147.01 | 035.05 | 126.04 | 232.06 | 332.16 | 430.21 |
| 149.15 | 035.15 | 126.21 | 232.10 | 335.12 | 431.21 |
| 160.10 | 035.20 | 126.22 | 232.16 | 335.13 | 432.14 |
| 175.19 | 036.01 | 130.22 | 234.08 | 335.15 | |

| | | | | | |
|---|---|---|---|---|---|
| 434.13 | 551.20 | 661.08 | 108.11 | 095.08 | 385.06 |
| 435.11 | 552.02 | 662.05 | 115.17 | 096.11 | 392.04 |
| 436.11 | 552.04 | 662.13 | 117.07 | 100.10 | 392.08 |
| 437.13 | 552.18 | 665.04 | 121.18 | 101.03 | 395.17 |
| 441.02 | 555.15 | 665.15 | 126.06 | 105.20 | 400.03 |
| 441.10 | 556.08 | 666.18 | 133.07 | 110.14 | 405.03 |
| 442.05 | 556.19 | 667.18 | 149.11 | 119.08 | 405.15 |
| 442.21 | 557.07 | 671.21 | 178.11 | 121.10 | 407.15 |
| 443.15 | 557.18 | 672.12 | 215.18 | 121.19 | 407.16 |
| 446.21 | 559.16 | 676.08 | 219.10 | 125.10 | 409.03 |
| 449.21 | 559.20 | 678.19 | 243.13 | 125.18 | 410.15 |
| 450.04 | 563.05 | 680.06 | 266.06 | 126.22 | 411.13 |
| 451.10 | 565.22 | 682.07 | 272.15 | 128.04 | 414.09 |
| 452.21 | 568.08 | 682.10 | 283.03 | 129.09 | 415.09 |
| 453.04 | 568.17 | 684.09 | 303.12 | 132.15 | 416.04 |
| 453.08 | 569.06 | 686.10 | 312.17 | 135.01 | 417.06 |
| 455.16 | 569.08 | 686.11 | 315.19 | 135.05 | 417.11 |
| 456.06 | 570.09 | 688.04 | 331.18 | 135.20 | 421.07 |
| 456.15 | 570.14 | 689.22 | 333.10 | 136.01 | 421.21 |
| 456.21 | 573.02 | 690.16 | 346.07 | 136.13 | 425.16 |
| 457.19 | 573.07 | 693.03 | 367.10 | 137.17 | 426.12 |
| 459.04 | 574.01 | 693.09 | 394.21 | 137.18 | 428.14 |
| 461.16 | 576.10 | 694.19 | 400.19 | 138.04 | 431.13 |
| 462.03 | 578.11 | 695.15 | 404.10 | 141.16 | 431.21 |
| 463.07 | 579.19 | 695.22 | 420.21 | 143.10 | 432.06 |
| 463.15 | 582.11 | 700.14 | 426.09 | 143.14 | 438.21 |
| 463.22 | 582.15 | 700.21 | 427.06 | 145.18 | 445.09 |
| 465.11 | 583.04 | 701.14 | 435.11 | 148.22 | 451.09 |
| 467.05 | 583.20 | 702.13 | 452.02 | 154.10 | 455.14 |
| 467.15 | 585.04 | 702.21 | 458.02 | 157.15 | 476.02 |
| 467.17 | 585.10 | 703.04 | 477.14 | 162.07 | 476.16 |
| 473.03 | 586.03 | 704.05 | 484.19 | 163.10 | 480.21 |
| 475.07 | 586.06 | 704.09 | 488.04 | 165.09 | 482.09 |
| 476.03 | 586.15 | 704.21 | 489.20 | 168.09 | 482.13 |
| 476.13 | 587.02 | 705.10 | 511.16 | 171.12 | 486.12 |
| 477.16 | 587.03 | 705.15 | 511.21 | 175.22 | 488.22 |
| 478.03 | 588.20 | 706.01 | 541.14 | 176.04 | 490.07 |
| 478.05 | 591.07 | 708.14 | 555.11 | 177.03 | 494.06 |
| 478.12 | 595.05 | 709.03 | 566.10 | 182.10 | 494.21 |
| 478.18 | 595.06 | 709.08 | 569.15 | 188.13 | 497.16 |
| 479.05 | 596.09 | 710.13 | 583.03 | 189.02 | 500.14 |
| 479.09 | 598.18 | 710.16 | 586.07 | 191.13 | 502.01 |
| 480.16 | 599.01 | 711.16 | 587.11 | 193.20 | 504.01 |
| 482.01 | 599.11 | 711.19 | 599.09 | 197.06 | 504.16 |
| 482.20 | 600.01 | 712.05 | 602.01 | 198.01 | 505.11 |
| 483.09 | 601.14 | 712.06 | 606.20 | 199.13 | 506.09 |
| 485.21 | 602.01 | 712.09 | 616.11 | 200.03 | 507.06 |
| 485.22 | 603.10 | 712.12 | 621.06 | 204.14 | 507.16 |
| 488.08 | 604.02 | 714.05 | 625.03 | 208.09 | 513.06 |
| 489.02 | 604.12 | 715.02 | 628.06 | 210.12 | 513.07 |
| 491.11 | 604.16 | 716.13 | 629.03 | 211.07 | 513.12 |
| 491.20 | 605.15 | 717.15 | 631.21 | 212.12 | 517.17 |
| 493.02 | 608.01 | 717.16 | 642.04 | 215.13 | 518.16 |
| 498.06 | 609.04 | 717.19 | 649.15 | 216.04 | 531.21 |
| 498.10 | 610.02 | 719.03 | 653.04 | 222.01 | 538.09 |
| 498.21 | 610.06 | 720.16 | 661.06 | 222.14 | 539.09 |
| 499.12 | 610.07 | 725.08 | 664.10 | 226.14 | 544.06 |
| 500.05 | 610.10 | 725.15 | 665.01 | 228.17 | 550.12 |
| 501.10 | 610.14 | 726.18 | 670.20 | 231.13 | 552.19 |
| 502.20 | 611.01 | 727.07 | 678.07 | 231.19 | 557.04 |
| 502.22 | 611.15 | 727.11 | 678.09 | 232.10 | 558.22 |
| 503.18 | 611.19 | 727.19 | 684.16 | 235.05 | 563.16 |
| 503.22 | 612.07 | 729.07 | 700.09 | 237.11 | 564.09 |
| 505.12 | 613.08 | 729.16 | 701.19 | 237.13 | 567.20 |
| 506.01 | 614.16 | 731.15 | 702.16 | 237.20 | 568.18 |
| 506.06 | 616.18 | 732.13 | 723.21 | 242.12 | 575.10 |
| 506.07 | 617.05 | 732.21 | 736.07 | 245.09 | 576.15 |
| 506.14 | 618.05 | 733.02 | 742.07 | 258.06 | 578.15 |
| 508.22 | 618.16 | 733.02 | one | 261.18 | 583.14 |
| 509.19 | 620.18 | 733.18 | 002.17 | 265.05 | 583.15 |
| 509.22 | 621.12 | 737.08 | 004.09 | 270.03 | 587.02 |
| 510.17 | 622.16 | 740.15 | 004.13 | 271.05 | 593.01 |
| 511.04 | 623.09 | 741.09 | 005.10 | 275.01 | 593.13 |
| 515.11 | 624.05 | 742.20 | 005.21 | 279.15 | 596.02 |
| 516.06 | 626.02 | 742.22 | 006.14 | 287.09 | 602.19 |
| 516.14 | 626.06 | 743.07 | 008.10 | 288.20 | 614.03 |
| 517.02 | 627.02 | 744.05 | 011.06 | 294.06 | 624.17 |
| 517.10 | 628.15 | 746.14 | 014.07 | 296.17 | 628.21 |
| 517.17 | 628.20 | 747.06 | 019.22 | 297.03 | 630.16 |
| 519.10 | 629.06 | 747.16 | 022.10 | 305.01 | 632.22 |
| 519.20 | 629.13 | 749.16 | 023.16 | 321.20 | 633.11 |
| 521.01 | 632.22 | 750.01 | 024.16 | 322.07 | 635.12 |
| 521.03 | 633.01 | 752.06 | 027.14 | 322.22 | 636.08 |
| 521.11 | 634.01 | 757.16 | 027.19 | 323.01 | 643.04 |
| 522.04 | 635.01 | 758.01 | 032.12 | 323.10 | 644.05 |
| 522.06 | 638.01 | 759.01 | 033.10 | 327.15 | 645.03 |
| 522.07 | 638.10 | 759.20 | 035.01 | 327.16 | 645.21 |
| 523.03 | 638.13 | 760.12 | 035.09 | 331.05 | 649.19 |
| 525.08 | 638.17 | 760.15 | 038.17 | 336.15 | 651.19 |
| 526.08 | 639.01 | 760.18 | 038.19 | 338.03 | 652.09 |
| 527.19 | 639.17 | 760.18 | 039.12 | 339.05 | 653.20 |
| 528.09 | 640.11 | 761.12 | 040.05 | 339.19 | 653.21 |
| 529.06 | 642.09 | 761.15 | 040.07 | 340.04 | 655.15 |
| 529.13 | 643.04 | 762.04 | 044.02 | 352.05 | 659.11 |
| 531.02 | 645.02 | 764.01 | 046.20 | 353.16 | 660.19 |
| 531.21 | 646.05 | on't | 047.20 | 355.03 | 661.13 |
| 532.06 | 649.02 | 233.01 | 048.01 | 357.04 | 669.06 |
| 534.09 | 649.18 | 321.06 | 049.07 | 358.13 | 670.10 |
| 534.11 | 651.03 | 322.08 | 054.09 | 362.21 | 670.11 |
| 539.11 | 652.08 | 497.06 | 056.05 | 365.06 | 671.15 |
| 541.09 | 652.21 | 696.17 | 061.13 | 365.16 | 671.17 |
| 541.20 | 654.08 | once | 061.16 | 365.17 | 678.06 |
| 542.09 | 654.09 | 018.21 | 065.19 | 372.01 | 681.14 |
| 543.02 | 654.17 | 060.14 | 066.05 | 372.04 | 683.01 |
| 544.01 | 655.10 | 079.02 | 072.04 | 376.01 | 685.08 |
| 544.01 | 655.19 | 082.08 | 073.04 | 376.20 | 686.10 |
| 544.13 | 658.08 | 083.15 | 074.11 | 378.15 | 690.11 |
| 547.20 | 659.12 | 084.05 | 075.21 | 378.17 | 692.18 |
| 548.04 | 659.15 | 090.18 | 083.16 | 381.07 | 693.20 |
| 550.04 | 660.03 | 091.18 | 087.10 | 382.11 | 700.18 |
| 551.18 | 660.14 | 106.08 | 092.19 | 383.19 | 703.04 |

| | | | | | |
|---|---|---|---|---|---|
| 704.05 | 340.07 | 219.02 | 378.20 | 182.13 | 451.16 |
| 713.20 | 341.20 | 226.21 | 412.16 | 183.19 | 459.07 |
| 714.05 | 343.19 | 274.14 | 419.03 | 185.07 | 467.12 |
| 726.20 | 349.07 | 283.04 | 465.10 | 186.22 | 469.08 |
| 734.01 | 352.15 | 283.05 | 501.07 | 188.19 | 472.13 |
| 734.04 | 359.16 | 283.10 | 598.02 | 189.02 | 475.20 |
| 736.10 | 370.02 | 287.17 | 620.10 | 195.16 | 476.13 |
| 741.16 | 377.04 | 294.22 | 698.01 | 196.06 | 477.19 |
| 743.07 | 383.04 | 315.05 | 739.10 | 196.08 | 480.15 |
| 744.01 | 383.19 | 315.19 | oppose | 200.08 | 481.02 |
| 747.18 | 390.21 | 350.19 | 344.07 | 203.10 | 481.18 |
| 750.19 | 396.13 | 351.05 | opposed | 203.11 | 488.04 |
| 750.22 | 405.01 | 355.08 | 653.13 | 203.13 | 489.20 |
| 751.14 | 405.15 | 396.20 | opposite | 204.21 | 490.16 |
| 754.06 | 407.01 | 431.11 | 009.09 | 212.15 | 492.03 |
| 756.08 | 411.16 | 433.21 | 154.14 | 214.09 | 496.12 |
| 756.12 | 413.09 | 476.04 | 215.01 | 214.22 | 499.04 |
| 758.01 | 420.14 | 485.13 | 240.18 | 218.17 | 513.06 |
| 758.08 | 426.14 | 495.17 | 272.09 | 228.01 | 513.07 |
| 759.07 | 440.20 | 497.15 | 314.14 | 230.03 | 516.10 |
| 759.11 | 444.15 | 513.03 | 385.01 | 230.04 | 516.14 |
| 760.21 | 450.06 | 523.06 | 393.01 | 231.13 | 517.11 |
| 764.02 | 469.13 | 523.18 | 414.18 | 231.19 | 518.10 |
| 764.10 | 477.16 | 532.15 | 538.19 | 234.01 | 518.12 |
| one's | 478.19 | 560.15 | 567.04 | 234.19 | 519.11 |
| 206.03 | 480.05 | 563.18 | 747.17 | 239.12 | 519.11 |
| 220.18 | 486.14 | 569.01 | opposition | 244.10 | 521.15 |
| 225.16 | 499.07 | 616.15 | 204.16 | 245.15 | 523.01 |
| 258.05 | 501.20 | 629.01 | 456.16 | 257.22 | 524.09 |
| ones | 516.10 | 638.11 | oppression | 259.14 | 531.11 |
| 006.15 | 522.10 | 654.19 | 241.06 | 261.18 | 535.05 |
| 018.10 | 531.16 | 661.07 | 391.10 | 262.03 | 535.15 |
| 275.21 | 535.20 | 673.08 | 442.18 | 265.06 | 542.10 |
| 510.03 | 546.19 | 693.11 | oppressions | 271.17 | 544.05 |
| 518.12 | 557.16 | 702.04 | 126.03 | 272.16 | 544.06 |
| 644.05 | 558.04 | 710.13 | oppressive | 276.19 | 547.04 |
| ongoings | 560.08 | 729.01 | 759.06 | 280.06 | 554.06 |
| 595.03 | 571.04 | 738.18 | oppressor | 280.20 | 559.08 |
| only | 573.03 | 743.12 | 082.01 | 280.22 | 560.09 |
| 003.15 | 576.18 | 756.20 | 726.11 | 284.01 | 561.13 |
| 008.09 | 578.20 | 757.06 | or | 285.14 | 576.21 |
| 011.15 | 583.10 | open-mouthed | 005.07 | 287.19 | 577.01 |
| 019.16 | 588.04 | 297.06 | 005.11 | 299.12 | 578.04 |
| 028.11 | 591.12 | opened | 005.19 | 300.01 | 581.16 |
| 037.09 | 593.09 | 017.20 | 006.14 | 303.10 | 582.18 |
| 047.18 | 605.10 | 054.13 | 007.05 | 306.09 | 583.02 |
| 055.03 | 619.01 | 062.12 | 008.01 | 306.21 | 583.08 |
| 059.09 | 623.05 | 063.07 | 014.09 | 313.17 | 589.18 |
| 060.02 | 638.10 | 101.14 | 019.13 | 313.19 | 589.21 |
| 063.15 | 646.16 | 126.21 | 021.01 | 314.07 | 591.08 |
| 067.07 | 652.11 | 126.22 | 027.06 | 327.08 | 597.08 |
| 074.11 | 655.16 | 190.19 | 029.15 | 331.20 | 597.19 |
| 076.10 | 662.05 | 209.05 | 030.04 | 332.18 | 602.19 |
| 078.05 | 663.03 | 234.20 | 031.06 | 333.21 | 604.01 |
| 081.06 | 672.10 | 250.02 | 031.15 | 336.10 | 604.14 |
| 083.11 | 678.07 | 262.16 | 032.07 | 338.08 | 605.11 |
| 085.07 | 682.06 | 269.05 | 032.11 | 342.01 | 609.01 |
| 092.03 | 691.20 | 311.05 | 033.06 | 342.09 | 609.05 |
| 094.04 | 700.05 | 353.22 | 037.09 | 343.15 | 609.13 |
| 100.05 | 702.10 | 364.22 | 044.17 | 343.19 | 610.17 |
| 103.21 | 712.10 | 378.15 | 047.08 | 343.19 | 611.01 |
| 117.17 | 713.05 | 379.07 | 047.12 | 344.10 | 612.15 |
| 121.19 | 721.10 | 382.08 | 056.19 | 345.02 | 614.03 |
| 123.08 | 729.21 | 405.04 | 056.19 | 346.09 | 615.11 |
| 133.18 | 730.08 | 446.01 | 057.19 | 347.03 | 616.04 |
| 134.02 | 730.13 | 466.04 | 058.04 | 350.06 | 618.13 |
| 141.14 | 732.08 | 507.17 | 059.16 | 352.10 | 620.06 |
| 144.06 | 733.06 | 522.03 | 062.17 | 352.20 | 621.08 |
| 147.13 | 735.07 | 610.03 | 063.16 | 353.08 | 622.02 |
| 152.22 | 737.19 | 621.16 | 064.06 | 353.11 | 622.20 |
| 159.21 | 741.04 | 622.10 | 066.06 | 353.14 | 624.09 |
| 169.11 | 743.16 | 649.15 | 066.16 | 355.17 | 625.06 |
| 174.18 | 746.14 | 654.19 | 067.22 | 363.07 | 626.02 |
| 175.08 | 750.19 | 681.14 | 070.03 | 367.03 | 629.03 |
| 175.11 | 752.20 | 751.08 | 071.05 | 368.08 | 629.19 |
| 175.17 | 759.07 | 763.08 | 080.01 | 368.09 | 633.19 |
| 178.18 | 764.03 | opening | 080.04 | 369.06 | 635.04 |
| 183.17 | onst | 034.10 | 081.05 | 371.07 | 636.10 |
| 190.17 | 322.05 | 077.17 | 087.10 | 371.13 | 639.22 |
| 195.05 | onto | 320.21 | 088.09 | 374.09 | 640.07 |
| 199.15 | 020.17 | 373.07 | 096.08 | 377.22 | 644.11 |
| 206.01 | 122.01 | 623.21 | 099.21 | 383.15 | 645.08 |
| 216.15 | 185.05 | openly | 100.08 | 384.09 | 646.10 |
| 223.15 | 189.09 | 147.17 | 101.05 | 387.17 | 650.19 |
| 224.01 | 400.08 | 314.13 | 103.03 | 390.10 | 654.15 |
| 227.07 | 401.13 | operation | 105.06 | 390.15 | 654.16 |
| 232.07 | 410.21 | 062.01 | 109.21 | 392.01 | 654.17 |
| 246.02 | 535.13 | 135.19 | 109.22 | 393.05 | 661.04 |
| 247.06 | 634.19 | 400.13 | 116.17 | 396.09 | 661.06 |
| 252.20 | 642.10 | opinion | 124.01 | 396.13 | 664.14 |
| 256.17 | 675.12 | 339.02 | 127.02 | 398.04 | 665.18 |
| 267.03 | 763.01 | 763.09 | 130.20 | 399.06 | 667.03 |
| 273.11 | ony | oppen | 134.20 | 399.21 | 668.20 |
| 276.16 | 185.13 | 233.12 | 135.01 | 406.13 | 670.14 |
| 280.09 | onybody | 624.12 | 145.20 | 412.13 | 671.01 |
| 285.11 | 232.20 | 696.11 | 149.04 | 413.03 | 671.14 |
| 286.07 | open | oppen't | 149.13 | 413.11 | 672.12 |
| 294.14 | 016.08 | 016.11 | 153.15 | 414.04 | 677.08 |
| 296.06 | 031.03 | opportunely | 153.16 | 414.22 | 678.15 |
| 299.19 | 039.17 | 180.06 | 153.19 | 425.18 | 681.09 |
| 301.06 | 054.01 | opportunities | 159.20 | 426.11 | 681.10 |
| 302.01 | 060.10 | 222.08 | 160.03 | 426.15 | 684.19 |
| 303.04 | 081.07 | opportunity | 161.01 | 430.01 | 690.15 |
| 306.11 | 107.16 | 065.13 | 162.07 | 430.11 | 694.07 |
| 313.11 | 124.15 | 130.20 | 162.09 | 430.13 | 695.04 |
| 321.17 | 137.22 | 155.11 | 168.19 | 433.08 | 696.20 |
| 322.18 | 157.22 | 193.13 | 170.18 | 433.15 | 698.08 |
| 330.20 | 163.19 | 195.11 | 171.20 | 434.11 | 700.09 |
| 333.08 | 186.03 | 289.21 | 172.06 | 443.01 | 701.08 |
| 335.16 | 207.07 | 344.04 | 179.14 | 443.03 | 701.10 |
| 338.02 | 218.10 | 367.22 | 180.02 | 445.03 | 701.19 |

703.18
704.13
721.03
724.10
727.17
728.11
728.20
730.20
734.03
739.15
741.10
741.16
741.20
743.19
745.13
750.21
753.04
757.10
763.02
orange
 245.21
 247.16
 519.12
oranges
 350.22
order
 003.13
 071.13
 100.07
 121.17
 152.10
 185.12
 199.09
 204.22
 250.05
 299.12
 383.05
 384.08
 419.11
 597.02
 640.22
 644.09
 744.03
ordered
 034.22
 110.07
 187.18
 196.18
 199.14
 281.19
 312.13
 421.17
 470.13
 633.11
 698.20
 721.14
ordering
 091.07
 448.12
 592.09
orders
 036.14
 045.11
 212.14
 261.02
 430.08
 446.22
 636.22
 686.15
ordinary
 048.06
 060.16
 160.11
 196.09
 216.18
 239.09
 255.21
 430.05
 517.06
 614.16
 715.03
 731.19
 745.06
origin
 332.14
original
 388.02
originally
 072.08
 477.07
orisons
 062.15
 391.02
ornament
 006.11
 721.19
ornamented
 045.19
 238.02
orphan
 370.01
orther
 565.14
ortherings
 318.12
other
 006.18
 006.19
 024.20
 025.19
 026.21

032.20
040.09
044.03
050.13
061.15
073.04
095.09
095.16
099.17
116.14
120.14
121.11
125.04
126.22
132.16
135.07
136.16
145.19
154.11
162.09
169.12
174.21
176.05
179.03
189.02
197.02
202.06
204.21
209.16
211.02
212.13
218.21
222.15
223.15
231.05
240.08
262.19
271.22
273.18
275.06
284.07
284.14
291.02
296.16
305.01
322.16
336.14
352.19
358.14
364.06
367.09
372.10
376.12
393.20
394.10
411.20
413.12
415.10
422.05
427.02
442.14
446.02
448.05
455.15
461.03
462.16
463.16
476.13
476.17
480.08
482.03
486.12
494.07
501.19
531.21
533.12
538.01
545.20
558.10
558.22
610.07
619.09
633.01
633.08
645.09
647.07
680.14
683.02
686.11
688.11
692.03
692.19
700.12
703.18
713.21
717.09
724.19
726.21
728.08
733.03
742.09
745.02
752.02
755.10
763.03
other's
 206.04
 258.05
 364.06
others
 082.16

182.08
204.14
310.06
357.16
374.09
377.16
589.03
754.21
otherwise
 311.07
 346.01
 371.11
 658.08
 734.13
ought
 059.17
 171.21
 197.20
 198.14
 220.20
 271.21
 387.07
 405.06
 418.09
 418.09
 543.12
 546.16
 570.17
 604.12
 653.18
 733.16
our
 023.08
 023.18
 024.20
 035.20
 041.02
 041.11
 042.14
 042.16
 043.06
 043.15
 045.12
 046.16
 061.16
 066.21
 073.11
 088.14
 090.08
 103.17
 110.21
 126.06
 131.09
 132.01
 133.01
 139.06
 147.20
 160.11
 164.14
 179.11
 183.11
 184.04
 193.13
 196.13
 197.03
 197.16
 209.15
 226.14
 227.17
 228.08
 262.14
 275.14
 276.15
 280.01
 285.13
 290.04
 297.09
 318.01
 325.09
 325.18
 326.21
 327.01
 334.13
 337.16
 374.19
 381.02
 387.14
 398.13
 407.04
 422.06
 424.05
 432.15
 438.12
 438.12
 454.16
 480.13
 485.10
 488.22
 495.04
 498.19
 501.18
 511.22
 515.04
 527.19
 528.08
 530.04
 532.04
 547.13
 547.16
 556.13
 570.10

585.04
585.08
586.08
586.10
586.15
589.06
594.02
594.15
595.03
598.03
612.07
615.21
621.22
622.07
622.15
623.01
632.17
634.16
635.22
643.04
644.15
660.13
663.08
671.10
680.06
689.16
699.05
700.03
716.20
718.04
727.14
740.18
ours
 199.05
 586.14
ourselves
 042.14
 098.15
 103.18
 104.11
 105.07
 205.21
 286.13
 439.15
 547.02
 646.03
 746.11
 748.12
ousels
 373.19
out
 003.06
 007.01
 008.04
 019.03
 019.20
 020.15
 025.01
 027.07
 028.19
 029.07
 030.11
 030.20
 034.03
 035.01
 038.04
 042.05
 045.10
 046.14
 048.22
 051.21
 055.03
 055.17
 056.09
 059.21
 060.19
 062.08
 064.03
 064.17
 065.06
 074.09
 074.21
 078.09
 078.17
 079.14
 080.09
 084.03
 084.14
 084.15
 085.07
 085.09
 090.20
 094.20
 099.16
 101.15
 102.15
 103.02
 106.02
 106.14
 107.04
 110.18
 118.07
 120.19
 127.05
 132.17
 134.03
 135.21
 136.17
 138.02
 139.10
 140.13

142.15
145.07
145.21
148.01
152.11
152.19
154.11
156.08
157.10
159.19
160.20
163.01
163.05
164.01
165.03
166.20
169.06
169.11
171.17
175.03
176.09
178.22
179.18
181.22
183.15
186.03
187.02
192.01
195.09
196.06
201.09
203.06
208.14
211.03
216.08
217.18
220.03
221.12
226.21
228.09
237.05
237.09
242.12
244.02
245.04
246.04
246.17
249.01
250.05
254.08
255.02
259.22
263.12
266.05
267.01
277.18
282.19
283.13
287.13
291.10
298.12
302.06
306.01
308.13
314.08
318.02
318.04
329.03
331.05
333.01
334.20
339.22
343.04
347.01
348.10
350.04
351.18
355.16
360.16
363.01
366.19
368.04
370.06
370.11
372.20
379.08
382.08
383.05
386.03
386.06
386.17
386.21
388.16
388.17
389.15
394.03
394.05
394.17
397.14
399.03
400.07
401.04
406.05
408.09
408.12
408.21
409.18
420.16
430.08
431.05
432.20

435.09
436.09
437.22
445.08
445.09
450.12
452.02
455.01
462.12
463.22
467.19
473.01
476.20
478.17
479.09
481.02
482.09
482.22
485.22
491.07
492.13
493.01
495.18
499.16
500.08
506.01
506.05
506.20
509.03
510.15
512.08
515.07
524.13
525.02
526.10
533.15
536.20
545.02
553.19
556.05
556.11
557.18
559.03
564.04
564.10
566.08
567.10
567.21
577.15
579.22
585.04
593.05
597.03
599.22
602.16
607.13
609.09
610.15
612.02
612.06
614.21
615.12
619.05
622.01
622.11
622.21
623.22
627.22
629.19
629.20
632.05
632.18
633.05
637.06
642.05
642.09
644.17
645.11
646.02
650.01
653.14
654.08
654.13
660.06
661.14
662.10
665.05
665.14
666.10
668.13
669.05
671.01
672.11
672.15
675.08
676.04
676.08
679.17
680.18
684.12
684.20
691.16
693.18
695.14
698.04
699.11
700.19
704.18
704.21
705.08
706.04

707.14
708.16
712.22
715.08
718.07
722.15
724.18
725.03
731.02
736.11
739.12
740.16
743.12
744.17
747.04
749.14
757.10
758.13
760.18
761.18
out-and-outer
107.14
out-matched
494.16
out-of-the-way
617.19
out-works
160.13
outcast
282.12
724.15
outcry
059.11
outdoor
628.17
outer
287.03
308.21
373.08
cutlive
169.04
outrage
719.03
outrageous
262.09
outright
105.04
188.19
440.16
720.19
outside
053.15
132.13
249.15
364.15
378.08
379.21
392.18
426.11
612.09
638.15
639.11
644.22
654.15
663.08
outstripped
244.15
294.19
480.14
outward
149.06
514.09
outweighs
341.02
oven
118.14
over
002.21
004.10
004.21
008.02
008.17
010.07
015.12
020.05
020.07
021.06
024.01
028.13
039.05
045.06
045.17
049.19
052.03
054.18
057.16
058.08
062.19
063.17
070.16
073.08
078.01
078.06
078.06
082.04
082.15
084.04
087.11
092.01
095.03
101.01

101.21
117.04
120.09
127.06
127.22
129.13
130.15
135.13
136.04
136.05
144.11
145.18
155.13
157.06
157.17
165.03
174.02
188.22
192.17
200.01
204.08
206.08
220.04
223.12
226.08
233.22
247.14
266.21
274.03
274.17
275.14
275.20
276.04
278.10
284.19
287.15
296.01
299.05
310.05
312.01
317.17
325.18
326.17
330.16
337.19
342.05
346.09
349.02
350.22
351.04
351.09
359.14
360.04
364.16
373.12
380.02
382.01
383.03
386.16
388.04
394.11
398.16
402.13
406.15
410.04
410.10
418.11
419.22
424.11
432.19
435.04
436.15
437.14
449.08
454.10
459.06
460.18
466.18
495.20
506.18
507.06
508.17
519.10
519.16
521.09
522.06
526.14
540.16
545.08
549.02
551.13
557.10
561.01
561.10
569.19
573.10
573.11
576.03
582.10
587.09
588.16
597.07
598.09
610.19
613.01
619.02
620.20
631.20
640.10
641.10
652.13

656.03
662.02
666.09
669.16
669.18
672.12
679.16
681.15
686.18
694.11
694.18
700.11
703.06
711.17
724.05
726.12
734.16
743.18
746.04
754.20
760.08
over-intent
249.14
over-looking
665.22
over-topped
442.11
overcame
027.09
258.19
601.16
overcast
123.19
456.20
overcome
085.19
overcoming
512.06
overdone
551.16
overflowing
636.07
overhead
737.17
overhear
180.10
260.06
overheard
471.13
498.03
711.15
overhearing
622.09
overlaid
712.12
overlook
060.22
overlooked
211.02
overpass
313.14
overreach
395.13
overtaking
295.10
299.13
overwhelmed
009.02
280.18
ow'd
719.21
ow't
758.18
owd
043.21
044.05
owe
405.14
owes
646.20
owing
055.06
082.22
136.07
261.18
293.20
393.18
534.20
704.18
owld
318.16
own
002.15
008.02
009.01
012.17
022.13
041.15
047.03
048.02
067.01
070.12
078.12
085.11
089.03
092.04
096.12
111.15
117.21
129.18
145.08

157.17
166.10
167.05
168.11
171.02
171.02
183.10
197.20
203.22
205.02
235.12
241.07
253.02
254.22
263.03
269.08
273.05
277.14
279.11
286.02
290.14
294.07
299.16
316.01
319.14
335.16
337.12
341.11
342.15
349.07
355.12
359.19
362.09
362.20
363.08
370.03
372.06
379.09
379.20
391.01
403.10
414.14
415.11
417.10
418.06
420.13
422.02
423.02
424.10
426.15
438.06
445.06
449.01
454.06
456.22
464.10
465.13
470.09
478.12
480.20
494.16
501.01
501.11
502.18
507.19
527.03
527.05
530.12
536.16
548.19
550.12
556.06
561.21
563.22
580.15
586.12
596.08
601.21
612.04
615.08
616.11
617.20
618.18
631.10
636.17
638.01
638.16
647.14
656.08
659.02
666.22
675.19
689.10
707.09
723.03
731.19
749.22
752.17
owned
422.16
owner
005.05
078.21
224.14
444.08
444.09
449.16
469.19
593.20
694.20
694.22

owner's
399.14
438.13
owners
278.21
445.17
owning
018.08
026.12
442.08
owt
310.12
472.01
692.11
oyster
230.01
pace
552.22
734.17
paced
186.10
314.06
pacified
474.10
655.03
pacify
279.17
pacing
067.22
pack
012.22
199.09
321.04
384.16
page
040.12
045.17
392.21
668.16
694.17
711.18
729.01
paid
112.05
196.16
351.01
658.02
pail
028.12
688.07
pain
107.07
134.04
238.06
297.02
343.07
399.20
539.13
591.09
634.07
730.10
749.04
pained
130.06
painful
236.10
369.09
433.16
513.04
617.02
655.14
painfully
087.11
217.17
296.02
344.22
351.22
pains
079.20
475.22
paint
038.21
painted
006.11
006.14
019.05
painting
105.14
239.10
pair
001.10
010.06
111.09
249.15
373.18
498.06
palace
253.01
palaver
042.13
pale
158.04
192.06
215.10
258.17
319.11
450.21
514.08
529.09
586.18
634.09
639.02

722.11
738.19
paleness
278.21
351.18
744.09
palms
055.14
paltry
346.02
490.09
525.09
605.08
pan
317.18
317.20
692.12
pane
052.18
panelled
038.14
745.07
panels
054.14
281.22
323.13
624.05
654.16
757.13
panes
051.04
110.17
705.16
pang
205.05
218.17
panted
139.10
211.13
434.07
537.19
587.06
605.10
panting
297.05
382.20
papa
106.01
106.01
108.18
425.20
428.03
428.04
435.03
435.21
439.19
440.13
449.12
449.17
449.17
451.22
461.10
479.08
481.09
481.15
481.19
488.14
497.14
499.10
500.03
500.05
501.17
505.09
510.12
510.20
510.20
513.17
518.21
519.18
520.01
520.05
520.18
521.13
524.02
532.11
533.18
534.19
535.07
536.05
536.09
536.12
537.01
537.01
537.03
546.20
546.20
555.21
567.08
570.17
573.03
587.17
591.16
592.18
606.02
613.15
613.17
615.14
617.10
617.13
618.11
618.13

620.17
629.20
632.14
633.06
633.09
633.21
638.18
**papa's**
499.03
521.12
535.20
**paper**
323.03
505.20
506.20
507.11
514.11
710.02
**papered**
098.17
**papers**
330.16
**paradise**
044.01
224.08
587.21
**paragon**
713.19
**paragraph**
040.19
**pardon**
020.03
049.05
073.13
092.11
123.05
164.05
223.16
269.08
331.22
405.20
408.16
**pardonable**
597.20
**pared**
619.19
**parent**
619.10
**parent's**
082.02
**parentage**
746.02
**parents**
074.08
461.12
761.16
**parings**
675.09
**parish**
074.11
083.15
090.17
196.08
**park**
033.03
066.20
103.13
209.08
229.15
269.02
308.08
373.14
413.08
426.09
428.08
428.09
430.09
451.11
509.16
517.03
547.15
552.17
554.01
555.17
588.08
692.20
**park-fence**
480.03
**parlor**
005.13
**parlour**
098.18
208.21
212.03
226.21
261.01
264.05
280.14
304.07
304.17
304.22
320.09
320.11
320.11
367.15
382.02
475.20
477.01
570.02
571.22
641.19

700.07
703.20
**parlours**
320.12
**paroxysm**
282.03
359.13
376.15
604.19
**parrying**
010.22
**parson**
095.05
095.17
**part**
043.18
051.01
057.10
060.08
065.09
091.12
136.19
141.13
163.21
177.04
183.01
184.22
214.22
258.14
267.16
272.03
313.13
344.17
409.22
437.12
476.16
580.14
583.17
593.22
608.18
622.07
645.18
704.01
708.13
708.17
**partake**
065.02
**parted**
166.03
359.17
363.08
385.06
529.05
758.10
**partial**
082.16
499.04
**partiality**
088.06
370.03
443.06
**partially**
304.04
**particular**
119.17
211.07
455.22
674.01
747.18
**particularly**
184.12
256.04
313.08
427.08
728.13
754.17
**parties**
024.15
637.03
**parting**
018.10
199.03
**partly**
031.07
256.17
351.06
387.20
388.01
559.16
559.17
570.06
684.14
732.11
**partner**
131.05
**partner's**
341.15
**partook**
312.19
330.09
371.01
594.21
**parts**
040.09
048.06
429.09
**party**
129.20
155.04
481.14

**pass**
046.09
138.10
158.11
209.11
225.16
234.16
284.12
429.02
480.07
480.11
540.07
569.20
616.16
658.05
672.17
683.12
689.09
698.22
761.10
**passage**
005.11
255.06
257.12
325.19
424.05
**passages**
060.03
**passed**
036.11
047.11
057.10
102.21
141.19
189.22
242.12
278.20
320.22
326.03
368.03
399.16
475.17
503.15
506.14
591.02
688.09
713.10
752.18
**passes**
030.06
**passing**
004.19
085.11
220.01
285.12
290.16
364.21
373.19
540.09
598.13
623.09
638.06
739.21
**passion**
060.12
101.10
128.14
156.15
234.11
256.13
263.18
292.20
339.18
376.16
502.19
537.19
543.17
564.01
600.10
608.21
724.10
**passionate**
188.20
197.04
263.10
474.04
**passionately**
290.06
366.13
397.08
569.04
**passionless**
651.06
**passive**
591.02
**past**
019.09
032.16
090.08
095.14
144.22
145.09
151.11
200.03
241.06
288.09
318.22
357.15
443.11
492.16
515.03

585.02
730.19
**pastor**
047.21
**paternal**
619.14
**paternity**
026.18
**path**
066.12
103.18
432.10
432.11
449.22
485.13
530.04
682.19
693.03
750.05
**pathos**
539.13
**paths**
516.16
**patience**
032.14
090.08
183.15
187.12
187.13
226.12
323.19
443.11
527.04
599.14
713.19
749.18
**patient**
081.03
091.13
196.13
196.14
250.18
291.21
430.22
543.05
591.19
624.03
**patiently**
301.08
449.22
453.10
**patriarchs**
189.10
**patted**
560.06
**pattering**
373.17
**pattern**
323.02
**paul**
232.15
**pause**
049.19
070.11
170.17
360.12
382.22
546.15
**paused**
004.19
183.13
284.22
655.08
703.22
**pausing**
441.20
519.10
**paved**
017.01
308.11
**pavement**
249.02
**paving**
494.07
**paw**
104.19
**paws**
034.17
**pawsed**
043.13
**pay**
064.10
133.16
155.05
270.06
368.08
616.05
713.09
**paying**
130.21
405.02
475.05
685.05
**payment**
222.10
298.18
**pays**
247.07
**peace**
011.03
079.10

089.01
223.17
253.13
274.04
359.06
359.08
370.20
372.03
398.13
558.02
701.03
762.14
**peace-offering**
445.05
**peaceful**
209.19
**pearl-containing**
229.22
**pears**
076.20
**peat**
017.06
380.02
**peaty**
047.14
**pebble**
693.02
**pebbles**
243.18
743.18
**peculiar**
008.07
010.21
025.16
137.08
351.20
421.05
430.06
582.13
655.13
**peculiarity**
371.10
**peculiarly**
226.15
**peep**
078.02
450.19
507.13
**peeped**
299.06
757.15
**peeping**
127.20
**peer**
145.06
**peering**
317.17
471.11
**peevish**
003.19
091.15
099.10
153.08
411.12
506.10
531.14
535.16
551.17
588.19
**peevishly**
172.09
193.03
**peevishness**
224.01
451.03
**peg**
667.01
**pen**
040.06
305.22
**penance**
592.09
**pencil**
305.14
505.21
**pendant**
107.04
**penetralium**
005.09
**peniston**
276.14
**penistone**
276.21
427.07
428.20
433.02
445.12
483.06
**penning**
582.13
**pennistow**
151.20
**penny**
048.02
**pensive**
146.02
425.11
**people**
007.15
022.04
025.19

072.01
089.09
123.03
132.02
133.21
136.03
136.04
154.01
175.16
199.15
231.21
235.03
242.06
250.08
262.13
273.20
292.13
313.11
314.02
336.14
356.21
372.09
389.03
406.12
421.01
437.11
440.18
445.03
455.07
461.03
499.01
536.10
536.14
573.03
579.10
603.20
686.08
699.02
718.21
**per**
047.18
**perceive**
012.21
136.03
252.02
273.09
338.21
419.10
512.16
652.18
**perceived**
038.07
130.18
170.18
243.17
364.20
374.10
456.06
491.22
589.04
711.16
725.01
748.21
763.16
**perceives**
472.17
**perceiving**
024.12
192.09
228.13
237.19
285.05
343.12
437.11
502.04
534.01
551.08
561.05
611.20
632.05
684.09
691.12
**perceptible**
352.07
**perdition**
168.14
443.21
**peremptorily**
227.01
267.12
**peremptory**
457.07
**perfect**
001.09
042.05
227.06
263.16
296.07
335.04
370.20
426.17
557.12
**perfectly**
008.10
083.10
142.05
162.11
175.16
314.07
426.18
434.16

| | | | | | |
|---|---|---|---|---|---|
| 611.03 | permitted | personated | petulant | piked | pity |
| 712.04 | 041.20 | 431.18 | 506.07 | 191.04 | 025.07 |
| 737.11 | 117.08 | personification | petulantly | pikes | 058.05 |
| 757.21 | 188.12 | 731.03 | 152.17 | 233.12 | 148.17 |
| perforce | 418.15 | personified | 352.19 | pile | 168.21 |
| 036.09 | 580.06 | 058.09 | pewter | 053.16 | 171.05 |
| 705.02 | permitting | persons | 006.01 | piled | 174.18 |
| perform | 590.10 | 012.04 | 098.20 | 038.19 | 343.03 |
| 592.05 | perpetual | 221.15 | 312.18 | 053.04 | 343.03 |
| performed | 015.18 | 406.11 | phalanx | 321.09 | 343.08 |
| 172.03 | 080.14 | 480.21 | 203.05 | pilgrim's | 346.03 |
| 289.10 | 224.10 | perspicacity | phantoms | 046.18 | 356.22 |
| performing | 410.13 | 339.03 | 761.14 | 050.07 | 374.08 |
| 062.14 | perpetually | perspiration | pharisee | pilgrimage | 386.09 |
| 209.19 | 234.02 | 054.04 | 089.12 | 445.12 | 476.14 |
| 715.09 | perplex | 655.09 | phase | pillow | 479.21 |
| perfuming | 177.07 | persuade | 252.10 | 045.05 | 500.09 |
| 039.13 | 414.16 | 031.15 | phases | 082.10 | 540.08 |
| perhaps | perplexed | 209.01 | 734.11 | 271.02 | 574.01 |
| 003.17 | 594.18 | 273.04 | pheasant | 274.12 | 594.19 |
| 007.12 | 738.02 | 285.21 | 108.19 | 276.05 | 600.19 |
| 022.08 | 739.09 | 304.15 | pheasants | 296.01 | 627.15 |
| 081.04 | 743.05 | 317.01 | 556.13 | 302.15 | 631.10 |
| 127.02 | 759.16 | 329.06 | phenix | 370.15 | 631.11 |
| 136.18 | perplexities | 343.15 | 437.02 | 462.03 | 661.10 |
| 167.22 | 148.13 | 462.08 | 437.06 | 597.08 | pitying |
| 170.15 | perplexity | 484.06 | 445.07 | 654.18 | 621.07 |
| 174.19 | 291.03 | 675.01 | philosopher | pillows | place |
| 195.10 | 362.12 | 722.22 | 713.18 | 275.10 | 005.05 |
| 195.11 | 460.12 | persuaded | philosophical | pills | 013.10 |
| 216.05 | persecuting | 009.03 | 274.09 | 202.06 | 027.08 |
| 230.14 | 081.11 | 085.22 | phlegm | pinafores | 028.16 |
| 256.01 | persecutions | 132.07 | 011.05 | 042.16 | 032.12 |
| 272.11 | 056.16 | 188.09 | phrase | pincers | 039.13 |
| 281.01 | persecutor | 198.20 | 048.10 | 389.16 | 043.13 |
| 337.10 | 222.04 | 242.05 | phraseology | pinch | 045.15 |
| 373.04 | perseverance | 527.11 | 401.17 | 606.16 | 049.16 |
| 393.02 | 002.11 | 583.01 | physical | 645.19 | 056.02 |
| 404.14 | 309.20 | 715.11 | 027.10 | pinched | 063.05 |
| 446.22 | 378.16 | 759.20 | 235.11 | 048.18 | 097.03 |
| 461.13 | persevere | persuading | 359.09 | 111.13 | 104.03 |
| 463.12 | 579.01 | 555.12 | 594.21 | 156.02 | 125.22 |
| 464.06 | persevered | 615.19 | 682.05 | 389.02 | 128.10 |
| 523.05 | 132.06 | persuasions | physically | 476.10 | 147.09 |
| 540.13 | 159.15 | 541.04 | 442.16 | pinches | 149.08 |
| 555.11 | 234.01 | pert | physiognomy | 081.06 | 150.21 |
| 567.19 | 265.02 | 498.11 | 010.13 | pined | 160.10 |
| 574.06 | 461.08 | pertinacious | 201.07 | 226.08 | 176.05 |
| 582.01 | 755.01 | 417.21 | 442.08 | pines | 181.21 |
| 601.12 | persevering | 590.06 | pick | 527.06 | 203.11 |
| 603.11 | 703.13 | pertinaciously | 055.02 | pining | 212.06 |
| 622.19 | persist | 269.09 | 109.18 | 238.19 | 222.16 |
| 645.09 | 345.02 | pertly | picked | 324.15 | 250.10 |
| 669.02 | 346.13 | 537.02 | 078.20 | 616.07 | 278.21 |
| 678.17 | 396.19 | pertness | 245.04 | pinkness | 287.14 |
| 686.04 | persisted | 205.04 | 275.18 | 549.02 | 290.17 |
| 702.05 | 084.05 | 234.14 | 437.10 | pint | 291.18 |
| 702.21 | 142.20 | 524.14 | picture | 036.04 | 295.13 |
| 713.13 | 152.11 | 670.21 | 146.04 | 168.03 | 304.03 |
| 728.05 | 158.16 | peruse | 230.12 | 699.14 | 308.09 |
| 730.17 | 280.21 | 354.12 | 358.04 | pious | 312.01 |
| 735.08 | 338.17 | perused | 409.08 | 004.01 | 318.16 |
| 762.08 | 365.19 | 328.02 | 561.19 | 046.01 | 320.09 |
| peril | 587.12 | 509.10 | 576.02 | 089.16 | 321.12 |
| 035.01 | 615.18 | 550.11 | 583.22 | pipe | 323.20 |
| 263.08 | 707.03 | 676.10 | 632.20 | 062.02 | 330.06 |
| 319.01 | person | perusing | 634.03 | 476.07 | 334.14 |
| perilous | 020.12 | 057.12 | 647.17 | 531.04 | 344.03 |
| 205.15 | 020.18 | 703.04 | 655.19 | 690.17 | 350.04 |
| perils | 035.09 | pervading | pictured | 691.11 | 378.02 |
| 576.16 | 114.02 | 330.09 | 066.03 | 706.13 | 379.17 |
| period | 135.02 | perverse | 095.18 | pistol | 386.17 |
| 024.16 | 135.05 | 025.18 | pictures | 315.14 | 392.22 |
| 144.20 | 146.10 | 425.16 | 555.04 | 316.12 | 397.05 |
| 197.10 | 182.11 | perverseness | 632.21 | 398.08 | 402.13 |
| 243.02 | 208.10 | 541.10 | 649.05 | pistols | 411.21 |
| 318.20 | 210.03 | perversity | 668.14 | 260.05 | 422.02 |
| 325.03 | 211.06 | 709.05 | 705.15 | 344.08 | 428.08 |
| 335.14 | 229.01 | perverted | 712.01 | pit | 433.10 |
| 340.20 | 263.17 | 388.14 | picturing | 031.06 | 463.03 |
| 355.21 | 291.11 | pet | 338.13 | 490.09 | 469.20 |
| 424.03 | 333.07 | 009.20 | 746.05 | 695.17 | 483.12 |
| 548.01 | 340.07 | 020.14 | piece | pitch | 513.03 |
| 552.20 | 348.09 | 272.11 | 019.04 | 075.03 | 526.03 |
| 597.04 | 352.02 | 443.07 | 029.04 | 389.14 | 535.01 |
| 655.18 | 382.08 | 453.18 | 060.08 | pitched | 585.08 |
| 735.06 | 408.02 | 479.16 | 062.04 | 402.05 | 588.03 |
| 754.03 | 409.12 | 545.17 | 160.21 | pitcher | 617.19 |
| perishable | 465.07 | 612.04 | 244.02 | 270.17 | 618.10 |
| 243.20 | 521.07 | peter | 339.07 | 319.16 | 628.22 |
| perished | 525.12 | 232.15 | 374.01 | 534.09 | 641.01 |
| 067.16 | 542.01 | petition | 420.20 | pitchfork | 649.01 |
| 182.20 | 588.16 | 580.12 | 722.03 | 016.20 | 661.11 |
| 376.18 | 597.17 | 642.03 | 749.14 | piteous | 665.18 |
| perishing | 609.07 | 711.02 | pieces | 326.02 | 672.16 |
| 614.06 | 616.18 | petrified | 323.03 | pitied | 685.05 |
| permanent | 626.04 | 553.13 | 513.20 | 356.21 | 691.10 |
| 188.13 | 645.06 | petted | 531.03 | 456.21 | 721.13 |
| 296.09 | 684.08 | 105.04 | 680.17 | 600.18 | 731.08 |
| permission | 695.18 | 500.02 | 724.01 | 631.10 | 742.10 |
| 175.13 | 721.10 | petting | piercing | pitiful | 747.14 |
| 222.11 | 750.22 | 081.15 | 191.19 | 152.12 | 754.11 |
| 289.20 | 753.01 | pettish | 278.12 | 340.09 | placed |
| 311.17 | personal | 218.11 | pigeon | 497.19 | 038.18 |
| 341.09 | 149.22 | pettishly | 017.02 | 534.20 | 065.06 |
| 597.02 | 257.14 | 540.19 | pigeon's | 614.01 | 075.10 |
| 643.08 | 582.13 | pettishness | 275.09 | pitiless | 108.14 |
| permit | 636.09 | 588.11 | pigeons | 230.02 | 186.08 |
| 032.11 | personally | petulance | 248.13 | pits | 453.04 |
| 360.06 | 580.11 | 223.07 | pigeons' | 065.22 | 471.02 |
| 672.02 | | 436.04 | 275.09 | | 542.07 |

| | | | | |
|---|---|---|---|---|
| 667.20 | playfulness | 219.14 | pocket-handkerchief | possessed |
| 703.04 | 235.15 | 470.13 | 129.07 | 072.11 |
| places | playing | 541.21 | 081.12 | 011.22 |
| 446.02 | 065.09 | 630.07 | 094.19 | 144.19 |
| placidly | 075.17 | pleasure | 120.05 | 149.11 |
| 352.15 | 118.13 | 019.11 | 124.09 | 160.01 |
| placing | 160.21 | 059.16 | 132.09 | 174.17 |
| 367.10 | 344.16 | 098.19 | 138.05 | 225.09 |
| plague | 430.13 | 099.04 | 142.18 | 262.07 |
| 064.11 | 599.21 | 104.22 | 157.13 | 358.18 |
| 541.11 | 604.05 | 115.18 | 162.10 | 442.09 |
| 607.15 | 655.01 | 131.09 | 164.22 | 468.20 |
| 646.16 | playmate | 150.06 | 196.21 | 587.11 |
| 660.12 | 148.11 | 168.14 | 514.15 | possesses |
| plagued | 243.21 | 183.08 | poetry | 160.02 |
| 080.20 | playmate's | 183.09 | 678.11 | 718.08 |
| plaguing | 130.10 | 216.05 | poignant | possessing |
| 090.14 | playmates | 224.16 | 149.18 | 316.07 |
| 708.15 | 454.14 | 248.11 | point | possession |
| plaid | playthings | 302.17 | 030.20 | 205.19 |
| 114.19 | 512.18 | 342.08 | 152.13 | 323.15 |
| plain | 512.19 | 389.20 | 152.20 | 382.02 |
| 238.22 | plea | 389.21 | 163.21 | 422.13 |
| 292.03 | 226.13 | 395.10 | 170.22 | 555.18 |
| 298.21 | plead | 449.16 | 199.22 | 664.20 |
| 380.05 | 085.01 | 460.10 | 228.09 | possessor |
| 665.13 | 580.16 | 479.20 | 263.07 | 026.01 |
| plainer | 685.05 | 493.11 | 342.14 | possibility |
| 166.08 | 685.09 | 500.19 | 387.16 | 295.10 |
| 407.06 | pleaded | 558.18 | 393.03 | possible |
| plainly | 340.01 | 592.08 | 428.12 | 002.09 |
| 054.07 | 365.16 | 608.01 | 573.07 | 027.21 |
| 108.09 | 418.03 | 648.15 | 641.04 | 051.07 |
| 356.02 | 646.14 | 682.13 | 652.08 | 051.15 |
| 471.09 | pleasant | 682.15 | 668.13 | 092.05 |
| 755.17 | 027.08 | 694.16 | 713.20 | 136.11 |
| plan | 044.15 | 739.19 | 717.16 | 225.14 |
| 100.19 | 126.05 | 749.03 | 733.03 | 328.08 |
| 113.06 | 173.09 | pledge | pointed | 333.12 |
| 134.03 | 236.21 | 012.20 | 153.01 | 333.13 |
| 161.03 | 322.11 | 372.07 | 321.17 | 429.17 |
| 216.03 | 350.18 | pledged | 354.15 | 484.13 |
| 252.17 | 376.10 | 172.13 | 395.03 | 516.09 |
| 263.17 | 463.03 | 447.03 | 482.03 | 576.05 |
| 457.05 | 478.04 | pledging | pointer | 636.03 |
| plank | 561.12 | 294.15 | 006.17 | 701.11 |
| 028.06 | 592.11 | plentiful | pointers | 726.13 |
| planned | 647.17 | 017.07 | 431.19 | 758.07 |
| 556.21 | 703.20 | plentifully | 432.09 | possibly |
| planning | pleasanter | 221.18 | 433.19 | 007.14 |
| 285.06 | 727.16 | plenty | pointing | 174.22 |
| 716.02 | pleasantest | 131.19 | 066.13 | 340.04 |
| plans | 557.05 | 144.13 | 518.15 | 552.14 |
| 503.02 | 588.04 | 204.09 | poised | 578.04 |
| 584.05 | please | 287.11 | 020.06 | 609.06 |
| plant | 059.21 | 431.16 | poison | 753.07 |
| 346.04 | 064.18 | 479.13 | 256.20 | post |
| 721.09 | 074.18 | 577.10 | 290.01 | 024.08 |
| plantation | 118.05 | 611.10 | 476.07 | 217.01 |
| 294.11 | 159.11 | 611.11 | poisoned | 248.03 |
| 432.14 | 163.15 | 693.17 | 612.05 | 279.19 |
| planted | 171.06 | pliable | poisoning | 415.04 |
| 103.18 | 212.14 | 182.03 | 387.14 | 716.21 |
| 456.13 | 214.18 | plight | poisonous | postern |
| plants | 216.17 | 387.04 | 230.20 | 034.05 |
| 380.01 | 239.20 | plisky | poker | postpone |
| 716.03 | 253.15 | 324.21 | 011.01 | 466.01 |
| plase | 265.05 | plodding | 261.07 | postponed |
| 713.08 | 287.18 | 322.19 | 385.10 | 587.03 |
| plash | 306.19 | plotted | 513.04 | pot |
| 188.17 | 334.17 | 745.10 | 692.02 | 020.07 |
| plate | 337.14 | plottered | policy | 044.08 |
| 154.20 | 354.04 | 187.09 | 263.09 | potatoes |
| 717.12 | 397.03 | plough-boy | polished | 084.10 |
| 718.15 | 437.03 | 041.10 | 119.14 | potent |
| 740.05 | 452.12 | 210.15 | 494.07 | 474.11 |
| 741.09 | 532.15 | ploughboy | politeness | 646.05 |
| plateful | 550.10 | 214.11 | 147.13 | 731.11 |
| 111.06 | 562.14 | pluck | 216.19 | pots |
| platefuls | 563.03 | 064.01 | 674.17 | 324.13 |
| 130.03 | 581.07 | 518.21 | pondered | pounds |
| plausible | 600.06 | plucked | 217.17 | 047.18 |
| 249.19 | 754.16 | 049.10 | 281.13 | 166.05 |
| play | pleased | 509.03 | pondering | pour |
| 041.21 | 017.08 | plump | 417.18 | 624.19 |
| 045.09 | 034.21 | 487.05 | ponies | poured |
| 061.21 | 075.11 | plundered | 656.06 | 050.17 |
| 091.04 | 093.11 | 510.01 | pony | 168.04 |
| 187.11 | 100.14 | plundering | 114.01 | 319.15 |
| 232.06 | 133.01 | 481.01 | 120.13 | 512.07 |
| 272.11 | 175.19 | plunge | 187.08 | 612.02 |
| 417.19 | 198.07 | 317.21 | 428.12 | 757.04 |
| 451.18 | 227.18 | poacher | 430.21 | pouring |
| 524.11 | 270.11 | 481.05 | 432.08 | 238.20 |
| 548.12 | 299.18 | pocket | 437.02 | 434.22 |
| 558.13 | 412.19 | 203.06 | 437.05 | 557.17 |
| 558.19 | 421.09 | 233.10 | 440.01 | pouting |
| 619.16 | 453.22 | 245.21 | 441.15 | 435.14 |
| play-things | 499.08 | 326.22 | 459.04 | powders |
| 507.09 | 501.20 | 350.05 | 529.08 | 203.02 |
| played | 518.03 | 399.17 | 553.02 | power |
| 051.01 | 534.15 | 420.16 | 556.02 | 004.09 |
| 099.21 | 544.10 | 509.03 | 598.18 | 092.01 |
| 148.03 | 574.04 | 523.05 | 632.16 | 101.01 |
| 260.07 | 633.15 | 685.12 | 656.02 | 156.15 |
| 290.05 | 651.04 | pocket-book | 656.05 | 160.01 |
| 311.22 | 666.19 | 330.17 | poor | 160.02 |
| 421.10 | 700.10 | 712.13 | 009.01 | 177.16 |
| playfellow | 741.04 | pocket-handherchief | 032.11 | 181.22 |
| 449.11 | pleases | 325.17 | 035.22 | 225.16 |
| | 219.13 | | 045.06 | 235.12 |
| | | | 063.21 | 305.19 |

342.05
389.05
598.02
632.07
729.13
powerful
199.04
316.06
582.21
powerfully
040.15
058.05
powerless
565.05
607.08
powers
336.04
practicable
234.22
practically
755.08
practice
350.15
practise
147.13
practised
245.16
praise
147.15
praised
083.01
218.22
praiseworthy
562.08
praising
218.19
677.06
prattled
099.06
pray
085.04
094.14
181.06
229.20
285.20
342.06
376.19
413.14
439.13
521.17
525.07
560.20
697.17
prayed
144.01
374.13
577.20
prayer
053.06
118.21
185.15
376.20
401.16
624.19
prayer-books
041.11
prayer-meeting
556.12
prayers
092.10
094.06
274.04
praying
030.11
390.20
651.10
pre-eminent
313.18
preach
047.06
preached
048.04
preacher
047.07
preaching
191.11
precarious
457.17
precaution
248.21
precautions
501.12
precede
656.17
preceded
003.07
320.20
preceding
415.21
485.12
precept
443.04
precepts
754.09
precincts
755.03
precious
081.14
166.15
306.03
324.16

340.07
391.02
434.20
512.06
646.10
660.18
719.03
precipitating
410.11
precise
729.15
precisely
041.16
728.06
precluding
683.10
predecessor's
072.17
predicament
036.13
067.06
383.10
preeminently
005.12
preferable
407.18
461.17
preference
225.12
240.14
preferred
071.09
259.11
556.06
701.02
747.03
prejucial
254.14
prejudice
488.21
prejudiced
499.02
prematurely
027.18
premises
567.13
690.11
preparation
317.22
preparations
023.03
062.22
416.01
prepare
345.12
451.12
460.05
472.14
555.04
691.17
prepared
068.04
118.16
128.03
294.16
304.18
612.05
746.22
preparing
097.04
151.02
466.09
674.12
preposterously
049.12
presence
054.10
062.03
097.04
148.06
151.14
155.13
155.15
172.03
179.16
180.02
184.13
213.08
256.20
296.20
313.03
341.02
368.13
372.05
378.21
387.18
404.18
419.09
569.22
573.11
581.01
646.04
653.04
730.13
present
013.10
022.07
066.11
116.12
119.03
136.02

149.07
167.19
175.09
175.12
175.17
194.18
203.08
239.21
261.19
280.07
288.06
293.19
295.15
304.21
322.15
331.21
342.10
358.07
416.07
443.14
444.08
457.17
504.05
506.04
522.11
528.14
543.14
592.03
608.05
609.11
616.05
639.10
672.05
698.05
710.06
728.08
730.05
750.22
752.15
760.09
presentable
580.05
666.13
presented
330.05
409.08
455.11
presentiment
217.21
416.05
733.13
presently
026.06
050.13
075.08
166.14
193.01
238.02
325.07
362.14
403.01
454.16
482.10
491.09
553.01
589.07
648.17
671.08
681.06
706.02
717.02
presents
079.12
099.08
preserve
216.18
296.06
302.04
307.04
470.15
preserved
449.14
preserving
271.11
presiding
024.01
press
277.02
277.03
277.08
pressed
166.15
294.16
325.20
759.10
pressing
763.05
presume
030.18
198.01
524.15
presumed
149.01
presuming
567.04
presumptuous
250.06
293.20
405.07
pretence
069.09

670.07
pretend
342.02
397.06
444.13
483.17
570.09
600.17
722.17
pretended
091.22
216.05
477.18
500.09
528.11
pretending
276.15
487.16
600.16
631.13
675.10
preter-human
400.05
preternaturally
267.02
prettier
167.17
pretty
071.03
099.19
144.16
167.16
294.09
330.10
388.03
422.04
435.08
439.12
486.05
509.13
511.22
536.01
545.16
559.09
560.02
565.02
604.07
609.20
632.16
676.18
679.13
prevail
192.13
347.16
prevailing
023.07
149.19
prevent
101.22
195.02
216.07
249.04
256.22
279.10
344.09
400.04
485.05
539.07
602.04
638.02
prevented
084.20
180.01
347.04
383.19
527.19
573.01
previous
005.08
266.17
421.03
740.06
previously
017.10
048.14
274.22
596.05
prey
107.10
price
181.13
pricked
048.18
pride
007.16
088.08
117.04
198.10
269.12
325.05
326.09
375.16
444.05
470.20
489.11
494.01
512.20
666.22
671.10
707.11
732.05

prime
091.14
135.04
431.03
585.02
primitive
006.14
primrose
737.18
primroses
381.09
717.12
prince
125.15
princess
667.11
principal
004.21
222.02
principles
240.20
print
045.18
printed
057.14
511.07
678.20
printer
040.08
prior
241.02
548.01
prison
360.21
545.09
567.08
prisoner
133.04
620.06
637.20
private
048.09
118.21
131.01
155.05
342.20
privilege
026.12
105.12
644.13
privileges
082.03
probability
596.10
probable
071.05
429.14
465.08
probably
013.04
040.12
056.14
096.07
103.07
141.03
174.16
240.07
269.10
308.09
318.01
330.13
365.01
373.06
377.15
393.11
414.08
495.06
532.01
562.10
580.14
582.08
686.07
733.16
754.02
761.14
proceed
112.02
178.03
203.21
209.02
565.19
745.06
proceeded
058.06
121.01
134.12
155.21
318.04
372.14
453.03
455.15
513.03
662.11
669.04
689.18
proceeding
010.17

305.16
389.19
401.15
553.10
644.10
proceedings
509.22
706.02
process
270.12
proclaimant
297.03
procure
737.18
produce
258.12
591.10
604.21
712.14
produced
054.15
058.09
061.03
097.14
118.11
205.14
304.03
528.20
683.03
profaned
680.15
profiting
224.09
profound
062.09
profusely
383.20
progess
445.04
prognosticate
135.10
progress
270.13
462.10
763.17
progressed
029.18
prohibition
101.16
project
044.20
308.17
428.16
projected
016.02
projecting
206.10
prolong
478.11
prolonged
156.03
326.01
360.12
498.19
promise
021.18
127.03
142.07
142.16
183.21
184.02
275.22
333.20
341.21
355.11
395.16
446.16
474.10
512.14
513.01
554.14
563.11
574.02
599.19
617.13
618.08
promised
076.19
079.12
099.22
129.08
247.15
346.19
428.17
504.22
544.06
559.11
promises
089.13
462.16
582.20
promising
327.11
prompt
222.13
263.03
prompted
030.13
443.07
709.06
734.01

prompters 641.08, 682.21
promptly 203.14, 664.09
prone 239.22
pronounce 375.03, 759.16
pronounced 154.16, 196.02
pronouncing 206.20
pronouns 013.07
pronunciation 497.04
proof 056.02, 223.16, 345.21
proofs 021.11, 352.04
prop 457.19
propensity 425.15
proper 020.12, 267.20, 288.14, 332.11, 508.18, 518.05, 665.21, 739.10, 743.08
properly 043.21, 103.06, 172.19, 564.19, 569.14
property 225.15, 300.03, 418.10, 419.01, 443.16, 466.13, 485.04, 502.08, 636.09, 664.12, 752.09
prophecy 178.01, 672.09
prophesy 044.16
propitiate 245.21, 441.16
proportion 343.06
proposal 482.21, 589.08
propose 672.11
proposed 185.10, 465.08, 488.18, 522.13, 673.03, 692.06
proposes 044.12
proposing 589.07
propriety 255.18
prose 680.13
prosecute 503.01
prospect 356.06, 447.02, 457.03, 577.02, 583.11, 644.02, 681.03
prospective 469.19
prostrate 604.18
protect 646.09
protected 383.17
protector 342.16
protestations 235.18, 529.04

protested 344.16
protract 217.10
protracted 185.12, 372.22, 546.15, 749.11
proud 123.02, 123.03, 148.16, 173.18, 235.06, 494.04, 494.05, 726.20
proudly 664.08
prove 070.01, 253.10, 261.22, 521.22, 529.11, 755.08
proved 008.09, 040.03, 196.01, 422.14, 422.15, 431.12
proves 521.19
provided 143.19, 319.15, 323.20, 484.19, 637.01, 677.20, 739.19
providence 223.04, 579.07
provident 619.09
providential 029.22
province 672.06
provincial 004.05
provincialisms 137.05
provision 431.16
provoke 091.16, 256.05, 263.08, 342.03, 535.17, 590.20, 621.02
provoked 009.15, 161.01, 197.07, 338.21, 602.13, 717.16, 723.16
provokes 392.08
provoking 029.14, 223.16, 280.15, 542.15
provokingly 572.15, 681.18
prowled 241.08
proximity 373.21, 459.11, 712.08
proxy 327.12
prudence 342.07, 389.18
prudential 013.04
prudently 221.21, 718.21
prying 656.16, 743.03
psalmody 133.01
public-house 688.06
publicly 047.09

puffed 062.06, 322.15
puffs 531.18
puling 468.03, 614.10
pull 003.06, 042.07, 127.18, 160.10, 522.12, 565.18, 649.22, 694.07
pulled 036.04, 038.15, 042.09, 052.17, 060.11, 104.21, 108.13, 257.17, 399.15, 676.07, 721.03, 721.06
pulling 116.06, 163.02, 218.04, 235.02, 275.03, 315.13, 389.15, 409.17, 610.06, 623.21
pulpit 048.02, 050.18
pulse 143.07, 376.01, 640.02
pump 017.02, 259.17
punch 009.18
punctually 686.04
punish 133.21, 168.14, 239.02, 645.17
punishing 633.21
punishment 057.01, 091.01, 100.12, 272.15, 589.05
puny 336.04, 369.04, 414.01
pupil 695.19, 726.14
puppies 006.18, 410.05
pure 004.07, 104.04, 215.10, 340.15, 372.20, 462.19, 479.18, 526.07, 616.07, 744.14
purgatory 130.18, 410.07
purification 129.07
purity 119.17
purple 107.03, 156.18
purport 400.17
purpose 011.14, 040.05, 066.09, 165.11, 226.22, 239.01, 251.02, 256.10, 264.02, 290.01, 308.20, 342.04, 390.05, 422.11, 509.19, 524.05, 539.11, 570.09, 588.20, 599.11, 620.18, 662.05, 759.21
purposely 572.09, 582.19
purposes 047.15, 636.08
pursue 058.04, 295.11, 437.16, 503.06
pursued 171.09, 219.05, 247.11, 277.16, 295.10, 358.18, 427.16, 440.13, 456.04, 703.18, 722.06, 733.10, 749.08
pursuing 034.07, 583.21, 629.07
pursuit 149.12
pursuits 682.21
push 063.16, 259.17, 281.22, 352.21, 401.13, 538.09, 539.17
pushed 020.15, 032.15, 044.09, 054.01, 067.01, 110.09, 163.20, 263.04, 325.12, 468.04, 527.01, 613.05, 633.04
pushing 003.05, 271.15, 433.04, 436.07, 456.13, 482.12, 607.13, 633.21, 675.05, 747.22, 757.14
puss's 135.20
put 028.06, 030.09, 034.14, 037.05, 064.09, 064.13, 077.04, 080.02, 081.01, 084.03, 090.07, 095.04, 101.15, 102.15, 103.20, 108.17, 117.03, 126.16, 135.20, 143.02, 143.14, 162.12, 169.20, 173.03, 208.14, 209.21, 216.08, 229.15

242.04, 247.16, 249.06, 250.07, 254.08, 274.09, 275.09, 294.15, 298.17, 302.15, 316.15, 320.17, 326.06, 329.16, 332.09, 341.16, 343.12, 347.17, 362.14, 374.04, 384.05, 385.01, 394.06, 397.14, 410.18, 435.11, 435.19, 452.15, 452.21, 462.22, 479.09, 489.02, 494.06, 506.05, 513.02, 519.20, 530.11, 539.13, 542.11, 553.09, 555.05, 563.13, 567.08, 610.15, 610.20, 611.15, 636.17, 638.13, 662.05, 669.05, 676.01, 676.11, 703.07, 721.08, 747.15, 758.02
puts 042.04
putting 012.05, 067.21, 094.17, 107.16, 118.14, 141.22, 190.08, 441.18, 443.11, 452.07, 505.12, 519.16, 724.09, 742.15, 742.17
puzzle 636.12
puzzled 137.02, 329.16, 392.12, 590.09, 709.21, 716.18
pyramid 053.04
quaker 665.13
qualified 425.05
qualities 442.09, 494.11, 620.05
quality 322.21
qualm 085.20, 514.04
quantities 099.07, 481.10
quantity 004.20, 133.09
quarrel 105.01, 160.12, 184.08, 219.02, 253.14, 253.14

264.07, 292.19, 489.07, 489.15, 545.18, 571.15
quarrelled 280.15, 488.22, 501.21
quarrelling 235.16, 499.10, 557.05, 701.02
quarrels 720.05
quarries 066.02
quart 531.02
quarter 005.16, 039.21, 053.07, 098.15, 185.15, 539.10, 586.12, 639.11, 661.20
quarters 222.05
quean 720.13
queen 125.17, 145.06, 446.12
queer 037.10, 176.16, 199.18, 446.02, 491.18, 627.14, 699.18, 742.14
quelled 374.13, 538.18
quenched 404.13
querulous 061.11
quest 187.04
question 028.10, 117.03, 172.19, 209.21, 210.06, 249.06, 265.01, 267.13, 294.02, 307.08, 329.03, 372.12, 376.05, 417.19, 428.21, 482.22, 531.08, 534.15, 742.15, 742.17
questioned 313.15, 496.13
questioner 438.17
questioning 221.12, 354.17, 711.02
questions 307.02, 332.09, 402.15, 434.21, 462.22, 465.11, 551.02, 563.14, 676.11
quick 098.03, 172.10, 215.04, 283.05, 322.17, 365.06, 426.05, 434.08, 437.03, 562.17, 594.12, 596.08, 604.04

661.09
705.18
744.16
quicker
319.02
quickly
036.06
126.16
211.05
259.18
291.07
545.12
728.19
757.14
quiescence
344.06
quiet
033.15
054.12
067.19
090.21
129.13
142.10
162.11
282.18
288.14
353.08
372.07
377.22
396.03
404.02
430.14
451.20
485.12
541.18
611.17
615.12
632.01
661.22
669.16
764.11
quieter
392.07
540.14
quietest
082.14
quietly
077.11
092.19
110.19
241.02
256.15
375.19
409.10
503.13
637.20
701.09
710.18
quietness
719.15
quilt
321.20
quit
060.05
185.01
289.17
316.21
372.19
377.18
550.02
578.14
618.10
636.13
637.14
641.02
700.22
743.06
quite
040.12
059.15
098.13
110.02
114.08
123.12
126.05
142.04
152.19
167.21
181.01
181.04
202.08
213.20
214.07
221.05
230.09
285.19
303.03
313.03
330.18
333.12
333.13
344.14
388.05
423.03
428.15
434.08
449.14
463.09
477.18
485.01
496.19

501.16
544.03
568.21
593.09
618.20
620.08
628.04
631.16
636.03
668.22
669.03
709.11
727.12
732.19
748.16
quitted
165.14
210.10
290.14
498.18
499.01
506.08
555.15
570.04
641.13
692.08
692.19
747.13
quitting
080.06
263.09
285.07
410.09
429.06
quiver
098.04
659.20
quivered
332.06
quivering
158.04
564.13
719.02
quoting
191.06
rabbit
490.16
rabbits
018.20
442.07
rabid
160.10
race
103.14
248.02
517.12
racked
318.22
539.16
654.21
radiance
017.05
radiant
479.19
640.01
711.17
rafters
027.12
rage
034.14
058.02
088.12
156.14
162.07
237.04
367.08
389.14
497.21
610.16
rages
198.06
265.17
324.17
ragged
078.02
raging
280.20
rahm
321.01
321.07
326.09
456.04
712.18
rahnd
016.06
raight
029.02
187.09
232.21
472.06
696.14
rail
494.20
rails
165.07
rain
041.04
044.18
095.08
124.08
188.07

193.11
275.17
353.09
381.05
516.20
527.16
585.08
757.07
757.20
rainbow
239.11
rained
101.15
408.03
raining
151.06
579.20
rains
152.06
rainy
530.02
760.19
raise
050.09
113.07
124.18
203.19
215.04
355.01
601.15
604.01
642.07
683.02
709.21
726.08
727.14
729.19
raised
077.11
108.15
143.14
145.22
207.21
237.20
245.10
246.15
248.03
256.08
299.10
317.16
334.16
374.02
473.09
480.08
560.16
617.01
627.08
639.17
655.11
674.15
759.01
761.14
raises
237.14
raising
015.02
274.12
358.12
517.14
532.08
651.03
rake
089.13
140.10
raked
061.07
rally
288.15
rallying
583.19
ramble
022.03
060.02
102.18
227.18
428.06
478.17
516.21
586.20
rambled
185.21
ramblers
762.18
rambles
413.09
463.15
580.11
699.04
rambling
337.20
431.04
509.16
604.11
692.16
739.02
ramparts
523.03
ran
052.19
075.08
085.15

095.11
097.07
099.06
101.21
103.12
126.08
139.09
162.07
165.05
185.05
210.21
248.01
294.20
299.06
319.03
366.11
433.21
437.14
448.07
449.19
466.18
499.12
531.06
541.16
566.01
611.14
623.18
704.12
757.13
rang
387.01
range
004.12
032.12
138.03
303.05
426.09
456.05
ranged
041.12
119.15
ranges
066.01
ranging
275.04
rankled
446.10
rankness
442.11
ranks
006.01
ransacked
089.13
rapid
237.16
249.07
368.10
596.03
598.09
657.02
rapidly
055.20
416.18
429.13
516.19
557.15
672.09
713.15
718.03
727.01
747.10
rappings
050.14
rapt
640.01
raptured
749.05
rapturously
141.11
rare
012.16
232.19
426.11
741.04
rarely
093.12
rascal
029.06
233.13
249.17
654.22
rascally
417.09
rascals
108.01
rash
032.03
295.08
rate
017.21
067.08
134.07
237.09
664.19
705.06
739.14
rather
007.12
007.14
019.13

026.17
035.09
047.22
058.19
073.20
075.05
076.18
082.01
097.20
125.14
128.16
148.01
150.07
156.05
163.15
163.16
186.19
190.18
198.08
200.05
209.16
211.11
234.06
240.10
260.09
263.12
263.15
271.20
280.06
285.01
289.18
319.14
323.05
339.15
388.07
391.18
396.17
405.12
410.13
460.14
490.20
512.09
521.18
531.11
533.07
536.07
544.07
550.08
554.08
565.09
579.03
589.05
608.02
621.10
626.02
636.10
643.12
645.07
664.07
671.02
698.08
716.18
725.14
728.10
730.17
732.10
736.06
739.06
741.18
745.11
748.05
754.12
ratified
711.19
rating
255.11
rational
035.10
338.16
676.12
rationally
175.09
731.07
rattle
285.10
rattled
051.04
402.04
624.05
744.22
rattling
188.22
raves
293.02
raving
060.21
233.04
238.20
ravings
283.20
366.12
ray
043.07
207.16
rayther
420.08
471.16
567.17
696.06
720.01

re-appeared
514.07
566.18
681.06
685.20
re-appearing
122.02
re-ascended
641.21
re-ascending
522.20
re-commenced
178.05
717.22
re-enter
185.21
526.20
606.05
606.06
736.12
re-entered
491.10
615.22
699.13
741.10
re-entering
187.07
242.09
re-entrance
299.09
637.08
747.06
re-establishing
011.03
re-fastened
312.14
re-filled
653.05
re-lock
641.22
re-locking
508.19
re-secured
616.20
reach
019.20
167.21
246.04
285.06
290.16
318.04
350.10
355.17
386.06
409.14
433.12
436.09
480.08
577.05
586.09
668.03
705.01
713.23
718.07
753.09
reached
044.08
049.01
065.17
149.03
165.06
195.18
215.11
243.02
394.09
419.06
426.08
449.20
478.04
485.10
487.04
547.13
586.11
594.17
607.10
653.10
690.09
734.08
749.15
reaching
019.04
060.18
487.20
522.06
635.01
read
043.03
052.11
112.06
137.21
191.15
202.09
247.10
299.10
306.01
353.17
354.01
354.07
393.12
443.01
496.02

| | | | | | |
|---|---|---|---|---|---|
| 496.03 | 361.04 | receive | 477.20 | redemption | 411.14 |
| 496.04 | 399.05 | 012.18 | 493.06 | 144.22 | 450.09 |
| 528.11 | 406.12 | 043.06 | 522.21 | redoubled | 516.22 |
| 550.05 | 482.10 | 103.09 | 545.01 | 165.01 | 526.04 |
| 560.19 | 487.17 | 131.14 | 588.02 | redoubling | 596.08 |
| 563.16 | 499.07 | 151.02 | 694.06 | 584.04 | 607.05 |
| 668.21 | 512.10 | 308.13 | recollected | redounded | 633.12 |
| 669.19 | 524.19 | 348.02 | 057.04 | 308.14 | 661.05 |
| 670.01 | 530.11 | 482.18 | 242.07 | reduce | 755.03 |
| 679.12 | 543.21 | 512.15 | 377.19 | 045.14 | 758.14 |
| 679.18 | 561.13 | 514.13 | recollecting | 405.18 | refuses |
| 681.09 | 600.12 | received | 491.14 | reduced | 218.10 |
| 681.15 | 724.10 | 017.04 | 638.09 | 422.21 | refusing |
| 682.10 | 759.08 | 112.10 | recollection | reed | 190.02 |
| 694.11 | reaming | 147.19 | 083.07 | 611.02 | 456.06 |
| 694.13 | 699.14 | 154.08 | 274.19 | reentrance | refute |
| 696.22 | reaped | 250.13 | 354.10 | 506.01 | 156.18 |
| 702.16 | 688.08 | 263.14 | recommence | reference | refuted |
| 703.21 | reapers | 267.15 | 697.04 | 004.01 | 352.03 |
| 710.08 | 515.07 | 307.18 | recommenced | refering | regained |
| 745.14 | reappeared | 403.04 | 110.06 | 191.06 | 403.01 |
| 746.14 | 128.14 | 429.03 | 255.07 | refinement | 444.19 |
| readily | 553.01 | 472.14 | 317.15 | 229.13 | regaining |
| 113.09 | reappearing | 533.12 | 389.11 | reflect | 416.18 |
| 144.09 | 306.20 | 568.14 | 505.11 | 221.22 | regard |
| 336.07 | rear | 598.22 | 528.13 | 234.03 | 081.21 |
| 507.15 | 164.19 | 636.22 | recommend | 358.20 | 089.22 |
| 684.15 | 547.12 | 645.20 | 096.08 | 745.15 | 136.19 |
| reading | reared | 651.05 | 229.16 | reflected | 207.20 |
| 041.09 | 092.12 | 677.08 | recommended | 005.22 | 220.18 |
| 058.08 | 467.05 | 686.15 | 037.02 | 152.01 | 332.22 |
| 063.11 | 680.03 | 695.11 | 152.01 | 208.04 | 334.19 |
| 093.03 | rearing | 740.05 | 619.12 | 309.08 | 338.16 |
| 103.03 | 421.21 | receiving | recompense | 348.01 | 468.17 |
| 352.10 | reason | 023.16 | 080.08 | 433.14 | 480.16 |
| 392.15 | 037.07 | 224.16 | 302.01 | 444.01 | 589.02 |
| 430.13 | 056.04 | 506.06 | reconciled | 472.16 | 593.13 |
| 506.18 | 117.03 | recent | 223.02 | 552.13 | regarded |
| 509.19 | 122.22 | 170.10 | 264.13 | 686.19 | 143.21 |
| 516.06 | 123.01 | 197.17 | 571.17 | 727.16 | 230.16 |
| 556.02 | 180.17 | 234.09 | reconciliation | 740.01 | 528.02 |
| 568.18 | 193.08 | 553.17 | 269.09 | reflecting | 748.22 |
| 668.20 | 196.22 | recently | 305.16 | 493.11 | regarding |
| 678.03 | 221.01 | 507.10 | recounting | reflection | 171.01 |
| reads | 222.03 | reception | 431.07 | 003.12 | 185.03 |
| 678.05 | 227.12 | 108.03 | recover | 025.10 | 242.06 |
| ready | 240.15 | 121.17 | 155.18 | 072.15 | 303.20 |
| 020.16 | 255.15 | 214.17 | 272.16 | 111.15 | 315.02 |
| 022.20 | 281.06 | 529.12 | 305.03 | 122.03 | 373.21 |
| 075.19 | 301.10 | recess | 460.10 | 176.17 | 391.09 |
| 078.09 | 341.06 | 351.05 | 522.14 | 244.19 | 444.10 |
| 091.19 | 346.12 | 537.21 | 545.12 | 272.08 | 617.03 |
| 119.15 | 385.06 | recesses | 706.16 | 325.03 | regardless |
| 123.11 | 581.04 | 006.19 | recovered | 372.04 | 018.01 |
| 141.21 | 592.08 | recipient | 129.20 | 441.02 | 118.18 |
| 160.10 | 599.12 | 710.06 | 281.03 | 502.15 | 414.01 |
| 180.12 | 631.14 | reciprocation | 314.16 | 563.19 | 609.15 |
| 269.11 | 648.03 | 226.04 | 351.20 | reflections | 624.18 |
| 338.03 | 726.01 | reckless | 369.05 | 291.16 | 732.12 |
| 384.16 | 732.20 | 100.21 | 388.06 | 397.16 | regardlessly |
| 409.05 | 742.12 | 144.03 | 391.12 | 407.07 | 546.12 |
| 453.02 | reasonable | 221.20 | 506.15 | reflective | regions |
| 492.11 | 080.21 | 401.19 | 559.07 | 137.11 | 061.05 |
| 497.07 | 137.15 | 521.06 | 609.11 | reform | 136.03 |
| 535.18 | reasoned | 722.07 | 635.22 | 113.07 | 410.14 |
| 567.01 | 396.13 | reckon | 737.12 | reformed | 695.18 |
| 589.02 | reasons | 111.21 | recovering | 221.04 | regret |
| 610.17 | 008.04 | 412.10 | 159.09 | refrain | 025.08 |
| 612.01 | 247.05 | 569.06 | 167.18 | 029.14 | 149.18 |
| 647.01 | 298.02 | reckoned | 332.20 | 252.22 | 333.02 |
| 656.01 | 307.12 | 029.22 | 411.03 | 315.22 | 396.09 |
| 712.22 | 315.21 | 150.19 | 441.13 | 322.11 | 464.15 |
| 723.22 | 499.20 | reclined | 532.12 | 442.01 | 470.17 |
| 729.12 | 500.01 | 532.10 | 551.20 | 569.16 | 494.13 |
| 740.10 | 548.07 | 587.19 | 579.18 | 743.02 | 571.11 |
| real | 700.04 | 690.16 | 672.10 | refrained | 571.12 |
| 008.13 | rebel | reclining | recovery | 413.01 | 594.19 |
| 092.01 | 041.02 | 039.12 | 356.07 | 597.20 | regrets |
| 130.02 | rebellion | recluse | recriminate | refresh | 314.10 |
| 212.18 | 223.03 | 426.17 | 262.04 | 688.07 | regretted |
| 294.08 | rebuffing | recognise | recurred | refreshing | 371.22 |
| 425.01 | 473.02 | 071.07 | 759.05 | 372.20 | regular |
| 431.01 | rebuke | 109.02 | recurring | refreshment | 040.10 |
| 448.10 | 347.08 | 307.06 | 281.05 | 068.05 | 070.01 |
| 503.21 | 532.22 | 475.03 | 281.06 | 132.11 | 125.09 |
| 579.13 | rebuked | recognised | red | 552.15 | 411.05 |
| reality | 443.01 | 245.08 | 020.15 | refuge | regularly |
| 243.20 | 614.18 | 325.08 | 029.20 | 323.21 | 090.02 |
| 372.22 | recall | 376.07 | 045.19 | 441.03 | 612.13 |
| 623.12 | 281.16 | 552.18 | 104.16 | 695.20 | reinstate |
| 738.13 | 318.22 | 763.11 | 128.15 | refusal | 437.10 |
| realization | 486.16 | recognising | 156.14 | 275.01 | reiterated |
| 686.20 | 731.13 | 697.05 | 163.14 | 329.18 | 430.07 |
| really | recalled | recognition | 237.16 | refuse | 462.17 |
| 047.12 | 240.08 | 286.21 | 238.03 | 064.14 | reiterating |
| 078.16 | 359.09 | 353.13 | 276.02 | 066.02 | 534.15 |
| 086.04 | 413.17 | recognized | 389.16 | 172.04 | reject |
| 089.06 | 541.08 | 165.12 | 408.22 | 333.21 | 670.06 |
| 106.02 | 609.10 | recoil | 514.08 | 368.04 | rejected |
| 148.16 | 682.13 | 395.02 | 531.17 | 612.19 | 445.05 |
| 172.01 | 694.19 | recoiled | 537.19 | 673.05 | 542.08 |
| 205.19 | recalling | 150.12 | 655.10 | 699.07 | rejecting |
| 208.02 | 214.16 | 226.01 | 693.13 | 710.09 | 226.15 |
| 216.11 | 315.21 | 669.14 | 727.18 | refused | rejoice |
| 234.12 | 456.22 | recollect | 751.18 | 079.22 | 270.12 |
| 253.04 | recantation | 026.06 | reddened | 105.03 | 357.17 |
| 262.15 | 290.09 | 202.11 | 561.17 | 110.08 | rejoicing |
| 276.20 | recapitulation | 210.13 | reddening | 199.05 | 478.06 |
| 304.01 | 402.12 | 281.12 | 142.03 | 293.01 | rekindle |
| 329.05 | receipt | 388.09 | redeemed | 346.16 | 061.08 |
| 332.22 | 350.09 | 407.19 | 370.08 | 387.05 | 744.20 |

related
061.02
254.12
635.22
relating
498.09
573.13
575.06
relation
033.06
197.12
414.13
417.15
504.17
536.21
relations
072.22
379.21
relationship
268.04
440.17
relax
609.19
relaxed
012.13
013.06
053.03
367.01
533.02
654.05
724.03
release
236.08
371.22
483.13
624.02
723.20
released
291.07
362.02
610.20
releasing
164.03
relent
360.15
685.07
relented
340.14
512.12
relentless
089.20
756.09
relic
306.02
relief
050.20
433.17
653.01
relieve
615.09
relieved
021.14
362.13
462.20
734.12
relieving
003.19
681.01
religious
091.20
323.22
relinquished
653.02
relish
273.08
315.11
436.18
476.17
relished
156.05
relishing
498.10
reluctance
462.09
490.22
732.09
reluctant
213.14
294.04
377.18
418.02
430.04
460.03
reluctantly
192.07
209.19
402.14
456.07
544.18
585.03
remain
050.16
100.12
255.19
264.09
303.14
341.10
387.07
396.02
410.21
431.05

457.16
459.10
523.11
543.03
580.13
581.14
589.11
598.18
606.13
620.06
643.11
686.02
733.17
remainder
065.10
129.06
195.12
307.01
465.14
remained
011.15
017.13
119.11
121.12
133.13
144.11
162.11
169.14
182.20
182.21
188.17
214.10
217.22
234.20
301.02
325.01
373.02
378.03
498.06
498.19
509.09
531.08
547.21
552.01
609.03
624.21
625.02
640.10
653.05
659.18
663.16
684.11
692.22
749.16
remaining
387.05
709.07
715.04
remains
067.18
293.02
379.12
remark
062.05
098.01
128.01
296.18
406.08
remarkable
224.20
remarkably
618.02
remarked
012.05
017.15
026.02
066.05
070.20
087.09
110.01
226.07
294.06
301.10
333.12
337.08
411.15
419.13
495.10
520.18
549.01
592.20
676.21
684.06
688.09
728.06
738.12
740.09
remarking
180.01
701.10
remarks
118.11
434.21
remedy
128.14
166.12
562.13
672.04
703.17
remember
046.09

076.01
083.14
093.10
168.19
177.12
189.10
202.13
231.14
239.22
280.14
318.19
342.12
359.22
385.07
420.14
422.05
451.17
465.02
469.10
499.10
521.22
544.10
588.09
653.12
653.13
730.07
746.06
remembered
051.09
119.20
207.19
347.08
486.06
562.05
576.17
remembering
313.09
679.22
remembrance
136.20
305.15
318.21
333.09
335.06
580.09
763.05
remind
263.09
302.21
718.10
733.20
733.20
754.13
reminded
100.07
418.06
425.08
609.06
749.11
reminding
243.11
remnant
722.03
remorse
503.02
remorselessly
650.13
removal
223.07
663.09
remove
015.11
072.12
191.10
215.03
237.22
325.06
422.03
452.15
453.03
507.07
649.14
663.15
675.03
675.05
679.22
removed
001.08
093.02
114.18
120.04
132.22
145.20
169.13
184.05
304.04
318.03
351.06
384.05
393.09
495.05
558.14
651.08
705.22
710.17
755.07
removing
161.03
276.06
640.13

render
027.06
257.03
581.11
732.12
rendered
457.07
477.05
487.10
494.12
508.06
621.17
719.08
rendering
437.15
renders
693.14
705.18
753.11
renew
187.03
renewed
255.09
270.17
539.13
rent
108.02
685.01
698.06
rents
275.03
repaid
083.07
659.06
repair
120.08
repairing
433.04
repassing
373.19
repay
435.14
repaying
682.07
repayment
394.21
repeal
305.19
repeat
051.12
056.10
156.13
168.19
228.08
253.07
327.03
341.20
376.20
396.22
458.03
537.06
557.02
679.14
680.17
718.15
732.07
761.17
repeated
020.10
038.22
078.06
157.05
177.18
184.02
192.15
230.18
267.13
298.01
321.14
329.17
416.20
422.07
436.03
471.11
496.17
519.09
526.11
531.10
541.01
544.09
609.17
638.12
662.08
662.20
689.01
710.11
repeatedly
097.11
291.13
320.02
400.02
704.02
repeating
019.01
523.10
685.17
repeatng
746.03
repelled
273.22
664.09
repelling
589.01

repellingly
018.13
repent
196.22
398.04
571.11
571.12
723.18
752.13
753.12
repented
312.10
502.20
repenting
269.07
495.07
505.18
753.11
repents
707.21
repetition
013.16
059.14
377.16
473.05
repidly
426.06
replaced
354.03
replacing
379.08
replied
018.14
029.11
032.08
052.10
055.19
059.12
084.12
102.13
107.13
114.13
117.09
125.06
129.10
140.11
141.21
142.12
153.08
155.03
158.14
170.01
172.02
174.12
176.03
184.18
187.20
189.17
192.20
202.20
208.03
210.13
221.08
222.19
233.18
246.08
251.07
252.15
267.12
271.18
277.06
280.05
289.17
293.09
303.04
309.16
310.10
311.14
315.13
331.17
333.23
336.22
365.17
386.19
394.22
398.06
406.04
408.16
417.01
421.18
427.18
432.17
434.09
437.05
438.03
439.10
460.17
461.20
463.08
468.15
469.07
481.17
484.12
488.16
491.01
491.16
493.09
505.05
519.01
520.07
520.21

521.21
533.14
534.18
539.01
540.19
543.04
543.22
573.08
577.04
589.20
593.09
603.13
606.12
615.08
617.09
624.03
627.06
628.13
629.15
632.09
647.09
650.07
663.22
677.13
680.09
685.13
691.03
697.20
721.03
721.17
733.12
738.11
739.18
744.13
748.11
751.19
753.05
755.06
replies
267.22
402.18
reply
020.03
027.01
028.10
186.04
305.20
322.18
354.15
495.02
547.11
554.04
569.04
684.13
711.01
report
469.03
583.15
691.13
reported
047.22
411.12
441.08
reports
292.11
repose
188.12
323.21
371.14
378.09
640.12
752.19
reposed
006.16
repossess
611.05
represent
231.20
263.08
421.02
representatives
729.16
represented
064.06
238.21
repress
224.21
repressing
211.22
reprimanded
100.05
reproached
397.12
598.12
reproaches
046.17
reproachful
500.14
reproachfully
723.08
reprobate
030.03
090.01
reproofs
091.15
121.10
reprove
144.13
reproved
425.20
703.14

596.12
rider's
523.21
ridge
605.05
ridicule
091.20
ridiculing
528.16
ridiculous
061.02
409.06
437.15
511.11
680.11
riding
159.20
318.05
384.10
416.03
553.19
583.19
672.12
676.15
686.19
right
007.06
012.07
045.14
051.13
066.16
096.04
117.19
128.17
134.16
142.04
156.10
158.06
171.12
175.15
175.16
175.16
221.06
224.18
235.01
250.10
251.04
251.05
299.17
302.11
309.10
336.16
340.21
347.03
355.15
363.03
363.04
372.16
373.09
387.10
397.15
423.03
496.12
500.06
528.21
558.09
605.17
619.22
628.13
664.18
666.21
680.10
710.06
732.05
739.12
746.21
762.15
763.20
righteous
189.12
righteously
415.11
rightly
477.20
rights
196.17
759.03
rigidly
089.22
rigs
187.09
ring
202.15
385.12
763.12
ringing
353.01
662.04
663.07
ringlets
019.12
114.02
479.17
695.01
rings
323.08
512.18
riot
415.05
444.21
ripening
596.10
ripples
743.18
rise
049.03
059.04
167.03
179.18
181.21
191.10
357.05
406.13
407.12
494.17
586.16
600.21
risen
223.03
235.16
285.17
296.19
365.20
623.17
645.10
rises
065.21
439.02
648.06
rising
019.04
028.08
124.13
172.09
250.11
297.17
502.19
504.21
692.18
713.02
risk
022.04
152.08
226.11
477.13
598.19
641.15
724.01
rival
128.05
235.21
riven
043.16
720.17
road
022.06
031.01
046.16
066.05
066.18
101.19
112.07
126.08
180.07
185.20
188.14
233.11
243.04
248.01
260.20
290.16
295.03
298.03
342.21
364.21
410.08
414.22
429.01
433.05
436.15
450.04
483.17
517.17
522.04
529.07
552.21
628.15
667.04
686.20
689.06
720.02
761.12
road-side
567.14
roads
028.01
201.05
299.03
roadside
688.06
roamed
751.21
roar
095.03
roared
092.22
roaring
531.02
roasted
039.14
roasting
005.19
rob
678.18
robbers
107.15
robbing
556.13
578.19
robert
107.10
107.22
110.07
rocked
623.08
rocking
169.15
382.05
434.13
556.19
557.13
rocks
183.05
427.05
rod
323.09
rode
002.02
126.13
299.01
559.20
690.14
rogue
709.09
roll
180.06
541.21
rolled
450.11
527.13
rolling
105.08
410.10
romance
338.13
516.03
romantic
686.21
roof
006.04
036.10
047.16
058.01
061.18
132.15
189.04
303.09
303.15
386.17
410.15
618.06
689.10
713.13
729.14
756.02
763.20
room
014.12
028.18
032.08
036.12
038.10
055.13
059.09
080.01
095.12
098.18
103.19
104.15
105.09
118.08
127.05
141.14
155.10
157.05
169.20
193.01
195.15
209.17
211.02
217.04
231.09
267.05
274.01
277.08
277.19
280.16
283.12
284.06
295.05
299.07
304.18
320.08
326.07
326.21
343.01
350.12
355.15
370.13
372.19
382.02
403.10
437.13
448.05
458.06
470.09
475.15
503.17
528.05
531.15
548.09
551.16
555.03
556.10
558.12
563.22
568.12
569.05
570.04
573.12
616.11
621.19
626.04
628.01
629.18
632.02
632.17
637.14
638.22
644.18
646.02
649.04
653.15
654.16
659.18
660.06
662.12
678.10
681.05
697.21
700.07
705.06
717.07
722.16
724.20
730.08
734.17
741.11
743.14
747.13
750.10
751.17
rooms
047.19
322.16
691.05
roots
517.19
518.16
737.19
rose
051.15
121.22
134.12
154.03
209.14
215.12
226.02
277.15
313.18
320.19
330.17
361.14
390.07
393.21
402.06
410.18
424.05
474.03
479.19
491.06
517.17
522.08
544.18
553.12
593.21
611.21
624.01
635.20
640.09
667.14
681.01
722.11
740.16
746.17
rosebushes
522.19
rotten
260.12
rough
017.15
021.04
073.20
073.22
128.13
146.20
229.22
243.07
284.11
292.03
299.03
319.14
323.07
425.05
476.15
482.07
517.18
682.18
689.06
706.07
rough-headed
116.03
roughly
467.20
roughness
214.08
400.12
round
007.04
016.03
023.06
027.11
028.11
032.19
038.01
050.08
078.01
078.06
092.21
094.17
108.22
115.05
180.04
184.17
191.13
207.13
211.14
221.07
291.12
304.11
311.01
319.03
330.13
360.06
373.17
379.06
386.14
393.20
404.04
417.14
428.11
430.20
432.14
437.13
441.16
463.10
471.03
483.15
492.08
509.04
517.16
523.02
554.12
560.04
586.08
587.09
597.01
614.20
628.05
635.20
649.04
651.16
653.16
668.01
669.08
695.20
711.16
748.11
757.05
758.21
764.06
rounds
131.13
rouse
070.02
094.06
099.12
218.04
295.12
327.08
457.09
722.18
744.04
roused
010.17
088.11
408.02
452.04
460.03
507.12
589.08
rousing
039.10
102.14
281.20
310.01
389.14
row
006.03
006.03
041.12
051.02
720.17
rubbed
048.18
052.18
rubbidge
191.04
rubbing
551.18
564.13
ruddy
070.16
244.18
429.08
rude
021.02
099.22
146.21
562.17
rude-bred
441.12
rudely
040.15
rudeness
310.16
710.20
763.07
rue
092.12
290.08
ruffian
147.10
255.03
320.05
400.01
567.03
617.22
ruffianly
010.05
309.05
ruffling
204.19
rug
135.18
215.12
528.09
ruin
033.18
199.16
302.04
366.14
395.13
501.06
ruined
443.21
ruining
335.04
ruling
089.21
rullers
696.19
rumbling
126.07
rummaged
062.17
rumour
603.09
627.18
run
022.04
079.02
095.04
100.11
106.09
106.09
141.21
152.08
185.20
195.20
199.15
202.13
205.22
212.16
235.14
250.01
297.16
346.17
350.22
382.21
386.10
396.14
398.15
430.17
449.18
449.18
451.18
477.13
519.07
523.02
533.13
618.16
628.04
638.21
659.15
737.17
runaway
213.02
rung
265.14
running
008.01
015.12
032.16

| | | | | | |
|---|---|---|---|---|---|
| 077.06 | safe | 237.07 | 469.13 | 648.18 | salubrious |
| 104.16 | 095.21 | 239.06 | 472.03 | 649.06 | 486.07 |
| 139.07 | 165.19 | 240.02 | 472.09 | 649.18 | salutation |
| 164.06 | 434.06 | 246.10 | 475.11 | 650.20 | 062.13 |
| 193.12 | 470.07 | 246.17 | 477.16 | 651.22 | salutations |
| 269.12 | 490.08 | 249.03 | 478.17 | 656.03 | 500.04 |
| 280.16 | 507.15 | 249.13 | 479.07 | 656.14 | salute |
| 435.07 | 618.12 | 250.11 | 480.01 | 658.05 | 325.13 |
| 483.02 | 623.01 | 250.21 | 481.07 | 659.14 | 411.01 |
| 517.10 | 635.04 | 251.17 | 481.20 | 660.04 | 452.14 |
| 576.07 | 638.20 | 254.05 | 484.14 | 660.11 | 487.20 |
| runnings | 662.21 | 255.17 | 485.03 | 662.01 | saluted |
| 645.13 | 685.17 | 256.15 | 486.11 | 662.17 | 061.10 |
| runs | safely | 257.08 | 489.13 | 663.21 | salvation |
| 135.06 | 429.19 | 257.19 | 494.19 | 664.04 | 043.17 |
| 209.12 | safer | 259.09 | 495.05 | 667.10 | 166.14 |
| 233.10 | 064.20 | 264.01 | 496.08 | 670.02 | 526.08 |
| rush | safety | 264.04 | 496.22 | 670.21 | same |
| 141.06 | 258.14 | 264.10 | 500.15 | 671.03 | 043.13 |
| 283.01 | sagacity | 266.14 | 501.02 | 675.05 | 080.20 |
| 409.22 | 022.13 | 277.09 | 501.19 | 677.01 | 090.15 |
| rushed | sahnd | 283.09 | 504.13 | 677.04 | 134.18 |
| 011.12 | 042.21 | 286.03 | 506.04 | 678.04 | 136.21 |
| 034.04 | said | 286.17 | 510.09 | 679.06 | 143.09 |
| 050.07 | 002.06 | 287.08 | 512.22 | 683.17 | 163.10 |
| 067.13 | 012.14 | 289.19 | 519.22 | 684.13 | 179.12 |
| 267.04 | 018.03 | 292.08 | 524.05 | 685.04 | 187.05 |
| 279.18 | 018.12 | 293.11 | 526.19 | 694.04 | 197.15 |
| 415.05 | 019.03 | 294.14 | 532.04 | 696.08 | 219.19 |
| 610.10 | 020.11 | 297.13 | 532.08 | 698.03 | 252.21 |
| 644.06 | 021.22 | 299.04 | 532.11 | 699.21 | 265.08 |
| 653.10 | 022.22 | 299.22 | 533.04 | 702.09 | 267.13 |
| rushing | 025.15 | 303.13 | 534.13 | 702.19 | 267.15 |
| 113.10 | 026.13 | 309.14 | 534.21 | 703.07 | 280.08 |
| 399.02 | 028.07 | 311.20 | 535.19 | 704.14 | 304.21 |
| rustic | 030.17 | 315.05 | 537.10 | 706.13 | 356.04 |
| 023.06 | 032.13 | 315.10 | 537.13 | 710.08 | 359.18 |
| 230.01 | 033.04 | 316.14 | 538.03 | 711.12 | 375.14 |
| 673.12 | 047.15 | 320.09 | 538.15 | 712.16 | 380.04 |
| rustle | 053.01 | 321.01 | 539.15 | 712.21 | 393.02 |
| 602.20 | 054.07 | 322.05 | 540.10 | 713.06 | 414.21 |
| 710.17 | 059.05 | 326.08 | 541.02 | 721.06 | 415.16 |
| rustling | 070.22 | 328.10 | 541.20 | 721.22 | 421.08 |
| 516.16 | 076.06 | 329.17 | 542.12 | 722.14 | 429.11 |
| 557.14 | 077.17 | 331.12 | 542.22 | 723.05 | 475.15 |
| sabbath | 078.22 | 332.21 | 543.18 | 723.15 | 502.11 |
| 042.20 | 081.14 | 335.10 | 545.08 | 724.07 | 524.04 |
| 108.06 | 081.14 | 337.12 | 547.10 | 725.11 | 526.07 |
| 666.04 | 083.18 | 341.04 | 548.16 | 732.16 | 540.11 |
| sack | 085.03 | 342.10 | 554.14 | 733.06 | 546.20 |
| 041.13 | 088.20 | 343.09 | 557.05 | 734.19 | 562.02 |
| sackless | 093.20 | 344.22 | 558.04 | 739.01 | 598.14 |
| 519.06 | 094.05 | 350.01 | 558.05 | 740.19 | 644.18 |
| sacks | 094.16 | 351.18 | 558.06 | 742.02 | 644.20 |
| 321.09 | 095.09 | 353.16 | 558.18 | 744.18 | 644.21 |
| sacrifice | 102.08 | 354.18 | 560.07 | 751.09 | 645.07 |
| 513.04 | 103.11 | 356.15 | 560.17 | 751.15 | 654.17 |
| 682.11 | 107.22 | 359.13 | 561.07 | 752.05 | 674.17 |
| sacrificed | 117.06 | 362.17 | 563.07 | 753.21 | 681.20 |
| 302.03 | 117.14 | 365.08 | 563.22 | 754.13 | 712.05 |
| sad | 120.16 | 366.13 | 564.21 | 754.20 | 713.20 |
| 025.07 | 122.09 | 367.12 | 565.10 | 755.04 | 727.07 |
| 123.03 | 123.03 | 374.03 | 566.12 | 755.21 | 735.07 |
| 141.13 | 131.20 | 376.08 | 569.17 | 762.02 | 741.12 |
| 199.03 | 133.20 | 376.18 | 570.01 | 762.13 | 741.14 |
| 284.11 | 137.16 | 376.22 | 575.02 | sail | 747.11 |
| 310.21 | 151.08 | 384.09 | 576.20 | 114.05 | samples |
| 393.12 | 152.05 | 384.20 | 580.18 | sailors | 258.06 |
| 430.13 | 153.10 | 388.18 | 582.01 | 125.21 | sanctimonious |
| 452.21 | 154.18 | 394.16 | 588.01 | saint | 455.13 |
| 474.02 | 156.05 | 396.01 | 589.13 | 095.03 | sanctum |
| 528.01 | 158.06 | 398.09 | 590.19 | 144.18 | 062.03 |
| 555.12 | 159.08 | 401.22 | 592.14 | 265.16 | sand |
| 559.16 | 163.16 | 403.05 | 593.03 | 375.01 | 205.09 |
| 579.01 | 164.03 | 408.01 | 593.22 | saints | sand-pillar |
| 590.15 | 166.19 | 408.02 | 599.04 | 050.05 | 243.07 |
| 603.14 | 168.11 | 408.12 | 599.17 | 189.20 | sane |
| 627.15 | 170.11 | 412.09 | 601.09 | sake | 228.07 |
| sadder | 172.20 | 413.22 | 602.10 | 041.15 | sang |
| 176.14 | 174.09 | 416.03 | 603.06 | 056.10 | 537.20 |
| 347.15 | 176.17 | 416.15 | 603.18 | 141.14 | sanguine |
| 516.04 | 180.11 | 417.03 | 605.06 | 182.09 | 302.09 |
| saddest | 183.17 | 418.04 | 605.15 | 182.10 | 448.09 |
| 352.18 | 184.22 | 418.22 | 609.01 | 212.01 | 467.07 |
| saddle | 186.02 | 419.10 | 609.12 | 238.06 | sank |
| 431.21 | 186.15 | 420.13 | 611.05 | 238.19 | 046.05 |
| 569.17 | 188.05 | 421.19 | 612.03 | 264.16 | 094.01 |
| 594.12 | 190.20 | 429.05 | 612.17 | 264.17 | 271.01 |
| saddled | 192.21 | 431.14 | 614.19 | 299.06 | 462.03 |
| 656.02 | 193.07 | 434.04 | 616.01 | 322.16 | sarcastic |
| saddles | 197.19 | 435.11 | 617.22 | 359.19 | 759.11 |
| 085.18 | 199.10 | 436.10 | 619.22 | 365.05 | sarcastically |
| sadly | 210.07 | 438.01 | 620.12 | 408.18 | 481.20 |
| 077.09 | 210.19 | 438.14 | 622.09 | 447.03 | sartin |
| 210.19 | 212.03 | 438.20 | 623.21 | 513.08 | 696.17 |
| 235.03 | 212.21 | 439.19 | 624.11 | 581.13 | sarve |
| 254.08 | 214.15 | 451.13 | 627.20 | 594.06 | 564.15 |
| 337.07 | 218.06 | 452.07 | 629.14 | 600.04 | sarved |
| 386.16 | 219.20 | 454.03 | 632.21 | 612.18 | 719.12 |
| 415.02 | 220.17 | 455.05 | 633.02 | 699.22 | sat |
| 445.09 | 220.20 | 455.17 | 634.11 | 719.15 | 010.10 |
| 499.16 | 221.09 | 457.18 | 636.02 | 748.08 | 034.01 |
| 517.10 | 222.17 | 458.03 | 637.06 | 748.10 | 039.16 |
| 594.01 | 227.15 | 459.05 | 638.09 | sall | 048.19 |
| 700.20 | 227.20 | 461.13 | 639.04 | 324.12 | 054.03 |
| 709.21 | 228.13 | 462.02 | 644.06 | sallied | 076.05 |
| sadness | 229.04 | 464.03 | 645.12 | 479.09 | 093.05 |
| 404.16 | 230.21 | 465.04 | 647.03 | sallow | 097.10 |
| 635.09 | 231.16 | 466.20 | 647.22 | 207.17 | 099.02 |
| 676.20 | 232.09 | 467.19 | | sallower | 103.01 |
| 759.06 | 236.03 | 468.12 | | 645.07 | 104.18 |

| | | | | | |
|---|---|---|---|---|---|
| 110.19 | 144.23 | say | 711.03 | 195.18 | scouring |
| 121.16 | 203.20 | 008.08 | 713.12 | 209.18 | 109.09 |
| 124.07 | 282.20 | 023.21 | 718.14 | 254.12 | 155.09 |
| 151.22 | 377.11 | 030.06 | 728.20 | 262.20 | 435.15 |
| 169.08 | 608.08 | 057.12 | 738.03 | 304.05 | scowl |
| 188.21 | 759.11 | 070.05 | 739.15 | 330.04 | 023.13 |
| 192.12 | savagely | 080.19 | 760.16 | 377.15 | 251.09 |
| 209.06 | 022.21 | 082.13 | 760.16 | 392.22 | 561.10 |
| 253.19 | 358.19 | 089.11 | sayhave | 406.14 | scowled |
| 304.09 | 723.01 | 092.08 | 497.03 | 597.12 | 617.05 |
| 314.04 | savages | 092.10 | saying | 610.19 | 709.01 |
| 330.15 | 099.22 | 092.15 | 043.05 | 729.07 | scowling |
| 351.03 | save | 122.11 | 066.21 | scenery | 174.09 |
| 367.15 | 171.02 | 122.17 | 093.12 | 690.03 | scowls |
| 390.09 | 197.12 | 123.07 | 143.11 | scenes | 108.09 |
| 392.15 | 316.04 | 123.07 | 151.22 | 444.20 | scrambling |
| 393.01 | 415.05 | 129.09 | 168.03 | scent | 522.14 |
| 397.16 | 464.17 | 135.22 | 192.03 | 119.12 | scrape |
| 417.14 | 526.09 | 142.15 | 568.14 | scented | 751.06 |
| 430.12 | 602.12 | 152.10 | 572.19 | 378.04 | scraped |
| 453.17 | 615.04 | 153.16 | 644.14 | scents | 652.05 |
| 495.04 | 627.03 | 154.02 | 661.15 | 193.02 | scratched |
| 503.12 | 689.12 | 166.11 | 676.01 | sceptre | 038.20 |
| 509.19 | saved | 170.03 | 749.22 | 414.05 | 057.16 |
| 554.17 | 301.11 | 172.04 | sayings | scheme | 383.21 |
| 556.18 | 392.12 | 172.10 | 498.11 | 672.06 | 495.21 |
| 570.04 | saving | 172.15 | says | schemes | scratching |
| 587.19 | 160.04 | 173.08 | 042.03 | 316.01 | 053.15 |
| 634.04 | 667.04 | 173.19 | 045.09 | scholar | scrawled |
| 640.08 | saw | 177.13 | 139.12 | 426.06 | 040.10 |
| 640.09 | 003.05 | 178.19 | 139.12 | 679.08 | scream |
| 654.07 | 015.01 | 179.19 | 140.20 | school-boy | 055.06 |
| 667.22 | 027.17 | 186.13 | 142.02 | 508.13 | 541.08 |
| 669.15 | 028.11 | 196.11 | 142.09 | scintillating | 606.17 |
| 690.15 | 041.18 | 206.16 | 169.03 | 358.09 | screamed |
| 696.01 | 045.19 | 208.10 | 174.03 | scissors | 094.20 |
| 704.05 | 067.19 | 210.16 | 203.01 | 164.12 | 156.08 |
| 705.13 | 074.19 | 224.11 | 247.08 | scold | 279.04 |
| 717.01 | 081.02 | 227.09 | 298.07 | 436.01 | 513.13 |
| 740.04 | 083.06 | 230.02 | 342.04 | 499.10 | 531.11 |
| 759.08 | 089.10 | 230.04 | 366.14 | 512.11 | 632.03 |
| satan | 090.07 | 232.02 | 472.05 | 518.05 | screaming |
| 085.08 | 093.19 | 232.21 | 483.03 | 553.18 | 104.14 |
| 163.06 | 095.13 | 234.02 | 492.06 | 554.18 | 164.07 |
| 253.09 | 097.01 | 243.12 | 512.04 | 555.06 | screen |
| 363.07 | 104.02 | 261.20 | 524.02 | 562.04 | 396.08 |
| 762.21 | 107.01 | 273.05 | 524.04 | 592.06 | screwed |
| satellites | 111.16 | 277.13 | 536.05 | 699.03 | 122.06 |
| 067.13 | 143.19 | 279.05 | 537.07 | 727.18 | 310.10 |
| satisfaction | 160.12 | 282.04 | 587.17 | scolded | screws |
| 134.01 | 165.18 | 292.19 | 630.01 | 035.07 | 652.07 |
| 182.08 | 179.17 | 309.03 | 630.03 | 152.08 | scripture |
| 236.20 | 185.01 | 310.13 | 632.10 | 196.17 | 103.05 |
| 259.14 | 191.19 | 310.14 | 632.14 | 227.03 | 191.05 |
| 344.19 | 195.07 | 318.15 | 646.07 | 262.17 | scroop |
| 387.15 | 196.02 | 329.01 | scale | 637.16 | 043.10 |
| 403.20 | 204.21 | 329.20 | 523.03 | scolding | scrubbed |
| 419.09 | 234.16 | 333.22 | scalping | 078.17 | 128.16 |
| 443.19 | 240.09 | 333.23 | 419.22 | 091.17 | scruple |
| 618.04 | 249.22 | 337.03 | scamper | 255.09 | 292.04 |
| 726.21 | 255.13 | 337.11 | 044.11 | 324.22 | 589.07 |
| satisfactorily | 275.19 | 339.15 | scampering | sconses | scruples |
| 414.17 | 290.18 | 341.08 | 483.15 | 050.13 | 335.03 |
| satisfactory | 295.17 | 342.19 | scandal | scooping | 606.09 |
| 499.20 | 298.09 | 345.12 | 699.09 | 244.02 | scrutinizing |
| satisfied | 298.21 | 345.19 | 760.01 | scope | 717.21 |
| 468.10 | 329.21 | 347.21 | scandalous | 484.14 | scutter |
| 493.12 | 337.04 | 356.01 | 029.11 | score | 326.01 |
| 508.15 | 339.21 | 357.12 | scarcely | 208.04 | scuttle |
| 541.22 | 350.03 | 357.19 | 010.11 | 216.06 | 532.18 |
| 556.06 | 352.03 | 359.02 | 019.09 | scorn | sea |
| 587.19 | 356.02 | 382.14 | 028.02 | 019.17 | 011.16 |
| satisfy | 358.16 | 391.17 | 040.05 | 088.10 | 322.07 |
| 182.09 | 361.20 | 406.17 | 057.03 | 471.07 | 336.07 |
| 402.16 | 369.03 | 421.16 | 096.09 | 494.02 | 427.02 |
| 753.15 | 373.18 | 439.05 | 114.09 | 570.19 | sea-coast |
| sattan | 408.03 | 440.12 | 148.11 | 682.20 | 008.12 |
| 696.12 | 412.04 | 450.07 | 165.17 | 696.04 | seal |
| saturnine | 412.19 | 455.22 | 217.08 | scorned | 353.19 |
| 686.09 | 432.17 | 459.07 | 240.03 | 106.14 | sealed |
| saucepans | 444.16 | 468.14 | 265.12 | 600.07 | 404.16 |
| 005.20 | 446.04 | 492.12 | 282.06 | 680.07 | search |
| saucer | 451.05 | 497.15 | 286.10 | 708.06 | 054.12 |
| 217.08 | 461.19 | 510.20 | 325.18 | scornful | 067.18 |
| 453.22 | 466.12 | 519.08 | 336.09 | 195.14 | 187.03 |
| saucers | 471.06 | 521.15 | 352.07 | 440.09 | 432.11 |
| 612.01 | 495.02 | 535.05 | 373.19 | 467.02 | 754.05 |
| saucier | 498.04 | 535.15 | 412.22 | 602.10 | searched |
| 197.03 | 500.04 | 544.05 | 415.19 | 667.18 | 048.08 |
| sauciness | 500.06 | 546.20 | 431.10 | scornfully | 101.08 |
| 121.11 | 520.13 | 548.02 | 442.01 | 018.19 | 457.04 |
| 239.03 | 541.14 | 556.21 | 490.11 | 336.19 | 507.15 |
| 707.22 | 561.17 | 570.11 | 526.17 | 408.06 | 678.07 |
| saucy | 570.02 | 571.03 | 577.05 | 511.18 | searching |
| 091.18 | 583.15 | 577.06 | 586.12 | 648.21 | 079.11 |
| 231.07 | 587.13 | 589.21 | 594.14 | scorning | 312.04 |
| 425.16 | 591.12 | 590.04 | 689.08 | 497.02 | 394.11 |
| 439.10 | 602.21 | 594.22 | 733.18 | 671.12 | 534.08 |
| 668.15 | 645.11 | 599.09 | scared | scorns | season |
| 682.02 | 649.16 | 604.11 | 248.03 | 537.03 | 201.12 |
| saunter | 666.11 | 611.18 | scares | scoundrel | 353.09 |
| 186.22 | 671.08 | 619.03 | 186.20 | 035.17 | 391.09 |
| sauntered | 703.12 | 631.07 | scarlet | 202.01 | 535.14 |
| 227.18 | 715.11 | 631.21 | 522.07 | 249.09 | 739.14 |
| 365.01 | 717.02 | 639.05 | 626.05 | 421.19 | seasoned |
| 750.04 | 735.05 | 665.18 | scattered | 493.21 | 121.10 |
| sauntering | 740.17 | 669.21 | 577.18 | 611.05 | seasons |
| 519.09 | 748.08 | 670.09 | scene | 627.06 | 150.10 |
| savage | 761.11 | 671.16 | 011.17 | scoured | 205.11 |
| 057.21 | saw-edge | 699.01 | 035.08 | 119.18 | 372.04 |
| 113.10 | 073.22 | 708.15 | 063.21 | | |

| | | | | |
|---|---|---|---|---|
| seat | 345.04 | 469.04 | seek | 652.09 | 147.16 |
| 009.08 | 345.06 | 475.01 | 103.15 | 654.08 | 371.11 |
| 017.12 | 485.04 | 477.13 | 120.11 | 663.10 | 475.17 |
| 049.13 | 636.09 | 479.02 | 185.05 | 691.22 | 734.22 |
| 065.08 | secured | 481.10 | 252.15 | 700.10 | select |
| 075.10 | 110.12 | 483.21 | 254.03 | 722.10 | 022.02 |
| 184.05 | 305.08 | 484.03 | 269.09 | 723.22 | 040.03 |
| 203.04 | 313.22 | 486.17 | 290.07 | 731.03 | 221.20 |
| 215.01 | 493.21 | 488.02 | 290.13 | 736.08 | selected |
| 218.03 | 610.04 | 488.15 | 297.20 | 741.04 | 550.12 |
| 236.13 | securely | 490.19 | 356.10 | 749.01 | 598.15 |
| 277.09 | 659.07 | 494.04 | 383.07 | 757.18 | 680.16 |
| 299.09 | securing | 499.15 | 385.18 | 758.10 | self |
| 332.07 | 267.08 | 501.13 | 386.01 | seeming | 262.12 |
| 362.04 | 370.03 | 504.09 | 392.01 | 088.01 | 302.12 |
| 366.05 | security | 505.09 | 396.16 | 730.15 | 615.02 |
| 404.05 | 090.11 | 512.04 | 439.14 | seemingly | self-absorbed |
| 467.16 | 397.22 | 521.02 | 441.11 | 564.07 | 588.21 |
| 491.04 | see | 526.01 | 443.12 | 742.03 | self-complacent |
| 538.19 | 021.17 | 527.09 | 445.02 | seemly | 223.19 |
| 541.09 | 025.21 | 529.09 | 520.19 | 712.19 | self-defence |
| 563.21 | 030.07 | 533.03 | 591.09 | seems | 050.09 |
| 591.05 | 032.18 | 533.11 | 612.06 | 072.03 | self-denial |
| 608.04 | 035.21 | 534.14 | 622.08 | 176.01 | 400.05 |
| 667.12 | 063.19 | 543.20 | 629.04 | 280.12 | self-love |
| 712.15 | 073.07 | 546.04 | 679.16 | 404.19 | 681.21 |
| 725.02 | 077.18 | 547.11 | 695.20 | 417.10 | self-preservation |
| 747.14 | 084.15 | 561.16 | 701.05 | 511.04 | 389.22 |
| seated | 093.12 | 564.03 | seeking | 604.03 | self-respect |
| 007.03 | 097.14 | 570.12 | 059.15 | 608.09 | 113.07 |
| 042.10 | 102.02 | 574.05 | 105.07 | 664.03 | 315.02 |
| 092.19 | 102.20 | 575.10 | 327.05 | seen | self-righteous |
| 135.17 | 109.03 | 577.11 | 365.08 | 007.05 | 089.12 |
| 176.13 | 112.02 | 580.04 | 400.15 | 024.13 | selfish |
| 191.20 | 116.11 | 580.19 | 434.04 | 070.20 | 130.12 |
| 243.22 | 124.10 | 589.15 | 493.01 | 100.04 | 181.18 |
| 313.08 | 127.17 | 591.21 | 646.18 | 115.20 | 206.01 |
| 324.07 | 140.13 | 592.01 | 668.20 | 175.04 | 218.12 |
| 384.21 | 141.10 | 603.07 | 708.06 | 207.02 | 477.06 |
| 434.12 | 145.20 | 604.10 | 724.14 | 215.17 | 546.08 |
| 449.21 | 153.05 | 611.04 | seem | 254.06 | 615.20 |
| 453.05 | 154.12 | 619.07 | 025.10 | 291.08 | 631.17 |
| 522.05 | 156.01 | 621.02 | 178.19 | 311.15 | 659.04 |
| 552.10 | 164.03 | 630.15 | 183.01 | 324.03 | 684.14 |
| 597.08 | 167.03 | 631.12 | 333.13 | 386.10 | 754.01 |
| 623.08 | 175.05 | 633.15 | 412.22 | 416.18 | selfishness |
| 643.03 | 180.17 | 633.18 | 464.05 | 432.15 | 231.02 |
| 662.12 | 181.17 | 635.02 | 465.06 | 454.19 | 264.03 |
| 694.14 | 187.02 | 637.15 | 496.19 | 465.01 | 344.18 |
| 710.18 | 187.14 | 637.22 | 528.02 | 475.09 | 359.05 |
| 712.05 | 198.11 | 645.20 | 617.07 | 482.02 | 371.20 |
| seats | 208.11 | 653.07 | 674.21 | 482.13 | 472.16 |
| 129.15 | 210.03 | 653.17 | 699.06 | 483.04 | 572.05 |
| secluded | 219.13 | 654.19 | 704.09 | 484.05 | send |
| 475.08 | 242.04 | 656.11 | seemed | 504.17 | 034.03 |
| 731.01 | 245.06 | 662.06 | 003.03 | 512.01 | 042.01 |
| seclusion | 260.09 | 663.03 | 026.06 | 552.08 | 127.05 |
| 413.08 | 261.01 | 666.04 | 034.16 | 557.18 | 195.03 |
| second | 261.20 | 669.01 | 048.10 | 572.10 | 227.03 |
| 011.06 | 265.12 | 669.02 | 053.07 | 574.08 | 236.01 |
| 018.06 | 274.03 | 670.11 | 058.05 | 655.03 | 297.01 |
| 116.18 | 276.11 | 672.04 | 063.13 | 658.03 | 300.03 |
| 200.04 | 277.06 | 684.02 | 076.22 | 661.08 | 306.10 |
| 261.05 | 277.11 | 684.12 | 081.03 | 673.12 | 386.20 |
| 292.05 | 278.17 | 693.02 | 122.04 | 674.15 | 391.06 |
| 295.16 | 281.03 | 693.21 | 128.04 | 690.03 | 397.15 |
| 307.08 | 287.12 | 695.03 | 142.12 | 709.09 | 430.20 |
| 312.10 | 291.21 | 698.13 | 143.10 | 709.20 | 456.17 |
| 316.10 | 303.04 | 699.12 | 170.04 | 715.09 | 490.04 |
| 321.17 | 306.12 | 700.09 | 204.08 | 719.05 | 504.22 |
| 348.10 | 307.14 | 714.01 | 213.20 | 748.05 | 512.15 |
| 424.11 | 316.16 | 716.14 | 224.02 | 760.17 | 512.19 |
| 484.18 | 321.13 | 724.13 | 224.13 | sees | 514.12 |
| 556.08 | 321.15 | 730.16 | 229.10 | 646.06 | 524.15 |
| 569.08 | 328.06 | 738.15 | 240.18 | seize | 581.05 |
| 595.01 | 329.04 | 743.01 | 249.03 | 051.21 | 599.19 |
| 599.10 | 333.22 | 746.18 | 256.10 | 239.04 | 618.11 |
| 662.04 | 334.12 | 752.21 | 275.02 | 606.21 | 624.03 |
| 672.11 | 342.09 | 756.18 | 291.13 | seized | 638.11 |
| seconds | 343.16 | 760.06 | 296.20 | 016.17 | 646.14 |
| 266.05 | 345.10 | seearch | 304.14 | 034.02 | 656.03 |
| 279.18 | 354.18 | 712.19 | 330.20 | 088.11 | 691.09 |
| secret | 360.04 | seed | 339.15 | 106.12 | 702.08 |
| 171.08 | 360.15 | 194.04 | 351.11 | 117.13 | 724.14 |
| 176.10 | 364.02 | 194.05 | 354.11 | 128.05 | 752.04 |
| 179.03 | 365.10 | 401.11 | 362.03 | 157.12 | 754.06 |
| 234.10 | 371.14 | seeght | 364.08 | 213.13 | sending |
| 252.08 | 384.11 | 184.16 | 372.06 | 215.12 | 168.14 |
| 331.15 | 385.02 | 401.11 | 383.10 | 261.07 | 189.05 |
| 397.11 | 387.11 | seeing | 392.17 | 295.04 | 250.19 |
| 484.06 | 408.19 | 078.18 | 393.13 | 319.17 | sends |
| 554.19 | 413.03 | 124.21 | 407.05 | 343.01 | 331.21 |
| 573.19 | 414.20 | 127.01 | 413.22 | 357.05 | 477.03 |
| 596.09 | 419.07 | 137.17 | 434.15 | 395.22 | sensation |
| 602.11 | 421.07 | 157.09 | 441.14 | 483.14 | 367.18 |
| 634.16 | 439.01 | 200.02 | 475.11 | 538.10 | 594.18 |
| 678.09 | 439.06 | 205.06 | 482.06 | 563.20 | 617.02 |
| 682.17 | 439.08 | 222.08 | 492.19 | 609.04 | sensations |
| secretly | 439.11 | 326.07 | 502.16 | 610.05 | 243.13 |
| 755.07 | 449.16 | 361.02 | 531.01 | 676.01 | 730.14 |
| secrets | 450.04 | 373.01 | 551.19 | 689.07 | sense |
| 183.21 | 450.19 | 469.22 | 556.08 | 706.18 | 060.09 |
| 331.15 | 452.01 | 489.04 | 569.15 | seizing | 080.02 |
| 511.11 | 452.19 | 494.19 | 583.20 | 044.02 | 120.08 |
| sections | 455.09 | 501.18 | 598.05 | 094.12 | 146.21 |
| 061.12 | 460.09 | 612.12 | 601.03 | seldom | 149.13 |
| secure | 460.20 | 625.02 | 607.09 | 024.17 | 153.09 |
| 038.16 | 463.09 | 634.20 | 629.01 | 086.03 | 183.16 |
| 212.17 | 464.22 | 666.18 | 639.17 | 090.19 | 187.20 |
| 253.12 | 466.14 | 700.06 | 643.12 | 109.03 | 210.01 |
| 340.07 | 468.22 | 743.22 | 648.13 | 115.17 | 225.17 |

**SENSE (continued)**
281.02
333.11
333.15
359.09
389.21
403.20
466.01
477.09
514.02
625.05
641.17
653.01
680.20
694.02
720.19
745.19
746.16

**senseless**
265.16
338.22
390.21
399.20

**senses**
009.01
376.07
521.15
567.21
628.05
728.14
732.18

**sensible**
046.13
059.17
179.15
270.03

**sensitive**
413.01
425.06
492.01
524.13
682.04

**sent**
059.11
080.09
088.18
102.09
201.11
228.15
305.10
328.04
364.12
368.10
379.13
420.01
449.12
460.01
512.17
569.05
582.12
622.08
641.16
646.02
659.21
661.03
663.18
725.02

**sentence**
045.01
170.08
217.17
228.14
356.09
409.17
491.21
497.13
621.18

**sentences**
040.09
218.15
247.06

**sententiously**
172.20

**sentiment**
002.20
019.17
189.13
226.04
267.20
307.06
360.11
388.01
471.08
576.13

**sentiments**
148.10
236.14
728.02

**sentinel**
060.01
312.01
398.07

**separate**
044.07
048.08
091.02
181.06
445.18

**separated**
181.04
593.12

**separating**
115.10

**separation**
181.01
183.11
281.18
340.21
521.09
581.03
700.03

**september**
206.05
688.02

**sequel**
168.18
200.06
699.17

**series**
062.15
137.18

**serious**
075.06
118.09
122.18
146.06
159.14
198.05
509.08
525.01
546.11
570.06
717.20

**seriously**
030.04
135.20
230.13
261.22
387.16
496.12

**sermon**
048.05

**sermonizing**
089.15

**sermons**
103.04

**serpent**
327.08

**servant**
021.01
055.19
063.15
068.04
089.10
106.20
111.03
184.07
197.13
204.21
213.03
289.11
297.21
311.04
350.14
366.18
383.07
400.16
417.16
420.06
423.02
425.18
434.02
436.10
438.15
439.06
441.05
441.14
446.07
455.02
466.06
471.06
631.13
637.04
644.05
689.14

**servant's**
017.17
289.12
299.08
317.13
387.01

**servant-girl**
015.01

**servants**
093.04
099.14
116.14
137.10
144.04
155.08
224.09
226.16
255.05
296.13
344.07
347.01
364.20
372.20
379.15
411.20
451.12
552.07
622.08
635.02
641.02

**serve**
066.09
338.03
347.21
440.08
656.08

**served**
014.10
038.12
080.16
128.17
224.21
253.21

**serves**
243.09

**service**
041.16
115.20
289.17
350.17
364.16
494.08
533.12
600.14

**serviceable**
637.02

**services**
418.05
646.21

**serving**
264.02

**ses**
191.05

**set**
004.16
007.01
012.11
014.02
025.18
033.14
046.14
057.18
067.17
075.20
076.21
078.05
094.12
094.22
096.03
098.03
100.14
103.05
126.15
130.14
131.18
133.08
137.17
156.16
159.14
168.01
196.17
206.11
207.18
212.11
232.17
270.19
275.20
299.01
304.07
308.05
309.19
318.13
340.17
350.18
384.16
399.04
402.07
445.08
506.06
508.18
527.06
547.11
583.06
585.04
591.20
645.22
670.05
671.09
672.03
684.20
696.11
721.04
741.09
745.15
747.04
749.18
750.02

**setting**
055.11
136.13
165.21
238.05
244.18
250.09
427.09

**settle**
032.22
116.01
133.16
158.01
169.12
180.01
184.09
185.05
190.06
216.06
302.10
317.19
322.17
346.07
394.17
400.09
409.12
419.22
429.18
541.20
542.20
544.01
563.05
611.17
629.06
667.14
669.15
685.11
698.08

**settled**
222.09
411.07
469.05
479.02
561.14
753.06

**settles**
175.11

**settling**
515.11

**seven**
045.20
047.07
049.10
049.11
049.20
049.21
066.06
116.17
201.11
281.15
369.04
596.02
623.16
763.17

**seventeen**
024.21
545.11

**seventeenth**
579.19

**seventy**
045.19
045.20
047.06
047.08
049.09
049.11
049.20
049.21

**seventy-first**
049.01
050.03

**sever**
742.22

**several**
035.02
050.12
174.21
191.06
196.16
197.10
224.08
238.19
377.13
462.13
485.14
597.15
605.01
692.03
726.14

**severe**
076.18
590.22
680.20

**severely**
323.12
614.12

**severity**
511.01

**sewing**
074.18
134.12
696.02

**sexton**
649.13
649.22
746.09
754.17
760.03

**sha'n't**
235.14
259.05

**shaamed**
699.12

**shabby**
020.18
022.16

**shade**
006.15
296.02

**shaded**
404.12

**shadow**
427.11
449.10
504.01
567.14
730.05

**shadow's**
059.06

**shadowing**
522.08

**shadowless**
371.16

**shadows**
206.09
598.09
598.10

**shaft**
235.22

**shaggy**
010.06
311.08

**shaime**
696.10

**shake**
117.06
117.15
181.15
282.15
309.09
372.21
614.12
709.15

**shaken**
301.09
451.06

**shaking**
021.22
052.17
104.19
110.22
238.05
294.06
513.17
614.15
762.13

**shall**
001.05
013.17
020.08
021.19
029.19
030.06
030.07
054.14
059.21
064.10
074.15
076.09
076.11
083.20
094.16
107.20
117.09
117.10
117.11
118.05
123.12
127.13
133.16
134.02
158.14
158.17
163.06
163.11
163.17
167.13
167.17
168.10
168.13
173.16
173.18
175.14
177.15
179.09
195.03
195.05
195.17
200.08
212.02
214.22
215.15
215.16
220.07
222.08
236.19
239.19
246.10
251.10
255.02
256.22
258.03
260.14
261.19
264.11
286.17
287.11
287.12
289.17
303.12
303.14
307.18
309.17
316.04
317.06
320.08
320.15
327.17
329.11
329.12
333.16
334.01
334.08
344.05
344.08
345.02
345.08
353.18
354.21
356.21
357.17
357.18
359.06
359.08
360.18
361.08
361.09
365.15
366.03
367.13
368.04
368.05
368.07
383.03
384.06
384.09
385.16
397.01
402.01
408.18
425.19
428.13
435.07
437.03
439.19
453.09
455.05
457.12
458.01
459.06
462.01
470.08
480.08
482.18
483.10
484.01
485.08
489.16
490.01
493.18
494.09
500.07
505.09
506.05
511.10
519.08
520.01
525.22
526.15
528.22
529.02
540.02
540.12
541.20
543.06
547.05
554.15
559.21
562.04
563.02
571.12
586.10
600.15
601.07
604.14
605.11
607.20
609.13
611.08
611.10
611.12
612.14
613.21
616.08
618.02
618.04
618.09
618.10
618.14
627.07
627.08
630.06

| | | | | | |
|---|---|---|---|---|---|
| 632.11 | 629.19 | 093.07 | 146.22 | 200.03 | 266.17 |
| 637.22 | **sharpness** | 093.15 | 147.01 | 200.07 | 266.20 |
| 639.22 | 238.01 | 093.19 | 147.05 | 202.12 | 266.20 |
| 647.03 | **shattered** | 093.20 | 147.09 | 202.19 | 267.03 |
| 647.11 | 325.15 | 093.20 | 147.11 | 204.06 | 267.07 |
| 648.05 | 360.21 | 093.21 | 147.12 | 204.07 | 267.09 |
| 648.17 | **shattering** | 094.02 | 148.03 | 204.09 | 267.10 |
| 649.07 | 110.17 | 094.19 | 148.07 | 205.15 | 267.12 |
| 650.08 | **shaume** | 096.06 | 148.09 | 208.06 | 268.02 |
| 672.14 | 233.06 | 096.06 | 148.14 | 208.08 | 269.09 |
| 678.17 | **shawl** | 096.07 | 148.16 | 208.12 | 270.18 |
| 681.12 | 101.21 | 096.11 | 148.17 | 208.13 | 270.18 |
| 684.20 | 277.15 | 097.01 | 148.19 | 210.07 | 271.01 |
| 685.02 | 278.13 | 097.01 | 148.21 | 210.10 | 271.04 |
| 697.12 | 351.04 | 097.06 | 150.19 | 210.20 | 271.14 |
| 702.14 | 410.19 | 097.07 | 150.20 | 211.13 | 272.03 |
| 703.07 | 626.05 | 097.10 | 150.21 | 211.16 | 272.05 |
| 707.07 | **shawlless** | 097.13 | 151.06 | 211.21 | 272.08 |
| 707.09 | 190.04 | 097.17 | 151.17 | 212.04 | 273.04 |
| 707.10 | **she** | 097.18 | 152.02 | 212.10 | 273.12 |
| 714.04 | 008.14 | 097.20 | 152.05 | 212.19 | 274.08 |
| 716.13 | 008.17 | 098.04 | 152.17 | 213.12 | 274.10 |
| 722.08 | 010.14 | 099.04 | 153.13 | 213.13 | 274.21 |
| 724.10 | 011.15 | 099.05 | 154.02 | 215.02 | 274.22 |
| 733.05 | 015.03 | 099.09 | 155.06 | 215.03 | 275.02 |
| 733.17 | 017.11 | 099.20 | 155.17 | 215.15 | 275.04 |
| 740.01 | 017.12 | 103.14 | 156.01 | 217.01 | 275.07 |
| 755.08 | 017.20 | 104.13 | 156.07 | 217.06 | 276.06 |
| 761.20 | 017.20 | 106.08 | 156.13 | 218.06 | 276.11 |
| **shalln't** | 017.21 | 106.09 | 156.14 | 219.05 | 277.05 |
| 564.03 | 018.18 | 106.13 | 156.19 | 220.08 | 277.11 |
| **shallow** | 019.03 | 106.14 | 157.05 | 220.14 | 277.16 |
| 346.07 | 019.08 | 106.15 | 157.12 | 221.08 | 278.01 |
| **shame** | 019.21 | 107.06 | 158.12 | 222.19 | 278.06 |
| 008.20 | 020.01 | 108.22 | 158.16 | 223.19 | 278.19 |
| 043.01 | 020.04 | 109.11 | 159.09 | 224.06 | 279.01 |
| 117.04 | 020.10 | 109.18 | 159.13 | 225.07 | 279.12 |
| 133.20 | 020.13 | 110.19 | 159.20 | 226.09 | 279.20 |
| 230.18 | 022.18 | 111.01 | 170.02 | 226.13 | 280.04 |
| 230.18 | 024.05 | 111.11 | 170.03 | 226.15 | 280.08 |
| 278.22 | 025.05 | 111.13 | 170.06 | 226.17 | 280.13 |
| 436.05 | 026.13 | 111.17 | 170.07 | 226.19 | 283.09 |
| 468.16 | 026.14 | 111.18 | 170.11 | 227.02 | 283.12 |
| 511.11 | 028.15 | 112.14 | 170.20 | 228.07 | 283.18 |
| 512.20 | 029.11 | 112.15 | 170.21 | 228.11 | 284.04 |
| 682.19 | 029.16 | 113.08 | 170.22 | 228.16 | 284.04 |
| 727.18 | 031.01 | 114.04 | 171.03 | 229.09 | 284.05 |
| **shameful** | 033.19 | 114.05 | 171.09 | 230.19 | 284.22 |
| 062.04 | 035.13 | 114.11 | 172.09 | 231.08 | 285.19 |
| 170.20 | 035.16 | 114.13 | 172.16 | 231.10 | 286.11 |
| 630.02 | 035.18 | 114.22 | 173.01 | 231.11 | 286.21 |
| **shamefully** | 036.03 | 115.03 | 176.13 | 231.12 | 287.04 |
| 080.21 | 036.12 | 115.05 | 176.17 | 231.18 | 287.08 |
| 340.16 | 037.02 | 116.05 | 178.03 | 231.20 | 288.13 |
| **shameless** | 037.05 | 116.16 | 178.03 | 233.18 | 288.21 |
| 005.01 | 037.08 | 117.03 | 178.04 | 233.22 | 290.05 |
| **shan't** | 037.08 | 117.14 | 178.16 | 234.02 | 290.11 |
| 170.22 | 037.08 | 117.20 | 178.18 | 234.10 | 291.09 |
| 220.08 | 037.10 | 117.21 | 180.04 | 234.13 | 292.05 |
| 251.09 | 045.02 | 118.01 | 180.11 | 234.16 | 292.06 |
| 307.11 | 045.04 | 121.18 | 181.04 | 234.16 | 292.20 |
| 342.05 | 055.22 | 121.19 | 182.07 | 234.21 | 292.22 |
| 385.07 | 056.01 | 122.10 | 183.12 | 235.14 | 293.01 |
| 386.22 | 056.14 | 122.12 | 184.01 | 235.21 | 293.02 |
| 471.18 | 056.20 | 122.17 | 184.03 | 236.08 | 294.07 |
| 504.11 | 056.20 | 122.17 | 184.22 | 236.14 | 294.10 |
| 537.11 | 056.21 | 122.19 | 185.02 | 236.15 | 294.14 |
| 630.05 | 056.22 | 122.22 | 185.04 | 237.01 | 296.18 |
| 630.05 | 063.12 | 123.06 | 185.07 | 237.02 | 296.19 |
| **shant** | 065.08 | 128.21 | 185.09 | 237.03 | 296.21 |
| 524.01 | 069.12 | 130.10 | 186.02 | 237.08 | 298.04 |
| 634.15 | 070.01 | 130.13 | 186.06 | 237.15 | 298.14 |
| **shape** | 070.08 | 130.13 | 188.10 | 237.20 | 298.15 |
| 178.01 | 070.11 | 130.15 | 188.17 | 237.21 | 298.16 |
| 325.08 | 070.16 | 130.18 | 188.19 | 237.22 | 298.20 |
| **shaped** | 070.22 | 131.20 | 190.04 | 238.18 | 298.21 |
| 061.12 | 071.04 | 131.22 | 190.06 | 238.18 | 299.04 |
| 731.15 | 071.14 | 132.02 | 190.07 | 239.16 | 299.16 |
| **share** | 072.08 | 132.06 | 192.09 | 240.03 | 299.17 |
| 032.06 | 072.09 | 132.19 | 192.10 | 240.17 | 299.17 |
| 127.11 | 073.14 | 132.20 | 192.12 | 240.17 | 299.19 |
| 127.13 | 073.15 | 137.16 | 192.20 | 240.18 | 299.20 |
| 261.12 | 075.08 | 139.09 | 192.21 | 245.08 | 300.03 |
| 307.07 | 075.12 | 139.10 | 193.05 | 248.14 | 302.11 |
| 371.13 | 076.14 | 140.02 | 193.08 | 248.15 | 302.13 |
| 468.03 | 076.15 | 140.09 | 195.12 | 249.03 | 302.19 |
| 489.15 | 076.15 | 140.11 | 195.16 | 249.05 | 302.21 |
| 642.12 | 077.04 | 140.11 | 195.18 | 249.06 | 303.20 |
| 651.05 | 077.08 | 140.12 | 195.19 | 250.09 | 304.01 |
| **shared** | 078.09 | 140.12 | 196.03 | 251.01 | 304.09 |
| 010.06 | 079.16 | 140.22 | 196.05 | 251.04 | 304.14 |
| 471.06 | 081.01 | 141.10 | 196.14 | 253.22 | 304.22 |
| **sharing** | 090.06 | 142.08 | 196.19 | 254.15 | 305.03 |
| 591.10 | 090.07 | 142.09 | 196.22 | 254.22 | 305.04 |
| **sharp** | 090.09 | 142.09 | 197.07 | 255.14 | 305.17 |
| 137.19 | 090.10 | 142.12 | 197.10 | 255.14 | 305.18 |
| 195.05 | 090.11 | 143.04 | 197.11 | 257.17 | 314.20 |
| 294.18 | 090.15 | 143.06 | 197.15 | 257.19 | 329.05 |
| 398.02 | 090.16 | 143.09 | 197.15 | 258.14 | 329.06 |
| 509.09 | 090.18 | 143.12 | 197.19 | 261.11 | 329.20 |
| 582.10 | 090.19 | 143.12 | 197.20 | 261.14 | 330.01 |
| 638.07 | 090.20 | 143.14 | 198.04 | 261.18 | 330.08 |
| 662.04 | 090.23 | 143.16 | 198.07 | 264.01 | 330.13 |
| 758.11 | 091.02 | 145.05 | 198.13 | 265.14 | 331.04 |
| **sharpen** | 091.04 | 145.06 | 198.13 | 265.17 | 331.06 |
| 647.20 | 091.06 | 145.07 | 199.06 | 265.19 | 331.19 |
| **sharply** | 091.16 | 145.10 | 199.07 | 266.02 | 332.07 |
| 033.19 | 091.18 | 145.11 | 199.21 | 266.03 | 332.15 |
| 204.21 | 092.06 | 145.21 | 199.22 | 266.05 | 332.21 |
| 318.03 | 092.14 | 146.14 | | 266.14 | 333.10 |
| 609.20 | 092.15 | 146.19 | | | 334.11 |

| | | | | | |
|---|---|---|---|---|---|
| 334.19 | 382.22 | 450.01 | 520.18 | 589.11 | |
| 335.06 | 383.09 | 450.03 | 520.21 | 590.18 | |
| 335.09 | 383.12 | 450.13 | 520.22 | 591.11 | |
| 335.10 | 383.13 | 452.19 | 522.13 | 591.12 | |
| 335.12 | 384.09 | 453.17 | 522.15 | 591.14 | |
| 335.12 | 384.13 | 453.18 | 522.15 | 592.15 | |
| 336.02 | 384.14 | 453.19 | 523.11 | 593.22 | |
| 336.12 | 384.20 | 453.20 | 526.20 | 594.08 | |
| 336.22 | 384.21 | 459.08 | 528.02 | 594.11 | |
| 337.13 | 385.11 | 459.11 | 528.03 | 596.12 | |
| 337.14 | 385.13 | 461.08 | 528.06 | 597.06 | |
| 337.16 | 385.15 | 461.14 | 528.09 | 597.13 | |
| 337.19 | 386.19 | 461.18 | 528.10 | 598.16 | |
| 338.01 | 387.04 | 474.03 | 528.12 | 599.17 | |
| 338.07 | 387.05 | 474.12 | 528.13 | 601.17 | |
| 338.08 | 387.08 | 475.01 | 528.18 | 601.19 | |
| 338.12 | 388.21 | 475.03 | 528.21 | 607.05 | |
| 338.17 | 389.10 | 475.11 | 532.13 | 607.11 | |
| 338.19 | 405.10 | 477.16 | 534.08 | 608.07 | 6..20 |
| 338.20 | 406.09 | 478.01 | 534.13 | 608.20 | 660.21 |
| 339.07 | 406.10 | 478.17 | 534.14 | 608.22 | 661.13 |
| 339.15 | 406.13 | 478.17 | 536.09 | 609.07 | 661.19 |
| 339.20 | 409.07 | 478.21 | 536.19 | 609.08 | 662.19 |
| 339.21 | 409.08 | 479.07 | 537.02 | 609.15 | 662.21 |
| 340.01 | 410.18 | 479.10 | 537.08 | 609.17 | 662.22 |
| 340.04 | 410.21 | 479.20 | 537.10 | 609.20 | 663.01 |
| 340.06 | 411.04 | 479.21 | 537.12 | 610.04 | 663.05 |
| 340.13 | 411.09 | 480.14 | 537.17 | 610.09 | 663.18 |
| 340.13 | 411.11 | 480.15 | 537.18 | 610.21 | 663.19 |
| 340.16 | 411.14 | 480.16 | 537.20 | 611.01 | 663.21 |
| 341.01 | 411.16 | 480.17 | 537.20 | 614.19 | 664.03 |
| 341.01 | 411.17 | 480.19 | 538.06 | 614.22 | 665.05 |
| 341.06 | 412.01 | 481.06 | 538.06 | 615.08 | 665.06 |
| 341.08 | 413.19 | 481.16 | 538.06 | 615.18 | 665.10 |
| 343.20 | 424.06 | 482.03 | 538.07 | 615.18 | 665.11 |
| 343.21 | 424.08 | 482.15 | 538.13 | 616.03 | 665.13 |
| 344.13 | 424.12 | 482.20 | 538.14 | 616.08 | 665.20 |
| 344.22 | 425.08 | 483.01 | 538.15 | 617.09 | 666.03 |
| 345.13 | 425.09 | 483.14 | 539.01 | 620.03 | 666.06 |
| 345.15 | 425.10 | 484.18 | 539.15 | 620.05 | 666.18 |
| 345.16 | 425.14 | 485.03 | 540.12 | 623.07 | 667.06 |
| 345.19 | 426.06 | 485.08 | 540.12 | 623.18 | 667.10 |
| 345.19 | 426.08 | 485.14 | 541.01 | 626.08 | 667.13 |
| 346.19 | 426.08 | 486.11 | 541.04 | 628.03 | 667.15 |
| 349.07 | 426.14 | 487.01 | 541.06 | 628.05 | 667.17 |
| 350.01 | 426.17 | 487.19 | 541.16 | 628.06 | 667.19 |
| 351.07 | 426.20 | 491.01 | 542.07 | 628.13 | 667.20 |
| 351.11 | 427.06 | 492.06 | 542.11 | 629.14 | 667.22 |
| 351.20 | 427.16 | 492.12 | 542.17 | 630.02 | 667.22 |
| 352.01 | 428.01 | 492.22 | 542.19 | 630.03 | 668.02 |
| 352.09 | 428.10 | 497.11 | 544.09 | 630.04 | 668.07 |
| 352.14 | 428.16 | 499.01 | 544.18 | 630.05 | 668.09 |
| 352.19 | 428.17 | 499.03 | 544.20 | 630.05 | 668.11 |
| 353.10 | 428.18 | 499.12 | 544.21 | 630.06 | 668.12 |
| 353.11 | 429.03 | 499.14 | 545.04 | 630.06 | 668.16 |
| 353.12 | 429.07 | 499.15 | 545.08 | 630.07 | 668.20 |
| 353.20 | 429.14 | 499.21 | 546.14 | 630.13 | 669.02 |
| 354.02 | 429.16 | 500.03 | 547.11 | 630.15 | 669.08 |
| 354.11 | 429.17 | 500.12 | 548.09 | 630.17 | 669.10 |
| 354.12 | 429.18 | 500.15 | 548.11 | 631.03 | 669.16 |
| 354.13 | 429.21 | 500.16 | 548.12 | 631.04 | 670.04 |
| 354.13 | 430.08 | 500.18 | 548.13 | 631.05 | 671.04 |
| 354.15 | 430.14 | 500.19 | 548.14 | 631.10 | 671.07 |
| 355.15 | 430.18 | 500.22 | 548.20 | 631.19 | 671.10 |
| 356.07 | 431.01 | 502.04 | 548.22 | 631.20 | 671.14 |
| 357.05 | 431.03 | 502.13 | 550.07 | 631.22 | 671.15 |
| 357.07 | 431.05 | 503.03 | 550.11 | 632.01 | 671.19 |
| 357.17 | 431.09 | 503.14 | 550.12 | 632.14 | 671.20 |
| 358.06 | 431.14 | 503.16 | 551.08 | 632.15 | 672.05 |
| 358.10 | 431.22 | 504.08 | 551.14 | 632.18 | 674.13 |
| 358.11 | 432.17 | 504.21 | 551.18 | 632.20 | 674.15 |
| 359.13 | 432.19 | 505.11 | 551.19 | 633.04 | 674.21 |
| 359.14 | 433.01 | 505.15 | 551.21 | 633.06 | 675.05 |
| 360.05 | 433.13 | 506.01 | 552.03 | 633.06 | 675.06 |
| 360.13 | 434.02 | 506.09 | 552.14 | 633.08 | 675.07 |
| 360.20 | 434.04 | 506.15 | 553.02 | 633.12 | 675.13 |
| 361.10 | 434.09 | 506.18 | 553.09 | 633.20 | 675.20 |
| 361.14 | 434.15 | 507.01 | 553.14 | 633.22 | 676.11 |
| 362.02 | 435.06 | 507.03 | 554.01 | 634.03 | 676.18 |
| 362.05 | 435.20 | 507.04 | 554.11 | 634.05 | 677.10 |
| 362.14 | 437.05 | 507.05 | 554.14 | 634.06 | 677.14 |
| 364.19 | 437.12 | 507.06 | 554.20 | 634.08 | 680.09 |
| 365.13 | 437.17 | 507.07 | 556.16 | 635.17 | 681.11 |
| 365.17 | 438.01 | 507.08 | 558.16 | 636.19 | 681.14 |
| 365.21 | 438.07 | 507.14 | 560.07 | 638.21 | 681.18 |
| 366.01 | 438.20 | 509.02 | 563.01 | 638.21 | 686.04 |
| 366.13 | 438.21 | 509.15 | 564.03 | 639.05 | 686.05 |
| 366.14 | 439.16 | 509.17 | 566.02 | 639.06 | 686.06 |
| 366.15 | 440.01 | 510.04 | 566.03 | 639.08 | 686.08 |
| 367.04 | 440.13 | 510.12 | 566.05 | 639.08 | 687.01 |
| 367.19 | 440.15 | 510.16 | 566.19 | 639.15 | 690.20 |
| 367.19 | 441.01 | 512.06 | 566.21 | 640.08 | 691.03 |
| 368.03 | 441.20 | 512.07 | 569.18 | 640.09 | 691.07 |
| 371.01 | 445.11 | 513.01 | 570.02 | 641.14 | 691.11 |
| 371.02 | 445.13 | 513.05 | 573.19 | 641.16 | 691.17 |
| 371.05 | 445.19 | 513.12 | 573.21 | 641.17 | 691.22 |
| 372.02 | 445.20 | 513.20 | 574.01 | 642.06 | 692.01 |
| 372.03 | 446.04 | 514.02 | 576.06 | 642.07 | 692.11 |
| 372.13 | 446.06 | 514.07 | 576.12 | 642.09 | 695.02 |
| 372.16 | 446.11 | 514.07 | 577.09 | 645.11 | 697.05 |
| 374.06 | 446.14 | 514.13 | 578.07 | 648.13 | 698.08 |
| 374.20 | 446.16 | 516.07 | 579.10 | 648.21 | 698.09 |
| 374.21 | 446.20 | 516.22 | 579.17 | 650.12 | 698.13 |
| 375.08 | 446.21 | 517.03 | 580.18 | 650.18 | 699.07 |
| 375.20 | 447.02 | 517.04 | 581.12 | 651.09 | 699.09 |
| 376.03 | 447.04 | 517.10 | 583.08 | 651.14 | 699.13 |
| 376.07 | 448.12 | 518.06 | 588.01 | 652.01 | 699.16 |
| 376.09 | 449.04 | 518.08 | 588.10 | 652.03 | 699.18 |
| 376.12 | 449.08 | 519.09 | 588.12 | 653.08 | 699.20 |
| 376.13 | 449.19 | 519.20 | 588.14 | 653.21 | 700.02 |
| 376.17 | 449.21 | 519.22 | 589.06 | 653.21 | 700.10 |

| | | | | | |
|---|---|---|---|---|---|
| .18 | 286.09 | 041.14 | 383.15 | 272.01 | 618.21 |
| 01.01 | 294.06 | **shivered** | 414.08 | 274.21 | 618.22 |
| 701.02 | 294.08 | 599.13 | 451.17 | 275.13 | 619.06 |
| 701.08 | 297.15 | **shivering** | 462.15 | 276.20 | 621.19 |
| 701.12 | 297.15 | 041.13 | 478.20 | 276.21 | 622.10 |
| 701.19 | 342.13 | 074.19 | 486.15 | 282.17 | 630.02 |
| 702.03 | 344.22 | 097.10 | 508.04 | 282.18 | 632.21 |
| 702.05 | 345.17 | 102.21 | 531.04 | 283.02 | 636.21 |
| 702.13 | 367.03 | 191.11 | 583.09 | 289.10 | 639.05 |
| 702.21 | 374.03 | 259.11 | 597.04 | 290.21 | 641.05 |
| 703.04 | 374.15 | 741.15 | 599.04 | 292.13 | 642.02 |
| 703.04 | 376.16 | **shiveringly** | 655.18 | 293.08 | 642.06 |
| 703.05 | 408.19 | 052.10 | 689.21 | 297.01 | 644.08 |
| 703.07 | 434.05 | **shivers** | 720.04 | 299.15 | 651.04 |
| 703.09 | 452.08 | 741.16 | **shorter** | 305.10 | 653.07 |
| 703.13 | 483.12 | **shock** | 626.03 | 308.02 | 654.08 |
| 703.15 | 622.12 | 054.20 | **shot** | 310.06 | 654.09 |
| 703.20 | 629.15 | 301.04 | 105.21 | 315.22 | 656.02 |
| 703.22 | 629.15 | 316.17 | 160.20 | 316.07 | 658.08 |
| 704.02 | 630.01 | 417.13 | 163.15 | 316.22 | 661.03 |
| 704.14 | 631.07 | **shocked** | 275.19 | 318.02 | 662.22 |
| 705.07 | 634.07 | 110.04 | 366.07 | 318.08 | 666.22 |
| 705.08 | 662.01 | 157.02 | 397.02 | 319.20 | 671.12 |
| 705.22 | 667.02 | 401.18 | 410.09 | 327.02 | 675.18 |
| 706.10 | 675.02 | 503.03 | **should** | 327.12 | 676.02 |
| 706.13 | 756.09 | 700.02 | 002.16 | 329.05 | 676.15 |
| 706.19 | **sheaves** | 755.04 | 008.08 | 332.03 | 676.16 |
| 707.03 | 515.08 | **shocking** | 019.03 | 333.14 | 678.02 |
| 707.21 | **shed** | 245.17 | 022.02 | 334.05 | 679.20 |
| 708.03 | 566.04 | 607.09 | 031.12 | 334.06 | 680.07 |
| 708.17 | 631.11 | **shockingly** | 037.03 | 337.12 | 685.10 |
| 708.22 | **shedding** | 262.01 | 042.13 | 345.14 | 695.15 |
| 709.07 | 081.05 | 446.14 | 044.12 | 346.19 | 696.20 |
| 709.10 | 120.09 | 565.18 | 047.02 | 347.01 | 697.10 |
| 709.13 | **sheep** | **shodld** | 048.11 | 347.12 | 699.09 |
| 710.04 | 010.06 | 151.10 | 055.21 | 348.03 | 700.14 |
| 710.08 | 028.04 | **shoe** | 064.17 | 348.08 | 706.05 |
| 710.16 | 064.06 | 298.11 | 071.04 | 352.03 | 707.20 |
| 710.17 | 241.07 | **shoes** | 072.01 | 354.04 | 709.14 |
| 711.12 | 689.21 | 103.16 | 073.14 | 359.17 | 709.20 |
| 713.01 | 761.02 | 114.20 | 087.12 | 361.12 | 713.09 |
| 713.10 | 761.11 | 455.16 | 088.18 | 367.04 | 716.15 |
| 713.12 | **sheep-dog** | 486.02 | 089.01 | 368.02 | 725.04 |
| 715.08 | 473.03 | 490.18 | 089.02 | 371.12 | 728.20 |
| 715.09 | **sheer** | 547.18 | 091.12 | 375.15 | 733.14 |
| 715.11 | 025.06 | 553.10 | 094.02 | 385.19 | 741.20 |
| 716.07 | 378.13 | **shone** | 094.04 | 390.03 | 742.01 |
| 717.01 | **sheet** | 114.18 | 097.09 | 391.16 | 756.17 |
| 717.03 | 153.01 | 243.11 | 099.16 | 397.13 | 763.09 |
| 717.04 | 275.05 | 302.18 | 101.11 | 397.15 | **shoulder** |
| 717.10 | **sheets** | 398.14 | 101.17 | 401.01 | 084.02 |
| 717.11 | 691.20 | 427.09 | 104.11 | 402.09 | 094.08 |
| 717.15 | **shelf** | 431.03 | 105.01 | 403.05 | 143.11 |
| 717.17 | 029.17 | 552.12 | 110.04 | 411.17 | 190.10 |
| 717.20 | 044.09 | 577.16 | 110.11 | 417.03 | 294.02 |
| 717.22 | **shelter** | 638.15 | 112.12 | 418.19 | 467.17 |
| 720.06 | 021.20 | 644.20 | 114.09 | 419.14 | 519.17 |
| 721.10 | 044.14 | **shoo** | 115.01 | 422.19 | 542.20 |
| 722.01 | 058.12 | 193.19 | 118.11 | 428.11 | 683.15 |
| 722.14 | 190.03 | 690.21 | 120.03 | 428.17 | 694.18 |
| 723.10 | 313.21 | 720.09 | 124.10 | 433.13 | 702.06 |
| 723.16 | 326.06 | 720.10 | 126.02 | 436.13 | 702.10 |
| 724.18 | 386.02 | 720.11 | 128.21 | 436.14 | 712.06 |
| 725.14 | 396.16 | **shoo'll** | 132.20 | 438.14 | **shouldering** |
| 725.15 | 398.15 | 016.10 | 133.21 | 447.01 | 016.19 |
| 725.19 | 519.01 | **shoo's** | 134.06 | 456.09 | **shoulders** |
| 725.20 | **sheltered** | 033.20 | 135.22 | 459.11 | 123.15 |
| 726.04 | 002.02 | 193.19 | 140.15 | 460.10 | 157.12 |
| 726.07 | 019.06 | 690.21 | 140.15 | 460.19 | 266.21 |
| 726.09 | 431.22 | 696.14 | 141.05 | 462.14 | 276.13 |
| 727.22 | **shew** | 719.17 | 143.12 | 464.21 | 283.14 |
| 728.11 | 311.04 | **shook** | 148.17 | 466.12 | 311.09 |
| 730.13 | 320.16 | 016.01 | 153.12 | 469.20 | 351.04 |
| 732.01 | 324.18 | 088.12 | 158.18 | 472.03 | 383.11 |
| 737.11 | **shewn** | 157.13 | 166.20 | 474.07 | 397.21 |
| 738.01 | 716.09 | 189.15 | 166.20 | 477.01 | 406.16 |
| 738.05 | **shielders** | 331.06 | 171.17 | 480.02 | 443.15 |
| 738.11 | 109.16 | 393.07 | 172.15 | 484.18 | 621.13 |
| 738.14 | **shift** | 402.04 | 174.18 | 493.13 | **shouldn't** |
| **she'd** | 085.11 | 418.18 | 175.01 | 494.18 | 104.10 |
| 210.19 | 720.09 | 438.17 | 178.06 | 494.20 | 135.03 |
| 340.22 | 761.21 | 465.20 | 180.17 | 496.11 | 141.01 |
| 436.12 | **shifted** | 509.13 | 181.20 | 501.12 | 179.07 |
| **she'll** | 381.04 | 565.06 | 182.13 | 521.19 | 181.12 |
| 140.03 | 718.21 | 621.13 | 182.20 | 525.12 | 195.16 |
| 142.04 | 724.03 | 709.12 | 183.01 | 533.05 | 337.11 |
| 142.07 | 737.13 | 727.01 | 184.08 | 535.16 | 357.08 |
| 202.15 | **shifting** | **shoon** | 185.10 | 536.08 | 357.10 |
| 288.15 | 022.16 | 708.05 | 186.21 | 545.18 | 378.22 |
| 329.03 | **shilling** | **shoot** | 190.15 | 545.19 | 414.21 |
| 332.21 | 119.22 | 235.22 | 199.12 | 558.06 | 438.14 |
| 337.17 | **shillings** | 275.22 | 223.14 | 558.16 | 546.21 |
| 341.08 | 166.04 | 276.02 | 224.11 | 562.19 | 566.12 |
| 483.21 | **shimmering** | 396.18 | 227.02 | 566.16 | 721.18 |
| 484.18 | 104.07 | **shooting** | 230.05 | 567.08 | **shout** |
| 605.16 | **shine** | 535.13 | 230.13 | 570.19 | 635.05 |
| 671.16 | 277.02 | 704.10 | 235.05 | 571.15 | 748.10 |
| 671.17 | 364.13 | **shop** | 239.18 | 575.05 | **shouted** |
| 677.06 | **shining** | 298.11 | 244.10 | 576.05 | 009.21 |
| **she's** | 119.13 | **shore** | 244.11 | 578.19 | 016.05 |
| 009.18 | 284.04 | 753.09 | 247.12 | 579.06 | 034.07 |
| 122.10 | 557.11 | **short** | 248.10 | 581.13 | 043.15 |
| 139.12 | 694.22 | 005.04 | 250.16 | 582.18 | 053.10 |
| 140.13 | **ship** | 041.15 | 251.15 | 591.16 | 186.04 |
| 142.02 | 415.03 | 178.05 | 254.22 | 592.06 | 458.08 |
| 143.04 | **shirk** | 194.22 | 255.14 | 592.20 | 480.14 |
| 193.07 | 355.11 | 240.04 | 261.18 | 600.19 | 604.16 |
| 239.16 | **shirt** | 305.12 | 262.04 | 602.18 | **shouting** |
| 254.07 | 054.17 | 311.05 | 262.05 | 604.10 | 106.21 |
| 254.08 | **shiver** | 337.09 | 262.20 | 608.11 | **shoved** |
| 286.01 | 015.10 | 353.22 | 270.10 | 617.14 | 127.03 |

666.10
shovel
062.18
514.01
652.12
744.22
show
029.18
031.15
043.07
058.18
084.01
085.07
126.19
146.20
153.10
166.06
205.01
211.10
219.04
235.06
315.04
382.13
401.20
405.21
445.21
458.04
463.17
477.02
490.15
499.08
512.09
518.21
562.11
620.01
664.10
709.16
734.14
754.08
showed
021.09
055.13
060.16
079.18
204.09
208.05
246.04
296.21
369.10
568.15
634.01
653.21
695.18
726.04
763.18
shower
015.08
050.17
104.05
124.08
192.11
398.12
610.07
showers
516.22
737.04
757.09
showing
057.08
091.21
124.09
156.17
339.20
352.16
462.09
551.09
571.11
shown
027.01
292.06
415.02
511.09
582.12
604.09
621.19
shows
108.11
435.18
570.18
showy
007.19
shrank
209.19
225.21
313.05
491.04
759.11
shriek
278.13
shrieked
167.10
366.01
450.12
565.10
565.18
633.05
shrieking
104.15
566.20
shrieks
646.07

shrink
577.22
756.08
shrinking
452.14
540.19
606.21
shrubs
719.04
shrugged
621.13
shrunk
008.20
147.18
193.05
611.16
shudder
231.04
390.12
shuddered
317.12
568.06
shuddering
054.03
266.14
590.19
shudders
277.22
605.20
shuffled
758.13
shuffling
061.17
534.21
shun
261.17
332.23
499.21
shunned
350.04
412.17
701.09
736.03
shunning
590.09
shut
040.01
132.01
160.07
169.01
193.04
207.01
269.04
276.08
280.03
286.04
312.13
316.12
326.03
370.16
396.02
397.04
437.06
505.17
532.15
564.10
607.17
607.19
624.07
634.19
644.17
659.17
661.09
690.07
697.09
750.10
758.09
762.10
shutters
103.21
191.20
233.02
shutting
056.04
250.21
373.08
642.01
743.22
shuttle-cocks
558.21
shyed
483.17
sich
187.12
324.19
326.12
566.16
sick
036.08
082.09
093.06
107.06
133.10
159.12
159.20
218.13
218.14
258.09
403.14
510.13
551.04

555.20
566.01
587.17
618.22
630.07
631.07
sick-chamber
304.13
sickly
451.03
546.01
628.13
sickness
193.10
201.03
289.01
298.06
514.05
side
056.18
066.20
073.05
121.11
126.22
145.19
146.20
151.19
169.05
169.12
188.14
193.22
207.06
209.16
211.02
240.15
243.08
278.18
323.10
339.19
355.18
382.20
394.10
427.02
427.23
431.21
435.07
453.16
456.14
479.11
480.08
483.18
499.03
517.13
517.17
522.09
523.03
529.07
553.03
557.18
565.14
578.08
586.01
591.05
597.08
632.22
649.19
649.20
696.01
704.06
707.14
712.19
712.21
side-board
331.07
side-door
009.21
sides
038.14
220.05
364.08
610.08
711.20
sideways
707.13
sidled
717.11
sigh
062.09
170.07
352.17
375.20
623.05
652.09
652.14
676.19
sighed
123.19
279.02
354.13
367.19
393.13
539.09
551.14
577.14
683.19
704.11
sighing
314.12
318.19
339.14

sighs
270.07
408.05
712.11
752.01
sight
027.17
064.11
129.21
140.16
166.20
213.02
244.14
249.01
264.21
285.17
408.12
432.21
450.11
480.18
506.01
598.19
666.10
692.22
722.21
727.17
742.21
sign
060.17
083.08
244.11
579.15
signal
390.02
signature
354.12
signed
257.13
656.17
signet
012.11
significant
004.05
signified
285.15
296.08
signify
725.13
signing
165.12
729.02
signs
005.18
077.05
213.09
392.13
478.06
694.20
silence
009.10
023.07
042.06
051.14
105.22
152.06
194.10
205.11
205.12
239.17
250.05
336.17
345.18
393.15
505.13
517.08
552.09
617.22
655.17
680.19
722.04
750.17
silenced
610.14
silent
149.18
169.14
215.20
234.08
255.14
269.03
286.05
314.07
360.08
364.05
370.13
375.05
381.10
404.01
453.17
456.19
528.13
590.14
616.22
639.15
649.03
671.01
701.11
silently
062.05
104.17
438.17

538.18
676.03
718.18
silk
114.19
151.07
321.05
383.16
626.06
silky
669.01
sill
352.06
676.19
758.01
silly
097.06
137.13
152.12
173.21
218.11
240.03
325.03
338.21
494.03
503.20
509.13
529.05
557.03
600.11
614.11
703.01
silver
006.02
104.06
119.15
379.04
494.08
678.13
694.05
699.14
silvery
209.14
similar
312.19
409.08
411.01
414.18
679.22
728.06
simple
193.17
380.05
496.12
509.11
580.14
simpleton
194.17
simply
083.09
351.08
simultaneously
531.14
sin
048.08
048.11
049.04
230.11
since
013.02
046.10
056.09
061.03
070.18
080.17
086.02
115.14
130.01
133.05
146.18
155.18
172.05
192.17
195.01
197.05
199.17
216.02
216.13
232.03
237.03
244.21
244.22
270.08
271.04
271.21
278.05
280.03
309.04
329.21
330.14
337.05
357.16
389.04
416.18
434.03
448.12
451.17
502.12
516.05
524.09
527.12

533.18
535.13
540.09
548.02
555.01
572.01
572.20
613.07
627.15
634.06
646.04
653.22
655.03
658.03
671.13
698.16
700.02
707.21
726.11
760.19
sincere
030.11
727.03
sincerely
070.01
229.10
366.21
576.22
sincerity
263.16
334.09
603.05
sinewy
003.17
sing
093.20
544.04
544.04
629.19
629.20
singer
696.21
singers
131.13
132.11
singing
090.13
093.21
103.01
118.17
120.06
303.06
479.14
518.09
557.10
696.02
713.11
single
136.14
231.10
248.19
300.01
304.02
334.07
335.02
341.16
342.08
443.03
443.04
465.02
493.05
510.05
637.04
694.12
734.04
746.12
singular
007.07
038.07
207.18
498.06
728.13
singularly
019.18
508.10
sinister
061.20
sink
124.13
149.22
679.10
sinking
067.06
089.07
366.05
375.21
407.12
537.20
692.17
sinner
049.04
169.06
758.19
sinners
178.09
189.21
sins
048.11
sip
476.13

sipping
  613.16
sir
  002.08
  002.15
  012.02
  012.19
  021.17
  023.05
  026.10
  049.06
  055.03
  057.10
  070.07
  071.14
  072.09
  073.10
  074.06
  074.17
  089.06
  107.12
  107.21
  109.16
  127.09
  134.21
  135.12
  159.18
  202.18
  210.14
  214.15
  254.07
  256.15
  285.16
  288.12
  311.15
  329.09
  337.21
  345.02
  372.10
  421.14
  575.02
  577.04
  579.05
  579.22
  684.18
  698.03
sister
  073.06
  099.05
  104.09
  128.18
  144.08
  204.09
  251.13
  253.16
  299.19
  328.03
  331.19
  379.12
  407.16
  412.19
  489.09
sister's
  415.18
sister-in
  121.09
sister-in-law
  112.13
  227.15
  230.16
  235.10
  248.15
  296.21
sister-in-law's
  252.07
sisters
  536.11
sit
  012.21
  018.03
  023.11
  043.02
  043.03
  045.08
  069.12
  074.16
  074.18
  118.16
  120.20
  134.15
  134.15
  158.17
  188.06
  192.21
  202.05
  212.11
  214.15
  232.04
  302.07
  385.01
  391.18
  395.09
  453.08
  456.02
  469.02
  476.11
  483.02
  490.20
  518.01
  528.07
  544.01

  544.03
  563.09
  570.15
  597.05
  607.17
  628.12
  639.01
  666.03
  667.15
  685.15
  698.16
  698.21
  701.16
  722.14
  726.15
  729.05
  755.15
sits
  193.19
  284.08
sitting
  049.06
  058.13
  085.19
  153.12
  157.08
  179.22
  221.15
  234.07
  318.09
  382.04
  403.14
  475.15
  531.01
  547.18
  550.04
  558.11
  589.14
  628.17
  661.08
  677.01
  696.20
  700.07
  701.03
  719.01
  737.09
sitting-room
  005.10
  101.04
  691.18
sittings
  349.04
situation
  001.07
  071.10
  120.05
  136.08
  188.13
  328.06
  671.22
six
  007.05
  059.02
  066.06
  076.14
  305.11
  308.07
  344.01
  390.06
  415.19
  424.08
  449.07
  466.05
  525.01
  548.18
  555.07
  589.17
  659.10
  672.14
  760.03
  760.05
sixteen
  070.05
  149.03
  478.04
  486.04
sixty
  076.11
  520.13
  719.12
sizer's
  203.11
sizes
  010.19
skeletons
  275.20
sketch
  502.06
sketched
  040.15
skies
  201.05
skift
  564.19
skill
  377.22
  528.19
skin
  124.02
  163.02
  219.07

  358.17
  425.03
  758.02
skinned
  007.09
skirmishes
  701.04
skirts
  463.07
skittish
  761.04
skulk
  116.01
skulked
  561.18
  695.20
skulker
  106.22
  107.12
  108.04
  109.06
  111.12
  325.09
skulker's
  107.02
skull
  166.13
  257.09
skurrying
  692.12
sky
  027.18
  303.06
  516.17
  557.11
  585.07
  764.07
skylight
  132.15
  132.16
  622.21
slam
  193.15
slammed
  257.18
slander
  236.06
slanders
  233.18
slant
  004.11
slap
  223.14
  506.07
  694.19
slapped
  156.21
slapping
  091.07
slaps
  610.07
slate
  244.02
  729.13
slates
  763.19
slattenly
  194.07
slattern
  331.03
slaver
  107.05
slavered
  320.07
slavering
  259.11
slaves
  198.14
  252.17
slavish
  340.10
sleep
  032.08
  055.06
  059.11
  070.03
  079.08
  093.21
  169.09
  177.10
  233.07
  277.04
  279.08
  295.21
  315.01
  321.12
  375.21
  457.10
  461.17
  551.17
  618.06
  632.04
  642.02
  650.16
  652.03
  662.03
  663.20
  691.19
  750.08
  753.03

sleeper
  452.03
  650.16
sleepers
  764.11
sleeping
  191.13
  279.06
  650.15
sleepless
  378.06
sleeplessness
  404.13
sleeps
  701.20
  760.11
sleepy
  218.13
sleet
  381.05
sleet-laden
  652.16
sleeve
  400.10
sleeves
  383.15
slender
  019.08
  213.20
  468.05
  487.05
  549.02
slept
  191.12
  296.18
  326.15
  654.12
slid
  038.14
  541.09
slide
  650.01
sliding
  283.11
  654.16
slight
  137.06
  143.14
  179.16
  214.12
  454.11
  487.09
  502.18
  530.11
  545.16
  574.09
  614.15
  629.04
  710.16
  726.12
slighter
  259.20
  548.07
slightest
  340.21
  378.21
  501.06
  674.19
  734.01
slightly
  146.05
  332.06
slights
  087.07
  492.01
slim
  464.16
slinging
  416.11
slip
  090.15
  119.22
  312.11
  416.07
  514.11
  546.01
slipped
  057.06
  130.15
  385.11
  433.13
  473.01
  506.01
  553.09
slippers
  111.10
  383.18
slitting
  399.15
slop
  217.07
  476.13
slope
  379.22
  598.21
  764.01
slouching
  150.02
slough
  524.18

slovenly
  007.12
  311.07
slow
  143.07
  191.16
  270.12
  285.03
  429.12
  608.12
slowly
  365.01
  453.14
  458.08
  492.13
  614.20
  750.04
slumber
  326.16
  592.22
slumbers
  764.10
slung
  020.17
  431.21
slut
  337.14
  468.19
  721.21
sly
  294.06
  492.21
smacked
  035.04
small
  019.12
  039.01
  098.17
  101.01
  147.12
  171.01
  237.18
  397.05
  425.03
  449.01
  468.06
  475.19
  492.21
  507.04
  534.12
  546.05
  568.16
  694.18
smart
  120.18
  219.17
  384.12
  445.17
  694.19
smartly
  050.19
smash
  385.13
smashed
  261.07
smashing
  166.13
smelling
  039.19
  321.08
smelt
  119.12
smile
  090.16
  141.22
  177.04
  234.18
  240.09
  285.01
  370.22
  376.09
  454.02
  481.13
  534.16
  560.13
  575.11
  649.11
  730.18
  741.15
  744.08
  748.06
  757.18
smiled
  026.17
  397.21
  412.04
  485.16
  498.04
  545.04
  627.19
  748.04
smiles
  177.10
  338.21
  352.18
smiling
  020.11
  442.01
  711.13
  713.10

smiths'
  261.16
smiting
  695.07
smitten
  381.11
smoked
  705.20
smoking
  068.04
  075.08
  690.16
  704.04
smooth
  006.13
  124.17
  152.02
  176.01
  347.09
  370.20
  522.18
  558.12
  760.09
smoothing
  120.12
  355.02
smote
  189.12
  286.06
smothered
  026.07
  126.11
  705.17
  718.01
smothering
  325.05
smouldered
  743.14
smuggled
  700.11
snail
  008.21
snail-shells
  243.18
snails
  467.05
snake
  621.11
snap
  042.08
  671.17
snapped
  020.01
snapping
  226.09
snappish
  558.08
snappishly
  471.18
snarled
  531.11
snatch
  009.14
  168.12
snatched
  053.03
  128.11
  156.02
  246.01
  316.11
  395.21
  409.14
  471.20
  609.08
  628.17
snatching
  118.04
  704.03
sneaking
  009.12
  193.18
  249.17
  537.04
sneer
  024.04
  374.21
  404.15
  562.14
  758.10
sneered
  708.14
  758.11
sneering
  256.09
  467.13
sneeringly
  320.11
  756.05
snivel
  374.05
snivelling
  604.07
  616.02
snoozled
  063.17
snorting
  106.13
  419.21
snow
  015.08
  016.17

027.20
031.06
046.15
051.11
060.17
067.06
276.09
303.01
303.02
303.03
381.06
383.12
392.18
398.01
398.12
414.02
427.21
552.13
630.15
651.15
snow-storm
022.02
snowy
553.10
snuffed
039.15
snuffers
393.09
snuffing
295.02
snug
042.14
so
001.08
002.01
003.21
010.04
010.14
012.16
013.14
016.01
022.21
023.11
031.09
032.17
036.01
037.10
041.05
041.14
043.05
044.06
045.04
046.22
050.19
051.14
053.19
055.01
057.15
058.01
058.05
059.10
060.05
068.03
071.10
072.01
074.15
075.11
077.19
080.02
081.18
083.06
084.20
086.03
088.06
091.06
091.08
091.17
094.09
095.18
097.18
099.03
099.17
100.03
108.09
110.07
111.17
113.09
115.14
117.19
120.17
123.11
124.01
124.14
126.04
130.12
131.19
132.02
135.19
148.16
151.22
156.07
160.06
163.17
171.06
171.06
172.08
172.15
176.20
178.21
179.06
179.08

182.03
183.10
185.07
192.05
192.19
199.13
208.07
210.16
212.16
215.09
218.13
218.17
230.12
230.12
239.18
250.06
254.04
254.15
256.14
260.15
262.05
265.19
268.03
270.20
272.01
272.18
274.01
276.18
277.14
282.04
282.22
286.12
290.07
291.11
296.09
296.21
298.06
303.10
305.04
307.10
308.10
309.03
313.04
313.05
315.08
317.11
318.02
319.22
320.05
324.06
324.22
326.20
330.22
333.07
337.18
338.17
341.09
344.11
347.12
349.02
350.18
354.05
355.11
356.11
357.19
358.14
360.04
362.11
363.11
366.07
367.03
371.21
375.15
377.19
379.13
380.01
384.07
385.04
386.12
388.09
388.15
388.15
389.22
392.12
392.17
392.22
399.05
402.10
403.11
404.10
404.11
405.14
407.01
408.09
409.13
412.22
414.09
414.18
417.21
420.04
421.16
421.21
422.11
426.11
427.15
429.03
433.11
435.08
435.17
437.03
437.07

439.17
439.22
443.14
446.14
447.01
451.01
451.15
451.16
456.07
456.12
460.09
460.18
463.08
463.09
463.17
464.06
470.18
473.11
475.02
476.02
477.06
478.21
480.10
484.11
485.04
486.16
488.03
489.14
493.07
493.08
493.14
496.14
499.05
499.08
499.12
500.09
501.11
503.03
504.10
505.09
505.15
506.07
507.14
509.16
510.19
511.03
518.06
519.07
523.10
525.06
525.18
528.01
531.08
532.17
532.21
536.07
538.12
540.02
541.15
544.13
546.12
548.15
548.15
551.05
554.13
554.19
556.04
556.20
556.21
562.20
565.18
567.02
569.07
569.11
570.10
570.16
570.22
571.07
572.18
573.09
575.11
580.13
582.12
583.20
586.17
586.18
587.18
588.05
588.14
590.04
592.11
592.12
594.14
594.15
598.05
598.20
600.05
600.18
603.07
605.19
606.04
613.10
613.19
614.11
621.06
627.04
627.05
627.18
631.09
631.19
633.20

634.07
634.09
639.20
640.04
649.19
650.02
651.11
652.20
654.19
655.21
663.02
665.09
666.05
666.13
667.06
674.21
677.03
678.05
684.02
684.11
686.17
692.15
693.16
694.10
695.04
700.02
703.01
703.11
706.06
706.07
710.13
711.04
711.12
716.22
718.21
722.14
723.08
726.16
727.22
730.05
730.18
731.01
734.07
734.07
736.06
738.05
742.13
743.16
748.06
748.10
752.02
752.11
752.16
757.01
757.17
760.16
761.12
763.09
soa
187.14
232.13
322.05
401.09
457.23
472.06
713.07
720.11
soaked
052.19
190.07
373.15
547.18
soap
115.18
sob
195.08
539.13
707.19
sobbed
052.06
060.13
095.20
129.05
157.10
167.08
227.14
231.09
315.01
363.16
435.20
453.08
511.15
567.02
601.05
sobbing
105.08
179.02
615.03
638.17
sober
192.10
390.05
390.05
449.20
728.03
sobered
166.17
sobriety
042.05
sobs
374.16

519.21
603.03
sociable
013.18
027.14
social
069.04
594.21
society
001.08
059.16
237.05
237.09
271.22
334.18
392.01
495.08
516.12
581.16
597.12
670.14
704.17
732.09
756.12
sod
525.04
sods
760.08
sofa
110.19
261.15
265.18
304.17
453.09
552.04
568.18
655.20
soft
104.07
159.22
206.14
254.11
302.22
365.03
394.19
425.09
479.18
535.19
588.05
630.01
737.16
764.08
soft-featured
146.01
soften
329.18
softened
083.02
370.12
460.06
485.17
594.18
694.09
softer
154.17
676.07
softly
440.04
505.19
563.13
softness
339.21
351.14
soil
346.06
442.13
517.20
solace
024.19
443.12
509.18
591.09
sold
640.16
soldered
051.17
649.21
soldier
208.17
sole
419.01
470.03
629.06
651.21
solemn
049.19
268.02
465.19
solemnly
062.10
274.03
538.20
712.11
solicited
756.12
soliciting
002.12
solidity
263.14
soliloquised
003.18

058.20
soliloquized
577.20
soliloquy
312.07
676.14
solitary
001.04
119.11
413.09
431.04
579.02
651.17
solitude
069.08
177.12
242.03
313.09
548.04
581.15
671.08
683.18
701.03
735.07
743.07
solitudes
690.05
some
002.14
003.10
007.13
010.13
011.02
020.21
021.15
030.20
035.14
039.21
040.09
054.21
074.03
074.20
078.07
100.19
108.04
115.08
117.03
120.09
132.11
135.13
150.22
154.20
163.11
165.09
168.04
169.06
175.05
176.17
184.08
189.13
202.06
204.22
208.10
210.12
218.07
221.15
221.17
226.07
237.02
248.13
249.06
250.03
262.13
266.02
267.11
267.20
270.21
273.08
281.11
291.14
293.20
305.11
311.03
315.22
320.18
328.08
330.11
330.12
330.16
350.21
352.12
355.03
355.21
382.08
384.16
392.16
396.21
401.19
405.21
406.02
411.20
412.12
419.03
433.15
445.15
450.04
453.10
460.07
466.08
469.16
472.15

475.13
475.22
476.12
477.13
486.04
490.07
493.07
496.01
498.14
506.13
508.10
509.08
509.20
513.14
513.16
517.21
522.07
534.08
542.08
545.16
556.16
563.15
567.13
573.09
575.09
604.06
607.22
608.03
612.20
613.16
628.21
640.11
650.08
652.09
652.19
658.12
659.08
674.12
677.01
678.10
678.11
689.17
699.01
703.20
704.20
705.11
709.16
709.19
713.04
715.10
721.09
734.13
736.02
737.18
739.01
740.21
742.12
744.22
746.02
747.08
747.22
750.20
752.05
752.19
752.19
753.18
754.06
754.06

**somebody**
033.10
054.01
106.05
235.07
298.07
306.10
638.11
755.16

**somebody's**
337.09

**somehow**
388.13

**something**
018.17
064.10
074.14
094.11
106.02
125.11
138.02
144.20
145.20
164.11
164.12
170.03
177.22
202.10
206.19
207.03
220.04
226.08
240.21
249.03
257.16
285.07
290.18
307.16
337.01
342.19
372.13
420.21
455.22

468.21
472.10
492.07
507.04
509.02
509.03
517.14
519.22
534.17
537.13
552.22
587.21
603.07
624.11
658.07
668.21
686.20
695.07
711.06
739.16
749.01
756.01

**sometime**
184.13
260.14
428.13
489.14
501.14
724.10

**sometimes**
076.18
092.06
098.05
152.13
219.10
242.02
327.06
340.14
374.08
426.18
488.14
536.10
543.20
568.05
568.05
580.11
634.06
653.22
654.01
660.20

**somewhat**
036.14
137.02
191.18
255.11
686.11

**somewhere**
186.03
322.17
350.08
396.16
612.08
654.11

**son**
026.14
026.16
072.03
076.07
080.15
081.11
108.18
140.22
162.04
233.11
325.09
411.09
438.13
440.06
440.15
457.01
457.12
467.01
468.18
469.19
476.19
482.02
482.11
483.04
486.11
489.21
494.04
521.07
524.07
528.17
578.15
581.10
606.13
616.16
617.20
636.10
645.16
648.01
661.16

**son's**
370.04
620.01

**song**
169.16
170.09
544.04
696.02

**songs**
118.20
131.18
132.10
518.09
559.09
559.09
589.16
630.14
705.17

**sooin**
719.21

**soon**
002.09
018.04
029.19
054.14
071.19
083.17
084.14
093.19
099.06
120.07
139.07
149.10
154.18
180.20
196.02
209.10
229.15
244.11
248.20
259.03
262.10
272.13
280.17
283.17
302.11
304.22
307.15
326.17
328.02
344.13
359.04
361.07
372.19
383.04
402.19
409.08
450.13
454.07
474.07
484.01
484.05
507.14
528.12
538.11
542.04
545.15
547.17
556.03
558.09
566.03
578.03
582.18
591.21
610.15
613.09
635.22
639.06
641.20
664.03
665.10
672.02
675.06
691.12
697.16
698.05
723.05
725.01
734.08
746.17
753.06
755.10
762.03
763.22

**sooner**
295.07
453.05
751.07

**soot**
189.06

**sooth**
474.06

**soothed**
541.17
588.21
726.16

**soothing**
245.11
295.22

**soothingly**
353.03

**sore**
406.06
454.10

**sorrow**
143.22
237.04
313.17
328.05

369.10
420.18
449.04
452.20
456.20
504.01
529.09
571.19
597.09
726.07

**sorrowful**
027.17
264.11

**sorrowfully**
554.05

**sorrows**
123.03

**sorry**
031.12
036.13
055.07
092.15
122.10
155.20
170.20
216.11
239.18
257.10
293.06
293.08
329.01
357.18
361.07
361.08
417.05
446.19
452.19
499.17
501.14
539.15
571.19
592.11
621.07
648.17
703.13

**sort**
007.18
038.07
135.15
171.10
292.13
468.20
475.22
531.01
550.09
609.05
651.02
759.06

**sorts**
293.04
397.10
440.19
445.09

**sotto**
062.15

**sough**
046.03
209.12

**sought**
044.06
313.21
509.20
763.22

**soul**
025.20
050.01
056.21
078.21
142.18
147.04
148.20
168.11
176.06
176.06
231.13
235.22
253.09
270.03
288.07
317.07
360.19
363.14
377.08
410.07
413.15
415.08
443.21
467.06
640.03
707.13
735.03
751.02
758.16

**soul's**
089.21
753.14

**souls**
095.15
179.12

**sound**
031.04

051.12
063.04
079.20
126.07
132.22
206.20
279.08
291.18
296.18
393.06
393.16
408.11
475.14
523.13
621.21
644.15
663.07
733.03

**sounded**
092.22
131.21
353.07

**sounding**
279.13
557.21

**soundly**
760.11

**sounds**
148.15
729.20

**sour**
467.05

**source**
183.06
225.04
302.02
508.09
726.21

**sourest**
455.14

**sourly**
003.21

**south**
303.02
381.04
411.08
461.06

**south-west**
243.09

**southern**
737.06

**sovereign**
298.17
310.22
763.13

**sow**
472.07

**souls**
043.04

**space**
021.21
099.01
135.14
205.08
225.03
321.10
693.17
700.17
715.12
748.18
752.03
754.05

**spade**
062.17
063.04
652.04

**spake**
016.07
455.19

**spaniel**
616.17

**spanish**
109.22

**spare**
022.10
055.04
098.18
189.11
251.17
295.15
349.05
450.17
488.06
513.06
516.10
600.08
689.11

**spared**
140.22
294.22
297.02
332.22
520.12
638.03
752.13

**sparely**
577.18

**sparer**
098.12
684.07

**sparing**
329.12

**spark**
111.14

**sparkle**
558.02

**sparkled**
097.21
114.21

**sparkling**
341.13
464.19
487.06

**sparks**
063.16
401.07

**sparrow's**
230.06

**spat**
164.01

**spatters**
325.16

**speak**
058.01
083.12
084.07
100.22
121.18
129.04
142.16
155.17
170.06
175.09
186.01
187.01
194.20
197.14
208.08
214.14
229.10
231.01
247.18
251.20
264.08
273.04
292.04
297.12
309.01
331.18
367.13
394.15
418.14
426.02
436.17
439.17
444.15
455.03
461.07
492.12
524.01
539.21
540.01
546.12
553.21
560.08
568.19
593.14
602.15
618.02
634.06
656.15
677.04
702.02
706.20
717.14
723.08
725.19
730.11
735.06
750.22
760.14
762.15

**speaker**
064.19
257.06
382.19
482.01
526.22
694.13

**speaker's**
128.08

**speaking**
076.07
154.15
238.16
266.02
272.17
410.17
412.16
471.01
599.04
620.04
711.04
739.06
741.05
749.09

**speaks**
341.17
702.12

**spears**
377.12

| | | | | | |
|---|---|---|---|---|---|
| 395.03 | 478.08 | splitting | 546.04 | 552.06 | stared |
| special | 640.06 | 257.08 | 579.12 | 555.15 | 017.20 |
| 029.15 | sperrit | spoiled | 700.21 | 622.17 | 017.21 |
| 185.15 | 324.18 | 009.19 | 733.22 | 629.15 | 078.06 |
| 507.06 | 564.16 | 219.15 | 737.15 | 638.05 | 192.14 |
| species | spices | 582.08 | springer | 653.15 | 237.10 |
| 007.22 | 119.13 | spoils | 291.05 | 669.12 | 244.06 |
| 015.19 | spider | 540.11 | springing | 702.09 | 298.08 |
| 030.14 | 136.05 | spoilt | 399.14 | 705.06 | 356.11 |
| 275.05 | 136.05 | 129.01 | 594.12 | 710.09 | 408.06 |
| 362.09 | spies | spoke | springs | 713.11 | 434.18 |
| specimen | 124.16 | 025.16 | 007.19 | 715.08 | 467.01 |
| 032.19 | 345.16 | 052.14 | 759.13 | 736.11 | 495.21 |
| speckless | spilling | 058.13 | sprinkled | 745.05 | 518.22 |
| 119.17 | 319.18 | 098.12 | 266.04 | 751.13 | 561.09 |
| spectacle | spilt | 112.11 | sprinkling | 751.15 | 627.17 |
| 015.04 | 509.06 | 142.14 | 552.12 | stairs' | 639.06 |
| 712.04 | spirit | 205.03 | sprung | 132.03 | staring |
| 738.17 | 024.08 | 207.01 | 399.19 | 661.08 | 207.12 |
| spectacles | 088.19 | 231.17 | 439.22 | stairs-head | 272.08 |
| 108.14 | 111.14 | 296.05 | 638.17 | 324.08 | 310.09 |
| 111.14 | 122.04 | 297.21 | spur | stale | 394.01 |
| spectator | 124.09 | 314.11 | 727.04 | 720.10 | 439.16 |
| 358.03 | 146.16 | 354.22 | spurn | staling | 663.11 |
| spectre | 156.21 | 355.20 | 600.19 | 034.06 | 669.05 |
| 060.16 | 231.06 | 362.10 | spurred | stall | 695.07 |
| 655.06 | 253.21 | 374.02 | 641.15 | 085.11 | 701.17 |
| spectre's | 280.01 | 422.09 | spy | stalled | stark |
| 060.16 | 330.09 | 502.10 | 110.15 | 669.20 | 420.04 |
| spectres | 371.08 | 541.06 | 298.14 | 676.17 | 758.04 |
| 039.09 | 397.10 | 563.13 | squalling | stalwart | stars |
| speculation | 408.01 | 571.14 | 164.22 | 007.01 | 069.04 |
| 749.20 | 425.04 | 576.14 | square | stammer | start |
| speech | 454.06 | 576.15 | 043.05 | 414.03 | 071.03 |
| 021.02 | 464.20 | 593.08 | 244.01 | stammered | 102.02 |
| 085.12 | 502.22 | 616.15 | 281.09 | 151.09 | 354.09 |
| 108.22 | 571.02 | 632.12 | squares | 298.04 | 506.18 |
| 137.02 | 578.22 | 635.15 | 038.04 | 554.01 | 744.07 |
| 159.09 | 596.08 | 639.22 | 054.03 | 679.03 | started |
| 179.15 | 605.08 | 648.12 | squealing | stammering | 022.21 |
| 237.02 | 647.14 | 725.02 | 006.18 | 245.13 | 039.08 |
| 245.11 | 648.14 | 738.01 | squeeze | stamp | 097.15 |
| 256.09 | 651.11 | 744.06 | 113.11 | 409.01 | 156.07 |
| 270.19 | 678.16 | 747.10 | 211.16 | stamped | 180.03 |
| 399.11 | 684.19 | spoken | 616.19 | 156.19 | 244.04 |
| 421.10 | 726.08 | 087.12 | squeezed | 352.04 | 266.20 |
| 438.17 | 727.05 | 128.21 | 162.08 | stamping | 433.02 |
| 467.11 | spirited | 215.17 | squint | 264.17 | 500.05 |
| 546.12 | 674.14 | 248.14 | 308.16 | 376.14 | 552.21 |
| 608.19 | spirits | 272.01 | squire | stanchions | 588.12 |
| 661.19 | 012.01 | 282.17 | 007.11 | 397.20 | 592.22 |
| 677.10 | 069.08 | 393.04 | squire's | stand | 607.19 |
| 683.10 | 090.12 | 481.18 | 628.09 | 028.21 | 669.08 |
| 696.09 | 142.12 | 526.01 | stab | 077.13 | 718.03 |
| 719.08 | 168.17 | 634.05 | 205.04 | 081.04 | 757.17 |
| 740.09 | 205.16 | 750.22 | stable | 117.10 | startled |
| speeches | 224.02 | spontaneously | 076.15 | 198.01 | 054.20 |
| 218.11 | 390.08 | 600.14 | 084.06 | 211.06 | 262.01 |
| speechless | 391.12 | spoon | 120.13 | 222.22 | startles |
| 286.06 | 402.21 | 020.13 | 170.13 | 235.20 | 344.21 |
| 721.17 | 434.17 | spoonful | 490.18 | 252.09 | startling |
| speed | 487.07 | 020.06 | 553.05 | 265.12 | 224.21 |
| 410.04 | 556.09 | 534.11 | 555.05 | 284.15 | 731.08 |
| 483.16 | 599.02 | spoons | stable-boys | 332.08 | starve |
| speedily | spiritual | 678.13 | 438.22 | 401.04 | 048.01 |
| 047.19 | 027.09 | sport | stables | 427.06 | 272.14 |
| 160.18 | spite | 654.02 | 042.18 | 438.05 | 318.08 |
| 318.21 | 101.16 | spot | 101.09 | 495.15 | 392.01 |
| 609.11 | 140.16 | 069.05 | 308.20 | 511.02 | starved |
| 715.05 | 200.09 | 158.03 | 310.08 | 579.08 | 519.05 |
| speedy | 237.14 | 243.15 | staff | 594.03 | 532.03 |
| 005.07 | 271.12 | 380.04 | 046.19 | 605.15 | 667.16 |
| spell | 375.11 | 598.15 | stage | 609.12 | 667.17 |
| 076.12 | 385.14 | 719.06 | 143.01 | 648.18 | starving |
| 561.21 | 396.06 | spots | staggered | 668.12 | 078.18 |
| 593.18 | 572.06 | 303.05 | 084.18 | 719.19 | 193.04 |
| 679.12 | 671.09 | 463.18 | 610.16 | 725.14 | 279.10 |
| spelling | 695.05 | sprang | stagnates | standing | 609.02 |
| 039.05 | spiteful | 064.20 | 059.02 | 020.08 | 753.02 |
| 057.16 | 498.11 | 213.17 | staid | 084.12 | state |
| spelt | 539.02 | 225.04 | 121.20 | 102.21 | 021.16 |
| 561.01 | 616.19 | 259.19 | 179.21 | 104.01 | 040.03 |
| spend | 633.04 | 367.07 | 290.20 | 136.13 | 136.13 |
| 014.03 | spitefully | 409.18 | 498.16 | 190.03 | 167.16 |
| 023.20 | 128.16 | 414.12 | stained | 248.22 | 188.11 |
| 119.06 | 156.03 | 431.22 | 377.15 | 267.01 | 286.13 |
| 352.11 | spitted | 480.16 | stair's-foot | 274.02 | 351.21 |
| 460.07 | 106.15 | 512.06 | 165.10 | 373.17 | 415.21 |
| 535.14 | spitting | 554.11 | stairs | 402.13 | 422.21 |
| 536.01 | 079.18 | 623.12 | 014.11 | 454.21 | 430.14 |
| 588.03 | 400.12 | spread | 041.07 | 505.20 | 574.07 |
| 660.03 | splashed | 039.17 | 059.10 | 524.22 | 589.10 |
| 672.14 | 036.03 | 248.08 | 076.02 | 564.13 | 596.04 |
| spended | splashes | 321.06 | 080.02 | 613.01 | 735.01 |
| 645.02 | 377.13 | 352.06 | 090.10 | stands | 744.17 |
| spending | spleen | 712.11 | 098.02 | 398.07 | 752.01 |
| 557.06 | 612.03 | spreading | 127.14 | staple | stated |
| spends | 682.12 | 519.12 | 196.06 | 051.17 | 203.17 |
| 335.12 | splendid | 527.15 | 261.11 | stare | 368.12 |
| 335.13 | 104.03 | spring | 297.06 | 027.05 | statement |
| spent | 115.02 | 165.15 | 304.20 | 109.01 | 299.08 |
| 153.04 | 693.04 | 201.09 | 326.01 | 216.04 | 420.06 |
| 153.05 | splendidly | 241.10 | 342.19 | 314.15 | 481.08 |
| 267.16 | 005.22 | 287.15 | 365.06 | 375.07 | 738.15 |
| 325.09 | splinter | 288.05 | 366.10 | 492.10 | stating |
| 378.05 | 704.22 | 303.08 | 454.18 | 531.18 | 460.07 |
| 378.08 | splinters | 303.14 | 458.02 | 608.08 | station |
| 413.07 | 265.20 | 315.15 | 477.03 | 718.09 | 004.06 |
| 419.18 | split | 349.03 | 507.15 | 738.07 | 060.19 |
| 431.07 | 189.02 | 361.21 | 533.20 | 748.08 | 110.15 |
| 445.11 | | 478.15 | 552.05 | | 522.11 |
| 475.18 | | | | | |

| | | | | | |
|---|---|---|---|---|---|
| stretch | stronger | 517.18 | success | 669.08 | sufficient |
| 049.07 | 415.01 | stupid | 223.20 | 670.18 | 042.01 |
| 398.16 | 593.11 | 079.19 | 341.14 | 683.04 | 059.17 |
| 654.03 | 593.13 | 111.16 | successfully | 685.15 | 109.02 |
| stretched | 725.22 | 172.06 | 420.20 | 692.15 | 173.07 |
| 061.14 | strongly | 258.07 | succession | 694.20 | 359.05 |
| 266.05 | 231.17 | 493.08 | 237.16 | 711.17 | 369.06 |
| 375.20 | strove | 496.14 | 277.22 | 716.12 | 391.12 |
| 403.09 | 148.14 | 560.17 | 434.21 | 731.05 | 419.08 |
| 450.12 | struck | 590.14 | 523.09 | 745.14 | 470.07 |
| 527.20 | 025.11 | 637.16 | 598.10 | 747.19 | 599.15 |
| 749.14 | 058.02 | 707.06 | successor | 762.11 | 610.08 |
| stretching | 120.07 | stupidity | 414.01 | sucked | 685.14 |
| 004.13 | 158.21 | 526.07 | 469.21 | 629.13 | 736.08 |
| 034.17 | 211.18 | 701.14 | 478.01 | sucking | sufficiently |
| 051.21 | 245.12 | stupified | 484.19 | 062.08 | 029.05 |
| 467.19 | 259.19 | 037.12 | succinct | 259.06 | 281.03 |
| 522.12 | 282.01 | style | 415.20 | 320.06 | 603.02 |
| 551.11 | 292.20 | 007.08 | succour | 629.06 | suffocate |
| 668.03 | 314.05 | 013.06 | 402.21 | 683.06 | 610.17 |
| strewn | 316.06 | 134.18 | such | sug | suffocating |
| 378.04 | 331.01 | 252.21 | 001.10 | 187.19 | 027.19 |
| stricken | 372.13 | 319.05 | 007.02 | 326.10 | 408.04 |
| 356.05 | 374.12 | 349.09 | 011.14 | 420.09 | 538.10 |
| 607.15 | 399.18 | 470.10 | 022.06 | 564.18 | suffused |
| strict | 409.16 | 668.16 | 023.19 | 691.09 | 370.13 |
| 091.11 | 415.03 | suall | 031.13 | 719.14 | sugar |
| 608.10 | 433.01 | 713.05 | 046.09 | sudden | 140.05 |
| strictly | 508.10 | subdue | 047.02 | 049.02 | sugar-candy |
| 340.19 | 539.03 | 055.15 | 050.04 | 098.03 | 629.07 |
| stride | 544.14 | 615.19 | 056.06 | 127.04 | 631.02 |
| 355.17 | 608.14 | subdued | 060.20 | 165.14 | suggested |
| strides | 621.03 | 158.14 | 074.04 | 225.06 | 003.12 |
| 657.02 | 623.10 | 214.06 | 077.14 | 242.03 | 050.21 |
| striding | 633.12 | 224.02 | 086.04 | 265.21 | 151.17 |
| 009.21 | 633.15 | 279.21 | 090.06 | 336.15 | 212.05 |
| strike | 649.19 | 514.09 | 098.19 | 376.15 | 213.21 |
| 069.09 | 668.13 | subduing | 112.07 | 393.18 | 244.20 |
| 088.12 | 669.07 | 471.12 | 116.02 | 653.01 | 273.07 |
| 181.18 | 687.02 | subject | 118.11 | 689.07 | 472.13 |
| 259.12 | 745.10 | 013.08 | 134.07 | 724.02 | 749.06 |
| 406.18 | structure | 045.01 | 139.10 | suddenly | suggestion |
| 539.06 | 038.06 | 046.05 | 140.14 | 010.14 | 044.15 |
| 633.19 | structures | 071.02 | 141.06 | 036.03 | suggestive |
| 710.14 | 006.14 | 133.14 | 146.08 | 087.04 | 351.22 |
| 722.13 | struggle | 171.02 | 146.22 | 176.17 | suicidal |
| 722.13 | 069.07 | 178.04 | 150.14 | 280.04 | 390.08 |
| 722.16 | 236.04 | 202.06 | 164.19 | 315.06 | suing |
| 723.10 | 261.06 | 205.15 | 173.18 | 356.16 | 385.21 |
| strikes | 354.10 | 239.21 | 177.13 | 460.01 | suit |
| 395.17 | 375.10 | 294.05 | 181.13 | 506.17 | 032.11 |
| striking | 407.13 | 299.22 | 185.09 | 553.12 | 337.17 |
| 137.04 | 640.05 | 347.10 | 211.19 | 561.14 | 342.14 |
| 176.04 | 663.02 | 352.12 | 220.09 | 567.13 | 550.09 |
| 278.07 | struggled | 369.09 | 224.06 | 610.03 | 577.12 |
| 385.13 | 058.16 | 393.02 | 225.16 | 740.14 | suitable |
| 728.14 | 149.16 | 421.20 | 233.16 | 758.22 | 001.10 |
| 729.18 | 167.11 | 465.12 | 240.18 | sudn't | 212.06 |
| 751.12 | 216.14 | 503.07 | 248.08 | 720.09 | suited |
| string | 290.11 | 521.04 | 264.21 | suffer | 092.03 |
| 090.02 | 396.12 | 570.14 | 265.16 | 034.19 | 530.06 |
| 245.14 | 546.01 | 655.15 | 270.20 | 120.03 | 705.05 |
| 262.03 | struggling | 712.09 | 289.01 | 186.07 | suitor |
| striving | 052.08 | 733.02 | 291.15 | 215.09 | 268.04 |
| 216.18 | 105.03 | subjects | 292.14 | 223.13 | sulkily |
| 594.07 | 483.13 | 010.21 | 298.02 | 231.08 | 171.14 |
| strode | 676.06 | 307.21 | 307.21 | 252.05 | 547.09 |
| 466.16 | 753.08 | 588.12 | 316.07 | 295.18 | sulkiness |
| stroke | stubborn | 717.19 | 330.04 | 334.10 | 703.13 |
| 134.21 | 006.22 | submissive | 334.06 | 336.22 | sulking |
| 282.10 | 346.13 | 292.05 | 338.10 | 357.10 | 012.22 |
| stroked | stubbornly | subsequent | 340.12 | 397.21 | 125.13 |
| 421.11 | 132.05 | 198.19 | 345.05 | 454.19 | sulky |
| 669.06 | studied | 254.13 | 372.09 | 473.10 | 117.16 |
| stroking | 070.14 | 283.19 | 386.08 | 493.18 | 186.22 |
| 093.11 | 649.05 | 411.10 | 387.04 | 602.18 | 218.09 |
| 318.10 | 711.22 | subsided | 404.18 | 637.15 | 674.14 |
| 453.20 | studies | 011.14 | 418.13 | 649.02 | sullen |
| 535.19 | 149.17 | 613.09 | 431.04 | 725.11 | 081.03 |
| stroll | 271.20 | 728.19 | 436.05 | 732.11 | 083.06 |
| 517.02 | 503.05 | substance | 440.12 | suffered | 361.12 |
| strolled | 509.17 | 422.07 | 440.17 | 205.06 | 392.09 |
| 449.08 | 548.12 | substantial | 461.16 | 357.09 | 493.09 |
| strong | 682.17 | 504.01 | 463.15 | 405.12 | 666.10 |
| 004.15 | 695.02 | 652.19 | 474.04 | 429.16 | 701.11 |
| 131.11 | study | substitute | 476.01 | 484.09 | sullenly |
| 222.20 | 014.03 | 040.21 | 483.13 | 528.15 | 003.07 |
| 274.15 | 068.02 | 353.04 | 488.01 | 641.11 | 283.09 |
| 304.22 | 462.04 | 516.10 | 494.10 | 642.11 | sullenness |
| 309.05 | 463.20 | 647.20 | 496.10 | 759.08 | 144.23 |
| 321.08 | 511.06 | 674.10 | 504.05 | suffering | sultry |
| 338.07 | 573.09 | succeed | 511.12 | 046.11 | 585.06 |
| 357.01 | 668.22 | 115.09 | 512.04 | 279.09 | summer |
| 363.12 | studying | 536.19 | 518.06 | 327.12 | 008.09 |
| 388.02 | 492.19 | succeeded | 522.17 | 539.10 | 075.21 |
| 418.06 | stuff | 256.12 | 525.08 | 750.21 | 138.10 |
| 434.18 | 401.06 | 295.22 | 545.17 | sufferings | 138.10 |
| 451.02 | 494.11 | 339.08 | 547.18 | 357.10 | 188.04 |
| 451.16 | 566.16 | 351.13 | 567.03 | 376.19 | 224.06 |
| 508.12 | 719.14 | 389.14 | 568.20 | 405.13 | 243.12 |
| 517.21 | stuffing | 430.15 | 592.16 | 572.06 | 335.16 |
| 520.10 | 062.02 | 438.18 | 600.19 | 582.13 | 353.05 |
| 546.17 | stumble | 509.07 | 604.21 | 592.16 | 365.03 |
| 647.18 | 680.07 | 609.09 | 605.19 | 631.10 | 381.08 |
| 651.11 | stumbled | 640.13 | 611.12 | suffers | 398.13 |
| 732.19 | 680.05 | 757.12 | 618.07 | 125.03 | 427.21 |
| 741.17 | stunned | succeeding | 631.14 | 493.16 | 431.03 |
| 759.13 | 759.04 | 325.03 | 645.18 | suffice | 465.09 |
| strong-hold | stunted | 412.15 | 651.03 | 405.06 | 465.09 |
| 108.06 | 004.11 | 547.20 | 654.03 | sufficed | 476.06 |
| | 427.14 | 752.02 | 656.13 | 215.05 | 515.02 |

517.22
525.04
557.01
578.07
582.01
585.02
690.06
summit
522.08
summon
200.08
602.15
710.21
summoned
217.02
278.12
367.16
668.06
699.19
712.15
summoning
400.04
summons
154.08
510.14
640.18
summut
094.15
310.17
324.13
565.14
sun
004.14
243.11
308.05
364.14
427.09
432.02
486.08
557.11
577.16
640.08
692.17
737.05
sun-dahn
233.01
sunbeams
191.19
sunday
040.19
041.20
101.03
102.21
350.12
390.13
455.13
572.10
665.04
671.06
sundays
100.04
665.16
sundry
006.09
119.02
sung
131.17
630.13
sunk
203.21
369.10
604.18
626.10
635.21
sunny
355.01
sunrise
372.19
sunset
690.09
sunshine
205.16
205.17
224.10
302.22
304.08
425.01
462.20
479.15
522.05
585.06
588.06
598.09
598.11
628.22
sup
180.12
298.20
319.08
691.18
720.02
superfluous
227.22
superintend
695.02
superior
111.17
322.21
470.16
superiority
021.03

145.15
149.14
403.21
superstition
060.08
244.08
444.09
745.22
superstitious
177.20
supped
121.08
supper
069.12
100.09
101.06
119.16
180.12
184.06
318.01
320.08
323.18
698.20
742.07
743.10
745.02
supper-time
077.03
supplicated
513.05
supplicating
599.14
supplication
185.16
supplications
402.06
653.20
supplied
221.18
supply
131.06
270.17
408.18
422.01
422.17
493.03
516.08
684.15
support
126.02
375.10
383.22
542.21
587.08
supported
275.01
361.14
639.16
supporter
391.20
supporting
323.09
602.14
suppose
003.12
044.20
056.01
061.19
070.21
082.11
111.01
127.10
193.08
211.04
255.20
260.10
287.11
289.18
306.08
311.17
322.01
335.09
340.06
364.07
393.18
405.04
412.02
481.19
504.02
511.08
520.12
524.07
538.04
590.13
604.20
651.01
664.18
696.21
728.17
731.10
supposed
009.02
013.08
132.13
355.10
382.11
445.21
528.12
547.14
695.15

747.17
761.03
supposing
156.01
170.03
221.11
244.09
244.11
249.08
282.06
388.04
629.10
755.01
suppress
680.22
suppressed
591.08
suppressing
059.05
352.17
sure
030.19
044.05
098.01
124.21
137.08
155.14
164.20
172.02
174.18
180.08
185.01
196.17
221.02
237.01
273.11
283.02
310.21
339.12
356.07
372.01
387.15
392.10
395.10
422.04
442.11
455.22
476.16
496.16
511.06
563.09
564.15
579.17
593.08
593.09
605.12
610.21
627.02
646.20
653.07
653.08
661.11
661.17
667.15
690.04
726.20
748.16
sure-ly
466.20
surely
059.03
109.11
182.12
186.20
192.16
227.11
260.19
398.18
405.06
416.14
579.22
surer
618.05
surface
115.21
136.10
surgeons
201.06
surlily
675.03
surly
005.05
044.15
071.06
124.17
625.04
710.20
surmise
025.15
surmised
211.11
surname
080.17
746.10
surpassed
283.18
surpressed
488.17
surprise
192.14
208.13

214.09
216.05
228.20
257.20
263.06
291.03
314.16
345.01
379.18
439.09
486.19
553.13
609.05
surprised
063.19
085.16
313.07
507.22
563.01
698.11
721.14
738.14
surprising
336.20
345.11
surrendered
348.09
637.20
surrounded
006.17
015.01
023.22
273.21
731.18
survey
028.18
248.21
surveyed
316.05
441.20
465.17
486.12
560.13
586.22
718.04
surveying
310.19
426.19
456.05
464.15
681.03
747.18
surviving
292.04
398.21
susceptibility
442.19
susceptible
019.16
suspect
007.15
507.21
suspected
017.10
087.07
241.04
492.01
616.17
suspecting
124.19
257.15
suspend
065.05
suspended
291.05
suspense
311.05
433.16
450.10
568.09
615.09
suspicion
150.12
745.11
suspicions
295.05
507.12
suspiciously
002.01
360.10
sustain
333.08
sustaining
588.11
sustenance
736.08
swallow
163.07
258.02
swallowed
217.08
282.03
390.10
534.12
734.10
759.18
swallowing
023.16
599.08
swamp
047.14
141.09

swamps
066.11
swarm
006.18
swarmed
039.10
swarming
056.03
swayed
013.04
swaying
284.07
swear
064.17
246.18
246.20
252.08
343.17
526.08
526.11
622.11
666.17
760.12
swearing
119.10
476.16
696.06
swears
045.14
236.21
sweat
366.10
653.18
sweep
748.17
sweeping
234.17
248.21
691.19
sweet
146.04
154.15
193.02
206.14
252.03
326.16
353.04
376.09
447.04
479.15
559.15
571.05
578.02
601.11
638.16
647.14
689.22
694.04
711.13
737.04
763.12
sweeter
413.16
sweetest
008.19
090.16
131.21
463.18
sweetheart
508.14
604.11
sweetly
177.10
177.11
303.11
sweetness
224.07
sweets
476.08
swelled
433.20
564.02
swells
065.20
275.16
449.09
557.20
690.08
swept
061.22
282.01
330.07
743.04
swerved
158.11
swine
011.22
swing
187.08
swinging
518.02
757.06
switch
432.18
swoon
635.21
swopped
466.21
swore
101.11
141.09

327.02
397.08
443.17
534.20
564.05
608.15
706.17
sworn
163.04
711.20
swung
189.09
317.18
563.20
626.07
762.17
syllable
100.22
341.21
493.05
528.03
621.20
711.01
726.10
syllables
561.01
sympathetic
007.16
sympathies
307.05
sympathise
385.09
493.15
632.07
sympathised
082.05
150.01
sympathize
098.07
sympathizing
002.22
205.12
sympathy
220.21
240.20
371.18
375.06
394.11
477.05
567.04
symptoms
098.06
495.06
t'
016.05
016.10
029.02
034.06
035.22
042.20
042.21
043.18
043.19
187.07
187.10
187.10
187.11
187.22
188.01
190.21
191.02
191.05
194.08
232.14
232.22
233.01
233.03
233.08
233.11
233.12
318.15
319.11
319.12
321.04
321.06
321.15
323.17
324.12
324.16
391.19
457.21
472.07
691.07
691.10
696.11
696.12
696.13
699.11
707.14
712.16
719.13
719.14
719.15
720.17
720.18
758.17
761.09
t'boards
193.16
t'doctor
420.08

t'door
079.02
624.12
t'father
565.13
t'fields
194.01
t'fowld
016.06
t'grand
232.14
t'kitchen
193.20
t'lads
193.12
t'maister
420.09
564.18
t'maister's
194.08
t'other
193.21
232.12
t'raight
564.16
t'road
194.09
t'soart
194.04
420.11
t'sowl
720.10
taan
719.18
table
007.04
010.16
012.07
017.07
023.07
038.13
093.04
104.18
121.12
136.17
216.17
277.01
281.08
330.16
392.04
394.10
403.17
409.15
421.04
453.04
454.21
456.14
466.07
505.20
509.19
531.03
534.11
558.14
608.14
609.04
611.03
694.15
703.08
710.16
712.12
716.22
740.15
743.05
747.05
747.16
749.16
table-top
282.01
tables
104.04
212.11
330.08
tacit
010.11
taciturn
023.11
tacked
185.17
taen
420.09
tail
018.07
325.20
355.03
tails
034.18
tak
457.23
624.15
tak'
712.16
713.05
take
003.09
012.08
012.15
017.12
031.01
041.11
050.01
059.20
077.20

242.11
258.15
271.06
293.22
358.13
379.05
402.12
414.21
441.14
451.01
451.09
454.17
472.21
481.06
552.14
663.11
721.20
758.12
takes
494.01
532.11
620.03
754.11
taking
029.17
150.19
178.04
185.06
193.07
202.18
218.03
224.04
252.12
252.13
263.06
272.18
275.11
295.18
309.13
318.05
326.13
331.05
337.19
341.12
342.13
345.03
345.06
360.19
374.18
374.20
377.04
378.01
383.06
386.15
387.08
405.16
421.17
426.10
428.13
459.03
462.06
463.05
471.19
481.09
488.12
490.17
499.03
502.05
506.03
507.13
519.07
545.05
564.02
569.15
570.15
605.15
606.09
608.04
613.22
614.01
618.09
620.22
622.06
637.18
656.07
656.13
670.02
671.22
672.16
677.20
678.01
681.09
685.16
698.17
703.02
706.13
707.08
710.07
724.16
729.19
730.05
744.19
751.13
752.19
761.12
762.07
763.02
taken
014.08
024.08
059.01
166.21

659.10
663.08
693.21
704.12
707.04
711.16
717.05
723.02
730.21
752.11
755.18
talked
152.04
153.18
242.06
438.11
461.09
522.03
533.07
556.20
588.10
671.07
talking
029.01
042.12
057.20
202.16
213.10
277.04
285.13
288.13
451.20
541.03
632.09
653.09
677.05
701.13
talks
140.12
570.18
tall
207.04
213.19
311.06
486.03
taller
123.14
464.05
486.20
tallest
428.12
talons
238.07
tame
108.19
tangible
352.03
tankards
006.02
tapers
104.07
taps
050.18
tarnish
312.20
tarry
290.13
tartly
266.16
421.12
tarts
127.07
task
121.01
384.20
592.05
680.21
695.09
746.07
tasks
660.13
taste
259.10
319.22
388.14
405.01
431.04
589.18
611.12
tasted
164.01
tastes
023.18
608.11
taught
099.20
137.20
223.10
246.05
442.22
494.02
taunting
399.10
tauntingly
496.18
tea
020.04
020.13
022.15
023.16
025.01

046.07
210.08
216.16
267.14
270.21
384.22
386.15
410.18
431.06
432.06
453.02
453.10
453.21
454.18
472.13
514.08
518.08
528.08
548.21
559.20
607.20
611.21
612.20
716.21
tea-canister
028.16
teach
079.20
164.08
199.03
246.16
247.10
289.13
339.05
362.18
470.12
544.06
702.16
710.08
teacher
726.15
teachers
680.06
teaches
246.20
teaching
088.15
426.07
tear
059.07
081.06
249.22
406.22
498.16
503.22
567.01
631.15
677.17
723.22
tears
042.18
060.12
120.09
130.15
157.09
199.04
220.16
237.17
269.04
279.20
303.21
356.13
361.03
363.02
364.06
374.06
389.07
408.03
416.15
439.22
452.16
474.04
519.21
554.11
593.15
602.13
613.02
631.11
640.06
tease
385.18
486.16
563.12
710.10
teased
350.06
428.16
704.11
teases
588.20
teasing
051.12
238.15
280.21
540.20
717.15
teazing
226.10
tedious
546.07

teens
546.02
teeth
002.20
009.14
055.15
163.21
193.05
247.13
265.19
274.12
358.02
398.02
402.04
407.01
609.20
619.18
634.02
741.14
748.05
758.11
teething
343.05
tell
016.13
022.06
031.14
048.09
074.14
083.20
084.13
102.13
125.13
125.14
134.17
140.02
141.02
142.06
142.09
145.01
151.17
171.20
171.21
172.08
177.03
178.13
186.15
194.18
202.03
212.02
220.09
227.13
229.11
246.09
247.17
251.11
261.17
273.03
281.04
307.11
310.13
313.16
316.14
331.19
334.10
336.23
340.11
340.17
342.21
347.19
365.15
367.09
383.07
387.10
390.15
395.09
411.15
422.05
425.20
428.04
435.08
437.07
439.19
457.11
457.15
459.12
462.06
468.18
486.10
488.21
489.14
501.20
504.20
510.20
514.04
520.06
529.01
537.01
537.13
543.08
554.02
561.06
567.07
570.11
572.13
573.03
573.05
576.22
590.02
590.04
591.15

592.18
600.20
601.07
601.20
602.09
605.12
612.14
612.17
612.21
619.20
627.11
628.01
634.15
639.04
649.12
660.04
660.16
661.16
661.18
663.18
664.03
677.14
694.06
697.14
698.17
707.03
709.19
710.07
716.18
722.08
730.21
742.13
746.10
748.11
754.20

telled
322.06

telling
046.19
252.07
289.11
337.01
466.08
553.20
572.18
755.17

tells
007.17
233.09
630.19

temper
042.05
046.08
118.12
129.01
135.21
158.18
171.11
198.08
219.12
225.10
263.10
265.16
289.09
437.08
502.19
506.15
532.22
568.21
571.01
588.19
611.13

temperate
733.15

tempered
425.18
546.01
759.14

teapers
088.08

tempest
011.07
292.20

temples
146.05
351.09
610.20
655.12

temporary
282.05
486.07
530.03
713.16

tempt
246.02
375.17

temptation
065.06
146.19
442.17
476.22
576.08
686.05

tempted
027.05
517.12
690.04
702.11

tempter
315.16

tempting
355.09
731.02

ten
115.13
135.02
135.03
135.06
217.05
244.21
317.07
419.16
437.01
465.05
538.22
591.06
635.12
690.15

tenacious
052.21

tenant
002.08
013.05
033.18
071.20
629.06
646.18
672.16
696.08
760.11

tenants
144.11
379.15
444.18
518.11

tend
082.06

tended
301.07
470.08
745.16

tendency
707.19

tender
195.01
370.14
413.18
425.13

tenderly
225.11

tenderness
339.16
576.15
601.16

tending
713.20

tends
470.09

tenour
517.20

tension
655.15

tent
420.09

term
220.05
396.21
750.21

termed
147.10
443.13

terminating
168.18

termination
296.06
729.08

terms
222.13
234.08
316.16

terrible
046.09
201.08
373.11
734.17
744.07

terribly
082.17

terrier
441.17
445.06

terrific
610.07

terrified
195.19
266.09
273.22
641.20
716.04

terrify
106.03
525.20

terror
052.15
147.17
162.05
167.08
242.03

327.09
399.10
541.16
566.01
593.01
601.04
613.07
615.15
744.10

testament
039.18

text
043.07
047.06

texts
191.06

tg
243.09

th
326.10

th-
016.06
022.15
043.17
043.17
043.21
184.15
187.07
187.19
191.04
194.08
318.16
324.05
472.01
586.01
689.05
690.21
691.03
696.06
713.06
719.18
719.20
720.02
758.16

thah
319.07

than
003.04
011.06
012.01
018.13
026.03
027.04
027.10
030.22
033.09
033.12
034.18
035.10
035.10
044.18
048.01
051.08
071.17
078.04
079.02
081.20
082.01
091.03
091.14
092.01
092.09
095.17
104.14
111.20
112.03
120.09
122.12
122.22
125.11
137.09
137.21
141.05
144.09
147.11
150.07
154.17
166.06
166.08
167.04
167.10
168.09
175.01
179.05
179.11
183.09
189.19
191.18
197.04
197.21
199.05
199.20
201.07
202.06
204.07
205.05
206.01
213.17
214.02
215.22
222.09

222.22
229.05
230.19
231.19
231.20
234.06
235.07
245.20
258.01
260.09
271.20
280.02
290.19
291.04
292.06
293.10
293.18
301.06
313.08
317.08
336.03
336.10
347.15
355.22
359.15
360.01
361.06
367.05
371.01
371.03
371.11
373.21
382.10
383.14
385.05
388.20
389.17
391.15
391.19
392.08
393.17
395.04
401.08
407.19
408.01
409.19
410.14
413.16
414.13
417.12
418.21
421.15
427.18
442.09
449.07
449.13
453.05
454.17
464.09
467.06
480.20
486.06
486.20
493.20
494.12
494.14
497.18
498.13
499.19
500.14
501.02
509.12
510.04
512.09
516.13
517.05
518.13
520.14
520.17
521.16
521.19
521.20
535.03
535.08
536.06
536.09
543.06
545.13
546.14
548.07
554.09
565.10
567.21
570.17
571.07
571.09
572.11
573.17
575.03
578.02
581.10
587.05
587.13
586.06
589.05
589.14
589.17
592.03
593.11
611.19
615.14

618.07
623.15
663.12
670.20
671.02
674.14
684.16
686.21
690.07
705.07
713.12
714.06
716.15
717.04
717.19
725.15
726.01
741.18
743.05
748.05
751.07
754.12
756.07

thank
012.09
056.05
191.02
236.05
252.07
340.22
412.01
604.04
617.18
668.10
708.19
720.10

thanked
069.04
638.20

thankful
504.06
519.18
548.02

thanks
258.06
274.04
339.11
442.16
533.12
590.10
590.11
595.04
647.16
759.02

that
001.04
001.07
002.10
003.01
003.21
007.10
007.17
009.09
010.14
011.13
011.14
011.19
012.17
012.21
013.03
014.10
015.09
019.11
021.21
022.03
022.21
023.13
023.22
024.07
024.11
024.15
024.19
025.06
025.07
025.13
025.18
026.19
027.08
029.04
030.14
030.19
031.07
031.21
032.17
032.22
034.03
035.03
035.14
036.02
037.03
040.08
041.14
041.14
042.06
042.13
043.06
044.12
045.03
046.08
046.10
046.18

047.01
047.22
048.14
049.02
049.04
049.16
050.06
050.19
050.21
051.03
051.14
055.01
056.01
056.02
056.10
056.18
057.17
058.05
058.16
058.18
060.21
060.21
061.03
061.17
062.22
063.05
063.17
065.11
067.10
067.16
067.19
069.04
071.03
071.06
072.05
072.20
073.21
074.11
075.16
075.19
076.12
078.07
078.10
078.17
079.05
081.14
082.12
082.14
084.13
085.04
085.08
086.04
088.02
088.06
088.13
088.17
089.06
089.13
090.11
090.20
090.21
092.12
092.13
092.17
093.06
094.06
094.15
095.03
095.06
096.03
096.11
097.03
097.07
098.02
098.03
098.04
099.02
099.15
100.07
101.03
101.12
104.22
106.03
107.18
108.01
108.19
109.16
109.16
109.19
110.04
110.10
112.08
112.11
113.03
113.09
114.05
117.07
117.17
118.07
118.18
119.09
119.10
120.01
120.04
123.11
123.13
123.16
123.21
124.12
124.13
125.01

| | | | | | |
|---|---|---|---|---|---|
| 125.06 | 192.17 | 262.16 | 330.06 | 376.05 | 445.18 |
| 125.12 | 194.02 | 262.20 | 330.20 | 377.02 | 446.05 |
| 126.20 | 195.01 | 263.03 | 331.01 | 378.22 | 446.16 |
| 128.06 | 197.10 | 263.09 | 331.19 | 379.14 | 446.21 |
| 128.09 | 197.17 | 263.11 | 332.02 | 380.01 | 447.01 |
| 129.08 | 197.19 | 265.03 | 332.16 | 381.02 | 447.02 |
| 129.16 | 198.05 | 265.04 | 333.02 | 381.08 | 450.01 |
| 131.04 | 199.11 | 265.19 | 333.04 | 381.12 | 450.07 |
| 132.20 | 199.20 | 268.02 | 333.12 | 382.19 | 451.03 |
| 133.06 | 200.07 | 268.03 | 333.14 | 385.08 | 453.17 |
| 134.01 | 201.08 | 269.05 | 333.16 | 385.19 | 454.10 |
| 134.04 | 202.02 | 269.07 | 333.20 | 386.07 | 454.11 |
| 134.09 | 203.05 | 269.10 | 334.04 | 386.20 | 454.12 |
| 134.17 | 203.06 | 270.02 | 334.11 | 387.13 | 454.20 |
| 135.05 | 203.17 | 270.03 | 334.15 | 387.15 | 455.02 |
| 135.13 | 204.18 | 270.19 | 335.11 | 388.01 | 456.09 |
| 135.19 | 205.02 | 271.06 | 335.19 | 388.03 | 457.12 |
| 136.03 | 205.04 | 271.14 | 336.02 | 388.10 | 457.15 |
| 136.04 | 205.18 | 272.03 | 336.07 | 388.16 | 457.20 |
| 137.04 | 206.03 | 272.10 | 336.16 | 391.16 | 460.05 |
| 137.07 | 206.17 | 272.12 | 336.23 | 391.20 | 460.07 |
| 138.01 | 207.13 | 272.15 | 337.03 | 392.11 | 462.14 |
| 138.02 | 209.12 | 273.01 | 337.22 | 392.21 | 462.15 |
| 138.03 | 210.13 | 273.08 | 338.01 | 393.19 | 463.16 |
| 138.11 | 211.02 | 274.06 | 338.07 | 394.12 | 464.18 |
| 139.06 | 211.18 | 274.13 | 338.21 | 394.14 | 464.21 |
| 139.11 | 212.14 | 274.21 | 339.01 | 395.01 | 467.13 |
| 142.06 | 215.11 | 275.22 | 339.04 | 395.16 | 467.22 |
| 142.16 | 215.16 | 276.04 | 339.06 | 396.22 | 468.01 |
| 142.19 | 217.10 | 276.16 | 339.08 | 397.04 | 468.10 |
| 142.22 | 217.22 | 276.20 | 339.18 | 397.07 | 469.10 |
| 143.01 | 218.09 | 277.03 | 340.02 | 397.09 | 470.03 |
| 143.22 | 219.14 | 277.10 | 340.04 | 398.11 | 470.06 |
| 143.22 | 220.10 | 277.11 | 340.09 | 398.20 | 470.17 |
| 144.06 | 220.17 | 278.16 | 340.10 | 399.08 | 472.10 |
| 144.20 | 221.18 | 279.13 | 340.11 | 399.21 | 474.02 |
| 145.17 | 222.08 | 280.09 | 340.18 | 401.01 | 474.05 |
| 145.21 | 223.05 | 281.08 | 341.06 | 401.06 | 474.09 |
| 146.15 | 224.20 | 281.09 | 341.07 | 402.01 | 475.03 |
| 147.05 | 225.07 | 281.16 | 342.06 | 402.03 | 475.09 |
| 147.13 | 225.15 | 281.18 | 342.10 | 402.10 | 477.04 |
| 148.15 | 225.18 | 282.09 | 342.13 | 402.17 | 477.10 |
| 148.20 | 225.20 | 283.14 | 343.12 | 402.20 | 477.20 |
| 149.06 | 226.02 | 284.09 | 343.16 | 403.03 | 478.08 |
| 149.08 | 226.08 | 284.13 | 343.17 | 403.10 | 479.04 |
| 151.07 | 226.16 | 285.02 | 343.22 | 404.10 | 480.07 |
| 151.09 | 226.17 | 285.15 | 344.16 | 404.11 | 480.07 |
| 152.13 | 226.19 | 287.05 | 345.06 | 405.06 | 480.11 |
| 152.14 | 227.02 | 287.09 | 345.10 | 405.09 | 481.18 |
| 153.01 | 227.06 | 288.01 | 345.13 | 405.14 | 482.01 |
| 153.09 | 227.21 | 288.04 | 345.20 | 406.09 | 482.09 |
| 153.10 | 228.22 | 288.07 | 346.01 | 406.10 | 482.11 |
| 153.18 | 229.01 | 289.08 | 347.11 | 407.14 | 482.20 |
| 153.19 | 229.15 | 289.09 | 347.11 | 408.10 | 484.08 |
| 155.11 | 229.19 | 291.01 | 348.07 | 408.19 | 484.15 |
| 156.17 | 229.20 | 291.13 | 348.09 | 409.03 | 486.09 |
| 156.22 | 230.03 | 291.16 | 350.03 | 411.15 | 486.16 |
| 157.17 | 230.12 | 291.18 | 350.10 | 412.10 | 486.19 |
| 158.18 | 231.06 | 292.12 | 350.17 | 412.19 | 487.10 |
| 160.09 | 233.20 | 294.09 | 350.18 | 413.01 | 487.16 |
| 160.11 | 235.07 | 294.16 | 350.21 | 413.03 | 487.16 |
| 161.03 | 235.20 | 296.11 | 353.05 | 414.02 | 489.10 |
| 163.04 | 235.22 | 296.21 | 353.11 | 415.21 | 490.05 |
| 163.05 | 236.05 | 297.17 | 353.16 | 417.07 | 490.09 |
| 164.03 | 236.09 | 298.03 | 354.04 | 417.20 | 494.16 |
| 165.04 | 236.21 | 299.22 | 354.05 | 417.21 | 494.20 |
| 165.09 | 236.22 | 301.09 | 355.03 | 418.07 | 495.02 |
| 165.16 | 237.04 | 301.11 | 355.10 | 418.18 | 495.07 |
| 165.18 | 237.15 | 302.03 | 356.02 | 419.04 | 496.19 |
| 167.05 | 237.19 | 302.10 | 356.06 | 419.07 | 497.11 |
| 169.04 | 238.10 | 303.11 | 356.10 | 419.11 | 497.13 |
| 169.11 | 238.15 | 304.02 | 356.11 | 419.13 | 499.02 |
| 169.16 | 239.08 | 304.16 | 357.17 | 419.17 | 499.06 |
| 169.18 | 240.02 | 305.06 | 357.18 | 420.15 | 499.14 |
| 170.21 | 240.19 | 305.07 | 357.19 | 421.13 | 499.21 |
| 171.10 | 241.06 | 305.10 | 358.05 | 422.01 | 500.01 |
| 172.05 | 242.05 | 305.17 | 358.16 | 422.10 | 500.19 |
| 172.19 | 243.02 | 306.06 | 358.19 | 422.15 | 501.07 |
| 174.16 | 243.21 | 306.12 | 358.20 | 422.19 | 501.12 |
| 175.11 | 244.05 | 306.13 | 359.03 | 423.05 | 502.04 |
| 175.13 | 244.17 | 307.14 | 359.05 | 424.03 | 502.12 |
| 176.21 | 245.07 | 307.21 | 359.22 | 424.12 | 502.22 |
| 177.13 | 246.07 | 308.06 | 360.16 | 425.07 | 503.05 |
| 177.22 | 247.15 | 308.14 | 360.17 | 425.16 | 504.02 |
| 178.11 | 247.17 | 311.08 | 360.20 | 427.12 | 504.06 |
| 178.12 | 248.06 | 312.13 | 361.01 | 427.22 | 505.09 |
| 178.19 | 250.16 | 312.15 | 361.08 | 428.05 | 505.16 |
| 178.22 | 251.14 | 313.05 | 361.15 | 428.12 | 506.03 |
| 179.02 | 251.21 | 313.09 | 362.09 | 429.08 | 506.13 |
| 179.09 | 252.02 | 313.10 | 363.07 | 429.20 | 507.09 |
| 180.14 | 253.03 | 313.22 | 363.11 | 430.08 | 507.16 |
| 180.17 | 253.06 | 315.05 | 365.02 | 430.13 | 507.22 |
| 180.20 | 254.19 | 315.21 | 366.16 | 431.05 | 508.13 |
| 181.19 | 254.22 | 315.22 | 366.17 | 431.14 | 510.05 |
| 182.13 | 255.14 | 316.02 | 367.01 | 432.10 | 512.08 |
| 183.18 | 255.20 | 317.07 | 367.04 | 433.10 | 513.05 |
| 183.19 | 256.15 | 317.18 | 368.01 | 434.14 | 514.04 |
| 184.01 | 256.18 | 317.22 | 368.11 | 435.11 | 515.04 |
| 184.11 | 256.20 | 319.20 | 369.02 | 435.14 | 515.10 |
| 184.14 | 256.21 | 319.21 | 369.12 | 437.11 | 517.04 |
| 184.21 | 257.02 | 320.02 | 371.04 | 440.15 | 518.06 |
| 185.09 | 257.10 | 322.15 | 371.14 | 441.09 | 518.19 |
| 185.15 | 258.12 | 322.20 | 371.20 | 442.13 | 520.13 |
| 185.19 | 258.18 | 324.20 | 373.08 | 442.18 | 521.04 |
| 186.21 | 259.10 | 326.21 | 373.15 | 442.19 | 521.09 |
| 188.16 | 259.20 | 327.07 | 373.18 | 443.20 | 521.17 |
| 189.13 | 260.10 | 327.09 | 373.21 | 443.21 | 521.19 |
| 189.16 | 261.01 | 327.11 | 374.04 | 444.01 | 521.19 |
| 189.19 | 261.21 | 328.03 | 374.08 | 444.04 | 522.03 |
| 190.13 | 262.06 | 328.07 | 374.11 | 444.09 | 522.07 |
| 190.17 | 262.12 | 329.01 | 374.12 | 445.11 | 522.21 |

| | | | | | |
|---|---|---|---|---|---|
| 523.10 | 589.21 | 661.03 | 747.20 | 004.14 | 019.16 |
| 523.11 | 589.22 | 661.16 | 748.01 | 004.14 | 019.20 |
| 523.17 | 590.04 | 662.07 | 749.01 | 004.15 | 020.06 |
| 524.05 | 590.05 | 662.08 | 749.06 | 004.16 | 020.07 |
| 524.07 | 590.13 | 663.03 | 750.01 | 004.17 | 020.11 |
| 524.12 | 594.01 | 664.14 | 752.14 | 004.19 | 020.13 |
| 525.10 | 594.03 | 665.01 | 753.04 | 004.21 | 020.17 |
| 525.12 | 594.08 | 665.06 | 753.18 | 004.21 | 020.19 |
| 527.03 | 596.04 | 666.02 | 753.20 | 005.02 | 020.20 |
| 527.05 | 597.07 | 667.04 | 753.22 | 005.02 | 020.21 |
| 527.11 | 597.13 | 668.08 | 754.13 | 005.05 | 021.03 |
| 527.21 | 597.16 | 668.09 | 754.17 | 005.05 | 021.10 |
| 529.01 | 598.01 | 668.11 | 754.21 | 005.06 | 021.11 |
| 529.02 | 598.05 | 670.06 | 755.02 | 005.09 | 021.14 |
| 529.05 | 598.12 | 672.03 | 755.06 | 005.10 | 021.18 |
| 529.11 | 598.16 | 672.06 | 755.09 | 005.12 | 021.22 |
| 531.09 | 599.10 | 672.14 | 755.17 | 005.15 | 022.02 |
| 532.05 | 602.01 | 675.14 | 758.01 | 005.19 | 022.04 |
| 532.08 | 603.10 | 677.02 | 758.07 | 005.21 | 022.09 |
| 534.05 | 604.03 | 677.03 | 759.02 | 006.03 | 022.16 |
| 536.07 | 604.06 | 677.08 | 759.08 | 006.04 | 022.17 |
| 536.14 | 604.11 | 677.14 | 759.11 | 006.09 | 022.20 |
| 538.11 | 605.07 | 678.16 | 759.12 | 006.12 | 022.21 |
| 538.12 | 605.12 | 679.20 | 760.13 | 006.13 | 022.22 |
| 539.17 | 605.13 | 680.17 | 760.16 | 006.15 | 023.03 |
| 539.18 | 606.05 | 681.14 | 762.04 | 006.16 | 023.06 |
| 540.02 | 606.16 | 682.11 | 762.17 | 006.20 | 023.07 |
| 542.01 | 607.03 | 682.12 | 764.06 | 007.04 | 023.09 |
| 542.02 | 608.09 | 683.04 | 764.11 | 007.06 | 023.13 |
| 542.12 | 608.22 | 683.21 | that's | 007.18 | 023.15 |
| 542.22 | 609.03 | 684.11 | 109.05 | 008.05 | 023.19 |
| 544.12 | 609.13 | 684.21 | 116.21 | 008.12 | 023.20 |
| 545.06 | 609.19 | 685.17 | 152.19 | 008.12 | 024.01 |
| 546.01 | 609.21 | 686.18 | 154.16 | 008.16 | 024.08 |
| 546.06 | 610.16 | 689.02 | 156.09 | 008.18 | 024.09 |
| 546.19 | 611.10 | 689.09 | 158.06 | 008.22 | 024.14 |
| 546.19 | 611.18 | 691.13 | 167.14 | 009.06 | 024.14 |
| 548.01 | 612.09 | 691.14 | 168.01 | 009.08 | 024.18 |
| 548.13 | 613.03 | 692.22 | 173.07 | 009.08 | 024.19 |
| 551.14 | 613.12 | 693.03 | 176.08 | 009.11 | 024.20 |
| 552.13 | 614.04 | 693.07 | 181.11 | 009.13 | 024.22 |
| 554.08 | 614.05 | 693.16 | 181.11 | 009.16 | 025.04 |
| 555.09 | 614.07 | 694.02 | 182.04 | 010.02 | 025.10 |
| 555.16 | 614.20 | 694.05 | 192.08 | 010.03 | 025.19 |
| 556.06 | 615.18 | 695.22 | 193.08 | 010.05 | 025.21 |
| 556.09 | 618.07 | 696.15 | 204.04 | 010.13 | 026.01 |
| 556.11 | 618.18 | 697.14 | 227.20 | 010.16 | 026.03 |
| 557.02 | 618.20 | 699.09 | 232.13 | 010.17 | 026.07 |
| 557.12 | 618.21 | 700.12 | 235.01 | 010.20 | 026.11 |
| 559.01 | 619.01 | 702.20 | 239.03 | 010.22 | 026.18 |
| 559.07 | 621.03 | 704.01 | 252.16 | 011.01 | 026.21 |
| 559.17 | 621.19 | 705.02 | 275.07 | 011.03 | 027.02 |
| 560.04 | 622.11 | 705.08 | 276.17 | 011.04 | 027.05 |
| 561.05 | 623.07 | 705.21 | 278.07 | 011.07 | 027.08 |
| 561.17 | 623.13 | 706.04 | 284.05 | 011.09 | 027.10 |
| 562.01 | 627.08 | 706.04 | 292.21 | 011.12 | 027.13 |
| 562.05 | 627.11 | 706.05 | 315.16 | 011.14 | 027.15 |
| 562.08 | 627.16 | 706.13 | 322.07 | 011.17 | 028.01 |
| 562.18 | 628.07 | 707.07 | 342.20 | 011.18 | 028.04 |
| 562.19 | 630.02 | 708.13 | 357.13 | 011.18 | 028.05 |
| 563.12 | 630.04 | 709.06 | 398.11 | 011.21 | 028.12 |
| 564.12 | 630.17 | 709.16 | 415.16 | 011.22 | 028.13 |
| 565.19 | 631.06 | 709.17 | 417.10 | 012.05 | 028.15 |
| 566.13 | 632.03 | 709.20 | 467.06 | 012.06 | 028.16 |
| 566.20 | 632.06 | 711.04 | 472.11 | 012.07 | 028.17 |
| 567.02 | 632.21 | 711.18 | 489.13 | 012.12 | 028.18 |
| 567.06 | 633.02 | 712.09 | 491.15 | 012.20 | 029.06 |
| 567.07 | 633.05 | 713.09 | 538.03 | 012.22 | 029.07 |
| 567.08 | 635.03 | 713.12 | 542.15 | 013.01 | 029.13 |
| 568.01 | 636.08 | 715.02 | 544.02 | 013.05 | 029.18 |
| 568.04 | 636.20 | 716.09 | 565.13 | 013.06 | 029.20 |
| 569.02 | 637.10 | 716.16 | 565.13 | 013.09 | 030.01 |
| 569.13 | 637.13 | 718.22 | 605.17 | 013.12 | 030.02 |
| 570.10 | 637.17 | 719.03 | 619.14 | 014.07 | 030.05 |
| 570.12 | 638.01 | 719.17 | 630.21 | 014.09 | 030.06 |
| 570.13 | 639.17 | 723.21 | 683.04 | 014.11 | 030.09 |
| 571.05 | 640.01 | 725.04 | thaw | 014.12 | 031.01 |
| 571.08 | 640.10 | 725.20 | 235.04 | 015.03 | 031.03 |
| 571.19 | 640.17 | 726.07 | 302.22 | 015.07 | 031.10 |
| 572.01 | 641.04 | 726.17 | 353.08 | 015.09 | 031.10 |
| 572.19 | 641.07 | 728.01 | the | 015.10 | 031.13 |
| 573.07 | 641.14 | 728.06 | 001.04 | 015.12 | 031.19 |
| 573.19 | 643.12 | 728.10 | 001.08 | 015.12 | 032.04 |
| 574.02 | 644.06 | 729.19 | 001.11 | 015.15 | 032.12 |
| 574.04 | 644.09 | 730.06 | 002.07 | 015.21 | 032.12 |
| 574.08 | 645.20 | 730.10 | 002.09 | 016.01 | 032.13 |
| 576.05 | 646.20 | 731.05 | 002.10 | 016.03 | 032.16 |
| 576.18 | 648.03 | 731.09 | 002.12 | 016.08 | 032.18 |
| 578.01 | 648.06 | 732.01 | 002.19 | 016.16 | 033.01 |
| 578.03 | 649.07 | 732.01 | 002.20 | 016.17 | 033.03 |
| 578.10 | 650.16 | 733.05 | 002.21 | 016.18 | 033.07 |
| 578.17 | 651.02 | 733.22 | 002.22 | 016.20 | 033.10 |
| 579.10 | 651.04 | 734.02 | 003.02 | 017.03 | 033.18 |
| 580.08 | 651.07 | 734.07 | 003.06 | 017.05 | 034.01 |
| 580.12 | 651.12 | 734.19 | 003.07 | 017.07 | 034.02 |
| 580.14 | 651.17 | 736.02 | 003.08 | 017.08 | 034.04 |
| 580.18 | 652.02 | 737.13 | 003.11 | 017.16 | 034.04 |
| 581.08 | 652.09 | 737.20 | 003.12 | 017.16 | 034.07 |
| 582.12 | 652.20 | 738.06 | 003.14 | 018.03 | 034.10 |
| 582.17 | 653.12 | 738.20 | 003.14 | 018.05 | 034.12 |
| 583.08 | 654.02 | 740.04 | 003.15 | 018.07 | 034.14 |
| 583.11 | 654.03 | 743.06 | 003.18 | 018.10 | 034.16 |
| 583.12 | 654.08 | 743.16 | 004.03 | 018.12 | 034.22 |
| 583.18 | 654.13 | 744.08 | 004.06 | 018.21 | 035.06 |
| 585.12 | 654.22 | 744.14 | 004.09 | 019.01 | 035.08 |
| 586.11 | 655.01 | 745.03 | 004.09 | 019.02 | 035.11 |
| 586.18 | 656.01 | 745.07 | 004.10 | 019.04 | 035.13 |
| 588.14 | 656.03 | 745.10 | 004.10 | 019.05 | 035.13 |
| 588.17 | 656.18 | 745.19 | 004.11 | 019.06 | 035.17 |
| 589.04 | 660.01 | 746.12 | 004.12 | 019.10 | |
| 589.08 | 660.14 | 746.14 | | 019.11 | |

| | | | | | |
|---|---|---|---|---|---|
| 036.05 | 051.11 | 063.11 | 080.12 | 098.15 | 111.14 |
| 036.12 | 051.11 | 063.11 | 080.15 | 098.16 | 111.22 |
| 037.02 | 051.12 | 063.12 | 080.19 | 098.19 | 112.03 |
| 037.03 | 051.13 | 063.15 | 080.20 | 098.20 | 112.06 |
| 037.05 | 051.16 | 063.20 | 080.22 | 098.21 | 112.07 |
| 037.07 | 051.16 | 064.01 | 081.11 | 099.03 | 112.07 |
| 038.01 | 051.17 | 064.08 | 081.15 | 099.08 | 112.11 |
| 038.02 | 051.20 | 064.11 | 081.18 | 099.13 | 113.05 |
| 038.04 | 051.21 | 064.14 | 081.19 | 099.14 | 113.06 |
| 038.09 | 052.02 | 064.19 | 081.21 | 099.14 | 113.10 |
| 038.10 | 052.03 | 065.02 | 082.05 | 099.15 | 114.02 |
| 038.11 | 052.04 | 065.02 | 082.06 | 099.17 | 114.18 |
| 038.14 | 052.13 | 065.03 | 082.07 | 099.21 | 114.21 |
| 038.16 | 052.15 | 065.09 | 082.09 | 100.01 | 115.04 |
| 038.18 | 052.17 | 065.10 | 082.14 | 100.05 | 115.10 |
| 038.21 | 052.18 | 065.12 | 082.15 | 100.11 | 115.15 |
| 039.05 | 052.19 | 065.13 | 082.16 | 100.11 | 115.21 |
| 039.09 | 052.19 | 065.17 | 082.21 | 100.12 | 116.01 |
| 039.09 | 053.03 | 065.17 | 083.02 | 100.13 | 116.03 |
| 039.11 | 053.04 | 065.18 | 083.06 | 100.17 | 116.14 |
| 039.12 | 053.04 | 065.19 | 083.10 | 100.18 | 116.18 |
| 039.13 | 053.06 | 065.20 | 083.12 | 101.01 | 117.03 |
| 039.16 | 053.08 | 065.22 | 083.15 | 101.01 | 117.09 |
| 039.17 | 053.09 | 066.01 | 083.16 | 101.04 | 117.12 |
| 039.19 | 053.12 | 066.02 | 083.17 | 101.05 | 117.20 |
| 040.07 | 053.16 | 066.02 | 083.21 | 101.08 | 118.08 |
| 040.08 | 053.21 | 066.05 | 084.02 | 101.09 | 118.08 |
| 040.10 | 054.03 | 066.07 | 084.04 | 101.11 | 118.08 |
| 040.11 | 054.03 | 066.08 | 084.06 | 101.13 | 118.09 |
| 040.17 | 054.03 | 066.10 | 084.06 | 101.16 | 118.13 |
| 040.19 | 054.04 | 066.11 | 084.17 | 101.19 | 118.14 |
| 041.06 | 054.05 | 066.12 | 084.21 | 101.19 | 118.15 |
| 041.10 | 054.14 | 066.16 | 085.10 | 101.20 | 118.19 |
| 041.16 | 054.16 | 066.17 | 085.16 | 102.07 | 119.03 |
| 041.17 | 054.18 | 066.18 | 085.20 | 102.10 | 119.06 |
| 042.04 | 054.19 | 066.20 | 085.20 | 102.14 | 119.07 |
| 042.04 | 054.19 | 067.02 | 085.21 | 102.16 | 119.12 |
| 042.12 | 054.20 | 067.03 | 085.22 | 102.17 | 119.12 |
| 042.15 | 055.04 | 067.03 | 086.01 | 102.19 | 119.13 |
| 042.15 | 055.05 | 067.05 | 087.02 | 102.20 | 119.14 |
| 042.18 | 055.10 | 067.06 | 087.05 | 103.03 | 119.14 |
| 043.06 | 055.11 | 067.09 | 088.01 | 103.09 | 119.17 |
| 043.07 | 055.15 | 067.10 | 088.04 | 103.12 | 119.18 |
| 043.08 | 055.17 | 067.11 | 088.04 | 103.12 | 120.05 |
| 043.09 | 055.20 | 067.18 | 088.05 | 103.13 | 120.10 |
| 043.10 | 056.02 | 068.01 | 088.07 | 103.14 | 120.12 |
| 043.11 | 056.09 | 068.03 | 088.11 | 103.16 | 120.13 |
| 043.13 | 056.13 | 068.04 | 088.15 | 103.17 | 120.13 |
| 044.02 | 056.13 | 069.10 | 088.15 | 103.19 | 120.14 |
| 044.02 | 056.15 | 070.07 | 088.17 | 103.19 | 120.16 |
| 044.03 | 056.17 | 070.09 | 089.02 | 103.20 | 120.20 |
| 044.03 | 056.18 | 071.01 | 089.04 | 103.21 | 121.11 |
| 044.03 | 056.22 | 071.05 | 089.10 | 104.01 | 121.12 |
| 044.09 | 057.04 | 071.06 | 089.12 | 104.01 | 121.13 |
| 044.10 | 057.05 | 071.12 | 089.13 | 104.06 | 121.17 |
| 044.13 | 057.09 | 071.21 | 089.14 | 104.15 | 121.18 |
| 044.14 | 057.10 | 072.02 | 089.17 | 104.15 | 121.20 |
| 044.15 | 057.10 | 073.01 | 089.18 | 104.17 | 121.22 |
| 044.18 | 057.11 | 073.02 | 089.18 | 104.18 | 122.01 |
| 045.01 | 057.16 | 073.04 | 090.05 | 104.18 | 122.02 |
| 045.05 | 058.07 | 073.04 | 090.05 | 104.22 | 122.14 |
| 045.10 | 058.12 | 073.07 | 090.09 | 105.04 | 122.15 |
| 045.17 | 058.13 | 073.08 | 090.10 | 105.08 | 123.01 |
| 045.20 | 058.18 | 073.10 | 090.15 | 105.09 | 123.15 |
| 045.20 | 058.20 | 073.12 | 090.16 | 105.12 | 124.09 |
| 046.01 | 058.21 | 073.19 | 090.17 | 105.13 | 124.13 |
| 046.02 | 059.06 | 074.01 | 090.23 | 105.14 | 124.17 |
| 046.07 | 059.09 | 074.01 | 091.04 | 105.20 | 124.19 |
| 046.15 | 059.11 | 074.10 | 092.02 | 105.21 | 124.22 |
| 046.19 | 059.13 | 074.10 | 092.08 | 106.05 | 125.01 |
| 047.05 | 059.20 | 074.22 | 092.17 | 106.05 | 125.02 |
| 047.06 | 059.22 | 075.01 | 092.20 | 106.07 | 125.03 |
| 047.07 | 059.22 | 075.02 | 092.21 | 106.10 | 125.10 |
| 047.08 | 060.01 | 075.05 | 092.22 | 106.12 | 126.01 |
| 047.08 | 060.02 | 075.10 | 093.02 | 106.15 | 126.03 |
| 047.11 | 060.05 | 075.10 | 093.04 | 107.02 | 126.08 |
| 047.15 | 060.06 | 075.17 | 093.04 | 107.06 | 126.08 |
| 047.16 | 060.08 | 075.19 | 093.05 | 107.11 | 126.09 |
| 047.16 | 060.10 | 075.21 | 093.08 | 107.15 | 126.09 |
| 047.17 | 060.11 | 076.02 | 093.10 | 107.16 | 126.10 |
| 047.21 | 060.16 | 076.04 | 094.06 | 107.17 | 126.10 |
| 048.01 | 060.17 | 076.15 | 094.09 | 107.17 | 126.12 |
| 048.07 | 060.19 | 076.22 | 094.12 | 107.20 | 126.14 |
| 048.10 | 060.20 | 077.03 | 094.12 | 107.22 | 126.15 |
| 048.11 | 061.05 | 077.04 | 094.19 | 108.01 | 126.16 |
| 048.13 | 061.06 | 077.06 | 095.05 | 108.04 | 126.21 |
| 049.01 | 061.10 | 077.07 | 095.05 | 108.06 | 126.21 |
| 049.01 | 061.13 | 077.10 | 095.06 | 108.09 | 126.22 |
| 049.04 | 061.15 | 077.11 | 095.08 | 108.10 | 127.01 |
| 049.04 | 061.18 | 077.15 | 095.09 | 108.13 | 127.05 |
| 049.08 | 061.18 | 077.16 | 095.09 | 108.15 | 127.05 |
| 049.13 | 061.20 | 077.22 | 095.12 | 108.17 | 127.06 |
| 049.16 | 061.21 | 078.11 | 095.15 | 108.18 | 127.07 |
| 049.18 | 061.22 | 078.15 | 095.18 | 108.18 | 127.08 |
| 050.02 | 062.01 | 078.15 | 096.02 | 108.22 | 127.11 |
| 050.03 | 062.01 | 078.19 | 096.03 | 109.08 | 127.16 |
| 050.04 | 062.05 | 079.05 | 096.09 | 109.09 | 127.20 |
| 050.06 | 062.07 | 079.08 | 096.12 | 109.10 | 128.03 |
| 050.11 | 062.08 | 079.12 | 097.01 | 109.16 | 128.06 |
| 050.11 | 062.13 | 079.13 | 097.01 | 110.02 | 128.08 |
| 050.13 | 062.18 | 079.15 | 097.04 | 110.09 | 128.10 |
| 050.18 | 062.19 | 079.16 | 097.04 | 110.09 | 128.11 |
| 050.18 | 062.19 | 079.17 | 097.04 | 110.12 | 128.14 |
| 050.21 | 062.21 | 079.19 | 097.05 | 110.14 | 128.15 |
| 051.02 | 063.03 | 080.02 | 097.09 | 110.19 | 129.05 |
| 051.02 | 063.05 | 080.02 | 097.14 | 110.20 | 129.06 |
| 051.03 | 063.07 | 080.03 | 097.17 | 110.20 | 129.06 |
| 051.04 | 063.07 | 080.09 | 098.02 | 111.03 | 129.18 |
| 051.06 | 063.09 | | 098.03 | 111.10 | 129.20 |
| 051.09 | 063.10 | | 098.11 | 111.12 | 129.21 |
| 051.10 | | | 098.13 | 111.14 | 130.04 |

| | | | | | |
|---|---|---|---|---|---|
| 130.07 | 146.02 | 165.15 | 186.04 | 205.16 | 222.11 |
| 130.14 | 146.04 | 165.18 | 186.05 | 205.22 | 222.13 |
| 130.16 | 146.05 | 165.20 | 186.11 | 205.22 | 222.15 |
| 130.16 | 146.05 | 166.01 | 186.22 | 206.01 | 222.18 |
| 130.19 | 146.06 | 166.02 | 187.01 | 206.03 | 223.01 |
| 130.22 | 146.13 | 166.05 | 187.05 | 206.03 | 223.09 |
| 131.03 | 146.18 | 166.07 | 188.04 | 206.04 | 223.14 |
| 131.06 | 146.21 | 166.09 | 188.06 | 206.06 | 223.14 |
| 131.08 | 147.01 | 166.10 | 188.11 | 206.08 | 223.15 |
| 131.09 | 147.03 | 166.12 | 188.11 | 206.08 | 223.20 |
| 131.10 | 147.03 | 166.13 | 188.14 | 206.09 | 223.21 |
| 131.10 | 147.05 | 167.07 | 188.14 | 206.10 | 224.05 |
| 131.13 | 147.09 | 167.09 | 188.15 | 206.10 | 224.08 |
| 131.14 | 147.20 | 167.15 | 188.16 | 206.11 | 224.09 |
| 131.17 | 148.01 | 167.18 | 188.21 | 206.12 | 224.12 |
| 131.19 | 148.03 | 168.01 | 188.22 | 206.12 | 224.19 |
| 131.21 | 149.02 | 168.04 | 189.02 | 206.14 | 225.04 |
| 131.21 | 149.03 | 168.12 | 189.03 | 206.15 | 225.07 |
| 131.22 | 149.08 | 168.13 | 189.03 | 206.15 | 225.13 |
| 132.01 | 149.09 | 168.15 | 189.04 | 206.19 | 225.14 |
| 132.03 | 149.14 | 168.17 | 189.05 | 207.01 | 225.21 |
| 132.04 | 149.20 | 169.01 | 189.06 | 207.02 | 226.04 |
| 132.08 | 150.06 | 169.05 | 189.08 | 207.03 | 226.05 |
| 132.09 | 150.07 | 169.07 | 189.10 | 207.06 | 226.11 |
| 132.10 | 150.15 | 169.08 | 189.10 | 207.07 | 226.13 |
| 132.11 | 150.16 | 169.10 | 189.12 | 207.09 | 226.16 |
| 132.12 | 150.21 | 169.12 | 189.12 | 207.12 | 226.17 |
| 132.14 | 151.10 | 169.12 | 189.14 | 207.16 | 226.18 |
| 132.15 | 151.14 | 169.13 | 189.15 | 207.18 | 226.20 |
| 132.15 | 151.19 | 169.13 | 189.21 | 207.18 | 226.21 |
| 132.16 | 151.22 | 169.17 | 190.06 | 207.19 | 227.04 |
| 132.16 | 152.03 | 169.17 | 190.07 | 208.04 | 227.10 |
| 132.17 | 152.05 | 169.18 | 190.18 | 208.13 | 227.10 |
| 132.21 | 152.08 | 169.18 | 190.19 | 208.20 | 227.17 |
| 132.22 | 152.13 | 169.19 | 191.07 | 208.21 | 228.04 |
| 133.04 | 152.20 | 170.02 | 191.09 | 209.04 | 228.11 |
| 133.08 | 152.22 | 170.04 | 191.16 | 209.05 | 228.14 |
| 133.14 | 153.02 | 170.13 | 191.19 | 209.07 | 228.17 |
| 134.01 | 153.03 | 170.19 | 191.19 | 209.08 | 228.22 |
| 134.02 | 153.03 | 170.22 | 191.20 | 209.08 | 229.04 |
| 134.11 | 153.04 | 171.12 | 191.21 | 209.11 | 229.15 |
| 134.13 | 153.04 | 171.12 | 191.21 | 209.12 | 231.05 |
| 134.17 | 153.09 | 172.02 | 192.01 | 209.12 | 231.07 |
| 134.17 | 154.05 | 172.13 | 192.10 | 209.13 | 231.09 |
| 134.18 | 154.07 | 173.03 | 192.11 | 209.13 | 232.01 |
| 134.21 | 154.09 | 173.17 | 192.12 | 209.16 | 233.17 |
| 134.21 | 154.10 | 173.17 | 192.15 | 209.17 | 233.20 |
| 135.01 | 154.11 | 174.01 | 192.16 | 209.17 | 234.03 |
| 135.03 | 154.19 | 174.01 | 192.22 | 210.01 | 234.04 |
| 135.04 | 154.20 | 174.09 | 193.01 | 210.07 | 234.07 |
| 135.07 | 154.21 | 174.10 | 193.01 | 210.10 | 234.08 |
| 135.10 | 155.08 | 174.14 | 193.02 | 210.12 | 234.09 |
| 135.15 | 155.09 | 174.17 | 193.04 | 210.15 | 234.11 |
| 135.16 | 155.16 | 174.22 | 193.06 | 210.15 | 234.17 |
| 135.17 | 155.18 | 175.09 | 193.08 | 211.01 | 234.17 |
| 135.18 | 156.02 | 175.12 | 193.11 | 211.02 | 234.20 |
| 135.19 | 156.04 | 175.17 | 194.20 | 211.02 | 235.01 |
| 136.01 | 156.13 | 175.19 | 195.05 | 211.06 | 235.02 |
| 136.04 | 156.20 | 176.02 | 195.12 | 211.08 | 235.04 |
| 136.07 | 156.21 | 176.05 | 195.20 | 211.08 | 235.05 |
| 136.08 | 157.02 | 176.06 | 196.01 | 211.22 | 235.15 |
| 136.08 | 157.05 | 177.02 | 196.07 | 212.03 | 235.20 |
| 136.16 | 157.08 | 178.21 | 196.08 | 212.05 | 236.04 |
| 136.18 | 157.13 | 178.22 | 196.09 | 212.11 | 236.06 |
| 136.21 | 157.16 | 179.01 | 196.12 | 212.13 | 236.12 |
| 137.06 | 157.20 | 179.01 | 196.21 | 212.14 | 236.18 |
| 137.09 | 157.21 | 179.03 | 197.01 | 212.17 | 236.22 |
| 137.17 | 158.03 | 179.05 | 197.05 | 213.01 | 237.02 |
| 138.10 | 158.10 | 179.12 | 197.06 | 213.02 | 237.03 |
| 138.10 | 158.16 | 179.18 | 197.07 | 213.05 | 237.05 |
| 139.02 | 159.16 | 179.22 | 197.08 | 213.08 | 237.10 |
| 139.03 | 159.22 | 180.01 | 197.12 | 213.08 | 237.12 |
| 139.03 | 159.22 | 180.01 | 197.14 | 213.10 | 237.14 |
| 139.05 | 160.01 | 180.06 | 197.19 | 213.11 | 237.15 |
| 139.06 | 160.02 | 180.06 | 198.11 | 213.16 | 237.17 |
| 139.08 | 160.07 | 180.08 | 198.12 | 213.18 | 237.18 |
| 139.08 | 160.07 | 180.10 | 198.17 | 213.22 | 237.22 |
| 139.11 | 160.10 | 180.12 | 198.18 | 213.22 | 238.02 |
| 139.11 | 160.12 | 180.19 | 199.08 | 214.05 | 238.08 |
| 140.12 | 160.13 | 181.01 | 199.09 | 214.11 | 238.14 |
| 140.16 | 160.15 | 181.02 | 199.10 | 215.06 | 238.15 |
| 140.18 | 160.20 | 181.07 | 199.12 | 215.12 | 238.16 |
| 140.19 | 160.20 | 181.09 | 199.14 | 216.03 | 238.22 |
| 140.20 | 160.22 | 181.09 | 199.21 | 216.07 | 239.09 |
| 141.02 | 160.22 | 182.04 | 199.22 | 216.17 | 239.10 |
| 141.07 | 161.02 | 182.05 | 200.01 | 217.01 | 239.10 |
| 141.10 | 161.04 | 182.07 | 200.02 | 217.02 | 239.11 |
| 141.17 | 161.04 | 182.08 | 200.03 | 217.03 | 239.21 |
| 141.19 | 162.03 | 182.08 | 200.05 | 217.05 | 240.02 |
| 141.20 | 162.04 | 182.10 | 201.06 | 217.19 | 240.04 |
| 142.01 | 162.09 | 182.15 | 201.07 | 217.21 | 240.08 |
| 142.02 | 162.09 | 182.18 | 201.12 | 218.01 | 240.09 |
| 142.03 | 162.10 | 182.22 | 201.12 | 218.01 | 240.09 |
| 143.01 | 162.10 | 183.02 | 202.14 | 218.04 | 240.12 |
| 143.09 | 163.02 | 183.03 | 202.19 | 218.14 | 240.14 |
| 143.11 | 163.02 | 183.04 | 203.01 | 219.06 | 240.17 |
| 143.17 | 163.06 | 183.05 | 203.07 | 219.07 | 240.22 |
| 143.17 | 163.07 | 183.13 | 203.08 | 219.08 | 241.01 |
| 144.04 | 163.09 | 183.18 | 203.09 | 219.08 | 241.05 |
| 144.05 | 163.10 | 184.03 | 203.14 | 219.15 | 241.07 |
| 144.06 | 163.13 | 184.06 | 203.19 | 219.18 | 241.09 |
| 144.15 | 163.20 | 184.10 | 203.20 | 220.07 | 242.04 |
| 144.17 | 164.10 | 184.16 | 203.21 | 220.12 | 242.10 |
| 144.19 | 164.20 | 184.18 | 204.11 | 220.18 | 242.12 |
| 145.02 | 165.03 | 185.01 | 204.12 | 220.19 | 243.02 |
| 145.05 | 165.04 | 185.05 | 204.12 | 221.06 | 243.03 |
| 145.06 | 165.07 | 185.15 | 204.13 | 221.19 | 243.04 |
| 145.18 | 165.10 | 185.17 | 204.14 | 221.22 | 243.05 |
| 145.19 | 165.11 | 185.17 | 205.04 | 222.05 | 243.06 |
| 145.22 | 165.13 | 185.20 | 205.08 | 222.06 | 243.07 |
| 146.02 | | 186.02 | 205.09 | | 243.08 |

| | | | | | |
|---|---|---|---|---|---|
| 243.09 | 259.19 | 279.15 | 298.03 | 314.02 | 329.22 |
| 243.10 | 259.22 | 279.17 | 298.05 | 314.04 | 330.04 |
| 243.11 | 260.01 | 280.08 | 298.13 | 314.09 | 330.06 |
| 243.16 | 260.01 | 280.14 | 298.15 | 314.10 | 330.07 |
| 243.17 | 260.13 | 280.17 | 298.18 | 314.19 | 330.08 |
| 243.22 | 260.18 | 280.18 | 299.02 | 315.07 | 330.09 |
| 244.02 | 260.19 | 281.09 | 299.03 | 315.11 | 330.20 |
| 244.05 | 260.20 | 281.09 | 299.03 | 315.15 | 331.05 |
| 244.08 | 261.01 | 281.10 | 299.07 | 315.20 | 331.07 |
| 244.13 | 261.03 | 281.14 | 299.09 | 316.03 | 331.11 |
| 244.13 | 261.05 | 281.18 | 299.10 | 316.04 | 331.18 |
| 244.15 | 261.07 | 281.20 | 299.17 | 316.05 | 332.01 |
| 244.16 | 261.08 | 281.22 | 299.22 | 316.08 | 332.02 |
| 244.19 | 261.08 | 282.01 | 300.03 | 316.09 | 332.07 |
| 245.07 | 261.12 | 282.01 | 301.02 | 316.12 | 332.08 |
| 245.12 | 261.15 | 282.08 | 301.04 | 316.12 | 332.13 |
| 245.13 | 262.10 | 282.11 | 301.08 | 316.16 | 333.07 |
| 245.13 | 262.12 | 282.12 | 301.11 | 316.21 | 333.09 |
| 246.06 | 262.15 | 282.14 | 302.02 | 317.10 | 334.02 |
| 246.07 | 262.20 | 283.03 | 302.08 | 317.13 | 334.06 |
| 246.15 | 263.08 | 283.04 | 302.09 | 317.16 | 334.11 |
| 246.20 | 263.14 | 283.11 | 302.13 | 317.16 | 334.12 |
| 247.06 | 263.18 | 283.12 | 302.14 | 317.17 | 334.19 |
| 247.10 | 264.02 | 283.14 | 302.14 | 317.19 | 335.14 |
| 247.12 | 264.04 | 284.06 | 302.15 | 317.20 | 335.15 |
| 247.14 | 264.05 | 284.06 | 302.20 | 317.20 | 335.17 |
| 247.16 | 264.06 | 284.07 | 303.02 | 317.21 | 335.19 |
| 247.18 | 264.16 | 284.10 | 303.03 | 318.03 | 336.03 |
| 247.20 | 264.21 | 284.15 | 303.05 | 318.04 | 336.07 |
| 247.22 | 265.08 | 284.19 | 303.05 | 318.07 | 336.20 |
| 248.01 | 265.14 | 285.09 | 303.06 | 318.10 | 337.04 |
| 248.02 | 265.15 | 285.10 | 303.06 | 318.11 | 337.07 |
| 248.08 | 265.18 | 285.10 | 303.10 | 318.21 | 337.16 |
| 248.09 | 265.18 | 285.12 | 303.13 | 319.01 | 337.18 |
| 248.12 | 266.07 | 285.13 | 303.18 | 319.02 | 338.09 |
| 248.13 | 266.10 | 285.16 | 303.19 | 319.02 | 338.16 |
| 248.18 | 266.10 | 285.17 | 303.20 | 319.03 | 338.19 |
| 248.22 | 266.19 | 285.18 | 303.21 | 319.04 | 338.21 |
| 248.22 | 266.21 | 285.18 | 304.06 | 319.15 | 338.22 |
| 249.02 | 267.05 | 286.04 | 304.06 | 319.17 | 339.17 |
| 249.08 | 267.06 | 286.05 | 304.08 | 319.19 | 339.18 |
| 249.09 | 267.13 | 286.16 | 304.08 | 319.22 | 339.21 |
| 249.09 | 267.14 | 287.02 | 304.10 | 319.22 | 339.22 |
| 249.15 | 267.15 | 287.03 | 304.11 | 320.02 | 340.02 |
| 249.17 | 267.17 | 287.16 | 304.12 | 320.05 | 340.03 |
| 249.19 | 268.01 | 287.16 | 304.17 | 320.07 | 340.08 |
| 250.01 | 269.02 | 287.17 | 304.19 | 320.19 | 340.13 |
| 250.02 | 269.10 | 287.21 | 304.20 | 320.20 | 340.19 |
| 250.06 | 270.02 | 288.05 | 304.21 | 320.22 | 340.19 |
| 250.09 | 270.07 | 288.05 | 304.21 | 321.07 | 340.20 |
| 250.14 | 270.15 | 288.13 | 305.01 | 321.10 | 341.01 |
| 250.17 | 270.16 | 289.11 | 305.06 | 321.17 | 341.02 |
| 250.21 | 271.15 | 289.16 | 305.09 | 321.18 | 341.04 |
| 251.07 | 272.03 | 290.01 | 305.14 | 321.19 | 341.09 |
| 251.11 | 272.06 | 290.13 | 305.22 | 322.02 | 341.14 |
| 251.17 | 272.06 | 290.14 | 306.01 | 322.02 | 341.19 |
| 252.05 | 272.09 | 290.16 | 306.02 | 322.12 | 342.08 |
| 252.08 | 272.16 | 290.16 | 306.06 | 322.12 | 342.10 |
| 252.16 | 272.17 | 290.17 | 306.11 | 322.13 | 342.14 |
| 252.17 | 272.20 | 290.19 | 306.12 | 322.14 | 342.18 |
| 252.21 | 273.20 | 290.21 | 306.20 | 322.15 | 342.20 |
| 253.06 | 274.01 | 291.02 | 307.01 | 322.19 | 342.21 |
| 253.11 | 274.06 | 291.07 | 307.01 | 322.21 | 343.01 |
| 253.16 | 274.08 | 291.08 | 307.02 | 322.22 | 343.03 |
| 253.19 | 274.12 | 291.12 | 307.04 | 323.01 | 343.04 |
| 253.20 | 274.14 | 291.12 | 307.08 | 323.07 | 343.06 |
| 253.20 | 274.14 | 291.13 | 307.20 | 323.08 | 343.08 |
| 254.01 | 274.15 | 291.16 | 307.21 | 323.10 | 344.01 |
| 254.03 | 274.15 | 291.19 | 308.01 | 323.11 | 344.03 |
| 254.07 | 274.17 | 291.21 | 308.03 | 323.11 | 344.18 |
| 254.12 | 274.18 | 291.22 | 308.04 | 323.13 | 344.21 |
| 254.12 | 274.20 | 292.10 | 308.05 | 323.22 | 345.01 |
| 254.13 | 275.03 | 292.16 | 308.05 | 323.22 | 345.16 |
| 254.16 | 275.03 | 292.17 | 308.06 | 324.01 | 345.22 |
| 254.19 | 275.04 | 292.22 | 308.08 | 324.01 | 346.06 |
| 255.02 | 275.10 | 293.12 | 308.08 | 324.02 | 346.17 |
| 255.03 | 275.11 | 293.15 | 308.09 | 324.07 | 347.02 |
| 255.05 | 275.15 | 293.16 | 308.11 | 324.08 | 347.10 |
| 255.06 | 275.15 | 293.17 | 308.11 | 325.01 | 347.13 |
| 255.07 | 275.16 | 293.18 | 308.13 | 325.02 | 347.17 |
| 255.10 | 275.16 | 293.19 | 308.19 | 325.03 | 348.01 |
| 255.13 | 275.18 | 294.02 | 308.20 | 325.04 | 348.02 |
| 255.15 | 275.18 | 294.05 | 308.20 | 325.08 | 348.03 |
| 255.19 | 275.19 | 294.11 | 308.21 | 325.10 | 348.06 |
| 256.03 | 275.21 | 294.11 | 309.02 | 325.13 | 348.10 |
| 256.04 | 276.05 | 294.20 | 309.05 | 325.15 | 348.11 |
| 256.08 | 276.06 | 294.21 | 309.11 | 325.15 | 349.05 |
| 256.09 | 276.06 | 294.21 | 309.22 | 325.16 | 349.08 |
| 256.21 | 276.09 | 294.22 | 310.05 | 325.19 | 350.01 |
| 257.05 | 276.13 | 295.01 | 310.05 | 325.20 | 350.01 |
| 257.06 | 277.01 | 295.02 | 310.08 | 325.21 | 350.02 |
| 257.12 | 277.01 | 295.03 | 310.15 | 325.21 | 350.04 |
| 257.13 | 277.03 | 295.12 | 310.20 | 326.04 | 350.10 |
| 257.15 | 277.05 | 295.12 | 310.21 | 326.07 | 350.11 |
| 257.18 | 277.08 | 295.13 | 311.01 | 326.14 | 350.11 |
| 257.21 | 277.10 | 295.22 | 311.02 | 326.15 | 350.13 |
| 258.02 | 277.12 | 296.04 | 311.18 | 326.20 | 350.14 |
| 258.05 | 277.19 | 296.04 | 311.21 | 326.21 | 350.16 |
| 258.11 | 278.02 | 296.08 | 312.01 | 327.01 | 350.16 |
| 258.12 | 278.06 | 296.13 | 312.02 | 327.16 | 350.17 |
| 258.13 | 278.09 | 296.13 | 312.03 | 328.03 | 350.21 |
| 258.14 | 278.11 | 296.14 | 312.04 | 328.04 | 350.22 |
| 258.15 | 278.13 | 297.02 | 312.08 | 329.03 | 351.01 |
| 258.20 | 278.13 | 297.02 | 312.14 | 329.06 | 351.04 |
| 259.04 | 278.15 | 297.03 | 312.15 | 329.07 | 351.05 |
| 259.08 | 278.16 | 297.06 | 312.16 | 329.15 | 351.07 |
| 259.10 | 278.17 | 297.12 | 312.17 | 329.15 | 351.12 |
| 259.16 | 278.20 | 297.16 | 312.21 | 329.20 | 351.13 |
| 259.16 | 279.11 | 297.18 | 313.11 | 329.22 | 351.15 |
| | 279.13 | 297.21 | 313.13 | | 351.15 |
| | 279.14 | 297.21 | | | 351.18 |

| | | | | | |
|---|---|---|---|---|---|
| 351.20 | 372.05 | 387.14 | 402.17 | 419.03 | 435.15 |
| 352.01 | 372.10 | 387.16 | 402.17 | 419.06 | 436.03 |
| 352.06 | 372.15 | 387.18 | 403.03 | 419.12 | 436.08 |
| 352.07 | 372.18 | 387.21 | 403.09 | 419.12 | 436.08 |
| 352.18 | 372.19 | 388.12 | 403.14 | 419.14 | 436.10 |
| 353.02 | 372.20 | 389.10 | 403.15 | 419.17 | 436.11 |
| 353.02 | 372.20 | 389.15 | 403.17 | 419.18 | 436.15 |
| 353.03 | 372.21 | 389.17 | 404.02 | 419.18 | 436.16 |
| 353.04 | 373.02 | 389.18 | 404.03 | 419.22 | 436.21 |
| 353.05 | 373.03 | 389.21 | 404.04 | 420.02 | 437.01 |
| 353.06 | 373.03 | 390.04 | 404.05 | 420.06 | 437.05 |
| 353.06 | 373.04 | 390.05 | 404.14 | 420.12 | 437.05 |
| 353.12 | 373.05 | 390.08 | 404.18 | 420.15 | 437.11 |
| 353.19 | 373.07 | 390.10 | 405.01 | 420.15 | 437.12 |
| 353.20 | 373.07 | 390.13 | 405.01 | 420.22 | 437.13 |
| 354.11 | 373.08 | 390.14 | 405.14 | 421.01 | 437.15 |
| 354.12 | 373.10 | 390.21 | 405.19 | 421.01 | 437.17 |
| 354.15 | 373.14 | 391.06 | 405.20 | 421.02 | 438.10 |
| 354.19 | 373.15 | 391.14 | 406.21 | 421.04 | 438.13 |
| 355.01 | 373.16 | 391.14 | 407.03 | 421.04 | 438.21 |
| 355.03 | 374.09 | 392.01 | 407.06 | 421.08 | 438.22 |
| 355.07 | 374.11 | 392.02 | 407.06 | 421.09 | 439.01 |
| 355.08 | 374.14 | 392.03 | 407.11 | 421.15 | 439.02 |
| 355.08 | 375.02 | 392.04 | 407.13 | 421.19 | 439.03 |
| 355.14 | 375.03 | 392.11 | 407.15 | 421.20 | 439.04 |
| 355.15 | 375.10 | 392.13 | 407.21 | 422.01 | 439.07 |
| 355.17 | 375.14 | 392.17 | 407.22 | 422.05 | 439.22 |
| 356.04 | 376.04 | 392.19 | 408.01 | 422.08 | 440.01 |
| 356.05 | 376.08 | 392.19 | 408.01 | 422.12 | 440.02 |
| 356.09 | 376.12 | 392.21 | 408.04 | 422.12 | 440.04 |
| 356.12 | 376.16 | 393.02 | 408.07 | 422.14 | 440.06 |
| 356.20 | 377.01 | 393.06 | 408.08 | 422.18 | 440.16 |
| 356.21 | 377.09 | 393.06 | 408.13 | 422.20 | 440.20 |
| 357.12 | 377.14 | 393.07 | 409.06 | 422.20 | 441.04 |
| 357.13 | 377.14 | 393.08 | 409.12 | 423.02 | 441.05 |
| 358.03 | 377.15 | 393.08 | 409.12 | 424.02 | 441.08 |
| 358.11 | 377.17 | 393.08 | 409.15 | 424.03 | 441.11 |
| 358.13 | 377.19 | 393.10 | 409.17 | 424.08 | 441.15 |
| 358.15 | 378.02 | 393.10 | 409.18 | 424.10 | 441.16 |
| 358.17 | 378.04 | 393.14 | 409.21 | 424.12 | 441.17 |
| 359.06 | 378.12 | 393.15 | 409.22 | 425.02 | 442.02 |
| 359.09 | 378.15 | 393.16 | 410.02 | 425.03 | 442.06 |
| 359.11 | 378.17 | 393.16 | 410.03 | 426.08 | 442.06 |
| 359.13 | 378.19 | 393.18 | 410.06 | 426.09 | 442.18 |
| 359.18 | 378.21 | 393.20 | 410.08 | 426.09 | 443.08 |
| 360.03 | 379.01 | 394.01 | 410.09 | 426.13 | 443.08 |
| 360.07 | 379.02 | 394.05 | 410.12 | 426.14 | 443.09 |
| 360.16 | 379.02 | 394.06 | 410.12 | 426.19 | 443.11 |
| 360.20 | 379.03 | 394.07 | 410.14 | 427.01 | 443.14 |
| 361.03 | 379.07 | 394.07 | 410.15 | 427.02 | 443.15 |
| 361.15 | 379.09 | 394.09 | 411.02 | 427.02 | 443.15 |
| 361.15 | 379.12 | 394.10 | 411.08 | 427.07 | 443.17 |
| 362.04 | 379.12 | 394.12 | 411.11 | 427.09 | 443.20 |
| 362.08 | 379.14 | 394.17 | 411.13 | 427.09 | 444.08 |
| 363.05 | 379.17 | 394.20 | 411.20 | 427.10 | 444.08 |
| 363.11 | 379.17 | 395.11 | 411.21 | 427.20 | 444.14 |
| 363.14 | 379.18 | 395.11 | 411.22 | 427.22 | 444.16 |
| 364.07 | 379.18 | 395.14 | 412.03 | 428.05 | 444.18 |
| 364.11 | 379.19 | 395.14 | 412.11 | 428.06 | 444.20 |
| 364.11 | 379.19 | 395.19 | 412.12 | 428.08 | 445.01 |
| 364.13 | 379.20 | 395.21 | 412.15 | 428.08 | 445.05 |
| 364.13 | 379.22 | 396.02 | 412.21 | 428.09 | 445.06 |
| 364.14 | 379.22 | 396.05 | 413.06 | 428.11 | 445.11 |
| 364.21 | 380.02 | 396.13 | 413.08 | 428.14 | 445.12 |
| 364.21 | 380.04 | 396.15 | 413.10 | 428.14 | 445.14 |
| 364.22 | 380.06 | 396.20 | 413.10 | 428.17 | 445.14 |
| 365.02 | 381.02 | 397.01 | 413.18 | 428.21 | 445.21 |
| 365.06 | 381.03 | 397.04 | 414.01 | 429.01 | 446.01 |
| 365.07 | 381.03 | 397.05 | 414.01 | 429.02 | 446.01 |
| 365.19 | 381.04 | 397.07 | 414.03 | 429.03 | 446.04 |
| 365.21 | 381.07 | 397.09 | 414.07 | 429.08 | 446.10 |
| 366.02 | 381.09 | 397.10 | 414.07 | 429.11 | 446.13 |
| 366.04 | 381.10 | 397.16 | 414.09 | 429.13 | 446.16 |
| 366.10 | 381.10 | 397.17 | 414.11 | 429.14 | 446.18 |
| 366.10 | 381.11 | 397.18 | 414.14 | 430.01 | 446.19 |
| 366.16 | 382.02 | 397.20 | 415.01 | 430.08 | 446.21 |
| 366.20 | 382.04 | 398.03 | 415.02 | 430.11 | 448.02 |
| 366.20 | 382.06 | 398.09 | 415.03 | 430.12 | 448.07 |
| 367.04 | 382.07 | 398.13 | 415.03 | 430.20 | 448.09 |
| 367.09 | 382.07 | 398.14 | 415.04 | 431.03 | 448.11 |
| 367.11 | 382.11 | 398.17 | 415.07 | 431.06 | 449.05 |
| 367.15 | 382.19 | 398.19 | 415.08 | 431.08 | 449.09 |
| 367.22 | 382.19 | 398.20 | 415.10 | 431.08 | 449.10 |
| 368.03 | 382.21 | 399.02 | 415.16 | 431.15 | 449.20 |
| 368.03 | 383.01 | 399.10 | 415.17 | 431.21 | 449.21 |
| 368.05 | 383.05 | 399.13 | 415.20 | 432.02 | 449.22 |
| 368.10 | 383.05 | 399.13 | 416.01 | 432.05 | 450.04 |
| 368.11 | 383.09 | 399.16 | 416.01 | 432.06 | 450.08 |
| 368.13 | 383.12 | 399.18 | 416.02 | 432.08 | 450.10 |
| 369.03 | 383.16 | 399.20 | 416.03 | 432.08 | 450.14 |
| 369.05 | 383.19 | 400.01 | 416.07 | 432.14 | 451.02 |
| 369.08 | 384.08 | 400.02 | 416.11 | 432.14 | 451.05 |
| 369.10 | 384.12 | 400.08 | 416.12 | 432.19 | 451.06 |
| 370.01 | 384.15 | 400.09 | 416.16 | 433.04 | 451.07 |
| 370.03 | 384.18 | 400.10 | 417.07 | 433.05 | 451.11 |
| 370.08 | 384.22 | 400.11 | 417.13 | 433.07 | 451.12 |
| 370.12 | 385.09 | 400.12 | 417.15 | 433.09 | 451.14 |
| 370.13 | 385.10 | 400.16 | 417.17 | 433.11 | 451.15 |
| 370.13 | 385.10 | 400.17 | 417.19 | 433.18 | 452.03 |
| 370.15 | 385.11 | 400.18 | 418.01 | 433.18 | 452.03 |
| 370.18 | 385.12 | 401.03 | 418.01 | 433.19 | 452.04 |
| 370.19 | 385.15 | 401.07 | 418.03 | 433.21 | 452.10 |
| 370.21 | 385.16 | 401.12 | 418.07 | 433.21 | 452.13 |
| 371.02 | 386.03 | 401.14 | 418.08 | 434.03 | 453.01 |
| 371.05 | 386.03 | 401.18 | 418.10 | 434.06 | 453.04 |
| 371.12 | 386.06 | 401.20 | 418.11 | 434.13 | 453.06 |
| 371.13 | 386.13 | 401.20 | 418.16 | 434.15 | 453.08 |
| 371.16 | 386.14 | 401.22 | 418.19 | 434.17 | 453.09 |
| 371.16 | 387.01 | 402.07 | 418.22 | 434.20 | 453.11 |
| 372.01 | 387.08 | 402.14 | 419.01 | 435.04 | 454.03 |
| | 387.09 | | 419.02 | 435.14 | 454.05 |

| | | | | | |
|---|---|---|---|---|---|
| 454.17 | 473.04 | 492.16 | 511.19 | 530.07 | 553.13 |
| 454.20 | 473.05 | 492.16 | 511.20 | 530.09 | 554.01 |
| 454.21 | 473.09 | 492.19 | 511.21 | 530.09 | 554.01 |
| 454.21 | 474.05 | 493.03 | 512.02 | 531.03 | 554.04 |
| 455.01 | 475.04 | 493.05 | 512.03 | 531.06 | 554.15 |
| 455.03 | 475.07 | 494.06 | 513.02 | 531.07 | 554.17 |
| 455.04 | 475.14 | 494.07 | 513.04 | 531.09 | 555.05 |
| 455.07 | 475.15 | 494.10 | 513.04 | 531.15 | 555.08 |
| 455.09 | 475.19 | 494.14 | 513.09 | 531.18 | 555.10 |
| 455.10 | 476.02 | 494.17 | 513.11 | 531.20 | 555.16 |
| 455.12 | 476.04 | 494.19 | 513.11 | 531.21 | 555.17 |
| 455.15 | 476.04 | 494.19 | 513.13 | 532.04 | 555.17 |
| 455.16 | 476.06 | 494.21 | 513.15 | 532.09 | 555.18 |
| 456.04 | 476.10 | 494.21 | 513.17 | 532.09 | 555.18 |
| 456.05 | 476.12 | 495.01 | 513.18 | 532.15 | 555.21 |
| 456.07 | 476.13 | 495.08 | 513.18 | 532.17 | 556.02 |
| 456.08 | 476.16 | 495.10 | 513.20 | 532.18 | 556.05 |
| 456.13 | 476.17 | 495.11 | 513.21 | 532.19 | 556.18 |
| 456.14 | 476.21 | 495.11 | 513.22 | 533.10 | 556.19 |
| 456.14 | 477.01 | 495.15 | 514.04 | 534.04 | 556.19 |
| 456.15 | 477.02 | 495.15 | 514.08 | 534.09 | 557.05 |
| 456.21 | 477.14 | 495.15 | 514.10 | 534.11 | 557.08 |
| 457.03 | 477.15 | 495.16 | 514.14 | 534.16 | 557.08 |
| 457.05 | 478.03 | 495.17 | 515.03 | 535.02 | 557.08 |
| 457.07 | 478.05 | 495.19 | 515.07 | 535.02 | 557.09 |
| 457.14 | 478.07 | 495.20 | 515.07 | 535.13 | 557.10 |
| 457.15 | 478.09 | 496.06 | 515.08 | 535.13 | 557.10 |
| 457.19 | 478.18 | 496.09 | 515.09 | 536.06 | 557.18 |
| 458.05 | 478.18 | 496.21 | 516.01 | 536.11 | 557.21 |
| 458.06 | 478.20 | 497.02 | 516.01 | 537.10 | 557.22 |
| 458.06 | 479.05 | 497.06 | 516.14 | 537.21 | 558.09 |
| 458.07 | 479.05 | 497.06 | 516.16 | 538.01 | 558.11 |
| 459.02 | 479.10 | 497.09 | 516.17 | 538.01 | 558.14 |
| 459.04 | 479.14 | 497.13 | 516.19 | 538.08 | 558.22 |
| 459.12 | 479.15 | 497.13 | 517.02 | 538.14 | 559.01 |
| 460.06 | 480.02 | 497.20 | 517.03 | 538.16 | 559.02 |
| 460.10 | 480.07 | 498.03 | 517.08 | 538.20 | 559.03 |
| 460.16 | 480.08 | 498.06 | 517.11 | 539.14 | 559.11 |
| 461.04 | 480.09 | 498.07 | 517.13 | 540.09 | 559.16 |
| 461.06 | 481.01 | 498.07 | 517.17 | 540.11 | 559.20 |
| 461.08 | 481.02 | 498.10 | 517.20 | 540.20 | 560.04 |
| 461.18 | 481.03 | 498.12 | 517.20 | 541.07 | 560.06 |
| 462.08 | 481.04 | 498.21 | 518.02 | 541.09 | 560.15 |
| 462.13 | 481.05 | 498.21 | 518.03 | 541.10 | 560.16 |
| 462.18 | 481.08 | 499.06 | 518.10 | 541.20 | 560.16 |
| 462.19 | 481.11 | 499.14 | 518.16 | 542.01 | 561.02 |
| 462.19 | 481.13 | 499.17 | 518.18 | 542.08 | 561.04 |
| 462.20 | 482.01 | 499.21 | 518.18 | 542.09 | 561.09 |
| 463.05 | 482.03 | 499.22 | 518.22 | 542.15 | 561.17 |
| 463.07 | 482.05 | 500.03 | 519.12 | 542.20 | 561.18 |
| 463.07 | 482.15 | 500.05 | 520.04 | 543.01 | 562.02 |
| 463.10 | 482.18 | 501.06 | 520.11 | 543.07 | 563.04 |
| 463.10 | 482.21 | 502.01 | 521.07 | 543.09 | 563.05 |
| 463.12 | 482.22 | 502.07 | 521.09 | 544.01 | 563.08 |
| 463.13 | 483.02 | 502.09 | 522.01 | 544.09 | 563.18 |
| 463.14 | 483.05 | 502.10 | 522.04 | 544.10 | 563.20 |
| 463.15 | 483.10 | 502.20 | 522.06 | 544.14 | 563.21 |
| 463.18 | 483.14 | 502.21 | 522.06 | 544.15 | 564.06 |
| 463.22 | 483.15 | 503.07 | 522.07 | 545.02 | 564.11 |
| 464.15 | 483.17 | 503.15 | 522.08 | 545.08 | 564.22 |
| 465.11 | 484.01 | 503.15 | 522.09 | 545.09 | 565.05 |
| 465.13 | 484.06 | 503.16 | 522.09 | 545.21 | 565.06 |
| 465.14 | 484.07 | 503.19 | 522.10 | 546.07 | 565.22 |
| 465.14 | 484.08 | 504.04 | 522.13 | 546.07 | 566.01 |
| 465.15 | 484.15 | 504.05 | 522.17 | 546.16 | 566.03 |
| 465.17 | 485.01 | 504.06 | 522.17 | 546.18 | 566.04 |
| 465.18 | 485.04 | 505.08 | 522.19 | 546.20 | 566.08 |
| 465.21 | 485.10 | 505.20 | 523.01 | 547.06 | 566.09 |
| 466.05 | 485.13 | 506.06 | 523.02 | 547.12 | 566.11 |
| 466.05 | 485.13 | 506.06 | 523.03 | 547.15 | 566.11 |
| 466.06 | 485.18 | 506.09 | 523.08 | 547.19 | 566.15 |
| 466.07 | 485.21 | 506.11 | 523.08 | 547.19 | 566.18 |
| 466.10 | 485.22 | 506.13 | 523.09 | 547.20 | 566.22 |
| 466.16 | 486.07 | 506.18 | 523.14 | 548.05 | 567.03 |
| 466.18 | 486.12 | 506.21 | 523.15 | 548.08 | 567.13 |
| 466.19 | 486.13 | 507.02 | 523.18 | 548.12 | 567.14 |
| 467.07 | 486.19 | 507.02 | 523.21 | 548.17 | 567.14 |
| 467.09 | 486.22 | 507.03 | 524.04 | 548.18 | 568.02 |
| 467.11 | 487.02 | 507.05 | 524.05 | 549.03 | 568.06 |
| 467.13 | 487.03 | 507.08 | 524.10 | 549.04 | 568.08 |
| 467.21 | 487.14 | 507.09 | 524.12 | 549.04 | 568.11 |
| 468.04 | 487.15 | 507.17 | 524.16 | 549.05 | 568.13 |
| 468.08 | 487.17 | 507.18 | 525.04 | 550.02 | 568.14 |
| 468.10 | 487.17 | 508.03 | 525.06 | 550.03 | 569.02 |
| 468.20 | 487.22 | 508.06 | 525.07 | 550.04 | 569.02 |
| 469.04 | 488.16 | 508.06 | 525.09 | 550.04 | 569.05 |
| 469.04 | 488.18 | 508.12 | 525.15 | 550.06 | 569.08 |
| 469.08 | 488.19 | 508.19 | 525.19 | 550.07 | 569.08 |
| 469.09 | 489.13 | 508.21 | 525.21 | 550.10 | 569.15 |
| 469.16 | 489.16 | 508.22 | 526.07 | 551.18 | 569.19 |
| 469.22 | 489.21 | 508.22 | 526.10 | 551.19 | 569.20 |
| 470.03 | 490.02 | 509.01 | 526.19 | 551.20 | 569.21 |
| 470.04 | 490.04 | 509.04 | 526.21 | 552.04 | 570.01 |
| 470.06 | 490.07 | 509.05 | 526.22 | 552.05 | 570.02 |
| 470.16 | 490.12 | 509.06 | 527.13 | 552.07 | 570.04 |
| 470.16 | 490.14 | 509.07 | 527.14 | 552.11 | 570.04 |
| 470.18 | 490.17 | 509.10 | 527.16 | 552.12 | 570.06 |
| 470.19 | 490.18 | 509.14 | 527.17 | 552.13 | 570.14 |
| 470.21 | 491.02 | 509.16 | 527.17 | 552.15 | 571.14 |
| 471.03 | 491.04 | 509.17 | 527.19 | 552.16 | 571.16 |
| 471.06 | 491.06 | 509.18 | 528.04 | 552.17 | 571.18 |
| 471.07 | 491.07 | 509.18 | 528.07 | 552.18 | 572.02 |
| 471.08 | 491.09 | 509.19 | 528.09 | 552.19 | 572.03 |
| 471.20 | 491.10 | 509.21 | 528.19 | 552.20 | 572.04 |
| 472.02 | 491.11 | 510.05 | 529.06 | 552.21 | 572.07 |
| 472.09 | 491.14 | 510.08 | 529.07 | 553.04 | 572.08 |
| 472.13 | 491.20 | 510.11 | 529.11 | 553.05 | 572.13 |
| 472.18 | 492.03 | 510.11 | 529.12 | 553.05 | 572.15 |
| 472.20 | 492.05 | 511.08 | 530.02 | 553.06 | 572.20 |
| 473.02 | 492.08 | 511.12 | 530.04 | 553.06 | 573.04 |
| 473.03 | 492.10 | | 530.06 | 553.09 | 573.13 |

| | | | | | |
|---|---|---|---|---|---|
| 573.13 | 606.10 | 631.01 | 646.18 | 666.04 | 689.22 |
| 573.17 | 606.16 | 631.02 | 647.04 | 666.08 | 690.01 |
| 573.21 | 606.21 | 632.01 | 647.11 | 666.09 | 690.02 |
| 574.03 | 607.10 | 632.02 | 647.12 | 666.14 | 690.09 |
| 575.06 | 607.12 | 632.06 | 647.18 | 667.09 | 690.10 |
| 576.09 | 607.15 | 632.09 | 648.06 | 667.12 | 690.11 |
| 576.12 | 607.17 | 632.11 | 648.08 | 667.14 | 690.12 |
| 576.13 | 607.22 | 632.17 | 648.14 | 667.15 | 690.14 |
| 576.15 | 608.05 | 633.01 | 648.15 | 667.18 | 690.14 |
| 576.18 | 608.14 | 633.04 | 649.01 | 668.02 | 690.16 |
| 577.01 | 608.18 | 633.07 | 649.03 | 668.08 | 690.18 |
| 577.07 | 609.03 | 633.07 | 649.04 | 668.09 | 691.01 |
| 577.14 | 609.04 | 633.08 | 649.05 | 668.15 | 691.04 |
| 577.16 | 609.07 | 633.10 | 649.09 | 668.16 | 691.12 |
| 577.17 | 609.08 | 633.10 | 649.13 | 668.19 | 692.01 |
| 577.18 | 609.10 | 633.13 | 649.14 | 668.22 | 692.01 |
| 577.18 | 609.18 | 633.22 | 649.18 | 669.15 | 692.02 |
| 577.21 | 610.03 | 634.01 | 649.19 | 670.05 | 692.06 |
| 578.01 | 610.05 | 634.03 | 649.22 | 670.07 | 692.08 |
| 578.01 | 610.07 | 634.03 | 650.02 | 670.13 | 692.09 |
| 578.03 | 610.08 | 634.05 | 650.06 | 671.09 | 692.10 |
| 578.10 | 610.14 | 634.10 | 650.15 | 671.16 | 692.14 |
| 578.11 | 610.16 | 634.22 | 651.03 | 671.18 | 692.17 |
| 578.12 | 610.19 | 635.01 | 651.14 | 671.19 | 692.17 |
| 579.04 | 611.03 | 635.05 | 651.15 | 671.20 | 692.19 |
| 579.08 | 611.05 | 635.06 | 651.15 | 672.09 | 692.20 |
| 579.14 | 611.06 | 635.19 | 651.18 | 672.10 | 692.20 |
| 579.20 | 611.07 | 635.21 | 651.21 | 672.14 | 693.02 |
| 580.04 | 611.09 | 636.01 | 652.04 | 672.16 | 693.03 |
| 580.09 | 611.17 | 636.09 | 652.06 | 673.03 | 693.05 |
| 580.22 | 611.18 | 636.10 | 652.06 | 673.06 | 693.08 |
| 581.16 | 611.21 | 636.13 | 652.07 | 673.08 | 693.10 |
| 581.19 | 612.01 | 636.18 | 652.08 | 673.08 | 693.10 |
| 582.14 | 612.08 | 637.01 | 652.10 | 673.10 | 693.12 |
| 582.15 | 612.10 | 637.04 | 652.10 | 673.11 | 693.13 |
| 583.04 | 613.06 | 637.06 | 652.12 | 674.02 | 693.13 |
| 583.04 | 613.08 | 637.10 | 652.15 | 674.09 | 693.14 |
| 583.09 | 613.08 | 637.12 | 652.16 | 674.10 | 693.14 |
| 583.12 | 613.16 | 637.16 | 652.18 | 674.13 | 693.15 |
| 583.14 | 613.19 | 637.19 | 652.19 | 674.17 | 693.16 |
| 583.20 | 614.02 | 637.20 | 652.21 | 674.19 | 693.20 |
| 584.04 | 614.07 | 638.03 | 653.05 | 675.04 | 694.05 |
| 585.09 | 614.16 | 638.03 | 653.10 | 675.07 | 694.13 |
| 585.09 | 614.22 | 638.07 | 653.11 | 675.09 | 694.17 |
| 586.04 | 615.05 | 638.08 | 653.14 | 675.11 | 694.19 |
| 586.06 | 615.09 | 638.11 | 653.18 | 675.15 | 695.06 |
| 586.15 | 615.12 | 638.13 | 653.19 | 675.16 | 695.09 |
| 587.01 | 615.15 | 638.13 | 654.01 | 676.08 | 695.10 |
| 587.02 | 615.16 | 638.15 | 654.05 | 676.08 | 695.13 |
| 587.09 | 616.08 | 638.16 | 654.07 | 676.12 | 695.15 |
| 587.10 | 616.13 | 639.08 | 654.09 | 676.13 | 695.17 |
| 587.17 | 616.15 | 639.11 | 654.11 | 676.19 | 695.17 |
| 588.02 | 616.16 | 639.12 | 654.14 | 677.20 | 695.21 |
| 588.03 | 616.18 | 640.03 | 654.15 | 678.01 | 696.01 |
| 588.07 | 616.20 | 640.07 | 654.16 | 678.12 | 696.08 |
| 588.12 | 616.21 | 640.08 | 654.16 | 678.14 | 696.08 |
| 588.17 | 617.04 | 640.14 | 654.17 | 678.15 | 696.21 |
| 588.19 | 617.18 | 640.17 | 655.02 | 679.16 | 697.20 |
| 588.21 | 617.22 | 640.20 | 655.06 | 679.17 | 698.04 |
| 589.02 | 617.22 | 641.01 | 655.10 | 679.19 | 698.06 |
| 589.11 | 618.06 | 641.02 | 655.11 | 680.02 | 699.02 |
| 589.22 | 618.10 | 641.04 | 655.11 | 680.06 | 699.17 |
| 591.10 | 618.19 | 641.06 | 655.12 | 680.17 | 700.07 |
| 592.05 | 619.04 | 641.06 | 655.12 | 681.03 | 700.13 |
| 593.05 | 619.17 | 641.10 | 655.19 | 681.03 | 700.16 |
| 593.07 | 620.03 | 641.12 | 655.20 | 681.05 | 700.19 |
| 593.15 | 621.11 | 641.15 | 656.20 | 681.15 | 700.22 |
| 593.18 | 621.18 | 641.16 | 656.21 | 681.19 | 701.02 |
| 593.18 | 621.18 | 641.17 | 657.01 | 682.03 | 701.05 |
| 594.12 | 621.20 | 641.17 | 657.03 | 682.06 | 701.06 |
| 595.06 | 621.22 | 641.19 | 658.02 | 682.06 | 701.06 |
| 596.03 | 622.09 | 641.21 | 658.03 | 682.07 | 701.07 |
| 596.04 | 622.14 | 641.22 | 658.06 | 682.09 | 701.16 |
| 596.06 | 622.17 | 642.01 | 658.07 | 682.10 | 701.17 |
| 596.09 | 622.20 | 642.06 | 659.12 | 682.13 | 702.08 |
| 596.12 | 622.22 | 642.06 | 659.14 | 682.14 | 702.13 |
| 597.03 | 623.01 | 642.07 | 659.15 | 682.16 | 703.07 |
| 597.04 | 623.04 | 642.10 | 659.19 | 683.02 | 703.11 |
| 597.12 | 623.05 | 642.11 | 659.20 | 683.03 | 703.18 |
| 597.21 | 623.11 | 642.12 | 659.21 | 683.04 | 703.20 |
| 598.03 | 623.12 | 643.02 | 660.06 | 683.06 | 704.01 |
| 598.05 | 623.18 | 643.02 | 660.06 | 683.11 | 704.06 |
| 598.08 | 624.01 | 643.03 | 660.09 | 683.13 | 704.06 |
| 598.10 | 624.05 | 643.05 | 660.12 | 683.14 | 704.08 |
| 598.11 | 624.05 | 643.07 | 660.20 | 684.01 | 704.10 |
| 598.14 | 624.15 | 643.09 | 661.01 | 684.04 | 704.12 |
| 598.18 | 624.21 | 644.02 | 661.08 | 684.10 | 704.13 |
| 598.20 | 624.22 | 644.05 | 661.21 | 684.11 | 704.19 |
| 598.21 | 624.22 | 644.07 | 662.04 | 685.01 | 704.20 |
| 599.01 | 626.02 | 644.08 | 662.04 | 685.04 | 704.21 |
| 599.10 | 626.04 | 644.13 | 662.06 | 685.18 | 705.02 |
| 600.16 | 626.04 | 644.15 | 662.07 | 686.02 | 705.03 |
| 601.03 | 626.11 | 644.16 | 662.13 | 686.11 | 705.11 |
| 601.15 | 627.03 | 644.17 | 662.14 | 686.13 | 705.12 |
| 601.20 | 627.11 | 644.18 | 663.07 | 686.16 | 705.13 |
| 602.07 | 627.12 | 644.20 | 663.07 | 686.19 | 705.16 |
| 602.17 | 627.18 | 644.20 | 663.09 | 687.03 | 705.19 |
| 602.20 | 627.19 | 644.21 | 663.12 | 687.04 | 705.20 |
| 602.22 | 627.21 | 645.01 | 663.15 | 688.03 | 706.01 |
| 603.03 | 628.02 | 645.01 | 663.18 | 688.03 | 706.17 |
| 603.05 | 628.02 | 645.02 | 664.01 | 688.06 | 707.01 |
| 603.08 | 628.06 | 645.02 | 664.11 | 689.09 | 707.16 |
| 603.09 | 628.08 | 645.03 | 664.13 | 689.12 | 708.16 |
| 603.19 | 628.15 | 645.05 | 664.15 | 689.13 | 708.22 |
| 604.05 | 628.18 | 645.07 | 665.02 | 689.15 | 709.03 |
| 604.09 | 628.20 | 645.12 | 665.03 | 689.15 | 709.09 |
| 604.12 | 628.22 | 645.18 | 665.07 | 689.16 | 709.11 |
| 604.13 | 628.22 | 645.22 | 665.07 | 689.18 | 709.18 |
| 604.16 | 629.05 | 646.02 | 665.16 | 689.19 | 710.06 |
| 605.02 | 629.06 | 646.07 | 665.18 | 689.20 | 710.11 |
| 605.18 | 630.19 | 646.08 | 665.22 | 689.21 | 710.16 |

| | | | | | |
|---|---|---|---|---|---|
| 710.16 | 734.10 | 753.09 | 321.15 | 415.11 | 130.02 |
| 710.17 | 734.17 | 753.22 | 565.13 | 424.04 | 130.04 |
| 711.10 | 735.04 | 754.03 | **theafe** | 427.13 | 130.15 |
| 711.11 | 735.06 | 754.04 | 712.17 | 440.21 | 131.16 |
| 711.17 | 735.06 | 754.04 | **thee** | 441.06 | 131.18 |
| 711.18 | 736.10 | 754.13 | 092.09 | 442.12 | 133.03 |
| 711.19 | 736.11 | 754.15 | 092.12 | 443.13 | 146.19 |
| 711.20 | 737.01 | 754.15 | 164.08 | 445.08 | 152.07 |
| 711.22 | 737.03 | 754.17 | 164.18 | 445.17 | 160.09 |
| 712.04 | 737.04 | 754.18 | 245.01 | 448.11 | 160.14 |
| 712.05 | 737.05 | 755.03 | 246.07 | 452.07 | 164.15 |
| 712.09 | 737.06 | 755.03 | 439.06 | 461.12 | 165.06 |
| 712.10 | 737.10 | 755.09 | 468.01 | 470.01 | 175.02 |
| 712.12 | 737.10 | 755.10 | 468.03 | 470.02 | 183.22 |
| 712.13 | 737.10 | 755.11 | 497.19 | 470.02 | 191.03 |
| 712.14 | 737.14 | 755.12 | 564.03 | 479.03 | 191.08 |
| 713.03 | 737.15 | 755.14 | 565.16 | 485.06 | 205.13 |
| 713.15 | 737.16 | 755.15 | **their** | 517.19 | 213.14 |
| 713.20 | 737.18 | 755.19 | 002.01 | 518.11 | 219.03 |
| 713.21 | 738.15 | 755.19 | 004.13 | 536.10 | 219.18 |
| 713.23 | 738.15 | 756.07 | 010.09 | 536.11 | 221.16 |
| 714.03 | 738.18 | 756.12 | 022.05 | 536.14 | 226.17 |
| 714.04 | 738.21 | 756.14 | 023.14 | 556.09 | 230.04 |
| 715.02 | 739.08 | 756.14 | 032.19 | 560.03 | 230.05 |
| 715.05 | 739.16 | 756.20 | 034.17 | 579.11 | 230.05 |
| 715.09 | 739.19 | 757.01 | 034.18 | 583.02 | 235.04 |
| 716.03 | 740.10 | 757.03 | 034.20 | 585.03 | 237.08 |
| 716.04 | 740.13 | 757.05 | 035.01 | 587.03 | 238.12 |
| 716.06 | 740.15 | 757.06 | 035.03 | 619.18 | 245.15 |
| 716.08 | 740.15 | 757.06 | 041.09 | 619.19 | 252.19 |
| 716.09 | 740.17 | 757.13 | 048.02 | 635.02 | 254.03 |
| 716.10 | 741.07 | 757.14 | 050.07 | 635.03 | 257.17 |
| 716.12 | 741.09 | 757.20 | 057.14 | 639.10 | 260.20 |
| 716.13 | 741.11 | 757.22 | 057.14 | 642.08 | 261.04 |
| 716.21 | 741.12 | 758.01 | 064.08 | 662.11 | 264.22 |
| 717.07 | 741.13 | 758.02 | 065.11 | 679.18 | 265.20 |
| 717.11 | 741.19 | 758.05 | 066.14 | 695.13 | 275.04 |
| 717.16 | 742.09 | 758.19 | 078.11 | 699.04 | 276.03 |
| 717.18 | 742.15 | 758.22 | 079.11 | 701.04 | 278.10 |
| 718.14 | 742.17 | 759.02 | 080.01 | 712.01 | 282.22 |
| 718.16 | 742.20 | 759.02 | 093.05 | 713.19 | 284.15 |
| 718.20 | 743.04 | 759.04 | 095.12 | 714.05 | 287.18 |
| 719.01 | 743.04 | 759.07 | 095.19 | 726.14 | 292.14 |
| 719.03 | 743.06 | 759.07 | 099.13 | 727.06 | 292.18 |
| 719.06 | 743.11 | 759.08 | 100.04 | 727.19 | 295.10 |
| 720.06 | 743.13 | 759.10 | 100.10 | 727.20 | 295.11 |
| 721.01 | 743.13 | 759.17 | 102.21 | 728.04 | 298.15 |
| 721.04 | 743.14 | 759.17 | 102.22 | 728.06 | 299.03 |
| 721.07 | 743.15 | 759.21 | 103.02 | 729.16 | 299.11 |
| 721.10 | 743.15 | 759.22 | 103.04 | 730.02 | 302.18 |
| 721.12 | 743.16 | 760.01 | 104.20 | 749.16 | 302.19 |
| 721.13 | 743.16 | 760.01 | 104.22 | 755.13 | 308.02 |
| 721.17 | 743.18 | 760.03 | 107.18 | 759.03 | 308.19 |
| 722.03 | 743.19 | 760.03 | 108.07 | 760.12 | 313.14 |
| 722.07 | 743.22 | 760.04 | 110.17 | 762.20 | 323.09 |
| 722.10 | 744.01 | 760.05 | 115.07 | **theirs** | 323.12 |
| 722.11 | 744.05 | 760.06 | 119.04 | 095.01 | 324.12 |
| 722.15 | 744.07 | 760.08 | 124.15 | 322.14 | 338.12 |
| 722.19 | 744.11 | 760.11 | 126.12 | 747.02 | 344.08 |
| 723.07 | 744.11 | 760.14 | 126.17 | **theirseln** | 344.10 |
| 723.20 | 744.15 | 760.15 | 130.01 | 719.15 | 350.18 |
| 724.02 | 744.18 | 760.17 | 133.04 | **them** | 355.02 |
| 724.19 | 744.20 | 760.21 | 136.06 | 012.01 | 357.19 |
| 724.20 | 744.22 | 761.01 | 146.20 | 012.18 | 375.16 |
| 725.06 | 745.02 | 761.01 | 158.01 | 017.18 | 375.17 |
| 725.07 | 745.05 | 761.04 | 185.14 | 020.02 | 379.08 |
| 725.13 | 745.07 | 761.06 | 193.16 | 028.06 | 379.10 |
| 725.21 | 745.20 | 761.11 | 215.08 | 035.14 | 395.04 |
| 726.10 | 746.07 | 761.12 | 217.03 | 038.15 | 408.21 |
| 726.21 | 746.09 | 761.14 | 217.10 | 042.16 | 408.21 |
| 727.01 | 746.11 | 761.15 | 219.16 | 048.08 | 415.12 |
| 727.07 | 746.13 | 761.16 | 220.01 | 053.07 | 415.19 |
| 727.07 | 746.14 | 761.18 | 220.02 | 055.17 | 427.06 |
| 727.09 | 746.17 | 761.21 | 231.21 | 064.08 | 427.19 |
| 727.11 | 746.22 | 762.01 | 238.01 | 067.19 | 428.01 |
| 727.13 | 747.02 | 762.07 | 240.06 | 073.11 | 431.21 |
| 727.13 | 747.04 | 762.09 | 255.08 | 076.06 | 433.12 |
| 727.18 | 747.09 | 762.09 | 263.02 | 077.08 | 433.14 |
| 727.20 | 747.11 | 762.11 | 263.21 | 077.13 | 437.18 |
| 728.02 | 747.13 | 762.14 | 264.07 | 079.12 | 439.03 |
| 728.08 | 747.14 | 762.17 | 273.21 | 080.01 | 440.12 |
| 728.10 | 747.16 | 762.18 | 275.05 | 082.07 | 445.18 |
| 728.12 | 747.17 | 762.20 | 284.04 | 083.03 | 449.08 |
| 728.18 | 748.18 | 763.01 | 294.16 | 084.08 | 454.04 |
| 728.20 | 748.22 | 763.02 | 295.18 | 091.11 | 464.18 |
| 728.22 | 749.05 | 763.05 | 296.16 | 094.13 | 472.03 |
| 729.01 | 749.07 | 763.07 | 299.02 | 095.15 | 475.18 |
| 729.07 | 749.16 | 763.08 | 308.03 | 100.21 | 480.02 |
| 729.10 | 750.01 | 763.12 | 311.10 | 101.06 | 481.07 |
| 729.13 | 750.02 | 763.15 | 314.03 | 101.07 | 481.09 |
| 729.15 | 750.03 | 763.15 | 323.08 | 101.12 | 486.06 |
| 729.18 | 750.04 | 763.19 | 330.22 | 101.16 | 488.07 |
| 729.19 | 750.05 | 763.20 | 341.14 | 101.22 | 493.16 |
| 729.20 | 750.06 | 763.22 | 343.05 | 104.21 | 495.14 |
| 730.01 | 750.10 | 764.01 | 344.10 | 105.05 | 499.02 |
| 730.02 | 750.16 | 764.01 | 351.22 | 106.04 | 503.11 |
| 730.08 | 750.17 | 764.01 | 352.16 | 107.16 | 505.02 |
| 730.08 | 750.19 | 764.03 | 364.05 | 108.03 | 507.19 |
| 730.19 | 750.20 | 764.07 | 373.20 | 109.04 | 508.10 |
| 731.08 | 751.01 | 764.07 | 377.01 | 111.18 | 508.18 |
| 731.10 | 751.04 | 764.08 | 380.06 | 115.01 | 508.19 |
| 731.12 | 751.05 | 764.09 | 389.04 | 115.08 | 510.16 |
| 731.15 | 751.07 | 764.11 | 392.01 | 119.06 | 510.18 |
| 731.16 | 751.08 | **the'** | 395.04 | 120.10 | 511.05 |
| 731.18 | 751.17 | 233.06 | 402.21 | 124.16 | 512.07 |
| 731.20 | 751.18 | **thear** | 404.15 | 125.07 | 512.09 |
| 732.03 | 751.20 | 028.21 | 406.13 | 125.18 | 512.10 |
| 732.10 | 752.10 | 319.07 | 407.07 | 126.15 | 512.14 |
| 733.02 | 752.10 | 319.09 | 414.17 | 126.15 | 513.02 |
| 734.01 | 752.17 | 319.11 | 414.20 | 127.08 | 513.10 |
| | 753.08 | 321.04 | 415.06 | 127.18 | 514.01 |

| | | | | | |
|---|---|---|---|---|---|
| 514.13 | 073.02 | 363.03 | 659.18 | 148.02 | 420.14 |
| 522.12 | 074.18 | 367.13 | 660.11 | 148.20 | 421.14 |
| 524.15 | 076.13 | 372.05 | 661.09 | 149.19 | 427.20 |
| 534.03 | 076.20 | 374.20 | 661.10 | 150.13 | 432.13 |
| 534.07 | 077.07 | 377.01 | 664.02 | 155.02 | 434.03 |
| 561.06 | 079.11 | 378.03 | 674.02 | 159.16 | 437.06 |
| 575.06 | 084.13 | 381.05 | 676.11 | 160.04 | 439.11 |
| 581.12 | 085.03 | 385.14 | 679.17 | 163.01 | 440.06 |
| 583.01 | 085.19 | 387.02 | 679.21 | 165.17 | 444.03 |
| 587.09 | 088.14 | 393.08 | 681.16 | 170.17 | 446.20 |
| 591.11 | 092.13 | 394.09 | 691.01 | 172.18 | 451.02 |
| 608.16 | 093.05 | 399.17 | 694.08 | 173.15 | 454.11 |
| 610.03 | 094.01 | 402.06 | 695.12 | 174.05 | 456.02 |
| 631.10 | 095.07 | 404.14 | 695.19 | 174.21 | 457.08 |
| 632.16 | 097.13 | 405.20 | 698.07 | 175.03 | 462.01 |
| 633.03 | 105.22 | 405.21 | 699.10 | 178.08 | 466.02 |
| 637.15 | 106.04 | 409.04 | 702.03 | 178.12 | 472.01 |
| 640.08 | 111.03 | 410.08 | 703.09 | 179.06 | 474.08 |
| 646.15 | 112.05 | 410.18 | 708.13 | 182.13 | 475.17 |
| 646.15 | 115.05 | 416.20 | 709.12 | 187.02 | 476.11 |
| 651.19 | 116.18 | 418.14 | 710.17 | 189.01 | 478.02 |
| 654.20 | 119.20 | 428.02 | 717.17 | 190.15 | 480.10 |
| 656.20 | 120.19 | 430.17 | 718.17 | 192.12 | 481.09 |
| 657.04 | 121.14 | 431.06 | 723.12 | 199.11 | 483.21 |
| 662.02 | 121.21 | 432.19 | 724.05 | 204.13 | 485.03 |
| 662.07 | 123.18 | 434.07 | 725.20 | 206.19 | 487.09 |
| 664.18 | 128.05 | 438.07 | 728.13 | 211.06 | 488.05 |
| 665.13 | 130.13 | 439.20 | 729.01 | 211.19 | 494.16 |
| 668.03 | 131.04 | 441.21 | 733.10 | 216.12 | 496.05 |
| 668.12 | 132.11 | 444.01 | 735.07 | 219.21 | 496.22 |
| 671.16 | 137.21 | 446.10 | 737.03 | 221.11 | 497.01 |
| 675.05 | 140.20 | 449.21 | 738.12 | 221.15 | 504.10 |
| 675.06 | 149.03 | 452.13 | 740.16 | 222.09 | 505.19 |
| 677.19 | 149.22 | 453.09 | 741.06 | 228.06 | 508.07 |
| 678.03 | 151.01 | 454.11 | 741.15 | 233.20 | 517.10 |
| 678.13 | 151.07 | 460.21 | 744.21 | 234.03 | 518.06 |
| 678.15 | 156.06 | 463.20 | 745.15 | 241.07 | 520.08 |
| 678.16 | 156.17 | 464.12 | 747.16 | 243.19 | 523.12 |
| 678.19 | 156.20 | 465.20 | 753.10 | 249.07 | 525.14 |
| 680.15 | 164.16 | 467.21 | 756.03 | 251.11 | 531.16 |
| 681.09 | 172.12 | 468.18 | 757.17 | 260.03 | 533.15 |
| 681.10 | 173.03 | 473.09 | 759.20 | 261.03 | 539.04 |
| 681.11 | 176.19 | 476.22 | 762.01 | 265.17 | 542.04 |
| 681.12 | 177.20 | 481.20 | 762.06 | 266.10 | 542.05 |
| 681.13 | 179.20 | 486.12 | thence | 276.10 | 553.02 |
| 682.10 | 184.10 | 487.19 | 103.20 | 276.22 | 555.12 |
| 682.16 | 188.18 | 489.16 | 260.01 | 277.08 | 558.18 |
| 683.05 | 188.18 | 489.19 | 491.07 | 277.16 | 562.05 |
| 686.08 | 191.16 | 492.22 | thenceforth | 278.18 | 564.02 |
| 693.21 | 191.17 | 500.15 | 098.15 | 281.07 | 566.05 |
| 693.21 | 193.21 | 501.01 | 282.13 | 282.06 | 570.03 |
| 696.12 | 196.07 | 503.14 | 514.14 | 283.21 | 577.02 |
| 699.01 | 197.18 | 504.04 | 711.20 | 284.18 | 585.10 |
| 699.03 | 199.17 | 505.06 | 726.04 | 287.15 | 588.04 |
| 699.11 | 205.11 | 506.08 | theology | 291.10 | 588.19 |
| 712.02 | 213.13 | 512.07 | 678.08 | 291.15 | 592.19 |
| 715.11 | 215.05 | 512.21 | ther | 292.10 | 597.22 |
| 716.08 | 216.07 | 516.12 | 688.11 | 295.09 | 600.11 |
| 718.10 | 217.02 | 526.03 | there | 303.01 | 604.17 |
| 721.06 | 220.05 | 528.15 | 004.08 | 303.12 | 604.20 |
| 726.15 | 220.07 | 536.03 | 016.08 | 305.04 | 605.16 |
| 726.17 | 229.08 | 537.14 | 019.19 | 306.15 | 607.07 |
| 727.18 | 230.21 | 538.17 | 020.21 | 312.15 | 613.12 |
| 732.13 | 233.03 | 541.01 | 022.07 | 313.12 | 616.09 |
| 740.15 | 236.19 | 542.04 | 024.13 | 315.05 | 617.18 |
| 747.05 | 242.07 | 542.17 | 028.10 | 319.01 | 619.22 |
| 757.15 | 245.13 | 543.08 | 030.22 | 322.15 | 622.02 |
| 760.08 | 246.01 | 547.10 | 031.17 | 323.01 | 622.20 |
| 760.12 | 247.01 | 551.01 | 031.19 | 326.19 | 624.21 |
| 762.15 | 247.11 | 551.13 | 035.09 | 330.03 | 626.09 |
| 763.04 | 249.02 | 552.21 | 036.02 | 330.15 | 629.21 |
| 764.06 | 250.17 | 555.08 | 037.06 | 330.20 | 631.08 |
| themes | 267.04 | 555.10 | 037.09 | 334.05 | 631.16 |
| 582.14 | 271.07 | 556.01 | 039.02 | 334.12 | 634.17 |
| themselves | 274.03 | 558.09 | 042.11 | 341.13 | 640.08 |
| 002.03 | 274.12 | 565.02 | 043.14 | 342.10 | 641.06 |
| 079.09 | 278.07 | 566.09 | 047.04 | 344.02 | 643.11 |
| 100.06 | 282.02 | 567.05 | 047.16 | 346.12 | 645.06 |
| 104.09 | 285.02 | 570.22 | 053.09 | 346.22 | 647.19 |
| 123.04 | 285.12 | 572.20 | 060.01 | 350.14 | 648.19 |
| 136.09 | 289.19 | 576.08 | 060.20 | 351.11 | 649.16 |
| 160.16 | 298.01 | 579.16 | 063.05 | 352.09 | 650.01 |
| 374.09 | 298.07 | 580.17 | 063.19 | 354.09 | 650.11 |
| 401.20 | 303.13 | 580.22 | 064.07 | 356.06 | 651.11 |
| 450.17 | 304.09 | 586.04 | 066.13 | 356.07 | 651.19 |
| 693.19 | 305.18 | 586.17 | 066.21 | 361.02 | 652.14 |
| 725.06 | 308.19 | 588.05 | 070.11 | 365.21 | 652.21 |
| then | 311.18 | 592.13 | 076.11 | 366.04 | 653.07 |
| 003.07 | 312.06 | 601.11 | 077.05 | 366.09 | 654.14 |
| 009.21 | 315.01 | 606.18 | 079.03 | 367.12 | 669.10 |
| 022.12 | 317.06 | 612.20 | 080.05 | 371.20 | 671.12 |
| 024.22 | 319.11 | 618.11 | 080.07 | 373.13 | 674.11 |
| 031.05 | 320.15 | 620.02 | 094.11 | 376.17 | 676.16 |
| 031.21 | 320.21 | 622.17 | 095.21 | 378.06 | 676.16 |
| 033.16 | 322.05 | 623.11 | 097.10 | 379.01 | 684.05 |
| 034.21 | 324.07 | 623.21 | 099.01 | 381.08 | 684.07 |
| 036.11 | 324.13 | 630.17 | 100.12 | 382.03 | 685.02 |
| 039.03 | 325.13 | 632.19 | 102.01 | 383.03 | 689.18 |
| 042.09 | 334.21 | 634.03 | 102.06 | 385.16 | 691.05 |
| 043.14 | 334.22 | 635.21 | 104.08 | 388.19 | 691.10 |
| 044.15 | 335.18 | 637.08 | 105.21 | 390.20 | 693.19 |
| 047.03 | 337.02 | 639.03 | 108.03 | 393.05 | 695.22 |
| 051.06 | 344.12 | 639.13 | 111.20 | 398.10 | 697.11 |
| 057.13 | 347.07 | 646.04 | 113.11 | 399.01 | 697.21 |
| 059.13 | 351.18 | 649.03 | 114.18 | 400.10 | 703.22 |
| 061.16 | 352.16 | 650.02 | 120.07 | 401.05 | 705.05 |
| 063.16 | 352.21 | 650.20 | 129.15 | 402.03 | 714.05 |
| 066.22 | 355.02 | 653.14 | 129.15 | 411.09 | 716.09 |
| 070.19 | 356.01 | 653.18 | 140.08 | 415.19 | 717.14 |
| 072.12 | 359.14 | 653.22 | 141.18 | 417.03 | 721.09 |
| 072.16 | 361.20 | 656.04 | 142.14 | 419.21 | 727.16 |

| | | | | | |
|---|---|---|---|---|---|
| 728.21 | 010.10 | 238.12 | 552.07 | thickly | 027.21 |
| 730.04 | 011.06 | 239.12 | 567.12 | 016.17 | 043.04 |
| 733.17 | 012.04 | 239.14 | 582.01 | thief | 052.11 |
| 742.12 | 018.12 | 240.01 | 583.01 | 107.19 | 073.16 |
| 744.14 | 019.14 | 240.01 | 587.11 | 391.15 | 089.02 |
| 746.18 | 019.15 | 240.06 | 588.05 | thin | 103.03 |
| 746.19 | 019.17 | 252.18 | 600.04 | 097.20 | 120.02 |
| 750.13 | 023.10 | 252.18 | 603.02 | 383.18 | 125.13 |
| 751.17 | 023.13 | 261.02 | 603.11 | 565.03 | 137.10 |
| 756.03 | 023.13 | 261.04 | 612.10 | 627.04 | 141.09 |
| 756.08 | 024.15 | 261.09 | 615.21 | 690.12 | 148.01 |
| 757.16 | 028.02 | 262.19 | 624.08 | thing | 149.03 |
| 760.13 | 031.09 | 263.16 | 627.11 | 072.11 | 164.10 |
| 763.19 | 034.19 | 264.07 | 627.21 | 079.19 | 175.20 |
| there'd | 037.09 | 270.10 | 627.21 | 094.19 | 181.17 |
| 505.07 | 039.07 | 270.11 | 632.19 | 096.03 | 182.04 |
| there's | 042.11 | 271.20 | 633.01 | 100.13 | 194.03 |
| 107.13 | 048.13 | 273.18 | 633.02 | 108.17 | 199.18 |
| 121.04 | 050.20 | 273.19 | 635.03 | 128.06 | 203.22 |
| 135.03 | 067.15 | 273.20 | 637.13 | 159.22 | 215.15 |
| 164.17 | 067.17 | 275.09 | 646.15 | 162.10 | 215.20 |
| 190.13 | 067.17 | 276.02 | 651.12 | 177.14 | 219.17 |
| 208.16 | 067.19 | 276.16 | 652.12 | 218.09 | 221.03 |
| 230.11 | 072.02 | 280.14 | 654.04 | 223.14 | 231.01 |
| 238.04 | 072.22 | 281.16 | 654.04 | 237.15 | 233.15 |
| 254.10 | 073.09 | 284.18 | 658.08 | 259.11 | 237.07 |
| 260.18 | 077.09 | 287.12 | 660.16 | 270.20 | 239.18 |
| 276.08 | 078.11 | 296.16 | 665.17 | 283.21 | 250.08 |
| 278.03 | 079.22 | 296.18 | 668.04 | 330.20 | 252.03 |
| 292.09 | 080.14 | 298.14 | 668.14 | 339.21 | 254.09 |
| 353.15 | 084.06 | 299.01 | 678.14 | 340.13 | 255.21 |
| 400.22 | 094.14 | 299.01 | 682.12 | 345.19 | 258.10 |
| 452.17 | 094.22 | 302.21 | 682.13 | 360.20 | 271.19 |
| 494.06 | 095.13 | 306.03 | 690.13 | 370.05 | 273.03 |
| 496.21 | 095.14 | 306.18 | 695.12 | 385.10 | 276.21 |
| 518.17 | 095.19 | 306.18 | 695.14 | 412.08 | 293.22 |
| 526.01 | 097.12 | 306.19 | 697.21 | 414.03 | 303.16 |
| 617.18 | 098.09 | 307.22 | 699.04 | 421.09 | 318.15 |
| 698.10 | 099.01 | 323.06 | 704.05 | 424.12 | 322.12 |
| thereat | 099.21 | 351.14 | 711.22 | 429.11 | 324.19 |
| 053.15 | 100.02 | 351.16 | 713.22 | 432.05 | 326.10 |
| 676.03 | 100.02 | 356.13 | 716.01 | 449.02 | 329.02 |
| therefore | 100.03 | 356.14 | 716.17 | 462.13 | 334.08 |
| 026.14 | 100.06 | 361.19 | 719.14 | 465.02 | 338.20 |
| 115.19 | 100.16 | 361.20 | 726.13 | 467.04 | 349.09 |
| 136.02 | 100.17 | 361.22 | 726.18 | 469.05 | 352.03 |
| 264.04 | 100.18 | 364.05 | 727.10 | 470.15 | 357.01 |
| 304.01 | 101.03 | 366.09 | 728.04 | 490.12 | 359.18 |
| 388.05 | 101.09 | 371.17 | 728.07 | 491.20 | 361.05 |
| 399.08 | 101.17 | 374.01 | 734.06 | 506.08 | 372.16 |
| 406.01 | 102.06 | 380.04 | 734.13 | 517.06 | 385.03 |
| 451.18 | 103.03 | 391.03 | 747.03 | 534.21 | 387.11 |
| 478.12 | 103.06 | 395.03 | 749.15 | 539.02 | 387.13 |
| 489.03 | 103.07 | 404.09 | 752.15 | 542.16 | 391.16 |
| 547.15 | 103.20 | 412.06 | 755.02 | 548.20 | 398.21 |
| 715.04 | 104.10 | 412.06 | 755.06 | 566.09 | 404.11 |
| 751.05 | 104.21 | 412.07 | 758.09 | 593.13 | 412.07 |
| thereto | 105.21 | 412.10 | 758.09 | 603.14 | 415.15 |
| 694.01 | 106.02 | 414.18 | 760.05 | 611.02 | 416.08 |
| these | 106.10 | 414.21 | 761.20 | 633.04 | 434.10 |
| 007.06 | 107.18 | 415.10 | 762.01 | 634.08 | 435.16 |
| 018.15 | 108.02 | 425.18 | 762.04 | 652.17 | 455.09 |
| 022.05 | 108.21 | 427.12 | 762.09 | 656.13 | 463.12 |
| 032.03 | 109.02 | 427.15 | 762.19 | 659.14 | 471.17 |
| 036.03 | 110.18 | 427.17 | 762.21 | 660.12 | 482.14 |
| 049.07 | 111.01 | 427.19 | 763.01 | 700.18 | 483.04 |
| 056.22 | 111.08 | 428.05 | 763.08 | 722.07 | 485.16 |
| 057.03 | 111.16 | 429.11 | they'll | 745.21 | 486.14 |
| 061.13 | 115.01 | 431.10 | 028.05 | 760.20 | 488.20 |
| 066.08 | 115.09 | 434.10 | 181.06 | things | 490.08 |
| 082.04 | 119.06 | 438.06 | 319.08 | 079.07 | 494.03 |
| 084.07 | 124.21 | 440.20 | 363.02 | 105.04 | 496.14 |
| 086.04 | 126.12 | 440.21 | 363.02 | 114.15 | 500.18 |
| 098.05 | 126.22 | 445.07 | 454.15 | 121.16 | 503.11 |
| 119.11 | 127.19 | 445.17 | they're | 132.09 | 511.08 |
| 134.05 | 127.21 | 450.03 | 476.15 | 133.09 | 511.16 |
| 136.03 | 129.21 | 450.04 | 688.10 | 136.10 | 526.03 |
| 140.01 | 131.13 | 450.05 | they's | 155.13 | 526.16 |
| 155.13 | 131.19 | 450.16 | 016.10 | 172.18 | 535.16 |
| 180.15 | 131.22 | 450.18 | 043.02 | 180.15 | 543.06 |
| 201.04 | 136.08 | 451.14 | 298.07 | 191.10 | 562.02 |
| 203.15 | 152.07 | 455.08 | 318.11 | 196.17 | 570.09 |
| 216.08 | 152.08 | 464.19 | 320.13 | 239.08 | 572.02 |
| 242.02 | 152.13 | 465.07 | 320.14 | 242.02 | 573.10 |
| 263.14 | 152.15 | 467.04 | 321.03 | 243.20 | 575.04 |
| 272.14 | 155.10 | 469.18 | 324.04 | 287.09 | 576.22 |
| 273.13 | 158.01 | 473.09 | 326.08 | 291.15 | 589.13 |
| 288.21 | 167.14 | 475.19 | 627.14 | 292.15 | 589.21 |
| 302.20 | 175.03 | 479.03 | 691.09 | 338.04 | 592.13 |
| 344.08 | 178.22 | 479.05 | 696.18 | 353.14 | 603.16 |
| 391.02 | 185.11 | 487.02 | 761.08 | 384.06 | 615.10 |
| 397.16 | 185.13 | 488.07 | they've | 387.09 | 618.14 |
| 415.15 | 194.03 | 494.12 | 176.22 | 411.07 | 618.15 |
| 427.04 | 204.10 | 495.14 | thible | 415.15 | 620.03 |
| 429.09 | 204.16 | 498.12 | 319.02 | 440.12 | 631.04 |
| 455.11 | 205.12 | 501.06 | thick | 442.10 | 634.06 |
| 484.04 | 205.18 | 502.21 | 021.04 | 530.08 | 634.07 |
| 487.10 | 208.06 | 504.17 | 022.02 | 572.21 | 652.02 |
| 488.01 | 209.04 | 505.03 | 080.18 | 575.02 | 666.20 |
| 518.01 | 209.06 | 507.22 | 115.21 | 627.14 | 677.04 |
| 530.07 | 209.18 | 508.05 | 124.12 | 628.18 | 681.10 |
| 575.02 | 211.04 | 508.15 | 271.15 | 648.20 | 684.14 |
| 589.17 | 215.08 | 508.16 | 293.14 | 675.03 | 697.08 |
| 616.15 | 218.20 | 515.08 | 351.06 | 685.19 | 698.01 |
| 712.16 | 219.14 | 520.03 | 468.05 | 732.21 | 702.15 |
| 732.07 | 219.15 | 528.01 | 669.01 | 734.18 | 708.04 |
| 750.03 | 219.21 | 533.19 | 726.13 | 748.19 | 730.12 |
| 752.18 | 219.22 | 534.07 | 752.02 | 750.02 | 730.17 |
| they | 232.02 | 536.15 | thickening | think | 739.12 |
| 004.08 | 232.04 | 544.13 | 364.14 | 003.01 | 755.21 |
| 005.12 | 238.09 | | | 011.06 | 757.19 |

| | | | | |
|---|---|---|---|---|
| thinking | 180.09 | 391.09 | 733.19 | thou´rt |
| 017.11 | 182.10 | 392.03 | 734.22 | 092.09 |
| 095.02 | 182.16 | 394.08 | 739.14 | though |
| 115.07 | 184.15 | 396.10 | 742.10 | 003.17 |
| 134.04 | 186.14 | 400.22 | 742.12 | 011.07 |
| 289.03 | 187.22 | 401.12 | 744.03 | 040.04 |
| 310.15 | 190.16 | 402.09 | 751.14 | 059.22 |
| 331.17 | 190.22 | 403.08 | 760.15 | 061.03 |
| 353.10 | 195.03 | 403.12 | 761.19 | 064.16 |
| 479.10 | 199.22 | 404.20 | thither | 076.18 |
| 518.13 | 201.06 | 411.05 | 347.15 | 077.21 |
| 539.20 | 202.02 | 417.02 | 429.01 | 082.18 |
| 567.18 | 202.08 | 417.12 | thorn | 083.10 |
| 618.03 | 204.02 | 419.20 | 204.11 | 088.19 |
| 648.06 | 209.14 | 420.06 | 204.13 | 095.13 |
| 663.12 | 215.19 | 421.09 | thorns | 097.08 |
| 761.15 | 216.03 | 422.02 | 004.13 | 101.15 |
| thinks | 217.14 | 422.06 | thorough | 106.16 |
| 332.01 | 217.17 | 428.16 | 331.03 | 109.03 |
| 345.16 | 223.01 | 430.06 | thoroughly | 123.10 |
| 556.03 | 223.19 | 431.04 | 113.04 | 141.13 |
| 614.03 | 225.12 | 432.10 | 190.02 | 145.11 |
| 628.14 | 228.21 | 432.22 | 236.13 | 149.18 |
| 658.10 | 230.03 | 434.10 | 413.13 | 182.03 |
| thinner | 233.01 | 435.02 | 467.10 | 186.04 |
| 587.14 | 233.22 | 436.07 | 530.05 | 186.19 |
| third | 236.08 | 437.21 | 541.13 | 189.12 |
| 027.12 | 238.20 | 438.17 | 601.17 | 194.21 |
| 077.03 | 239.23 | 439.21 | those | 196.11 |
| 155.04 | 244.09 | 440.03 | 008.06 | 196.13 |
| 235.03 | 244.20 | 442.01 | 012.01 | 214.08 |
| 270.15 | 245.19 | 445.03 | 021.07 | 219.17 |
| 326.12 | 248.05 | 451.20 | 025.19 | 222.14 |
| 385.12 | 250.11 | 452.06 | 027.12 | 224.02 |
| 551.20 | 252.10 | 453.22 | 028.04 | 225.09 |
| 568.08 | 254.02 | 459.02 | 031.20 | 225.18 |
| 694.05 | 254.12 | 469.05 | 057.12 | 240.02 |
| thirsty | 254.21 | 474.10 | 067.07 | 248.09 |
| 216.21 | 255.17 | 477.04 | 070.13 | 266.12 |
| 612.20 | 257.01 | 478.14 | 124.11 | 270.11 |
| thirteen | 257.07 | 482.16 | 124.12 | 271.19 |
| 412.12 | 258.22 | 486.13 | 127.17 | 273.17 |
| 426.08 | 261.17 | 488.12 | 138.04 | 291.17 |
| 436.05 | 262.07 | 494.06 | 152.12 | 293.16 |
| 753.22 | 263.06 | 497.19 | 153.04 | 301.10 |
| thirty | 263.07 | 501.13 | 210.18 | 304.12 |
| 067.22 | 264.14 | 503.04 | 220.05 | 306.17 |
| thirty-nine | 273.09 | 503.22 | 238.07 | 315.20 |
| 635.11 | 275.08 | 521.17 | 246.05 | 326.16 |
| this | 275.08 | 523.03 | 252.18 | 334.14 |
| 001.05 | 275.12 | 525.22 | 283.04 | 347.04 |
| 003.13 | 275.17 | 526.15 | 284.02 | 351.21 |
| 009.05 | 276.13 | 531.17 | 287.09 | 362.10 |
| 010.17 | 279.09 | 531.19 | 293.03 | 386.02 |
| 011.20 | 280.06 | 535.03 | 301.03 | 389.06 |
| 012.16 | 280.16 | 540.03 | 303.10 | 396.10 |
| 014.11 | 286.11 | 546.11 | 306.17 | 402.08 |
| 015.04 | 286.19 | 553.19 | 307.07 | 408.15 |
| 018.06 | 288.03 | 564.04 | 313.13 | 411.19 |
| 026.03 | 292.05 | 570.10 | 358.21 | 417.02 |
| 026.15 | 292.09 | 571.04 | 363.21 | 417.07 |
| 029.04 | 292.19 | 577.05 | 363.22 | 425.05 |
| 032.08 | 294.19 | 579.15 | 368.07 | 436.18 |
| 032.14 | 299.05 | 580.02 | 370.07 | 438.06 |
| 035.11 | 303.08 | 581.02 | 370.17 | 440.05 |
| 035.21 | 303.09 | 584.03 | 395.04 | 463.13 |
| 038.06 | 303.15 | 586.01 | 408.14 | 468.21 |
| 038.21 | 304.03 | 586.20 | 427.01 | 471.07 |
| 041.03 | 304.20 | 587.21 | 427.05 | 474.11 |
| 043.05 | 305.20 | 588.04 | 428.10 | 475.12 |
| 043.20 | 306.15 | 592.09 | 444.14 | 476.15 |
| 044.08 | 307.09 | 599.01 | 460.17 | 477.08 |
| 050.01 | 307.12 | 599.15 | 477.02 | 482.14 |
| 050.02 | 309.08 | 600.20 | 479.21 | 486.06 |
| 051.09 | 312.10 | 601.20 | 487.15 | 487.21 |
| 054.13 | 313.18 | 604.17 | 501.06 | 493.18 |
| 055.13 | 315.18 | 610.10 | 504.22 | 500.13 |
| 055.17 | 316.20 | 615.09 | 518.19 | 502.10 |
| 057.20 | 317.22 | 620.13 | 532.16 | 506.15 |
| 058.03 | 318.18 | 626.04 | 532.16 | 507.21 |
| 060.15 | 320.01 | 627.22 | 533.06 | 517.11 |
| 060.21 | 321.12 | 635.19 | 540.07 | 524.22 |
| 063.02 | 322.06 | 647.16 | 544.06 | 535.09 |
| 071.08 | 322.18 | 652.02 | 578.09 | 538.15 |
| 071.17 | 323.16 | 652.11 | 581.16 | 544.07 |
| 074.11 | 323.18 | 659.05 | 608.12 | 548.21 |
| 075.04 | 324.15 | 659.12 | 622.22 | 559.07 |
| 080.11 | 325.03 | 661.17 | 635.08 | 571.10 |
| 081.10 | 326.13 | 661.19 | 678.21 | 571.15 |
| 082.13 | 327.16 | 669.09 | 680.13 | 578.22 |
| 084.01 | 328.02 | 671.21 | 690.07 | 579.13 |
| 087.09 | 328.12 | 674.01 | 690.08 | 581.11 |
| 107.20 | 332.02 | 675.21 | 706.20 | 581.19 |
| 109.18 | 333.01 | 677.10 | 712.01 | 583.06 |
| 109.18 | 333.19 | 679.02 | 714.04 | 592.10 |
| 111.20 | 337.18 | 684.15 | 718.09 | 594.02 |
| 122.20 | 338.11 | 688.02 | 719.07 | 594.22 |
| 128.01 | 339.06 | 689.04 | 728.07 | 598.06 |
| 138.01 | 340.20 | 697.01 | 730.07 | 599.02 |
| 140.22 | 341.04 | 697.08 | 744.08 | 603.02 |
| 142.05 | 342.21 | 697.18 | 752.06 | 608.02 |
| 142.11 | 351.18 | 700.10 | 757.08 | 612.05 |
| 151.03 | 354.20 | 707.14 | 760.13 | 617.19 |
| 152.05 | 360.21 | 709.06 | thou | 630.19 |
| 168.03 | 362.22 | 712.18 | 049.18 | 631.20 |
| 168.07 | 364.09 | 713.02 | 049.20 | 632.03 |
| 169.05 | 377.05 | 723.16 | 093.13 | 635.11 |
| 172.03 | 383.18 | 725.17 | 439.10 | 646.06 |
| 177.02 | 385.10 | 726.12 | 468.02 | 647.04 |
| 178.18 | 386.17 | 728.17 | 497.18 | 652.19 |
| 179.15 | 389.06 | 731.14 | 564.03 | 657.01 |

| | |
|---|---|
| 661.02 |  |
| 663.10 |  |
| 672.10 |  |
| 677.20 |  |
| 682.04 |  |
| 691.22 |  |
| 701.07 |  |
| 701.10 |  |
| 713.16 |  |
| 727.21 |  |
| 732.17 |  |
| 734.22 |  |
| 743.09 |  |
| 759.14 |  |
| thought |  |
| 023.09 |  |
| 030.13 |  |
| 035.14 |  |
| 046.13 |  |
| 051.15 |  |
| 062.20 |  |
| 071.02 |  |
| 079.01 |  |
| 086.04 |  |
| 091.22 |  |
| 094.11 |  |
| 097.06 |  |
| 099.02 |  |
| 102.19 |  |
| 104.11 |  |
| 108.02 |  |
| 122.12 |  |
| 123.08 |  |
| 130.09 |  |
| 137.09 |  |
| 140.12 |  |
| 143.12 |  |
| 151.12 |  |
| 160.04 |  |
| 169.10 |  |
| 179.07 |  |
| 182.19 |  |
| 189.08 |  |
| 195.19 |  |
| 197.17 |  |
| 207.08 |  |
| 215.22 |  |
| 228.02 |  |
| 230.13 |  |
| 244.10 |  |
| 258.10 |  |
| 270.14 |  |
| 273.16 |  |
| 279.01 |  |
| 279.02 |  |
| 281.05 |  |
| 281.07 |  |
| 291.17 |  |
| 298.06 |  |
| 305.03 |  |
| 314.04 |  |
| 317.13 |  |
| 330.21 |  |
| 332.11 |  |
| 335.12 |  |
| 347.04 |  |
| 347.06 |  |
| 353.11 |  |
| 356.12 |  |
| 361.11 |  |
| 362.01 |  |
| 367.03 |  |
| 372.21 |  |
| 375.13 |  |
| 397.12 |  |
| 404.10 |  |
| 414.22 |  |
| 417.11 |  |
| 425.21 |  |
| 431.09 |  |
| 436.14 |  |
| 438.12 |  |
| 441.10 |  |
| 442.07 |  |
| 444.04 |  |
| 449.15 |  |
| 450.16 |  |
| 454.12 |  |
| 461.13 |  |
| 464.15 |  |
| 477.12 |  |
| 481.17 |  |
| 487.20 |  |
| 489.09 |  |
| 499.17 |  |
| 504.14 |  |
| 508.08 |  |
| 508.17 |  |
| 511.13 |  |
| 531.09 |  |
| 552.01 |  |
| 558.13 |  |
| 560.01 |  |
| 568.06 |  |
| 573.11 |  |
| 577.22 |  |
| 588.03 |  |
| 593.06 |  |
| 599.06 |  |
| 612.07 |  |
| 620.18 |  |

622.04
623.14
626.10
627.17
635.13
640.19
649.15
661.02
663.10
665.20
674.21
679.19
693.07
709.09
718.11
734.02
740.20
741.19
746.20
752.06
757.08
758.21

**thoughtless**
297.04
536.18

**thoughtlessly**
157.14

**thoughtlessness**
502.20

**thoughts**
002.14
095.17
126.01
133.15
206.04
231.15
240.07
254.02
261.06
308.01
392.18
517.17
582.15
732.07

**thousand**
105.10
166.05
261.16
275.13
335.13
730.19

**thowt**
719.12
719.17

**thrang**
658.06

**thrash**
100.16
671.19

**thrashing**
476.18

**thrashings**
083.21

**thread**
379.04

**threat**
309.19
439.21
459.02
610.09
615.01
621.18

**threaten**
344.08
585.08

**threatened**
227.03
250.05
350.06
584.05
602.07
631.22
664.13
713.09

**threatening**
047.19
084.09
296.08
509.08
760.22

**threatens**
045.10
257.07

**threats**
035.02
198.05
312.07

**three**
006.11
041.17
059.01
076.22
077.15
083.21
098.11
115.20
135.13
138.09
196.08
198.19
202.14

215.20
248.15
257.03
261.07
273.13
288.21
350.11
373.19
381.08
393.05
395.17
430.11
431.17
453.01
465.04
466.19
470.11
477.18
482.09
516.10
524.09
547.21
550.02
554.09
559.08
572.02
622.02
622.08
624.09
635.04
638.05
688.11
689.17
698.16
721.03
727.14
742.22
752.18
763.22

**three-inch**
062.02

**threshold**
004.19
031.13
097.01
247.14
260.13
310.05
435.04
607.10
680.06
742.20

**threw**
077.12
084.17
087.07
101.21
117.04
192.22
283.13
385.12
413.05
505.15
554.12
589.09
595.06
681.07
681.11
691.11

**thrice**
047.12
088.09
555.02

**thrill**
165.18

**thrilling**
741.18

**thrive**
088.22
346.05

**thriven**
357.01

**throat**
034.11
056.12
106.20
247.13
253.05
259.19
391.04
396.10
757.20

**throbbing**
359.10

**throstles**
557.16

**throttled**
107.02

**throttler**
309.19
309.22
325.08

**through**
014.04
015.11
017.01
025.12
051.20
052.15
053.03
054.02
060.18
061.18
062.18
066.07
075.03
082.21
095.07
101.20
103.16
107.16
132.08
159.22
169.10
173.03
176.22
177.01
177.01
187.09
192.12
192.15
196.15
216.13
244.16
279.18
285.02
285.13
292.14
296.14
311.01
329.21
334.01
361.03
361.03
368.10
370.12
383.22
393.06
397.20
398.03
407.07
410.03
410.10
411.20
433.04
449.05
455.10
527.16
531.12
547.15
552.21
568.20
578.06
578.10
597.20
622.17
622.20
630.14
638.06
644.07
644.20
650.13
653.02
655.06
678.07
684.10
742.15
742.17
743.19
745.09
745.17
750.05
752.17
753.05
756.13
757.09
762.20
763.07
764.09

**throughout**
130.19
462.18
516.01

**throw**
084.12
196.06
275.11
284.19

**throwing**
064.15
261.15
564.06

**thrown**
008.12
025.05
133.11
478.12
488.07
601.02
695.06

**thrushcross**
002.12
002.14
066.20
071.09
071.19
102.05
102.11
105.11
113.02
125.19
196.20
204.05
224.12
282.11
306.14
421.14
428.07
463.04
481.16
581.07
620.14
637.11
665.08
684.22
689.07
697.09

**thrust**
043.08
053.16
063.03
106.18
127.04
193.14
260.20
343.01
399.16
458.10
536.17
621.15
692.01
720.06

**thrusting**
335.05
472.02
624.15

**thud**
457.18

**thumped**
624.05

**thunder**
188.05
188.16
189.02
192.16
709.01
760.22

**thunder-cloud**
438.16

**thunder-storm**
197.10

**thundered**
057.21
260.11
316.22
377.20
400.22
722.16

**thundering**
567.20

**thur**
233.05
233.05
400.20
400.20

**thursday**
280.06
590.08
594.11
597.01

**thus**
036.09
057.06
083.03
134.11
546.18
615.21
629.11
659.06
672.08
689.12
713.15

**thwart**
316.01
683.20

**thwarting**
166.10
248.10

**thy**
049.21
092.09
092.10
092.11
164.17
245.03
245.06
319.08
439.06
468.01
468.02
563.22

**ticket**
166.04

**tidied**
119.21

**tidy**
154.20
338.04
568.16

**tie**
436.03
614.05

**tied**
386.14
493.04
508.18
710.03

**ties**
725.22

**tiger**
327.08

**tigers**
012.03

**tight**
236.05

**tight-stretched**
741.17

**tightened**
211.16

**tigress**
238.04

**till**
008.22
015.15
016.11
022.09
033.18
034.20
039.06
040.02
045.05
052.19
057.06
059.13
069.07
079.10
090.10
093.21
100.16
102.09
113.03
120.21
121.13
122.02
127.06
127.14
127.17
132.10
135.02
135.03
135.10
142.18
148.17
151.20
157.13
163.12
179.19
184.09
190.16
201.09
208.19
214.13
233.03
234.20
248.02
262.18
265.14
281.06
284.09
284.20
286.11
304.17
310.05
314.13
327.12
334.21
334.22
344.03
344.14
345.08
350.07
354.03
357.08
357.21
359.13
365.07
375.17
376.20
378.03
384.04
384.15
386.10
390.14
391.03
392.16
402.04
403.17
420.02
426.08
431.06
433.07
435.03
437.19
446.06
454.20
456.09
460.10
465.14
469.20
470.02
478.04
490.11
498.16
499.12
500.15
503.05
506.13
511.17
515.08
520.11
520.13
522.21
526.15
528.22
536.19
538.16
541.17
551.15
555.07
557.07
559.15
566.18
571.12
586.16
591.19
598.03
607.11
618.10
620.07
620.22
622.16
626.12
628.05
636.11
640.02
640.08
640.09
641.12
650.14
651.05
654.22
659.18
664.01
667.22
682.19
686.03
697.17
705.04
710.16
712.03
717.15
720.15
724.20
733.05
733.17
734.18
742.07
743.08
744.01
745.04
749.20
750.07
757.04

**timber**
374.01

**time**
007.06
015.07
015.21
027.12
044.10
051.09
059.02
060.15
070.04
079.01
087.02
100.20
113.03
122.09
123.11
126.09
129.17
135.05
142.05
149.08
151.11
154.03
155.17
165.17
178.05
183.03
184.15
195.01
205.03
207.13
215.06
216.10
225.08
226.07
234.02
241.09
242.12
248.12
254.09
265.08
267.16
280.09
281.20
282.09
289.13
289.14
289.16
302.13

| | | | | | |
|---|---|---|---|---|---|
| 303.08 | timidly | 016.08 | 045.17 | 070.08 | 093.15 |
| 306.06 | 473.02 | 016.17 | 045.18 | 071.02 | 093.21 |
| 314.04 | 587.09 | 016.18 | 046.04 | 071.03 | 094.01 |
| 316.03 | tin | 016.21 | 046.12 | 071.04 | 094.13 |
| 318.14 | 005.21 | 017.08 | 046.12 | 071.12 | 094.15 |
| 323.18 | 494.07 | 017.18 | 046.21 | 071.16 | 095.01 |
| 332.02 | tingled | 018.07 | 047.02 | 071.18 | 095.03 |
| 339.05 | 015.15 | 018.16 | 047.05 | 071.18 | 095.04 |
| 349.05 | tingling | 018.21 | 047.09 | 071.20 | 095.04 |
| 354.20 | 156.13 | 019.19 | 047.11 | 073.12 | 095.11 |
| 366.02 | tiny | 019.21 | 047.15 | 073.14 | 095.12 |
| 373.18 | 414.03 | 019.23 | 047.20 | 074.04 | 095.15 |
| 376.08 | tip | 020.03 | 048.06 | 074.14 | 096.02 |
| 396.11 | 018.07 | 020.04 | 048.20 | 074.15 | 096.08 |
| 400.15 | tiptoe | 020.08 | 049.03 | 074.16 | 097.02 |
| 405.01 | 491.20 | 020.12 | 049.11 | 074.20 | 097.14 |
| 412.12 | tired | 020.16 | 049.12 | 075.03 | 097.19 |
| 413.15 | 077.06 | 020.22 | 049.15 | 075.04 | 098.01 |
| 424.11 | 099.09 | 021.12 | 050.09 | 075.11 | 098.06 |
| 444.21 | 250.13 | 021.17 | 050.16 | 075.12 | 098.08 |
| 451.17 | 314.18 | 022.03 | 050.19 | 075.13 | 098.09 |
| 456.11 | 337.14 | 022.12 | 051.13 | 075.17 | 099.01 |
| 460.08 | 360.22 | 022.15 | 051.14 | 075.18 | 099.02 |
| 474.10 | 360.22 | 022.17 | 051.16 | 075.20 | 099.06 |
| 478.03 | 457.14 | 022.18 | 051.21 | 076.04 | 099.11 |
| 480.07 | 469.02 | 022.19 | 052.04 | 076.05 | 099.12 |
| 486.14 | 483.01 | 023.01 | 052.05 | 076.07 | 099.14 |
| 487.02 | 533.06 | 023.10 | 052.09 | 076.08 | 099.17 |
| 488.22 | 551.03 | 023.10 | 052.16 | 076.19 | 099.22 |
| 493.06 | 551.06 | 023.21 | 052.18 | 076.22 | 100.04 |
| 496.13 | 551.12 | 024.13 | 052.18 | 077.07 | 100.07 |
| 506.14 | 587.15 | 024.15 | 053.02 | 077.07 | 100.11 |
| 518.05 | 618.15 | 025.13 | 053.05 | 077.08 | 100.11 |
| 518.22 | 634.17 | 026.02 | 053.07 | 077.09 | 100.13 |
| 526.15 | 676.17 | 026.06 | 053.18 | 077.09 | 100.15 |
| 535.03 | 685.03 | 026.09 | 053.21 | 077.16 | 100.20 |
| 536.01 | 700.06 | 026.18 | 054.05 | 077.16 | 100.20 |
| 543.02 | 704.14 | 026.19 | 054.06 | 078.03 | 100.22 |
| 555.10 | tiresome | 026.21 | 054.10 | 078.09 | 101.06 |
| 557.04 | 438.10 | 027.05 | 054.21 | 078.10 | 101.06 |
| 564.05 | 475.10 | 027.06 | 055.04 | 078.12 | 101.10 |
| 570.10 | 532.20 | 027.07 | 055.06 | 078.13 | 101.13 |
| 571.18 | 541.05 | 027.11 | 055.06 | 078.15 | 101.14 |
| 577.11 | 660.12 | 027.15 | 055.12 | 078.21 | 101.15 |
| 578.12 | tiresomely | 027.21 | 055.13 | 079.02 | 101.16 |
| 583.09 | 136.01 | 028.10 | 055.15 | 079.07 | 101.21 |
| 597.04 | 270.11 | 028.16 | 055.17 | 079.15 | 102.02 |
| 599.10 | 417.21 | 029.05 | 055.20 | 079.20 | 102.07 |
| 605.02 | titan | 029.14 | 056.01 | 079.22 | 102.07 |
| 626.04 | 752.19 | 029.19 | 056.15 | 080.05 | 102.11 |
| 628.08 | title | 030.07 | 056.18 | 080.07 | 102.15 |
| 630.14 | 045.19 | 030.15 | 057.09 | 080.08 | 102.18 |
| 644.10 | 239.20 | 030.22 | 057.12 | 080.11 | 103.05 |
| 645.05 | 409.07 | 030.23 | 057.18 | 080.19 | 103.13 |
| 649.04 | titter | 030.23 | 057.21 | 080.22 | 103.15 |
| 650.02 | 042.01 | 031.10 | 058.01 | 081.04 | 103.22 |
| 661.17 | tittered | 031.12 | 058.03 | 081.06 | 104.01 |
| 662.04 | 497.14 | 031.12 | 058.16 | 081.09 | 104.09 |
| 674.01 | to | 031.14 | 058.18 | 081.13 | 104.22 |
| 677.02 | 001.03 | 031.15 | 059.03 | 081.21 | 105.02 |
| 694.05 | 001.10 | 031.15 | 059.11 | 082.06 | 105.03 |
| 699.02 | 002.10 | 031.16 | 059.17 | 082.12 | 105.03 |
| 699.10 | 002.17 | 031.21 | 060.05 | 082.13 | 105.06 |
| 723.16 | 002.20 | 032.01 | 060.07 | 082.16 | 105.21 |
| 726.18 | 002.22 | 032.02 | 060.10 | 082.22 | 106.03 |
| 729.15 | 003.02 | 032.02 | 061.01 | 083.06 | 106.14 |
| 729.21 | 003.06 | 032.05 | 061.05 | 083.07 | 106.17 |
| 749.22 | 003.22 | 032.11 | 061.08 | 083.09 | 106.19 |
| 753.22 | 004.02 | 033.02 | 061.19 | 083.12 | 107.16 |
| time-piece | 004.06 | 033.05 | 061.21 | 083.13 | 107.17 |
| 200.01 | 004.15 | 033.07 | 062.05 | 083.13 | 107.20 |
| times | 004.19 | 034.04 | 062.18 | 083.18 | 108.02 |
| 004.09 | 005.06 | 034.20 | 063.02 | 084.02 | 108.05 |
| 045.19 | 005.08 | 034.21 | 063.15 | 084.06 | 108.10 |
| 047.07 | 005.09 | 034.22 | 063.16 | 084.07 | 108.10 |
| 049.09 | 005.15 | 035.01 | 063.19 | 084.20 | 109.02 |
| 049.10 | 006.03 | 035.12 | 063.21 | 085.10 | 109.05 |
| 049.11 | 006.05 | 035.15 | 063.22 | 085.11 | 109.15 |
| 049.12 | 006.21 | 035.20 | 064.04 | 085.14 | 109.21 |
| 049.20 | 007.01 | 036.09 | 064.10 | 085.16 | 110.07 |
| 049.21 | 007.05 | 036.10 | 064.20 | 085.19 | 110.08 |
| 052.12 | 007.08 | 036.11 | 064.22 | 085.22 | 110.16 |
| 070.18 | 007.19 | 036.15 | 065.02 | 087.02 | 110.17 |
| 090.08 | 007.20 | 037.11 | 065.05 | 087.05 | 111.10 |
| 115.13 | 007.22 | 037.12 | 065.08 | 087.09 | 111.18 |
| 123.21 | 008.06 | 038.07 | 065.16 | 087.10 | 111.18 |
| 189.11 | 008.08 | 038.09 | 065.18 | 087.12 | 112.01 |
| 214.16 | 009.01 | 038.10 | 066.01 | 088.01 | 112.02 |
| 317.07 | 009.03 | 039.02 | 066.09 | 088.03 | 112.05 |
| 346.16 | 009.11 | 039.03 | 066.15 | 088.04 | 112.06 |
| 352.19 | 009.13 | 039.11 | 066.16 | 088.05 | 112.11 |
| 449.20 | 009.19 | 040.04 | 066.16 | 088.07 | 112.13 |
| 470.11 | 009.21 | 040.13 | 066.22 | 088.11 | 113.07 |
| 477.17 | 010.04 | 040.18 | 067.01 | 088.12 | 113.11 |
| 490.05 | 010.09 | 041.01 | 067.03 | 088.18 | 114.04 |
| 512.01 | 010.16 | 041.02 | 067.04 | 089.02 | 114.10 |
| 572.02 | 010.19 | 041.05 | 067.04 | 089.13 | 114.22 |
| 630.18 | 011.02 | 041.11 | 067.06 | 089.14 | 115.05 |
| 654.20 | 011.14 | 041.18 | 067.14 | 089.16 | 115.08 |
| 708.13 | 012.07 | 041.20 | 067.20 | 089.22 | 115.09 |
| 728.13 | 012.17 | 041.21 | 067.22 | 090.04 | 115.11 |
| 759.05 | 012.18 | 042.01 | 068.01 | 090.10 | 115.15 |
| timid | 012.21 | 042.03 | 068.02 | 090.21 | 115.19 |
| 442.19 | 012.21 | 043.05 | 068.03 | 091.02 | 116.04 |
| 499.20 | 013.01 | 043.07 | 069.03 | 091.04 | 116.11 |
| 520.18 | 013.09 | 043.13 | 069.06 | 091.06 | 116.12 |
| 642.13 | 013.14 | 043.19 | 069.08 | 091.16 | 116.16 |
| timidity | 014.03 | 044.07 | 069.12 | 092.06 | 116.22 |
| 160.14 | 014.05 | 044.09 | 070.02 | 092.15 | 117.03 |
| | 015.07 | 045.10 | 070.03 | 092.16 | 117.10 |
| | 015.11 | 045.14 | | 093.12 | 117.14 |

| | | | | | |
|---|---|---|---|---|---|
| 118.06 | 140.18 | 165.12 | 192.21 | 215.16 | 237.22 |
| 118.09 | 140.19 | 165.13 | 193.03 | 215.17 | 238.07 |
| 118.13 | 140.22 | 165.17 | 193.06 | 215.19 | 238.08 |
| 118.16 | 141.05 | 166.01 | 193.09 | 215.20 | 239.02 |
| 118.20 | 141.10 | 166.12 | 193.09 | 216.04 | 239.04 |
| 118.21 | 141.11 | 166.15 | 193.14 | 216.16 | 239.06 |
| 119.03 | 141.12 | 167.03 | 194.06 | 216.17 | 239.18 |
| 119.03 | 141.18 | 167.07 | 194.13 | 216.18 | 239.22 |
| 119.06 | 141.21 | 167.16 | 194.14 | 217.12 | 240.09 |
| 119.15 | 142.01 | 167.17 | 195.02 | 217.13 | 240.12 |
| 119.19 | 142.07 | 168.12 | 195.05 | 217.20 | 240.13 |
| 119.21 | 142.11 | 168.14 | 195.08 | 218.04 | 240.14 |
| 120.02 | 142.17 | 168.14 | 195.15 | 218.08 | 240.15 |
| 120.05 | 143.02 | 168.16 | 195.17 | 218.10 | 240.18 |
| 120.06 | 143.10 | 168.19 | 195.20 | 218.11 | 240.21 |
| 120.08 | 143.12 | 169.05 | 196.04 | 218.13 | 241.03 |
| 120.10 | 144.03 | 169.08 | 196.08 | 218.14 | 241.04 |
| 120.14 | 144.07 | 169.09 | 196.16 | 218.16 | 241.04 |
| 120.20 | 144.11 | 169.10 | 196.17 | 218.17 | 241.07 |
| 121.13 | 144.12 | 169.19 | 196.19 | 218.19 | 241.09 |
| 121.15 | 144.13 | 170.03 | 196.22 | 218.21 | 242.04 |
| 121.17 | 144.18 | 170.06 | 197.03 | 218.22 | 242.06 |
| 121.18 | 144.21 | 170.19 | 197.08 | 219.13 | 242.10 |
| 121.18 | 145.04 | 170.22 | 197.11 | 219.22 | 243.01 |
| 121.20 | 145.10 | 171.05 | 197.18 | 220.01 | 243.05 |
| 122.04 | 145.11 | 171.10 | 197.20 | 220.02 | 243.06 |
| 122.04 | 145.12 | 171.12 | 198.01 | 220.04 | 243.10 |
| 122.07 | 145.15 | 171.17 | 198.01 | 220.07 | 244.08 |
| 122.15 | 145.18 | 171.18 | 198.07 | 220.11 | 244.09 |
| 122.22 | 146.09 | 171.21 | 198.11 | 220.12 | 244.13 |
| 123.01 | 146.12 | 172.02 | 198.11 | 220.15 | 245.06 |
| 123.06 | 146.20 | 172.04 | 198.18 | 220.19 | 245.10 |
| 123.07 | 146.21 | 172.09 | 198.19 | 220.20 | 245.20 |
| 123.10 | 147.06 | 172.18 | 198.21 | 220.22 | 245.21 |
| 123.11 | 147.07 | 173.10 | 199.02 | 221.01 | 246.02 |
| 124.09 | 147.11 | 173.16 | 199.05 | 221.02 | 246.17 |
| 124.17 | 147.12 | 174.08 | 199.07 | 221.03 | 246.20 |
| 124.18 | 147.16 | 174.10 | 199.09 | 221.06 | 247.05 |
| 124.19 | 148.02 | 174.18 | 199.11 | 221.09 | 247.07 |
| 125.01 | 148.04 | 175.08 | 199.14 | 221.12 | 247.10 |
| 125.07 | 148.09 | 175.11 | 199.15 | 221.15 | 247.18 |
| 125.08 | 148.12 | 175.16 | 199.15 | 221.17 | 248.06 |
| 125.18 | 148.14 | 177.03 | 199.18 | 221.19 | 248.08 |
| 125.21 | 148.17 | 177.04 | 199.21 | 221.20 | 248.13 |
| 126.02 | 148.19 | 177.07 | 199.21 | 221.22 | 248.21 |
| 126.05 | 149.01 | 177.15 | 200.01 | 222.04 | 249.02 |
| 126.08 | 149.05 | 177.16 | 200.05 | 222.06 | 249.04 |
| 126.09 | 149.16 | 178.08 | 200.07 | 222.10 | 249.07 |
| 126.09 | 149.20 | 178.13 | 200.09 | 222.11 | 249.09 |
| 126.13 | 150.11 | 178.14 | 201.02 | 222.13 | 249.15 |
| 126.18 | 150.16 | 178.17 | 201.09 | 222.16 | 249.19 |
| 127.02 | 150.18 | 178.19 | 202.03 | 223.02 | 249.20 |
| 127.03 | 150.20 | 178.21 | 202.04 | 223.06 | 250.03 |
| 128.03 | 150.21 | 178.21 | 202.09 | 223.08 | 250.05 |
| 128.04 | 150.22 | 179.03 | 202.11 | 223.10 | 250.07 |
| 128.10 | 151.02 | 179.04 | 202.15 | 223.13 | 250.08 |
| 128.12 | 151.22 | 179.05 | 202.18 | 224.04 | 250.14 |
| 128.14 | 152.02 | 179.08 | 202.21 | 224.05 | 250.19 |
| 128.18 | 152.10 | 179.20 | 203.08 | 224.16 | 251.03 |
| 128.21 | 153.01 | 179.21 | 203.11 | 224.18 | 251.04 |
| 129.02 | 153.10 | 180.12 | 203.19 | 224.21 | 251.05 |
| 129.04 | 153.16 | 180.13 | 204.05 | 225.17 | 251.19 |
| 129.09 | 154.04 | 181.01 | 204.06 | 225.18 | 251.20 |
| 129.15 | 154.19 | 181.06 | 204.07 | 225.22 | 251.21 |
| 130.06 | 155.04 | 181.10 | 204.09 | 226.12 | 252.19 |
| 130.09 | 155.05 | 181.13 | 204.10 | 226.18 | 252.20 |
| 130.11 | 155.12 | 181.21 | 204.12 | 226.22 | 252.21 |
| 130.13 | 155.15 | 182.09 | 205.03 | 227.03 | 253.04 |
| 130.16 | 155.17 | 182.11 | 205.07 | 227.05 | 253.11 |
| 130.17 | 155.18 | 182.21 | 205.07 | 227.18 | 253.12 |
| 130.19 | 156.10 | 182.22 | 205.10 | 228.05 | 253.13 |
| 130.21 | 156.10 | 183.09 | 205.13 | 228.08 | 254.03 |
| 131.01 | 156.13 | 183.17 | 205.15 | 228.12 | 254.09 |
| 131.01 | 156.15 | 183.21 | 206.03 | 228.14 | 254.11 |
| 131.06 | 156.18 | 184.03 | 206.10 | 228.17 | 254.15 |
| 131.16 | 157.11 | 184.05 | 206.13 | 229.10 | 254.19 |
| 131.18 | 157.15 | 184.08 | 206.15 | 229.11 | 255.03 |
| 132.04 | 157.20 | 184.08 | 206.21 | 229.16 | 255.06 |
| 132.07 | 157.22 | 184.10 | 207.07 | 230.02 | 255.10 |
| 132.10 | 158.03 | 184.12 | 207.10 | 230.04 | 255.18 |
| 132.11 | 158.06 | 184.21 | 207.20 | 230.05 | 255.20 |
| 132.12 | 158.07 | 185.05 | 208.04 | 230.13 | 255.22 |
| 132.22 | 158.10 | 185.06 | 208.08 | 231.07 | 256.01 |
| 132.22 | 158.11 | 185.12 | 208.11 | 233.18 | 256.05 |
| 133.02 | 159.05 | 185.15 | 208.21 | 233.19 | 256.10 |
| 133.03 | 159.05 | 185.17 | 209.01 | 233.19 | 256.11 |
| 133.11 | 159.14 | 186.01 | 209.04 | 234.01 | 256.12 |
| 133.16 | 159.16 | 186.01 | 209.10 | 234.03 | 256.16 |
| 133.21 | 159.21 | 186.07 | 210.02 | 234.05 | 256.22 |
| 133.22 | 160.01 | 186.15 | 210.03 | 234.14 | 257.13 |
| 134.12 | 160.02 | 186.22 | 210.14 | 234.15 | 257.17 |
| 134.16 | 160.05 | 187.01 | 210.16 | 234.21 | 257.18 |
| 134.22 | 160.09 | 187.03 | 210.20 | 235.02 | 257.19 |
| 134.22 | 160.10 | 188.05 | 210.22 | 235.04 | 257.21 |
| 135.13 | 160.15 | 188.07 | 211.01 | 235.06 | 257.22 |
| 136.06 | 160.18 | 188.10 | 211.10 | 235.08 | 258.04 |
| 136.08 | 160.18 | 188.11 | 211.16 | 235.12 | 258.07 |
| 136.14 | 160.19 | 188.16 | 211.20 | 235.20 | 258.09 |
| 136.17 | 160.20 | 189.10 | 212.02 | 235.21 | 258.11 |
| 137.01 | 160.22 | 190.03 | 212.18 | 236.04 | 258.13 |
| 137.07 | 162.02 | 190.04 | 212.19 | 236.05 | 259.11 |
| 137.08 | 162.08 | 190.07 | 212.22 | 236.06 | 259.15 |
| 137.11 | 162.11 | 190.12 | 213.06 | 236.07 | 260.01 |
| 137.19 | 163.04 | 190.14 | 213.13 | 236.10 | 260.20 |
| 138.07 | 163.11 | 191.07 | 213.17 | 236.16 | 261.01 |
| 138.10 | 164.06 | 191.09 | 214.11 | 236.22 | 261.06 |
| 138.10 | 164.08 | 191.12 | 214.13 | 237.08 | 261.12 |
| 140.03 | 164.14 | 192.10 | 214.18 | 237.09 | 261.13 |
| 140.05 | 165.05 | 192.13 | 215.03 | 237.13 | 261.17 |
| 140.05 | 165.07 | 192.18 | 215.04 | 237.18 | 261.18 |
| 140.13 | 165.07 | | 215.09 | | |

| | | | | | |
|---|---|---|---|---|---|
| 261.20 | 289.08 | 313.13 | 340.21 | 361.13 | 387.16 |
| 262.02 | 289.09 | 314.06 | 341.01 | 361.16 | 388.01 |
| 262.08 | 289.13 | 314.09 | 341.03 | 362.02 | 388.02 |
| 262.12 | 289.16 | 314.18 | 341.10 | 362.05 | 388.06 |
| 262.19 | 289.20 | 314.19 | 341.15 | 362.07 | 388.14 |
| 263.02 | 289.21 | 314.20 | 342.01 | 362.10 | 389.02 |
| 263.04 | 290.01 | 314.20 | 342.03 | 362.14 | 389.03 |
| 263.05 | 290.08 | 314.20 | 342.03 | 362.15 | 389.05 |
| 263.06 | 290.11 | 315.06 | 342.04 | 363.04 | 389.07 |
| 263.07 | 290.12 | 315.08 | 342.08 | 363.12 | 389.09 |
| 263.18 | 290.13 | 315.15 | 342.09 | 363.14 | 389.12 |
| 263.20 | 290.16 | 315.16 | 342.15 | 363.21 | 389.13 |
| 263.21 | 290.20 | 316.01 | 342.19 | 363.21 | 389.18 |
| 264.06 | 291.03 | 316.13 | 342.19 | 364.03 | 389.19 |
| 264.08 | 291.05 | 316.18 | 343.04 | 365.09 | 389.20 |
| 264.12 | 291.09 | 316.19 | 343.06 | 366.12 | 390.02 |
| 264.13 | 291.13 | 316.21 | 343.09 | 366.12 | 390.12 |
| 264.14 | 291.16 | 317.01 | 343.13 | 366.15 | 390.18 |
| 265.01 | 291.21 | 317.02 | 343.15 | 366.21 | 391.05 |
| 265.07 | 292.01 | 317.03 | 343.16 | 367.06 | 391.09 |
| 265.09 | 292.04 | 317.04 | 343.18 | 367.07 | 391.12 |
| 265.10 | 292.06 | 317.12 | 343.19 | 367.09 | 391.13 |
| 265.15 | 292.10 | 317.20 | 343.20 | 367.13 | 391.22 |
| 265.20 | 293.01 | 317.21 | 343.21 | 367.17 | 392.08 |
| 266.01 | 293.11 | 318.04 | 343.22 | 367.18 | 392.12 |
| 266.12 | 293.20 | 318.06 | 344.05 | 367.18 | 392.17 |
| 266.17 | 294.05 | 318.07 | 344.06 | 368.01 | 392.19 |
| 267.06 | 294.12 | 318.11 | 344.09 | 368.04 | 393.14 |
| 267.06 | 294.16 | 318.19 | 345.02 | 369.06 | 393.18 |
| 267.09 | 294.17 | 318.19 | 345.04 | 369.09 | 393.20 |
| 267.09 | 294.18 | 318.21 | 345.06 | 370.03 | 394.01 |
| 267.10 | 294.22 | 318.22 | 345.09 | 370.10 | 394.10 |
| 267.19 | 295.01 | 320.01 | 345.10 | 372.01 | 394.15 |
| 268.01 | 295.03 | 320.05 | 345.11 | 372.07 | 394.15 |
| 268.03 | 295.05 | 320.18 | 345.14 | 372.10 | 394.17 |
| 269.08 | 295.14 | 320.20 | 345.14 | 372.16 | 394.19 |
| 269.11 | 295.15 | 320.21 | 346.05 | 372.19 | 394.20 |
| 270.01 | 295.17 | 321.12 | 346.06 | 372.20 | 394.20 |
| 270.07 | 295.18 | 321.13 | 346.08 | 372.21 | 395.04 |
| 270.08 | 295.20 | 322.15 | 346.08 | 373.05 | 395.08 |
| 270.12 | 296.05 | 322.18 | 346.17 | 373.07 | 395.16 |
| 270.21 | 296.08 | 322.22 | 346.18 | 373.10 | 395.20 |
| 272.14 | 296.12 | 323.03 | 346.18 | 373.11 | 396.08 |
| 272.16 | 296.18 | 323.10 | 346.20 | 373.12 | 396.11 |
| 273.15 | 297.01 | 323.14 | 347.09 | 374.04 | 396.14 |
| 273.19 | 297.05 | 324.22 | 347.17 | 374.16 | 396.18 |
| 273.21 | 297.21 | 325.04 | 347.21 | 374.17 | 396.19 |
| 274.01 | 298.01 | 325.06 | 348.02 | 374.19 | 396.22 |
| 274.02 | 298.10 | 325.11 | 348.04 | 375.03 | 397.05 |
| 274.03 | 298.14 | 325.13 | 348.09 | 375.09 | 397.06 |
| 274.04 | 299.04 | 325.14 | 350.02 | 375.11 | 397.15 |
| 274.05 | 299.13 | 325.20 | 350.06 | 375.15 | 397.17 |
| 274.05 | 299.17 | 325.22 | 350.07 | 375.17 | 397.20 |
| 274.06 | 300.02 | 326.06 | 350.13 | 375.21 | 397.21 |
| 274.11 | 300.03 | 326.06 | 350.14 | 376.05 | 399.02 |
| 274.18 | 302.04 | 327.05 | 350.19 | 376.06 | 400.03 |
| 274.19 | 302.08 | 327.09 | 350.22 | 376.10 | 400.22 |
| 275.02 | 302.10 | 327.16 | 351.01 | 376.16 | 401.02 |
| 275.02 | 302.17 | 328.02 | 351.16 | 377.12 | 401.03 |
| 275.05 | 303.08 | 328.06 | 351.22 | 377.18 | 401.06 |
| 275.06 | 303.15 | 328.07 | 352.02 | 377.20 | 401.15 |
| 275.07 | 303.19 | 328.11 | 352.02 | 377.21 | 401.15 |
| 275.11 | 304.02 | 329.01 | 352.05 | 377.22 | 401.18 |
| 275.15 | 304.06 | 329.04 | 352.09 | 378.01 | 402.11 |
| 275.16 | 304.07 | 329.05 | 352.12 | 378.09 | 402.15 |
| 276.15 | 304.16 | 329.07 | 352.12 | 378.11 | 402.16 |
| 276.17 | 304.16 | 329.16 | 352.22 | 378.14 | 402.20 |
| 277.14 | 304.16 | 329.17 | 354.04 | 378.16 | 403.07 |
| 278.10 | 304.19 | 329.18 | 354.10 | 378.19 | 403.07 |
| 278.11 | 304.22 | 330.01 | 354.11 | 378.21 | 403.10 |
| 278.21 | 305.01 | 331.04 | 354.12 | 379.05 | 403.16 |
| 279.17 | 305.05 | 331.05 | 354.14 | 379.11 | 404.09 |
| 279.19 | 305.10 | 331.07 | 354.15 | 379.12 | 404.20 |
| 280.10 | 305.19 | 331.08 | 354.18 | 379.17 | 405.06 |
| 280.19 | 305.20 | 331.09 | 354.20 | 380.06 | 405.07 |
| 281.02 | 306.05 | 331.14 | 355.02 | 381.04 | 405.07 |
| 281.02 | 306.08 | 331.18 | 355.09 | 382.05 | 405.15 |
| 281.03 | 306.09 | 332.07 | 355.10 | 382.19 | 405.18 |
| 281.04 | 306.10 | 332.09 | 355.11 | 382.20 | 405.19 |
| 281.13 | 306.12 | 333.08 | 355.11 | 383.05 | 405.20 |
| 281.22 | 306.13 | 333.13 | 355.16 | 383.06 | 406.09 |
| 282.16 | 306.20 | 333.15 | 356.03 | 383.06 | 406.18 |
| 292.17 | 307.02 | 333.17 | 356.07 | 383.07 | 406.22 |
| 282.18 | 307.04 | 333.19 | 356.10 | 383.17 | 407.03 |
| 283.16 | 307.13 | 334.07 | 356.20 | 383.18 | 407.05 |
| 283.17 | 307.14 | 334.08 | 356.20 | 383.22 | 407.10 |
| 284.11 | 307.19 | 334.10 | 356.21 | 384.02 | 407.10 |
| 284.13 | 307.20 | 334.15 | 357.02 | 384.07 | 407.12 |
| 284.14 | 308.06 | 335.05 | 357.04 | 384.07 | 407.18 |
| 284.15 | 308.07 | 335.15 | 357.05 | 384.10 | 407.21 |
| 285.02 | 308.08 | 336.01 | 357.15 | 384.15 | 408.10 |
| 285.05 | 308.13 | 336.10 | 357.16 | 384.16 | 408.21 |
| 285.07 | 308.15 | 336.11 | 357.18 | 384.18 | 409.02 |
| 285.09 | 308.15 | 336.16 | 358.02 | 385.02 | 409.03 |
| 285.14 | 308.16 | 337.03 | 358.05 | 385.06 | 409.05 |
| 285.17 | 309.01 | 337.14 | 358.12 | 385.08 | 409.14 |
| 285.21 | 309.01 | 337.17 | 358.15 | 385.18 | 409.18 |
| 285.21 | 309.10 | 337.22 | 358.19 | 385.18 | 410.13 |
| 286.01 | 309.13 | 338.03 | 358.19 | 386.01 | 410.20 |
| 286.03 | 309.19 | 338.04 | 359.02 | 386.05 | 410.21 |
| 286.07 | 310.05 | 338.10 | 359.09 | 386.06 | 411.05 |
| 287.01 | 310.08 | 338.20 | 359.16 | 386.11 | 411.10 |
| 287.18 | 310.08 | 339.04 | 359.22 | 386.20 | 411.12 |
| 287.19 | 310.09 | 339.11 | 360.03 | 387.01 | 411.15 |
| 287.21 | 310.14 | 339.14 | 360.04 | 387.03 | 411.16 |
| 288.10 | 310.17 | 339.17 | 360.06 | 387.05 | 411.18 |
| 288.19 | 311.02 | 339.22 | 360.07 | 387.07 | 412.06 |
| 288.20 | 311.16 | 340.03 | 361.01 | 387.08 | 412.07 |
| 289.03 | 312.11 | 340.10 | 361.02 | 387.11 | |
| 289.04 | 312.18 | 340.17 | 361.11 | 387.12 | |
| 289.06 | 312.22 | 340.20 | 361.11 | 387.16 | |

| | | | | | |
|---|---|---|---|---|---|
| 412.16 | 437.10 | 461.09 | 488.06 | 515.09 | 541.04 |
| 412.19 | 437.16 | 461.10 | 488.07 | 516.08 | 541.07 |
| 412.22 | 437.21 | 461.14 | 488.10 | 516.12 | 541.09 |
| 413.02 | 438.02 | 461.15 | 488.11 | 516.21 | 541.11 |
| 413.06 | 438.11 | 461.17 | 488.11 | 517.02 | 541.15 |
| 413.10 | 439.01 | 461.18 | 488.14 | 517.02 | 541.20 |
| 413.13 | 439.02 | 462.06 | 488.18 | 517.12 | 541.22 |
| 413.15 | 439.13 | 462.08 | 489.02 | 518.01 | 542.01 |
| 413.18 | 439.13 | 462.09 | 489.09 | 518.05 | 542.03 |
| 414.01 | 439.14 | 462.11 | 489.16 | 518.08 | 542.05 |
| 414.10 | 439.17 | 462.22 | 489.18 | 518.10 | 542.06 |
| 414.13 | 439.18 | 463.05 | 490.02 | 518.12 | 542.11 |
| 414.15 | 439.21 | 464.06 | 490.04 | 518.15 | 542.14 |
| 414.16 | 440.02 | 464.21 | 490.15 | 518.21 | 542.19 |
| 414.20 | 440.07 | 465.06 | 490.18 | 518.21 | 543.05 |
| 415.05 | 440.13 | 465.07 | 490.22 | 519.10 | 543.11 |
| 415.11 | 441.08 | 465.09 | 491.02 | 519.14 | 543.12 |
| 415.13 | 441.11 | 465.16 | 491.02 | 520.07 | 543.20 |
| 415.22 | 441.16 | 466.01 | 491.04 | 520.09 | 544.02 |
| 416.02 | 441.16 | 466.12 | 491.07 | 520.11 | 544.06 |
| 416.02 | 442.02 | 466.16 | 492.01 | 520.15 | 545.13 |
| 416.04 | 442.11 | 467.14 | 492.11 | 520.19 | 545.19 |
| 416.06 | 442.16 | 468.01 | 493.01 | 520.20 | 546.05 |
| 417.04 | 442.17 | 468.08 | 493.03 | 520.22 | 546.12 |
| 417.12 | 442.20 | 468.17 | 493.19 | 521.01 | 546.16 |
| 417.16 | 442.21 | 468.19 | 494.02 | 521.01 | 547.03 |
| 417.16 | 442.22 | 468.22 | 494.06 | 521.08 | 547.12 |
| 417.17 | 443.05 | 469.04 | 494.08 | 521.09 | 547.17 |
| 417.22 | 443.07 | 469.08 | 494.13 | 521.10 | 547.22 |
| 417.22 | 443.12 | 469.12 | 494.17 | 521.15 | 548.01 |
| 418.01 | 443.19 | 469.14 | 494.20 | 522.07 | 548.02 |
| 418.02 | 443.21 | 469.15 | 495.05 | 522.12 | 548.04 |
| 418.09 | 444.09 | 469.17 | 495.06 | 522.14 | 548.06 |
| 418.10 | 444.10 | 469.20 | 495.11 | 523.01 | 548.15 |
| 418.13 | 444.13 | 470.02 | 496.04 | 523.02 | 548.15 |
| 418.14 | 444.18 | 470.11 | 496.08 | 523.06 | 548.22 |
| 418.15 | 445.02 | 470.12 | 497.08 | 523.07 | 549.04 |
| 418.17 | 445.13 | 470.13 | 497.11 | 523.12 | 550.02 |
| 419.02 | 445.15 | 470.14 | 497.12 | 523.21 | 550.05 |
| 419.04 | 445.20 | 470.15 | 497.15 | 523.22 | 550.05 |
| 419.07 | 445.21 | 470.19 | 497.16 | 523.23 | 550.07 |
| 419.15 | 446.10 | 471.08 | 498.02 | 524.01 | 551.10 |
| 419.19 | 446.13 | 471.10 | 498.13 | 524.05 | 551.16 |
| 420.14 | 446.15 | 471.12 | 498.13 | 524.09 | 552.04 |
| 421.02 | 446.18 | 471.21 | 498.14 | 524.10 | 552.09 |
| 421.03 | 446.20 | 472.09 | 499.13 | 524.15 | 552.15 |
| 421.04 | 447.01 | 472.14 | 499.16 | 525.02 | 553.07 |
| 421.08 | 448.04 | 472.17 | 500.09 | 525.06 | 553.09 |
| 421.13 | 449.05 | 473.04 | 500.16 | 525.18 | 553.11 |
| 421.17 | 449.05 | 473.10 | 500.18 | 525.20 | 553.17 |
| 421.20 | 449.11 | 473.11 | 501.05 | 526.05 | 553.20 |
| 422.01 | 449.16 | 474.03 | 501.13 | 526.05 | 554.01 |
| 422.02 | 449.22 | 474.06 | 501.18 | 526.08 | 554.07 |
| 422.03 | 450.07 | 475.04 | 501.19 | 526.17 | 554.08 |
| 422.04 | 450.16 | 475.06 | 502.01 | 526.20 | 554.14 |
| 422.05 | 450.19 | 475.09 | 502.02 | 526.22 | 554.15 |
| 422.06 | 451.06 | 475.11 | 502.06 | 527.03 | 554.21 |
| 422.10 | 451.10 | 475.13 | 502.09 | 527.09 | 555.04 |
| 422.14 | 451.12 | 475.14 | 503.06 | 527.13 | 555.05 |
| 422.15 | 451.18 | 476.13 | 503.09 | 527.16 | 555.09 |
| 422.17 | 452.01 | 476.14 | 503.10 | 527.18 | 555.13 |
| 422.21 | 452.04 | 476.16 | 503.13 | 528.04 | 555.13 |
| 423.03 | 452.09 | 476.18 | 503.14 | 528.05 | 555.14 |
| 424.06 | 452.11 | 476.20 | 503.17 | 528.07 | 555.20 |
| 425.06 | 452.13 | 477.11 | 503.17 | 528.10 | 555.21 |
| 425.15 | 452.15 | 477.13 | 503.18 | 528.11 | 556.01 |
| 425.15 | 452.15 | 477.14 | 503.21 | 528.15 | 556.03 |
| 425.19 | 452.22 | 477.18 | 504.09 | 528.19 | 556.05 |
| 426.02 | 453.01 | 478.17 | 504.20 | 529.07 | 556.21 |
| 426.07 | 453.03 | 479.01 | 504.21 | 529.09 | 557.21 |
| 426.12 | 453.05 | 479.02 | 505.01 | 529.09 | 558.01 |
| 427.01 | 453.09 | 479.11 | 505.02 | 530.10 | 558.02 |
| 427.14 | 453.16 | 479.14 | 505.06 | 531.06 | 558.07 |
| 427.20 | 453.18 | 480.07 | 506.03 | 531.06 | 558.08 |
| 428.10 | 453.19 | 480.11 | 506.11 | 531.16 | 558.13 |
| 428.11 | 454.03 | 480.11 | 506.16 | 532.04 | 558.14 |
| 428.15 | 454.09 | 480.14 | 506.19 | 532.07 | 558.15 |
| 428.20 | 454.19 | 480.17 | 507.07 | 532.17 | 558.16 |
| 428.20 | 455.03 | 481.07 | 507.13 | 533.03 | 558.17 |
| 429.02 | 455.07 | 481.09 | 507.19 | 533.07 | 558.19 |
| 429.14 | 455.16 | 481.10 | 507.22 | 533.08 | 559.01 |
| 429.17 | 455.21 | 482.03 | 508.02 | 533.13 | 559.06 |
| 429.17 | 455.22 | 482.06 | 508.14 | 533.13 | 559.10 |
| 429.18 | 456.03 | 482.21 | 508.16 | 533.16 | 559.11 |
| 429.18 | 456.07 | 483.09 | 508.22 | 533.18 | 560.01 |
| 429.22 | 456.11 | 483.12 | 509.05 | 533.19 | 560.04 |
| 430.05 | 456.11 | 483.13 | 509.18 | 533.20 | 560.08 |
| 430.05 | 457.02 | 483.17 | 510.01 | 533.21 | 560.08 |
| 430.06 | 457.06 | 484.03 | 510.19 | 534.01 | 560.09 |
| 430.17 | 457.08 | 484.05 | 511.06 | 534.14 | 560.14 |
| 430.20 | 457.09 | 484.06 | 511.07 | 534.15 | 560.15 |
| 431.05 | 457.12 | 484.09 | 511.15 | 534.17 | 560.16 |
| 431.13 | 457.14 | 484.11 | 511.21 | 534.20 | 561.05 |
| 431.15 | 457.16 | 484.16 | 512.03 | 535.07 | 561.15 |
| 432.03 | 458.03 | 485.04 | 512.04 | 535.18 | 561.16 |
| 432.18 | 459.02 | 485.05 | 512.10 | 536.17 | 561.20 |
| 433.05 | 459.03 | 485.05 | 512.14 | 536.18 | 562.08 |
| 433.11 | 459.08 | 485.06 | 512.15 | 537.06 | 562.09 |
| 433.17 | 459.10 | 485.13 | 513.03 | 537.06 | 562.11 |
| 433.21 | 459.12 | 485.15 | 513.04 | 537.07 | 562.13 |
| 434.17 | 460.02 | 485.18 | 513.07 | 537.15 | 562.14 |
| 435.07 | 460.03 | 486.01 | 513.16 | 538.01 | 563.03 |
| 435.08 | 460.05 | 486.01 | 513.17 | 538.09 | 563.04 |
| 435.16 | 460.07 | 486.10 | 513.18 | 538.13 | 563.06 |
| 435.17 | 460.09 | 486.16 | 513.21 | 539.07 | 563.16 |
| 436.08 | 460.09 | 486.17 | 514.03 | 539.11 | 563.17 |
| 436.14 | 460.19 | 487.13 | 514.04 | 539.21 | 563.19 |
| 436.17 | 460.20 | 487.16 | 514.06 | 540.01 | 563.22 |
| 436.20 | 461.04 | 487.20 | 514.12 | 540.06 | 564.03 |
| 437.07 | 461.06 | 488.01 | 514.12 | 540.07 | 564.05 |
| 437.09 | 461.07 |  | 515.02 | 540.16 |  |

| | | | | | |
|---|---|---|---|---|---|
| 564.08 | 588.20 | 616.13 | 638.14 | 660.15 | 680.15 |
| 564.21 | 589.02 | 616.16 | 638.21 | 661.01 | 680.17 |
| 565.17 | 589.06 | 617.01 | 638.22 | 661.04 | 680.21 |
| 566.05 | 589.07 | 617.13 | 639.01 | 661.05 | 681.09 |
| 566.06 | 589.20 | 617.14 | 639.05 | 661.06 | 682.02 |
| 566.08 | 590.10 | 617.15 | 639.07 | 661.07 | 682.04 |
| 566.17 | 590.13 | 617.15 | 639.10 | 661.10 | 682.11 |
| 567.01 | 590.22 | 617.17 | 639.21 | 661.11 | 682.12 |
| 567.05 | 591.02 | 617.22 | 639.22 | 662.01 | 682.17 |
| 567.10 | 591.09 | 618.01 | 640.07 | 662.03 | 682.21 |
| 567.12 | 591.11 | 618.08 | 640.15 | 662.06 | 683.02 |
| 568.02 | 591.20 | 618.08 | 640.16 | 662.06 | 683.11 |
| 568.03 | 591.21 | 618.11 | 640.17 | 662.10 | 683.12 |
| 568.04 | 592.01 | 618.19 | 640.20 | 662.11 | 683.16 |
| 568.11 | 592.05 | 619.10 | 640.22 | 662.15 | 683.18 |
| 568.12 | 592.07 | 619.13 | 641.02 | 662.16 | 684.02 |
| 568.16 | 592.07 | 619.13 | 641.04 | 663.02 | 684.04 |
| 568.19 | 592.09 | 619.17 | 641.07 | 663.13 | 684.10 |
| 569.01 | 592.12 | 619.20 | 641.11 | 663.15 | 684.12 |
| 569.03 | 592.18 | 620.01 | 641.15 | 663.16 | 684.13 |
| 569.04 | 592.20 | 620.09 | 641.19 | 663.16 | 684.19 |
| 569.09 | 593.04 | 620.14 | 641.22 | 663.18 | 684.22 |
| 569.11 | 593.07 | 620.19 | 642.02 | 663.19 | 685.01 |
| 569.15 | 593.19 | 620.20 | 642.02 | 663.20 | 685.05 |
| 569.16 | 594.03 | 621.02 | 643.05 | 664.02 | 685.09 |
| 569.16 | 594.06 | 621.16 | 643.09 | 664.06 | 685.14 |
| 569.20 | 594.07 | 622.05 | 643.10 | 664.10 | 685.15 |
| 569.20 | 594.09 | 622.08 | 643.11 | 664.13 | 686.05 |
| 569.21 | 594.12 | 622.12 | 644.01 | 665.08 | 686.13 |
| 569.21 | 594.22 | 622.12 | 644.02 | 665.15 | 686.15 |
| 570.05 | 595.07 | 622.15 | 644.09 | 665.21 | 686.16 |
| 570.07 | 595.08 | 622.16 | 644.13 | 666.04 | 688.02 |
| 570.09 | 596.08 | 622.18 | 644.16 | 666.11 | 688.04 |
| 570.12 | 596.12 | 622.19 | 645.01 | 666.13 | 688.07 |
| 570.17 | 597.02 | 622.20 | 645.05 | 666.15 | 689.07 |
| 570.19 | 597.05 | 623.06 | 645.10 | 666.22 | 689.11 |
| 571.11 | 597.10 | 623.07 | 645.14 | 667.05 | 689.15 |
| 571.22 | 598.02 | 623.08 | 645.16 | 667.08 | 689.15 |
| 572.07 | 598.02 | 623.18 | 645.17 | 667.14 | 689.16 |
| 573.01 | 598.17 | 624.01 | 646.02 | 668.01 | 690.04 |
| 573.09 | 598.20 | 624.07 | 646.03 | 668.03 | 691.05 |
| 573.12 | 599.12 | 624.11 | 646.08 | 668.06 | 691.06 |
| 573.17 | 599.15 | 624.14 | 646.12 | 668.08 | 691.17 |
| 573.20 | 599.19 | 624.19 | 646.14 | 668.12 | 691.18 |
| 573.22 | 600.12 | 625.05 | 646.16 | 668.13 | 691.19 |
| 574.01 | 601.15 | 626.07 | 646.20 | 668.21 | 691.22 |
| 574.03 | 601.19 | 627.13 | 646.21 | 669.03 | 692.14 |
| 574.03 | 601.19 | 627.19 | 647.02 | 669.04 | 692.21 |
| 574.05 | 602.15 | 628.01 | 647.04 | 669.05 | 693.05 |
| 574.08 | 602.19 | 628.05 | 647.05 | 669.18 | 693.05 |
| 575.06 | 603.03 | 628.06 | 647.06 | 669.19 | 693.06 |
| 575.08 | 603.04 | 628.08 | 647.06 | 669.19 | 694.06 |
| 576.02 | 603.07 | 628.21 | 647.07 | 669.21 | 694.13 |
| 576.07 | 603.07 | 629.03 | 647.08 | 670.01 | 694.18 |
| 576.09 | 604.01 | 629.05 | 647.11 | 670.06 | 695.02 |
| 576.10 | 604.03 | 629.16 | 647.13 | 670.08 | 695.12 |
| 576.16 | 604.04 | 629.18 | 647.17 | 670.09 | 695.14 |
| 576.18 | 604.10 | 629.21 | 647.20 | 670.09 | 695.17 |
| 576.20 | 604.12 | 630.01 | 648.02 | 670.11 | 695.20 |
| 577.05 | 604.21 | 630.03 | 648.04 | 670.12 | 696.09 |
| 577.07 | 605.01 | 630.04 | 648.13 | 670.13 | 697.02 |
| 577.11 | 605.04 | 630.09 | 648.14 | 670.16 | 697.04 |
| 577.13 | 605.19 | 630.11 | 648.17 | 670.22 | 697.06 |
| 577.14 | 605.19 | 630.15 | 648.22 | 671.04 | 697.11 |
| 577.22 | 606.02 | 630.15 | 649.01 | 671.08 | 697.16 |
| 578.04 | 606.06 | 630.18 | 649.03 | 671.08 | 697.16 |
| 578.20 | 606.13 | 631.03 | 649.09 | 671.10 | 697.21 |
| 578.21 | 606.16 | 631.05 | 649.14 | 671.10 | 698.09 |
| 578.22 | 606.19 | 631.09 | 649.17 | 671.16 | 698.18 |
| 579.03 | 607.01 | 631.14 | 649.22 | 671.19 | 698.22 |
| 579.05 | 607.02 | 631.22 | 650.02 | 671.22 | 699.03 |
| 579.08 | 607.12 | 632.07 | 650.05 | 672.01 | 699.07 |
| 579.14 | 607.16 | 632.09 | 650.08 | 672.07 | 699.10 |
| 580.03 | 607.17 | 632.15 | 651.10 | 672.13 | 699.12 |
| 580.04 | 607.22 | 632.19 | 651.10 | 672.13 | 699.13 |
| 580.06 | 608.02 | 633.03 | 651.15 | 672.16 | 699.19 |
| 580.08 | 608.06 | 633.09 | 651.19 | 673.03 | 700.09 |
| 580.10 | 608.09 | 633.11 | 651.22 | 673.04 | 700.19 |
| 580.19 | 608.11 | 633.12 | 652.05 | 673.05 | 700.20 |
| 580.20 | 608.15 | 633.15 | 652.06 | 674.02 | 700.20 |
| 580.20 | 609.10 | 633.18 | 652.15 | 674.15 | 700.22 |
| 580.21 | 609.18 | 633.22 | 652.19 | 674.17 | 701.03 |
| 580.21 | 609.18 | 634.04 | 653.09 | 675.01 | 701.05 |
| 581.02 | 610.02 | 634.05 | 653.11 | 675.04 | 701.06 |
| 581.04 | 610.08 | 634.07 | 653.14 | 675.07 | 701.07 |
| 581.06 | 610.09 | 634.17 | 653.15 | 675.08 | 702.02 |
| 581.15 | 610.12 | 634.20 | 653.18 | 675.10 | 702.08 |
| 581.20 | 610.17 | 635.02 | 653.20 | 676.05 | 702.11 |
| 582.02 | 610.17 | 635.04 | 653.22 | 676.07 | 702.16 |
| 582.03 | 610.20 | 636.02 | 654.11 | 676.11 | 702.16 |
| 583.02 | 611.04 | 636.06 | 654.19 | 676.15 | 703.01 |
| 583.09 | 611.05 | 636.07 | 654.20 | 676.16 | 703.08 |
| 583.15 | 611.07 | 636.09 | 655.05 | 677.04 | 703.09 |
| 583.17 | 611.07 | 636.10 | 655.09 | 677.10 | 703.12 |
| 584.03 | 611.14 | 636.12 | 655.17 | 677.19 | 703.17 |
| 585.03 | 612.06 | 636.17 | 655.20 | 677.20 | 703.21 |
| 585.05 | 612.07 | 636.20 | 656.04 | 678.05 | 704.04 |
| 585.07 | 613.05 | 637.01 | 656.04 | 678.08 | 704.07 |
| 586.02 | 613.15 | 637.02 | 656.14 | 678.15 | 704.09 |
| 586.02 | 613.19 | 637.07 | 656.15 | 678.18 | 704.09 |
| 586.14 | 613.20 | 637.14 | 656.17 | 679.06 | 704.12 |
| 586.14 | 614.05 | 637.15 | 658.02 | 679.10 | 704.12 |
| 587.02 | 614.12 | 637.17 | 658.04 | 679.12 | 704.17 |
| 587.04 | 614.16 | 637.17 | 659.01 | 679.12 | 704.18 |
| 587.10 | 615.05 | 637.18 | 659.15 | 679.16 | 705.03 |
| 588.02 | 615.16 | 637.19 | 659.16 | 679.21 | 705.05 |
| 588.07 | 615.19 | 637.21 | 660.04 | 680.09 | 705.07 |
| 588.09 | 616.03 | 638.02 | 660.11 | 680.10 | 705.10 |
| 588.13 | 616.04 | 638.05 | 660.13 | 680.12 | 705.22 |
| 588.13 | 616.05 | 638.10 | | 680.14 | 706.05 |
| 588.18 | 616.09 | 638.11 | | | 706.07 |

| | | | | | |
|---|---|---|---|---|---|
| 706.16 | 729.13 | 751.13 | **toast** | 451.10 | 240.06 |
| 706.19 | 729.15 | 751.15 | 270.22 | 460.13 | **too** |
| 707.01 | 729.19 | 751.17 | 476.12 | 477.14 | 008.01 |
| 707.04 | 729.21 | 751.21 | **toasted** | 480.12 | 024.14 |
| 707.04 | 730.03 | 752.02 | 531.04 | 481.09 | 026.18 |
| 707.04 | 730.07 | 752.05 | **tobacco** | 483.21 | 037.12 |
| 707.05 | 730.09 | 752.08 | 062.02 | 497.14 | 041.14 |
| 707.10 | 730.11 | 752.13 | **today** | 505.03 | 045.13 |
| 707.12 | 730.12 | 752.20 | 075.06 | 510.20 | 049.14 |
| 707.16 | 730.17 | 753.11 | 171.17 | 528.09 | 059.12 |
| 707.18 | 730.18 | 754.05 | 607.16 | 537.01 | 062.04 |
| 707.19 | 730.19 | 754.06 | **together** | 543.22 | 068.03 |
| 708.01 | 731.02 | 754.08 | 038.15 | 555.19 | 070.22 |
| 708.04 | 731.02 | 754.14 | 042.16 | 556.11 | 075.18 |
| 708.20 | 731.05 | 754.14 | 045.09 | 560.09 | 081.16 |
| 708.22 | 731.06 | 754.14 | 061.07 | 572.20 | 090.23 |
| 709.17 | 731.08 | 754.17 | 072.13 | 585.11 | 099.04 |
| 709.22 | 731.11 | 755.03 | 093.02 | 592.17 | 101.13 |
| 710.04 | 731.13 | 755.11 | 095.21 | 598.16 | 102.06 |
| 710.05 | 731.14 | 755.19 | 100.17 | 611.07 | 108.06 |
| 710.06 | 732.04 | 756.02 | 120.20 | 626.12 | 131.20 |
| 710.08 | 732.07 | 756.03 | 125.20 | 627.18 | 139.07 |
| 710.15 | 732.08 | 756.07 | 172.17 | 632.18 | 141.04 |
| 711.01 | 732.09 | 756.11 | 209.06 | 637.09 | 146.06 |
| 711.01 | 732.12 | 756.15 | 222.07 | 641.14 | 153.19 |
| 712.02 | 732.18 | 756.16 | 232.04 | 658.07 | 154.18 |
| 712.08 | 732.19 | 756.20 | 237.22 | 659.01 | 161.02 |
| 712.23 | 733.16 | 757.13 | 264.07 | 659.13 | 167.21 |
| 713.12 | 733.19 | 757.18 | 284.14 | 663.15 | 168.19 |
| 713.14 | 733.20 | 757.22 | 302.19 | 665.07 | 182.09 |
| 713.17 | 733.21 | 758.03 | 379.10 | 700.05 | 186.06 |
| 713.20 | 734.06 | 758.06 | 410.01 | 738.04 | 186.22 |
| 713.21 | 734.17 | 758.07 | 413.03 | 747.01 | 191.21 |
| 713.22 | 734.18 | 758.10 | 431.20 | **tolerable** | 198.09 |
| 713.23 | 734.18 | 758.14 | 451.11 | 590.03 | 202.08 |
| 714.02 | 734.20 | 758.21 | 452.07 | 700.14 | 211.10 |
| 715.03 | 736.04 | 759.03 | 461.03 | **tolerably** | 212.18 |
| 715.06 | 736.05 | 759.05 | 475.16 | 025.13 | 214.08 |
| 715.10 | 736.06 | 759.16 | 512.01 | 089.08 | 215.08 |
| 715.11 | 736.07 | 759.19 | 528.08 | 192.10 | 221.20 |
| 715.12 | 737.12 | 760.01 | 544.03 | 263.20 | 225.10 |
| 716.09 | 737.13 | 760.03 | 583.03 | 271.19 | 234.20 |
| 716.11 | 737.18 | 760.06 | 598.21 | 390.05 | 239.03 |
| 716.15 | 738.01 | 760.14 | 636.14 | 472.19 | 239.06 |
| 717.02 | 738.04 | 760.20 | 646.08 | 511.04 | 239.21 |
| 717.10 | 738.07 | 760.21 | 660.16 | 592.17 | 249.12 |
| 717.11 | 738.14 | 761.21 | 674.11 | 616.13 | 254.11 |
| 717.14 | 738.15 | 762.01 | 687.03 | **tolerate** | 256.02 |
| 717.16 | 738.17 | 762.08 | 716.02 | 181.15 | 272.13 |
| 718.08 | 739.03 | 762.11 | 728.04 | **tolerated** | 278.18 |
| 719.09 | 739.04 | 762.15 | 732.13 | 225.07 | 289.03 |
| 721.04 | 739.07 | 762.17 | 747.21 | **tombs** | 296.19 |
| 721.09 | 739.10 | 763.02 | 762.21 | 379.20 | 302.09 |
| 721.10 | 739.12 | 763.04 | **togither** | **tome** | 306.09 |
| 721.11 | 740.01 | 763.20 | 191.03 | 039.17 | 306.09 |
| 721.12 | 740.04 | 764.08 | **toil** | **tomorrow** | 310.21 |
| 721.15 | 740.06 | **to't** | 547.12 | 143.12 | 311.09 |
| 721.15 | 740.09 | 719.20 | **toiled** | **tone** | 317.05 |
| 721.19 | 740.10 | **to-bed** | 481.07 | 022.21 | 326.17 |
| 722.16 | 740.10 | 227.02 | **toilette** | 153.08 | 336.19 |
| 722.18 | 740.13 | 390.06 | 058.19 | 172.16 | 347.06 |
| 722.22 | 740.14 | **to-day** | **token** | 206.18 | 355.08 |
| 722.23 | 740.17 | 076.09 | 018.08 | 216.18 | 363.18 |
| 723.02 | 741.06 | 151.15 | 328.08 | 256.04 | 369.09 |
| 723.02 | 741.09 | 303.17 | **told** | 262.16 | 378.20 |
| 723.09 | 742.01 | 390.14 | 008.15 | 315.07 | 385.05 |
| 723.15 | 742.08 | 416.17 | 036.10 | 321.14 | 397.05 |
| 723.20 | 742.09 | 539.04 | 056.21 | 356.10 | 397.20 |
| 723.21 | 742.10 | 589.15 | 076.03 | 396.18 | 408.17 |
| 723.22 | 742.10 | 593.22 | 079.06 | 456.16 | 412.06 |
| 724.01 | 742.22 | 717.01 | 086.02 | 490.21 | 413.13 |
| 724.02 | 743.02 | 742.20 | 092.15 | 510.10 | 416.04 |
| 724.04 | 743.09 | 746.21 | 094.01 | 570.06 | 417.02 |
| 724.06 | 743.10 | **to-morn** | 095.04 | 603.04 | 417.05 |
| 724.07 | 743.13 | 187.11 | 098.14 | 603.10 | 420.14 |
| 724.09 | 743.14 | **to-morrow** | 101.10 | 669.11 | 424.10 |
| 724.12 | 744.02 | 013.15 | 105.17 | 681.16 | 427.19 |
| 724.12 | 744.03 | 103.16 | 105.19 | **tones** | 428.02 |
| 724.13 | 744.09 | 135.09 | 112.11 | 028.19 | 430.13 |
| 724.19 | 744.18 | 215.15 | 122.19 | 532.01 | 430.16 |
| 724.20 | 744.19 | 273.09 | 133.03 | 694.09 | 430.16 |
| 724.22 | 745.03 | 345.08 | 134.09 | **tongue** | 436.17 |
| 725.02 | 745.04 | 368.06 | 143.09 | 011.13 | 445.02 |
| 725.02 | 745.09 | 457.13 | 153.18 | 064.17 | 452.19 |
| 725.10 | 745.15 | 504.10 | 159.07 | 084.03 | 457.13 |
| 725.11 | 745.17 | 544.16 | 175.14 | 090.13 | 465.10 |
| 725.12 | 745.19 | 544.17 | 185.01 | 107.03 | 472.07 |
| 725.15 | 745.19 | 545.01 | 194.13 | 107.19 | 473.03 |
| 725.18 | 745.19 | 573.08 | 196.04 | 117.10 | 482.13 |
| 725.19 | 745.21 | 581.06 | 199.14 | 142.08 | 488.04 |
| 725.22 | 746.02 | 611.09 | 221.12 | 193.14 | 489.09 |
| 726.02 | 746.11 | 656.03 | 226.17 | 230.14 | 489.17 |
| 726.02 | 746.16 | 697.13 | 227.17 | 250.07 | 495.05 |
| 726.06 | 746.18 | 713.04 | 232.08 | 280.22 | 499.20 |
| 726.07 | 747.02 | **to-night** | 247.12 | 295.17 | 513.04 |
| 726.15 | 747.05 | 167.22 | 249.20 | 362.11 | 517.20 |
| 726.17 | 748.19 | 177.17 | 266.01 | 376.20 | 526.22 |
| 727.04 | 749.09 | 216.21 | 266.17 | 395.16 | 537.15 |
| 727.06 | 749.12 | 261.21 | 293.11 | 396.01 | 538.04 |
| 727.09 | 749.14 | 344.02 | 298.09 | 434.22 | 542.15 |
| 727.14 | 749.18 | 384.07 | 299.04 | 483.08 | 543.02 |
| 727.18 | 749.21 | 396.17 | 304.06 | 493.04 | 553.16 |
| 728.01 | 750.07 | 435.08 | 326.20 | 499.09 | 567.17 |
| 728.04 | 750.10 | 452.09 | 327.10 | 536.18 | 575.08 |
| 728.08 | 750.12 | 455.18 | 332.11 | 538.05 | 576.06 |
| 728.15 | 750.22 | 458.01 | 339.19 | 682.03 | 585.07 |
| 728.18 | 751.03 | 543.07 | 341.18 | 683.08 | 587.16 |
| 729.04 | 751.04 | 563.07 | 350.20 | 721.08 | 600.07 |
| 729.09 | 751.06 | 579.22 | 351.10 | 725.18 | 601.06 |
| 729.10 | | 616.09 | 373.11 | **tongues** | 610.02 |
| 729.11 | | 635.18 | 445.19 | 005.17 | 612.10 |

| | | | | | |
|---|---|---|---|---|---|
| true | 679.12 | 308.17 | tutored | 143.15 | 190.22 |
| 138.07 | 679.21 | 313.16 | 198.04 | 144.06 | 193.22 |
| 181.16 | 739.07 | 315.08 | twang | 148.04 | 194.02 |
| 231.13 | 749.18 | 352.19 | 265.14 | 163.10 | 324.04 |
| 233.15 | tube | 394.01 | twelve | 170.18 | ugly |
| 261.22 | 062.05 | 416.06 | 014.07 | 187.08 | 125.11 |
| 272.02 | tucked | 417.09 | 067.09 | 196.08 | 174.19 |
| 278.07 | 011.10 | 422.14 | 190.12 | 200.08 | uh |
| 297.17 | 325.20 | 433.07 | 194.01 | 212.11 | 029.01 |
| 368.12 | 509.02 | 450.08 | 278.07 | 214.22 | 043.04 |
| 375.01 | tuesday | 472.20 | 282.07 | 235.03 | 043.17 |
| 415.08 | 378.12 | 476.20 | 284.18 | 239.12 | 043.18 |
| 417.04 | tuft | 482.16 | 369.02 | 255.02 | 043.21 |
| 495.22 | 519.11 | 497.11 | 390.07 | 258.06 | 187.09 |
| 524.19 | tuh | 569.07 | 392.16 | 260.19 | 188.02 |
| 528.03 | 016.07 | 586.08 | 412.13 | 272.14 | 193.18 |
| 570.07 | 028.20 | 598.02 | 424.02 | 277.01 | 232.13 |
| 603.14 | 029.02 | 615.19 | 544.14 | 291.18 | 232.14 |
| 627.06 | 187.20 | 621.01 | 575.05 | 294.12 | 232.15 |
| 636.03 | 188.01 | 709.22 | twelvemonths | 298.12 | 321.04 |
| 675.02 | 191.01 | 722.15 | 685.01 | 301.02 | 321.05 |
| 691.13 | 191.03 | 731.02 | twentieth | 301.03 | 322.05 |
| 746.12 | 232.14 | 748.11 | 478.14 | 303.05 | 322.06 |
| truer | 232.17 | 761.01 | twenty | 303.10 | 324.16 |
| 112.03 | 232.22 | turned | 044.11 | 307.02 | 420.09 |
| truly | 233.04 | 019.21 | 047.18 | 308.19 | 420.09 |
| 144.19 | 233.08 | 025.16 | 052.12 | 318.12 | 420.11 |
| 433.16 | 233.08 | 035.16 | 053.11 | 335.20 | 457.21 |
| 593.11 | 233.12 | 051.06 | 053.12 | 336.14 | 565.14 |
| 632.10 | 310.02 | 054.13 | 053.13 | 355.17 | 699.11 |
| trumpet | 318.11 | 076.04 | 053.13 | 358.03 | 719.14 |
| 131.11 | 318.12 | 093.15 | 056.22 | 369.04 | 719.15 |
| trunk | 318.14 | 121.01 | 123.20 | 379.09 | 720.10 |
| 377.10 | 318.15 | 160.06 | 189.22 | 387.09 | uh't |
| trunks | 319.08 | 169.11 | 202.18 | 393.05 | 042.21 |
| 518.01 | 321.03 | 179.17 | 230.19 | 399.18 | ultimate |
| trust | 324.05 | 206.21 | 243.15 | 400.18 | 356.06 |
| 022.12 | 324.14 | 236.15 | 357.12 | 419.17 | umbrella |
| 285.08 | 324.15 | 247.22 | 446.02 | 430.12 | 517.01 |
| 339.11 | 326.11 | 266.06 | 470.12 | 432.08 | 527.15 |
| 347.11 | 400.20 | 273.19 | 490.05 | 456.14 | umph |
| 355.11 | 400.21 | 308.06 | 518.02 | 477.21 | 022.14 |
| 435.04 | 458.09 | 317.21 | 520.15 | 480.19 | un |
| 509.06 | 472.07 | 334.15 | 546.03 | 482.05 | 028.21 |
| trusted | 696.07 | 348.10 | twenty-four | 484.15 | 187.06 |
| 409.05 | 696.12 | 361.16 | 306.14 | 491.09 | 187.09 |
| 415.09 | 712.16 | 395.21 | 618.06 | 497.09 | 232.19 |
| 426.12 | 712.17 | 404.09 | 736.08 | 504.17 | 233.04 |
| trustees | 719.11 | 428.15 | twenty-seven | 513.06 | 233.07 |
| 636.18 | 719.14 | 438.09 | 417.09 | 513.07 | 319.10 |
| trustful | 719.16 | 492.22 | twenty-three | 516.10 | 322.05 |
| 240.16 | 719.20 | 624.01 | 138.11 | 524.09 | 326.09 |
| trusting | 719.21 | 634.18 | 727.22 | 535.15 | 326.11 |
| 067.01 | tull | 649.09 | twenty-two | 558.20 | 420.10 |
| truth | 016.07 | 653.03 | 173.04 | 559.08 | 456.17 |
| 057.10 | 455.19 | 662.16 | twice | 573.02 | 471.15 |
| 080.19 | tum'le | 667.13 | 047.12 | 577.17 | 720.16 |
| 081.15 | 324.12 | 676.03 | 088.09 | 588.02 | 758.18 |
| 167.15 | tumbler | 681.15 | 123.14 | 603.20 | un' |
| 194.20 | 111.05 | 692.15 | 142.15 | 604.14 | 043.17 |
| 200.05 | 168.05 | 717.22 | 477.16 | 608.12 | 233.06 |
| 236.06 | 534.10 | 734.20 | 488.04 | 610.19 | 233.07 |
| 238.17 | tumblerfuls | 745.07 | 489.20 | 610.20 | 233.07 |
| 251.11 | 390.10 | 747.10 | 496.13 | 615.03 | 310.12 |
| 272.17 | tumult | turning | 504.17 | 616.04 | 319.11 |
| 331.18 | 004.06 | 018.16 | 555.02 | 622.02 | 320.13 |
| 339.17 | 051.01 | 026.02 | 620.03 | 624.09 | 322.08 |
| 386.19 | 283.02 | 064.04 | 661.06 | 632.21 | 324.13 |
| 408.01 | 335.07 | 091.19 | 664.06 | 635.04 | 458.09 |
| 418.19 | tumultuously | 109.14 | 700.09 | 637.08 | 696.12 |
| 526.01 | 067.14 | 174.09 | 717.16 | 645.08 | 696.14 |
| 543.09 | tune | 190.07 | 741.05 | 646.03 | 696.15 |
| 554.15 | 493.02 | 217.18 | twined | 651.20 | 712.17 |
| 571.14 | 697.02 | 239.11 | 542.19 | 672.12 | 713.06 |
| 738.15 | 707.18 | 263.18 | twinkle | 711.17 | 719.12 |
| try | tunes | 264.06 | 159.06 | 714.04 | 719.13 |
| 212.22 | 118.19 | 276.05 | twinkling | 718.20 | 719.14 |
| 231.05 | tureen | 330.16 | 123.16 | 721.03 | 719.18 |
| 250.16 | 128.05 | 360.07 | 244.07 | 725.06 | 720.14 |
| 263.02 | turf | 410.20 | twist | 727.19 | 720.17 |
| 265.15 | 243.22 | 438.01 | 421.08 | 729.10 | 720.17 |
| 281.02 | 449.09 | 440.02 | twisted | 730.07 | 761.09 |
| 299.13 | 516.16 | 463.04 | 330.14 | 737.05 | unable |
| 421.21 | 518.19 | 486.10 | 379.09 | 741.10 | 015.11 |
| 452.09 | 605.05 | 488.19 | 518.16 | 749.02 | 423.03 |
| 460.20 | 689.21 | 508.17 | twisting | 754.18 | 569.04 |
| 488.11 | 764.03 | 513.18 | 237.08 | 760.17 | 715.03 |
| 497.16 | turkey's | 533.17 | twitched | 761.02 | unacceptable |
| 553.20 | 275.07 | 560.03 | 702.06 | tying | 237.06 |
| 558.08 | turn | 564.12 | 702.10 | 020.05 | unaccompanied |
| 558.16 | 009.05 | 656.04 | twitches | 140.10 | 430.10 |
| 560.14 | 010.13 | 669.16 | 702.07 | type | 637.12 |
| 588.08 | 013.03 | 679.16 | two | 039.18 | unaccountable |
| 623.07 | 019.22 | 721.15 | 006.15 | 259.06 | 734.13 |
| 624.07 | 045.10 | 724.07 | 019.04 | tyrannical | unachieved |
| 642.06 | 055.17 | 756.03 | 034.10 | 099.10 | 062.13 |
| 691.17 | 071.01 | turnip | 037.09 | 144.04 | unalterably |
| 703.03 | 084.14 | 675.09 | 042.11 | tyrannically | 145.14 |
| 714.03 | 084.15 | turns | 047.13 | 584.01 | unannoyed |
| 730.19 | 124.05 | 171.11 | 047.19 | tyrannies | 062.07 |
| trying | 125.10 | 336.20 | 060.04 | 616.06 | unanswered |
| 113.07 | 145.07 | 524.13 | 061.12 | tyrant | 531.08 |
| 133.16 | 152.11 | tush | 081.20 | 042.04 | unavailing |
| 145.10 | 182.22 | 336.09 | 089.09 | 252.17 | 494.12 |
| 279.10 | 194.22 | tut | 104.21 | 401.22 | unavenged |
| 315.18 | 195.09 | 467.19 | 115.10 | 619.17 | 020.22 |
| 337.14 | 223.15 | 467.19 | 124.11 | ud | unavoidably |
| 352.12 | 252.18 | tutor | 126.10 | 043.21 | 759.05 |
| 415.05 | 260.08 | 470.11 | 133.12 | uf | unbarred |
| 569.21 | 262.08 | | 135.01 | 187.15 | 270.15 |
| 638.02 | 294.01 | | 141.14 | 187.21 | |

unbeliever
136.12
unbidden
367.07
uncared
115.12
uncarpeted
558.12
unceremoniously
034.02
uncertain
207.20
485.01
517.19
561.11
uncertainly
283.13
unchain
003.06
unchained
059.22
673.11
unchangeable
225.19
unchanged
225.19
unchristian
489.01
754.01
uncivil
491.20
uncle
452.05
453.10
460.15
461.09
461.21
462.05
463.20
464.02
464.09
487.19
488.13
488.16
491.13
499.09
499.09
581.05
586.05
590.02
604.04
619.20
621.05
632.10
633.01
664.15
uncle's
580.09
uncle-in-law's
502.05
uncleared
515.04
unclose
757.13
unclosed
191.22
uncombed
115.21
uncomfortable
021.15
075.05
089.03
180.13
364.10
uncommonly
337.15
741.22
uncomplaining
082.18
uncompromising
706.11
unconscious
553.11
683.21
unconsciously
279.05
unconsciousness
746.01
uncontrollable
060.12
195.12
uncovered
378.03
uncoveted
754.22
uncultivated
021.15
682.05
uncurled
330.11
uncurtained
382.07
und
042.21
184.14
187.22
191.01
193.21
233.02
401.09
457.22

471.15

undecided
709.07
undefined
206.09

undeniable
386.19
under
002.01
006.16
007.21
027.12
036.10
039.15
044.14
057.22
058.10
069.09
085.13
103.19
108.13
119.11
124.16
128.07
130.16
174.01
197.13
213.05
217.20
237.05
263.21
269.10
276.14
276.21
282.22
287.16
290.10
303.09
303.15
308.17
324.17
338.12
359.11
368.07
379.19
381.09
383.19
386.17
427.06
427.22
429.16
430.09
433.19
435.02
437.14
442.14
444.20
449.09
457.16
472.02
509.10
514.01
518.16
525.04
539.09
542.07
578.09
579.07
583.03
593.18
603.20
604.12
607.08
618.06
644.02
652.21
657.01
680.20
689.10
690.14
713.12
722.22
737.10
741.13
746.19
747.04
756.02
761.09
764.06
under-bred
007.16
under-drawn
006.04
under-lip
020.15
undergo
592.09
undergone
137.19
underground
359.19
650.10
underlined
306.17
underlings
261.07
471.09
underneath
165.19
527.16

understand
010.11
078.07
091.09
331.06
343.08
362.10
496.14
496.15
670.06
704.07
707.05
719.09
understanding
309.11
understood
008.18
046.21
104.20
109.15
122.16
undertake
047.20
183.18
619.17
undertone
003.19
undertook
112.13
undeserved
009.07
undisguised
215.06
undisputed
422.04
undisturbed
451.07
undone
135.07
undress
503.18
616.10
undressed
102.15
663.19
undulating
557.20
unearthly
351.11
748.08
uneasily
542.09
uneasiness
225.01
495.06
uneasy
186.19
436.13
594.20
unequal
359.10
unexpected
004.02
154.07
325.07
412.15
unexpectedly
589.08
688.04
727.12
unfastened
211.03
unfeeling
130.09
130.18
584.05
unfit
110.02
418.13
754.10
unfixed
365.20
unfledged
074.09
unflinching
375.07
unfold
295.13
unformed
040.11
unfortunate
074.10
168.07
180.19
421.04
695.18
unfortunately
010.11
032.13
unfriended
101.01
ungenerous
230.04
ungodly
189.12
ungovernable
376.15
ungraciously
676.09
ungrateful
252.13
612.19

unhappy
026.10
041.10
171.04
175.18
227.08
413.13
568.21
unharmed
190.01
unhasp
051.16
unheard
696.09
unheeding
303.22
unhesitatingly
677.13
uniform
312.17
uninhabited
392.02
union
096.09
485.06
583.11
714.04
unison
009.17
universal
023.13
734.04
universe
182.22
unjustly
562.20
unknotted
513.09
unknown
040.17
438.21
unless
025.17
056.11
070.12
098.08
110.18
138.02
145.03
167.22
169.06
174.16
216.16
219.01
250.13
254.15
272.15
292.05
314.07
358.06
367.12
373.04
395.12
405.11
437.03
455.21
464.18
489.04
490.09
512.22
525.04
540.19
547.05
572.14
577.08
593.03
619.08
637.20
651.05
672.05
754.10
unlikely
387.04
455.06
unlimited
338.14
unlock
641.22
unluckily
018.20
431.12
unlucky
157.12
unmanned
720.19
unmannerly
032.13
unmistakably
027.07
unmolested
132.09
unmoved
712.02
unnatural
019.18
164.07
308.04
646.16
741.12
741.12

unnecessary
099.02
248.19
503.06
unnerved
399.09
unnoticed
675.12
unobserved
344.13
568.12
unobstructed
695.22
unperilous
733.16
unpleasing
487.11
unprincipled
183.20
unquiet
764.10
unreasonable
227.11
262.16
unreclaimed
229.12
unreconciled
385.06
unresting
327.05
unrestrained
582.07
unrevenged
252.05
unripped
509.20
unruly
147.14
unsaid
209.21
unsatisfactorily
268.01
unseasonable
456.08
unseen
249.08
unsettle
282.16
unsettled
345.22
unslinging
671.05
unsociable
121.10
150.05
495.18
unsolicited
226.02
unspeakable
050.19
404.16
unspeakably
653.04
unsubstantial
426.13
unsuccessful
325.22
unsummoned
743.09
unsuspecting
421.09
untenanted
067.02
untidy
309.02
untie
114.16
untied
553.10
until
544.13
untold
148.14
untroubled
371.04
untruth
159.07
554.07
590.07
untying
291.12
unusual
177.21
404.03
unutterable
377.06
unutterably
756.10
unvalued
754.22
unwarrantable
345.05
unwashed
025.02
unwaveringly
734.07
unwearied
749.08
unwelcome
691.15

unwelcomed
370.05
unwell
589.21
unwilling
050.16
533.13
unwillingly
516.22
550.08
713.02
unwittingly
147.01
unwonted
728.15
unworthy
008.10
578.20
581.11
up
002.02
003.07
003.10
003.14
004.08
009.10
009.13
011.10
014.06
015.12
038.19
039.17
040.01
041.06
042.17
044.01
045.01
048.19
049.10
053.04
053.18
055.02
055.13
056.04
062.09
063.09
064.01
066.13
067.06
067.15
077.09
077.18
078.09
078.20
081.15
084.18
085.17
089.11
090.07
092.06
093.15
094.05
094.22
099.22
101.18
103.17
103.20
106.21
107.06
109.17
109.18
110.14
111.21
114.04
114.22
120.10
121.16
122.06
123.06
125.18
126.07
128.11
130.07
130.22
131.22
132.12
139.08
140.19
143.12
144.03
146.17
149.16
154.03
156.18
166.01
170.04
177.06
178.04
180.06
185.04
186.10
188.13
188.21
190.18
192.16
192.21
194.07
194.09
198.01
199.09
202.10

| | | | | | |
|---|---|---|---|---|---|
| 208.04 | 525.08 | 165.02 | 096.03 | 591.17 | ushered |
| 210.08 | 532.18 | 186.02 | 096.07 | 593.07 | 036.15 |
| 212.02 | 533.20 | 211.09 | 098.09 | 595.01 | 213.07 |
| 212.21 | 539.10 | 291.09 | 101.10 | 598.22 | 530.02 |
| 218.18 | 541.06 | 320.15 | 103.22 | 599.12 | 644.19 |
| 228.16 | 542.19 | 342.20 | 105.07 | 602.22 | using |
| 232.04 | 547.20 | 342.21 | 105.20 | 603.09 | 091.05 |
| 232.13 | 550.04 | 351.02 | 107.18 | 603.14 | usual |
| 233.01 | 551.05 | 390.17 | 109.03 | 611.20 | 011.06 |
| 236.03 | 552.05 | 392.17 | 112.06 | 612.15 | 067.11 |
| 239.05 | 552.06 | 510.13 | 113.11 | 613.12 | 131.17 |
| 242.03 | 553.07 | 566.10 | 131.19 | 613.15 | 185.15 |
| 245.05 | 555.15 | 634.12 | 137.01 | 613.17 | 191.18 |
| 247.20 | 557.10 | 634.13 | 145.03 | 614.03 | 234.06 |
| 256.18 | 560.03 | 638.22 | 151.13 | 614.09 | 296.14 |
| 259.05 | 560.16 | 664.05 | 159.21 | 622.16 | 351.05 |
| 261.11 | 562.16 | upbraid | 168.18 | 622.17 | 393.17 |
| 265.05 | 563.06 | 363.19 | 175.17 | 623.03 | 472.11 |
| 265.06 | 568.12 | uplands | 177.07 | 637.21 | 503.16 |
| 266.06 | 569.05 | 530.04 | 181.06 | 638.20 | 572.11 |
| 266.20 | 569.12 | upon | 187.01 | 639.22 | 587.05 |
| 267.02 | 570.05 | 019.21 | 189.09 | 643.04 | 705.13 |
| 267.11 | 573.07 | 024.22 | 189.14 | 647.06 | 738.06 |
| 269.04 | 578.04 | 025.06 | 190.01 | 648.05 | 747.01 |
| 274.13 | 593.07 | 043.08 | 191.07 | 650.03 | usuald |
| 275.18 | 593.19 | 050.04 | 192.14 | 651.13 | 193.12 |
| 277.09 | 597.05 | 087.10 | 192.18 | 651.21 | usually |
| 278.16 | 602.21 | 115.01 | 196.16 | 652.13 | 099.02 |
| 284.08 | 604.15 | 161.02 | 196.18 | 666.03 | 139.06 |
| 291.22 | 604.16 | 182.03 | 197.03 | 667.21 | 408.08 |
| 292.11 | 604.17 | 185.19 | 198.13 | 669.19 | 693.12 |
| 293.01 | 605.08 | 323.10 | 219.13 | 670.02 | 717.01 |
| 295.02 | 608.20 | 333.16 | 228.01 | 671.15 | usurped |
| 296.13 | 609.04 | 342.11 | 232.22 | 676.04 | 392.22 |
| 297.05 | 615.01 | 354.14 | 235.05 | 680.07 | 548.11 |
| 298.14 | 616.22 | 502.09 | 241.02 | 685.16 | usurper |
| 303.10 | 620.21 | 602.22 | 246.09 | 697.10 | 082.02 |
| 304.20 | 621.15 | 640.22 | 249.18 | 699.20 | 443.15 |
| 310.10 | 622.17 | 668.02 | 253.13 | 712.19 | ut |
| 313.01 | 624.03 | 678.09 | 260.06 | 725.03 | 043.20 |
| 315.17 | 624.07 | 713.03 | 262.09 | 727.12 | 187.07 |
| 319.02 | 628.02 | 727.12 | 264.18 | 736.03 | 188.01 |
| 320.06 | 629.15 | upper | 286.03 | 737.20 | 193.17 |
| 322.13 | 631.08 | 020.18 | 286.11 | 740.04 | 194.04 |
| 326.05 | 634.03 | 522.11 | 290.08 | 756.21 | 318.15 |
| 326.20 | 635.05 | uppermost | 308.13 | usage | 321.06 |
| 329.22 | 635.20 | 582.14 | 313.13 | 323.07 | 322.06 |
| 332.05 | 637.18 | upright | 320.14 | use | 586.01 |
| 338.02 | 641.19 | 066.06 | 324.01 | 029.01 | 696.10 |
| 340.01 | 644.02 | 213.21 | 324.02 | 095.06 | 696.13 |
| 340.20 | 646.04 | uproar | 331.16 | 167.04 | 713.05 |
| 342.18 | 648.13 | 035.13 | 341.01 | 182.15 | 720.17 |
| 350.07 | 649.20 | 189.22 | 346.07 | 190.13 | ut' |
| 362.14 | 651.18 | 261.17 | 359.16 | 218.19 | 016.07 |
| 364.14 | 653.15 | 569.03 | 360.09 | 238.01 | 194.02 |
| 364.21 | 660.10 | ups | 363.08 | 343.22 | ut's |
| 365.01 | 661.17 | 074.03 | 366.02 | 435.14 | 232.13 |
| 365.18 | 662.05 | upset | 371.07 | 492.09 | 720.13 |
| 366.15 | 662.14 | 440.16 | 387.06 | 494.07 | utensils |
| 377.10 | 663.11 | 691.14 | 390.16 | 497.06 | 005.18 |
| 382.07 | 664.02 | upstairs | 394.18 | 497.13 | 119.13 |
| 383.07 | 664.10 | 120.17 | 403.08 | 508.14 | utmost |
| 384.16 | 665.05 | 470.09 | 416.07 | 529.04 | 132.17 |
| 389.18 | 666.08 | 659.15 | 427.20 | 569.21 | 169.02 |
| 390.07 | 667.11 | 724.22 | 436.04 | 636.18 | 248.08 |
| 391.14 | 667.13 | upward | 439.14 | 678.15 | 609.18 |
| 399.16 | 668.04 | 149.21 | 445.09 | 702.11 | 682.03 |
| 400.11 | 669.12 | urge | 449.18 | 729.18 | utter |
| 401.15 | 670.04 | 294.17 | 460.02 | 762.11 | 218.11 |
| 404.08 | 670.21 | urged | 461.15 | used | 280.17 |
| 407.03 | 672.03 | 126.18 | 461.18 | 008.08 | 477.04 |
| 408.12 | 675.20 | 244.09 | 466.14 | 011.13 | 511.19 |
| 409.01 | 676.16 | 248.06 | 471.21 | 040.04 | 569.02 |
| 413.05 | 681.02 | 310.04 | 476.10 | 041.20 | 639.07 |
| 416.12 | 683.14 | 344.18 | 477.10 | 075.17 | 711.01 |
| 417.04 | 686.15 | 387.03 | 483.03 | 084.10 | uttered |
| 427.17 | 687.02 | 426.05 | 483.09 | 116.22 | 002.19 |
| 430.17 | 690.21 | 473.11 | 485.13 | 119.21 | 022.21 |
| 431.22 | 696.11 | urges | 486.16 | 145.18 | 032.15 |
| 435.07 | 697.09 | 316.01 | 488.02 | 210.14 | 057.03 |
| 437.10 | 702.09 | urging | 488.15 | 224.12 | 231.11 |
| 451.11 | 705.04 | 063.08 | 492.05 | 256.01 | 286.15 |
| 454.18 | 705.06 | 106.07 | 495.05 | 312.18 | 340.02 |
| 456.07 | 705.12 | urn | 502.02 | 318.12 | 356.09 |
| 457.04 | 710.09 | 217.01 | 509.07 | 392.08 | 371.05 |
| 465.06 | 711.14 | us | 519.07 | 406.09 | 408.14 |
| 466.16 | 712.17 | 001.11 | 520.07 | 414.15 | 455.11 |
| 467.21 | 713.11 | 003.18 | 520.09 | 430.20 | 467.02 |
| 468.21 | 719.13 | 005.10 | 527.18 | 439.13 | 553.14 |
| 471.20 | 719.16 | 010.17 | 529.12 | 475.06 | 565.12 |
| 477.03 | 720.17 | 011.12 | 536.12 | 486.16 | 591.07 |
| 477.18 | 721.03 | 020.22 | 546.06 | 525.01 | 621.20 |
| 479.04 | 721.06 | 026.11 | 548.10 | 544.02 | 636.03 |
| 481.10 | 722.11 | 030.02 | 548.16 | 545.19 | 661.19 |
| 485.13 | 724.01 | 041.15 | 556.10 | 558.17 | 696.04 |
| 485.15 | 740.05 | 041.18 | 556.11 | 608.02 | 718.01 |
| 487.20 | 747.18 | 042.01 | 558.15 | 666.04 | 725.12 |
| 495.13 | 749.21 | 043.05 | 558.16 | 719.20 | 743.21 |
| 495.21 | 750.13 | 043.07 | 560.20 | 719.21 | 750.03 |
| 501.08 | 751.13 | 043.08 | 563.19 | 725.15 | uttering |
| 505.17 | 751.15 | 044.02 | 564.05 | useful | 027.14 |
| 507.15 | 752.18 | 044.05 | 564.10 | 674.12 | 299.12 |
| 510.07 | 757.10 | 045.08 | 565.15 | useless | 327.15 |
| 511.02 | 758.13 | 045.08 | 570.11 | 052.16 | 409.17 |
| 513.11 | 762.10 | 061.15 | 571.17 | 143.01 | 554.07 |
| 513.22 | 764.04 | 073.11 | 581.01 | 420.04 | utterly |
| 518.18 | up-stairs | 076.22 | 583.16 | 685.06 | 272.18 |
| 518.21 | 037.02 | 088.05 | 585.11 | 704.15 | 405.22 |
| 519.08 | 067.21 | 090.08 | 586.02 | uselessness | 580.13 |
| 520.18 | 094.14 | 091.03 | 586.06 | 352.16 | vacancy |
| 522.05 | 142.06 | 091.18 | 587.16 | | 062.01 |

vacant
111.14
468.12
508.19
514.14
725.01
748.18
757.14
vagabond
045.07
127.15
vagaries
163.22
vague
269.06
353.12
594.19
vaguely
303.20
vain
041.16
069.02
079.03
083.01
131.06
285.05
573.21
vainly
015.14
148.14
191.09
749.11
valances
323.07
valley
154.13
209.09
353.03
364.14
463.05
689.19
valorously
509.05
valour
258.01
valuable
494.09
value
136.04
220.12
260.15
490.03
526.04
valued
306.03
336.02
vampire
745.13
vane
356.17
vanish
215.03
vanished
061.18
066.14
200.07
244.06
351.19
393.13
483.18
661.19
729.14
763.07
vanishing
016.16
vanity
156.06
339.16
512.12
561.19
vanquish
058.16
vanquished
259.02
259.02
vapid
039.04
490.12
vapour
209.15
variations
746.05
varied
039.02
413.09
variety
731.05
various
010.18
136.06
321.08
varrah
458.08
varry
233.06
varying
356.18
705.16
vast
006.03

vastly
320.01
619.12
vegetables
674.12
vehemence
035.05
057.22
376.14
vehemently
016.02
252.16
433.22
veil
432.01
vein
399.22
veins
264.20
vengeance
107.09
venom
563.18
venomous
327.08
671.20
vent
622.15
ventilation
004.08
venture
023.21
284.17
431.10
493.05
576.07
603.21
713.11
ventured
027.12
128.01
142.01
224.04
372.18
404.03
639.12
668.11
venturesome
172.06
venturing
643.05
verbs
013.07
verdant
760.09
verge
317.11
verging
263.10
verified
044.17
verse
680.13
681.19
verses
191.07
very
003.17
006.04
013.12
019.12
035.20
038.08
039.15
067.20
071.17
073.10
073.15
073.16
073.16
080.18
081.18
093.21
098.02
098.13
099.09
107.15
114.01
116.20
122.18
134.14
135.04
140.09
141.13
143.13
146.12
153.07
156.03
169.02
171.03
174.11
176.08
188.04
195.03
196.21
199.18
204.10
209.10
219.14
220.05
223.04

223.05
235.05
239.07
252.06
254.14
260.21
261.10
283.12
298.12
298.21
306.07
307.15
337.16
349.08
350.21
353.22
356.12
361.07
364.10
375.11
393.12
393.12
415.20
435.01
451.17
454.03
454.04
455.06
456.07
457.05
457.17
460.03
465.06
469.12
479.07
483.19
487.08
492.01
492.07
505.15
508.16
509.12
509.13
513.16
525.21
532.14
534.13
537.06
540.08
554.15
558.07
562.15
573.05
576.05
577.04
578.06
589.21
590.21
592.18
598.17
599.05
599.17
600.19
606.15
614.12
621.22
635.10
637.04
647.19
650.04
659.22
666.03
669.15
670.03
676.04
677.13
677.21
686.04
688.08
695.19
709.19
725.03
729.03
738.10
742.18
754.08
757.03
vessel
318.04
415.07
vestige
464.19
veto
489.02
vex
226.22
250.22
288.16
425.19
521.15
vexation
601.16
632.03
vexatious
011.05
vexed
061.01
087.06
093.19
145.09
178.03

186.14
205.06
212.05
324.06
441.05
534.19
746.07
vials
203.05
vibrates
741.17
vice
443.04
vicious
124.22
victim
396.15
victuals
131.02
472.01
view
019.07
433.07
470.05
503.04
572.20
675.11
727.13
744.08
viewing
526.21
552.20
vigilance
038.16
430.07
749.08
vigilant
012.07
248.07
vigorous
054.02
531.18
616.06
vigour
024.17
255.09
346.06
vile
525.11
680.12
village
243.10
291.21
299.02
350.22
411.14
413.06
418.06
477.15
506.13
627.11
637.10
689.15
villagers
379.18
444.16
villain
018.05
108.01
164.04
250.17
312.03
329.06
395.14
397.09
494.03
525.15
610.12
610.12
villanous
006.09
vindictive
086.05
vindictiveness
358.08
vinegar-faced
016.02
viol
131.13
violence
157.03
265.03
389.19
395.02
395.06
395.07
610.10
violent
035.15
058.17
085.20
128.02
189.01
255.11
274.22
292.18
359.10
538.08
729.09
viper
402.02

virtue
443.03
virtuous
256.21
virulency
035.04
vis-a-vis
010.05
visage
049.21
visible
183.06
284.03
310.07
432.09
491.11
645.01
741.14
visibly
359.11
vision
291.04
748.09
visions
177.07
visit
001.03
013.14
112.06
129.02
130.21
147.16
331.20
350.02
368.08
412.16
459.12
462.16
484.06
487.22
499.14
543.08
555.20
556.08
569.09
579.20
580.19
636.01
658.02
673.09
685.17
689.07
visitation
190.22
503.02
613.11
visitations
029.22
visited
113.05
483.06
488.04
508.21
583.14
642.07
664.06
visiter
158.03
207.21
456.08
visiters
032.06
488.18
visiting
224.12
428.06
526.17
visits
145.04
155.05
196.16
241.02
254.10
293.15
413.10
489.03
572.04
573.20
713.14
vivacity
224.03
336.15
vivid
039.09
vividly
553.17
vivifisection
608.12
vixen
238.07
vocal
035.16
vocally
008.15
vocation
144.12
vocations
203.15
296.16
voce
062.15

vociferate
189.18
vociferated
106.16
vociferating
162.02
voice
032.04
052.05
053.12
080.04
132.14
154.14
158.15
206.16
206.18
207.09
216.14
249.13
264.10
270.09
281.02
314.09
382.16
391.04
408.15
409.11
425.10
471.12
475.14
485.17
523.20
531.14
534.18
539.04
539.14
563.22
593.19
609.06
624.12
644.15
671.02
694.04
744.14
voices
621.22
volume
043.10
564.09
703.21
volumes
039.13
057.12
669.17
681.07
volunteer
013.14
vouchsafed
313.01
vowed
637.22
637.22
vowing
043.11
402.06
vulgar
147.10
560.11
wading
014.04
410.10
wafted
693.09
wag
355.03
wage
719.10
wager
169.04
433.06
wages
199.09
289.12
423.03
470.03
wah
233.06
472.04
waif
053.13
wail
095.01
386.20
540.08
622.16
wailed
051.03
052.20
370.06
wailing
280.02
waistcoat
002.04
315.14
676.01
wait
070.08
127.17
133.17
185.10
255.06

| | | | | | |
|---|---|---|---|---|---|
| 260.19 | 691.17 | 694.17 | warld | 050.21 | 107.02 |
| 284.10 | 695.14 | wanderings | 696.13 | 051.09 | 107.06 |
| 310.05 | 751.03 | 067.09 | warm | 051.17 | 108.01 |
| 314.22 | 757.05 | 241.08 | 017.03 | 053.09 | 109.16 |
| 318.06 | 763.14 | wanders | 105.01 | 053.21 | 110.07 |
| 436.20 | walked | 288.12 | 111.04 | 055.01 | 111.01 |
| 449.22 | 065.08 | want | 213.09 | 055.16 | 112.08 |
| 504.11 | 120.10 | 020.01 | 302.22 | 055.19 | 112.10 |
| 509.04 | 157.20 | 031.14 | 306.16 | 056.02 | 113.04 |
| 521.01 | 169.10 | 053.02 | 350.18 | 056.17 | 114.04 |
| 548.04 | 186.09 | 137.11 | 450.20 | 056.20 | 115.03 |
| 563.02 | 211.01 | 143.05 | 479.15 | 057.12 | 115.11 |
| 591.19 | 259.22 | 163.11 | 531.06 | 060.07 | 115.22 |
| 613.18 | 311.01 | 171.17 | 548.14 | 060.20 | 117.17 |
| 636.11 | 313.01 | 175.13 | 556.16 | 061.04 | 119.21 |
| 637.08 | 360.07 | 180.13 | 652.15 | 061.09 | 120.12 |
| 660.13 | 367.15 | 186.01 | 667.22 | 061.16 | 121.19 |
| 742.07 | 433.06 | 193.09 | 689.22 | 062.03 | 121.20 |
| 750.01 | 451.11 | 208.08 | 690.01 | 062.14 | 122.01 |
| waited | 478.09 | 210.05 | 726.22 | 063.01 | 122.14 |
| 017.11 | 498.20 | 218.07 | 737.04 | 063.05 | 122.17 |
| 102.15 | 568.10 | 250.09 | 741.09 | 063.19 | 123.19 |
| 121.07 | 569.05 | 251.21 | warmed | 065.11 | 124.02 |
| 130.05 | 586.17 | 262.02 | 001.13 | 065.18 | 125.16 |
| 207.11 | 590.01 | 266.11 | 129.17 | 065.19 | 126.01 |
| 305.04 | 607.10 | 271.10 | 386.04 | 066.17 | 126.06 |
| 338.01 | 654.09 | 288.09 | warmly | 069.05 | 128.03 |
| 374.03 | 667.10 | 307.02 | 249.16 | 069.08 | 128.22 |
| 403.17 | 684.04 | 314.18 | warms | 070.08 | 130.05 |
| 485.10 | 697.18 | 321.21 | 525.21 | 070.11 | 130.18 |
| waiting | 728.18 | 350.06 | warmth | 072.10 | 131.06 |
| 075.13 | walking | 363.12 | 065.02 | 072.16 | 131.09 |
| 190.13 | 056.22 | 412.09 | warn | 072.17 | 132.02 |
| 213.04 | 222.05 | 415.13 | 029.14 | 072.19 | 132.04 |
| 216.02 | 283.12 | 439.01 | 066.15 | 073.03 | 132.16 |
| 241.09 | 294.10 | 452.01 | 132.12 | 074.07 | 133.10 |
| 247.18 | 355.09 | 461.14 | 242.06 | 075.02 | 134.14 |
| 284.09 | 384.09 | 469.22 | 344.11 | 075.14 | 136.12 |
| 354.03 | 434.08 | 479.02 | 396.14 | 075.16 | 139.04 |
| 538.22 | 485.22 | 484.03 | 742.08 | 075.21 | 140.17 |
| 607.11 | 492.16 | 496.04 | warn't | 076.04 | 141.10 |
| 618.15 | 553.03 | 533.16 | 420.10 | 076.14 | 141.13 |
| 635.10 | 570.05 | 540.16 | 699.09 | 076.18 | 141.20 |
| 674.07 | 573.12 | 543.19 | warned | 077.11 | 143.06 |
| 748.02 | 577.14 | 599.09 | 142.22 | 077.13 | 143.06 |
| wake | 583.19 | 614.09 | 527.17 | 077.19 | 143.16 |
| 094.02 | 587.16 | 618.01 | warning | 078.05 | 143.20 |
| 190.16 | 740.17 | 646.19 | 158.07 | 078.08 | 143.22 |
| 248.10 | walks | 656.15 | 168.07 | 078.08 | 144.12 |
| 278.16 | 047.12 | 663.14 | 268.02 | 078.16 | 144.17 |
| 376.12 | 579.13 | 681.09 | 293.13 | 078.18 | 145.05 |
| 376.13 | 760.13 | 697.21 | 374.18 | 079.03 | 145.09 |
| 670.22 | wall | 698.20 | 374.20 | 079.05 | 145.17 |
| waken | 004.16 | 706.04 | 499.18 | 079.10 | 145.21 |
| 468.17 | 054.19 | 709.17 | 609.15 | 079.13 | 146.15 |
| wakened | 153.01 | 741.07 | 684.21 | 080.07 | 147.05 |
| 091.15 | 162.10 | 742.06 | warrant | 080.09 | 147.19 |
| 218.01 | 169.13 | 751.13 | 316.20 | 080.11 | 148.02 |
| 352.01 | 188.14 | wanted | was | 080.15 | 148.03 |
| 420.01 | 206.09 | 056.01 | 002.07 | 081.08 | 148.16 |
| 663.07 | 209.07 | 086.03 | 002.19 | 081.16 | 148.20 |
| 728.15 | 272.09 | 105.06 | 003.12 | 082.08 | 149.15 |
| wakens | 277.05 | 146.16 | 003.16 | 082.12 | 149.19 |
| 327.09 | 290.18 | 184.11 | 006.12 | 082.14 | 150.04 |
| wakes | 325.20 | 199.10 | 008.12 | 082.18 | 150.18 |
| 591.19 | 380.01 | 228.12 | 008.17 | 082.22 | 151.01 |
| 646.07 | 434.15 | 240.21 | 009.01 | 083.01 | 155.20 |
| waking | 509.10 | 275.15 | 009.12 | 083.08 | 157.08 |
| 101.22 | 522.06 | 287.01 | 011.01 | 083.09 | 157.15 |
| 281.12 | 545.08 | 287.10 | 011.07 | 085.11 | 157.22 |
| 302.18 | 634.05 | 386.05 | 013.13 | 085.16 | 159.01 |
| 746.03 | 645.02 | 406.02 | 015.09 | 086.02 | 160.06 |
| walk | 693.09 | 419.11 | 017.04 | 086.05 | 160.21 |
| 002.17 | 737.06 | 505.02 | 017.08 | 087.04 | 162.05 |
| 002.19 | 744.11 | 558.01 | 018.20 | 087.09 | 163.22 |
| 015.06 | 747.17 | 558.02 | 019.06 | 087.11 | 164.22 |
| 059.12 | 748.22 | 560.08 | 019.08 | 088.04 | 165.17 |
| 066.03 | walls | 638.21 | 021.08 | 088.07 | 165.19 |
| 076.11 | 005.21 | 666.13 | 022.20 | 088.10 | 166.14 |
| 077.15 | 049.07 | 669.21 | 023.09 | 088.21 | 169.01 |
| 078.03 | 270.03 | 700.05 | 023.12 | 089.07 | 169.15 |
| 216.20 | 321.19 | 701.06 | 023.14 | 089.11 | 169.17 |
| 221.15 | 323.13 | 721.09 | 024.13 | 089.20 | 170.03 |
| 227.17 | 361.04 | 739.03 | 024.16 | 090.15 | 170.13 |
| 237.04 | 445.01 | 745.04 | 025.11 | 090.23 | 171.20 |
| 247.20 | 763.16 | 755.16 | 025.13 | 091.02 | 172.11 |
| 314.15 | wan | wanting | 026.03 | 091.14 | 173.04 |
| 317.15 | 330.11 | 288.09 | 026.13 | 091.16 | 173.11 |
| 424.09 | 597.09 | 486.03 | 027.01 | 092.15 | 177.13 |
| 427.01 | wander | 591.17 | 028.10 | 093.01 | 177.20 |
| 449.05 | 376.10 | wants | 029.05 | 093.05 | 178.03 |
| 458.02 | 430.08 | 202.18 | 032.14 | 093.08 | 178.12 |
| 460.18 | 651.18 | 353.18 | 032.17 | 094.11 | 178.18 |
| 463.21 | 739.12 | 374.06 | 034.20 | 095.12 | 179.22 |
| 463.22 | wandered | 395.17 | 035.11 | 095.13 | 180.20 |
| 482.17 | 032.18 | 455.05 | 036.08 | 096.06 | 183.15 |
| 483.10 | 045.18 | 577.12 | 036.14 | 096.06 | 184.03 |
| 488.12 | 088.22 | 613.15 | 038.20 | 096.11 | 184.07 |
| 489.18 | 377.03 | 630.04 | 038.21 | 097.06 | 184.10 |
| 500.05 | 587.08 | 679.10 | 039.18 | 097.16 | 184.22 |
| 515.07 | 593.19 | war | 040.03 | 097.20 | 185.07 |
| 517.03 | wanderers | 028.21 | 040.13 | 098.10 | 185.09 |
| 526.14 | 413.12 | 187.06 | 042.06 | 099.01 | 186.06 |
| 552.15 | wandering | 187.06 | 043.14 | 100.10 | 186.14 |
| 561.15 | 102.10 | wardrobe | 046.03 | 102.01 | 187.04 |
| 583.03 | 188.10 | 383.08 | 046.11 | 103.15 | 188.04 |
| 605.19 | 276.08 | wark | 046.13 | 104.02 | 189.01 |
| 634.13 | 276.19 | 322.06 | 047.04 | 104.22 | 189.14 |
| 644.13 | 432.11 | warks | 048.22 | 105.21 | 190.07 |
| 656.20 | 495.11 | 191.03 | 049.03 | 106.05 | 191.21 |
| 660.06 | 547.14 | | 050.15 | 106.07 | 192.03 |

| | | | | | |
|---|---|---|---|---|---|
| 192.17 | 281.16 | 351.11 | 414.06 | 480.16 | 562.17 |
| 192.22 | 281.17 | 352.14 | 414.10 | 480.19 | 563.05 |
| 194.13 | 281.19 | 352.22 | 414.17 | 480.22 | 563.09 |
| 195.19 | 282.03 | 353.03 | 415.17 | 481.05 | 563.13 |
| 196.09 | 282.09 | 353.10 | 415.19 | 481.15 | 563.17 |
| 196.13 | 283.18 | 353.22 | 415.22 | 482.21 | 564.08 |
| 196.18 | 283.21 | 354.05 | 417.12 | 483.14 | 565.01 |
| 197.21 | 285.06 | 354.09 | 417.20 | 485.18 | 565.01 |
| 198.08 | 286.05 | 355.08 | 418.02 | 485.22 | 565.06 |
| 198.16 | 287.01 | 355.10 | 418.07 | 486.01 | 566.03 |
| 198.20 | 287.02 | 355.18 | 418.10 | 487.05 | 566.05 |
| 199.01 | 287.05 | 356.06 | 418.13 | 487.09 | 566.09 |
| 199.11 | 288.21 | 356.07 | 419.11 | 489.10 | 567.01 |
| 199.14 | 290.03 | 356.09 | 419.21 | 489.11 | 567.06 |
| 199.20 | 291.01 | 356.17 | 420.03 | 491.11 | 567.11 |
| 200.02 | 291.17 | 357.14 | 420.04 | 492.01 | 568.03 |
| 202.04 | 291.20 | 357.17 | 420.22 | 492.06 | 568.05 |
| 202.15 | 292.03 | 358.14 | 421.09 | 495.17 | 568.15 |
| 203.20 | 292.20 | 359.14 | 422.06 | 495.19 | 569.01 |
| 204.11 | 294.02 | 360.05 | 422.12 | 497.08 | 569.03 |
| 205.15 | 294.10 | 364.07 | 422.18 | 498.01 | 569.08 |
| 205.17 | 294.17 | 364.22 | 422.21 | 499.02 | 569.11 |
| 206.03 | 294.21 | 365.21 | 424.12 | 499.17 | 569.14 |
| 206.05 | 295.06 | 366.11 | 425.05 | 499.19 | 569.20 |
| 206.18 | 295.09 | 366.21 | 425.11 | 500.10 | 569.21 |
| 206.19 | 295.14 | 367.19 | 425.12 | 500.18 | 570.03 |
| 209.15 | 296.09 | 368.02 | 425.16 | 500.21 | 571.19 |
| 209.20 | 296.17 | 368.12 | 425.19 | 501.03 | 572.15 |
| 210.11 | 297.02 | 369.02 | 426.13 | 501.16 | 572.19 |
| 210.20 | 298.16 | 369.11 | 426.17 | 502.14 | 573.16 |
| 212.19 | 299.22 | 370.02 | 428.21 | 502.21 | 574.02 |
| 213.17 | 300.04 | 370.05 | 429.10 | 505.19 | 576.10 |
| 214.01 | 301.04 | 370.09 | 429.20 | 506.11 | 576.12 |
| 214.06 | 301.07 | 370.19 | 430.04 | 507.21 | 576.13 |
| 214.07 | 302.06 | 371.03 | 430.11 | 509.11 | 577.15 |
| 216.12 | 302.13 | 373.01 | 430.15 | 513.04 | 578.03 |
| 217.06 | 303.08 | 373.09 | 431.14 | 513.22 | 578.07 |
| 217.18 | 304.01 | 373.13 | 432.13 | 514.05 | 579.15 |
| 218.01 | 304.22 | 374.07 | 433.04 | 515.03 | 579.16 |
| 218.12 | 305.04 | 374.13 | 433.16 | 515.03 | 579.20 |
| 218.13 | 305.04 | 374.14 | 434.15 | 516.13 | 580.06 |
| 219.16 | 305.14 | 377.16 | 436.07 | 516.18 | 580.14 |
| 220.17 | 308.03 | 377.22 | 437.07 | 516.21 | 582.04 |
| 222.13 | 308.04 | 378.01 | 440.07 | 517.05 | 582.19 |
| 223.07 | 308.10 | 378.11 | 441.05 | 517.10 | 582.21 |
| 223.21 | 308.15 | 379.11 | 442.02 | 517.20 | 583.11 |
| 224.20 | 309.04 | 379.16 | 442.22 | 518.07 | 583.12 |
| 225.07 | 309.17 | 379.18 | 443.08 | 519.14 | 585.02 |
| 225.12 | 310.06 | 379.21 | 443.20 | 519.21 | 585.06 |
| 225.18 | 311.05 | 382.03 | 443.21 | 520.17 | 586.11 |
| 225.19 | 311.14 | 382.10 | 444.17 | 522.13 | 588.19 |
| 226.03 | 312.11 | 383.09 | 445.02 | 522.17 | 590.07 |
| 226.13 | 312.15 | 383.12 | 445.12 | 523.12 | 592.05 |
| 227.06 | 312.15 | 383.16 | 445.19 | 523.14 | 594.15 |
| 227.07 | 312.19 | 384.01 | 445.20 | 524.06 | 595.04 |
| 227.21 | 313.04 | 384.20 | 446.03 | 524.19 | 596.05 |
| 227.22 | 313.22 | 384.21 | 446.11 | 525.14 | 598.08 |
| 232.07 | 314.13 | 385.08 | 447.04 | 527.22 | 598.11 |
| 234.03 | 315.02 | 386.03 | 448.03 | 528.06 | 598.16 |
| 234.04 | 315.06 | 386.08 | 449.13 | 528.10 | 599.15 |
| 234.17 | 316.10 | 389.13 | 450.01 | 528.20 | 602.17 |
| 234.20 | 316.11 | 389.17 | 450.10 | 529.13 | 604.21 |
| 235.18 | 317.08 | 390.22 | 450.19 | 530.06 | 605.02 |
| 235.19 | 317.11 | 391.04 | 451.02 | 534.13 | 605.18 |
| 238.18 | 317.17 | 391.08 | 451.02 | 534.20 | 607.06 |
| 240.16 | 317.22 | 391.09 | 452.04 | 536.20 | 607.07 |
| 241.05 | 319.01 | 392.03 | 453.02 | 536.21 | 610.01 |
| 242.04 | 319.14 | 393.05 | 453.05 | 538.10 | 610.19 |
| 242.06 | 319.16 | 393.12 | 453.06 | 539.03 | 612.07 |
| 243.01 | 320.02 | 393.15 | 454.01 | 540.04 | 612.09 |
| 244.04 | 321.07 | 393.19 | 454.11 | 543.13 | 612.18 |
| 244.17 | 323.01 | 396.14 | 454.18 | 543.15 | 613.07 |
| 245.08 | 323.02 | 397.17 | 454.20 | 546.07 | 615.01 |
| 246.12 | 323.09 | 398.20 | 454.21 | 547.11 | 615.17 |
| 247.12 | 323.14 | 399.09 | 455.03 | 547.20 | 616.20 |
| 247.18 | 323.18 | 401.18 | 455.12 | 548.10 | 621.17 |
| 248.21 | 324.06 | 401.19 | 456.06 | 548.12 | 621.21 |
| 248.22 | 325.10 | 402.08 | 456.19 | 548.19 | 622.02 |
| 249.07 | 325.22 | 402.10 | 457.08 | 550.02 | 622.08 |
| 253.21 | 326.16 | 402.17 | 457.09 | 551.14 | 622.22 |
| 254.03 | 326.19 | 402.20 | 460.03 | 552.09 | 623.01 |
| 255.09 | 327.02 | 403.03 | 460.07 | 552.17 | 623.12 |
| 256.15 | 330.04 | 403.13 | 462.13 | 553.02 | 623.13 |
| 258.08 | 330.10 | 403.17 | 465.13 | 553.10 | 624.06 |
| 258.15 | 330.15 | 404.11 | 466.05 | 554.04 | 625.03 |
| 261.04 | 330.20 | 404.19 | 466.06 | 555.06 | 626.05 |
| 261.10 | 332.21 | 405.01 | 466.09 | 555.08 | 628.19 |
| 261.13 | 333.10 | 405.14 | 467.07 | 555.09 | 628.22 |
| 262.09 | 336.01 | 405.19 | 467.13 | 555.10 | 630.17 |
| 262.18 | 337.03 | 406.03 | 467.14 | 555.17 | 631.22 |
| 263.15 | 337.12 | 406.08 | 468.19 | 555.20 | 633.02 |
| 265.15 | 337.16 | 406.19 | 469.21 | 556.11 | 633.09 |
| 267.13 | 338.03 | 407.21 | 470.19 | 556.12 | 633.20 |
| 267.22 | 339.01 | 408.01 | 471.01 | 557.06 | 633.21 |
| 269.11 | 339.03 | 408.02 | 471.07 | 557.12 | 635.02 |
| 270.11 | 339.18 | 408.09 | 473.01 | 557.13 | 635.04 |
| 270.18 | 339.22 | 408.15 | 473.03 | 558.18 | 635.11 |
| 274.22 | 340.08 | 409.17 | 473.09 | 558.22 | 636.03 |
| 275.17 | 341.13 | 409.21 | 474.06 | 559.08 | 636.09 |
| 275.18 | 344.01 | 410.05 | 474.11 | 559.10 | 636.11 |
| 276.06 | 344.13 | 411.04 | 475.08 | 559.16 | 637.06 |
| 276.21 | 346.22 | 411.06 | 475.10 | 559.19 | 637.13 |
| 277.09 | 347.03 | 411.08 | 475.21 | 560.03 | 638.03 |
| 277.13 | 347.03 | 411.11 | 477.08 | 560.07 | 638.06 |
| 278.03 | 347.14 | 411.15 | 478.01 | 560.14 | 638.12 |
| 278.12 | 350.03 | 412.13 | 478.07 | 561.13 | 638.16 |
| 279.01 | 350.10 | 412.17 | 478.12 | 562.01 | 638.21 |
| 279.02 | 350.12 | 413.01 | 478.14 | 562.06 | 639.14 |
| 280.01 | 350.14 | 413.02 | 479.12 | 562.07 | 639.15 |
| 280.05 | 350.17 | 413.13 | 479.20 | 562.08 | 640.04 |
| 281.09 | 351.10 | 413.19 | 480.06 | 562.15 | 640.13 |

| | | | | | |
|---|---|---|---|---|---|
| 640.17 | 709.19 | 240.13 | 117.07 | 072.12 | 320.20 |
| 641.06 | 709.21 | 274.02 | 134.03 | 078.01 | 320.22 |
| 641.10 | 711.22 | 277.10 | 148.01 | 080.20 | 329.04 |
| 641.11 | 712.04 | 316.15 | 149.20 | 088.06 | 331.15 |
| 641.20 | 712.10 | 329.20 | 152.03 | 088.14 | 347.21 |
| 642.03 | 713.17 | 344.14 | 157.17 | 089.01 | 350.15 |
| 644.07 | 713.18 | 372.22 | 163.06 | 089.08 | 357.08 |
| 644.12 | 714.01 | 393.17 | 175.03 | 090.10 | 366.17 |
| 644.18 | 716.04 | 443.19 | 197.21 | 091.01 | 367.18 |
| 645.01 | 716.22 | 541.22 | 218.06 | 091.17 | 370.08 |
| 645.06 | 717.12 | 551.15 | 233.01 | 092.12 | 372.16 |
| 645.17 | 717.16 | 582.10 | 243.01 | 093.01 | 374.07 |
| 649.13 | 717.18 | 703.09 | 253.11 | 094.03 | 374.17 |
| 650.14 | 718.13 | 726.17 | 262.07 | 094.18 | 374.18 |
| 650.15 | 719.04 | watchdog | 263.03 | 095.02 | 385.06 |
| 651.08 | 721.17 | 674.10 | 285.02 | 095.21 | 387.13 |
| 651.14 | 723.13 | watched | 286.01 | 098.07 | 393.19 |
| 651.16 | 724.01 | 082.15 | 294.20 | 098.14 | 394.17 |
| 651.21 | 724.18 | 115.07 | 300.02 | 101.08 | 394.18 |
| 652.08 | 725.17 | 182.18 | 325.12 | 102.19 | 398.12 |
| 652.14 | 725.22 | 465.16 | 329.15 | 102.19 | 407.20 |
| 652.17 | 726.12 | 492.16 | 332.23 | 103.12 | 415.20 |
| 652.21 | 726.20 | 508.22 | 342.20 | 103.16 | 417.03 |
| 653.05 | 727.16 | 548.13 | 346.08 | 104.02 | 419.20 |
| 653.07 | 727.21 | 623.04 | 347.02 | 104.11 | 419.20 |
| 653.08 | 728.13 | 656.20 | 382.21 | 104.20 | 427.18 |
| 653.08 | 728.21 | 710.12 | 386.03 | 105.03 | 436.11 |
| 653.11 | 729.04 | 745.16 | 404.07 | 105.04 | 445.08 |
| 653.21 | 732.03 | 764.07 | 420.14 | 105.19 | 449.08 |
| 654.12 | 732.17 | watching | 424.10 | 106.03 | 450.05 |
| 654.13 | 732.19 | 193.19 | 445.21 | 106.04 | 454.05 |
| 654.15 | 734.18 | 249.14 | 450.06 | 106.06 | 454.09 |
| 655.01 | 735.01 | 261.01 | 462.18 | 106.06 | 459.06 |
| 655.04 | 735.06 | 296.01 | 464.07 | 109.03 | 465.15 |
| 656.01 | 737.01 | 301.08 | 478.04 | 110.21 | 466.14 |
| 658.06 | 737.03 | 371.12 | 480.03 | 127.12 | 472.06 |
| 658.06 | 737.13 | 377.20 | 480.15 | 131.03 | 474.02 |
| 658.09 | 737.15 | 382.05 | 481.18 | 131.08 | 478.05 |
| 659.15 | 737.20 | 454.04 | 499.06 | 131.15 | 478.19 |
| 659.21 | 738.14 | 479.16 | 508.13 | 131.17 | 480.02 |
| 660.13 | 738.18 | 518.10 | 511.12 | 133.21 | 480.12 |
| 660.22 | 739.07 | 597.09 | 526.10 | 136.21 | 482.09 |
| 661.04 | 740.12 | 598.14 | 530.10 | 139.05 | 482.10 |
| 661.21 | 741.11 | 668.05 | 545.07 | 141.01 | 484.01 |
| 662.03 | 741.12 | 762.20 | 562.08 | 141.18 | 485.09 |
| 662.07 | 742.20 | water | 563.15 | 145.02 | 488.22 |
| 662.12 | 743.11 | 036.04 | 575.09 | 154.17 | 490.10 |
| 662.19 | 743.13 | 108.05 | 588.03 | 165.18 | 495.05 |
| 663.09 | 743.14 | 111.04 | 615.12 | 166.13 | 498.16 |
| 663.11 | 743.17 | 115.18 | 618.05 | 181.04 | 498.20 |
| 663.21 | 745.03 | 156.22 | 628.18 | 181.19 | 499.01 |
| 664.13 | 745.19 | 177.01 | 655.04 | 184.09 | 509.06 |
| 665.03 | 747.01 | 190.04 | 658.07 | 184.10 | 510.18 |
| 665.07 | 748.13 | 196.05 | 666.12 | 184.11 | 512.19 |
| 667.15 | 748.21 | 266.02 | 683.12 | 184.12 | 522.03 |
| 667.15 | 749.03 | 270.16 | 686.13 | 185.10 | 522.03 |
| 667.22 | 749.07 | 280.11 | 689.15 | 188.06 | 527.20 |
| 668.02 | 750.12 | 298.20 | 697.08 | 188.21 | 528.04 |
| 668.09 | 750.19 | 319.04 | 709.16 | 189.08 | 528.08 |
| 668.15 | 756.03 | 383.12 | 727.13 | 190.15 | 529.05 |
| 670.16 | 756.16 | 389.10 | 740.21 | 191.07 | 530.09 |
| 671.10 | 756.21 | 406.02 | 752.17 | 192.19 | 532.01 |
| 673.02 | 757.03 | 417.03 | ways | 195.18 | 540.14 |
| 673.06 | 757.14 | 476.12 | 029.01 | 196.21 | 541.08 |
| 673.09 | 757.15 | 534.08 | 090.06 | 199.03 | 541.21 |
| 674.06 | 757.21 | 542.08 | 144.15 | 205.21 | 543.03 |
| 674.11 | 758.04 | 557.22 | 242.07 | 216.16 | 543.04 |
| 678.03 | 759.07 | 638.06 | 324.19 | 219.09 | 544.14 |
| 679.15 | 759.16 | 688.07 | 374.19 | 220.07 | 545.02 |
| 680.21 | 759.20 | 753.08 | 443.13 | 220.08 | 545.18 |
| 682.06 | 759.21 | watered | 477.02 | 222.07 | 545.19 |
| 682.11 | 760.21 | 406.22 | 720.14 | 226.07 | 545.19 |
| 683.21 | 761.03 | watering | 731.05 | 226.12 | 547.01 |
| 684.05 | 763.14 | 009.14 | wayward | 226.21 | 547.13 |
| 684.18 | was'nt | watery | 081.17 | 227.22 | 547.14 |
| 688.02 | 080.21 | 516.15 | 159.18 | 235.05 | 550.06 |
| 688.06 | wash | wavered | 226.15 | 235.16 | 554.17 |
| 689.08 | 079.07 | 156.19 | waywardness | 241.02 | 555.14 |
| 689.22 | 115.16 | waves | 289.04 | 243.19 | 556.14 |
| 691.13 | 117.17 | 557.21 | we | 248.17 | 556.15 |
| 692.06 | 401.06 | waving | 003.08 | 251.21 | 556.20 |
| 692.14 | 612.03 | 455.20 | 003.11 | 259.02 | 556.21 |
| 693.01 | wash-house | wax | 013.12 | 259.02 | 557.01 |
| 694.13 | 102.17 | 030.05 | 017.02 | 262.05 | 557.01 |
| 695.03 | washed | waxed | 023.06 | 262.20 | 557.04 |
| 695.09 | 111.04 | 045.02 | 023.08 | 274.14 | 558.08 |
| 695.22 | 364.06 | 157.13 | 026.11 | 275.19 | 558.09 |
| 696.03 | 386.04 | 437.18 | 030.14 | 284.12 | 558.13 |
| 697.04 | 639.02 | 475.02 | 035.19 | 286.12 | 558.19 |
| 699.19 | 757.20 | 546.11 | 041.02 | 286.13 | 564.21 |
| 700.06 | washhouse | waxen | 041.04 | 287.11 | 571.17 |
| 700.08 | 017.01 | 239.09 | 041.12 | 287.12 | 571.17 |
| 700.18 | washing | waxing | 041.20 | 288.15 | 572.02 |
| 700.22 | 125.12 | 725.17 | 041.21 | 288.16 | 572.03 |
| 701.05 | 491.10 | way | 042.13 | 296.06 | 577.17 |
| 701.11 | wasn't | 004.13 | 042.14 | 296.12 | 579.06 |
| 702.17 | 520.21 | 006.10 | 043.06 | 297.08 | 581.02 |
| 702.21 | waste | 008.05 | 044.05 | 298.05 | 586.06 |
| 703.13 | 213.07 | 030.21 | 044.06 | 299.13 | 586.09 |
| 703.17 | 503.21 | 031.15 | 044.12 | 299.15 | 586.11 |
| 703.22 | 690.05 | 037.02 | 044.17 | 304.01 | 586.13 |
| 704.02 | wasted | 043.19 | 044.18 | 304.11 | 586.13 |
| 704.14 | 270.05 | 046.14 | 045.11 | 304.20 | 586.16 |
| 704.15 | 271.16 | 052.13 | 046.16 | 305.06 | 588.02 |
| 705.02 | 363.22 | 057.21 | 047.04 | 308.05 | 591.16 |
| 705.02 | 543.02 | 059.09 | 047.11 | 308.10 | 591.18 |
| 705.12 | watch | 067.11 | 059.02 | 308.21 | 593.12 |
| 705.14 | 058.20 | 076.12 | 061.15 | 311.20 | 593.22 |
| 706.17 | 100.20 | 095.03 | 066.19 | 314.02 | 594.14 |
| 708.18 | 135.19 | 103.17 | 069.02 | 314.21 | 594.17 |
| 709.05 | 158.01 | 106.03 | | 316.16 | 596.07 |

| | | | | |
|---|---|---|---|---|
| 598.03 | 611.11 | weeks | 190.09 | 085.17 | 019.20 |
| 598.14 | weakness | 113.03 | 197.10 | 090.10 | 020.04 |
| 598.20 | 050.02 | 238.19 | 205.21 | 095.07 | 020.10 |
| 600.17 | 090.04 | 305.11 | 210.07 | 097.07 | 020.21 |
| 607.06 | 219.04 | 381.08 | 211.17 | 101.06 | 021.01 |
| 607.10 | 359.09 | 430.11 | 211.17 | 101.13 | 021.02 |
| 609.17 | 404.21 | 506.14 | 216.12 | 120.02 | 021.04 |
| 612.08 | 597.20 | 525.01 | 219.22 | 121.21 | 021.06 |
| 612.09 | 647.19 | 547.21 | 220.22 | 131.22 | 022.22 |
| 612.12 | 741.16 | 550.02 | 228.12 | 133.08 | 023.03 |
| 613.18 | wealthy | 578.04 | 239.03 | 154.11 | 024.15 |
| 613.19 | 175.22 | 659.11 | 251.18 | 160.08 | 026.17 |
| 617.19 | 442.13 | 678.07 | 253.07 | 160.19 | 028.02 |
| 618.14 | weaned | weeks' | 262.22 | 169.08 | 030.15 |
| 621.21 | 287.03 | 146.18 | 271.19 | 184.20 | 040.09 |
| 622.01 | 749.09 | 201.03 | 280.12 | 199.07 | 040.20 |
| 622.14 | weapon | weel | 284.10 | 217.12 | 041.11 |
| 622.19 | 011.13 | 187.11 | 289.13 | 247.20 | 041.12 |
| 623.02 | 047.02 | 321.02 | 293.11 | 255.06 | 042.11 |
| 623.03 | 050.08 | 324.10 | 308.10 | 267.10 | 044.05 |
| 629.16 | 316.05 | 324.11 | 312.03 | 270.01 | 047.05 |
| 643.07 | 399.12 | 458.08 | 313.12 | 276.10 | 047.09 |
| 644.09 | weapons | 564.17 | 315.10 | 279.12 | 048.13 |
| 644.10 | 637.02 | weel's | 335.11 | 291.09 | 055.10 |
| 644.22 | wearied | 232.20 | 337.21 | 295.19 | 056.12 |
| 646.02 | 046.17 | weep | 346.04 | 296.12 | 057.03 |
| 648.05 | 352.17 | 364.08 | 346.15 | 299.02 | 061.15 |
| 659.12 | wearies | 452.18 | 350.02 | 299.16 | 063.08 |
| 660.01 | 677.05 | 504.16 | 354.18 | 318.19 | 065.22 |
| 660.13 | weariness | 619.07 | 358.04 | 320.17 | 066.08 |
| 661.06 | 430.16 | weeping | 360.17 | 324.22 | 066.22 |
| 662.05 | wearing | 097.16 | 386.12 | 328.02 | 067.08 |
| 663.13 | 370.21 | 104.17 | 388.15 | 331.08 | 067.17 |
| 674.11 | wearisome | 128.18 | 396.12 | 350.08 | 074.07 |
| 676.21 | 196.13 | 159.14 | 406.12 | 351.02 | 077.05 |
| 680.04 | 226.09 | 178.20 | 415.14 | 360.03 | 078.13 |
| 680.07 | 324.03 | 259.14 | 416.03 | 361.11 | 080.07 |
| 689.16 | 548.06 | 281.21 | 421.19 | 367.22 | 080.18 |
| 696.20 | wearisomest | 314.12 | 435.01 | 378.14 | 084.06 |
| 700.14 | 089.12 | 337.17 | 437.20 | 409.19 | 085.14 |
| 712.19 | weary | 364.07 | 454.03 | 432.11 | 090.12 |
| 712.21 | 048.16 | 374.07 | 454.05 | 441.02 | 091.17 |
| 716.12 | 204.01 | 391.13 | 469.07 | 456.07 | 093.01 |
| 716.14 | 280.12 | 404.14 | 480.01 | 466.04 | 095.14 |
| 716.20 | 394.22 | 528.13 | 492.07 | 478.19 | 095.16 |
| 717.07 | 480.12 | 611.16 | 498.04 | 487.13 | 095.21 |
| 718.20 | 524.16 | 614.17 | 511.04 | 491.06 | 099.12 |
| 720.11 | 528.10 | 618.12 | 511.20 | 503.17 | 100.17 |
| 721.09 | 591.01 | 759.09 | 513.16 | 509.04 | 101.04 |
| 727.14 | 591.13 | weighed | 517.12 | 509.14 | 101.09 |
| 737.03 | 618.22 | 315.02 | 521.01 | 517.10 | 103.21 |
| 740.01 | 699.06 | weighing | 521.22 | 533.18 | 103.22 |
| 740.17 | 746.02 | 084.10 | 524.17 | 544.13 | 104.08 |
| 740.18 | wearying | weighs | 527.06 | 551.16 | 104.12 |
| 740.20 | 130.19 | 602.01 | 533.01 | 555.09 | 104.16 |
| 745.05 | 269.05 | weight | 536.03 | 559.13 | 107.15 |
| 745.11 | 361.01 | 064.21 | 537.13 | 568.10 | 107.17 |
| 746.10 | weasel's | 084.10 | 541.01 | 570.03 | 110.14 |
| 746.11 | 490.16 | weighty | 547.01 | 572.19 | 111.16 |
| 746.13 | weather | 640.07 | 547.01 | 619.05 | 115.12 |
| 748.11 | 004.07 | welcome | 554.13 | 624.08 | 119.01 |
| 748.14 | 008.11 | 067.14 | 562.21 | 627.15 | 122.02 |
| 756.14 | 017.15 | 114.22 | 581.18 | 634.04 | 122.19 |
| 760.01 | 027.16 | 116.14 | 582.05 | 638.10 | 125.09 |
| 760.06 | 350.17 | 164.06 | 586.08 | 651.15 | 125.20 |
| we'd | 381.03 | 215.19 | 589.04 | 654.10 | 125.21 |
| 558.15 | 463.19 | 216.08 | 591.18 | 662.14 | 129.21 |
| we'll | 558.09 | 252.19 | 592.17 | 664.10 | 131.06 |
| 240.04 | 589.22 | 390.02 | 602.10 | 666.18 | 132.10 |
| 372.17 | 689.22 | 482.19 | 606.12 | 673.03 | 133.11 |
| 421.07 | 704.04 | 563.06 | 610.04 | 697.16 | 135.17 |
| 421.19 | 737.03 | 685.18 | 617.07 | 702.21 | 139.05 |
| 484.05 | weather-bound | welcomed | 619.17 | 705.10 | 140.07 |
| 505.13 | 021.19 | 205.17 | 626.09 | 713.11 | 140.14 |
| 512.04 | weather-cocks | welcoming | 635.17 | 715.10 | 143.01 |
| 520.08 | 069.02 | 213.02 | 636.09 | 717.15 | 144.05 |
| 543.19 | weather-worn | 448.08 | 637.16 | 725.03 | 144.19 |
| 547.11 | 243.16 | well | 640.13 | 740.16 | 146.05 |
| 586.08 | weathered | 012.02 | 647.10 | 745.01 | 148.11 |
| 588.07 | 196.14 | 022.12 | 662.22 | 746.17 | 150.09 |
| 606.08 | wed | 024.07 | 664.01 | 756.13 | 151.12 |
| we're | 489.09 | 035.18 | 666.22 | 757.02 | 154.05 |
| 164.15 | wedding | 040.04 | 677.13 | wenting | 154.14 |
| 177.06 | 337.16 | 056.03 | 689.09 | 322.03 | 164.07 |
| 467.22 | 697.02 | 057.14 | 691.04 | wept | 170.05 |
| 618.14 | wedding-day | 065.19 | 692.09 | 144.01 | 174.19 |
| we's | 714.05 | 073.15 | 694.10 | 228.04 | 178.06 |
| 232.09 | weeds | 074.13 | 703.07 | 389.07 | 178.21 |
| 324.13 | 442.10 | 079.05 | 703.19 | 417.15 | 180.08 |
| 324.14 | week | 099.19 | 709.13 | 440.18 | 181.12 |
| we've | 084.01 | 102.08 | 718.07 | 467.18 | 182.08 |
| 125.12 | 115.17 | 108.12 | 722.14 | 538.13 | 182.15 |
| 294.13 | 142.05 | 116.01 | 727.16 | 567.02 | 182.15 |
| 292.10 | 142.18 | 117.01 | 732.03 | 573.21 | 182.22 |
| 320.12 | 232.07 | 122.21 | 741.01 | 602.14 | 185.11 |
| 565.14 | 280.08 | 124.03 | 753.07 | 630.15 | 185.13 |
| weak | 349.02 | 125.02 | 753.10 | 708.08 | 189.16 |
| 069.06 | 390.16 | 127.11 | 756.08 | wer | 194.15 |
| 202.09 | 392.03 | 129.10 | well-formed | 193.21 | 194.19 |
| 220.05 | 470.12 | 135.12 | 213.19 | 319.10 | 195.13 |
| 258.05 | 489.20 | 142.05 | well-made | 320.13 | 196.12 |
| 279.04 | 525.22 | 142.15 | 442.02 | 471.15 | 196.21 |
| 306.21 | 526.16 | 143.04 | well-swept | 471.15 | 197.15 |
| 475.10 | 555.11 | 159.10 | 119.18 | 472.06 | 199.04 |
| 494.03 | 583.03 | 164.16 | went | 472.06 | 204.10 |
| 550.06 | 588.06 | 173.09 | 013.13 | 564.15 | 204.13 |
| weaker | 672.11 | 175.11 | 016.07 | 586.01 | 205.12 |
| 415.03 | 684.20 | 179.03 | 030.12 | 696.13 | 205.19 |
| weakling | week's | 180.18 | 042.10 | 696.18 | 206.14 |
| 454.12 | 125.18 | 183.03 | 057.15 | were | 207.01 |
| | 664.15 | 189.01 | 080.20 | 006.09 | 207.16 |

| | | | | | |
|---|---|---|---|---|---|
| 209.01 | 504.03 | 728.14 | 175.01 | 433.03 | 730.21 |
| 211.04 | 504.03 | 730.13 | 175.18 | 433.13 | 731.12 |
| 215.03 | 505.03 | 733.03 | 180.16 | 435.20 | 731.13 |
| 215.08 | 507.03 | 734.15 | 181.11 | 439.08 | 732.15 |
| 216.11 | 507.10 | 736.10 | 181.11 | 439.19 | 738.03 |
| 216.11 | 507.12 | 737.03 | 182.14 | 443.04 | 739.18 |
| 221.15 | 507.15 | 739.10 | 184.15 | 443.13 | 740.02 |
| 234.07 | 507.22 | 742.14 | 184.22 | 449.15 | 741.19 |
| 235.16 | 508.04 | 746.11 | 186.13 | 453.06 | 744.07 |
| 238.16 | 508.08 | 746.13 | 186.15 | 454.14 | 745.18 |
| 238.17 | 510.18 | 746.18 | 186.18 | 455.05 | 753.20 |
| 240.01 | 515.04 | 746.19 | 186.19 | 455.18 | 758.18 |
| 241.03 | 516.16 | 747.07 | 190.11 | 458.03 | 759.16 |
| 243.19 | 520.12 | 748.16 | 192.03 | 464.01 | 761.06 |
| 244.11 | 521.05 | 749.09 | 192.15 | 465.07 | **what´s** |
| 245.15 | 522.18 | 753.22 | 193.10 | 466.14 | 156.17 |
| 250.08 | 524.09 | 755.13 | 195.18 | 467.03 | 311.12 |
| 256.17 | 525.14 | 757.20 | 207.20 | 467.03 | 340.22 |
| 261.03 | 528.01 | 759.03 | 208.01 | 468.16 | 439.04 |
| 263.16 | 528.18 | 761.04 | 208.13 | 469.03 | 683.16 |
| 268.03 | 529.04 | 762.18 | 210.05 | 470.13 | 720.04 |
| 273.11 | 530.05 | **wern´t** | 210.15 | 471.15 | **whatever** |
| 274.14 | 530.10 | 298.05 | 218.19 | 472.03 | 033.06 |
| 276.20 | 531.07 | 497.18 | 219.21 | 472.11 | 067.08 |
| 279.11 | 531.20 | **west** | 221.03 | 481.21 | 179.11 |
| 282.19 | 536.02 | 516.19 | 221.13 | 485.15 | 198.06 |
| 282.20 | 536.06 | 557.14 | 222.14 | 486.18 | 338.05 |
| 283.03 | 536.07 | 693.02 | 226.17 | 488.02 | 342.02 |
| 284.03 | 536.11 | **westering** | 227.16 | 492.06 | 417.19 |
| 286.13 | 541.08 | 364.13 | 229.12 | 493.16 | 554.18 |
| 290.03 | 542.10 | **wet** | 233.19 | 493.18 | 592.08 |
| 291.03 | 545.02 | 102.12 | 236.10 | 495.05 | 749.02 |
| 291.15 | 545.18 | 191.10 | 236.14 | 495.19 | **whear** |
| 292.05 | 545.19 | 192.07 | 238.14 | 510.08 | 323.22 |
| 294.10 | 548.16 | 361.17 | 240.13 | 511.07 | 324.02 |
| 295.06 | 550.06 | 383.17 | 246.16 | 512.04 | 531.13 |
| 296.13 | 550.06 | 404.14 | 247.07 | 520.01 | **wheare** |
| 298.14 | 552.03 | 509.15 | 250.11 | 528.02 | 719.11 |
| 302.03 | 557.04 | 655.09 | 251.03 | 528.20 | **wheedle** |
| 303.09 | 558.10 | 704.04 | 252.10 | 529.04 | 085.06 |
| 303.16 | 559.17 | 757.03 | 254.04 | 537.07 | **wheedling** |
| 304.12 | 561.12 | **wetted** | 255.18 | 540.04 | 339.14 |
| 306.03 | 562.18 | 491.12 | 262.07 | 540.18 | **wheeled** |
| 311.08 | 563.03 | 530.05 | 262.19 | 548.20 | 111.10 |
| 311.09 | 565.04 | **wh** | 271.14 | 550.10 | **wheeling** |
| 314.02 | 565.20 | 243.07 | 274.06 | 556.05 | 275.14 |
| 321.09 | 566.17 | **what** | 276.17 | 556.14 | **whelp** |
| 323.11 | 567.02 | 008.19 | 277.13 | 557.01 | 192.05 |
| 325.18 | 571.17 | 011.18 | 278.15 | 560.01 | 441.17 |
| 340.02 | 572.03 | 011.21 | 280.08 | 561.13 | 470.04 |
| 340.07 | 572.04 | 013.08 | 281.05 | 566.05 | 604.05 |
| 350.13 | 573.20 | 030.07 | 281.05 | 568.21 | **whelphood** |
| 353.01 | 577.09 | 035.08 | 281.13 | 576.22 | 325.10 |
| 353.06 | 579.17 | 035.19 | 282.13 | 577.21 | **when** |
| 356.21 | 583.18 | 041.19 | 285.15 | 578.13 | 001.13 |
| 357.08 | 584.05 | 046.04 | 287.20 | 582.04 | 002.02 |
| 361.22 | 586.13 | 046.08 | 288.06 | 588.09 | 003.05 |
| 362.08 | 587.04 | 048.04 | 291.11 | 590.07 | 008.05 |
| 364.05 | 588.14 | 050.21 | 292.09 | 595.07 | 011.16 |
| 366.09 | 591.20 | 051.01 | 295.09 | 595.08 | 016.18 |
| 370.17 | 592.04 | 056.07 | 297.08 | 597.10 | 023.03 |
| 377.15 | 593.10 | 056.08 | 297.12 | 597.21 | 024.10 |
| 379.14 | 600.12 | 057.19 | 297.13 | 600.03 | 028.17 |
| 381.09 | 603.02 | 064.17 | 300.03 | 600.17 | 028.21 |
| 381.10 | 603.20 | 067.05 | 301.04 | 601.19 | 039.08 |
| 383.17 | 609.01 | 069.02 | 301.11 | 602.17 | 040.12 |
| 387.13 | 610.21 | 071.15 | 306.10 | 607.06 | 041.18 |
| 393.11 | 611.01 | 072.14 | 306.19 | 608.05 | 042.17 |
| 394.18 | 612.01 | 076.04 | 307.13 | 608.08 | 051.18 |
| 395.15 | 612.10 | 076.09 | 312.07 | 610.15 | 057.03 |
| 398.01 | 612.12 | 076.10 | 316.18 | 612.13 | 058.10 |
| 398.12 | 615.21 | 078.12 | 316.19 | 615.10 | 060.06 |
| 398.16 | 617.20 | 079.14 | 321.21 | 616.02 | 066.10 |
| 399.08 | 619.02 | 083.05 | 326.19 | 617.15 | 066.16 |
| 404.13 | 623.02 | 085.08 | 329.17 | 618.14 | 069.12 |
| 404.14 | 626.10 | 086.02 | 331.10 | 627.01 | 070.07 |
| 407.20 | 627.02 | 086.02 | 333.10 | 627.10 | 072.01 |
| 411.07 | 632.19 | 091.21 | 333.22 | 631.09 | 077.02 |
| 413.12 | 633.01 | 095.02 | 336.12 | 633.09 | 078.05 |
| 414.19 | 633.02 | 096.06 | 336.22 | 634.14 | 078.11 |
| 415.11 | 633.15 | 097.16 | 340.16 | 647.05 | 079.13 |
| 417.11 | 635.04 | 098.05 | 343.08 | 647.17 | 079.16 |
| 418.20 | 637.04 | 099.20 | 345.19 | 649.10 | 081.01 |
| 421.01 | 637.20 | 100.02 | 346.11 | 649.12 | 081.11 |
| 424.03 | 640.07 | 102.10 | 354.21 | 650.19 | 082.05 |
| 427.12 | 643.03 | 104.12 | 356.15 | 656.07 | 083.18 |
| 429.07 | 647.18 | 105.06 | 357.09 | 659.13 | 085.12 |
| 431.06 | 650.04 | 107.10 | 363.03 | 660.08 | 087.04 |
| 431.09 | 650.05 | 109.13 | 363.04 | 662.07 | 090.18 |
| 432.09 | 655.10 | 115.09 | 363.12 | 664.02 | 091.17 |
| 437.20 | 659.19 | 116.11 | 364.02 | 664.12 | 092.03 |
| 438.06 | 664.08 | 117.16 | 366.14 | 667.01 | 097.16 |
| 444.21 | 666.10 | 121.20 | 367.08 | 668.13 | 099.09 |
| 452.20 | 668.04 | 123.07 | 368.12 | 669.03 | 100.06 |
| 454.16 | 669.06 | 124.10 | 370.02 | 670.15 | 101.06 |
| 467.12 | 674.04 | 125.03 | 382.14 | 675.13 | 105.06 |
| 468.10 | 680.14 | 126.01 | 386.05 | 680.11 | 106.08 |
| 469.18 | 682.21 | 127.15 | 387.02 | 682.11 | 107.01 |
| 474.08 | 691.21 | 141.07 | 389.12 | 684.16 | 112.14 |
| 476.19 | 693.11 | 145.01 | 393.21 | 686.20 | 114.21 |
| 477.06 | 693.19 | 145.21 | 397.12 | 693.18 | 119.21 |
| 478.20 | 695.04 | 152.15 | 397.14 | 698.03 | 122.19 |
| 480.10 | 700.08 | 152.20 | 402.12 | 701.21 | 123.05 |
| 481.04 | 702.19 | 153.13 | 405.10 | 702.02 | 126.06 |
| 481.10 | 711.20 | 153.14 | 406.17 | 702.15 | 132.19 |
| 486.04 | 716.02 | 154.11 | 408.01 | 707.04 | 137.01 |
| 487.08 | 716.06 | 155.01 | 415.17 | 708.20 | 139.06 |
| 487.21 | 716.17 | 164.17 | 416.15 | 709.14 | 140.08 |
| 488.05 | 717.06 | 165.08 | 427.01 | 716.11 | 140.22 |
| 493.13 | 725.13 | 171.17 | 427.05 | 718.08 | 141.18 |
| 502.21 | 726.13 | 172.12 | 429.09 | 718.14 | 142.22 |

| | | | | | |
|---|---|---|---|---|---|
| 146.15 | 428.02 | 697.04 | 428.06 | 561.11 | 327.09 |
| 147.14 | 428.18 | 701.06 | 432.20 | 561.12 | 330.10 |
| 148.05 | 431.01 | 702.12 | 437.01 | 566.16 | 342.14 |
| 148.08 | 434.14 | 703.21 | 437.02 | 570.20 | 348.03 |
| 149.21 | 443.10 | 707.05 | 439.01 | 577.11 | 352.01 |
| 154.01 | 445.14 | 708.03 | 445.20 | 587.04 | 352.13 |
| 155.08 | 450.05 | 708.13 | 453.02 | 611.01 | 353.05 |
| 160.08 | 455.01 | 709.21 | 459.08 | 629.03 | 353.13 |
| 165.02 | 460.18 | 715.10 | 460.14 | 640.06 | 355.21 |
| 165.13 | 466.11 | 719.01 | 462.06 | 640.07 | 359.10 |
| 169.01 | 469.18 | 721.19 | 468.03 | 646.09 | 360.05 |
| 169.12 | 471.14 | 723.17 | 477.02 | 676.21 | 362.01 |
| 169.19 | 474.12 | 724.02 | 478.10 | 699.08 | 371.02 |
| 171.11 | 475.04 | 726.12 | 479.01 | 703.09 | 372.06 |
| 177.13 | 478.15 | 729.12 | 479.01 | 709.18 | 372.13 |
| 180.12 | 485.16 | 735.05 | 480.01 | 728.11 | 379.04 |
| 181.16 | 492.10 | 737.17 | 483.05 | 739.09 | 383.19 |
| 184.03 | 492.12 | 740.13 | 484.06 | whey | 393.07 |
| 184.13 | 492.12 | 741.02 | 485.10 | 196.05 | 393.22 |
| 192.04 | 498.04 | 741.11 | 497.06 | whey-faced | 395.19 |
| 195.18 | 500.09 | 747.13 | 497.13 | 470.21 | 396.15 |
| 196.18 | 501.20 | 748.22 | 517.18 | which | 401.16 |
| 197.07 | 503.16 | 750.08 | 523.04 | 002.21 | 408.08 |
| 199.05 | 505.02 | 752.04 | 533.09 | 004.06 | 408.18 |
| 199.06 | 507.07 | 756.19 | 553.07 | 004.22 | 409.19 |
| 204.16 | 510.18 | 758.02 | 553.18 | 008.06 | 412.01 |
| 206.02 | 511.08 | 760.05 | 553.20 | 009.09 | 412.21 |
| 206.16 | 513.03 | 761.20 | 554.03 | 022.22 | 418.04 |
| 208.21 | 516.16 | 763.15 | 556.21 | 024.17 | 424.06 |
| 210.01 | 517.05 | whence | 564.21 | 026.08 | 429.16 |
| 210.21 | 520.01 | 067.21 | 568.16 | 027.02 | 430.18 |
| 213.11 | 520.05 | 463.05 | 576.17 | 028.14 | 433.04 |
| 214.18 | 523.13 | whenever | 597.03 | 030.21 | 434.22 |
| 215.11 | 526.05 | 029.13 | 608.10 | 031.18 | 442.17 |
| 217.14 | 533.02 | 240.11 | 616.21 | 034.02 | 443.02 |
| 218.13 | 535.10 | 539.12 | 629.09 | 038.12 | 443.06 |
| 226.15 | 540.14 | 546.05 | 634.15 | 046.21 | 456.04 |
| 227.12 | 543.14 | 694.20 | 645.13 | 049.16 | 462.17 |
| 232.22 | 545.02 | where | 675.07 | 050.18 | 468.06 |
| 238.13 | 545.17 | 006.06 | 683.11 | 052.01 | 470.04 |
| 249.20 | 546.18 | 017.04 | 685.19 | 057.05 | 483.13 |
| 254.05 | 548.14 | 024.05 | 709.22 | 058.09 | 490.21 |
| 257.16 | 548.22 | 038.18 | 715.09 | 060.09 | 502.07 |
| 262.15 | 553.12 | 044.04 | 724.14 | 061.10 | 505.21 |
| 263.04 | 555.14 | 048.08 | 725.07 | 061.21 | 507.05 |
| 263.10 | 559.09 | 059.20 | 729.18 | 066.03 | 507.09 |
| 264.04 | 560.04 | 060.06 | 739.03 | 067.07 | 508.07 |
| 265.05 | 563.17 | 061.06 | 742.01 | 068.04 | 510.02 |
| 274.07 | 567.11 | 063.05 | 742.14 | 077.17 | 517.03 |
| 275.11 | 569.01 | 063.07 | 745.20 | 081.20 | 532.10 |
| 277.18 | 574.03 | 065.08 | where's | 084.02 | 569.08 |
| 285.09 | 576.01 | 069.05 | 170.11 | 085.20 | 579.0c |
| 287.10 | 578.12 | 072.08 | whereas | 091.22 | 581.11 |
| 287.10 | 579.02 | 074.07 | 181.20 | 104.19 | 588.20 |
| 291.09 | 583.19 | 078.20 | 573.03 | 110.21 | 591.06 |
| 293.17 | 585.02 | 088.22 | whereby | 113.08 | 594.21 |
| 294.17 | 586.09 | 096.06 | 036.14 | 114.04 | 603.05 |
| 299.07 | 586.11 | 099.01 | whereupon | 115.19 | 611.06 |
| 300.04 | 587.13 | 102.03 | 258.15 | 118.01 | 616.17 |
| 302.05 | 593.12 | 108.06 | wherever | 126.16 | 623.10 |
| 307.05 | 597.01 | 109.18 | 162.11 | 135.17 | 636.02 |
| 307.14 | 599.19 | 124.21 | 185.20 | 136.15 | 637.17 |
| 308.01 | 602.20 | 128.13 | 216.20 | 137.20 | 643.07 |
| 308.10 | 607.13 | 132.04 | 300.04 | 148.14 | 644.18 |
| 311.21 | 617.11 | 144.13 | whet | 157.03 | 650.03 |
| 312.19 | 617.11 | 146.22 | 016.05 | 157.11 | 650.03 |
| 316.03 | 619.02 | 147.09 | 191.05 | 160.21 | 663.21 |
| 318.12 | 619.13 | 153.09 | 310.13 | 170.18 | 665.19 |
| 318.20 | 619.20 | 155.10 | 400.20 | 171.11 | 668.14 |
| 319.14 | 627.13 | 158.03 | 400.20 | 171.21 | 668.16 |
| 323.15 | 628.02 | 158.09 | 691.08 | 178.01 | 674.08 |
| 325.18 | 630.12 | 176.02 | 720.12 | 188.12 | 677.17 |
| 329.17 | 630.13 | 179.02 | whether | 189.18 | 680.02 |
| 330.17 | 633.01 | 186.12 | 021.01 | 196.20 | 680.21 |
| 335.06 | 633.21 | 186.12 | 058.03 | 203.20 | 681.07 |
| 339.01 | 634.12 | 188.14 | 071.04 | 206.07 | 693.14 |
| 340.01 | 635.03 | 191.07 | 078.13 | 206.20 | 694.18 |
| 344.12 | 637.07 | 196.08 | 084.15 | 208.04 | 695.11 |
| 346.21 | 638.07 | 197.09 | 085.14 | 209.13 | 696.02 |
| 351.10 | 642.01 | 203.08 | 102.20 | 214.21 | 716.04 |
| 353.06 | 644.04 | 208.06 | 125.13 | 221.19 | 718.06 |
| 354.12 | 645.11 | 208.21 | 171.20 | 223.08 | 726.02 |
| 357.12 | 645.17 | 212.04 | 172.10 | 224.20 | 727.02 |
| 358.20 | 647.08 | 222.07 | 172.15 | 227.07 | 730.08 |
| 363.13 | 648.10 | 226.03 | 175.15 | 229.19 | 731.10 |
| 371.21 | 649.16 | 227.18 | 180.08 | 234.21 | 734.03 |
| 374.10 | 649.22 | 243.05 | 207.20 | 237.13 | 734.14 |
| 378.13 | 650.11 | 246.09 | 228.01 | 240.21 | 735.06 |
| 382.07 | 652.08 | 262.05 | 233.22 | 243.19 | 737.13 |
| 384.02 | 654.07 | 264.09 | 245.14 | 245.14 | 743.19 |
| 384.20 | 654.09 | 277.03 | 264.06 | 249.06 | 745.11 |
| 387.18 | 654.10 | 282.14 | 264.13 | 253.21 | 746.06 |
| 390.22 | 654.12 | 287.14 | 267.10 | 255.14 | 754.08 |
| 391.22 | 654.18 | 290.17 | 287.18 | 255.19 | 759.13 |
| 392.02 | 656.01 | 304.20 | 298.05 | 259.17 | whichever |
| 399.11 | 656.14 | 313.15 | 312.21 | 263.14 | 176.05 |
| 403.12 | 658.04 | 314.19 | 334.10 | 265.09 | while |
| 405.01 | 658.12 | 315.01 | 368.08 | 267.19 | 003.19 |
| 406.18 | 659.12 | 331.08 | 371.07 | 274.08 | 008.11 |
| 407.19 | 664.15 | 360.08 | 372.03 | 281.12 | 023.07 |
| 411.07 | 665.05 | 371.17 | 390.14 | 285.17 | 032.12 |
| 412.03 | 666.14 | 374.17 | 425.17 | 293.21 | 034.12 |
| 412.09 | 667.07 | 376.17 | 452.20 | 304.12 | 036.12 |
| 412.13 | 670.09 | 376.18 | 467.12 | 305.21 | 037.02 |
| 412.18 | 674.14 | 377.05 | 477.15 | 307.07 | 041.07 |
| 415.03 | 678.03 | 379.22 | 479.02 | 311.02 | 046.03 |
| 419.06 | 679.01 | 383.01 | 508.15 | 312.18 | 062.17 |
| 420.10 | 683.22 | 387.04 | 520.06 | 314.11 | 069.12 |
| 420.22 | 686.08 | 411.14 | 530.10 | 319.17 | 076.22 |
| 427.05 | 688.08 | 413.02 | 546.04 | 321.09 | 082.09 |
| 427.09 | 692.08 | 413.19 | 552.03 | 322.20 | 088.10 |

```
095.20        whining       072.20        632.10        412.20        721.06
097.07          220.15      072.21        641.19        434.01        732.08
101.18          470.21      074.07        647.13        477.21        733.14
102.15        whinstone     080.15        649.13        480.21        738.09
102.22          073.22      081.16        658.08        500.04        740.19
108.21          229.14      083.07        658.09        609.07        742.04
114.20        whip          085.01        663.06      whose           742.13
122.05          076.16      088.15        664.06        017.09        744.15
132.06          079.17      090.14        704.16        047.14        749.21
134.04          567.18      105.01        705.16        083.03        762.07
143.10        whipping      107.14        708.07        111.12      wi
150.17          614.09      109.18        708.07        165.12        194.02
160.08        whirl         118.10        721.12        209.06      wi'
168.02          027.19      124.14        721.14        213.09        187.12
180.11        whirled       125.15        730.07        246.10        188.03
184.06          060.18      128.08        737.11        312.16        232.11
185.09        whiskers      130.21        737.17        337.10        233.08
188.21          021.05      135.02        741.20        437.21        297.16
191.15          207.17      135.05        756.03        438.07        466.21
207.12          421.10      157.07        756.04        442.11        564.04
212.10        whisper       161.01        756.08        507.06        688.11
216.02          031.07      165.09        760.13        657.03        706.11
227.18          331.09      166.03        762.06        699.15        707.10
233.11          471.13      167.07      who's           717.18        720.02
237.16          572.21      169.19        416.07      why             720.14
242.02        whispered     173.01      whoever         016.13      wi't
251.20          094.13      181.06        598.06        052.11        016.15
252.06          106.09      182.10      whoiver         061.03        319.12
259.21          109.05      184.08        691.08        071.08      wick
263.20          155.06      190.01      whole           072.09        039.12
266.06          169.21      191.12        003.11        091.12        090.15
269.02          184.21      194.13        010.17        093.12        393.10
271.07          236.15      202.04        019.08        093.17      wick'
276.16          266.11      204.15        038.02        114.08        688.11
278.04          309.22      205.13        047.17        116.20      wicked
284.10          406.21      206.21        050.06        129.03        030.01
291.12          440.18      207.08        050.13        147.22        030.01
298.20          452.17      210.11        065.19        151.07        030.12
304.10          482.20      210.14        066.07        173.06        056.21
305.07          491.21      215.01        105.09        173.08        110.01
325.14          523.17      221.12        120.20        174.06        125.21
344.07          523.19      225.11        136.19        180.04        133.21
358.12          544.22      232.08        150.21        185.07        157.10
359.06          591.14      235.16        156.16        192.05        179.05
362.16          606.01      246.05        207.12        202.10        183.20
371.03          622.18      247.01        213.01        210.16        231.01
371.11          635.16      249.13        237.22        232.01        241.08
393.12          656.09      254.03        254.13        236.20        265.16
403.04          669.18      256.08        281.14        243.13        289.04
417.03          703.09      261.10        288.13        250.22        385.20
426.18          705.17      263.17        303.05        272.20        399.05
450.18          709.13      270.07        313.05        278.15        417.01
451.11          717.06      277.17        336.08        282.04        439.19
462.21          723.12      278.15        349.08        282.22        468.19
469.05        whispers      287.05        382.21        283.01        488.11
471.01          296.15      297.04        394.05        283.05        524.03
473.01        whistle       298.14        398.20        286.04        537.05
497.21          188.02      311.13        419.01        298.03        537.07
498.08        whistled      313.19        420.15        315.10        650.04
506.17          594.09      333.07        427.10        321.11        704.07
509.01        white         339.18        443.14        334.07        723.04
514.06          006.13      350.20        446.18        342.21        758.18
521.14          009.14      352.03        484.14        343.21      wickedly
523.08          022.01      394.01        487.06        357.10        584.01
528.15          039.08      395.04        503.15        362.19        612.19
532.13          054.18      400.16        507.18        362.20      wickedness
540.05          065.20      402.05        516.01        375.15        144.13
541.05          084.19      407.04        544.02        376.16      wickednesses
547.19          098.19      408.02        557.22        405.20        696.13
552.02          104.05      410.05        568.20        414.17      wicket
555.16          114.19      411.03        571.18        416.10        311.02
563.04          126.17      416.09        573.13        427.15        433.21
579.01          237.16      416.20        588.16        461.01      wide
581.14          239.10      417.10        597.06        461.02        098.21
587.08          290.18      419.08        615.10        461.07        189.19
598.17          303.05      422.14        619.15        465.04        240.19
615.21          351.03      422.19        624.21        483.01        283.04
621.15          358.09      434.01        624.22        487.21        321.10
624.04          383.20      434.18        637.18        489.07        350.18
653.05          464.15      438.10        664.11        496.05        361.17
655.21          468.22      442.02        670.05        497.06        431.11
659.18          557.15      445.16        701.17        500.16        469.10
666.06          565.01      445.19        720.17        503.08        629.01
668.06          660.19      446.11        727.14        504.21        745.08
676.07          694.18      450.22        729.20        511.06      wide-brimmed
686.19          710.02      460.08        734.05        519.15        432.01
689.14          758.11      481.15        738.21        533.04      wider
697.20        whitened      482.04        745.18        546.21        718.21
701.12          116.07      486.09        756.14        553.19      widow
703.18          398.01      487.14        760.01        575.11        071.03
704.21        whiteness     495.04        760.04        576.02        072.06
706.20          219.07      496.18      wholesome       576.03      wielded
719.07        who           498.06        162.05        586.18        414.04
722.12          003.03      500.08        348.05        591.15      wife
727.10          009.11      506.12      wholly          592.01        024.06
729.07          010.06      509.05        143.18        599.07        024.16
740.18          012.04      511.21        339.18        599.08        041.07
748.02          016.13      521.07        379.15        599.17        077.19
752.06          018.06      523.17      whom            599.18        096.05
752.07          025.01      538.02        033.21        606.03        098.18
752.12          030.05      540.11        078.22        614.02        114.13
755.12          031.17      564.18        128.04        617.14        140.21
whim            033.07      575.07        213.20        624.06        141.15
684.18          035.12      579.11        222.01        636.11        143.09
684.19          042.04      581.16        232.02        639.07        182.05
whimper         052.08      594.09        310.07        646.13        233.08
539.05          055.13      603.20        325.08        669.10        253.08
whims           055.16      608.18        338.03        692.13        254.20
182.08          063.22      616.18        345.14        697.06        282.12
220.01          067.07      622.06        355.04        702.12        286.19
                069.02      631.08        364.11        708.12        331.03
```

| | | | | | |
|---|---|---|---|---|---|
| 341.05 | 175.20 | 513.16 | wince | 302.22 | 329.05 |
| 413.10 | 175.20 | 514.13 | 468.21 | 517.21 | 334.09 |
| 536.07 | 176.10 | 518.20 | wincing | wine | 340.02 |
| 630.02 | 179.02 | 519.22 | 002.16 | 003.10 | 343.20 |
| 641.05 | 180.07 | 520.04 | wind | 012.08 | 357.07 |
| 653.13 | 181.16 | 520.05 | 004.10 | 012.15 | 359.16 |
| wife's | 183.03 | 532.14 | 011.16 | 177.01 | 387.07 |
| 145.19 | 195.01 | 533.09 | 027.19 | 534.11 | 399.07 |
| 267.18 | 198.16 | 535.10 | 051.11 | 556.16 | 406.04 |
| 418.07 | 203.06 | 535.16 | 060.18 | 663.06 | 412.06 |
| 664.18 | 203.22 | 543.07 | 092.21 | wing | 412.07 |
| wih | 208.12 | 544.16 | 095.07 | 130.08 | 469.20 |
| 441.21 | 208.13 | 546.16 | 189.01 | 364.21 | 477.09 |
| wild | 208.14 | 546.20 | 274.15 | wink | 479.01 |
| 090.15 | 210.22 | 560.02 | 279.13 | 133.06 | 499.21 |
| 092.22 | 212.14 | 562.21 | 290.19 | 289.10 | 503.09 |
| 113.09 | 216.20 | 573.05 | 303.02 | 633.18 | 523.18 |
| 114.14 | 222.12 | 573.05 | 352.07 | winked | 535.05 |
| 209.08 | 222.20 | 579.10 | 381.04 | 633.18 | 536.02 |
| 211.09 | 235.21 | 581.17 | 393.07 | winking | 539.01 |
| 261.20 | 238.10 | 590.03 | 421.08 | 010.12 | 543.20 |
| 314.10 | 247.09 | 591.16 | 517.11 | 081.05 | 570.12 |
| 358.08 | 249.19 | 600.14 | 557.14 | 720.12 | 576.21 |
| 392.18 | 250.12 | 601.12 | 630.15 | winning | 592.01 |
| 411.03 | 252.13 | 601.21 | 652.02 | 424.12 | 617.14 |
| 417.02 | 257.03 | 602.20 | 652.16 | 683.02 | 622.05 |
| 436.15 | 258.01 | 603.14 | 764.08 | winsome | 630.03 |
| 448.07 | 260.21 | 603.16 | winding | 171.10 | 649.21 |
| 479.19 | 262.05 | 605.10 | 209.10 | winter | 652.12 |
| 521.05 | 263.01 | 605.12 | windings | 059.04 | 656.14 |
| 522.08 | 263.03 | 605.20 | 066.17 | 126.13 | 661.11 |
| 558.01 | 263.19 | 608.22 | 410.09 | 140.04 | 679.13 |
| 634.09 | 265.05 | 609.13 | window | 141.02 | 680.09 |
| 651.09 | 265.06 | 609.17 | 016.03 | 183.04 | 685.11 |
| 732.04 | 271.04 | 612.19 | 027.15 | 274.15 | 686.17 |
| 738.10 | 273.01 | 614.05 | 038.12 | 275.19 | 691.06 |
| 750.21 | 273.04 | 617.10 | 039.05 | 398.14 | 713.18 |
| 755.14 | 273.06 | 618.03 | 052.15 | 427.19 | 730.12 |
| wild-beast's | 273.09 | 619.07 | 056.13 | 450.21 | 734.05 |
| 162.06 | 277.18 | 620.02 | 103.19 | 476.10 | 734.15 |
| wild-duck's | 279.09 | 628.08 | 107.16 | 516.01 | 742.09 |
| 275.08 | 282.15 | 631.06 | 126.09 | 518.17 | 742.10 |
| wildered | 284.16 | 635.17 | 153.02 | 575.02 | 751.15 |
| 660.21 | 284.21 | 636.15 | 160.01 | 575.04 | 752.05 |
| wilderness | 288.07 | 641.07 | 193.04 | 578.07 | 752.09 |
| 004.22 | 289.13 | 647.13 | 196.07 | 593.12 | wished |
| 229.14 | 292.16 | 647.19 | 209.06 | 630.12 | 013.16 |
| 338.11 | 293.06 | 648.10 | 211.01 | 651.16 | 110.16 |
| 442.10 | 306.21 | 653.07 | 234.17 | 672.17 | 192.18 |
| wildly | 307.20 | 656.08 | 249.01 | 690.05 | 198.10 |
| 060.18 | 315.04 | 660.05 | 255.10 | winter's | 228.05 |
| 282.04 | 317.05 | 664.11 | 274.14 | 229.16 | 239.02 |
| 362.17 | 317.07 | 667.01 | 281.09 | wintry | 253.04 |
| 602.14 | 318.07 | 669.19 | 283.04 | 381.10 | 289.08 |
| wildness | 324.18 | 670.06 | 286.04 | wipe | 350.21 |
| 019.01 | 333.08 | 670.08 | 288.06 | 154.19 | 361.11 |
| 587.10 | 333.22 | 683.20 | 304.08 | 708.04 | 373.10 |
| wile | 342.10 | 699.06 | 332.07 | wiped | 429.18 |
| 347.21 | 346.07 | 702.08 | 351.05 | 330.08 | 455.03 |
| wilful | 346.10 | 707.01 | 365.12 | 613.05 | 460.09 |
| 191.09 | 347.21 | 708.06 | 382.07 | 655.08 | 470.18 |
| 529.08 | 357.11 | 714.04 | 397.04 | 743.04 | 481.10 |
| wilfully | 357.11 | 716.09 | 426.19 | wiping | 555.19 |
| 579.10 | 357.12 | 717.07 | 433.19 | 054.04 | 556.05 |
| will | 357.19 | 719.20 | 450.14 | 466.07 | 559.01 |
| 015.21 | 358.21 | 722.13 | 476.04 | wisdom | 559.17 |
| 022.20 | 359.22 | 723.08 | 492.17 | 137.20 | 562.13 |
| 025.18 | 361.08 | 724.15 | 495.11 | 536.16 | 568.03 |
| 028.01 | 363.08 | 727.17 | 509.21 | wise | 582.02 |
| 032.02 | 363.13 | 728.11 | 552.11 | 172.04 | 599.20 |
| 032.11 | 364.17 | 729.13 | 577.14 | 739.14 | 605.11 |
| 033.16 | 365.18 | 732.08 | 622.20 | wisely | 697.15 |
| 033.17 | 366.02 | 734.08 | 622.22 | 721.08 | 721.11 |
| 035.21 | 366.14 | 739.01 | 633.22 | wiser | 760.02 |
| 045.14 | 385.22 | 741.19 | 644.20 | 316.21 | wishes |
| 047.20 | 398.10 | 752.08 | 654.15 | 545.14 | 083.13 |
| 056.05 | 415.15 | 752.12 | 656.20 | 589.16 | 210.03 |
| 071.06 | 425.16 | 754.10 | 675.07 | wish | 237.08 |
| 074.13 | 426.21 | 755.19 | 684.10 | 040.20 | 331.22 |
| 082.13 | 429.08 | 756.06 | 705.16 | 055.10 | 342.03 |
| 084.07 | 433.03 | 762.04 | 709.11 | 072.11 | 354.18 |
| 084.15 | 435.19 | 762.06 | 740.16 | 088.05 | 457.01 |
| 086.06 | 437.01 | 762.07 | 745.08 | 116.13 | 484.16 |
| 102.08 | 449.11 | 762.09 | 746.19 | 124.01 | 613.21 |
| 108.07 | 450.05 | 762.10 | 757.06 | 124.10 | 670.01 |
| 111.20 | 451.21 | willing | 758.05 | 124.17 | 714.04 |
| 112.01 | 454.06 | 012.17 | 760.18 | 125.04 | 744.19 |
| 114.16 | 454.12 | 394.20 | 762.20 | 134.02 | wishing |
| 117.18 | 460.22 | 422.11 | 763.17 | 140.07 | 095.21 |
| 118.06 | 463.12 | 502.02 | window-ledge | 175.09 | 105.06 |
| 124.04 | 463.15 | 606.18 | 057.17 | 186.16 | 218.13 |
| 125.08 | 463.17 | 691.22 | window-seat | 186.16 | 256.18 |
| 125.10 | 465.12 | willingly | 554.17 | 220.11 | 359.15 |
| 129.19 | 469.10 | 037.06 | 707.17 | 222.04 | 454.07 |
| 133.18 | 476.03 | 126.19 | windows | 233.19 | 486.17 |
| 138.09 | 482.08 | 214.22 | 004.16 | 250.14 | 578.12 |
| 140.07 | 482.16 | 571.07 | 038.05 | 258.08 | 659.16 |
| 141.03 | 483.09 | 589.19 | 124.15 | 259.08 | wisht |
| 142.06 | 483.21 | 617.15 | 191.22 | 261.22 | 035.22 |
| 143.22 | 485.04 | 659.03 | 208.04 | 263.11 | 035.22 |
| 151.17 | 489.06 | willow | 261.01 | 263.21 | 164.16 |
| 151.20 | 489.17 | 626.07 | 378.15 | 264.13 | 441.19 |
| 155.14 | 490.03 | willut | 393.07 | 271.05 | 567.05 |
| 159.20 | 490.10 | 319.08 | 399.18 | 282.19 | 696.22 |
| 160.04 | 500.02 | wilt | 408.07 | 282.20 | 723.07 |
| 168.09 | 503.08 | 310.02 | 569.20 | 303.09 | 723.07 |
| 170.21 | 504.18 | win | 612.10 | 310.14 | wit |
| 170.22 | 511.08 | 259.01 | 642.08 | 321.12 | 082.12 |
| 171.08 | 512.14 | 546.03 | 693.20 | 324.20 | 109.02 |
| 173.16 | 512.22 | 714.02 | winds | 324.21 | 225.10 |
| 175.19 | 513.12 | | 201.04 | 328.07 | 366.15 |

| | | | | | |
|---|---|---|---|---|---|
| 716.15 | 078.16 | 185.19 | 310.22 | 402.18 | 500.08 |
| witch | 079.02 | 190.05 | 311.10 | 404.12 | 501.08 |
| 030.09 | 079.08 | 191.12 | 313.02 | 406.06 | 501.09 |
| 194.07 | 079.10 | 193.02 | 313.15 | 406.22 | 501.21 |
| 290.07 | 079.22 | 193.10 | 314.01 | 407.11 | 502.17 |
| 439.10 | 080.21 | 194.19 | 314.10 | 411.03 | 504.05 |
| 648.19 | 082.04 | 195.10 | 314.18 | 411.17 | 505.05 |
| 722.17 | 083.19 | 197.12 | 315.12 | 412.20 | 505.14 |
| 723.16 | 084.08 | 197.18 | 315.18 | 413.17 | 505.20 |
| witched | 084.10 | 198.12 | 317.07 | 414.12 | 507.19 |
| 696.16 | 085.17 | 201.10 | 317.09 | 415.01 | 508.07 |
| 720.13 | 088.12 | 202.20 | 319.05 | 416.05 | 509.16 |
| witches | 088.19 | 203.03 | 320.19 | 417.07 | 511.01 |
| 104.16 | 090.06 | 203.21 | 321.20 | 421.03 | 512.03 |
| with | 091.11 | 205.12 | 321.21 | 421.05 | 513.03 |
| 001.05 | 091.18 | 206.06 | 322.14 | 421.08 | 514.02 |
| 002.03 | 093.09 | 207.05 | 323.03 | 421.10 | 514.14 |
| 002.19 | 095.08 | 207.17 | 323.04 | 421.13 | 516.09 |
| 004.17 | 095.16 | 208.09 | 323.20 | 422.02 | 516.16 |
| 006.02 | 096.05 | 209.09 | 325.01 | 424.07 | 517.19 |
| 006.07 | 097.08 | 212.07 | 325.16 | 425.02 | 518.03 |
| 006.22 | 097.13 | 213.10 | 326.05 | 426.10 | 518.12 |
| 007.13 | 098.07 | 215.10 | 327.06 | 427.13 | 518.20 |
| 008.20 | 099.07 | 216.06 | 328.07 | 428.07 | 519.08 |
| 0C9.02 | 099.21 | 216.09 | 329.11 | 428.15 | 520.18 |
| 009.18 | 104.03 | 222.03 | 329.12 | 429.20 | 521.13 |
| 010.07 | 104.07 | 222.14 | 330.08 | 429.21 | 523.07 |
| 010.09 | 105.14 | 222.15 | 332.13 | 430.04 | 524.18 |
| 011.01 | 105.20 | 223.07 | 332.18 | 430.07 | 525.10 |
| 011.05 | 106.19 | 223.17 | 333.21 | 430.22 | 526.21 |
| 011.10 | 106.21 | 224.05 | 334.04 | 431.15 | 527.04 |
| 012.03 | 107.05 | 224.06 | 334.14 | 432.02 | 527.05 |
| 012.04 | 109.10 | 225.14 | 336.03 | 433.20 | 527.20 |
| 013.19 | 110.22 | 226.20 | 336.15 | 434.08 | 528.07 |
| 014.09 | 112.15 | 226.22 | 336.20 | 434.19 | 531.03 |
| 014.11 | 113.08 | 227.19 | 338.11 | 436.14 | 531.15 |
| 015.03 | 114.02 | 228.01 | 340.12 | 436.16 | 532.20 |
| 015.10 | 114.04 | 228.12 | 341.07 | 438.08 | 535.15 |
| 015.13 | 114.11 | 228.15 | 341.10 | 439.01 | 535.16 |
| 018.10 | 114.15 | 230.11 | 343.06 | 439.14 | 536.01 |
| 020.06 | 116.07 | 230.16 | 344.08 | 439.22 | 536.12 |
| 022.05 | 118.02 | 231.19 | 344.10 | 440.09 | 537.19 |
| 023.04 | 118.07 | 233.17 | 347.10 | 440.17 | 538.13 |
| 023.22 | 118.15 | 234.12 | 350.15 | 444.14 | 540.03 |
| 024.03 | 119.16 | 235.15 | 351.04 | 445.02 | 542.12 |
| 025.02 | 120.20 | 238.02 | 352.10 | 445.04 | 543.01 |
| 026.04 | 121.01 | 238.05 | 352.18 | 446.03 | 545.15 |
| 027.02 | 121.08 | 239.08 | 354.16 | 446.13 | 547.04 |
| 028.08 | 121.10 | 240.15 | 355.13 | 448.02 | 547.06 |
| 028.14 | 121.20 | 243.07 | 356.14 | 448.07 | 548.21 |
| 029.07 | 123.02 | 243.19 | 356.16 | 449.03 | 551.16 |
| 030.10 | 125.18 | 244.02 | 358.06 | 449.05 | 556.02 |
| 030.19 | 127.04 | 244.09 | 358.13 | 451.19 | 556.13 |
| 031.02 | 127.08 | 245.09 | 358.13 | 455.04 | 557.08 |
| 032.01 | 128.22 | 245.16 | 358.18 | 455.13 | 557.14 |
| 032.07 | 129.07 | 247.18 | 360.05 | 456.14 | 558.01 |
| 032.14 | 130.04 | 248.05 | 360.08 | 457.18 | 558.12 |
| 032.22 | 130.06 | 253.15 | 360.19 | 458.05 | 558.19 |
| 033.03 | 132.08 | 254.01 | 361.04 | 459.09 | 559.08 |
| 033.05 | 132.16 | 255.03 | 362.07 | 460.08 | 560.13 |
| 034.22 | 132.19 | 255.09 | 362.16 | 460.14 | 560.17 |
| 035.02 | 135.16 | 256.13 | 363.14 | 461.14 | 561.09 |
| 036.03 | 139.05 | 256.14 | 366.07 | 461.18 | 563.19 |
| 036.12 | 140.05 | 257.06 | 367.08 | 462.13 | 564.01 |
| 038.03 | 145.14 | 258.16 | 367.16 | 463.01 | 566.01 |
| 038.14 | 146.09 | 259.12 | 370.14 | 464.08 | 566.20 |
| 038.20 | 146.10 | 259.13 | 371.08 | 464.15 | 567.04 |
| 039.10 | 146.18 | 260.03 | 371.14 | 465.07 | 567.18 |
| 039.13 | 147.20 | 260.05 | 372.17 | 465.11 | 572.05 |
| 041.04 | 148.10 | 260.10 | 373.15 | 465.13 | 572.06 |
| 044.10 | 149.16 | 261.04 | 375.05 | 465.19 | 572.07 |
| 045.08 | 149.17 | 263.06 | 375.06 | 467.15 | 573.13 |
| 045.08 | 150.01 | 263.14 | 376.09 | 468.12 | 573.14 |
| 046.10 | 150.12 | 264.10 | 376.14 | 470.07 | 575.06 |
| 046.15 | 151.15 | 264.15 | 377.03 | 470.15 | 577.11 |
| 046.17 | 152.01 | 265.14 | 377.12 | 470.21 | 578.06 |
| 047.19 | 152.16 | 269.06 | 378.04 | 471.04 | 579.14 |
| 050.01 | 153.04 | 273.08 | 378.10 | 472.20 | 580.22 |
| 050.06 | 153.05 | 274.07 | 379.04 | 474.02 | 581.03 |
| 050.10 | 153.12 | 274.12 | 382.04 | 475.15 | 582.09 |
| 050.14 | 154.07 | 276.04 | 382.19 | 475.16 | 582.19 |
| 052.22 | 155.19 | 277.15 | 383.11 | 477.09 | 583.11 |
| 054.01 | 155.21 | 278.11 | 383.14 | 477.10 | 584.05 |
| 054.13 | 156.03 | 279.06 | 383.17 | 478.18 | 585.07 |
| 054.17 | 156.14 | 281.07 | 384.22 | 479.08 | 586.22 |
| 056.03 | 156.22 | 281.11 | 385.09 | 479.16 | 591.11 |
| 057.04 | 157.21 | 284.06 | 385.14 | 479.19 | 592.19 |
| 057.21 | 158.04 | 284.20 | 387.05 | 481.12 | 594.02 |
| 058.02 | 160.21 | 284.22 | 389.04 | 481.13 | 594.19 |
| 058.06 | 162.05 | 286.20 | 389.16 | 483.10 | 597.09 |
| 060.03 | 163.06 | 287.08 | 390.16 | 483.11 | 598.01 |
| 061.11 | 165.01 | 287.17 | 391.01 | 484.19 | 598.22 |
| 062.02 | 166.03 | 292.17 | 391.14 | 485.09 | 599.05 |
| 062.21 | 166.15 | 292.20 | 391.18 | 486.06 | 601.01 |
| 062.21 | 167.08 | 293.04 | 391.19 | 486.17 | 601.03 |
| 063.03 | 167.13 | 293.14 | 392.07 | 487.02 | 601.13 |
| 063.09 | 168.18 | 294.14 | 392.17 | 487.06 | 602.10 |
| 063.15 | 168.21 | 294.19 | 393.21 | 487.13 | 604.08 |
| 064.21 | 171.10 | 295.04 | 394.12 | 487.22 | 604.11 |
| 066.09 | 173.10 | 295.13 | 394.17 | 488.10 | 605.03 |
| 066.12 | 174.16 | 295.19 | 396.12 | 488.16 | 605.06 |
| 067.05 | 175.08 | 296.14 | 396.13 | 489.01 | 605.20 |
| 069.07 | 175.12 | 302.09 | 397.04 | 490.06 | 606.13 |
| 070.15 | 176.21 | 304.21 | 398.01 | 492.08 | 607.02 |
| 071.08 | 178.20 | 305.12 | 398.07 | 492.19 | 607.06 |
| 072.21 | 180.07 | 305.14 | 399.20 | 493.10 | 607.15 |
| 074.01 | 180.13 | 307.07 | 400.03 | 493.15 | 607.22 |
| 075.17 | 181.05 | 308.14 | 400.11 | 495.13 | 608.21 |
| 076.06 | 182.01 | 308.16 | 402.01 | 497.21 | 609.05 |
| 077.19 | 183.15 | 309.06 | 402.02 | 499.11 | 610.05 |
| 078.13 | 183.21 | 310.14 | 402.13 | 499.21 | 610.06 |

| | | | | | |
|---|---|---|---|---|---|
| 610.16 | 731.18 | 317.03 | won't | 526.14 | 473.06 |
| 613.11 | 731.20 | 330.03 | 083.20 | 532.16 | 492.09 |
| 613.22 | 732.08 | 343.17 | 127.18 | 540.10 | 492.13 |
| 614.01 | 733.14 | 353.20 | 158.19 | 613.03 | 497.15 |
| 614.10 | 734.04 | 369.12 | 164.18 | 616.09 | 518.13 |
| 616.06 | 737.09 | 377.07 | 175.05 | 620.16 | 520.03 |
| 617.04 | 738.01 | 377.07 | 253.07 | 629.16 | 521.21 |
| 618.01 | 739.16 | 391.13 | 283.06 | 629.17 | 576.17 |
| 620.07 | 739.19 | 419.14 | 283.08 | 631.20 | 581.01 |
| 621.14 | 740.04 | 440.20 | 284.20 | 698.05 | 601.21 |
| 624.14 | 741.16 | 445.13 | 336.16 | 707.03 | 616.15 |
| 626.06 | 742.02 | 462.05 | 339.13 | 711.12 | 679.17 |
| 626.11 | 742.18 | 487.16 | 385.21 | 742.05 | 696.04 |
| 628.22 | 743.15 | 497.16 | 394.04 | 755.06 | 750.03 |
| 629.08 | 745.02 | 498.11 | 421.07 | 756.08 | 750.19 |
| 630.01 | 745.07 | 501.09 | 462.05 | wood | wordy |
| 631.18 | 746.02 | 503.02 | 469.05 | 006.06 | 508.13 |
| 632.07 | 746.04 | 516.02 | 502.01 | 017.07 | wore |
| 633.14 | 746.11 | 547.04 | 510.22 | 542.10 | 023.14 |
| 634.02 | 747.19 | 576.14 | 542.22 | 652.07 | 351.08 |
| 634.04 | 747.19 | 606.06 | 545.01 | wooden | 364.11 |
| 637.02 | 748.17 | 606.11 | 562.21 | 061.17 | 383.13 |
| 638.07 | 749.08 | 617.21 | 594.01 | 317.19 | 478.03 |
| 638.20 | 749.13 | 622.15 | 599.07 | 322.19 | work |
| 639.03 | 750.13 | 634.20 | 615.03 | woods | 017.18 |
| 639.06 | 750.20 | 640.05 | 631.11 | 183.03 | 075.09 |
| 639.18 | 751.11 | 642.01 | 660.03 | 556.13 | 093.05 |
| 641.06 | 753.02 | 644.14 | 670.12 | 557.21 | 121.13 |
| 642.03 | 753.02 | 656.05 | 677.04 | wool | 135.06 |
| 645.10 | 755.14 | 659.16 | 681.11 | 276.17 | 149.10 |
| 648.12 | 755.16 | 671.17 | 685.06 | woonder | 151.15 |
| 649.10 | 756.01 | 677.19 | 714.06 | 028.20 | 155.03 |
| 650.16 | 757.13 | 694.11 | 723.10 | word | 170.13 |
| 650.21 | 757.20 | 729.02 | 730.11 | 027.14 | 217.20 |
| 652.05 | 758.12 | 730.15 | wonder | 050.06 | 292.14 |
| 652.06 | 758.14 | 753.17 | 003.13 | 065.09 | 310.18 |
| 653.05 | 759.06 | witness | 022.01 | 081.01 | 318.19 |
| 653.08 | 759.12 | 060.07 | 035.18 | 087.12 | 402.03 |
| 654.07 | 760.07 | 085.16 | 073.18 | 112.11 | 420.20 |
| 655.06 | 761.02 | 144.21 | 127.21 | 129.09 | 446.15 |
| 655.09 | 762.15 | 156.18 | 167.02 | 142.14 | 469.17 |
| 657.02 | withdraw | 213.02 | 186.12 | 172.14 | 474.02 |
| 659.06 | 002.01 | 529.09 | 186.12 | 174.03 | 509.20 |
| 659.10 | withdrawing | witnessed | 190.21 | 203.17 | 532.01 |
| 660.12 | 693.17 | 166.14 | 249.19 | 208.09 | 555.12 |
| 662.11 | withdrew | 377.16 | 275.10 | 228.09 | 566.05 |
| 662.13 | 648.21 | 406.14 | 327.06 | 228.09 | 649.17 |
| 662.22 | withered | 729.08 | 361.10 | 242.11 | 652.06 |
| 663.11 | 243.22 | witnessing | 391.06 | 248.14 | 666.06 |
| 664.16 | 276.20 | 395.11 | 406.08 | 294.15 | 701.20 |
| 666.01 | 516.17 | 601.14 | 427.01 | 299.12 | 703.17 |
| 666.03 | withhold | wits | 487.02 | 312.04 | 710.15 |
| 668.07 | 250.03 | 290.03 | 533.09 | 341.17 | 711.22 |
| 668.17 | 574.08 | 622.01 | 540.06 | 343.08 | 715.10 |
| 672.01 | within | 647.20 | 677.10 | 359.17 | 726.16 |
| 674.16 | 005.18 | 661.14 | 691.05 | 362.21 | 737.09 |
| 676.19 | 007.17 | 691.14 | 701.15 | 368.06 | 755.13 |
| 677.07 | 034.01 | 733.03 | 716.14 | 414.04 | worked |
| 677.21 | 040.16 | wives | wondered | 426.02 | 099.21 |
| 680.12 | 049.06 | 402.09 | 083.05 | 447.03 | 264.19 |
| 681.12 | 116.17 | 536.10 | 221.08 | 502.05 | 389.17 |
| 682.18 | 132.14 | 536.15 | 291.09 | 511.19 | 719.07 |
| 683.07 | 142.18 | wod | 663.21 | 521.15 | 724.01 |
| 685.11 | 156.21 | 191.01 | 684.16 | 527.07 | 763.20 |
| 685.16 | 197.02 | woke | 734.20 | 547.03 | working |
| 686.01 | 208.06 | 050.20 | 741.06 | 555.13 | 432.13 |
| 686.09 | 340.19 | 179.02 | 764.09 | 563.10 | 442.05 |
| 689.12 | 373.09 | 360.11 | wonderful | 620.10 | 729.11 |
| 689.15 | 387.17 | 389.21 | 560.20 | 620.12 | world |
| 692.12 | 404.02 | wold | wonderfully | 637.13 | 020.21 |
| 692.17 | 413.08 | 324.02 | 116.07 | 644.14 | 023.20 |
| 694.16 | 445.01 | wolf | wondering | 649.10 | 072.02 |
| 695.01 | 466.03 | 034.08 | 067.17 | 660.07 | 095.18 |
| 696.16 | 478.20 | 311.19 | 254.03 | 667.18 | 102.10 |
| 697.22 | 586.16 | wolfish | 320.04 | 670.10 | 121.16 |
| 698.07 | 620.13 | 230.02 | 590.06 | 671.16 | 125.02 |
| 698.08 | 672.06 | wolfishly | wondrous | 691.09 | 171.12 |
| 699.15 | 688.05 | 009.12 | 145.12 | 711.05 | 174.22 |
| 699.17 | 690.18 | wollsome | 336.18 | 725.11 | 181.02 |
| 700.01 | 696.03 | 320.04 | 506.15 | 746.12 | 182.17 |
| 700.08 | 699.20 | woman | wondrously | words | 199.21 |
| 701.02 | 742.21 | 074.22 | 209.18 | 003.01 | 219.16 |
| 704.04 | 749.02 | 082.07 | wont | 022.22 | 233.21 |
| 705.11 | 753.08 | 111.03 | 012.04 | 036.03 | 266.10 |
| 705.15 | 760.15 | 173.17 | 031.07 | 057.03 | 282.13 |
| 705.21 | without | 197.16 | 045.07 | 091.19 | 291.02 |
| 706.11 | 005.11 | 247.17 | 112.02 | 099.11 | 306.12 |
| 707.20 | 016.19 | 276.12 | 125.06 | 112.03 | 322.13 |
| 710.03 | 027.22 | 345.07 | 134.01 | 125.04 | 336.20 |
| 712.05 | 046.20 | 348.02 | 142.16 | 134.10 | 351.18 |
| 712.12 | 057.08 | 395.18 | 172.08 | 150.12 | 361.01 |
| 713.17 | 081.05 | 428.03 | 177.18 | 154.16 | 372.10 |
| 716.12 | 085.13 | 434.01 | 177.18 | 166.08 | 376.12 |
| 716.20 | 103.13 | 437.17 | 178.13 | 195.13 | 393.14 |
| 717.05 | 110.08 | 440.02 | 228.15 | 213.07 | 398.18 |
| 717.21 | 128.01 | 476.02 | 230.21 | 246.05 | 413.19 |
| 718.04 | 147.07 | 545.11 | 236.18 | 251.20 | 421.15 |
| 718.09 | 149.04 | 631.12 | 251.11 | 252.04 | 428.08 |
| 718.10 | 164.15 | 659.04 | 314.20 | 254.19 | 469.10 |
| 721.02 | 174.15 | 673.06 | 329.08 | 283.02 | 470.19 |
| 722.12 | 177.06 | 690.16 | 360.01 | 303.19 | 494.21 |
| 722.18 | 188.07 | 692.10 | 361.10 | 306.17 | 504.04 |
| 724.07 | 212.22 | 714.06 | 363.19 | 335.20 | 520.05 |
| 724.11 | 213.07 | 761.08 | 365.11 | 340.02 | 536.06 |
| 724.11 | 229.13 | woman's | 434.10 | 349.07 | 557.22 |
| 726.15 | 229.13 | 044.13 | 435.14 | 358.21 | 576.09 |
| 727.11 | 251.18 | 314.09 | 456.01 | 360.01 | 597.06 |
| 727.20 | 264.10 | 436.21 | 476.22 | 371.05 | 616.08 |
| 728.11 | 285.07 | women | 488.14 | 408.14 | 619.04 |
| 731.09 | 299.11 | 199.10 | 520.06 | 439.12 | 636.14 |
| 731.13 | 311.06 | 731.19 | 525.10 | 455.11 | 647.04 |

| | | | | | |
|---|---|---|---|---|---|
| 685.04 | 035.08 | 235.20 | 441.10 | 602.02 | 389.08 |
| 731.21 | 037.05 | 235.22 | 442.19 | 605.17 | 391.15 |
| worldly | 041.14 | 235.22 | 444.02 | 606.21 | 395.01 |
| 207.21 | 044.05 | 239.09 | 444.06 | 614.08 | 399.06 |
| 640.19 | 045.03 | 240.01 | 446.16 | 614.22 | 409.09 |
| worms | 046.05 | 251.13 | 446.20 | 615.10 | 443.17 |
| 343.04 | 047.22 | 256.20 | 446.22 | 617.03 | 481.18 |
| worn't | 048.20 | 258.22 | 449.16 | 617.13 | 490.20 |
| 190.22 | 056.14 | 259.03 | 451.09 | 618.08 | 499.05 |
| worried | 057.13 | 259.04 | 453.19 | 619.04 | 514.07 |
| 281.13 | 070.01 | 259.12 | 454.19 | 622.06 | 534.19 |
| 708.16 | 072.12 | 259.20 | 456.21 | 623.07 | 535.18 |
| worries | 075.20 | 262.14 | 457.06 | 628.03 | 554.07 |
| 171.16 | 077.02 | 264.07 | 461.14 | 629.20 | 558.17 |
| worrying | 077.08 | 265.19 | 462.15 | 630.16 | 560.12 |
| 011.08 | 077.14 | 266.03 | 475.01 | 632.17 | 563.10 |
| 046.04 | 079.04 | 267.10 | 476.17 | 635.12 | 569.07 |
| 089.20 | 081.04 | 268.04 | 476.20 | 636.13 | 598.19 |
| 449.04 | 082.10 | 269.07 | 477.13 | 637.10 | 599.06 |
| worse | 083.12 | 271.09 | 478.10 | 637.15 | 599.20 |
| 012.01 | 084.13 | 272.15 | 482.15 | 637.17 | 601.10 |
| 026.03 | 084.20 | 273.11 | 484.08 | 639.08 | 602.02 |
| 092.09 | 088.21 | 274.01 | 485.01 | 640.09 | 602.03 |
| 125.11 | 089.05 | 274.13 | 485.03 | 641.03 | 609.01 |
| 147.10 | 090.14 | 278.01 | 485.05 | 643.08 | 613.17 |
| 167.04 | 090.20 | 279.08 | 489.18 | 645.13 | 633.04 |
| 201.07 | 091.07 | 286.11 | 494.04 | 645.19 | 648.10 |
| 205.05 | 092.02 | 295.03 | 494.13 | 647.18 | 658.05 |
| 222.22 | 092.08 | 299.03 | 497.03 | 649.02 | 662.08 |
| 230.19 | 093.20 | 302.01 | 497.19 | 649.15 | 709.15 |
| 231.20 | 094.08 | 302.07 | 498.20 | 649.18 | 709.15 |
| 232.03 | 095.06 | 302.10 | 499.18 | 650.19 | 725.11 |
| 232.03 | 095.09 | 302.11 | 499.21 | 651.07 | wound |
| 256.22 | 096.09 | 303.11 | 501.10 | 651.18 | 384.18 |
| 262.15 | 096.11 | 305.07 | 501.21 | 654.04 | 395.03 |
| 313.08 | 098.17 | 309.03 | 502.04 | 660.22 | 400.11 |
| 337.07 | 100.03 | 311.22 | 504.04 | 664.07 | 429.01 |
| 359.22 | 102.06 | 312.08 | 504.16 | 666.03 | wounded |
| 363.11 | 102.20 | 313.19 | 505.06 | 666.15 | 546.13 |
| 388.19 | 105.05 | 318.20 | 505.16 | 670.01 | wounds |
| 395.04 | 106.14 | 328.07 | 506.18 | 670.10 | 339.16 |
| 415.02 | 108.10 | 330.07 | 507.05 | 672.02 | wrangle |
| 440.20 | 112.15 | 331.01 | 507.17 | 672.03 | 264.12 |
| 467.06 | 115.04 | 332.17 | 511.13 | 672.17 | wrap |
| 475.12 | 115.08 | 334.03 | 512.08 | 674.05 | 285.07 |
| 493.09 | 116.12 | 334.10 | 513.05 | 675.01 | wrapped |
| 494.12 | 117.12 | 334.11 | 515.06 | 675.20 | 450.20 |
| 517.05 | 120.08 | 334.16 | 518.08 | 677.15 | 476.11 |
| 519.19 | 125.22 | 334.18 | 520.13 | 679.13 | wrapping |
| 519.22 | 126.20 | 334.20 | 520.14 | 681.21 | 710.01 |
| 525.03 | 133.06 | 335.01 | 521.07 | 686.12 | wrapt |
| 540.20 | 135.19 | 335.18 | 521.18 | 686.21 | 133.13 |
| 543.07 | 135.20 | 335.20 | 523.10 | 690.04 | wrath |
| 551.14 | 137.21 | 335.22 | 523.11 | 691.16 | 034.22 |
| 587.04 | 141.17 | 339.15 | 526.04 | 692.13 | 325.05 |
| 587.12 | 142.08 | 342.14 | 526.17 | 695.04 | 398.03 |
| 587.13 | 144.06 | 343.22 | 527.07 | 702.03 | 613.11 |
| 592.21 | 144.10 | 344.15 | 528.18 | 703.02 | 680.21 |
| 650.19 | 147.13 | 350.09 | 532.12 | 703.06 | wreath |
| 756.07 | 147.15 | 350.20 | 535.02 | 703.10 | 062.08 |
| worship | 150.21 | 351.17 | 535.05 | 703.20 | 690.12 |
| 631.14 | 158.01 | 352.11 | 536.03 | 704.08 | wrench |
| worst | 164.02 | 352.19 | 536.05 | 705.07 | 156.03 |
| 082.10 | 164.10 | 356.12 | 536.12 | 707.22 | 238.12 |
| 173.19 | 164.19 | 358.05 | 536.12 | 708.01 | 405.17 |
| 182.04 | 165.04 | 360.06 | 540.06 | 710.13 | 405.18 |
| 301.04 | 166.12 | 360.15 | 541.14 | 715.05 | wrenched |
| 417.07 | 167.11 | 362.01 | 543.20 | 717.03 | 060.10 |
| 443.20 | 169.03 | 362.10 | 544.11 | 725.13 | 282.07 |
| 506.09 | 172.04 | 363.08 | 545.12 | 725.14 | 323.08 |
| 545.21 | 174.15 | 363.14 | 553.19 | 725.19 | 399.12 |
| worth | 175.09 | 365.20 | 554.18 | 726.02 | 633.13 |
| 171.14 | 178.09 | 373.02 | 555.12 | 726.21 | 652.13 |
| 257.11 | 179.07 | 373.06 | 555.21 | 729.15 | wrenching |
| 398.18 | 179.20 | 376.05 | 556.04 | 731.06 | 358.01 |
| 428.05 | 182.22 | 382.14 | 557.01 | 734.21 | wrest |
| 563.04 | 184.11 | 384.14 | 557.01 | 735.04 | 258.13 |
| 608.06 | 185.07 | 388.03 | 557.02 | 736.04 | wretch |
| 660.02 | 185.17 | 388.13 | 558.04 | 738.16 | 032.13 |
| worthless | 186.04 | 388.16 | 558.05 | 740.19 | 069.06 |
| 064.03 | 186.17 | 389.06 | 558.13 | 744.04 | 165.19 |
| 249.16 | 188.07 | 391.05 | 560.10 | 749.21 | 181.18 |
| 268.03 | 188.09 | 395.10 | 562.07 | 750.22 | 288.01 |
| 508.16 | 190.17 | 395.20 | 562.16 | 752.11 | 310.01 |
| 534.21 | 193.08 | 396.09 | 566.14 | 752.14 | 375.13 |
| 570.21 | 194.14 | 397.13 | 566.19 | 753.17 | 470.22 |
| 571.01 | 197.14 | 402.07 | 567.07 | 753.18 | 513.12 |
| 600.06 | 197.19 | 404.17 | 567.19 | 755.05 | 600.06 |
| worthy | 200.04 | 405.09 | 568.19 | 757.01 | 682.03 |
| 074.22 | 205.01 | 406.11 | 571.06 | 757.09 | wretch's |
| 220.17 | 209.04 | 407.09 | 573.17 | 758.09 | 564.22 |
| 470.20 | 211.11 | 407.16 | 574.02 | 760.12 | 613.06 |
| 525.15 | 214.16 | 409.07 | 574.08 | 761.04 | wretched |
| 673.06 | 215.03 | 410.13 | 576.06 | 761.12 | 015.17 |
| would | 218.21 | 411.19 | 576.17 | 762.21 | 282.04 |
| 005.03 | 219.02 | 412.22 | 576.21 | wouldn't | 327.14 |
| 006.20 | 219.22 | 416.15 | 577.08 | 031.10 | 357.15 |
| 008.05 | 220.18 | 417.10 | 577.12 | 090.11 | 409.01 |
| 010.10 | 221.19 | 417.20 | 578.02 | 123.21 | 555.10 |
| 012.11 | 223.10 | 418.20 | 580.06 | 129.08 | 621.06 |
| 012.21 | 224.14 | 419.22 | 581.08 | 167.22 | 632.06 |
| 013.08 | 226.01 | 425.21 | 582.08 | 174.16 | wretchedness |
| 014.09 | 226.18 | 426.10 | 589.11 | 220.11 | 315.03 |
| 015.20 | 228.02 | 426.20 | 590.18 | 229.08 | wretches |
| 017.11 | 229.06 | 427.03 | 591.12 | 316.20 | 534.04 |
| 019.15 | 230.03 | 428.04 | 595.01 | 331.06 | wring |
| 024.07 | 231.20 | 429.22 | 596.07 | 338.08 | 363.01 |
| 030.23 | 233.15 | 431.10 | 597.11 | 344.09 | 375.17 |
| 031.18 | 233.16 | 432.18 | 597.13 | 346.22 | 445.10 |
| 034.03 | 233.22 | 433.12 | 597.17 | 386.10 | wringing |
| 034.19 | 234.21 | 438.21 | 597.22 | 387.10 | 279.12 |

| | | | | | |
|---|---|---|---|---|---|
| 031.01 | 118.03 | 164.10 | 216.11 | 252.01 | 287.18 |
| 031.05 | 120.18 | 166.19 | 216.12 | 252.01 | 287.20 |
| 031.09 | 120.19 | 166.20 | 216.14 | 252.02 | 287.21 |
| 031.12 | 121.03 | 167.04 | 216.15 | 252.03 | 288.01 |
| 031.12 | 121.04 | 167.13 | 219.02 | 252.04 | 288.04 |
| 031.14 | 122.09 | 167.14 | 219.09 | 252.04 | 288.06 |
| 031.18 | 122.11 | 167.14 | 219.10 | 252.05 | 288.06 |
| 032.02 | 122.13 | 167.15 | 219.21 | 252.07 | 288.08 |
| 032.06 | 122.19 | 167.20 | 219.22 | 252.09 | 288.09 |
| 032.07 | 123.01 | 167.21 | 220.03 | 252.12 | 288.09 |
| 032.22 | 123.04 | 167.22 | 220.05 | 252.13 | 288.10 |
| 033.14 | 123.05 | 168.08 | 220.06 | 252.14 | 288.11 |
| 033.16 | 123.06 | 169.22 | 220.09 | 252.15 | 288.17 |
| 036.01 | 123.07 | 171.08 | 221.03 | 252.19 | 288.18 |
| 042.03 | 123.08 | 171.20 | 221.09 | 252.22 | 288.19 |
| 042.06 | 123.11 | 171.21 | 221.10 | 253.04 | 289.08 |
| 042.07 | 123.13 | 172.03 | 221.11 | 253.10 | 289.11 |
| 049.12 | 123.13 | 172.05 | 222.17 | 253.13 | 289.14 |
| 052.08 | 123.14 | 172.08 | 227.09 | 253.15 | 289.16 |
| 053.02 | 123.15 | 172.08 | 227.09 | 254.06 | 289.16 |
| 053.02 | 123.16 | 172.12 | 227.11 | 255.18 | 290.02 |
| 053.10 | 123.17 | 172.13 | 227.17 | 255.20 | 290.07 |
| 053.11 | 124.07 | 172.21 | 227.18 | 255.21 | 290.07 |
| 055.08 | 124.08 | 173.06 | 228.01 | 255.22 | 292.16 |
| 055.09 | 124.10 | 173.08 | 228.04 | 256.03 | 292.17 |
| 055.10 | 124.10 | 173.19 | 228.05 | 256.14 | 294.17 |
| 055.13 | 124.11 | 174.07 | 228.09 | 256.17 | 303.09 |
| 055.22 | 125.08 | 174.12 | 228.10 | 257.01 | 303.09 |
| 056.04 | 125.09 | 174.14 | 228.16 | 257.10 | 303.11 |
| 056.05 | 125.13 | 174.15 | 228.19 | 257.20 | 303.16 |
| 056.05 | 125.14 | 174.16 | 228.22 | 258.01 | 304.21 |
| 056.07 | 125.20 | 175.02 | 229.01 | 258.02 | 306.11 |
| 056.08 | 127.15 | 175.05 | 229.02 | 258.03 | 307.02 |
| 056.09 | 127.16 | 175.09 | 229.04 | 258.08 | 307.04 |
| 056.11 | 127.16 | 175.11 | 229.05 | 258.09 | 307.05 |
| 056.18 | 128.21 | 175.14 | 229.06 | 259.01 | 307.13 |
| 057.20 | 129.04 | 175.18 | 229.08 | 259.03 | 307.13 |
| 057.22 | 129.14 | 175.20 | 229.16 | 259.05 | 307.14 |
| 059.08 | 129.19 | 175.22 | 230.06 | 259.08 | 307.15 |
| 059.14 | 134.06 | 176.01 | 230.07 | 259.10 | 307.18 |
| 059.20 | 134.08 | 176.10 | 230.13 | 259.11 | 309.03 |
| 059.21 | 134.10 | 176.12 | 230.14 | 260.07 | 309.15 |
| 060.02 | 134.18 | 176.16 | 230.19 | 260.09 | 309.17 |
| 060.03 | 134.19 | 177.12 | 230.20 | 260.10 | 310.14 |
| 064.03 | 135.03 | 177.15 | 230.21 | 260.15 | 311.13 |
| 064.03 | 135.12 | 178.08 | 231.01 | 261.20 | 313.16 |
| 064.07 | 135.16 | 178.13 | 231.03 | 262.05 | 314.21 |
| 064.08 | 135.17 | 180.11 | 231.04 | 262.06 | 315.04 |
| 064.10 | 135.18 | 180.13 | 231.17 | 262.09 | 316.02 |
| 064.11 | 135.18 | 180.18 | 233.15 | 263.08 | 316.03 |
| 064.12 | 135.20 | 180.18 | 233.16 | 263.11 | 316.14 |
| 064.13 | 137.01 | 180.20 | 233.17 | 264.09 | 316.16 |
| 064.16 | 137.03 | 180.22 | 233.19 | 264.14 | 316.17 |
| 070.04 | 137.06 | 181.17 | 235.04 | 265.02 | 316.18 |
| 070.05 | 137.08 | 181.19 | 235.06 | 265.04 | 316.19 |
| 073.12 | 137.10 | 182.03 | 235.07 | 265.05 | 317.02 |
| 073.19 | 137.21 | 182.12 | 235.08 | 265.05 | 318.08 |
| 074.01 | 137.22 | 182.14 | 235.13 | 265.06 | 320.09 |
| 074.04 | 138.05 | 183.18 | 235.17 | 265.07 | 320.09 |
| 074.18 | 140.04 | 183.18 | 236.01 | 265.09 | 327.07 |
| 074.19 | 140.07 | 183.19 | 236.05 | 265.12 | 327.17 |
| 074.20 | 140.22 | 186.20 | 236.09 | 265.12 | 328.11 |
| 076.09 | 141.02 | 187.06 | 236.19 | 265.12 | 328.12 |
| 076.09 | 141.05 | 187.16 | 236.20 | 265.19 | 329.08 |
| 076.10 | 142.06 | 187.16 | 237.01 | 271.10 | 331.13 |
| 077.20 | 142.06 | 187.17 | 237.07 | 271.18 | 331.14 |
| 083.19 | 143.04 | 190.10 | 238.08 | 272.11 | 331.14 |
| 083.20 | 143.05 | 190.11 | 238.10 | 272.17 | 332.01 |
| 084.07 | 144.07 | 190.11 | 238.15 | 273.01 | 332.22 |
| 084.13 | 145.20 | 192.03 | 238.16 | 273.03 | 333.02 |
| 084.13 | 145.21 | 192.04 | 238.17 | 273.03 | 333.03 |
| 084.15 | 151.03 | 192.05 | 238.18 | 273.05 | 333.16 |
| 085.05 | 151.04 | 193.11 | 238.20 | 273.07 | 333.18 |
| 085.08 | 151.07 | 194.14 | 239.04 | 273.08 | 333.19 |
| 086.06 | 151.10 | 194.15 | 239.21 | 273.09 | 333.20 |
| 089.06 | 151.12 | 194.16 | 240.05 | 273.15 | 333.22 |
| 089.10 | 151.16 | 194.17 | 245.19 | 276.11 | 333.23 |
| 090.19 | 152.08 | 194.19 | 246.05 | 276.12 | 334.01 |
| 090.20 | 152.10 | 194.20 | 246.09 | 276.14 | 334.02 |
| 090.21 | 152.20 | 195.04 | 246.10 | 276.18 | 334.09 |
| 090.21 | 153.03 | 195.06 | 246.13 | 276.20 | 334.12 |
| 093.17 | 153.05 | 203.01 | 246.16 | 277.04 | 334.16 |
| 102.08 | 153.12 | 203.08 | 246.20 | 277.11 | 334.17 |
| 102.10 | 153.14 | 203.22 | 247.10 | 277.18 | 334.21 |
| 102.13 | 153.14 | 204.01 | 249.11 | 278.04 | 334.22 |
| 103.03 | 153.15 | 204.01 | 249.12 | 278.17 | 335.03 |
| 103.09 | 153.16 | 206.17 | 249.21 | 279.08 | 335.07 |
| 103.11 | 153.18 | 207.14 | 250.08 | 281.05 | 335.09 |
| 105.05 | 153.19 | 208.01 | 250.08 | 282.13 | 335.10 |
| 105.16 | 154.12 | 208.02 | 250.09 | 282.15 | 335.11 |
| 105.19 | 154.16 | 208.07 | 250.11 | 282.16 | 336.18 |
| 107.19 | 155.01 | 208.07 | 250.12 | 282.16 | 336.20 |
| 107.19 | 155.15 | 208.15 | 250.12 | 282.17 | 337.01 |
| 107.20 | 156.09 | 208.16 | 250.13 | 283.05 | 337.02 |
| 109.03 | 156.12 | 208.19 | 250.15 | 283.06 | 337.02 |
| 110.03 | 156.12 | 209.11 | 250.22 | 283.08 | 337.03 |
| 111.21 | 158.08 | 209.11 | 251.02 | 283.08 | 338.03 |
| 111.22 | 158.09 | 210.04 | 251.03 | 284.16 | 338.05 |
| 114.08 | 158.12 | 210.13 | 251.04 | 284.16 | 338.06 |
| 114.09 | 158.17 | 210.16 | 251.06 | 284.17 | 338.11 |
| 114.09 | 158.20 | 210.18 | 251.07 | 284.17 | 339.10 |
| 114.15 | 158.21 | 210.20 | 251.08 | 284.20 | 339.12 |
| 116.09 | 159.03 | 211.11 | 251.09 | 285.03 | 339.12 |
| 116.13 | 159.07 | 211.21 | 251.09 | 285.03 | 339.13 |
| 116.20 | 159.10 | 212.01 | 251.10 | 286.12 | 339.13 |
| 117.01 | 163.04 | 212.15 | 251.10 | 286.17 | 339.16 |
| 117.14 | 163.07 | 212.21 | 251.11 | 287.07 | 341.06 |
| 117.16 | 163.08 | 214.17 | 251.12 | 287.07 | 341.07 |
| 117.17 | 163.11 | 215.17 | 251.19 | 287.08 | 341.08 |
| 117.17 | 163.15 | 215.18 | 251.21 | 287.10 | 341.09 |
| 117.19 | 163.17 | 215.22 | 251.22 | 287.17 | 341.10 |

| | | | | | |
|---|---|---|---|---|---|
| 342.11 | 382.15 | 456.01 | 501.01 | 535.17 | 570.17 |
| 342.17 | 383.22 | 457.14 | 501.07 | 535.18 | 571.02 |
| 342.21 | 384.04 | 458.01 | 501.10 | 536.01 | 571.03 |
| 343.08 | 384.06 | 459.07 | 501.12 | 536.02 | 571.06 |
| 343.10 | 385.01 | 460.18 | 501.14 | 536.03 | 571.09 |
| 343.13 | 385.03 | 460.19 | 501.20 | 536.05 | 571.11 |
| 343.15 | 385.07 | 460.19 | 501.21 | 536.06 | 572.22 |
| 344.11 | 386.05 | 460.20 | 502.01 | 536.07 | 573.05 |
| 344.11 | 386.14 | 460.21 | 502.01 | 536.11 | 573.06 |
| 344.12 | 387.10 | 460.22 | 502.03 | 536.12 | 573.09 |
| 344.15 | 387.11 | 461.05 | 503.08 | 536.13 | 575.11 |
| 345.07 | 389.12 | 461.13 | 503.09 | 537.06 | 575.11 |
| 345.07 | 390.03 | 461.15 | 503.20 | 537.10 | 576.02 |
| 345.11 | 391.15 | 462.06 | 503.22 | 537.13 | 576.22 |
| 345.12 | 394.04 | 463.09 | 504.03 | 537.18 | 579.06 |
| 345.16 | 394.05 | 463.11 | 504.04 | 537.18 | 580.21 |
| 345.18 | 394.16 | 463.11 | 504.07 | 538.05 | 581.03 |
| 345.19 | 394.19 | 463.14 | 504.13 | 538.21 | 581.03 |
| 345.21 | 394.20 | 463.18 | 504.14 | 539.06 | 581.04 |
| 346.08 | 395.08 | 463.18 | 504.14 | 539.15 | 581.06 |
| 346.10 | 395.10 | 463.21 | 504.19 | 539.18 | 581.07 |
| 346.10 | 395.10 | 464.06 | 505.06 | 539.19 | 581.08 |
| 346.13 | 395.13 | 464.07 | 506.04 | 539.20 | 581.13 |
| 347.20 | 395.20 | 464.09 | 510.08 | 540.01 | 581.13 |
| 351.17 | 396.01 | 464.09 | 510.16 | 540.03 | 586.19 |
| 353.15 | 396.06 | 465.07 | 510.20 | 540.06 | 586.21 |
| 353.17 | 396.07 | 466.14 | 510.21 | 540.09 | 587.12 |
| 354.18 | 396.18 | 468.09 | 511.03 | 540.13 | 587.13 |
| 356.18 | 396.19 | 468.17 | 511.04 | 540.14 | 587.13 |
| 356.20 | 396.20 | 468.18 | 511.05 | 540.16 | 588.02 |
| 356.21 | 397.02 | 468.19 | 511.08 | 540.18 | 588.07 |
| 356.22 | 398.04 | 468.20 | 511.10 | 540.20 | 589.15 |
| 356.22 | 398.15 | 468.22 | 511.11 | 541.22 | 589.16 |
| 357.01 | 398.16 | 469.01 | 512.01 | 542.01 | 589.17 |
| 357.02 | 398.19 | 469.01 | 512.14 | 542.03 | 589.19 |
| 357.07 | 398.21 | 469.02 | 512.16 | 543.02 | 590.01 |
| 357.09 | 399.05 | 469.03 | 512.22 | 543.10 | 590.03 |
| 357.10 | 401.03 | 469.05 | 518.20 | 543.11 | 590.04 |
| 357.11 | 401.04 | 469.09 | 519.06 | 543.12 | 590.05 |
| 357.11 | 401.22 | 469.10 | 519.08 | 543.12 | 590.10 |
| 357.12 | 401.22 | 469.12 | 519.15 | 543.13 | 590.12 |
| 357.19 | 402.01 | 469.17 | 519.17 | 543.13 | 590.12 |
| 358.18 | 402.01 | 480.08 | 520.01 | 543.14 | 590.15 |
| 358.20 | 402.02 | 481.17 | 520.05 | 543.19 | 590.22 |
| 358.20 | 402.03 | 481.18 | 520.06 | 543.22 | 591.20 |
| 359.01 | 405.04 | 481.19 | 520.14 | 544.04 | 592.13 |
| 359.02 | 405.06 | 481.21 | 520.20 | 544.04 | 592.16 |
| 359.02 | 405.21 | 482.13 | 521.01 | 544.05 | 592.19 |
| 359.03 | 406.10 | 482.15 | 521.02 | 544.06 | 593.04 |
| 359.03 | 406.11 | 482.16 | 521.05 | 544.16 | 593.08 |
| 359.04 | 406.15 | 482.18 | 521.05 | 545.01 | 593.11 |
| 359.06 | 406.18 | 483.07 | 521.09 | 545.03 | 593.12 |
| 359.15 | 406.20 | 483.08 | 522.01 | 545.03 | 593.14 |
| 359.18 | 406.21 | 483.10 | 523.04 | 545.06 | 594.03 |
| 359.20 | 406.22 | 483.20 | 523.18 | 545.10 | 599.06 |
| 359.21 | 407.15 | 483.20 | 523.21 | 545.14 | 599.07 |
| 360.01 | 408.20 | 484.10 | 524.01 | 545.20 | 599.09 |
| 360.15 | 409.02 | 484.14 | 524.02 | 546.08 | 599.09 |
| 361.05 | 409.06 | 486.10 | 524.03 | 546.20 | 599.10 |
| 361.05 | 412.07 | 486.14 | 524.08 | 547.03 | 599.18 |
| 361.07 | 415.15 | 486.15 | 524.10 | 551.03 | 599.20 |
| 361.08 | 416.08 | 486.15 | 524.11 | 551.03 | 600.05 |
| 361.10 | 416.15 | 486.16 | 524.12 | 553.18 | 600.12 |
| 361.12 | 417.11 | 486.20 | 524.12 | 553.19 | 600.16 |
| 362.17 | 421.06 | 487.19 | 524.14 | 553.21 | 600.18 |
| 362.19 | 425.21 | 487.21 | 524.16 | 554.06 | 600.19 |
| 362.20 | 427.06 | 487.21 | 524.17 | 554.06 | 601.07 |
| 362.21 | 427.18 | 487.22 | 524.17 | 554.07 | 601.09 |
| 362.22 | 428.01 | 488.02 | 524.20 | 554.09 | 601.09 |
| 362.22 | 428.04 | 488.05 | 525.04 | 554.13 | 601.10 |
| 363.02 | 428.06 | 488.06 | 525.06 | 554.15 | 601.10 |
| 363.03 | 429.08 | 488.14 | 525.08 | 555.01 | 601.12 |
| 363.03 | 432.22 | 488.21 | 525.10 | 555.03 | 601.13 |
| 363.04 | 434.04 | 489.01 | 525.11 | 555.05 | 601.21 |
| 363.05 | 434.11 | 489.03 | 525.16 | 555.13 | 602.01 |
| 363.08 | 435.04 | 489.04 | 525.18 | 555.15 | 602.02 |
| 363.09 | 435.04 | 489.05 | 526.04 | 557.02 | 602.02 |
| 363.10 | 435.09 | 489.05 | 526.05 | 558.16 | 602.03 |
| 363.13 | 435.12 | 489.06 | 526.09 | 558.17 | 602.04 |
| 363.14 | 435.16 | 489.07 | 526.14 | 559.17 | 603.07 |
| 363.18 | 435.17 | 490.05 | 526.14 | 560.21 | 603.08 |
| 363.19 | 435.17 | 490.15 | 527.03 | 560.21 | 603.16 |
| 363.19 | 435.18 | 490.18 | 527.07 | 561.07 | 605.07 |
| 364.02 | 435.19 | 490.20 | 527.10 | 562.05 | 605.08 |
| 365.10 | 436.02 | 491.13 | 527.11 | 562.07 | 605.11 |
| 365.10 | 436.05 | 491.17 | 527.12 | 562.11 | 605.12 |
| 365.13 | 436.13 | 492.06 | 528.21 | 562.14 | 605.16 |
| 365.14 | 437.03 | 492.07 | 531.16 | 562.15 | 605.17 |
| 365.15 | 437.03 | 492.11 | 532.08 | 562.16 | 605.20 |
| 366.12 | 437.07 | 492.12 | 532.11 | 562.18 | 606.03 |
| 366.14 | 437.08 | 492.15 | 532.14 | 562.21 | 606.03 |
| 366.15 | 437.20 | 493.06 | 532.15 | 563.01 | 606.07 |
| 366.17 | 438.22 | 494.03 | 532.15 | 563.02 | 606.15 |
| 367.12 | 439.03 | 495.13 | 533.02 | 563.08 | 606.18 |
| 367.13 | 439.11 | 496.09 | 533.03 | 563.09 | 607.20 |
| 368.06 | 439.11 | 497.01 | 533.04 | 563.10 | 607.20 |
| 369.03 | 439.18 | 497.01 | 533.05 | 563.11 | 608.05 |
| 372.09 | 439.19 | 497.03 | 533.07 | 565.08 | 608.17 |
| 374.04 | 440.01 | 497.03 | 533.09 | 565.08 | 609.13 |
| 374.05 | 440.08 | 497.14 | 533.21 | 565.09 | 610.12 |
| 375.13 | 451.16 | 497.15 | 534.05 | 565.09 | 610.12 |
| 375.15 | 451.19 | 499.03 | 534.14 | 565.11 | 611.04 |
| 375.16 | 451.21 | 499.04 | 534.19 | 565.11 | 611.08 |
| 376.08 | 452.08 | 499.04 | 534.21 | 567.03 | 611.10 |
| 376.18 | 452.08 | 499.08 | 535.03 | 568.01 | 611.11 |
| 376.18 | 452.11 | 500.05 | 535.04 | 570.08 | 611.11 |
| 376.21 | 452.12 | 500.06 | 535.05 | 570.08 | 612.13 |
| 376.22 | 452.19 | 500.07 | 535.07 | 570.09 | 612.14 |
| 376.22 | 453.10 | 500.08 | 535.08 | 570.12 | 612.17 |
| 377.05 | 455.18 | 500.08 | 535.14 | 570.16 | 612.19 |
| 382.13 | 455.21 | 500.21 | 535.16 | | 612.21 |

| | | | | | |
|---|---|---|---|---|---|
| 613.01 | 646.08 | 698.19 | 746.13 | 573.05 | 174.13 |
| 613.02 | 646.09 | 698.21 | 748.08 | 575.07 | 174.22 |
| 613.20 | 646.10 | 699.01 | 751.12 | 577.10 | 175.06 |
| 613.21 | 646.12 | 699.01 | 751.13 | 579.21 | 177.14 |
| 613.22 | 646.15 | 699.06 | 752.20 | 601.10 | 182.06 |
| 614.01 | 647.02 | 699.06 | 752.21 | 606.12 | 185.18 |
| 614.02 | 647.04 | 702.01 | 753.05 | 606.16 | 194.04 |
| 614.04 | 647.05 | 702.01 | 753.07 | 611.09 | 197.03 |
| 614.06 | 647.06 | 702.02 | 753.17 | 616.05 | 222.16 |
| 614.06 | 647.07 | 702.09 | 753.19 | 619.19 | 225.08 |
| 614.08 | 647.08 | 702.09 | 753.21 | 620.10 | 228.04 |
| 614.09 | 647.09 | 702.15 | 753.22 | 621.02 | 248.12 |
| 614.12 | 647.10 | 702.19 | 754.01 | 645.15 | 297.09 |
| 615.04 | 647.11 | 703.02 | 754.03 | 645.20 | 297.13 |
| 615.06 | 647.13 | 703.02 | 754.04 | 650.09 | 330.06 |
| 615.07 | 648.04 | 706.05 | 754.08 | 656.06 | 333.05 |
| 615.07 | 648.04 | 706.06 | 754.09 | 685.13 | 337.07 |
| 615.13 | 648.05 | 706.09 | 754.10 | 711.07 | 348.09 |
| 615.14 | 648.07 | 706.19 | 754.11 | 711.09 | 370.16 |
| 616.03 | 648.08 | 707.01 | 754.13 | 730.16 | 381.10 |
| 616.07 | 648.09 | 707.04 | 754.15 | 730.21 | 384.03 |
| 616.08 | 648.10 | 707.04 | 754.16 | 739.15 | 416.16 |
| 616.10 | 648.10 | 707.06 | 754.20 | 739.19 | 421.21 |
| 616.12 | 648.11 | 707.07 | 755.01 | 743.01 | 432.16 |
| 616.12 | 648.17 | 707.07 | 755.03 | 746.13 | 439.13 |
| 617.06 | 648.18 | 707.08 | 755.05 | 752.12 | 464.02 |
| 617.07 | 649.12 | 707.09 | 755.07 | 760.16 | 464.03 |
| 617.14 | 650.04 | 707.10 | 755.08 | you're | 475.07 |
| 617.17 | 650.05 | 707.14 | 755.08 | 102.09 | 477.05 |
| 618.01 | 650.19 | 707.20 | 755.21 | 125.15 | 478.16 |
| 618.04 | 651.01 | 707.22 | 756.06 | 129.11 | 479.12 |
| 618.09 | 651.08 | 708.01 | 756.06 | 140.05 | 484.17 |
| 618.10 | 652.18 | 708.07 | 756.07 | 167.04 | 485.14 |
| 618.15 | 653.06 | 708.07 | 760.12 | 167.16 | 488.20 |
| 618.17 | 653.07 | 708.09 | you'a | 171.05 | 489.13 |
| 618.18 | 656.04 | 708.14 | 009.16 | 173.21 | 491.10 |
| 618.20 | 656.07 | 708.16 | 033.14 | 219.20 | 492.10 |
| 618.22 | 656.08 | 708.17 | 084.05 | 276.08 | 495.04 |
| 619.03 | 656.13 | 708.20 | 151.18 | 276.19 | 508.20 |
| 619.05 | 656.15 | 708.20 | 159.19 | 342.15 | 510.03 |
| 619.06 | 659.11 | 711.03 | 163.16 | 395.17 | 514.04 |
| 619.21 | 660.09 | 711.03 | 239.07 | 519.07 | 516.20 |
| 619.21 | 660.09 | 711.11 | 289.18 | 539.18 | 518.11 |
| 620.07 | 661.12 | 711.12 | 337.15 | 575.08 | 520.09 |
| 620.08 | 662.17 | 712.22 | 396.16 | 611.11 | 522.04 |
| 620.09 | 662.20 | 714.01 | 396.20 | 615.13 | 529.08 |
| 620.16 | 663.01 | 714.03 | 437.21 | 616.06 | 535.06 |
| 620.22 | 665.16 | 716.11 | 503.21 | 620.15 | 537.12 |
| 621.02 | 666.19 | 716.14 | 535.17 | 620.15 | 544.17 |
| 621.03 | 667.03 | 717.05 | 535.17 | 627.04 | 552.17 |
| 621.03 | 669.09 | 717.09 | 540.04 | 628.13 | 570.01 |
| 621.04 | 669.10 | 718.07 | 540.11 | 631.17 | 575.08 |
| 621.05 | 669.12 | 718.08 | 589.13 | 666.21 | 583.07 |
| 621.06 | 669.12 | 718.12 | 626.12 | 667.03 | 590.06 |
| 621.09 | 669.19 | 718.14 | 646.15 | 685.03 | 598.15 |
| 621.11 | 670.01 | 720.05 | 683.08 | 708.11 | 601.14 |
| 621.12 | 670.05 | 720.06 | 743.01 | you've | 603.20 |
| 622.08 | 670.07 | 721.02 | you'll | 070.20 | 614.04 |
| 622.10 | 670.08 | 721.06 | 030.07 | 074.19 | 627.16 |
| 622.12 | 670.09 | 721.12 | 033.05 | 083.21 | 628.08 |
| 624.11 | 670.11 | 721.15 | 035.19 | 129.01 | 633.02 |
| 626.09 | 670.12 | 721.17 | 059.09 | 134.16 | 634.22 |
| 626.10 | 670.14 | 721.19 | 084.08 | 152.18 | 635.10 |
| 626.11 | 670.17 | 721.21 | 102.08 | 159.02 | 637.03 |
| 627.01 | 670.19 | 722.09 | 103.15 | 163.03 | 639.06 |
| 627.01 | 670.23 | 722.13 | 121.05 | 182.05 | 643.02 |
| 627.03 | 677.02 | 722.13 | 180.22 | 260.03 | 644.04 |
| 627.03 | 677.04 | 722.14 | 182.02 | 260.07 | 658.11 |
| 627.05 | 677.06 | 722.15 | 184.01 | 311.15 | 665.21 |
| 627.10 | 677.08 | 722.17 | 195.10 | 317.09 | 666.20 |
| 628.01 | 677.08 | 722.19 | 216.10 | 322.10 | 673.05 |
| 628.02 | 677.12 | 722.20 | 252.12 | 362.18 | 679.19 |
| 628.05 | 677.14 | 723.02 | 253.16 | 435.08 | 694.14 |
| 628.12 | 677.18 | 723.04 | 260.19 | 435.13 | 699.02 |
| 629.17 | 678.12 | 723.06 | 276.17 | 466.13 | 713.18 |
| 629.19 | 678.15 | 723.08 | 303.13 | 468.14 | 718.20 |
| 629.20 | 678.15 | 723.10 | 303.15 | 500.06 | 721.04 |
| 629.20 | 678.16 | 723.15 | 303.16 | 540.02 | 723.07 |
| 630.11 | 678.20 | 724.09 | 313.07 | 540.18 | 724.18 |
| 630.11 | 679.13 | 724.10 | 332.23 | 543.16 | 728.20 |
| 630.12 | 679.14 | 724.13 | 333.01 | 616.13 | 737.17 |
| 630.12 | 679.15 | 724.17 | 333.20 | 627.04 | younger |
| 630.13 | 679.16 | 726.18 | 337.21 | 634.17 | 035.17 |
| 630.14 | 679.18 | 728.05 | 341.21 | 752.17 | 104.14 |
| 630.15 | 681.12 | 730.21 | 342.12 | young | 123.13 |
| 630.16 | 683.05 | 731.10 | 365.05 | 016.19 | 449.07 |
| 630.17 | 684.12 | 732.08 | 386.13 | 018.03 | 451.01 |
| 630.18 | 684.17 | 732.08 | 399.04 | 020.17 | 493.07 |
| 630.19 | 684.21 | 732.15 | 415.13 | 022.17 | 520.17 |
| 630.20 | 685.04 | 733.07 | 415.14 | 026.15 | 546.14 |
| 630.20 | 685.05 | 733.07 | 415.15 | 033.01 | 635.13 |
| 631.04 | 685.06 | 733.10 | 416.13 | 064.14 | 704.08 |
| 631.06 | 685.11 | 735.04 | 420.04 | 072.05 | youngsters |
| 631.06 | 685.11 | 735.05 | 439.08 | 073.02 | 497.09 |
| 631.07 | 685.14 | 739.01 | 440.05 | 081.21 | your |
| 631.08 | 685.19 | 739.02 | 452.18 | 085.03 | 002.08 |
| 631.09 | 686.01 | 739.15 | 469.03 | 088.17 | 012.18 |
| 631.11 | 691.01 | 739.16 | 469.07 | 097.20 | 015.19 |
| 631.12 | 694.05 | 740.10 | 469.08 | 098.10 | 015.19 |
| 631.13 | 694.06 | 741.06 | 482.17 | 100.01 | 017.17 |
| 631.15 | 697.07 | 741.21 | 492.04 | 111.01 | 018.15 |
| 633.15 | 697.08 | 741.22 | 494.16 | 112.07 | 020.01 |
| 634.10 | 697.09 | 742.05 | 506.03 | 116.11 | 020.03 |
| 634.10 | 697.13 | 742.08 | 523.01 | 145.14 | 022.08 |
| 634.15 | 697.16 | 742.13 | 532.03 | 146.02 | 023.05 |
| 638.20 | 697.17 | 742.14 | 540.04 | 147.10 | 023.22 |
| 639.21 | 697.18 | 742.16 | 540.13 | 154.06 | 024.01 |
| 645.14 | 698.07 | 743.02 | 542.22 | 155.16 | 024.02 |
| 645.14 | 698.12 | 743.02 | 551.04 | 157.16 | 024.06 |
| | 698.17 | 744.15 | 571.03 | 173.12 | 026.10 |
| | 698.18 | 744.19 | 573.03 | 174.09 | 026.12 |

| | | | | |
|---|---|---|---|---|
| 029.15 | 264.18 | 490.15 | 627.06 | 575.09 |
| 029.21 | 264.19 | 490.18 | 627.12 | 581.05 |
| 031.06 | 272.21 | 490.19 | 628.01 | 589.20 |
| 031.07 | 273.05 | 491.16 | 630.19 | 600.21 |
| 032.22 | 276.08 | 492.11 | 631.05 | 602.05 |
| 033.13 | 277.04 | 492.12 | 631.10 | 602.12 |
| 049.09 | 278.18 | 492.13 | 646.10 | 616.10 |
| 055.03 | 279.10 | 492.13 | 646.11 | 620.02 |
| 055.19 | 282.15 | 497.15 | 646.16 | 631.05 |
| 056.12 | 283.06 | 499.09 | 647.15 | 631.16 |
| 056.16 | 286.01 | 501.08 | 648.01 | 648.17 |
| 059.10 | 288.10 | 501.11 | 648.06 | 675.05 |
| 064.07 | 288.18 | 503.10 | 648.07 | 752.20 |
| 064.09 | 289.20 | 505.14 | 648.20 | yourseln |
| 064.17 | 289.21 | 506.05 | 656.05 | 669.22 |
| 083.21 | 294.11 | 511.06 | 656.07 | 713.08 |
| 085.05 | 297.10 | 511.10 | 656.16 | yourselves |
| 085.09 | 297.13 | 512.02 | 666.20 | 120.21 |
| 102.09 | 297.19 | 512.04 | 670.11 | youth |
| 103.09 | 308.12 | 513.12 | 670.14 | 023.06 |
| 104.12 | 309.04 | 519.06 | 671.02 | 026.03 |
| 107.19 | 311.12 | 520.03 | 675.15 | 129.05 |
| 107.21 | 311.17 | 521.01 | 678.10 | 442.03 |
| 114.16 | 311.22 | 524.08 | 678.17 | 486.22 |
| 114.16 | 315.08 | 524.14 | 679.08 | 731.04 |
| 117.18 | 315.09 | 524.15 | 683.08 | 745.17 |
| 117.18 | 317.09 | 524.21 | 684.15 | youth-like |
| 123.04 | 331.22 | 525.16 | 685.06 | 213.21 |
| 124.11 | 333.04 | 526.02 | 685.14 | youthful |
| 124.18 | 333.14 | 526.04 | 685.16 | 160.14 |
| 125.16 | 334.04 | 526.05 | 686.01 | 448.06 |
| 125.17 | 336.18 | 526.16 | 694.07 | zeal |
| 125.22 | 338.06 | 533.21 | 696.22 | 050.17 |
| 129.01 | 339.11 | 535.03 | 697.22 | zealous |
| 129.15 | 340.11 | 536.04 | 698.17 | 141.11 |
| 129.18 | 341.05 | 537.14 | 699.20 | zest |
| 134.08 | 341.11 | 537.14 | 707.11 | 442.19 |
| 135.08 | 342.15 | 538.04 | 707.11 | zillah |
| 137.08 | 342.16 | 538.05 | 707.20 | 031.17 |
| 137.11 | 343.10 | 540.11 | 708.12 | 035.11 |
| 137.12 | 344.14 | 541.03 | 711.10 | 036.10 |
| 140.21 | 345.03 | 544.01 | 717.06 | 055.19 |
| 155.07 | 346.13 | 547.06 | 718.11 | 063.08 |
| 163.19 | 357.10 | 555.03 | 720.04 | 063.21 |
| 164.04 | 359.05 | 559.09 | 721.21 | 533.09 |
| 166.19 | 359.21 | 562.04 | 724.12 | 533.17 |
| 167.05 | 362.20 | 562.06 | 724.15 | 556.09 |
| 168.11 | 363.08 | 563.10 | 742.04 | 558.15 |
| 172.13 | 363.09 | 570.15 | 751.11 | 566.02 |
| 175.13 | 363.14 | 571.08 | 752.12 | 566.10 |
| 175.18 | 364.02 | 571.09 | 752.13 | 568.14 |
| 178.13 | 365.11 | 573.10 | 752.14 | 570.01 |
| 182.01 | 368.06 | 576.03 | 752.17 | 607.22 |
| 183.16 | 374.04 | 581.01 | 752.21 | 616.09 |
| 190.10 | 374.06 | 581.10 | 753.01 | 626.05 |
| 194.11 | 375.14 | 587.21 | 754.02 | 627.10 |
| 203.04 | 375.16 | 591.20 | 755.01 | 627.22 |
| 203.04 | 382.13 | 593.10 | your're | 628.11 |
| 203.06 | 384.05 | 593.13 | 619.22 | 628.11 |
| 203.06 | 386.15 | 599.05 | yours | 634.17 |
| 203.21 | 386.17 | 600.01 | 012.02 | 647.17 |
| 208.09 | 394.19 | 600.08 | 140.07 | 658.07 |
| 212.12 | 395.12 | 600.14 | 152.12 | 659.03 |
| 213.02 | 395.16 | 601.08 | 182.14 | 659.10 |
| 216.01 | 396.08 | 601.21 | 236.08 | 664.06 |
| 216.04 | 398.20 | 602.01 | 257.07 | 664.22 |
| 216.08 | 401.01 | 602.05 | 258.08 | 667.05 |
| 216.13 | 401.07 | 602.11 | 321.21 | 669.19 |
| 220.02 | 405.05 | 605.14 | 364.03 | 671.21 |
| 227.12 | 405.05 | 605.16 | 398.11 | 697.15 |
| 227.20 | 405.07 | 606.10 | 416.06 | zillah's |
| 227.22 | 406.15 | 606.13 | 421.15 | 622.18 |
| 228.03 | 407.16 | 606.17 | 463.17 | 648.22 |
| 229.17 | 408.16 | 608.04 | 501.02 | |
| 229.19 | 409.09 | 611.08 | 526.03 | |
| 230.10 | 416.12 | 611.08 | 534.18 | |
| 231.06 | 416.22 | 611.13 | 537.03 | |
| 231.07 | 417.10 | 612.03 | 537.05 | |
| 231.15 | 422.01 | 612.04 | 588.04 | |
| 233.18 | 434.05 | 612.06 | 605.08 | |
| 235.11 | 435.03 | 612.13 | 677.03 | |
| 235.12 | 435.10 | 612.15 | yourself | |
| 235.22 | 438.01 | 612.15 | 125.14 | |
| 237.05 | 438.07 | 612.18 | 155.07 | |
| 238.06 | 440.07 | 613.02 | 167.19 | |
| 238.11 | 451.15 | 613.17 | 166.08 | |
| 238.19 | 452.06 | 614.10 | 171.07 | |
| 238.22 | 456.02 | 614.13 | 177.08 | |
| 239.20 | 458.03 | 614.13 | 228.18 | |
| 239.22 | 460.21 | 616.01 | 231.05 | |
| 243.06 | 461.13 | 616.10 | 252.02 | |
| 246.09 | 462.01 | 616.11 | 253.17 | |
| 246.10 | 463.20 | 617.06 | 257.22 | |
| 249.16 | 463.20 | 618.01 | 273.01 | |
| 250.10 | 468.16 | 618.03 | 278.04 | |
| 251.05 | 468.17 | 618.05 | 278.17 | |
| 251.08 | 468.18 | 618.08 | 287.18 | |
| 252.07 | 469.17 | 618.18 | 289.15 | |
| 252.20 | 469.19 | 618.21 | 307.01 | |
| 253.02 | 470.08 | 619.01 | 314.22 | |
| 253.09 | 480.01 | 619.02 | 335.05 | |
| 253.12 | 482.02 | 619.08 | 357.21 | |
| 254.06 | 482.14 | 619.09 | 362.22 | |
| 256.16 | 484.10 | 620.01 | 396.06 | |
| 256.19 | 484.16 | 620.07 | 437.04 | |
| 256.20 | 485.09 | 620.21 | 452.12 | |
| 257.02 | 486.11 | 620.22 | 504.03 | |
| 259.06 | 486.16 | 621.05 | 510.09 | |
| 259.10 | 489.02 | 621.08 | 525.11 | |
| 263.12 | 489.05 | 622.04 | 526.15 | |
| 264.15 | 489.15 | 624.04 | 543.16 | |

# WORD FREQUENCY TABLE

| Count | Word |
|---|---|
| 1 | 'bacca |
| 2 | 'baht |
| 1 | 'bide |
| 1 | 'but |
| 1 | 'cahnt |
| 13 | 'em |
| 2 | 'em's |
| 1 | 'feard |
| 1 | 'munn't |
| 1 | 'quest |
| 1 | 'sizes |
| 1 | 'ud |
| 3 | 'ull |
| 1 | 1500 |
| 1 | 1778 |
| 1 | 1801 |
| 1 | 1802 |
| 2 | [10] |
| 2 | [11] |
| 2 | [12] |
| 2 | [13] |
| 2 | [14] |
| 1 | [15] |
| 1 | [16] |
| 1 | [17] |
| 1 | [18] |
| 1 | [19] |
| 17 | [1] |
| 1 | [20] |
| 22 | [2] |
| 2 | [3] |
| 2 | [4] |
| 2 | [5] |
| 2 | [6] |
| 2 | [7] |
| 2 | [8] |
| 2 | [9] |
| 34 | [chapter] |
| 2 | [end] |
| 2 | [heights] |
| 1 | [of] |
| 2 | [the] |
| 35 | [vol] |
| 2 | [wuthering] |
| 2321 | a |
| 2 | a'most |
| 1 | a-day |
| 1 | a-night |
| 2 | abaht |
| 1 | abandon |
| 4 | abandoned |
| 1 | abandonment |
| 1 | abashed |
| 1 | abduction |
| 1 | abetted |
| 2 | abhorred |
| 1 | abhorrence |
| 1 | abhors |
| 2 | abide |
| 2 | abject |
| 1 | abjured |
| 16 | able |
| 7 | abode |
| 3 | abominable |
| 157 | about |
| 29 | above |
| 2 | abroad |
| 1 | abrupt |
| 5 | abruptly |
| 21 | absence |
| 1 | absences |
| 7 | absent |
| 1 | absented |
| 2 | absolute |
| 4 | absolutely |
| 1 | absolve |
| 1 | absolved |
| 9 | absorbed |
| 1 | absorbing |
| 2 | abstain |
| 1 | abstaining |
| 1 | abstinence |
| 1 | abstract |
| 2 | abstracted |
| 2 | abstracting |
| 1 | abstraction |
| 4 | absurd |
| 1 | absurdities |
| 2 | absurdity |
| 1 | abundant |
| 6 | abuse |
| 1 | abused |
| 1 | abusing |
| 2 | abyss |
| 1 | accede |
| 2 | accent |
| 3 | accents |
| 4 | accept |
| 5 | accepted |
| 1 | accepting |
| 3 | access |
| 5 | accident |
| 1 | accidental |
| 1 | accommodate |
| 1 | accommodated |
| 1 | accommodation |
| 2 | accommodations |
| 5 | accompanied |
| 12 | accompany |
| 1 | accompanying |
| 1 | accomplice |
| 5 | accomplished |
| 5 | accord |
| 6 | according |
| 1 | accordingly |
| 1 | accosted |
| 26 | account |
| 1 | accumulations |
| 4 | accursed |
| 3 | accusations |
| 1 | accuse |
| 1 | accused |
| 1 | accusing |
| 5 | accustomed |
| 2 | ached |
| 2 | aches |
| 2 | achieved |
| 3 | aching |
| 1 | acknowledge |
| 2 | acknowledged |
| 2 | acknowledgment |
| 12 | acquaintance |
| 1 | acquaintances |
| 7 | acquainted |
| 1 | acquainting |
| 1 | acquiesce |
| 2 | acquiesced |
| 2 | acquire |
| 1 | acquired |
| 1 | acquirements |
| 1 | acquisition |
| 1 | acquisitions |
| 11 | across |
| 17 | act |
| 4 | acted |
| 2 | acting |
| 4 | action |
| 3 | actions |
| 6 | active |
| 1 | activity |
| 2 | acts |
| 2 | actual |
| 6 | actually |
| 1 | actuate |
| 5 | add |
| 27 | added |
| 2 | adding |
| 3 | addition |
| 2 | address |
| 5 | addressed |
| 10 | addressing |
| 1 | adhere |
| 3 | adieu |
| 1 | adieux |
| 2 | adjective |
| 1 | adjourned |
| 1 | adjuration |
| 1 | administer |
| 2 | administered |
| 1 | admirable |
| 6 | admiration |
| 4 | admire |
| 2 | admired |
| 1 | admission |
| 6 | admit |
| 6 | admittance |
| 1 | admitted |
| 1 | admonition |
| 1 | ado |
| 1 | adopt |
| 1 | adoration |
| 1 | adored |
| 1 | adrift |
| 1 | adroitly |
| 2 | advance |
| 8 | advanced |
| 3 | advances |
| 2 | advancing |
| 5 | advantage |
| 3 | advantages |
| 3 | advent |
| 2 | adventure |
| 1 | adventures |
| 1 | adversary |
| 6 | advice |
| 3 | advise |
| 5 | advised |
| 1 | adviser |
| 1 | advising |
| 1 | afeard |
| 2 | affair |
| 4 | affairs |
| 1 | affect |
| 1 | affectation |
| 2 | affectations |
| 6 | affected |
| 1 | affecting |
| 14 | affection |
| 2 | affectionate |
| 4 | affections |
| 2 | affirm |
| 1 | affirmation |
| 1 | affirmations |
| 10 | affirmed |
| 9 | affirming |
| 4 | affirms |
| 1 | afflict |
| 1 | affliction |
| 3 | afford |
| 2 | afore |
| 29 | afraid |
| 3 | afresh |
| 166 | after |
| 1 | after-thought |
| 25 | afternoon |
| 2 | afternoons |
| 1 | afterward |
| 24 | afterwards |
| 137 | again |
| 69 | against |
| 1 | agait |
| 16 | age |
| 3 | agean |
| 2 | aged |
| 1 | agent |
| 2 | ages |
| 2 | aggravate |
| 1 | aggravating |
| 1 | aggravation |
| 1 | aggressor |
| 2 | aghast |
| 1 | aght |
| 1 | agility |
| 1 | agitated |
| 12 | agitation |
| 12 | ago |
| 12 | agony |
| 6 | agreeable |
| 5 | agreed |
| 2 | agreement |
| 1 | ague |
| 23 | ah |
| 2 | aha |
| 2 | ahr |
| 7 | aht |
| 13 | aid |
| 1 | aided |
| 2 | aiding |
| 1 | ail |
| 3 | ailing |
| 4 | ails |
| 2 | aim |
| 2 | aimed |
| 22 | air |
| 4 | ajar |
| 2 | akin |
| 1 | al |
| 1 | alacrity |
| 9 | alarm |
| 6 | alarmed |
| 3 | alas |
| 4 | ale |
| 3 | alert |
| 1 | alienation |
| 1 | alighted |
| 1 | alike |
| 12 | alive |
| 283 | all |
| 1 | all's |
| 4 | allas |
| 1 | allayed |
| 1 | alleviation |
| 1 | alley |
| 2 | alliance |
| 1 | allies |
| 17 | allow |
| 11 | allowed |
| 1 | allowing |
| 1 | allus |
| 1 | allusion |
| 3 | ally |
| 1 | almanack |
| 47 | almost |
| 1 | alms |
| 61 | alone |
| 12 | along |
| 1 | aloof |
| 16 | aloud |
| 15 | already |
| 43 | also |
| 2 | alter |
| 3 | alteration |
| 1 | alterations |
| 15 | altered |
| 1 | altering |
| 1 | alternately |
| 12 | altogether |
| 54 | always |
| 90 | am |
| 3 | amang |
| 4 | amazed |
| 3 | amazement |
| 1 | ambassadress |
| 1 | amber |
| 2 | ambition |
| 2 | amends |
| 1 | america |
| 1 | american |
| 8 | amiable |
| 3 | amid |
| 2 | amiss |
| 43 | among |
| 3 | amongst |
| 1 | amongst' |
| 1 | amount |
| 1 | amounted |
| 1 | amounting |
| 1 | ample |
| 12 | amuse |
| 2 | amused |
| 14 | amusement |
| 2 | amusements |
| 2 | amuses |
| 2 | amusing |
| 316 | an |
| 2 | an' |
| 1 | anatomy |
| 2 | ancestors |
| 8 | ancient |
| 4747 | and |
| 1 | anecdote |
| 1 | anecdotes |
| 3 | anew |
| 8 | angel |
| 1 | angel's |
| 4 | angels |
| 12 | anger |
| 1 | angered |
| 1 | angle |
| 8 | angrily |
| 27 | angry |
| 13 | anguish |
| 2 | anguished |
| 5 | animal |
| 1 | animals |
| 4 | animated |
| 5 | animation |
| 3 | ankle |
| 1 | annie's |
| 2 | annihilate |
| 4 | annihilated |
| 1 | annihiliate |
| 2 | anniversary |
| 1 | annum |
| 2 | anon |
| 85 | another |
| 1 | another's |
| 1 | anquish |
| 49 | answer |
| 156 | answered |
| 5 | answering |
| 1 | answers |
| 2 | anticipate |
| 4 | anticipated |
| 3 | anticipating |
| 2 | anticipation |
| 2 | anticipations |
| 5 | antipathy |
| 1 | antique |
| 5 | anxiety |
| 13 | anxious |
| 6 | anxiously |
| 146 | any |
| 11 | anybody |
| 1 | anyone |
| 36 | anything |
| 8 | anywhere |
| 1 | apart |
| 18 | apartment |
| 1 | apartments |
| 2 | apathetic |
| 2 | apathy |
| 1 | ape |
| 3 | apology |
| 1 | appal |
| 2 | appalled |
| 2 | appalling |
| 2 | apparent |
| 17 | apparently |
| 3 | apparition |
| 3 | appeal |
| 3 | appealing |
| 5 | appear |
| 17 | appearance |
| 35 | appeared |
| 2 | appears |
| 2 | appellation |
| 3 | appetite |
| 1 | applause |
| 2 | apple |
| 1 | apple-sauce |
| 2 | apples |
| 5 | applied |
| 1 | applying |
| 3 | appointed |
| 1 | apppeared |
| 3 | appreciate |
| 11 | approach |
| 15 | approached |
| 10 | approaching |
| 1 | approbation |
| 2 | appropriate |
| 1 | approval |
| 2 | approve |
| 1 | approved |
| 2 | april |
| 5 | apron |
| 1 | apt |
| 1 | arabian |
| 1 | arc |
| 3 | arch |
| 1 | arched |
| 1 | archer |
| 1 | architect |
| 2 | ardent |

| Count | Word | Count | Word | Count | Word | Count | Word |
|---|---|---|---|---|---|---|---|
| 1 | ardently | 4 | attack | 2 | bang | 4 | behold |
| 1 | ardour | 1 | attacked | 1 | banged | 3 | beholding |
| 299 | are | 1 | attain | 1 | banish | 117 | being |
| 1 | area | 1 | attained | 5 | banished | 1 | beings |
| 3 | argue | 1 | attaining | 2 | banishment | 1 | belie |
| 1 | argued | 1 | attainments | 4 | bank | 1 | belied |
| 2 | argument | 16 | attempt | 1 | bank-notes | 1 | belief |
| 1 | arguments | 14 | attempted | 2 | banks | 40 | believe |
| 1 | arid | 4 | attempting | 1 | banning | 5 | believed |
| 2 | arising | 5 | attempts | 3 | bannister | 1 | believing |
| 34 | arm | 4 | attend | 1 | baptists' | 6 | bell |
| 1 | arm's | 6 | attendance | 11 | bare | 2 | bellows |
| 3 | arm-chair | 2 | attendant | 1 | barefoot | 1 | bells |
| 25 | arms | 3 | attended | 2 | barely | 2 | belonged |
| 1 | arms-length | 6 | attending | 1 | bargain | 2 | belonging |
| 2 | army | 15 | attention | 1 | bargin | 1 | beloved |
| 1 | arn | 5 | attentive | 2 | bark | 15 | below |
| 2 | arose | 1 | attenuated | 7 | barn | 2 | bemoaned |
| 7 | around | 1 | attire | 2 | barred | 5 | bench |
| 10 | arrange | 2 | attired | 1 | barrel | 1 | benches |
| 2 | arranged | 1 | attitude | 1 | barren | 5 | bend |
| 3 | arrangement | 3 | attorney | 2 | barrier | 7 | bending |
| 2 | arrangements | 2 | attract | 2 | bars | 16 | beneath |
| 2 | arrest | 5 | attracted | 1 | barthens | 1 | benefactor |
| 5 | arrested | 2 | attraction | 2 | base | 1 | beneficent |
| 2 | arresting | 1 | attractions | 1 | basely | 6 | benefit |
| 10 | arrival | 1 | attractive | 1 | basement | 1 | benefiting |
| 1 | arrive | 1 | attribute | 1 | baseness | 1 | benevolence |
| 9 | arrived | 1 | attributes | 1 | bashfully | 1 | benevolent |
| 1 | arriving | 1 | atween | 1 | bashfulness | 1 | benign |
| 1 | arrogance | 1 | audacity | 1 | basilisk | 16 | bent |
| 1 | arrows | 2 | audible | 7 | basin | 1 | benumbed |
| 5 | art | 3 | audibly | 1 | basins | 1 | bequeath |
| 1 | artery | 1 | audience | 1 | basked | 1 | bequeathed |
| 1 | artful | 1 | aught | 4 | basket | 1 | bereavement |
| 2 | article | 2 | august | 1 | bass | 1 | beseech |
| 3 | articles | 7 | aunt | 1 | bassoons | 1 | beseeching |
| 1 | artillery | 1 | aunt's | 1 | bathed | 1 | besetting |
| 1 | artist's | 1 | austere | 1 | bathos | 16 | beside |
| 934 | as | 1 | author | 1 | battle | 25 | besides |
| 1 | ascended | 1 | authoritative | 1 | battledoors | 1 | besought |
| 2 | ascending | 1 | authoritative- | 1 | bay | 1 | bespeak |
| 1 | ascent |  | ly | 728 | be | 1 | bespoke |
| 5 | ascertain | 3 | authority | 1 | beacon | 20 | best |
| 1 | ascertained | 1 | automatons | 1 | beaded | 1 | bestir |
| 1 | ascertaining | 3 | autumn | 1 | beamless | 1 | bestirring |
| 2 | ascribed | 1 | auxiliary | 42 | bear | 3 | bestow |
| 1 | ash | 2 | avail | 1 | beard | 5 | bestowed |
| 12 | ashamed | 1 | availed | 8 | bearing | 3 | bestowing |
| 7 | ashes | 1 | avarice | 1 | bearishly | 1 | betook |
| 14 | aside | 1 | avaricious | 7 | beast | 2 | betray |
| 35 | ask | 1 | averred | 6 | beasts | 2 | betrayal |
| 1 | askance | 14 | aversion | 7 | beat | 1 | betrayed |
| 104 | asked | 1 | avert | 6 | beaten | 1 | betrayer |
| 8 | asking | 3 | averted | 1 | beating | 82 | better |
| 16 | asleep | 1 | averting | 13 | beautiful | 50 | between |
| 19 | aspect | 14 | avoid | 2 | beautifully | 1 | bevy |
| 1 | aspirations | 6 | avoided | 9 | beauty | 1 | bewail |
| 1 | aspiring | 2 | avoiding | 1 | beaver | 8 | beware |
| 1 | ass | 1 | avoids | 11 | became | 5 | bewildered |
| 1 | assailant | 42 | aw | 97 | because | 1 | bewilderment |
| 1 | assassin | 7 | aw'd | 3 | beck | 1 | bewilders |
| 2 | assault | 1 | aw'll | 1 | becks | 1 | bewitched |
| 1 | assembly | 4 | aw'm | 1 | beclouded | 20 | beyond |
| 2 | assent | 3 | aw's | 5 | become | 7 | bible |
| 2 | assert | 2 | await | 1 | becomes | 1 | bibles |
| 4 | asserted | 2 | awaited | 1 | becoming | 46 | bid |
| 1 | asserting | 1 | awaiting | 60 | bed | 6 | bidding |
| 7 | assertion | 4 | awake | 2 | bed-clothes | 7 | bide |
| 2 | assertions | 3 | awakened | 4 | bed-room | 2 | big |
| 1 | asses | 1 | awakens | 1 | bed-rume | 1 | bigger |
| 1 | asseverated | 20 | aware | 1 | bed-rumes | 1 | bilberries |
| 1 | assiduity | 87 | away | 2 | bed-side | 1 | bilberry |
| 1 | assiduously | 2 | awe | 2 | beds | 1 | billowy |
| 3 | assist | 6 | awful | 4 | bedside | 2 | bind |
| 6 | assistance | 1 | awfully | 1 | bedtime | 1 | binding |
| 1 | assistant | 1 | awhile | 1 | beef | 1 | birches |
| 1 | assistants | 2 | awkward | 222 | been | 6 | bird |
| 1 | assisting | 1 | awkwardly | 1 | bees | 5 | birds |
| 1 | associate | 2 | awkwardness | 1 | befall | 3 | birth |
| 1 | associated | 2 | awn | 1 | befallen | 1 | birthday |
| 1 | associates | 1 | awoke | 3 | befitting | 21 | bit |
| 2 | association | 2 | ay | 155 | before | 2 | bitch |
| 5 | associations | 4 | aye | 1 | before-named | 1 | bite |
| 1 | assume | 1 | b | 2 | beforehand | 1 | biter |
| 6 | assumed | 1 | babies | 1 | befriend | 1 | biting |
| 3 | assuming | 9 | baby | 11 | beg | 4 | bits |
| 2 | assurance | 1 | baby-work | 73 | began | 3 | bitten |
| 1 | assurances | 1 | babyish | 3 | beggar | 18 | bitter |
| 6 | assure | 117 | back | 1 | beggarly | 7 | bitterly |
| 4 | assured | 3 | back-kitchen | 1 | beggars | 2 | bitterness |
| 1 | assuredly | 43 | bad | 7 | begged | 40 | black |
| 1 | assuring | 1 | bad-natured | 1 | begging | 1 | black-haired |
| 1 | astir | 1 | bad-tempered | 13 | begin | 1 | blackberry |
| 5 | astonished | 4 | bade | 1 | beginner | 1 | blackbirds |
| 1 | astonishing | 3 | badly | 14 | beginning | 3 | blackened |
| 8 | astonishment | 1 | bahn | 2 | begins | 1 | blacker |
| 5 | asunder | 1 | baht | 11 | begone | 2 | blackguard |
| 1 | asylum | 2 | bairn | 1 | beguile | 2 | blackhorse |
| 780 | at | 1 | bairnies | 1 | beguiled | 3 | blackness |
| 8 | ate | 1 | bairns | 1 | beguiling | 2 | blacksmith's |
| 2 | athletic | 1 | bait | 1 | beguilnig | 2 | blade |
| 1 | atlantic | 1 | baiting | 2 | begun | 10 | blame |
| 3 | atmosphere | 1 | baking | 3 | behalf | 1 | blameable |
| 1 | atmospheric | 1 | balance | 5 | behave | 3 | blamed |
| 1 | atom | 1 | balancing | 8 | behaved | 1 | blaming |
| 1 | atoms | 1 | ball | 1 | behaving | 3 | blanched |
| 2 | atrocious | 1 | ballad | 12 | behaviour | 5 | blank |
| 3 | attached | 1 | ban | 14 | beheld | 1 | blanker |
| 6 | attachment | 1 | band | 1 | behest | 1 | blasphemer |
| 3 | attachments | 1 | bane | 28 | behind | 3 | blast |

| | | | |
|---|---|---|---|
| 3 blaze | 37 boy | 1 buries | 1 castle |
| 1 blazing | 1 boy's | 5 burn | 8 cat |
| 5 bleak | 1 boyhood | 2 burned | 2 catastrophe |
| 1 bled | 2 boys | 8 burning | 11 catch |
| 1 bleed | 2 brace | 1 burnished | 7 catching |
| 3 bleeding | 1 brach | 1 burnt | 1 catechised |
| 1 bleeds | 1 bracing | 9 burst | 1 catechism |
| 1 blended | 8 brain | 2 bursting | 1 catgut |
| 1 blending | 2 brains | 1 bursts | 1 catharine |
| 3 bless | 1 bran | 2 bury | 338 catherine |
| 2 blessed | 2 branch | 4 bushes | 43 catherine's |
| 8 blessing | 5 branches | 22 business | 1 catherines |
| 1 blest | 1 branching | 1 business-visi- | 117 cathy |
| 3 blew | 1 branded |    ts | 7 cathy's |
| 1 blight | 6 branderham | 2 bustled | 3 cats |
| 1 blighted | 5 brandy | 1 bustling | 3 cattle |
| 1 blightingly | 1 brass | 10 busy | 19 caught |
| 5 blind | 1 brat | 676 but | 19 cause |
| 1 blind-man's | 1 brat's | 3 buy | 11 caused |
| 1 blinds | 1 brave | 450 by | 4 causes |
| 2 bliss | 1 braved | 1 by-road | 4 causeway |
| 1 blissfully | 1 bravely | 5 bye | 3 causing |
| 1 blisters | 1 brazened | 3 c | 1 cautions |
| 3 block | 6 bread | 1 cabinet | 4 cautious |
| 23 blood | 2 breadth | 1 cahnt | 5 cautiously |
| 1 blood-shot | 14 break | 4 cake | 3 cave |
| 1 blood-vessel | 16 breakfast | 2 cakes | 1 cawlf |
| 3 bloodless | 1 breakfasts | 4 calamity | 1 cease |
| 1 bloody | 6 breaking | 3 calculate | 10 ceased |
| 3 bloom | 1 breaks | 2 calculated | 1 ceiling |
| 1 bloomed | 8 breast | 1 calf | 4 cellar |
| 1 blooming | 21 breath | 1 calf-skin | 1 cemented |
| 1 blossom | 3 breathe | 34 call | 1 centipede |
| 1 blossomed | 5 breathed | 34 called | 2 centre |
| 2 blotted | 4 breathing | 15 calling | 2 centred |
| 8 blow | 6 breathless | 9 calls | 1 century |
| 4 blowing | 1 breathlessly | 7 calm | 2 ceremony |
| 1 blown | 1 breaths | 2 calmer | 31 certain |
| 4 blows | 3 bred | 3 calmly | 16 certainly |
| 2 blubbered | 1 breead | 1 calmness | 1 certainty |
| 1 blubbering | 2 breed | 1 cambric | 2 chafing |
| 1 bludgeon | 1 breeding | 107 came | 1 chagrin |
| 12 blue | 1 breeze | 1 camels | 3 chain |
| 1 blue-bells | 1 breeze-rocked | 133 can | 2 chains |
| 2 bluff | 1 brethren | 1 can'le | 46 chair |
| 1 blunder | 1 bribed | 46 can't | 4 chairs |
| 2 blunders | 1 bride | 1 canary | 2 cham'er |
| 1 blush | 1 bridegroom | 1 candid | 35 chamber |
| 3 blushed | 3 bridle | 28 candle | 1 chamber-door |
| 2 blushing | 2 bridles | 1 candle-light | 2 chambers |
| 1 blustered | 8 brief | 3 candles | 1 champion |
| 1 board | 1 briefly | 2 canine | 19 chance |
| 2 boards | 14 bright | 3 canisters | 5 chanced |
| 1 boast | 2 brightened | 1 cannibal | 1 chandelier |
| 2 boasted | 2 brightening | 75 cannot | 22 change |
| 1 boastful | 1 brighter | 3 cannut | 17 changed |
| 1 boastfully | 1 brightness | 1 canst | 1 changeling |
| 2 boath | 3 brilliant | 3 cant | 2 changes |
| 5 bodily | 1 brim | 1 canter | 1 changing |
| 1 boding | 1 brim-ful | 1 canty | 1 channel |
| 19 body | 1 brindled | 4 cap | 2 chap |
| 2 bog | 34 bring | 7 capable | 12 chapel |
| 1 bog-hoile | 7 bringing | 2 capacity | 1 chapel-roof |
| 1 bog-water | 1 brings | 1 caper | 1 chaplain |
| 1 boil | 1 brink | 1 capering | 2 chapter |
| 1 boiled | 1 brisk | 2 capital | 2 chapters |
| 2 boiling | 3 briskly | 1 caprice | 16 character |
| 4 bold | 1 bristling | 2 caprices | 2 characters |
| 3 boldly | 2 broad | 1 caps | 13 charge |
| 1 boldness | 1 brocken | 1 captain | 2 charged |
| 5 bolt | 11 broke | 1 captured | 3 charitable |
| 2 bolts | 16 broken | 1 caravan | 5 charity |
| 1 bonds | 1 brooad | 1 carcass | 3 charlie |
| 2 bones | 2 brood | 1 cards | 2 charm |
| 8 bonnet | 2 brooded | 47 care | 1 charmed |
| 1 bonnetless | 3 brooding | 4 cared | 3 charming |
| 2 bonniest | 2 brooks | 5 careful | 1 chart |
| 14 bonny | 33 brother | 3 carefully | 3 chase |
| 1 bony | 5 brother's | 8 careless | 1 chased |
| 26 book | 1 brother-in-law | 2 carelessly | 1 chastened |
| 1 book-larning | 1 brothers | 3 carelessness | 1 chastise |
| 32 books | 48 brought | 5 cares | 1 chastisement |
| 2 boor | 6 brow | 2 caress | 1 chat |
| 1 border | 6 brown | 1 caressed | 3 chatter |
| 2 bordered | 1 brown-eyed | 5 caresses | 3 chattered |
| 1 bordering | 7 brows | 1 caricature | 3 chattering |
| 1 borders | 2 bruised | 1 caring | 1 cheap |
| 5 bore | 1 bruises | 1 carn | 1 cheat |
| 12 born | 1 brush | 2 carols | 4 cheated |
| 5 borne | 1 brushes | 2 carpet | 1 cheating |
| 4 borrowed | 1 brushing | 3 carpeted | 3 check |
| 1 borrowing | 1 brusts | 8 carriage | 5 checked |
| 76 both | 3 brutal | 15 carried | 3 checking |
| 2 bother | 1 brutality | 1 carrion | 19 cheek |
| 1 bothered | 2 brutally | 9 carry | 1 cheeking |
| 2 bothom | 8 brute | 2 carrying | 12 cheeks |
| 3 bottle | 1 brutishness | 1 cart | 7 cheer |
| 7 bottom | 16 bud | 1 cart-horse | 15 cheerful |
| 1 bough | 1 budding | 1 cartwheels | 2 cheerfully |
| 2 bought | 1 bugbear | 1 carve | 1 cheerfulness |
| 4 bound | 2 build | 4 carved | 2 cheerless |
| 2 bounded | 5 building | 4 carving | 1 cheese |
| 2 bounding | 1 bulk | 12 case | 2 cherish |
| 1 boundless | 1 bull | 3 casement | 4 cherished |
| 2 bounds | 3 bull-dog | 1 casement-wind- | 1 cherishing |
| 1 bountiful | 5 bundle |    ow | 1 cheritably |
| 2 bow | 1 bundled | 1 casements | 1 cherub |
| 2 bowed | 1 buoyant | 2 cash | 3 chest |
| 3 bowl | 6 burden | 11 cast | 1 chevy |
| 4 box | 1 burial | 2 castaway | 3 chewing |
| 1 boxes | 12 buried | 3 casting | 1 chicken |

| | | | | | | |
|---|---|---|---|---|---|---|
| 1 | chide | 5 | closer | 8 | companions | 3 | connection |
| 1 | chided | 2 | closet | 2 | companionship | 1 | conned |
| 6 | chief | 2 | closing | 31 | company | 1 | conquered |
| 51 | child | 3 | cloth | 1 | comparatively | 10 | conscience |
| 5 | child's | 12 | clothes | 3 | compare | 10 | conscious |
| 1 | childer | 1 | clothes-press | 3 | compared | 1 | consciously |
| 2 | childhood | 7 | cloud | 2 | comparison | 3 | consciousness |
| 1 | childhood's | 4 | clouded | 4 | compassion | 1 | consecrated |
| 9 | childish | 1 | cloudless | 1 | compassionate | 12 | consent |
| 30 | children | 1 | cloudlessly | 5 | compel | 3 | consented |
| 1 | children's | 7 | clouds | 19 | compelled | 11 | consequence |
| 6 | chill | 2 | cloudy | 2 | compelling | 7 | consequences |
| 1 | chillness | 4 | clown | 1 | compensation | 3 | consequently |
| 1 | chills | 1 | clowns | 1 | competent | 7 | consider |
| 1 | chimbley | 1 | clubs | 1 | complacently | 6 | considerable |
| 1 | chimed | 1 | clump | 3 | complain | 4 | considerably |
| 11 | chimney | 7 | clung | 6 | complained | 5 | consideration |
| 1 | chimney-corner | 1 | clusters | 6 | complaining | 1 | considerations |
| 2 | chimney-piece | 2 | clutch | 1 | complainings | 11 | considered |
| 1 | chimney-stack | 1 | clutched | 1 | complaint | 4 | considering |
| 2 | chin | 1 | coach | 4 | complaints | 1 | consisted |
| 1 | china | 3 | coachman | 1 | compelled | 8 | consolation |
| 1 | chinks | 3 | coal | 6 | complete | 5 | console |
| 1 | chipping | 1 | coal-hole | 14 | completely | 4 | consoled |
| 1 | chirping | 1 | coal-scuttles | 3 | complexion | 1 | conspire |
| 2 | chit | 1 | coal-shed | 1 | complexioned | 1 | constable |
| 1 | chivalrous | 5 | coals | 3 | compliance | 1 | constancy |
| 7 | choice | 1 | coarseness | 1 | complied | 11 | constant |
| 1 | choke | 6 | coat | 1 | compliment | 7 | constantly |
| 2 | choked | 1 | coat-laps | 2 | comply | 2 | consternation |
| 3 | choking | 1 | coax | 2 | complying | 6 | constitution |
| 8 | choose | 1 | coaxed | 6 | composed | 1 | constrained |
| 1 | chooses | 2 | coaxing | 1 | composing | 1 | constructed |
| 1 | chord | 1 | cobweb | 1 | composition | 1 | consulting |
| 9 | chose | 1 | cockatrice | 2 | composure | 2 | consumed |
| 1 | chosen | 2 | coffee | 1 | compound | 1 | consuming |
| 1 | chosing | 5 | coffin | 1 | compounded | 2 | consumption |
| 1 | chozzen | 1 | coffins | 1 | compounds | 4 | contact |
| 1 | christendom | 1 | cogitating | 8 | comprehend | 3 | contained |
| 2 | christened | 1 | cogitations | 3 | comprehended | 2 | containing |
| 5 | christian | 2 | coincide | 3 | comprehending | 1 | contaminate |
| 5 | christmas | 36 | cold | 1 | comprehends | 1 | contemplate |
| 2 | chubby | 2 | colder | 2 | comprehension | 1 | contemplated |
| 1 | chuck | 1 | coldly | 1 | compressing | 2 | contemplating |
| 1 | chucked | 2 | coldness | 2 | compulsion | 1 | contemplation |
| 1 | chuckled | 1 | colds | 1 | compulsory | 9 | contempt |
| 12 | church | 1 | cole | 2 | compunction | 2 | contemptible |
| 4 | churchyard | 1 | collar | 10 | conceal | 2 | contemptuously |
| 1 | churl | 2 | collect | 9 | concealed | 9 | content |
| 1 | churlish | 1 | collected | 1 | concealing | 6 | contented |
| 1 | churstmas | 2 | collecting | 2 | concealment | 1 | contentedly |
| 4 | cinders | 1 | collection | 1 | conceals | 10 | contents |
| 1 | cipher | 2 | college | 2 | conceit | 1 | continent |
| 3 | circle | 2 | colony | 2 | conceited | 3 | continual |
| 1 | circuit | 2 | colossal | 3 | conceive | 10 | continually |
| 5 | circumstance | 6 | colour | 1 | conceived | 12 | continue |
| 8 | circumstances | 2 | coloured | 1 | concentrate | 67 | continued |
| 4 | civil | 1 | colourless | 1 | concentrated | 1 | contort |
| 1 | civilities | 2 | colours | 3 | concern | 1 | contracted |
| 3 | civility | 1 | colt | 1 | concernedly | 5 | contradict |
| 1 | civilized | 1 | colt's | 15 | concerning | 1 | contradiction |
| 4 | claim | 1 | colts | 3 | concerns | 1 | contrariety |
| 1 | claimant | 1 | column | 1 | concessions | 8 | contrary |
| 2 | claimed | 1 | comb | 6 | concluded | 2 | contrast |
| 1 | clamber | 2 | combat | 3 | concluding | 2 | contribute |
| 1 | clambered | 1 | combatants | 6 | conclusion | 1 | contributed |
| 1 | clambering | 5 | combed | 2 | conclusions | 1 | contributes |
| 1 | clamorously | 1 | combine | 1 | concourse | 1 | contributing |
| 1 | clamour | 1 | combing | 4 | condemned | 1 | contributions |
| 1 | clamourous | 188 | come | 1 | condensed | 1 | contrite |
| 1 | clane | 1 | comed | 1 | condescend | 1 | contrivances |
| 1 | clapped | 1 | comer | 1 | condescending-ly | 4 | contrive |
| 1 | clarionets | 13 | comes | | | 6 | contrived |
| 1 | clasp | 16 | comfort | 17 | condition | 1 | contrives |
| 2 | clasped | 5 | comfortable | 1 | condoled | 1 | control |
| 2 | clasping | 3 | comfortably | 1 | condolences | 5 | convalescence |
| 2 | class | 3 | comforted | 20 | conduct | 1 | convalescent |
| 3 | clatter | 1 | comforting | 2 | conducted | 1 | convenience |
| 1 | clause | 1 | comfortless | 1 | conducting | 1 | convenient |
| 1 | claws | 3 | comforts | 1 | cones | 1 | conveniently |
| 1 | clay | 56 | coming | 8 | confess | 1 | conversant |
| 4 | clean | 8 | command | 1 | confessed | 16 | conversation |
| 1 | cleaner | 1 | commanded | 2 | confession | 1 | conversations |
| 1 | cleaning | 1 | commanding | 1 | confessions | 1 | converse |
| 13 | clear | 1 | commands | 1 | confidant | 1 | conversing |
| 3 | cleared | 5 | commence | 1 | confide | 3 | converted |
| 1 | clearing | 28 | commenced | 3 | confidence | 1 | converting |
| 3 | clearly | 6 | commencement | 1 | confident | 3 | convey |
| 1 | cleaved | 2 | commencing | 2 | confidently | 3 | conveyed |
| 1 | clefts | 1 | commendation | 1 | confiding | 2 | conveying |
| 5 | clenched | 3 | commendations | 1 | confine | 4 | conviction |
| 1 | clenching | 1 | commending | 5 | confined | 8 | convince |
| 1 | clergy | 2 | comment | 2 | confinement | 15 | convinced |
| 1 | clergyman | 2 | commentary | 5 | confirmed | 2 | convulsed |
| 1 | clergyman's | 1 | commenting | 1 | confirming | 2 | convulsions |
| 2 | clever | 1 | comments | 1 | conflagration | 1 | convulsively |
| 1 | cleverly | 1 | comminations | 1 | conflict | 1 | cooked |
| 2 | click | 1 | commissioned | 1 | confluence | 1 | cookery |
| 1 | climax | 1 | commit | 2 | confound | 1 | cooks |
| 5 | climb | 6 | committed | 10 | confounded | 6 | cool |
| 5 | climbed | 1 | committing | 2 | confused | 3 | coolly |
| 1 | climbing | 12 | common | 6 | confusion | 1 | coolness |
| 1 | clinging | 1 | commonest | 1 | congratulating | 3 | coom |
| 8 | cloak | 1 | commonly | 1 | congratulation | 1 | coorting |
| 1 | cloaks | 2 | communicated | 2 | congregation | 1 | copestone |
| 7 | clock | 4 | communication | 3 | conjecture | 1 | copious |
| 1 | cloes | 1 | communion | 7 | conjectured | 1 | copper |
| 1 | cloised | 1 | compactly | 2 | conjectures | 1 | coquette |
| 25 | close | 38 | companion | 2 | conjuring | 1 | cord |
| 1 | close-handed | 1 | companion's | 1 | connect | 4 | cordial |
| 23 | closed | 1 | companionable | 4 | connected | 1 | cordiality |

| | | | |
|---|---|---|---|
| 5 corn | 1 croaker | 32 dark | 1 deigned |
| 21 corner | 1 croaking | 2 darkened | 1 deity |
| 5 corners | 1 croaks | 6 darkness | 1 dejected |
| 3 corpse | 2 crocuses | 18 darling | 6 delay |
| 1 corpse's | 2 crooked | 1 darlings | 3 delayed |
| 1 corpses | 1 crooked-legged | 1 darnut | 1 delectably |
| 3 correct | 1 cropped | 2 darr | 1 delegated |
| 2 correcting | 1 cropping | 2 dart | 1 delf-case |
| 1 correction | 1 crops | 1 darting | 6 deliberate |
| 4 correctly | 15 cross | 2 dash | 5 deliberately |
| 1 correspond | 1 cross-examina-<br> tion | 9 dashed | 5 delicate |
| 2 correspondence | | 3 dashing | 10 delight |
| 1 corresponding | 2 cross-roads | 1 dastardly | 7 delighted |
| 1 corroborating | 9 crossed | 3 date | 1 delightedly |
| 1 corroboration | 1 crosser | 1 dated | 5 delightful |
| 2 corrugated | 1 crosses | 1 daubed | 2 delightfully |
| 1 costly | 1 crossest | 11 daughter | 1 delighting |
| 1 cotch | 2 crossing | 1 daughter's | 1 delights |
| 1 cote | 3 crossly | 5 daughter-in-l-<br> aw | 2 delirious |
| 4 cottage | 1 crouched | | 1 deliriously |
| 3 couch | 1 crowded | 1 daunted | 2 delirium |
| 5 cough | 1 crown | 8 dawn | 4 deliver |
| 2 coughed | 14 cruel | 88 day | 2 deliverance |
| 2 coughing | 2 cruelly | 2 day's | 10 delivered |
| 1 coughs | 2 cruelty | 1 day-dawn | 1 dells |
| 281 could | 1 crumbling | 2 daylight | 1 delude |
| 38 couldn't | 6 crush | 34 days | 2 deluded |
| 5 counsel | 3 crushed | 40 dead | 1 deluge |
| 4 counselled | 1 crushing | 1 deadens | 3 delusion |
| 1 counsellor | 1 crust | 2 deadly | 1 delusive |
| 1 count | 29 cry | 5 deaf | 1 delve |
| 1 counted | 23 crying | 15 deal | 7 demand |
| 1 countenanance | 1 cub | 1 dealing | 21 demanded |
| 37 countenance | 1 cuckoo's | 43 dean | 2 demolish |
| 1 countenances | 1 cuckoos | 6 dean's | 1 demolished |
| 1 counter-rappi-<br> ngs | 1 cud | 29 dear | 1 demon |
| | 1 cudgel | 2 dearer | 1 demons |
| 1 counteract | 1 cuffed | 1 dearly | 3 demonstrations |
| 1 counterpart | 1 culinary | 1 dearth | 1 demurely |
| 2 counting | 1 cullenders | 46 death | 5 den |
| 19 country | 1 culpable | 2 death-bed | 3 denial |
| 1 country-side | 1 culpably | 1 death-like | 2 denied |
| 8 couple | 1 culprit | 1 deaved | 2 denominated |
| 1 coupled | 1 cultivate | 1 debased | 1 denomination |
| 12 courage | 1 cultivation | 2 debt | 1 denounce |
| 21 course | 2 cunning | 1 debts | 1 dens |
| 1 coursed | 1 cunningly | 1 decamp | 3 deny |
| 17 court | 8 cup | 1 decanter | 1 denying |
| 2 courtesy | 2 cupboard | 2 decay | 9 depart |
| 1 courting | 1 cups | 1 decayed | 18 departed |
| 60 cousin | 1 cur | 3 decease | 9 departure |
| 5 cousin's | 12 curate | 1 deceit | 1 depended |
| 2 cousins | 1 curbed | 1 deceitful | 1 dependence |
| 5 cover | 3 cure | 3 deceive | 1 deplorable |
| 11 covered | 3 cured | 2 deceived | 1 deportment |
| 5 covering | 8 curiosity | 1 deceiver | 2 deposited |
| 3 covet | 8 curious | 1 deceiving | 1 depreciated |
| 2 coveting | 2 curiousity | 7 decent | 1 depreciation |
| 2 covetousness | 3 curiously | 2 decently | 3 depressed |
| 3 cow | 4 curl | 1 decide | 1 depression |
| 4 coward | 4 curled | 3 decided | 1 depressions |
| 1 coward's | 2 curling | 1 decidedly | 1 deprive |
| 3 cowardice | 6 curls | 2 decision | 3 deprived |
| 4 cowardly | 3 currant | 2 decisively | 1 dept |
| 1 cowards | 1 currently | 1 decked | 2 depth |
| 1 cowed | 1 curs | 1 declare | 2 depths |
| 2 cows | 3 curse | 4 declared | 1 deranged |
| 1 coxcomb | 4 cursed | 4 declined | 1 derangement |
| 1 cracked | 9 curses | 2 declining | 1 derelictions |
| 1 cracking | 6 cursing | 1 decorum | 1 deriding |
| 1 crackling | 3 curtain | 1 decoying | 2 derision |
| 1 cracky | 1 curtainless | 1 decypher | 1 derived |
| 1 cradle | 4 curtains | 1 dee | 1 derives |
| 1 craft | 4 cushion | 1 deead | 1 desarve |
| 3 crag | 2 custody | 6 deed | 2 descend |
| 5 craggs | 4 custom | 3 deeds | 12 descended |
| 2 crags | 1 customary | 1 deem | 1 descendent |
| 1 crahnr's | 19 cut | 5 deemed | 5 descending |
| 1 cram | 2 cutting | 25 deep | 2 descent |
| 1 crammed | 1 cynic | 1 deep-rooted | 4 describe |
| 1 cramming | 1 dacent | 1 deepened | 1 described |
| 1 cranky | 1 dad | 4 deeper | 1 describing |
| 1 crash | 5 daddy | 4 deeply | 1 description |
| 1 crater | 6 dahn | 1 default | 1 descriptive |
| 1 craters | 1 daht | 1 defeat | 2 desert |
| 1 craving | 11 daily | 1 defective | 5 deserted |
| 1 creak | 3 dainties | 2 defects | 1 desertion |
| 1 create | 1 daintiness | 2 defend | 7 deserve |
| 1 created | 3 dainty | 1 defended | 4 deserved |
| 1 creating | 4 dairy | 1 defending | 3 deserves |
| 2 creation | 1 dam'n | 1 defensive | 3 design |
| 21 creature | 2 damaged | 3 defer | 1 designed |
| 3 creatures | 7 dame | 1 deferred | 2 designing |
| 3 credit | 12 damn | 1 defiance | 3 designs |
| 1 creditor's | 3 damnable | 1 deficiencies | 1 desirable |
| 1 credulity | 2 damnably | 1 deficiency | 24 desire |
| 3 creep | 2 damnation | 2 deficient | 14 desired |
| 3 creeping | 7 damned | 1 defied | 2 desires |
| 7 crept | 4 damp | 1 defies | 8 desiring |
| 1 crescents | 1 damper | 1 definite | 4 desirous |
| 1 crest-fallen | 1 damsel | 1 deformed | 1 desisted |
| 1 crew | 8 dance | 2 defy | 1 desisting |
| 115 cried | 1 dancing | 2 defying | 1 desolate |
| 3 cries | 12 danger | 1 defyingly | 2 desolation |
| 4 crimson | 1 dangerous | 1 degenerates | 6 despair |
| 1 crimson-cover-<br> ed | 2 dangerously | 7 degradation | 1 despaired |
| | 1 dappled | 3 degrade | 1 despairing |
| 1 cringing | 37 dare | 1 degraded | 2 despairingly |
| 3 crisis | 10 dared | 3 degrading | 4 despatched |
| 2 critical | 1 dares | 3 degree | 7 desperate |
| 1 croaked | 3 daring | 4 degrees | 2 desperately |

2 desperation
8 despise
4 despised
1 despond
3 despondency
1 despot's
1 destination
1 destined
2 destiny
1 destitute
4 destroy
1 destroyed
1 destroying
2 destruction
2 detached
1 details
3 detain
1 detainer's
8 detect
8 detected
1 detention
2 deterioration
1 determination
2 determine
14 determined
3 detest
3 detestable
2 detestably
2 detestation
2 detested
2 detests
1 deuce
1 devastate
1 devastation
32 devil
3 devil's
2 devilish
3 devoid
1 devotedly
3 devotion
2 devour
1 devoured
1 devouring
1 dew
1 dewy
8 diabolical
1 diamond
1 diamonds
1 diary
1 dice
1 dictating
1 dictionary
241 did
52 didn't
1 didst
29 die
20 died
1 dies
1 differ
4 difference
11 different
2 differently
1 differing
3 difficult
5 difficulty
3 dig
1 digest
1 digging
2 dignified
3 dignity
1 dilapidation
2 dilating
1 dilatory
5 dim
1 diminishing
4 dimly
1 dimmed
2 din
4 dine
2 dingy
19 dinner
3 dinner-time
1 dins
1 dip
1 dips
5 direct
4 directed
3 directing
6 direction
7 directions
27 directly
1 directs
1 dirtily
9 dirty
1 dis-relish
1 disadvantage
1 disadvantages
5 disagreeable
1 disagreebly
2 disagreement
1 disagreements
1 disappearance
3 disappeared
2 disappoint
8 disappointed
6 disappointment
2 disapproved
1 disapprovingly
1 disarm
1 disarmed
1 disarrange

1 disarrangement
1 discarded
4 discerned
3 discerning
1 discharge
1 discharged
1 discipline
1 disclosure
1 discomfited
1 discomfiture
2 discontent
1 discord
6 discourse
1 discoursing
13 discover
17 discovered
1 discoverer
2 discovering
1 discovery
1 discreet
1 discretion
2 discussed
4 discussing
2 discussion
1 disdainfully
1 disdaining
1 disease
1 disenchanted
2 disengage
1 disengaged
2 disgrace
2 disgraceful
1 disgraces
4 disguise
1 disguised
1 disguising
5 disgust
3 disgusted
1 dish
1 dishcloth
3 dishes
1 disinclined
5 dislike
3 disliked
1 dislikes
13 dismal
1 dismally
3 dismiss
1 dismissal
2 dismissed
1 dismisses
2 dismount
3 dismounted
1 dismounting
2 disobedience
2 disobey
3 disorder
1 disordered
1 disorderly
1 disown
1 disowned
1 disparagement
1 disparity
1 dispatch
2 dispel
1 displaced
1 displacing
1 display
2 displayed
1 displaying
1 displays
5 displeasure
1 disposal
2 disposed
8 disposition
1 dispositions
1 disputant
6 dispute
1 disputed
1 disputes
2 disputing
1 disquietude
2 disregard
1 disregarded
3 disregarding
1 disrespect
1 dissented
1 dissimilar
1 dissipation
1 dissolve
1 dissolved
1 dissolving
18 distance
2 distant
2 distasteful
4 distinct
4 distinction
3 distinctly
3 distinguish
2 distinguishab-
le
6 distinguished
3 distorted
1 distract
2 distracted
2 distraction
1 distraught
9 distress
4 distressed
2 distresses
1 distressing

1 district
7 disturb
4 disturbance
7 disturbed
1 disturber
2 disturbing
1 diurnal
3 dived
4 diversion
1 diversions
4 divert
2 diverted
2 diverting
1 divested
1 divide
7 divided
3 dividing
4 divil
2 divil's
4 divine
6 divined
1 division
1 dizzily
1 dizzy
256 do
20 doctor
3 doctor's
1 documents
56 does
4 doesn't
23 dog
1 dog's
2 dog-kennel
1 dogged
2 doggedly
12 dogs
26 doing
3 doleful
1 dolefully
2 doll
1 domestic
1 domestic's
1 domestics
1 domineer
2 domineering
180 don't
62 done
4 donned
1 donning
2 dont
4 doomed
119 door
1 door-handle
1 door-latch
5 door-stones
3 door-way
27 doors
1 doorstones
2 doorway
6 dose
1 dosed
1 dot
1 dote
2 doted
1 dotes
1 dots
1 dotted
7 double
25 doubt
2 doubted
2 doubtfully
3 doubting
1 doubtingly
4 doubtless
4 doubts
1 dour
1 dove
1 dove's
174 down
2 downright
2 downs
1 doze
1 dozed
2 dozen
1 dozing
2 drag
3 dragged
4 dragging
5 drank
2 drapery
1 draughts
14 draw
5 drawer
1 drawers
9 drawing
2 drawing-room
2 drawled
1 drawling
2 drawn
10 dread
3 dreaded
7 dreadful
4 dreadfully
1 dreading
14 dream
2 dreamily
5 dreaming
9 dreams
9 dreamt
2 dreamy
13 dreary

1 dree
1 dree'
1 drench
1 drenched
12 dress
8 dressed
7 dresser
2 dressing
30 drew
2 dried
2 drifts
14 drink
5 drinking
1 dripped
3 dripping
8 drive
6 driven
3 driving
1 drizzle
1 droll
5 drop
18 dropped
3 dropping
2 drops
1 dropt
4 drove
3 drowned
2 drowsily
1 drowsiness
1 drowsy
5 drunk
12 dry
1 dry-eyed
1 dryer
4 drying
1 duck
7 due
2 dug
3 dull
1 duller
1 duly
9 dumb
4 dunce
1 dungeon
1 dunnock
1 dunnot
3 dunnut
1 duration
28 during
1 durst
6 dusk
2 dusky
7 dust
1 duster
1 dusters
1 dusting
5 duties
1 dutiful
13 duty
1 dwarf
1 dwell
5 dwelling
1 dwelt
1 dwindling
17 dying
1 e
1 e'en
46 each
8 eager
12 eagerly
4 eagerness
15 ear
1 ear-shot
6 earlier
3 earliest
22 early
3 earn
1 earned
13 earnest
8 earnestly
2 earnestness
1 earning
116 earnshaw
16 earnshaw's
2 earnshaws
1 earnshaws'
16 ears
1 earshot
23 earth
1 earthenware
2 earthly
1 earthy
14 ease
7 easily
2 east
1 easter
7 easy
1 easy-chair
18 eat
1 eatable
3 eaten
9 eating
1 eats
1 eaves-droppers
1 eavesdropper
1 eccentric
10 ech
1 echo
2 echoed
1 ecstacy
1 ecstasy

| | | | |
|---|---|---|---|
| 104 edgar | 10 ended | 2 events | 3 expostulated |
| 12 edgar's | 1 endless | 68 ever | 1 expostulating |
| 4 edge | 2 ends | 87 every | 3 expostulations |
| 2 edged | 1 endurable | 8 everybody | 8 express |
| 1 edges | 3 endurance | 1 everyone | 11 expressed |
| 1 edition | 15 endure | 8 everything | 5 expressing |
| 4 education | 5 endured | 1 everywhere | 25 expression |
| 1 ee | 2 enduring | 2 evidence | 3 expressions |
| 2 eea | 8 enemies | 1 evident | 1 expressive |
| 1 eedle | 6 enemy | 16 evidently | 3 exquisite |
| 1 een | 1 enemy's | 14 evil | 2 extended |
| 5 effect | 2 energetically | 2 evince | 2 extent |
| 7 effects | 1 energies | 7 evinced | 3 exterior |
| 3 effectually | 2 energy | 2 evincing | 4 external |
| 1 effeminate | 5 eneugh | 2 exact | 1 extinct |
| 1 efficient | 2 engage | 1 exacting | 1 extinguish |
| 1 efficiently | 6 engaged | 13 exactly | 6 extinguished |
| 4 effort | 1 engagement | 1 exaggerate | 1 extinguisher |
| 4 efforts | 1 engaging | 3 exaggerated | 2 extinguishing |
| 1 eft's | 5 england | 1 exaggeratedly | 1 extorted |
| 1 egg | 2 english | 1 exalting | 3 extra |
| 1 eggs | 1 engrossing | 3 examination | 1 extra-animal |
| 1 egotism | 1 enigmatical | 8 examine | 2 extract |
| 1 egress | 11 enjoy | 5 examined | 1 extraordinary |
| 5 eh | 8 enjoying | 1 examining | 2 extreme |
| 1 eht | 1 enjoyment | 3 example | 12 extremely |
| 8 eight | 1 enjoyments | 2 exasperate | 2 extremes |
| 8 eighteen | 1 enlarge | 1 exasperating | 1 extremities |
| 2 eighty | 1 enlightened | 1 exceeded | 1 extremity |
| 34 either | 1 enlightening | 1 exceeding | 1 extricate |
| 5 ejaculated | 1 enlisted | 13 exceedingly | 1 exuberance |
| 1 ejaculating | 1 enormous | 1 excellencies | 2 exultation |
| 4 ejaculation | 55 enough | 1 excellent | 1 exulting |
| 1 ejaculations | 7 enquired | 1 excellently | 22 eye |
| 1 elapsed | 3 enraged | 28 except | 1 eye-sight |
| 2 elastic | 1 ensconcing | 3 excepting | 1 eyed |
| 1 elation | 2 ensued | 4 exception | 2 eyeing |
| 2 elbow | 2 ensure | 3 excess | 117 eyes |
| 1 elbows | 1 entangled | 2 excessive | 1 f'r |
| 4 elder | 16 enter | 3 exchange | 1 fabulous |
| 1 elder's | 44 entered | 2 exchanged | 101 face |
| 3 elderly | 9 entering | 5 exchanging | 12 faces |
| 1 electric | 1 enters | 1 excite | 1 facial |
| 1 elegance | 4 entertain | 7 excited | 1 facing |
| 1 elegancies | 2 entertained | 2 excitement | 12 fact |
| 2 elegant | 1 entertainer | 2 exciting | 1 facts |
| 1 elevate | 2 entertaining | 2 exclaim | 3 faculties |
| 2 elevated | 3 entertainment | 74 exclaimed | 1 faculty |
| 2 elevation | 1 entertains | 8 exclaiming | 2 faded |
| 4 eleven | 2 entice | 3 exclamation | 3 fading |
| 2 elf-bolts | 1 enticed | 2 exclude | 1 fagots |
| 1 elf-locked | 5 entire | 1 excluded | 2 fahl |
| 1 elicit | 20 entirely | 1 excommunicated | 2 fail |
| 99 ellen | 1 entrails | 6 excursion | 3 failed |
| 2 eloquence | 17 entrance | 1 excursions | 1 failing |
| 1 eloquent | 7 entreated | 12 excuse | 1 failings |
| 2 eloquently | 7 entreaties | 3 excused | 1 failure |
| 47 else | 1 entreating | 1 execrated | 8 fain |
| 2 elsewhere | 2 entreaty | 2 execrations | 10 faint |
| 1 elysium | 1 entrust | 4 execute | 1 faint-hearted |
| 1 em | 1 envied | 1 executed | 2 fainted |
| 1 embalming | 3 envious | 3 execution | 15 fair |
| 4 embarrassed | 4 envy | 1 exelaimed | 1 fairies |
| 1 embarrassing | 1 envying | 2 exercise | 1 fairishes |
| 2 embarrassment | 2 epistle | 1 exerted | 6 fairly |
| 1 embellishment | 2 epistles | 2 exerting | 8 fairy |
| 2 embers | 1 epithet | 1 exertions | 1 faishion |
| 1 embodies | 6 equal | 4 exhausted | 6 faith |
| 7 embrace | 1 equality | 1 exhausting | 5 faithful |
| 1 embracing | 1 equalled | 2 exhaustion | 1 faithfully |
| 1 embrowned | 6 equally | 3 exhibit | 18 fall |
| 1 emerge | 2 equanimity | 2 exhibited | 8 fallen |
| 1 emerging | 1 equipping | 1 exhibiting | 1 falling |
| 1 emissaries | 1 erase | 3 exhibition | 2 falls |
| 7 emotion | 16 ere | 3 exile | 4 false |
| 1 emperor | 4 erect | 4 exist | 3 falsehood |
| 1 emphasis | 1 erected | 1 existed | 4 falsehoods |
| 1 emphatically | 1 erecting | 19 existence | 6 familiar |
| 1 employed | 5 errand | 4 exit | 1 familiarity |
| 1 employer | 1 errands | 1 exotic | 30 family |
| 1 employer's | 1 erred | 1 expanded | 1 famous |
| 1 employers | 4 error | 1 expanding | 11 fancied |
| 2 employing | 14 escape | 1 expansive | 2 fancies |
| 4 employment | 9 escaped | 15 expect | 2 fanciful |
| 3 employments | 3 escaping | 2 expectation | 25 fancy |
| 1 empower | 3 escort | 3 expectations | 3 fancying |
| 3 emptied | 2 escorted | 16 expected | 1 fangs |
| 5 empty | 9 especially | 4 expecting | 2 fanny |
| 1 emulated | 1 espionage | 1 expects | 1 fantastic |
| 1 emulous | 2 essay | 3 expedient | 45 far |
| 1 enable | 1 essayed | 1 expedition | 1 far-off |
| 2 enabled | 1 essence | 1 expeditions | 6 farm |
| 1 enacted | 2 establish | 1 expeditiously | 4 farm-house |
| 1 enah | 3 established | 1 expences | 2 farmer |
| 1 enchanting | 2 establishment | 4 expense | 2 farmhouse |
| 7 enclosed | 3 estate | 1 expensive | 2 farming |
| 1 encompassed | 1 estates | 5 experience | 8 farther |
| 6 encounter | 5 esteem | 9 experienced | 2 farthing |
| 5 encountered | 7 esteemed | 1 experiments | 1 fascinating |
| 3 encountering | 1 estimating | 1 expire | 1 fascination |
| 6 encourage | 3 eternal | 1 expiring | 8 fashion |
| 4 encouraged | 6 eternally | 12 explain | 23 fast |
| 2 encouraging | 1 eternity | 6 explained | 2 fasted |
| 1 encouragingly | 1 evaporated | 3 explaining | 4 fasten |
| 1 encroached | 1 evasive | 6 explanation | 11 fastened |
| 29 end | 1 eve | 2 explanations | 2 fastening |
| 1 endearment | 49 even | 1 explode | 4 faster |
| 1 endeavour | 57 evening | 1 exploded | 1 fastidiousness |
| 6 endeavoured | 3 evening's | 2 explosion | 2 fasting |
| 8 endeavouring | 8 evenings | 4 exposed | 1 fat |
| 4 endeavours | 7 event | 2 exposing | 4 fate |

| | | | |
|---|---|---|---|
| 1 fated | 4 filling | 1 foe | 1 fourth |
| 101 father | 1 final | 3 foes | 1 fowks |
| 22 father's | 18 finally | 1 foil | 1 fowling |
| 3 father-in-law | 25 find | 3 fold | 1 fox |
| 1 father-in-law-'s | 10 finding | 4 folded | 1 fractions |
| | 1 finds | 1 folds | 1 fragile |
| 1 fatherless | 22 fine | 3 foliage | 2 fragments |
| 1 fathers' | 1 finer | 3 folk | 1 fragrance |
| 1 fathur's | 2 finest | 3 folks | 1 fragrant |
| 7 fatigue | 6 finger | 17 follow | 1 frail |
| 1 fatigued | 1 finger-ends | 23 followed | 15 frame |
| 8 fault | 32 fingers | 1 followers | 2 framed |
| 5 faults | 7 finish | 13 following | 1 framing |
| 1 favour | 11 finished | 2 follows | 4 frances |
| 5 favourable | 4 finishing | 7 folly | 1 frangrance |
| 2 favoured | 3 fir | 13 fond | 2 frank |
| 7 favourite | 1 fir-tree | 2 fonder | 2 frankly |
| 1 favourite's | 1 firbough | 2 fondest | 6 frantic |
| 3 favourites | 69 fire | 2 fondling | 1 fraternal |
| 1 favours | 1 fire-flushed | 6 fondness | 16 free |
| 1 fawn | 5 fire-place | 9 food | 1 freeing |
| 1 fawning | 2 fire-side | 1 fooil | 2 freely |
| 39 fear | 1 firelight | 1 fooit | 1 freer |
| 1 feard | 2 fireplace | 16 fool | 3 french |
| 9 feared | 2 fires | 1 fool's | 1 frenzied |
| 5 fearful | 1 firing | 1 fool's-craving | 5 frenzy |
| 4 fearfully | 2 firm | 16 foolish | 3 frequent |
| 1 fearing | 1 firmer | 3 foolishly | 13 frequently |
| 1 fearless | 1 firmly | 1 foolishness | 9 fresh |
| 4 fears | 3 firs | 1 fools | 1 fresher |
| 1 feast | 111 first | 14 foot | 3 fret |
| 1 feather | 2 first-rate | 1 foot-stool | 3 fretful |
| 1 feathered | 1 firstly | 1 footing | 1 fretfully |
| 2 feathers | 7 fist | 1 footmarks | 1 frets |
| 1 feathery | 4 fists | 1 footmen | 5 fretted |
| 1 feature | 32 fit | 2 footstep | 1 fretting |
| 24 features | 3 fits | 3 footsteps | 3 friday |
| 1 february | 1 fitted | 832 for | 31 friend |
| 1 fed | 20 five | 1 forbearance | 2 friendless |
| 7 feeble | 4 fix | 1 forbearing | 1 friendlessness |
| 1 feebleness | 19 fixed | 3 forbid | 4 friendly |
| 1 feebly | 1 fixing | 3 forbidden | 21 friends |
| 3 feed | 3 fixture | 1 forbidding | 2 friendship |
| 2 feeding | 1 flagged | 1 forbids | 3 fright |
| 1 feeing | 5 flags | 9 force | 7 frighten |
| 38 feel | 4 flakes | 11 forced | 11 frightened |
| 17 feeling | 4 flame | 1 forces | 1 frightening |
| 18 feelings | 2 flames | 1 forcibly | 1 frightens |
| 3 feels | 1 flaming | 2 forcing | 9 frightful |
| 25 feet | 1 flapping | 1 forebodingly | 1 fringes |
| 1 feigned | 1 flash | 1 forebodings | 1 frittering |
| 1 feigning | 7 flashed | 1 foregathered | 2 frivolous |
| 32 fell | 2 flashing | 1 forego | 12 fro |
| 1 fellies | 1 flatly | 12 forehead | 9 frock |
| 17 fellow | 1 flatness | 1 foreign | 485 from |
| 2 fellow-servant | 4 flatter | 1 foreigners | 16 front |
| 1 fellow-servan-t's | 5 flattered | 2 foremost | 1 froo |
| | 2 flattering | 1 foresee | 2 froo' |
| 1 fellows | 1 flattery | 1 foresight | 5 frost |
| 1 fellowship | 3 flaxen | 1 forged | 3 frosty |
| 1 felony | 2 flaying | 15 forget | 1 frothing |
| 62 felt | 6 flaysome | 1 forgetful | 5 frough |
| 1 female | 2 flee | 1 forgetfulness | 3 frown |
| 1 females | 1 fleecy | 1 forgets | 4 frowned |
| 2 fence | 1 flees | 4 forgetting | 2 frowning |
| 1 fend | 7 flesh | 1 forgie | 1 frozen |
| 1 fender | 8 flew | 19 forgive | 4 fruit |
| 4 ferocious | 1 flies | 2 forgiven | 1 fryingpan |
| 1 ferociously | 3 flight | 2 forgiveness | 1 fugitives |
| 4 ferocity | 1 flighted | 4 forgot | 4 fulfil |
| 1 ferret | 1 flights | 10 forgotten | 6 fulfilled |
| 1 fertile | 2 flighty | 2 fork | 2 fulfilling |
| 1 fervently | 1 flinched | 1 forks | 1 fulfilment |
| 1 fervour | 4 fling | 1 forlorn | 35 full |
| 1 festoons | 7 flinging | 6 form | 4 fully |
| 13 fetch | 1 flings | 1 form's | 1 fulness |
| 2 fetched | 1 flint | 1 formal | 3 fun |
| 1 fetches | 1 flinty | 1 formally | 11 funeral |
| 1 fetching | 1 flippant | 11 formed | 1 fungus |
| 1 feud | 2 flit | 26 former | 2 funny |
| 9 fever | 5 flitting | 6 formerly | 13 fur |
| 2 feverish | 1 floating | 2 forming | 1 fur-lined |
| 1 fevers | 1 flock | 3 forms | 7 furious |
| 42 few | 1 flog | 1 forrard | 3 furiously |
| 1 ffin | 2 flogged | 2 forsake | 1 furnace-heat |
| 1 fickleness | 4 flogging | 1 forsaken | 1 furnish |
| 2 fiddle | 1 flooding | 13 forth | 2 furnished |
| 2 fidgetting | 24 floor | 1 forthwith | 4 furniture |
| 3 fie | 1 floundered | 3 fortnight | 1 furred |
| 3 field | 1 flour | 1 fortunate | 1 furs |
| 3 fields | 3 flourishing | 7 fortunately | 38 further |
| 12 fiend | 3 flow | 4 fortune | 7 fury |
| 1 fiend's | 2 flowed | 1 fortune-teller | 1 furze |
| 2 fiendish | 2 flower | 1 fortunes | 8 future |
| 3 fiends | 1 flower-plot | 2 forty | 1 g |
| 6 fierce | 1 flower-pot | 1 forty-five | 1 gable |
| 2 fiercely | 5 flowers | 20 forward | 1 gadding |
| 2 fiercer | 1 flown | 2 forwarded | 2 gaily |
| 1 fiercest | 1 flows | 1 forwardly | 4 gain |
| 2 fiery | 1 fluent | 2 forwards | 8 gained |
| 3 fifteen | 17 flung | 4 foster | 1 gaining |
| 1 fifth | 2 flurried | 1 fostered | 4 gait |
| 4 fifty | 1 flurry | 2 fought | 1 gaiters |
| 5 fight | 4 flushed | 1 foul | 2 gall |
| 1 fighting | 1 fluttered | 1 foul-mouthed | 1 gallon |
| 1 figuratively | 1 fluttering | 48 found | 2 gallop |
| 7 figure | 1 flutterings | 1 founded | 3 galloped |
| 2 figures | 2 fly | 24 four | 2 galloping |
| 2 filial | 1 fly-leaf | 1 four-footed | 1 gallops |
| 1 fill | 6 flying | 2 fourteen | 1 galloway |
| 14 filled | 1 foamed | | 2 gallows |

| | |
|---:|:---|
| 5 | game |
| 1 | gaming |
| 4 | gang |
| 1 | ganging |
| 1 | gangs |
| 2 | gap |
| 3 | gaping |
| 1 | gapingly |
| 1 | gaps |
| 1 | garb |
| 35 | garden |
| 1 | garden-wall |
| 2 | gardeners |
| 1 | gardens |
| 1 | garment |
| 5 | garments |
| 11 | garret |
| 1 | garrets |
| 1 | gasp |
| 7 | gasped |
| 2 | gasping |
| 24 | gate |
| 1 | gates |
| 7 | gather |
| 16 | gathered |
| 4 | gathering |
| 1 | gathers |
| 1 | gaudily |
| 1 | gaumless |
| 3 | gaunt |
| 1 | gauze |
| 46 | gave |
| 4 | gay |
| 17 | gaze |
| 13 | gazed |
| 6 | gazing |
| 4 | general |
| 1 | generality |
| 17 | generally |
| 1 | generosity |
| 3 | generous |
| 2 | generously |
| 2 | genial |
| 2 | genius |
| 8 | gentle |
| 12 | gentleman |
| 1 | gentleman's |
| 1 | gentlemanly |
| 2 | gentleness |
| 7 | gently |
| 1 | gentry |
| 3 | genuine |
| 120 | get |
| 7 | gets |
| 4 | getten |
| 16 | getting |
| 3 | ghastly |
| 3 | ghost |
| 2 | ghostly |
| 6 | ghosts |
| 1 | ghoul |
| 1 | ghoulish |
| 1 | gibberish |
| 1 | giddiness |
| 1 | giddy |
| 2 | gie |
| 1 | gies |
| 1 | gift |
| 2 | gifts |
| 1 | giggled |
| 1 | gimmerden |
| 36 | gimmerton |
| 1 | gin |
| 1 | gingerbread |
| 5 | gipsy |
| 24 | girl |
| 1 | girlhood |
| 3 | girlish |
| 1 | girls |
| 1 | girn |
| 1 | girned |
| 1 | girnning |
| 1 | girt |
| 69 | give |
| 13 | given |
| 1 | gives |
| 11 | giving |
| 32 | glad |
| 1 | gladdened |
| 5 | gladly |
| 1 | gladness |
| 20 | glance |
| 10 | glanced |
| 2 | glances |
| 2 | glancing |
| 2 | glare |
| 1 | glared |
| 1 | glaring |
| 2 | glaringly |
| 13 | glass |
| 1 | glass-drops |
| 4 | gleam |
| 3 | gleamed |
| 1 | glee |
| 1 | gleefully |
| 1 | glees |
| 2 | glen |
| 1 | glens |
| 2 | glided |
| 1 | gliding |
| 2 | glimmered |
| 10 | glimpse |
| 1 | glimpses |
| 1 | glinting |
| 1 | glisten |
| 2 | glitter |
| 2 | glittering |
| 6 | gloom |
| 3 | gloomy |
| 1 | glories |
| 2 | glorious |
| 1 | glory |
| 1 | glossy |
| 1 | gloves |
| 4 | glow |
| 5 | glowed |
| 1 | glowered |
| 2 | glowing |
| 1 | gnarl |
| 1 | gnash |
| 1 | gnashed |
| 1 | gnasher |
| 175 | go |
| 6 | goa |
| 7 | goaded |
| 2 | goal |
| 4 | goan |
| 1 | goas |
| 5 | goblin |
| 1 | goblins |
| 37 | god |
| 5 | god's |
| 1 | goddess |
| 1 | godless |
| 7 | goes |
| 88 | going |
| 2 | goings |
| 6 | gold |
| 5 | golden |
| 51 | gone |
| 1 | gong |
| 107 | good |
| 2 | good-bye |
| 1 | good-evening |
| 2 | good-hearted |
| 1 | good-humoured |
| 3 | good-night |
| 1 | goodnatured |
| 1 | goodness |
| 2 | goods |
| 6 | gooid |
| 1 | gooid-fur-nowt |
| 1 | goold |
| 1 | goose |
| 1 | goose-berry |
| 2 | gooseberry |
| 1 | gospel |
| 4 | gossip |
| 1 | gossip's |
| 1 | gossipping |
| 79 | got |
| 1 | gouge |
| 2 | gown |
| 3 | grace |
| 3 | graceful |
| 1 | graceless |
| 1 | gracious |
| 1 | graden |
| 1 | gradual |
| 7 | gradually |
| 1 | grain |
| 6 | grand |
| 1 | grandest |
| 87 | grange |
| 1 | grant |
| 1 | granted |
| 1 | grappling |
| 5 | grasp |
| 3 | grasped |
| 2 | grasping |
| 1 | grasps |
| 9 | grass |
| 1 | grassy |
| 1 | grat |
| 3 | grate |
| 1 | grated |
| 1 | grateful |
| 1 | grates |
| 4 | gratification |
| 4 | gratified |
| 3 | gratitude |
| 23 | grave |
| 2 | gravely |
| 1 | graver |
| 3 | graves |
| 1 | gravestones |
| 2 | gravity |
| 1 | graze |
| 1 | grazed |
| 63 | great |
| 9 | greater |
| 5 | greatest |
| 10 | greatly |
| 3 | greedy |
| 2 | greek |
| 16 | green |
| 1 | greet |
| 3 | greeting |
| 34 | grew |
| 10 | grey |
| 1 | greyer |
| 1 | greyhound |
| 15 | grief |
| 2 | griefs |
| 2 | grievance |
| 5 | grieve |
| 12 | grieved |
| 2 | grieving |
| 1 | grievous |
| 1 | grievously |
| 1 | griffins |
| 9 | grim |
| 1 | grimace |
| 1 | grimaces |
| 1 | grimalkin |
| 3 | grimly |
| 3 | grin |
| 1 | grind |
| 3 | grinding |
| 1 | grinds |
| 1 | grinned |
| 1 | grinning |
| 4 | gripe |
| 5 | groan |
| 4 | groaned |
| 5 | groaning |
| 1 | grooms |
| 2 | groped |
| 1 | grotesque |
| 20 | ground |
| 8 | grounds |
| 1 | group |
| 2 | grouse |
| 1 | grovel |
| 1 | grovelled |
| 11 | grow |
| 9 | growing |
| 7 | growled |
| 1 | growling |
| 11 | grown |
| 3 | grows |
| 1 | growth |
| 1 | grudge |
| 1 | grudged |
| 4 | gruel |
| 1 | gruff |
| 1 | gruffly |
| 1 | gruffness |
| 3 | grumbled |
| 2 | grumbling |
| 1 | grumblings |
| 1 | guaged |
| 3 | guard |
| 1 | guarded |
| 4 | guardian |
| 4 | guardianship |
| 1 | guarding |
| 1 | guards |
| 23 | guess |
| 13 | guessed |
| 2 | guesses |
| 2 | guessing |
| 13 | guest |
| 1 | guests |
| 1 | guffaw |
| 1 | guidance |
| 9 | guide |
| 1 | guide-post |
| 1 | guide-stone |
| 2 | guided |
| 1 | guides |
| 1 | guilp |
| 1 | guiltily |
| 1 | guiltless |
| 1 | guilty |
| 1 | gullet |
| 4 | gun |
| 2 | gunpowder |
| 2 | guns |
| 2 | gurgling |
| 2 | gush |
| 4 | gushed |
| 1 | gusto |
| 1 | gusty |
| 1 | guttural |
| 1 | gypsy |
| 1 | h |
| 2 | ha' |
| 11 | habit |
| 2 | habits |
| 3 | habitual |
| 2 | habituated |
| 686 | had |
| 1 | had'nt |
| 5 | hadn't |
| 3 | hae |
| 1 | hag |
| 3 | haggard |
| 1 | haggardness |
| 1 | hagh |
| 4 | hah |
| 3 | hahse |
| 2 | hahsiver |
| 1 | hahsomdiver |
| 1 | hailed |
| 1 | hailing |
| 38 | hair |
| 1 | hair-breadths |
| 1 | hairy |
| 1 | haks |
| 1 | hale |
| 67 | half |
| 1 | half-a-day |
| 5 | half-a-dozen |
| 3 | half-an-hour |
| 1 | half-bred |
| 1 | half-civilized |
| 2 | half-hour |
| 1 | half-open |
| 4 | half-past |
| 1 | half-way |
| 1 | half-whisper |
| 5 | hall |
| 2 | hallo |
| 3 | hallooed |
| 4 | halt |
| 7 | halted |
| 1 | halting |
| 1 | ham |
| 1 | hammer |
| 1 | hammers |
| 92 | hand |
| 3 | handed |
| 1 | handful |
| 2 | handfuls |
| 5 | handkerchief |
| 1 | handkerchir |
| 4 | handle |
| 59 | hands |
| 19 | handsome |
| 2 | handsomer |
| 1 | handsomest |
| 1 | handywork |
| 4 | hang |
| 1 | hanged |
| 9 | hanging |
| 6 | happen |
| 8 | happened |
| 1 | happening |
| 4 | happier |
| 3 | happiest |
| 6 | happily |
| 10 | happiness |
| 28 | happy |
| 2 | harass |
| 2 | harassed |
| 2 | harassing |
| 1 | harboured |
| 28 | hard |
| 2 | hardened |
| 1 | hardihood |
| 44 | hardly |
| 2 | hardness |
| 1 | hardy |
| 1 | hare-bells |
| 169 | hareton |
| 10 | hareton's |
| 1 | hark |
| 1 | harken |
| 12 | harm |
| 1 | harmed |
| 1 | harming |
| 3 | harmless |
| 1 | harmlessly |
| 1 | harmonized |
| 1 | harped |
| 1 | harried |
| 8 | harsh |
| 3 | harshness |
| 4 | harvest |
| 165 | has |
| 3 | hasn't |
| 1 | hasped |
| 9 | haste |
| 1 | hasten |
| 14 | hastened |
| 3 | hastening |
| 8 | hastily |
| 5 | hasty |
| 17 | hat |
| 38 | hate |
| 15 | hated |
| 2 | hateful |
| 6 | hates |
| 3 | hathecliff |
| 1 | hathecliff's |
| 2 | hatless |
| 6 | hatred |
| 1 | hauding |
| 1 | haughtier |
| 4 | haughty |
| 1 | haulf |
| 5 | haunt |
| 5 | haunted |
| 1 | haunts |
| 634 | have |
| 1 | haven |
| 2 | haven't |
| 78 | having |
| 1 | havoc |
| 4 | hay |
| 1 | hay-field |
| 1 | hay-loft |
| 2 | hazard |
| 1 | hazarding |
| 1 | hazel |
| 1 | hazel-nut |
| 1 | hazels |
| 1 | hazy |
| 1959 | he |
| 23 | he'd |
| 60 | he'll |
| 103 | he's |

| | |
|---|---|
| 91 | head |
| 2 | head-ache |
| 1 | head-downmost |
| 1 | head-stone |
| 1 | head-stones |
| 1 | headache |
| 6 | heads |
| 2 | headstone |
| 3 | headstrong |
| 20 | health |
| 1 | healthier |
| 6 | healthy |
| 3 | heap |
| 1 | heaped |
| 1 | heaping |
| 2 | heaps |
| 72 | hear |
| 79 | heard |
| 15 | hearing |
| 4 | hearken |
| 1 | hearsay |
| 79 | heart |
| 1 | heart's |
| 2 | heart-breaking |
| 1 | heart-broken |
| 27 | hearth |
| 1 | hearth-brush |
| 2 | hearth-stone |
| 5 | hearthstone |
| 1 | hearthstun |
| 6 | heartily |
| 1 | heartiness |
| 3 | heartless |
| 1 | heartlessness |
| 2 | hearts |
| 5 | hearty |
| 6 | heat |
| 13 | heath |
| 420 | heathcliff |
| 53 | heathcliff's |
| 1 | heathen |
| 1 | heathenism |
| 1 | heather |
| 1 | heather-scent- |
|  | ed |
| 1 | heating |
| 1 | heave |
| 3 | heaved |
| 21 | heaven |
| 5 | heaven's |
| 1 | heavens |
| 1 | heavier |
| 1 | heaviest |
| 3 | heaving |
| 9 | heavy |
| 1 | heavy-headed |
| 1 | hector |
| 1 | hed |
| 2 | hedge |
| 1 | hedge-cutters |
| 2 | heead |
| 1 | heed |
| 1 | heeding |
| 1 | heedless |
| 2 | heels |
| 1 | heen |
| 1 | heifers |
| 3 | height |
| 98 | heights |
| 6 | heir |
| 1 | heirs |
| 33 | held |
| 20 | hell |
| 2 | hellish |
| 1 | helmet |
| 32 | help |
| 3 | helped |
| 1 | helping |
| 2 | helpless |
| 2 | hemmed |
| 2 | hence |
| 1 | henceforth |
| 2 | hend |
| 1548 | her |
| 3 | her's |
| 1 | herbs |
| 2 | hercules |
| 1 | herd |
| 1 | herd-boy |
| 135 | here |
| 2 | here's |
| 12 | hereafter |
| 1 | heretofore |
| 2 | hermit |
| 1 | hermit's |
| 3 | hero |
| 1 | heroine |
| 1 | herrings |
| 14 | hers |
| 71 | herself |
| 3 | hesitate |
| 3 | hesitated |
| 1 | hesitating |
| 1 | hesitation |
| 1 | heterodox |
| 7 | hev |
| 1 | hev'em |
| 4 | hey |
| 4 | hia |
| 4 | hidden |
| 12 | hide |

| | |
|---|---|
| 3 | hideous |
| 1 | hieroglyphics |
| 17 | high |
| 1 | high-backed |
| 1 | high-water |
| 3 | higher |
| 1 | highest |
| 2 | highly |
| 2 | highway |
| 1 | highways |
| 1 | higs |
| 1 | hilarity |
| 1 | hill |
| 1 | hill-back |
| 1 | hillock |
| 1 | hillocks |
| 1 | hilltop |
| 1 | hilly |
| 19 | hills |
| 927 | him |
| 1 | him's |
| 125 | himself |
| 14 | hinder |
| 2 | hindered |
| 1 | hindering |
| 74 | hindley |
| 6 | hindley's |
| 2 | hinges |
| 5 | hint |
| 1 | hips |
| 1 | hired |
| 1 | hiring |
| 1424 | his |
| 7 | hisseln |
| 9 | history |
| 7 | hit |
| 4 | hither |
| 3 | hitherto |
| 1 | hitting |
| 1 | hive |
| 1 | hives |
| 1 | hivin |
| 1 | ho |
| 1 | hoard |
| 2 | hoarse |
| 1 | hoary |
| 2 | hob |
| 1 | hoile |
| 1 | hoile's |
| 38 | hold |
| 11 | holding |
| 1 | holds |
| 4 | hole |
| 1 | holes |
| 3 | holiday |
| 1 | holier |
| 2 | holld |
| 7 | hollow |
| 1 | hollowness |
| 1 | hollows |
| 5 | holly |
| 91 | home |
| 3 | homely |
| 1 | homeward |
| 1 | homily |
| 3 | honest |
| 1 | honey |
| 1 | honeymoon |
| 2 | honeysuckles |
| 7 | honour |
| 2 | honourable |
| 1 | honoured |
| 1 | honours |
| 4 | hook |
| 1 | hoops |
| 41 | hope |
| 4 | hoped |
| 2 | hopeful |
| 1 | hopefully |
| 1 | hopeless |
| 1 | hopelessly |
| 6 | hopes |
| 6 | hoping |
| 2 | hor |
| 1 | horizontal |
| 1 | horizontally |
| 2 | horns |
| 2 | horrible |
| 3 | horrid |
| 2 | horrified |
| 12 | horror |
| 25 | horse |
| 3 | horse's |
| 1 | horse-pistols |
| 1 | horse-steps |
| 1 | horse-trough |
| 3 | horseback |
| 7 | horses |
| 2 | horses' |
| 2 | hospitable |
| 9 | host |
| 1 | hostess |
| 2 | hostile |
| 1 | hostilities |
| 1 | hostility |
| 1 | hostler |
| 9 | hot |
| 1 | hottest |
| 3 | hound |
| 50 | hour |
| 4 | hour's |

| | |
|---|---|
| 29 | hours |
| 131 | house |
| 2 | house-door |
| 2 | house-front |
| 1 | house-keeper |
| 1 | house-keeper's |
| 9 | household |
| 18 | housekeeper |
| 2 | housekeeper's |
| 1 | houseless |
| 2 | houses |
| 1 | housewife |
| 1 | hovel |
| 1 | hovered |
| 1 | hovering |
| 223 | how |
| 66 | however |
| 2 | howl |
| 2 | howled |
| 2 | hubbub |
| 2 | hue |
| 1 | hug |
| 6 | huge |
| 1 | hugged |
| 10 | human |
| 6 | humanity |
| 5 | humiliation |
| 1 | humility |
| 3 | humming |
| 16 | humour |
| 2 | humoured |
| 3 | humouring |
| 2 | humours |
| 12 | hundred |
| 1 | hundreds |
| 11 | hung |
| 3 | hunger |
| 6 | hungry |
| 1 | hunter |
| 1 | hunting |
| 1 | hurl |
| 3 | hurled |
| 10 | hurried |
| 4 | hurriedly |
| 8 | hurry |
| 4 | hurrying |
| 33 | hurt |
| 1 | hurtful |
| 25 | husband |
| 3 | husband's |
| 1 | husbands |
| 22 | hush |
| 1 | hypocricy |
| 2 | hypocrisy |
| 3 | hypocrite |
| 1 | hysterical |
| 3534 | i |
| 15 | i' |
| 52 | i'd |
| 188 | i'll |
| 190 | i'm |
| 93 | i've |
| 3 | ice |
| 1 | ice-cold |
| 1 | ice-water |
| 1 | icicle |
| 1 | icily |
| 1 | icy |
| 25 | idea |
| 1 | ideal |
| 9 | ideas |
| 4 | idiocy |
| 7 | idiot |
| 1 | idiotic |
| 1 | idiots |
| 13 | idle |
| 3 | idleness |
| 3 | idol |
| 1 | idols |
| 447 | if |
| 2 | ignoble |
| 1 | ignominious |
| 11 | ignorance |
| 7 | ignorant |
| 39 | ill |
| 1 | ill-bred |
| 1 | ill-founded |
| 1 | ill-humour |
| 1 | ill-meaning |
| 2 | ill-nature |
| 3 | ill-natured |
| 2 | ill-temper |
| 1 | ill-tempered |
| 2 | ill-treatment |
| 1 | ill-turn |
| 15 | illness |
| 1 | illnesses |
| 1 | illumined |
| 1 | illusion |
| 1 | illusions |
| 5 | image |
| 2 | imaginable |
| 2 | imaginary |
| 4 | imagination |
| 17 | imagine |
| 11 | imagined |
| 1 | imagines |
| 5 | imagining |
| 1 | imbecile |
| 1 | immeasurably |
| 2 | immediate |

| | |
|---|---|
| 20 | immediately |
| 4 | immense |
| 1 | imminent |
| 1 | imminently |
| 1 | immolation |
| 1 | immortal |
| 1 | immovable |
| 1 | immoveable |
| 1 | imp |
| 1 | impalpable |
| 1 | imparted |
| 1 | imparting |
| 1 | impassable |
| 2 | impatience |
| 8 | impatient |
| 6 | impatiently |
| 2 | impelled |
| 1 | imperceptibly |
| 1 | imperfect |
| 1 | imperious |
| 1 | imperiously |
| 2 | impertinence |
| 2 | impertinent |
| 1 | implements |
| 1 | implore |
| 3 | implored |
| 1 | imploring |
| 1 | imploringly |
| 1 | implying |
| 1 | import |
| 1 | important |
| 1 | importation |
| 1 | importunate |
| 1 | importunately |
| 1 | importuned |
| 1 | importunity |
| 2 | impose |
| 1 | imposed |
| 12 | impossible |
| 3 | impracticable |
| 1 | imprecations |
| 7 | impressed |
| 7 | impression |
| 3 | impressions |
| 1 | imprisoned |
| 1 | improper |
| 2 | improve |
| 2 | improved |
| 2 | improvement |
| 1 | improving |
| 1 | imps |
| 2 | impudence |
| 5 | impulse |
| 1468 | in |
| 1 | in-door |
| 1 | inadequacy |
| 1 | inadequate |
| 1 | inanimate |
| 4 | inarticulate |
| 1 | inattention |
| 1 | inaudible |
| 1 | incapability |
| 4 | incapable |
| 1 | incapacitated |
| 1 | incapacity |
| 2 | incarnate |
| 1 | incautiously |
| 1 | incessantly |
| 1 | inch |
| 2 | inches |
| 2 | incidents |
| 1 | incipient |
| 1 | incitement |
| 6 | inclination |
| 11 | inclined |
| 1 | includes |
| 1 | including |
| 1 | incoherent |
| 2 | income |
| 2 | incomparably |
| 1 | incomprehensi- |
|  | ble |
| 1 | inconsiderati- |
|  | on |
| 1 | inconvenience |
| 1 | inconvenienced |
| 1 | incorporeal |
| 2 | increase |
| 4 | increased |
| 1 | increases |
| 3 | increasing |
| 1 | incredible |
| 1 | incredulous |
| 1 | incur |
| 2 | incurable |
| 32 | indeed |
| 2 | indefinite |
| 2 | indentations |
| 2 | independent |
| 1 | indian |
| 1 | indicating |
| 1 | indications |
| 1 | indicative |
| 1 | indies |
| 3 | indifference |
| 4 | indifferent |
| 1 | indigenae |
| 6 | indignant |
| 2 | indignantly |
| 5 | indignation |

| | | | | | | | |
|---:|---|---:|---|---:|---|---:|---|
| 1 | indigo-colour-ed | 2 | instilled | 1 | irregular | 39 | kind |
| 1 | indiscretion | 3 | instinct | 1 | irregularly | 2 | kinder |
| 1 | indiscretions | 3 | instinctively | 2 | irrepressible | 1 | kindest |
| 1 | indispensable | 2 | instructed | 3 | irresistible | 1 | kindle |
| 1 | indisposition | 5 | instructions | 2 | irresistibly | 4 | kindled |
| 1 | indistinctly | 1 | instructors | 1 | irresolutely | 1 | kindliness |
| 6 | individual | 3 | instrument | 1 | irrevocably | 4 | kindling |
| 1 | individuals | 1 | instruments | 4 | irritable | 4 | kindly |
| 1 | indolence | 1 | insufferable | 7 | irritated | 18 | kindness |
| 1 | indoors | 6 | insult | 1 | irritating | 1 | kindred |
| 3 | induced | 3 | insulted | 4 | irritation | 1 | kinds |
| 2 | indulge | 2 | insults | 654 | is | 3 | king |
| 5 | indulged | 3 | intellect | 57 | isabella | 1 | kingdom |
| 3 | indulgence | 7 | intelligence | 7 | isabella's | 1 | kingdoms |
| 1 | indulgences | 4 | intelligent | 1 | island | 1 | kinsman |
| 3 | indulgent | 4 | intelligible | 10 | isn't | 5 | kirk |
| 1 | indulging | 4 | intend | 2 | isolation | 5 | kirkyard |
| 1 | industry | 8 | intended | 2 | issue | 13 | kiss |
| 1 | inefficient | 3 | intending | 5 | issued | 13 | kissed |
| 1 | inexperienced | 5 | intense | 1 | issuing | 6 | kisses |
| 1 | inexpressible | 1 | intensest | 1309 | it | 4 | kissing |
| 1 | infamous | 4 | intensity | 81 | it's | 63 | kitchen |
| 2 | infancy | 1 | intent | 1 | iteration | 2 | kitten |
| 3 | infant | 13 | intention | 157 | its | 1 | knack |
| 1 | infantile | 1 | intentions | 11 | itself | 1 | knave |
| 2 | infatuated | 2 | intently | 2 | itseln | 4 | knaw |
| 1 | infatuation | 1 | intentness | 4 | iver | 2 | knaws |
| 1 | inferior | 1 | intercepted | 7 | jabes | 14 | knee |
| 1 | inferiority | 1 | intercepting | 1 | jabes' | 1 | knee-breeches |
| 9 | infernal | 1 | intercommunic-ation | 1 | jacket | 2 | kneel |
| 4 | infernally | 1 | intercourse | 1 | jade | 3 | kneeling |
| 1 | infinite | 1 | interdict | 4 | jailer | 12 | knees |
| 1 | infinitely | 18 | interest | 1 | january | 4 | knelt |
| 1 | inflexions | 4 | interested | 1 | jargon | 40 | knew |
| 3 | inflict | 6 | interesting | 3 | jaws | 12 | knife |
| 1 | inflicted | 3 | interfere | 10 | jealous | 1 | knighthood |
| 1 | inflicter | 2 | interference | 1 | jealously | 1 | knitted |
| 2 | inflicting | 2 | interfering | 1 | jealousy | 3 | knitting |
| 7 | influence | 1 | interim | 1 | jenny | 2 | knives |
| 15 | inform | 1 | interior | 2 | jerked | 9 | knock |
| 2 | informant | 1 | interloper | 1 | jerking | 8 | knocked |
| 1 | informant's | 1 | intermeddling | 6 | jest | 9 | knocking |
| 7 | information | 1 | interment | 1 | jesting | 1 | knocks |
| 9 | informed | 1 | intermission | 1 | jet | 1 | knot |
| 1 | informing | 1 | internally | 1 | jewel | 1 | knotted |
| 1 | infringement | 1 | interpose | 1 | jocks | 122 | know |
| 2 | ingenious | 7 | interposed | 2 | john | 5 | knowing |
| 1 | ingenuity | 1 | interpret | 10 | join | 5 | knowledge |
| 2 | ingratitude | 1 | interpreter | 6 | joined | 6 | known |
| 1 | inhabit | 1 | interpreting | 1 | joining | 1 | known't |
| 1 | inhabitant | 1 | interred | 1 | joins | 12 | knows |
| 2 | inhabitants | 2 | interrogative-ly | 2 | joint | 3 | knuckles |
| 1 | inherited | 1 | interrupt | 1 | joke | 9 | labour |
| 2 | inhospitable | 29 | interrupted | 1 | joked | 2 | laboured |
| 1 | inhospitality | 2 | interrupting | 1 | jokes | 2 | labourer |
| 1 | inhumanity | 1 | interruptions | 1 | jonah | 1 | labourers |
| 1 | initiatory | 1 | interspersed | 128 | joseph | 1 | labouring |
| 1 | injudicious | 8 | interval | 10 | joseph's | 1 | labours |
| 2 | injunction | 11 | intervals | 19 | journey | 1 | laced |
| 1 | injunctions | 7 | interview | 1 | journeying | 1 | lachrymose |
| 2 | injure | 4 | intimacy | 1 | journeys | 8 | lack |
| 4 | injured | 4 | intimate | 1 | journies | 1 | lacked |
| 3 | injuries | 1 | intimated | 25 | joy | 2 | laconic |
| 4 | injury | 1 | intimately | 2 | joyful | 39 | lad |
| 3 | injustice | 4 | intimating | 2 | joyfully | 2 | lad's |
| 2 | injustices | 4 | intimation | 2 | jubilee | 3 | ladder |
| 2 | ink | 264 | into | 1 | judas | 3 | laden |
| 1 | inmate | 1 | intolerable | 5 | judge | 3 | lads |
| 6 | inmates | 1 | intolerance | 5 | judged | 62 | lady |
| 1 | inn | 1 | intoxicated | 2 | judges | 8 | lady's |
| 1 | innate | 1 | intractable | 2 | judging | 28 | laid |
| 6 | inner | 3 | introduce | 5 | judgment | 1 | laiking |
| 6 | innocent | 1 | introduced | 2 | judicious | 1 | lair |
| 1 | innumerable | 1 | introducing | 3 | jug | 1 | laith |
| 8 | inquire | 3 | introduction | 1 | jugs | 6 | lamb |
| 22 | inquired | 1 | introductory | 3 | july | 2 | lambs |
| 3 | inquiries | 1 | intruded | 2 | jump | 2 | lame |
| 4 | inquiring | 3 | intruder | 4 | jumped | 1 | lamed |
| 3 | inquiry | 5 | intrusion | 2 | jumping | 2 | lament |
| 1 | inquisitive | 1 | intrusions | 3 | june | 1 | lamentable |
| 1 | inquisitively | 8 | intuh | 1 | junior | 1 | lamentation |
| 1 | inroads | 1 | inuendo's | 3 | juno | 5 | lamentations |
| 3 | insane | 1 | invaded | 76 | just | 1 | lamented |
| 1 | insanity | 1 | invading | 6 | justice | 1 | lamenting |
| 1 | inscribed | 5 | invalid | 1 | justice-meeti-ng | 10 | land |
| 4 | inscription | 1 | invariable | | | 1 | landed |
| 4 | insensible | 6 | invariably | 1 | justified | 1 | landing |
| 1 | inserting | 3 | invent | 1 | justly | 7 | landlord |
| 8 | inside | 1 | invented | 1 | jutted | 1 | landlord's |
| 1 | insipid | 1 | invention | 1 | jutting | 1 | landmarks |
| 2 | insist | 1 | investing | 5 | keen | 3 | lands |
| 14 | insisted | 1 | inveterate | 69 | keep | 4 | landscape |
| 1 | insisting | 5 | invisible | 1 | keeper | 1 | lane |
| 5 | insolence | 4 | invitation | 12 | keeping | 1 | lang |
| 3 | insolent | 6 | invited | 2 | keeps | 1 | langs |
| 2 | inspect | 1 | invoked | 1 | kennel | 8 | language |
| 1 | inspected | 1 | invokes | 24 | kenneth | 3 | languid |
| 1 | inspecting | 4 | involuntarily | 37 | kept | 1 | lankly |
| 1 | inspection | 1 | involuntary | 15 | key | 6 | lantern |
| 1 | inspector | 1 | involving | 3 | keys | 6 | lap |
| 2 | inspiration | 4 | inward | 5 | kick | 2 | lapse |
| 1 | install | 1 | irefully | 5 | kicked | 1 | lapsed |
| 3 | instance | 1 | irks | 1 | kicker | 1 | lapwing |
| 1 | instanced | 1 | irksome | 2 | kicking | 1 | lapwing's |
| 15 | instant | 3 | iron | 1 | kicks | 1 | lapwings |
| 1 | instantaneous-ly | 1 | ironed | 1 | kidnapped | 2 | larch |
| | | 1 | ironing | 15 | kill | 1 | larches |
| 12 | instantly | 1 | irrational | 13 | killed | 22 | large |
| 34 | instead | 1 | irrationality | 3 | killing | 2 | largely |
| 1 | instil | | | 1 | kills | 1 | larger |
| | | | | 3 | kin | 5 | larks |

| | | | |
|---|---|---|---|
| 1 lascar | 1 life-like | 1 loosed | 1 mania |
| 4 lashes | 1 lifeless-look- | 2 loosen | 1 maniac's |
| 14 lass | ing | 2 loosened | 2 manifestations |
| 107 last | 1 lifetime | 11 lord | 3 manifested |
| 3 lasted | 5 lift | 1 lore | 1 manly |
| 1 lasts | 16 lifted | 6 lose | 27 manner |
| 10 latch | 3 lifting | 1 loses | 8 manners |
| 27 late | 1 lig | 7 losing | 1 manoeuvres |
| 2 lately | 40 light | 10 loss | 2 mantle |
| 1 later | 9 lighted | 1 losses | 1 manual |
| 1 latest | 1 lightened | 23 lost | 1 manuscript |
| 1 lath | 1 lightening | 2 lot | 32 many |
| 2 latin | 3 lighter | 1 lots | 1 many-week's |
| 1 latitude | 1 lightest | 1 lottery | 5 march |
| 18 latter | 2 lighting | 7 loud | 1 marched |
| 4 latter's | 1 lightly | 2 louder | 1 marching |
| 15 lattice | 1 lightning | 1 lounged | 1 marcy |
| 2 lattices | 3 lights | 1 lounging | 4 mare |
| 1 lauded | 154 like | 89 love | 4 mark |
| 26 laugh | 1 like's | 23 loved | 3 marked |
| 21 laughed | 7 liked | 2 lovely | 1 marking |
| 19 laughing | 13 likely | 2 lover | 4 marks |
| 1 laughs | 2 likeness | 1 lovers | 3 marred |
| 2 laughter | 1 liker | 6 loves | 2 marriage |
| 1 launched | 2 likes | 12 loving | 16 married |
| 1 lave | 2 likewise | 13 low | 18 marry |
| 1 lavish | 2 liking | 1 low-browed | 4 marrying |
| 3 lavished | 1 likker | 1 low-spirited | 5 marsh |
| 1 lavishing | 1 lilac | 8 lower | 3 marshes |
| 8 law | 1 lilting | 1 lowering | 1 martyrs |
| 1 lawful | 5 limb | 2 lowest | 1 marvel |
| 1 laws | 4 limbs | 1 loyal | 1 marvelled |
| 4 lawyer | 2 lime | 2 luck | 1 marvelling |
| 42 lay | 1 limit | 1 luckily | 2 marvellous |
| 2 laying | 3 limited | 3 luckless | 3 marvellously |
| 2 laziness | 4 limits | 3 lucky | 2 mary |
| 2 lazy | 4 limping | 1 lug | 1 mass |
| 4 lead | 4 line | 1 lught | 2 masses |
| 4 leading | 1 lineage | 2 lugs | 185 master |
| 1 leads | 1 linen | 3 lull | 20 master's |
| 3 leaf | 2 lines | 1 lumber | 2 masters |
| 1 league | 1 ling | 1 lumber-hole | 1 mat |
| 1 leagued | 2 linger | 1 lumps | 1 match |
| 3 lean | 9 lingered | 1 lunatic | 1 matches |
| 1 leaned | 5 lingering | 1 lungs | 3 mate |
| 10 leaning | 1 linked | 2 lurk | 3 material |
| 18 leant | 1 linnets | 1 lurked | 1 materials |
| 1 leap | 349 linton | 3 lurking | 1 mathew |
| 2 leaped | 58 linton's | 1 lurks | 1 matronly |
| 1 leaping | 10 lintons | 1 lustre | 31 matter |
| 2 leapt | 2 lintons' | 1 lusty | 6 matters |
| 1 lear | 12 lip | 1 luxuriant | 1 mattocks |
| 13 learn | 19 lips | 2 luxury | 1 mattress |
| 3 learning | 2 liquid | 11 lying | 1 mature |
| 1 learns | 1 lisping | 8 ma'am | 1 maturity |
| 14 learnt | 13 listen | 21 mad | 2 maw |
| 39 least | 16 listened | 2 madam | 1 mawkish |
| 67 leave | 1 listener | 3 maddening | 1 maxillary |
| 5 leaves | 6 listening | 1 madder | 105 may |
| 17 leaving | 2 listless | 99 made | 1068 me |
| 3 lecture | 1 listlessness | 1 madling | 2 meadow |
| 1 lectures | 1 lit | 1 madman | 11 meal |
| 14 led | 1 literally | 1 madman's | 4 meals |
| 6 ledge | 1 literary | 4 madness | 23 mean |
| 1 leeches | 1 litter | 1 magically | 1 mean-minded |
| 1 lees | 178 little | 1 magisterial | 1 meanest |
| 72 left | 32 live | 3 magistrate | 6 meaning |
| 1 leg | 14 lived | 2 magnanimity | 21 means |
| 3 legal | 1 liveliness | 1 magpie | 15 meant |
| 1 legally | 6 lively | 7 maid | 10 meantime |
| 1 legion | 1 liver-coloured | 1 maid-servant | 7 meanwhile |
| 1 legions | 3 liverpool | 1 maiden | 1 measles |
| 1 legitimate | 9 lives | 3 maids | 8 measure |
| 3 legs | 3 livid | 1 main | 3 measured |
| 5 leisure | 30 living | 3 maintained | 4 measures |
| 5 leisurely | 2 lo | 1 maintaining | 1 measuring |
| 3 lend | 1 loaded | 1 maintains | 1 meat |
| 25 length | 1 loading | 1 maintenance | 7 meddle |
| 1 lengthened | 1 loath | 19 maister | 1 meddling |
| 1 lengthening | 1 lobbies | 3 maister's | 1 mediation |
| 1 lengths | 2 lobby | 2 maisters | 1 medical |
| 1 leniently | 3 locality | 2 mak | 2 medicine |
| 36 less | 15 lock | 105 make | 2 medicines |
| 1 lesson | 11 locked | 2 maker | 1 meditate |
| 5 lessons | 1 locket | 6 makes | 3 meditated |
| 10 lest | 3 locking | 29 making | 3 meditating |
| 140 let | 8 locks | 2 makking | 4 meditation |
| 2 lethargy | 18 lockwood | 2 maks | 2 meditations |
| 1 lets | 1 lockwood's | 1 mal-appropria- | 1 meditative |
| 20 letter | 7 lodge | ted | 1 medium |
| 9 letters | 3 lodged | 2 malady | 1 meek |
| 5 letting | 1 lodging | 2 male | 13 meet |
| 4 level | 1 loggings | 1 malefactors | 1 meeterly |
| 2 levelled | 6 loike | 4 malevolence | 11 meeting |
| 1 leveret | 6 london | 2 malice | 3 meets |
| 1 levers | 1 lonelier | 3 malignant | 6 melancholy |
| 1 levity | 1 loneliness | 1 malignantly | 4 mellow |
| 4 liar | 5 lonely | 3 malignity | 1 mells |
| 1 liberal | 97 long | 1 malt | 2 melt |
| 2 liberally | 2 longed | 2 mama | 3 melted |
| 2 liberated | 27 longer | 9 mamma | 1 melting |
| 1 liberating | 2 longest | 89 man | 1 member |
| 1 liberties | 4 longing | 3 man's | 1 members |
| 8 liberty | 99 look | 1 man-servant | 1 memoranda |
| 20 library | 75 looked | 7 manage | 1 memories |
| 1 licking | 1 looker-on | 7 managed | 11 memory |
| 2 lid | 38 looking | 1 management | 11 men |
| 7 lids | 15 looks | 1 mane | 3 menaced |
| 29 lie | 1 looped | 1 manes | 2 mend |
| 8 lies | 1 looping | 2 manger | 1 mended |
| 54 life | 10 loose | 1 manhood | 1 mending |

| | | | |
|---|---|---|---|
| 2 mensful | 48 mistress | 1 moveable | 4 neeght |
| 7 mental | 4 mistress's | 17 moved | 7 neglect |
| 2 mentally | 1 mistrusting | 8 movement | 4 neglected |
| 18 mention | 4 misty | 4 movements | 1 neglecting |
| 7 mentioned | 1 misunderstood | 2 moves | 2 negligence |
| 1 mentioning | 1 misused | 7 moving | 2 negligent |
| 1 mentions | 3 mitch | 310 mr | 1 negotiated |
| 1 merchant | 1 mither | 133 mrs | 1 negus |
| 2 mercy | 1 mitigated | 95 much | 1 neigbourhood |
| 2 mercy's | 1 mitigating | 2 mucky | 5 neighbour |
| 11 mere | 1 mixed | 1 muckying | 5 neighbour's |
| 12 merely | 1 mixture | 4 mud | 9 neighbourhood |
| 1 merest | 2 moan | 2 mug | 4 neighbours |
| 1 merit | 4 moaned | 1 mugs | 39 neither |
| 2 merited | 6 moaning | 7 muh | 3 nell |
| 3 merrily | 1 moans | 1 mule | 88 nelly |
| 3 merriment | 3 mock | 1 mulled | 1 nelly's |
| 10 merry | 4 mockery | 1 multiply | 9 nephew |
| 5 mess | 2 mocking | 2 multitude | 2 nephew's |
| 6 message | 3 mode | 1 multitudes | 1 nephews |
| 3 messenger | 3 model | 1 mumbled | 1 nerve |
| 14 met | 1 moderate | 1 mumbling | 1 nerveless |
| 4 method | 1 modern | 1 mummy | 8 nerves |
| 1 methodist | 1 modlled | 1 mumn't | 1 nervous |
| 1 methodists' | 2 moist | 8 mun | 1 nervously |
| 1 mew | 1 moisture | 1 mun'n't | 1 nervousness |
| 2 mice | 1 molest | 1 munching | 5 nest |
| 3 michael | 37 moment | 1 munificent | 1 nesting |
| 1 michaelmas | 2 momentary | 9 murder | 2 nests |
| 13 middle | 1 moments | 2 murdered | 1 neutralized |
| 6 midnight | 3 monday | 2 murderer | 180 never |
| 3 midst | 13 money | 1 murderers | 1 never |
| 131 might | 3 monkey | 1 murderess | 2 nevertheless |
| 1 mightily | 1 monomania | 1 murderous | 27 new |
| 2 mighty | 1 monopolized | 3 murmur | 2 newly |
| 1 migrated | 1 monopolizing | 15 murmured | 12 news |
| 4 mild | 1 monotonous | 1 murmuring | 49 next |
| 1 mildewed | 3 monster | 1 murthering | 10 nice |
| 1 mildness | 1 monsters | 4 muscles | 3 nicely |
| 9 mile | 7 month | 1 muse | 2 nicer |
| 1 mile' | 2 month's | 4 mused | 1 nicest |
| 13 miles | 20 months | 3 music | 1 nicety |
| 10 milk | 2 months' | 1 musical | 1 nick |
| 1 milk-blood | 2 monument | 4 musing | 1 nigh |
| 1 milk-fetcher | 3 mood | 1 musingly | 83 night |
| 1 milk-porridge | 1 moodily | 2 musn't | 1 night-walking |
| 2 milking | 3 moods | 187 must | 4 nightmare |
| 1 miller | 1 moody | 1 mustered | 7 nights |
| 1 million | 1 mools | 1 mustering | 1 nimbly |
| 1 milo | 10 moon | 7 mustn't | 5 nine |
| 3 mim | 1 moonbeam | 1 musty | 2 ninety |
| 1 minching | 1 moonlight | 4 mute | 1 ninety-first |
| 75 mind | 1 moons | 1 mutely | 1 ninny |
| 2 minded | 15 moor | 1 mutsn't | 3 nip |
| 2 minding | 1 moor-cock's | 1 mutter | 6 niver |
| 1 minds | 1 moor-game | 32 muttered | 1 nivir |
| 55 mine | 23 moors | 5 muttering | 391 no |
| 1 mine's | 1 moped | 1 mutton | 1 no-where |
| 5 mingled | 3 moral | 6 mutual | 6 noa |
| 3 minister | 1 moralizing | 1101 my | 1 noah |
| 1 ministering | 1 morally | 115 myself | 7 noan |
| 11 minny | 1 morbid | 1 mysteries | 3 nob'dy |
| 1 minny's | 217 more | 1 mysterious | 4 nobbut |
| 1 minor | 3 moreover | 1 mystery | 1 nobility |
| 38 minute | 3 morn | 2 n't | 1 noble |
| 3 minute's | 60 morning | 2 na | 39 nobody |
| 1 minute-hand | 2 morning's | 3 nab | 2 nod |
| 1 minutely | 2 morose | 7 nah | 3 nodded |
| 24 minutes | 4 moroseness | 3 nails | 3 nodding |
| 2 minutes' | 14 morrow | 1 naked | 13 noise |
| 1 minx | 3 morsel | 39 name | 2 noiselessly |
| 1 mire | 1 morsels | 3 named | 1 noises |
| 3 mirror | 1 mortagaged | 1 nameless | 1 noisily |
| 3 mirth | 8 mortal | 3 names | 1 noisy |
| 1 mis-pronuncia-<br>      tions | 1 mortally | 1 nap | 24 none |
| 1 misanthropical | 1 mortgaged | 2 narrative | 15 nonsense |
| 1 misanthropist-<br>      's | 1 mortgagee | 1 narrator | 1 nooin |
| 1 misanthropists | 2 mortification | 7 narrow | 3 nook |
| 1 misbehaviour | 1 mortified | 1 narrow-minded | 4 noon |
| 9 mischief | 1 mortifying | 2 nasty | 61 nor |
| 3 mischievous | 2 moss | 1 native | 1 nor-ne |
| 1 miscreants | 1 mossy | 10 natural | 6 north |
| 1 misdoubting | 35 most | 4 naturally | 1 north-east |
| 2 miser | 1 mostly | 19 nature | 2 northeast |
| 15 miserable | 29 mother | 9 naught | 6 norther |
| 3 miseries | 10 mother's | 1 naughtiness | 2 northern |
| 9 misery | 1 moths | 17 naughty | 10 nose |
| 1 misery-maker | 5 motion | 1 nausea | 1 nostril |
| 4 misfortune | 2 motioned | 1 nave | 2 nostrils |
| 1 misfortunes | 1 motioning | 26 nay | 936 not |
| 3 misgivings | 2 motionless | 1 nb | 1 notable |
| 1 misguided | 3 motive | 44 near | 9 note |
| 1 misplaced | 1 motives | 1 neared | 1 notebook |
| 129 miss | 3 mould | 11 nearer | 2 notes |
| 2 miss's | 1 mound | 5 nearest | 110 nothing |
| 3 missed | 2 mounds | 30 nearly | 27 notice |
| 2 missile | 3 mount | 1 neat | 12 noticed |
| 1 missing | 7 mounted | 2 neatly | 2 noticing |
| 5 missis | 6 mounting | 1 necessarily | 2 noting |
| 1 missis's | 1 mounts | 7 necessary | 22 notion |
| 2 missive | 1 mourn | 1 necessities | 2 notions |
| 1 missy | 1 mourned | 6 necessity | 9 notwithstandi-<br>      ng |
| 1 missy's | 3 mourner | 23 neck | |
| 3 mist | 2 mourners | 1 neckerchief | 1 nourish |
| 1 mista'en | 1 mournful | 25 need | 1 nourishment |
| 6 mistake | 1 mournfully | 2 needed | 2 novelty |
| 5 mistaken | 3 mourning | 2 needful | 1 november |
| 1 mistakes | 3 mouse | 1 needles | 229 now |
| 1 mistaking | 21 mouth | 2 needless | 1 now't |
| | 2 mouthful | 19 needn't | 2 nowhere |
| | 13 move | 1 needs | 15 nowt |

| | | | |
|---|---|---|---|
| 1 nud | 4 one's | 1 pacify | 1 peaceful |
| 1 nudged | 6 ones | 1 pacing | 1 pearl-contain- |
| 1 nuh | 1 ongoings | 4 pack |     ing |
| 1 nuisance | 149 only | 7 page | 1 pears |
| 6 number | 1 onst | 4 paid | 2 peat |
| 3 numerous | 12 onto | 2 pail | 1 peaty |
| 7 nur | 1 ony | 11 pain | 1 Pebble |
| 11 nurse | 1 onybody | 1 pained | 2 pebbles |
| 4 nursed | 55 open | 6 painful | 9 peculiar |
| 4 nursery | 1 open-mouthed | 5 painfully | 1 peculiarity |
| 4 nursing | 32 opened | 2 pains | 1 peculiarly |
| 1 nursling | 5 opening | 1 paint | 3 peep |
| 1 nurture | 2 openly | 3 painted | 2 peeped |
| 5 nut | 3 operation | 2 painting | 1 peeping |
| 8 o | 2 opinion | 6 pair | 1 peer |
| 20 o'clock | 3 oppen | 1 palace | 2 peering |
| 4 o'er | 1 oppen't | 1 palaver | 10 peevish |
| 5 oak | 1 opportunely | 13 pale | 2 peevishly |
| 1 oak-bedstead | 1 opportunities | 3 paleness | 2 peevishness |
| 1 oak-panelled | 17 opportunity | 1 palms | 1 peg |
| 1 oaks | 1 oppose | 4 paltry | 2 pen |
| 1 oat | 1 opposed | 3 pan | 1 penance |
| 1 oatcakes | 12 opposite | 1 pane | 2 pencil |
| 3 oath | 2 opposition | 2 panelled | 1 pendant |
| 1 oaths | 3 oppression | 6 panels | 1 penetralium |
| 1 oatmeal | 1 oppressions | 3 panes | 1 peniston |
| 1 oats | 1 oppressive | 2 pang | 6 penistone |
| 1 obdurate | 2 oppressor | 6 panted | 1 penning |
| 1 obedient | 311 or | 2 panting | 1 pennistow |
| 10 obey | 3 orange | 71 papa | 1 penny |
| 14 obeyed | 1 oranges | 3 papa's | 2 pensive |
| 1 obeying | 17 order | 6 paper | 42 people |
| 1 obeys | 12 ordered | 1 papered | 1 per |
| 18 object | 3 ordering | 1 papers | 8 perceive |
| 4 objected | 8 orders | 3 paradise | 13 perceived |
| 3 objection | 13 ordinary | 1 paragon | 1 perceives |
| 1 objections | 1 origin | 1 paragraph | 15 perceiving |
| 6 objects | 1 original | 11 pardon | 1 perceptible |
| 1 obleeged | 2 originally | 1 pardonable | 2 perdition |
| 2 obligation | 2 orisons | 1 pared | 2 peremptorily |
| 4 oblige | 2 ornament | 1 parent | 1 peremptory |
| 19 obliged | 2 ornamented | 1 parent's | 9 perfect |
| 1 obliterated | 1 orphan | 1 parentage | 12 perfectly |
| 1 oblivion | 1 orther | 3 parents | 2 perforce |
| 2 obscure | 1 ortherings | 1 parings | 1 perform |
| 1 obscurely | 110 other | 4 parish | 2 performed |
| 1 obscurity | 3 other's | 22 park | 3 performing |
| 1 observable | 9 others | 1 park-fence | 1 perfuming |
| 2 observation | 5 otherwise | 1 parlor | 44 perhaps |
| 1 observations | 16 ought | 22 parlour | 3 peril |
| 5 observe | 111 our | 1 parlours | 1 perilous |
| 41 observed | 2 ours | 4 paroxysm | 1 perils |
| 4 observing | 12 ourselves | 1 parrying | 16 period |
| 1 obstacle | 1 ousels | 2 parson | 1 perishable |
| 1 obstinacy | 302 out | 30 part | 3 perished |
| 5 obstinate | 1 out-and-outer | 1 partake | 1 perishing |
| 3 obstinately | 1 out-matched | 6 parted | 2 permanent |
| 6 obtain | 1 out-of-the-way | 2 partial | 7 permission |
| 1 obtained | 1 out-works | 3 partiality | 3 permit |
| 1 obtaining | 2 outcast | 1 partially | 5 permitted |
| 1 obtrusive | 1 outcry | 5 particular | 1 permitting |
| 3 obviate | 1 outdoor | 6 particularly | 4 perpetual |
| 2 obvious | 3 outer | 2 parties | 1 perpetually |
| 5 obviously | 1 outlive | 2 parting | 2 perplex |
| 15 occasion | 1 outrage | 10 partly | 5 perplexed |
| 4 occasioned | 1 outrageous | 1 partner | 1 perplexities |
| 3 occasions | 4 outright | 1 partner's | 3 perplexity |
| 1 occupant | 14 outside | 4 partook | 1 persecuting |
| 3 occupants | 3 outstripped | 3 parts | 1 persecutions |
| 8 occupation | 2 outward | 3 party | 1 persecutor |
| 8 occupations | 1 outweighs | 19 pass | 3 perseverance |
| 5 occupied | 1 oven | 5 passage | 1 persevere |
| 5 occupy | 166 over | 1 passages | 6 persevered |
| 1 occurrence | 1 over-intent | 19 passed | 1 persevering |
| 1 occurs | 1 over-looking | 1 passes | 3 persist |
| 1 ocean | 1 over-topped | 12 passing | 10 persisted |
| 3 october | 3 overcame | 17 passion | 36 person |
| 16 odd | 2 overcast | 4 passionate | 4 personal |
| 2 oddly | 1 overcome | 4 passionately | 1 personally |
| 3 odious | 1 overcoming | 1 passionless | 1 personated |
| 1 odour | 1 overdone | 1 passive | 1 personificati- |
| 1 oe'red | 1 overflowing | 17 past |     on |
| 2217 of | 1 overhead | 1 pastor | 1 personified |
| 126 off | 2 overhear | 1 paternal | 4 persons |
| 1 offald | 3 overheard | 1 paternity | 1 perspicacity |
| 1 offalld | 1 overhearing | 10 path | 2 perspiration |
| 3 offence | 1 overlaid | 1 pathos | 12 persuade |
| 1 offend | 1 overlook | 1 paths | 10 persuaded |
| 3 offended | 1 overlooked | 12 patience | 2 persuading |
| 3 offending | 1 overpass | 10 patient | 1 persuasions |
| 11 offer | 1 overreach | 3 patiently | 1 pert |
| 15 offered | 2 overtaking | 1 patriarchs | 2 pertinacious |
| 7 offering | 2 overwhelmed | 1 patted | 1 pertinaciously |
| 1 offers | 1 ow'd | 1 pattering | 1 pertly |
| 2 office | 1 ow't | 1 pattern | 4 pertness |
| 1 offspring | 2 owd | 1 paul | 1 peruse |
| 1 offspring's | 1 owe | 6 pause | 4 perused |
| 33 often | 1 owes | 5 paused | 2 perusing |
| 1 oftener | 8 owing | 2 pausing | 1 pervading |
| 100 oh | 1 owld | 2 paved | 2 perverse |
| 1 oho | 117 own | 1 pavement | 1 perverseness |
| 81 old | 1 owned | 1 paving | 1 perversity |
| 1 old-fashioned | 10 owner | 1 paw | 1 perverted |
| 5 older | 2 owner's | 1 paws | 8 pet |
| 1 omen | 1 owners | 1 pawsed | 1 peter |
| 1 ominous | 3 owning | 7 pay | 3 petition |
| 2 omit | 3 owt | 4 paying | 1 petrified |
| 801 on | 1 oyster | 2 payment | 2 petted |
| 5 on't | 2 pace | 1 pays | 1 petting |
| 77 once | 2 paced | 14 peace | 1 pettish |
| 288 one | 2 pacified | 1 peace-offering | 1 pettishly |

| | | | |
|---|---|---|---|
| 1 pettishness | 2 pleasantest | 3 prayers | 1 progressed |
| 2 petulance | 28 please | 3 praying | 1 prohibition |
| 1 petulant | 25 pleased | 1 pre-eminent | 3 project |
| 2 petulantly | 5 pleases | 1 preach | 1 projected |
| 3 pewter | 33 pleasure | 1 preached | 1 projecting |
| 1 phalanx | 2 pledge | 1 preacher | 1 prolong |
| 1 phantoms | 2 pledged | 1 preaching | 4 prolonged |
| 1 pharisee | 1 pledging | 1 precarious | 21 promise |
| 1 phase | 1 plentiful | 1 precaution | 10 promised |
| 1 phases | 1 plentifully | 1 precautions | 3 promises |
| 1 pheasant | 10 plenty | 1 precede | 1 promising |
| 1 pheasants | 1 pliable | 2 preceded | 2 prompt |
| 3 phenix | 1 plight | 2 preceding | 4 prompted |
| 1 philosopher | 1 plisky | 1 precept | 1 prompters |
| 1 philosophical | 1 plodding | 1 precepts | 2 promptly |
| 1 phlegm | 1 plotted | 1 precincts | 1 prone |
| 1 phrase | 1 plottered | 11 precious | 2 pronounce |
| 1 phraseology | 2 plough-boy | 1 precipitating | 2 pronounced |
| 5 physical | 1 ploughboy | 1 precise | 1 pronouncing |
| 1 physically | 2 pluck | 2 precisely | 1 pronouns |
| 3 physiognomy | 2 plucked | 1 precluding | 1 pronunciation |
| 2 pick | 1 plump | 1 predecessor's | 3 proof |
| 4 picked | 1 plundered | 3 predicament | 2 proofs |
| 11 picture | 1 plundering | 1 preeminently | 1 prop |
| 2 pictured | 1 plunge | 2 preferable | 1 propensity |
| 6 pictures | 1 poacher | 2 preference | 9 proper |
| 2 picturing | 10 pocket | 5 preferred | 5 properly |
| 11 piece | 2 pocket-book | 1 prejucial | 11 property |
| 5 pieces | 1 pocket-handhe- | 1 prejudice | 2 prophecy |
| 2 piercing |    rchief | 1 prejudiced | 1 prophesy |
| 1 pigeon | 2 pocket-handke- | 1 prematurely | 2 propitiate |
| 1 pigeon's |    rchief | 2 premises | 1 proportion |
| 1 pigeons | 1 pocketful | 1 preparation | 2 proposal |
| 1 pigeons' | 7 pockets | 3 preparations | 1 propose |
| 1 piked | 1 poetry | 6 prepare | 6 proposed |
| 1 pikes | 1 poignant | 7 prepared | 2 proposes |
| 1 pile | 19 point | 4 preparing | 1 proposing |
| 3 piled | 5 pointed | 1 preposterously | 1 propriety |
| 2 pilgrim's | 1 pointer | 28 presence | 1 prose |
| 1 pilgrimage | 3 pointers | 46 present | 1 prosecute |
| 11 pillow | 2 pointing | 2 presentable | 7 prospect |
| 1 pillows | 1 poised | 3 presented | 1 prospective |
| 1 pills | 3 poison | 3 presentiment | 1 prostrate |
| 1 pinafores | 1 poisoned | 19 presently | 1 protect |
| 1 pincers | 1 poisoning | 2 presents | 1 protected |
| 2 pinch | 1 poisonous | 5 preserve | 1 protector |
| 5 pinched | 5 poker | 1 preserved | 3 protestations |
| 1 pinches | 1 policy | 1 preserving | 1 protested |
| 1 pined | 2 polished | 1 presiding | 1 protract |
| 1 pines | 3 politeness | 3 press | 4 protracted |
| 3 pining | 2 pondered | 4 pressed | 8 proud |
| 1 pinkness | 1 pondering | 1 pressing | 1 proudly |
| 3 pint | 1 ponies | 3 presume | 6 prove |
| 3 pious | 18 pony | 1 presumed | 6 proved |
| 6 pipe | 52 poor | 1 presuming | 1 proves |
| 3 pistol | 1 poorer | 3 presumptuous | 7 provided |
| 2 pistols | 4 poorly | 2 pretence | 2 providence |
| 3 pit | 7 porch | 7 pretend | 1 provident |
| 2 pitch | 7 porridge | 5 pretended | 1 providential |
| 1 pitched | 1 portended | 5 pretending | 1 province |
| 3 pitcher | 2 porter's | 1 preter-human | 1 provincial |
| 1 pitchfork | 6 portion | 1 preternatural- | 1 provincialisms |
| 1 piteous | 1 portions |    ly | 1 provision |
| 4 pitied | 3 portrait | 1 prettier | 7 provoke |
| 5 pitiful | 2 portraits | 23 pretty | 7 provoked |
| 1 pitiless | 6 position | 2 prevail | 1 provokes |
| 1 pits | 2 positions | 2 prevailing | 4 provoking |
| 24 pity | 4 positive | 12 prevent | 2 provokingly |
| 1 pitying | 3 possess | 6 prevented | 1 prowled |
| 74 place | 11 possessed | 4 previous | 3 proximity |
| 10 placed | 2 possesses | 4 previously | 1 proxy |
| 1 places | 1 possessing | 1 prey | 1 prudence |
| 1 placidly | 6 possession | 1 price | 1 prudential |
| 1 placing | 1 possessor | 1 pricked | 2 prudently |
| 5 plague | 1 possibility | 17 pride | 2 prying |
| 1 plagued | 18 possible | 4 prime | 1 psalmody |
| 2 plaguing | 7 possibly | 1 primitive | 1 public-house |
| 1 plaid | 6 post | 1 primrose | 1 publicly |
| 5 plain | 1 postern | 2 primroses | 1 puffed |
| 2 plainer | 1 postpone | 1 prince | 1 puffs |
| 5 plainly | 1 postponed | 1 princess | 2 puling |
| 8 plan | 2 pot | 2 principal | 8 pull |
| 1 plank | 1 potatoes | 1 principles | 12 pulled |
| 1 planned | 3 potent | 1 print | 10 pulling |
| 2 planning | 1 pots | 3 printed | 2 pulpit |
| 2 plans | 2 pounds | 1 printer | 3 pulse |
| 2 plant | 1 pour | 2 prior | 1 pump |
| 2 plantation | 6 poured | 3 prison | 1 punch |
| 2 planted | 3 pouring | 3 prisoner | 1 punctually |
| 2 plants | 1 pouting | 9 private | 4 punish |
| 1 plase | 1 powders | 3 privilege | 1 punishing |
| 1 plash | 16 power | 1 privileges | 5 punishment |
| 5 plate | 3 powerful | 1 probability | 3 puny |
| 1 plateful | 2 powerfully | 3 probable | 2 pupil |
| 1 platefuls | 2 powerless | 26 probably | 2 puppies |
| 1 plausible | 1 powers | 6 proceed | 10 pure |
| 14 play | 1 practicable | 12 proceeded | 2 purgatory |
| 1 play-things | 1 practically | 6 proceeding | 1 purification |
| 7 played | 1 practice | 2 proceedings | 1 purity |
| 1 playfellow | 1 practise | 1 process | 2 purple |
| 1 playfulness | 1 practised | 1 proclaimant | 1 purport |
| 9 playing | 1 praise | 1 procure | 24 purpose |
| 2 playmate | 2 praised | 4 produce | 2 purposely |
| 1 playmate's | 1 praiseworthy | 9 produced | 2 purposes |
| 1 playmates | 2 praising | 1 profaned | 4 pursue |
| 2 playthings | 1 prattled | 1 profiting | 13 pursued |
| 1 plea | 13 pray | 1 profound | 3 pursuing |
| 4 plead | 3 prayed | 1 profusely | 1 pursuit |
| 4 pleaded | 6 prayer | 1 progess | 1 pursuits |
| 14 pleasant | 1 prayer-books | 1 prognosticate | 7 push |
| 1 pleasanter | 1 prayer-meeting | 3 progress | 13 pushed |

| | | | |
|---|---|---|---|
| 11 pushing | 2 rash | 1 redeemed | 1 renew |
| 1 puss´s | 7 rate | 1 redemption | 3 renewed |
| 84 put | 75 rather | 1 redoubled | 3 rent |
| 1 puts | 1 ratified | 1 redoubling | 1 rents |
| 15 putting | 1 rating | 1 redounded | 2 repaid |
| 1 puzzle | 3 rational | 2 reduce | 1 repair |
| 6 puzzled | 2 rationally | 1 reduced | 1 repairing |
| 1 pyramid | 1 rattle | 1 reed | 1 repassing |
| 1 quaker | 4 rattled | 1 reentrance | 1 repay |
| 1 qualified | 1 rattling | 1 reference | 1 repaying |
| 3 qualities | 1 raves | 1 refering | 1 repayment |
| 1 quality | 3 raving | 1 refinement | 1 repeal |
| 2 qualm | 2 ravings | 4 reflect | 18 repeat |
| 2 quantities | 2 ray | 12 reflected | 28 repeated |
| 2 quantity | 5 rayther | 1 reflecting | 5 repeatedly |
| 12 quarrel | 4 re-appeared | 13 reflection | 3 repeating |
| 3 quarrelled | 1 re-appearing | 3 reflections | 1 repeatng |
| 4 quarrelling | 1 re-ascended | 1 reflective | 1 repelled |
| 1 quarrels | 1 re-ascending | 1 reform | 2 repelling |
| 1 quarries | 2 re-commenced | 1 reformed | 1 repellingly |
| 1 quart | 5 re-enter | 7 refrain | 7 repent |
| 9 quarter | 4 re-entered | 2 refrained | 2 repented |
| 1 quarters | 2 re-entering | 1 refresh | 4 repenting |
| 1 quean | 3 re-entrance | 1 refreshing | 1 repents |
| 3 queen | 1 re-establishi-<br>ng | 3 refreshment | 4 repetition |
| 8 queer | | 3 refuge | 1 repidly |
| 2 quelled | 1 re-fastened | 2 refusal | 1 replaced |
| 1 quenched | 1 re-filled | 9 refuse | 1 replacing |
| 1 querulous | 1 re-lock | 17 refused | 117 replied |
| 1 quest | 1 re-locking | 1 refuses | 2 replies |
| 20 question | 1 re-secured | 2 refusing | 13 reply |
| 2 questioned | 20 reach | 1 refute | 3 report |
| 1 questioner | 23 reached | 1 refuted | 3 reported |
| 3 questioning | 5 reaching | 2 regained | 1 reports |
| 9 questions | 37 read | 1 regaining | 6 repose |
| 16 quick | 5 readily | 12 regard | 1 reposed |
| 1 quicker | 15 reading | 4 regarded | 1 repossess |
| 8 quickly | 1 reads | 9 regarding | 3 represent |
| 1 quiescence | 28 ready | 6 regardless | 1 representativ-<br>es |
| 24 quiet | 10 real | 1 regardlessly | |
| 2 quieter | 4 reality | 4 regions | 2 represented |
| 1 quietest | 1 realization | 10 regret | 1 repress |
| 11 quietly | 31 really | 1 regrets | 1 repressing |
| 1 quietness | 1 reaming | 1 regretted | 1 reprimanded |
| 1 quilt | 1 reaped | 4 regular | 2 reproached |
| 14 quit | 1 reapers | 2 regularly | 1 reproaches |
| 48 quite | 2 reappeared | 1 reinstate | 1 reproachful |
| 12 quitted | 1 reappearing | 2 reiterated | 1 reproachfully |
| 5 quitting | 2 rear | 1 reiterating | 2 reprobate |
| 2 quiver | 3 reared | 1 reject | 2 reproofs |
| 1 quivered | 1 rearing | 2 rejected | 1 reprove |
| 3 quivering | 26 reason | 1 rejecting | 2 reproved |
| 1 quoting | 2 reasonable | 2 rejoice | 1 reprover |
| 1 rabbit | 1 reasoned | 1 rejoicing | 1 reproving |
| 2 rabbits | 9 reasons | 2 rekindle | 1 reprovingly |
| 1 rabid | 1 rebel | 3 related | 1 reptile |
| 3 race | 1 rebellion | 3 relating | 1 repulsed |
| 3 racked | 1 rebuffing | 6 relation | 1 repulsing |
| 1 radiance | 2 rebuke | 2 relations | 3 repulsive |
| 3 radiant | 2 rebuked | 2 relationship | 1 repulsiveness |
| 1 rafters | 4 recall | 1 relax | 3 reputation |
| 10 rage | 7 recalled | 7 relaxed | 6 request |
| 3 rages | 3 recalling | 5 release | 7 requested |
| 1 ragged | 1 recantation | 3 released | 1 requesting |
| 1 raging | 1 recapitulation | 1 releasing | 4 require |
| 5 rahm | 1 receipt | 2 relent | 3 required |
| 1 rahnd | 10 receive | 2 relented | 1 requirements |
| 5 raight | 21 received | 2 relentless | 4 requires |
| 1 rail | 3 receiving | 1 relic | 4 rescue |
| 1 rails | 4 recent | 3 relief | 1 researches |
| 14 rain | 1 recently | 1 relieve | 6 resemblance |
| 1 rainbow | 4 reception | 4 relieved | 4 resemble |
| 2 rained | 2 recess | 2 relieving | 3 resembled |
| 2 raining | 1 recesses | 2 religious | 2 resembles |
| 1 rains | 1 recipient | 1 relinquished | 3 resembling |
| 2 rainy | 1 reciprocation | 4 relish | 2 resent |
| 14 raise | 6 reckless | 1 relished | 1 resentment |
| 24 raised | 3 reckon | 1 relishing | 2 reserve |
| 1 raises | 2 reckoned | 3 reluctance | 4 reserved |
| 6 raising | 3 reclined | 6 reluctant | 1 reside |
| 2 rake | 1 reclining | 6 reluctantly | 2 resided |
| 1 raked | 1 recluse | 23 remain | 6 residence |
| 1 rally | 4 recognise | 5 remainder | 1 resident |
| 1 rallying | 5 recognised | 34 remained | 5 resign |
| 8 ramble | 1 recognising | 3 remaining | 3 resignation |
| 1 rambled | 2 recognition | 3 remains | 1 resigned |
| 1 ramblers | 1 recognized | 5 remark | 3 resist |
| 4 rambles | 1 recoil | 1 remarkable | 2 resisted |
| 6 rambling | 3 recoiled | 1 remarkably | 1 resolute |
| 1 ramparts | 12 recollect | 24 remarked | 2 resolutely |
| 33 ran | 3 recollected | 2 remarking | 9 resolution |
| 1 rang | 2 recollecting | 2 remarks | 1 resolutions |
| 6 range | 3 recollection | 5 remedy | 2 resolve |
| 2 ranged | 1 recommence | 28 remember | 17 resolved |
| 1 ranges | 6 recommenced | 7 remembered | 2 resolving |
| 1 ranging | 2 recommend | 2 remembering | 2 resort |
| 1 rankled | 2 recommended | 7 remembrance | 1 resorted |
| 1 rankness | 2 recompense | 6 remind | 1 resorting |
| 1 ranks | 3 reconciled | 5 reminded | 1 resounded |
| 1 ransacked | 2 reconciliation | 1 reminding | 3 resource |
| 6 rapid | 1 recounting | 1 remnant | 2 resources |
| 10 rapidly | 7 recover | 1 remorse | 4 respect |
| 1 rappings | 12 recovered | 1 remorselessly | 5 respectable |
| 1 rapt | 9 recovering | 2 removal | 1 respectably |
| 1 raptured | 1 recovery | 15 remove | 3 respected |
| 1 rapturously | 1 recriminate | 19 removed | 1 respecting |
| 4 rare | 1 recurred | 3 removing | 1 respired |
| 1 rarely | 2 recurring | 4 render | 1 respite |
| 4 rascal | 19 red | 7 rendered | 5 responded |
| 1 rascally | 1 reddened | 1 rendering | 2 response |
| 1 rascals | 1 reddening | 1 renders | 1 responsibility |

| | | | |
|---|---|---|---|
| 1 responsible | 1 roasting | 4 sank | 3 seasons |
| 1 responsively | 1 rob | 1 sarcastic | 27 seat |
| 35 rest | 1 robbers | 1 sarcastically | 22 seated |
| 7 rested | 2 robbing | 1 sartin | 1 seats |
| 3 resting | 3 robert | 1 sarve | 2 secluded |
| 1 resting-place | 1 rocked | 1 sarved | 1 seclusion |
| 7 restless | 5 rocking | 52 sat | 20 second |
| 1 restlessly | 2 rocks | 5 satan | 2 seconds |
| 1 restoration | 1 rod | 1 satellites | 15 secret |
| 4 restore | 5 rode | 11 satisfaction | 1 secretly |
| 7 restored | 1 rogue | 1 satisfactorily | 3 secrets |
| 2 restoring | 2 roll | 1 satisfactory | 1 sections |
| 1 restrain | 2 rolled | 6 satisfied | 8 secure |
| 1 restrained | 2 rolling | 3 satisfy | 5 secured |
| 1 restrains | 2 romance | 1 sattan | 1 securely |
| 3 restraint | 1 romantic | 1 saturnine | 2 securing |
| 2 result | 17 roof | 1 saucepans | 2 security |
| 1 resulting | 95 room | 2 saucer | 172 see |
| 4 resume | 3 rooms | 1 saucers | 1 seearch |
| 14 resumed | 3 roots | 1 saucier | 3 seed |
| 3 resuming | 34 rose | 3 sauciness | 2 seeght |
| 1 resurrection | 1 rosebushes | 6 saucy | 21 seeing |
| 6 retain | 1 rotten | 1 saunter | 27 seek |
| 5 retained | 20 rough | 3 sauntered | 11 seeking |
| 2 retaining | 1 rough-headed | 1 sauntering | 13 seem |
| 1 retains | 1 roughly | 8 savage | 69 seemed |
| 2 retaliate | 2 roughness | 3 savagely | 2 seeming |
| 2 retaliation | 63 round | 1 savages | 2 seemingly |
| 3 retire | 1 rounds | 10 save | 1 seemly |
| 11 retired | 9 rouse | 2 saved | 9 seems |
| 1 retirement | 7 roused | 2 saving | 40 seen |
| 11 retorted | 5 rousing | 79 saw | 1 sees |
| 1 retrace | 5 row | 1 saw-edge | 3 seize |
| 1 retracing | 2 rubbed | 118 say | 23 seized |
| 3 retract | 1 rubbidge | 1 sayhave | 2 seizing |
| 4 retreat | 2 rubbing | 13 saying | 9 seldom |
| 3 retreated | 3 ruddy | 1 sayings | 3 select |
| 2 retreating | 4 rude | 28 says | 3 selected |
| 1 retrieval | 1 rude-bred | 1 scale | 3 self |
| 1 retrieving | 1 rudely | 1 scalping | 1 self-absorbed |
| 42 return | 3 rudeness | 1 scamper | 1 self-complace- |
| 62 returned | 2 rue | 1 scampering |      nt |
| 8 returning | 6 ruffian | 2 scandal | 1 self-defence |
| 2 returns | 2 ruffianly | 1 scandalous | 1 self-denial |
| 2 reveal | 1 ruffling | 29 scarcely | 1 self-love |
| 12 revealed | 3 rug | 1 scared | 1 self-preserva- |
| 1 revealing | 6 ruin | 1 scares |      tion |
| 2 revelation | 1 ruined | 2 scarlet | 2 self-respect |
| 1 revelations | 1 ruining | 1 scattered | 1 self-righteous |
| 1 revelling | 1 ruling | 15 scene | 11 selfish |
| 10 revenge | 1 rullers | 1 scenery | 7 selfishness |
| 1 revenged | 1 rumbling | 1 scenes | 32 send |
| 1 revenging | 1 rummaged | 1 scent | 3 sending |
| 2 reverend | 2 rumour | 1 scented | 2 sends |
| 1 reverie | 36 run | 1 scents | 3 sensation |
| 1 reverting | 1 runaway | 1 sceptre | 2 sensations |
| 1 revisit | 1 rung | 1 scheme | 27 sense |
| 1 revive | 14 running | 1 schemes | 4 senseless |
| 6 revived | 1 runnings | 2 scholar | 7 senses |
| 1 revives | 3 runs | 1 school-boy | 4 sensible |
| 2 reviving | 3 rush | 1 scintillating | 5 sensitive |
| 1 revolted | 10 rushed | 1 scissors | 24 sent |
| 1 reward | 2 rushing | 11 scold | 9 sentence |
| 4 rewarded | 3 rustic | 6 scolded | 3 sentences |
| 1 rheumatism | 2 rustle | 4 scolding | 1 sententiously |
| 1 riband | 2 rustling | 1 sconses | 10 sentiment |
| 1 ribband | 3 sabbath | 1 scooping | 3 sentiments |
| 1 ribbed | 1 sack | 1 scope | 3 sentinel |
| 2 ribs | 1 sackless | 2 score | 5 separate |
| 13 rich | 1 sacks | 7 scorn | 2 separated |
| 1 richer | 2 sacrifice | 4 scorned | 1 separating |
| 1 richly | 1 sacrificed | 5 scornful | 7 separation |
| 7 rid | 17 sad | 5 scornfully | 2 september |
| 1 ridden | 3 sadder | 2 scorning | 3 sequel |
| 12 ride | 1 saddest | 1 scorns | 2 series |
| 1 rider's | 3 saddle | 7 scoundrel | 11 serious |
| 1 ridge | 1 saddled | 1 scoured | 6 seriously |
| 1 ridicule | 1 saddles | 3 scouring | 1 sermon |
| 1 ridiculing | 13 sadly | 3 scowl | 1 sermonizing |
| 5 ridiculous | 4 sadness | 2 scowled | 1 sermons |
| 9 riding | 12 safe | 1 scowling | 1 serpent |
| 52 right | 1 safely | 1 scowls | 30 servant |
| 1 righteous | 1 safer | 1 scrambling | 5 servant's |
| 1 righteously | 1 safety | 1 scrape | 1 servant-girl |
| 1 rightly | 1 sagacity | 1 scraped | 21 servants |
| 2 rights | 1 sahnd | 4 scratched | 5 serve |
| 1 rigidly | 374 said | 1 scratching | 6 served |
| 1 rigs | 1 sail | 1 scrawled | 1 serves |
| 3 ring | 1 sailors | 3 scream | 8 service |
| 3 ringing | 4 saint | 6 screamed | 1 serviceable |
| 4 ringlets | 2 saints | 2 screaming | 2 services |
| 2 rings | 25 sake | 1 screen | 1 serving |
| 2 riot | 1 sall | 2 screwed | 1 ses |
| 1 ripening | 1 sallied | 1 screws | 63 set |
| 1 ripples | 1 sallow | 2 scripture | 7 setting |
| 12 rise | 1 sallower | 1 scroop | 29 settle |
| 7 risen | 1 salubrious | 1 scrubbed | 6 settled |
| 3 rises | 1 salutation | 2 scruple | 1 settles |
| 10 rising | 1 salutations | 2 scruples | 1 settling |
| 7 risk | 4 salute | 1 scrutinizing | 14 seven |
| 2 rival | 1 saluted | 1 scutter | 2 seventeen |
| 2 riven | 3 salvation | 1 scuttle | 1 seventeenth |
| 37 road | 48 same | 4 sea | 1 seventy |
| 1 road-side | 1 samples | 1 sea-coast | 8 seventy |
| 3 roads | 1 sanctimonious | 1 seal | 2 seventy-first |
| 1 roadside | 1 sanctum | 1 sealed | 1 sever |
| 1 roamed | 1 sand | 5 search | 15 several |
| 1 roar | 1 sand-pillar | 5 searched | 3 severe |
| 1 roared | 1 sane | 4 searching | 2 severely |
| 1 roaring | 1 sang | 5 season | 1 severity |
| 1 roasted | 3 sanguine | 1 seasoned | 3 sewing |
| | | | 5 sexton |

| | | | |
|---|---|---|---|
| 2 sha'n't | 5 shrank | 6 skin | 2 sneered |
| 1 shaamed | 1 shriek | 1 skinned | 2 sneering |
| 2 shabby | 6 shrieked | 1 skirmishes | 2 sneeringly |
| 2 shade | 2 shrieking | 1 skirts | 1 snivel |
| 1 shaded | 1 shrieks | 1 skittish | 2 snivelling |
| 5 shadow | 2 shrink | 1 skulk | 1 snoozled |
| 1 shadow's | 3 shrinking | 2 skulked | 2 snorting |
| 1 shadowing | 1 shrubs | 6 skulker | 22 snow |
| 1 shadowless | 1 shrugged | 1 skulker's | 1 snow-storm |
| 3 shadows | 4 shrunk | 2 skull | 1 snowy |
| 1 shaft | 2 shudder | 1 skurrying | 1 snuffed |
| 2 shaggy | 2 shuddered | 6 sky | 1 snuffers |
| 1 shaime | 3 shuddering | 3 skylight | 1 snuffing |
| 8 shake | 2 shudders | 1 slam | 1 snug |
| 2 shaken | 1 shuffled | 1 slammed | 358 so |
| 9 shaking | 2 shuffling | 1 slander | 8 soa |
| 195 shall | 3 shun | 1 slanders | 4 soaked |
| 1 shalln't | 4 shunned | 1 slant | 1 soap |
| 1 shallow | 1 shunning | 3 slap | 3 sob |
| 13 shame | 32 shut | 1 slapped | 15 sobbed |
| 3 shameful | 3 shutters | 1 slapping | 4 sobbing |
| 2 shamefully | 5 shutting | 1 slaps | 5 sober |
| 1 shameless | 1 shuttle-cocks | 2 slate | 1 sobered |
| 12 shan't | 1 shyed | 1 slates | 1 sobriety |
| 2 shant | 4 sich | 1 slattenly | 3 sobs |
| 2 shape | 19 sick | 1 slattern | 2 sociable |
| 2 shaped | 1 sick-chamber | 1 slaver | 2 social |
| 10 share | 3 sickly | 1 slavered | 15 society |
| 2 shared | 5 sickness | 1 slavering | 1 sod |
| 1 sharing | 53 side | 2 slaves | 1 sods |
| 9 sharp | 1 side-board | 1 slavish | 8 sofa |
| 1 sharpen | 1 side-door | 28 sleep | 14 soft |
| 5 sharply | 5 sides | 2 sleeper | 1 soft-featured |
| 1 sharpness | 1 sideways | 1 sleepers | 1 soften |
| 2 shattered | 1 sidled | 3 sleeping | 6 softened |
| 1 shattering | 8 sigh | 1 sleepless | 2 softer |
| 1 shaume | 10 sighed | 1 sleeplessness | 3 softly |
| 6 shawl | 3 sighing | 2 sleeps | 2 softness |
| 1 shawlless | 4 sighs | 1 sleepy | 3 soil |
| 1280 she | 21 sight | 1 sleet | 4 solace |
| 3 she'd | 4 sign | 1 sleet-laden | 1 sold |
| 15 she'll | 1 signal | 1 sleeve | 2 soldered |
| 37 she's | 1 signature | 1 sleeves | 1 soldier |
| 1 sheaves | 2 signed | 5 slender | 4 sole |
| 2 shed | 1 signet | 4 slept | 3 solemn |
| 2 shedding | 1 significant | 2 slid | 4 solemnly |
| 7 sheep | 2 signified | 1 slide | 1 solicited |
| 1 sheep-dog | 1 signify | 2 sliding | 1 soliciting |
| 2 sheer | 2 signing | 14 slight | 1 solidity |
| 2 sheet | 6 signs | 2 slighter | 2 soliloquised |
| 1 sheets | 22 silence | 5 slightest | 1 soliloquized |
| 2 shelf | 1 silenced | 2 slightly | 2 soliloquy |
| 10 shelter | 23 silent | 2 slights | 6 solitary |
| 3 sheltered | 6 silently | 1 slim | 11 solitude |
| 3 shew | 5 silk | 1 slinging | 1 solitudes |
| 1 shewn | 1 silky | 6 slip | 151 some |
| 1 shielders | 3 sill | 7 slipped | 8 somebody |
| 3 shift | 16 silly | 2 slippers | 1 somebody's |
| 4 shifted | 8 silver | 1 slitting | 1 somehow |
| 1 shifting | 1 silvery | 2 slop | 51 something |
| 1 shilling | 6 similar | 3 slope | 6 sometime |
| 1 shillings | 5 simple | 1 slouching | 20 sometimes |
| 1 shimmering | 1 simpleton | 1 slough | 5 somewhat |
| 2 shine | 2 simply | 2 slovenly | 6 somewhere |
| 4 shining | 1 simultaneously | 6 slow | 39 son |
| 1 ship | 4 sin | 6 slowly | 2 son's |
| 1 shirk | 62 since | 2 slumber | 4 song |
| 1 shirt | 2 sincere | 1 slumbers | 9 songs |
| 2 shiver | 4 sincerely | 2 slung | 1 sooin |
| 1 shivered | 3 sincerity | 3 slut | 73 soon |
| 7 shivering | 1 sinewy | 2 sly | 3 sooner |
| 1 shiveringly | 5 sing | 1 smacked | 1 soot |
| 1 shivers | 1 singer | 18 small | 1 sooth |
| 4 shock | 2 singers | 5 smart | 3 soothed |
| 6 shocked | 11 singing | 1 smartly | 2 soothing |
| 2 shocking | 18 single | 1 smash | 1 soothingly |
| 3 shockingly | 5 singular | 1 smashed | 2 sore |
| 1 shodld | 2 singularly | 1 smashing | 14 sorrow |
| 1 shoe | 1 sinister | 2 smelling | 2 sorrowful |
| 7 shoes | 3 sink | 1 smelt | 1 sorrowfully |
| 10 shone | 7 sinking | 19 smile | 1 sorrows |
| 5 shoo | 3 sinner | 8 smiled | 27 sorry |
| 1 shoo'll | 2 sinners | 3 smiles | 12 sort |
| 5 shoo's | 1 sins | 4 smiling | 4 sorts |
| 15 shook | 1 sip | 1 smiths' | 1 sotto |
| 1 shoon | 1 sipping | 1 smiting | 2 sough |
| 4 shoot | 43 sir | 1 smitten | 4 sought |
| 2 shooting | 15 sister | 1 smoked | 29 soul |
| 1 shop | 1 sister's | 4 smoking | 2 soul's |
| 1 shore | 1 sister-in | 9 smooth | 2 souls |
| 23 short | 6 sister-in-law | 2 smoothing | 19 sound |
| 1 shorter | 1 sister-in-law-'s | 2 smote | 3 sounded |
| 7 shot | 1 sisters | 4 smothered | 2 sounding |
| 246 should | 50 sit | 1 smothering | 1 soundly |
| 13 shoulder | 2 sits | 1 smouldered | 2 sounds |
| 1 shouldering | 25 sitting | 1 smuggled | 1 sour |
| 12 shoulders | 3 sitting-room | 1 snail | 5 source |
| 15 shouldn't | 1 sittings | 1 snail-shells | 1 sourest |
| 2 shout | 7 situation | 1 snails | 1 sourly |
| 9 shouted | 20 six | 1 snake | 4 south |
| 1 shouting | 4 sixteen | 2 snap | 1 south-west |
| 2 shoved | 3 sixty | 1 snapped | 1 southern |
| 4 shovel | 1 sizer's | 1 snapping | 3 sovereign |
| 32 show | 1 sizes | 1 snappish | 1 sow |
| 15 showed | 1 skeletons | 1 snappishly | 1 sowls |
| 7 shower | 1 sketch | 1 snarled | 12 space |
| 3 showers | 1 sketched | 2 snatch | 3 spade |
| 9 showing | 1 skies | 10 snatched | 2 spake |
| 7 shown | 1 skift | 2 snatching | 1 spaniel |
| 3 shows | 2 skill | 4 sneaking | 1 spanish |
| 1 showy | | 5 sneer | 13 spare |

| | | | |
|---|---|---|---|
| 7 spared | 1 stained | 3 straining | 1 suggestive |
| 1 sparely | 1 stair's-foot | 28 strange | 1 suicidal |
| 2 sparer | 38 stairs | 3 strangely | 1 suing |
| 1 sparing | 2 stairs' | 20 stranger | 5 suit |
| 1 spark | 1 stairs-head | 2 stranger's | 2 suitable |
| 1 sparkle | 1 stale | 1 strangest | 3 suited |
| 2 sparkled | 1 staling | 3 strangle | 1 suitor |
| 3 sparkling | 1 stall | 2 strangled | 2 sulkily |
| 2 sparks | 2 stalled | 3 stray | 1 sulkiness |
| 1 sparrow's | 1 stalwart | 1 strayed | 2 sulking |
| 1 spat | 1 stammer | 1 stream | 4 sulky |
| 1 spatters | 4 stammered | 1 streamed | 7 sullen |
| 59 speak | 1 stammering | 1 streamers | 2 sullenly |
| 6 speaker | 1 stamp | 3 streaming | 1 sullenness |
| 1 speaker's | 2 stamped | 1 street | 1 sultry |
| 14 speaking | 2 stamping | 1 streets | 25 summer |
| 2 speaks | 1 stanchions | 1 strengh | 1 summit |
| 2 spears | 25 stand | 15 strength | 3 summon |
| 3 special | 16 standing | 1 strenuous | 6 summoned |
| 5 species | 1 stands | 3 stretch | 1 summoning |
| 1 specimen | 1 staple | 7 stretched | 3 summons |
| 1 speckless | 11 stare | 7 stretching | 4 summut |
| 3 spectacle | 16 stared | 1 strewn | 12 sun |
| 1 spectacles | 9 staring | 2 stricken | 1 sun-dahn |
| 1 spectator | 2 stark | 2 strict | 1 sunbeams |
| 2 spectre | 1 stars | 1 strictly | 10 sunday |
| 1 spectre's | 5 start | 1 stride | 2 sundays |
| 1 spectres | 16 started | 1 strides | 2 sundry |
| 1 speculation | 2 startled | 1 striding | 2 sung |
| 22 speech | 1 startles | 12 strike | 5 sunk |
| 1 speeches | 2 startling | 1 strikes | 1 sunny |
| 2 speechless | 4 starve | 7 striking | 1 sunrise |
| 2 speed | 4 starved | 3 string | 1 sunset |
| 5 speedily | 5 starving | 2 striving | 14 sunshine |
| 1 speedy | 16 state | 1 strode | 5 sup |
| 4 spell | 2 stated | 2 stroke | 1 superfluous |
| 2 spelling | 4 statement | 2 stroked | 1 superintend |
| 1 spelt | 1 stating | 4 stroking | 3 superior |
| 10 spend | 7 station | 1 stroll | 4 superiority |
| 1 spended | 1 stationary | 1 strolled | 4 superstition |
| 1 spending | 1 stationed | 24 strong | 1 superstitious |
| 2 spends | 1 statue | 1 strong-hold | 1 supped |
| 13 spent | 1 staunch | 4 stronger | 13 supper |
| 2 sperrit | 1 staunchily | 1 strongly | 1 supper-time |
| 1 spices | 1 staves | 1 strove | 1 supplicated |
| 2 spider | 49 stay | 31 struck | 1 supplicating |
| 2 spies | 13 stayed | 1 structure | 1 supplication |
| 1 spilling | 7 staying | 1 structures | 2 supplications |
| 1 spilt | 1 steadfastly | 8 struggle | 1 supplied |
| 29 spirit | 4 steadily | 7 struggled | 8 supply |
| 1 spirited | 5 steady | 5 struggling | 5 support |
| 14 spirits | 4 steal | 2 stubborn | 3 supported |
| 1 spiritual | 4 stealing | 1 stubbornly | 1 supporter |
| 11 spite | 2 stealthily | 3 studied | 2 supporting |
| 4 spiteful | 1 stealthy | 7 studies | 36 suppose |
| 2 spitefully | 2 steel | 7 study | 12 supposed |
| 1 spitted | 2 steep | 1 studying | 10 supposing |
| 2 spitting | 1 steeped | 4 stuff | 1 suppress |
| 1 splashed | 1 steer | 1 stuffing | 1 suppressed |
| 1 splashes | 1 steering | 1 stumble | 2 suppressing |
| 2 spleen | 21 step | 1 stumbled | 46 sure |
| 3 splendid | 12 stepped | 1 stunned | 1 sure-ly |
| 1 splendidly | 2 stepping | 3 stunted | 11 surely |
| 1 splinter | 14 steps | 10 stupid | 1 surer |
| 1 splinters | 2 stept | 2 stupidity | 2 surface |
| 1 split | 5 stern | 1 stupified | 1 surgeons |
| 1 splitting | 1 sterner | 8 style | 1 surlily |
| 3 spoiled | 1 sterness | 1 suall | 6 surly |
| 1 spoils | 4 sternly | 2 subdue | 1 surmise |
| 1 spoilt | 5 stick | 5 subdued | 1 surmised |
| 33 spoke | 4 sticking | 1 subduing | 2 surname |
| 11 spoken | 4 stiff | 24 subject | 1 surpassed |
| 1 spontaneously | 1 stiffens | 4 subjects | 1 surpressed |
| 1 spoon | 2 stifled | 1 submissive | 15 surprise |
| 2 spoonful | 99 still | 4 subsequent | 8 surprised |
| 1 spoons | 1 stinging | 3 subsided | 2 surprising |
| 1 sport | 1 stipend | 1 substance | 2 surrendered |
| 6 spot | 12 stir | 2 substantial | 5 surrounded |
| 2 spots | 11 stirred | 5 substitute | 2 survey |
| 12 sprang | 4 stirring | 2 succeed | 7 surveyed |
| 5 spread | 1 stirs | 11 succeeded | 6 surveying |
| 2 spreading | 6 stock | 4 succeeding | 2 surviving |
| 16 spring | 2 stockings | 2 success | 1 susceptibility |
| 1 springer | 1 stocks | 1 successfully | 1 susceptible |
| 2 springing | 1 stoical | 5 succession | 2 suspect |
| 2 springs | 8 stole | 4 successor | 5 suspected |
| 1 sprinkled | 1 stomach | 1 succinct | 2 suspecting |
| 1 sprinkling | 11 stone | 1 succour | 1 suspend |
| 3 sprung | 8 stones | 102 such | 1 suspended |
| 1 spur | 1 stony | 1 sucked | 5 suspense |
| 1 spurn | 43 stood | 5 sucking | 2 suspicion |
| 1 spurred | 2 stool | 6 sud | 2 suspicions |
| 2 spy | 1 stoop | 13 sudden | 2 suspiciously |
| 1 squalling | 4 stooped | 15 suddenly | 1 sustain |
| 3 square | 1 stooping | 1 sudn't | 1 sustaining |
| 2 squares | 14 stop | 20 suffer | 1 sustenance |
| 1 squealing | 17 stopped | 9 suffered | 2 swallow |
| 3 squeeze | 4 stopping | 5 suffering | 6 swallowed |
| 1 squeezed | 4 store | 7 sufferings | 2 swallowing |
| 1 squint | 1 stories | 2 suffers | 1 swamp |
| 1 squire | 1 storing | 1 suffice | 1 swamps |
| 1 squire's | 6 storm | 1 sufficed | 1 swarm |
| 1 stab | 1 storms | 13 sufficient | 1 swarmed |
| 7 stable | 3 stormy | 3 sufficiently | 1 swarming |
| 1 stable-boys | 11 story | 1 suffocate | 1 swayed |
| 4 stables | 4 stout | 3 suffocating | 1 swaying |
| 1 staff | 1 stowing | 1 suffused | 10 swear |
| 1 stage | 1 stragglers | 1 sugar | 3 swearing |
| 2 staggered | 2 straggling | 2 sugar-candy | 2 swears |
| 1 stagnates | 8 straight | 9 suggested | 2 sweat |
| 4 staid | 1 strained | 1 suggestion | 1 sweep |

| | | | | | | |
|---|---|---|---|---|---|---|
| 3 | sweeping | 8 | telling | 118 | thought | |
| 21 | sweet | 3 | tells | 2 | thoughtless | |
| 1 | sweeter | 21 | temper | 1 | thoughtlessly | |
| 4 | sweetest | 1 | temperate | 1 | thoughtlessne-ss | |
| 2 | sweetheart | 3 | tempered | 14 | thoughts | |
| 3 | sweetly | 1 | tempers | 6 | thousand | |
| 1 | sweetness | 2 | tempest | 2 | thowt | |
| 1 | sweets | 4 | temples | 1 | thrang | |
| 2 | swelled | 4 | temporary | 2 | thrash | |
| 5 | swells | 2 | tempt | 1 | thrashing | |
| 4 | swept | 6 | temptation | 1 | thrashings | |
| 1 | swerved | 4 | tempted | 1 | thread | |
| 1 | swine | 1 | tempter | 6 | threat | |
| 1 | swing | 2 | tempting | 2 | threaten | |
| 2 | swinging | 14 | ten | 8 | threatened | |
| 1 | switch | 1 | tenacious | 5 | threatening | |
| 1 | swoon | 9 | tenant | 2 | threatens | |
| 1 | swopped | 4 | tenants | 3 | threats | |
| 9 | swore | 1 | tend | 52 | three | |
| 2 | sworn | 3 | tended | 1 | three-inch | |
| 5 | swung | 1 | tendency | 10 | threshold | |
| 7 | syllable | 4 | tender | 16 | threw | |
| 1 | syllables | 1 | tenderly | 3 | thrice | |
| 1 | sympathetic | 3 | tenderness | 1 | thrill | |
| 1 | sympathies | 1 | tending | 1 | thrilling | |
| 3 | sympathise | 1 | tends | 2 | thrive | |
| 2 | sympathised | 1 | tenour | 1 | thriven | |
| 1 | sympathize | 1 | tension | 9 | throat | |
| 2 | sympathizing | 1 | tent | 1 | throbbing | |
| 7 | sympathy | 3 | term | 1 | throstles | |
| 2 | symptoms | 2 | termed | 1 | throttled | |
| 53 | t' | 1 | terminating | 3 | throttler | |
| 1 | t'boards | 2 | termination | 86 | through | |
| 1 | t'doctor | 3 | terms | 3 | throughout | |
| 1 | t'door | 5 | terrible | 4 | throw | |
| 1 | t'father | 4 | terribly | 3 | throwing | |
| 1 | t'fields | 2 | terrier | 7 | thrown | |
| 1 | t'fowld | 1 | terrific | 26 | thrushcross | |
| 1 | t'grand | 5 | terrified | 14 | thrust | |
| 1 | t'kitchen | 2 | terrify | 3 | thrusting | |
| 1 | t'lads | 14 | terror | 1 | thud | |
| 2 | t'maister | 1 | testament | 1 | thumped | |
| 1 | t'maister's | 2 | text | 6 | thunder | |
| 2 | t'other | 1 | texts | 1 | thunder-cloud | |
| 1 | t'raight | 1 | tg | 1 | thunder-storm | |
| 1 | t'road | 1 | th | 6 | thundered | |
| 2 | t'soart | 23 | th' | 1 | thundering | |
| 1 | t'sowl | 1 | thah | 4 | thur | |
| 1 | taan | 198 | than | 4 | thursday | |
| 41 | table | 12 | thank | 11 | thus | |
| 1 | table-top | 2 | thanked | 2 | thwart | |
| 3 | tables | 3 | thankful | 2 | thwarting | |
| 1 | tacit | 10 | thanks | 12 | thy | |
| 1 | taciturn | 1195 | that | 1 | ticket | |
| 1 | tacked | 46 | that's | 1 | tidied | |
| 1 | taen | 3 | thaw | 3 | tidy | |
| 3 | tail | 4573 | the | 2 | tie | |
| 1 | tails | 1 | the' | 4 | tied | |
| 2 | tak | 7 | thear | 1 | ties | |
| 2 | tak' | 1 | theare | 1 | tiger | |
| 115 | take | 12 | thee | 1 | tigers | |
| 22 | taken | 148 | their | 1 | tight | |
| 4 | takes | 3 | theirs | 1 | tight-stretch-ed | |
| 24 | taking | 1 | theirseln | | | |
| 14 | tale | 232 | them | 1 | tightened | |
| 8 | tales | 1 | themes | 1 | tigress | |
| 49 | talk | 12 | themselves | 151 | till | |
| 10 | talked | 289 | then | 1 | timber | |
| 14 | talking | 3 | thence | 117 | time | |
| 2 | talks | 5 | thenceforth | 1 | time-piece | |
| 4 | tall | 1 | theology | 31 | times | |
| 3 | taller | 1 | ther | 4 | timid | |
| 1 | tallest | 288 | there | 1 | timidity | |
| 1 | talons | 1 | there'd | 2 | timidly | |
| 1 | tame | 22 | there's | 2 | tin | |
| 1 | tangible | 2 | thereat | 1 | tingled | |
| 1 | tankards | 14 | therefore | 1 | tingling | |
| 1 | tapers | 1 | thereto | 1 | tiny | |
| 1 | taps | 48 | these | 1 | tip | |
| 1 | tarnish | 292 | they | 1 | tiptoe | |
| 1 | tarry | 6 | they'll | 21 | tired | |
| 2 | tartly | 2 | they're | 5 | tiresome | |
| 1 | tarts | 13 | they's | 3 | tiresomely | |
| 6 | task | 1 | they've | 1 | titan | |
| 1 | tasks | 1 | thible | 3 | title | |
| 7 | taste | 12 | thick | 1 | titter | |
| 1 | tasted | 1 | thickening | 1 | tittered | |
| 2 | tastes | 1 | thickly | 3438 | to | |
| 6 | taught | 2 | thief | 1 | to't | |
| 1 | taunting | 5 | thin | 2 | to-bed | |
| 1 | tauntingly | 57 | thing | 11 | to-day | |
| 29 | tea | 38 | things | 1 | to-morn | |
| 1 | tea-canister | 113 | think | 18 | to-morrow | |
| 12 | teach | 16 | thinking | 16 | to-night | |
| 1 | teacher | 6 | thinks | 2 | toast | |
| 1 | teachers | 1 | thinner | 1 | toasted | |
| 1 | teaches | 10 | third | 1 | tobacco | |
| 2 | teaching | 2 | thirsty | 3 | today | |
| 10 | tear | 4 | thirteen | 41 | together | |
| 29 | tears | 1 | thirty | 1 | togither | |
| 4 | tease | 1 | thirty-nine | 1 | toil | |
| 3 | teased | 292 | this | 1 | toiled | |
| 1 | teases | 2 | thither | 1 | toilette | |
| 5 | teasing | 2 | thorn | 2 | token | |
| 1 | teazing | 1 | thorns | 79 | told | |
| 1 | tedious | 1 | thorough | 2 | tolerable | |
| 1 | teens | 8 | thoroughly | 10 | tolerably | |
| 18 | teeth | 74 | those | 1 | tolerate | |
| 1 | teething | 7 | thou | 1 | tolerated | |
| 122 | tell | 1 | thou'rt | 1 | tombs | |
| 1 | telled | 122 | though | | | |

| | |
|---|---|
| 1 | tome |
| 1 | tomorrow |
| 19 | tone |
| 3 | tones |
| 27 | tongue |
| 2 | tongues |
| 136 | too |
| 96 | took |
| 1 | tool |
| 1 | toolhouse |
| 1 | tools |
| 2 | tooth |
| 1 | toothless |
| 15 | top |
| 1 | top-most |
| 2 | topic |
| 1 | topics |
| 1 | tops |
| 1 | torch |
| 2 | tore |
| 5 | torment |
| 1 | tormented |
| 1 | tormenter |
| 1 | tormenting |
| 1 | torments |
| 1 | torn |
| 2 | torrent |
| 6 | torture |
| 1 | tortures |
| 2 | tossed |
| 2 | tossing |
| 1 | total |
| 2 | totter |
| 1 | tottered |
| 18 | touch |
| 15 | touched |
| 3 | touches |
| 2 | touchiness |
| 4 | touching |
| 1 | touchy |
| 2 | tough |
| 44 | towards |
| 1 | towel |
| 1 | towering |
| 3 | town |
| 1 | towns |
| 1 | toys |
| 2 | traces |
| 1 | tracing |
| 1 | tracked |
| 1 | trail |
| 1 | trailed |
| 2 | train |
| 1 | train-oil |
| 1 | trait |
| 3 | traitor |
| 1 | tramped |
| 1 | trample |
| 2 | trampled |
| 4 | tranquil |
| 8 | tranquillity |
| 1 | transactions |
| 1 | transcient |
| 1 | transfigured |
| 2 | transformation |
| 1 | transformed |
| 1 | transforming |
| 1 | transgress |
| 2 | transgressions |
| 1 | transient |
| 1 | transmit |
| 1 | transmuted |
| 1 | transplanted |
| 4 | trap |
| 5 | trash |
| 1 | travel |
| 1 | traveller |
| 4 | travelling |
| 1 | travels |
| 2 | traversed |
| 7 | tray |
| 1 | treacherous |
| 4 | treachery |
| 2 | tread |
| 3 | treasure |
| 2 | treasures |
| 6 | treat |
| 10 | treated |
| 4 | treating |
| 5 | treatment |
| 1 | treaty |
| 9 | tree |
| 20 | trees |
| 10 | trembled |
| 1 | trembles |
| 11 | trembling |
| 1 | tremendous |
| 2 | trepidation |
| 1 | tresses |
| 1 | trial |
| 2 | trick |
| 1 | trickle |
| 1 | trickled |
| 5 | tricks |
| 23 | tried |
| 3 | trifle |
| 3 | trifles |
| 2 | trifling |
| 1 | trim |
| 1 | trinket |
| 1 | trinkets |

| | |
|---|---|
| 1 | trio |
| 1 | tripped |
| 4 | triumph |
| 1 | triumphant |
| 1 | triumphed |
| 1 | trodden |
| 1 | trombone |
| 3 | trot |
| 3 | trotted |
| 30 | trouble |
| 8 | troubled |
| 5 | troubles |
| 1 | troublesome |
| 1 | troublesomely |
| 2 | troubling |
| 2 | trousers |
| 22 | true |
| 1 | truer |
| 4 | truly |
| 1 | trumpet |
| 1 | trunk |
| 1 | trunks |
| 7 | trust |
| 3 | trusted |
| 1 | trustees |
| 1 | trustful |
| 1 | trusting |
| 20 | truth |
| 24 | try |
| 14 | trying |
| 1 | tube |
| 3 | tucked |
| 1 | tuesday |
| 1 | tuft |
| 38 | tuh |
| 2 | tull |
| 1 | tum'le |
| 3 | tumbler |
| 1 | tumblerfuls |
| 4 | tumult |
| 1 | tumultuously |
| 3 | tune |
| 1 | tunes |
| 1 | tureen |
| 7 | turf |
| 1 | turkey's |
| 45 | turn |
| 40 | turned |
| 31 | turning |
| 1 | turnip |
| 3 | turns |
| 1 | tush |
| 2 | tut |
| 1 | tutor |
| 1 | tutored |
| 1 | twang |
| 14 | twelve |
| 1 | twelvemonths |
| 1 | twentieth |
| 20 | twenty |
| 3 | twenty-four |
| 1 | twenty-seven |
| 2 | twenty-three |
| 1 | twenty-two |
| 16 | twice |
| 1 | twined |
| 1 | twinkle |
| 2 | twinkling |
| 1 | twist |
| 3 | twisted |
| 1 | twisting |
| 2 | twitched |
| 1 | twitches |
| 106 | two |
| 2 | tying |
| 2 | type |
| 2 | tyrannical |
| 1 | tyrannically |
| 1 | tyrannies |
| 4 | tyrant |
| 1 | ud |
| 6 | uf |
| 2 | ugly |
| 25 | uh |
| 1 | uh't |
| 1 | ultimate |
| 2 | umbrella |
| 1 | umph |
| 15 | un |
| 23 | un' |
| 4 | unable |
| 1 | unacceptable |
| 2 | unaccompanied |
| 1 | unaccountable |
| 1 | unachieved |
| 1 | unalterably |
| 1 | unannoyed |
| 1 | unanswered |
| 1 | unavailing |
| 1 | unavenged |
| 1 | unavoidably |
| 1 | unbarred |
| 1 | unbeliever |
| 1 | unbidden |
| 1 | uncared |
| 1 | uncarpeted |
| 1 | unceremonious- |
| | ly |
| 4 | uncertain |
| 1 | uncertainly |
| 1 | unchain |

| | |
|---|---|
| 2 | unchained |
| 1 | unchangeable |
| 1 | unchanged |
| 2 | unchristian |
| 1 | uncivil |
| 24 | uncle |
| 1 | uncle's |
| 1 | uncle-in-law's |
| 1 | uncleared |
| 1 | unclose |
| 1 | unclosed |
| 1 | uncombed |
| 5 | uncomfortable |
| 2 | uncommonly |
| 1 | uncomplaining |
| 1 | uncompromising |
| 2 | unconscious |
| 1 | unconsciously |
| 1 | unconsciousne- |
| | ss |
| 2 | uncontrollable |
| 1 | uncovered |
| 1 | uncoveted |
| 2 | uncultivated |
| 1 | uncurled |
| 1 | uncurtained |
| 9 | und |
| 1 | undecided |
| 1 | undefined |
| 1 | undeniable |
| 81 | under |
| 1 | under-bred |
| 1 | under-drawn |
| 1 | under-lip |
| 1 | undergo |
| 1 | undergone |
| 2 | underground |
| 1 | underlined |
| 2 | underlings |
| 2 | underneath |
| 12 | understand |
| 1 | understanding |
| 5 | understood |
| 3 | undertake |
| 1 | undertone |
| 1 | undertook |
| 1 | undeserved |
| 1 | undisguised |
| 1 | undisputed |
| 1 | undisturbed |
| 1 | undone |
| 2 | undress |
| 2 | undressed |
| 1 | undulating |
| 2 | unearthly |
| 1 | uneasily |
| 2 | uneasiness |
| 3 | uneasy |
| 1 | unequal |
| 4 | unexpected |
| 3 | unexpectedly |
| 1 | unfastened |
| 3 | unfeeling |
| 3 | unfit |
| 1 | unfixed |
| 1 | unfledged |
| 1 | unflinching |
| 1 | unfold |
| 1 | unformed |
| 5 | unfortunate |
| 1 | unfortunately |
| 1 | unfriended |
| 1 | ungenerous |
| 1 | ungodly |
| 1 | ungovernable |
| 1 | ungraciously |
| 2 | ungrateful |
| 7 | unhappy |
| 1 | unharmed |
| 1 | unhasp |
| 1 | unheard |
| 1 | unheeding |
| 1 | unhesitatingly |
| 1 | uniform |
| 1 | uninhabited |
| 4 | union |
| 1 | unison |
| 2 | universal |
| 1 | universe |
| 1 | unjustly |
| 1 | unknotted |
| 2 | unknown |
| 39 | unless |
| 2 | unlikely |
| 1 | unlimited |
| 1 | unlock |
| 2 | unluckily |
| 1 | unlucky |
| 1 | unmanned |
| 1 | unmannerly |
| 1 | unmistakably |
| 1 | unmolested |
| 1 | unmoved |
| 6 | unnatural |
| 3 | unnecessary |
| 1 | unnerved |
| 1 | unnoticed |
| 2 | unobserved |
| 1 | unobstructed |
| 1 | unperilous |
| 1 | unpleasing |

| | |
|---|---|
| 1 | unprincipled |
| 1 | unquiet |
| 2 | unreasonable |
| 1 | unreclaimed |
| 1 | unreconciled |
| 1 | unresting |
| 1 | unrestrained |
| 1 | unrevenged |
| 1 | unripped |
| 1 | unruly |
| 1 | unsaid |
| 1 | unsatisfactor- |
| | ily |
| 1 | unseasonable |
| 1 | unseen |
| 1 | unsettle |
| 1 | unsettled |
| 1 | unslinging |
| 3 | unsociable |
| 1 | unsolicited |
| 2 | unspeakable |
| 1 | unspeakably |
| 1 | unsubstantial |
| 1 | unsuccessful |
| 1 | unsummoned |
| 1 | unsuspecting |
| 1 | untenanted |
| 1 | untidy |
| 1 | untie |
| 1 | untied |
| 1 | until |
| 1 | untold |
| 1 | untroubled |
| 3 | untruth |
| 1 | untying |
| 1 | unusual |
| 1 | unutterable |
| 1 | unutterably |
| 1 | unvalued |
| 1 | unwarrantable |
| 1 | unwashed |
| 1 | unwaveringly |
| 1 | unwearied |
| 1 | unwelcome |
| 1 | unwelcomed |
| 1 | unwell |
| 2 | unwilling |
| 3 | unwillingly |
| 1 | unwittingly |
| 1 | unwonted |
| 3 | unworthy |
| 308 | up |
| 20 | up-stairs |
| 1 | upbraid |
| 1 | uplands |
| 21 | upon |
| 2 | upper |
| 1 | uppermost |
| 2 | upright |
| 4 | uproar |
| 2 | ups |
| 2 | upset |
| 4 | upstairs |
| 1 | upward |
| 1 | urge |
| 8 | urged |
| 1 | urges |
| 2 | urging |
| 1 | urn |
| 181 | us |
| 1 | usage |
| 21 | use |
| 30 | used |
| 1 | useful |
| 5 | useless |
| 1 | uselessness |
| 4 | ushered |
| 1 | using |
| 16 | usual |
| 1 | usuald |
| 5 | usually |
| 2 | usurped |
| 2 | usurper |
| 13 | ut |
| 2 | ut' |
| 2 | ut's |
| 2 | utensils |
| 5 | utmost |
| 7 | utter |
| 23 | uttered |
| 5 | uttering |
| 3 | utterly |
| 1 | vacancy |
| 7 | vacant |
| 2 | vagabond |
| 1 | vagaries |
| 3 | vague |
| 1 | vaguely |
| 7 | vain |
| 4 | vainly |
| 1 | valances |
| 6 | valley |
| 1 | valorously |
| 1 | valour |
| 1 | valuable |
| 5 | value |
| 2 | valued |
| 1 | vampire |
| 1 | vane |
| 1 | vanish |
| 10 | vanished |

| | |
|---|---|
| 1 | vanishing |
| 4 | vanity |
| 1 | vanquish |
| 2 | vanquished |
| 2 | vapid |
| 1 | vapour |
| 1 | variations |
| 2 | varied |
| 1 | variety |
| 3 | various |
| 1 | varrah |
| 1 | varry |
| 2 | varying |
| 1 | vast |
| 2 | vastly |
| 1 | vegetables |
| 3 | vehemence |
| 3 | vehemently |
| 1 | veil |
| 1 | vein |
| 1 | veins |
| 1 | vengeance |
| 1 | venom |
| 2 | venomous |
| 1 | vent |
| 1 | ventilation |
| 7 | venture |
| 8 | ventured |
| 1 | venturesome |
| 1 | venturing |
| 1 | verbs |
| 1 | verdant |
| 1 | verge |
| 1 | verging |
| 1 | verified |
| 2 | verse |
| 1 | verses |
| 131 | very |
| 2 | vessel |
| 1 | vestige |
| 1 | veto |
| 5 | vex |
| 2 | vexation |
| 1 | vexatious |
| 12 | vexed |
| 1 | vials |
| 1 | vibrates |
| 1 | vice |
| 1 | vicious |
| 1 | victim |
| 2 | victuals |
| 8 | view |
| 2 | viewing |
| 3 | vigilance |
| 2 | vigilant |
| 3 | vigorous |
| 3 | vigour |
| 2 | vile |
| 12 | village |
| 2 | villagers |
| 12 | villain |
| 1 | villanous |
| 1 | vindictive |
| 1 | vindictiveness |
| 1 | vinegar-faced |
| 1 | viol |
| 7 | violence |
| 11 | violent |
| 1 | viper |
| 1 | virtue |
| 1 | virtuous |
| 1 | virulency |
| 1 | vis-a-vis |
| 1 | visage |
| 7 | visible |
| 1 | visibly |
| 2 | vision |
| 1 | visions |
| 26 | visit |
| 3 | visitation |
| 1 | visitations |
| 7 | visited |
| 3 | visiter |
| 2 | visiters |
| 3 | visiting |
| 11 | visits |
| 2 | vivacity |
| 1 | vivid |
| 1 | vividly |
| 1 | vivifisection |
| 1 | vixen |
| 1 | vocal |
| 1 | vocally |
| 1 | vocation |
| 2 | vocations |
| 1 | voce |
| 1 | vociferate |
| 1 | vociferated |
| 1 | vociferating |
| 37 | voice |
| 1 | voices |
| 3 | volume |
| 4 | volumes |
| 1 | volunteer |
| 1 | vouchsafed |
| 2 | vowed |
| 2 | vowing |
| 2 | vulgar |
| 2 | wading |
| 1 | wafted |
| 1 | wag |

| | | | | | | |
|---|---|---|---|---|---|---|
| 1 | wage | 18 | week | 1 | wile | 1 | wrapping |
| 2 | wager | 2 | week's | 2 | wilful | 1 | wrapt |
| 4 | wages | 12 | weeks | 1 | wilfully | 5 | wrath |
| 2 | wah | 2 | weeks' | 242 | will | 2 | wreath |
| 1 | waif | 6 | weel | 6 | willing | 4 | wrench |
| 4 | wail | 1 | weel's | 7 | willingly | 6 | wrenched |
| 3 | wailed | 4 | weep | 1 | willow | 1 | wrenching |
| 1 | wailing | 18 | weeping | 1 | willut | 1 | wrest |
| 3 | waistcoat | 1 | weighed | 3 | win | 11 | wretch |
| 24 | wait | 1 | weighing | 1 | wince | 2 | wretch's |
| 10 | waited | 1 | weighs | 1 | wincing | 8 | wretched |
| 14 | waiting | 2 | weight | 22 | wind | 1 | wretchedness |
| 7 | wake | 1 | weighty | 1 | winding | 1 | wretches |
| 1 | waken | 11 | welcome | 2 | windings | 3 | wring |
| 6 | wakened | 1 | welcomed | 56 | window | 1 | wringing |
| 1 | wakens | 2 | welcoming | 1 | window-ledge | 1 | wrinkles |
| 2 | wakes | 131 | well | 2 | window-seat | 3 | wrist |
| 4 | waking | 1 | well-formed | 14 | windows | 14 | write |
| 43 | walk | 1 | well-made | 3 | winds | 1 | writer |
| 25 | walked | 1 | well-swept | 7 | wine | 2 | writhe |
| 16 | walking | 88 | went | 2 | wing | 2 | writhed |
| 3 | walks | 1 | wenting | 3 | wink | 2 | writhing |
| 24 | wall | 12 | wept | 1 | winked | 10 | writing |
| 8 | walls | 11 | wer | 3 | winking | 5 | written |
| 2 | wan | 355 | were | 2 | winning | 20 | wrong |
| 4 | wander | 2 | wern't | 1 | winsome | 5 | wronged |
| 6 | wandered | 3 | west | 21 | winter | 2 | wrongs |
| 1 | wanderers | 1 | westering | 1 | winter's | 4 | wrote |
| 8 | wandering | 10 | wet | 1 | wintry | 3 | wrought |
| 2 | wanderings | 2 | wetted | 2 | wipe | 4 | wrung |
| 1 | wanders | 1 | wh | 4 | wiped | 3 | wur |
| 51 | want | 300 | what | 2 | wiping | 61 | wuthering |
| 27 | wanted | 6 | what's | 2 | wisdom | 37 | yah |
| 3 | wanting | 10 | whatever | 2 | wise | 2 | yah'll |
| 9 | wants | 3 | whear | 1 | wisely | 6 | yah're |
| 3 | war | 1 | wheare | 3 | wiser | 2 | yah's |
| 1 | wardrobe | 1 | wheedle | 78 | wish | 15 | yard |
| 1 | wark | 1 | wheedling | 28 | wished | 9 | yards |
| 1 | warks | 1 | wheeled | 12 | wishes | 1 | yate |
| 1 | warld | 1 | wheeling | 9 | wishing | 1 | yawn |
| 19 | warm | 4 | whelp | 8 | wisht | 2 | yawned |
| 3 | warmed | 1 | whelphood | 5 | wit | 2 | yawning |
| 1 | warmly | 308 | when | 7 | witch | 25 | ye |
| 1 | warms | 2 | whence | 2 | witched | 1 | ye'll |
| 1 | warmth | 5 | whenever | 1 | witches | 10 | year |
| 7 | warn | 122 | where | 803 | with | 4 | year's |
| 2 | warn't | 1 | where's | 1 | withdraw | 1 | yearly |
| 2 | warned | 2 | whereas | 1 | withdrawing | 1 | yearn |
| 9 | warning | 1 | whereby | 1 | withdrew | 2 | yearned |
| 1 | warrant | 1 | whereupon | 3 | withered | 5 | yearning |
| 1125 | was | 4 | wherever | 2 | withhold | 46 | years |
| 1 | was'nt | 7 | whet | 30 | within | 2 | yell |
| 5 | wash | 55 | whether | 61 | without | 1 | yelled |
| 1 | wash-house | 1 | whey | 6 | witness | 1 | yelling |
| 5 | washed | 1 | whey-faced | 4 | witnessed | 4 | yellow |
| 1 | washhouse | 183 | which | 2 | witnessing | 1 | yells |
| 2 | washing | 1 | whichever | 6 | wits | 1 | yelped |
| 1 | wasn't | 116 | while | 3 | wives | 4 | yelping |
| 3 | waste | 2 | whim | 1 | wod | 10 | yer |
| 4 | wasted | 1 | whimper | 4 | woke | 1 | yerseln |
| 18 | watch | 2 | whims | 1 | wold | 56 | yes |
| 1 | watchdog | 2 | whining | 2 | wolf | 1 | yester |
| 12 | watched | 2 | whinstone | 1 | wolfish | 1 | yester-evening |
| 15 | watching | 3 | whip | 1 | wolfishly | 17 | yesterday |
| 24 | water | 1 | whipping | 1 | wollsome | 3 | yesterday's |
| 1 | watered | 1 | whirl | 23 | woman | 2 | yesternight |
| 1 | watering | 1 | whirled | 3 | woman's | 105 | yet |
| 1 | watery | 3 | whiskers | 2 | women | 8 | yield |
| 1 | wavered | 4 | whisper | 33 | won't | 7 | yielded |
| 1 | waves | 28 | whispered | 23 | wonder | 2 | yielding |
| 1 | waving | 1 | whispers | 8 | wondered | 1 | yoak |
| 1 | wax | 1 | whistle | 1 | wonderful | 6 | yon |
| 5 | waxed | 1 | whistled | 1 | wonderfully | 1 | yon' |
| 1 | waxen | 26 | white | 4 | wondering | 3 | yon's |
| 1 | waxing | 2 | whitened | 3 | wondrous | 10 | yonder |
| 78 | way | 1 | whiteness | 1 | wondrously | 1 | yorkshire |
| 10 | ways | 152 | who | 43 | wont | 1739 | you |
| 4 | wayward | 1 | who's | 4 | wood | 22 | you'd |
| 1 | waywardness | 1 | whoever | 3 | wooden | 80 | you'll |
| 318 | we | 1 | whoiver | 3 | woods | 28 | you're |
| 1 | we'd | 61 | whole | 1 | wool | 27 | you've |
| 13 | we'll | 2 | wholesome | 1 | woonder | 107 | young |
| 4 | we're | 3 | wholly | 47 | word | 10 | younger |
| 3 | we's | 18 | whom | 45 | words | 1 | youngsters |
| 5 | we've | 17 | whose | 1 | wordy | 406 | your |
| 9 | weak | 96 | why | 5 | wore | 1 | your're |
| 1 | weaker | 1 | wi | 33 | work | 21 | yours |
| 2 | weakling | 12 | wi' | 6 | worked | 42 | yourself |
| 8 | weakness | 2 | wi't | 3 | working | 2 | yourseln |
| 2 | wealthy | 3 | wick | 44 | world | 1 | yourselves |
| 2 | weaned | 1 | wick' | 2 | worldly | 7 | youth |
| 5 | weapon | 27 | wicked | 1 | worms | 1 | youth-like |
| 1 | weapons | 2 | wickedly | 1 | worn't | 2 | youthful |
| 2 | wearied | 1 | wickedness | 2 | worried | 1 | zeal |
| 1 | wearies | 1 | wickednesses | 1 | worries | 1 | zealous |
| 1 | weariness | 2 | wicket | 4 | worrying | 1 | zest |
| 1 | wearing | 11 | wide | 40 | worse | 32 | zillah |
| 4 | wearisome | 1 | wide-brimmed | 1 | worship | 2 | zillah's |
| 1 | wearisomest | 1 | wider | 8 | worst | | |
| 12 | weary | 2 | widow | 7 | worth | | |
| 3 | wearying | 1 | wielded | 8 | worthless | | |
| 1 | weasel's | 23 | wife | 5 | worthy | | |
| 12 | weather | 4 | wife's | 444 | would | | |
| 1 | weather-bound | 1 | wih | 47 | wouldn't | | |
| 1 | weather-cocks | 24 | wild | 4 | wound | | |
| 1 | weather-worn | 1 | wild-beast's | 1 | wounded | | |
| 1 | weathered | 1 | wild-duck's | 1 | wounds | | |
| 1 | wed | 1 | wildered | 1 | wrangle | | |
| 2 | wedding | 4 | wilderness | 1 | wrap | | |
| 1 | wedding-day | 4 | wildly | 2 | wrapped | | |
| 1 | weeds | 2 | wildness | | | | |

# FIELD OF REFERENCE

1.01 [WUTHERING HEIGHTS
1.02 VOL. 1 CHAPTER 1]
1.03 1801 -- I have just returned from a visit to
1.04 my landlord -- the solitary neighbour that I
1.05 shall be troubled with. This is certainly, a
1.06 beautiful country! In all England, I do not
1.07 believe that I could have fixed on a situation
1.08 so completely removed from the stir of society.
1.09 A perfect misanthropist's Heaven -- and Mr.
1.10 Heathcliff and I are such a suitable pair to
1.11 divide the desolation between us.  A capital
1.12 fellow! He little imagined how my heart
1.13 warmed towards him when I beheld his black
2.01 eyes withdraw so suspiciously under their
2.02 brows, as I rode up, and when his fingers shel-
2.03 tered themselves, with a jealous resolution, still
2.04 further in his waistcoat, as I announced my
2.05 name.
2.06 "Mr. Heathcliff?" I said.
2.07 A nod was the answer.
2.08 "Mr. Lockwood your new tenant, sir -- I do
2.09 myself the honour of calling as soon as possible,
2.10 after my arrival, to express the hope that I
2.11 have not inconvenienced you by my perseve-
2.12 rance in soliciting the occupation of Thrush-
2.13 cross Grange: I heard, yesterday, you had
2.14 had some thoughts --"
2.15 "Thrushcross Grange is my own, sir," he
2.16 interrupted wincing, "I should not allow any
2.17 one to inconvenience me, if I could hinder it --
2.18 walk in!"
2.19 The "walk in," was uttered with closed
2.20 teeth and expressed the sentiment, "Go to the
2.21 Deuce!" even the gate over which he leant
2.22 manifested no sympathizing movement to the
3.01 words; and I think that circumstance deter-
3.02 mined me to accept the invitation: I felt in-
3.03 terested in a man who seemed more exagge-
3.04 rately reserved than myself.
3.05 when he saw my horse's breast fairly push-
3.06 ing the barrier, he did pull out his hand to un-
3.07 chain it, and then sullenly preceded me up the
3.08 causeway, calling, as we entered the court:
3.09 "Joseph, take Mr. Lockwood's horse; and
3.10 bring up some wine."
3.11 "Here we have the whole establishment of
3.12 domestics, I suppose," was the reflection, sug-
3.13 gested by this compound order, "No wonder
3.14 the grass grows up between the flags, and
3.15 cattle are the only hedge-cutters."
3.16 Joseph was an elderly, nay, an old man,
3.17 very old, perhaps, though hale and sinewy.
3.18 "The Lord help us!" he soliloquised in an
3.19 undertone of peevish displeasure, while reliev-
3.20 ing me of my horse: looking, meantime, in my
3.21 face so sourly that I charitably conjectured he
3.22 must have need of divine aid to digest his dinner,
4.01 and his pious ejaculation had no reference
4.02 to my unexpected advent.
4.03 Wuthering Heights is the name of Mr.
4.04 Heathcliff's dwelling. "wuthering" being a
4.05 significant provincial adjective, descriptive of
4.06 the atmospheric tumult to which its station is
4.07 exposed, in stormy weather. Pure, bracing
4.8 ventilation they must have up there, at all
4.09 times, indeed: one may guess the power of the
4.10 north wind, blowing over the edge, by the
4.11 excessive slant of a few, stunted firs at the
4.12 end of the house; and by a range of gaunt
4.13 thorns all stretching their limbs one way, as
4.14 if craving alms of the sun. Happily, the ar-
4.15 chitect had foresight to build it strong: the
4.16 narrow windows are deeply set in the wall;
4.17 and the corners defended with large jutting
4.18 stones.
4.19 Before passing the threshold, I paused to
4.20 admire a quantity of grotesque carving lavished
4.21 over the front, and especially about the princi-
4.22 pal door, above which, among a wilderness of
5.01 crumbling griffins, and shameless little boys, I
5.02 detected the date "1500," and the name
5.03 "Hareton Earnshaw," I would have made a
5.04 few comments, and requested a short history
5.05 of the place, from the surly owner, but his
5.06 attitude at the door appeared to demand my
5.07 speedy entrance, or complete departure, and I
5.08 had no desire to aggravate his impatience, pre-
5.09 vious to inspecting the penetralium.
5.10 One step brought us into the family sitting--
5.11 room, without any introductory lobby, or pas-
5.12 sage: they call it here "the house" preemi-
5.13 nently. It includes kitchen, and parlor, ge-
5.14 nerally, but I believe at Wuthering Heights,
5.15 the kitchen is forced to retreat altogether, into
5.16 another quarter, at least I distinguished a
5.17 chatter of tongues, and a clatter of culinary
5.18 utensils, deep within; and I observed no signs
5.19 of roasting, boiling, or baking, about the huge
5.20 fire-place; nor any glitter of copper saucepans
5.21 and tin cullenders on the walls. One end,
5.22 indeed, reflected splendidly both light and heat,
6.01 from ranks of immense pewter dishes; inter-
6.02 spersed with silver jugs, and tankards, tower-
6.03 ing row after row, in a vast oak dresser, to the
6.04 very roof. The latter had never been under--
6.05 drawn, its entire anatomy lay bare to an in-
6.06 quiring eye, except where a frame of wood
6.07 laden with oatcakes, and clusters of legs of
6.08 beef, mutton and ham, concealed it. Above
6.09 the chimney were sundry villanous old guns,
6.10 and a couple of horse-pistols, and, by way of

6.11 ornament, three gaudily painted canisters dis-
6.12 posed along its ledge. The floor was of
6.13 smooth, white stone: the chairs, high-backed,
6.14 primitive structures, painted green: one or
6.15 two heavy black ones lurking in the shade.
6.16 In an arch, under the dresser, reposed a huge,
6.17 liver-coloured bitch pointer surrounded by a
6.18 swarm of squealing puppies, and other dogs,
6.19 haunted other recesses.
6.20 The apartment, and furniture would have
6.21 been nothing extraordinary as belonging to a
6.22 homely, northern farmer with a stubborn countenance,
7.01 and stalwart limbs, set out to advan-
7.02 tage in knee-breeches, and gaiters. Such an
7.03 individual, seated in his arm-chair, his mug of
7.04 ale frothing on the round table before him, is
7.05 to be seen in any circuit of five or six miles
7.06 among these hills, if you go at the right time,
7.07 after dinner. But, Mr. Heathcliff forms a sin-
7.08 gular contrast to his abode and style of living.
7.09 He is a dark skinned gypsy, in aspect, in
7.10 dress, and manners, a gentleman, that is, as
7.11 much a gentleman as many a country squire:
7.12 rather slovenly, perhaps, yet not looking amiss,
7.13 with his negligence, because he has an erect
7.14 and handsome figure -- and rather morose -- pos-
7.15 sibly, some people might suspect him of a de-
7.16 gree of under-bred pride -- I have a sympathe-
7.17 tic chord within that tells me it is nothing of
7.18 the sort; I know, by instinct, his reserve
7.19 springs from an aversion to showy displays of
7.20 feeling -- to manifestations of mutual kindliness.
7.21 He'll love and hate, equally under cover, and
7.22 esteem it a species of impertinence, to be loved
8.01 or hated again -- No, I'm running on too fast --
8.02 I bestow my own attributes over liberally on
8.03 him. Mr. Heathcliff may have entirely dis-
8.04 similar reasons for keeping his hand out of
8.05 the way, when he meets a would be acquaint-
8.06 ance, to those which actuate me. Let me hope my
8.07 constitution is almost peculiar: my dear mo-
8.08 ther used to say I should never have a com-
8.09 fortable home, and only last summer, I proved
8.10 myself perfectly unworthy of one.
8.11 While enjoying a month of fine weather at
8.12 the sea-coast, I was thrown into the company
8.13 of a most fascinating creature, a real goddess,
8.14 in my eyes, as long as she took no notice of
8.15 me. I "never told my love" vocally; still, if
8.16 looks have language, the merest idiot might
8.17 have guessed I was over head and ears: she
8.18 understood me, at last, and looked a return --
8.19 the sweetest of all imaginable looks -- and what
8.20 did I do? I confess it with shame -- shrunk
8.21 icily into myself, like a snail, at every glance
8.22 retired colder and farther; till, finally, the
9.01 poor innocent was led to doubt her own senses,
9.02 and, overwhelmed with confusion at her sup-
9.03 posed mistake, persuaded her mamma to de-
9.04 camp.
9.05 By this curious turn of disposition I have
9.06 gained the reputation of deliberate heartless-
9.07 ness, how undeserved, I alone can appreciate.
9.08 I took a seat at the end of the hearthstone
9.09 opposite that towards which my landlord ad-
9.10 vanced, and filled up an interval of silence by
9.11 attempting to caress the canine mother, who
9.12 had left her nursery, and was sneaking wolf-
9.13 ishly to the back of my legs, her lip curled up,
9.14 and her white teeth watering for a snatch.
9.15 My caress provoked a long, guttural gnarl.
9.16 "you'd better let the dog alone," growled
9.17 Mr. Heathcliff, in unison, checking fiercer de-
9.18 monstrations with a punch of his foot. "She's
9.19 not accustomed to be spoiled -- not kept for a
9.20 pet."
9.21 Then, striding to a side-door, he shouted
9.22 again.
10.01 "Joseph!"
10.02 Joseph mumbled indistinctly in the depths
10.03 of the cellar, but, gave no intimation of as-
10.04 cending; so, his master dived down to him,
10.05 leaving me \vis-a-vis# the ruffianly bitch, and a
10.06 pair of grim, shaggy sheep dogs, who shared
10.07 with her a jealous guardianship over all my
10.08 movements.
10.09 Not anxious to come in contact with their
10.10 fangs, I sat still -- but, imagining they would
10.11 scarcely understand tacit insults, I unfortu-
10.12 nately indulged in winking and making faces
10.13 at the trio, and some turn of my physiognomy
10.14 so irritated madam, that she suddenly broke
10.15 into fury, and leapt on my knees. I flung
10.16 her back, and hastened to interpose the table
10.17 between us. This proceeding roused the whole
10.18 hive. Half-a-dozen four-footed fiends, of va-
10.19 rious sizes, and ages, issued from hidden dens to
10.20 the common centre. I felt my heels, and
10.21 coat-laps peculiar subjects of assault; and,
10.22 parrying off the larger combatants, as effectually
11.01 as I could, with the poker, I was con-
11.02 strained to demand, aloud, assistance from some
11.03 of the household, in re-establishing peace.
11.04 Mr. Heathcliff and his man climbed the
11.05 cellar steps with vexatious phlegm. I don't
11.06 think they moved one second faster than usual,
11.07 though the hearth was an absolute tempest of
11.08 worrying and yelping.
11.09 Happily, an inhabitant of the kitchen made
11.10 more dispatch; a lusty dame, with tucked up
11.11 gown, bare arms, and fire-flushed cheeks,

11.12 rushed into the midst of us flourishing a fry-
11.13 ingpan; and used that weapon, and her tongue
11.14 to such purpose, that the storm subsided magi-
11.15 cally, and she only remained, heaving like a
11.16 sea after a high wind, when her master entered
11.17 on the scene.
11.18 "What the devil is the matter?" he asked,
11.19 eyeing me in a manner that I could ill endure
11.20 after this inhospitable treatment.
11.21 "What the devil, indeed!" I muttered.
11.22 "The herd of possessed swine could have had
12.01 no worse spirits in them than those animals of
12.02 yours, sir. You might as well leave a stranger
12.03 with a brood of tigers!"
12.04 "They wont meddle with persons who
12.05 touch nothing," he remarked, putting the
12.06 bottle before me, and restoring the displaced
12.07 table. "The dogs do right to be vigilant.
12.08 Take a glass of wine?"
12.09 "No, thank you."
12.10 "Not bitten, are you?"
12.11 "If I had been, I would have set my signet
12.12 on the biter."
12.13 Heathcliff's countenance relaxed into a grin.
12.14 "Come, come," he said, "you are flurried,
12.15 Mr. Lockwood. Here, take a little wine.
12.16 Guests are so exceedingly rare in this house
12.17 that I and my dogs, I am willing to own,
12.18 hardly know how to receive them. Your
12.19 health, sir!"
12.20 I bowed and returned the pledge; beginning
12.21 to perceive that it would be foolish to sit
12.22 sulking for the misbehaviour of a pack of curs:
13.01 besides, I felt loath to yield the fellow further
13.02 amusement, at my expense; since his humour
13.03 took that turn.
13.04 He -- probably swayed by prudential consider-
13.05 ations of the folly of offending a good tenant
13.06 -- relaxed, a little, in the laconic style of chip-
13.07 ping of his pronouns, and auxiliary verbs; and
13.08 introduced, what he supposed would be a sub-
13.09 ject of interest to me, a discourse on the ad-
13.10 vantages and disadvantages of my present place
13.11 of retirement.
13.12 I found him very intelligent on the topics we
13.13 touched; and, before I went home, I was en-
13.14 couraged so far as to volunteer another visit,
13.15 to-morrow.
13.16 He evidently wished no repetition of my in-
13.17 trusion. I shall go, notwithstanding. It is
13.18 astonishing how sociable I feel myself compared
13.19 with him.
14.01 [VOL. 1 CHAPTER 2]
14.02 YESTERDAY afternoon set in misty and cold. I
14.03 had half a mind to spend it by my study
14.04 fire, instead of wading through heath and mud
14.05 to Wuthering Heights.
14.06 On coming up from dinner, however, /N.B.
14.07 I dine between twelve and one o'clock; the
14.08 housekeeper, a matronly lady taken as a fixture
14.09 along with the house, could not, or would not
14.10 comprehend my request that I might be served
14.11 at five.// On mounting the stairs with this
14.12 lazy intention, and stepping into the room, I
15.01 saw a servant-girl on her knees, surrounded by
15.02 brushes, and coal-scuttles; and raising an in-
15.03 fernal dust as she extinguished the flames with
15.04 heaps of cinders. This spectacle drove me
15.05 back immediately; I took my hat, and, after a
15.06 four miles walk, arrived at Heathcliff's garden
15.07 gate just in time to escape the first feathery
15.08 flakes of a snow shower.
15.09 On that bleak hill top the earth was hard
15.10 with a black frost, and the air made me shiver
15.11 through every limb. Being unable to remove
15.12 the chain, I jumped over, and, running up the
15.13 flagged causeway bordered with straggling
15.14 gooseberry bushes, knocked vainly for admit-
15.15 tance, till my knuckles tingled, and the dogs
15.16 howled.
15.17 "Wretched inmates!" I ejaculated, men-
15.18 tally, "you deserve perpetual isolation from
15.19 your species for your churlish inhospitality.
15.20 At least, I would not keep my doors barred
15.21 in the day time -- I don't care -- I will get in!"
16.01 So resolved, I grasped the latch, and shook
16.02 it vehemently. Vinegar-faced Joseph pro-
16.03 jected his head from a round window of the
16.04 barn.
16.05 "whet are ye for?" he shouted. "T'
16.06 maister's dahn i' t'fowld. Goa rahnd by th'
16.07 end ut' laith, if yah went tuh spake tull him."
16.08 "Is there nobody inside to open the door?"
16.09 I hallooed, responsively.
16.10 "They's nobbut t' missis; and shoo'll nut
16.11 oppen't an ye mak yer flaysome dins till
16.12 neeght."
16.13 "Why? cannot you tell her who I am, eh,
16.14 Joseph?"
16.15 "Nor-ne me! Aw'll hae noa hend wi't,"
16.16 muttered the head vanishing.
16.17 The snow began to drive thickly. I seized
16.18 the handle to essay another trial; when a
16.19 young man, without coat, and shouldering a
16.20 pitchfork, appeared in the yard behind. He
16.21 hailed me to follow him; and, after marching
17.01 through a washhouse, and a paved area con-
17.02 taining a coal-shed, pump, and pigeon cote, we
17.03 at length arrived in the large, warm, cheerful
17.04 apartment, where I was formerly received.
17.05 It glowed delightfully in the radiance of an

17.06 immense fire, compounded of coal, peat, and
17.07 wood: and near the table, laid for a plentiful
17.08 evening meal, I was pleased to observe the
17.09 "missis," an individual whose existence I had
17.10 never previously suspected.
17.11 I bowed and waited, thinking she would bid
17.12 me take a seat. She looked at me, leaning
17.13 back in her chair, and remained motionless and
17.14 mute.
17.15 "Rough weather!" I remarked. "I'm
17.16 afraid, Mrs. Heathcliff, the floor must bear the
17.17 consequence of your servant's leisure attend-
17.18 ance: I had hard work to make them hear
17.19 me!"
17.20 She never opened her mouth. I stared --
17.21 she stared also. At any rate, she kept her eyes
18.01 on me, in a cool, regardless manner, exceed-
18.02 ingly embarrassing and disagreeable.
18.03 "Sit down," said the young man, gruffly.
18.04 "He'll be in soon."
18.05 I obeyed; and hemmed, and called the vil-
18.06 lain Juno, who deigned, at this second inter-
18.07 view, to move the extreme tip of her tail, in
18.08 token of owning my acquaintance.
18.09 "A beautiful animal!" I commenced again.
18.10 "Do you intend parting with the little ones,
18.11 madam?"
18.12 "They are not mine," said the amiable
18.13 hostess more repellingly than Heathcliff him-
18.14 self could have replied.
18.15 "Ah, your favourites are among these!" I
18.16 continued, turning to an obscure cushion full
18.17 of something like cats.
18.18 "A strange choice of favourites," she ob-
18.19 served scornfully.
18.20 Unluckily, it was a heap of dead rabbits --
18.21 I hemmed once more, and drew closer to the
19.01 hearth, repeating my comment on the wildness
19.02 of the evening.
19.03 "You should not have come out," she said,
19.04 rising and reaching from the chimney piece two
19.05 of the painted canisters.
19.06 Her position before was sheltered from the
19.07 light: now, I had a distinct view of her
19.08 whole figure and countenance. She was slender,
19.09 and apparently scarcely past girlhood: an ad-
19.10 mirable form, and the most exquisite little face
19.11 that I have ever had the pleasure of behold-
19.12 ing: small features, very fair; flaxen ringlets,
19.13 or rather golden, hanging loose on her delicate
19.14 neck; and eyes -- had they been agreeable in
19.15 expression, they would have been irresistible --
19.16 fortunately for my susceptible heart, the only
19.17 sentiment they evinced hovered between scorn
19.18 and a kind of desperation, singularly unnatural
19.19 to be detected there.
19.20 The canisters were almost out of her reach;
19.21 I made a motion to aid her; she turned upon
19.22 me as a miser might turn, if any one at-
19.23 tempted to assist him in counting his gold.
20.01 "I don't want your help," she snapped, "I
20.02 can get them for myself."
20.03 "I beg your pardon," I hastened to reply.
20.04 "Were you asked to tea?" she demanded,
20.05 tying an apron over her neat black frock, and
20.06 standing with a spoonful of the leaf poised
20.07 over the pot.
20.08 "I shall be glad to have a cup," I an-
20.09 swered.
20.10 "Were you asked?" she repeated.
20.11 "No;" I said, half smiling. "You are the
20.12 proper person to ask me."
20.13 She flung the tea back, spoon and all; and
20.14 resumed her chair in a pet, her forehead cor-
20.15 rugated, and her red under-lip pushed out,
20.16 like a child's, ready to cry.
20.17 Meanwhile, the young man had slung onto
20.18 his person a decidedly shabby upper garment,
20.19 and, erecting himself before the blaze, looked
20.20 down on me, from the corner of his eyes, for
20.21 all the world as if there were some mortal
20.22 feud unavenged between us. I began to doubt
21.01 whether he were a servant or not; his dress
21.02 and speech were both rude, entirely devoid of
21.03 the superiority observable in Mr. and Mrs.
21.04 Heathcliff; his thick, brown curls were rough
21.05 and uncultivated, his whiskers encroached
21.06 bearishly over his cheeks, and his hands were
21.07 embrowned like those of a common labourer,
21.08 still his bearing was free, almost haughty;
21.09 and he showed none of a domestic's assiduity
21.10 in attending on the lady of the house.
21.11 In the absence of clear proofs of his con-
21.12 dition, I deemed it best to abstain from no-
21.13 ticing his curious conduct, and, five minutes
21.14 afterwards, the entrance of Heathcliff relieved
21.15 me, in some measure, from my uncomfortable
21.16 state.
21.17 "You see, sir, I am come according to
21.18 promise!" I exclaimed, assuming the cheerful
21.19 "and I fear I shall be weather-bound for
21.20 half an hour, if you can afford me shelter dur-
21.21 ing that space."
21.22 "Half an hour?" he said, shaking the
22.01 white flakes from his clothes; "I wonder
22.02 you should select the thick of a snow-storm
22.03 to ramble about in. Do you know that you
22.04 run a risk of being lost in the marshes? People
22.05 familiar with these moors often miss their
22.06 road on such evenings, and, I can tell you,
22.07 there is no chance of a change at present."

22.08 "Perhaps I can get a guide among your
22.09 lads, and he might stay at the Grange till
22.10 morning -- could you spare me one?"
22.11 "No, I could not."
22.12 "Oh, indeed! Well then, I must trust to
22.13 my own sagacity."
22.14 "Umph."
22.15 "Are you going to mak th' tea?" demanded
22.16 he of the shabby coat, shifting his ferocious
22.17 gaze from me to the young lady.
22.18 "Is \he# to have any?" she asked, appealing
22.19 to Heathcliff.
22.20 "Get it ready, will you?" was the answer,
22.21 uttered so savagely that I started. The tone
22.22 in which the words were said, revealed a genuine
23.01 bad nature. I no longer felt inclined to
23.02 call Heathcliff a capital fellow.
23.03 When the preparations were finished, he
23.04 invited me with --
23.05 "Now, sir, bring forward your chair." And
23.06 we all, including the rustic youth, drew round
23.07 the table, an austere silence prevailing while
23.08 we discussed our meal.
23.09 I thought, if I had caused the cloud, it was
23.10 my duty to make an effort to dispel it. They
23.11 could not every day sit so grim and taciturn,
23.12 and it was impossible, however ill-tempered
23.13 they might be, that the universal scowl they
23.14 wore was their every day countenance.
23.15 "It is strange," I began in the interval of
23.16 swallowing one cup of tea, and receiving
23.17 another, "it is strange how custom can mould
23.18 our tastes and ideas; many could not imagine
23.19 the existence of happiness in a life of such
23.20 complete exile from the world as you spend,
23.21 Mr. Heathcliff; yet, I'll venture to say,
23.22 that, surrounded by your family, and with
24.01 your amiable lady as the presiding genius over
24.02 your home and heart --"
24.03 "My amiable lady!" he interrupted, with
24.04 an almost diabolical sneer on his face.
24.05 "Where is she -- my amiable lady?"
24.06 "Mrs. Heathcliff, your wife, I mean."
24.07 "Well, yes -- Oh! you would intimate that
24.08 her spirit has taken the post of ministering
24.09 angel, and guards the fortunes of Wuthering
24.10 Heights, even when her body is gone. Is
24.11 that it?"
24.12 Perceiving myself in a blunder, I attempted
24.13 to correct it. I might have seen there was
24.14 too great a disparity between the ages of the
24.15 parties to make it likely that they were man
24.16 and wife. One was about forty; a period of
24.17 mental vigour at which men seldom cherish
24.18 the delusion of being married for love, by
24.19 girls: that dream is reserved for the solace
24.20 of our declining years. The other did not look
24.21 seventeen.
24.22 Then it flashed upon me; "the clown at
25.01 my elbow, who is drinking his tea out of a
25.02 basin, and eating his bread with unwashed
25.03 hands, may be her husband. Heathcliff,
25.04 junior, of course. Here is the consequence of
25.05 being buried alive: she has thrown herself
25.06 away upon that boor, from sheer ignorance
25.07 that better individuals existed! A sad pity --
25.08 I must beware how I cause her to regret her
25.09 choice."
25.10 The last reflection may seem conceited; it
25.11 was not. My neighbour struck me as bor-
25.12 dering on repulsive. I knew, through expe-
25.13 rience, that I was tolerably attractive.
25.14 "Mrs. Heathcliff is my daughter-in-law,"
25.15 said Heathcliff, corroborating my surmise. He
25.16 turned, as he spoke, a peculiar look in her di-
25.17 rection, a look of hatred unless he has a most
25.18 perverse set of facial muscles that will not,
25.19 like those of other people, interpret the langu-
25.20 age of his soul.
25.21 "Ah, certainly -- I see now; you are the
26.01 favoured possessor of the beneficent fairy," I
26.02 remarked, turning to my neighbour.
26.03 This was worse than before: the youth grew
26.04 crimson, and clenched his fist with every ap-
26.05 pearance of a meditated assault. But he
26.06 seemed to recollect himself, presently, and
26.07 smothered the storm in a brutal curse, muttered
26.08 on my behalf, which, however, I took care not
26.09 to notice."
26.10 "Unhappy in your conjectures, sir!" ob-
26.11 served my host; "we neither of us have the
26.12 privilege of owning your good fairy; her mate
26.13 is dead. I said she was my daughter-in-law,
26.14 therefore, she must have married my son."
26.15 "And this young man is --"
26.16 "Not my son, assuredly!"
26.17 Heathcliff smiled again, as if it were rather
26.18 too bold a jest to attribute the paternity of
26.19 that bear to him.
26.20 "My name is Hareton Earnshaw," growled
26.21 the other; "and I'd counsel you to respect
26.22 it!"
27.01 "I've shown no disrespect," was my reply,
27.02 laughing internally at the dignity with which
27.03 he announced himself.
27.04 He fixed his eye on me longer than I cared
27.05 to return the stare, for fear I might be tempted
27.06 either to box his ears, or render my hilarity
27.07 audible. I began to feel unmistakably out of
27.08 place in that pleasant family circle. The dis-
27.09 mal spiritual atmosphere overcame, and more

27.10 than neutralized the glowing physical comforts
27.11 round me; and I resolved to be cautious how
27.12 I ventured under those rafters a third time.
27.13 The business of eating being concluded, and
27.14 no one uttering a word of sociable conversa-
27.15 tion, I approached a window to examine the
27.16 weather.
27.17 A sorrowful sight I saw; dark night coming
27.18 down prematurely, and sky and hills mingled
27.19 in one bitter whirl of wind and suffocating
27.20 snow.
27.21 "I don't think it possible for me to get home
27.22 now, without a guide," I could not help exclaiming.
28.01 "The roads will be buried already;
28.02 and, if they were bare, I could scarcely dis-
28.03 tinguish a foot in advance."
28.04 "Hareton, drive those dozen sheep into the
28.05 barn porch. They'll be covered if left in the
28.06 fold all night; and put a plank before them,"
28.07 said Heathcliff.
28.08 "How must I do?" I continued, with rising
28.09 irritation.
28.10 There was no reply to my question; and,
28.11 on looking round, I saw only Joseph bringing
28.12 in a pail of porridge for the dogs; and Mrs.
28.13 Heathcliff, leaning over the fire, diverting her-
28.14 self with burning a bundle of matches which
28.15 had fallen from the chimney-piece as she re-
28.16 stored the tea-canister to its place.
28.17 The former, when he had deposited his bur-
28.18 den, took a critical survey of the room; and,
28.19 in cracked tones, grated out:
28.20 "Aw woonder hagh yah can faishion tuh
28.21 stand thear i' idleness un war, when all on 'em's
28.22 goan ayht! Bud yah're a nowt, and it's noa
29.01 use talking -- yah'll niver mend uh yer ill ways;
29.02 bud, goa raight tuh t' divil, like yer mother
29.03 afore ye!"
29.04 I imagined, for a moment, that this piece of
29.05 eloquence was addressed to me; and, suffici-
29.06 ently enraged, stepped towards the aged rascal
29.07 with an intention of kicking him out of the
29.08 door.
29.09 Mrs. Heathcliff, however, checked me by her
29.10 answer.
29.11 "You scandalous old hypocrite!" she re-
29.12 plied. "Are you not afraid of being carried
29.13 away bodily, whenever you mention the devil's
29.14 name? I warn you to refrain from provoking
29.15 me, or I'll ask your abduction as a special
29.16 favour. Stop, look here, Joseph," she con-
29.17 tinued, taking a long, dark book from a shelf.
29.18 "I'll show you how far I've progressed in the
29.19 Black Art -- I shall soon be competent to make
29.20 a clear house of it. The red cow didn't die
29.21 by chance; and your rheumatism can hardly
29.22 be reckoned among providential visitations!"
30.01 "Oh, wicked, wicked!" gasped the elder,
30.02 "may the Lord deliver us from evil!"
30.03 "No, reprobate! you are a castaway -- be
30.04 off, or I'll hurt you seriously! I'll have you
30.05 all modlled in wax and clay; and the first who
30.06 passes the limits, I fix, shall -- I'll not say
30.07 what he shall be done to -- but, you'll see! Go,
30.08 I'm looking at you!"
30.09 The little witch put a mock malignity into
30.10 her beautiful eyes, and Joseph, trembling with
30.11 sincere horror, hurried out praying and ejacu-
30.12 lating "wicked" as he went.
30.13 I thought her conduct must be prompted
30.14 by a species of dreary fun; and, now that we
30.15 were alone, I endeavoured to interest her in
30.16 my distress.
30.17 "Mrs. Heathcliff," I said, earnestly, "you
30.18 must excuse me for troubling you -- I presume,
30.19 because, with that face, I'm sure you cannot
30.20 help being good-hearted. Do point out some
30.21 landmarks by which I may know my way home
30.22 -- I have no more idea how to get there than
30.23 you would have how to get to London!"
31.01 "Take the road you came," she answered,
31.02 ensconcing herself in a chair, with a candle,
31.03 and the long book open before her. "It is
31.04 brief advice; but, as sound as I can give."
31.05 "Then, if you hear of me being discovered
31.06 dead in a bog, or a pit full of snow, your con-
31.07 science wont whisper that it is partly your
31.08 fault?"
31.09 "How so? I cannot escort you. They
31.10 wouldn't let me go to the end of the garden--
31.11 wall."
31.12 "\You#! I should be sorry to ask you to cross
31.13 the threshold, for my convenience, on such a
31.14 night," I cried. "I want you to \tell# me my
31.15 way, not to \show# it; or else to persuade Mr.
31.16 Heathcliff to give me a guide."
31.17 "Who? There is himself, Earnshaw, Zillah,
31.18 Joseph, and I. Which would you have?"
31.19 "Are there no boys at the farm?"
31.20 "No, those are all."
31.21 "Then, it follows that I am compelled to
31.22 stay."
32.01 have nothing to do with it."
32.02 "I hope it will be a lesson to you, to make
32.03 no more rash journeys on these hills," cried
32.04 Heathcliff's stern voice from the kitchen en-
32.05 trance. "As to staying here, I don't keep
32.06 accommodations for visiters; you must share a
32.07 bed with Hareton, or Joseph, if you do."
32.08 "I can sleep on a chair in this room," I re-
32.09 plied.

32.10 "No, no! A stranger is a stranger, be he
32.11 rich or poor -- it will not suit me to permit any
32.12 one the range of the place while I am off
32.13 guard!" said the unmannerly wretch.
32.14 With this insult my patience was at an end.
32.15 I uttered an expression of disgust, and pushed
32.16 past him into the yard, running against Earn-
32.17 shaw in my haste. It was so dark that I could
32.18 not see the means of exit, and, as I wandered
32.19 round, I heard another specimen of their civil
32.20 behaviour amongst each other.
33.01 At first, the young man appeared about
33.02 to befriend me.
33.03 "I'll go with him as far as the park," he
33.04 said.
33.05 "You'll go with him to hell!" exclaimed
33.06 his master, or whatever relation he bore.
33.07 "And who is to look after the horses,
33.08 eh?"
33.09 "A man's life is of more consequence than
33.10 one evening's neglect of the horses; somebody
33.11 must go," murmured Mrs. Heathcliff, more
33.12 kindly than I expected.
33.13 "Not at your command!" retorted Hareton.
33.14 "If you set store on him, you'd better be
33.15 quiet."
33.16 "Then I hope his ghost will haunt you;
33.17 and I hope Mr. Heathcliff will never get
33.18 another tenant, till the Grange is a ruin!"
33.19 she answered sharply.
33.20 "Hearken, hearken, shoo's cursing on em!"
33.21 muttered Joseph, towards whom I had been
33.22 steering.
34.01 He sat within earshot, milking the cows,
34.02 by the aid of a lantern which I seized uncere-
34.03 moniously, and calling out that I would send
34.04 it back on the morrow, rushed to the nearest
34.05 postern.
34.06 "Maister, maister, he's staling t' lantern!"
34.07 shouted the ancient, pursuing my retreat.
34.08 "Hey, Gnasher! Hey, dog! Hey, wolf,
34.09 holld him, holld him!"
34.10 On opening the little door, two hairy
34.11 monsters flew at my throat, bearing me
34.12 down, and extinguishing the light, while a
34.13 mingled guffaw, from Heathcliff and Hareton,
34.14 put the copestone on my rage and humi-
34.15 liation.
34.16 Fortunately, the beasts seemed more bent
34.17 on stretching their paws, and yawning, and
34.18 flourishing their tails, than devouring me alive;
34.19 but, they would suffer no resurrection, and I
34.20 was forced to lie till their malignant masters
34.21 pleased to deliver me: then hatless, and trem-
34.22 bling with wrath, I ordered the miscreants to
35.01 let me out -- on their peril to keep me one
35.02 minute longer -- with several incoherent threats
35.03 of retaliation, that in their indefinite depth of
35.04 virulency, smacked of King Lear.
35.05 The vehemence of my agitation brought on
35.06 a copious bleeding at the nose, and still Heath-
35.07 cliff laughed, and still I scolded. I don't know
35.08 what would have concluded the scene had
35.09 there not been one person at hand rather more
35.10 rational than myself, and more benevolent than
35.11 my entertainer. This was Zillah, the stout
35.12 housewife; who at length issued forth to in-
35.13 quire into the nature of the uproar. She
35.14 thought that some of them had been laying
35.15 violent hands on me; and, not daring to at-
35.16 tack her master, she turned her vocal artillery
35.17 against the younger scoundrel.
35.18 "Well, Mr. Earnshaw," she cried, "I won-
35.19 der what you'll have agait next! Are we
35.20 going to murder folk on our very door-stones?
35.21 I see this house will never do for me -- look at
35.22 t' poor lad, he's fair choking! Wisht, wisht!
36.01 you mun'n't go on so -- come in, and I'll cure
36.02 that. There now, hold ye still."
36.03 With these words she suddenly splashed a
36.04 pint of icy water down my neck, and pulled
36.05 me into the kitchen. Mr. Heathcliff followed,
36.06 his accidental merriment expiring quickly in
36.07 his habitual moroseness.
36.08 I was sick exceedingly, and dizzy and faint;
36.09 and thus compelled, perforce, to accept lodg-
36.10 ings under his roof. He told Zillah to give
36.11 me a glass of brandy, and then passed on to
36.12 the inner room, while she condoled with me on
36.13 my sorry predicament, and having obeyed his
36.14 orders, whereby I was somewhat revived,
36.15 ushered me to bed.
37.01 [VOL. 1 CHAPTER 3]
37.02 WHILE leading the way up-stairs, she recom-
37.03 mended that I should hide the candle, and not
37.04 make a noise, for her master had an odd notion
37.05 about the chamber she would put me in; and
37.06 never let anybody lodge there willingly.
37.07 I asked the reason.
37.08 She did not know, she answered; she had
37.09 only lived there a year or two; and they had
37.10 so many queer goings on, she could not begin
37.11 to be curious.
37.12 Too stupified to be curious myself, I fastened
38.01 my door and glanced round for the bed.
38.02 The whole furniture consisted of a chair, a
38.03 clothes-press, and a large oak case, with
38.04 squares cut out near the top, resembling coach
38.05 windows.
38.06 Having approached this structure, I looked
38.07 inside, and perceived it to be a singular sort

38.08 of old-fashioned couch, very conveniently de-
38.09 signed to obviate the necessity for every mem-
38.10 ber of the family having a room to himself.
38.11 In fact, it formed a little closet, and the ledge
38.12 of a window, which it enclosed, served as a
38.13 table.
38.14 I slid back the panelled sides, got in with
38.15 my light, pulled them together again, and felt
38.16 secure against the vigilance of Heathcliff, and
38.17 every one else."
38.18 The ledge, where I placed my candle, had a
38.19 few mildewed books piled up in one corner;
38.20 and it was covered with writing scratched on
38.21 the paint. This writing, however, was nothing
38.22 but a name repeated in all kinds of characters,
39.01 large and small -- \Catherine# \Earnshaw#; here
39.02 and there varied to \Catherine# \Heathcliff#, and
39.03 then again to \Catherine# \Linton#."
39.04 In vapid listlessness I leant my head against
39.05 the window, and continued spelling over
39.06 Catherine Earnshaw -- Heathcliff -- Linton, till
39.07 my eyes closed; but they had not rested five
39.08 minutes when a glare of white letters started
39.09 from the dark, as vivid as spectres -- the air
39.10 swarmed with Catherines; and rousing myself
39.11 to dispel the obtrusive name, I discovered my
39.12 candle wick reclining on one of the antique
39.13 volumes, and perfuming the place with an
39.14 odour of roasted calf-skin.
39.15 I snuffed it off, and, very ill at ease, under
39.16 the influence of cold and lingering nausea, sat
39.17 up, and spread open the injured tome on my
39.18 knee. It was a Testament, in lean type, and
39.19 smelling dreadfully musty: a fly-leaf bore the
39.20 inscription -- "Catherine Earnshaw, her book,"
39.21 and a date some quarter of a century back.
40.01 I shut it, and took up another, and another,
40.02 till I had examined all. Catherine's library
40.03 was select; and its state of dilapidation proved
40.04 it to have been well used, though not altogether
40.05 for a legitimate purpose; scarcely one chapter
40.06 had escaped a pen and ink commentary, at
40.07 least, the appearance of one, covering every
40.08 morsel of blank that the printer had left.
40.09 Some were detached sentences; other parts
40.10 took the form of a regular diary, scrawled in
40.11 an unformed, childish hand. At the top of an
40.12 extra page, quite a treasure probably when
40.13 first lighted on, I was greatly amused to behold
40.14 an excellent caricature of my friend Joseph,
40.15 rudely yet powerfully sketched.
40.16 An immediate interest kindled within me for
40.17 the unknown Catherine, and I began, forth-
40.18 with, to decypher her faded hieroglyphics.
40.19 "An awful Sunday!" commenced the para-
40.20 graph beneath. "I wish my father were back
40.21 again. Hindley is a detestable substitute --
41.01 his conduct to Heathcliff is atrocious -- H. and
41.02 I are going to rebel -- we took our initiatory
41.03 step this evening.
41.04 "All day had been flooding with rain; we
41.05 could not go to church, so Joseph must needs
41.06 get up a congregation in the garret; and,
41.07 while Hindley and his wife basked down stairs
41.08 before a comfortable fire, doing anything but
41.09 reading their bibles, I'll answer for it; Heath-
41.10 cliff, myself, and the unhappy plough-boy,
41.11 were commanded to take our Prayer-books,
41.12 and mount -- we were ranged in a row, on a
41.13 sack of corn, groaning and shivering, and hop-
41.14 ing that Joseph would shiver too, so that he
41.15 might give us a short homily for his own sake.
41.16 A vain idea! The service lasted precisely
41.17 three hours; and yet my brother had the face
41.18 to exclaim, when he saw us descending,
41.19 "'What, done already?'"
41.20 "On Sunday evenings we used to be permitted
41.21 to play, if we did not make much noise; now
42.01 a mere titter is sufficient to send us into
42.02 corners!
42.03 "'You forget to have a master here," says
42.04 the tyrant. 'I'll demolish the first who puts
42.05 me out of temper! I insist on perfect sobri-
42.06 ety and silence. Oh, boy! was that you?
42.07 Frances, darling, pull his hair as you go by; I
42.08 heard him snap his fingers.'
42.09 "Frances pulled his hair heartily; and then
42.10 went and seated herself on her husband's knee,
42.11 and there they were, like two babies, kissing
42.12 and talking nonsense by the hour -- foolish
42.13 palaver that we should be ashamed of.
42.14 "We made ourselves as snug as our means
42.15 allowed in the arch of the dresser. I had just
42.16 fastened our pinafores together, and hung them
42.17 up for a curtain; when in comes Joseph, on an
42.18 errand from the stables. He tears down my
42.19 handywork, boxes my ears, and croaks:
42.20 "'T' maister nobbut just buried, and Sab-
42.21 bath nut oe'red, und t' sahnd, uh't gospel still i'
43.01 yer lugs, and yah darr be laiking! shame on
43.02 ye! sit ye dahn, ill childer! they's good books
43.03 enough if ye'll read 'em; sit ye dahn, and
43.04 think uh yer sowls!'
43.05 Saying this, he compelled us so to square
43.06 our positions that we might receive, from the
43.07 far-off fire, a dull ray to show us the text of
43.08 the lumber he thrust upon us.
43.09 "I could not bear the employment. I took
43.10 my dingy volume by the scroop, and hurled it
43.11 into the dog-kennel, vowing I hated a good
43.12 book.

43.13 "Heathcliff kicked his to the same place.
43.14 "Then there was a hubbub!
43.15 "`Maister Hindley!` shouted our chaplain.
43.16 `Maister, coom hither! Miss Cathy's riven
43.17 th` back off `Th` Helmet uh Salvation,` un`
43.18 Heathcliff's pawsed his fit intuh t` first part uh
43.19 `T` Brooad Way to Destruction!` It's fair
43.20 flaysome ut yah let `em goa on this gait. Ech!
43.21 th` owd man ud uh laced `em properly -- bud
43.22 he's goan!`

44.01 "Hindley hurried up from his paradise on
44.02 the hearth, and seizing one of us by the collar,
44.03 and the other by the arm, hurled both into the
44.04 back-kitchen; where, Joseph asseverated,
44.05 "owd Nick" would fetch us as sure as we were
44.06 living; and, so comforted, we each sought a
44.07 separate nook to await his advent.
44.08 "I reached this book, and a pot of ink from
44.09 a shelf, and pushed the house-door ajar to give
44.10 me light, and I have got the time on with
44.11 writing for twenty minutes; but my companion
44.12 is impatient and proposes that we should ap-
44.13 propriate the dairy woman's cloak, and have a
44.14 scamper on the moors, under its shelter. A
44.15 pleasant suggestion -- and then, if the surly old
44.16 man come in, he may believe his prophesy
44.17 verified -- we cannot be damper, or colder, in
44.18 the rain than we are here."
44.19 + + + +
44.20 I suppose Catherine fulfilled her project,
45.01 for the next sentence took up another subject;
45.02 she waxed lachrymose.
45.03 "How little did I dream that Hindley would
45.04 ever make me cry so!" she wrote. "My head
45.05 aches, till I cannot keep it on the pillow; and
45.06 still I can't give over. Poor Heathcliff!
45.07 Hindley calls him a vagabond, and wont let
45.08 him sit with us, nor eat with us any more;
45.09 and, he says, he and I must not play together,
45.10 and threatens to turn him out of the house if
45.11 we break his orders.
45.12 "He has been blaming our father /how
45.13 dare he?// for treating H. too liberally;
45.14 and swears he will reduce him to his right
45.15 place --"
45.16 + + + +
45.17 I began to nod drowsily over the dim page;
45.18 my eye wandered from manuscript to print. I
45.19 saw a red ornamented title ... "Seventy Times
45.20 Seven, and the First of the Seventy First.
46.01 A Pious Discourse delivered by the Reverend
46.02 Jabes Branderham, in the Chapel of Gimmer-
46.03 den Sough." And while I was, half consciously,
46.04 worrying my brain to guess what Jabes Bran-
46.05 derham would make of his subject, I sank back
46.06 in bed, and fell asleep.
46.07 Alas, for the effects of bad tea and bad
46.08 temper! what else could it be that made me
46.09 pass such a terrible night? I don't remember
46.10 another that I can at all compare with it since
46.11 I was capable of suffering.
46.12 I began to dream, almost before I ceased to
46.13 be sensible of my locality. I thought it was
46.14 morning; and I had set out on my way home,
46.15 with Joseph for a guide. The snow lay yards
46.16 deep in our road; and, as we floundered on,
46.17 my companion wearied me with constant re-
46.18 proaches that I had not brought a pilgrim's
46.19 staff: telling me I could never get into the
46.20 house without one, and boastfully flourishing
46.21 a heavy-headed cudgel, which I understood to
46.22 be so denominated.
47.01 For a moment I considered it absurd that I
47.02 should need such a weapon to gain admittance
47.03 into my own residence. Then, a new idea
47.04 flashed across me. I was not going there; we
47.05 were journeying to hear the famous Jabes
47.06 Branderham preach from the text -- "Seventy
47.07 Times Seven;" and either Joseph, the preacher,
47.08 or I had committed the "First of the Seventy
47.09 First," and were to be publicly exposed and ex-
47.10 communicated.
47.11 We came to the chapel -- I have passed it
47.12 really in my walks, twice or thrice: it lies in
47.13 a hollow, between two hills -- an elevated hol-
47.14 low -- near a swamp, whose peaty moisture is
47.15 said to answer all the purposes of embalming on
47.16 the few corpses deposited there. The roof has
47.17 been kept whole hitherto, but, as the clergyman's
47.18 stipend is only twenty pounds per annum, and
47.19 a house with two rooms, threatening speedily
47.20 to determine into one, no clergyman will un-
47.21 dertake the duties of pastor, especially, as it is
47.22 currently reported that his flock would rather
48.01 let him starve than increase the living by one
48.02 penny from their own pockets. However, in
48.03 my dream, Jabes had a full and attentive con-
48.04 gregation: and he preached -- good God -- what
48.05 a sermon! Divided into \four# \hundred# \and#
48.06 \ninety# parts -- each fully equal to an ordinary
48.07 address from the pulpit -- and each discussing a
48.08 separate sin! where he searched for them, I
48.09 cannot tell; he had his private manner of in-
48.10 terpreting the phrase, and it seemed necessary
48.11 the brother should sin different sins on every
48.12 occasion.
48.13 They were of the most curious character --
48.14 odd transgressions that I never imagined previ-
48.15 ously.
48.16 Oh, how weary I grew. How I writhed,
48.17 and yawned, and nodded, and revived! How

48.18 I pinched and pricked myself, and rubbed my
48.19 eyes, and stood up, and sat down again, and
48.20 nudged Joseph to inform me if he would \ever#
48.21 have done!"
48.22 I was condemned to hear all out -- finally, he
49.01 reached the "\First# \of# \the# \Seventy-First#." At
49.02 that crisis, a sudden inspiration descended on
49.03 me; I was moved to rise and denounce Jabes
49.04 Branderham as the sinner of the sin that no
49.05 christian need pardon.
49.06 "Sir," I exclaimed, "sitting here, within
49.07 these four walls, at one stretch, I have endured
49.08 and forgiven the four hundred and ninety
49.09 heads of your discourse. Seventy times
49.10 seven times have I plucked up my hat, and
49.11 been about to depart -- Seventy times seven
49.12 times have you preposterously forced me to re-
49.13 sume my seat. The four hundred and ninety--
49.14 first is too much. Fellow martyrs, have at
49.15 him! Drag him down, and crush him to
49.16 atoms, that the place which knows him may
49.17 know him no more!"
49.18 "\Thou# \art# \the# \Man#!" cried Jabes, after a
49.19 solemn pause, leaning over his cushion.
49.20 "Seventy times seven times didst thou gapingly
49.21 contort thy visage -- seventy times seven did I
50.01 take counsel with my soul -- Lo, this is human
50.02 weakness; this also may be absolved! The
50.03 First of the Seventy-First is come. Brethren,
50.04 execute upon him the judgment written! such
50.05 honour have all His saints!"
50.06 with that concluding word, the whole as-
50.07 sembly, exalting their pilgrim's staves, rushed
50.08 round me in a body; and, I, having no weapon
50.09 to raise in self-defence, commenced grappling
50.10 with Joseph, my nearest and most ferocious as-
50.11 sailant, for his. In the confluence of the mul-
50.12 titude, several clubs crossed; blows, aimed at
50.13 me, fell on other sconces. Presently the whole
50.14 chapel resounded with rappings and counter--
50.15 rappings. Every man's hand was against his
50.16 neighbour; and Branderham, unwilling to re-
50.17 main idle, poured forth his zeal in a shower of
50.18 loud taps on the boards of the pulpit which
50.19 responded so smartly, that, at last, to my un-
50.20 speakable relief, they woke me.
50.21 And what was it that had suggested the tremendous
51.01 tumult, what had played Jabes' part in
51.02 the row? Merely, the branch of a fir-tree
51.03 that touched my lattice, as the blast wailed by,
51.04 and rattled its dry cones against the panes!
51.05 I listened doubtingly an instant; detected
51.06 the disturber, then turned and dosed, and
51.07 dreamt again; if possible, still more disagree-
51.08 bly than before.
51.09 This time, I remembered I was lying in the
51.10 oak closet, and I heard distinctly the gusty
51.11 wind, and the driving of the snow; I heard
51.12 also, the firbough repeat its teasing sound, and
51.13 ascribed it to the right cause: but, it annoyed
51.14 me so much, that I resolved to silence it, if
51.15 possible; and, I thought, I rose and endea-
51.16 voured to unhasp the casement. The hook
51.17 was soldered into the staple, a circumstance
51.18 observed by me, when awake, but forgotten.
51.19 "I must stop it, nevertheless!" I muttered,
51.20 knocking my knuckles through the glass, and
51.21 stretching an arm out to seize the importunate
52.01 branch: instead of which, my fingers closed on
52.02 the fingers of a little, ice-cold hand!
52.03 The intense horror of nightmare came over
52.04 me; I tried to draw back my arm, but, the
52.05 hand clung to it, and a most melancholy voice,
52.06 sobbed,
52.07 "Let me in -- let me in!"
52.08 "Who are you?" I asked struggling, mean-
52.09 while, to disengage myself.
52.10 "Catherine Linton," it replied, shiveringly,
52.11 /why did I think of \Linton#? I had read \Earn-
52.12 shaw#, twenty times for Linton// "I'm come
52.13 home, I'd lost my way on the moor!"
52.14 As it spoke, I discerned, obscurely, a child's
52.15 face looking through the window -- Terror
52.16 made me cruel; and, finding it useless to at-
52.17 tempt shaking the creature off, I pulled its
52.18 wrist on to the broken pane, and rubbed it to
52.19 and fro till the blood ran down and soaked the
52.20 bed-clothes: still it wailed, "Let me in!" and
52.21 maintained its tenacious gripe, almost madden-
52.22 ing me with fear.
53.01 "How can I?" I said at length. "Let \me#
53.02 go, if you want me to let you in!"
53.03 The fingers relaxed, I snatched mine through
53.04 the hole, hurriedly piled the books up in a py-
53.05 ramid against it, and stopped my ears to ex-
53.06 clude the lamentable prayer.
53.07 I seemed to keep them closed above a quar-
53.08 ter of an hour, yet, the instant I listened,
53.09 again, there was the doleful cry moaning on!
53.10 "Begone!" I shouted, "I'll never let you in,
53.11 not if you beg for twenty years!"
53.12 "It's twenty years," mourned the voice,
53.13 "twenty years, I've been a waif for twenty
53.14 years!"
53.15 Thereat began a feeble scratching outside,
53.16 and the pile of books moved as if thrust for-
53.17 ward.
53.18 I tried to jump up; but, could not stir a
53.19 limb; and so, yelled aloud, in a frenzy of
53.20 fright.
53.21 To my confusion, I discovered the yell was

53.22 not ideal. Hasty footsteps approached my
54.01 chamber door: somebody pushed it open, with
54.02 a vigorous hand, and a light glimmered through
54.03 the squares at the top of the bed. I sat shud-
54.04 dering, yet, and wiping the perspiration from
54.05 my forehead: the intruder appeared to hesitate
54.06 and muttered to himself.
54.07 At last, he said in a half-whisper, plainly
54.08 not expecting an answer,
54.09 "Is any one here?"
54.10 I considered it best to confess my presence,
54.11 for I knew Heathcliff's accents, and feared he
54.12 might search further, if I kept quiet.
54.13 With this intention, I turned and opened
54.14 the panels -- I shall not soon forget the effect
54.15 my action produced.
54.16 Heathcliff stood near the entrance, in his
54.17 shirt and trousers; with a candle dripping
54.18 over his fingers, and his face as white as the
54.19 wall behind him. The first creak of the oak
54.20 startled him like an electric shock: the light
54.21 leaped from his hold to a distance of some
55.01 feet, and his agitation was so extreme, that he
55.02 could hardly pick it up.
55.03 "It is only your guest, sir," I called out,
55.04 desirous to spare him the humiliation of ex-
55.05 posing his cowardice further. "I had the
55.06 misfortune to scream in my sleep, owing to a
55.07 frightful nightmare. I'm sorry I disturbed
55.08 you."
55.09 "Oh, God confound you, Mr. Lockwood! I
55.10 wish you were at the --" commenced my host
55.11 setting the candle on a chair, because he found
55.12 it impossible to hold it steady.
55.13 "And who showed you up to this room?"
55.14 he continued, crushing his nails into his palms,
55.15 and grinding his teeth to subdue the maxillary
55.16 convulsions. "Who was it? I've a good
55.17 mind to turn them out of the house, this
55.18 moment!"
55.19 "It was your servant, Zillah," I replied
55.20 flinging myself, on to the floor, and rapidly
55.21 resuming my garments. "I should not care
55.22 if you did, Mr. Heathcliff; she richly deserves
56.01 it. I suppose that she wanted to get another
56.02 proof that the place was haunted, at my ex-
56.03 pense -- Well, it is -- swarming with ghosts and
56.04 goblins! You have reason in shutting it up,
56.05 I assure you. No one will thank you for a
56.06 dose in such a den!"
56.07 "What do you mean?" asked Heathcliff,
56.08 "and what are you doing? Lie down and
56.09 finish out the night, since you \are# here; but,
56.10 for Heaven's sake! don't repeat that horrid
56.11 noise -- Nothing could excuse it, unless you
56.12 were having your throat cut!"
56.13 "If the little fiend had got in at the win-
56.14 dow, she probably would have strangled me!"
56.15 I returned. "I'm not going to endure the
56.16 persecutions of your hospitable ancestors, again
56.17 -- was not the Reverend Jabes Branderham
56.18 akin to you on the mother's side? And that
56.19 minx, Catherine Linton, or Earnshaw, or how-
56.20 ever she was called -- she must have been a
56.21 changling -- wicked little soul! She told me
56.22 she had been walking the earth these twenty
57.01 years: a just punishment for her mortal trans-
57.02 gressions, I've no doubt!"
57.03 Scarcely were these words uttered, when I
57.04 recollected the association of Heathcliff's with
57.05 Catherine's name in the book, which had com-
57.06 pletely slipped from my memory till thus
57.07 awakened. I blushed at my inconsideration;
57.08 but without showing further consciousness of
57.09 the offence, I hastened to add,
57.10 "The truth is, sir, I passed the first part of
57.11 the night in --" Here, I stopped afresh -- I
57.12 was about to say "perusing those old vo-
57.13 lumes," then it would have revealed my know-
57.14 ledge of their written, as well as their printed
57.15 contents; so correcting myself, I went on,
57.16 "In spelling over the name scratched on
57.17 that window-ledge. A monotonous occupa-
57.18 tion, calculated to set me asleep, like counting,
57.19 or --"
57.20 "What \can# you mean, by talking in this
57.21 way to \me#!" thundered Heathcliff with savage
57.22 vehemence. "How -- how \dare# you, under my
58.01 roof -- God! he's mad to speak so!" And he
58.02 struck his forehead with rage.
58.03 I did not know whether to resent this lan-
58.04 guage, or pursue my explanation; but he
58.05 seemed so powerfully affected that I took pity
58.06 and proceeded with my dreams; affirming
58.07 I had never heard the appellation of "Cathe-
58.08 rine Linton," before, but, reading it often over
58.09 produced an impression which personified itself
58.10 when I had no longer my imagination under
58.11 control.
58.12 Heathcliff gradually fell back into the shel-
58.13 ter of the bed, as I spoke, finally, sitting down
58.14 almost concealed behind it. I guessed, how-
58.15 ever, by his irregular and intercepted breath-
58.16 ing, that he struggled to vanquish an access of
58.17 violent emotion.
58.18 Not liking to show him that I heard the
58.19 conflict, I continued my toilette rather noisily,
58.20 looked at my watch, and soliloquised on the
58.21 length of the night:
59.01 "Not three o'clock, yet! I could have taken
59.02 oath it had been six -- time stagnates here -- we

59.03 must surely have retired to rest at eight!"
59.04 "Always at nine in winter, and always rise
59.05 at four," said my host, suppressing a groan;
59.06 and, as I fancied, by the motion of his shadow's
59.07 arm, dashing a tear from his eyes.
59.08 "Mr. Lockwood," he added, "you may go
59.09 into my room; you'll only be in the way, com-
59.10 ing down stairs so early: and your childish
59.11 outcry has sent sleep to the devil for me."
59.12 "And for me too," I replied. "I'll walk
59.13 in the yard till daylight, and then I'll be off;
59.14 and you need not dread a repetition of my in-
59.15 trusion. I am now quite cured of seeking
59.16 pleasure in society, be it country or town. A
59.17 sensible man ought to find sufficient company
59.18 in himself."
59.19 "Delightful company!" muttered Heath-
59.20 cliff. "Take the candle, and go where you
59.21 please. I shall join you directly. Keep out
59.22 of the yard though the dogs are unchained;
60.01 and the house -- Juno mounts sentinel there --
60.02 and -- nay, you can only ramble about the steps
60.03 and passages -- but, away with you! I'll come
60.04 in two minutes."
60.05 I obeyed, so far as to quit the chamber;
60.06 when, ignorant where the narrow lobbies led,
60.07 I stood still, and was witness, involuntarily, to
60.08 a piece of superstition on the part of my land-
60.09 lord, which belied, oddly, his apparent sense.
60.10 He got on to the bed, and wrenched open
60.11 the lattice, bursting, as he pulled at it, into an
60.12 uncontrollable passion of tears.
60.13 "Come in! come in!" he sobbed. "Cathy,
60.14 do come. Oh do -- \once# more! Oh! my heart's
60.15 darling, hear me \this# time -- Catherine, at last!"
60.16 The spectre showed a spectre's ordinary ca-
60.17 price; it gave no sign of being; but the snow
60.18 and wind whirled wildly through, even reach-
60.19 ing my station, and blowing out the light.
60.20 There was such anguish in the gush of grief
60.21 that accompanied this raving, that my com-
60.22 passion made me overlook its folly, and I drew
61.01 off, half angry to have listened at all, and vexed
61.02 at having related my ridiculous nightmare,
61.03 since it produced that agony; though \why#,
61.04 was beyond my comprehension.
61.05 I descended cautiously to the lower regions
61.06 and landed in the back-kitchen, where a gleam
61.07 of fire, raked compactly together, enabled me
61.08 to rekindle my candle.
61.09 Nothing was stirring except a brindled, grey
61.10 cat, which crept from the ashes, and saluted me
61.11 with a querulous mew.
61.12 Two benches, shaped in sections of a circle,
61.13 nearly enclosed the hearth; on one of these
61.14 I stretched myself, and Grimalkin mounted
61.15 the other. We were both of us nodding, ere
61.16 any one invaded our retreat; and then it was
61.17 Joseph shuffling down a wooden ladder that
61.18 vanished in the roof, through a trap, the assent
61.19 to his garret, I suppose.
61.20 He cast a sinister look at the little flame
61.21 which I had enticed to play between the ribs,
61.22 swept the cat from its elevation, and bestowing
62.01 himself in the vacancy, commenced the opera-
62.02 tion of stuffing a three-inch pipe with tobacco;
62.03 my presence in his sanctum was evidently es-
62.04 teemed a piece of impudence too shameful for
62.05 remark. He silently applied the tube to his
62.06 lips, folded his arms, and puffed away.
62.07 I let him enjoy the luxury, unannoyed; and
62.08 after sucking out the last wreath, and heaving
62.09 a profound sigh, he got up, and departed as
62.10 solemnly as he came.
62.11 A more elastic footstep entered next, and
62.12 now I opened my mouth for a "good morn-
62.13 ing," but closed it again, the salutation un-
62.14 achieved; for Hareton Earnshaw was perform-
62.15 ing his orisons, \sotto# \voce#, in a series of curses
62.16 directed against every object he touched,
62.17 while he rummaged a corner, for a spade or
62.18 shovel to dig through the drifts. He glanced
62.19 over the back of the bench dilating his nostrils,
62.20 and thought as little of exchanging civilities
62.21 with me, as with my companion, the cat.
62.22 I guessed by his preparations that egress
63.01 was allowed, and leaving my hard couch, made
63.02 a movement to follow him. He noticed this,
63.03 and thrust at an inner door with the end of
63.04 his spade, intimating by an inarticulate sound,
63.05 that there was the place where I must go, if I
63.06 changed my locality.
63.07 It opened into the house, where the females
63.08 were already astir. Zillah urging flakes of
63.09 flame up the chimney with a colossal bellows;
63.10 and Mrs. Heathcliff, kneeling on the hearth,
63.11 reading a book by the aid of the blaze.
63.12 She held her hand interposed between the
63.13 furnace-heat and her eyes; and seemed ab-
63.14 sorbed in her occupation: desisting from it
63.15 only to chide the servant for covering her with
63.16 sparks, or to push away a dog, now and then,
63.17 that snoozled its nose over forwardly into her
63.18 face.
63.19 I was surprised to see Heathcliff there also.
63.20 He stood by the fire, his back towards me,
63.21 just finishing a stormy scene to poor Zillah,
63.22 who ever and anon interrupted her labour to
64.01 pluck up the corner of her apron, and heave an
64.02 indignant groan.
64.03 "And you, you worthless --" he broke out

64.04 as I entered, turning to his daughter-in-law,
64.05 and employing an epithet as harmless as duck,
64.06 or sheep, but generally represented by a dash.
64.07 "There you are at your idle tricks again!
64.08 The rest of them do earn their bread -- you live
64.09 on my charity! Put your trash away, and
64.10 find something to do. You shall pay me for
64.11 the plague of having you eternally in my sight
64.12 -- do you hear, damnable jade?"
64.13 "I'll put my trash away, because you can
64.14 make me, if I refuse," answered the young
64.15 lady, closing her book, and throwing it on a
64.16 chair. "But I'll not do anything, though you
64.17 should swear your tongue out, except what I
64.18 please!"
64.19 Heathcliff lifted his hand, and the speaker
64.20 sprang to a safer distance, obviously acquainted
64.21 with its weight.
64.22 Having no desire to be entertained by a cat
65.01 and dog combat, I stepped forward briskly,
65.02 as if eager to partake the warmth of the
65.03 hearth, and innocent of any knowledge of the
65.04 interrupted dispute. Each had enough de-
65.05 corum to suspend further hostilities; Heath-
65.06 cliff placed his fists, out of temptation, in his
65.07 pockets: Mrs. Heathcliff curled her lip, and
65.08 walked to a seat far off; where she kept her
65.09 word by playing the part of a statue during
65.10 the remainder of my stay.
65.11 That was not long. I declined joining their
65.12 breakfast, and, at the first gleam of dawn, took
65.13 an opportunity of escaping into the free air,
65.14 now clear, and still, and cold as impalpable
65.15 ice.
65.16 My landlord hallooed for me to stop ere I
65.17 reached the bottom of the garden, and offered
65.18 to accompany me across the moor. It was
65.19 well he did, for the whole hill-back was one
65.20 billowy, white ocean; the swells and falls not
65.21 indicating corresponding rises and depressions
65.22 in the ground -- many pits, at least, were filled
66.01 to a level; and entire ranges of mounds, the
66.02 refuse of the quarries, blotted from the chart
66.03 which my yesterday's walk left pictured in my
66.04 mind.
66.05 I had remarked on one side of the road, at
66.06 intervals of six or seven yards, a line of up-
66.07 right stones, continued through the whole
66.08 length of the barren: these were erected, and
66.09 daubed with lime, on purpose to serve as guides
66.10 in the dark, and also, when a fall, like the
66.11 present, confounded the deep swamps on
66.12 either hand with the firmer path: but, except-
66.13 ing a dirty dot pointing up, here and there, all
66.14 traces of their existence had vanished; and my
66.15 companion found it necessary to warn me fre-
66.16 quently to steer to the right, or left, when I
66.17 imagined I was following, correctly, the wind-
66.18 ings of the road.
66.19 We exchanged little conversation, and he
66.20 halted at the entrance of Thrushcross park,
66.21 saying, I could make no error there. Our
66.22 adieux were limited to a hasty bow, and then
67.01 I pushed forward, trusting to my own resources,
67.02 for the porter's lodge is untenanted as yet.
67.03 The distance from the gate to the Grange is
67.04 two miles: I believe I managed to make it four;
67.05 what with losing myself among the trees, and
67.06 sinking up to the neck in snow, a predicament
67.07 which only those who have experienced it can
67.08 appreciate. At any rate, whatever were my
67.09 wanderings, the clock chimed twelve as I en-
67.10 tered the house; and that gave exactly an
67.11 hour for every mile of the usual way from
67.12 Wuthering Heights.
67.13 My human fixture, and her satellites rushed
67.14 to welcome me; exclaiming, tumultuously,
67.15 they had completely given me up; everybody
67.16 conjectured that I perished last night; and
67.17 they were wondering how they must set about
67.18 the search for my remains.
67.19 I bid them be quiet, now that they saw me
67.20 returned, and, benumbed to my very heart, I
67.21 dragged up-stairs whence, after putting on
67.22 dry clothes, and pacing to and fro, thirty or
68.01 forty minutes, to restore the animal heat, I am
68.02 adjourned to my study, feeble as a kitten, al-
68.03 most too much so to enjoy the cheerful fire, and
68.04 smoking coffee which the servant has prepared
68.05 for my refreshment.
69.01 [VOL. 1 CHAPTER 4]
69.02 WHAT vain weather-cocks we are! I, who had
69.03 determined to hold myself independent of all
69.04 social intercourse, and thanked my stars that,
69.05 at length, I had lighted on a spot where it was
69.06 next to impracticable, I, weak wretch, after
69.07 maintaining till dusk a struggle with low
69.08 spirits, and solitude, was finally compelled to
69.09 strike my colours; and, under pretence of
69.10 gaining information concerning the necessities
69.11 of my establishment, I desired Mrs. Dean,
69.12 when she brought in supper, to sit down while
70.01 I ate it, hoping sincerely she would prove a re-
70.02 gular gossip, and either rouse me to animation,
70.03 or lull me to sleep by her talk.
70.04 "You have lived here a considerable time,"
70.05 I commenced; "did you not say sixteen
70.06 years?"
70.07 "Eighteen, sir; I came, when the mistress
70.08 was married, to wait on her; after she died,
70.09 the master retained me for his house-keeper."

70.10 "Indeed."
70.11 There ensued a pause. She was not a gos-
70.12 sip, I feared, unless about her own affairs, and
70.13 those could hardly interest me.
70.14 However, having studied for an interval,
70.15 with a fist on either knee, and a cloud of me-
70.16 ditation over her ruddy countenance, she eja-
70.17 culated --
70.18 "Ah, times are greatly changed since
70.19 then!"
70.20 "Yes," I remarked, "you've seen a good
70.21 many alterations, I suppose?"
70.22 "I have: and troubles too," she said.
71.01 "Oh, I'll turn the talk on my landlord's
71.02 family!" I thought to myself. "A good sub-
71.03 ject to start -- and that pretty girl -- widow, I
71.04 should like to know her history; whether she
71.05 be a native of the country, or, as is more pro-
71.06 bable, an exotic that the surly indigenae will
71.07 not recognise for kin."
71.08 With this intention I asked Mrs. Dean why
71.09 Heathcliff let Thrushcross Grange, and pre-
71.10 ferred living in a situation and residence so
71.11 much inferior.
71.12 "Is he not rich enough to keep the estate
71.13 in good order?" I enquired.
71.14 "Rich sir!" she returned. "He has, no-
71.15 body knows what money, and every year it in-
71.16 creases. Yes, yes, he's rich enough to live in
71.17 a finer house than this; but he's very near --
71.18 close-handed; and, if he had meant to flit to
71.19 Thrushcross Grange, as soon as he heard of a
71.20 good tenant, he could not have borne to miss
71.21 the chance of getting a few hundreds more. It
72.01 is strange people should be so greedy, when
72.02 they are alone in the world!"
72.03 "He had a son, it seems?"
72.04 "Yes, he had one -- he is dead."
72.05 "And that young lady, Mrs. Heathcliff, is
72.06 his widow?"
72.07 "Yes."
72.08 "Where did she come from originally?"
72.09 "Why, sir, she is my late master's daughter;
72.10 Catherine Linton was her maiden name. I
72.11 nursed her, poor thing! I did wish Mr. Heath-
72.12 cliff would remove here, and then we might
72.13 have been together again."
72.14 "What, Catherine Linton!" I exclaimed,
72.15 astonished. But a minute's reflection convinced
72.16 me it was not my ghostly Catherine. "Then,"
72.17 I continued, "my predecessor's name was
72.18 Linton?"
72.19 "It was."
72.20 "And who is that Earnshaw, Hareton
72.21 Earnshaw, who lives with Mr. Heathcliff? are
72.22 they relations?"
73.01 "No; he is the late Mrs. Linton's nephew."
73.02 "The young lady's cousin then?"
73.03 "Yes; and her husband was her cousin
73.04 also -- one, on the mother's -- the other, on the
73.05 father's side -- Heathcliff married Mr. Linton's
73.06 sister."
73.07 "I see the house at Wuthering Heights has
73.08 'Earnshaw' carved over the front door. Are
73.09 they an old family?"
73.10 "Very old, sir; and Hareton is the last of
73.11 them, as our Miss Cathy is of us -- I mean, of
73.12 the Lintons. Have you been to Wuthering
73.13 Heights? I beg pardon for asking; but I
73.14 should like to hear how she is!"
73.15 "Mrs. Heathcliff? she looked very well,
73.16 and very handsome; yet, I think, not very
73.17 happy."
73.18 "Oh dear, I don't wonder! And how did
73.19 you like the master?"
73.20 "A rough fellow, rather, Mrs. Dean. Is
73.21 not that his character?"
73.22 "Rough as a saw-edge, and hard as whinstone!
74.01 The less you meddle with him the
74.02 better."
74.03 "He must have had some ups and downs in
74.04 life to make him such a churl. Do you know
74.05 anything of his history?"
74.06 "It's a cuckoo's; sir -- I know all about it;
74.07 except where he was born, and who were his
74.08 parents, and how he got his money, at first --
74.09 And Hareton has been cast out like an un-
74.10 fledged dunnock -- The unfortunate lad is the
74.11 only one, in all this parish, that does not guess
74.12 how he has been cheated!"
74.13 "Well, Mrs. Dean, it will be a charitable
74.14 deed to tell me something of my neighbours --
74.15 I feel I shall not rest, if I go to bed; so, be
74.16 good enough to sit, and chat an hour."
74.17 "Oh, certainly, sir! I'll just fetch a little
74.18 sewing, and then I'll sit as long as you please
74.19 but you've caught cold, I saw you shivering,
74.20 and you must have some gruel to drive it
74.21 out."
74.22 The worthy woman bustled off; and I
75.01 crouched nearer the fire: my head felt hot,
75.02 and the rest of me chill: moreover I was ex-
75.03 cited, almost to a pitch of foolishness through
75.04 my nerves and brain. This caused me to feel,
75.05 not uncomfortable, but rather fearful, as I am
75.06 still, of serious effects from the incidents of to-
75.07 day and yesterday.
75.08 She returned presently, bringing a smoking
75.09 basin, and a basket of work; and, having
75.10 placed the former on the hob, drew in her seat,
75.11 evidently pleased to find me so companionable.

75.12     "Before I came to live here," she com-
75.13 menced, waiting no further invitation to her
75.14 story; "I was almost always at Wuthering
75.15 Heights; because, my mother had nursed Mr.
75.16 Hindley Earnshaw, that was Hareton's father,
75.17 and I got used to playing with the children --
75.18 I ran errands too, and helped to make hay, and
75.19 hung about the farm ready for anything that
75.20 anybody would set me to.
75.21     "One fine summer morning -- it was the beginning
76.01 of harvest, I remember -- Mr. Earn-
76.02 shaw, the old master, came down stairs, dressed
76.03 for a journey; and, after he had told Joseph
76.04 what was to be done during the day, he turn-
76.05 ed to Hindley, and Cathy, and me -- for I sat
76.06 eating my porridge, with them, and he said,
76.07 speaking to his son,
76.08     "Now my bonny man, I'm going to Liver-
76.09 pool, to-day ... What shall I bring you? You
76.10 may choose what you like; only let it be little,
76.11 for I shall walk there and back; sixty miles
76.12 each way, that is a long spell!"
76.13     Hindley named a fiddle, and then he asked
76.14 Miss Cathy; she was hardly six years old, but
76.15 she could ride any horse in the stable, and she
76.16 chose a whip.
76.17     He did not forget me, for, he had a kind
76.18 heart, though he was rather severe, sometimes.
76.19 He promised to bring me a pocketful of apples,
76.20 and pears, and then he kissed his children,
76.21 good bye, and set off.
76.22     It seemed a long while to us all -- the three
77.01 days of his absence -- and often did little Cathy
77.02 ask when he would be home: Mrs. Earnshaw,
77.03 expected him by supper-time, on the third
77.04 evening; and she put the meal off hour after
77.05 hour; there were no signs of his coming, how-
77.06 ever, and at last the children got tired of run-
77.07 ning down to the gate to look -- Then it grew
77.08 dark, she would have had them to bed, but
77.09 they begged sadly to be allowed to stay up
77.10 and, just about eleven o'clock, the door-latch
77.11 was raised quietly and in stept the master.
77.12 He threw himself into a chair, laughing and
77.13 groaning, and bid them all stand off, for he was
77.14 nearly killed -- he would not have such another
77.15 walk for the three kingdoms.
77.16     "And at the end of it, to be flighted to
77.17 death!" he said opening his great coat, which
77.18 he held bundled up in his arms, "See here,
77.19 wife; I was never so beaten with anything in
77.20 my life; but you must e'en take it as a gift
77.21 of God; though it's as dark almost as if it
77.22 came from the devil."
78.01     We crowded round, and, over Miss Cathy's
78.02 head, I had a peep at a dirty, ragged, black--
78.03 haired child; big enough both to walk and
78.04 talk -- indeed, its face looked older than Cathe-
78.05 rine's -- yet, when it was set on its feet, it only
78.06 stared round, and repeated over and over again,
78.07 some gibberish that nobody could understand.
78.08 I was frightened, and Mrs. Earnshaw was
78.09 ready to fling it out of doors: she did fly up --
78.10 asking how he could fashion to bring that gip-
78.11 sy brat into the house, when they had their
78.12 own bairns to feed, and fend for? What he
78.13 meant to do with it, and whether he were
78.14 mad?
78.15     The master tried to explain the matter; but,
78.16 he was really half dead with fatigue, and all
78.17 that I could make out, amongst her scold-
78.18 ing, was a tale of his seeing it starving, and
78.19 houseless, and as good as dumb in the streets
78.20 of Liverpool where he picked it up and in-
78.21 quired for its owner -- Not a soul knew to
78.22 whom it belonged, he said, and his money and
79.01 time, being both limited, he thought it better,
79.02 to take it home with him, at once, than run,
79.03 into vain expences there; because he was de-
79.04 termined he would not leave as he found it.
79.05     Well, the conclusion was that my mistress
79.06 grumbled herself calm; and Mr Earnshaw told
79.07 me to wash it, and give it clean things, and let
79.08 it sleep with the children.
79.09     Hindley and Cathy contented themselves
79.10 with looking and listening till peace was res-
79.11 tored: then, both began searching their father's
79.12 pockets for the presents he had promised them.
79.13 The former was a boy of fourteen, but when
79.14 he drew out, what had been a fiddle crushed
79.15 to morsels in the great coat, he blubbered
79.16 aloud, and Cathy, when she learnt the master
79.17 had lost her whip in attending on the stran-
79.18 ger, showed her humour by grinning and spit-
79.19 ting at the stupid little thing, earning for her
79.20 pains, a sound blow from her father to teach
79.21 her cleaner manners.
79.22     They entirely refused to have it in bed with
80.01 them, or even in their room, and I had no more
80.02 sense, so, I put it on the landing of the stairs,
80.03 hoping it might be gone on the morrow. By
80.04 chance, or else attracted by hearing his voice,
80.05 it crept to Mr. Earnshaw's door and there he
80.06 found it on quitting his chamber. Inquiries
80.07 were made as to how it got there; I was obli-
80.08 ged to confess, and in recompense for my co-
80.09 wardice and inhumanity was sent out of the
80.10 house.
80.11     This was Heathcliff's first introduction to
80.12 the family: on coming back a few days after-
80.13 wards, for I did not consider my banishment

80.14 perpetual, I found they had christened him
80.15 "Heathcliff," it was the name of a son who
80.16 died in childhood, and it has served him ever
80.17 since, both for christian and surname.
80.18     Miss Cathy and he were now very thick;
80.19 but Hindley hated him, and to say the truth
80.20 I did the same; and we plagued and went on
80.21 with him shamefully, for I was'nt reasonable
80.22 enough to feel my injustice, and the mistress
81.01 never put in a word on his behalf, when she
81.02 saw him wronged.
81.03     He seemed a sullen, patient child; hardened,
81.04 perhaps, to ill-treatment: he would stand
81.05 Hindley's blows without winking or shedding
81.06 a tear, and my pinches moved him only to
81.07 draw in a breath, and open his eyes as if he
81.08 had hurt himself by accident, and nobody was
81.09 to blame.
81.10     This endurance made old Earnshaw furious
81.11 when he discovered his son persecuting the
81.12 poor, fatherless, child, as he called him. He
81.13 took to Heathcliff strangely, believing, all he
81.14 said, /for that matter, he said precious little,
81.15 and generally the truth,// and petting him up
81.16 far above Cathy, who was too mischievous and
81.17 wayward for a favourite.
81.18     So, from the very beginning, he bred bad
81.19 feeling in the house; and at Mrs Earnshaw's
81.20 death, which happened in less than two years
81.21 after, the young master had learnt to regard
82.01 his father as an oppressor rather than a friend,
82.02 and Heathcliff as a usurper of his parent's
82.03 affections, and his privileges, and he grew bit-
82.04 ter with brooding over these injuries.
82.05     I sympathised awhile, but, when the chil-
82.06 dren fell ill of the measles and I had to tend
82.07 them, and take on me the cares of a woman,
82.08 at once, I changed my ideas. Heathcliff was
82.09 dangerously sick, and while he lay at the
82.10 worst he would have me constantly by his pil-
82.11 low; I suppose he felt I did a good deal for
82.12 him, and he had'nt wit to guess that I was
82.13 compelled to do it. However, I will say this,
82.14 he was the quietest child that ever nurse
82.15 watched over. The difference between him
82.16 and the others forced me to be less partial:
82.17 Cathy and her brother harassed me terribly:
82.18 \he# was as uncomplaining as a lamb; though
82.19 hardness, not gentleness, made him give little
82.20 trouble.
82.21     He got through, and the doctor affirmed it
82.22 was in a great measure owing to me, and
83.01 praised me for my care. I was vain of his
83.02 commendations, and softened towards the being
83.03 by whose means, I earned them, and thus
83.04 Hindley lost his last ally; still I couldn't dote
83.05 on Heathcliff, and I wondered often what my
83.06 master saw to admire so much in the sullen
83.07 boy who never, to recollection, repaid his
83.08 indulgence by any sign of gratitude. He was
83.09 not insolent to his benefactor; he was simply
83.10 insensible, though knowing perfectly the hold
83.11 he had on his heart, and conscious he had only
83.12 to speak and all the house would be obliged
83.13 to bend to his wishes.
83.14     As an instance, I remember Mr. Earnshaw
83.15 once bought a couple of colts at the parish
83.16 fair, and gave the lads each one. Heathcliff
83.17 took the handsomest, but it soon fell lame, and
83.18 when he discovered it, he said to Hindley,
83.19     "You must exchange horses with me; I
83.20 don't like mine, and, if you won't I shall tell
83.21 your father of the three thrashings you've
84.01 given me this week, and show him my arm
84.02 which is black to the shoulder."
84.03     Hindley put out his tongue, and cuffed him
84.04 over the ears.
84.05     "You'd better do it, at once," he persisted
84.06 escaping to the porch, /they were in the stable//
84.07 "you will have to, and, if I speak, of these
84.08 blows, you'll get them again with interest."
84.09     "Off dog!" cried Hindley, threatening him
84.10 with an iron weight, used for weighing pota-
84.11 toes, and hay.
84.12     "Throw it," he replied, standing still, "and
84.13 then I'll tell how you boasted that you would
84.14 turn me out of doors as soon as he died, and
84.15 see whether he will not turn you out direct-
84.16 ly."
84.17     Hindley threw it, hitting him on the breast
84.18 and down he fell but staggered up, imme-
84.19 diately, breathless and white, and had not I
84.20 prevented it he would have gone just so to
84.21 the master, and got full revenge by letting
85.01 his condition plead for him, intimating who
85.02 had caused it."
85.03     "Take my colt, gipsy, then!" said young
85.04 Earnshaw, "And I pray that he may break
85.05 your neck, take him, and be damned, you
85.06 beggarly interloper! and wheedle my father
85.07 out of all he has, only, afterwards, show him
85.08 what you are, imp of Satan -- And take that,
85.09 I hope he'll kick out your brains!"
85.10     Heathcliff had gone to loose the beast, and
85.11 shift it to his own stall -- He was passing be-
85.12 hind it, when Hindley finished his speech by
85.13 knocking him under its feet, and without stop-
85.14 ping to examine whether his hopes were ful-
85.15 filled, ran away as fast as he could.
85.16     I was surprised to witness how coolly the
85.17 child gathered himself up, and went on with

85.18 his intention, exchanging saddles and all; and
85.19 then sitting down on a bundle of hay to over-
85.20 come the qualm which the violent blow occa-
85.21 sioned, before he entered the house.
85.22 I persuaded him easily to let me lay the
86.01 blame of his bruises on the horse; he minded
86.02 little what tale was told since he had what he
86.03 wanted. He complained so seldom, indeed, of
86.04 such stirs as these, that I really thought him
86.05 not vindictive -- I was deceived, completely, as
86.06 you will hear.
87.01 [VOL. 1 CHAPTER 5]
87.02 IN the course of time, Mr. Earnshaw began to
87.03 fail. He had been active and healthy, yet his
87.04 strength left him suddenly; and when he was
87.05 confined to the chimney-corner he grew griev-
87.06 ously irritable. A nothing vexed him, and
87.07 suspected slights of his authority nearly threw
87.08 him into fits.
87.09 This was especially to be remarked if any
87.10 one attempted to impose upon, or domineer
87.11 over his favourite: he was painfully jealous
87.12 lest a word should be spoken amiss to him,
88.01 seeming to have got into his head the notion
88.02 that, because he liked Heathcliff, all hated, and
88.03 longed to do him an ill-turn.
88.04 It was a disadvantage to the lad, for the
88.05 kinder among us did not wish to fret the mas-
88.06 ter, so we humoured his partiality; and that
88.07 humouring was rich nourishment to the child's
88.08 pride and black tempers. Still it became in a
88.09 manner necessary; twice, or thrice, Hindley's
88.10 manifestations of scorn, while his father was
88.11 near, roused the old man to a fury. He seized
88.12 his stick to strike him, and shook with rage
88.13 that he could not do it.
88.14 At last, our curate, /we had a curate then
88.15 who made the living answer by teaching the
88.16 little Lintons and Earnshaws, and farming his
88.17 bit of land himself,// he advised that the young
88.18 man should be sent to college, and Mr. Earn-
88.19 shaw agreed, though with a heavy spirit, for he
88.20 said --
88.21 "Hindley was naught, and would never
88.22 thrive as where he wandered."
89.01 I hoped heartily we should have peace now.
89.02 It hurt me to think the master should be made
89.03 uncomfortable by his own good deed. I fan-
89.04 cied the discontent of age and disease arose
89.05 from his family disagreements, and he would
89.06 have it that it did -- really, you know, sir, it
89.07 was in his sinking frame.
89.08 We might have got on tolerably, notwith-
89.09 standing; but, for two people, Miss Cathy,
89.10 and Joseph, the servant; you saw him, I dare
89.11 say, up yonder. He was, and is yet, most
89.12 likely, the wearisomest, self-righteous pharisee
89.13 that ever ransacked a bible to rake the pro-
89.14 mises to himself, and fling the curses on his
89.15 neighbours. By his knack of sermonizing and
89.16 pious discoursing, he contrived to make a great
89.17 impression on Mr. Earnshaw, and, the more
89.18 feeble the master became, the more influence
89.19 he gained.
89.20 He was relentless in worrying him about his
89.21 soul's concerns, and about ruling his children
89.22 rigidly. He encouraged him to regard Hindley
90.01 as a reprobate; and, night after night, he
90.02 regularly grumbled out a long string of tales
90.03 against Heathcliff and Catherine; always
90.04 minding to flatter Earnshaw's weakness by
90.05 heaping the heaviest blame on the last.
90.06 Certainly, she had ways with her such as I
90.07 never saw a child take up before; and she put
90.08 all of us past our patience fifty times and of-
90.09 tener in a day: from the hour she came down
90.10 stairs, till the hour she went to bed, we had
90.11 not a minute's security that she wouldn't be in
90.12 mischief. Her spirits were always at high-water
90.13 mark, her tongue always going -- singing, laugh-
90.14 ing, and plaguing everybody who would not do
90.15 the same. A wild, wick slip she was -- but,
90.16 she had the bonniest eye, and the sweetest smile,
90.17 and lightest foot in the parish; and, after all,
90.18 I believe she meant no harm; for when once
90.19 she made you cry in good earnest, it seldom
90.20 happened that she would not keep you com-
90.21 pany, and oblige you to be quiet that you
90.22 might comfort her.
90.23 She was much too fond of Heathcliff. The
91.01 greatest punishment we could invent for her
91.02 was to keep her separate from him: yet, she
91.03 got chided more than any of us on his account.
91.04 In play, she liked, exceedingly, to act the
91.05 little mistress; using her hands freely, and com-
91.06 manding her companions: she did so to me,
91.07 but I would not bear slapping, and ordering;
91.08 and so I let her know.
91.09 Now, Mr. Earnshaw did not understand
91.10 jokes from his children: he had always been
91.11 strict and grave with them; and Catherine, on
91.12 her part, had no idea why her father should be
91.13 crosser and less patient in his ailing condition,
91.14 than he was in his prime.
91.15 His peevish reproofs wakened in her a
91.16 naughty delight to provoke him: she was never
91.17 so happy as when we were all scolding her at
91.18 once, and she defying us with her bold, saucy
91.19 look, and her ready words; turning Joseph's
91.20 religious curses into ridicule, baiting me, and
91.21 doing just what her father hated most, showing

91.22 how her pretended insolence, which he thought
92.01 real, had more power over Heathcliff than his
92.02 kindness. How the boy would do \her# bidding
92.03 in anything, and \his# only when it suited his
92.04 own inclination.
92.05 After behaving as badly as possible all day,
92.06 she sometimes came fondling to make it up at
92.07 night.
92.08 "Nay, Cathy," the old man would say," I
92.09 cannot love thee; thou'rt worse than thy
92.10 brother. Go, say thy prayers, child, and ask
92.11 God's pardon. I doubt thy mother and I must
92.12 rue that we ever reared thee!"
92.13 That made her cry, at first; and then, being
92.14 repulsed continually hardened her, and she
92.15 laughed if I told her to say she was sorry for
92.16 her faults, and beg to be forgiven.
92.17 But the hour came, at last, that ended Mr.
92.18 Earnshaw's troubles on earth. He died
92.19 quietly in his chair one October evening, seated
92.20 by the fire-side.
92.21 A high wind blustered round the house, and
92.22 roared in the chimney: it sounded wild and
93.01 stormy, yet it was not cold, and we were all
93.02 together -- I, a little removed from the hearth,
93.03 busy at my knitting, and Joseph reading his
93.04 Bible near the table, /for the servants generally
93.05 sat in the house then, after their work was
93.06 done.// Miss Cathy had been sick, and that
93.07 made her still; she leant against her father's
93.08 knee, and Heathcliff was lying on the floor
93.09 with his head on her lap.
93.10 I remember the master, before he fell into a
93.11 doze, stroking her bonny hair -- it pleased him
93.12 rarely to see her gentle -- and saying --
93.13 "Why canst thou not always be a good
93.14 lass, Cathy?"
93.15 And she turned her face up to his, and
93.16 laughed, and answered,
93.17 "Why cannot you always be a good man,
93.18 father?"
93.19 But as soon as she saw him vexed again,
93.20 she kissed his hand, and said she would sing
93.21 him to sleep. She began singing very low, till
93.22 his fingers dropped from hers, and his head
94.01 sank on his breast. Then I told her to hush,
94.02 and not stir, for fear she should wake him.
94.03 we all kept as mute as mice for a full half-hour,
94.04 and should have done longer, only Joseph,
94.05 having finished his chapter, got up and said
94.06 that he must rouse the master for prayers and
94.07 bed. He stepped forward, and called him by
94.08 name, and touched his shoulder, but he would
94.09 not move -- so he took the candle and looked at
94.10 him.
94.11 I thought there was something wrong as he
94.12 set down the light; and seizing the children
94.13 each by an arm, whispered them to "frame
94.14 up-stairs, and make little din -- they might pray
94.15 alone that evening -- he had summut to do."
94.16 "I shall bid father good-night first," said
94.17 Catherine, putting her arms round his neck,
94.18 before we could hinder her.
94.19 The poor thing discovered her loss directly --
94.20 she screamed out --
94.21 "Oh, he's dead, Heathcliff! he's dead!"
94.22 And they both set up a heart-breaking cry.
95.01 I joined my wail to theirs, loud and bitter;
95.02 but Joseph asked what we could be thinking
95.03 of to roar in that way over a saint in Heaven.
95.04 He told me to put on my cloak and run to
95.05 Gimmerton for the doctor and the parson. I
95.06 could not guess the use that either would be
95.07 of, then. However, I went, through wind and
95.08 rain, and brought one, the doctor, back with
95.09 me; the other said he would come in the
95.10 morning.
95.11 Leaving Joseph to explain matters, I ran
95.12 to the children's room; their door was ajar, I
95.13 saw they had never laid down, though it was
95.14 past midnight; but they were calmer, and did
95.15 not need me to console them. The little souls
95.16 were comforting each other with better
95.17 thoughts than I could have hit on; no parson
95.18 in the world ever pictured Heaven so beauti-
95.19 fully as they did, in their innocent talk; and,
95.20 while I sobbed, and listened, I could not help
95.21 wishing we were all there safe together.
96.01 [VOL. 1 CHAPTER 6]
96.02 MR. HINDLEY came home to the funeral; and
96.03 -- a thing that amazed us, and set the neigh-
96.04 bours gossiping right and left -- he brought a
96.05 wife with him.
96.06 What she was, and where she was born he
96.07 never informed us; probably, she had neither
96.08 money nor name to recommend her, or he
96.09 would scarcely have kept the union from his
96.10 father.
96.11 She was not one that would have disturbed
96.12 the house much on her own account. Every object
97.01 she saw, the moment she crossed the thres-
97.02 hold, appeared to delight her; and every cir-
97.03 cumstance that took place about her, except
97.04 the preparing for the burial, and the presence
97.05 of the mourners.
97.06 I thought she was half silly from her be-
97.07 haviour while that went on; she ran into her
97.08 chamber, and made me come with her, though
97.09 I should have been dressing the children; and
97.10 there she sat shivering and clasping her hands,
97.11 and asking repeatedly --

97.12 "Are they gone yet?"
97.13 Then she began describing with hysterical
97.14 emotion the effect it produced on her to see
97.15 black; and started, and trembled, and, at last,
97.16 fell a weeping -- and when I asked what was
97.17 the matter? answered, she didn't know; but
97.18 she felt so afraid of dying!
97.19 I imagined her as little likely to die as my-
97.20 self. She was rather thin, but young, and
97.21 fresh complexioned, and her eyes sparkled as
98.01 bright as diamonds. I did remark, to be sure,
98.02 that mounting the stairs made her breathe very
98.03 quick, that the least sudden noise set her all in
98.04 a quiver, and that she coughed troublesomely
98.05 sometimes: but, I knew nothing of what these
98.06 symptoms portended, and had no impulse to
98.07 sympathize with her. We don't in general
98.08 take to foreigners here, Mr. Lockwood, unless
98.09 they take to us first.
98.10 Young Earnshaw was altered considerably in
98.11 the three years of his absence. He had grown
98.12 sparer, and lost his colour, and spoke and
98.13 dressed quite differently: and, on the very day
98.14 of his return, he told Joseph and me we must
98.15 thenceforth quarter ourselves in the back-kit-
98.16 chen, and leave the house for him. Indeed
98.17 he would have carpeted and papered a small
98.18 spare room for a parlour; but his wife ex-
98.19 pressed such pleasure at the white floor, and
98.20 huge glowing fire-place, at the pewter dishes,
98.21 and delf-case, and dog-kennel, and the wide
99.01 space there was to move about in, where they
99.02 usually sat, that he thought it unnecessary to
99.03 her comfort, and so dropped the intention.
99.04 She expressed pleasure, too, at finding a
99.05 sister among her new acquaintance, and she
99.06 prattled to Catherine, and kissed her, and ran
99.07 about with her, and gave her quantities of
99.08 presents, at the beginning. Her affection
99.09 tired very soon, however, and when she grew
99.10 peevish, Hindley became tyrannical. A few
99.11 words from her, evincing a dislike to Heath-
99.12 cliff, were enough to rouse in him all his old
99.13 hatred of the boy. He drove him from their
99.14 company to the servants, deprived him of the
99.15 instructions of the curate, and insisted that he
99.16 should labour out of doors instead, compelling
99.17 him to do so, as hard as any other lad on the
99.18 farm.
99.19 He bore his degradation pretty well at first,
99.20 because Cathy taught him what she learnt, and
99.21 worked or played with him in the fields. They
99.22 both promised fair to grow up as rude as savages,
100.01 the young master being entirely negli-
100.02 gent how they behaved, and what they did,
100.03 so they kept clear of him. He would not even
100.04 have seen after their going to church on Sun-
100.05 days, only Joseph and the curate reprimanded
100.06 his carelessness when they absented themselves,
100.07 and that reminded him to order Heathcliff a
100.08 flogging, and Catherine a fast from dinner or
100.09 supper.
100.10 But it was one of their chief amusements
100.11 to run away to the moors in the morning and
100.12 remain there all day, and the after punishment
100.13 grew a mere thing to laugh at. The curate
100.14 might set as many chapters as he pleased for
100.15 Catherine to get by heart, and Joseph might
100.16 thrash Heathcliff till his arm ached; they
100.17 forgot everything the minute they were to-
100.18 gether again, at least the minute they had
100.19 contrived some naughty plan of revenge, and
100.20 many a time I've cried to myself to watch
100.21 them growing more reckless daily, and I not
100.22 daring to speak a syllable for fear of losing
101.01 the small power I still retained over the un-
101.02 friended creatures.
101.03 One Sunday evening, it chanced that they
101.04 were banished from the sitting-room, for
101.05 making a noise, or a light offence of the kind,
101.06 and when I went to call them to supper, I
101.07 could discover them nowhere.
101.08 We searched the house, above and below,
101.09 and the yard, and the stables, they were invisible;
101.10 and, at last, Hindley in a passion told us to
101.11 bolt the doors, and swore nobody should let
101.12 them in that night.
101.13 The household went to bed; and I, too
101.14 anxious to lie down, opened my lattice and
101.15 put my head out to hearken, though it rained,
101.16 determined to admit them in spite of the pro-
101.17 hibition, should they return.
101.18 In a while, I distinguished steps coming up
101.19 the road, and the light of a lantern glimmered
101.20 through the gate.
101.21 I threw a shawl over my head and ran to
101.22 prevent them from waking Mr. Earnshaw by
102.01 knocking. There was Heathcliff, by himself;
102.02 it gave me a start to see him alone.
102.03 "Where is Miss Catherine?" I cried hur-
102.04 riedly. "No accident, I hope?"
102.05 "At Thrushcross Grange," he answered,
102.06 "and I would have been there too, but they
102.07 had not the manners to ask me to stay."
102.08 "Well, you will catch it!" I said, "you'll
102.09 never be content till you're sent about your
102.10 business. What in the world led you wan-
102.11 dering to Thrushcross Grange?"
102.12 "Let me get off my wet clothes, and I'll
102.13 tell you all about it, Nelly," he replied.
102.14 I bid him beware of rousing the master, and

102.15 while he undressed, and I waited to put out
102.16 the candle, he continued --
102.17 "Cathy and I escaped from the wash-house
102.18 to have a ramble at liberty, and getting a
102.19 glimpse of the Grange lights, we thought we
102.20 would just go and see whether the Lintons
102.21 passed their Sunday evenings standing shiver-
102.22 ing in corners, while their father and mother
103.01 sat eating and drinking, and singing and
103.02 laughing, and burning their eyes out before
103.03 the fire. Do you think they do? Or reading
103.04 sermons, and being catechised by their man-
103.05 servant, and set to learn a column of Scripture
103.06 names, if they don't answer properly?"
103.07 "Probably not," I responded. "They are
103.08 good children, no doubt, and don't deserve
103.09 the treatment you receive, for your bad
103.10 conduct."
103.11 "Don't you cant, Nelly," he said "non-
103.12 sense! We ran from the top of the Heights
103.13 to the park, without stopping -- Catherine
103.14 completely beaten in the race, because she
103.15 was barefoot. You'll have to seek for her
103.16 shoes in the bog to-morrow. We crept through
103.17 a broken hedge, groped our way up the
103.18 path, and planted ourselves on a flower-plot
103.19 under the drawing room window. The light
103.20 came from thence; they had not put up the
103.21 shutters, and the curtains were only half
103.22 closed. Both of us were able to look in by
104.01 standing on the basement, and clinging to the
104.02 ledge, and we saw -- ah! it was beautiful -- a
104.03 splendid place carpeted with crimson, and
104.04 crimson-covered chairs and tables, and a pure
104.05 white ceiling bordered by gold, a shower of
104.06 glass-drops hanging in silver chains from the
104.07 centre, and shimmering with little soft tapers.
104.08 Old Mr. and Mrs Linton were not there.
104.09 Edgar and his sister had it entirely to them-
104.10 selves; shouldn't they have been happy?
104.11 We should have thought ourselves in heaven!
104.12 And now, guess what your good children were
104.13 doing? Isabella, I believe she is eleven, a
104.14 year younger than Cathy, lay screaming at
104.15 the farther end of the room, shrieking as if
104.16 witches were running red hot needles into
104.17 her. Edgar stood on the hearth weeping si-
104.18 lently, and in the middle of the table sat a
104.19 little dog shaking its paw and yelping, which,
104.20 from their mutual accusations, we understood
104.21 they had nearly pulled in two between them.
104.22 The idiots! That was their pleasure! to
105.01 quarrel who should hold a heap of warm hair,
105.02 and each begin to cry because both, after
105.03 struggling to get it, refused to take it. We
105.04 laughed outright at the petted things, we did
105.05 despise them! When would you catch me
105.06 wishing to have what Catherine wanted? or
105.07 find us by ourselves, seeking entertainment
105.08 in yelling, and sobbing, and rolling on the
105.09 ground, divided by the whole room? I'd not
105.10 exchange, for a thousand lives, my condition
105.11 here, for Edgar Linton's at Thrushcross
105.12 Grange -- not if I might have the privilege of
105.13 flinging Joseph off the highest gable, and
105.14 painting the house-front with Hindley's
105.15 blood!"
105.16 "Hush, hush!" I interrupted. "Still you
105.17 have not told me, Heathcliff, how Catherine
105.18 is left behind?"
105.19 "I told you we laughed," he answered.
105.20 The Linton's heard us, and with one accord,
105.21 they shot like arrows to the door; there was
105.22 silence, and then a cry, 'Oh, mamma, mamma!
106.01 Oh, papa! Oh, mamma, come here. Oh papa,
106.02 oh!' They really did howl out, something in
106.03 that way. We made frightful noises to ter-
106.04 rify them still more, and then we dropped off
106.05 the ledge, because somebody was drawing the
106.06 bars, and we felt we had better flee. I had
106.07 Cathy by the hand, and was urging her on,
106.08 when all at once she fell down.
106.09 "Run, Heathcliff, run!" she whispered.
106.10 "They have let the bull-dog loose, and he
106.11 holds me!"
106.12 "The devil had seized her ankle, Nelly; I
106.13 heard his abominable snorting. She did not
106.14 yell out -- no! She would have scorned to do
106.15 it, if she had been spitted on the horns of a
106.16 mad cow. I did, though, I vociferated curses
106.17 enough to annihilate any fiend in Christendom,
106.18 and I got a stone and thrust it between his
106.19 jaws, and tried with all my might to cram it
106.20 down his throat. A beast of a servant came
106.21 up with a lantern, at last, shouting --
106.22 "Keep fast, Skulker, keep fast!"
107.01 "He changed his note, however, when he saw
107.02 Skulker's game. The dog was throttled off,
107.03 his huge, purple tongue hanging half a foot
107.04 out of his mouth, and his pendant lips stream-
107.05 ing with bloody slaver.
107.06 "The man took Cathy up; she was sick;
107.07 not from fear, I'm certain, but from pain. He
107.08 carried her in; I followed grumbling exe-
107.09 crations and vengeance."
107.10 "What prey, Robert?" hallooed Linton from
107.11 the entrance."
107.12 "Skulker has caught a little girl, sir," he
107.13 replied, and there's a lad here," he added,
107.14 making a clutch at me, "who looks an out--
107.15 and-outer! Very like, the robbers were for

107.16 putting them through the window, to open
107.17 the doors to the gang, after all were asleep,
107.18 that they might murder us at their ease. Hold
107.19 your tongue, you foul-mouthed thief, you!
107.20 you shall go to the gallows for this. Mr.
107.21 Linton, sir, don't lay by your gun!"
107.22 "No, no, Robert!" said the old fool.
108.01 "The rascals knew that yesterday was my
108.02 rent day; they thought to take me cleverly.
108.03 Come in; I'll furnish them a reception. There,
108.04 John, fasten the chain. Give Skulker some
108.05 water, Jenny. To beard a magistrate in his
108.06 strong-hold, and on the Sabbath, too! where
108.07 will their insolence stop? Oh, my dear Mary,
108.08 look here! Don't be afraid, it is but a boy --
108.09 yet, the villain scowls so plainly in his face,
108.10 would it not be a kindness to the country to
108.11 hang him at once, before he shows his nature
108.12 in acts, as well as features?"
108.13 He pulled me under the chandelier, and
108.14 Mrs. Linton placed her spectacles on her nose
108.15 and raised her hands in horror. The cowardly
108.16 children crept nearer also, Isabella lisping --
108.17 "Frightful thing! put him in the cellar,
108.18 papa. He's exactly like the son of the fortune--
108.19 teller, that stole my tame pheasant. Isn't he,
108.20 Edgar?"
108.21 "While they examined me, Cathy came
108.22 round; she heard the last speech, and laughed.
109.01 Edgar Linton, after an inquisitive stare, col-
109.02 lected sufficient wit to recognise her. They
109.03 see us at church, you know, though we sel-
109.04 dom meet them elsewhere."
109.05 "That's Miss Earnshaw!" he whispered to
109.06 his mother, "and look how Skulker has bitten
109.07 her -- how her foot bleeds!"
109.08 "Miss Earnshaw? Nonsense!" cried the
109.09 dame, "Miss Earnshaw scouring the country
109.10 with a gipsy! And yet, my dear, the child
109.11 is in mourning -- surely it is -- and she may be
109.12 lamed for life!"
109.13 "What culpable carelessness in her bro-
109.14 ther!" exclaimed Mr. Linton, turning from
109.15 me to Catherine. "I've understood from
109.16 Shielders /that was the curate sir// that he lets
109.17 her grow up in absolute heathenism. But
109.18 who is this? Where did she pick up this com-
109.19 panion? Oho! I declare he is that strange
109.20 acquisition my late neighbour made in his
109.21 journey to Liverpool -- a little Lascar, or an
109.22 American or Spanish castaway."
110.01 "A wicked boy, at all events," remarked
110.02 the old lady, "and quite unfit for a decent
110.03 house! Did you notice his language, Linton?
110.04 I'm shocked that my children should have
110.05 heard it."
110.06 "I recommenced cursing -- don't be angry
110.07 Nelly -- and so Robert was ordered to take me
110.08 off -- I refused to go without Cathy -- he drag-
110.09 ged me into the garden, pushed the lantern
110.10 into my hand, assured me that Mr. Earnshaw
110.11 should be informed of my behaviour, and bid-
110.12 ding me march, directly, secured the door
110.13 again.
110.14 "The curtains were still looped up at one
110.15 corner; and I resumed my station as spy, be-
110.16 cause, if Catherine had wished to return, I
110.17 intended shattering their great glass panes to
110.18 a million fragments, unless they let her out.
110.19 "She sat on the sofa quietly, Mrs. Linton
110.20 took off the grey cloak of the dairy maid
110.21 which we had borrowed for our excursion,
110.22 shaking her head, and expostulating with her,
111.01 I suppose; she was a young lady and they
111.02 made a distinction between her treatment, and
111.03 mine. Then the woman servant brought a
111.04 basin of warm water, and washed her feet;
111.05 and Mr. Linton mixed a tumbler of negus, and
111.06 Isabella emptied a plateful of cakes into her
111.07 lap, and Edgar, stood gaping at a distance.
111.08 Afterwards, they dried and combed her beau-
111.09 tiful hair, and gave her a pair of enormous
111.10 slippers, and wheeled her to the fire, and I left
111.11 her, as merry as she could be, dividing her
111.12 food, between the little dog and Skulker whose
111.13 nose she pinched as he ate; and kindling a
111.14 spark of spirit in the vacant blue eyes of the
111.15 Lintons -- a dim reflection from her own en-
111.16 chanting face -- I saw they were full of stupid
111.17 admiration; she is so immeasurably superior
111.18 to them -- to everybody on earth; is she not
111.19 Nelly?"
111.20 "There will more come of this business than
111.21 you reckon on." I answered covering him up
111.22 and extinguishing the light, "You are incurable
112.01 Heathcliff, and Mr. Hindley will have to
112.02 proceed to extremities, see if he won't."
112.03 My words came truer than I desired. The
112.04 luckless adventure made Earnshaw furious --
112.05 And then, Mr. Linton, to mend matters, paid
112.06 us a visit himself, on the morrow; and read
112.07 the young master such a lecture on the road
112.08 he guided his family, that he was stirred to
112.09 look about him, in earnest.
112.10 Heathcliff received no flogging, but he was
112.11 told that the first word he spoke to Miss Ca-
112.12 therine should ensure a dismissal; and Mrs.
112.13 Earnshaw undertook to keep her sister-in-law
112.14 in due restraint, when she returned home em-
112.15 ploying art, not force -- with force she would
112.16 have found it impossible.

113.01 [VOL. 1 CHAPTER 7]
113.02 CATHY stayed at Thrushcross Grange five
113.03 weeks, till Christmas. By that time her an-
113.04 kle was thoroughly cured, and her manners
113.05 much improved. The mistress visited her of-
113.06 ten, in the interval, and commenced her plan
113.07 of reform, by trying to raise her self-respect
113.08 with fine clothes, and flattery, which she took
113.09 readily: so that, instead of a wild, hatless
113.10 little savage jumping into the house, and rush-
113.11 ing to squeeze us all breathless, there lighted
114.01 from a handsome black pony a very dignified
114.02 person with brown ringlets falling from the
114.03 cover of a feathered beaver, and a long cloth
114.04 habit which she was obliged to hold up with
114.05 both hands that she might sail in.
114.06 Hindley lifted her from her horse exclaiming
114.07 delightedly,
114.08 "Why Cathy, you are quite a beauty! I
114.09 should scarcely have known you -- you look
114.10 like a lady now -- Isabella Linton is not to be
114.11 be compared with her, is she Frances?"
114.12 "Isabella has not her natural advantages,"
114.13 replied his wife, "but she must mind and not
114.14 grow wild again here. Ellen, help Miss Ca-
114.15 therine off with her things -- Stay, dear, you
114.16 will disarrange your curls -- let me untie your
114.17 hat."
114.18 I removed the habit, and there shone
114.19 forth, beneath a grand plaid silk frock, white
114.20 trousers, and burnished shoes; and, while her
114.21 eyes sparkled joyfully when the dogs came
114.22 bounding up to welcome her, she dare hardly
115.01 touch them lest they should fawn upon her
115.02 splendid garments.
115.03 She kissed me gently, I was all flour making
115.04 the christmas cake, and it would not have done
115.05 to give me a hug; and, then, she looked round
115.06 for Heathcliff. Mr. and Mrs. Earnshaw
115.07 watched anxiously their meeting, thinking it
115.08 would enable them to judge, in some measure,
115.09 what grounds they had for hoping to succeed
115.10 in separating the two friends.
115.11 Heathcliff was hard to discover, at first -- If
115.12 he were careless, and uncared for, before Ca-
115.13 therine's absence, he had been ten times more
115.14 so, since.
115.15 Nobody, but I even did him the kindness to
115.16 call him a dirty boy, and bid him wash him-
115.17 self, once a week; and children of his age, sel-
115.18 dom have a natural pleasure in soap and water.
115.19 Therefore, not to mention his clothes, which
115.20 had seen three month's service, in mire and
115.21 dust, and his thick uncombed hair; the surface
115.22 of his face and hands was dismally beclouded.
116.01 He might well skulk behind the settle, on be-
116.02 holding such a bright, graceful damsel enter
116.03 the house, instead of a rough-headed counter-
116.04 part to himself, as he expected.
116.05 "Is Heathcliff not here?" she demanded
116.06 pulling off her gloves, and displaying fingers
116.07 wonderfully whitened with doing nothing, and
116.08 staying in doors.
116.09 "Heathcliff you may come forward," cried
116.10 Mr. Hindley enjoying his discomfiture and
116.11 gratified to see what a forbidding young black-
116.12 guard he would be compelled to present him-
116.13 self. "You may come and wish Miss Cathe-
116.14 rine welcome, like the other servants."
116.15 Cathy, catching a glimpse of her friend in
116.16 his concealment, flew to embrace him, she bes-
116.17 towed seven or eight kisses on his cheek within
116.18 the second, and, then, stopped, and drawing
116.19 back, burst into a laugh, exclaiming,
116.20 "Why, how very black and cross you look!
116.21 and how -- how funny and grim! But that's
116.22 because I'm used to Edgar, and Isabella Linton,
117.01 Well, Heathcliff, have you forgotten
117.02 me?"
117.03 She had some reason to put the question,
117.04 for shame, and pride threw double gloom over
117.05 his countenance, and kept him immoveable.
117.06 "Shake hands, Heathcliff," said Mr. Earn-
117.07 shaw, condescendingly; "once in a way, that
117.08 is permitted."
117.09 "I shall not!" replied the boy finding his
117.10 tongue at last, "I shall not stand to be laughed
117.11 at, I shall not bear it!"
117.12 And he would have broken from the circle,
117.13 but Miss Cathy seized him again.
117.14 "I did not mean to laugh at you," she said,
117.15 "I could not hinder myself, Heathcliff, shake
117.16 hands, at least! What are you sulky for? It
117.17 was only that you looked odd -- If you wash
117.18 your face, and brush your hair it will be all
117.19 right. But you are so dirty!"
117.20 She gazed concernedly at the dusky fingers
117.21 she held in her own, and also at her dress
118.01 which she feared had gained no embellishment
118.02 from its contact with his.
118.03 "You needn't have touched me!" He an-
118.04 swered, following her eye and snatching away
118.05 his hand. I shall be as dirty as I please, and
118.06 I like to be dirty, and I will be dirty."
118.07 With that he dashed head foremost out of
118.08 the room, amid the merriment of the master
118.09 and mistress, and to the serious disturbance of
118.10 Catherine who could not comprehend how her
118.11 remarks should have produced such an exhi-
118.12 bition of bad temper.
118.13 After playing lady's maid to the new comer,

118.14 and putting my cakes in the oven, and making
118.15 the house and kitchen cheerful with great fires
118.16 befitting Christmas eve, I prepared to sit down
118.17 and amuse myself by singing carols, all alone;
118.18 regardless of Joseph's affirmations that he con-
118.19 sidered the merry tunes I chose as next door
118.20 to songs.
118.21 He had retired to private prayer in his
119.01 chamber, and Mr. and Mrs. Earnshaw were
119.02 engaging Missy's attention by sundry gay tri-
119.03 fles bought for her to present to the little
119.04 Lintons, as an acknowledgment of their kind-
119.05 ness
119.06 They had invited them to spend the morrow
119.07 at Wuthering Heights, and the invitation had
119.08 been accepted, on one condition, Mrs. Linton
119.09 begged that her darlings might be kept care-
119.10 fully apart from that "naughty, swearing boy."
119.11 Under these circumstances I remained soli-
119.12 tary. I smelt the rich scent of the heating
119.13 spices; and admired the shining kitchen uten-
119.14 sils, the polished clock, decked in holly, the
119.15 silver mugs ranged on a tray ready to be
119.16 filled with mulled ale for supper; and, above
119.17 all, the speckless purity of my particular care
119.18 -- the scoured and well-swept floor.
119.19 I gave due inward applause to every object
119.20 and, then, I remembered how old Earnshaw
119.21 used to come in when all was tidied, and call
119.22 me a cant lass, and slip a shilling into my
120.01 hand, as a christmas box: and, from that, I
120.02 went on to think of his fondness for Heathcliff,
120.03 and his dread lest he should suffer neglect after
120.04 death had removed him; and that naturally
120.05 led me to consider the poor lad's situation
120.06 now, and from singing I changed my mind to
120.07 crying. It struck me soon, however, there
120.08 would be more sense in endeavouring to repair
120.09 some of his wrongs than shedding tears over
120.10 them -- I got up and walked into the court to
120.11 seek him.
120.12 He was not far, I found him smoothing the
120.13 glossy coat of the new pony in the stable,
120.14 and feeding the other beasts, according to
120.15 custom.
120.16 "Make haste, Heathcliff!" I said "the
120.17 kitchen is so comfortable -- and Joseph is up-
120.18 stairs; make haste, and let me dress you smart
120.19 before Miss Cathy comes out -- and then you
120.20 can sit together, with the whole hearth to
120.21 yourselves, and have a long chatter till bed-
120.22 time."
121.01 He proceeded with his task and never turned
121.02 his head towards me.
121.03 "Come -- are you coming?" I continued,
121.04 "There's a little cake for each of you, nearly
121.05 enough; and you'll need half an hour's don-
121.06 ning."
121.07 I waited five minutes, but getting no answer
121.08 left him ... Catherine supped with her brother
121.09 and sister-in law: Joseph and I joined at an
121.10 unsociable meal seasoned with reproofs on one
121.11 side, and sauciness on the other. His cake
121.12 and cheese remained on the table all night, for
121.13 the fairies. He managed to continue work till
121.14 nine o'clock, and, then, marched dumb and
121.15 dour, to his chamber.
121.16 Cathy sat up late; having a world of things
121.17 to order for the reception of her new friends:
121.18 she came into the kitchen, once, to speak to
121.19 her old one, but he was gone, and she only
121.20 staid to ask what was the matter with him, and
121.21 then went back.
121.22 "In the morning, he rose early; and, as it
122.01 was a holiday, carried his ill-humour onto the
122.02 moors; not re-appearing till the family were
122.03 departed for church. Fasting, and reflection
122.04 seemed to have brought him to a better spirit.
122.05 He hung about me, for a while, and having
122.06 screwed up his courage, exclaimed abruptly,
122.07 "Nelly, make me decent, I'm going to be
122.08 good."
122.09 "High time, Heathcliff," I said, "you \have#
122.10 grieved Catherine; she's sorry she ever came
122.11 home, I dare say! It looks as if you envied
122.12 her, because she is more thought of than
122.13 you."
122.14 The notion of \envying# Catherine was in-
122.15 comprehensible to him, but the notion of griev-
122.16 ing her, he understood clearly enough.
122.17 "Did she say she was grieved?" he inquired
122.18 looking very serious.
122.19 "She cried when I told her you were off
122.20 again this morning."
122.21 "Well, \I# cried last night" he returned,
122.22 "and I had more reason to cry than she."
123.01 "Yes, you had the reason of going to bed,
123.02 with a proud heart, and an empty stomach,"
123.03 said I, "Proud people breed sad sorrows for
123.04 themselves -- But, if you be ashamed of your
123.05 touchiness, you must ask pardon, mind, when
123.06 she comes in. You must go up, and offer to
123.07 kiss her, and say -- you know best what to say,
123.08 only, do it heartily, and not as if you thought
123.09 her converted into a stranger by her grand
123.10 dress. And now, though I have dinner to get
123.11 ready, I'll steal time to arrange you so that
123.12 Edgar Linton shall look quite a doll beside
123.13 you: and that he does -- You are younger, and
123.14 yet, I'll be bound, you are taller and twice as
123.15 broad across the shoulders -- you could knock

123.16 him down in a twinkling; don't you feel that
123.17 you could?"
123.18 Heathcliff's face brightened a moment; then,
123.19 it was overcast afresh, and he sighed.
123.20 "But, Nelly, if I knocked him down twenty
123.21 times, that wouldn't make him less handsome,
124.01 or me more so. I wish I had light hair and a
124.02 fair skin, and was dressed, and behaved as
124.03 well, and had a chance of being as rich as he
124.04 will be!"
124.05 "And cried for mamma, at every turn --" I
124.06 added, "and trembled if a country lad heaved
124.07 his fist against you, and sat at home all day
124.08 for a shower of rain. -- O, Heathcliff, you are
124.09 showing a poor spirit! Come to the glass,
124.10 and I'll let you see what you should wish.
124.11 Do you mark those two lines between your
124.12 eyes, and those thick brow, that instead of
124.13 rising arched, sink in the middle, and that cou-
124.14 ple of black fiends, so deeply buried, who
124.15 never open their windows boldly, but lurk
124.16 glinting under them, like devil's spies?
124.17 Wish and learn to smooth away the surly
124.18 wrinkles, to raise your lids frankly, and change
124.19 the fiends to confident, innocent angels, sus-
124.20 pecting and doubting nothing, and always
124.21 seeing friends where they are not sure of
124.22 foes -- Don't get the expression of a vicious
125.01 cur that appears to know the kicks it gets are
125.02 its desert, and yet, hates all the world, as well
125.03 as the kicker, for what it suffers."
125.04 "In other words, I must wish for Edgar
125.05 Linton's great blue eyes, and even forehead,"
125.06 he replied. "I do -- and that wont help me
125.07 to them."
125.08 "A good heart will help you to a bonny
125.09 face my lad," I continued, "if you were a re-
125.10 gular black; and a bad one will turn the bon-
125.11 niest into something worse than ugly. And
125.12 now that we've done washing, and combing,
125.13 and sulking -- tell me whether you don't think
125.14 yourself rather handsome? I'll tell you, I do.
125.15 You're fit for a prince in disguise. Who
125.16 knows, but your father was Emperor of China,
125.17 and your mother an Indian queen, each of
125.18 them able to buy up, with one week's income,
125.19 wuthering Heights and Thrushcross Grange
125.20 together? And you were kidnapped by
125.21 wicked sailors, and brought to England. Were
125.22 I in your place, I would frame high notions of
126.01 my birth; and, the thoughts of what I was
126.02 should give me courage and dignity to support
126.03 the oppressions of a little farmer!"
126.04 So I chattered on; and Heathcliff gradually
126.05 lost his frown, and began to look quite plea-
126.06 sant; when, all at once, our conversation was
126.07 interrupted by a rumbling sound moving up
126.08 the road and entering the court. He ran to
126.09 the window, and I to the door, just in time to
126.10 behold the two Lintons descend from the family
126.11 carriage, smothered in cloaks and furs, and
126.12 the Earnshaws dismount from their horses --
126.13 they often rode to church in winter. Cathe-
126.14 rine took a hand of each of the children, and
126.15 brought them into the house, and set them
126.16 before the fire which quickly put colour into
126.17 their white faces.
126.18 I urged my companion to hasten now, and
126.19 show his amiable humour; and he willingly
126.20 obeyed: but ill luck would have it, that as he
126.21 opened the door leading from the kitchen on
126.22 one side, Hindley opened it on the other; they
127.01 met, and the master irritated at seeing him
127.02 clean and cheerful, or, perhaps, eager to keep
127.03 his promise to Mrs. Linton shoved him back
127.04 with a sudden thrust, and angrily bade Joseph
127.05 "keep the fellow out of the room -- send him
127.06 into the garret till dinner is over. He'll be
127.07 cramming his fingers in the tarts, and stealing
127.08 the fruit, if left alone with them a minute."
127.09 "Nay, sir," I could not avoid answering,
127.10 "he'll touch nothing, not he -- and, I suppose,
127.11 he must have his share of the dainties as well
127.12 as we."
127.13 "He shall have his share of my hand, if I
127.14 catch him down stairs again till dark," cried
127.15 Hindley. "Begone, you vagabond! what,
127.16 you are attempting the coxcomb, are you?
127.17 wait till I get hold of those elegant locks -- see
127.18 if I won't pull them a bit longer!"
127.19 "They are long enough already," observed
127.20 Master Linton, peeping from the door-way,
127.21 "I wonder they don't make his head-ache.
127.22 It's like a colt's mane over his eyes!"
128.01 He ventured this remark without any inten-
128.02 tion of insult; but, Heathcliff's violent nature
128.03 was not prepared to endure the appearance of
128.04 impertinence from one whom he seemed to
128.05 hate, even then, as a rival. He seized a tu-
128.06 reen of hot apple-sauce, the first thing that
128.07 came under his gripe, and dashed it full against
128.08 the speaker's face and neck -- who instantly
128.09 commenced a lament that brought Isabella
128.10 and Catherine hurrying to the place.
128.11 Mr. Earnshaw snatched up the culprit di-
128.12 rectly and conveyed him to his chamber,
128.13 where, doubtless, he administered a rough
128.14 remedy to cool the fit of passion, for he re-
128.15 appeared red and breathless. I got the dish-
128.16 cloth, and, rather spitefully, scrubbed Edgar's
128.17 nose and mouth, affirming, it served him right

128.18 for meddling. His sister began weeping to go
128.19 home, and Cathy stood by confounded, blush-
128.20 ing for all.
128.21 "You should not have spoken to him!" she
128.22 expostulated with Master Linton. "He was
129.01 in a bad temper, and now you've spoilt your
129.02 visit, and he'll be flogged -- I hate him to be
129.03 flogged! I can't eat my dinner. Why did
129.04 you speak to him, Edgar?"
129.05 "I didn't," sobbed the youth, escaping from
129.06 my hands, and finishing the remainder of the
129.07 purification with his cambric pocket-handker-
129.08 chief. "I promised mamma that I wouldn't
129.09 say one word to him, and I didn't!"
129.10 "Well, don't cry!" replied Catherine, con-
129.11 temptuously. "You're not killed -- don't
129.12 make more mischief -- my brother is coming --
129.13 be quiet! Give over, Isabella! Has any body
129.14 hurt \you#?"
129.15 "There, there, children -- to your seats!"
129.16 cried Hindley, bustling in. "That brute of
129.17 a lad has warmed me nicely. Next time, Master
129.18 Edgar, take the law into your own fists -- it
129.19 will give you an appetite!"
129.20 The little party recovered its equanimity at
129.21 sight of the fragrant feast. They were hungry,
130.01 after their ride, and easily consoled, since
130.02 no real harm had befallen them.
130.03 Mr. Earnshaw carved bountiful platefuls;
130.04 and the mistress made them merry with lively
130.05 talk. I waited behind her chair, and was
130.06 pained to behold Catherine, with dry eyes and
130.07 an indifferent air, commence cutting up the
130.08 wing of a goose before her.
130.09 "An unfeeling child," I thought to myself,
130.10 "how lightly she dismisses her old playmate's
130.11 troubles. I could not have imagined her to be
130.12 so selfish."
130.13 She lifted a mouthful to her lips; then, she
130.14 set it down again: her cheeks flushed, and the
130.15 tears gushed over them. She slipped her fork
130.16 to the floor, and hastily dived under the cloth
130.17 to conceal her emotion. I did not call her
130.18 unfeeling long, for, I perceived she was in pur-
130.19 gatory throughout the day, and wearying to
130.20 find an opportunity of getting by herself, or
130.21 paying a visit to Heathcliff, who had been
130.22 locked up by the master, as I discovered, on
131.01 endeavouring to introduce to him a private
131.02 mess of victuals.
131.03 In the evening we had a dance. Cathy
131.04 begged that she might be liberated then, as
131.05 Isabella Linton had no partner; her entreaties
131.06 were vain, and I was appointed to supply the
131.07 deficiency.
131.08 We got rid of all gloom in the excitement
131.09 of the exercise, and our pleasure was increased
131.10 by the arrival of the Gimmerton band, mus-
131.11 tering fifteen strong; a trumpet, a trombone,
131.12 clarionets, bassoons, French horns, and a bass
131.13 viol, besides singers. They go the rounds of
131.14 all the respectable houses, and receive contribu-
131.15 tions every Christmas, and we esteemed it a
131.16 first-rate treat to hear them.
131.17 After the usual carols had been sung, we
131.18 set them to songs and glees. Mrs. Earnshaw
131.19 loved the music, and, so, they gave us plenty.
131.20 Catherine loved it too; but she said it
131.21 sounded sweetest at the top of the steps, and
131.22 she went up in the dark: I followed. They
132.01 shut the house door below, never noting our
132.02 absence, it was so full of people. She made
132.03 no stay at the stairs' head, but mounted far-
132.04 ther, to the garret where Heathcliff was con-
132.05 fined; and called him. He stubbornly de-
132.06 clined answering for a while -- she persevered,
132.07 and finally persuaded him to hold communion
132.08 with her through the boards.
132.09 I let the poor things converse unmolested,
132.10 till I supposed the songs were going to cease;
132.11 and the singers to get some refreshment: then,
132.12 I clambered up the ladder to warn her.
132.13 Instead of finding her outside, I heard her
132.14 voice within. The little monkey had crept by
132.15 the skylight of one garret, along the roof,
132.16 into the skylight of the other, and it was with
132.17 the utmost difficulty I could coax her out
132.18 again.
132.19 When she did come, Heathcliff came with
132.20 her; and she insisted that I should take him
132.21 into the kitchen, as my fellow-servant had gone
132.22 to a neighbour's to be removed from the sound
133.01 of our "devil's psalmody," as it pleased him
133.02 to call it.
133.03 I told them I intended, by no means, to en-
133.04 courage their tricks; but as the prisoner had
133.05 never broken his fast since yesterday's dinner,
133.06 I would wink at his cheating Mr. Hindley that
133.07 once.
133.08 He went down; I set him a stool by the
133.09 fire, and offered him a quantity of good things;
133.10 but, he was sick and could eat little: and my
133.11 attempts to entertain him were thrown away.
133.12 He leant his two elbows on his knees, and his
133.13 chin on his hands, and remained wrapt in dumb
133.14 meditation. On my inquiring the subject of
133.15 his thoughts, he answered gravely --
133.16 "I'm trying to settle how I shall pay Hind-
133.17 ley back. I don't care how long I wait, if I
133.18 can only do it, at last. I hope he will not die
133.19 before I do!"

133.20 "For shame, Heathcliff!" said I. "It is for
133.21 God to punish wicked people; we should learn
133.22 to forgive."
134.01 "No, God wont have the satisfaction that I
134.02 shall," he returned. "I only wish I knew the
134.03 best way! Let me alone, and I'll plan it out:
134.04 while I'm thinking of that, I don't feel pain."
134.05 "But, Mr. Lockwood, I forget these tales
134.06 cannot divert you. I'm annoyed how I should
134.07 dream of chattering on at such a rate; and
134.08 your gruel cold, and you nodding for bed! I
134.09 could have told Heathcliff's history, all that
134.10 you need hear, in half-a-dozen words."
134.11 Thus interrupting herself, the housekeeper
134.12 rose, and proceeded to lay aside her sewing;
134.13 but I felt incapable of moving from the hearth,
134.14 and I was very far from nodding.
134.15 "Sit still, Mrs. Dean," I cried, "do sit still,
134.16 another half hour! You've done just right to
134.17 tell the story leisurely. That is the method I
134.18 like; and you must finish in the same style. I
134.19 am interested in every character you have
134.20 mentioned, more or less."
134.21 "The clock is on the stroke of eleven, sir."
134.22 "No matter -- I'm not accustomed to go to
135.01 bed in the long hours. One or two is early
135.02 enough for a person who lies till ten."
135.03 "You shouldn't lie till ten. There's the
135.04 very prime of the morning gone long before
135.05 that time. A person who has not done one
135.06 half his day's work by ten o'clock, runs a
135.07 chance of leaving the other half undone."
135.08 "Nevertheless, Mrs. Dean, resume your
135.09 chair; because to-morrow I intend lengthen-
135.10 ing the night till afternoon. I prognosticate
135.11 for myself an obstinate cold, at least."
135.12 "I hope not, sir. Well, you must allow me
135.13 to leap over some three years, during that
135.14 space, Mrs. Earnshaw --"
135.15 "No, no, I'll allow nothing of the sort!
135.16 Are you acquainted with the mood of mind in
135.17 which, if you were seated alone, and the cat
135.18 licking its kitten on the rug before you, you
135.19 would watch the operation so intently that
135.20 puss's neglect of one ear would put you seri-
135.21 ously out of temper?"
135.22 "A terribly lazy mood, I should say."
136.01 "On the contrary, a tiresomely active one.
136.02 It is mine, at present; and, therefore, continue
136.03 minutely. I perceive that people in these re-
136.04 gions acquire over people in towns the value that
136.05 a spider in a dungeon does over a spider in a
136.06 cottage, to their various occupants; and yet
136.07 the deepened attraction is not entirely owing
136.08 to the situation of the looker-on. They \do# live
136.09 more in earnest, more in themselves, and less in
136.10 surface change, and frivolous external things.
136.11 I could fancy a love for life here almost possi-
136.12 ble; and I was a fixed unbeliever in any love
136.13 of a year's standing -- one state resembles set-
136.14 ting a hungry man down to a single dish on
136.15 which he may concentrate his entire appetite,
136.16 and do it justice -- the other, introducing him
136.17 to a table laid out by French cooks; he can
136.18 perhaps extract as much enjoyment from the
136.19 whole; but each part is a mere atom in his re-
136.20 gard and remembrance."
136.21 "Oh! here we are the same as anywhere
137.01 else, when you get to know us," observed Mrs.
137.02 Dean, somewhat puzzled at my speech.
137.03 "Excuse me," I responded; "you, my good
137.04 friend, are a striking evidence against that as-
137.05 sertion. Excepting a few provincialisms of
137.06 slight consequence; you have no marks of the
137.07 manners that I am habituated to consider as
137.08 peculiar to your class. I am sure you have
137.09 thought a great deal more than the generality
137.10 of servants think. You have been compelled
137.11 to cultivate your reflective faculties, for want
137.12 of occasions for frittering your life away in
137.13 silly trifles."
137.14 Mrs. Dean laughed.
137.15 "I certainly esteem myself a steady, reason-
137.16 able kind of body," she said, "not exactly
137.17 from living among the hills, and seeing one set
137.18 of faces, and one series of actions, from year's
137.19 end to year's end: but I have undergone sharp
137.20 discipline which has taught me wisdom; and
137.21 then, I have read more than you would fancy,
137.22 Mr. Lockwood. You could not open a book
138.01 in this library that I have not looked into, and
138.02 got something out of also; unless it be that
138.03 range of Greek and Latin, and that of French
138.04 -- and those I know one from another, it is as
138.05 much as you can expect of a poor man's
138.06 daughter."
138.07 However, if I am to follow my story in true
138.08 gossip's fashion, I had better go on; and in-
138.09 stead of leaping three years, I will be content
138.10 to pass to the next summer -- the summer of
138.11 1778, that is nearly twenty-three years ago.
139.01 [VOL. 1 CHAPTER 8]
139.02 ON the morning of a fine June day, my first
139.03 bonny little nursling, and the last of the anci-
139.04 ent Earnshaw stock was born.
139.05 We were busy with the hay in a far away
139.06 field, when the girl that usually brought our
139.07 breakfasts came running, an hour too soon,
139.08 across the meadow and up the lane, calling me
139.09 as she ran.
139.10 "Oh, such a grand bairn!" she panted out.

139.11 "The finest lad that ever breathed! but the
139.12 doctor says missis must go; he says she's been
140.01 in a consumption these many months. I heard
140.02 him tell Mr. Hindley -- and now she has
140.03 nothing to keep her, and she'll be dead before
140.04 winter. You must come home directly.
140.05 You're to nurse it, Nelly -- to feed it with sugar
140.06 and milk, and take care of it, day and night --
140.07 I wish I were you, because it will be all yours
140.08 when there is no missis!"
140.09 "But is she very ill?" I asked, flinging down
140.10 my rake, and tying my bonnet.
140.11 "I guess she is; yet she looks bravely," re-
140.12 plied the girl, "and she talks as if she thought
140.13 of living to see it grow a man. She's out of
140.14 her head for joy, it's such a beauty! If I were
140.15 her I'm certain I should not die. I should get
140.16 better at the bare sight of it, in spite of Ken-
140.17 neth. I was fairly mad at him. Dame Ar-
140.18 cher brought the cherub down to master, in
140.19 the house, and his face just began to light up,
140.20 then the old croaker steps forward, and, says
140.21 he: -- `Earnshaw, it's a blessing your wife has
140.22 been spared to leave you this son. When she
141.01 came, I felt convinced we shouldn't keep her
141.02 long; and now, I must tell you, the winter
141.03 will probably finish her. Don't take on, and
141.04 fret about it too much, it can't be helped. And
141.05 besides, you should have known better than to
141.06 choose such a rush of a lass!"
141.07 "And what did the master answer?" I en-
141.08 quired.
141.09 "I think he swore -- but, I didn't mind him,
141.10 I was straining to see the bairn," and she began
141.11 again to describe it rapturously. I, as zealous
141.12 as herself, hurried eagerly home to admire, on
141.13 my part, though I was very sad for Hindley's
141.14 sake; he had room in his heart only for two
141.15 idols -- his wife and himself -- he doted on
141.16 both, and adored one, and I couldn't conceive
141.17 how he would bear the loss.
141.18 When we got to Wuthering Heights, there
141.19 he stood at the front door; and, as I passed in,
141.20 I asked, how was the baby?"
141.21 "Nearly ready to run about, Nell!" he re-
141.22 plied, putting on a cheerful smile.
142.01 "And the mistress?" I ventured to inquire,
142.02 "the doctor says she's --"
142.03 "Damn the doctor!" he interrupted, red-
142.04 dening. "Frances is quite right -- she'll be
142.05 perfectly well by this time next week. Are
142.06 you going up-stairs? will you tell her that I'll
142.07 come, if she'll promise not to talk. I left her
142.08 because she would not hold her tongue; and
142.09 she must -- tell her Mr. Kenneth says she must
142.10 be quiet."
142.11 I delivered this message to Mrs. Earnshaw;
142.12 she seemed in flighty spirits, and replied mer-
142.13 rily --
142.14 "I hardly spoke a word, Ellen, and there
142.15 he has gone out twice, crying. Well, say I
142.16 promise I wont speak; but that does not bind
142.17 me not to laugh at him!"
142.18 Poor soul! Till within a week of her death
142.19 that gay heart never failed her; and her hus-
142.20 band persisted doggedly, nay, furiously, in
142.21 affirming her health improved every day.
142.22 When Kenneth warned him that his medicines
143.01 were useless at that stage of the malady, and
143.02 he needn't put him to further expense by at-
143.03 tending her, he retorted --
143.04 "I know you need not -- she's well -- she
143.05 does not want any more attendance from you!
143.06 She never was in a consumption. It was a
143.07 fever; and it is gone -- her pulse is as slow as
143.08 mine now, and her cheek as cool."
143.09 He told his wife the same story, and she
143.10 seemed to believe him; but one night, while
143.11 leaning on his shoulder, in the act of saying
143.12 she thought she should be able to get up to-
143.13 morrow, a fit of coughing took her -- a very
143.14 slight one -- he raised her in his arms; she put
143.15 her two hands about his neck, her face changed,
143.16 and she was dead.
143.17 As the girl had anticipated; the child
143.18 Hareton, fell wholly into my hands. Mr.
143.19 Earnshaw, provided he saw him healthy, and
143.20 never heard him cry, was contented, as far as
143.21 regarded him. For himself, he grew desper-
143.22 ate; his sorrow was of that kind that will not
144.01 lament, he neither wept nor prayed -- he cursed
144.02 and defied -- execrated God and man, and gave
144.03 himself up to reckless dissipation.
144.04 The servants could not bear his tyrannical
144.05 and evil conduct long: Joseph and I were the
144.06 only two that would stay. I had not the
144.07 heart to leave my charge; and besides, you
144.08 know, I had been his foster sister, and excused
144.09 his behaviour more readily than a stranger
144.10 would.
144.11 Joseph remained to hector over tenants and
144.12 labourers; and because it was his vocation to
144.13 be where he had plenty of wickedness to re-
144.14 prove.
144.15 The master's bad ways and bad companions
144.16 formed a pretty example for Catherine and
144.17 Heathcliff. His treatment of the latter was
144.18 enough to make a fiend of a saint. And,
144.19 truly, it appeared as if the lad \were possessed
144.20 of something diabolical at that period. He
144.21 delighted to witness Hindley degrading himself

144.22 past redemption; and became daily more
144.23 notable for savage sullenness and ferocity.
145.01 I could not tell what an infernal house
145.02 we had. The curate dropped calling, and no-
145.03 body decent came near us, at last; unless,
145.04 Edgar Linton's visits to Miss Cathy might
145.05 be an exception. At fifteen she was the
145.06 queen of the country-side; she had no peer:
145.07 and she did turn out a haughty, headstrong
145.08 creature! I own I did not like her, after her
145.09 infancy was past; and I vexed her frequently
145.10 by trying to bring down her arrogance; she
145.11 never took an aversion to me though. She
145.12 had wondrous constancy to old attachments;
145.13 even Heathcliff kept his hold on her affections
145.14 unalterably, and young Linton, with all his
145.15 superiority, found it difficult to make an
145.16 equally deep impression.
145.17 He was my late master; that is his portrait
145.18 over the fireplace. It used to hang on one
145.19 side, and his wife's on the other; but her's has
145.20 been removed, or else you might see something
145.21 of what she was. Can you make that out?
145.22 Mrs. Dean raised the candle, and I discerned
146.01 a soft-featured face, exceedingly resembling
146.02 the young lady at the Heights, but more pen-
146.03 sive and amiable in expression. It formed a
146.04 sweet picture. The long light hair curled
146.05 slightly on the temples; the eyes were large
146.06 and serious; the figure almost too graceful. I
146.07 did not marvel how Catherine Earnshaw could
146.08 forget her first friend for such an individual.
146.09 I marvelled much how he, with a mind to cor-
146.10 respond with his person, could fancy my idea
146.11 of Catherine Earnshaw.
146.12 "A very agreeable portrait," I observed to
146.13 the housekeeper. "Is it like?"
146.14 "Yes," she answered; "but he looked
146.15 better when he was animated, that is his every
146.16 day countenance; he wanted spirit in general."
146.17 Catherine had kept up her acquaintance
146.18 with the Lintons since her five weeks' residence
146.19 among them; and as she had no temptation
146.20 to show her rough side in their company, and
146.21 had the sense to be ashamed of being rude
146.22 where she experienced such invariable courtesy,
147.01 she imposed un-wittingly on the old lady
147.02 and gentleman, by her ingenious cordiality;
147.03 gained the admiration of Isabella, and the
147.04 heart and soul of her brother -- acquisitions
147.05 that flattered her from the first, for she was
147.06 full of ambition -- and led her to adopt a double
147.07 character without exactly intending to deceive
147.08 anyone.
147.09 In the place where she heard Heathcliff
147.10 termed a "vulgar young ruffian," and "worse
147.11 than a brute," she took care not to act like
147.12 him; but at home she had small inclination to
147.13 practise politeness that would only be laughed
147.14 at, and restrain an unruly nature when it
147.15 would bring her neither credit, nor praise.
147.16 Mr. Edgar seldom mustered courage to visit
147.17 Wuthering Heights openly. He had a terror
147.18 of Earnshaw's reputation, and shrunk from en-
147.19 countering him, and yet, he was always re-
147.20 ceived with our best attempts at civility: the
147.21 master himself, avoided offending him -- know-
147.22 ing why he came, and if he could not be gracious,
148.01 kept out of the way. I rather think his
148.02 appearance there was distasteful to Catherine;
148.03 she was not artful, never played the coquette,
148.04 and had evidently an objection to her two
148.05 friends meeting at all: for when Heathcliff
148.06 expressed contempt of Linton, in his presence,
148.07 she could not half coincide, as she did in his
148.08 absence; and when Linton evinced disgust,
148.09 and antipathy to Heathcliff, she dare not treat
148.10 his sentiments with indifference, as if depre-
148.11 ciation of her playmate were of scarcely any
148.12 consequence to her.
148.13 I've had many a laugh at her perplexities,
148.14 and untold troubles, which she vainly strove to
148.15 hide from my mockery. That sounds ill-na-
148.16 tured -- but she was so proud, it became really
148.17 impossible to pity her distresses, till she should
148.18 be chastened into more humility.
148.19 She did bring herself, finally, to confess, and
148.20 confide in me. There was not a soul else that
148.21 she might fashion into an adviser.
148.22 Mr. Hindley had gone from home, one afternoon;
149.01 and Heathcliff presumed to give him-
149.02 self a holiday, on the strength of it. He had
149.03 reached the age of sixteen then, I think, and
149.04 without having bad features or being deficient
149.05 in intellect, he contrived to convey an impres-
149.06 sion of inward and outward repulsiveness that
149.07 his present aspect retains no traces of.
149.08 In the first place, he had, by that time, lost
149.09 the benefit of his early education; continual
149.10 hard work, begun soon and concluded late, had
149.11 extinguished any curiosity he once possessed
149.12 in pursuit of knowledge, and any love for
149.13 books, or learning. His childhood's sense of
149.14 superiority, instilled into him by the favours
149.15 of old Mr. Earnshaw, was faded away. He
149.16 struggled long to keep up an equality with
149.17 Catherine in her studies and yielded with
149.18 poignant though silent regret: but, he yielded
149.19 completely; and there was no prevailing on
149.20 him to take a step in the way of moving
149.21 upward, when he found he must, necessarily,

149.22   sink beneath his former level. Then personal
150.01   appearance sympathised with mental deterio-
150.02   ration; he acquired a slouching gait, and ig-
150.03   noble look; his naturally reserved disposition
150.04   was exaggerated into an almost idiotic excess
150.05   of unsociable moroseness; and he took a grim
150.06   pleasure, apparently, in exciting the aversion
150.07   rather than the esteem of his few acquaint-
150.08   ance.
150.09     Catherine and he were constant companions
150.10   still, at his seasons of respite from labour; but,
150.11   he had ceased to express his fondness for her
150.12   in words, and recoiled with angry suspicion
150.13   from her girlish caresses, as if conscious there
150.14   could be no gratification in lavishing such
150.15   marks of affection on him. On the before--
150.16   named occasion he came into the house to
150.17   announce his intention of doing nothing, while
150.18   I was assisting Miss Cathy to arrange her
150.19   dress -- she had not reckoned on his taking it
150.20   into his head to be idle, and imagining she
150.21   would have the whole place to herself, she
150.22   managed, by some means, to inform Mr.
151.01   Edgar of her brother's absence, and was then
151.02   preparing to receive him.
151.03     "Cathy, are you busy, this afternoon?"
151.04   asked Heathcliff. "Are you going any-
151.05   where?"
151.06     "No, it is raining," she answered.
151.07     "Why have you that silk frock on, then?"
151.08   he said, "Nobody coming here I hope?"
151.09     "Not that I know of;" stammered Miss,
151.10   "but you shodld be in the field now, Heath-
151.11   cliff. It is an hour past dinner time; I
151.12   thought you were gone."
151.13     "Hindley does not often free us from his
151.14   accursed presence;" observed the boy, "I'll
151.15   not work any more to-day, I'll stay with
151.16   you."
151.17     "O, but Joseph will tell;" she suggested,
151.18   "you'd better go!"
151.19     "Joseph is loading lime on the farther side
151.20   of Pennistow Crag, it will take him till dark,
151.21   and he'll never know."
151.22     So saying he lounged to the fire, and sat
152.01   down, Catherine reflected an instant, with
152.02   knitted brows -- she found it needful to smooth
152.03   the way for an intrusion.
152.04     "Isabella, and Edgar Linton talked of
152.05   calling this afternoon;" she said at the con-
152.06   clusion of a minute's silence. "As it rains, I
152.07   hardly expect them; but, they may come, and
152.08   if they do, you run the risk of being scolded
152.09   for no good."
152.10     "Order Ellen to say you are engaged,
152.11   Cathy," he persisted, "Don't turn me out for
152.12   those pitiful, silly friends of yours! I'm on
152.13   the point, sometimes, of complaining that they
152.14   -- but I'll not --"
152.15     "That they what?" cried Catherine, gazing
152.16   at him with a troubled countenance. "Oh
152.17   Nelly!" she added petulantly jerking her head
152.18   away from my hands, "you've combed my
152.19   hair quite out of curl! That's enough, let me
152.20   alone. What are you on the point of com-
152.21   plaining about, Heathcliff?"
152.22     "Nothing -- only look at the almanack, on
153.01   that wall," he pointed to a framed sheet hang-
153.02   ing near the window, and continued;
153.03     "The crosses are for the evenings you have
153.04   spent with the Lintons, the dots for those
153.05   spent with me -- Do you see, I've marked every
153.06   day?"
153.07     "Yes -- very foolish; as if I took notice!"
153.08   replied Catherine in a peevish tone. "And
153.09   where is the sense of that?"
153.10     "To show that I \do# take notice." said
153.11   Heathcliff.
153.12     "And should I always be sitting with you,"
153.13   she demanded, growing more irritated. "What
153.14   good do I get -- What do you talk about? You
153.15   might be dumb or a baby for anything you
153.16   say to amuse me, or for anything you do,
153.17   either!"
153.18     "You never told me, before, that I talked
153.19   too little, or that you disliked my company,
153.20   Cathy!" exclaimed Heathcliff in much agita-
153.21   tion.
154.01     "It is no company at all, when people know
154.02   nothing and say nothing," she muttered.
154.03     Her companion rose up, but he hadn't time
154.04   to express his feelings further, for a horse's
154.05   feet were heard on the flags, and, having
154.06   knocked gently, young Linton entered, his
154.07   face brilliant with delight at the unexpected
154.08   summons he had received.
154.09     Doubtless Catherine marked the difference
154.10   between her friends as one came in, and the
154.11   other went out. The contrast resembled what
154.12   you see in exchanging a bleak, hilly, coal coun-
154.13   try, for a beautiful fertile valley; and his
154.14   voice, and greeting were as opposite as his
154.15   aspect -- He had a sweet, low manner of speak-
154.16   ing, and pronounced his words as you do, that's
154.17   less gruff than we talk here and softer.
154.18     "I'm not come too soon, am I?" he said,
154.19   casting a look at me, I had begun to wipe the
154.20   plate, and tidy some drawers at the far end in
154.21   the dresser.
155.01     "No," answered Catherine. "What are you
155.02   doing there, Nelly?"

155.03     "My work, Miss," I replied. /Mr. Hindley
155.04   had given me direction to make a third party
155.05   in any private visits Linton chose to pay.//
155.06     She stepped behind me and whispered cross-
155.07   ly, "Take yourself and your dusters off!
155.08   when company are in the house, servants
155.09   don't commence scouring and cleaning in the
155.10   room where they are!"
155.11     "It's a good opportunity, now that master
155.12   is away," I answered aloud, "he hates me to
155.13   be fidgetting over these things in his presence
155.14   -- I'm sure Mr. Edgar will excuse me."
155.15     "I hate you to be fidgetting in \my# pre-
155.16   sence," exclaimed the young lady imperiously,
155.17   not allowing her guest time to speak -- she had
155.18   failed to recover her equanimity since the little
155.19   dispute with Heathcliff.
155.20     "I'm sorry for it, Miss Catherine!" was my
155.21   response; and I proceeded assiduously with
155.22   my occupation.
156.01     She, supposing Edgar could not see her,
156.02   snatched the cloth from my hand, and pinched
156.03   me, with a prolonged wrench, very spitefully
156.04   on the arm.
156.05     I've said I did not love her; and rather re-
156.06   lished mortifying her vanity, now and then;
156.07   besides, she hurt me extremely, so I started
156.08   up from my knees, and screamed out.
156.09     "O, Miss, that's a nasty trick! you have no
156.10   right to nip me, and I'm not going to bear
156.11   it!"
156.12     "I didn't touch you, you lying creature!"
156.13   cried she, her fingers tingling to repeat the
156.14   act, and her ears red with rage. She never
156.15   had power to conceal her passion, it always
156.16   set her whole complexion in a blaze.
156.17     "What's that then?" I retorted showing a
156.18   decided purple witness to refute her.
156.19     She stamped her foot, wavered a moment,
156.20   and then, irresistibly impelled by the naughty
156.21   spirit within her, slapped me on the cheek a
156.22   stinging blow that filled both eyes with water.
157.01     "Catherine, love! Catherine!" interposed
157.02   Linton, greatly shocked at the double fault of
157.03   falsehood, and violence which his idol had com-
157.04   mitted.
157.05     "Leave the room, Ellen!" she repeated,
157.06   trembling all over.
157.07     Little Hareton, who followed me every-
157.08   where, and was sitting near me on the floor,
157.09   at seeing my tears commenced crying himself,
157.10   and sobbed out complaints against "wicked
157.11   aunt Cathy," which drew her fury on to his
157.12   unlucky head: she seized his shoulders, and
157.13   shook him till the poor child waxed livid,
157.14   and Edgar thoughtlessly laid hold of her hands
157.15   to deliver him. In an instant one was wrung
157.16   free, and the astonished young man felt it ap-
157.17   plied over his own ear in a way that could not
157.18   be mistaken for jest.
157.19     He drew back in consternation -- I lifted
157.20   Hareton in my arms, and walked off to the
157.21   kitchen with him; leaving the door of com-
157.22   munication open, for I was curious to
158.01   watch how they would settle their disagree-
158.02   ment.
158.03     The insulted visiter moved to the spot where
158.04   he had laid his hat, pale and with a quivering
158.05   lip.
158.06     "That's right!" I said to myself, "Take
158.07   warning and begone! It's a kindness to let
158.08   you have a glimpse of her genuine disposition."
158.09     "Where are you going?" demanded Cathe-
158.10   rine, advancing to the door.
158.11     He swerved aside and attempted to pass.
158.12     "You must not go!" she exclaimed ener-
158.13   getically.
158.14     "I must and shall!" he replied in a subdued
158.15   voice.
158.16     "No," she persisted, grasping the handle;
158.17   "not yet, Edgar Linton -- sit down, you shall
158.18   not leave me in that temper. I should be
158.19   miserable, all night, and I won't be misera-
158.20   ble for you!"
158.21     "Can I stay after you have struck me?"
158.22   asked Linton.
159.01     Catherine was mute.
159.02     "You've made me afraid, and ashamed of
159.03   you;" he continued; "I'll not come here
159.04   again!"
159.05     Her eyes began to glisten and her lids to
159.06   twinkle.
159.07     "And you told a deliberate untruth!" he
159.08   said.
159.09     "I didn't!" she cried, recovering her speech
159.10   "I did nothing deliberately -- well, go, if you
159.11   please -- get away! And now I'll cry -- I'll cry
159.12   myself sick!"
159.13     She dropped down on her knees by a chair
159.14   and set to weeping in serious earnest.
159.15     Edgar persevered in his resolution as far as
159.16   the court; there, he lingered. I resolved to
159.17   encourage him.
159.18     "Miss is dreadfully wayward, sir!" I called
159.19   out. "As bad as any marred child -- you'd
159.20   better be riding home, or else she will be sick,
159.21   only to grieve us."
159.22     The soft thing looked askance through the
160.01   window -- he possessed the power to depart,
160.02   as much as a cat possesses the power to leave
160.03   a mouse half killed, or a bird half eaten --

160.04 Ah, I thought; there will be no saving him
160.05 -- He's doomed, and flies to his fate!
160.06 And, so it was; he turned abruptly, has-
160.07 tened into the house again, shut the door be-
160.08 hind him; and, when I went in a while after
160.09 to inform them that Earnshaw had come home
160.10 rabid drunk, ready to pull the old place about
160.11 our ears, /his ordinary frame of mind in that
160.12 condition// I saw the quarrel had merely af-
160.13 fected a closer intimacy -- had broken the out--
160.14 works of youthful timidity, and enabled them
160.15 to forsake the disguise of friendship, and con-
160.16 fess themselves lovers.
160.17 Intelligence of Mr. Hindley's arrival drove
160.18 Linton speedily to his horse, and Catherine to
160.19 her chamber. I went to hide little Hareton,
160.20 and to take the shot out of the master's fow-
160.21 ling piece which he was fond of playing with
160.22 in his insane excitement, to the hazard of the
161.01 lives of any who provoked, or even, attracted
161.02 his notice too much; and I had hit upon the
161.03 plan of removing it, that he might do less mis-
161.04 chief, if he did go the length of firing the
161.05 gun.
162.01 [VOL. 1 CHAPTER 9]
162.02 HE entered, vociferating oaths dreadful to
162.03 hear; and caught me in the act of stowing
162.04 his son away in the kitchen cupboard. Hare-
162.05 ton was impressed with a wholesome terror of
162.06 encountering either his wild-beast's fondness,
162.07 or his madman's rage -- for in one he ran a
162.08 chance of being squeezed and kissed to death,
162.09 and in the other of being flung into the fire, or
162.10 dashed against the wall -- and the poor thing
162.11 remained perfectly quiet wherever I chose to
162.12 put him.
163.01 "There I've found it out at last!" cried Hind-
163.02 ley, pulling me back by the skin of the neck,
163.03 like a dog, "By Heaven and Hell, you've
163.04 sworn between you to murder that child! I
163.05 know how it is, now, that he is always out of
163.06 my way. But, with the help of Satan, I shall
163.07 make you swallow the carving knife, Nelly!
163.08 you needn't laugh; for I've just crammed
163.09 Kenneth head-downmost, in the Blackhorse
163.10 marsh; and two is the same as one -- and I
163.11 want to kill some of you, I shall have no rest
163.12 till I do!"
163.13 "But I don't like the carving knife, Mr.
163.14 Hindley;" I answered, it has been cutting red
163.15 herrings -- I'd rather be shot if you please."
163.16 "You'd rather be damned!" he said, "and
163.17 so you shall -- no law in England can hinder a
163.18 man from keeping his house decent, and mine's
163.19 abominable! open your mouth."
163.20 He held the knife in his hand, and pushed
163.21 its point between my teeth: but, for my part
163.22 I was never much afraid of his vagaries. I
164.01 spat out, and affirmed it tasted detestably -- I
164.02 would not take it on any account."
164.03 "Oh!" said he releasing me, I see that hi-
164.04 deous little villain is not Hareton -- I beg your
164.05 pardon, Nell -- if it be he deserves flaying alive
164.06 for not running to welcome me, and for
164.07 screaming as if I were a goblin. Unnatural
164.08 cub, come hither! I'll teach thee to impose on
164.09 a good-hearted, deluded father -- Now, don't
164.10 you think the lad would be handsomer crop-
164.11 ped? It makes a dog fiercer, and I love some-
164.12 thing fierce -- Get me a scissors -- something
164.13 fierce and trim! Besides, it's infernal affecta-
164.14 tion -- devilish conceit, it is to cherish our ears
164.15 -- we're asses enough without them. Hush,
164.16 child, hush! well then, it is my darling! wisht,
164.17 dry thy eyes -- there's a joy; kiss me; what it
164.18 won't? kiss me, Hareton! Dam'n thee, kiss
164.19 me! By God, as if I would rear such a mon-
164.20 ster! As sure as I'm living, I'll break the
164.21 brat's neck."
164.22 Poor Hareton was squalling and kicking in
165.01 his father's arms with all his might, and re-
165.02 doubled his yells when he carried him up-stairs
165.03 and lifted him over the bannister. I cried out
165.04 that he would frighten the child into fits, and
165.05 ran to rescue him.
165.06 As I reached them, Hindley leant forward
165.07 on the rails to listen to a noise below; almost
165.08 forgetting what he had in his hands.
165.09 "Who is that?" he asked, hearing some one
165.10 approaching the stair's-foot.
165.11 I leant forward, also, for the purpose of
165.12 signing to Heathcliff, whose step I recognized,
165.13 not to come further; and, at the instant when
165.14 my eye quitted Hareton, he gave a sudden
165.15 spring, delivered himself from the careless
165.16 grasp that held him, and fell.
165.17 There was scarcely time to experience a
165.18 thrill of horror before we saw that the little
165.19 wretch was safe. Heathcliff arrived under-
165.20 neath just at the critical moment; by a natu-
165.21 ral impulse, he arrested his descent, and setting
166.01 him on his feet, looked up to discover the au-
166.02 thor of the accident.
166.03 A miser who has parted with a lucky lottery
166.04 ticket for five shillings and finds next day he
166.05 has lost in the bargain five thousand pounds,
166.06 could not show a blanker countenance than he
166.07 did on beholding the figure of Mr. Earnshaw
166.08 above -- It expressed, plainer than words could
166.09 do, the intensest anguish at having made him-
166.10 self the instrument of thwarting his own re-

166.11 venge. Had it been dark, I dare say, he
166.12 would have tried to remedy the mistake by
166.13 smashing Hareton's skull on the steps; but, we
166.14 witnessed his salvation; and I was presently
166.15 below with my precious charge pressed to my
166.16 heart.
166.17 Hindley descended more leisurely, sobered
166.18 and abashed.
166.19 "It is your fault, Ellen," he said, "you
166.20 should have kept him out of sight; you should
166.21 have taken him from me! Is he injured any-
166.22 where?"
167.01 "Injured!" I cried angrily, "If he's not
167.02 killed, he'll be an idiot! Oh! I wonder his
167.03 mother does not rise from her grave to see how
167.04 you use him. You're worse than a heathen --
167.05 treating your own flesh and blood in that man-
167.06 ner!"
167.07 He attempted to touch the child, who on
167.08 finding himself with me sobbed off his terror
167.09 directly. At the first finger his father laid on
167.10 him, however, he shrieked again louder than
167.11 before, and struggled as if he would go into
167.12 convulsions.
167.13 "You shall not meddle with him!" I conti-
167.14 nued, "He hates you -- they all hate you --
167.15 that's the truth! A happy family you have;
167.16 and a pretty state you're come to!"
167.17 "I shall come to a prettier, yet! Nelly,"
167.18 laughed the misguided man, recovering his
167.19 hardness. "At present, convey yourself and
167.20 him away -- And, hark you, Heathcliff! clear
167.21 you too, quite from my reach and hearing ... I
167.22 wouldn't murder you to-night, unless, perhaps
168.01 I set the house on fire; but that's as my fancy
168.02 goes --"
168.03 while saying this he took a pint bottle of
168.04 brandy from the dresser, and poured some into
168.05 a tumbler.
168.06 "Nay don't!" I entreated, "Mr. Hindley
168.07 do take warning. Have mercy on this unfor-
168.08 tunate boy, if you care nothing for yourself!"
168.09 "Any one will do better for him, than I
168.10 shall," he answered.
168.11 "Have mercy on your own soul!" I said,
168.12 endeavouring to snatch the glass from his hand.
168.13 "Not I! on the contrary, I shall have great
168.14 pleasure in sending it to perdition, to punish
168.15 its maker," exclaimed the blasphemer, "Here's
168.16 to its hearty damnation!"
168.17 He drank the spirits, and impatiently bade
168.18 us go; terminating his command with a sequel
168.19 of horrid imprecations, too bad to repeat, or re-
168.20 member.
168.21 "It's a pity he cannot kill himself with
168.22 drink," observed Heathcliff, muttering an
169.01 echo of curses back when the door was shut.
169.02 "He's doing his very utmost; but his consti-
169.03 tution defies him -- Mr. Kenneth says he would
169.04 wager his mare, that he'll outlive any man on
169.05 this side Gimmerton, and go to the grave a
169.06 hoary sinner; unless, some happy chance out
169.07 of the common course befall him."
169.08 I went into the kitchen and sat down to lull
169.09 my little lamb to sleep. Heathcliff, as I
169.10 thought, walked through to the barn. It
169.11 turned out, afterwards, that he only got as far
169.12 as the other side the settle, when he flung him-
169.13 self on a bench by the wall, removed from the
169.14 fire, and remained silent.
169.15 I was rocking Hareton on my knee, and
169.16 humming a song that began;
169.17 "It was far in the night, and the bairnies grat,
169.18 The mither beneath the mools heard that."
169.19 when Miss Cathy, who had listened to the
169.20 hubbub from her room, put her head in, and
169.21 whispered,
169.22 "Are you alone, Nelly?"
170.01 "Yes, miss," I replied.
170.02 She entered and approached the hearth. I,
170.03 supposing she was going to say something,
170.04 looked up. The expression of her face seem-
170.05 ed disturbed and anxious. Her lips were
170.06 half asunder as if she meant to speak; and
170.07 she drew a breath, but it escaped in a sigh,
170.08 instead of a sentence.
170.09 I resumed my song: not having forgotten
170.10 her recent behaviour.
170.11 "Where's Heathcliff?" she said, interrupt-
170.12 ing me.
170.13 "About his work in the stable," was my
170.14 answer.
170.15 He did not contradict me; perhaps, he had
170.16 fallen into a doze.
170.17 There followed another long pause, during
170.18 which I perceived a drop or two trickle from
170.19 Catherine's cheek to the flags.
170.20 Is she sorry for her shameful conduct? I
170.21 asked myself. That will be a novelty, but, she
170.22 may come to the point as she will -- I shan't
170.23 help her!
171.01 No, she felt small trouble regarding any
171.02 subject, save her own own concerns.
171.03 "Oh, dear!" she cried at last. "I'm very
171.04 unhappy!"
171.05 "A pity," observed I, "you're hard to
171.06 please -- so many friends and so few cares, and
171.07 can't make yourself, content!"
171.08 "Nelly, will you keep a secret for me?"
171.09 she pursued, kneeling down by me, and lifting
171.10 her winsome eyes to my face with that sort of

171.11 look which turns off bad temper, even, when
171.12 one has all the right in the world to indulge
171.13 it.
171.14 "Is it worth keeping?" I inquired less sulk-
171.15 ily.
171.16 "Yes, and it worries me, and I must let it
171.17 out! I want to know what I should do -- To-
171.18 day, Edgar Linton has asked me to marry
171.19 him, and I've given him an answer -- Now, be-
171.20 fore I tell you whether it was a consent, or
171.21 denial -- you tell me which it ought to have
171.22 been."
172.01 "Really, Miss Catherine, how can I know?"
172.02 I replied. "To be sure, considering the ex-
172.03 hibition you performed in his presence, this
172.04 afternoon, I might say it would be wise to re-
172.05 fuse him -- since he asked you after that, he
172.06 must either be hopelessly stupid, or a venture-
172.07 some fool."
172.08 "If you talk so, I wont tell you any more,"
172.09 she returned, peevishly, rising to her feet, "I
172.10 accepted him, Nelly; be quick, and say whe-
172.11 ther I was wrong!"
172.12 "You accepted him? then, what good is it
172.13 discussing the matter? You have pledged your
172.14 word, and cannot retract."
172.15 "But, say whether I should have done so --
172.16 do!" she exclaimed in an irritated tone; chafing
172.17 her hands together, and frowning.
172.18 "There are many things to be considered,
172.19 before that question can be answered pro-
172.20 perly." I said sententiously, "First and fore-
172.21 most, do you love Mr. Edgar?"
173.01 "Who can help it? of course I do," she an-
173.02 swered.
173.03 Then I put her through the following cate-
173.04 chism -- for a girl of twenty-two it was not in-
173.05 judicious.
173.06 "Why do you love him, Miss Cathy?"
173.07 "Nonsense, I do -- that's sufficient."
173.08 "By no means; you must say why?"
173.09 "Well, because he is handsome, and pleasant
173.10 to be with."
173.11 "Bad," was my commentary.
173.12 "And because he is young and cheerful."
173.13 "Bad, still."
173.14 "And, because he loves me."
173.15 "Indifferent, coming there."
173.16 "And he will be rich, and I shall like to be
173.17 the greatest woman of the neighbourhood, and
173.18 I shall be proud of having such a husband."
173.19 "Worst of all! And, now, say how you love
173.20 him?"
173.21 "As every body loves -- You're silly, Nelly."
173.22 "Not at all -- Answer."
174.01 "I love the ground under his feet, and the
174.02 air over his head, and everything he touches,
174.03 and every word he says -- I love all his looks,
174.04 and all his actions, and him entirely, and al-
174.05 together. There now!"
174.06 "And why?"
174.07 "Nay -- you are making a jest of it; it is
174.08 exceedingly ill-natured! It's no jest to me!"
174.09 said the young lady scowling, and turning her
174.10 face to the fire.
174.11 "I'm very far from jesting, Miss Cathe-
174.12 rine," I replied, "you love Mr. Edgar, because
174.13 he is handsome, and young, and cheerful, and
174.14 rich, and loves you. The last, however, goes
174.15 for nothing -- You would love him without
174.16 that, probably, and with it, you wouldn't un-
174.17 less he possessed the four former attractions."
174.18 "No, to be sure not -- I should only pity
174.19 him -- hate him, perhaps, if he were ugly, and
174.20 a clown."
174.21 "But, there are several other handsome, rich
174.22 young men in the world; handsomer, possibly,
175.01 and richer than he is -- What should hinder
175.02 you from loving them?"
175.03 "If there be any, they are out of my way --
175.04 I've seen none like Edgar."
175.05 "You may see some; and he won't always
175.06 be handsome, and young, and may not always
175.07 be rich."
175.08 "He is now; and I have only to do with
175.09 the present -- I wish you would speak ration-
175.10 ally."
175.11 "Well, that settles it -- if you have only to
175.12 do with the present, marry Mr. Linton."
175.13 "I don't want your permission for that -- I
175.14 \shall# marry him; and yet, you have not told
175.15 me whether I'm right."
175.16 "Perfectly right; if people be right to
175.17 marry only for the present. And now, let us
175.18 hear what you are unhappy about. Your bro-
175.19 ther will be pleased ... The old lady and gen-
175.20 tleman will not object, I think -- you will escape
175.21 from a disorderly, comfortless home into a
175.22 wealthy respectable one; and you love Edgar,
176.01 and Edgar loves you. All seems smooth and
176.02 easy -- where is the obstacle?"
176.03 "\Here#! and \here#!" replied Catherine,
176.04 striking one hand on her forehead, and
176.05 the other on her breast. "In whichever place
176.06 the soul lives -- in my soul, and in my heart,
176.07 I'm convinced I'm wrong!"
176.08 "That's very strange! I cannot make it
176.09 out."
176.10 "It's my secret; but if you will not mock
176.11 at me, I'll explain it; I can't do it distinctly
176.12 -- but I'll give you a feeling of how I feel."

176.13 She seated herself by me again: her coun-
176.14 tenance grew sadder and graver, and her
176.15 clasped hands trembled.
176.16 "Nelly, do you never dream queer dreams?"
176.17 she said, suddenly, after some minutes' reflec-
176.18 tion.
176.19 "Yes, now and then," I answered.
176.20 "And so do I. I've dreamt in my life
176.21 dreams that have stayed with me ever after,
176.22 and changed my ideas; they've gone through
177.01 and through me, like wine through water, and
177.02 altered the colour of my mind. And this is
177.03 one -- I'm going to tell it -- but take care not
177.04 to smile at any part of it."
177.05 "Oh! don't, Miss Catherine!" I cried.
177.06 "We're dismal enough without conjuring up
177.07 ghosts, and visions to perplex us. Come,
177.08 come, be merry, and like yourself! Look at
177.09 little Hareton -- \he's# dreaming nothing dreary.
177.10 How sweetly he smiles in his sleep!"
177.11 "Yes; and how sweetly his father curses
177.12 in his solitude! You remember him, I dare
177.13 say, when he was just such another as that
177.14 chubby thing -- nearly as young and innocent.
177.15 However, Nelly, I shall oblige you to listen
177.16 -- it's not long; and I've no power to be
177.17 merry to-night."
177.18 "I wont hear it, I wont hear it!" I repeated,
177.19 hastily.
177.20 I was superstitious about dreams then, and
177.21 am still; and Catherine had an unusual gloom
177.22 in her aspect, that made me dread something
178.01 from which I might shape a prophecy, and
178.02 foresee a fearful catastrophe.
178.03 She was vexed, but she did not proceed.
178.04 Apparently taking up another subject, she
178.05 re-commenced in a short time.
178.06 "If I were in heaven, Nelly, I should be
178.07 extremely miserable."
178.08 "Because you are not fit to go there," I
178.09 answered. "All sinners would be miserable
178.10 in heaven."
178.11 "But it is not for that. I dreamt, once,
178.12 that I was there."
178.13 "I tell you I wont harken to your dreams,
178.14 Miss Catherine! I'll go to bed," I interrupted
178.15 again.
178.16 She laughed, and held me down, for I
178.17 made a motion to leave my chair.
178.18 "This is nothing," cried she; "I was only
178.19 going to say that heaven did not seem to be
178.20 my home; and I broke my heart with weeping
178.21 to come back to earth; and the angels were so
178.22 angry that they flung me out, into the middle
179.01 of the heath on the top of Wuthering Heights;
179.02 where I woke sobbing for joy. That will do
179.03 to explain my secret, as well as the other.
179.04 I've no more business to marry Edgar Linton
179.05 than I have to be in heaven; and if the wicked
179.06 man in there, had not brought Heathcliff so
179.07 low I shouldn't have thought of it. It would
179.08 degrade me to marry Heathcliff, now; so he
179.09 shall never know how I love him; and that,
179.10 not because he's handsome, Nelly, but because
179.11 he's more myself than I am. Whatever our
179.12 souls are made of, his and mine are the same,
179.13 and Linton's is as different as a moonbeam
179.14 from lightning, or frost from fire."
179.15 Ere this speech ended I became sensible of
179.16 Heathcliff's presence. Having noticed a slight
179.17 movement, I turned my head, and saw him
179.18 rise from the bench, and steal out, noiselessly.
179.19 He had listened till he heard Catherine say it
179.20 would degrade her to marry him, and then he
179.21 staid to hear no farther.
179.22 My companion, sitting on the ground, was
180.01 prevented by the back of the settle from re-
180.02 marking his presence or departure; but I
180.03 started, and bade her hush!
180.04 "Why?" she asked, gazing nervously round.
180.05 "Joseph is here," I answered, catching,
180.06 opportunely, the roll of his cartwheels up the
180.07 road; "and Heathcliff will come in with him.
180.08 I'm not sure whether he were not at the door
180.09 this moment."
180.10 "Oh, he couldn't overhear me at the door!"
180.11 said she. "Give me Hareton, while you get
180.12 the supper, and when it is ready ask me to sup
180.13 with you. I want to cheat my uncomfortable
180.14 conscience, and be convinced that Heathcliff
180.15 has no notion of these things -- he has not, has
180.16 he? He does not know what being in love is?"
180.17 "I see no reason that he should not know,
180.18 as well as you," I returned; "and if \you# are
180.19 his choice, he'll be the most unfortunate crea-
180.20 ture that ever was born! As soon as you be-
180.21 come Mrs. Linton, he loses friend, and love,
180.22 and all! Have you considered how you'll bear
181.01 the separation, and how he'll bear to be quite
181.02 deserted in the world? Because, Miss
181.03 Catherine --"
181.04 "He quite deserted! we separated!" she
181.05 exclaimed, with an accent of indignation.
181.06 "Who is to separate us, pray? They'll meet
181.07 the fate of Milo! Not as long as I live, Ellen
181.08 -- for no mortal creature. Every Linton on
181.09 the face of the earth might melt into nothing,
181.10 before I could consent to forsake Heathcliff.
181.11 Oh, that's not what I intend -- that's not what
181.12 I mean! I shouldn't be Mrs. Linton were
181.13 such a price demanded! He'll be as much to

181.14 me as he has been all his lifetime. Edgar must
181.15 shake off his antipathy, and tolerate him, at
181.16 least. He will when he learns my true feelings
181.17 towards him. Nelly, I see now, you think
181.18 me a selfish wretch, but, did it never strike
181.19 you that, if Heathcliff and I married, we
181.20 should be beggars? whereas, if I marry
181.21 Linton, I can aid Heathcliff to rise, and place
181.22 him out of my brother's power."
182.01    "With your husband's money, Miss
182.02 Catherine?" I asked. "You'll find him not
182.03 so pliable as you calculate upon: and, though
182.04 I'm hardly a judge, I think that's the worst
182.05 motive you've given yet for being the wife of
182.06 young Linton."
182.07    "It is not," retorted she, "it is the best!
182.08 The others were the satisfaction of my whims;
182.09 and for Edgar's sake, too, to satisfy him.
182.10 This is for the sake of one who comprehends
182.11 in his person my feelings to Edgar and myself.
182.12 I cannot express it; but surely you and every
182.13 body have a notion that there is, or should be
182.14 an existence of yours beyond you. What
182.15 were the use of my creation if I were entirely
182.16 contained here? My great miseries in this
182.17 world have been Heathcliff's miseries, and I
182.18 watched and felt each from the beginning; my
182.19 great thought in living is himself. If all else
182.20 perished, and \he# remained, I should still con-
182.21 tinue to be; and, if all else remained, and he
182.22 were annihilated, the Universe would turn to
183.01 a mighty stranger. I should not seem a part
183.02 of it. My love for Linton is like the foliage
183.03 in the woods. Time will change it, I'm well
183.04 aware, as winter changes the trees -- my love
183.05 for Heathcliff resembles the eternal rocks be-
183.06 neath -- a source of little visible delight, but
183.07 necessary. Nelly, I \am# Heathcliff -- he's al-
183.08 ways, always in my mind -- not as a pleasure,
183.09 any more than I am always a pleasure to my-
183.10 self -- but, as my own being -- so, don't talk of
183.11 our separation again -- it is impracticable;
183.12 and --"
183.13    She paused, and hid her face in the folds of
183.14 my gown; but I jerked it forcibly away. I
183.15 was out of patience with her folly!
183.16    "If I can make any sense of your nonsense,
183.17 Miss," I said, "it only goes to convince me
183.18 that you are ignorant of the duties you under-
183.19 take in marrying; or else, that you are a
183.20 wicked, unprincipled girl. But, trouble me
183.21 with no more secrets. I'll not promise to keep
183.22 them."
184.01    "You'll keep that?" she asked, eagerly.
184.02    "No, I'll not promise," I repeated.
184.03    She was about to insist, when the entrance
184.04 of Joseph finished our conversation; and
184.05 Catherine removed her seat to a corner, and
184.06 nursed Hareton, while I made the supper.
184.07    After it was cooked, my fellow servant and
184.08 I began to quarrel who should carry some to
184.09 Mr. Hindley; and we didn't settle it till all
184.10 was nearly cold. Then we came to the agree-
184.11 ment that we would let him ask, if he wanted
184.12 any, for we feared particularly to go into his
184.13 presence when he had been sometime alone.
184.14    "Und hah isn't that nowt comed in frough
184.15 th' field, be this time? What is he abaht?
184.16 girt eedle seeght!" demanded the old man,
184.17 looking round for Heathcliff.
184.18    "I'll call him," I replied. "He's in the
184.19 barn, I've no doubt."
184.20    I went and called, but got no answer. On
184.21 returning, I whispered to Catherine that he
184.22 had heard a good part of what she said, I was
185.01 sure; and told how I saw him quit the kitchen
185.02 just as she complained of her brother's conduct
185.03 regarding him.
185.04    She jumped up in a fine fright -- flung Hare-
185.05 ton onto the settle, and ran to seek for her
185.06 friend herself, not taking leisure to consider
185.07 why she was so flurried, or how her talk would
185.08 have affected him.
185.09    She was absent such a while that Joseph
185.10 proposed we should wait no longer. He cun-
185.11 ningly conjectured they were staying away in
185.12 order to avoid hearing his protracted blessing.
185.13 They were "ill enough for ony fahl manners,"
185.14 he affirmed. And, on their behalf, he added,
185.15 that night a special prayer to the usual quar-
185.16 ter of an hour's supplication before meat, and
185.17 would have tacked another to the end of the
185.18 grace, had not his young mistress broken in
185.19 upon him with a hurried command, that he
185.20 must run down the road, and, wherever
185.21 Heathcliff had rambled, find and make him re--
185.22 enter directly!
186.01    "I want to speak to him, and I \must#, before
186.02 I go up-stairs, she said. "And the gate is
186.03 open, he is somewhere out of hearing; for he
186.04 would not reply, though I shouted at the top
186.05 of the fold as loud as I could."
186.06    Joseph objected at first; she was too much
186.07 in earnest, however, to suffer contradiction;
186.08 and, at last, he placed his hat on his head, and
186.09 walked grumbling forth.
186.10    Meantime, Catherine paced up and down
186.11 the floor, exclaiming --
186.12    "I wonder where he is -- I wonder where he
186.13 \can# be!" What did I say, Nelly? I've forgot-
186.14 ten. Was he vexed at my bad humour this

186.15 afternoon? Dear! tell me what I've said to
186.16 grieve him? I do wish he'd come. I do wish
186.17 he would!"
186.18    "What a noise for nothing!" I cried,
186.19 though rather uneasy myself. "What a trifle
186.20 scares you! It's surely no great cause of
186.21 alarm that Heathcliff should take a moonlight
186.22 saunter on the moors, or, even lie too sulky to
187.01 speak to us, in the hay-loft. I'll engage he's
187.02 lurking there. See, if I don't ferret him out!"
187.03    I departed to renew my search; its result
187.04 was disappointment, and Joseph's quest ended
187.05 in the same.
187.06    "Yon lad gets war un war!" observed he
187.07 on re-entering. "He's left th' yate ut t' full
187.08 swing, and miss's pony has trodden dahn two
187.09 rigs uh corn, un plottered through, raight o'er
187.10 intuh t' meadow! Hahsomdiver, t' maister
187.11 'ull play t' divil to-morn, and he'll do weel.
187.12 He's patience itsseln wi' sich careless, offald
187.13 craters -- patience itsseln he is! Bud he'll nut
187.14 be soa allus -- yah's see, all on ye! Yah
187.15 munn't drive him aht uf his heead fur nowt!"
187.16    "Have you found Heathcliff, you ass?"
187.17 interrupted Catherine. "Have you been
187.18 looking for him, as I ordered?"
187.19    "Aw sud more likker look for th' horse," he
187.20 replied. "It 'ud be tuh more sense. Bud, aw
187.21 can look for norther horse, nur man uf a neeght
187.22 loike this -- as black as t' chimbley! und
188.01 Hathecliff's noan t' chap tuh coom ut \maw#
188.02 whistle -- happen he'll be less hard uh hearing
188.03 wi' \ye#!"
188.04    It \was# a very dark evening for summer: the
188.05 clouds appeared inclined to thunder, and I said
188.06 we had better all sit down; the approaching
188.07 rain would be certain to bring him home with-
188.08 out further trouble.
188.09    However, Catherine would not be persuaded
188.10 into tranquillity. She kept wandering to and
188.11 fro, from the gate to the door, in a state of agi-
188.12 tation, which permitted no repose: and, at
188.13 length, took up a permanent situation on one
188.14 side of the wall, near the road; where, heed-
188.15 less of expostulations, and the growling
188.16 thunder, and the great drops that began to
188.17 plash around her, she remained calling, at in-
188.18 tervals, and then listening, and then crying
188.19 outright. She beat Hareton, or any child, at
188.20 a good, passionate fit of crying.
188.21    About midnight, while we still sat up, the
188.22 storm came rattling over the Heights in full
189.01 fury. There was a violent wind, as well as
189.02 thunder, and either one or the other split a
189.03 tree off at the corner of the building; a huge
189.04 bough fell across the roof, and knocked down a
189.05 portion of the east chimney-stack, sending a
189.06 clatter of stones and soot into the kitchen
189.07 fire.
189.08    We thought a bolt had fallen in the middle
189.09 of us, and Joseph swung onto his knees, be-
189.10 seeching the Lord to remember the Patriarchs
189.11 Noah and Lot; and, as in former times, spare
189.12 the righteous, though he smote the ungodly.
189.13 I felt some sentiment that it must be judg-
189.14 ment on us also. The Jonah, in my mind, was
189.15 Mr. Earnshaw, and I shook the handle of his
189.16 den that I might ascertain if he were yet
189.17 living. He replied audibly enough, in a fash-
189.18 ion which made my companion vociferate
189.19 more clamorously than before that a wide dis-
189.20 tinction might be drawn between saints like
189.21 himself, and sinners like his master. But, the
189.22 uproar passed away in twenty minutes, leaving
190.01 us all unharmed, excepting Cathy, who got
190.02 thoroughly drenched for her obstinacy in re-
190.03 fusing to take shelter, and standing bonnetless
190.04 and shawlless to catch as much water as she
190.05 could with her hair and clothes.
190.06    She came in, and lay down on the settle, all
190.07 soaked as she was, turning her face to the
190.08 back, and putting her hands before it.
190.09    "Well Miss!" I exclaimed, touching her
190.10 shoulder. "You are not bent on getting your
190.11 death, are you? Do you know what o'clock
190.12 it is? Half-past twelve. Come! come to
190.13 bed; there's no use waiting longer on that
190.14 foolish boy -- he'll be gone to Gimmerton, and
190.15 he'll stay there now. He guesses we should
190.16 n't wake for him till this late hour; at least,
190.17 he guesses that only Mr. Hindley would be
190.18 up; and he'd rather avoid having the door
190.19 opened by the master."
190.20    "Nay, nay, he's noan at Gimmerton!" said
190.21 Joseph. "Aw's niver wonder, bud he's at t'
190.22 bothom uf a bog-hoile. This visitation worn't
191.01 for nowt, und aw wod hev ye tuh look aht,
191.02 Miss, -- yah muh be t' next. Thank Hivin
191.03 for all! All warks togither for gooid tuh them
191.04 as is chozzen, and piked aht froo' th' rubbidge!
191.05 Yah knaw whet t' Scripture ses --"
191.06    And he began quoting several texts; refer-
191.07 ing us to the chapters and verses, where we
191.08 might find them.
191.09    I having vainly begged the wilful girl to
191.10 rise and remove her wet things, left him
191.11 preaching, and her shivering, and betook my-
191.12 self to bed with little Hareton; who slept as
191.13 fast as if every one had been sleeping round
191.14 him.
191.15    I heard Joseph read on a while afterwards;

191.16 then, I distinguished his slow step on the lad-
191.17 der, and then I dropt asleep.
191.18 Coming down somewhat later than usual, I
191.19 saw, by the sunbeams piercing the chinks of
191.20 the shutters, Miss Catherine still seated near
191.21 the fire-place. The house door was ajar, too
191.22 light entered from its unclosed windows,
192.01 Hindley had come out, and stood on the kit-
192.02 chen hearth, haggard and drowsy.
192.03 "what ails you, Cathy?" he was saying
192.04 when I entered; "You look as dismal as a
192.05 drowned whelp -- Why are you so damp and
192.06 pale child?"
192.07 "I've been wet;" she answered reluctantly
192.08 "and I'm cold, that's all."
192.09 "Oh, she is naughty!" I cried, perceiving
192.10 the master to be tolerably sober; "She got
192.11 steeped in the shower of yesterday evening,
192.12 and there she has sat, the night through, and
192.13 I couldn't prevail on her to stir."
192.14 Mr. Earnshaw stared at us in surprise.
192.15 "The night through," he repeated, "what
192.16 kept her up, not fear of the thunder, surely?
192.17 That was over, hours since."
192.18 Neither of us wished to mention Heathcliff's
192.19 absence, as long as we could conceal it; so, I
192.20 replied, I didn't know how she took it into
192.21 her head to sit up; and she said nothing.
192.22 The morning was fresh and cool; I threw
193.01 back the lattice, and presently the room filled
193.02 with sweet scents from the garden: but Ca-
193.03 therine called peevishly to me.
193.04 "Ellen, shut the window. I'm starving!"
193.05 And her teeth chattered as she shrunk closer
193.06 to the almost extinguished embers.
193.07 "She's ill --" said Hindley, taking her
193.08 wrist, "I suppose that's the reason she would
193.09 not go to bed -- Damn it! I don't want to be
193.10 troubled with more sickness, here -- What took
193.11 you into the rain?"
193.12 "Running after t'lads, as usuald!" croaked
193.13 Joseph, catching an opportunity, from our he-
193.14 sitation, to thrust in his evil tongue.
193.15 "If Aw wur yah, maister, Aw'd just slam
193.16 t'boards i' their faces all on 'em, gentle and
193.17 simple! Never a day ut yah're off, but yon
193.18 cat uh Linton comes sneaking hither -- and
193.19 Miss Nelly shoo's a fine lass! shoo sits watch-
193.20 ing for ye i' t'kitchen; and as yah're in at one
193.21 door, he's aht at t'other -- Und, then, wer grand
193.22 lady goes a coorting uf hor side! It's bonny
194.01 benaviour, lurking amang t'fields, after twelve
194.02 ut' night, wi that fahl, flaysome divil uf a gip-
194.03 sy, Heathcliff,! They think \Aw'm# blind; but
194.04 Aw'm noan, now't ut t'soart! Aw seed young
194.05 Linton, boath coming and going, and Aw seed
194.06 \yah# /directing his discourse to me.// Yah gooid
194.07 fur nowt, slattenly witch! nip up nud bolt intuh
194.08 th' haks, t' minute yah heard t'maister's horse
194.09 fit clatter up t'road.
194.10 "Silence, eavesdropper!" cried Catherine,
194.11 "None of your insolence, before me!" That
194.12 Linton, came yesterday, by chance, Hindley;
194.13 and it was \I# who told him to be off: because,
194.14 I knew you would not like to have met him as
194.15 you were."
194.16 "You lie, Cathy, no doubt," answered her
194.17 brother, "and you are a confounded simpleton!
194.18 But, never mind Linton, at present -- Tell me,
194.19 were you not with Heathcliff, last night?
194.20 Speak the truth, now. You need not be
194.21 afraid of harming him -- Though I hate him as
194.22 much as ever, he did me a good turn, a short
195.01 time since, that will make my conscience ten-
195.02 der of breaking his neck. To prevent it, I
195.03 shall send him about his business, this very
195.04 morning; and after he's gone, I'd advise you
195.05 all to look sharp, I shall only have the more
195.06 humour for you!"
195.07 "I never saw Heathcliff last night," an-
195.08 swered Catherine, beginning to sob bitterly:
195.09 "and if you do turn him out of doors, I'll go
195.10 with him. But, perhaps, you'll never have
195.11 an opportunity -- perhaps, he's gone." Here
195.12 she burst into uncontrollable grief, and the re-
195.13 mainder of her words were inarticulate.
195.14 Hindley lavished on her a torrent of scorn-
195.15 ful abuse, and bid her go to her room imme-
195.16 diately, or she shouldn't cry for nothing! I
195.17 obliged her to obey; and I shall never forget
195.18 what a scene she acted, when we reached her
195.19 chamber. It terrified me -- I thought she was
195.20 going mad, and I begged Joseph to run for the
195.21 doctor.
196.01 It proved the commencement of delirium;
196.02 Mr. Kenneth, as soon as he saw her, pronoun-
196.03 ced her dangerously ill; she had a fever.
196.04 He bled her, and he told me to let her live
196.05 on whey, and water gruel; and take care she
196.06 did not throw herself down stairs, or out of
196.07 the window; and then he left; for, he had
196.08 enough to do in the parish where two or three
196.09 miles was the ordinary distance between cot-
196.10 tage and cottage.
196.11 Though I cannot say I made a gentle nurse,
196.12 and Joseph and the master were no better;
196.13 and, though our patient was as wearisome and
196.14 headstrong as a patient could be, she weather-
196.15 ed it through.
196.16 Old Mrs. Linton paid us several visits, to be
196.17 sure; and set things to rights, and scolded and

196.18 ordered us all; and when Catherine was con-
196.19 valescent, she insisted on conveying her to
196.20 Thrushcross Grange; for which deliverance
196.21 we were very grateful. But, the poor dame
196.22 had reason to repent of her kindness; she, and
197.01 her husband, both took the fever, and died
197.02 within a few days of each other.
197.03 Our young lady returned to us, saucier,
197.04 and more passionate, and haughtier than ever.
197.05 Heathcliff had never been heard of since the
197.06 evening of the thunder-storm, and, one day,
197.07 I had the misfortune, when she had provoked
197.08 me exceedingly, to lay the blame of his dis-
197.09 appearance on her /where indeed it belonged,
197.10 as she well knew.// From that period for seve-
197.11 ral months, she ceased to hold any communi-
197.12 cation with me save in the relation of a mere
197.13 servant. Joseph fell under a ban also; he
197.14 \would# speak his mind, and lecture her all the
197.15 same as if she were a little girl; and she es-
197.16 teemed herself a woman, and our mistress; and
197.17 thought that her recent illness gave her a
197.18 claim to be treated with consideration. Then
197.19 the doctor had said that she would not bear
197.20 crossing much, she ought to have her own
197.21 way; and it was nothing less than murder, in
198.01 her eyes, for any one, to presume to stand up
198.02 and contradict her.
198.03 From Mr. Earnshaw, and his companions
198.04 she kept aloof, and tutored by Kenneth, and
198.05 serious threats of a fit that often attended
198.06 her rages, her brother allowed her whatever
198.07 she pleased to demand, and generally avoided
198.08 aggravating her fiery temper. He was rather
198.09 \too# indulgent in humouring her caprices; not
198.10 from affection, but pride; he wished
198.11 earnestly to see her bring honour to the family
198.12 by an alliance with the Lintons, and, as long
198.13 as she let him alone, she might trample us like
198.14 slaves for ought he cared!
198.15 Edgar Linton, as multitudes have been be-
198.16 fore, and will be after him, was infatuated;
198.17 and believed himself the happiest man alive
198.18 on the day he led her to Gimmerton chapel,
198.19 three years subsequent to his father's death.
198.20 Much against my inclination, I was per-
198.21 suaded to leave Wuthering Heights and accompany
199.01 her here. Little Hareton was near-
199.02 ly five years old, and I had just began to
199.03 teach him his letters: we made a sad part-
199.04 ing, but Catherine's tears were more power-
199.05 ful than ours -- When I refused to go, and
199.06 when she found her entreaties did not move
199.07 me, she went lamenting to her husband, and
199.08 brother. The former offered me munificent
199.09 wages; the latter order me to pack up -- he
199.10 wanted no women in the house, he said, now
199.11 that there was no mistress; and as to Hare-
199.12 ton, the curate should take him in hand, by
199.13 and bye. And so, I had but one choice left,
199.14 to do as I was ordered -- I told the master he
199.15 got rid of all decent people only to run to
199.16 ruin a little faster; I kissed Hareton good
199.17 bye; and, since then, he has been a stranger,
199.18 and it's very queer to think it, but I've no
199.19 doubt, he has completely forgotten all about
199.20 Ellen Dean and that he was ever more than
199.21 all the world to her, and she to him!
199.22 At this point of the housekeeper's story she
200.01 chanced to glance towards the time-piece over
200.02 the chimney; and was in amazement, on seeing
200.03 the minute-hand measure half past one. She
200.04 would not hear of staying a second longer --
200.05 In truth, I felt rather disposed to defer the
200.06 sequel of her narrative, myself: and now,
200.07 that she is vanished to her rest, and I have
200.08 meditated for another hour or two, I shall sum-
200.09 mon courage to go, also, in spite of aching la-
200.10 ziness of head and limbs.
201.01 [VOL. 1 CHAPTER 10]
201.02 A CHARMING introduction to a hermit's life!
201.03 Four weeks' torture, tossing and sickness!
201.04 Oh, these bleak winds, and bitter, northern
201.05 skies, and impassable roads, and dilatory coun-
201.06 try surgeons! And, oh, this dearth of the
201.07 human physiognomy, and, worse than all, the
201.08 terrible intimation of Kenneth that I need not
201.09 expect to be out of doors till spring!
201.10 Mr. Heathcliff has just honoured me with a
201.11 call. About seven days ago he sent me a
201.12 brace of grouse -- the last of the season.
202.01 Scoundrel! He is not altogether guiltless in
202.02 this illness of mine; and that I had a great
202.03 mind to tell him. But, alas! how could I
202.04 offend a man who was charitable enough to
202.05 sit at my bedside a good hour, and talk on
202.06 some other subject than pills, and draughts,
202.07 blisters, and leeches?
202.08 This is quite an easy interval. I am too
202.09 weak to read, yet I feel as if I could enjoy
202.10 something interesting. Why not have up Mrs.
202.11 Dean to finish her tale? I can recollect its
202.12 chief incidents, as far as she had gone. Yes,
202.13 I remember her hero had run off, and never
202.14 been heard of for three years: and the heroine
202.15 was married. I'll ring; she'll be delighted to
202.16 find me capable of talking cheerfully.
202.17 Mrs. Dean came.
202.18 "It wants twenty minutes, sir, to taking
202.19 the medicine," she commenced.
202.20 "Away, away with it!" I replied; !I de-

202.21 sire to have --"
203.01 "The doctor says you must drop the
203.02 powders."
203.03 "With all my heart! Don't interrupt me.
203.04 Come and take your seat here. Keep your
203.05 fingers from that bitter phalanx of vials. Draw
203.06 your knitting out of your pocket -- that will do
203.07 -- now continue the history of Mr. Heathcliff,
203.08 from where you left off, to the present day.
203.09 Did he finish his education on the Continent,
203.10 and come back a gentleman? or did he get a
203.11 sizer's place at college? or escape to America,
203.12 and earn honours by drawing blood from his
203.13 foster country? or make a fortune more
203.14 promptly, on the English highways?"
203.15 "He may have done a little in all these vo-
203.16 cations, Mr. Lockwood; but I couldn't give
203.17 my word for any. I stated before that I didn't
203.18 know how he gained his money; neither am I
203.19 aware of the means he took to raise his mind
203.20 from the savage ignorance into which it was
203.21 sunk; but, with your leave, I'll proceed in
203.22 my own fashion, if you think it will amuse,
204.01 and not weary you. Are you feeling better
204.02 this morning?"
204.03 "Much."
204.04 "That's good news. I got Miss Cathe-
204.05 rine and myself to Thrushcross Grange: and
204.06 to my agreeable disappointment, she behaved
204.07 infinitely better than I dared to expect. She
204.08 seemed almost over fond of Mr. Linton; and
204.09 even to his sister, she showed plenty of affec-
204.10 tion. They were both very attentive to her
204.11 comfort, certainly. It was not the thorn bend-
204.12 ing to the honeysuckles, but the honeysuckles
204.13 embracing the thorn. There were no mutual
204.14 concessions; one stood erect, and the others
204.15 yielded; and who \can# be ill-natured, and bad--
204.16 tempered, when they encounter neither oppo-
204.17 sition, nor indifference?
204.18 "I observed that Mr. Edgar had a deep--
204.19 rooted fear of ruffling her humour. He con-
204.20 cealed it from her; but if ever he heard me
204.21 answer sharply, or saw any other servant grow
204.22 cloudy at some imperious order of hers, he
205.01 would show his trouble by a frown of displea-
205.02 sure that never darkened on his own account.
205.03 He, many a time, spoke sternly to me about
205.04 my pertness; and averred that the stab of a
205.05 knife could not inflict a worse pang than he
205.06 suffered at seeing his lady vexed.
205.07 "Not to grieve a kind master I learnt to be
205.08 less touchy; and, for the space of half a year,
205.09 the gunpowder lay as harmless as sand, be-
205.10 cause no fire came near to explode it. Catherine
205.11 had seasons of gloom and silence, now and then,
205.12 they were respected with sympathizing silence
205.13 by her husband, who ascribed them to an al-
205.14 teration in her constitution, produced by her
205.15 perilous illness, as she was never subject to de-
205.16 pression of spirits before. The return of sun-
205.17 shine was welcomed by answering sunshine
205.18 from him. I believe I may assert that they
205.19 were really in possession of deep and growing
205.20 happiness.
205.21 "It ended. Well, we \must# be for our-
205.22 selves in the long run; the mild and generous
206.01 are only more justly selfish than the domineer-
206.02 ing -- and it ended when circumstances caused
206.03 each to feel that the one's interest was not the
206.04 chief consideration in the other's thoughts.
206.05 "On a mellow evening in September, I was
206.06 coming from the garden with a heavy basket
206.07 of apples which I had been gathering. It had
206.08 got dusk, and the moon looked over the high
206.09 wall of the court, causing undefined shadows
206.10 to lurk in the corners of the numerous project-
206.11 ing portions of the building. I set my burden
206.12 on the house steps by the kitchen door, and
206.13 lingered to rest, and draw in a few more
206.14 breaths of the soft, sweet air; my eyes were
206.15 on the moon, and my back to the entrance,
206.16 when I heard a voice behind me say --
206.17 "'Nelly, is that you?'
206.18 "It was a deep voice, and foreign in tone;
206.19 yet, there was something in the manner of
206.20 pronouncing my name which made it sound
206.21 familiar. I turned about to discover who
207.01 spoke, fearfully, for the doors were shut, and
207.02 I had seen nobody on approaching the steps.
207.03 "Something stirred in the porch; and mov-
207.04 ing nearer, I distinguished a tall man dressed
207.05 in dark clothes, with dark face and hair. He
207.06 leant against the side, and held his fingers on
207.07 the latch, as if intending to open for himself.
207.08 "'Who can it be?' I thought. 'Mr.
207.09 Earnshaw? Oh, no! The voice has no re-
207.10 semblance to his.'
207.11 "'I have waited here an hour,' he resumed,
207.12 while I continued staring; 'and the whole of
207.13 that time all round has been as still as death.
207.14 I dared not enter. You do not know me?
207.15 Look, I'm not a stranger!'
207.16 "A ray fell on his features; the cheeks were
207.17 sallow, and half covered with black whiskers;
207.18 the brows lowering, the eyes deep set and sin-
207.19 gular. I remembered the eyes."
207.20 "What!" I cried, uncertain whether to re-
207.21 gard him as a worldly visiter, and I raised my
208.01 hands in amazement. "What! you come
208.02 back? Is it really you? Is it?"

208.03 "Yes, Heathcliff," he replied, glancing from
208.04 me up to the windows which reflected a score
208.05 of glittering moons, but showed no lights from
208.06 within. "Are they at home -- where is she?
208.07 Nelly, you are not glad -- you needn't be so
208.08 disturbed. Is she here? Speak! I want to
208.09 have one word with her -- your mistress. Go,
208.10 and say some person from Gimmerton desires
208.11 to see her."
208.12 "How will she take it?" I exclaimed,
208.13 "what will she do? The surprise bewilders
208.14 me -- it will put her out of her head! And
208.15 you \are# Heathcliff! But altered! Nay,
208.16 there's no comprehending it. Have you been
208.17 for a soldier?"
208.18 "Go, and carry my message," he interrupted
208.19 impatiently; I'm in hell till you do!"
208.20 He lifted the latch, and I entered; but
208.21 when I got to the parlour where Mr. and Mrs.
209.01 Linton were, I could not persuade myself to
209.02 proceed.
209.03 At length, I resolved on making an excuse
209.04 to ask if they would have the candles lighted,
209.05 and I opened the door.
209.06 They sat together in a window whose lattice
209.07 lay back against the wall, and displayed beyond
209.08 the garden trees, and the wild green park, the
209.09 valley of Gimmerton, with a long line of mist
209.10 winding nearly to its top, /for very soon after
209.11 you pass the chapel, as you may have no-
209.12 ticed, the sough that runs from the marshes
209.13 joins a beck which follows the bend of the
209.14 glen//, wuthering Heights rose above this sil-
209.15 very vapour,; but our old house was invisible
209.16 -- it rather dips down on the other side.
209.17 Both the room, and its occupants, and the
209.18 scene they gazed on, looked wondrously
209.19 peaceful. I shrank reluctantly from perform-
209.20 ing my errand: and was actually going away,
209.21 leaving it unsaid, after having put my question
210.01 about the candles, when a sense of my
210.02 folly compelled me to return, and mutter:
210.03 "A person from Gimmerton wishes to see
210.04 you, ma'am."
210.05 "what does he want?" asked Mrs. Linton.
210.06 "I did not question him," I answered.
210.07 "well, close the curtains, Nelly," she said;
210.08 "and bring up tea. I'll be back again di-
210.09 rectly."
210.10 She quitted the apartment; Mr. Edgar in-
210.11 quired carelessly, who it was?
210.12 "Some one the mistress does not expect,"
210.13 I replied. "That Heathcliff, you recollect
210.14 him, sir, who used to live at Mr. Earnshaw's."
210.15 "what, the gipsy -- the plough-boy?" he
210.16 cried. "why did you not say so to Cathe-
210.17 rine?"
210.18 "Hush! you must not call him by those
210.19 names, master," I said. "She'd be sadly
210.20 grieved to hear you. She was nearly heart--
210.21 broken when he ran off; I guess his return
210.22 will make a jubilee to her."
211.01 Mr. Linton walked to a window on the
211.02 other side of the room that overlooked the
211.03 court. He unfastened it, and leant out. I
211.04 suppose they were below, for he exclaimed,
211.05 quickly:--
211.06 "Don't stand there love! Bring the person
211.07 in, if it be any one particular."
211.08 Ere long, I heard the click of the latch, and
211.09 Catherine flew up-stairs, breathless and wild,
211.10 too excited to show gladness; indeed, by her
211.11 face, you would rather have surmised an awful
211.12 calamity.
211.13 "Oh, Edgar, Edgar!" she panted, flinging
211.14 her arms round his neck. "Oh, Edgar, darl-
211.15 ing! Heathcliff's come back -- he is!" And
211.16 she tightened her embrace to a squeeze.
211.17 "well, well," cried her husband, crossly,
211.18 "don't strangle me for that! He never struck
211.19 me as such a marvellous treasure. There is
211.20 no need to be frantic!"
211.21 "I know you didn't like him," she an-
211.22 swered, repressing a little the intensity of her
212.01 delight. "yet for my sake, you must be
212.02 friends now. Shall I tell him to come up?"
212.03 "Here," he said, "into the parlour?"
212.04 "where else?" she asked.
212.05 He looked vexed, and suggested the kitchen
212.06 as a more suitable place for him.
212.07 Mrs. Linton eyed him with a droll expres-
212.08 sion -- half angry, half laughing at his fastidi-
212.09 ousness.
212.10 "No," she added, after a while; "I cannot
212.11 sit in the kitchen. Set two tables here, Ellen;
212.12 one for your master and Miss Isabella, being
212.13 gentry; the other for Heathcliff and myself,
212.14 being of the lower orders. Will that please
212.15 you dear? Or must I have a fire lighted else-
212.16 where? If so, give directions. I'll run down
212.17 and secure my guest. I'm afraid the joy is
212.18 too great to be real!"
212.19 She was about to dart off again; but Edgar
212.20 arrested her.
212.21 "\You# bid him step up," he said, addressing
212.22 me; "and, Catherine, try to be glad, without
213.01 being absurd! The whole household need not
213.02 witness the sight of your welcoming a runaway
213.03 servant as a brother."
213.04 I descended and found Heathcliff waiting
213.05 under the porch, evidently anticipating an in-

213.06 vitation to enter. He followed my guidance
213.07 without waste of words, and I ushered him
213.08 into the presence of the master and mistress,
213.09 whose flushed cheeks betrayed signs of warm
213.10 talking. But the lady's glowed with another
213.11 feeling when her friend appeared at the door;
213.12 she sprang forward, took both his hands, and
213.13 led him to Linton; and then she seized Lin-
213.14 ton's reluctant fingers and crushed them into
213.15 his.
213.16    Now fully revealed by the fire and candle--
213.17 light, I was amazed, more than ever, to behold
213.18 the transformation of Heathcliff. He had
213.19 grown a tall, athletic, well-formed man; be-
213.20 side whom, my master seemed quite slender
213.21 and youth-like. His upright carriage sug-
213.22 gested the idea of his having been in the army.
214.01 His countenance was much older in expression,
214.02 and decision of feature than Mr. Linton's; it
214.03 looked intelligent, and retained no marks of
214.04 former degradation. A half-civilized ferocity
214.05 lurked yet in the depressed brows, and eyes
214.06 full of black fire, but it was subdued; and his
214.07 manner was even dignified, quite divested of
214.08 roughness though too stern for grace.
214.09    My master's surprise equalled or exceeded
214.10 mine: he remained for a minute at a loss how
214.11 to address the ploughboy, as he had called
214.12 him; Heathcliff dropped his slight hand, and
214.13 stood looking at him coolly till he chose to
214.14 speak.
214.15    "Sit down, sir," he said, at length. "Mrs.
214.16 Linton, recalling old times, would have me
214.17 give you a cordial reception, and, of course, I
214.18 am gratified when anything occurs to please
214.19 her."
214.20    "And I also," answered Heathcliff, "espe-
214.21 cially if it be anything in which I have a
214.22 part. I shall stay an hour or two willingly."
215.01    He took a seat opposite Catherine, who kept
215.02 her gaze fixed on him as if she feared he
215.03 would vanish were she to remove it. He did
215.04 not raise his to her, often; a quick glance now
215.05 and then sufficed; but it flashed back, each
215.06 time, more confidently, the undisguised delight
215.07 he drank from hers.
215.08    They were too much absorbed in their mu-
215.09 tual joy to suffer embarrassment; not so Mr.
215.10 Edgar, he grew pale with pure annoyance, a
215.11 feeling that reached its climax when his lady
215.12 rose -- and stepping across the rug, seized
215.13 Heathcliff's hands again, and laughed like one
215.14 beside herself.
215.15    "I shall think it a dream to-morrow!" she
215.16 cried. "I shall not be able to believe that I
215.17 have seen, and touched, and spoken to you
215.18 once more -- and yet, cruel Heathcliff! you
215.19 don't deserve this welcome. To be absent and
215.20 silent for three years, and never to think of
215.21 me!"
215.22    "A little more than you have thought of
216.01 me!" he murmured. "I heard of your mar-
216.02 riage, Cathy, not long since; and, while wait-
216.03 ing in the yard below, I meditated this plan --
216.04 just to have one glimpse of your face -- a stare
216.05 of surprise, perhaps, and pretended pleasure;
216.06 afterwards settle my score with Hindley; and
216.07 then prevent the law by doing execution on
216.08 myself. Your welcome has put these ideas out
216.09 of my mind; but beware of meeting me with
216.10 another aspect next time! Nay, you'll not drive
216.11 me off again -- you were really sorry for me, were
216.12 you? Well, there was cause. I've fought
216.13 through a bitter life since I last heard your
216.14 voice, and you must forgive me, for I struggled
216.15 only for you!"
216.16    "Catherine, unless we are to have cold tea,
216.17 please to come to the table," interrupted Lin-
216.18 ton, striving to preserve his ordinary tone, and
216.19 a due measure of politeness. "Mr. Heath-
216.20 cliff will have a long walk, wherever he may
216.21 lodge to-night; and I'm thirsty."
217.01    She took her post before the urn; and Miss
217.02 Isabella came, summoned by the bell; then,
217.03 having handed their chairs forward, I left the
217.04 room.
217.05    The meal hardly endured ten minutes -- Ca-
217.06 therine's cup was never filled, she could nei-
217.07 ther eat, nor drink. Edgar had made a slop
217.08 in his saucer, and scarcely swallowed a mouth-
217.09 ful.
217.10    Their guest did not protract his stay, that
217.11 evening, above an hour longer. I asked, as he
217.12 departed, if he went to Gimmerton?
217.13    "No, to Wuthering Heights," he answered,
217.14 "Mr. Earnshaw invited me when I called this
217.15 morning."
217.16    Mr. Earnshaw invited \him#! and \he# called on
217.17 Mr. Earnshaw! I pondered this sentence pain-
217.18 fully, after he was gone. Is he turning out a
217.19 bit of a hypocrite, and coming into the country
217.20 to work mischief under a cloak? I mused -- I
217.21 had a presentiment, in the bottom of my heart,
217.22 that he had better have remained away.
218.01    About the middle of the night, I was wa-
218.02 kened from my first nap by Mrs. Linton glid-
218.03 ing into my chamber, taking a seat on my
218.04 bed-side, and pulling me by the hair to rouse
218.05 me.
218.06    "I cannot rest, Ellen," she said by way of
218.07 apology. "And I want some living creature

218.08 to keep me company in my happiness! Edgar
218.09 is sulky, because I'm glad of a thing that does
218.10 not interest him -- He refuses to open his
218.11 mouth, except to utter pettish, silly speeches;
218.12 and he affirmed I was cruel and selfish for
218.13 wishing to talk when he was so sick and sleepy.
218.14 He always contrives to be sick at the least
218.15 cross! I gave a few sentences of commenda-
218.16 tion to Heathcliff, and he, either for a head-
218.17 ache or a pang of envy, began to cry: so I got
218.18 up and left him."
218.19    "What use is it praising Heathcliff to
218.20 him?" I answered, "As lads they had an aver-
218.21 sion to each other, and Heathcliff would hate
218.22 just as much to hear him praised -- it's human
219.01 nature. Let Mr. Linton alone about him, un-
219.02 less you would like an open quarrel between
219.03 them."
219.04    "But does it not show great weakness?"
219.05 pursued she. "I'm not envious -- I never feel
219.06 hurt at the brightness of Isabella's yellow hair,
219.07 and the whiteness of her skin; at her dainty
219.08 elegance, and the fondness all the family ex-
219.09 hibit for her. Even you Nelly, if we have a
219.10 dispute sometimes, you back Isabella, at once;
219.11 and I yield like a foolish mother -- I call her a
219.12 darling, and flatter her into a good temper.
219.13 It pleases her brother to see us cordial, and
219.14 that pleases me. But, they are very much
219.15 alike they are spoiled children, and fancy the
219.16 world was made for their accommodation;
219.17 and, though I humour both, I think a smart
219.18 chastisement might improve them, all the
219.19 same."
219.20    "You're mistaken, Mrs. Linton," said I,
219.21 "They humour you -- I know what there
219.22 would be to do if they did not! You can well
220.01 afford to indulge their passing whims, as long
220.02 as their business is to anticipate all your de-
220.03 sires -- You may, however, fall out, at last,
220.04 over something of equal consequence to both
220.05 sides; and, then those you term weak are very
220.06 capable of being as obstinate as you!"
220.07    "And then we shall fight to the death,
220.08 shan't we, Nelly?" she returned laughing,
220.09 "No! I tell you, I have such faith in Linton's
220.10 love that I believe I might kill him, and he
220.11 wouldn't wish to retaliate."
220.12    I advised her to value him the more for his
220.13 affection.
220.14    "I do," she answered, "but, he needn't re-
220.15 sort to whining for trifles. It is childish;
220.16 and, instead of melting into tears, because
220.17 I said that Heathcliff was now worthy of any
220.18 one's regard, and it would honour the first
220.19 gentleman in the country to be his friend;
220.20 he ought to have said it for me, and been de-
220.21 lighted from sympathy -- He must get accus-
220.22 tomed to him, and he may as well like him --
221.01 considering how Heathcliff has reason to object
221.02 to him, I'm sure he behaved excellently!"
221.03    "What do you think of his going to Wu-
221.04 thering Heights?" I inquired. "He is reform-
221.05 ed in every respect, apparently -- quite a chris-
221.06 tian -- offering the right hand of fellowship to
221.07 his enemies all round!"
221.08    "He explained it," she replied, "I won-
221.09 dered as much as you -- He said he called to
221.10 gather information concerning me, from you,
221.11 supposing you resided there still; and Joseph
221.12 told Hindley who came out, and fell to ques-
221.13 tioning him of what he had been doing, and
221.14 how he had been living: and finally, desired
221.15 him to walk in -- There were some persons sit-
221.16 ting at cards -- Heathcliff joined them; my bro-
221.17 ther lost some money to him; and, finding him
221.18 plentifully supplied, he requested that he
221.19 would come again in the evening, to which he
221.20 consented. Hindley is too reckless to select
221.21 his acquaintance prudently; he doesn't trouble
221.22 himself to reflect on the causes he might have
222.01 for mistrusting one whom he has basely in-
222.02 jured -- But, Heathcliff affirms his principal
222.03 reason for resuming a connection with his
222.04 ancient persecutor is a wish to install himself
222.05 in quarters at walking distance from the
222.06 Grange, and an attachment to the house
222.07 where we lived together, and, likewise a hope
222.08 that I should have more opportunities of seeing
222.09 him there than I could have if he settled in
222.10 Gimmerton. He means to offer liberal pay-
222.11 ment for permission to lodge at the Heights;
222.12 and doubtless my brother's covetousness will
222.13 prompt him to accept the terms; he was al-
222.14 ways greedy, though what he grasps with one
222.15 hand, he flings away with the other."
222.16    "It's a nice place for a young man to fix
222.17 his dwelling in!" said I, "Have you no fear
222.18 of the consequences, Mrs. Linton?"
222.19    "None for my friend," she replied, "his
222.20 strong head will keep him from danger -- a lit-
222.21 tle for Hindley; but, he can't be made moral-
222.22 ly worse than he is; and I stand between
223.01 him and bodily harm -- The event of this
223.02 evening has reconciled me to God, and hu-
223.03 manity! I had risen in angry rebellion
223.04 against providence -- Oh, I've endured very,
223.05 very bitter misery, Nelly! If that creature
223.06 knew how bitter, he'd be ashamed to cloud
223.07 its removal with idle petulance -- It was kind-
223.08 ness for him which induced me to bear it

223.09 alone: had I expressed the agony I frequently
223.10 felt, he would have been taught to long for
223.11 its alleviation as ardently as I -- However, it's
223.12 over, and I'll take no revenge on his folly --
223.13 I can afford to suffer anything, hereafter!
223.14 should the meanest thing alive slap me on the
223.15 cheek, I'd not only turn the other, but, I'd
223.16 ask pardon for provoking it -- and, as a proof,
223.17 I'll go make my peace with Edgar instantly
223.18 -- Good night -- I'm an angel!"
223.19  In this self-complacent conviction she de-
223.20 parted; and the success of her fulfilled reso-
223.21 lution was obvious on the morrow -- Mr. Linton
224.01 had not only abjured his peevishness
224.02 /though his spirits seemed still subdued by
224.03 Catherine's exuberance of vivacity// but he
224.04 ventured no objection to her taking Isabella
224.05 with her to Wuthering Heights, in the after-
224.06 noon; and she rewarded him with such a sum-
224.07 mer of sweetness and affection, in return, as
224.08 made the house a paradise for several days;
224.09 both master, and servants profiting from the
224.10 perpetual sunshine.
224.11  Heathcliff -- Mr. Heathcliff I should say in
224.12 future, used the liberty of visiting at Thrush-
224.13 cross Grange cautiously, at first: he seemed
224.14 estimating how far its owner would bear his
224.15 intrusion. Catherine also, deemed it judicious
224.16 to moderate her expressions of pleasure in re-
224.17 ceiving him; and he gradually established his
224.18 right to be expected.
224.19  He retained a great deal of the reserve for
224.20 which his boyhood was remarkable, and that
224.21 served to repress all startling demonstrations
225.01 of feeling. My master's uneasiness experienced
225.02 a lull, and further circumstances diverted it in-
225.03 to another channel for a space.
225.04  His new source of trouble sprang from the
225.05 not anticipated misfortune of Isabella Linton
225.06 evincing a sudden and irresistible attraction
225.07 towards the tolerated guest -- She was at that
225.08 time a charming young lady of eighteen; in-
225.09 fantile in manners though possessed of keen
225.10 wit, keen feelings, and a keen temper, too, if
225.11 irritated. Her brother, who loved her tender-
225.12 ly, was appalled at this fantastic preference.
225.13 Leaving aside the degradation of an alliance
225.14 with a nameless man, and the possible fact
225.15 that his property, in default of heirs male,
225.16 might pass into such a one's power, he had
225.17 sense to comprehend Heathcliff's disposition
225.18 -- to know that, though his exterior was alter-
225.19 ed, his mind was unchangeable, and unchan-
225.20 ged. And he dreaded that mind; it revolted
225.21 him; he shrank forebodingly from the idea of
225.22 committing Isabella to its keeping.
226.01  He would have recoiled still more had he
226.02 been aware that her attachment rose unsoli-
226.03 cited, and was bestowed where it awakened no
226.04 reciprocation of sentiment; for the minute he
226.05 discovered its existence, he laid the blame on
226.06 Heathcliff's deliberate designing.
226.07  We had all remarked, during some time,
226.08 that Miss Linton fretted and pined over some-
226.09 thing. She grew cross and wearisome, snap-
226.10 ping at and teazing Catherine, continually, at
226.11 the imminent risk of exhausting her limited
226.12 patience. We excused her to a certain extent,
226.13 on the plea of ill health -- she was dwindling
226.14 and fading before our eyes -- But, one day
226.15 when she had been peculiarly wayward, reject-
226.16 ing her breakfast, complaining that the ser-
226.17 vants did not do what she told them; that the
226.18 mistress would allow her to be nothing in the
226.19 house, and Edgar neglected her; that she
226.20 had caught a cold with the doors being left
226.21 open, and we let the parlour fire go out on
226.22 purpose to vex her; with a hundred yet more
227.01 frivolous accusations; Mrs. Linton perempto-
227.02 rily insisted that she should get to-bed; and,
227.03 having scolded her heartily, threatened to send
227.04 for the doctor.
227.05  Mention of Kenneth, caused her to exclaim,
227.06 instantly, that her health was perfect, and it
227.07 was only Catherine's harshness which made
227.08 her unhappy.
227.09  "How can you say I am harsh, you naughty
227.10 fondling?" cried the mistress, amazed at the
227.11 unreasonable assertion. "You are surely
227.12 losing your reason. When have I been harsh,
227.13 tell me?"
227.14  "Yesterday," sobbed Isabella, "and now!"
227.15  "Yesterday!" said her sister-in-law. "On
227.16 what occasion?"
227.17  "In our walk along the moor; you told me
227.18 to ramble where I pleased, while you sauntered
227.19 on with Mr. Heathcliff!"
227.20  "And that's your notion of harshness?" said
227.21 Catherine, laughing. "It was no hint that
227.22 your company was superfluous; we didn't care
228.01 whether you kept with us or not; I merely
228.02 thought Heathcliff's talk would have nothing
228.03 entertaining for your ears."
228.04  "Oh, no," wept the young lady, "you
228.05 wished me away, because you knew I liked to
228.06 be there!"
228.07  "Is she sane?" asked Mrs. Linton, appeal-
228.08 ing to me. "I'll repeat our conversation,
228.09 word for word, Isabella; and you point out
228.10 any charm it could have had for you."
228.11  "I don't mind the conversation," she an-

228.12 swered: "I wanted to be with --"
228.13  "Well!" said Catherine, perceiving her
228.14 hesitate to complete the sentence.
228.15  "With him; and I wont be always sent off!"
228.16 she continued, kindling up. "You are a dog
228.17 in the manger, Cathy, and desire no one to
228.18 be loved but yourself!"
228.19  "You are an impertinent little monkey!"
228.20 exclaimed Mrs. Linton, in surprise. "But
228.21 I'll not believe this idiocy! It is impossible
228.22 that you can covet the admiration of Heathcliff
229.01 -- that you can consider him an agreeable per-
229.02 son! I hope I have misunderstood you,
229.03 Isabella?"
229.04  "No, you have not," said the infatuated
229.05 girl. "I love him more than ever you loved
229.06 Edgar; and he might love me if you would
229.07 let him!"
229.08  "I wouldn't be you for a kingdom, then!"
229.09 Catherine declared, emphatically -- and she
229.10 seemed to speak sincerely. "Nelly, help me
229.11 to convince her of her madness. Tell her
229.12 what Heathcliff is -- an unreclaimed creature,
229.13 without refinement -- without cultivation; an
229.14 arid wilderness of furze and whinstone. I'd
229.15 as soon put that little canary into the park on
229.16 a winter's day as recommend you to bestow
229.17 your heart on him! It is deplorable ignorance
229.18 of his character, child, and nothing else,
229.19 which makes that dream enter your head.
229.20 pray don't imagine that he conceals depths of
229.21 benevolence and affection beneath a stern ex-
229.22 terior! He's not a rough diamond -- a pearl-containing
230.01 oyster of a rustic; he's a fierce,
230.02 pitiless, wolfish man. I never say to him let
230.03 this or that enemy alone, because it would be
230.04 ungenerous or cruel to harm them -- I say let
230.05 them alone, because I/# should hate them to be
230.06 wronged: and he'd crush you, like a sparrow's
230.07 egg, Isabella, if he found you a troublesome
230.08 charge. I know he couldn't love a Linton;
230.09 and yet, he'd be quite capable of marrying
230.10 your fortune, and expectations. Avarice is
230.11 growing with him a besetting sin. There's my
230.12 picture; and I'm his friend -- so much so, that
230.13 had he thought seriously to catch you, I should,
230.14 perhaps, have held my tongue, and let you
230.15 fall into his trap."
230.16  Miss Linton regarded her sister-in-law with
230.17 indignation.
230.18  "For shame! for shame!" she repeated,
230.19 angrily. "You are worse than twenty foes,
230.20 you poisonous friend!"
230.21  "Ah! you wont believe me, then?" said
231.01 Catherine. "You think I speak from wicked
231.02 selfishness?"
231.03  "I'm certain you do," retorted Isabella;
231.04 "and I shudder at you!"
231.05  "Good!" cried the other. "Try for your-
231.06 self, if that be your spirit; I have done, and
231.07 yield the argument to your saucy insolence."
231.08  "And I must suffer for her egotism!" she
231.09 sobbed, as Mrs. Linton left the room. "All,
231.10 all is against me; she has blighted my single
231.11 consolation. But she uttered falsehoods,
231.12 didn't she? Mr. Heathcliff is not a fiend; he
231.13 has an honourable soul, and a true one, or how
231.14 could he remember her?"
231.15  "Banish him from your thoughts, miss," I
231.16 said. "He's a bird of bad omen; no mate for
231.17 you. Mrs. Linton spoke strongly, and yet, I
231.18 can't contradict her. She is better acquainted
231.19 with his heart than I, or any one besides; and
231.20 she never would represent him as worse than
231.21 he is. Honest people don't hide their deeds.
231.22 How has he been living? how has he got rich?
232.01 Why is he staying at Wuthering Heights, the
232.02 house of a man whom he abhors? They say
232.03 Mr. Earnshaw is worse and worse since he
232.04 came. They sit up all night together continu-
232.05 ally: and Hindley has been borrowing money
232.06 on his land; and does nothing but play and
232.07 drink, I heard only a week ago; it was Joseph
232.08 who told me -- I met him at Gimmerton."
232.09  "Nelly," he said, "we's hae a Crahnr's
232.10 'quest enah, at ahr folks. One on 'em's
232.11 a'most getten his finger cut off wi' hauding
232.12 t'other froo' sticking hisseln loike a cawlf.
232.13 That's maister, yah knaw, ut's soa up uh going
232.14 tuh t'grand 'sizes. He's noan feard uh t'
232.15 Bench uh judges, norther Paul, nur Peter,
232.16 nur John, nor Mathew, nor noan on 'em, nut
232.17 he! He fair like's he langs tuh set his braz-
232.18 ened face agean 'em! And yon bonny lad
232.19 Heathcliff, yah mind, he's a rare un! He
232.20 can girn a laugh, as weel's onybody at a
232.21 raight divil's jest. Does he niver say nowt of
232.22 his fine living amang us, when he goas tuh t'
233.01 Grange? This is t' way on't -- up at sun-dahn;
233.02 dice, brandy, cloised shutters, und can'le
233.03 lught till next day, at nooin -- then, t' fooil
233.04 gangs banning un raving tuh his cham'er,
233.05 makking dacent fowks dig thur fingers i' thur
233.06 higs fur varry shaume; un' the knave, wah
233.07 he carn cahnt his brass, un ate, un' sleep, un'
233.08 off tuh his neighbour's tuh gossip wi' t' wife.
233.09 I' course, he tells Dame Catherine hah her
233.10 father's goold runs intuh his pocket, and her
233.11 fathur's son gallops dahn t' Broad road, while
233.12 he flees afore tuh oppen t' pikes?" Now,
233.13 Miss Linton, Joseph is an old rascal, but no

233.14 liar; and, if his account of Heathcliff's con-
233.15 duct be true, you would never think of desir-
233.16 ing such a husband, would you?"
233.17 "You are leagued with the rest, Ellen!"
233.18 she replied. "I'll not listen to your slanders.
233.19 what malevolence you must have to wish to
233.20 convince me that there is no happiness in the
233.21 world!"
233.22 whether she would have got over this fancy
234.01 if left to herself, or persevered in nursing it
234.02 perpetually, I cannot say; she had little time
234.03 to reflect. The day after, there was a justice--
234.04 meeting at the next town; my master was
234.05 obliged to attend; and Mr. Heathcliff, aware of
234.06 his absence, called rather earlier than usual.
234.07 Catherine and Isabella were sitting in the
234.08 library, on hostile terms, but silent, The lat-
234.09 ter alarmed at her recent indiscretion, and the
234.10 disclosure she had made of her secret feelings
234.11 in a transient fit of passion; the former, on
234.12 mature consideration, really offended with her
234.13 companion; and, if she laughed again at her
234.14 pertness, inclined to make it no laughing mat-
234.15 ter to \her#.
234.16 She did laugh as she saw Heathcliff pass
234.17 the window. I was sweeping the hearth, and
234.18 I noticed a mischievous smile on her lips. Isa-
234.19 bella, absorbed in her meditations, or a book,
234.20 remained till the door opened, and it was too
234.21 late to attempt an escape, which she would
234.22 gladly have done had it been practicable.
235.01 "Come in, that's right!" exclaimed the
235.02 mistress, gaily, pulling a chair to the fire.
235.03 "Here are two people sadly in need of a third
235.04 to thaw the ice between them; and you are
235.05 the very one we should both of us choose.
235.06 Heathcliff, I'm proud to show you, at last,
235.07 somebody that dotes on you more than myself.
235.08 I expect you to feel flattered -- nay, it's not
235.09 Nelly; don't look at her! My poor little
235.10 sister-in-law is breaking her heart by mere
235.11 contemplation of your physical and moral
235.12 beauty. It lies in your own power to be
235.13 Edgar's brother! No, no, Isabella, you
235.14 sha'n't run off," she continued, arresting,
235.15 with feigned playfulness, the confounded girl
235.16 who had risen indignantly. "we were quar-
235.17 relling like cats about you, Heathcliff; and I
235.18 was fairly beaten in protestations of devotion,
235.19 and admiration; and, moreover, I was informed
235.20 that if I would but have the manners to stand
235.21 aside, my rival, as she will have herself to be,
235.22 would shoot a shaft into your soul that would
236.01 fix you for ever, and send my image into eter-
236.02 nal oblivion!"
236.03 "Catherine," said Isabella, calling up her
236.04 dignity, and disdaining to struggle from the
236.05 tight grasp that held her. "I'd thank you to
236.06 adhere to the truth and not slander me, even
236.07 in joke! Mr. Heathcliff, be kind enough to
236.08 bid this friend of yours release me -- she forgets
236.09 that you and I are not intimate acquaintances,
236.10 and what amuses her is painful to me beyond
236.11 expression."
236.12 As the guest answered nothing, but took
236.13 his seat, and looked thoroughly indifferent
236.14 what sentiments she cherished concerning him,
236.15 she turned, and whispered an earnest appeal
236.16 for liberty to her tormenter.
236.17 "By no means!" cried Mrs. Linton in
236.18 answer. "I wont be named a dog in the
236.19 manger again. You \shall# stay, now then!
236.20 Heathcliff, why don't you evince satisfaction
236.21 at my pleasant news? Isabella swears that
236.22 the love Edgar has for me, is nothing to that
237.01 she entertains for you. I'm sure she made
237.02 some speech of the kind, did she not, Ellen?
237.03 And she has fasted ever since the day before
237.04 yesterday's walk, from sorrow and rage that I
237.05 despatched her out of your society, under the
237.06 idea of its being unacceptable."
237.07 "I think you belie her," said Heathcliff,
237.08 twisting his chair to face them. "She wishes
237.09 to be out of my society now, at any rate!"
237.10 And he stared hard at the object of dis-
237.11 course, as one might do at a strange repulsive
237.12 animal, a centipede from the Indies, for in-
237.13 stance, which curiosity leads one to examine in
237.14 spite of the aversion it raises.
237.15 The poor thing couldn't bear that; she grew
237.16 white and red in rapid succession, and, while
237.17 tears beaded her lashes, bent the strength of
237.18 her small fingers to loosen the firm
237.19 clutch of Catherine, and perceiving that,
237.20 as fast as she raised one finger off
237.21 her arm, another closed down, and she could
237.22 not remove the whole together, she began to
238.01 make use of her nails, and their sharpness
238.02 presently ornamented the detainer's with cres-
238.03 cents of red.
238.04 "There's a tigress!" exclaimed Mrs. Linton,
238.05 setting her free, and shaking her hand with
238.06 pain. "Begone, for God's sake, and hide your
238.07 vixen face! How foolish to reveal those talons
238.08 to \him#. Can't you fancy the conclusions he'll
238.09 draw? Look, Heathcliff! they are instruments
238.10 that will do execution -- you must beware of
238.11 your eyes."
238.12 "I'd wrench them off her fingers, if they
238.13 ever menaced me," he answered, brutally, when
238.14 the door had closed after her. "But, what

238.15 did you mean by teasing the creature in that
238.16 manner, Cathy? You were not speaking the
238.17 truth, were you?"
238.18 "I assure you I was," she returned. "She
238.19 has been pining for your sake several weeks;
238.20 and raving about you this morning, and pour-
238.21 ing forth a deluge of abuse, because I repre-
238.22 sented your failings in a plain light for the
239.01 purpose of mitigating her adoration. But
239.02 don't notice it further. I wished to punish
239.03 her sauciness, that's all -- I like her too well,
239.04 my dear Heathcliff, to let you absolutely seize
239.05 and devour her up."
239.06 "And I like her too ill to attempt it," said
239.07 he, "except in a very ghoulish fashion. you'd
239.08 hear of odd things, if I lived alone with that
239.09 mawkish, waxen face; the most ordinary would
239.10 be painting on its white the colours of the
239.11 rainbow, and turning the blue eyes, black,
239.12 every day or two; they detestably resemble
239.13 Linton's."
239.14 "Delectably," observed Catherine. "They
239.15 are dove's eyes -- angel's!"
239.16 "She's her brother's heir, is she not?" he
239.17 asked, after a brief silence.
239.18 "I should be sorry to think so," returned
239.19 his companion. "Half-a-dozen nephews shall
239.20 erase her title, please Heaven! Abstract your
239.21 mind from the subject, at present -- you are too
239.22 prone to covet your neighbour's goods: re-
239.23 member \this# neighbour's goods are mine."
240.01 "If they were \mine#, they would be none
240.02 the less that," said Heathcliff, "but though
240.03 Isabella Linton may be silly, she is scarcely
240.04 mad; and -- in short we'll dismiss the matter as
240.05 you advise."
240.06 From their tongues, they did dismiss it;
240.07 and Catherine, probably, from her thoughts.
240.08 The other, I felt certain, recalled it often in
240.09 the course of the evening; I saw him smile to
240.10 himself -- grin rather -- and lapse into ominous
240.11 musing whenever Mrs. Linton had occasion
240.12 to be absent from the apartment.
240.13 I determined to watch his movements. My
240.14 heart invariably cleaved to the master's, in pre-
240.15 ference to Catherine's side; with reason, I im-
240.16 agined, for he was kind, and trustful, and hon-
240.17 ourable: and she -- she could not be called the
240.18 \opposite#, yet, she seemed to allow herself such
240.19 wide latitude, that I had little faith in her
240.20 principles, and still less sympathy for her feel-
240.21 ings. I wanted something to happen which
240.22 might have the effect of freeing both wuthering
241.01 Heights and the Grange of Mr. Heath-
241.02 cliff, quietly, leaving us as we had been prior
241.03 to his advent. His visits were a continual
241.04 nightmare to me; and, I suspected, to my
241.05 master also. His abode at the Heights was
241.06 an oppression past explaining. I felt that God
241.07 had forsaken the stray sheep there to its own
241.08 wicked wanderings, and an evil beast prowled
241.09 between it and the fold, waiting his time to
241.10 spring and destroy.
242.01 [VOL. 1 CHAPTER 11]
242.02 SOMETIMES, while meditating on these things
242.03 in solitude, I've got up in a sudden terror, and
242.04 put on my bonnet to go see how all was at the
242.05 farm; I've persuaded my conscience that it
242.06 was a duty to warn him how people talked re-
242.07 garding his ways; and then I've recollected
242.08 his confirmed bad habits, and, hopeless of
242.09 benefiting him, have flinched from re-entering
242.10 the dismal house, doubting if I could bear to
242.11 be taken at my word.
242.12 One time, I passed the old gate, going out of
243.01 my way, on a journey to Gimmerton. It was
243.02 about the period that my narrative has reached
243.03 -- a bright, frosty afternoon; the ground bare,
243.04 and the road hard and dry.
243.05 I came to a stone where the highway
243.06 branches off on to the moor at your left hand;
243.07 a rough sand-pillar, with the letters W.H.
243.08 cut on its north side, on the east, G., and on
243.09 the south-west, T.G. It serves as a guide-post
243.10 to the Grange, and Heights, and village.
243.11 The sun shone yellow on its grey head, re-
243.12 minding me of summer; and I cannot say
243.13 why, but all at once, a gush of child's sensa-
243.14 tions flowed into my heart. Hindley and I
243.15 held it a favourite spot twenty years before.
243.16 I gazed long at the weather-worn block;
243.17 and, stooping down, perceived a hole near the
243.18 bottom still full of snail-shells and pebbles
243.19 which we were fond of storing there with
243.20 more perishable things -- and, as fresh as rea-
243.21 lity, it appeared that I beheld my early play-
243.22 mate seated on the withered turf; his dark,
244.01 square head bent forward, and his little hand
244.02 scooping out the earth with a piece of slate.
244.03 "Poor Hindley!" I exclaimed, involuntarily.
244.04 I started -- my bodily eye was cheated into a
244.05 momentary belief that the child lifted its face
244.06 and stared straight into mine! It vanished in
244.07 a twinkling; but, immediately, I felt an irre-
244.08 sistible yearning to be at the Heights. Super-
244.09 stition urged me to comply with this impulse --
244.10 supposing he should be dead! I thought -- or
244.11 should die soon! -- supposing it were a sign of
244.12 death!
244.13 The nearer I got to the house the more agi-
244.14 tated I grew: and on catching sight of it, I

244.15 trembled every limb. The apparition had out-
244.16 stripped me; it stood looking through the
244.17 gate. That was my first idea on observing an
244.18 elf-locked, brown-eyed boy setting his ruddy
244.19 countenance against the bars. Further reflec-
244.20 tion suggested this must be Hareton, \my# Hare-
244.21 ton, not altered greatly since I left him, ten
244.22 months since.
245.01 "God bless thee, darling!" I cried, forget-
245.02 ting instantaneously my foolish fears. "Hare-
245.03 ton, it's Nelly -- Nelly, thy nurse."
245.04 He retreated out of arm's length, and picked
245.05 up a large flint.
245.06 "I am come to see thy father, Hareton," I
245.07 added, guessing from the action that Nelly, if
245.08 she lived in his memory at all, was not recog-
245.09 nised as one with me.
245.10 He raised his missile to hurl it; I com-
245.11 menced a soothing speech, but could not stay
245.12 his hand. The stone struck my bonnet, and
245.13 then ensued, from the stammering lips of the
245.14 little fellow, a string of curses which, whether
245.15 he comprehended them or not, were delivered
245.16 with practised emphasis, and distorted his baby
245.17 features into a shocking expression of malig-
245.18 nity.
245.19 You may be certain this grieved, more
245.20 than angered me. Fit to cry, I took an
245.21 orange from my pocket, and offered it to pro-
245.22 pitiate him.
246.01 He hesitated, and then snatched it from my
246.02 hold, as if he fancied I only intended to tempt,
246.03 and disappoint him.
246.04 I showed another keeping it out of his reach.
246.05 "who has taught you those fine words, my
246.06 barn," I inquired. "The curate?"
246.07 "Damn the curate, and thee! Gie me that,"
246.08 he replied.
246.09 "Tell us where you got your lessons, and
246.10 you shall have it," said I. "Whose your mas-
246.11 ter?"
246.12 "Devil daddy," was his answer.
246.13 "And what do you learn from Daddy?" I
246.14 continued.
246.15 He jumped at the fruit; I raised it higher.
246.16 "what does he teach you?" I asked.
246.17 "Naught," said he, "but to keep out of his
246.18 gait -- Daddy cannot bide me, because I swear
246.19 at him."
246.20 "Ah! and the devil teaches you to swear at
246.22 Daddy?" I observed.
246.22 "Aye -- nay," he drawled.
247.01 "who then?"
247.02 "Heathcliff."
247.03 I asked if he liked Mr. Heathcliff?
247.04 "Aye!" he answered again.
247.05 Desiring to have his reasons for liking him,
247.06 I could only gather the sentences. I known't
247.07 -- he pays Dad back what he gies to me -- he
247.08 curses Daddy for cursing me -- He says I mun
247.09 do as I will."
247.10 "And the curate does not teach you to read
247.11 and write, then?" I pursued.
247.12 "No, I was told the curate should have his
247.13 ---- teeth dashed down his ---- throat, if he
247.14 stepped over the threshold -- Heathcliff, had
247.15 promised that!"
247.16 I put the orange in his hand; and bade him
247.17 tell his father that a woman called Nelly Dean,
247.18 was waiting to speak with him, by the garden
247.19 gate.
247.20 He went up the walk, and entered the
247.21 house; but, instead of Hindley, Heathcliff ap-
247.22 peared on the door stones, and I turned directly
248.01 and ran down the road as hard as ever I could
248.02 race, making no halt till I gained the guide
248.03 post, and feeling as scared as if I had raised a
248.04 goblin.
248.05 This is not much connected with Miss Isa-
248.06 bella's affair; except, that it urged me to re-
248.07 solve further, on mounting vigilant guard, and
248.08 doing my utmost to check the spread of such
248.09 bad influence at the Grange, even though I
248.10 should wake a domestic storm, by thwarting
248.11 Mrs. Linton's pleasure.
248.12 The next time Heathcliff came, my young
248.13 lady chanced to be feeding some pigeons in the
248.14 court. She had never spoken a word to her
248.15 sister-in-law, for three days; but, she had
248.16 likewise dropped her fretful complaining, and
248.17 we found it a great comfort.
248.18 Heathcliff had not the habit of bestowing a
248.19 single unnecessary civility on Miss Linton, I
248.20 knew. Now, as soon as he beheld her, his
248.21 first precaution was to take a sweeping survey
248.22 of the house-front. I was standing by the
249.01 kitchen window, but I drew out of sight. He
249.02 then stept across the pavement to her, and
249.03 said something: she seemed embarrassed, and
249.04 desirous of getting away; to prevent it, he laid
249.05 his hand on her arm: she averted her face;
249.06 he apparently put some question which she had
249.07 no mind to answer. There was another rapid
249.08 glance at the house, and supposing himself un-
249.09 seen, the scoundrel had the impudence to em-
249.10 brace her.
249.11 "Judas! Traitor!" I ejaculated "you are a
249.12 hypocrite too, are you? A deliberate deceiver."
249.13 "who is Nelly?" said Catherine's voice at
249.14 my elbow -- I had been over-intent on watching
249.15 the pair outside to mark her entrance.

249.16 "Your worthless friend!" I answered warm-
249.17 ly, "the sneaking rascal yonder -- Ah, he has
249.18 caught a glimpse of us -- he is coming in! I
249.19 wonder will he have the art to find a plausible
249.20 excuse, for making love to Miss, when he told
249.21 you he hated her?"
249.22 Mrs. Linton saw Isabella tear herself free,
250.01 and run into the garden; and a minute after,
250.02 Heathcliff opened the door.
250.03 I couldn't withhold giving some loose to
250.04 my indignation; but Catherine angrily insisted
250.05 on silence, and threatened to order me out of
250.06 the kitchen, if I dared be so presumptuous as
250.07 to put in my insolent tongue.
250.08 "To hear you, people might think \you# were
250.09 the mistress!" She cried. "You want set-
250.10 ting down in your right place! Heathcliff,
250.11 what are you about, rising this stir? I said
250.12 you must let Isabella alone! -- I beg you will
250.13 unless you are tired of being received here, and
250.14 wish Linton to draw the bolts against
250.15 you!"
250.16 "God forbid that he should try!" answered
250.17 the black villain -- I detested him just then.
250.18 "God keep him meek and patient! Every
250.19 day I grow madder after sending him to hea-
250.20 ven!"
250.21 "Hush!" said Catherine shutting the inner
250.22 door! "Don't vex me. Why have you disregarded
251.01 my request? Did she come across
251.02 you on purpose?"
251.03 "what is it to you?" he growled, "I have
251.04 a right to kiss her, if she chooses, and you
251.05 have no right to object -- I'm not \your# husband
251.06 \you# needn't be jealous of me!"
251.07 "I'm not jealous of you;" replied the mis-
251.08 tress, "I'm jealous for you. Clear your face,
251.09 you shan't scowl at me! If you like Isabella,
251.10 you shall marry her. But, do you like her,
251.11 tell the truth, Heathcliff? There, you wont
251.12 answer. I'm certain you don't!"
251.13 "And would Mr. Linton approve of his sis-
251.14 ter marrying that man?" I inquired.
251.15 "Mr. Linton should approve," returned my
251.16 lady decisively.
251.17 "He might spare himself the trouble," said
251.18 Heathcliff, "I could do as well without his
251.19 approbation -- And, as to you, Catherine, I
251.20 have a mind to speak a few words, now, while
251.21 we are at it -- I want you to be aware that I
251.22 \know# you have treated me infernally -- infernally!
252.01 Do you hear? And, if you flatter
252.02 yourself that I don't perceive it you are a fool
252.03 -- and if you think I can be consoled by sweet
252.04 words you are an idiot -- and if you fancy I'll
252.05 suffer unrevenged, I'll convince you of the
252.06 contrary, in a very little while! Meantime,
252.07 thank you for telling me your sister-in-law's
252.08 secret -- I swear I'll make the most of it, and
252.09 stand you aside!"
252.10 "What new phase of his character is this?"
252.11 exclaimed Mrs. Linton, in amazement. "I've
252.12 treated you infernally -- and you'll take re-
252.13 venge! How will you take it, ungrateful
252.14 brute? How have I treated you infernally?"
252.15 "I seek no revenge on you," replied
252.16 Heathcliff less vehemently. "That's not the
252.17 plan -- The tyrant grinds down his slaves and
252.18 they don't turn against him, they crush those
252.19 beneath them -- You are welcome to torture me
252.20 to death for your amusement, only, allow me
252.21 to amuse myself a little in the same style --
252.22 And refrain from insult, as much as you are
253.01 able. Having levelled my palace, don't erect
253.02 a hovel and complacently admire your own
253.03 charity in giving me that for a home. If I
253.04 imagined you really wished me to marry Isa-
253.05 bella, I'd cut my throat!"
253.06 "Oh the evil is that I am \not# jealous, is
253.07 it?" cried Catherine. "Well, I won't repeat
253.08 my offer of a wife -- It is as bad as offering
253.09 Satan a lost soul -- Your bliss lies, like his, in
253.10 inflicting misery -- You prove it -- Edgar is res-
253.11 tored from the ill-temper he gave way to at
253.12 your coming; I begin to be secure and tran-
253.13 quil; and, you, restless to know us at peace,
253.14 appear resolved on exciting a quarrel -- quarrel
253.15 with Edgar if you please, Heathcliff, and de-
253.16 ceive his sister; you'll hit on exactly the most
253.17 efficient method of revenging yourself on
253.18 me."
253.19 The conversation ceased -- Mrs. Linton sat
253.20 down by the fire, flushed and gloomy. The
253.21 spirit which served her was growing intracta-
253.22 ble: she could neither lay nor control it. He
254.01 stood on the hearth, with folded arms brooding
254.02 on his evil thoughts; and in this position I
254.03 left them, to seek the master who was wonder-
254.04 ing what kept Catherine below so long.
254.05 "Ellen," said he, when I entered, "have
254.06 you seen your mistress?"
254.07 "Yes, she's in the kitchen, sir," I answered.
254.08 "She's sadly put out by Mr. Heathcliff's be-
254.09 haviour; and, indeed, I do think it's time to
254.10 arrange his visits on another footing. There's
254.11 harm in being too soft, and now it's come to
254.12 this --." And I related the scene in the court,
254.13 and, as near as I dared, the whole subsequent
254.14 dispute. I fancied it could not be very preju-
254.15 cial to Mrs. Linton, unless she made it so, af-
254.16 terwards, by assuming the defensive for her

254.17  guest.
254.18      Edgar Linton had difficulty in hearing me
254.19  to the close -- His first words revealed that he
254.20  did not clear his wife of blame.
254.21      "This is insufferable!" he exclaimed. "It
254.22  is disgraceful that she should own him for a
255.01  friend, and force his company on me! Call me
255.02  two men out of the hall, Ellen -- Catherine shall
255.03  linger no longer to argue with the low ruffian
255.04  -- I have humoured her enough."
255.05      He descended, and, bidding the servants
255.06  wait in the passage, went, followed by me, to
255.07  the kitchen. Its occupants had recommenced
255.08  their angry discussion; Mrs. Linton, at least,
255.09  was scolding with renewed vigour; Heathcliff
255.10  had moved to the window, and hung his head
255.11  somewhat cowed by her violent rating ap-
255.12  parently.
255.13      He saw the master first, and made a hasty
255.14  motion that she should be silent; which she
255.15  obeyed, abruptly, on discovering the reason of
255.16  his intimation.
255.17      "How is this?" said Linton, addressing her;
255.18  "what notion of propriety must you have to
255.19  remain here, after the language which has been
255.20  held to you by that blackguard? I suppose,
255.21  because it is his ordinary talk, you think no-
255.22  thing of it -- you are habituated to his baseness,
256.01  and, perhaps, imagine I can get used to it
256.02  too!"
256.03      "Have you been listening at the door,
256.04  Edgar?" asked the mistress, in a tone parti-
256.05  cularly calculated to provoke her husband, im-
256.06  plying both carelessness and contempt of his
256.07  irritation.
256.08      Heathcliff, who had raised his eyes at the
256.09  former speech, gave a sneering laugh at the
256.10  latter, on purpose, it seemed, to draw Mr.
256.11  Linton's attention to him.
256.12      He succeeded; but Edgar did not mean to
256.13  entertain him with any high flights of passion.
256.14      "I have been so far forbearing with you,
256.15  sir," he said, quietly; "not that I was igno-
256.16  rant of your miserable, degraded character,
256.17  but, I felt you were only partly responsible
256.18  for that; and Catherine, wishing to keep up
256.19  your acquaintance, I acquiesced -- foolishly.
256.20  Your presence is a moral poison that would
256.21  contaminate the most virtuous -- for that cause,
256.22  and to prevent worse consequences, I shall deny
257.01  you, hereafter, admission into this house, and
257.02  give notice, now, that I require your instant
257.03  departure. Three minutes' delay will render
257.04  it involuntary and ignominious."
257.05      Heathcliff measured the height and breadth
257.06  of the speaker with an eye full of derision.
257.07      "Cathy, this lamb of yours threatens like
257.08  a bull!" he said. "It is in danger of splitting
257.09  its skull against my knuckles. By God, Mr.
257.10  Linton, I'm mortally sorry that you are not
257.11  worth knocking down!"
257.12      My master glanced towards the passage,
257.13  and signed me to fetch the men -- he had no in-
257.14  tention of hazarding a personal encounter.
257.15      I obeyed the hint; but Mrs. Linton sus-
257.16  pecting something, followed, and when I at-
257.17  tempted to call them, she pulled me back,
257.18  slammed the door to, and locked it.
257.19      "Fair means!" she said, in answer to her
257.20  husband's look of angry surprise. "If you
257.21  have not the courage to attack him, make an
257.22  apology, or allow yourself to be beaten. It
258.01  will correct you of feigning more valour than
258.02  you possess. No, I'll swallow the key before
258.03  you shall get it! I'm delightfully rewarded
258.04  for my kindness to each! After constant in-
258.05  dulgence of one's weak nature, and the other's
258.06  bad one, I earn, for thanks, two samples of
258.07  blind ingratitude, stupid to absurdity! Edgar,
258.08  I was defending you, and yours; and I wish
258.09  Heathcliff may flog you sick, for daring to
258.10  think an evil thought of me!"
258.11      It did not need the medium of a flogging to
258.12  produce that effect on the master. He tried
258.13  to wrest the key from Catherine's grasp; and
258.14  for safety she flung it into the hottest part of
258.15  the fire; whereupon Mr. Edgar was taken
258.16  with a nervous trembling, and his counten-
258.17  ance grew deadly pale. For his life he could
258.18  not avert that access of emotion -- mingled
258.19  anguish and humiliation overcame him com-
258.20  pletely. He leant on the back of a chair, and
258.21  covered his face.
258.22      "Oh! Heavens! In old days this would
259.01  win you knighthood!" exclaimed Mrs. Linton.
259.02  "We are vanquished! we are vanquished!
259.03  Heathcliff would as soon lift a finger at you
259.04  as the king would march his army against a
259.05  colony of mice. Cheer up, you sha'n't be
259.06  hurt! Your type is not a lamb, it's a suck-
259.07  ing leveret."
259.08      "I wish you joy of the milk-blood
259.09  coward, Cathy!" said her friend. "I com-
259.10  pliment you on your taste: and that is the
259.11  slavering, shivering thing you preferred to me!
259.12  I would not strike him with my fist, but I'd
259.13  kick him with my foot, and experience consider-
259.14  able satisfaction. Is he weeping, or is he
259.15  going to faint for fear?"
259.16      The fellow approached and gave the chair
259.17  on which Linton rested a push. He'd better

259.18  have kept his distance: my master quickly
259.19  sprang erect, and struck him full on the throat
259.20  a blow that would have levelled a slighter man.
259.21      It took his breath for a minute; and, while
259.22  he choked, Mr. Linton walked out by the back
260.01  door into the yard, and from thence, to the
260.02  front entrance.
260.03      "There! you've done with coming here,"
260.04  cried Catherine. "Get away, now -- he'll re-
260.05  turn with a brace of pistols, and half-a-dozen
260.06  assistants. If he did overhear us, of course,
260.07  he'd never forgive you. You've played me an
260.08  ill turn, Heathcliff! But, go -- make haste! I'd
260.09  rather see Edgar at bay than you."
260.10      "Do you suppose I'm going with that blow
260.11  burning in my gullet?" he thundered. "By
260.12  Hell, no! I'll crush his ribs in like a rotten
260.13  hazel-nut, before I cross the threshold! If I
260.14  don't floor him now, I shall murder him some-
260.15  time, so, as you value his existence, let me
260.16  get at him!"
260.17      "He is not coming," I interposed, fram-
260.18  ing a bit of a lie. "There's the coachman,
260.19  and the two gardeners; you'll surely not wait
260.20  to be thrust into the road by them! Each has
260.21  a bludgeon, and master will, very likely, be
261.01  watching from the parlour windows to see that
261.02  they fulfil his orders."
261.03      The gardeners, and coachman were# there;
261.04  but Linton was with them. They had already
261.05  entered the court -- Heathcliff, on second
261.06  thoughts resolved to avoid a struggle against
261.07  three underlings; he seized the poker, smashed
261.08  the lock from the inner door, and made his
261.09  escape as they tramped in.
261.10      Mrs. Linton who was very much excited,
261.11  bid me accompany her up stairs. She did not
261.12  know my share in contributing to the disturb-
261.13  ance, and I was anxious to keep her in ignorance.
261.14      "I'm nearly distracted, Nelly!" she ex-
261.15  claimed, throwing herself on the sofa. "A
261.16  thousand smiths' hammers are beating in my
261.17  head! Tell Isabella to shun me -- this uproar
261.18  is owing to her; and should she or any one else
261.19  aggravate my anger at present, I shall get
261.20  wild. And, Nelly, say to Edgar, if you see
261.21  him again to-night, that I'm in danger of being
261.22  seriously ill -- I wish it may prove true. He
262.01  has startled and distressed me shockingly! I
262.02  want to frighten him. Besides, he might come
262.03  and begin a string of abuse, or complainings:
262.04  I'm certain I should recriminate, and God
262.05  knows where we should end! Will you do so,
262.06  my good Nelly? You are aware that I am
262.07  no way blameable in this matter. What pos-
262.08  sessed him to turn listener? Heathcliff's talk
262.09  was outrageous, after you left us; but I could
262.10  soon have diverted him from Isabella, and the
262.11  rest meant nothing. Now, all is dashed wrong
262.12  by the fool's-craving to hear evil of self that
262.13  haunts some people like a demon! Had Edgar
262.14  never gathered our conversation, he would
262.15  never have been the worse for it. Really, when
262.16  he opened on me in that unreasonable tone
262.17  of displeasure, after I had scolded Heathcliff
262.18  till I was hoarse for him#; I did not care, hardly,
262.19  what they did to each other, especially as I
262.20  felt that, however the scene closed, we should
262.21  all be driven asunder for nobody knows how
262.22  long! Well, if I cannot keep Heathcliff for
263.01  my friend -- if Edgar will be mean and jealous,
263.02  I'll try to break their hearts by breaking my
263.03  own. That will be a prompt way of finishing
263.04  all, when I am pushed to extremity! But it's
263.05  a deed to be reserved for a forlorn hope -- I'd
263.06  not take Linton by surprise with it. To this
263.07  point he has been discreet in dreading to
263.08  provoke me; you must represent the peril of
263.09  quitting that policy; and remind him of my
263.10  passionate temper, verging, when kindled, on
263.11  frenzy -- I wish you could dismiss that apathy
263.12  out of your countenance, and look rather more
263.13  anxious about me!"
263.14      The solidity with which I received these
263.15  instructions was, no doubt, rather exasperat-
263.16  ing; for they were delivered in perfect sincer-
263.17  ity, but I believe a person who could plan
263.18  the turning of her fits of passion to account,
263.19  beforehand, might, by exerting her will,
263.20  manage to control herself tolerably even while
263.21  under their influence; and I did not wish to
264.01  "frighten" her husband, as she said, and mul-
264.02  tiply his annoyances for the purpose of serving
264.03  her selfishness.
264.04      Therefore I said nothing when I met the
264.05  master coming towards the parlour; but I took
264.06  the liberty of turning back to listen whether
264.07  they would resume their quarrel together.
264.08      He began to speak first.
264.09      "Remain where you are, Catherine," he
264.10  said, without any anger in his voice, but with
264.11  much sorrowful despondency. "I shall not
264.12  stay. I am neither come to wrangle, nor be
264.13  reconciled; but I wish just to learn whether,
264.14  after this evening's events, you intend to con-
264.15  tinue your intimacy with --"
264.16      "Oh, for mercy's sake," interrupted the
264.17  mistress, stamping her foot, "for mercy's sake,
264.18  let us hear no more of it now! Your cold
264.19  blood cannot be worked into a fever -- your
264.20  veins are full of ice-water -- but mine are

244

264.21 boiling, and the sight of such chillness makes
264.22 them dance."
265.01 "To get rid of me -- answer my question,"
265.02 persevered Mr. Linton. "You \must# answer
265.03 it; and that violence does not alarm me. I
265.04 have found that you can be as stoical as any
265.05 one, when you please. Will you give up
265.06 Heathcliff hereafter, or will you give up me?
265.07 It is impossible for you to be \my# friend, and
265.08 \his# at the same time; and I absolutely \require#
265.09 to know which you choose."
265.10 "I require to be let alone!" exclaimed
265.11 Catherine, furiously. "I demand it! Don't
265.12 you see I can scarcely stand? Edgar, you --
265.13 you leave me!"
265.14 She rung the bell till it broke with a twang:
265.15 I entered leisurely. It was enough to try the
265.16 temper of a saint, such senseless wicked
265.17 rages! There she lay dashing her head
265.18 against the arm of the sofa, and grinding her
265.19 teeth, so that you might fancy she would crash
265.20 them to splinters!
265.21 Mr. Linton stood looking at her in sudden
266.01 compunction and fear. He told me to fetch
266.02 some water. She had no breath for speaking.
266.03 I brought a glass full; and, as she would not
266.04 drink, I sprinkled it on her face. In a few
266.05 seconds she stretched herself out stiff, and
266.06 turned up her eyes, while her cheeks, at once
266.07 blanched and livid, assumed the aspect of
266.08 death.
266.09 Linton looked terrified.
266.10 "There is nothing in the world the
266.11 matter," I whispered. I did not want him
266.12 to yield, though I could not help being afraid
266.13 in my heart.
266.14 "She has blood on her lips!" he said, shud-
266.15 dering.
266.16 "Never mind!" I answered, tartly. And I
266.17 told him how she had resolved, previous to
266.18 his coming, on exhibiting a fit of frenzy.
266.19 I incautiously gave the account aloud, and
266.20 she heard me, for she started up -- her hair
266.21 flying over her shoulders, here eyes flashing, the
267.01 muscles of her neck and arms standing out
267.02 preternaturally. I made up my mind for
267.03 broken bones, at least; but she only glared
267.04 about her, for an instant, and then rushed from
267.05 the room.
267.06 The master directed me to follow; I did, to
267.07 her chamber door; she hindered me from
267.08 going farther by securing it against me.
267.09 As she never offered to descend to breakfast
267.10 next morning, I went to ask whether she would
267.11 have some carried up.
267.12 "No!" she replied, peremptorily.
267.13 The same question was repeated at dinner,
267.14 and tea; and again on the morrow after, and
267.15 received the same answer.
267.16 Mr. Linton, on his part, spent his time in
267.17 the library, and did not inquire concerning his
267.18 wife's occupations. Isabella and he had had an
267.19 hour's interview, during which he tried to elicit
267.20 from her some sentiment of proper horror for
267.21 Heathcliff's advances; but he could make
267.22 nothing of her evasive replies, and was obliged
268.01 to close the examination, unsatisfactorily;
268.02 adding, however, a solemn warning, that if she
268.03 were so insane as to encourage that worthless
268.04 suitor, it would dissolve all bonds of relation-
268.05 ship between herself and him.
269.01 [VOL. 1 CHAPTER 12]
269.02 WHILE Miss Linton moped about the park and
269.03 garden, always silent, and almost always in
269.04 tears; and her brother shut himself up among
269.05 books that he never opened; wearying, I
269.06 guessed, with a continual vague expectation
269.07 that Catherine, repenting her conduct, would
269.08 come of her own accord to ask pardon, and
269.09 seek a reconciliation; and \she# fasted pertina-
269.10 ciously, under the idea, probably, that at every
269.11 meal, Edgar was ready to choke for her ab-
269.12 sence, and pride alone held him from running
270.01 to cast himself at her feet; I went about my
270.02 household duties, convinced that the Grange
270.03 had but one sensible soul in its walls, and that
270.04 lodged in my body.
270.05 I wasted no condolences on miss, nor any
270.06 expostulations on my mistress, nor did I pay
270.07 attention to the sighs of my master who
270.08 yearned to hear his lady's name, since he might
270.09 not hear her voice.
270.10 I determined they should come about as
270.11 they pleased for me; and though it was a tire-
270.12 somely slow process, I began to rejoice at
270.13 length in a faint dawn of its progress, as I
270.14 thought at first.
270.15 Mrs. Linton, on the third day, unbarred her
270.16 door; and having finished the water in her
270.17 pitcher and decanter, desired a renewed supply,
270.18 and a basin of gruel, for she believed she was
270.19 dying. That I set down as a speech meant
270.20 for Edgar's ears, I believed no such thing, so
270.21 I kept it to myself, and brought her some tea
270.22 and dry toast.
271.01 She eat and drank eagerly; and sank back
271.02 on her pillow again clenching her hands and
271.03 groaning.
271.04 "Oh, I will die," she exclaimed, "since no
271.05 one cares anything about me. I wish I had
271.06 not taken that."

271.07 Then a good while after I heard her murmur,
271.08 "No, I'll not die -- he'd be glad -- he does
271.09 not love me at all -- he would never miss me!"
271.10 "Did you want anything, ma'am?" I en-
271.11 quired, still preserving my external composure,
271.12 in spite of her ghastly countenance, and
271.13 strange exaggerated manner.
271.14 "What is that apathetic being doing?" she
271.15 demanded, pushing the thick entangled locks
271.16 from her wasted face. "Has he fallen into a
271.17 lethargy, or is he dead?"
271.18 "Neither," replied I; "if you mean Mr.
271.19 Linton. He's tolerably well, I think, though
271.20 his studies occupy him rather more than they
271.21 ought; he is continually among his books, since
271.22 he has no other society."
272.01 I should not have spoken so, if I had known
272.02 her true condition, but I could not get rid of
272.03 the notion that she acted a part of her dis-
272.04 order.
272.05 "Among his books!" she cried, confounded.
272.06 "And I dying! I on the brink of the grave!
272.07 My God! does he know how I'm altered?"
272.08 continued she, staring at her reflection in a
272.09 mirror, hanging against the opposite wall. "Is
272.10 that Catherine Linton? He imagines me in
272.11 a pet -- in play, perhaps. Cannot you inform
272.12 him that it is frightful earnest? Nelly, if it be
272.13 not too late, as soon as I learn how he feels,
272.14 I'll choose between these two -- either to starve,
272.15 at once, that would be no punishment unless
272.16 he had a heart -- or to recover and leave the
272.17 country. Are you speaking the truth about
272.18 him now? Take care. Is he actually so ut-
272.19 terly indifferent for my life?"
272.20 "Why, ma'am," I answered, "the master
272.21 has no idea of your being deranged; and, of
273.01 course, he does not fear that you will let your-
273.02 self die of hunger."
273.03 "You think not? Cannot you tell him I
273.04 will?" she returned; "persuade him -- speak
273.05 of your own mind -- say you are certain I
273.06 will!"
273.07 "No, you forget, Mrs. Linton," I suggested,
273.08 "that you have eaten some food with a relish
273.09 this evening, and to-morrow you will perceive
273.10 its good effects."
273.11 "If I were only sure it would kill him,"
273.12 she interrupted, "I'd kill myself directly!
273.13 These three awful nights, I've never closed my
273.14 lids -- and oh, I've been tormented! I've been
273.15 haunted, Nelly! But I begin to fancy you
273.16 don't like me. How strange! I thought,
273.17 though everybody hated and despised each
273.18 other, they could not avoid loving me -- and
273.19 they have all turned to enemies in a few hours.
273.20 \They# have, I'm positive; the people \here#.
273.21 How dreary to meet death, surrounded by their
273.22 cold faces! Isabella, terrified and repelled,
274.01 afraid to enter the room, it would be so dread-
274.02 ful to watch Catherine go. And Edgar stand-
274.03 ing solemnly by to see it over; then offering
274.04 prayers of thanks to God for restoring peace
274.05 to his house, and going back to his \books#!
274.06 What in the name of all that feels, has he to
274.07 do with \books#, when I am dying?"
274.08 She could not bear the notion which I had
274.09 put into her head of Mr. Linton's philosophi-
274.10 cal resignation. Tossing about, she increased
274.11 her feverish bewilderment to madness, and
274.12 tore the pillow with her teeth, then raising
274.13 herself up all burning, desired that I would
274.14 open the window. We were in the middle of
274.15 winter, the wind blew strong from the north-
274.16 east, and I objected.
274.17 Both the expressions flitting over her face,
274.18 and the changes of her moods, began to alarm
274.19 me terribly; and brought to my recollection
274.20 her former illness, and the doctor's injunction
274.21 that she should not be crossed.
274.22 A minute previously she was violent; now,
275.01 supported on one arm, and not noticing my re-
275.02 fusal to obey her, she seemed to find childish
275.03 diversion in pulling the feathers from the rents
275.04 she had just made, and ranging them on the
275.05 sheet according to their different species: her
275.06 mind had strayed to other associations.
275.07 "That's a turkey's," she murmured to her-
275.08 self; "and this is a wild-duck's; and this is a
275.09 pigeon's. Ah, they put pigeons' feathers in
275.10 the pillows -- no wonder I couldn't die! Let me
275.11 take care to throw it on the floor when I lie
275.12 down. And here is a moor-cock's; and this --
275.13 I should know it among a thousand -- it's a lap-
275.14 wing's. Bonny bird; wheeling over our heads
275.15 in the middle of the moor. It wanted to get
275.16 to its nest, for the clouds touched the swells,
275.17 and it felt rain coming. This feather was
275.18 picked up from the heath, the bird was not
275.19 shot -- we saw its nest in the winter, full of
275.20 little skeletons. Heathcliff set a trap over it,
275.21 and the old ones dare not come. I made him
275.22 promise he'd never shoot a lapwing, after that,
276.01 and he didn't. Yes, here are more! Did he
276.02 shoot my lapwings, Nelly? Are they red, any
276.03 of them? Let me look."
276.04 "Give over with that baby-work!" I inter-
276.05 rupted, dragging the pillow away, and turning
276.06 the holes towards the mattress, for she was re-
276.07 moving its contents by handfuls. "Lie down
276.08 and shut your eyes, you're wandering. There's

276.09 a mess! The down is flying about like snow!"
276.10 I went here and there collecting it.
276.11 "I see in you, Nelly," she continued,
276.12 dreamily, "an aged woman -- you have grey
276.13 hair, and bent shoulders. This bed is the
276.14 fairy cave under Peniston Crag, and you are
276.15 gathering elf-bolts to hurt our heifers; pre-
276.16 tending, while I am near, that they are only
276.17 locks of wool. That's what you'll come to
276.18 fifty years hence; I know you are not so now.
276.19 I'm not wandering, you're mistaken, or else I
276.20 should believe you really \were# that withered
276.21 hag, and I should think I \was# under Penistone
276.22 Crag, and I'm conscious it's night, and there
277.01 are two candles on the table making the black
277.02 press shine like jet.
277.03 "The black press? where is that?" I asked.
277.04 "you are talking in your sleep!"
277.05 "It's against the wall, as it always is," she
277.06 replied. "It \does# appear odd -- I see a face in
277.07 it!"
277.08 "There is no press in the room, and never
277.09 was," said I, resuming my seat, and looping up
277.10 the curtain that I might watch her.
277.11 "Don't \you# see that face?" she enquired,
277.12 gazing earnestly in the mirror.
277.13 And say what I could, I was incapable of
277.14 making her comprehend it to be her own; so
277.15 I rose and covered it with a shawl.
277.16 "It's behind there still!" she pursued, anxi-
277.17 ously. "And it stirred. Who is it?" I hope
277.18 it will not come out when you are gone! Oh!
277.19 Nelly, the room is haunted! I'm afraid of being
277.20 alone!"
277.21 I took her hand in mine, and bid her be com-
277.22 posed, for a succession of shudders convulsed
278.01 her frame, and she \would# keep straining her
278.02 gaze towards the glass.
278.03 "There's nobody here!" I insisted. "It was
278.04 \yourself#, Mrs. Linton; you knew it a while
278.05 since."
278.06 "Myself," she gasped, "and the clock is
278.07 striking twelve! It's true then; that's dread-
278.08 ful!"
278.09 Her fingers clutched the clothes, and gath-
278.10 ered them over her eyes. I attempted to steal
278.11 to the door with an intention of calling her
278.12 husband; but I was summoned back by a pierc-
278.13 ing shriek. The shawl had dropped from the
278.14 frame.
278.15 "why what \is# the matter?" cried I. "who
278.16 is coward now? wake up! That is the glass
278.17 -- the mirror, Mrs. Linton; and you see your-
278.18 self in it, and there am I too by your side."
278.19 Trembling and bewildered, she held me fast,
278.20 but the horror gradually passed from her coun-
278.21 tenance; its paleness gave place to a glow of
278.22 shame.
279.01 "Oh, dear! I thought I was at home," she
279.02 sighed. "I thought I was lying in my cham-
279.03 ber at Wuthering Heights. Because I'm
279.04 weak, my brain got confused, and I screamed
279.05 unconsciously. Don't say anything; but
279.06 stay with me. I dread sleeping, my dreams
279.07 appal me."
279.08 "A sound sleep would do you good, ma'am,"
279.09 I answered; "and I hope this suffering will
279.10 prevent your trying starving again."
279.11 "Oh, if I were but in my own bed in the
279.12 old house!" she went on bitterly, wringing her
279.13 hands. "And that wind sounding in the firs
279.14 by the lattice. Do let me feel it -- it comes
279.15 straight down the moor -- do let me have one
279.16 breath!"
279.17 To pacify her, I held the casement ajar, a
279.18 few seconds. A cold blast rushed through, I
279.19 closed it, and returned to my post.
279.20 She lay still, now: her face bathed in tears
279.21 -- exhaustion of body had entirely subdued
280.01 her spirit; our fiery Catherine was no better
280.02 than a wailing child!
280.03 "How long is it since I shut myself in
280.04 here?" she asked suddenly reviving.
280.05 "It was Monday evening," I replied, "and
280.06 this is Thursday night, or rather Friday morn-
280.07 ing, at present."
280.08 "what! of the same week?" she exclaimed.
280.09 "Only that brief time?"
280.10 "Long enough to live on nothing but cold
280.11 water, and ill-temper," observed I.
280.12 "well, it seems a weary number of hours,"
280.13 she muttered doubtfully, "it must be more -- I
280.14 remember being in the parlour, after they had
280.15 quarrelled; and Edgar being cruelly provok-
280.16 ing, and me running into this room desperate
280.17 -- As soon as ever I had barred the door, utter
280.18 blackness overwhelmed me, and I fell on the
280.19 floor -- I couldn't explain to Edgar how cer-
280.20 tain I felt of having a fit, or going raging
280.21 mad, if he persisted in teasing me! I had no
280.22 command of tongue, or brain, and he did not
281.01 guess my agony, perhaps; it barely left me
281.02 sense to try to escape from him and his voice
281.03 -- Before I recovered, sufficiently to see, and
281.04 hear, it began to be dawn; and Nelly, I'll tell
281.05 you what I thought, and what has kept recurring
281.06 and recurring till I feared for my reason -- I
281.07 thought as I lay there with my head against
281.08 that table leg, and my eyes dimly discerning
281.09 the grey square of the window, that I was
281.10 enclosed in the oak-panelled bed at home;

281.11 and my heart ached with some great grief
281.12 which, just waking, I could not recollect -- I
281.13 pondered, and worried myself to discover what
281.14 it could be; and most strangely, the whole
281.15 last seven years of my life grew blank! I
281.16 did not recall that they had been at all. I was
281.17 a child; my father was just buried, and my misery
281.18 arose from the separation that Hindley had
281.19 ordered between me, and Heathcliff -- I was
281.20 laid alone, for the first time, and rousing from
281.21 a dismal doze after a night of weeping -- I
281.22 lifted my hand to push the panels aside, it
282.01 struck the table-top! I swept it along the
282.02 carpet, and then, memory burst in -- my late
282.03 anguish was swallowed in a paroxysm of des-
282.04 pair -- I cannot say why I felt so wildly wretch-
282.05 ed -- it must have been temporary derangement
282.06 for there is scarcely cause -- But, supposing at
282.07 twelve years old, I had been wrenched from
282.08 the Heights, and every early association, and
282.09 my all in all, as Heathcliff was at that time,
282.10 and been converted, at a stroke into Mrs.
282.11 Linton, the lady of Thrushcross Grange, and
282.12 the wife of a stranger; an exile, and outcast,
282.13 thenceforth, from what had been my world --
282.14 You may fancy a glimpse of the abyss where
282.15 I grovelled! Shake your head, as you will,
282.16 Nelly, \you# have helped to unsettle me! You
282.17 should have spoken to Edgar, indeed you
282.18 should, and compelled him to leave me quiet!
282.19 Oh, I'm burning! I wish I were out of doors
282.20 -- I wish I were a girl again, half savage and
282.21 hardy, and free ... and laughing at injuries, not
282.22 maddening under them! why am I so
283.01 changed? why does my blood rush into a hell
283.02 of tumult at a few words? I'm sure I should
283.03 be myself were I once among the heather on
283.04 those hills ... Open the window again wide, fas-
283.05 ten it open! Quick, why don't you move?"
283.06 "Because, I won't give you your death of
283.07 cold," I answered.
283.08 "You won't give me a chance of life, you
283.09 mean," she said sullenly. "However, I'm not
283.10 helpless yet; I'll open it myself."
283.11 And sliding from the bed before I could hin-
283.12 der her, she crossed the room, walking very
283.13 uncertainly, threw it back, and bent out, care-
283.14 less of the frosty air that cut about her shoul-
283.15 ders as keen as a knife.
283.16 I entreated, and finally attempted to force
283.17 her to retire. But I soon found her delirious
283.18 strengh much surpassed mine; /she \was#
283.19 delirious I became convinced by her subsequent
283.20 actions, and ravings.//
283.21 There was no moon, and every thing be-
283.22 neath lay in misty darkness; not a light
284.01 gleamed from any house, far or near; all had
284.02 been extinguished long ago; and those at
284.03 wuthering Heights were never visible ... still
284.04 she asserted she caught their shining.
284.05 "Look!" she cried eagerly, "that's my
284.06 room, with the candle in it, and the trees
284.07 swaying before it ... and the other candle is in
284.08 Joseph's garret ... Joseph sits up late, doesn't
284.09 he? He's waiting till I come home that he
284.10 may lock the gate ... Well, he'll wait a while
284.11 yet. It's a rough journey, and a sad heart to
284.12 travel it; and we must pass by Gimmerton
284.13 Kirk, to go that journey! we've braved it's
284.14 ghosts often together, and dared each other to
284.15 stand among the graves and ask them to come
284.16 ...But Heathcliff, if I dare you now, will you
284.17 venture? If you do, I'll keep you. I'll not lie
284.18 there by myself; they may bury me twelve
284.19 feet deep, and throw the church down over
284.20 me; but I won't rest till you are with me ... I
284.21 never will!"
284.22 she paused, and resumed with a strange
285.01 smile, "He's considering ... he'd rather I'd come
285.02 to him! Find a way, then! not through that
285.03 kirkyard ... You are slow! Be content, you
285.04 always followed me!"
285.05 Perceiving it vain to argue against her in-
285.06 sanity, I was planning how I could reach
285.07 something to wrap about her, without quit-
285.08 ting my hold of herself; for I could not trust
285.09 her alone by the gaping lattice; when to my
285.10 consternation, I heard the rattle of the door--
285.11 handle, and Mr. Linton entered. He had on-
285.12 ly then come from the library; and, in passing
285.13 through the lobby, had noticed our talking
285.14 and been attracted by curiosity, or fear to ex-
285.15 amine what it signified, at that late hour.
285.16 "Oh, sir!" I cried, checking the exclama-
285.17 tion risen to his lips at the sight which met
285.18 him, and the bleak atmosphere of the chamber.
285.19 "My poor Mistress is ill, and she quite
285.20 masters me; I cannot manage her at all, pray,
285.21 come and persuade her to go to bed. Forget
286.01 your anger, for she's hard to guide any way
286.02 but her own."
286.03 "Catherine ill?" he said hastening to us.
286.04 "Shut the window, Ellen! Catherine! why..."
286.05 He was silent; the haggardness of Mrs.
286.06 Linton's appearance smote him speechless, and
286.07 he could only glance from her to me in hor-
286.08 rified astonishment.
286.09 "She's been fretting here," I continued, "and
286.10 eating scarcely anything, and never complain-
286.11 ing, she would admit none of us till this even-
286.12 ing, and so we couldn't inform you of her

286.13 state, as we were not aware of it ourselves,"
286.14 but it is nothing."
286.15 I felt I uttered my explanations awkwardly;
286.16 the master frowned. "It is nothing is it,
286.17 Ellen Dean?" he said sternly. "You shall
286.18 account more clearly for keeping me ignorant
286.19 of this!" And he took his wife in his arms,
286.20 and looked at her with anguish.
286.21 At first she gave him no glance of recognition
287.01 ... he was invisible to her abstracted gaze.
287.02 The delirium was not fixed, however; having
287.03 weaned her eyes from contemplating the outer
287.04 darkness; by degrees, she centred her atten-
287.05 tion on him, and discovered who it was that
287.06 held her.
287.07 "Ah! you are come, are you, Edgar Lin-
287.08 ton?" she said with angry animation... "You
287.09 are one of those things that are ever found
287.10 when least wanted, and when you are wanted
287.11 never! I suppose we shall have plenty of la-
287.12 mentations, now ... I see we shall ... but they
287.13 can't keep me from my narrow home out yon-
287.14 der -- My resting place where I'm bound be-
287.15 fore Spring is over! There it is, not among
287.16 the Lintons, mind, under the chapel-roof;
287.17 but in the open air with a head-stone, and you
287.18 may please yourself, whether you go to them,
287.19 or come to me!"
287.20 "Catherine, what have you done?" com-
287.21 menced the master. "Am I nothing to you,
288.01 any more? Do you love that wretch,
288.02 Heath --"
288.03 "Hush!" cried Mrs. Linton. "Hush, this
288.04 moment! You mention that name and I end
288.05 the matter, instantly, by a spring from the
288.06 window! what you touch at present, you
288.07 may have; but my soul will be on that hill-
288.08 top before you lay hands on me again. I don't
288.09 want you, Edgar; I'm past wanting you...
288.10 Return to your books ... I'm glad you possess
288.11 a consolation, for all you had in me is gone."
288.12 "Her mind wanders, sir," I interposed.
288.13 "She has been talking nonsense the whole
288.14 evening; but, let her have quiet and proper
288.15 attendance, and she'll rally ... Hereafter, we
288.16 must be cautious how we vex her."
288.17 "I desire no further advice from you," an-
288.18 swered Mr. Linton. "You knew your mis-
288.19 tress's nature, and you encouraged me to ha-
288.20 rass her. And not to give me one hint of how
288.21 she has been these three days! It was heartless!
289.01 months of sickness could not cause such a
289.02 change!"
289.03 I began to defend myself, thinking it too bad
289.04 to be blamed for another's wicked wayward-
289.05 ness!
289.06 "I knew Mrs. Linton's nature to be head-
289.07 strong and domineering," cried I; "but I
289.08 didn't know that you wished to foster her fierce
289.09 temper! I didn't know that, to humour her, I
289.10 should wink at Mr. Heathcliff. I performed
289.11 the duty of a faithful servant in telling you,
289.12 and I have got a faithful servant's wages!
289.13 well, it will teach me to be careful next time.
289.14 Next time you may gather intelligence for
289.15 yourself!"
289.16 "The next time you bring a tale to me, you
289.17 shall quit my service, Ellen Dean," he replied.
289.18 "You'd rather hear nothing about it, I sup-
289.19 pose, then, Mr. Linton?" said I. "Heathcliff
289.20 has your permission to come a courting Miss
289.21 and to drop in at every opportunity your absence
290.01 offers, on purpose to poison the mistress
290.02 against you?"
290.03 Confused as Catherine was, her wits were
290.04 alert at applying our conversation.
290.05 "Ah! Nelly has played traitor," she ex-
290.06 claimed, passionately. "Nelly is my hidden
290.07 enemy -- you witch! so you do seek elf-bolts
290.08 to hurt us! Let me go, and I'll make her rue!
290.09 I'll make her howl a recantation!"
290.10 A maniac's fury kindled under her brows;
290.11 she struggled desperately to disengage herself
290.12 from Linton's arms. I felt no inclination to
290.13 tarry the event; and resolving to seek medical
290.14 aid on my own responsibility, I quitted the
290.15 chamber.
290.16 In passing the garden to reach the road, at a
290.17 place where a bridle hook is driven into the
290.18 wall, I saw something white moved irregularly
290.19 evidently by another agent than the wind.
290.20 Notwithstanding my hurry, I staid to examine
290.21 it, lest ever after I should have the conviction
291.01 impressed on my imagination that it was a
291.02 creature of the other world.
291.03 My surprise and perplexity were great to
291.04 discover, by touch more than vision, Miss Isa-
291.05 bella's springer Fanny, suspended to a hand-
291.06 kerchief, and nearly at its last gasp.
291.07 I quickly released the animal, and lifted it
291.08 into the garden. I had seen it follow its mis-
291.09 tress up-stairs, when she went to bed, and won-
291.10 dered much how it could have got out there,
291.11 and what mischievous person had treated it so.
291.12 While untying the knot round the hook, it
291.13 seemed to me that I repeatedly caught the
291.14 beat of horses' feet galloping at some dis-
291.15 tance; but there were such a number of things
291.16 to occupy my reflections that I hardly gave the
291.17 circumstance a thought, though it was a
291.18 strange sound, in that place, at two o'clock in

291.19 the morning.
291.20 Mr. Kenneth was fortunately just issuing
291.21 from his house to see a patient in the village
291.22 as I came up the street; and my account of
292.01 Catherine Linton's malady induced him to ac-
292.02 company me back immediately.
292.03 He was a plain, rough man; and he made
292.04 no scruple to speak his doubts of her surviving
292.05 this second attack; unless she were more sub-
292.06 missive to his directions than she had shown
292.07 herself before.
292.08 "Nelly Dean," said he, "I can't help fan-
292.09 cying there's an extra cause for this. What
292.10 has there been to do at the Grange? We've
292.11 odd reports up here. A stout, hearty lass like
292.12 Catherine does not fall ill for a trifle; and that
292.13 sort of people should not either. It's hard
292.14 work bringing them through fevers, and such
292.15 things. How did it begin?"
292.16 "The master will inform you," I answered;
292.17 "but you are acquainted with the Earnshaw's
292.18 violent dispositions, and Mrs. Linton caps them
292.19 all. I may say this; it commenced in a quarrel.
292.20 She was struck during a tempest of passion with
292.21 a kind of fit. That's her account, at least; for
292.22 she flew off in the height of it, and locked
293.01 herself up. Afterwards, she refused to eat,
293.02 and now she alternately raves, and remains in
293.03 a half dream, knowing those about her, but
293.04 having her mind filled with all sorts of strange
293.05 ideas and illusions."
293.06 "Mr. Linton will be sorry?" observed Ken-
293.07 neth, interrogatively.
293.08 "Sorry? he'll break his heart should any-
293.09 thing happen!" I replied. "Don't alarm him
293.10 more than necessary."
293.11 "well, I told him to beware," said my com-
293.12 panion, "and he must bide the consequences
293.13 of neglecting my warning! Hasn't he been
293.14 thick with Mr. Heathcliff lately?"
293.15 "Heathcliff frequently visits at the Grange,"
293.16 answered I, "though more on the strength of
293.17 the mistress having known him when a boy,
293.18 than because the master likes his company.
293.19 At present, he's discharged from the trouble of
293.20 calling; owing to some presumptuous aspira-
293.21 tions after Miss Linton which he manifested.
293.22 I hardly think he'll be taken in again."
294.01 "And does Miss Linton turn a cold
294.02 shoulder on him?" was the doctor's next ques-
294.03 tion.
294.04 "I'm not in her confidence," returned I, re-
294.05 luctant to continue the subject.
294.06 "No, she's a sly one," he remarked, shak-
294.07 ing his head. "She keeps her own counsel!
294.08 But she's a real little fool. I have it from
294.09 good authority that, last night, and a pretty
294.10 night it was! she and Heathcliff were walking
294.11 in the plantation at the back of your house,
294.12 above two hours; and he pressed her not to
294.13 go in again, but just mount his horse and away
294.14 with him! My informant said she could only
294.15 put him off by pledging her word of honour
294.16 to be prepared on their first meeting after that,
294.17 when it was to be, he didn't hear, but you urge
294.18 Mr. Linton to look sharp!"
294.19 This news filled me with fresh fears; I out-
294.20 stripped Kenneth, and ran most of the way
294.21 back. The little dog was yelping in the gar-
294.22 den yet. I spared a minute to open the gate
295.01 for it, but instead of going to the house door,
295.02 it coursed up and down snuffing the grass, and
295.03 would have escaped to the road, had I not
295.04 seized and conveyed it in with me.
295.05 On ascending to Isabella's room, my sus-
295.06 picions were confirmed; it was empty. Had
295.07 I been a few hours sooner, Mrs. Linton's ill-
295.08 ness might have arrested her rash step. But
295.09 what could be done now? There was a bare
295.10 possibility of overtaking them if pursued in-
295.11 stantly. \I# could not pursue them, however;
295.12 and I dare not rouse the family, and fill the
295.13 place with confusion; still less unfold the busi-
295.14 ness to my master, absorbed as he was in his
295.15 present calamity, and having no heart to spare
295.16 for a second grief!
295.17 I saw nothing for it, but to hold my tongue,
295.18 and suffer matters to take their course; and
295.19 Kenneth being arrived, I went with a badly
295.20 composed countenance to announce him.
295.21 Catherine lay in a troubled sleep; her hus-
295.22 band had succeeded in soothing the access of
296.01 frenzy; he now hung over her pillow, watching
296.02 every shade, and every change of her painfully
296.03 expressive features.
296.04 The doctor, on examining the case for him-
296.05 self, spoke hopefully to him of its having a
296.06 favourable termination, if we could only pre-
296.07 serve around her perfect and constant tran-
296.08 quility. To me, he signified the threatening
296.09 danger was, not so much death, as permanent
296.10 alienation of intellect.
296.11 I did not close my eyes that night, nor did
296.12 Mr. Linton; indeed, we never went to bed:
296.13 and the servants were all up long before the
296.14 usual hour, moving through the house with
296.15 stealthy tread and exchanging whispers as
296.16 they encountered each other in their vocations.
296.17 Every one was active, but Miss Isabella; and
296.18 they began to remark how sound she slept --
296.19 her brother too asked if she has risen, and

296.20 seemed impatient for her presence, and hurt
296.21 that she showed so little anxiety for her sister--
296.22 in-law.
297.01 I trembled lest he should send me to call
297.02 her; but I was spared the pain of being the
297.03 first proclaimant of her flight. One of the
297.04 maids, a thoughtless girl, who had been on an
297.05 early errand to Gimmerton, came panting up
297.06 stairs, open-mouthed, and dashed into the
297.07 chamber, crying.
297.08 "Oh, dear, dear! What mun we have
297.09 next? Master, master, our young lady -- "
297.10 "Hold your noise!" cried I hastily, enraged
297.11 at her clamourous manner.
297.12 "Speak lower, Mary -- what is the matter?"
297.13 said Mr. Linton. "What ails your young
297.14 lady?"
297.15 "She's gone, she's gone! Yon' Heathcliff's
297.16 run off wi' her!" gasped the girl.
297.17 "That is not true!" exclaimed Linton, rising
297.18 in agitation. "It cannot be -- how has the
297.19 idea entered your head? Ellen Dean, go and
297.20 seek her -- it is incredible -- it cannot be."
297.21 As he spoke he took the servant to the door,
298.01 and, then, repeated his demand to know her
298.02 reasons for such an assertion.
298.03 "Why, I met on the road a lad that fetches
298.04 milk here," she stammered, "and he asked
298.05 whether we wern't in trouble at the Grange --
298.06 I thought he meant for Missis's sickness, so I
298.07 answered, yes. Then says he, they's some-
298.08 body gone after 'em I guess?" I stared. He
298.09 saw I knew naught about it, and he told how
298.10 a gentleman and lady had stopped to have a
298.11 horse's shoe fastened at a blacksmith's shop,
298.12 two miles out of Gimmerton, not very long
298.13 after midnight! and how the blacksmith's lass
298.14 had got up to spy who they were: she knew
298.15 them both directly -- And she noticed the man,
298.16 Heathcliff it was, she felt certain, nob'dy
298.17 could mistake him, besides -- put a sovereign
298.18 in her father's hand for payment. The lady
298.19 had a cloak about her face; but having desired
298.20 a sup of water, while she drank, it fell back,
298.21 and she saw her very plain -- Heathcliff held
299.01 both bridles as they rode on, and they set
299.02 their faces from the village, and went as fast
299.03 as the rough roads would let them. The lass
299.04 said nothing to her father, but she told it al
299.05 over Gimmerton this morning."
299.06 I ran and peeped, for form's sake into Isa-
299.07 bella's room: confirming, when I returned, the
299.08 servant's statement -- Mr. Linton had resumed
299.09 his seat by the bed; on my re-entrance, he
299.10 raised his eyes, read the meaning of my blank
299.11 aspect, and dropped them without giving an
299.12 order, or uttering a word.
299.13 "Are we to try any measures for overtaking
299.14 and bringing her back," I inquired. "How
299.15 should we do?"
299.16 "She went of her own accord," answered
299.17 the master; "she had a right to go if she
299.18 pleased -- Trouble me no more about her --
299.19 Hereafter she is only my sister in name; not
299.20 because I disown her, but because she has dis-
299.21 owned me."
299.22 And that was all he said on the subject; he
300.01 did not make a single inquiry further, or men-
300.02 tion her in any way, except directing me to
300.03 send what property she had in the house to
300.04 her fresh home, wherever it was, when I knew
300.05 it.
301.01 [VOL. 1 CHAPTER 13]
301.02 FOR two months the fugitives remained absent,
301.03 in those two months, Mrs. Linton encountered
301.04 and conquered the worst shock of what was
301.05 denominated a brain fever. No mother could
301.06 have nursed an only child more devotedly than
301.07 Edgar tended her. Day and night, he was
301.08 watching, and patiently enduring all the an-
301.09 noyances that irritable nerves and a shaken
301.10 reason could inflict: and, though Kenneth re-
301.11 marked that what he saved from the grave
302.01 would only recompense his care by forming
302.02 the source of constant future anxiety, in fact,
302.03 that his health and strength were being sacri-
302.04 ficed to preserve a mere ruin of humanity, he
302.05 knew no limits in gratitude and joy, when
302.06 Catherine's life was declared out of danger;
302.07 and hour after hour, he would sit beside her,
302.08 tracing the gradual return to bodily health,
302.09 and flattering his too sanguine hopes with the
302.10 illusion that her mind would settle back to its
302.11 right balance also, and she would soon be en-
302.12 tirely her former self.
302.13 The first time she left her chamber, was at
302.14 the commencement of the following March.
302.15 Mr. Linton had put on her pillow, in the
302.16 morning, a handful of golden crocuses; her
302.17 eye, long stranger to any gleam of pleasure,
302.18 caught them in waking, and shone delighted as
302.19 she gathered them eagerly together.
302.20 "These are the earliest flowers at the
302.21 Heights!" she exclaimed. "They remind me
302.22 of soft thaw winds, and warm sunshine, and
303.01 nearly melted snow -- Edgar, is there not a
303.02 south wind, and is not the snow almost gone?"
303.03 "The snow is quite gone; down here, dar-
303.04 ling!" replied her husband, "and I only see
303.05 two white spots on the whole range of moors --
303.06 The sky is blue, and the larks are singing, and the

303.07 becks and brooks are all brim full. Catherine;
303.08 last spring at this time, I was longing to have
303.09 you under this roof -- now, I wish you were a
303.10 mile or two up those hills, the air blows so
303.11 sweetly, I feel that it would cure you."
303.12 "I shall never be there, but once more!"
303.13 said the invalid; "and then you'll leave me,
303.14 and I shall remain, for ever. Next spring
303.15 you'll long again to have me under this roof,
303.16 and you'll look back and think you were happy
303.17 to-day."
303.18 Linton lavished on her the kindest caresses,
303.19 and tried to cheer her by the fondest words;
303.20 but vaguely regarding the flowers, she let
303.21 the tears collect on her lashes, and stream
303.22 down her cheeks unheeding.
304.01 We knew she was really better, and there-
304.02 fore, decided that long confinement to a single
304.03 place produced much of this despondency, and
304.04 it might be partially removed by a change of
304.05 scene.
304.06 The master told me to light a fire in the
304.07 many-week's deserted parlour, and to set an
304.08 easy-chair in the sunshine by the window;
304.09 and then he brought her down, and she sat a
304.10 long while enjoying the genial heat, and, as
304.11 we expected, revived by the objects round her,
304.12 which, though familiar, were free from the
304.13 dreary associations investing her hated sick--
304.14 chamber. By evening, she seemed greatly ex-
304.15 hausted; yet no arguments could persuade her
304.16 to return to that apartment, and I had to ar-
304.17 range the parlour sofa for her bed, till another
304.18 room could be prepared.
304.19 To obviate the fatigue of mounting and de-
304.20 scending the stairs, we fitted up this, where
304.21 you lie at present; on the same floor with the
304.22 parlour: and she was soon strong enough to
305.01 move from one to the other, leaning on Edgar's
305.02 arm.
305.03 Ah, I thought myself, she might recover,
305.04 so waited on as she was. And there was dou-
305.05 ble cause to desire it, for on her existence de-
305.06 pended that of another; we cherished the hope
305.07 that in a little while, Mr. Linton's heart would
305.08 be gladdened, and his lands secured from a
305.09 stranger's gripe, by the birth of an heir.
305.10 I should mention that Isabella sent to her
305.11 brother, some six weeks from her departure a
305.12 short note, announcing her marriage with
305.13 Heathcliff. It appeared dry and cold; but at
305.14 the bottom, was dotted in with pencil, an ob-
305.15 scure apology, and an entreaty for kind remem-
305.16 brance, and reconciliation, if her proceeding
305.17 had offended him; asserting that she could not
305.18 help it then, and being done, she had now no
305.19 power to repeal it.
305.20 Linton did not reply to this, I believe; and,
305.21 in a fortnight more, I got a long letter which
305.22 I considered odd coming from the pen of a
306.01 bride just out of the honeymoon, I'll read it,
306.02 for I keep it yet. Any relic of the dead is
306.03 precious, if they were valued living.
306.04 "DEAR ELLEN," it begins.
306.05 "I came, last night, to Wuthering Heights,
306.06 and heard, for the first time, that Catherine
306.07 has been, and is yet, very ill. I must not
306.08 write to her I suppose, and my brother is ei-
306.09 ther too angry, or too distressed to answer
306.10 what I send him. Still, I must write to some-
306.11 body, and the only choice left me is you.
306.12 Inform Edgar that I'd give the world to see
306.13 his face again -- that my heart returned to
306.14 Thrushcross Grange in twenty-four hours
306.15 after I left it, and is there at this moment, full
306.16 of warm feelings for him, and Catherine! \I#
306.17 \can't# \follow# \it# \though# -- /those words are under-
306.18 lined// they need not expect me, and they may
306.19 draw what conclusions they please; taking
306.20 care however, to lay nothing at the door of
306.21 my weak will, or deficient affection.
307.01 The remainder of the letter is for yourself,
307.02 alone. I want to ask you two questions: the
307.03 first is,
307.04 How did you contrive to preserve the com-
307.05 mon sympathies of human nature when you
307.06 resided here? I cannot recognise any senti-
307.07 ment which those around, share with me.
307.08 The second question, I have great interest
307.09 in; it is this --
307.10 Is Mr. Heathcliff a man? If so, is he mad?
307.11 And if not, is he a devil? I shan't tell my
307.12 reasons for making this inquiry; but, I be-
307.13 seech you to explain, if you can, what I have
307.14 married -- that is, when you call to see me;
307.15 and you must call Ellen, very soon. Don't
307.16 write, but come, and bring me something from
307.17 Edgar.
307.18 Now, you shall hear how I have been re-
307.19 ceived in my new home, as I am led to ima-
307.20 gine the Heights will be. It is to amuse my-
307.21 self that I dwell on such subjects as the lack
307.22 of external comforts; they never occupy my
308.01 thoughts, except at the moment when I miss
308.02 them -- I should laugh and dance for joy, if I
308.03 found their absence was the total of my mise-
308.04 ries, and the rest was an unnatural dream!
308.05 The sun set behind the Grange, as we
308.06 turned on to the moors; by that, I judged it
308.07 to be six o'clock; and my companion halted
308.08 half-an-hour, to inspect the park, and the

308.09 gardens, and, probably, the place itself, as
308.10 well as he could; so it was dark when we
308.11 dismounted in the paved yard of the farm-
308.12 house, and your old fellow-servant, Joseph,
308.13 issued out to receive us by the light of a dip
308.14 candle. He did it with a courtesy that re-
308.15 dounded to his credit. His first act was to
308.16 elevate his torch to a level with my face, squint
308.17 malignantly, project his under lip, and turn
308.18 away.
308.19     Then he took the two horses, and led them
308.20 into the stables; reappearing for the purpose
308.21 of locking the outer gate, as if we lived in an
308.22 ancient castle.
309.01     Heathcliff stayed to speak to him, and I
309.02 entered the kitchen -- a dingy, untidy hole; I
309.03 dare say you would not know it, it is so
309.04 changed since it was in your charge.
309.05     By the fire stood a ruffianly child, strong
309.06 in limb, and dirty in garb, with a look of
309.07 Catherine in his eyes, and about his mouth.
309.08     "This is Edgar's legal nephew," I reflected
309.09 -- "mine in a manner; I must shake hands,
309.10 and -- yes -- I must kiss him. It is right to
309.11 establish a good understanding at the begin-
309.12 ning."
309.13     I approached, and, attempting to take his
309.14 chubby fist, said --
309.15     "How do you do, my dear?"
309.16     He replied in a jargon I did not comprehend.
309.17     "Shall you and I be friends, Hareton?" was
309.18 my next essay at conversation.
309.19     An oath, and a threat to set Throttler on me
309.20 if I did not "frame off" rewarded my perse-
309.21 verance.
309.22     "Hey, Throttler, lad!" whispered the little
310.01 wretch, rousing a half-bred bull-dog from its
310.02 lair in a corner. "Now, wilt tuh be ganging?"
310.03 he asked authoritatively.
310.04     Love for my life urged a compliance; I
310.05 stepped over the threshold to wait till the
310.06 others should enter. Mr. Heathcliff was no-
310.07 where visible; and Joseph, whom I followed
310.08 to the stables, and requested to accompany me
310.09 in, after staring and muttering to himself,
310.10 screwed up his nose and replied --
310.11     "Mim! mim! mim! Did iver Christian
310.12 body hear owt like it? Minching un' munch-
310.13 ing! Hah can Aw tell whet ye say?"
310.14     "I say, I wish you to come with me into
310.15 the house!" I cried, thinking him deaf, yet
310.16 highly disgusted at his rudeness.
310.17     "Nor nuh me! Aw getten summut else to
310.18 do," he answered, and continued his work, mov-
310.19 ing his lantern jaws meanwhile, and surveying
310.20 my dress and countenance /the former a great
310.21 deal too fine, but the latter, I'm sure, as sad
310.22 as he could desire// with sovereign contempt.
311.01     I walked round the yard, and through a
311.02 wicket, to another door, at which I took the
311.03 liberty of knocking, in hopes some more civil
311.04 servant might shew himself.
311.05     After a short suspense it was opened by a
311.06 tall, gaunt man, without neckerchief, and
311.07 otherwise extremely slovenly; his features
311.08 were lost in masses of shaggy hair that hung
311.09 on his shoulders; and \his# eyes, too, were like
311.10 a ghostly Catherine's, with all their beauty
311.11 annihilated.
311.12     "What's your business here?" he demanded,
311.13 grimly. "Who are you?"
311.14     "My name \was# Isabella Linton," I replied.
311.15 "You've seen me before, sir. I'm lately
311.16 married to Mr. Heathcliff; and he has brought
311.17 me here -- I suppose by your permission."
311.18     "Is he come back, then?" asked the hermit,
311.19 glaring like a hungry wolf.
311.20     "Yes -- we came just now," I said; "but
311.21 he left me by the kitchen door; and when I
311.22 would have gone in, your little boy played
312.01 sentinel over the place, and frightened me off
312.02 by the help of a bull-dog."
312.03     "It's well the hellish villain has kept his
312.04 word!" growled my future host, searching the
312.05 darkness beyond me in expectation of discover-
312.06 ing Heathcliff, and then he indulged in a
312.07 soliloquy of execrations, and threats of what
312.08 he would have done had the "fiend" deceived
312.09 him.
312.10     I repented having tried this second entrance;
312.11 and was almost inclined to slip away before
312.12 he finished cursing, but ere I could execute
312.13 that intention, he ordered me in, and shut and
312.14 re-fastened the door.
312.15     There was a great fire, and that was all the
312.16 light in the huge apartment, whose floor had
312.17 grown a uniform grey; and the once brilliant
312.18 pewter dishes which used to attract my gaze
312.19 when I was a girl partook of a similar obscurity,
312.20 created by tarnish and dust.
312.21     I inquired whether I might call the maid,
312.22 and be conducted to a bed-room? Mr. Earnshaw
313.01 vouchsafed no answer. He walked up
313.02 and down, with his hands in his pockets, ap-
313.03 parently quite forgetting my presence; and
313.04 his abstraction was evidently so deep, and his
313.05 whole aspect so misanthropical, that I shrank
313.06 from disturbing him again.
313.07     "You'll not be surprised, Ellen, at my feeling
313.08 particularly cheerless, seated in worse than
313.09 solitude, on that inhospitable hearth, and re-

313.10 membering that four miles distant lay my
313.11 delightful home, containing the only people I
313.12 loved on earth: and there might as well be
313.13 the Atlantic to part us, instead of those four
313.14 miles, I could not overpass them!
313.15     I questioned with myself -- where must I
313.16 turn for comfort? and -- mind you don't tell
313.17 Edgar, or Catherine -- above every sorrow
313.18 beside, this rose pre-eminent -- despair at find-
313.19 ing nobody who could or would be my ally
313.20 against Heathcliff!
313.21     I had sought shelter at Wuthering Heights,
313.22 almost gladly, because I was secured by that
314.01 arrangement from living alone with him; but
314.02 he knew the people we were coming amongst,
314.03 and he did not fear their intermeddling.
314.04     I sat and thought a doleful time; the clock
314.05 struck eight, and nine, and still my companion
314.06 paced to and fro, his head bent on his breast,
314.07 and perfectly silent, unless a groan, or a bitter
314.08 ejaculation forced itself out at intervals.
314.09     I listened to detect a woman's voice in the
314.10 house, and filled the interim with wild regrets,
314.11 and dismal anticipations, which, at last, spoke
314.12 audibly in irrepressible sighing, and weeping.
314.13     I was not aware how openly I grieved, till
314.14 Earnshaw halted opposite, in his measured
314.15 walk, and gave me a stare of newly awakened
314.16 surprise. Taking advantage of his recovered
314.17 attention, I exclaimed --
314.18     "I'm tired with my journey, and I want to
314.19 go to bed! Where is the maid-servant?
314.20 Direct me to her, as she wont come to to me!"
314.21     "We have none," he answered; "you must
314.22 wait on yourself!"
315.01     "Where must I sleep, then?" I sobbed -- I
315.02 was beyond regarding self-respect, weighed
315.03 down by fatigue and wretchedness.
315.04     Joseph will show you Heathcliff's chamber,"
315.05 said he; "open that door -- he's in there."
315.06     "I was going to obey, but he suddenly
315.07 arrested me, and added in the strangest tone --
315.08     "Be so good as to turn your lock, and draw
315.09 your bolt -- don't omit it!"
315.10     "Well!" I said. "But why, Mr. Earn-
315.11 shaw?" I did not relish the notion of deli-
315.12 berately fastening myself in with Heathcliff.
315.13     Look here!" he replied, pulling from his
315.14 waistcoat a curiously constructed pistol, having
315.15 a double edged spring knife attached to the
315.16 barrel. "That's a great tempter to a despe-
315.17 rate man, is it not? I cannot resist going up
315.18 with this, every night, and trying his door.
315.19 if once I find it open he's done for! I do it
315.20 invariably, even though the minute before I
315.21 have been recalling a hundred reasons that
315.22 should make me refrain -- it is some devil that
316.01 urges me to thwart my own schemes by killing
316.02 him -- you fight against that devil, for love, as
316.03 as long as you may; when the time comes, not
316.04 all the angels in heaven shall save him!
316.05     I surveyed the weapon inquisitively; a hi-
316.06 deous notion struck me. How powerful I
316.07 should be possessing such an instrument! I
316.08 took it from his hand, and touched the blade.
316.09 He looked astonished at the expression my
316.10 face assumed during a brief second. It was
316.11 not horror, it was covetousness. He snatched
316.12 the pistol back, jealously; shut the knife, and
316.13 returned it to its concealment.
316.14     "I don't care if you tell him," said he.
316.15 Put him on his guard, and watch for him.
316.16 You know the terms we are on, I see; his
316.17 danger does not shock you."
316.18     "What has Heathcliff done to you?" I
316.19 asked. "In what has he wronged you to
316.20 warrant this appalling hatred? Wouldn't it
316.21 be wiser to bid him quit the house?"
316.22     "No," thundered Earnshaw, "should he
317.01 offer to leave me, he's a dead man, persuade
317.02 him to attempt it, and you are a murderess!
317.03 Am I to lose \all#, without a chance of retrieval?
317.04 Is Hareton to be a beggar? Oh, damnation!
317.05 I \will# have it back; and I'll have \his# gold too;
317.06 and then his blood; and hell shall have his
317.07 soul! It will be ten times blacker with that
317.08 guest than ever it was before!"
317.09     "You've acquainted me, Ellen, with your
317.10 old master's habits. He is clearly on the
317.11 verge of madness -- he was so last night, at
317.12 least. I shuddered to be near him, and
317.13 thought on the servant's ill-bred moroseness as
317.14 comparatively agreeable.
317.15     He now recommenced his moody walk, and
317.16 I raised the latch, and escaped into the kitchen.
317.17 Joseph was bending over the fire, peering
317.18 into a large pan that swung above it; and a
317.19 wooden bowl of oatmeal stood on the settle
317.20 close by. The contents of the pan began to
317.21 boil, and he turned to plunge his hand into the
317.22 bowl; I conjectured that this preparation was
318.01 probably for our supper, and, being hungry, I
318.02 resolved it should be eatable -- so crying out,
318.03 sharply -- "\I'll# make the porridge!" I removed
318.04 the vessel out of his reach, and proceeded to
318.05 take off my hat and riding habit. "Mr.
318.06 Earnshaw," I continued, "directs me to wait
318.07 on myself -- I will -- I'm not going to act the
318.08 lady among you, for fear I should starve."
318.09     "Good Lord!" he muttered, sitting down,
318.10 and stroking his ribbed stockings from the

318.11 knee to the ankle. "If they's tuh be fresh
318.12 ortherings -- just when Aw getten used tuh two
318.13 maisters, if aw mun hev a \mistress# set o˝er my
318.14 heead, it's loike time tuh be flitting. Aw
318.15 niver \did# think tuh say t˝ day ut aw mud lave
318.16 th˝ owld place -- but aw daht it's nigh at
318.17 hend!"
318.18 This lamentation drew no notice from me; I
318.19 went briskly to work; sighing to remember a
318.20 period when it would have been all merry fun;
318.21 but compelled speedily to drive off the re-
318.22 membrance. It racked me to recall past happiness,
319.01 and the greater peril there was of con-
319.02 juring up its apparition, the quicker the thible
319.03 ran round, and the faster the handfuls of meal
319.04 fell into the water.
319.05 Joseph beheld my style of cookery with
319.06 growing indignation.
319.07 "Thear!" he ejaculated. "Hareton, thah
319.08 willut sup thy porridge tuh neeght; they'll be
319.09 nowt bud lumps as big as maw nave. Thear,
319.10 agean! Aw'd fling in bowl un all, if aw wer
319.11 yah! Thear, pale t˝ guilp off, un˝ then yah'll
319.12 hae done wi˝t. Bang, bang. It's a marcy t˝
319.13 bothom isn't deaved aht!"
319.14 It \was# rather a rough mess, I own, when
319.15 poured into the basins; four had been pro-
319.16 vided, and a gallon pitcher of new milk was
319.17 brought from the dairy, which Hareton seized
319.18 and commenced drinking and spilling from
319.19 the expansive lip.
319.20 I expostulated, and desired that he should
319.21 have his in a mug; affirming that I could not
319.22 taste the liquid treated so dirtily. The old
320.01 cynic chose to be vastly offended at this nicety;
320.02 assuring me, repeatedly, that "the barn was
320.03 every bit as gooid" as I, "and every bit as
320.04 wollsome," and wondering how I could fashion
320.05 to be so conceited; meanwhile, the infant ruf-
320.06 fian continued sucking; and glowered up at
320.07 me defyingly, as he slavered into the jug.
320.08 "I shall have my supper in another room,"
320.09 I said. "Have you no place you call a par-
320.10 lour?"
320.11 "\Parlour#!" he echoed, sneeringly, "\par-
320.12 lour#! Nay, we've noa \parlours#. If yah dun-
320.13 nut loike wer company, they's maister's; un˝
320.14 if yah dunnut loike maister, they's us."
320.15 "Then I shall go up-stairs," I answered;
320.16 "shew me a chamber!"
320.17 I put my basin on a tray, and went myself
320.18 to fetch some more milk.
320.19 With great grumblings, the fellow rose, and
320.20 preceded me in my ascent: we mounted to the
320.21 garrets; he opening a door, now and then, to
320.22 look into the apartments we passed.
321.01 "Here's a rahm," he said, at last, flinging
321.02 back a cranky board on hinges. "It's weel
321.03 enough tuh ate a few porridge in. They's a
321.04 pack uh corn i˝ t˝ corner, thear, meeterly clane;
321.05 if yah're feared uh muckying yer grand silk
321.06 cloes, spread yer handkerchir ut t˝ top on't."
321.07 The "rahm" was a kind of lumber-hole
321.08 smelling strong of malt and grain; various
321.09 sacks of which articles were piled around,
321.10 leaving a wide, bare space in the middle.
321.11 "Why, man!" I exclaimed, facing him an-
321.12 grily, "this is not a place to sleep in. I wish
321.13 to see my bed-room."
321.14 "\Bed-rume#!" he repeated, in a tone of
321.15 mockery. "Yah's see all t˝ \bed-rumes# thear
321.16 is -- yon's mine."
321.17 He pointed into the second garret, only dif-
321.18 fering from the first in being more naked about
321.19 the walls, and having a large, low, curtainless
321.20 bed, with an indigo-coloured quilt, at one end.
321.21 "What do I want with yours?" I retorted.
322.01 "I suppose Mr. Heathcliff does not lodge at
322.02 the top of the house, does he?"
322.03 "Oh! it's Maister \Heathcliff's# yah're went-
322.04 ing?" cried he, as if making a new discovery.
322.05 "Couldn't ye uh said soa, at onst? un then,
322.06 aw mud uh telled ye, baht all this wark, ut
322.07 that's just one yah cannut sea -- he allas keeps
322.08 it locked, un˝ nob'dy iver mells on't but his-
322.09 seln."
322.10 "You've a nice house, Joseph," I could not
322.11 refrain from observing, "and pleasant inmates;
322.12 and I think the concentrated essence of all the
322.13 madness in the world took up its abode in my
322.14 brain the day I linked my fate with theirs!
322.15 However this is not to the present purpose --
322.16 there are other rooms. For heaven's sake, be
322.17 quick, and let me settle somewhere!"
322.18 He made no reply to this adjuration; only
322.19 plodding doggedly down the wooden steps, and
322.20 halting before an apartment which, from that
322.21 halt, and the superior quality of its furniture,
322.22 I conjectured to be the best one.
323.01 There was a carpet, a good one; but the
323.02 pattern was obliterated by dust; a fire-place
323.03 hung with cut paper dropping to pieces; a
323.04 handsome oak-bedstead with ample crimson
323.05 curtains of rather expensive material, and
323.06 modern make. But they had evidently expe-
323.07 rienced rough usage, the valances hung in
323.08 festoons, wrenched from their rings; and the
323.09 iron rod supporting them was bent in an arc,
323.10 on one side, causing the drapery to trail upon
323.11 the floor. The chairs were also damaged,
323.12 many of them severely; and deep indentations

323.13 deformed the panels of the walls.
323.14 I was endeavouring to gather resolution for
323.15 entering, and taking possession, when my fool
323.16 of a guide announced --
323.17 "This here is t˝ maister's."
323.18 My supper by this time was cold, my appe-
323.19 tite gone, and my patience exhausted. I in-
323.20 sisted on being provided instantly with a place
323.21 of refuge, and means of repose.
323.22 "Whear the divil," began the religious
324.01 elder. "The Lord bless us! The Lord forgie
324.02 us! Whear the \hell#, wold ye gang? ye mar-
324.03 red, wearisome nowt! Yah seen all bud Hare-
324.04 ton's bit uf a cham˝er. They's nut another
324.05 hoile tuh lig dahn in i˝ th˝ hahse!"
324.06 I was so vexed, I flung my tray, and its
324.07 contents on the ground; and then seated my-
324.08 self on the stairs-head, hid my face in my
324.09 hands, and cried.
324.10 "Ech! ech!" exclaimed Joseph. "Weel
324.11 done, Miss Cathy! weel done, Miss Cathy!
324.12 Hahsiver, t˝ maister sall just tum˝le o˝er them
324.13 brocken pots; un˝ then we's hear summut;
324.14 we's hear hah it's tuh be. Gooid-fur-nowt
324.15 madling! yah desarve pining froo this tuh
324.16 Churstmas, flinging t˝ precious gifts uh God
324.17 under fooit i˝ yer flaysome rages! Bud, aw'm
324.18 mista˝en if yah shew yer sperrit lang. Will
324.19 Hathecliff bide sich bonny ways, think ye?
324.20 Aw nobbut wish he muh cotch ye i˝ that
324.21 plisky. Aw nobbut wish he may."
324.22 And so he went scolding to his den beneath,
325.01 taking the candle with him; and I remained in
325.02 the dark.
325.03 The period of reflection succeeding this silly
325.04 action, compelled me to admit the necessity of
325.05 smothering my pride, and choking my wrath,
325.06 and bestirring myself to remove its effects.
325.07 An unexpected aid presently appeared in
325.08 the shape of Throttler, whom I now recog-
325.09 nised as a son of our old Skulker; it had spent
325.10 its whelphood at the Grange, and was given
325.11 by my father to Mr. Hindley. I fancy it knew
325.12 me -- it pushed its nose against mine by way of
325.13 salute, and then hastened to devour the por-
325.14 ridge, while I groped from step to step, collect-
325.15 ing the shattered earthenware, and drying the
325.16 spatters of milk from the bannister with my
325.17 pocket-handkerchief.
325.18 Our labours were scarcely over when I heard
325.19 Earnshaw's tread in the passage; my assistant
325.20 tucked in his tail, and pressed to the wall; I
325.21 stole into the nearest doorway. The dog's en-
325.22 deavour to avoid him was unsuccessful; as I
326.01 guessed by a scutter down stairs, and a pro-
326.02 longed, piteous yelping. I had better luck.
326.03 He passed on, entered his chamber, and shut
326.04 the door.
326.05 Directly after Joseph came up with Hare-
326.06 ton, to put him to bed. I had found shelter in
326.07 Hareton's room, and the old man on seeing me,
326.08 said --
326.09 "They's rahm fur boath yah, un yer pride,
326.10 nah, aw sud think i˝ th hahse. It's empty;
326.11 yah muh hev it all tuh yerseln, un Him as allas
326.12 maks a third, i˝ sich ill company!"
326.13 Gladly did I take advantage of this intima-
326.14 tion; and the minute I flung myself into a
326.15 chair, by the fire, I nodded, and slept.
326.16 My slumber was deep, and sweet; though
326.17 over far too soon, Mr. Heathcliff awoke me;
326.18 he had just come in, and demanded, in his
326.19 loving manner, what I was doing there?
326.20 I told him the cause of my staying up so
326.21 late -- that he had the key of our room in his
326.22 pocket.
327.01 The adjective \our# gave mortal offence. He
327.02 swore it was not, nor ever should be mine; and
327.03 he'd -- but I'll not repeat his language, nor des-
327.04 cribe his habitual conduct; he is ingenious and
327.05 unresting in seeking to gain my abhorrence! I
327.06 sometimes wonder at him with an intensity
327.07 that deadens my fear: yet, I assure you, a
327.08 tiger, or a venomous serpent could not rouse
327.09 terror in me equal to that which he wakens.
327.10 He told me of Catherine's illness, and accused
327.11 my brother of causing it; promising that I
327.12 should be Edgar's proxy in suffering, till he
327.13 could get a hold of him.
327.14 "I do hate him -- I am wretched --
327.15 I have been a fool! Beware of uttering one
327.16 breath of this to any one at the Grange. I
327.17 shall expect you every day -- don't disappoint
327.18 me!
327.19 "ISABELLA."
328.01 [VOL. 1 CHAPTER 14]
328.02 AS soon as I had perused this epistle, I went to
328.03 the master, and informed him that his sister
328.04 had arrived at the Heights, and sent me a
328.05 a letter expressing her sorrow for Mrs. Linton's
328.06 situation, and her ardent desire to see him;
328.07 with a wish that he would transmit to her, as
328.08 early as possible, some token of forgiveness by
328.09 me.
328.10 "Forgiveness?" said Linton. "I have
328.11 nothing to forgive her, Ellen -- you may call at
328.12 Wuthering Heights this afternoon, if you like,
329.01 and say that I am not \angry#, but I'm \sorry# to
329.02 have lost her: especially as I can never think
329.03 she'll be happy. It is out of the question my
329.04 going to see her, however; we are eternally

329.05 divided; and should she really wish to oblige
329.06 me, let her persuade the villain she has mar-
329.07 ried to leave the country."
329.08 "And you wont write her a little note,
329.09 sir?" I asked, imploringly.
329.10 "No," he answered. "It is needless. My
329.11 communication with Heathcliff's family shall
329.12 be as sparing as his with mine. It shall not
329.13 exist!"
329.14 Mr. Edgar's coldness depressed me exceed-
329.15 ingly; and all the way from the Grange, I
329.16 puzzled my brains how to put more heart into
329.17 what he said, when I repeated it; and how to
329.18 soften his refusal of even a few lines to con-
329.19 sole Isabella.
329.20 I dare say she had been on the watch for
329.21 me since morning: I saw her looking through
329.22 the lattice, as I came up the graden causeway
330.01 and I nodded to her; but she drew back, as if
330.02 afraid of being observed.
330.03 I entered without knocking. There never
330.04 was such a dreary, dismal scene as the formerly
330.05 cheerful house presented! I must confess
330.06 that, if I had been in the young lady's place,
330.07 I would, at least, have swept the hearth, and
330.08 wiped the tables with a duster. But she al-
330.09 ready partook of the pervading spirit of neglect
330.10 which encompassed her. Her pretty face was
330.11 wan and listless; her hair uncurled; some
330.12 locks hanging lankly down, and some care-
330.13 lessly twisted round her head. Probably she
330.14 had not touched her dress since yester evening.
330.15 Hindley was not there. Mr. Heathcliff sat
330.16 at a table, turning over some papers in his
330.17 pocket-book; but he rose when I appeared,
330.18 asked me how I did, quite friendly, and offered
330.19 me a chair.
330.20 He was the only thing there that seemed
330.21 decent, and I thought he never looked better.
330.22 So much had circumstances altered their positions,
331.01 that he would certainly have struck a
331.02 stranger as a born and bred gentleman, and his
331.03 wife as a thorough little slattern!
331.04 She came forward eagerly to greet me; and
331.05 held out one hand to take the expected letter.
331.06 I shook my head. She wouldn't under-
331.07 stand the hint, but followed me to a side--
331.08 board, where I went to lay my bonnet, and
331.09 importuned me in a whisper to give her di-
331.10 rectly what I had brought.
331.11 Heathcliff guessed the meaning of her
331.12 manoeuvres, and said --
331.13 "If you have got anything for Isabella, as
331.14 no doubt you have, Nelly, give it to her. You
331.15 needn't make a secret of it; we have no secrets
331.16 between us."
331.17 "Oh, I have nothing," I replied, thinking
331.18 it best to speak the truth at once. "My
331.19 master bid me tell his sister that she must not
331.20 expect either a letter or a visit from him at
331.21 present. He sends his love, ma'am, and his
331.22 wishes for your happiness, and his pardon for
332.01 the grief you have occasioned; but he thinks
332.02 that after this time, his household, and the
332.03 household here, should drop intercommunica-
332.04 tion; as nothing good could come of keeping
332.05 it up.
332.06 Mrs. Heathcliff's lip quivered slightly, and
332.07 she returned to her seat in the window. Her
332.08 husband took his stand on the hearthstone,
332.09 near me, and began to put questions concern-
332.10 ing Catherine.
332.11 I told him as much as I thought proper of
332.12 her illness, and he extorted from me, by cross--
332.13 examination, most of the facts connected with
332.14 its origin.
332.15 I blamed her, as she deserved, for bringing
332.16 it all on herself; and ended by hoping that he
332.17 would follow Mr. Linton's example, and avoid
332.18 future interference with his family, for good or
332.19 evil.
332.20 "Mrs Linton is now just recovering," I
332.21 said, "she'll never be like she was, but her
332.22 life is spared, and if you really have a regard
332.23 for her, you'll shun crossing her way again.
333.01 Nay you'll move out of this country entirely;
333.02 and that you may not regret it, I'll inform
333.03 you Catherine Linton is as different now, from
333.04 your old friend Catherine Earnshaw, as that
333.05 young lady is different from me! Her appear-
333.06 ance is changed greatly, her character much
333.07 more so; and the person, who is compelled, of
333.08 necessity, to be her companion, will only sus-
333.09 tain his affection hereafter, by the remembrance
333.10 of what she once was, by common humanity,
333.11 and a sense of duty!"
333.12 "That is quite possible," remarked Heath-
333.13 cliff forcing himself to seem calm, "quite pos-
333.14 sible that your master should have nothing but
333.15 common humanity, and a sense of duty to fall
333.16 back upon. But do you imagine that I shall
333.17 leave Catherine to his \duty# and \humanity#? and
333.18 can you compare my feelings respecting Cathe-
333.19 rine, to his? Before you leave this house, I
333.20 must exact a promise from you, that you'll get
333.21 me an interview with her -- consent, or refuse,
333.22 I \will# see her! what do you say?"
333.23 "I say Mr. Heathcliff," I replied, "you
334.01 must not -- you never shall through my means.
334.02 Another encounter between you and the mas-
334.03 ter, would kill her altogether!"

334.04 "with your aid that may be avoided;" he
334.05 continued, "and should there be danger of
334.06 such an event -- should he be the cause of add-
334.07 ing a single trouble more to her existence --
334.08 Why, I think, I shall be justified in going to
334.09 extremes! I wish you had sincerity enough
334.10 to tell me whether Catherine would suffer
334.11 greatly from his loss. The fear that she would
334.12 restrains me: and there you see the distinction
334.13 between our feelings -- Had he been in my
334.14 place, and I in his, though I hated him with a
334.15 hatred that turned my life to gall, I never
334.16 would have raised a hand against him. You
334.17 may look incredulous, if you please! I never
334.18 would have banished him from her society, as
334.19 long as she desired his. The moment her re-
334.20 gard ceased, I would have torn his heart out,
334.21 and drank his blood! But, till then, if you
334.22 don't believe me, you don't know me -- till then,
335.01 I would have died by inches before I touched
335.02 a single hair of his head!"
335.03 "And yet, I interrupted, you have no scru-
335.04 ples in completely ruining all hopes of her per-
335.05 fect restoration, by thrusting yourself in to
335.06 her remembrance, now, when she has nearly
335.07 forgotten you, and involving her in a new tu-
335.08 mult of discord, and distress."
335.09 "You suppose she has nearly forgotten
335.10 me?" he said. "Oh Nelly! you know she
335.11 has not! You know as well as I do, that for
335.12 every thought she spends on Linton, she
335.13 spends a thousand on me! At a most misera-
335.14 ble period of my life, I had a notion of the
335.15 kind, it haunted me on my return to the
335.16 neighbourhood, last summer, but only her own
335.17 assurance, could make me admit the horrible
335.18 idea again. And then, Linton would be no-
335.19 thing, nor Hindley, nor all the dreams that
335.20 ever I dreamt. Two words would comprehend
335.21 my future \death# and \hell# -- existence, after losing
335.22 her would be hell.
336.01 "Yet I was a fool to fancy for a moment
336.02 that she valued Edgar Linton's attachment
336.03 more than mine -- If he loved with all the
336.04 powers of his puny being, he couldn't love as
336.05 much in eighty years, as I could in a day.
336.06 And Catherine has a heart as deep as I have;
336.07 the sea could be as readily contained in that
336.08 horse-trough, as her whole affection be mo-
336.09 nopolized by him -- Tush! He is scarcely a
336.10 degree dearer to her than her dog, or her
336.11 horse -- It is not in him to be loved like me,
336.12 how can she love in him what he has not?"
336.13 "Catherine and Edgar are as fond of each
336.14 other, as any two people can be!" cried Isa-
336.15 bella with sudden vivacity. "No one has a
336.16 right to talk in that manner, and I won't hear
336.17 my brother depreciated in silence!"
336.18 "Your brother is wondrous fond of you
336.19 too, isn't he?" observed Heathcliff scornfully.
336.20 "He turns you adrift on the world with sur-
336.21 prising alacrity."
336.22 "He is not aware of what I suffer," she re-
336.23 plied. "I didn't tell him that."
337.01 "You have been telling him something,
337.02 then -- you have written, have you?"
337.03 "To say that I was married, I did write --
337.04 you saw the note."
337.05 "And nothing since?"
337.06 "No."
337.07 "My young lady is looking sadly the worse,
337.08 for her change of condition," I remarked.
337.09 "Somebody's love comes short in her case,
337.10 obviously -- whose I may guess; but, perhaps,
337.11 I shouldn't say."
337.12 "I should guess it was her own," said
337.13 Heathcliff. "She degenerates into a mere
337.14 slut! She is tired of trying to please me,
337.15 uncommonly early -- You'd hardly credit it,
337.16 but the very morrow of our wedding, she was
337.17 weeping to go home. However, she'll suit
337.18 this house so much the better for not being
337.19 over nice, and I'll take care she does not dis-
337.20 grace me by rambling abroad."
337.21 "Well, sir;" returned I, "I hope you'll
337.22 consider that Mrs. Heathcliff is accustomed to
338.01 be looked after, and waited on; and that she
338.02 has been brought up like an only daughter
338.03 whom every one was ready to serve -- You
338.04 must let her have a maid to keep things tidy
338.05 about her, and you must treat her kindly --
338.06 whatever be your notion of Mr. Edgar, you
338.07 cannot doubt that she has a capacity for strong
338.08 attachments or she wouldn't have abandoned
338.09 the elegancies, and comforts, and friends of
338.10 her former home, to fix contentedly, in such a
338.11 wilderness as this, with you."
338.12 "She abandoned them under a delusion;"
338.13 he answered, "picturing in me a hero of ro-
338.14 mance, and expecting unlimited indulgences
338.15 from my chivalrous devotion. I can hardly
338.16 regard her in the light of a rational creature,
338.17 so obstinately has she persisted in forming a
338.18 fabulous notion of my character, and acting on
338.19 the false impressions she cherished. But at
338.20 last, I think she begins to know me -- I don't
338.21 perceive the silly smiles and grimaces that pro-
338.22 voked me, at first; and the senseless incapability
339.01 of discerning that I was in earnest when
339.02 I gave her my opinion of her infatuation, and
339.03 herself -- It was a marvellous effort of perspic-

339.04 acity to discover that I did not love her. I
339.05 believed at one time, no lessons could teach
339.06 her that! and yet it is poorly learnt; for this
339.07 morning she announced, as a piece of appal-
339.08 ling intelligence, that I had actually succeed-
339.09 ed in making her hate me! A positive labour
339.10 of Hercules, I assure you! If it be achieved,
339.11 I have cause to return thanks -- Can I trust your
339.12 assertion, Isabella, are you sure you hate me?
339.13 If I let you alone for half-a-day, won't you
339.14 come sighing and wheedling to me again? I
339.15 dare say she would rather I had seemed all
339.16 tenderness before you; it wounds her vanity
339.17 to have the truth exposed. But, I don't care
339.18 who knows that the passion was wholly on
339.19 one side, and I never told her a lie about it.
339.20 She cannot accuse me of showing a bit of de-
339.21 ceitful softness. The first thing she saw me
339.22 do, on coming out of the Grange, was to hang
340.01 up her little dog, and when she pleaded for it,
340.02 the first words I uttered, were a wish that I
340.03 had the hanging of every being belonging to
340.04 her, except one: possibly, she took that ex-
340.05 ception for herself -- But no brutality disgusted
340.06 her -- I suppose, she has an innate admiration
340.07 of it, if only her precious person were secure
340.08 from injury! Now, was it not the depth of
340.09 absurdity -- of genuine idiocy, for that pitiful,
340.10 slavish, mean-minded brach to dream that I
340.11 could love her? Tell your master, Nelly, that
340.12 I never, in all my life, met with such an ab-
340.13 ject thing as she is -- She even disgraces the name
340.14 of Linton; and I've sometimes relented, from
340.15 pure lack of invention, in my experiments on
340.16 what she could endure, and still creep shame-
340.17 fully cringing back! But tell him also, to set
340.18 his fraternal and magisterial heart at ease, that
340.19 I keep strictly within the limits of the law -- I
340.20 have avoided, up to this period, giving her the
340.21 slightest right to claim a separation; and
340.22 what's more, she'd thank nobody for dividing
341.01 us -- if she desired to go she might -- the nui-
341.02 sance of her presence outweighs the gratifica-
341.03 tion to be derived from tormenting her!"
341.04 "Mr. Heathcliff," said I, "this is the talk
341.05 of a madman, and your wife, most likely is con-
341.06 vinced you are mad; and, for that reason, she
341.07 has borne with you hitherto: but now that
341.08 you say she may go, she'll doubtless avail her-
341.09 self of the permission -- You are not so be-
341.10 witched ma'am, are you, as to remain with him,
341.11 of your own accord?"
341.12 "Take care, Ellen!" answered Isabella, her
341.13 eyes sparkling irefully -- there was no mis-
341.14 doubting by their expression, the full success
341.15 of her partner's endeavours to make himself
341.16 detested. "Don't put faith in a single
341.17 word he speaks. He's a lying fiend, a mon-
341.18 ster, and not a human being! I've been told
341.19 I might leave him before; and I've made the
341.20 attempt, but I dare not repeat it! Only
341.21 Ellen, promise you'll not mention a syllable of
342.01 his infamous conversation to my brother or
342.02 Catherine -- whatever he may pretend, he
342.03 wishes to provoke Edgar to desperation -- he
342.04 says he has married me on purpose to obtain
342.05 power over him; and he shan't obtain it -- I'll
342.06 die first! I just hope, I pray that he may
342.07 forget his diabolical prudence, and kill me!
342.08 The single pleasure I can imagine is, is to die,
342.09 or to see him dead!"
342.10 "There -- that will do for the present!" said
342.11 Heathcliff. "If you are called upon in a court
342.12 of law, you'll remember her language, Nelly!
342.13 And take a good look at that countenance --
342.14 she's near the point which would suit me.
342.15 No, you're not fit to be your own guardian,
342.16 Isabella now; and I, being your legal pro-
342.17 tector, must retain you in my custody, how-
342.18 ever distasteful the obligation may be -- Go up
342.19 stairs; I have something to say to Ellen Dean,
342.20 in private. That's not the way -- up-stairs, I
342.21 tell you! why this is the road up-stairs,
342.22 child!"
343.01 He seized, and thrust her from the room;
343.02 and returned muttering,
343.03 "I have no pity! I have no pity! The
343.04 worms writhe, the more I yearn to crush out
343.05 their entrails! It is a moral teething, and I
343.06 grind with greater energy, in proportion to the
343.07 increase of pain."
343.08 "Do you understand what the word pity
343.09 means?" I said hastening to resume my bon-
343.10 net. "Did you ever feel a touch of it in your
343.11 life?"
343.12 "Put that down!" he interrupted, perceiving
343.13 my intention to depart. "You are not going
343.14 yet -- Come here now, Nelly -- I must either
343.15 persuade, or compel you to aid me in fulfilling
343.16 my determination to see Catherine, and that
343.17 without delay -- I swear that I meditate no
343.18 harm; I don't desire to cause any disturbance,
343.19 or to exasperate, or insult Mr. Linton; I only
343.20 wish to hear from herself how she is, and
343.21 why she has been ill; and to ask, if anything
343.22 that I could do would be of use to her. Last
344.01 night, I was in the Grange garden six hours,
344.02 and I'll return there to-night; and every night
344.03 I'll haunt the place, and every day, till I find
344.04 an opportunity of entering. If Edgar Linton
344.05 meets me, I shall not hesitate to knock him

344.06 down, and give him enough to ensure his qui-
344.07 escence while I stay -- If his servants oppose
344.08 me, I shall threaten them off with these pistols
344.09 -- But wouldn't it be better to prevent my
344.10 coming in contact with them, or their master.
344.11 And you could do it so easily! I'd warn you
344.12 when I came, and then you might let me in
344.13 unobserved, as soon as she was alone, and
344.14 watch till I departed -- your conscience quite
344.15 calm, you would be hindering mischief."
344.16 I protested against playing that treacherous
344.17 part in my employer's house; and besides, I
344.18 urged the cruelty, and selfishness of his destroy-
344.19 ing Mrs. Linton's tranquillity, for his satisfac-
344.20 tion.
344.21 "The commonest occurrence startles her
344.22 painfully," I said. "She's all nerves, and she
345.01 couldn't bear the surprise, I'm positive -- Don't
345.02 persist, sir! or else, I shall be obliged to in-
345.03 form my master of your designs, and he'll take
345.04 measures to secure his house and its inmates
345.05 from any such unwarrantable intrusions!
345.06 In that case, I'll take measures to secure
345.07 you, woman!" exclaimed Heathcliff, "you
345.08 shall not leave wuthering Heights till to-mor-
345.09 row morning. It is a foolish story to assert
345.10 that Catherine could not bear to see me; and
345.11 as to surprising her, I don't desire it, you must
345.12 prepare her -- ask her if I may come. You say
345.13 she never mentions my name, and that I am
345.14 never mentioned to her. To whom should
345.15 she mention me if I am a forbidden topic in
345.16 the house? She thinks you are all spies for
345.17 her husband -- Oh, I've no doubt she's in hell
345.18 among you! I guess, by her silence as much
345.19 as any thing, what she feels. You say she is
345.20 often restless, and anxious looking -- is that a
345.21 proof of tranquillity? You talk of her mind,
345.22 being unsettled -- How the devil could it be
346.01 otherwise, in her frightful isolation. And that
346.02 insipid, paltry creature attending her from
346.03 \duty# and \humanity#! From \pity# and \charity#.
346.04 He might as well plant an oak in a flower-
346.05 pot, and expect it to thrive, as imagine he
346.06 can restore her to vigour in the soil of his
346.07 shallow cares! Let us settle it at once; will
346.08 you stay here, and am I to fight my way to
346.09 Catherine over Linton, and his footmen? Or
346.10 will you be my friend, as you have been hi-
346.11 therto, and do what I request? Decide! be-
346.12 cause there is no reason for my lingering ano-
346.13 ther minute, if you persist in your stubborn
346.14 ill-nature!"
346.15 Well, Mr. Lockwood, I argued, and com-
346.16 plained, and flatly refused him fifty times; but
346.17 in the long run he forced me to an agreement
346.18 -- I engaged to carry a letter from him to my
346.19 mistress; and should she consent, I promised
346.20 to let him have intelligence of Linton's next
346.21 absence from home, when he might come, and
346.22 get in as he was able -- I wouldn't be there,
347.01 and my fellow servants should be equally out
347.02 of the way.
347.03 was it right, or wrong? I fear it was
347.04 wrong, though expedient. I thought I pre-
347.05 vented another explosion by my compliance;
347.06 and I thought too, it might create a favourable
347.07 crisis in Catherine's mental illness: and then
347.08 I remembered Mr. Edgar's stern rebuke of my
347.09 carrying tales; and I tried to smooth away all
347.10 disquietude on the subject, by affirming, with
347.11 frequent iteration, that, that betrayal of trust,
347.12 if it merited so harsh an appellation, should
347.13 be the last.
347.14 Notwithstanding my journey homeward was
347.15 sadder than my journey thither; and many
347.16 misgivings I had, ere I could prevail on my-
347.17 self to put the missive into Mrs. Linton's
347.18 hand.
347.19 But here is Kenneth -- I'll go down, and tell
347.20 him how much better you are. My history
347.21 is \dree# as we say, and will serve to wile away
347.22 another morning.
348.01 Dree, and dreary! I reflected as the good
348.02 woman descended to receive the doctor; and
348.03 not exactly of the kind which I should have
348.04 chosen to amuse me; but never mind! I'll ex-
348.05 tract wholesome medicines from Mrs. Dean's
348.06 bitter herbs; and firstly, let me beware of the
348.07 fascination that lurks in Catherine Heathcliff's
348.08 brilliant eyes. I should be in a curious taking
348.09 if I surrendered my heart to that young per-
348.10 son, and the daughter turned out a second edi-
348.11 tion of the mother!
348.12 [THE END OF VOL. 1]
349.01 VOL. 2 CHAPTER 1]
349.02 ANOTHER week over -- and I am so many days
349.03 nearer health, and spring! I have now heard
349.04 all my neighbour's history, at different sittings,
349.05 as the housekeeper could spare time from more
349.06 important occupations. I'll continue it in her
349.07 own words, only a little condensed. She is,
349.08 on the whole, a very fair narrator and I don't
349.09 think I could improve her style.
350.01 "In the evening," she said, "the evening
350.02 of my visit to the Heights, I knew as well as
350.03 if I saw him, that Mr. Heathcliff was about
350.04 the place; and I shunned going out, because I
350.05 still carried his letter in my pocket, and didn't
350.06 want to be threatened, or teased any more.
350.07 I had made up my mind not to give it till

350.08 my master went somewhere; as I could not
350.09 guess how its receipt would affect Catherine.
350.10 The consequence was, that it did not reach
350.11 her before the lapse of three days. The fourth
350.12 was Sunday, and I brought it into her room,
350.13 after the family were gone to church.
350.14    There was a man servant left to keep the
350.15 house with me, and we generally made a prac-
350.16 tice of locking the doors during the hours of
350.17 service; but on that occasion, the weather was
350.18 so warm and pleasant that I set them wide
350.19 open; and to fulfil my engagement, as I knew
350.20 who would be coming, I told my companion
350.21 that the mistress wished very much for some
350.22 oranges, and he must run over to the village,
351.01 and get a few, to be paid for on the morrow.
351.02 He departed, and I went up-stairs.
351.03    Mrs. Linton sat in a loose, white dress,
351.04 with a light shawl over her shoulders, in the
351.05 recess of the open window, as usual. Her
351.06 thick, long hair had been partly removed at
351.07 the beginning of her illness; and now, she
351.08 wore it simply combed in its natural tresses
351.09 over her temples and neck. Her appearance
351.10 was altered, as I had told Heathcliff, but when
351.11 she was calm, there seemed unearthly beauty
351.12 in the change.
351.13    The flash of her eyes had been succeeded by
351.14 a dreamy and melancholy softness: they no
351.15 longer gave the impression of looking at the
351.16 objects around her; they appeared always to
351.17 gaze beyond, and far beyond -- you would have
351.18 said out of this world -- Then, the paleness of
351.19 her face, its haggard aspect having vanished
351.20 she recovered flesh, and the peculiar expres-
351.21 sion arising from her mental state, though
351.22 painfully suggestive of their causes, added to
352.01 the touching interest, which she wakened, and
352.02 invariably to me, I know, and to any person
352.03 who saw her, I should think, refuted more tan-
352.04 gible proofs of convalescence and stamped her
352.05 as one doomed to decay.
352.06    A book lay spread on the sill before her, and
352.07 the scarcely perceptible wind fluttered its
352.08 leaves at intervals. I believe Linton had
352.09 laid it there, for she never endeavoured to
352.10 divert herself with reading, or occupation of
352.11 any kind; and he would spend many an hour
352.12 in trying to entice her attention to some sub-
352.13 ject which had formerly been her amusement.
352.14    She was conscious of his aim, and in her
352.15 better moods, endured his efforts placidly; only
352.16 showing their uselessness by now and then
352.17 suppressing a wearied sigh, and checking him
352.18 at last, with the saddest of smiles and kisses.
352.19 At other times, she would turn petulantly
352.20 away, and hide her face in her hands, or even
352.21 push him off angrily; and then he took care
352.22 to let her alone, for he was certain of doing
352.23 no good.
353.01    Gimmerton chapel bells were still ringing;
353.02 and the full, mellow flow of the beck in the
353.03 valley, came soothingly on the ear. It was a
353.04 sweet substitute for the yet absent murmur of
353.05 the summer foliage which drowned that music
353.06 about the Grange, when the trees were in leaf.
353.07 At Wuthering Heights it always sounded on
353.08 quiet days, following a great thaw, or a
353.09 season of steady rain -- and, of Wuthering
353.10 Heights, Catherine was thinking as she lis-
353.11 tened; that is, if she thought, or listened, at
353.12 all; but she had the vague, distant look, I
353.13 mentioned before, which expressed no recogni-
353.14 tion of material things either by ear or eye.
353.15    "There's a letter for you, Mrs. Linton," I
353.16 said, gently inserting it in one hand that rested
353.17 on her knee. "You must read it immedi-
353.18 ately, because it wants an answer. Shall I
353.19 break the seal?"
353.20    "Yes," she answered, without altering the
353.21 direction of her eyes.
353.22    I opened it -- it was very short.
354.01    "Now," I continued, "read it."
354.02 She drew away her hand, and let it fall. I
354.03 replaced it in her lap, and stood waiting till it
354.04 should please her to glance down; but that
354.05 movement was so long delayed that at last I
354.06 resumed --
354.07    "Must I read it, ma'am? It is from Mr.
354.08 Heathcliff."
354.09    There was a start, and a troubled gleam of
354.10 recollection, and a struggle to arrange her
354.11 ideas. She lifted the letter, and seemed to
354.12 peruse it; and when she came to the signature
354.13 she sighed; yet still I found she had not
354.14 gathered its import; for upon my desiring to
354.15 hear her reply she merely pointed to the
354.16 name, and gazed at me with mournful and
354.17 questioning eagerness.
354.18    "Well, he wishes to see you," said I, guess-
354.19 ing her need of an interpreter. "He's in the
354.20 garden by this time, and impatient to know
354.21 what answer I shall bring."
354.22    As I spoke, I observed a large dog lying on
355.01 the sunny grass beneath, raise its ears, as if
355.02 about to bark; and then smoothing them back,
355.03 announce by a wag of the tail that some one
355.04 approached whom it did not consider a
355.05 stranger.
355.06    Mrs. Linton bent forward, and listened
355.07 breathlessly. The minute after a step tra-

355.08 versed the hall; the open house was too
355.09 tempting for Heathcliff to resist walking in:
355.10 most likely he supposed that I was inclined to
355.11 shirk my promise, and so resolved to trust to his
355.12 own audacity.
355.13    With straining eagerness Catherine gazed
355.14 towards the entrance of her chamber. He did
355.15 not hit the right room directly; she motioned
355.16 me to admit him; but he found it out, ere I
355.17 could reach the door, and in a stride or two
355.18 was at her side, and had her grasped in his
355.19 arms.
355.20    He neither spoke, nor loosed his hold, for
355.21 some five minutes, during which period he be-
355.22 stowed more kisses than ever he gave in his
356.01 life before, I dare say; but then my mistress
356.02 had kissed him first, and I plainly saw that he
356.03 could hardly bear, for downright agony, to
356.04 look into her face! The same conviction had
356.05 stricken him as me, from the instant he beheld
356.06 her, that there was no prospect of ultimate
356.07 recovery there -- she was fated, sure to die.
356.08    "Oh, Cathy! Oh my life! how can I bear
356.09 it?" was the first sentence he uttered, in a
356.10 tone that did not seek to disguise his despair.
356.11    And now he stared at her so earnestly that
356.12 I thought the very intensity of his gaze would
356.13 bring tears into his eyes; but they burned
356.14 with anguish, they did not melt.
356.15    "What now?" said Catherine, leaning
356.16 back, and returning his look with a suddenly
356.17 clouded brow -- her humour was a mere vane
356.18 for constantly varying caprices. "You and
356.19 Edgar have broken my heart, Heathcliff! And
356.20 you both come to bewail the deed to me, as if
356.21 you were the people to be pitied! I shall not
356.22 pity you, not I. You have killed me -- and
357.01 thriven on it, I think. How strong you are!
357.02 How many years do you mean to live after I
357.03 am gone?"
357.04    Heathcliff had knelt on one knee to embrace
357.05 her; he attempted to rise, but she seized his
357.06 hair, and kept him down.
357.07    "I wish I could hold you," she continued,
357.08 bitterly, "till we were both dead! I shouldn't
357.09 care what you suffered. I care nothing for
357.10 your sufferings. Why shouldn't you suffer? I
357.11 do! Will you forget me -- will you be happy
357.12 when I am in the earth? Will you say twenty
357.13 years hence, `That's the grave of Catherine
357.14 Earnshaw. I loved her long ago, and was
357.15 wretched to lose her; but it is past. I've loved
357.16 many others since -- my children are dearer to
357.17 me that she was, and, at death, I shall not re-
357.18 joice that I am going to her, I shall be sorry
357.19 that I must leave them!` Will you say so,
357.20 Heathcliff?"
357.21    "Don't torture me till I'm as mad as yourself,"
358.01 cried he, wrenching his head free, and
358.02 grinding his teeth.
358.03    The two, to a cool spectator, made a strange
358.04 and fearful picture. Well might Catherine
358.05 deem that heaven would be a land of exile to
358.06 her, unless, with her mortal body, she cast
358.07 away her mortal character also. Her present
358.08 countenance had a wild vindictiveness in its
358.09 white cheek, and a bloodless lip, and scintillat-
358.10 ing eye; and she retained, in her closed fingers,
358.11 a portion of the locks she had been grasping.
358.12 As to her companion, while raising himself
358.13 with one hand, he had taken her arm with the
358.14 other; and so inadequate was his stock of gen-
358.15 tleness to the requirements of her condition,
358.16 that on letting go, I saw four distinct im-
358.17 pressions left blue in the colourless skin.
358.18    "Are you possessed with a devil," he pur-
358.19 sued, savagely, "to talk in that manner to me,
358.20 when you are dying? Do you reflect that all
358.21 those words will be branded in my memory,
359.01 and eating deeper eternally, after you have left
359.02 me? You know you lie to say I have killed
359.03 you; and, Catherine, you know that I could
359.04 as soon forget you, as my existence! Is it not
359.05 sufficient for your infernal selfishness, that
359.06 while you are at peace I shall writhe in the
359.07 torments of hell?"
359.08    "I shall not be at peace," moaned Catherine,
359.09 recalled to a sense of physical weakness by the
359.10 violent, unequal throbbing of her heart, which
359.11 beat visibly, and audibly under the excess of
359.12 agitation.
359.13    She said nothing further till the paroxysm
359.14 was over; then she continued, more kindly --
359.15    "I'm not wishing you greater torment than
359.16 I have, Heathcliff! I only wish us never to be
359.17 parted -- and should a word of mine distress
359.18 you hereafter, think I feel the same distress
359.19 underground, and for my own sake, forgive
359.20 me! Come here and kneel down again! You
359.21 never harmed me in your life. Nay, if you
359.22 nurse anger, that will be worse to remember
360.01 than my harsh words! Wont you come here
360.02 again? Do!"
360.03    Heathcliff went to the back of her chair,
360.04 and leant over, but not so far as to let her see
360.05 his face, which was livid with emotion. She
360.06 bent round to look at him; he would not per-
360.07 mit it; turning abruptly, he walked to the
360.08 fire-place, where he stood, silent, with his back
360.09 towards us.
360.10    Mrs. Linton's glance followed him suspici-

360.11 ously: every movement woke a new senti-
360.12 ment in her. After a pause, and a prolonged
360.13 gaze, she resumed, addressing me in accents of
360.14 indignant disappointment.
360.15 "Oh, you see, Nelly! he would not relent
360.16 a moment, to keep me out of the grave! \That#
360.17 is how I'm loved! well, never mind! That
360.18 is not \my# Heathcliff. I shall love mine yet;
360.19 and take him with me -- he's in my soul.
360.20 And," added she, musingly, "the thing that
360.21 irks me most is this shattered prison, after all.
360.22 I'm tired, tired of being enclosed here. I'm
361.01 wearying to escape into that glorious world,
361.02 and to be always there; not seeing it dimly
361.03 through tears, and yearning for it through the
361.04 walls of an aching heart; but really with it,
361.05 and in it. Nelly, you think you are better and
361.06 more fortunate than I; in full health and
361.07 strength -- you are sorry for me -- very soon
361.08 that will be altered. I shall be sorry for \you#.
361.09 I shall be incomparably beyond and above
361.10 you all. I \wonder# he wont be near me!" She
361.11 went on to herself. "I thought he wished it.
361.12 Heathcliff dear! you should not be sullen now.
361.13 Do come to me, Heathcliff."
361.14 In her eagerness she rose, and supported
361.15 herself on the arm of the chair. At that
361.16 earnest appeal, he turned to her, looking ab-
361.17 solutely desperate. His eyes wide, and wet,
361.18 at last, flashed fiercely on her; his breast
361.19 heaved convulsively. An instant they held
361.20 asunder; and then how they met I hardly saw,
361.21 but Catherine made a spring, and he caught
361.22 her, and they were locked in an embrace from
362.01 which I thought my mistress would never be
362.02 released alive. In fact, to my eyes, she
362.03 seemed directly insensible. He flung himself
362.04 into the nearest seat, and on my approaching
362.05 hurriedly to ascertain if she had fainted, he
362.06 gnashed at me, and foamed like a mad dog,
362.07 and gathered her to him with greedy jealousy.
362.08 I did not feel as if I were in the company of a
362.09 creature of my own species; it appeared that
362.10 he would not understand, though I spoke to
362.11 him; so, I stood off, and held my tongue, in
362.12 great perplexity.
362.13 A movement of Catherine's relieved me a
362.14 little presently: she put up her hand to clasp
362.15 his neck, and bring her cheek to his, as he held
362.16 her: while he, in return, covering her with
362.17 frantic caresses, said wildly --
362.18 "You teach me now how cruel you've been
362.19 -- cruel and false. \Why# did you despise me?
362.20 \Why# did you betray your own heart, Cathy?
362.21 I have not one word of comfort -- you deserve
362.22 this. You have killed yourself. Yes, you
363.01 may kiss me, and cry; and wring out my
363.02 kisses and tears. They'll blight you -- they'll
363.03 damn you. You loved me -- then what \right#
363.04 had you to leave me? What right -- answer
363.05 me -- for the poor fancy you felt for Linton?
363.06 Because misery, and degradation, and death,
363.07 and nothing that God or satan could inflict
363.08 would have parted us, \you#, of your own will,
363.09 did it. I have not broken your heart -- \you#
363.10 have broken it -- and in breaking it, you have
363.11 broken mine. So much the worse for me, that
363.12 I am strong. Do I want to live? What kind
363.13 of living will it be when you -- oh God!
363.14 would \you# like to live with your soul in the
363.15 grave?"
363.16 "Let me alone. Let me alone," sobbed
363.17 Catherine. "If I've done wrong, I'm dying
363.18 for it. It is enough! You left me too; but I
363.19 wont upbraid you! I forgive you. Forgive
363.20 me!"
363.21 "It is hard to forgive, and to look at those
363.22 eyes, and feel those wasted hands," he answered.
364.01 "Kiss me again; and don't let me
364.02 see your eyes! I forgive what you have done
364.03 to me. I love \my# murderer -- but \yours#! How
364.04 can I?"
364.05 They were silent -- their faces hid against
364.06 each other, and washed by each other's tears.
364.07 At least, I suppose the weeping was on both
364.08 sides; as it seemed Heathcliff \could# weep on a
364.09 great occasion like this.
364.10 I grew very uncomfortable, meanwhile; for
364.11 the afternoon wore fast away, the man whom I
364.12 had sent off returned from his errand, and I
364.13 could distinguish, by the shine of the wester-
364.14 ing sun up the valley, a concourse thickening
364.15 outside Gimmerton chapel porch.
364.16 "Service is over," I announced. "My
364.17 master will be here in half-an-hour."
364.18 Heathcliff groaned a curse, and strained
364.19 Catherine closer -- she never moved.
364.20 Ere long I perceived a group of servants
364.21 passing up the road towards the kitchen wing.
364.22 Mr. Linton was not far behind; he opened the
365.01 gate himself, and sauntered slowly up, proba-
365.02 bly enjoying the lovely afternoon that breathed
365.03 as soft as summer.
365.04 "Now he is here," I exclaimed. "For
365.05 Heaven's sake, hurry down! You'll not meet
365.06 any one on the front stairs. Do be quick;
365.07 and stay among the trees till he is fairly in."
365.08 "I must go, Cathy," said Heathcliff, seeking
365.09 to extricate himself from his companion's arms.
365.10 "But, if I live, I'll see you again before you
365.11 are asleep. I wont stray five yards from your

365.12 window."
365.13 "You must not go!" she answered, holding
365.14 him as firmly as her strength allowed. "You
365.15 shall not, I tell you."
365.16 "For one hour," he pleaded, earnestly.
365.17 "Not for one minute," she replied.
365.18 "I \must# -- Linton will be up immediately,"
365.19 persisted the alarmed intruder.
365.20 He would have risen, and unfixed her fingers
365.21 by the act -- she clung fast gasping; there was
365.22 mad resolution in her face.
366.01 "No!" she shrieked. "Oh, don't, don't go.
366.02 It is the last time! Edgar will not hurt us.
366.03 Heathcliff, I shall die! I shall die!"
366.04 "Damn the fool. There he is," cried Heath-
366.05 cliff, sinking back into his seat. "Hush, my
366.06 darling! Hush, hush, Catherine! I'll stay.
366.07 If he shot me so, I'd expire with a blessing on
366.08 my lips."
366.09 And there they were fast again. I heard
366.10 my master mounting the stairs -- the cold sweat
366.11 ran from my forehead; I was horrified.
366.12 "Are you going to listen to her ravings?"
366.13 I said, passionately. "She does not know
366.14 what she says. Will you ruin her, because
366.15 she has not wit to help herself? Get up! you
366.16 could be free instantly. That is the most dia-
366.17 bolical deed that ever you did. We are all
366.18 done for -- master, mistress, and servant."
366.19 I wrung my hands, and cried out; and Mr.
366.20 Linton hastened his step at the noise. In the
366.21 midst of my agitation, I was sincerely glad to
367.01 observe that Catherine's arms had fallen re-
367.02 laxed, and her head hung down.
367.03 "She's fainted or dead," I thought, "so
367.04 much the better. Far better that she should
367.05 be dead, than lingering a burden, and a misery--
367.06 maker to all about her."
367.07 Edgar sprang to his unbidden guest, blanched
367.08 with astonishment and rage. What he meant
367.09 to do, I cannot tell; however, the other
367.10 stopped all demonstrations, at once, by placing
367.11 the lifeless-looking form in his arms.
367.12 "Look there," he said, "unless you be a
367.13 fiend, help her first -- then you shall speak to
367.14 me!"
367.15 He walked into the parlour, and sat down.
367.16 Mr. Linton summoned me, and, with great
367.17 difficulty, and after resorting to many means,
367.18 we managed to restore her to sensation; but
367.19 she was all bewildered; she sighed, and
367.20 moaned, and knew nobody. Edgar, in his anx-
367.21 iety for her, forgot her hated friend. I did
367.22 not. I went, at the earliest opportunity, and
368.01 besought him to depart, affirming that Cathe-
368.02 rine was better, and he should hear from me
368.03 in the morning, how she passed the night.
368.04 "I shall not refuse to go out of doors," he
368.05 answered; "but I shall stay in the garden;
368.06 and, Nelly, mind you keep your word to-mor-
368.07 row. I shall be under those larch trees, mind!
368.08 or I pay another visit, whether Linton be in
368.09 or not."
368.10 He sent a rapid glance through the half-open
368.11 door of the chamber, and ascertaining that
368.12 what I stated was apparently true, delivered
368.13 the house of his luckless presence.
369.01 [VOL. 2 CHAPTER 2]
369.02 ABOUT twelve o'clock, that night, was born
369.03 the Catherine you saw at Wuthering Heights,
369.04 a puny, seven months' child; and two hours
369.05 after the mother died, having never recovered
369.06 sufficient consciousness to miss Heathcliff, or
369.07 know Edgar.
369.08 The latter's distraction at his bereavement
369.09 is a subject too painful to be dwelt on; his
369.10 after effects showed how deep the sorrow sunk.
369.11 A great addition, in my eyes, was his being
369.12 left without an heir. I bemoaned that, as I
370.01 gazed on the feeble orphan; and I mentally
370.02 abused old Linton for, what was only natural
370.03 partiality, the securing his estate to his own
370.04 daughter, instead of his son's.
370.05 An unwelcomed infant it was, poor thing!
370.06 It might have wailed out of life, and nobody
370.07 cared a morsel, during those first hours of ex-
370.08 istence. We redeemed the neglect afterwards;
370.09 but it's beginning was as friendless as its end
370.10 is likely to be.
370.11 Next morning -- bright and cheerful out of
370.12 doors -- stole softened in through the blinds of
370.13 the silent room, and suffused the couch and its
370.14 occupant with a mellow, tender glow.
370.15 Edgar Linton had his head laid on the pil-
370.16 low, and his eyes shut. His young and fair
370.17 features were almost as death-like as those of
370.18 the form beside him, and almost as fixed; but
370.19 \his# was the hush of exhausted anguish, and
370.20 \her's# of perfect peace. Her brow smooth, her
370.21 lids closed, her lips wearing the expression of
370.22 a smile. No angel in heaven could be more
371.01 beautiful than she appeared; and I partook of
371.02 the infinite calm in which she lay. My mind
371.03 was never in a holier frame, than while I gazed
371.04 on that untroubled image of Divine rest. I in-
371.05 stinctively echoed the words she had uttered,
371.06 a few hours before. "Incomparably beyond,
371.07 and above us all! whether still on earth or
371.08 now in Heaven her spirit is at home \with
371.09 God!"
371.10 I don't know if it be a peculiarity in me,

371.11 but I am seldom otherwise than happy while
371.12 watching in the chamber of death, should no
371.13 frenzied or despairing mourner share the duty
371.14 with me. I see a repose that neither earth nor
371.15 hell can break; and I feel an assurance of
371.16 the endless and shadowless hereafter -- the
371.17 Eternity they have entered -- where life is
371.18 boundless in its duration, and love in its sym-
371.19 pathy, and joy in its fulness. I noticed on
371.20 that occasion how much selfishness there is
371.21 even in a love like Mr. Linton's, when he so
371.22 regretted Catherine's blessed release!
372.01 To be sure one might have doubted, after the
372.02 wayward and impatient existence she had led,
372.03 whether she merited a haven of peace at last.
372.04 One might doubt in seasons of cold reflection,
372.05 but not then, in the presence of her corpse.
372.06 It asserted its own tranquillity, which seemed
372.07 a pledge of equal quiet to its former inhabi-
372.08 tants.
372.09 "Do you believe such people \are# happy in
372.10 the other world, sir? I'd give a great deal to
372.11 know."
372.12 I declined answering Mrs. Dean's question,
372.13 which struck me as something heterodox. She
372.14 proceeded:
372.15 "Retracing the course of Catherine Linton
372.16 I fear we have no right to think she is: but
372.17 we'll leave her with her Maker."
372.18 The master looked asleep, and I ventured
372.19 soon after sunrise to quit the room and steal
372.20 out to the pure, refreshing air. The servants
372.21 thought me gone to shake off the drowsiness of
372.22 my protracted watch; in reality my chief motive
373.01 motive was seeing Mr. Heathcliff. If he had
373.02 remained among the larches all night he would
373.03 have heard nothing of the stir at the Grange,
373.04 unless, perhaps, he might catch the gallop of
373.05 the messenger going to Gimmerton. If he
373.06 had come nearer he would probably be aware,
373.07 from the lights flitting to and fro, and the open-
373.08 ing and shutting of the outer doors, that all
373.09 was not right within.
373.10 I wished yet feared to find him. I felt the
373.11 terrible news must be told, and I longed to
373.12 get it over, but \how# to do it I did not know.
373.13 He was there -- at least a few yards further
373.14 in the park; leant against an old ash tree, his
373.15 hat off, and his hair soaked with the dew that
373.16 had gathered on the budding branches, and fell
373.17 pattering round him. He had been standing a
373.18 long time in that position, for I saw a pair of
373.19 ousels passing and repassing, scarcely three
373.20 feet from him busy in building their nest, and
373.21 regarding his proximity no more than that
374.01 of a piece of timber. They flew off at my
374.02 approach, and he raised his eyes and spoke:
374.03 "She's dead!" he said; "I've not waited for
374.04 you to learn that. Put your handkerchief
374.05 away -- don't snivel before me. Damn you all!
374.06 she wants none of \your# tears!"
374.07 I was weeping as much for him as her: we
374.08 do sometimes pity creatures that have none of
374.09 the feeling either for themselves or others; and
374.10 when I first looked into his face I perceived
374.11 that he had got intelligence of the catastrophe;
374.12 and a foolish notion struck me that his heart
374.13 was quelled, and he prayed, because his lips
374.14 moved, and his gaze was bent on the ground.
374.15 "Yes, she's dead!" I answered, checking
374.16 my sobs, and drying my cheeks. "Gone to
374.17 to heaven, I hope, where we may, everyone,
374.18 join her, if we take due warning, and leave
374.19 our evil ways to follow good!"
374.20 "Did \she# take due warning, then?" asked
374.21 Heathcliff, attempting a sneer. "Did she die
375.01 like a saint? Come, give me a true history
375.02 of the event. How did -- "
375.03 He endeavoured to pronounce the name, but
375.04 could not manage it; and compressing his
375.05 mouth, he held a silent combat with his inward
375.06 agony, defying, meanwhile, my sympathy with
375.07 an unflinching, ferocious stare.
375.08 "How did she die?" he resumed, at last --
375.09 fain, notwithstanding his hardihood, to have a
375.10 support behind him for, after the struggle, he
375.11 trembled, in spite of himself, to his very
375.12 finger-ends.
375.13 "Poor wretch!" I thought; "you have a
375.14 heart and nerves the same as your brother men!
375.15 Why should you be so anxious to conceal
375.16 them? Your pride cannot blind God! You
375.17 tempt him to wring them, till he forces a cry
375.18 of humiliation!"
375.19 "Quietly as a lamb!" I answered, aloud.
375.20 "She drew a sigh, and stretched herself, like
375.21 a child reviving, and sinking again to sleep;
376.01 and five minutes after I felt one little pulse at
376.02 her heart, and nothing more!"
376.03 "And -- and did she ever mention me?" he
376.04 asked, hesitating, as if he dreaded the answer
376.05 to his question would introduce details that he
376.06 could not bear to hear.
376.07 "Her senses never returned -- she recognised
376.08 nobody from the time you left her," I said.
376.09 "She lies with a sweet smile on her face; and
376.10 her latest ideas wander back to pleasant
376.11 early days. Her life closed in a gentle dream
376.12 -- may she wake as kindly in the other world!"
376.13 "May she wake in torment!" he cried,
376.14 with frightful vehemence, stamping his foot,

376.15 and groaning in a sudden paroxysm of ungo-
376.16 vernable passion. "Why, she's a liar to the
376.17 end! Where is she? Not \there# -- not in hea-
376.18 ven -- not perished -- where? Oh! you said you
376.19 cared nothing for my sufferings! And I pray
376.20 one prayer -- I repeat it till my tongue stiffens
376.21 -- Catherine Earnshaw, may you not rest, as
376.22 long as I am living! You said I killed you --
377.01 haunt me then! The murdered \do# haunt their
377.02 murderers. I believe -- I know that ghosts
377.03 \have# wandered on earth. Be with me always
377.04 -- take any form -- drive me mad! only \do# not
377.05 leave me in this abyss, where I cannot find you!
377.06 Oh, God! it is unutterable! I \cannot# live
377.07 without my life! I \cannot# live without my
377.08 soul!"
377.09 He dashed his head against the knotted
377.10 trunk; and, lifting up his eyes, howled, not
377.11 like a man, but like a savage beast getting
377.12 goaded to death with knives and spears.
377.13 I observed several splashes of blood about
377.14 the bark of the tree, and his hand and fore-
377.15 head were both stained; probably the scene I
377.16 witnessed was a repetition of others acted dur-
377.17 ing the night. It hardly moved my compassion
377.18 -- it appalled me; still I felt reluctant to quit
377.19 him so. But the moment he recollected him-
377.20 self enough to notice me watching, he thun-
377.21 dered a command for me to go, and I obeyed.
377.22 He was beyond my skill to quiet or console!
378.01 Mrs. Linton's funeral was appointed to take
378.02 place on the Friday following her decease; and
378.03 till then her coffin remained uncovered, and
378.04 strewn with flowers and scented leaves, in the
378.05 great drawing-room. Linton spent his days
378.06 and nights there, a sleepless guardian; and --
378.07 a circumstance concealed from all but me --
378.08 Heathcliff spent his nights, at least, outside,
378.09 equally a stranger to repose.
378.10 I held no communication with him; still I
378.11 was conscious of his design to enter, if he
378.12 could; and on the Tuesday, a little after dark,
378.13 when my master from sheer fatigue, had been
378.14 compelled to retire a couple of hours, I went
378.15 and opened one of the windows, moved by his
378.16 perseverance to give him a chance of bestow-
378.17 ing on the fading image of his idol one final
378.18 adieu.
378.19 He did not omit to avail himself of the
378.20 opportunity, cautiously and briefly; too cau-
378.21 tiously to betray his presence by the slightest
378.22 noise; indeed, I shouldn't have discovered that
379.01 he had been there, except for the disarrange-
379.02 ment of the drapery about the corpse's face,
379.03 and for observing on the floor a curl of light
379.04 hair, fastened with a silver thread, which, on
379.05 examination, I ascertained to have been taken
379.06 from a locket hung round Catherine's neck.
379.07 Heathcliff had opened the trinket, and cast
379.08 out its contents, replacing them by a black
379.09 lock of his own. I twisted the two, and en-
379.10 closed them together.
379.11 Mr. Earnshaw was, of course, invited to
379.12 attend the remains of his sister to the grave;
379.13 and he sent no excuse, but he never came; so
379.14 that besides her husband, the mourners were
379.15 wholly composed of tenants and servants.
379.16 Isabella was not asked.
379.17 The place of Catherine's interment, to the
379.18 surprise of the villagers, was neither in the
379.19 chapel, under the carved monument of the
379.20 Lintons', nor yet by the tombs of her own
379.21 relations, outside. It was dug on a green
379.22 slope, in a corner of the kirkyard, where the
380.01 wall is so low that heath and bilberry plants
380.02 have climbed over it from the moor; and peat
380.03 mould almost buries it. Her husband lies
380.04 in the same spot, now; and they have each a
380.05 simple headstone, above, and a plain grey
380.06 block at their feet, to mark the graves.
381.01 [VOL. 2 CHAPTER 3]
381.02 THAT Friday made the last of our fine days,
381.03 for a month. In the evening, the weather
381.04 broke; the wind shifted from south to north-
381.05 east, and brought rain, first, and then sleet,
381.06 and snow.
381.07 On the morrow one could hardly imagine
381.08 that there had been three weeks of summer:
381.09 the primroses and crocuses were hidden under
381.10 wintry drifts: the larks were silent, the young
381.11 leaves of the early trees smitten and blackened
381.12 -- And dreary, and chill, and dismal that morrow
382.01 did creep over! My master kept his
382.02 room -- I took possession of the lonely parlour,
382.03 converting it into a nursery; and there I was
382.04 sitting, with the moaning doll of a child laid
382.05 on my knee; rocking it to and fro, and watch-
382.06 ing, meanwhile the still driving flakes build
382.07 up the uncurtained window, when the door
382.08 opened, and some person entered out of breath,
382.09 and laughing!"
382.10 My anger was greater than my astonishment
382.11 for a minute; I supposed it one of the maids,
382.12 and I cried,
382.13 "Have done! How dare you show your
382.14 giddiness, here? What would Mr. Linton say
382.15 if he heard you?"
382.16 "Excuse me!" answered a familiar voice,
382.17 "but I know Edgar is in bed, and I cannot
382.18 stop myself."
382.19 With that, the speaker came forward to the

382.20 fire, panting and holding her hand, to her side.
382.21 "I have run the whole way from Wuthering
382.22 Heights!" she continued, after a pause. "Except
383.01 where I've flown -- I couldn't count the
383.02 number of falls I've had -- Oh, I'm aching all
383.03 over! Don't be alarmed -- There shall be an
383.04 explanation as soon as I can give it -- only just
383.05 have the goodness to step out, and order the
383.06 carriage to take me on to Gimmerton, and
383.07 tell a servant to seek up a few clothes in my
383.08 wardrobe."
383.09 The intruder was Mrs. Heathcliff -- she cer-
383.10 tainly seemed in no laughing predicament:
383.11 her hair streamed on her shoulders dripping with
383.12 snow and water; she was dressed in the girl-
383.13 ish dress she commonly wore, befitting her age
383.14 more than her position; a low frock, with
383.15 short sleeves, and nothing on either head, or
383.16 neck. The frock was of light silk, and clung
383.17 to her with wet; and her feet were protected
383.18 merely by thin slippers; add to this a deep
383.19 cut under one ear, which only the cold pre-
383.20 vented from bleeding profusely, a white face
383.21 scratched and bruised, and a frame hardly
383.22 able to support itself through fatigue, and you
384.01 may fancy my first fright was not much allay-
384.02 ed when I had leisure to examine her.
384.03 "My dear young lady," I exclaimed "I'll
384.04 stir no-where, and hear nothing, till you have
384.05 removed every article of your clothes, and put
384.06 on dry things; and certainly you shall not go
384.07 to Gimmerton to-night; so it is needless to
384.08 order the carriage."
384.09 "Certainly, I shall;" she said; "walking or
384.10 riding -- yet I've no objection to dress myself
384.11 decently; and -- ah, see how it flows down my
384.12 neck now! the fire does make it smart."
384.13 She insisted on my fulfilling her directions,
384.14 before she would let me touch her; and not
384.15 till after the coachman had been instructed to
384.16 get ready, and a maid set to pack up some ne-
384.17 cessary attire, did I obtain her consent for
384.18 binding the wound, and helping to change her
384.19 garments.
384.20 "Now Ellen," she said when my task was
384.21 finished, and she was seated in an easy chair
384.22 on the hearth, with a cup of tea before her,
385.01 "You sit down opposite me, and put poor
385.02 Catherine's baby away -- I don't like to see it!
385.03 You mustn't think I care little for Catherine,
385.04 because I behaved so foolishly on entering --
385.05 I've cried too, bitterly -- yes, more than any
385.06 one else has reason to cry -- we parted unre-
385.07 conciled, you remember, and I shan't forgive
385.08 myself. But for all that, I was not going to
385.09 sympathise with him -- the brute beast! O
385.10 give me the poker! This is the last thing of
385.11 his I have about me," she slipped the gold
385.12 ring from her third finger, and threw it on the
385.13 floor. "I'll smash it!" she continued striking
385.14 with childish spite. "And then I'll burn it!"
385.15 and she took and dropped the misused article
385.16 among the coals. "There! he shall buy ano-
385.17 ther, if he gets me back again. He'd be capa-
385.18 ble of coming to seek me, to tease Edgar -- I
385.19 dare not stay, lest that notion should possess
385.20 his wicked head! And besides, Edgar has not
385.21 been kind, has he? And I won't come suing
385.22 for his assistance; nor will I bring him into
386.01 more trouble -- Necessity compelled me to seek
386.02 shelter here; though if I had not learnt he
386.03 was out of the way, I'd have halted at the
386.04 kitchen, washed my face, warmed myself, got
386.05 you to bring what I wanted, and departed
386.06 again to anywhere out of the reach of my ac-
386.07 cursed -- of that incarnate goblin! Ah, he
386.08 was in such a fury -- if he had caught me! It's
386.09 a pity, Earnshaw is not his match in strength
386.10 -- I wouldn't have run, till I'd seen him all but
386.11 demolished, had Hindley been able to do it!"
386.12 "Well, don't talk so fast, Miss!" I inter-
386.13 rupted, "you'll disorder the handkerchief I
386.14 have tied round you face, and make the cut
386.15 bleed again -- Drink your tea, and take breath
386.16 and give over laughing -- Laughter is sadly
386.17 out of place under this roof, and in your con-
386.18 dition!"
386.19 "An undeniable truth," she replied, "Listen
386.20 to that child! It maintains a constant wail --
386.21 send it out of my hearing, for an hour; I
386.22 shan't stay any longer."
387.01 I rang the bell, and committed it to a ser-
387.02 vant's care; and then I inquired what had
387.03 urged her to escape from Wuthering Heights
387.04 in such an unlikely plight -- and where she
387.05 meant to go, as she refused remaining with
387.06 us?"
387.07 "I ought, and I wish to remain;" answered
387.08 she; "to cheer Edgar, and take care of the
387.09 baby, for two things, and because the Grange
387.10 is my right home -- but I tell you, he wouldn't
387.11 let me! Do you think he could bear to see
387.12 me grow fat, and merry; and could bear to
387.13 think that we were tranquil, and not resolve
387.14 on poisoning our comfort? Now, I have the
387.15 satisfaction of being sure that he detests me
387.16 to the point of its annoying him seriously to
387.17 have me within ear-shot, or eye-sight -- I no-
387.18 tice, when I enter his presence, the muscles of
387.19 his countenance are involuntarily distorted
387.20 into an expression of hatred; partly arising

387.21 from his knowledge of the good causes I have
388.01 to feel that sentiment for him, and partly
388.02 from original aversion -- It is strong enough to
388.03 make me feel pretty certain that he would not
388.04 chase me over England, supposing I contrived
388.05 a clear escape; and therefore I must get quite
388.06 away. I've recovered from my first desire to
388.07 be killed by him. I'd rather he'd kill himself!
388.08 He has extinguished my love effectually, and
388.09 so I'm at my ease. I can recollect yet how I
388.10 loved him; and can dimly imagine that I
388.11 could still be loving him, if -- No, no! Even,
388.12 if he had doted on me, the devilish nature
388.13 would have revealed its existence, somehow.
388.14 Catherine had an awfully perverted taste to
388.15 esteem him so dearly, knowing him so well --
388.16 Monster! would that he could be blotted out
388.17 of creation, and out of my memory!"
388.18 "Hush, hush! He's a human being," I said.
388.19 "Be more charitable; there are worse men
388.20 than he is yet!"
388.21 "He's not a human being:" she retorted;
389.01 "and he has no claim on my charity -- I gave
389.02 him my heart, and he took and pinched it to
389.03 death; and flung it back to me -- people feel
389.04 with their hearts, Ellen, and since he has de-
389.05 stroyed mine, I have not power to feel for him,
389.06 and I would not, though he groaned from this,
389.07 to his dying day; and wept tears of blood for
389.08 Catherine! No, indeed, indeed, I wouldn't!"
389.09 And here Isabella began to cry; but, imme-
389.10 diately dashing the water from her lashes, she
389.11 recommenced.
389.12 "You asked, what has driven me to flight
389.13 at last? I was compelled to attempt it, because,
389.14 I had succeeded in rousing his rage a pitch
389.15 above his malignity. Pulling out the nerves
389.16 with red pincers, requires more coolness
389.17 than knocking on the head. He was worked
389.18 up to forget the fiendish prudence he boasted
389.19 of, and proceeding to murderous violence: I
389.20 experienced pleasure in being able to exaspe-
389.21 rate him: the sense of pleasure woke my in-
389.22 stinct of self-preservation; so, I fairly broke
390.01 free, and if ever I come into his hands again
390.02 he is welcome to a signal revenge.
390.03 "Yesterday, you know, Mr. Earnshaw should
390.04 have been at the funeral. He kept himself
390.05 sober, for the purpose -- tolerably sober; not
390.06 going to-bed mad, at six o'clock and getting
390.07 up drunk, at twelve. Consequently, he rose,
390.08 in suicidal low spirits; as fit for the church,
390.09 as for a dance; and instead, he sat down by
390.10 the fire, and swallowed gin or brandy by tum-
390.11 blerfuls.
390.12 "Heathcliff -- I shudder to name him! has
390.13 been a stranger in the house from last Sunday
390.14 till to-day -- whether the angels have fed him,
390.15 or his kin beneath, I cannot tell; but, he has
390.16 not eaten a meal with us for nearly a week --
390.17 He has just come home at dawn, and gone up-
390.18 stairs to his chamber; locking himself in --- as if
390.19 anybody dreamt of coveting his company!
390.20 There he has continued, praying like a metho-
390.21 dist; only the deity he implored is senseless
390.22 dust and ashes; and God, when addressed, was
391.01 curiously confounded with his own black fa-
391.02 ther! After concluding these precious orisons
391.03 and they lasted generally till he grew hoarse,
391.04 and his voice was strangled in his throat, he
391.05 would be off again; always straight down to
391.06 the Grange! I wonder Edgar did not send
391.07 for a constable, and give him into custody!
391.08 For me, grieved as I was about Catherine, it
391.09 was impossible to avoid regarding this season
391.10 of deliverance from degrading oppression as a
391.11 holiday.
391.12 "I recovered spirits sufficient to hear Joseph's
391.13 eternal lectures without weeping; and to move
391.14 up and down the house, less with the foot of a
391.15 frightened thief, than formerly. You wouldn't
391.16 think that I should cry at anything Joseph
391.17 could say; but he and Hareton are detestable
391.18 companions. I'd rather sit with Hindley, and
391.19 hear his awful talk, than with 't' little maister,'
391.20 and his staunch supporter, that odious old
391.21 man!
391.22 "When Heathcliff is in, I'm often obliged to
392.01 seek the kitchen, and their society, or starve
392.02 among the damp, uninhabited chambers; when
392.03 he is not, as was the case this week, I esta-
392.04 blish a table, and chair, at one corner of the
392.05 house fire, and never mind how Mr. Earnshaw
392.06 may occupy himself; and he does not interfere
392.07 with my arrangements: he is quieter, now,
392.08 than he used to be, if no one provokes him;
392.09 more sullen and depressed, and less furious.
392.10 Joseph affirms he's sure he's an altered man;
392.11 that the Lord has touched his heart, and he is
392.12 saved "so as by fire." I'm puzzled to detect
392.13 signs of the favourable change, but it is not
392.14 my business.
392.15 "Yester-evening, I sat in my nook reading
392.16 some old books, till late on towards twelve.
392.17 It seemed so dismal to go up-stairs, with the
392.18 wild snow blowing outside, and my thoughts
392.19 continually reverting to the kirkyard, and the
392.20 new made grave! I dared hardly lift my eyes
392.21 from the page before me, that melancholy
392.22 scene so instantly usurped its place.
393.01 "Hindley sat opposite; his head leant on his

393.02 hand, perhaps meditating on the same subject.
393.03 He had ceased drinking at a point below irra-
393.04 tionality, and had neither stirred, nor spoken
393.05 during two or three hours. There was no
393.06 sound through the house, but the moaning
393.07 wind which shook the windows every now and
393.08 then: the faint crackling of the coals; and the
393.09 click of my snuffers as I removed at inter-
393.10 vals the long wick of the candle. Hareton
393.11 and Joseph were probably fast asleep in bed.
393.12 It was very, very sad, and while I read, I
393.13 sighed, for it seemed as if all joy had vanished
393.14 from the world, never to be restored.
393.15 The doleful silence was broken, at length,
393.16 by the sound of the kitchen latch -- Heathcliff
393.17 had returned from his watch earlier than usual,
393.18 owing, I suppose, to the sudden storm.
393.19 "That entrance was fastened; and we heard
393.20 him coming round to get in by the other. I
393.21 rose with an irrepressible expression of what I
393.22 felt on my lips, which induced my companion,
394.01 who had been staring towards the door, to turn
394.02 and look at me.
394.03 "I'll keep him out five minutes." He ex-
394.04 claimed. "You won't object?"
394.05 "No, you may keep him out the whole
394.06 night for me," I answered. "Do! put the key
394.07 in the lock, and draw the bolts."
394.08 Earnshaw accomplished this, ere his guest
394.09 reached the front; he then came, and brought
394.10 his chair to the other side of my table; lean-
394.11 ing over it, and searching in my eyes, a sym-
394.12 pathy with the burning hate that gleamed
394.13 from his: as he both looked, and felt like an
394.14 assassin, he couldn't exactly find that; but he
394.15 discovered enough to encourage him to speak.
394.16 "You, and I," he said, "have each a great
394.17 debt to settle with the man out yonder! If we
394.18 were neither of us cowards, we might com-
394.19 bine to discharge it. Are you as soft as your
394.20 brother? Are you willing to endure to the
394.21 last, and not once attempt a repayment?"
394.22 "I'm weary of enduring now;" I replied,
395.01 "and I'd be glad of a retaliation that wouldn't
395.02 recoil on myself; but treachery, and violence,
395.03 are spears pointed at both ends -- they wound
395.04 those who resort to them, worse than their
395.05 enemies."
395.06 "Treachery and violence are a just return
395.07 for treachery and violence!" cried Hindley.
395.08 "Mrs. Heathcliff, I'll ask you to do nothing,
395.09 but sit still, and be dumb -- Tell me now, can
395.10 you? I'm sure you would have as much plea-
395.11 sure as I, in witnessing the conclusion of the
395.12 fiend's existence, he'll be \your# death unless
395.13 you overreach him -- and he'll be \my# ruin --
395.14 Damn the hellish villain! He knocks at the
395.15 door, as if he were master here, already!
395.16 Promise to hold your tongue, and before that
395.17 clock strikes -- it wants three minutes of one --
395.18 you're a free woman!"
395.19 He took the implements which I described
395.20 to you in my letter from his breast, and would
395.21 have turned down the candle -- I snatched it
395.22 away, however, and seized his arm.
396.01 "I'll not hold my tongue!" I said, "You
396.02 mustn't touch him ... Let the door remain shut
396.03 and be quiet!"
396.04 "No! I've formed my resolution, and by
396.05 God, I'll execute it!" cried the desperate being,
396.06 "I'll do you a kindness, in spite of yourself,
396.07 and Hareton justice! And you needn't trou-
396.08 ble your head to screen me, Catherine is gone
396.09 -- Nobody alive would regret me, or be ashamed
396.10 though I cut my throat, this minute -- and it's
396.11 time to make an end!"
396.12 I might as well have struggled with a bear;
396.13 or reasoned with a lunatic. The only resource
396.14 left me was to run to a lattice, and warn his
396.15 intended victim of the fate which awaited him.
396.16 "You'd better seek shelter somewhere else
396.17 to-night!" I exclaimed in a rather triumphant
396.18 tone. "Mr. Earnshaw has a mind to shoot you,
396.19 if you persist in endeavouring to enter."
396.20 "You'd better open the door, you --" he an-
396.21 swered, addressing me by some elegant term
396.22 that I don't care to repeat.
397.01 "I shall not meddle in the matter," I re-
397.02 torted again. "Come in, and get shot, if you
397.03 please! I've done my duty."
397.04 With that I shut the window, and returned
397.05 to my place by the fire; having too small a
397.06 stock of hypocrisy at my command to pretend
397.07 any anxiety for the danger that menaced him.
397.08 Earnshaw swore passionately at me; affirm-
397.09 ing that I loved the villain yet; and calling
397.10 me all sorts of names for the base spirit I
397.11 evinced. And I, in my secret heart, /and con-
397.12 science never reproached me// thought what a
397.13 blessing it would be for \him#, should Heathcliff
397.14 put him out of misery: and what a blessing
397.15 for \me#, should he send Heathcliff to his right
397.16 abode! As I sat nursing these reflections, the
397.17 casement behind me, was banged on to the
397.18 floor by a blow from the latter individual; and
397.19 his black countenance looked blightingly
397.20 through. The stanchions stood too close to
397.21 suffer his shoulders to follow; and I smiled, ex-
397.22 ulting in my fancied security. His hair and
398.01 clothes were whitened with snow, and his
398.02 sharp cannibal teeth, revealed by cold and

398.03 wrath, gleamed through the dark.
398.04 "Isabella let me in, or I'll make you re-
398.05 pent!" he `girned`, as Joseph calls it. "Mr.
398.06 "I cannot commit murder;" I replied "Mr.
398.07 Hindley stands sentinel with a knife, and load-
398.08 ed pistol."
398.09 "Let me in by the kitchen door!" he said.
398.10 "Hindley will be there before me," I an-
398.11 swered. And that's a poor love of yours, that
398.12 cannot bear a shower of snow! We were left
398.13 at peace in our beds, as long as the summer
398.14 moon shone, but the moment a blast of winter
398.15 returns, you must run for shelter! Heathcliff,
398.16 if I were you, I'd stretch myself over
398.17 her grave, and die like a faithful dog ... The
398.18 world is surely not worth living in now, is it?
398.19 You had distinctly impressed on me, the idea
398.20 that Catherine was the whole joy of your life
398.21 -- I can't imagine how you think of surviving
398.22 her loss."
399.01 "He's there ... is he?" exclaimed my compa-
399.02 nion, rushing to the gap. "If I can get my
399.03 arm out I can hit him!"
399.04 "I'm afraid Ellen, you'll set me down, as
399.05 really wicked -- but you don't know all, so don't
399.06 judge! I wouldn't have aided or abetted an
399.07 attempt on even \his# life, for anything -- wish
399.08 that he were dead, I must; and therefore, I
399.09 was fearfully disappointed, and unnerved by
399.10 terror for the consequences of my taunting
399.11 speech when he flung himself on Earnshaw's
399.12 weapon and wrenched it from his grasp.
399.13 The charge exploded, and the knife, in
399.14 springing back, closed into its owner's wrist.
399.15 Heathcliff pulled it away by main force, slitting
399.16 up the flesh as it passed on, and thrust it drip-
399.17 ping into his pocket. He then took a stone,
399.18 struck down the division between two windows
399.19 and sprung in. His adversary had fallen
399.20 senseless with excessive pain, and the flow of
399.21 blood that gushed from an artery, or a large
399.22 vein.
400.01 The ruffian kicked and trampled on him,
400.02 and dashed his head repeatedly against the
400.03 flags; holding me with one hand, meantime, to
400.04 prevent my summoning Joseph.
400.05 He exerted preter-human self-denial in ab-
400.06 staining from finishing him, completely; but
400.07 getting out of breath, he finally desisted, and
400.08 dragged the apparently inanimate body onto
400.09 the settle.
400.10 There he tore off the sleeve of Earnshaw's
400.11 coat, and bound up the wound with brutal
400.12 roughness, spitting and cursing, during the
400.13 operation, as energetically as he had kicked
400.14 before.
400.15 Being at liberty, I lost no time in seeking
400.16 the old servant; who, having gathered by de-
400.17 grees the purport of my hasty tale, hurried
400.18 below, gasping, as he descended the steps two
400.19 at once.
400.20 "whet is thur tuh do, nah? whet is thur
400.21 tuh do, nah?"
400.22 "There's this to do," thundered Heathcliff,
401.01 "that your master's mad; and should he last
401.02 another month, I'll have him to an asylum.
401.03 And how the devil did you come to fasten me
401.04 out, you toothless hound? Don't stand mut-
401.05 tering and mumbling there. Come, I'm not
401.06 going to nurse him. Wash that stuff away;
401.07 and mind the sparks of your candle -- it is more
401.08 than half brandy!"
401.09 "Und soa, yah been murthering on him?"
401.10 exclaimed Joseph, lifting his hands and eyes
401.11 in horror. "If iver Aw seed a seeght loike
401.12 this! May the Lord --"
401.13 Heathcliff gave him a push onto his knees,
401.14 in the middle of the blood; and flung a towel
401.15 to him; but instead of proceeding to dry it up,
401.16 he joined his hands, and began a prayer which
401.17 excited my laughter from its odd phraseology.
401.18 I was in the condition of mind to be shocked
401.19 at nothing; in fact, I was as reckless as some
401.20 malefactors show themselves at the foot of the
401.21 gallows.
401.22 "Oh, I forgot you," said the tyrant, "you
402.01 shall do that. Down with you. And you
402.02 conspire with him against me, do you, viper?
402.03 There, that is work fit for you!"
402.04 He shook me till my teeth rattled, and
402.05 pitched me beside Joseph, who steadily con-
402.06 cluded his supplications, and then rose, vowing
402.07 he would set off for the Grange directly. Mr.
402.08 Linton was a magistrate, and though he had
402.09 fifty wives dead, he should inquire into this.
402.10 He was so obstinate in his resolution that
402.11 Heathcliff deemed it expedient to compel, from
402.12 my lips, a recapitulation of what had taken
402.13 place; standing over me, heaving with male-
402.14 volence, as I reluctantly delivered the account
402.15 in answer to his questions.
402.16 It required a great deal of labour to satisfy
402.17 the old man that he was not the aggressor;
402.18 especially with my hardly wrung replies.
402.19 However, Mr. Earnshaw soon convinced him
402.20 that he was alive still; he hastened to admin-
402.21 ister a dose of spirits, and by their succour his
403.01 master presently regained motion and consci-
403.02 ousness.
403.03 Heathcliff, aware that he was ignorant of the
403.04 treatment received while insensible, called him

403.05 deliriously intoxicated; and said he should not
403.06 notice his atrocious conduct further; but ad-
403.07 vised him to get to bed. To my joy, he left
403.08 us after giving this judicious counsel, and
403.09 Hindley stretched himself on the hearth-stone.
403.10 I departed to my own room, marvelling that I
403.11 had escaped so easily.
403.12 This morning, when I came down, about
403.13 half-an-hour before noon, Mr. Earnshaw was
403.14 sitting by the fire, deadly sick; his evil genius
403.15 almost as gaunt and ghastly, leant against the
403.16 chimney. Neither appeared inclined to dine,
403.17 and having waited till all was cold on the table,
403.18 I commenced alone.
403.19 Nothing hindered me from eating heartily;
403.20 and I experienced a certain sense of satisfac-
403.21 tion and superiority, as, at intervals, I cast a
404.01 look towards my silent companions, and felt
404.02 the comfort of quiet conscience within me.
404.03 After I had done, I ventured on the unusual
404.04 liberty of drawing near the fire; going round
404.05 Earnshaw's seat, and kneeling in the corner
404.06 beside him.
404.07 Heathcliff did not glance my way, and I
404.08 gazed up, and contemplated his features, almost
404.09 as confidently as if they had been turned to
404.10 stone. His forehead, that I once thought so
404.11 manly, and that I now think so diabolical, was
404.12 shaded with a heavy cloud; his basilisk eyes
404.13 were nearly quenched by sleeplessness -- and
404.14 weeping, perhaps, for the lashes were wet then:
404.15 his lips devoid of their ferocious sneer, and
404.16 sealed in an expression of unspeakable sadness.
404.17 Had it been another,, I would have covered
404.18 my face, in the presence of such grief. In \his#
404.19 case, I was gratified: and ignoble as it seems
404.20 to insult a fallen enemy, I couldn't miss this
404.21 chance of sticking in a dart; his weakness
405.01 was the only time when I could taste the de-
405.02 light of paying wrong for wrong.
405.03 "Fie, fie, Miss!" I interrupted. "One
405.04 might suppose you had never opened a Bible
405.05 in your life. If God afflict your enemies,
405.06 surely that ought to suffice you. It is both
405.07 mean and presumptuous to add your torture to
405.08 his!"
405.09 "In general, I'll allow that it would be,
405.10 Ellen," she continued. "But what misery
405.11 laid on Heathcliff could content me, unless I
405.12 have a hand in it? I'd rather he suffered \less#,
405.13 if I might cause his sufferings, and he might
405.14 \know# that I was the cause. Oh, I owe him so
405.15 much. On only one condition can I hope to
405.16 forgive him. It is, if I may take an eye for
405.17 an eye, a tooth for a tooth, for every wrench
405.18 of agony, return a wrench, reduce him to my
405.19 level. As he was the first to injure, make
405.20 him the first to implore pardon; and then --
405.21 why then, Ellen, I might show you some
405.22 generosity. But it is utterly impossible I can
406.01 ever be revenged, and therefore I cannot forgive
406.02 him. Hindley wanted some water, and I handed
406.03 him a glass, and asked him how he was."
406.04 "Not as ill as I wish," he replied. "But
406.05 leaving out my arm, every inch of me is as
406.06 sore as if I had been fighting with a legion of
406.07 imps!"
406.08 "Yes, no wonder," was my next remark.
406.09 "Catherine used to boast that she stood be-
406.10 tween you and bodily harm -- she meant that
406.11 certain persons would not hurt you, for fear of
406.12 offending her. It's well people don't \really#
406.13 rise from their grave, or, last night, she might
406.14 have witnessed a repulsive scene! Are not
406.15 you bruised, and cut over your chest and
406.16 shoulders?"
406.17 "I can't say," he answered; "but what do
406.18 you mean? Did he dare to strike me when I
406.19 was down?"
406.20 "He trampled on, and kicked you, and
406.21 dashed you on the ground," I whispered.
406.22 "And his mouth watered to tear you with his
407.01 teeth; because, he's only half a man -- not so
407.02 much."
407.03 Mr. Earnshaw looked up, like me, to the
407.04 countenance of our mutual foe; who, absorbed
407.05 in his anguish, seemed insensible to anything
407.06 around him; the longer he stood, the plainer
407.07 his reflections revealed their blackness through
407.08 his features.
407.09 "Oh, if God would but give me strength
407.10 to strangle him in my last agony, I'd go to
407.11 hell with joy," groaned the impatient man
407.12 writhing to rise, and sinking back in despair,
407.13 convinced of his inadequacy for the struggle.
407.14 "Nay, it's enough that he has murdered
407.15 one of you," I observed aloud. "At the
407.16 Grange, every one knows your sister would
407.17 have been living now, had it not been for Mr.
407.18 Heathcliff. After all, it is preferable to be
407.19 hated, than loved by him. When I recollect
407.20 how happy we were -- how happy Catherine
407.21 was before he came -- I'm fit to curse the day."
407.22 Most likely, Heathcliff noticed more the
408.01 truth of what was said, than the spirit of the
408.02 person who said it. His attention was roused,
408.03 I saw, for his eyes rained down tears among
408.04 the ashes, and he drew his breath in suffocat-
408.05 ing sighs.
408.06 I stared full at him, and laughed scornfully.
408.07 The clouded windows of hell flashed, a mo-

408.08 ment towards me; the fiend which usually
408.09 looked out, however, was so dimmed and
408.10 drowned that I did not fear to hazard another
408.11 sound of derision.
408.12 "Get up, and begone out of my sight," said
408.13 the mourner.
408.14 I guessed he uttered those words, at least,
408.15 though his voice was hardly intelligible.
408.16 "I beg your pardon," I replied. "But I
408.17 loved Catherine too; and her brother requires
408.18 attendance which, for her sake, I shall supply.
408.19 Now that she's dead, I see her in Hindley.
408.20 Hindley has exactly her eyes, if you had not
408.21 tried to gouge them out, and made them black
408.22 and red, and her --"
409.01 "Get up, wretched idiot, before I stamp
409.02 you to death!" he cried, making a movement
409.03 that caused me to make one also."
409.04 "But then," I continued, holding myself
409.05 ready to flee; "if poor Catherine had trusted
409.06 you, and assumed the ridiculous, contemptible,
409.07 degrading title of Mrs. Heathcliff, she would
409.08 soon have presented a similar picture! \She#
409.09 wouldn't have borne your abominable behavi-
409.10 our quietly; her detestation and disgust must
409.11 have found voice."
409.12 The back of the settle, and Earnshaw's per-
409.13 son interposed between me and him; so in-
409.14 stead of endeavouring to reach me, he snatched
409.15 a dinner knife from the table, and flung it at
409.16 my head. It struck beneath my ear, and
409.17 stopped the sentence I was uttering; but pull-
409.18 ing it out, I sprang to the door, and delivered
409.19 another which I hope went a little deeper than
409.20 his missile.
409.21 The last glimpse I caught of him was a fu-
409.22 rious rush, on his part, checked by the embrace
410.01 of his host; and both fell locked together on
410.02 the hearth.
410.03 In my flight through the kitchen I bid
410.04 Joseph speed his master; I knocked over
410.05 Hareton, who was hanging a litter of puppies
410.06 from a chair back in the doorway; and, blest
410.07 as a soul escaped from purgatory, I bounded,
410.08 leaped, and flew down the steep road: then,
410.09 quitting its windings, shot direct across the
410.10 moor, rolling over banks, and wading through
410.11 marshes; precipitating myself, in fact, towards
410.12 the beacon light of the Grange. And far
410.13 rather would I be condemned to a perpetual
410.14 dwelling in the infernal regions, than even for
410.15 one night abide beneath the roof of Wuthering
410.16 Heights again."
410.17 Isabella ceased speaking, and took a drink
410.18 of tea; then she rose, and bidding me put on
410.19 her bonnet, and a great shawl I had brought,
410.20 and turning a deaf ear to my entreaties for
410.21 her to remain another hour, she stepped onto
410.22 a chair, kissed Edgar's and Catherine's portraits,
411.01 bestowed a similar salute on me, and
411.02 descended to the carriage accompanied by
411.03 Fanny, who yelped wild with joy at recover-
411.04 ing her mistress, She was driven away, never
411.05 to revisit this neighbourhood; but a regular
411.06 correspondence was established between her
411.07 and my master when things were more settled.
411.08 I believe her new abode was in the south,
411.09 near London; there she had a son born, a
411.10 few months subsequent to her escape. He
411.11 was christened Linton, and, from the first, she
411.12 reported him to be an ailing, peevish creature.
411.13 Mr. Heathcliff, meeting me one day in the
411.14 village, inquired where she lived. I refused
411.15 to tell. He remarked that it was not of any
411.16 moment, only she must beware of coming to
411.17 her brother; she should not be with him, if he
411.18 had to keep her himself.
411.19 Though I would give no information, he
411.20 discovered, through some of the other servants,
411.21 both her place of residence, and the existence
411.22 of the child. Still he didn't molest her; for
412.01 which forbearance she might thank his aver-
412.02 sion, I suppose.
412.03 He often asked about the infant, when he
412.04 saw me; and on hearing its name, smiled
412.05 grimly, and observed:
412.06 "They wish me to hate it too, do they?"
412.07 "I don't think they wish you to know any
412.08 thing about it," I answered.
412.09 "But I'll have it," he said, "when I want
412.10 it. They may reckon on that!"
412.11 Fortunately, its mother died before the
412.12 time arrived, some thirteen years after the de-
412.13 cease of Catherine, when Linton was twelve, or
412.14 a little more.
412.15 On the day succeeding Isabella's unexpected
412.16 visit, I had no opportunity of speaking to my
412.17 master: he shunned conversation, and was fit
412.18 for discussing nothing. When I could get him
412.19 to listen, I saw it pleased him that his sister
412.20 had left her husband, whom he abhorred with
412.21 an intensity which the mildness of his nature
412.22 would scarcely seem to allow. So deep and
413.01 sensitive was his aversion, that he refrained
413.02 from going anywhere where he was likely to
413.03 see or hear of Heathcliff. Grief, and that to-
413.04 gether, transformed him into a complete her-
413.05 mit: he threw up his office of magistrate,
413.06 ceased even to attend church, avoided the vil-
413.07 lage on all occasions, and spent a life of entire
413.08 seclusion within the limits of his park and

258

413.09 grounds: only varied by solitary rambles on
413.10 the moors, and visits to the grave of his wife,
413.11 mostly at evening, or early morning, before
413.12 other wanderers were abroad.
413.13  But he was too good to be thoroughly un-
413.14 happy long. \He# didn't pray for Catherine's
413.15 soul to haunt him: Time brought resig-
413.16 nation, and a melancholy sweeter than com-
413.17 mon joy. He recalled her memory with ar-
413.18 dent, tender love, and hopeful aspiring to the
413.19 better world, where, he doubted not she was
413.20 gone.
413.21  And he had earthly consolation and affec-
413.22 tions, also. For a few days, I said, he seemed
414.01 regardless of the puny successor to the de-
414.02 parted: that coldness melted as fast as snow
414.03 in April, and ere the tiny thing could stammer
414.04 a word or totter a step, it wielded a despot's
414.05 sceptre in his heart.
414.06  It was named Catherine, but he never called
414.07 it the name in full, as he had never called the
414.08 first Catherine short, probably because Heath-
414.09 cliff, had a habit of doing so. The little one
414.10 was always Cathy, it formed to him a distinc-
414.11 tion from the mother, and yet, a connection
414.12 with her; and his attachment sprang from its
414.13 relation to her, far more than from its being
414.14 his own.
414.15  I used to draw a comparison between him,
414.16 and Hindley Earnshaw and perplex myself to
414.17 explain satisfactorily, why their conduct was
414.18 so opposite in similar circumstances. They
414.19 had both been fond husbands, and were both
414.20 attached to their children; and I could not see
414.21 how they shouldn't both have taken the same
414.22 road, for good or evil. But, I thought in my
415.01 mind, Hindley with apparently the stronger
415.02 head, has shown himself sadly the worse and
415.03 the weaker man. When his ship struck, the
415.04 captain abandoned his post; and the crew, in-
415.05 stead of trying to save her, rushed into riot,
415.06 and confusion, leaving no hope for their luck-
415.07 less vessel. Linton, on the contrary, displayed
415.08 the true courage of a loyal and faithful soul:
415.09 he trusted God; and God comforted him. One
415.10 hoped, and the other despaired: they chose
415.11 their own lots, and were righteously doomed to
415.12 endure them.
415.13  But you'll not want to hear my moralizing,
415.14 Mr. Lockwood: you'll judge as well as I can,
415.15 all these things; at least, you'll think you will
415.16 and that's the same.
415.17  The end of Earnshaw was what might have
415.18 been expected: it followed fast on his sister's,
415.19 there was scarcely six months between them.
415.20 We, at the Grange, never got a very succinct
415.21 account of his state preceding it; all that I
415.22 did learn, was on occasion of going to aid in
416.01 the preparations for the funeral. Mr. Kenneth
416.02 came to announce the event to my master.
416.03  "Well, Nelly;" said he, riding into the
416.04 yard, one morning, too early not to alarm me
416.05 with an instant presentiment of bad news.
416.06 "It's yours, and my turn to go into mourning
416.07 at present. who's given us the slip, now do
416.08 you think?"
416.09  "who?" I asked in a flurry.
416.10  "why, guess!" he returned, dismounting,
416.11 and slinging his bridle on a hook by the door.
416.12 "And nip up the corner of your apron; I'm
416.13 certain you'll need it."
416.14  "Not Mr. Heathcliff, surely? I exclaimed."
416.15  "What! would you have tears for him?" said
416.16 the doctor. No, Heathcliff's a tough young
416.17 fellow; he looks blooming to-day -- I've just
416.18 seen him. He's rapidly regaining flesh since he
416.19 lost his better half.
416.20  "who is it, then Mr. Kenneth?" I repeated
416.21 impatiently.
416.22  "Hindley Earnshaw! Your old friend Hindley -- "
417.01 he replied. "And my wicked gossip;
417.02 though he's been too wild for me this long
417.03 while. There! I said we should draw water --
417.04 But cheer up! He died true to his character
417.05 drunk as a lord; Poor lad; I'm sorry too.
417.06 One can't help missing an old companion;
417.07 though he had the worst tricks with him that
417.08 ever man imagined; and has done me many a
417.09 rascally turn -- He's barely twenty-seven, it
417.10 seems; that's your own age; who would have
417.11 thought you were born in one year!"
417.12  I confess this blow was greater to me than
417.13 the shock of Mrs. Linton's death: ancient as-
417.14 sociations lingered round my heart; I sat down
417.15 in the porch, and wept as for a blood relation,
417.16 desiring Kenneth to get another servant to in-
417.17 troduce him to the master.
417.18  I could not hinder myself from pondering on
417.19 the question -- "Had he had fair play?" What-
417.20 ever I did that idea would bother me: it was
417.21 so tiresomely pertinacious that I resolved on
417.22 requesting leave to go to Wuthering Heights,
418.01 and assist in the last duties to the dead. Mr.
418.02 Linton was extremely reluctant to consent; but
418.03 I pleaded eloquently for the friendless condi-
418.04 tion in which he lay; and I said my old mas-
418.05 ter, and foster brother had a claim on my ser-
418.06 vices as strong as his own. Besides, I remind-
418.07 ed him that the child, Hareton, was his wife's
418.08 nephew; and, in the absence of nearer kin,
418.09 he ought to act as its guardian; and he ought

418.10 to and must inquire how the property was left,
418.11 and look over the concerns of his brother-in--
418.12 law.
418.13  He was unfit for attending to such matters
418.14 then, but he bid me speak to his lawyer; and
418.15 at length, permitted me to go. His lawyer
418.16 had been Earnshaw's also: I called at the vil-
418.17 lage, and asked him to accompany me. He
418.18 shook his head, and advised that Heathcliff
418.19 should be let alone; affirming, if the truth
418.20 were known, Hareton would be found little else
418.21 than a beggar.
418.22  "His father died in debt;" he said; "the
419.01 whole property is mortgaged, and the sole
419.02 chance for the natural heir is to allow him an
419.03 opportunity of creating some interest in the
419.04 creditor's heart, that he may be inclined to
419.05 deal leniently towards him."
419.06  When I reached the Heights, I explained
419.07 that I had come to see everything carried on
419.08 decently, and Joseph, who appeared in suffi-
419.09 cient distress, expressed satisfaction at my pre-
419.10 sence. Mr. Heathcliff said he did not perceive
419.11 that I was wanted, but I might stay and order
419.12 the arrangements for the funeral, if I chose.
419.13  "correctly," he remarked, "that fool's body
419.14 should be buried at the cross-roads, without
419.15 ceremony of any kind -- I happened to leave
419.16 him ten minutes, yesterday afternoon; and,
419.17 in that interval, he fastened the two doors of
419.18 the house against me, and he has spent the
419.19 night in drinking himself to death deliberately!
419.20 we broke in this morning, for we heard him
419.21 snorting like a horse; and there he was, laid
419.22 over the settle -- flaying and scalping would not
420.01 have wakened him -- I sent for Kenneth, and
420.02 he came; but not till the beast had changed
420.03 into carrion -- he was both dead and cold, and
420.04 stark; and so you'll allow, it was useless mak-
420.05 ing more stir about him!"
420.06  The old servant confirmed this statement,
420.07 but muttered,
420.08  "Aw'd rayther he'd goan hisseln fur t'doc-
420.09 tor! Aw sud uh taen tent uh t'maister better
420.10 nur him -- un he warn't deead when Aw left,
420.11 nowt uh t'soart!"
420.12  I insisted on the funeral being respectable
420.13 -- Mr. Heathcliff said I might have my own
420.14 way there too; only, he desired me to remem-
420.15 ber, that the money for the whole affair came
420.16 out of his pocket.
420.17  He maintained a hard, careless deportment,
420.18 indicative of neither joy nor sorrow; if any-
420.19 thing, it expressed a flinty gratification at a
420.20 piece of difficult work, successfully executed.
420.21 I observed once, indeed, something like exul-
420.22 tation in his aspect. It was just when the
421.01 people were bearing the coffin from the house;
421.02 he had the hypocrisy to represent a mourner;
421.03 and previous to following with Hareton he
421.04 lifted the unfortunate child on to the table,
421.05 and muttered with peculiar gusto,
421.06  "Now my bonny lad you are \mine#! And
421.07 we'll see if one tree won't grow as crooked as
421.08 another, with the same wind to twist it!"
421.09  The unsuspecting thing was pleased at this
421.10 speech; he played with Heathcliff's whiskers,
421.11 and stroked his cheek, but I divined its mean-
421.12 ing and observed tartly,
421.13  "That boy must go back with me to
421.14 Thrushcross Grange, Sir -- There is nothing in
421.15 the world less yours than he is!"
421.16  "Does Linton say so?" he demanded.
421.17  "Of course -- he has ordered me to take
421.18 him." I replied.
421.19  "well," said the scoundrel, "We'll not ar-
421.20 gue the subject now; but I have a fancy to
421.21 try my hand at rearing a young one, so intimate
422.01 to your master, that I must supply the
422.02 place of this with my own, if he attempt to
422.03 remove it; I don't engage to let Hareton go,
422.04 undisputed; but, I'll be pretty sure to make
422.05 the other come! remember to tell him."
422.06  This hint was enough to bind our hands.
422.07 I repeated its substance, on my return, and
422.08 Edgar Linton, little interested at the com-
422.09 mencement, spoke no more of interfering. I'm
422.10 not aware that he could have done it to any
422.11 purpose, had he been ever so willing.
422.12  The guest was now the master of wuther-
422.13 ing Heights: he held firm possession, and
422.14 proved to the attorney; who, in his turn,
422.15 proved to Mr. Linton, that Earnshaw had
422.16 mortgaged every yard of land he owned for
422.17 cash to supply his mania for gaming: and he,
422.18 Heathcliff, was the mortgagee.
422.19  In that manner, Hareton, who should now
422.20 be the first gentleman in the neighbourhood,
422.21 was reduced to a state of complete dependence
423.01 on his father's inveterate enemy; and lives in
423.02 his own house as a servant deprived of the ad-
423.03 vantage of wages, and quite unable to right
423.04 himself, because of his friendlessness, and his
423.05 ignorance that he has been wronged.
424.01 [VOL. 2 CHAPTER 4]
424.02  "THE twelve years," continued Mrs. Dean,
424.03 "following that dismal period, were the hap-
424.04 piest of my life: my greatest troubles, in their
424.05 passage, rose from our little lady's trifling ill-
424.06 nesses which she had to experience in common
424.07 with all children, rich and poor."

424.08 For the rest, after the first six months, she
424.09 grew like a larch; and could walk and talk
424.10 too, in her own way, before the heath blossom-
424.11 ed a second time over Mrs. Linton's dust.
424.12 She was the most winning thing that ever
425.01 brought sunshine into a desolate house -- a real
425.02 beauty in face -- with the Earnshaws' handsome
425.03 dark eyes, but the Lintons' fair skin, and small
425.04 features, and yellow curling hair. Her spirit
425.05 was high, though not rough, and qualified by a
425.06 heart, sensitive and lively to excess in its af-
425.07 fections. That capacity for intense attach-
425.08 ments reminded me of her mother; still she
425.09 did not resemble her; for she could be soft
425.10 and mild as a dove, and she had a gentle voice,
425.11 and pensive expression: her anger was never
425.12 furious; her love never fierce; it was deep
425.13 and tender.
425.14 However, it must be acknowledged, she had
425.15 faults to foil her gifts. A propensity to be
425.16 saucy was one; and a perverse will that in-
425.17 dulged children invariably acquire, whether
425.18 they be good tempered or cross. If a servant
425.19 chanced to vex her, it was always: "I shall
425.20 tell papa!" And if he reproved her, even by
425.21 a look, you would have thought it a heart-breaking
426.01 business: I don't believe he ever did
426.02 speak a harsh word to her.
426.03 He took her education entirely on himself,
426.04 and made it an amusement: fortunately, curi-
426.05 osity, and a quick intellect urged her into an
426.06 apt scholar; she learnt rapidly and eagerly,
426.07 and did honour to his teaching.
426.08 Till she reached the age of thirteen, she had
426.09 not once been beyond the range of the park
426.10 by herself. Mr. Linton would take her with
426.11 him, a mile or so outside, on rare occasions;
426.12 but he trusted her to no one else: Gimmerton
426.13 was an unsubstantial name in her ears; the
426.14 chapel, the only building she had approached,
426.15 or entered, except her own home; Wuthering
426.16 Heights and Mr. Heathcliff did not exist for
426.17 her; she was a perfect recluse; and, apparently,
426.18 perfectly contented. Sometimes, indeed, while
426.19 surveying the country from her nursery win-
426.20 dow, she would observe --
426.21 "Ellen, how long will it be before I can
427.01 walk to the top of those hills? I wonder what
427.02 lies on the other side -- is it the sea?"
427.03 "No, Miss Cathy," I would answer, "it
427.04 is hills again just like these."
427.05 "And what are those golden rocks like, when
427.06 you stand under them?" she once asked.
427.07 The abrupt descent of Penistone Craggs
427.08 particularly attracted her notice, especially
427.09 when the setting sun shone on it, and the top--
427.10 most Heights; and the whole extent of land-
427.11 scape besides lay in shadow.
427.12 I explained that they were bare masses of
427.13 stone, with hardly enough earth in their clefts
427.14 to nourish a stunted tree.
427.15 "And why are they bright so long after it
427.16 is evening here?" she pursued.
427.17 "Because they are a great deal higher up
427.18 than we are," replied I; "you could not climb
427.19 them, they are too high and steep. In winter
427.20 the frost is always there before it comes to us;
427.21 and, deep into summer, I have found snow
427.22 under that black hollow on the north-east
427.23 side!"
428.01 "Oh, you have been on them!" she cried,
428.02 gleefully. "Then I can go, too, when I am
428.03 a woman. Has papa been, Ellen?"
428.04 "Papa would tell you, Miss," I answered,
428.05 hastily, "that they are not worth the trouble
428.06 of visiting. The moors, where you ramble
428.07 with him, are much nicer; and Thrushcross
428.08 park is the finest place in the world."
428.09 "But I know the park, and I don't know
428.10 those," she murmured to herself. "And I
428.11 should delight to look round me, from the
428.12 brow of that tallest point -- my little pony,
428.13 Minny, shall take me sometime."
428.14 One of the maids mentioning the Fairy cave,
428.15 quite turned her head with a desire to fulfil
428.16 this project; she teased Mr. Linton about it;
428.17 and he promised she should have the journey
428.18 when she got older: but Miss Catherine mea-
428.19 sured her age by months, and --
428.20 "Now, am I old enough to go to Peni-
428.21 stone Craggs?" was the constant question in
428.22 her mouth.
429.01 The road thither wound close by Wuthering
429.02 Heights. Edgar had not the heart to pass it;
429.03 so she received as constantly the answer,
429.04 "Not yet, love, not yet."
429.05 I said Mrs. Heathcliff lived above a dozen
429.06 years after quitting her husband. Her family
429.07 were of a delicate constitution: she and Edgar
429.08 both lacked the ruddy health that you will
429.09 generally meet in these parts. What her last
429.10 illness was, I am not certain; I conjecture,
429.11 they died of the same thing, a kind of fever,
429.12 slow at its commencement, but incurable, and
429.13 rapidly consuming life towards the close.
429.14 She wrote to inform her brother of the proba-
429.15 ble conclusion of a four months' indisposition,
429.16 under which she had suffered; and entreated
429.17 him to come to her, if possible, for she had
429.18 much to settle, and she wished to bid him
429.19 adieu, and deliver Linton safely into his hands.

429.20 Her hope was, that Linton might be left with
429.21 him, as he had been with her; his father, she
429.22 would fain convince herself, had no desire to
430.01 assume the burden of his maintenance or edu-
430.02 cation.
430.03 My master hesitated not a moment in com-
430.04 plying with her request; reluctant as he was
430.05 to leave home at ordinary calls, he flew to an-
430.06 swer this; commending Catherine to my pe-
430.07 culiar vigilance, in my absence; with reiterated
430.08 orders that she must not wander out of the
430.09 park, even under my escort; he did not calcu-
430.10 late on her going unaccompanied.
430.11 He was away three weeks: the first day or
430.12 two, my charge sat in a corner of the library,
430.13 too sad for either reading or playing: in that
430.14 quiet state she caused me little trouble; but it
430.15 was succeeded by an interval of impatient,
430.16 fretful weariness; and being too busy, and too
430.17 old then, to run up and down amusing her, I
430.18 hit on a method by which she might entertain
430.19 herself.
430.20 I used to send her on her travels round the
430.21 grounds -- now on foot, and now on a pony;
430.22 indulging her with a patient audience of all
431.01 her real and imaginary adventures, when she
431.02 returned.
431.03 The summer shone in full prime; and she
431.04 took such a taste for this solitary rambling
431.05 that she often contrived to remain out from
431.06 breakfast till tea; and then the evenings were
431.07 spent in recounting her fanciful tales. I did
431.08 not fear her breaking bounds, because the gates
431.09 were generally locked, and I thought she
431.10 would scarcely venture forth alone, if they had
431.11 stood wide open.
431.12 Unluckily, my confidence proved misplaced.
431.13 Catherine came to me, one morning, at eight
431.14 o'clock, and said she was that day an Arabian
431.15 merchant, going to cross the Desert with his
431.16 caravan; and I must give her plenty of provi-
431.17 sion for herself, and beasts, a horse, and three
431.18 camels, personated by a large hound, and a
431.19 couple of pointers.
431.20 I got together good store of dainties, and
431.21 slung them in a basket on one side of the sad-
431.22 dle; and she sprang up as gay as a fairy, sheltered
432.01 by her wide-brimmed hat and gauze veil
432.02 from the July sun, and trotted off with a merry
432.03 laugh, mocking my cautious counsel to avoid
432.04 galloping, and come back early.
432.05 The naughty thing never made her appear-
432.06 ance at tea. One traveller, the hound, being
432.07 an old dog, and fond of its ease, returned; but
432.08 neither Cathy, nor the pony, nor the two
432.09 pointers were visible in any direction; and I
432.10 despatched emissaries down this path, and that
432.11 path, and, at last, went wandering in search of
432.12 her myself.
432.13 There was a labourer working at a fence
432.14 round a plantation, on the borders of the
432.15 grounds. I enquired of him if he had seen our
432.16 young lady?
432.17 "I saw her at morn," he replied, "she
432.18 would have me to cut her a hazel switch; and
432.19 then she leapt her galloway over the hedge
432.20 yonder, where it is lowest, and galloped out
432.21 of sight."
432.22 You may guess how I felt at hearing this
433.01 news. It struck me directly she must have
433.02 started for Penistone Craggs.
433.03 "What will become of her?" I ejaculated,
433.04 pushing through a gap which the man was re-
433.05 pairing, and making straight to the high road.
433.06 I walked as if for a wager, mile after mile,
433.07 till a turn brought me in view of the Heights,
433.08 but no Catherine could I detect, far or near.
433.09 The Craggs lie about a mile and a half be-
433.10 yond Mr. Heathcliff's place, and that is four
433.11 from the Grange, so I began to fear night
433.12 would fall ere I could reach them.
433.13 "And what if she should have slipped in
433.14 clambering among them," I reflected, "and
433.15 been killed, or broken some of her bones?"
433.16 My suspense was truly painful; and, at
433.17 first, it gave me delightful relief to observe,
433.18 in hurrying by the farm-house, Charlie, the
433.19 fiercest of the pointers, lying under a window,
433.20 with swelled head, and bleeding ear.
433.21 I open the wicket, and ran to the door,
433.22 knocking vehemently for admittance. A
434.01 woman whom I knew, and who formerly lived
434.02 at Gimmerton, answered -- she had been ser-
434.03 vant there since the death of Mr Earnshaw.
434.04 "Ah," said she, "you are come a seeking
434.05 your little mistress! don't be frightened. She's
434.06 here safe -- but I'm glad it isn't the master."
434.07 "He is not at home then, is he?" I panted,
434.08 quite breathless with quick walking and alarm.
434.09 "No, no," she replied, "both he and Joseph
434.10 are off, and I think they wont return this hour
434.11 or more. Step in and rest you a bit."
434.12 I entered, and beheld my stray lamb, seated
434.13 on the hearth, rocking herself in a little chair
434.14 that had been her mother's, when a child. Her
434.15 hat was hung against the wall, and she seemed
434.16 perfectly at home, laughing and chattering, in
434.17 the best spirits imaginable, to Hareton, now a
434.18 great, strong lad of eighteen, who stared at
434.19 her with considerable curiosity and astonish-
434.20 ment; comprehending precious little of the

434.21 fluent succession of remarks and questions
434.22 which her tongue never ceased pouring forth.
435.01 "Very well, Miss," I exclaimed, concealing
435.02 my joy under an angry countenance. "This
435.03 is your last ride, till papa comes back. I'll not
435.04 trust you over the threshold again, you
435.05 naughty, naughty girl."
435.06 "Aha, Ellen!" she cried, gaily, jumping
435.07 up, and running to my side. "I shall have a
435.08 pretty story to tell to-night -- and so you've
435.09 found me out. Have you ever been here in
435.10 your life before?"
435.11 "Put that hat on, and home at once," said
435.12 I. "I'm dreadfully grieved at you, Miss
435.13 Cathy, you've done extremely wrong! It's no
435.14 use pouting and crying; that wont repay the
435.15 trouble I've had, scouring the country after
435.16 you. To think how Mr. Linton charged me
435.17 to keep you in; and you stealing off so; it
435.18 shows you are a cunning little fox, and nobody
435.19 will put faith in you any more."
435.20 "What have I done?" sobbed she, instantly
435.21 checked. "Papa charged me nothing -- he'll
436.01 not scold me, Ellen -- he's never cross, like
436.02 you!"
436.03 "Come, come!" I repeated. "I'll tie the
436.04 riband. Now, let us have no petulance. Oh,
436.05 for shame. You thirteen years old, and such a
436.06 baby!"
436.07 This exclamation was caused by her pushing
436.08 the hat from her head, and retreating to the
436.09 chimney out of my reach.
436.10 "Nay," said the servant, "don't be hard
436.11 on the bonny lass, Mrs. Dean. We made her
436.12 stop -- she'd fain have ridden forwards, afeard
436.13 you should be uneasy. But Hareton offered
436.14 to go with her, and I thought he should. It's
436.15 a wild road over the hills."
436.16 Hareton, during the discussion, stood with
436.17 his hands in his pockets, too awkward to speak,
436.18 though he looked as if he did not relish my in-
436.19 trusion.
436.20 "How long am I to wait?" I continued,
436.21 disregarding the woman's interference. "It
437.01 will be dark in ten minutes. Where is the
437.02 pony, Miss Cathy? And where is Phenix? I
437.03 shall leave you, unless you be quick, so please
437.04 yourself."
437.05 "The pony is in the yard," she replied,
437.06 "and Phenix is shut in there. He's bitten --
437.07 and so is Charlie. I was going to tell you all
437.08 about it; but you are in a bad temper, and
437.09 don't deserve to hear."
437.10 I picked up her hat, and approached to re-
437.11 instate it; but perceiving that the people of
437.12 the house took her part, she commenced ca-
437.13 pering round the room; and, on my giving
437.14 chase ran like a mouse, over and under, and
437.15 behind the furniture, rendering it ridiculous
437.16 for me to pursue.
437.17 Hareton and the woman laughed; and she
437.18 joined them, and waxed more impertinent still;
437.19 till I cried, in great irritation.
437.20 "Well, Miss Cathy, if you were aware
437.21 whose house this is, you'd be glad enough to
437.22 get out."
438.01 "It's \your# father's, isn't it?" said she, turn-
438.02 ing to Hareton.
438.03 "Nay," he replied, looking down, and
438.04 blushing bashfully.
438.05 He could not stand a steady gaze from her
438.06 eyes, though they were just his own.
438.07 "Whose then -- your master's?" she asked.
438.08 He coloured deeper, with a different feeling,
438.09 muttered an oath, and turned away.
438.10 "Who is his master?" continued the tire-
438.11 some girl, appealing to me. "He talked
438.12 about 'our house,' and 'our folk.' I thought
438.13 he had been the owner's son. And he never
438.14 said, Miss; he should have done, shouldn't he,
438.15 if he's a servant?"
438.16 Hareton grew black as a thunder-cloud, at
438.17 this childish speech. I silently shook my ques-
438.18 tioner, and, at last, succeeded in equipping her
438.19 for departure.
438.20 "Now, get my horse," she said, addressing
438.21 her unknown kinsman as she would one of the
438.22 stable-boys at the Grange. "And you may
439.01 come with me. I want to see where the goblin
439.02 hunter rises in the marsh, and to hear about
439.03 the \fairishes#, as you call them -- but, make
439.04 haste! What's the matter? Get my horse, I
439.05 say."
439.06 "I'll see thee damned, before I be \thy# ser-
439.07 vant!" growled the lad.
439.08 "You'll see me me \what#?" asked Catherine
439.09 in surprise.
439.10 "Damned -- thou saucy witch!" he replied.
439.11 "There, Miss Cathy! you see you have got
439.12 into pretty company," I interposed. "Nice words
439.13 to be used to a young lady! Pray don't begin
439.14 to dispute with him -- Come, let us seek for
439.15 Minny ourselves, and begone."
439.16 "But Ellen," cried she, staring, fixed in
439.17 astonishment. "How dare he speak so to me?
439.18 Musn't he be made to do as I ask him? You
439.19 wicked creature, I shall tell papa what you said
439.20 -- Now then!"
439.21 Hareton did not appear to feel this threat;
439.22 so the tears sprung into her eyes with indignation.
440.01 "You bring the pony," she exclaim-

440.02 ed, turning to the woman, "and let my dog
440.03 free this moment!"
440.04 "Softly, Miss," answered the addressed.
440.05 "You'll lose nothing, by being civil. Though
440.06 Mr. Hareton, there, be not the master's son,
440.07 he's your cousin; and I was never hired to
440.08 serve you."
440.09 "\He# my cousin!" cried Cathy with a scorn-
440.10 ful laugh.
440.11 "Yes, indeed," responded her reprover.
440.12 "Oh, Ellen! don't let them say such things,"
440.13 she pursued in great trouble. Papa is gone to
440.14 fetch my cousin from London -- my cousin is
440.15 a gentleman's son -- That my --" she stopped,
440.16 and wept outright; upset at the bare notion
440.17 of relationship with such a clown.
440.18 "Hush, hush!" I whispered, "people can
440.19 have many cousins and of all sorts, Miss Cathy,
440.20 without being any the worse for it; only they
440.21 needn't keep their company, if they be disa-
440.22 greeable, and bad."
441.01 "He's not, he's not my cousin, Ellen!" she
441.02 went on, gathering fresh grief from reflection,
441.03 and flinging herself into my arms for refuge
441.04 from the idea.
441.05 I was much vexed at her and the servant
441.06 for their mutual revelations; having no doubt
441.07 of Linton's approaching arrival, communicated
441.08 by the former, being reported to Mr. Heath-
441.09 cliff; and feeling as confident that Catherine's
441.10 first thought on her father's return, would be
441.11 to seek an explanation of the latter's assertion,
441.12 concerning her rude-bred kindred.
441.13 Hareton, recovering from his disgust at
441.14 being taken for a servant, seemed moved by
441.15 her distress; and, having fetched the pony
441.16 round to the door, he took, to propitiate her,
441.17 a fine crooked-legged terrier whelp from the
441.18 kennel; and putting it into her hand, bid her
441.19 wisht for he meant naught.
441.20 Pausing in her lamentations, she surveyed
441.21 him with a glance of awe, and horror, then
441.22 burst forth anew.
442.01 I could scarcely refrain from smiling at this
442.02 antipathy to the poor fellow; who was a well--
442.03 made, athletic youth, good looking in features,
442.04 and stout and healthy, but attired in garments
442.05 befitting his daily occupations of working on
442.06 the farm, and lounging among the moors after
442.07 rabbits and game. Still, I thought I could
442.08 detect in his physiognomy a mind owning
442.09 better qualities than his father ever possessed.
442.10 Good things lost amid a wilderness of weeds,
442.11 to be sure, whose rankness far over-topped
442.12 their neglected growth; yet notwithstanding,
442.13 evidence of a wealthy soil that might yield
442.14 luxuriant crops, under other and favourable
442.15 circumstances. Mr. Heathcliff, I believe, had
442.16 not treated him physically ill; thanks to his
442.17 fearless nature which offered no temptation to
442.18 that course of oppression; it had none of the
442.19 timid susceptibility that would have given zest
442.20 to ill-treatment, in Heathcliff's judgment. He
442.21 appeared to have bent his malevolence on
442.22 making him a brute: he was never taught to
443.01 read or write; never rebuked for any bad habit
443.02 which did not annoy his keeper; never led a
443.03 single step towards virtue, or guarded by a
443.04 single precept against vice. And from what I
443.05 heard, Joseph contributed much to his dete-
443.06 rioration by a narrow minded partiality which
443.07 prompted him to flatter, and pet him, as a boy,
443.08 because he was the head of the old family.
443.09 And as he had been in the habit of accusing
443.10 Catherine Earnshaw, and Heathcliff, when
443.11 children, of putting the master past his pa-
443.12 tience, and compelling him to seek solace in
443.13 drink, by what he termed, their "offalld ways,"
443.14 so at present, he laid the whole burden of
443.15 Hareton's faults on the shoulders of the usurper
443.16 of his property.
443.17 If the lad swore he wouldn't correct him;
443.18 nor however culpably he behaved. It gave
443.19 Joseph satisfaction, apparently, to watch him
443.20 go the worst lengths. He allowed that he was
443.21 ruined; that his soul was abandoned to perdition;
444.01 but then, he reflected that Heathcliff
444.02 must answer for it. Hareton's blood would be
444.03 required at his hands; and there lay immense
444.04 consolation in that thought.
444.05 Joseph had instilled into him a pride of
444.06 name, and of his lineage; he would had he
444.07 dared, have fostered hate between him and
444.08 the present owner of the Heights, but his
444.09 dread of that owner amounted to superstition;
444.10 and he confined his feelings, regarding him, to
444.11 muttered inuendo's and private commina-
444.12 tions.
444.13 I don't pretend to be intimately acquainted
444.14 with the mode of living customary in those
444.15 days, at Wuthering Heights. I only speak
444.16 from hearsay; for I saw little. The villagers
444.17 affirmed Mr. Heathcliff was \near#, and a cruel
444.18 hard landlord to his tenants; but the house,
444.19 inside had regained its ancient aspect of com-
444.20 fort under female management; and the scenes
444.21 of riot common in Hindley's time, were not
445.01 now enacted within its walls. The master
445.02 was too gloomy to seek companionship with
445.03 any people, good or bad, and he is yet --
445.04 This, however, is not making progress with

445.05 my story. Miss Cathy rejected the peace--
445.06 offering of the terrier, and demanded her own
445.07 dogs, Charlie and Phenix. They came limp-
445.08 ing, and hanging their heads; and we set out
445.09 for home, sadly out of sorts, every one of us.
445.10 I could not wring from my little lady how
445.11 she had spent the day; except that, as I sup-
445.12 posed, the goal of her pilgrimage was Penistone
445.13 Crags; and she arrived without adventure to
445.14 the gate of the farmhouse, when Hareton hap-
445.15 pened to issue forth, attended by some canine
445.16 followers who attacked her train.
445.17 They had a smart battle, before their owners
445.18 could separate them: that formed an intro-
445.19 duction. Catherine told Hareton who she was,
445.20 and where she was going; and asked him to
445.21 show her the way; finally, beguilnig him to
445.22 accompany her.
446.01 He opened the mysteries of the Fairy cave,
446.02 and twenty other queer places; but being in
446.03 disgrace, I was not favoured with a descrip-
446.04 tion of the interesting objects she saw.
446.05 I could gather however, that her guide had
446.06 been a favourite till she hurt his feelings by
446.07 addressing him as a servant, and Heathcliff's
446.08 housekeeper hurt hers, by calling him her
446.09 cousin.
446.10 Then the language he had held to her ran-
446.11 kled in her heart; she who was always "love,"
446.12 and "darling," and "queen," and "angel,"
446.13 with everybody at the Grange; to be insulted
446.14 so shockingly by a stranger! She did not
446.15 comprehend it; and hard work I had, to ob-
446.16 tain a promise that she would not lay the
446.17 grievance before her father.
446.18 I explained how he objected to the whole
446.19 household at the Heights, and how sorry he
446.20 would be to find she had been there; but, I
446.21 insisted most on the fact, that if she revealed
446.22 my negligence of his orders, he would perhaps,
447.01 be so angry that I should have to leave;
447.02 and Cathy couldn't bear that prospect: she
447.03 pledged her word, and kept it, for my sake --
447.04 after all, she was a sweet little girl.
448.01 [VOL. 2 CHAPTER 5]
448.02 A LETTER, edged with black, announced the
448.03 day of my master's return. Isabella was dead;
448.04 and he wrote to bid me get mourning for his
448.05 daughter, and arrange a room, and other ac-
448.06 commodations, for his youthful nephew.
448.07 Catharine ran wild with joy at the idea of
448.08 welcoming her father back: and indulged
448.09 most sanguine anticipations of the innumera-
448.10 ble excellencies of her "real" cousin.
448.11 The evening of their expected arrival came.
448.12 Since early morning, she had been busy, ordering
449.01 her own small affairs; and now, attired
449.02 in her new black frock -- poor thing! her
449.03 aunt's death impressed her with no definite
449.04 sorrow -- she obliged me, by constant worrying,
449.05 to walk with her, down through the grounds, to
449.06 meet them.
449.07 "Linton is just six months younger than I
449.08 am," she chattered as we strolled leisurely over
449.09 the swells and hollows of mossy turf, under
449.10 shadow of the trees. "How delightful it
449.11 will be to have him for a playfellow! Aunt
449.12 Isabella sent papa a beautiful lock of his hair;
449.13 it was lighter than mine -- more flaxen, and
449.14 quite as fine. I have it carefully preserved in
449.15 a little glass box; and I've often thought what
449.16 pleasure it would be to see its owner -- Oh!
449.17 I am happy -- and papa, dear, dear papa! come,
449.18 Ellen, let us run! come run!"
449.19 She ran, and returned and ran again, many
449.20 times before my sober footsteps reached the
449.21 gate, and then she seated herself on the grassy
449.22 bank beside the path, and tried to wait patiently;
450.01 but that was impossible; she couldn't
450.02 be still a minute.
450.03 "How long they are!" she exclaimed. "Ah,
450.04 I see some dust on the road -- they are coming!
450.05 No! When will they be here? May we not
450.06 go a little way -- half a mile, Ellen, only just
450.07 half a mile? Do say yes, to that clump of
450.08 birches at the turn!"
450.09 I refused staunchily: and, at length, her
450.10 suspense was ended: the travelling carriage
450.11 rolled in sight.
450.12 Miss Cathy shrieked, and stretched out her
450.13 arms, as soon as she caught her father's face,
450.14 looking from the window. He descended,
450.15 nearly as eager as herself; and a considerable
450.16 interval elapsed, ere they had a thought to
450.17 spare for any but themselves.
450.18 While they exchanged caresses, I took a
450.19 peep in to see after Linton. He was asleep,
450.20 in a corner, wrapped in a warm, fur-lined
450.21 cloak, as if it had been winter. A pale, deli-
450.22 cate, effeminate boy, who might have been
451.01 taken for my master's younger brother, so
451.02 strong was the resemblance; but there was a
451.03 sickly peevishness in his aspect, that Edgar
451.04 Linton never had.
451.05 The latter saw me looking; and having
451.06 shaken hands, advised me to close the door,
451.07 and leave him undisturbed; for the journey
451.08 had fatigued him.
451.09 Cathy would fain have taken one glance;
451.10 but her father told her to come on, and they
451.11 walked together up the park, while I hastened

451.12 before, to prepare the servants.
451.13 "Now, darling," said Mr. Linton, address-
451.14 ing his daughter, as they halted at the bottom
451.15 of the front steps. "Your cousin is not so
451.16 strong, or so merry as you are, and he has lost
451.17 his mother, remember, a very short time since,
451.18 therefore, don't expect him to play, and run
451.19 about with you directly. And don't harass
451.20 him much by talking -- let him be quiet this
451.21 evening, at least, will you?"
451.22 "Yes, yes, papa," answered Catherine;
452.01 "but I do want to see him; and he hasn't
452.02 once looked out."
452.03 The carriage stopped; and the sleeper,
452.04 being roused, was lifted to the ground by his
452.05 uncle.
452.06 "This is your cousin Cathy, Linton," he
452.07 said, putting their little hands together.
452.08 "She's fond of you already; and mind you
452.09 don't grieve her by crying to-night. Try to be
452.10 cheerful now; the travelling is at an end, and
452.11 you have nothing to do but rest and amuse
452.12 yourself as you please."
452.13 "Let me go to bed then," answered the
452.14 boy, shrinking from Catherine's salute; and
452.15 he put his fingers to his eyes to remove incipi-
452.16 ent tears.
452.17 "Come, come, there's a good child," I whis-
452.18 pered, leading him in. "You'll make her weep
452.19 too -- see how sorry she is for you!"
452.20 I do not know whether it were sorrow for
452.21 him, but his cousin put on as sad a counte-
452.22 nance as himself, and returned to her father.
453.01 All three entered, and mounted to the library
453.02 where tea was laid ready.
453.03 I proceeded to remove Linton's cap, and
453.04 mantle, and placed him on a chair by the table;
453.05 but he was no sooner seated than he began to
453.06 cry afresh. My master inquired what was the
453.07 matter.
453.08 ."I can't sit on a chair," sobbed the boy.
453.09 "Go to the sofa then; and Ellen shall bring
453.10 you some tea," answered his uncle, patiently.
453.11 He had been greatly tried during the jour-
453.12 ney, I felt convinced, by his fretful, ailing
453.13 charge.
453.14 Linton slowly trailed himself off, and lay
453.15 down. Cathy carried a foot-stool and her cup
453.16 to his side.
453.17 At first she sat silent; but that could not
453.18 last; she had resolved to make a pet of her
453.19 little cousin, as she would have him to be;
453.20 and she commenced stroking his curls, and
453.21 kissing his cheek, and offering him tea in her
453.22 saucer, like a baby. This pleased him, for he
454.01 was not much better; he dried his eyes, and
454.02 lightened into a faint smile.
454.03 "Oh, he'll do very well," said the master to
454.04 me, after watching them a minute. "Very
454.05 well, if we can keep him, Ellen. The company
454.06 of a child of his own age will instil new spirit
454.07 into him soon: and by wishing for strength
454.08 he'll gain it."
454.09 Aye, if we can keep him! I mused to my-
454.10 self; and sore misgivings came over me that
454.11 there was slight hope of that. And then, I
454.12 thought, however will that weakling live at
454.13 Wuthering Heights, between his father and
454.14 Hareton? what playmates and instructors
454.15 they'll be.
454.16 Our doubts were presently decided; even
454.17 earlier than I expected. I had just taken the
454.18 children up stairs, after tea was finished; and
454.19 seen Linton asleep -- he would not suffer me to
454.20 leave him, till that was the case -- I had come
454.21 down, and was standing by the table in the
454.22 hall, lighting a bed-room candle for Mr. Edgar,
455.01 when a maid stepped out of the kitchen, and
455.02 informed me that Mr. Heathcliff's servant,
455.03 Joseph, was at the door, and wished to speak
455.04 with the master.
455.05 "I shall ask him what he wants first," I said,
455.06 in considerable trepidation. "A very unlikely
455.07 hour to be troubling people, and the instant
455.08 they have returned from a long journey. I don't
455.09 think the master can see him."
455.10 Joseph had advanced through the kitchen,
455.11 as I uttered these words, and now present-
455.12 ed himself in the hall. He was donned in his
455.13 Sunday garments, with his most sanctimonious
455.14 and sourest face; and holding his hat in one
455.15 hand, and his stick in the other, he proceeded
455.16 to clean his shoes on the mat.
455.17 "Good evening, Joseph," I said, coldly.
455.18 "What business brings you here to-night?"
455.19 "It's Maister Linton Aw mun spake tull,"
455.20 he answered, waving me disdainfully aside.
455.21 "Mr. Linton is going to bed; unless you
455.22 have something particular to say, I'm sure he
456.01 wont hear it now," I continued. "You had
456.02 better sit down in there, and entrust your mes-
456.03 sage to me."
456.04 "Which is his rahm?" pursued the fellow,
456.05 surveying the range of closed doors.
456.06 I perceived he was bent on refusing my me-
456.07 diation; so very reluctantly, I went up to the
456.08 library, and announced the unseasonable visi-
456.09 ter; advising that he should be dismissed till
456.10 next day.
456.11 Mr. Linton had no time to empower me to
456.12 do so, for he mounted close at my heels, and

456.13 pushing into the apartment, planted himself
456.14 at the far side of the table, with his two fists
456.15 clapped on the head of his stick, and began in
456.16 an elevated tone, as if anticipating opposition.
456.17 "Hathecliff has send me for his lad, un Aw
456.18 'munn't goa back 'baht him."
456.19 Edgar Linton was silent a minute; an ex-
456.20 pression of exceeding sorrow overcast his fea-
456.21 tures; he would have pitied the child on his
456.22 own account; but, recalling Isabella's hopes
457.01 and fears, and anxious wishes for her son, and
457.02 her commendations of him to his care, he
457.03 grieved bitterly at the prospect of yielding
457.04 him up, and searched in his heart how it might
457.05 be avoided. No plan offered itself: the very
457.06 exhibition of any desire to keep him would
457.07 have rendered the claimant more peremptory:
457.08 there was nothing left but to resign him.
457.09 However, he was not going to rouse him from
457.10 his sleep.
457.11 "Tell Mr. Heathcliff," he answered, calmly,
457.12 "that his son shall come to Wuthering
457.13 Heights to-morrow. He is in bed, and too
457.14 tired to go the distance now. You may also
457.15 tell him that the mother of Linton desired him
457.16 to remain under my guardianship; and, at
457.17 present, his health is very precarious."
457.18 "Noa!" said Joseph, giving a thud with
457.19 his prop on the floor, and assuming an authori-
457.20 tative air. "Noa! that manes nowt -- Hathe-
457.21 cliff maks noa 'cahnt uh t' mother, nur yah
457.22 norther -- bud he'll hev his lad; und Aw mun
457.23 tak him -- soa nah yah knaw!"
458.01 "You shall not to-night!" answered Linton,
458.02 decisively. "Walk down stairs at once, and
458.03 repeat to your master what I have said. Ellen,
458.04 show him down. Go --"
458.05 And, aiding the indignant elder with a lift
458.06 by the arm, he rid the room of him, and closed
458.07 the door.
458.08 "Varrah weel!" shouted Joseph, as he slowly
458.09 drew off. "Tuh morn, he's come hisseln, un'
458.10 thrust \him# aht, if yah darr!"
459.01 [VOL. 2 CHAPTER 6]
459.02 To obviate the danger of this threat being
459.03 fulfilled, Mr. Linton commissioned me to take
459.04 the boy home early, on Catherine's pony, and,
459.05 said he --
459.06 "As we shall now have no influence over
459.07 his destiny, good or bad, you must say nothing
459.08 of where he is gone to my daughter; she can-
459.09 not associate with him hereafter; and it is
459.10 better for her to remain in ignorance of his
459.11 proximity, lest she should be restless, and an-
459.12 xious to visit the Heights -- merely tell her,
460.01 his father sent for him suddenly, and he has
460.02 been obliged to leave us."
460.03 Linton was very reluctant to be roused
460.04 from his bed, at five o'clock, and astonished
460.05 to be informed that he must prepare for fur-
460.06 ther travelling: but I softened off the matter
460.07 by stating that he was going to spend some
460.08 time with his father, Mr. Heathcliff, who
460.09 wished to see him so much, he did not like to
460.10 defer the pleasure till he should recover from
460.11 his late journey.
460.12 "My father?" he cried, in strange perplex-
460.13 ity. "Mamma never told me I had a father.
460.14 Where does he live? I'd rather stay with
460.15 uncle."
460.16 "He lives a little distance from the
460.17 Grange," I replied, "just beyond those hills --
460.18 not so far, but you may walk over here, when
460.19 you get hearty. And you should be glad to
460.20 go home, and see him. You must try to
460.21 love him, as you did your mother, and then he
460.22 will love you."
461.01 "But why have I not heard of him before?"
461.02 asked Linton; "why didn't mamma, and he
461.03 live together as other people do?"
461.04 "He had business to keep him in the
461.05 north," I answered; "and your mother's health
461.06 required her to reside in the south."
461.07 "And why didn't mamma speak to me
461.08 about him?" persevered the child. "She
461.09 often talked of uncle, and I learnt to love him
461.10 long ago. How am I to love papa? I don't
461.11 know him."
461.12 "Oh, all children love their parents," I
461.13 said. "Your mother, perhaps, thought you
461.14 would want to be with him, if she mentioned
461.15 him often to you. Let us make haste. An
461.16 early ride on such a beautiful morning is much
461.17 preferable to an hour's more sleep."
461.18 "Is \she# to go with us," he demanded. "The
461.19 little girl I saw yesterday?"
461.20 "Not now," replied I.
461.21 "Is uncle?" he continued.
462.01 "No, I shall be your companion there," I
462.02 said.
462.03 Linton sank back on his pillow, and fell into
462.04 a brown study.
462.05 "I won't go without uncle;" he cried at
462.06 length; "I can't tell where you mean to take
462.07 me."
462.08 I attempted to persuade him of the naughti-
462.09 ness of showing reluctance to meet his father:
462.10 still he obstinately resisted any progress to-
462.11 wards dressing; and I had to call for my mas-
462.12 ter's assistance, in coaxing him out of bed.
462.13 The poor thing was finally got off with seve-

462.14 ral delusive assurances that his absence should
462.15 be short; that Mr. Edgar and Cathy would
462.16 visit him; and other promises, equally ill--
462.17 founded, which I invented and reiterated, at
462.18 intervals, throughout the way.
462.19 The pure heather-scented air, and the bright
462.20 sunshine, and the gentle canter of Minny re-
462.21 lieved his despondency, after a while. He be-
462.22 gan to put questions concerning his new home,
463.01 and its inhabitants, with greater interest, and
463.02 liveliness.
463.03 "Is Wuthering Heights as pleasant a place
463.04 as Thrushcross Grange?" he inquired, turning
463.05 to take a last glance into the valley, whence
463.06 a light mist mounted, and formed fleecy cloud,
463.07 on the skirts of the blue.
463.08 "It is not so buried in trees," I replied,
463.09 "and it is not quite so large, but you can see
463.10 the country beautifully, all round; and the air
463.11 is healthier for you -- fresher, and dryer. You
463.12 will, perhaps, think the building old and dark,
463.13 at first -- though it is a respectable house, the
463.14 next best in the neighbourhood. And you
463.15 will have such nice rambles on the moors!
463.16 Hareton Earnshaw -- that is Miss Cathy's other
463.17 cousin; and so yours in a manner -- will show
463.18 you all the sweetest spots; and you can bring
463.19 a book in fine weather, and make a green hol-
463.20 low your study; and, now and then your un-
463.21 cle may join you in a walk; he does, fre-
463.22 quently, walk out on the hills."
464.01 "And what is my father like?" he asked.
464.02 "Is he as young and handsome as uncle?"
464.03 "He's as young," said I "but he has black
464.04 hair, and eyes; and looks sterner, and he is
464.05 taller and bigger altogether. He'll not seem
464.06 to you so gentle and kind at first, perhaps, be-
464.07 cause, it is not his way -- still, mind you be
464.08 frank and cordial with him; and naturally,
464.09 he'll be fonder of you than any uncle, for you
464.10 are his own."
464.11 "Black hair and eyes!" mused Linton. "I
464.12 can't fancy him. Then I am not like him, am
464.13 I?"
464.14 "Not much," I answered ... Not a morsel, I
464.15 thought: surveying with regret the white com-
464.16 plexion, and slim frame of my companion, and
464.17 his large languid eyes ... his mother's eyes save
464.18 that, unless a morbid touchiness kindled them,
464.19 a moment, they had not a vestige of her spark-
464.20 ling spirit.
464.21 "How strange that he should never come to
464.22 see mama, and me" he murmured. "Has he
465.01 ever seen me? If he have, I must have been
465.02 a baby -- I remember not a single thing about
465.03 him!"
465.04 "Why, Master Linton," said I, "three hun-
465.05 dred miles is a great distance: and ten years
465.06 seem very different in length, to a grown up
465.07 person, compared with what they do to you.
465.08 It is probable Mr. Heathcliff proposed going,
465.09 from summer to summer, but never found a
465.10 convenient opportunity: and now it is too late
465.11 -- Don't trouble him with questions on the
465.12 subject: it will disturb him for no good."
465.13 The boy was fully occupied with his own
465.14 cogitations for the remainder of the ride, till
465.15 we halted before the farm-house garden gate.
465.16 I watched to catch his impressions in his coun-
465.17 tenance. He surveyed the carved front,
465.18 and low-browed lattices; the straggling goose--
465.19 berry bushes, and crooked firs, with solemn in-
465.20 tentness, and then shook his head: his private
465.21 feelings entirely disapproved of the exterior of
466.01 his new abode; but he had sense to postpone
466.02 complaining -- there might be compensation
466.03 within.
466.04 Before he dismounted, I went and opened
466.05 the door. It was half-past six; the family had
466.06 just finished breakfast; the servant was clear-
466.07 ing and wiping down the table: Joseph stood
466.08 by his master's chair telling some tale concern-
466.09 ing a lame horse; and Hareton was preparing
466.10 for the hay-field.
466.11 "Hallo, Nelly!" cried Mr. Heathcliff, when
466.12 he saw me. "I feared I should have to come
466.13 down and fetch my property, myself -- You've
466.14 brought it have you? Let us see what we
466.15 can make of it."
466.16 He got up and strode to the door: Hareton
466.17 and Joseph followed in gaping curiosity. Poor
466.18 Linton ran a frightened eye over the faces of
466.19 the three.
466.20 "Sure-ly," said Joseph after a grave inspec-
466.21 tion, 'he's swopped wi' ye, maister, an' yon's
466.22 his lass!"
467.01 Heathcliff having stared his son into an ague
467.02 of confusion, uttered a scornful laugh.
467.03 "God! what a beauty! what a lovely, charm-
467.04 ing thing!" he exclaimed. "Haven't they
467.05 reared it on snails, and sour milk, Nelly? Oh,
467.06 damn my soul! but that's worse than I ex-
467.07 pected -- and the devil knows I was not san-
467.08 guine!"
467.09 I bid the trembling and bewildered child
467.10 get down, and enter. He did not thoroughly
467.11 comprehend the meaning of his father's speech,
467.12 or whether it were intended for him: indeed,
467.13 he was not yet certain that the grim, sneering
467.14 stranger was his father; but he clung to me
467.15 with growing trepidation; and on Mr. Heath-

467.16 cliff´s taking a seat, and bidding him "come
467.17 hither," he hid his face on my shoulder, and
467.18 wept.
467.19 "Tut, tut!" said Heathcliff, stretching out
467.20 a hand and dragging him roughly between his
467.21 knees, and then holding up his head by the
467.22 chin. "None of that nonsense! we´re not
468.01 going to hurt thee, Linton -- isn´t that thy
468.02 name? Thou art thy mother´s child, entirely!
468.03 where in thee, \my# share in thee, puling chicken?"
468.04 He took off the boy´s cap and pushed back
468.05 his thick flaxen curls, felt his slender arms, and
468.06 his small fingers; during which examination,
468.07 Linton ceased crying, and lifted his great blue
468.08 eyes to inspect the inspector.
468.09 "Do you know me?" asked Heathcliff, hav-
468.10 ing satisfied himself that the limbs were all
468.11 equally frail and feeble.
468.12 "No!" said Linton, with a gaze of vacant
468.13 fear.
468.14 "You´ve heard of me, I dare say?"
468.15 "No," he replied again.
468.16 "No? what a shame of your mother, never
468.17 to waken your filial regard for me! You are
468.18 my son, then, I´ll tell you; and your mother
468.19 was a wicked slut to leave you in ignorance of
468.20 the sort of father you possessed -- Now, don´t
468.21 wince, and colour up! Though it \is# some-
468.22 thing to see you have not white blood -- Be a
469.01 good lad; and I´ll do for you -- Nelly, if you
469.02 be tired you may sit down, if not get home
469.03 again -- I guess you´ll report what you hear,
469.04 and see, to the cipher at the Grange; and
469.05 this thing won´t be settled while you linger
469.06 about it."
469.07 "well," replied I, "I hope you´ll be kind
469.08 to the boy, Mr. Heathcliff, or you´ll not keep
469.09 him long, and he´s all you have akin, in the
469.10 wide world that you will ever know -- remem-
469.11 ber.
469.12 "I´ll be \very# kind to him you needn´t fear!"
469.13 he said laughing. "Only nobody else must
469.14 be kind to him -- I´m jealous of monopolizing
469.15 his affection -- And, to begin my kindness,
469.16 Joseph! bring the lad some breakfast -- Hare-
469.17 ton, you infernal calf, begone to your work.
469.18 Yes, Nell," he added when they were depart-
469.19 ed, "my son is prospective owner of your
469.20 place, and I should not wish him to die till I
469.21 was certain of being his successor. Besides,
469.22 he´s \mine#, and I want the triumph of seeing
470.01 \my# descendent fairly lord of their estates; my
470.02 child hiring their children, to till their fathers´
470.03 lands for wages -- That is the sole considera-
470.04 tion which can make me endure the whelp --
470.05 I despise him for himself, and hate him for
470.06 the memories he revives! But, that conside-
470.07 ration is sufficient; he´s as safe with me, and
470.08 shall be tended as carefully, as your master
470.09 tends his own -- I have a room upstairs, fur-
470.10 nished in handsome style -- I´ve en-
470.11 gaged a tutor, also, to come three times a
470.12 week, from twenty miles distance, to teach
470.13 him what he pleases to learn. I´ve ordered
470.14 Hareton to obey him: and in fact, I´ve ar-
470.15 ranged every thing with a view to preserve
470.16 the superior, and the gentleman in him, above
470.17 his associates -- I do regret however, that he
470.18 so little deserves the trouble -- if I wished any
470.19 blessing in the world, it was to find him a
470.20 worthy object of pride, and I´m bitterly dis-
470.21 appointed with the whey-faced whining
470.22 wretch!"
471.01 while he was speaking, Joseph returned,
471.02 bearing a basin of milk-porridge, and placed
471.03 it before Linton. He stirred round the home-
471.04 ly mess with a look of aversion, and affirmed
471.05 he could not eat it.
471.06 I saw the old man servant shared largely in
471.07 his master´s scorn of the child, though he was
471.08 compelled to retain the sentiment in his heart,
471.09 because Heathcliff plainly meant his underlings
471.10 to hold him in honour.
471.11 "Cannot ate it?" repeated he, peering in
471.12 Linton´s face, and subduing his voice to a
471.13 whisper, for fear of being overheard. "But
471.14 Maister Hareton nivir ate nowt else, when he
471.15 wer a little un: und what wer good enough
471.16 fur him´s good enough fur yah, Aw´s rayther
471.17 think!"
471.18 "I \shan´t# eat it!" answered Linton, snap-
471.19 pishly. "Take it away."
471.20 Joseph snatched up the food indignantly, and
471.21 brought it to us.
472.01 "Is there owt ails th´ victuals?" he asked,
472.02 thrusting the tray under Heathcliff´s nose.
472.03 "what should ail them?" he said.
472.04 "wah!" answered Joseph, "yon dainty
472.05 chap says he cannut ate ´em. Bud Aw guess
472.06 it´s raight! His mother wer just soa -- we wer
472.07 a´most too mucky tuh sow t´ corn fur makking
472.08 her breead."
472.09 "Don´t mention his mother to me," said the
472.10 master, angrily. "Get him something that
472.11 he can eat, that´s all. what is his usual food,
472.12 Nelly?"
472.13 I suggested boiled milk or tea; and the
472.14 housekeeper received instructions to prepare
472.15 some.
472.16 Come, I reflected, his father´s selfishness
472.17 may contribute to his comfort. He perceives

472.18 his delicate constitution, and the necessity of
472.19 treating him tolerably. I´ll console Mr. Edgar
472.20 by acquainting him with the turn Heathcliff´s
472.21 humour has taken.
472.22 Having no excuse for lingering longer, I
473.01 slipped out, while Linton was engaged in
473.02 timidly rebuffing the advances of a friendly
473.03 sheep-dog. But he was too much on the
473.04 alert to be cheated -- as I closed the door, I
473.05 heard a cry, and a frantic repetition of the
473.06 words --
473.07 "Don´t leave me! I´ll not stay here! I´ll
473.08 not stay here!"
473.09 Then the latch was raised and fell -- they
473.10 did not suffer him to come forth. I mounted
473.11 Minny, and urged her to a trot; and so my
473.12 brief guardianship ended.
474.01 [VOL. 2 CHAPTER 7]
474.02 WE had sad work with little Cathy that day:
474.03 she rose in high glee, eager to join her cousin;
474.04 and such passionate tears and lamentations
474.05 followed the news of her departure, that Ed-
474.06 gar, himself, was obliged to sooth her, by af-
474.07 firming he should come back soon; he added,
474.08 however, "if I can get him;" and there were
474.09 no hopes of that.
474.10 This promise poorly pacified her; but time
474.11 was more potent; and though still, at inter-
474.12 vals, she inquired of her father, when Linton
475.01 would return; before she did see him again,
475.02 his features had waxed so dim in her memory
475.03 that she did not recognise him.
475.04 when I chanced to encounter the house-
475.05 keeper of Wuthering Heights, in paying busi-
475.06 ness-visits to Gimmerton, I used to ask how
475.07 the young master got on; for he lived almost
475.08 as secluded as Catherine herself, and was never
475.09 to be seen. I could gather from her that he
475.10 continued in weak health, and was a tiresome
475.11 inmate. She said Mr. Heathcliff seemed to
475.12 dislike him ever longer and worse, though he
475.13 took some trouble to conceal it. He had an
475.14 antipathy to the sound of his voice, and could
475.15 not do at all with his sitting in the same room
475.16 with him many minutes together.
475.17 There seldom passed much talk between
475.18 them; Linton learnt his lessons, and spent his
475.19 evenings in a small apartment, they called the
475.20 parlour; or else lay in bed all day; for he
475.21 was constantly getting coughs, and colds, and
475.22 aches, and pains of some sort.
476.01 "And I never knew such a faint-hearted
476.02 creature," added the woman; "nor one so
476.03 careful of hisseln. He \will# go on, if I leave
476.04 the window open, a bit late in the evening.
476.05 Oh! it´s killing a breath of night air! And
476.06 he must have a fire in the middle of summer;
476.07 and Joseph´s ´bacca pipe is poison; and he
476.08 must always have sweets and dainties, and
476.09 always milk, milk for ever -- heeding naught
476.10 how the rest of us are pinched in winter -- and
476.11 there he´ll sit, wrapped in his furred cloak in
476.12 his chair by the fire, and some toast and water,
476.13 or other slop on the hob to sip at; and if
476.14 Hareton, for pity, comes to amuse him -- Hare-
476.15 ton is not bad-natured, though he´s rough --
476.16 they´re sure to part, one swearing, and the
476.17 other crying. I believe the master would re-
476.18 lish Earnshaw´s thrashing him to a mummy, if
476.19 he were not his son: and, I´m certain, he
476.20 would be fit to turn him out of doors, if he
476.21 knew half the nursing he gives hisseln. But
476.22 then, he wont go into danger of temptation;
477.01 he never enters the parlour, and should Linton
477.02 show those ways in the house where he is, he
477.03 sends him up stairs directly."
477.04 I divined, from this account, that utter lack
477.05 of sympathy had rendered young Heathcliff
477.06 selfish and disagreeable, if he were not so
477.07 originally; and my interest in him, conse-
477.08 quently, decayed; though still I was moved
477.09 with a sense of grief at his lot, and a wish
477.10 that he had been left with us.
477.11 Mr. Edgar encouraged me to gain informa-
477.12 tion; he thought a great deal about him, I
477.13 fancy, and would have run some risk to see
477.14 him; and he told me once to ask the house-
477.15 keeper whether he ever came into the village?
477.16 She said he had only been twice, on horse-
477.17 back, accompanying his father: and both times
477.18 he pretended to be quite knocked up for three
477.19 or four days afterwards.
477.20 That housekeeper left, if I recollect rightly,
477.21 two years after he came; and another, whom I
478.01 did not know, was her successor: she lives
478.02 there still.
478.03 Time wore on at the Grange in its former
478.04 pleasant way, till Miss Cathy reached sixteen.
478.05 on the anniversary of her birth we never
478.06 manifested any signs of rejoicing, because it
478.07 was, also, the anniversary of my late mistress´s
478.08 death. Her father invariably spent that day
478.09 alone in the library; and walked, at dusk, as
478.10 far as Gimmerton kirkyard, where he would
478.11 frequently prolong his stay beyond midnight.
478.12 Therefore Catherine was thrown on her own
478.13 resources for amusement.
478.14 This twentieth of March was a beautiful
478.15 spring day, and when her father had retired,
478.16 my young lady came down dressed for going
478.17 out, and she said she had asked to have a ramble

478.18 on the edge of the moors with me; and Mr.
478.19 Linton had given her leave, if we went only a
478.20 short distance, and were back within the hour.
478.21 "So make haste, Ellen!" she cried. "I
479.01 know where I wish to go; where a colony of
479.02 moor game are settled; I want to see whether
479.03 they have made their nests yet."
479.04 "That must be a good distance up," I an-
479.05 swered; "they don't breed on the edge of the
479.06 moor."
479.07 "No, it's not," she said. "I've gone very
479.08 near with papa."
479.09 I put on my bonnet, and sallied out;
479.10 thinking nothing more of the matter. She
479.11 bounded before me, and returned to my side,
479.12 and was off again like a young greyhound;
479.13 and, at first, I found plenty of entertainment
479.14 in listening to the larks singing far and near;
479.15 and enjoying the sweet, warm sunshine; and
479.16 watching her, my pet, and my delight, with
479.17 her golden ringlets flying loose behind, and her
479.18 bright cheek, as soft and pure in its bloom,
479.19 as a wild rose, and her eyes radiant with
479.20 cloudless pleasure. She was a happy creature,
479.21 and an angel, in those days. It's a pity she
479.22 could not be content.
480.01 "Well," said I, "where are your moor--
480.02 game, Miss Cathy? We should be at them --
480.03 the Grange park-fence is a great way off
480.04 now."
480.05 "Oh, a little further -- only a little further,
480.06 Ellen," was her answer, continually. "Climb
480.07 to that hillock, pass that bank, and by the time
480.08 you reach the other side, I shall have raised
480.09 the birds."
480.10 But there were so many hillocks and banks
480.11 to climb and pass, that, at length, I began to be
480.12 weary, and told her we must halt, and retrace
480.13 our steps.
480.14 I shouted to her, as she had outstripped me,
480.15 a long way; she either did not hear, or did not
480.16 regard, for she still sprang on, and I was com-
480.17 pelled to follow. Finally, she dived into a
480.18 hollow; and before I came in sight of her
480.19 again, she was two miles nearer Wuthering
480.20 Heights than her own home; and I beheld a
480.21 couple of persons arrest her, one of whom I
480.22 felt convinced was Mr. Heathcliff himself.
481.01 Cathy had been caught in the fact of plun-
481.02 dering, or, at least, hunting out the nests of
481.03 the grouse.
481.04 The Heights were Heathcliff's land, and he
481.05 was reproving the poacher.
481.06 "I've neither taken any nor found any," she
481.07 said, as I toiled to them, expanding her hands
481.08 in corroboration of the statement. "I didn't
481.09 mean to take them; but papa told me there
481.10 were quantities up here, and I wished to see
481.11 the eggs."
481.12 Heathcliff glanced at me with an ill-mean-
481.13 ing smile, expressing his acquaintance with the
481.14 party, and consequently, his malevolence to-
481.15 wards it, and demanded who "papa" was?
481.16 "Mr. Linton of Thrushcross Grange," she
481.17 replied. "I thought you did not know me,
481.18 or you wouldn't have spoken in that way."
481.19 "You suppose papa is highly esteemed and
481.21 respected then?" he said, sarcastically.
481.21 "And what are you?" inquired Catherine,
482.01 gazing curiously on the speaker. "That man
482.02 I've seen before. Is he your son?"
482.03 She pointed to Hareton, the other indivi-
482.04 dual; who had gained nothing but increased
482.05 bulk and strength by the addition of two
482.06 years to his age: he seemed as awkward and
482.07 rough as ever.
482.08 "Miss Cathy," I interrupted, "it will be
482.09 three hours instead of one, that we are out,
482.10 presently. We really must go back."
482.11 "No, that man is not my son," answered
482.12 Heathcliff, pushing me aside. "But I have
482.13 one, and you have seen him before too; and,
482.14 though your nurse is in a hurry, I think both
482.15 you and she would be the better for a little
482.16 rest. Will you just turn this nab of heath,
482.17 and walk into my house? You'll get home
482.18 earlier for the ease; and you shall receive a
482.19 kind welcome."
482.20 I whispered Catherine, that she mustn't, on
482.21 any account, accede to the proposal; it was
482.22 entirely out of the question.
483.01 "Why?" she asked, aloud. "I'm tired of
483.02 running, and the ground is dewy -- I can't sit
483.03 here. Let us go, Ellen; he says I
483.04 have seen his son. He's mistaken, I think;
483.05 but I guess where he lives, at the farm-house I
483.06 visited in coming from Penistone Craggs.
483.07 Don't you?"
483.08 "I do. Come, Nelly, hold you tongue -- it
483.09 will be a treat for her to look in on us. Hare-
483.10 ton get forwards with the lass. You shall walk
483.11 with me, Nelly."
483.12 "No, she's not going to any such place," I
483.13 cried, struggling to release my arm which
483.14 he had seized; but she was almost at the door--
483.15 stones already, scampering round the brow at
483.16 full speed. Her appointed companion did not
483.17 pretend to escort her; he shyed off by the road
483.18 side, and vanished.
483.19 "Mr. Heathcliff, it's very wrong," I con-
483.20 tinued, "you know you mean no good; and

483.21 there she'll see Linton, and all will be told, as
484.01 soon as ever we return; and I shall have the
484.02 blame."
484.03 "I want her to see Linton," he answered:
484.04 he's looking better these few days; it's not
484.05 not often he's fit to be seen. And we'll soon
484.06 persuade her to keep the visit secret -- where is
484.07 the harm of it?"
484.08 "The harm of it is, that her father would
484.09 hate me, if he found I suffered her to enter
484.10 your house; and I am convinced you have a
484.11 bad design in encouraging her to do so," I
484.12 replied.
484.13 "My design is as honest as possible. I'll
484.14 inform you of its whole scope," he said.
484.15 "That the two cousins may fall in love, and
484.16 get married. I'm acting generously to your
484.17 master; his young chit has no expectations,
484.18 and should she second my wishes, she'll be
484.19 provided for, at once, as joint successor with
484.20 Linton."
484.21 "If Linton died," I answered, "and his
485.01 life is quite uncertain, Catherine would be the
485.02 heir."
485.03 "No, she would not," he said. "There is
485.04 no clause in the will to secure it so; his pro-
485.05 perty would go to me; but, to prevent dis-
485.06 putes, I desire their union, and am resolved to
485.07 bring it about."
485.08 "And I'm resolved she shall never approach
485.09 your house with me again," I returned, as we
485.10 reached the gate, where Miss Cathy waited our
485.11 coming.
485.12 Heathcliff bid me be quiet; and preceding
485.13 us up the path, hastened to open the door. My
485.14 young lady gave him several looks, as if she
485.15 could not exactly make up her mind what to
485.16 think of him; but now he smiled when he met
485.17 her eye, and softened his voice in addressing
485.18 her, and I was foolish enough to imagine the
485.19 memory of her mother might disarm him from
485.20 desiring her injury.
485.21 Linton stood on the hearth. He had been
485.22 out, walking in the fields; for his cap was on,
486.01 and he was calling to Joseph to bring him dry
486.02 shoes.
486.03 He had grown tall of his age, still wanting
486.04 some months of sixteen. His features were
486.05 pretty yet, and his eye and complexion brighter
486.06 than I remembered them, though with merely
486.07 temporary lustre borrowed from the salubrious
486.08 air and genial sun.
486.09 "Now, who is that?" asked Mr. Heathcliff,
486.10 turning to Cathy. "Can you tell?"
486.11 "Your son?" she said, having doubtfully
486.12 surveyed, first one, and then the other.
486.13 "Yes, yes," answered he; "but is this the
486.14 only time you have beheld him? Think! Ah!
486.15 you have a short memory. Linton, don't you
486.16 recall your cousin, that you used to tease us so,
486.17 with wishing to see?"
486.18 "What, Linton!" cried Cathy, kindling
486.19 into joyful surprise at the name. "Is that
486.20 little Linton? He's taller than I am! Are you,
486.21 Linton?"
486.22 The youth stepped forward, and acknowledged
487.01 himself: she kissed him fervently, and
487.02 they gazed with wonder at the change time
487.03 had wrought in the appearance of each.
487.04 Catherine had reached her full height; her
487.05 figure was both plump and slender, elastic as
487.06 steel, and her whole aspect sparkling with
487.07 health and spirits. Linton's looks and move-
487.08 ments were very languid, and his form ex-
487.09 tremely slight; but there was a grace in his
487.10 manner that mitigated these defects, and ren-
487.11 dered him not unpleasing.
487.12 After exchanging numerous marks of fond-
487.13 ness with him, his cousin went to Mr. Heath-
487.14 cliff, who lingered by the door, dividing his at-
487.15 tention between the objects inside, and those
487.16 that lay without, pretending, that is, to ob-
487.17 serve the latter, and really noting the former
487.18 alone.
487.19 "And you are my uncle, then!" she cried,
487.20 reaching up to salute him. "I thought I liked
487.21 you, though you were cross, at first. Why
487.22 don't you visit at the Grange with Linton?
488.01 To live all these years such close neighbours,
488.02 and never see us, is odd; what have you done
488.03 so for?"
488.04 "I visited it once or twice too often before
488.05 you were born," he answered. "There --
488.06 damn it! If you have any kisses to spare,
488.07 give them to Linton -- they are thrown away
488.08 on me."
488.09 "Naughty Ellen!" exclaimed Catherine,
488.10 flying to attack me next with her lavish
488.11 caresses. "Wicked Ellen! to try to hinder
488.12 me from entering. But, I'll take this walk
488.13 every morning in future -- may I, uncle -- and
488.14 sometimes bring papa? Wont you be glad to
488.15 see us?"
488.16 "Of course!" replied the uncle, with a
488.17 hardly suppressed grimace, resulting from his
488.18 deep aversion to both the proposed visiters.
488.19 "But stay," he continued, turning towards the
488.20 young lady. "Now I think of it, I'd better
488.21 tell you. Mr. Linton has a prejudice against
488.22 me; we quarrelled at one time of our lives,
489.01 with unchristian ferocity; and, if you mention

489.02 coming here to him, he'll put a veto on your
489.03 visits altogether.   Therefore, you must not
489.04 mention it, unless you be careless of seeing
489.05 your cousin hereafter -- you may come, if you
489.06 will, but you must not mention it."
489.07    "Why did you quarrel?" asked Catherine,
489.08 considerably crest-fallen.
489.09    "He thought me too poor to wed his sister,"
489.10 answered Heathcliff, "and was grieved that I
489.11 got her -- his pride was hurt, and he'll never
489.12 forgive it."
489.13    "That's wrong!" said the young lady:
489.14 "sometime, I'll tell him so; but Linton and I
489.15 have no share in your quarrel.  I'll not come
489.16 here, then, he shall come to the Grange."
489.17    "It will be too far for me," murmured her
489.18 cousin, "to walk four miles would kill me.
489.19 No, come here, Miss Catherine, now and then,
489.20 not every morning, but once or twice a week."
489.21    The father launched towards his son a glance
489.22 of bitter contempt.
490.01    "I am afraid, Nelly, I shall lose my labour,"
490.02 he muttered to me.  "Miss Catherine, as the
490.03 ninny calls her, will discover his value, and
490.04 send him to the devil.  Now, if it had been
490.05 Hareton -- do you know that, twenty times a
490.06 day, I covet Hareton, with all his degradation?
490.07 I'd have loved the lad had he been some one
490.08 else.  But I think he's safe from \her# love.  I'll
490.09 pit him against that paltry creature, unless it
490.10 bestir itself briskly.  We calculate it will
490.11 scarcely last till it is eighteen.  Oh, confound
490.12 the vapid thing.  He's absorbed in drying his
490.13 feet, and never looks at her -- Linton!"
490.14    "Yes, father," answered the boy.
490.15    "Have you nothing to show your cousin,
490.16 anywhere about; not even a rabbit, or a wea-
490.17 sel's nest?  Take her into the garden, before
490.18 you change your shoes; and into the stable to
490.19 see your horse."
490.20    "Wouldn't you rather sit here?" asked
490.21 Linton, addressing Cathy in a tone which ex-
490.22 pressed reluctance to move again.
491.01    "I don't know," she replied, casting a long-
491.02 ing look to the door, and evidently eager to be
491.03 active.
491.04    He kept his seat, and shrank closer to the
491.05 fire.
491.06    Heathcliff rose, and went into the kitchen,
491.07 and from thence to the yard, calling out for
491.08 Hareton.
491.09    Hareton responded, and presently the two
491.10 re-entered.  The young man had been washing
491.11 himself, as was visible by the glow on his
491.12 cheeks, and his wetted hair.
491.13    "Oh, I'll ask \you#, uncle;" cried Miss Cathy,
491.14 recollecting the housekeeper's assertion.
491.15 "That's not my cousin, is he?"
491.16    "Yes," he replied, "your mother's nephew.
491.17 Don't you like him?"
491.18    Catherine looked queer.
491.19    "Is he not a handsome lad?" he continued.
491.20    The uncivil little thing stood on tiptoe, and
491.21 whispered a sentence in Heathcliff's ear.
491.22    He laughed; Hareton darkened; I perceived
492.01 he was very sensitive to suspected slights, and
492.02 had obviously a dim notion of his inferiority.
492.03 But his master or guardian chased the frown
492.04 by exclaiming --
492.05    "You'll be the favourite among us, Hare-
492.06 ton!  She says you are a -- what was it?
492.07 Well, something very flattering -- Here! you go
492.08 with her round the farm.  And behave like a
492.09 gentleman, mind!  Don't use any bad words;
492.10 and don't stare, when the young lady is not
492.11 looking at you, and be ready to hide your face
492.12 when she is; and, when you speak, say your
492.13 words slowly, and keep your hands out of your
492.14 pockets.  Be off, and entertain her as nicely
492.15 as you can."
492.16    He watched the couple walking past the
492.17 window.  Earnshaw had his countenance com-
492.18 pletely averted from his companion.  He
492.19 seemed studying the familiar landscape with a
492.20 stranger's, and an artist's interest.
492.21    Catherine took a sly look at him, expressing
492.22 small admiration.  She then turned her attention
493.01 to seeking out objects of amusement for
493.02 herself, and tripped merrily on; lilting a tune
493.03 to supply the lack of conversation.
493.04    "I've tied his tongue," observed Heathcliff.
493.05 "He'll not venture a single syllable, all the
493.06 time!  Nelly, you recollect me at his age --
493.07 nay, some years younger -- Did I ever look so
493.08 stupid, so 'gaumless,' as Joseph calls it."
493.09    "Worse," I replied, "because more sullen
493.10 with it."
493.11    "I've a pleasure in him!" he continued re-
493.12 flecting aloud.  "He has satisfied my expecta-
493.13 tions -- If he were a born fool I should not en-
493.14 joy it half so much -- But he's no fool; and I
493.15 can sympathise with all his feelings, having felt
493.16 them myself -- I know what he suffers now, for
493.17 instance, exactly -- it is merely a beginning of
493.18 what he shall suffer, though.  And he'll never
493.19 be able to emerge from his bathos of coarse-
493.20 ness, and ignorance.  I've got him faster than
493.21 his scoundrel of a father secured me, and
494.01 lower; for he takes a pride in his brutishness.
494.02 I've taught him to scorn everything, extra-ani-
494.03 mal, as silly and weak -- don't you think Hind-

494.04 ley would be proud of his son, if he could see
494.05 him? almost as proud as I am of mine -- But
494.06 there's this difference, one is gold put to the
494.07 use of paving stones; and the other is tin po-
494.08 lished to ape a service of silver -- \Mine# has
494.09 nothing valuable about it; yet I shall have
494.10 the merit, of making it go as far as such poor
494.11 stuff can go.  \His# had first-rate qualities, and
494.12 they are lost -- rendered worse than unavailing
494.13 -- I have nothing to regret; he would have
494.14 more than any, but I, are aware of -- And the
494.15 best of it is, Hareton is damnably fond of me!
494.16 You'll own that I've out-matched Hindley there
494.17 -- If the dead villain could rise from his grave to
494.18 abuse me for his offspring's wrongs, I should have
494.19 the fun of seeing the said offspring fight him back
494.20 again, indignant that he should dare to rail at
494.21 the one friend he has in the world!"
495.01    Heathcliff chuckled a fiendish laugh at the
495.02 idea; I made no reply, because I saw that he
495.03 expected none.
495.04    Meantime, our young companion, who sat
495.05 too removed from us to hear what we said,
495.06 began to evince symptoms of uneasiness: pro-
495.07 bably repenting that he had denied himself
495.08 the treat of Catherine's society, for fear of a
495.09 little fatigue.
495.10    His father remarked the restless glances
495.11 wandering to the window, and the hand irre-
495.12 solutely extended towards his cap.
495.13    "Get up, you idle boy!" he exclaimed with
495.14 assumed heartiness.  "Away after them ... they
495.15 are just at the corner, by the stand of the hives."
495.16    Linton gathered his energies, and left the
495.17 hearth.  The lattice was open and, as he step-
495.18 ped out, I heard Cathy inquiring of her un-
495.19 sociable attendant, what was the inscription
495.20 over the door?
495.21    Hareton stared up, and scratched his head
495.22 like a true clown.
496.01    "It's some damnable writing;" he answered.
496.02 "I cannot read it."
496.03    "Can't read it?" cried Catherine, "I can
496.04 read it ... It's English ... but I want to know,
496.05 why it is there."
496.06    Linton giggled -- the first appearance of mirth
496.07 he had exhibited.
496.08    "He does not know his letters," he said to
496.09 his cousin.  "Could you believe in the exis-
496.10 tence of such a colossal dunce?"
496.11    "Is he all as he should be?" asked Miss
496.12 Cathy seriously, "or is he simple ... not right?
496.13 I've questioned him twice now, and each time
496.14 he looked so stupid, I think he does not under-
496.15 stand me; I can hardly understand \him# I'm
496.16 sure!"
496.17    Linton repeated his laugh, and glanced at
496.18 Hareton tauntingly, who certainly, did not
496.19 seem quite clear of comprehension at that mo-
496.20 ment.
496.21    "There's nothing the matter, but laziness,
496.22 is there, Earnshaw?" he said.  "My cousin
497.01 fancies you are an idiot ... There you expe-
497.02 rience the consequence of scorning "book--
497.03 larning," as you would say...Have you no-
497.04 ticed, Catherine, his frightful Yorkshire pro-
497.05 nunciation?"
497.06    "Why, where the devil is the use on't?"
497.07 growled Hareton, more ready in answering his
497.08 daily companion.  He was about to enlarge
497.09 further, but the two youngsters broke into a
497.10 noisy fit of merriment; my giddy Miss being
497.11 delighted to discover that she might turn his
497.12 strange talk to matter of amusement.
497.13    "Where is the use of the devil in that sen-
497.14 tence?" tittered Linton.  "Papa told you not
497.15 to say any bad words, and you can't open your
497.16 mouth without one ... Do try to behave like a
497.17 gentleman, now do!"
497.18    "If thou wern't more a lass than a lad, I'd
497.19 fell thee this minute, I would; pitiful lath of
497.20 a crater!" retorted the angry boor retreating,
497.21 while his face burnt with mingled rage, and
498.01 mortification; for he was conscious of being
498.02 insulted, and embarrassed how to resent it.
498.03    Mr. Heathcliff having overheard the conver-
498.04 sation, as well as I, smiled when he saw him
498.05 go, but immediately afterwards, cast a look of
498.06 singular aversion on the flippant pair, who re-
498.07 mained chattering in the door-way.  The boy
498.08 finding animation enough while discussing
498.09 Hareton's faults, and deficiencies, and relating
498.10 anecdotes of his goings on; and the girl relish-
498.11 ing his pert and spiteful sayings, without con-
498.12 sidering the ill-nature they evinced:  but I
498.13 began to dislike, more than to compassionate,
498.14 Linton, and to excuse his father, in some mea-
498.15 sure, for holding him cheap.
498.16    We staid till afternoon: I could not tear
498.17 Miss Cathy away, before: but happily my
498.18 master had not quitted his apartment, and
498.19 remained ignorant  of our prolonged absence.
498.20    As we walked home, I would fain have en-
498.21 lightened my charge on the characters of the
499.01 people we had quitted; but she got it into her
499.02 head that I was prejudiced against them.
499.03    "Aha!" she cried, "you take papa's side,
499.04 Ellen -- you are partial ... I know, or else you
499.05 wouldn't have cheated me so many years, into
499.06 the notion that Linton lived a long way from
499.07 here.  I'm really extremely angry, only, I'm

499.08 so pleased, I can't show it! But you must hold
499.09 your tongue about my uncle ... he's \my# uncle
499.10 remember, and I'll scold papa for quarrelling
499.11 with him."
499.12 And so she ran on, till I dropped endea-
499.13 vouring to convince her of her mistake.
499.14 She did not mention the visit that night,
499.15 because she did not see Mr. Linton. Next
499.16 day it all came out, sadly to my chagrin; and
499.17 still I was not altogether sorry: I thought the
499.18 burden of directing and warning would be more
499.19 efficiently borne by him than me, but he was
499.20 too timid in giving satisfactory reasons for his
499.21 wish that she would shun connection with the
499.22 household of the Heights, and Catherine liked
500.01 good reasons for every restraint that harassed
500.02 her petted will.
500.03 "Papa!" she exclaimed after the morning's
500.04 salutations, "guess whom I saw yesterday, in
500.05 my walk on the moors ... Ah, papa, you started!
500.06 you've not done right, have you, now? I saw
500.07 -- But listen, and you shall hear how I found
500.08 you out, and Ellen, who is in league with you,
500.09 and yet pretended to pity me so, when I kept
500.10 hoping, and was always disappointed about
500.11 Linton's coming back!"
500.12 She gave a faithful account of her excursion
500.13 and its consequences; and my master, though
500.14 he cast more than one reproachful look at me,
500.15 said nothing, till she had concluded. Then he
500.16 drew her to him, and asked if she knew why
500.17 he had concealed Linton's near neighbourhood
500.18 from her? Could she think it was to deny
500.19 her a pleasure that she might harmlessly en-
500.20 joy?
500.21 "It was because you disliked Mr. Heath-
500.22 cliff," she answered.
501.01 "Then you believe I care more for my own
501.02 feelings than yours, Cathy?" he said. "No, it
501.03 was not because I disliked Mr. Heathcliff; but
501.04 because Mr. Heathcliff dislikes me; and is a
501.05 most diabolical man, delighting to wrong and
501.06 ruin those he hates, if they give him the slight-
501.07 est opportunity. I knew that you could not
501.08 keep up an acquaintance with your cousin,
501.09 without being brought into contact with him;
501.10 and I knew he would detest you, on my ac-
501.11 count; so, for your own good, and nothing
501.12 else, I took precautions that you should not
501.13 see Linton again -- I meant to explain this,
501.14 sometime as you grew older, and I'm sorry I
501.15 delayed it!"
501.16 "But Mr. Heathcliff was quite cordial,
501.17 papa," observed Catherine, not at all con-
501.18 vinced; "and \he# didn't object to our seeing each
501.19 other: he said I might come to his house,
501.20 when I pleased; only I must not tell you, be-
501.21 cause you had quarrelled with him, and would
501.22 not forgive him for marrying aunt Isabella. And
502.01 you won't -- \you# are the one to be blamed -- he
502.02 is willing to let \us# be friends, at least; Linton
502.03 and I -- and you are not."
502.04 My master, perceiving that she would not
502.05 take his word for his uncle-in-law's evil dispo-
502.06 sition, gave a hasty sketch of his conduct to
502.07 Isabella, and the manner in which Wuthering
502.08 Heights became his property. He could not
502.09 bear to discourse long upon the topic, for
502.10 though he spoke little of it, he still felt the
502.11 same horror, and detestation of his ancient ene-
502.12 my that had occupied his heart ever since Mrs.
502.13 Linton's death. "she might have been living
502.14 yet, if it had not been for him!" was his con-
502.15 stant bitter reflection; and, in his eyes, Heath-
502.16 cliff seemed a murderer.
502.17 Miss Cathy, conversant with no bad deeds
502.18 except her own slight acts of disobedience, in-
502.19 justice and passion, rising from hot tem-
502.20 per, and thoughtlessness, and repented of on the
502.21 day they were committed, was amazed at the
502.22 blackness of spirit that could brood on, and cover
503.01 revenge for years; and deliberately prose-
503.02 cute its plans without a visitation of remorse.
503.03 She appeared so deeply impressed and shocked
503.04 at this new view of human nature -- excluded
503.05 from all her studies and all her ideas till now --
503.06 that Mr. Edgar deemed it unnecessary to pur-
503.07 sue the subject. He merely added,
503.08 "You will know hereafter, darling, why I
503.09 wish you to avoid his house and family -- now,
503.10 return to your old employments and amuse-
503.11 ments, and think no more about them!"
503.12 Catherine kissed her father, and sat down
503.13 quietly to her lessons for a couple of hours,
503.14 according to custom: then she accompanied
503.15 him into the grounds, and the whole day pass-
503.16 ed as usual: but in the evening, when she had
503.17 retired to her room, and I went to help her
503.18 to undress, I found her crying, on her knees
503.19 by the bedside.
503.20 Oh, fie, silly child!" I exclaimed. "If you
503.21 had any real griefs, you'd be ashamed to waste
503.22 a tear on this little contrariety. You never
504.01 had one shadow of substantial sorrow, Miss
504.02 Catherine. Suppose, for a minute, that mas-
504.03 ter and I were dead, and you were by your-
504.04 self in the world -- how would you feel, then?
504.05 Compare the present occasion with such an
504.06 affliction as that, and be thankful for the
504.07 friends you have, instead of coveting more."
504.08 "I'm not crying for myself, Ellen," she an-

504.09 swered, "it's for him -- He expected to see me
504.10 again, to-morrow, and there, he'll be so disap-
504.11 pointed -- and he'll wait for me, and I shan't
504.12 come!"
504.13 "Nonsense!" said I, "do you imagine he
504.14 has thought as much of you, as you have of
504.15 him? Hasn't he Hareton, for a companion?
504.16 Not one in a hundred would weep at losing
504.17 a relation they had just seen twice, for two
504.18 afternoons -- Linton will conjecture how it is,
504.19 and trouble himself no further about you."
504.20 "But may I not write a note to tell him
504.21 why I cannot come?" she asked rising to her
504.22 feet. "And just send those books, I promised
505.01 to lend him -- his books are not as nice as mine,
505.02 and he wanted to have them extremely, when
505.03 I told him how interesting they were -- May I
505.04 not, Ellen?"
505.05 "No, indeed, no indeed!" replied I with de-
505.06 cision. "Then he would write to you, and
505.07 there'd never be an end of it -- No, Miss Cathe-
505.08 rine, the acquaintance must be dropped entire-
505.09 ly -- so papa expects, and I shall see that it is
505.10 done."
505.11 "But how can one little note -- " she recom-
505.12 menced, putting on an imploring countenance.
505.13 "Silence!" I interrupted. "We'll not be-
505.14 gin with your little notes -- Get into bed!"
505.15 She threw at me a very naughty look, so
505.16 naughty that I would not kiss her good-night
505.17 at first: I covered her up, and shut her door,
505.18 in great displeasure -- but, repenting half-way,
505.19 I returned softly, and lo! there was Miss,
505.20 standing at the table with a bit of blank paper
505.21 before her, and a pencil in her hand, which
506.01 she guiltily slipped out of sight, on my re-
506.02 entrance.
506.03 "You'll get nobody to take that, Cathe-
506.04 rine," I said, "if you write it; and at present
506.05 I shall put out your candle."
506.06 I set the extinguisher on the flame, receiv-
506.07 ing as I did so, a slap on my hand, and a petu-
506.08 lant "cross thing!" I then quitted her again,
506.09 and she drew the bolt in one of her worst, most
506.10 peevish humours.
506.11 The letter was finished and forwarded to its
506.12 destination by a milk-fetcher who came from
506.13 the village, but that I didn't learn till some
506.14 time afterwards. weeks passed on, and Cathy
506.15 recovered her temper, though she grew won-
506.16 drous fond of stealing off to corners by herself,
506.17 and often, if I came near her suddenly while
506.18 reading she would start, and bend over the
506.19 book, evidently desirous to hide it; and I de-
506.20 tected edges of loose paper sticking out beyond
506.21 the leaves.
507.01 She also got a trick of coming down early
507.02 in the morning, and lingering about the kit-
507.03 chen, as if she were expecting the arrival of
507.04 something; and she had a small drawer in a
507.05 cabinet in the library which she would trifle
507.06 over for hours, and whose key she took special
507.07 care to remove when she left it.
507.08 One day, as she inspected the drawer, I ob-
507.09 served that the play-things, and trinkets which
507.10 recently formed its contents, were transmuted
507.11 into bits of folded paper.
507.12 My curiosity and suspicions were roused; I
507.13 determined to take a peep at her mysterious
507.14 treasures; so, at night, as soon as she and my
507.15 master were safe up stairs, I searched and rea-
507.16 dily found among my house keys, one that
507.17 would fit the lock. Having opened, I emptied
507.18 the whole contents into my apron, and took
507.19 them with me to examine at leisure in my own
507.20 chamber.
507.21 Though I could not but suspect, I was still
507.22 surprised to discover that they were a mass of
508.01 correspondence, daily almost, it must have
508.02 been, from Linton Heathcliff, answers to docu-
508.03 ments forwarded by her. The earlier dated
508.04 were embarrassed and short; gradually how-
508.05 ever they expanded into copious love letters,
508.06 foolish as the age of the writer rendered natu-
508.07 ral, yet with touches, here and there, which
508.08 I thought, were borrowed from a more expe-
508.09 rienced source.
508.10 Some of them struck me as singularly odd
508.11 compounds of ardour, and flatness; commenc-
508.12 ing in strong feeling, and concluding in the
508.13 affected, wordy way that a school-boy might
508.14 use to a fancied, incorporeal sweetheart.
508.15 Whether they satisfied Cathy, I don't know,
508.16 but they appeared very worthless trash to me.
508.17 After turning over as many as I thought
508.18 proper, I tied them in a handkerchief, and set
508.19 them aside, re-locking the vacant drawer.
508.20 Following her habit, my young lady de-
508.21 scended early, and visited the kitchen: I
508.22 watched her go to the door, on the arrival
509.01 of a certain little boy; and, while the dairy
509.02 maid filled his can, she tucked something into
509.03 his jacket pocket, and plucked something out.
509.04 I went round by the garden, and laid wait
509.05 for the messenger; who fought valorously to
509.06 defend his trust, and we spilt the milk be-
509.07 tween us; but I succeeded in abstracting the
509.08 epistle; and threatening some serious consequences
509.09 if he did not look sharp home, I remained
509.10 under the wall, and perused Miss Cathy's af-
509.11 fectionate composition. It was more simple

509.12 and more eloquent than her cousin's, very
509.13 pretty and very silly.  I shook my head, and
509.14 went meditating into the house.
509.15 The day being wet, she could not divert
509.16 herself with rambling about the park; so, at
509.17 the conclusion of her morning studies, she re-
509.18 sorted to the solace of the drawer.  Her father
509.19 sat reading at the table; and I, on purpose,
509.20 had sought a bit of work in some unripped
509.21 fringes of the window curtain, keeping my eye
509.22 steadily fixed on her proceedings.
510.01 Never did any bird flying back to a plundered
510.02 nest which it had left brim-ful of chirping
510.03 young ones, express more complete despair in
510.04 its anguished cries, and flutterings, than she
510.05 by her single "Oh!" And the change that
510.06 transfigured her late happy countenance.  Mr.
510.07 Linton looked up.
510.08 "What is the matter, love?  Have you
510.09 hurt yourself?" he said.
510.10 His tone and look, assured her \he# had not
510.11 been the discoverer of the hoard.
510.12 "No papa --" she gasped.  "Ellen! Ellen!
510.13 come up-stairs -- I'm sick!"
510.14 I obeyed her summons, and accompanied her
510.15 out.
510.16 "Oh, Ellen! you have got them," she com-
510.17 menced immediately, dropping on her knees,
510.18 when we were enclosed alone.  "O, give them
510.19 to me, and I'll never never do so again!  Don't
510.20 tell papa -- You have not told papa, Ellen, say
510.21 you have not!  I've been exceedingly naughty,
510.22 but I won't do it any more!"
511.01 With a grave severity in my manner, I bid
511.02 her stand up.
511.03 "So, I exclaimed, Miss Catherine, you are
511.04 tolerably far on, it seems -- you may well be
511.05 ashamed of them!  A fine bundle of trash you
511.06 study in your leisure hours, to be sure -- Why
511.07 it's good enough to be printed!  And what
511.08 do you suppose the master will think, when I
511.09 display it before him?  I haven't shown it
511.10 yet, but you needn't imagine I shall keep your
511.11 ridiculous secrets -- For shame!  And you
511.12 must have led the way in writing such absur-
511.13 dities, he would not have thought of beginning,
511.14 I'm certain."
511.15 "I didn't!  I didn't!" sobbed Cathy, fit to
511.16 break her heart.  "I didn't once think of lov-
511.17 ing him till --"
511.18 "\Loving#!" cried I, as scornfully as I could
511.19 utter the word.  "\Loving!#  Did anybody ever
511.20 hear the like!  I might just as well talk of lov-
511.21 ing the miller who comes once a year to buy
511.22 our corn.  Pretty loving, indeed, and both
512.01 times together you have seen Linton hardly
512.02 four hours, in your life!  Now here is the
512.03 babyish trash.  I'm going with it to the libra-
512.04 ry; and we'll see what your father says to such
512.05 \loving#."
512.06 She sprang at her precious epistles, but I
512.07 held them above my head; and then she pour-
512.08 ed out further frantic entreaties that I would
512.09 burn them -- do anything rather than show
512.10 them.  And being really fully as inclined to
512.11 laugh as scold, for I esteemed it all girlish
512.12 vanity, I at length, relented in a measure, and
512.13 asked,
512.14 "If I consent to burn them, will you pro-
512.15 mise faithfully, neither to send, nor receive a
512.16 letter again, nor a book, for I perceive you
512.17 have sent him books, nor locks of hair, nor
512.18 rings, nor playthings?"
512.19 "We don't send playthings!" cried Cathe-
512.20 rine, her pride overcoming her shame.
512.21 "Nor anything at all, then, my lady!" I
512.22 said.  "Unless you will, here I go."
513.01 "I promise, Ellen!" she cried catching my
513.02 dress.  "Oh put them in the fire, do, do!"
513.03 But when I proceeded to open a place with
513.04 the poker, the sacrifice was too painful to be
513.05 borne -- She earnestly supplicated that I would
513.06 spare her one or two.
513.07 "One or two, Ellen, to keep for Linton's
513.08 sake!"
513.09 I unknotted the handkerchief, and com-
513.10 menced dropping them in from an angle, and
513.11 the flame curled up the chimney.
513.12 "I will have one, your cruel wretch!" she
513.13 screamed, darting her hand into the fire, and
513.14 drawing forth some half consumed fragments,
513.15 at the expense of her fingers.
513.16 "Very well -- and I will have some to ex-
513.17 hibit to papa!" I answered shaking back the
513.18 rest into the bundle, and turning anew to the
513.19 door.
513.20 "She emptied her blackened pieces into the
513.21 flames, and motioned me to finish the immola-
513.22 tion.  It was done; I stirred up the ashes, and
514.01 interred them under a shovel full of coals; and
514.02 she mutely, and with a sense of intense injury,
514.03 retired to her private apartment.  I descended
514.04 to tell my master that the young lady's qualm
514.05 of sickness was almost over, but I judged it
514.06 best for her to lie down a while.
514.07 She wouldn't dine; but she re-appeared at
514.08 tea, pale and red about the eyes, and marvel-
514.09 lously subdued in outward aspect.
514.10 Next morning I answered the letter by a
514.11 slip of paper inscribed, "Master Heathcliff is
514.12 requested to send no more notes to Miss Lin-

514.13 ton as she will not receive them."  And,
514.14 thenceforth the little boy came with vacant
514.15 pockets.
515.01 [VOL. 2 CHAPTER 8]
515.02 SUMMER drew to an end, and early Autumn --
515.03 it was past Michaelmas, but the harvest was late
515.04 that year, and a few of our fields were still un-
515.05 cleared.
515.06 Mr. Linton and his daughter would fre-
515.07 quently walk out among the reapers: at the
515.08 carrying of the last sheaves, they stayed till
515.09 dusk, and the evening happening to be chill
515.10 and damp, my master caught a bad cold, that
515.11 settling obstinately on his lungs, confined him
516.01 indoors throughout the whole of the winter,
516.02 nearly without intermission.
516.03 Poor Cathy, frightened from her little ro-
516.04 mance, had been considerably sadder and duller
516.05 since its abandonment: and her father insist-
516.06 ed on her reading less, and taking more exer-
516.07 cise.  She had his companionship no longer;
516.08 I esteemed it a duty to supply its lack, as
516.09 much as possible, with mine; an inefficient
516.10 substitute, for I could only spare two or three
516.11 hours, from my numerous diurnal occupations,
516.12 to follow her footsteps, and then, my society
516.13 was obviously less desirable than his.
516.14 On an afternoon in October, or the begin-
516.15 ning of November, a fresh watery afternoon,
516.16 when the turf and paths were rustling with
516.17 moist, withered leaves, and the cold, blue sky
516.18 was half hidden by clouds, dark grey stream-
516.19 ers, rapidly mounting from the west, and bod-
516.20 ing abundant rain; I requested my young
516.21 lady to forego her ramble because I was cer-
516.22 tain of showers.  She refused; and I unwillingly
517.01 donned a cloak, and took my umbrella
517.02 to accompany her on a stroll to the bottom of
517.03 the park; a formal walk which she generally
517.04 affected if low-spirited; and that she invari-
517.05 ably was when Mr. Edgar had been worse than
517.06 ordinary; a thing never known from his con-
517.07 fession, but guessed by both her and me from
517.08 his increased silence, and the melancholy of
517.09 his countenance.
517.10 She went sadly on; there was no running
517.11 or bounding now; though the chill wind might
517.12 well have tempted her to a race.  And often,
517.13 from the side of my eye, I could detect her
517.14 raising a hand, and brushing something off her
517.15 cheek.
517.16 I gazed round for a means of diverting her
517.17 thoughts.  On one side of the road rose a
517.18 high, rough bank, where hazels and stunted
517.19 oaks, with their roots half exposed, held un-
517.20 certain tenour: the soil was too loose for the
517.21 latter; and strong winds had blown some
517.22 nearly horizontal.  In summer, Miss Catherine
518.01 delighted to climb along these trunks, and sit
518.02 in the branches, swinging twenty feet above
518.03 the ground; and I pleased with her agility,
518.04 and her light, childish heart, still considered
518.05 it proper to scold every time I caught her at
518.06 such an elevation; but so that she knew there
518.07 was no necessity for descending.  From dinner
518.08 to tea she would lie in her breeze-rocked
518.09 cradle, doing nothing except singing old songs
518.10 -- my nursery lore -- to herself, or watching the
518.11 birds, joint tenants, feed and entice their young
518.12 ones to fly, or nesting with closed lids, half
518.13 thinking, half dreaming, happier than words
518.14 can express.
518.15 "Look, Miss!" I exclaimed, pointing to a
518.16 nook under the roots of one twisted tree.
518.17 "Winter is not here yet.  There's a little
518.18 flower, up yonder, the last bud from the multi-
518.19 tude of blue-bells that clouded those turf steps
518.20 in July with a lilac mist.  Will you clamber
518.21 up, and pluck it to show to papa?"
518.22 Cathy stared a long time at the lonely blossom
519.01 trembling in its earthy shelter, and re-
519.02 plied, at length --
519.03 "No, I'll not touch it -- but it looks melan-
519.04 choly, does it not, Ellen?"
519.05 "Yes," I observed, "about as starved and
519.06 sackless as you -- your cheeks are bloodless;
519.07 let us take hold of hands and run.  You're so
519.08 low, I dare say I shall keep up with you."
519.09 "No," she repeated, and continued saun-
519.10 tering on, pausing, at intervals, to muse over
519.11 a bit of moss, or a tuft of blanched grass, or a
519.12 fungus spreading its bright orange among the
519.13 heaps of brown foliage; and, ever and anon,
519.14 her hand was lifted to her averted face.
519.15 "Catherine, why are you crying, love?" I
519.16 asked, approaching and putting my arm over
519.17 her shoulder.  "You mustn't cry, because
519.18 papa has a cold; be thankful it is nothing
519.19 worse."
519.20 She now put no further restraint on her
519.21 tears; her breath was stifled by sobs.
519.22 "Oh, it \will# be something worse," she said.
520.01 "And what shall I do when papa and you
520.02 leave me, and I am by myself?  I can't forget
520.03 your words, Ellen, they are always in my ear.
520.04 How life will be changed, how dreary the
520.05 world will be, when papa and you are dead."
520.06 "None can tell, whether you wont die
520.07 before us," I replied.  "It's wrong to antici-
520.08 pate evil -- we'll hope there are years and years
520.09 to come before any of us go -- master is young,

520.10 and I am strong, and hardly forty-five. My
520.11 mother lived till eighty, a canty dame to the
520.12 last. And suppose Mr. Linton were spared
520.13 till he saw sixty, that would be more years
520.14 than you have counted, Miss. And would it
520.15 not be foolish to mourn a calamity above twenty
520.16 years beforehand?"
520.17 "But Aunt Isabella was younger than
520.18 papa," she remarked, gazing up with timid
520.19 hope to seek further consolation.
520.20 "Aunt Isabella had not you and me to
520.21 nurse her," I replied. "She wasn't as
520.22 happy as master; she hadn't as much to live
521.01 for. All you need to do, is to wait well on your
521.02 father, and cheer him by letting him see you
521.03 cheerful; and avoid giving him anxiety on any
521.04 subject -- mind that, Cathy! I'll not disguise,
521.05 but you might kill him, if you were wild and
521.06 reckless, and cherished a foolish, fanciful af-
521.07 fection for the son of a person who would be
521.08 glad to have him in his grave -- and allowed
521.09 him to discover that you fretted over the separa-
521.10 ation, he has judged it expedient to make."
521.11 "I fret about nothing on earth except
521.12 papa's illness," answered my companion. "I
521.13 care for nothing in comparison with papa. And
521.14 I'll never -- never -- oh, never, while I have my
521.15 senses, do an act, or say a word to vex him. I
521.16 love him better than myself, Ellen; and I
521.17 know it by this -- I pray every night that I
521.18 may live after him; because I would rather be
521.19 miserable than that he should be -- that proves
521.20 I love him better than myself."
521.21 "Good words," I replied. "But deeds
521.22 must prove it also; and after he is well, remember
522.01 you don't forget resolutions formed in the
522.02 hour of fear."
522.03 As we talked, we neared a door that opened
522.04 on the road: and my young lady, lightening
522.05 into sunshine again, climbed up, and seated
522.06 herself on the top of the wall, reaching over
522.07 to gather some hips that bloomed scarlet on the
522.08 summit branches of the wild rose trees, sha-
522.09 dowing the highway side, the lower fruit had
522.10 disappeared, but only birds could touch the
522.11 upper, except from Cathy's present station.
522.12 In stretching to pull them, her hat fell off;
522.13 and as the door was locked, she proposed
522.14 scrambling down to recover it. I bid her be
522.15 cautious lest she got a fall, and she nimbly dis-
522.16 appeared.
522.17 But the return was no such easy matter; the
522.18 stones were smooth and neatly cemented, and
522.19 the rosebushes, and blackberry stragglers could
522.20 yield no assistance in re-ascending. I, like a
522.21 fool, didn't recollect that till I heard her
522.22 laughing, and exclaiming --
523.01 "Ellen! you'll have to fetch the key, or
523.02 else I must run round to the porter's lodge.
523.03 I can't scale the ramparts on this side!"
523.04 "Stay where you are," I answered, "I have
523.05 my bundle of keys in my pocket; perhaps I
523.06 may manage to open it, if not, I'll go."
523.07 Catherine amused herself with dancing to
523.08 and fro before the door, while I tried all the
523.09 large keys in succession. I had applied the
523.10 last, and found that none would do; so, re-
523.11 peating my desire that she would remain
523.12 there, I was about to hurry home as fast as I
523.13 could, when an approaching sound arrested me.
523.14 It was the trot of a horse; Cathy's dance
523.15 stopped; and in a minute the horse stopped
523.16 also.
523.17 "Who is that?" I whispered.
523.18 "Ellen, I wish you could open the door,"
523.19 whispered back my companion, anxiously.
523.20 "Ho, Miss Linton!" cried a deep voice,
523.21 /the rider's.// "I'm glad to meet you. Don't
523.22 be in haste to enter; for I have an explanation
523.23 to ask and obtain."
524.01 "I shan't speak to you, Mr. Heathcliff!" an-
524.02 swered Catherine. "Papa says you are a
524.03 wicked man, and you hate both him and me;
524.04 and Ellen says the same."
524.05 "That is nothing to the purpose," said
524.06 Heathcliff. /He it was.// "I don't hate my
524.07 son, I suppose, and it is concerning him, that I
524.08 demand your attention. Yes! you have cause
524.09 to blush. Two or three months since, were
524.10 you not in the habit of writing to Linton?
524.11 making love in play, eh? You deserved, both
524.12 of you, flogging for that! You especially, the
524.13 elder, and less sensitive, as it turns out. I've
524.14 got your letters, and if you give me any pert-
524.15 ness, I'll send them to your father. I presume
524.16 you grew weary of the amusement, and
524.17 dropped it, didn't you? Well, you dropped
524.18 Linton with it, into a Slough of Despond. He
524.19 was in earnest -- in love -- really. As true as I
524.20 live, he's dying for you -- breaking his heart at
524.21 your fickleness, not figuratively, but actually.
524.22 Though Hareton has made him a standing jest
525.01 for six weeks, and I have used more serious
525.02 measures, and attempted to frighten him out
525.03 of his idiocy, he gets worse daily, and he'll
525.04 be under the sod before summer, unless you
525.05 restore him!"
525.06 "How can you lie so glaringly to the poor
525.07 child!" I called from the inside. "Pray ride
525.08 on! How can you deliberately get up such
525.09 paltry falsehoods? Miss Cathy, I'll knock the

525.10 lock off with a stone, you wont believe that
525.11 vile nonsense. You can feel in yourself, it is
525.12 impossible that a person should die for love of
525.13 a stranger."
525.14 "I was not aware there were eaves-drop-
525.15 pers," muttered the detected villain. "worthy
525.16 Mrs. Dean, I like you, but I don't like your
525.17 double dealing," he added, aloud. "How
525.18 could \you# lie so glaringly, as to affirm I hated
525.19 the `poor child?' And invent bugbear stories
525.20 to terrify her from my door-stones? Catherine
525.21 Linton, /the very name warms me//, my bonny
525.22 lass, I shall be from home all this week, go and
526.01 see if I have not spoken truth; do, there's a
526.02 darling! Just imagine your father in my
526.03 place, and Linton in yours; then think how
526.04 you would value your careless lover, if he re-
526.05 fused to stir a step to comfort you, when your
526.06 father, himself, entreated him; and don't, from
526.07 pure stupidity, fall into the same error. I
526.08 swear, on my salvation, he's going to his grave,
526.09 and none but you can save him!"
526.10 The lock gave way, and I issued out.
526.11 "I swear Linton is dying," repeated Heath-
526.12 cliff, looking hard at me. "And grief and
526.13 disappointment are hastening his death. Nelly,
526.14 if you wont let her go, you can walk over
526.15 yourself. But I shall not return till this time
526.16 next week; and I think your master himself
526.17 would scarcely object to her visiting her
526.18 cousin!"
526.19 "Come in," said I, taking Cathy by the arm
526.20 and half forcing her to re-enter, for she lin-
526.21 gered, viewing, with troubled eyes, the fea-
526.22 tures of the speaker, too stern to express his
526.23 inward deceit.
527.01 He pushed his horse close, and, bending
527.02 down, observed --
527.03 "Miss Catherine, I'll own to you that I have
527.04 little patience with Linton -- and Hareton and
527.05 Joseph have less. I'll own that he's with a
527.06 harsh set. He pines for kindness, as well as
527.07 love; and a kind word from you would be his
527.08 best medicine. Don't mind Mrs. Dean's cruel
527.09 cautions, but be generous, and contrive to see
527.10 him. He dreams of you day and night, and
527.11 cannot be persuaded that you don't hate him,
527.12 since you neither write nor call."
527.13 I closed the door, and rolled a stone to
527.14 assist the loosened lock in holding it; and
527.15 spreading my umbrella, I drew my charge
527.16 underneath, for the rain began to drive through
527.17 the moaning branches of the trees, and warned
527.18 us to avoid delay.
527.19 Our hurry prevented any comment on the
527.20 encounter with Heathcliff, as we stretched to-
527.21 wards home; but I divined instinctively that
527.22 Catherine's heart was clouded now in double
528.01 darkness. Her features were so sad, they did
528.02 not seem hers: she evidently regarded what
528.03 she had heard as every syllable true.
528.04 The master had retired to rest before we
528.05 came in. Cathy stole in his room to inquire
528.06 how he was; he had fallen asleep. She re-
528.07 turned, and asked me to sit with her in the
528.08 library. We took our tea together; and after-
528.09 wards she lay down on the rug, and told me
528.10 not to talk for she was weary.
528.11 I got a book, and pretended to read. As
528.12 soon as she supposed me absorbed in my occu-
528.13 pation, she recommenced her silent weeping:
528.14 it appeared, at present, her favourite diversion.
528.15 I suffered her to enjoy it a while; then, I ex-
528.16 postulated; deriding and ridiculing all Mr.
528.17 Heathcliff's assertions about his son, as if I
528.18 were certain she would coincide. Alas! I
528.19 hadn't skill to counteract the effect his account
528.20 had produced; it was just what he intended.
528.21 "You may be right, Ellen," she answered;
528.22 "but I shall never feel at ease till I know --
529.01 and I must tell Linton it is not my fault that I
529.02 don't write; and convince him that I shall not
529.03 change."
529.04 What use were anger and protestations
529.05 against her silly credulity? We parted that
529.06 night hostile -- but next day beheld me on the
529.07 road to wuthering Heights, by the side of my
529.08 wilful young mistress's pony. I couldn't bear
529.09 to witness her sorrow, to see her pale, dejected
529.10 countenance, and heavy eyes; and I yielded in
529.11 the faint hope that Linton himself might prove
529.12 by his reception of us, how little of the tale
529.13 was founded on fact.
530.01 [VOL. 2 CHAPTER 9]
530.02 THE rainy night had ushered in a misty morn-
530.03 ing -- half frost, half drizzle -- and temporary
530.04 brooks crossed our path, gurgling from the up-
530.05 lands. My feet were thoroughly wetted; I
530.06 was cross and low, exactly the humour suited
530.07 for making the most of these disagreeable
530.08 things.
530.09 We entered the farm-house by the kitchen
530.10 way to ascertain whether Mr. Heathcliff were
530.11 really absent; because I put slight faith in his
530.12 own affirmation.
531.01 Joseph seemed sitting in a sort of elysium
531.02 alone, beside a roaring fire; a quart of ale on
531.03 the table near him, bristling with large pieces
531.04 of toasted oat cake; and his black, short pipe
531.05 in his mouth.
531.06 Catherine ran to the hearth to warm herself.

531.07 I asked if the master were in?
531.08  My question remained so long unanswered,
531.09 that I thought the old man had grown deaf,
531.10 and repeated it louder.
531.11  "Na -- ay!" he snarled, or rather screamed
531.12 through his nose. "Na -- ay! yah muh goa
531.13 back whear yah coom frough."
531.14  "Joseph," cried a peevish voice, simultane-
531.15 ously with me, from the inner room. "How
531.16 often am I to call you? There are only a few
531.17 red ashes now. Joseph! come this moment."
531.18  Vigorous puffs, and a resolute stare into the
531.19 grate declared he had no ear for this appeal.
531.20 The housekeeper and Hareton were invisible;
531.21 one gone on an errand, and the other at his
532.01 work, probably. We knew Linton's tones and
532.02 entered.
532.03  "Oh, I hope you'll die in a garret! starved
532.04 to death," said the boy, mistaking our approach
532.05 for that of his negligent attendant.
532.06  He stopped, on observing his error; his cou-
532.07 sin flew to him.
532.08  "Is that you, Miss Linton? he said, rais-
532.09 ing his head from the arm of the great chair,
532.10 in which he reclined. "No -- don't kiss me.
532.11 It takes my breath -- dear me! Papa said you
532.12 would call," continued he, after recovering a
532.13 little from Catherine's embrace; while she
532.14 stood by looking very contrite. "Will you
532.15 shut the door, if you please? you left it open
532.16 -- and those \detestable# creatures wont
532.17 bring coals to the fire. It's so cold!"
532.18  I stirred up the cinders, and fetched a scuttle
532.19 full myself. The invalid complained of being
532.20 covered with ashes; but he had a tiresome
532.21 cough, and looked feverish and ill, so I did not
532.22 rebuke his temper.
533.01  "well, Linton," murmured Catherine,
533.02 when his corrugated brow relaxed. "Are you
533.03 glad to see me? Can I do you any good?"
533.04  "why didn't you come before?" he said.
533.05 "You should have come, instead of writing.
533.06 It tired me dreadfully, writing those long
533.07 letters. I'd far rather have talked to you.
533.08 Now, I can neither bear to talk, nor anything
533.09 else. I wonder where Zillah is! will you,
533.10 /looking at me,// step into the kitchen and
533.11 see?"
533.12  I had received no thanks for my other ser-
533.13 vice; and being unwilling to run to and fro at
533.14 his behest, I replied --
533.15  "Nobody is out there but Joseph."
533.16  "I want to drink," he exclaimed, fretfully
533.17 turning away. "Zillah is constantly gadding
533.18 off to Gimmerton since papa went. It's miser-
533.19 able! And I'm obliged to come down here --
533.20 they resolved never to hear me up stairs."
533.21  "Is your father attentive to you, Master
534.01 Heathcliff?" I asked, perceiving Catherine to
534.02 be checked in her friendly advances.
534.03  "Attentive? He makes \them# a little more
534.04 attentive, at least," he cried. "The wretches!
534.05 Do you know, Miss Linton, that brute Hare-
534.06 ton laughs at me -- I hate him -- indeed, I hate
534.07 them all -- they are odious beings."
534.08  Cathy began searching for some water; she
534.09 lighted on a pitcher in the dresser; filled a
534.10 tumbler, and brought it. He bid her add a
534.11 spoonful of wine from a bottle on the table;
534.12 and having swallowed a small portion, appeared
534.13 more tranquil, and said she was very kind.
534.14  "And are you glad to see me?" asked she,
534.15 reiterating her former question, and pleased to
534.16 detect the faint dawn of a smile.
534.17  "Yes, I am -- It's something new to hear a
534.18 voice like yours! he replied, "but I \have# been
534.19 vexed, because you wouldn't come -- And papa
534.20 swore it was owing to me; he called me a piti-
534.21 ful, shuffling, worthless thing; and said you
535.01 despised me; and if he had been in my place,
535.02 he would be more the master of the Grange
535.03 than your father, by this time, But you don't
535.04 despise me, do you Miss --"
535.05  "I wish you would say Catherine, or
535.06 Cathy!" interrupted my young lady. "Des-
535.07 pise you? No! Next to papa, and Ellen, I love
535.08 you better than anybody living. I don't love
535.09 Mr. Heathcliff, though; and I dare not come
535.10 when he returns; will he stay away many
535.11 days?"
535.12  "Not many:" answered Linton, but he goes
535.13 onto the moors frequently, since the shooting
535.14 season commenced, and you might spend an
535.15 hour or two with me, in his absence -- Do! say
535.16 you will! I think I should not be peevish with
535.17 you; you'd not provoke me, and you'd always
535.18 be ready to help me, wouldn't you?"
535.19  "Yes," said Catherine stroking his long soft
535.20 hair, "if I could only get papa's consent, I'd
536.01 spend half my time with you -- Pretty Linton!
536.02 I wish you were my brother!"
536.03  "And then you would like me as well as
536.04 your father?" observed he more cheerfully.
536.05 "But papa says you would love me better
536.06 than him, and all the world, if you were my
536.07 wife -- so I'd rather you were that!"
536.08  "No! I should never love anybody better
536.09 than papa," she returned gravely. "And
536.10 people hate their wives, sometimes; but not
536.11 their sisters and brothers, and if you were the
536.12 latter, you would live with us, and papa would

536.13 be as fond of you, as he is of me."
536.14  Linton denied that people ever hated their
536.15 wives; but Cathy affirmed they did, and in
536.16 her wisdom, instanced his own father's aver-
536.17 sion to her aunt.
536.18  I endeavoured to stop her thoughtless tongue
536.19 -- I couldn't succeed, till everything she knew
536.20 was out. Master Heathcliff, much irritated,
536.21 asserted her relation was false.
537.01  "Papa told me; and papa does not tell
537.02 falsehoods!" she answered pertly.
537.03  "\My# papa scorns yours!" cried Linton. "He
537.04 calls him a sneaking fool!"
537.05  "Yours is a wicked man," retorted Cathe-
537.06 rine, and you are very naughty to dare to re-
537.07 peat what he says -- He must be wicked, to
537.08 have made aunt Isabella leave him as she
537.09 did!"
537.10  "She didn't leave him," said the boy. "you
537.11 shan't contradict me!"
537.12  "She did!" cried my young lady.
537.13  "well I'll tell \you# something!" said Linton
537.14 "Your mother hated your father, now then."
537.15  "Oh!" exclaimed Catherine, too enraged to
537.16 continue.
537.17  "And she loved mine!" added he.
537.18  "You little liar! I hate you now," she
537.19 panted, and her face grew red with passion.
537.20  "She did! she did!" sang Linton sinking
537.21 into the recess of his chair, and leaning back
538.01 his head to enjoy the agitation of the other
538.02 disputant who stood behind.
538.03  "Hush, Master Heathcliff!" I said, "that's
538.04 your father's tale too, I suppose."
538.05  "it isn't -- you hold your tongue!" he an-
538.06 swered, "she did, she did, Catherine, she did,
538.07 she did!"
538.08  "Cathy, beside herself, gave the chair a vio-
538.09 lent push, and caused him to fall against one
538.10 arm. He was immediately seized by a suffo-
538.11 cating cough that soon ended his triumph.
538.12  It lasted so long, that it frightened even
538.13 me. As to his cousin, she wept with all her
538.14 might, aghast at the mischief she had done,
538.15 though she said nothing.
538.16  I held him, till the fit exhausted itself.
538.17 Then he thrust me away; and leant his head
538.18 down, silently -- Catherine quelled her lamen-
538.19 tations also, took a seat opposite, and looked
538.20 solemnly into the fire.
538.21  "How do you feel now, Master Heathcliff,"
538.22 I inquired after waiting ten minutes.
539.01  "I wish \she# felt as I do," he replied,
539.02 "spiteful, cruel thing! Hareton never touches
539.03 me, he never struck me in his life -- And I was
539.04 better to-day -- and there -- " his voice died in
539.05 a whimper.
539.06  "\I# didn't strike you!" muttered Cathy
539.07 chewing her lip to prevent another burst of
539.08 emotion.
539.09  He sighed and moaned like one under
539.10 great suffering, and kept it up for a quarter
539.11 of an hour, on purpose to distress his cousin,
539.12 apparently, for whenever he caught a stifled
539.13 sob from her, he put renewed pain and pathos
539.14 into the inflexions of his voice.
539.15  "I'm sorry I hurt you, Linton!" she said
539.16 at length, racked beyond endurance. "But I \I#
539.17 couldn't have been hurt by that little push;
539.18 and I had no idea that you could, either --
539.19 you're not much, are you, Linton? Don't let
539.20 me go home, thinking I've done you harm!
539.21 answer, speak to me."
540.01  "I can't speak to you," he murmured,
540.02 "you've hurt me so, that I shall lie awake all
540.03 night, choking with this cough! If you had
540.04 you'd know what it was -- but \you'll# be com-
540.05 fortably asleep, while I'm in agony -- and nobo-
540.06 dy near me! I wonder how you would like to
540.07 pass those fearful nights!" And he began to
540.08 wail aloud for very pity of himself.
540.09  "Since you are in the habit of passing
540.10 dreadful nights," I said, "it wont be Miss
540.11 who spoils your ease; you'd be the same, had
540.12 she never come -- However, she shall not dis-
540.13 turb you, again -- and perhaps, you'll get
540.14 quieter when we leave you,"
540.15  "Must I go? asked Catherine dolefully,
540.16 bending over him. "Do you want me to go,
540.17 Linton?"
540.18  "You can't alter what you've done?" he
540.19 replied pettishly, shrinking from her, "unless
540.20 you alter it for the worse, by teasing me into
540.21 a fever!"
541.01  "well, then I must go?" she repeated.
541.02  "Let me alone, at least," said he "I can't
541.03 bear your talking!"
541.04  She lingered, and resisted my persuasions to
541.05 departure, a tiresome while, but as he neither
541.06 looked up, nor spoke, she finally made a move-
541.07 ment to the door and I followed.
541.08  we were recalled by a scream -- Linton had
541.09 slid from his seat on to the hearthstone, and
541.10 lay writhing in the mere perverseness of an
541.11 indulged plague of a child, determined to be
541.12 as grievous and harassing as it can.
541.13  I thoroughly guaged his disposition from
541.14 his behaviour, and saw at once it would be
541.15 folly to attempt humouring him. Not so my
541.16 companion, she ran back in terror, knelt down,
541.17 and cried, and soothed, and entreated, till he

541.18 grew quiet from lack of breath, by no means
541.19 from compunction at distressing her.
541.20 "I shall lift him on to the settle," I said,
541.21 "and he may roll about as he pleases; we
541.22 can't stop to watch him -- I hope you are satisfied,
542.01 Miss Cathy that \you# are not the person to
542.02 benefit him, and that his condition of health
542.03 is not occasioned by attachment to you. Now
542.04 then, there he is! Come away, as soon as he
542.05 knows there is nobody by to care for his non-
542.06 sense, he'll be glad to lie still!"
542.07 She placed a cushion under his head, and
542.08 offered him some water, he rejected the lat-
542.09 ter, and tossed uneasily on the former, as if it
542.10 were a stone, or a block of wood.
542.11 She tried to put it more comfortably.
542.12 "I can't do with that," he said, "it's not
542.13 high enough!"
542.14 Catherine brought another to lay above it.
542.15 "That's \too# high!" murmured the provok-
542.16 ing thing.
542.17 "How must I arrange it, then?" she asked
542.18 despairingly.
542.19 He twined himself up to her, as she half
542.20 knelt by the settle, and converted her shoulder
542.21 into a support.
542.22 "No, that won't do!" I said. "You'll be
543.01 content with the cushion, Master Heathcliff!
543.02 Miss has wasted too much time on you, alrea-
543.03 dy; we cannot remain five minutes longer."
543.04 "Yes, yes, we can!" replied Cathy. "He's
543.05 good and patient, now -- He's beginning to
543.06 think I shall have far greater misery than he
543.07 will, to-night, if I believe he is the worse for
543.08 my visit; and then, I dare not come again --
543.09 Tell the truth about it, Linton -- for I mustn't
543.10 come, if I have hurt you."
543.11 "You must come, to cure me," he answered.
543.12 "You ought to come because you have hurt
543.13 me -- You know you have, extremely! I was
543.14 not as ill, when you entered, as I am at present
543.15 -- was I?"
543.16 "But you've made yourself ill by crying,
543.17 and being in a passion."
543.18 "I didn't do it all," said his cousin. "How-
543.19 ever, we'll be friends now. And you want me
543.20 -- you would wish to see me sometimes,
543.21 really?"
543.22 "I told you, I did!" he replied impatiently.
544.01 "Sit on the settle and let me lean on your
544.02 knee -- That's as mama used to do, whole af-
544.03 ternoons together -- Sit quite still, and don't
544.04 talk, but you may sing a song if you can sing,
544.05 or you may say a nice, long interesting ballad
544.06 -- one of those you promised to teach me, or a
544.07 story -- I'd rather have a ballad though, be-
544.08 gin."
544.09 Catherine repeated the longest she could
544.10 remember. The employment pleased both
544.11 mightily. Linton would have another, and
544.12 after that another; notwithstanding my stre-
544.13 nuous objections; and so, they went on, until
544.14 the clock struck twelve, and we heard Hare-
544.15 ton in the court, returning for his dinner.
544.16 "And to-morrow, Catherine, will you be
544.17 here to-morrow?" asked young Heathcliff,
544.18 holding her frock, as she rose reluctantly.
544.19 "No!" I answered, "nor next day neither,"
544.20 She however, gave a different response, evi-
544.21 dently, for his forehead cleared, as she stooped,
544.22 and whispered in his ear.
545.01 "You won't go to-morrow, recollect, Miss!"
545.02 I commenced when we were out of the house.
545.03 "You are not dreaming of it, are you?"
545.04 She smiled.
545.05 "Oh, I'll take good care!" I continued,
545.06 "I'll have that lock mended, and you can es-
545.07 cape by no way else."
545.08 "I can get over the wall," she said laugh-
545.09 ing. "The Grange is not a prison, Ellen,
545.10 and you are not my jailer. And besides I'm
545.11 almost seventeen. I'm a woman -- and I'm
545.12 certain Linton would recover quickly if he
545.13 had me to look after him -- I'm older than he
545.14 is, you know, and wiser, less childish, am I
545.15 not? And he'll soon do as I direct him with
545.16 some slight coaxing -- He's a pretty little dar-
545.17 ling when he's good. I'd make such a pet of
545.18 him, if he were mine -- we should never quar-
545.19 rel, should we, after we were used to each
545.20 other? Don't you like him, Ellen?"
545.21 "Like him?" I exclaimed. "The worst
546.01 tempered bit of a sickly slip that ever strug-
546.02 gled into its teens! Happily, as Mr. Heath-
546.03 cliff conjectured, he'll not win twenty! I
546.04 doubt whether he'll see spring indeed -- and
546.05 small loss to his family, whenever he drops off;
546.06 and lucky it is for us that his father took him
546.07 -- The kinder he was treated, the more tedious
546.08 and selfish he'd be! I'm glad you have no
546.09 chance of having him for a husband, Miss Ca-
546.10 therine!"
546.11 My companion waxed serious at hearing this
546.12 speech -- To speak of his death so regardlessly
546.13 wounded her feelings.
546.14 "He's younger than I," she answered, after
546.15 a protracted pause of meditation, "and he
546.16 ought to live the longest; he will -- he must
546.17 live as long as I do. He's as strong now as
546.18 when he first came into the North, I'm posi-
546.19 tive of that! It's only a cold that ails him,

546.20 the same as papa has -- You say papa will get
546.21 better, and why shouldn't he?"
547.01 "Well, well," I cried, "after all, we needn't
547.02 trouble ourselves; for listen, Miss, and mind,
547.03 I'll keep my word -- If you attempt going to
547.04 Wuthering Heights again, with, or without
547.05 me, I shall inform Mr. Linton, and unless he
547.06 allow it, the intimacy with your cousin must
547.07 not be revived."
547.08 "It has been revived!" muttered Cathy
547.09 sulkily.
547.10 "Must not be continued, then!" I said.
547.11 "We'll see!" was her reply, and she set off
547.12 at a gallop, leaving me to toil in the rear.
547.13 We both reached home before our dinner--
547.14 time: my master supposed we had been wan-
547.15 dering through the park, and therefore, he
547.16 demanded no explanation of our absence. As
547.17 soon as I entered, I hastened to change my
547.18 soaked shoes, and stockings; but sitting such
547.19 a while at the Heights, had done the mischief.
547.20 On the succeeding morning, I was laid up;
547.21 and during three weeks I remained incapaci-
547.22 tated for attending to my duties -- a calamity
548.01 never experienced prior to that period, and,
548.02 never I am thankful to say since.
548.03 My little mistress behaved like an angel in
548.04 coming to wait on me, and cheer my solitude:
548.05 the confinement brought me exceedingly low
548.06 -- It is wearisome, to a stirring active body --
548.07 but few have slighter reasons for complaint than
548.08 I had. The moment Catherine left Mr. Lin-
548.09 ton's room, she appeared at my bed-side. Her
548.10 day was divided between us; no amusement
548.11 usurped a minute: she neglected her meals,
548.12 her studies, and her play; and she was the
548.13 fondest nurse that ever watched: she must
548.14 have had a warm heart, when she loved her
548.15 father so, to give so much to me!
548.16 I said her days were divided between us;
548.17 but the master retired early, and I generally
548.18 needed nothing after six o'clock, thus the
548.19 evening was her own.
548.20 "Poor thing, I never considered what she
548.21 did with herself after tea. And though fre-
548.22 quently, when she looked in to bid me good
549.01 night I remarked a fresh colour in her cheeks,
549.02 and a pinkness over her slender fingers; in-
549.03 stead of fancying the hue borrowed from a cold
549.04 ride across the moors, I laid it to the charge
549.05 of a hot fire in the library.
550.01 [VOL. 2 CHAPTER 10]
550.02 AT the close of three weeks, I was able to quit
550.03 my chamber, and move about the house. And
550.04 on the first occasion of my sitting up in the
550.05 evening, I asked Catherine to read to me, be-
550.06 cause my eyes were weak. We were in the
550.07 library, the master having gone to bed: she
550.08 consented, rather unwillingly, I fancied; and
550.09 imagining my sort of books did not suit her, I
550.10 bid her please herself in the choice of what
550.11 she perused.
550.12 She selected one of her own favourites, and
551.01 got forward steadily about an hour; then came
551.02 frequent questions.
551.03 "Ellen, are not you tired? Hadn't you
551.04 better lie down now? you'll be sick, keeping
551.05 up so long, Ellen."
551.06 "No, no, dear, I'm not tired," I returned,
551.07 continually.
551.08 Perceiving me immovable, she essayed an-
551.09 other method of showing her dis-relish for her
551.10 occupation. It changed to yawning, and
551.11 stretching, and --
551.12 "Ellen, I'm tired."
551.13 "Give over then and talk," I answered.
551.14 That was worse; she fretted and sighed, and
551.15 looked at her watch till eight; and finally
551.16 went to her room, completely overdone with
551.17 sleep, judging by her peevish, heavy look, and
551.18 the constant rubbing she inflicted on her eyes.
551.19 The following night she seemed more impa-
551.20 tient still; and on the third from recovering
551.21 my company, she complained of a head-ache,
551.22 and left me.
552.01 I thought her conduct odd; and having re-
552.02 mained alone a long while, I resolved on
552.03 going, and inquiring whether she were better,
552.04 and asking her to come and lie on the sofa, in-
552.05 stead of up stairs, in the dark.
552.06 No Catherine could I discover up stairs, and
552.07 none below. The servants affirmed they had
552.08 not seen her. I listened at Mr. Edgar's door --
552.09 all was silence. I returned to her apartment,
552.10 extinguished my candle, and seated myself in
552.11 the window.
552.12 The moon shone bright; a sprinkling of
552.13 snow covered the ground, and I reflected that
552.14 she might, possibly, have taken it into her head
552.15 to walk about the garden, for refreshment. I
552.16 did detect a figure creeping along the inner
552.17 fence of the park; but it was not my young
552.18 mistress; on its emerging into the light, I re-
552.19 cognised one of the grooms.
552.20 He stood a considerable period, viewing the
552.21 carriage road through the grounds; then started
552.22 off at a brisk pace, as if he had detected something,
553.01 and reappeared, presently, leading
553.02 Miss's pony; and there she was, just dis-
553.03 mounted, and walking by its side.
553.04 The man took his charge stealthily across

553.05 the grass towards the stable. Cathy entered
553.06 by the casement-window of the drawing-room,
553.07 and glided noiselessly up to where I awaited
553.08 her.
553.09 She put the door gently to, slipped off her
553.10 snowy shoes, untied her hat, and was proceed-
553.11 ing, unconscious of my espionage, to lay aside
553.12 her mantle, when I suddenly rose, and revealed
553.13 myself. The surprise petrified her an instant:
553.14 she uttered an inarticulate exclamation, and
553.15 stood fixed.
553.16 "My dear Miss Catherine," I began, too
553.17 vividly impressed by her recent kindness to
553.18 break into a scold, "where have you been
553.19 riding out at this hour? And why would you
553.20 try to deceive me, by telling a tale. Where
553.21 have you been? Speak!"
554.01 "To the bottom of the park," she stam-
554.02 mered. "I didn't tell a tale."
554.03 "And no where else?" I demanded.
554.04 "No," was the muttered reply.
554.05 "Oh, Catherine," I cried, sorrowfully.
554.06 "You know you have been doing wrong, or
554.07 you wouldn't be driven to uttering an untruth
554.08 to me. That does grieve me. I'd rather be
554.09 three months ill, than hear you frame a deliber-
554.10 ate lie."
554.11 She sprang forward, and bursting into tears,
554.12 threw her arms round my neck.
554.13 "Well Ellen, I'm so afraid of you being an-
554.14 gry," she said. "Promise not to be angry,
554.15 and you shall know the very truth. I hate to
554.16 hide it."
554.17 We sat down in the window-seat; I as-
554.18 sured her I would not scold, whatever her
554.19 secret might be, and I guessed it, of course, so
554.20 she commenced --
554.21 "I've been to Wuthering Heights, Ellen,
555.01 and I've never missed going a day since you
555.02 fell ill; except thrice before, and twice after
555.03 you left your room. I gave Michael books and
555.04 pictures to prepare Minny every evening, and
555.05 to put her back in the stable; you mustn't
555.06 scold \him# either, mind. I was at the Heights
555.07 by half-past six, and generally stayed till half--
555.08 past eight, and then galloped home. It was
555.09 not to amuse myself that I went; I was often
555.10 wretched all the time. Now and then, I was
555.11 happy, once in a week perhaps. At first, I
555.12 expected there would be sad work persuading
555.13 you to let me keep my word to Linton, for I
555.14 had engaged to call again next day, when we
555.15 quitted him; but, as you stayed up stairs on
555.16 the morrow, I escaped that trouble; and while
555.17 Michael was fastening the lock of the park
555.18 door in the afternoon, I got possession of the
555.19 key, and told him how my cousin wished me
555.20 to visit him, because he was sick, and couldn't
555.21 come to the Grange; and how papa would object
556.01 to my going. And then I negotiated
556.02 with him about the pony. He is fond of read-
556.03 ing, and he thinks of leaving soon to get mar-
556.04 ried, so he offered, if I would lend him books
556.05 out of the library, to do what I wished; but
556.06 I preferred giving him my own, and that satis-
556.07 fied him better.
556.08 "On my second visit, Linton seemed in
556.09 lively spirits; and Zillah, that is their house-
556.10 keeper, made us a clean room, and a good fire,
556.11 and told us that as Joseph was out at a
556.12 prayer-meeting, and Hareton Earnshaw was
556.13 off with his dogs, robbing our woods of phea-
556.14 sants, as I heard afterwards, we might do what
556.15 we liked.
556.16 "She brought me some warm wine and gin-
556.17 gerbread; and appeared exceedingly good-
556.18 natured; and Linton sat in the arm-chair, and
556.19 I in the little rocking chair, on the hearth-
556.20 stone, and we laughed and talked so merrily,
556.21 and I found so much to say; we planned where
557.01 we would go, and what we would do in sum-
557.02 mer. I needn't repeat that, because you would
557.03 call it silly.
557.04 "One time, however, we were near
557.05 quarrelling. He said the pleasantest manner
557.06 of spending a hot July day was lying from
557.07 morning till evening on a bank of heath in
557.08 the middle of the moors, with the bees hum-
557.09 ming dreamily about among the bloom, and
557.10 the larks singing high up over head, and the
557.11 blue sky, and bright sun shining steadily and
557.12 cloudlessly. That was his most perfect idea
557.13 of heaven's happiness -- mine was rocking in a
557.14 rustling green tree, with a west wind blowing,
557.15 and bright, white clouds flitting rapidly
557.16 above; and not only larks, but throstles, and
557.17 blackbirds, and linnets, and cuckoos pouring
557.18 out music on every side, and the moors seen at
557.19 a distance, broken into cool dusky dells; but
557.20 close by great swells of long grass undulating
557.21 in waves to the breeze; and woods and sound-
557.22 ing water, and the whole world awake and
558.01 wild with joy. He wanted all to lie in an ec-
558.02 stacy of peace; I wanted all to sparkle, and
558.03 dance in a glorious jubilee.
558.04 "I said his heaven would be only half alive,
558.05 and he said mine would be drunk; I said I
558.06 should fall asleep in his, and he said he could
558.07 not breathe in mine, and began to grow very
558.08 snappish. At last, we agreed to try both as
558.09 soon as the right weather came; and then we

558.10 kissed each other and were friends. After
558.11 sitting still an hour, I looked at the great
558.12 room with its smooth, uncarpeted floor; and
558.13 thought how nice it would be to play in, if we
558.14 removed the table; and I asked Linton to call
558.15 Zillah in to help us -- and we'd have a game at
558.16 blind-man's bluff -- she should try to catch us --
558.17 you used to, you know, Ellen. He wouldn't;
558.18 there was no pleasure in it, he said; but he
558.19 consented to play at ball with me. We found
558.20 two, in a cupboard, among a heap of old toys;
558.21 tops, and hoops, and battledoors, and shuttle--
558.22 cocks. One was marked C., and the other
559.01 H; I wished to have the C., because that
559.02 stood for Catherine, and the H. might be for
559.03 Heathcliff, his name; but the bran came out of
559.04 H., and Linton didn't like it.
559.05 "I beat him constantly; and he got cross
559.06 again, and coughed, and returned to his chair:
559.07 that night, though, he easily recovered his good
559.08 humour; he was charmed with two or three
559.09 pretty songs -- \your# songs, Ellen; and when I
559.10 was obliged to go, he begged and entreated
559.11 me to come the following evening, and I pro-
559.12 mised.
559.13 "Minny and I went flying home as light as
559.14 air: and I dreamt of Wuthering Heights, and
559.15 my sweet, darling cousin, till morning.
559.16 "On the morrow, I was sad; partly be-
559.17 cause you were poorly, and partly that I wished
559.18 my father knew, and approved of my excur-
559.19 sions: but it was beautiful moonlight after
559.20 tea; and, as I rode on, the gloom cleared.
559.21 "I shall have another happy evening, I
560.01 thought to myself, and what delights me more,
560.02 my pretty Linton will.
560.03 "I trotted up their garden, and was turning
560.04 round to the back, when that fellow Earnshaw
560.05 met me, took my bridle, and bid me go in by
560.06 the front entrance. He patted Minny's neck,
560.07 and said she was a bonny beast, and appeared
560.08 as if he wanted me to speak to him. I only
560.09 told him to leave my horse alone, or else it
560.10 would kick him.
560.11 "He answered in his vulgar accent.
560.12 "'It wouldn't do mitch hurt if it did;` and
560.13 surveyed its legs with a smile.
560.14 "I was half inclined to make it try; how-
560.15 ever, he moved off to open the door, and, as he
560.16 raised the latch, he looked up to the inscrip-
560.17 tion above, and said, with a stupid mixture of
560.18 awkwardness, and elation:
560.19 "'Miss Catherine! I can read yon, nah."
560.20 "'Wonderful,` I exclaimed. `Pray let us
560.21 hear you -- you \are# grown clever!"
561.01 "He spelt, and drawled over by syllables,
561.02 the name --
561.03 "'Hareton Earnshaw."
561.04 "'And the figures?` I cried, encouragingly,
561.05 perceiving that he came to a dead halt.
561.06 "'I cannot tell them yet,` he answered.
561.07 "'Oh, you dunce!" I said, laughing heartily
561.08 at his failure.
561.09 "The fool stared, with a grin hovering about
561.10 his lips, and a scowl gathering over his eyes, as
561.11 if uncertain whether he might not join in my
561.12 mirth; whether it were not pleasant familiarity,
561.13 or what it really was, contempt.
561.14 "I settled his doubts by suddenly retrieving
561.15 my gravity, and desiring him to walk away, for
561.16 I came to see Linton not him.
561.17 "He reddened -- I saw that by the moonlight --
561.18 dropped his hand from the latch, and skulked
561.19 off, a picture of mortified vanity. He ima-
561.20 gined himself to be as accomplished as Linton, I
561.21 supposed, because he could spell his own name;
562.01 and was marvellously discomfited that I didn't
562.02 think the same.
562.03 "Stop Miss Catherine, dear!" I interrupted.
562.04 "I shall not scold, but I don't like your con-
562.05 duct there. If you had remembered that Hare-
562.06 ton was your cousin, as much as Master Heath-
562.07 cliff, you would have felt how improper it was
562.08 to behave in that way. At least, it was praise-
562.09 worthy ambition, for him to desire to be as
562.10 accomplished as Linton: and probably he did
562.11 not learn merely to show off; you had made
562.12 him ashamed of his ignorance, before: I have
562.13 no doubt; and he wished to remedy it and
562.14 please you. To sneer at his imperfect attempt
562.15 was very bad breeding -- had \you# been brought
562.16 up in his circumstances, would you be less
562.17 rude? he was as quick and as intelligent a
562.18 child as ever you were, and I'm hurt that he
562.19 should be despised now, because that base
562.20 Heathcliff has treated him so unjustly."
562.21 "Well, Ellen, you won't cry about it, will
563.01 you?" she exclaimed, surprised at my earnest-
563.02 ness. "But wait, and you shall hear if he
563.03 conned his a b c, to please me; and if it were
563.04 worth while being civil to the brute." I en-
563.05 tered, Linton was lying on the settle and half
563.06 got up to welcome me.
563.07 "I'm ill to-night Catherine, love;" he said,
563.08 "and you must have all the talk, and let me
563.09 listen. Come, and sit by me -- I was sure you
563.10 wouldn't break your word, and I'll make you
563.11 promise again, before you go."
563.12 "I knew now that I mustn't tease him, as
563.13 he was ill; and I spoke softly and put no
563.14 questions, and avoiding irritating him in any

563.15 way. I had brought some of my nicest books
563.16 for him; he asked me to read a little of one,
563.17 and I was about to comply, when Earnshaw
563.18 burst the door open, having gathered venom
563.19 with reflection. He advanced direct to us;
563.20 seized Linton by the arm, and swung him off
563.21 the seat.
563.22 "Get to thy own room!" he said in a voice
564.01 almost inarticulate with passion, and his face
564.02 looked swelled and furious. "Take her there
564.03 if she comes to see thee -- thou shalln't keep me
564.04 out of this. Begone, wi' ye both!"
564.05 He swore at us, and left Linton no time to
564.06 answer, nearly throwing him into the kitchen;
564.07 and he clenched his fist, as I followed, seem-
564.08 ingly longing to knock me down. I was
564.09 afraid, for a moment, and I let one volume
564.10 fall; he kicked it after me, and shut us out.
564.11 I heard a malignant, cracky laugh by the
564.12 fire, and turning beheld that odious Joseph,
564.13 standing rubbing his bony hands, and quiver-
564.14 ing.
564.15 "Aw wer sure he'd sarve ye eht! He's a
564.16 grand lad! He's getten t'raight sperrit in
564.17 him! \He# knaws -- Aye, he knaws, as weel
564.18 as Aw do, who sud be t'maister yonder -- Ech,
564.19 ech, ech! He mad ye skift properly! Ech,
564.20 ech, ech!"
564.21 "Where must we go?" I said to my cousin,
564.22 disregarding the old wretch's mockery.
565.01 "Linton was white and trembling. He was
565.02 not pretty then -- Ellen, Oh! no, he looked
565.03 frightful! for his thin face, and large eyes
565.04 were wrought into an expression of frantic,
565.05 powerless fury. He grasped the handle of
565.06 the door, and shook it -- it was fastened in-
565.07 side.
565.08 "'If you don't let me in I'll kill you; If
565.09 you don't let me in I'll kill you!" he rather
565.10 shrieked than said. "Devil! devil! I'll kill
565.11 you, I'll kill you!"
565.12 "Joseph uttered his croaking laugh again.
565.13 "'Thear that's t'father!" he cried. 'That's
565.14 father! We've allas summut uh orther side
565.15 in us -- Niver heed Hareton, lad -- dunnut be
565.16 'feard -- he cannot get at thee!"
565.17 "I took hold of Linton's hands, and tried to
565.18 pull him away; but he shrieked so shock-
565.19 ingly that I dared not proceed. At last, his
565.20 cries were choked by a dreadful fit of cough-
565.21 ing; blood gushed from his mouth, and he fell
565.22 on the ground.
566.01 "I ran into the yard, sick with terror; and
566.02 called for Zillah, as loud as I could. She
566.03 soon heard me; she was milking the cows in
566.04 a shed behind the barn; and hurrying from
566.05 her work, she inquired what there was to do?
566.06 "I hadn't breath to explain; dragging her
566.07 in, I looked about for Linton, Earnshaw had
566.08 come out to examine the mischief he had caus-
566.09 ed, and he was then conveying the poor thing
566.10 up-stairs, Zillah and I ascended after him;
566.11 but, he stopped me, at the top of the steps,
566.12 and said, I shouldn't go in, I must go home.
566.13 "I exclaimed that he had killed Linton and I
566.14 \would# enter.
566.15 "Joseph locked the door, and declared I
566.16 should do 'no sich stuff,' and asked me whe-
566.17 ther I were 'bahn to be as mad as him.'
566.18 "I stood crying, till the housekeeper re-ap-
566.19 peared; she affirmed he would be better in a
566.20 bit; but he couldn't do with that shrieking,
566.21 and din, and she took me, and nearly carried
566.22 me into the house.
567.01 "Ellen, I was ready to tear my hair off my
567.02 head! I sobbed and wept so that my eyes were
567.03 almost blind: and the ruffian you have such
567.04 sympathy with, stood opposite; presuming
567.05 every now and then, to bid me "wisht," and
567.06 denying that it was his fault; and finally,
567.07 frightened by my assertions that I would tell
567.08 papa, and that he should be put in prison, and
567.09 hanged, he commenced blubbering himself, and
567.10 hurried out to hide his cowardly agitation.
567.11 "Still, I was not rid of him: when at length
567.12 they compelled me to depart, and I had got
567.13 some hundred yards off the premises, he sud-
567.14 denly issued from the shadow of the road-side,
567.15 and checked Minny and took hold of me.
567.16 "'Miss Catherine, I'm ill grieved,' he began,
567.17 'but it's rayther too bad--'
567.18 "I gave him a cut with my whip, thinking,
567.19 perhaps he would murder me -- He let go,
567.20 thundering one of his horrid curses, and I gal-
567.21 lopped home more than half out of my senses.
568.01 "I didn't bid you good--night, that evening;
568.02 and I didn't go to Wuthering Heights, the
568.03 next -- I wished to, exceedingly; but I was
568.04 strangely excited, and dreaded to hear that
568.05 Linton was dead, sometimes; and sometimes
568.06 shuddered at the thought of encountering
568.07 Hareton.
568.08 "On the third day I took courage; at least, I
568.09 couldn't bear longer suspense and stole off,
568.10 once more. I went at five o'clock, and walked,
568.11 fancying I might manage to creep into the
568.12 house, and up to Linton's room, unobserved.
568.13 However, the dogs gave notice of my ap-
568.14 proach: Zillah received me, and saying "the
568.15 lad was mending nicely," showed me into a
568.16 small, tidy, carpeted apartment, where, to my

568.17 inexpressible joy, I beheld Linton laid on a
568.18 little sofa, reading one of my books. But he
568.19 would neither speak to me, nor look at me,
568.20 through a whole hour, Ellen -- He has such an
568.21 unhappy temper -- and what quite confounded
569.01 me, when he did open his mouth it was to
569.02 utter the falsehood, that I had occasioned the
569.03 uproar, and Hareton was not to blame!"
569.04 "Unable to reply, except passionately, I got
569.05 up, and walked from the room. He sent after
569.06 me a faint "Catherine!" he did not reckon on
569.07 being answered so -- but I wouldn't turn back;
569.08 and the morrow was the second day on which
569.09 I stayed at home, nearly determined to visit
569.10 him no more.
569.11 "But it was so miserable going to bed, and
569.12 getting up, and never hearing anything about
569.13 him, that my resolution melted into air, before
569.14 it was properly formed. It \had# appeared
569.15 wrong to take the journey once; now it seem-
569.16 ed wrong to refrain. Michael came to ask if
569.17 he must saddle Minny; I said "Yes," and
569.18 considered myself doing a duty as she bore me
569.19 over the hills.
569.20 "I was forced to pass the front windows to
569.21 get to the court; it was no use trying to con-
569.22 ceal my presence.
570.01 "'Young master is in the house,' said Zillah
570.02 as she saw me making for the parlour.
570.03 "I went in, Earnshaw was there also, but he
570.04 quitted the room directly. Linton sat in the
570.05 great arm chair half asleep; walking up to
570.06 the fire, I began in a serious tone, partly
570.07 meaning it to be true.
570.08 "As you don't like me Linton, and as you
570.09 think I come on purpose to hurt you, and pre-
570.10 tend that I do so every time, this is our last
570.11 meeting -- let us say good bye; and tell Mr.
570.12 Heathcliff that you have no wish to see me,
570.13 and that he mustn't invent any more falsehoods
570.14 on the subject.
570.15 "'Sit down and take your hat off, Catherine,'
570.16 he answered. 'You are so much happier
570.17 than I am, you ought to be better. Papa
570.18 talks enough of my defects, and shows enough
570.19 scorn of me, to make it natural I should doubt
570.20 myself -- I doubt whether I am not altogether
570.21 as worthless as he calls me, frequently; and
570.22 then I feel so cross and bitter, I hate everybody!
571.01 I \am# worthless, and bad in temper,
571.02 and bad in spirit, almost always -- and if you
571.03 choose, you \may# say good-bye -- you'll get rid
571.04 of an annoyance -- Only, Catherine, do me this
571.05 justice; believe that if I might be as sweet, and
571.06 as kind, and as good as you are, I would be, as
571.07 willingly, and more so, than as happy and as
571.08 healthy. And, believe that your kindness has
571.09 made me love you deeper than if I deserved your
571.10 love, and though I couldn't, and cannot help
571.11 showing my nature to you, I regret it, and re-
571.12 pent it, and shall regret, and repent it, till I
571.13 die!"
571.14 "I felt he spoke the truth; and I felt I must
571.15 forgive him; and, though he should quarrel
571.16 the next moment, I must forgive him again.
571.17 We were reconciled, but we cried, both of us,
571.18 the whole time I stayed. Not entirely for
571.19 sorrow, yet I \was# sorry Linton had that dis-
571.20 torted nature. He'll never let his friends be
571.21 at ease, and he'll never be at ease himself!
571.22 "I have always gone to his little parlour,
572.01 since that night; because his father returned
572.02 the day after. About three times, I think, we
572.03 have been merry, and hopeful, as we were the
572.04 first evening; the rest of my visits were
572.05 dreary and troubled -- now, with his selfishness
572.06 and spite; and now with his sufferings: but
572.07 I've learnt to endure the former with nearly as
572.08 little resentment as the latter.
572.09 "Mr. Heathcliff purposely avoids me. I
572.10 have hardly seen him at all. Last Sunday,
572.11 indeed, coming earlier than usual, I heard him
572.12 abusing poor Linton, cruelly, for his conduct
572.13 of the night before. I can't tell how he knew
572.14 of it, unless he listened. Linton had certainly
572.15 behaved provokingly; however, it was the
572.16 business of nobody but me; and I interrupted
572.17 Mr. Heathcliff's lecture, by entering, and
572.18 telling him so. He burst into a laugh, and
572.19 went away, saying he was glad I took that
572.20 view of the matter. Since then, I've told
572.21 Linton but whisper his bitter things.
572.22 "Now, Ellen, you have heard all; and I
573.01 can't be prevented from going to Wuthering
573.02 Heights, except by inflicting misery on two
573.03 people -- whereas, if you'll only not tell papa,
573.04 my going need disturb the tranquillity of none.
573.05 You'll not tell, will you? It will be very
573.06 heartless if you do."
573.07 "I'll make up my mind on that point by
573.08 to-morrow, Miss Catherine," I replied. "It
573.09 requires some study; and so I'll leave you to
573.10 your rest, and go think it over."
573.11 I thought it over aloud, in my master's pre-
573.12 sence; walking straight from her room to his,
573.13 and relating the whole story, with the excep-
573.14 tion of her conversations with her cousin; and
573.15 any mention of Hareton.
573.16 Mr. Linton was alarmed and distressed more
573.17 than he would acknowledge to me. In the
573.18 morning, Catherine learnt my betrayal of her

573.19 confidence, and she learnt also that her secret
573.20 visits were to end.
573.21   In vain she wept and writhed against the
573.22 interdict; and implored her father to have
574.01 pity on Linton: all she got to comfort her
574.02 was a promise that he would write, and give
574.03 him leave to come to the Grange when he
574.04 pleased; but explaining that he must no
574.05 longer expect to see Catherine at Wuthering
574.06 Heights.  Perhaps, had he been aware of his
574.07 nephew's disposition and state of health, he
574.08 would have seen fit to withhold even that
574.09 slight consolation.
575.01 [VOL. 2 CHAPTER 11]
575.02 "THESE things happened last winter, sir," said
575.03 Mrs. Dean; "hardly more than a year ago.
575.04 Last winter, I did not think, at another
575.05 twelve month's end, I should be amusing a
575.06 stranger to the family with relating them!
575.07 Yet, who knows how long you'll be a stranger?
575.08 You're too young to rest always contented,
575.09 living by yourself; and I some way fancy, no
575.10 one could see Catherine Linton, and not love
575.11 her.  You smile; but why do you look so
576.01 lively and interested, when I talk about her --
576.02 and why have you asked me to hang her pic-
576.03 ture over your fireplace?  and why -- "
576.04   "Stop, my good friend!" I cried.  "It
576.05 may be very possible that \I# should love her;
576.06 but would she love me?  I doubt it too much
576.07 to venture my tranquillity, by running into
576.08 temptation; and then my home is not here.
576.09 I'm of the busy world, and to its arms I must
576.10 return.  Go on.  Was Catherine obedient to
576.11 her father's commands?"
576.12   "She was," continued the housekeeper.
576.13 "Her affection for him was still the chief sen-
576.14 timent in her heart; and he spoke without
576.15 anger; he spoke in the deep tenderness of one
576.16 about to leave his treasure amid perils and
576.17 foes, where his remembered words would be
576.18 the only aid that he could bequeath to guide
576.19 her.
576.20   He said to me, a few days afterwards,
576.21   "I wish my nephew would write, Ellen, or
576.22 call.  Tell me, sincerely, what you think of
577.01 him -- is he changed for the better, or is
577.02 there a prospect of improvement, as he grows a
577.03 man?"
577.04   "He's very delicate, sir," I replied; "and
577.05 scarcely likely to reach manhood; but this I can
577.06 say, he does not resemble his father; and if
577.07 Miss Catherine had the misfortune to marry
577.08 him, he would not be beyond her control, un-
577.09 less she were extremely and foolishly indul-
577.10 gent.  However, master, you'll have plenty of
577.11 time to get acquainted with him, and see whe-
577.12 ther he would suit her -- it wants four years
577.13 and more to his being of age."
577.14   Edgar sighed; and, walking to the window,
577.15 looked out towards Gimmerton Kirk.  It was
577.16 a misty afternoon, but the February sun shone
577.17 dimly, and we could just distinguish the two
577.18 fir trees in the yard, and the sparely scattered
577.19 gravestones.
577.20   "I've prayed often," he half soliloquized,
577.21 "for the approach of what is coming; and
577.22 now I begin to shrink, and fear it.  I thought
578.01 the memory of the hour I came down that
578.02 glen a bridegroom, would be less sweet than
578.03 the anticipation that I was soon, in a few
578.04 months, or, possibly, weeks, to be carried up,
578.05 and laid in its lonely hollow! Ellen, I've been
578.06 very happy with my little Cathy.  Through
578.07 winter nights and summer days she was a liv-
578.08 ing hope at my side -- but I've been as happy
578.09 musing by myself among those stones, under
578.10 that old church -- lying, through the long June
578.11 evenings, on the green mound of her mother's
578.12 grave, and wishing, yearning for the time when
578.13 I might lie beneath it.  What can I do for
578.14 Cathy?  How must I quit her?  I'd not care
578.15 one moment for Linton being Heathcliff's son;
578.16 nor for his taking her from me, if he could
578.17 console her for my loss.  I'd not care that
578.18 Heathcliff gained his ends, and triumphed in
578.19 robbing me of my last blessing!  But should
578.20 Linton be unworthy -- only a feeble tool to his
578.21 father -- I cannot abandon her to him!  And,
578.22 hard though it be to crush her buoyant spirit,
579.01 I must persevere in making her sad while I
579.02 live, and leaving her solitary when I die.
579.03 Darling! I'd rather resign her to God, and lay
579.04 her in the earth before me."
579.05   "Resign her to God, as it is, sir," I an-
579.06 swered, "and if we should lose you -- which
579.07 may He forbid -- under His providence, I'll
579.08 stand her friend and counsellor to the last.
579.09 Miss Catherine is a good girl; I don't fear
579.10 that she will go wilfully wrong; and people
579.11 who do their duty are always finally rewarded."
579.12   Spring advanced; yet my master gathered
579.13 no real strength, though he resumed his walks
579.14 in the grounds, with his daughter.  To her in-
579.15 experienced notions, this itself was a sign of
579.16 convalescence; and then his cheek was often
579.17 flushed, and his eyes were bright, she felt sure
579.18 of his recovering.
579.19   On her seventeenth birthday, he did not
579.20 visit the churchyard, it was raining, and I ob-
579.21 served --

579.22   "You'll surely not go out to-night, sir?"
580.01   He answered --
580.02   "No, I'll defer it, this year, a little longer."
580.03   He wrote again to Linton, expressing his
580.04 great desire to see him; and, had the invalid
580.05 been presentable, I've no doubt his father
580.06 would have permitted him to come.  As it was,
580.07 being instructed, he returned an answer, inti-
580.08 mating that Mr. Heathcliff objected to his
580.09 calling at the Grange; but his uncle's kind re-
580.10 membrance delighted him, and he hoped to
580.11 meet him, sometimes, in his rambles, and per-
580.12 sonally petition that his cousin and he might
580.13 not remain long so utterly divided.
580.14   That part of his letter was simple, and, pro-
580.15 bably his own.  Heathcliff knew he could
580.16 plead eloquently enough for Catherine's com-
580.17 pany, then --
580.18   "I do not ask," he said, "that she may
580.19 visit here; but, am I never to see her, because
580.20 my father forbids me to go to her home, and
580.21 you forbid her to come to mine?  Do, now and
580.22 then, ride with her towards the Heights; and
581.01 let us exchange a few words, in your pre-
581.02 sence!  we have done nothing to deserve this
581.03 separation; and you are not angry with me --
581.04 you have no reason to dislike me -- you allow
581.05 yourself.  Dear uncle! send me a kind note
581.06 to-morrow; and leave to join you anywhere
581.07 you please, except at Thrushcross Grange.  I
581.08 believe an interview would convince you that
581.09 my father's character is not mine; he affirms
581.10 I am more your nephew than his son; and
581.11 though I have faults which render me un-
581.12 worthy of Catherine, she has excused them,
581.13 and, for her sake, you should also.  You inquired
581.14 after my health -- it is better; but while I re-
581.15 main cut off from all hope, and doomed to soli-
581.16 tude, or the society of those who never did,
581.17 and never will like me, how can I be cheerful
581.18 and well?"
581.19   Edgar, though he felt for the boy, could not
581.20 consent to grant his request; because he could
581.21 not accompany Catherine.
582.01   He said, in summer, perhaps, they might
582.02 meet: meantime, he wished him to continue
582.03 writing at intervals, and engaged to give him
582.04 what advice and comfort he was able by
582.05 letter; being well aware of his hard position
582.06 in his family.
582.07   Linton complied; and had he been unre-
582.08 strained, would probably have spoiled all by
582.09 filling his epistles with complaints and lamen-
582.10 tations; but his father kept a sharp watch over
582.11 him; and, of course, insisted on every line
582.12 that my master sent being shown; so, instead
582.13 of penning his peculiar personal sufferings, and
582.14 distresses, the themes constantly uppermost in
582.15 his thoughts, he harped on the cruel obligation
582.16 of being held asunder from his friend and
582.17 love; and gently intimated that Mr. Linton
582.18 must allow an interview soon, or he should fear
582.19 he was purposely deceiving him with empty
582.20 promises.
582.21   Cathy was a powerful ally at home; and,
583.01 between them, they, at length, persuaded my
583.02 master to acquiesce in their having a ride or a
583.03 walk together, about once a week, under my
583.04 guardianship, and on the moors nearest the
583.05 Grange; for June found him still declining;
583.06 and, though he had set aside, yearly, a portion
583.07 of his income for my young lady's fortune, he
583.08 had a natural desire that she might retain, or,
583.09 at least, return, in a short time, to the house
583.10 of her ancestors; and he considered her only
583.11 prospect of doing that was by a union with
583.12 his heir: he had no idea that the latter was
583.13 failing almost as fast as himself; nor had any
583.14 one, I believe; no doctor visited the Heights,
583.15 and no one saw Master Heathcliff to make re-
583.16 port of his condition, among us.
583.17   I, for my part, began to fancy my forebod-
583.18 ings were false, and that he must be actually
583.19 rallying, when he mentioned riding and walk-
583.20 ing on the moors, and seemed so earnest in
583.21 pursuing his object.
583.22   I could not picture a father treating a
584.01 dying child as tyrannically and wickedly as
584.02 I afterwards learnt Heathcliff had treated him,
584.03 to compel this apparent eagerness; his efforts
584.04 redoubling the more imminently his avarici-
584.05 ous and unfeeling plans were threatened with
584.06 defeat by death.
585.01 [VOL. 2 CHAPTER 12]
585.02 SUMMER was already past its prime, when
585.03 Edgar reluctantly yielded his assent to their
585.04 entreaties, and Catherine and I set out on our
585.05 first ride to join her cousin.
585.06   "It was a close, sultry day; devoid of sun-
585.07 shine, but with a sky too dappled and hazy to
585.08 threaten rain; and our place of meeting had
585.09 been fixed at the guide-stone, by the cross--
585.10 roads.  On arriving there, however, a little
585.11 herd-boy, despatched as a messenger, told us
585.12 that --
586.01   "Maister Linton wer just ut this side th'
586.02 Heights: and he'd be mitch obleeged to us to
586.03 gang on a bit further."
586.04   "Then Master Linton has forgot the first
586.05 injunction of his uncle," I observed: "He bid
586.06 us keep on the Grange land, and here we are,

586.07 off at once."
586.08 "Well, we'll turn our horses' heads round,
586.09 when we reach him," answered my companion,
586.10 "our excursion shall lie towards home."
586.11 But when we reached him, and that was
586.12 scarcely a quarter of a mile from his own door,
586.13 we found he had no horse, and we were forced
586.14 to dismount, and leave ours to graze.
586.15 He lay on the heath, awaiting our approach,
586.16 and did not rise till we came within a few
586.17 yards. Then, he walked so feebly, and looked
586.18 so pale, that I immediately exclaimed --
586.19 "Why, Master Heathcliff, you are not fit
586.20 for enjoying a ramble, this morning. How ill
586.21 you do look!"
586.22 Catherine surveyed him with grief and astonishment;
587.01 and changed the ejaculation of
587.02 joy on her lips, to one of alarm; and the con-
587.03 gratulation on their long postponed meeting,
587.04 to an anxious inquiry, whether he were worse
587.05 than usual?
587.06 "No -- better -- better!" he panted, trem-
587.07 bling, and retaining her hand as if he needed
587.08 its support, while his large blue eyes wandered
587.09 timidly over her; the hollowness round them,
587.10 transforming to haggard wildness, the languid
587.11 expression they once possessed.
587.12 "But you have been worse," persisted his
587.13 cousin; "worse than when I saw you last -- you
587.14 are thinner, and --"
587.15 "I'm tired," he interrupted, hurriedly. "It
587.16 is too hot for walking, let us rest here. And,
587.17 in the morning, I often feel sick -- papa says I
587.18 grow so fast."
587.19 Badly satisfied, Cathy sat down, and he re-
587.20 clined beside her.
587.21 "This is something like your paradise,"
588.01 said she, making an effort at cheerfulness.
588.02 "You recollect the two days we agreed to
588.03 spend, in the place and way, each thought
588.04 pleasantest? This is nearly yours, only there
588.05 are clouds; but then, they are so soft and
588.06 mellow, it is nicer than sunshine. Next week,
588.07 if you can, we'll ride down to the Grange
588.08 Park, and try mine."
588.09 Linton did not appear to remember what
588.10 she talked of; and he had evidently great dif-
588.11 ficulty in sustaining any kind of conversation.
588.12 His lack of interest in the subjects she started,
588.13 and his equal incapacity to contribute to her
588.14 entertainment were so obvious, that she could
588.15 not conceal her disappointment. An indefinite
588.16 alteration had come over his whole person and
588.17 manner. The pettishness that might be caress-
588.18 ed into fondness, had yielded to a listless apa-
588.19 thy; there was less of the peevish temper of a
588.20 child which frets and teases on purpose to be
588.21 soothed, and more of the self-absorbed moroseness
589.01 of a confirmed invalid, repelling con-
589.02 solation, and ready to regard the good-hu-
589.03 moured mirth of others, as an insult.
589.04 Catherine perceived, as well as I did, that
589.05 he held it rather a punishment, than a gratifi-
589.06 cation, to endure our company; and she made
589.07 no scruple of proposing, presently, to depart.
589.08 That proposal, unexpectedly, roused Linton
589.09 from his lethargy, and threw him into a strange
589.10 state of agitation. He glanced fearfully to-
589.11 wards the Heights, begging she would remain
589.12 another half-hour, at least.
589.13 "But, I think," said Cathy, "you'd be more
589.14 comfortable at home than sitting here; and I
589.15 cannot amuse you to-day, I see, by my tales,
589.16 and songs, and chatter; you have grown wiser
589.17 than I, in these six months; you have little
589.18 taste for my diversions now; or else, if I could
589.19 amuse you, I'd willingly stay."
589.20 "Stay to rest yourself," he replied. "And,
589.21 Catherine, don't think, or say that I'm \very# un-
589.22 well -- it is the heavy weather, and heat that
590.01 make me dull; and I walked about, before you
590.02 came, a great deal, for me. Tell uncle, I'm in
590.03 tolerable health, will you?"
590.04 "I'll tell him that \you# say so, Linton. I
590.05 couldn't affirm that you are," observed my
590.06 young lady, wondering at his pertinacious as-
590.07 sertion of what was evidently an untruth.
590.08 "And be here again next Thursday," con-
590.09 tinued he, shunning her puzzled gaze. "And
590.10 give him my thanks for permitting you to come
590.11 -- my best thanks, Catherine. And -- and, if
590.12 you \did# meet my father, and he asked you
590.13 about me, don't lead him to suppose that I've
590.14 been extremely silent and stupid -- don't look
590.15 sad and down cast, as you \are# doing -- he'll be
590.16 angry."
590.17 "I care nothing for his anger," exclaimed
590.18 Cathy, imagining she would be its object.
590.19 "But I do," said her cousin, shuddering.
590.20 "\Don't# provoke him against me, Catherine,
590.21 for he is very hard."
590.22 "Is he severe to you, Master Heathcliff?"
591.01 I inquired. "Has he grown weary of indul-
591.02 gence, and passed from passive, to active
591.03 hatred?"
591.04 Linton looked at me, but did not answer;
591.05 and, after keeping her seat by his side, an-
591.06 other ten minutes, during which his head fell
591.07 drowsily on his breast, and he uttered nothing
591.08 except suppressed moans of exhaustion, or
591.09 pain, Cathy began to seek solace in looking for

591.10 bilberries, and sharing the produce of her re-
591.11 searches with me: she did not offer them to
591.12 him, for she saw further notice would only
591.13 weary and annoy.
591.14 "Is it half an hour now, Ellen!" she whis-
591.15 pered in my ear, at last. "I can't tell why
591.16 we should stay. He's asleep, and papa will be
591.17 wanting us back."
591.18 "Well, we must not leave him asleep," I
591.19 answered; "wait till he wakes and be patient.
591.20 You were mighty eager to set off, but your
591.21 longing to see poor Linton has soon evapor-
591.22 ated!"
592.01 "Why did \he# wish to see me?" returned
592.02 Catherine. "In his crossest humours, for-
592.03 merly, I like him better than I do in his pre-
592.04 sent curious moods. It's just as if it were a
592.05 task he was compelled to perform -- this inter-
592.06 view -- for fear his father should scold him.
592.07 But, I'm hardly going to come to give Mr.
592.08 Heathcliff pleasure; whatever reason he may
592.09 have for ordering Linton to undergo this pen-
592.10 ance. And, though I'm glad he's better in
592.11 health, I'm sorry he's so much less pleasant,
592.12 and so much less affectionate to me."
592.13 "You think \he# \is# better in health, then?" I
592.14 said.
592.15 "Yes," she answered; "because he always
592.16 made such a great deal of his sufferings, you
592.17 know. He is not tolerably well, as he told me
592.18 to tell papa, but he's better, very likely."
592.19 "There you differ with me, Miss Cathy,"
592.20 I remarked; "I should conjecture him to be
592.21 far worse."
592.22 Linton here started from his slumber in bewildered
593.01 terror, and asked if any one had
593.02 called his name.
593.03 "No," said Catherine; "unless in dreams.
593.04 I cannot conceive how you manage to dose,
593.05 out of doors, in the morning."
593.06 "I thought I heard my father," he gasped,
593.07 glancing up to the frowning nab above us.
593.08 "You are sure nobody spoke?"
593.09 "Quite sure," replied his cousin. "Only
593.10 Ellen and I were disputing concerning your
593.11 health. Are you truly stronger, Linton, than
593.12 when we separated in winter? If you be, I'm
593.13 certain one thing is not stronger -- your regard
593.14 for me -- speak, are you?"
593.15 The tears gushed from Linton's eyes as he
593.16 answered --
593.17 "Yes, yes, I am!"
593.18 And still under the spell of the imaginary
593.19 voice, his gaze wandered up and down to de-
593.20 tect its owner.
593.21 Cathy rose.
593.22 "For to-day we must part," she said.
594.01 "And I won't conceal that I have been sadly
594.02 disappointed with our meeting, though I'll men-
594.03 tion it to nobody but you -- not that I stand in
594.04 awe of Mr. Heathcliff!"
594.05 "Hush," murmured Linton; "For God's
594.06 sake, hush! He's coming." And he clung to
594.07 Catherine's arm, striving to detain her; but, at
594.08 that announcement, she hastily disengaged
594.09 herself, and whistled to Minny, who obeyed
594.10 her like a dog.
594.11 "I'll be here next Thursday," she cried,
594.12 springing to the saddle. "Good bye. Quick,
594.13 Ellen!"
594.14 And so we left him, scarcely conscious of
594.15 our departure, so absorbed was he in antici-
594.16 pating his father's approach.
594.17 "Before we reached home, Catherine's dis-
594.18 pleasure softened into a perplexed sensation of
594.19 pity and regret largely blended with vague,
594.20 uneasy doubts about Linton's actual circum-
594.21 stances, physical and social; in which I par-
594.22 took, though I counselled her not to say much,
595.01 for a second journey would make us better
595.02 judges.
595.03 My master requested an account of our on-
595.04 goings: his nephew's offering of thanks was
595.05 duly delivered, Miss Cathy gently touching on
595.06 the rest: I also, threw little light on his in-
595.07 quiries, for I hardly knew what to hide, and
595.08 what to reveal.
596.01 [VOL. 2 CHAPTER 13]
596.02 SEVEN days glided away, every one marking
596.03 its course by the henceforth rapid alteration of
596.04 Edgar Linton's state. The havoc that months
596.05 had previously wrought, was now emulated by
596.06 the inroads of hours.
596.07 Catherine, we would fain have deluded, yet,
596.08 but her own quick spirit refused to delude her.
596.09 It divined, in secret, and brooded on the dread-
596.10 ful probability, gradually ripening into cer-
596.11 tainty.
596.12 She had not the heart to mention her ride,
597.01 when Thursday came round; I mentioned it
597.02 for her; and obtained permission to order her
597.03 out of doors; for the library, where her father
597.04 stopped a short time daily -- the brief period he
597.05 could bear to sit up, and his chamber had be-
597.06 come her whole world. She grudged each
597.07 moment that did not find her bending over his
597.08 pillow, or seated by his side. Her counte-
597.09 nance grew wan with watching and sorrow,
597.10 and my master gladly dismissed her to what
597.11 he flattered himself would be a happy change
597.12 of scene and society, drawing comfort from the

597.13 hope that she would not now be left entirely
597.14 alone after his death.
597.15 He had a fixed idea, I guessed by several
597.16 observations he let fall, that as his nephew
597.17 resembled him in person, he would resemble
597.18 him in mind; for Linton's letters bore few,
597.19 or no indications of his defective character.
597.20 And I through pardonable weakness refrained
597.21 from correcting the error; asking myself what
597.22 good there would be in disturbing his last moments
598.01 with information that he had neither
598.02 power nor opportunity to turn to account.
598.03 We deferred our excursion till the after-
598.04 noon; a golden afternoon of August -- every
598.05 breath from the hills so full of life, that it seemed
598.06 whoever respired it, though dying, might re-
598.07 vive.
598.08 Catherine's face was just like the landscape
598.09 -- shadows and sunshine flitting over it, in ra-
598.10 pid succession; but the shadows rested longer
598.11 and the sunshine was more transient, and her
598.12 poor little heart reproached itself for even that
598.13 passing forgetfulness of its cares.
598.14 We discerned Linton watching at the same
598.15 spot he had selected before. My young mis-
598.16 tress alighted, and told me that as she was re-
598.17 solved to stay a very little while, I had better
598.18 hold the pony and remain on horseback; but
598.19 I dissented, I wouldn't risk losing sight of
598.20 the charge committed to me a minute; so we
598.21 climbed the slope of heath, together.
598.22 Master Heathcliff received us with greater
599.01 animation on this occasion; not the animation
599.02 of high spirits though, nor yet of joy; it look-
599.03 ed more like fear.
599.04 "It is late!" he said, speaking short, and
599.05 with difficulty. "Is not your father very ill?
599.06 I thought you wouldn't come."
599.07 "Why# won't you be candid?" cried Cathe-
599.08 rine, swallowing her greeting. "Why cannot
599.09 you say at once, you don't want me? It is
599.10 strange Linton, that for the second time, you
599.11 have brought me here on purpose, apparently,
599.12 to distress us both, and for no reason besides!"
599.13 Linton shivered, and glanced at her, half
599.14 supplicating, half ashamed, but his cousin's pa-
599.15 tience was not sufficient to endure this enig-
599.16 matical behaviour.
599.17 "My father \is# very ill," she said, "and why
599.18 am I called from his bedside -- why don't you
599.19 send to absolve me from my promise, when
599.20 you wished I wouldn't keep it? Come! I de-
599.21 sire an explanation -- playing and trifling are
599.22 completely banished out of my mind: and I
600.01 can't dance attendance on your affectations,
600.02 now!"
600.03 "My affectations!" he murmured, "what are
600.04 they? For Heaven's sake Catherine, don't
600.05 look so angry! Despise me as much as you
600.06 please; I am a worthless, cowardly wretch -- I
600.07 can't be scorned enough! but I'm too mean for
600.08 your anger -- hate my father, and spare me, for
600.09 contempt!"
600.10 "Nonsense!" cried Catherine in a passion.
600.11 "Foolish, silly boy! And there! he trembles,
600.12 as if I were really going to touch him! You
600.13 needn't bespeak contempt, Linton; anybody
600.14 will have it spontaneously, at your service.
600.15 Get off! I shall return home -- it is folly drag-
600.16 ging you from the hearth-stone, and pretend-
600.17 ing -- what do we pretend? Let go my frock
600.18 -- if I pitied you for crying, and looking so
600.19 very frightened, you should spurn such pity!
600.20 Ellen, tell him how disgraceful this conduct is.
600.21 Rise, and don't degrade yourself into an abject
600.22 reptile -- \don't#."
601.01 With streaming face and an expression of
601.02 agony, Linton had thrown his nerveless frame
601.03 along the ground; he seemed convulsed with
601.04 exquisite terror.
601.05 "Oh!" he sobbed, "I cannot bear it! Ca-
601.06 therine, Catherine, I'm a traitor too, and I
601.07 dare not tell you! But leave me and I shall
601.08 be killed! \Dear# Catherine, my life is in your
601.09 hands; and you have said you loved me -- and
601.10 if you did, it wouldn't harm you. You'll not
601.11 go, then? kind, sweet, good Catherine! And
601.12 perhaps you \will# consent -- and he'll let me die
601.13 with you!"
601.14 My young lady, on witnessing his intense
601.15 anguish, stooped to raise him. The old feel-
601.16 ing of indulgent tenderness overcame her vex-
601.17 ation, and she grew thoroughly moved and
601.18 alarmed.
601.19 "Consent to what?" she asked. "To stay?
601.20 Tell me the meaning of this strange talk, and
601.21 I will. You contradict your own words, and
601.22 distract me! Be calm and frank, and confess
602.01 at once, all that weighs on your heart. You
602.02 wouldn't injure me, Linton, would you? You
602.03 wouldn't let any enemy hurt me, if you could
602.04 prevent it? I'll believe you are a coward, for
602.05 yourself, but not a cowardly betrayer of your
602.06 best friend."
602.07 "But my father threatened me," gasped the
602.08 boy, clasping his attenuated fingers, "and I
602.09 dread him -- I dread him! I \dare# not tell!"
602.10 "Oh well!" said Catherine, with scornful
602.11 compassion, "keep your secret, \I'm# no coward
602.12 -- save yourself, I'm not afraid!"
602.13 Her magnanimity provoked his tears; he

602.14 wept wildly, kissing her supporting hands,
602.15 and yet could not summon courage to speak
602.16 out.
602.17 I was cogitating what the mystery might be,
602.18 and determined Catherine should never suffer
602.19 to benefit him or any one else, by my good
602.20 will. When hearing a rustle among the ling,
602.21 I looked up, and saw Mr. Heathcliff almost
602.22 close upon us, descending the Heights. He
603.01 didn't cast a glance towards my companions,
603.02 though they were sufficiently near for Linton's
603.03 sobs to be audible; but hailing me in the al-
603.04 most hearty tone he assumed to none besides,
603.05 and the sincerity of which, I couldn't avoid
603.06 doubting, he said.
603.07 "It is something to see you so near to my
603.08 house, Nelly! How are you at the Grange?
603.09 Let us hear! The rumour goes," he added in
603.10 a lower tone, "that Edgar Linton is on his
603.11 death-bed -- perhaps they exaggerate his ill-
603.12 ness?"
603.13 "No; my master is dying," I replied, "it is
603.14 true enough. A sad thing it will be for us
603.15 all, but a blessing for him!"
603.16 "How long will he last, do you think?" he
603.17 asked.
603.18 "I don't know," I said.
603.19 "Because," he continued, looking at the
603.20 two young people, who were fixed under his
603.21 eye -- Linton appeared as if he could not venture
604.01 to stir, or raise his head, and Catherine
604.02 could not move, on his account -- "Because
604.03 that lad yonder, seems determined to beat me
604.04 -- and I'd thank his uncle to be quick, and go
604.05 before him -- Hallo! Has the whelp been play-
604.06 ing that game long? I \did# give him some
604.07 lessons about snivelling. Is he pretty lively
604.08 with Miss Linton generally?"
604.09 "Lively? no -- he has shown the greatest
604.10 distress;" I answered. "To see him, I should
604.11 say, that instead of rambling with his sweet-
604.12 heart on the hills, he ought to be in bed, under
604.13 the hands of a doctor."
604.14 "He shall be, in a day or two," muttered
604.15 Heathcliff. "But first -- get up, Linton! Get
604.16 up!" he shouted. "Don't grovel on the ground,
604.17 there -- up this moment!"
604.18 Linton had sunk prostrate again in another
604.19 paroxysm of helpless fear, caused by his fa-
604.20 ther's glance towards him, I suppose, there
604.21 was nothing else to produce such humiliation.
605.01 He made several efforts to obey, but his little
605.02 strength was annihilated, for the time, and he
605.03 fell back again with a moan.
605.04 Mr. Heathcliff advanced, and lifted him to
605.05 lean against a ridge of turf.
605.06 "Now," said he with curbed ferocity, "I'm
605.07 getting angry -- and if you don't command that
605.08 paltry spirit of yours -- \Damn# you! Get up,
605.09 directly!"
605.10 "I will, father!" he panted. "Only, let me
605.11 alone, or I shall faint! I've done as you wish-
605.12 ed -- I'm sure. Catherine will tell you that
605.13 I -- that I -- have been cheerful. Ah! keep by
605.14 me Catherine; give me your hand."
605.15 "Take mine," said his father, "stand on
605.16 your feet! There now -- she'll lend you her
605.17 arm ... that's right, look at \her#. You would
605.18 imagine I was the devil himself, Miss Linton,
605.19 to excite such horror. Be so kind as to walk
605.20 home with him, will you? He shudders, if I
605.21 touch him."
606.01 "Linton, dear!" whispered Catherine, "I
606.02 can't go to Wuthering Heights ... papa has for-
606.03 bidden me ... He'll not harm you, why are you
606.04 so afraid?"
606.05 "I can never re-enter that house," he an-
606.06 swered. "I am \not# to re-enter it without
606.07 you!"
606.08 "Stop...!" cried his father. "We'll respect
606.09 Catherine's filial scruples. Nelly, take him in,
606.10 and I'll follow your advice concerning the doc-
606.11 tor, without delay."
606.12 "You'll do well," replied I, "but I must
606.13 remain with my mistress. To mind your son
606.14 is not my business."
606.15 "You are very stiff!" said Heathcliff, "I
606.16 know that -- but you'll force me to pinch the
606.17 baby, and make it scream, before it moves your
606.18 charity. Come then, my hero. Are you wil-
606.19 ling to return, escorted by me?"
606.20 He approached once more, and made as if
606.21 he would seize the fragile being; but shrinking
607.01 back, Linton clung to his cousin, and im-
607.02 plored her to accompany him with a frantic
607.03 importunity that admitted no denial.
607.04 However I disapproved, I couldn't hinder
607.05 her; indeed how could she have refused him
607.06 herself? what was filling him with dread, we had
607.07 no means of discerning, but there he was,
607.08 powerless under its gripe, and any addition
607.09 seemed capable of shocking him into idiocy.
607.10 We reached the threshold; Catherine walk-
607.11 ed in; and I stood waiting till she had
607.12 conducted the invalid to a chair, expecting her
607.13 out, immediately; when Mr. Heathcliff push-
607.14 ing me forward, exclaimed --
607.15 "My house is not stricken with the plague,
607.16 Nelly; and I have a mind to be hospitable to-
607.17 day; sit down, and allow me to shut the
607.18 door."

607.19 He shut and locked it also, I started.
607.20 "You shall have tea, before you go home,"
607.21 he added. "I am by myself. Hareton is
607.22 gone with some cattle to the Lees -- and Zillah
608.01 and Joseph are off on a journey of pleasure.
608.02 And, though I'm used to being alone, I'd rather
608.03 have some interesting company, if I can get
608.04 it. Miss Linton, take your seat by \him#. I
608.05 give you what I have; the present is hardly
608.06 worth accepting; but, I have nothing else to
608.07 offer. It is Linton, I mean. How she does
608.08 stare! It's odd what a savage feeling I have
608.09 to anything that seems afraid of me! Had I
608.10 been born where laws are less strict, and
608.11 tastes less dainty, I should treat myself to a
608.12 slow vivifisection of those two, as an evening's
608.13 amusement."
608.14 He drew in his breath, struck the table, and
608.15 swore to himself.
608.16 "By hell! I hate them."
608.17 "I'm not afraid of you!" exclaimed Cathe-
608.18 rine, who could not hear the latter part of his
608.19 speech.
608.20 She stepped close up; her black eyes flash-
608.21 ing with passion and resolution.
608.22 "Give me that key -- I will have it!" she
609.01 said. "I wouldn't eat or drink here, if I were
609.02 starving."
609.03 Heathcliff had the key in his hand that re-
609.04 mained on the table. He looked up, seized
609.05 with a sort of surprise at her boldness; or,
609.06 possibly, reminded by her voice and glance, of
609.07 the person from whom she inherited it.
609.08 She snatched at the instrument, and half
609.09 succeeded in getting it out of his loosened
609.10 fingers; but her action recalled him to the
609.11 present; he recovered it speedily.
609.12 "Now, Catherine Linton," he said, "stand
609.13 off, or I shall knock you down; and that will
609.14 make Mrs. Dean mad."
609.15 Regardless of his warning, she captured
609.16 his closed hand, and its contents again.
609.17 "We \will# go!" she repeated, exerting
609.18 her utmost efforts to cause the iron muscles to
609.19 relax; and finding that her nails made no im-
609.20 pression, she applied her teeth pretty sharply.
609.21 Heathcliff glanced at me a glance that kept
610.01 me from interfering a moment. Catherine was
610.02 too intent on his fingers to notice his face. He
610.03 opened them, suddenly, and resigned the object
610.04 of dispute; but, ere she had well secured it,
610.05 he seized her with the liberated hand, and,
610.06 pulling her on his knee, administered, with
610.07 the other, a shower of terrific slaps on both
610.08 sides of the head, each sufficient to have ful-
610.09 filled his threat, had she been able to fall.
610.10 At this diabolical violence, I rushed on him
610.11 furiously.
610.12 "You villain!" I began to cry, "you vil-
610.13 lain!"
610.14 A touch on the chest silenced me; I am
610.15 stout, and soon put out of breath; and, what
610.16 with that and the rage, I staggered dizzily
610.17 back, and felt ready to suffocate, or to burst a
610.18 blood-vessel.
610.19 The scene was over in two minutes; Cathe-
610.20 rine, released, put her two hands to her tem-
610.21 ples, and looked just as if she were not sure
611.01 whether her ears were off or on. She trem-
611.02 bled like a reed, poor thing, and leant against
611.03 the table perfectly bewildered.
611.04 "I know how to chastise children, you see,"
611.05 said the scoundrel, grimly, as he stooped to re-
611.06 possess himself of the key, which had dropped
611.07 to the floor. "Go to Linton now, as I told
611.08 you; and cry at your ease! I shall be your
611.09 father to-morrow -- all the father you'll have in
611.10 a few days -- and you shall have plenty of that
611.11 -- you can bear plenty -- you're no weakling --
611.12 you shall have a daily taste, if I catch such a
611.13 devil of a temper in your eyes again!"
611.14 Cathy ran to me instead of Linton, and
611.15 knelt down, and put her burning cheek on my
611.16 lap, weeping aloud. Her cousin had shrunk
611.17 into a corner of the settle, as quiet as a mouse,
611.18 congratulating himself, I dare say, that the
611.19 correction had lighted on another than him.
611.20 Mr. Heathcliff, perceiving us all confounded,
611.21 rose, and expeditiously made the tea himself.
612.01 The cups and saucers were laid ready. He
612.02 poured it out, and handed me a cup.
612.03 "Wash away your spleen," he said. "And
612.04 help your own naughty pet and mine. It is
612.05 not poisoned, though I prepared it. I'm going
612.06 out to seek your horses."
612.07 Our first thought, on his departure, was to
612.08 force an exit somewhere. We tried the kit-
612.09 chen door, but that was fastened outside; we
612.10 looked at the windows -- they were too narrow
612.11 for even Cathy's little figure.
612.12 "Master Linton," I cried, seeing we were
612.13 regularly imprisoned. "You know what your
612.14 diabolical father is after, and you shall tell
612.15 us, or I'll box your ears, as he has done your
612.16 cousin's."
612.17 "Yes, Linton; you must tell," said Cathe-
612.18 rine. "It was for your sake I came; and it
612.19 will be wickedly ungrateful if you refuse."
612.20 "Give me some tea, I'm thirsty, and then
612.21 I'll tell you," he answered. "Mrs. Dean, go
613.01 away. I don't like you standing over me.

613.02 Now, Catherine, you are letting your tears
613.03 fall into my cup! I wont drink that. Give
613.04 me another."
613.05 Catherine pushed another to him, and wiped
613.06 her face. I felt disgusted at the little wretch's
613.07 composure, since he was no longer in terror for
613.08 himself. The anguish he had exhibited on the
613.09 moor subsided as soon as ever he entered
613.10 Wuthering Heights; so, I guess he had been
613.11 menaced with an awful visitation of wrath, if
613.12 he failed in decoying us there; and, that ac-
613.13 complished, he had no further immediate
613.14 fears.
613.15 "Papa wants us to be married," he con-
613.16 tinued, after sipping some of the liquid. "And
613.17 he knows your papa wouldn't let us marry
613.18 now; and he's afraid of my dying, if we wait;
613.19 so we are to be married in the morning, and
613.20 you are to stay here all night; and, if you do
613.21 as he wishes, you shall return home next day,
613.22 and take me with you."
614.01 "Take you with her, pitiful changeling?"
614.02 I exclaimed. "\You# marry? Why, the man is
614.03 mad, or he thinks us fools, every one. And,
614.04 do you imagine that beautiful young lady,
614.05 that healthy, hearty girl, will tie herself to a
614.06 little perishing monkey like you? Are you
614.07 cherishing the notion that \anybody#, let alone
614.08 Miss Catherine Linton, would have you for a
614.09 husband? You want a whipping for bringing us
614.10 in here at all, with your dastardly, puling
614.11 tricks; and -- don't look so silly now! I've a
614.12 very good mind to shake you severely, for
614.13 your contemptible treachery, and your imbe-
614.14 cile conceit."
614.15 I did give him a slight shaking, but it
614.16 brought on the cough, and he took to his ordi-
614.17 nary resource of moaning and weeping, and
614.18 Catherine rebuked me.
614.19 "Stay all night? No!" she said, looking
614.20 slowly round. "Ellen, I'll burn that door
614.21 down, but I'll get out."
614.22 And she would have commenced the execution
615.01 of her threat directly, but Linton was up
615.02 in alarm for his dear self, again. He clasped
615.03 her in his two feeble arms, sobbing --
615.04 "Won't you have me, and save me -- not let
615.05 me come to the Grange? Oh! darling Cathe-
615.06 rine! you musn't go, and leave me, after all.
615.07 You \must# obey my father, you \must#!"
615.08 "I must obey my own," she replied, " and
615.09 relieve him from this cruel suspense. The
615.10 whole night! what would he think? he'll
615.11 be distressed already. I'll either break or
615.12 burn a way out of the house. Be quiet!
615.13 You're in no danger -- but, if you hinder me
615.14 -- Linton, I love papa better than you!"
615.15 The mortal terror he felt of Mr. Heathcliff's
615.16 anger, restored to the boy his coward's elo-
615.17 quence. Catherine was near distraught -- still,
615.18 she persisted that she must go home, and tried
615.19 entreaty, in her turn, persuading him to sub-
615.20 due his selfish agony.
615.21 While they were thus occupied, our jailer
615.22 re-entered.
616.01 "Your beasts have trotted off;" he said,
616.02 "and -- now, Linton! snivelling again? What
616.03 has she been doing to you? Come, come --
616.04 have done, and get to bed. In a month or two,
616.05 my lad, you'll be able to pay her back her pre-
616.06 sent tyrannies, with a vigorous hand -- you're
616.07 pining for pure love, are you not? nothing
616.08 else in the world -- and she shall have you!
616.09 There, to bed! Zillah wont be here to-night;
616.10 you must undress yourself. Hush! hold your
616.11 noise! Once in your own room, I'll not come
616.12 near you, you needn't fear. By chance,
616.13 you've managed tolerably. I'll look to the
616.14 rest."
616.15 He spoke these words, holding the door open
616.16 for his son to pass; and the latter achieved his
616.17 exit exactly as a spaniel might which suspected
616.18 the person who attended on it of designing a
616.19 spiteful squeeze.
616.20 The lock was re-secured. Heathcliff ap-
616.21 proached the fire, where my mistress and I
616.22 stood silent. Catherine looked up, and instinctively
617.01 raised her hand to her cheek -- his neigh-
617.02 bourhood revived a painful sensation. Any-
617.03 body else would have been incapable of re-
617.04 garding the childish act with sternness, but he
617.05 scowled on her, and muttered --
617.06 "Oh, you are not afraid of me? Your cour-
617.07 age is well disguised -- you \seem# damnably
617.08 afraid!"
617.09 "I \am# afraid now," she replied; "because
617.10 if I stay, papa will be miserable; and how can
617.11 I endure making him miserable -- when he --
617.12 when he -- Mr. Heathcliff, \let# me go home! I
617.13 promise to marry Linton -- papa would like me
617.14 to, and I love him -- and why should you wish
617.15 to force me to do what I'll willingly do of my-
617.16 self?"
617.17 "Let him dare to force you!" I cried.
617.18 "There's law in the land, thank God, there
617.19 is! though we \be# in an out-of-the-way place.
617.20 I'd inform, if he were my own son, and it's
617.21 felony without benefit of clergy!"
617.22 "Silence!" said the ruffian. "To the
618.01 devil with your clamour! I don't want \you# to
618.02 speak. Miss Linton, I shall enjoy myself re-

618.03 markably in thinking your father will be miser-
618.04 able; I shall not sleep for satisfaction. You could
618.05 have hit on no surer way of fixing your resi-
618.06 dence under my roof, for the next twenty-four
618.07 hours, than informing me that such an event
618.08 would follow. As to your promise to marry
618.09 Linton; I'll take care you shall keep it, for
618.10 you shall not quit the place till it is fulfilled."
618.11 "Send Ellen then, to let papa know I'm
618.12 safe!" exclaimed Catherine, weeping bitterly.
618.13 "Or marry me now. Poor papa! Ellen, he'll
618.14 think we're lost. What shall we do?"
618.15 "Not he! He'll think you are tired of wait-
618.16 ing on him, and run off, for a little amuse-
618.17 ment," answered Heathcliff. "You cannot
618.18 deny that you entered my house of your own
618.19 accord, in contempt of his injunctions to the
618.20 contrary. And it is quite natural that you
618.21 should desire amusement at your age; and that
618.22 you should weary of nursing a sick man, and
619.01 that man, \only# your father. Catherine, his
619.02 happiest days were over when your days be-
619.03 gan. He cursed you, I dare say, for coming
619.04 into the world, /I did, at least//. And it would
619.05 just do if he cursed you as \he# went out of it.
619.06 I'd join him. I don't love you! How should
619.07 I? Weep away. As far as I can see, it will be
619.08 your chief diversion hereafter: unless Linton
619.09 make amends for other losses; and your provi-
619.10 dent parent appears to fancy he may. His let-
619.11 ters of advice and consolation entertained me
619.12 vastly. In his last, he recommended my jewel
619.13 to be careful of his; and kind to her when he
619.14 got her. Careful and kind -- that's paternal!
619.15 But Linton requires his whole stock of care
619.16 and kindness for himself. Linton can play
619.17 the little tyrant well. He'll undertake to tor-
619.18 ture any number of cats if their teeth be
619.19 drawn, and their claws pared. You'll be able
619.20 to tell his uncle fine tales of his \kindness#, when
619.21 you get home again, I assure you."
619.22 "You're right there!" I said, "explain
620.01 your son's character. Show his resemblance to
620.02 yourself; and then, I hope, Miss Cathy will
620.03 think twice, before she takes the cockatrice!"
620.04 "I don't much mind speaking of his amia-
620.05 ble qualities now," he answered, "because she
620.06 must either accept him, or remain a prisoner,
620.07 and you along with her, till your master dies.
620.08 I can detain you both, quite concealed, here.
620.09 If you doubt, encourage her to retract her
620.10 word, and you'll have an opportunity of judg-
620.11 ing!"
620.12 "I'll not retract my word," said Catherine.
620.13 "I'll marry him, within this hour, if I may
620.14 go to Thrushcross Grange afterwards. Mr.
620.15 Heathcliff, you're a cruel man, but you're not
620.16 a fiend; and you wont from \mere# malice, de-
620.17 stroy, irrevocably, all my happiness. If papa
620.18 thought I had left him, on purpose; and if he
620.19 died before I returned, could I bear to live?
620.20 I've given over crying; but I'm gong to kneel
620.21 here, at your knee; and I'll not get up, and
620.22 I'll not take my eyes from your face, till you
621.01 look back at me! No, don't turn away! \do#
621.02 look! You'll see nothing to provoke you. I
621.03 don't hate you. I'm not angry that you struck
621.04 me. Have you never loved \anybody#, in all
621.05 your life, uncle? \never#? Ah! you must look
621.06 once -- I'm so wretched -- you can't help being
621.07 sorry and pitying me."
621.08 "Keep your eft's fingers off; and move, or
621.09 I'll kick you!" cried Heathcliff, brutally re-
621.10 pulsing her. "I'd rather be hugged by a
621.11 snake. How the devil can you dream of fawn-
621.12 ing on me? I \detest# you!"
621.13 He shrugged his shoulders -- shook himself,
621.14 indeed, as if his flesh crept with aversion; and
621.15 thrust back his chair: while I got up, and
621.16 opened my mouth to commence a downright
621.17 torrent of abuse; but I was rendered dumb in
621.18 the middle of the first sentence, by a threat
621.19 that I should be shown into a room by myself,
621.20 the very next syllable I uttered.
621.21 It was growing dark -- we heard a sound of
621.22 voices at the garden gate. Our host hurried
622.01 out, instantly; \he# had his wits about him; \we#
622.02 had not. There was a talk of two or three
622.03 minutes, and he returned alone.
622.04 "I thought it had been your cousin Hare-
622.05 ton," I observed to Catherine. "I wish he
622.06 would arrive! Who knows but he might take
622.07 our part?"
622.08 "It was three servants sent to seek you
622.09 from the Grange," said Heathcliff, overhearing
622.10 me. "You should have opened a lattice, and
622.11 called out; but I could swear that chit is glad
622.12 you didn't. She's glad to be obliged to stay,
622.13 I'm certain."
622.14 At learning the chance we had missed, we
622.15 both gave vent to our grief without control;
622.16 and he allowed us to wail on till nine o'clock;
622.17 then he bid us go up stairs, through the kit-
622.18 chen, to Zillah's chamber; and I whispered my
622.19 companion to obey; perhaps, we might con-
622.20 trive to get through the window there, or into
622.21 a garret, and out by its skylight.
622.22 The window, however, was narrow like those
623.01 below, and the garret trap was safe from our
623.02 attempts; for we were fastened in as before.
623.03 We neither of us lay down: Catherine took

623.04 her station by the lattice, and watched anxi-
623.05 ously for morning -- a deep sigh being the only
623.06 answer I could obtain to my frequent en-
623.07 treaties that she would try to rest.
623.08 I seated myself in a chair, and rocked, to
623.09 and fro, passing harsh judgment on my many
623.10 derelictions of duty; from which, it struck me
623.11 then, all the misfortunes of my employers
623.12 sprang. It was not the case, in reality, I am
623.13 aware; but it was, in my imagination, that
623.14 dismal night, and I thought Heathcliff himself
623.15 less guilty than I.
623.16 At seven o'clock he came, and inquired if
623.17 Miss Linton had risen.
623.18 She ran to the door immediately, and an-
623.19 swered --
623.20 "Yes."
623.21 "Here then," he said, opening it, and pull-
623.22 ing her out.
624.01 I rose to follow, but he turned the lock
624.02 again. I demanded my release.
624.03 "Be patient," he replied; "I'll send up
624.04 your breakfast in a while."
624.05 I thumped on the panels, and rattled the
624.06 latch angrily; and Catherine asked why I was
624.07 still shut up? He answered, I must try to
624.08 endure it another hour, and they went away.
624.09 I endured it two or three hours; at length,
624.10 I heard a footstep, not Heathcliff's.
624.11 "I've brought you something to eat," said
624.12 a voice; "oppen t'door!"
624.13 Complying eagerly, I beheld Hareton, laden
624.14 with food enough to last me all day.
624.15 "Tak it!" he added, thrusting the tray
624.16 into my hand.
624.17 "Stay one minute," I began.
624.18 "Nay!" cried he, and retired, regardless
624.19 of any prayer I could pour forth to detain
624.20 him.
624.21 And there I remained enclosed, the whole
624.22 day, and the whole of the next night; and another,
625.01 and another. Five nights and four days
625.02 I remained, altogether, seeing nobody but
625.03 Hareton, once every morning, and he was a
625.04 model of a jailer -- surly, and dumb, and deaf
625.05 to every attempt at moving his sense of justice
625.06 or compassion.
626.01 [VOL. 2 CHAPTER 14]
626.02 ON the fifth morning, or rather afternoon, a
626.03 different step approached -- lighter and shorter
626.04 -- and, this time, the person entered the room.
626.05 It was Zillah; donned in her scarlet shawl,
626.06 with a black silk bonnet on her head, and a
626.07 willow basket swung to her arm.
626.08 "Eh, dear! Mrs. Dean," she exclaimed.
626.09 "Well! there is a talk about you at Gimmer-
626.10 ton. I never thought, but you were sunk in
626.11 the Blackhorse marsh, and Missy with you,
626.12 till master told me you'd been found, and he'd
627.01 lodged you here! What, and you must have
627.02 got on an island, sure? And how long were
627.03 you in the hole? Did master save you, Mrs.
627.04 Dean? But you're not so thin -- you've not
627.05 been so poorly, have you?"
627.06 "Your master is a true scoundrel!" I re-
627.07 plied. "But he shall answer for it. He
627.08 needn't have raised that tale -- it shall all be
627.09 laid bare!"
627.10 "What do you mean?" asked Zillah. "It's
627.11 not his tale -- they tell that in the village --
627.12 about your being lost in the marsh; and I
627.13 calls to Earnshaw, when I came in --"
627.14 "Eh, they's queer things, Mr. Hareton,
627.15 happened since I went off. It's a sad pity of
627.16 that likely young lass, and cant Nelly Dean."
627.17 "He stared. I thought he had not heard
627.18 aught, so I told him the rumour.
627.19 "The master listened, and he just smiled to
627.20 himself, and said --
627.21 "'If they have been in the marsh, they are
627.22 out now, Zillah. Nelly Dean is lodged, at this
628.01 minute, in your room. You can tell her to
628.02 flit, when you go up; here is the key. The
628.03 bog-water got into her head, and she would
628.04 have run home, quite flighty, but I fixed her,
628.05 till she came round to her senses. You can
628.06 bid her go to the Grange, at once, if she be
628.07 able, and carry a message from me, that her
628.08 young lady will follow in time to attend the
628.09 Squire's funeral."
628.10 "Mr. Edgar is not dead?" I gasped. "Oh!
628.11 Zillah, Zillah!"
628.12 "No, no -- sit you down, my good mistress,"
628.13 she replied, "you're right sickly yet. He's
628.14 not dead: Doctor Kenneth thinks he may last
628.15 another day -- I met him on the road and
628.16 asked."
628.17 Instead of sitting down, I snatched my out-
628.18 door things, and hastened below, for the way
628.19 was free.
628.20 On entering the house, I looked about for
628.21 some one to give information of Catherine.
628.22 The place was filled with sunshine, and the
629.01 door stood wide open, but nobody seemed at
629.02 hand.
629.03 As I hesitated whether to go off at once, or
629.04 return and seek my mistress, a slight cough
629.05 drew my attention to the hearth.
629.06 Linton lay on the settle, sole tenant, sucking
629.07 a stick of sugar-candy, and pursuing my move-
629.08 ments with apathetic eyes.

629.09 "where is Miss Catherine?" I demanded,
629.10 sternly, supposing I could frighten him into
629.11 giving intelligence, by catching him thus,
629.12 alone.
629.13 He sucked on like an innocent.
629.14 "Is she gone?" I said.
629.15 "No," he replied; "she's up stairs -- she's
629.16 not to go; we wont let her."
629.17 "You wont let her, little idiot!" I ex-
629.18 claimed. "Direct me to her room immediately,
629.19 or I'll make you sing out sharply."
629.20 "Papa would make you sing out, if you at-
629.21 tempted to get there," he answered. "He
630.01 says I'm not to be soft with Catherine -- she's
630.02 my wife, and it's shameful that she should
630.03 wish to leave me! He says, she hates me, and
630.04 wants me to die, that she may have my money,
630.05 but she shan't have it; and she shan't go
630.06 home! she never shall! she may cry, and be
630.07 sick as much as she pleases!"
630.08 He resumed his former occupation, closing
630.09 his lids, as if he meant to drop asleep.
630.10 "Master Heathcliff," I resumed, "have
630.11 you forgotten all Catherine's kindness to you,
630.12 last winter, when you affirmed you loved her,
630.13 and when she brought you books, and sung
630.14 you songs, and came many a time through
630.15 wind and snow to see you? She wept to miss
630.16 one evening, because you would be disap-
630.17 pointed; and you felt then, that she was a
630.18 hundred times too good to you; and now you
630.19 believe the lies your father tells, though you
630.20 know he detests you both! And you join
630.21 him against her. That's fine gratitude, is it
630.22 not?"
631.01 The corner, of Linton's mouth fell, and he
631.02 took the sugar-candy from his lips.
631.03 "Did she come to wuthering Heights, be-
631.04 cause she hated you?" I continued. "Think
631.05 for yourself! As to your money, she does not
631.06 even know that you will have any. And you
631.07 say she's sick; and yet, you leave her alone,
631.08 up there in a strange house! \You#, who have
631.09 felt what it is to be so neglected! You could
631.10 pity your own sufferings, and she pitied them,
631.11 too, but you won't pity hers! I shed tears
631.12 Master Heathcliff, you see -- an elderly woman,
631.13 and a servant merely -- and you, after pretend-
631.14 ing such affection, and having reason to wor-
631.15 ship her, almost, store every tear you have for
631.16 yourself, and lie there quite at ease. Ah!
631.17 you're a heartless, selfish boy!"
631.18 "I can't stay with her," he answered crossly.
631.19 "I'll not stay, by myself. She cries so I can't
631.20 bear it. And she wont give over, though I
631.21 say I'll call my father -- I did call him once;
631.22 and he threatened to strangle her, if she was
632.01 not quiet, but she began again, the instant he
632.02 left the room; moaning and grieving, all night
632.03 long, though I screamed for vexation that I
632.04 couldn't sleep."
632.05 "Is Mr. Heathcliff out," I inquired, per-
632.06 ceiving that the wretched creature had no
632.07 power to sympathise with his cousin's mental
632.08 tortures.
632.09 "He's in the court," he replied, "talking to
632.10 Doctor Kenneth who says uncle is dying, truly,
632.11 at last -- I'm glad for I shall be master of the
632.12 Grange after him -- and Catherine always spoke
632.13 of it, as \her# house. It isn't hers! It's mine
632.14 -- papa says everything she has is mine, All
632.15 her nice books are mine -- she offered to give
632.16 me them, and her pretty birds, and her pony
632.17 Minny, if I would get the key of our room,
632.18 and let her out: but I told her she had nothing
632.19 to give, they were all, all mine. And then
632.20 she cried, and took a little picture from her
632.21 neck, and said I should have that -- two pic-
632.22 tures in a gold case -- on one side her mother,
633.01 and on the other, uncle, when they were
633.02 young. That was yesterday -- I said \they# were
633.03 mine, too; and tried to get them from her.
633.04 The spiteful thing wouldn't let me; she pushed
633.05 me off, and hurt me. I shrieked out -- that
633.06 frightens her -- she heard papa coming, and she
633.07 broke the hinges, and divided the case and
633.08 gave me her mother's portrait, the other she
633.09 attempted to hide; but papa asked what was
633.10 the matter and I explained it. He took the
633.11 one I had away; and ordered her to resign
633.12 hers to me; she refused, and he -- he struck
633.13 her down, and wrenched it off the chain, and
633.14 crushed it with his foot."
633.15 "And were you pleased to see her struck?"
633.16 I asked: having my designs in encouraging his
633.17 talk.
633.18 "I winked," he answered. "I wink to see
633.19 my father strike a dog, or a horse, he does it
633.20 so hard -- yet I was glad at first -- she deserved
633.21 punishing for pushing me: but when papa was
633.22 gone, she made me come to the window and
634.01 showed me her cheek cut on the inside, against
634.02 her teeth, and her mouth filling with blood;
634.03 and then she gathered up the bits of the pic-
634.04 ture, and went and sat down with her face to
634.05 the wall, and she has never spoken to me
634.06 since; and I sometimes think she can't speak
634.07 for pain. I don't like to think so! but she's a
634.08 naughty thing for crying continually; and she
634.09 looks so pale and wild, I'm afraid of her!"
634.10 "And you can get the key if you choose?"

634.11 I said.
634.12 "Yes, when I am up-stairs," he answered
634.13 "but I can't walk up-stairs now."
634.14 "In what apartment is it?" I asked.
634.15 "Oh, he cried, I shant tell \you# where it is!
634.16 It is our secret. Nobody, neither Hareton, nor
634.17 Zillah are to know. There! you've tired me --
634.18 go away, go away!" And he turned his face
634.19 onto his arm, and shut his eyes, again.
634.20 I considered it best to depart without seeing
634.21 Mr. Heathcliff; and bring a rescue for my
634.22 young lady, from the Grange.
635.01 On reaching it the astonishment of my fel-
635.02 low servants to see me, and their joy also, was
635.03 intense; and when they heard that their little
635.04 mistress was safe, two or three were about to
635.05 hurry up, and shout the news at Mr. Edgar's
635.06 door: but I bespoke the announcement of it,
635.07 myself.
635.08 How changed I found him, even in those
635.09 few days! He lay an image of sadness, and
635.10 resignation, waiting his death. Very young
635.11 he looked: though his actual age was thirty--
635.12 nine; one would have called him ten years
635.13 younger, at least. He thought of Catherine
635.14 for he murmured her name. I touched his
635.15 hand, and spoke.
635.16 "Catherine is coming, dear master!" I whis-
635.17 pered, "she is alive, and well; and will be here
635.18 I hope to-night."
635.19 I trembled at the first effects of this intel-
635.20 ligence: he half rose up, looked eagerly round
635.21 the apartment, and then sunk back in a swoon.
635.22 As soon as he recovered, I related our compulsory
636.01 visit, and detention at the Heights:
636.02 I said Heathcliff forced me to go in, which
636.03 was not quite true; I uttered as little as pos-
636.04 sible against Linton; nor did I describe all
636.05 his father's brutal conduct -- my intentions
636.06 being to add no bitterness, if I could help it,
636.07 to his already overflowing cup.
636.08 He divined that one of his enemy's purposes
636.09 was to secure the personal property, as well as
636.10 the estate to his son, or rather himself; yet
636.11 why he did not wait till his decease, was a
636.12 puzzle to my master; because ignorant how
636.13 nearly he, and his nephew would quit the
636.14 world together.
636.15 However, he felt his will had better be alter-
636.16 ed -- instead of leaving Catherine's fortune at
636.17 her own disposal, he determined to put it in
636.18 the hands of trustees, for her use during life;
636.19 and for her children, if she had any, after her.
636.20 By that means, it could not fall to Mr. Heath-
636.21 cliff should Linton die.
636.22 Having received his orders, I despatched a
637.01 man to fetch the attorney, and four more, pro-
637.02 vided with serviceable weapons, to demand
637.03 my young lady of her jailer. Both parties
637.04 were delayed very late. The single servant
637.05 returned first.
637.06 He said Mr. Green, the lawyer, was out
637.07 when he arrived at his house, and he had to
637.08 wait two hours for his re-entrance: and then
637.09 Mr. Green told him he had a little business in
637.10 the village, that must be done, but he would
637.11 be at Thrushcross Grange before morning.
637.12 The four men came back unaccompanied,
637.13 also. They brought word that Catherine was
637.14 ill, too ill to quit her room, and Heathcliff
637.15 would not suffer them to see her.
637.16 I scolded the stupid fellows well, for listen-
637.17 ing to that tale, which I would not carry to
637.18 my master; resolving to take a whole bevy up
637.19 to the Heights, at daylight; and storm it,
637.20 literally, unless the prisoner were quietly sur-
637.21 rendered to us.
637.22 Her father \shall# see her, I vowed, and vowed
638.01 again, if that devil be killed on his own door-
638.02 stones, in trying to prevent it!
638.03 Happily, I was spared the journey, and the
638.04 trouble.
638.05 I had gone down stairs at three o'clock to
638.06 fetch a jug of water; and was passing through
638.07 the hall, with it in my hand, when a sharp
638.08 knock, at the front door, made me jump.
638.09 "Oh! it is Green -- I said recollecting myself
638.10 -- only Green," and I went on, intending to
638.11 send somebody else to open it; but the knock
638.12 was repeated, not loud, and still importunately.
638.13 I put the jug on the bannister, and hasten-
638.14 ed to admit him, myself.
638.15 The harvest moon shone clear outside. It
638.16 was not the attorney. My own sweet little mis-
638.17 tress sprung on my neck sobbing,
638.18 "Ellen! Ellen! Is papa alive?"
638.19 "Yes!" I cried, "yes my angel he is! God
638.20 be thanked, you are safe with us again!"
638.21 She wanted to run, breathless as she was,
638.22 up-stairs to Mr. Linton's room; but I compelled
639.01 her to sit down on a chair, and made
639.02 her drink, and washed her pale face, chafing
639.03 it into a faint colour with my apron. Then I
639.04 said I must go first, and tell of her arrival;
639.05 imploring her to say, she should be happy,
639.06 with young Heathcliff. She stared, but soon
639.07 comprehending why I counselled her to utter
639.08 the falsehood, she assured me she would not
639.09 complain.
639.10 I couldn't abide to be present at their meet-
639.11 ing. I stood outside the chamber-door, a quarter

639.12 of an hour, and hardly ventured near the bed,
639.13 then.
639.14 All was composed, however; Catherine's
639.15 despair was as silent as her father's joy.  She
639.16 supported him calmly, in appearance; and he
639.17 fixed on her features his raised eyes that seem-
639.18 ed dilating with ecstasy.
639.19 He died blissfully, Mr. Lockwood; he died
639.20 so, kissing her cheek, he murmured;
639.21 "I am going to her, and you darling child
639.22 shall come to us;" and never stirred or spoke
640.01 again, but continued that rapt, radiant gaze,
640.02 till his pulse imperceptibly stopped, and his
640.03 soul departed. None could have noticed the
640.04 exact minute of his death, it was so entirely
640.05 without a struggle.
640.06 Whether Catherine had spent her tears,
640.07 or whether the grief were too weighty to let
640.08 them flow, she sat there dry-eyed till the sun
640.09 rose -- she sat till noon, and would still have
640.10 remained, brooding over that death-bed, but I
640.11 insisted on her coming away, and taking some
640.12 repose.
640.13 It was well I succeeded in removing her,
640.14 for at dinner-time appeared the lawyer, hav-
640.15 ing called at Wuthering Heights to get his
640.16 instructions how to behave.  He had sold him-
640.17 self to Mr. Heathcliff, and that was the cause
640.18 of his delay in obeying my master's summons.
640.19 Fortunately, no thought of worldly affairs
640.20 crossed the latter's mind, to disturb him, after
640.21 his daughter's arrival.
640.22 Mr. Green took upon himself to order
641.01 everything and everybody about the place.
641.02 He gave all the servants but me, notice to quit.
641.03 He would have carried his delegated authority
641.04 to the point of insisting that Edgar Linton
641.05 should not be buried beside his wife, but in
641.06 the chapel, with his family.  There was the
641.07 will however, to hinder that, and my loud
641.08 protestations against any infringement of its
641.09 directions.
641.10 The funeral was hurried over; Catherine,
641.11 Mrs. Linton Heathcliff now, was suffered to
641.12 stay at the Grange, till her father's corpse had
641.13 quitted it.
641.14 She told me that her anguish had at last
641.15 spurred Linton to incur the risk of liberating
641.16 her.  She heard the men I sent, disputing at
641.17 the door, and she gathered the sense of Heath-
641.18 cliff's answer.  It drove her desperate -- Linton,
641.19 who had been conveyed up to the little par-
641.20 lour soon after I left, was terrified into fetch-
641.21 ing the key before his father re-ascended.
641.22 He had the cunning to unlock, and re-lock
642.01 the door, without shutting it; and when he
642.02 should have gone to bed, he begged to sleep
642.03 with Hareton, and his petition was granted,
642.04 for once.
642.05 Catherine stole out before break of day.
642.06 She dare not try the doors, lest the dogs should
642.07 raise an alarm; she visited the empty cham-
642.08 bers, and examined their windows; and, lucki-
642.09 ly, lighting on her mother's, she got easily out
642.10 of its lattice, and onto the ground, by means
642.11 of the fir tree, close by.  Her accomplice suf-
642.12 fered for his share in the escape, notwithstand-
642.13 ing his timid contrivances.
643.01 [VOL. 2 CHAPTER 15]
643.03 THE evening after the funeral, my young lady
643.03 and I were seated in the library; now musing
643.04 mournfully, one of us despairingly, on our
643.05 loss; now venturing conjectures as to the
643.06 gloomy future.
643.07 We had just agreed the best destiny which
643.08 could await Catherine, would be a permission
643.09 to continue resident at the Grange, at least,
643.10 during Linton's life: he being allowed to join
643.11 her there, and I to remain as housekeeper.
643.12 That seemed rather too favourable an arrangement
644.01 to be hoped for, and yet I did hope, and
644.02 began to cheer up under the prospect of re-
644.03 taining my home, and my employment, and,
644.04 above all, my beloved young mistress, when a
644.05 servant -- one of the discarded ones, not yet de-
644.06 parted -- rushed hastily in, and said, "that devil
644.07 Heathcliff" was coming through the court,
644.08 should he fasten the door in his face?
644.09 If we had been mad enough to order that
644.10 proceeding, we had not time.  He made no
644.11 ceremony of knocking, or announcing his
644.12 name; he was master, and availed himself of
644.13 the master's privilege to walk straight in,
644.14 without saying a word.
644.15 The sound of our informant's voice directed
644.16 him to the library: he entered; and motioning
644.17 him out, shut the door.
644.18 It was the same room into which he had
644.19 been ushered, as a guest, eighteen years be-
644.20 fore: the same moon shone through the win-
644.21 dow; and the same autumn landscape lay
644.22 outside.  We had not yet lighted a candle,
645.01 but all the apartment was visible, even to the
645.02 portraits on the wall -- the splended head of
645.03 Mrs. Linton, and the graceful one of her hus-
645.04 band.
645.05 Heathcliff advanced to the hearth.  Time
645.06 had little altered his person either.  There was
645.07 the same man; his dark face rather sallower,
645.08 and more composed, his frame a stone or two
645.09 heavier, perhaps, and no other difference.

645.10 Catherine had risen with an impulse to dash
645.11 out, when she saw him.
645.12 "Stop!" he said, arresting her by the arm.
645.13 "No more runnings away! Where would
645.14 you go? I'm come to fetch you home; and I
645.15 hope you'll be a dutiful daughter, and not en-
645.16 courage my son to further disobedience.  I
645.17 was embarrassed how to punish him, when I
645.18 discovered his part in the business -- he's such
645.19 a cobweb, a pinch would annihilate him -- but,
645.20 you'll see by his look that he has received
645.21 his due! I brought him down one evening,
645.22 the day before yesterday, and just set him in
646.01 a chair, and never touched him afterwards.  I
646.02 sent Hareton out, and we had the room to
646.03 ourselves.  In two hours, I called Joseph to
646.04 carry him up again; and, since then, my pre-
646.05 sence is as potent on his nerves, as a ghost;
646.06 and I fancy he sees me often, though I am not
646.07 near, Hareton says he wakes and shrieks in the
646.08 night by the hour together; and calls you to
646.09 protect him from me; and, whether you like
646.10 your precious mate or not, you must come --
646.11 he's your concern now; I yield all my interest
646.12 in him to you."
646.13 "Why not let Catherine continue here?" I
646.14 pleaded, "and send Master Linton to her.
646.15 As you hate them both, you'd not miss them --
646.16 they \can# only be a daily plague to your un-
646.17 natural heart."
646.18 "I'm seeking a tenant for the Grange," he
646.19 answered; "and I want my children about
646.20 me, to be sure -- besides that lass owes me her
646.21 services for her bread; I'm not going to nur-
646.22 ture her in luxury and idleness after Linton is
647.01 gone.  Make haste and get ready now.  And
647.02 don't oblige me to compel you."
647.03 "I shall," said Catherine.  "Linton is all
647.04 I have to love in the world, and though you
647.05 have done what you could to make him hate-
647.06 ful to me, and me to him, you \cannot# make us
647.07 hate each other! and I defy you to hurt him
647.08 when I am by, and I defy you to frighten me."
647.09 "You are a boastful champion!" replied
647.10 Heathcliff; "But I don't like you well enough
647.11 to hurt him -- you shall get the full benefit of
647.12 the torment, as long as it lasts.  It is not I
647.13 who will make him hateful to you -- it is his
647.14 own sweet spirit.  He's as bitter as gall at
647.15 your desertion, and its consequences -- don't
647.16 expect thanks for this noble devotion.  I heard
647.17 him draw a pleasant picture to Zillah of what
647.18 he would do, if he were as strong as I -- the
647.19 inclination is there, and his very weakness will
647.20 sharpen his wits to find a substitute for
647.21 strength."
647.22 "I know he has a bad nature," said Catherine;
648.01 "he's your son.  But I'm glad I've a
648.02 better, to forgive it; and I know he loves me
648.03 and for that reason I love him.  Mr. Heath-
648.04 cliff, \you# have \nobody# to love you; and, how-
648.05 ever miserable you make us, we shall still have
648.06 the revenge of thinking that your cruelty rises
648.07 from your greater misery! You \are# miserable,
648.08 are you not? Lonely, like the devil, and
648.09 envious like him? \Nobody# loves you -- \nobody#
648.10 will cry for you, when you die! I wouldn't
648.11 be you!"
648.12 Catherine spoke with a kind of dreary tri-
648.13 umph: she seemed to have made up her mind
648.14 to enter into the spirit of her future family,
648.15 and draw pleasure from the griefs of her ene-
648.16 mies.
648.17 "You shall be sorry to be yourself pre-
648.18 sently," said her father-in-law.  "If you stand
648.19 there another minute.  Begone, witch, and get
648.20 your things."
648.21 She scornfully withdrew.
648.22 In her absence, I began to beg for Zillah's
649.01 place at the Heights, offering to resign her
649.02 mine; but he would suffer it on no account.
649.03 He bid me to be silent, and then, for the first
649.04 time, allowed himself a glance round the room,
649.05 and a look at the pictures.  Having studied
649.06 Mrs. Linton, he said --
649.07 "I shall have that at home.  Not because I
649.08 need it, but --"
649.09 He turned abruptly to the fire, and con-
649.10 tinued, with what, for lack of a better word, I
649.11 must call a smile --
649.12 "I'll tell you what I did yesterday! I got
649.13 the sexton, who was digging Linton's grave,
649.14 to remove the earth off her coffin lid, and I
649.15 opened it.  I thought, once, I would have
649.16 stayed there, when I saw her face again -- it is
649.17 hers yet -- he had hard work to stir me; but
649.18 he said it would change, if the air blew on it,
649.19 and so I struck one side of the coffin loose --
649.20 and covered it up -- not Linton's side, damn
649.21 him! I wish he'd been soldered in lead -- and I
649.22 bribed the sexton to pull it away, when I'm
650.01 laid there, and slide mine out too, I'll have it
650.02 made so, and then, by the time Linton gets to
650.03 us, he'll not know which is which!"
650.04 "You were very wicked, Mr. Heathcliff!"
650.05 I exclaimed; "were you not ashamed to dis-
650.06 turb the dead?"
650.07 "I disturbed nobody, Nelly," he replied;
650.08 "and I gave some ease to myself.  I shall be
650.09 a great deal more comfortable now; and you'll
650.10 have a better chance of keeping me un-

650.11 derground, when I get there.  Disturbed her?
650.12 No! she has disturbed me, night and day,
650.13 through eighteen years -- incessantly -- remorse-
650.14 lessly -- till yesternight -- and yesternight, I was
650.15 tranquil.  I dreamt I was sleeping the last
650.16 sleep, by that sleeper, with my heart stopped,
650.17 and my cheek frozen against hers."
650.18   "And if she had been dissolved into earth,
650.19 or worse, what would you have dreamd of
650.20 then?" I said.
650.21   "Of dissolving with her, and being more
651.01 happy still!" he answered.  "Do you suppose
651.02 I dread any change of that sort?  I expected
651.03 such a transformation on raising the lid, but
651.04 I'm better pleased that it should not commence
651.05 till I share it.  Besides, unless I had received a
651.06 distinct impression of her passionless features,
651.07 that strange feeling would hardly have been
651.08 removed.  It began oddly.  You know, I was
651.09 wild after she died, and eternally, from dawn
651.10 to dawn, praying her to return to me -- her
651.11 spirit -- I have a strong faith in ghosts; I have
651.12 a conviction that they can, and do exist, among
651.13 us!
651.14   "The day she was buried there came a fall
651.15 of snow.  In the evening I went to the church-
651.16 yard.  It blew bleak as winter -- all round was
651.17 solitary: I didn't fear that her fool of a hus-
651.18 band would wander up the den so late -- and
651.19 no one else had business to bring them there.
651.20   "Being alone, and conscious two yards of
651.21 loose earth was the sole barrier between us, I
651.22 said to myself --
652.01   "`I'll have her in my arms again!  If she
652.02 be cold, I'll think it is this north wind that
652.03 chills \me#; and if she be motionless, it is sleep.`
652.04   "I got a spade from the toolhouse, and be-
652.05 gan to delve with all my might -- it scraped
652.06 the coffin; I fell to work with my hands; the
652.07 wood commenced cracking about the screws, I
652.08 was on the point of attaining my object, when
652.09 it seemed that I heard a sigh from some one
652.10 above, close at the edge of the grave, and
652.11 bending down. -- `If I can only get this off,`
652.12 muttered, `I wish they may shovel in the
652.13 earth over us both!` and I wrenched at it more
652.14 desperately still.  There was another sigh,
652.15 close at my ear.  I appeared to feel the warm
652.16 breath of it displacing the sleet-laden wind.
652.17 I knew no living thing in flesh and blood was
652.18 by -- but as certainly as you perceive the approach
652.19 to some substantial body in the dark, though
652.20 it cannot be discerned, so certainly I felt that
652.21 Cathy was there, not under me, but on the
652.22 earth.
653.01   "A sudden sense of relief flowed, from my
653.02 heart, through every limb.  I relinquished
653.03 my labour of agony, and turned consoled at
653.04 once, unspeakably consoled.  Her presence
653.05 was with me; it remained while I re-filled the
653.06 grave, and led me home.  You may laugh, if
653.07 you will, but I was sure I should see her there.
653.08 I was sure she was with me, and I could not
653.09 help talking to her.
653.10   "Having reached the Heights, I rushed
653.11 eagerly to the door.  It was fastened; and, I
653.12 remember, that accursed Earnshaw and my
653.13 wife opposed my entrance.  I remember stop-
653.14 ping to kick the breath out of him, and then
653.15 hurrying up stairs, to my room, and hers -- I
653.16 looked round impatiently -- I felt her by me --
653.17 I could \almost# see her, and yet I \could# \not#!  I
653.18 ought to have sweat blood then, from the an-
653.19 guish of my yearning, from the fervour of my
653.20 supplications to have but one glimpse!  I had
653.21 not one.  She showed herself, as she often was
653.22 in life, a devil to me!  And, since then, sometimes
654.01 more, and sometimes less, I've been the
654.02 sport of that intolerable torture!  Infernal --
654.03 keeping my nerves at such a stretch, that, if
654.04 they had not resembled catgut, they would,
654.05 long ago, have relaxed to the feebleness of
654.06 Linton's.
654.07   "When I sat in the house with Hareton, it
654.08 seemed that on going out, I should meet her;
654.09 when I walked on the moors I should meet her
654.10 coming in.  When I went from home, I has-
654.11 tened to return, she \must# be somewhere at the
654.12 Heights, I was certain!  And when I slept in
654.13 her chamber -- I was beaten out of that -- I
654.14 couldn't lie there; for the moment I closed my
654.15 eyes, she was either outside the window, or
654.16 sliding back the panels, or entering the room,
654.17 or even resting her darling head on the same
654.18 pillow as she did  when a child.  And I must
654.19 open my lids to see.  And so I opened and
654.20 closed them a hundred times a-night -- to be
654.21 always disappointed!  It racked me!  I've
654.22 often groaned aloud, till that old rascal Joseph,
655.01 no doubt believed that my conscience was play-
655.02 ing the fiend inside of me.
655.03   "Now since I've seen her, I'm pacified -- a
655.04 little.  It was a strange way of killing, not by
655.05 inches, but by fractions of hair-breadths, to be-
655.06 guile me with the spectre of a hope, through
655.07 eighteen years!"
655.08   Mr. Heathcliff paused and wiped his fore-
655.09 head -- his hair clung to it, wet with perspira-
655.10 tion; his eyes were fixed on the red embers of
655.11 the fire; the brows not contracted, but raised
655.12 next the temples, diminishing the grim aspect

655.13 of his countenance, but imparting a peculiar
655.14 look of trouble, and a painful appearance of
655.15 mental tension towards one absorbing subject.
655.16 He only half addressed me, and I maintained
655.17 silence -- I didn't like to hear him talk!
655.18   After a short period, he resumed his medi-
655.19 tation on the picture, took it down, and leant
655.20 it against the sofa to contemplate it at better
655.21 advantage; and while so occupied Catherine
656.01 entered, announcing that she was ready, when
656.02 her pony should be saddled.
656.03   "Send that over to-morrow," said Heathcliff
656.04 to me, then turning to her he added, "You
656.05 may do without your pony -- it is a fine even-
656.06 ing, and you'll need no ponies at Wuthering
656.07 Heights, for what journies you take, your
656.08 own feet will serve you -- Come along."
656.09   "Good-bye, Ellen!" whispered my dear lit-
656.10 tle mistress.  As she kissed me, her lips felt
656.11 like ice.  "Come and see me Ellen, don't for-
656.12 get."
656.13   "Take care you do no such thing, Mrs.
656.14 Dean!" said her new father.  "When I wish to
656.15 speak to you I'll come here.  I want none of
656.16 your prying at my house!"
656.17   He signed her to precede him; and
656.18 casting back a look that cut my heart, she
656.19 obeyed.
656.20   I watched them from the window, walk
656.21 down the garden.  Heathcliff fixed Catherine's
657.01 arm under his, though she disputed the act, at
657.02 first, evidently, and with rapid strides, he hur-
657.03 ried her into the alley, whose trees concealed
657.04 them.
658.01 [VOL. 2 CHAPTER 16]
658.02   I HAVE paid a visit to the Heights, but I have
658.03 not seen her since she left; Joseph held the
658.04 door in his hand, when I called to ask after
658.05 her, and wouldn't let me pass.  He said Mrs.
658.06 Linton was "thrang," and the master was not
658.07 in.  Zillah has told me something of the way
658.08 they go on, otherwise I should hardly know who
658.09 was dead, and who living.
658.10   She thinks Catherine, haughty, and does not
658.11 like her, I can guess by her talk.  My young
658.12 lady asked some aid of her, when she first
659.01 came, but Mr. Heathcliff told her to follow
659.02 her own business, and let his daughter-in-law
659.03 look after herself, and Zillah willingly acqui-
659.04 esced, being a narrow-minded selfish woman.
659.05 Catherine evinced a child's annoyance at this
659.06 neglect; repaid it with contempt, and thus en-
659.07 listed my informant among her enemies, as se-
659.08 curely as if she had done her some great
659.09 wrong.
659.10   I had a long talk with Zillah, about six
659.11 weeks ago, a little before you came, one day,
659.12 when we foregathered on the moor; and this
659.13 is what she told me.
659.14   "The first thing Mrs. Linton did," she said,
659.15 "on her arrival at the Heights, was to run up-
659.16 stairs without even wishing good-evening to
659.17 me and Joseph; she shut herself into Linton's
659.18 room, and remained till morning -- then, while
659.19 the master and Earnshaw were at breakfast,
659.20 she entered the house and asked all in a quiver
659.21 if the doctor might be sent for?  her cousin was
659.22 very ill."
660.01   "We know that!" answered Heathcliff,
660.02 "but his life is not worth a farthing, and I
660.03 won't spend a farthing on him."
660.04   "But I cannot tell how to do," she said,
660.05 "and if nobody will help me, he'll die!"
660.06   "Walk out of the room!" cried the master,
660.07 "and let me never hear a word more about
660.08 him!  None here care what becomes of him;
660.09 if you do, act the nurse; if you do not, lock
660.10 him up and leave him."
660.11   Then she began to bother me, and I said
660.12 I'd had enough plague with the tiresome thing;
660.13 we each had our tasks, and her's was to wait
660.14 on Linton, Mr. Heathcliff bid me leave that
660.15 labour to her.
660.16   How they managed together, I can't tell.
660.17 I fancy he fretted a great deal, and moaned
660.18 hisseln, night and day; and she had precious
660.19 little rest, one could guess by her white face,
660.20 and heavy eyes -- she sometimes came into the
660.21 kitchen all wildered like, and looked as if she
660.22 would fain beg assistance:  but I was not going
661.01 to disobey the master -- I never dare disobey
661.02 him, Mrs. Dean, and though I thought it
661.03 wrong that Kenneth should  not be sent for,
661.04 it was no concern of mine, either to advise or
661.05 complain; and I always refused to meddle.
661.06   Once or twice, after we had gone to bed,
661.07 I've happened to open my door again, and
661.08 seen her sitting crying, on the stairs' top; and
661.09 then I've shut myself in, quick, for fear of
661.10 being moved to interfere.  I did pity her then,
661.11 I'm sure; still I didn't wish to lose my place,
661.12 you know!
661.13   At last, one night she came boldly into my
661.14 chamber, and frightened me out of my wits, by
661.15 saying
661.16   "Tell Mr. Heathcliff that his son is dying --
661.17 I'm sure he is, this time -- Get up, instantly,
661.18 and tell him!"
661.19   Having uttered this speech, she vanished
661.20 again.  I lay a quarter of an hour listening
661.21 and trembling -- Nothing stirred -- the house was

661.22 quiet.
662.01 "She's mistaken, I said to myself. He's got
662.02 over it. I needn't disturb them." And I
662.03 began to dose. But my sleep was marred a
662.04 second time, by a sharp ringing of the bell --
662.05 the only bell we have, put up on purpose for
662.06 Linton, and the master called to me, to see
662.07 what was the matter, and inform them that
662.08 he wouldn't have that noise repeated.
662.09 "I delivered Catherine's message. He curs-
662.10 ed to himself, and in a few minutes, came out
662.11 with a lighted candle, and proceeded to their
662.12 room. I followed -- Mrs. Heathcliff was seated
662.13 by the bedside, with her hands folded on her
662.14 knees. Her father-in-law went up, held the
662.15 light to Linton's face, looked at him, and
662.16 touched him, afterwards he turned to her.
662.17 "`Now -- Catherine,` he said, `how do you
662.18 feel?`
662.19 "She was dumb.
662.20 "`How do you feel, Catherine?` he repeated.
662.21 "`He's safe, and I'm free,` she answered,
662.22 `I should feel well -- but,` she continued with
663.01 a bitterness she couldn't conceal, `You have
663.02 left me so long to struggle against death,
663.03 alone, that I feel and see only death! I feel
663.04 like death!
663.05 "And she looked like it, too! I gave her a
663.06 little wine. Hareton and Joseph who had been
663.07 wakened by the ringing, and the sound of feet,
663.08 and heard our talk from outside, now entered.
663.09 Joseph was fain, I believe, of the lad's removal:
663.10 Hareton seemed a thought bothered, though
663.11 he was more taken up with staring at Cathe-
663.12 rine than thinking of Linton. But the mas-
663.13 ter bid him get off to bed again -- we didn't
663.14 want his help. He afterwards made Joseph
663.15 remove the body to his chamber, and told me
663.16 to return to mine, and Mrs. Heathcliff re-
663.17 mained by herself.
663.18 "In the morning, he sent me to tell her she
663.19 must come down to breakfast -- she had un-
663.20 dressed, and appeared going to sleep; and
663.21 said she was ill; at which I hardly wondered.
663.22 I informed Mr. Heathcliff, and he replied,
664.01 "`Well, let her be till after the funeral;
664.02 and go up now and then to get her what is
664.03 needful; and as soon as she seems better, tell
664.04 me.`
664.05 Cathy stayed up-stairs a fortnight, accord-
664.06 ing to Zillah, who visited her twice a-day, and
664.07 would have been rather more friendly, but her
664.08 attempts at increasing kindness were proudly
664.09 and promptly repelled.
664.10 Heathcliff went up once, to show her Lin-
664.11 ton's will. He had bequeathed the whole of
664.12 his, and what had been her moveable property
664.13 to his father. The poor creature was threat-
664.14 ened, or coaxed into that act, during her
664.15 week's absence, when his uncle died. The
664.16 lands, being a minor he could not meddle with.
664.17 However, Mr. Heathcliff has claimed, and kept
664.18 them in his wife's right, and his also -- I sup-
664.19 pose legally, at any rate Catherine, destitute
664.20 of cash and friends, cannot disturb his pos-
664.21 session.
664.22 "Nobody," said Zillah, "ever approached
665.01 her door, except that once, but I ... and nobody
665.02 asked anything about her. The first occa-
665.03 sion of her coming down into the house, was
665.04 on a Sunday afternoon.
665.05 "She had cried out, when I carried up her
665.06 dinner that she couldn't bear any longer being in
665.07 the cold; and I told her the master was going
665.08 to Thrushcross Grange; and Earnshaw and I
665.09 needn't hinder her from descending; so, as
665.10 soon as she heard Heathcliff's horse trot off,
665.11 she made her appearance, donned in black, and
665.12 her yellow curls combed back behind her ears,
665.13 as plain as a quaker, she couldn't comb them
665.14 out.
665.15 "Joseph, and I generally go to chapel on
665.16 Sundays, /the Kirk, you know, has no minis-
665.17 ter, now, explained Mrs. Dean, and they call
665.18 the Methodists' or Baptists' place, I can't say
665.19 which it is, at Gimmerton, a chapel.// "Jo-
665.20 seph had gone," she continued, "but I thought
665.21 proper to bide at home. Young folks are al-
665.22 ways the better for an elder's over-looking, and
666.01 Hareton with all his bashfulness, isn't a model
666.02 of nice behaviour. I let him know that his
666.03 cousin would very likely sit with us, and she
666.04 had been always used to see the Sabbath
666.05 respected, so he had as good leave his guns,
666.06 and bits of in-door work alone, while she
666.07 stayed.
666.08 "He coloured up at the news; and cast his
666.09 eyes over his hands and clothes. The train--
666.10 oil, and gunpowder were shoved out of sight
666.11 in a minute. I saw he meant to give her his
666.12 company; and I guessed, by his way, he
666.13 wanted to be presentable; so, laughing, as I
666.14 durst not laugh when the master is by, I offer-
666.15 ed to help him, if he would, and joked at his
666.16 confusion. He grew sullen, and began to
666.17 swear.
666.18 "Now, Mrs. Dean," she went on, seeing
666.19 me not pleased by her manner, "you happen
666.20 think your young lady too fine for Mr.
666.21 Hareton, and happen you're right -- but, I
666.22 own, I should love well to bring her pride a

667.01 peg lower. And what will all her learning
667.02 and her daintiness do for her, now? She's as
667.03 poor as you, or I -- poorer -- I'll be bound, you're
667.04 saving -- and I'm doing my little all, that road."
667.05 Hareton allowed Zillah to give him her aid;
667.06 and she flattered him into a good humour; so,
667.07 when Catherine came, half forgetting her
667.08 former insults, he tried to make himself agree-
667.09 able, by the house-keeper's account.
667.10 "Miss walked in," she said, "as chill as
667.11 an icicle, and as high as a princess. I got up
667.12 and offered her my seat in the arm-chair. No,
667.13 she turned up her nose at my civility. Earn-
667.14 shaw rose too, and bid her come to the settle,
667.15 and sit close by the fire; he was sure she was
667.16 starved.
667.17 "`I've been starved a month and more,` she
667.18 answered, resting on the word, as scornful as
667.19 she could.
667.20 "And she got a chair for herself, and placed
667.21 it at a distance from both of us.
667.22 "Having sat till she was warm, she began
668.01 to look round, and discovered a number of
668.02 books in the dresser; she was instantly upon
668.03 her feet again, stretching to reach them, but
668.04 they were too high up.
668.05 "Her cousin, after watching her endeavours
668.06 a while, at last summoned courage to help
668.07 her; she held her frock, and he filled it with
668.08 the first that came to hand.
668.09 "That was a great advance for the lad --
668.10 she didn't thank him; still, he felt gratified
668.11 that she had accepted his assistance, and ven-
668.12 tured to stand behind as she examined them,
668.13 and even to stoop and point out what struck
668.14 his fancy in certain old pictures which they
668.15 contained -- nor was he daunted by the saucy
668.16 style in which she jerked the page from his
668.17 finger; he contented himself with going a bit
668.18 farther back, and looking at her, instead of
668.19 the book.
668.20 "She continued reading, or seeking for
668.21 something to read. His attention became, by
668.22 degrees, quite centred in the study of her
669.01 thick, silky curls -- her face he couldn't see,
669.02 and she couldn't see him. And perhaps, not
669.03 quite awake to what he did, but attracted like
669.04 a child to a candle, at last, he proceeded from
669.05 staring to touching; he put out his hand and
669.06 stroked one curl, as gently as if it were a bird.
669.07 He might have struck a knife into her neck,
669.08 she started round in such a taking.
669.09 "`Get away, this moment! How dare you
669.10 touch me? Why are you stopping there?` she
669.11 cried, in a tone of disgust. `I can't endure
669.12 you! I'll go up stairs again, if you come
669.13 near me.`
669.14 "Mr. Hareton recoiled, looking as foolish as
669.15 he could do; he sat down in the settle, very
669.16 quiet, and she continued turning over her
669.17 volumes, another half hour -- finally, Earnshaw
669.18 crossed over, and whispered to me.
669.19 "`Will you ask her to read to us, Zillah?
669.20 I'm stalled of doing naught -- and I do like -- I
669.21 could like to hear her! dunnot say I wanted it,
669.22 but ask of yourseln.`
670.01 "`Mr. Hareton wishes you would read to
670.02 us, ma'am,` I said, immediately. `He'd take
670.03 it very kind -- he'd be much obliged.`
670.04 "She frowned; and, looking up, answered,
670.05 "`Mr. Hareton, and the whole set of you
670.06 will be good enough to understand that I re-
670.07 ject any pretence at kindness you have the
670.08 hypocrisy to offer! I despise you, and will
670.09 have nothing to say to any of you! When I
670.10 would have given my life for one kind word,
670.11 even to see one of your faces, you all kept off.
670.12 But I won't complain to you! I'm driven
670.13 down here by the cold, not either to amuse
670.14 you, or enjoy your society.`
670.15 "`What could I ha' done?` began Earn-
670.16 shaw. `How was I to blame?`
670.17 "`Oh! you are an exception,` answered
670.18 Mrs. Heathcliff. `I never missed such a con-
670.19 cern as you.`
670.20 "`But, I offered more than once, and
670.21 asked,` he said, kindling up at her pertness,
670.22 `I asked Mr. Heathcliff to let me wake for
670.23 you --`
671.01 "`Be silent! I'll go out of doors, or any-
671.02 where, rather than have your disagreeable voice
671.03 in my ear!` said my lady.
671.04 "Hareton muttered, she might go to hell,
671.05 for him! and unslinging his gun, restrained
671.06 himself from his Sunday occupations, no longer.
671.07 "He talked now, freely enough; and she
671.08 presently saw fit to retreat to her solitude:
671.09 but the frost had set in, and, in spite of her
671.10 pride, she was forced to condescend to our
671.11 company, more and more. However, I took
671.12 care there should be no further scorning at my
671.13 good nature -- ever since, I've been as stiff as
671.14 herself -- and she has no lover, or liker among
671.15 us -- and she does not deserve one -- for, let
671.16 them say the least word to her, and she'll curl
671.17 back without respect of any one! She'll snap
671.18 at the master himself; and, as good as dares
671.19 him to thrash her; and the more hurt she gets,
671.20 the more venomous she grows."
671.21 At first, on hearing this account from Zillah,
671.22 I determined to leave my situation, take a cottage,

672.01 and get Catherine to come and live with
672.02 me; but Mr. Heathcliff would as soon permit
672.03 that, as he would set up Hareton in an inde-
672.04 pendent house; and I can see no remedy, at
672.05 present, unless she could marry again; and
672.06 that scheme, it does not come within my pro-
672.07 vince to arrange."
672.08    Thus ended Mrs. Dean's story. Notwith-
672.09 standing the doctor's prophecy, I am rapidly
672.10 recovering strength, and, though it be only the
672.11 second week in January, I propose getting out
672.12 on horseback, in a day or two, and riding over
672.13 to Wuthering Heights, to inform my landlord
672.14 that I shall spend the next six months in Lon-
672.15 don; and, if he likes, he may look out for
672.16 another tenant to take the place, after October
672.17 -- I would not pass another winter here, for
672.18 much.
673.01 [VOL. 2 CHAPTER 17]
673.02 YESTERDAY was bright, calm, and frosty. I
673.03 went to the Heights as I proposed; my house-
673.04 keeper entreated me to bear a little note from
673.05 her to her young lady, and I did not refuse,
673.06 for the worthy woman was not conscious of
673.07 anything odd in her request.
673.08    The front door stood open, but the jealous
673.09 gate was fastened, as at my last visit; I knocked
673.10 and invoked Earnshaw from among the garden
673.11 beds; he unchained it, and I entered. The
673.12 fellow is as handsome a rustic as need be seen.
674.01 I took particular notice of him this time; but
674.02 then, he does his best, apparently, to make the
674.03 least of his advantages.
674.04    I asked if Mr. Heathcliff were at home?
674.05 He answered, no; but he would be in at din-
674.06 ner-time. It was eleven o'clock, and I an-
674.07 nounced my intention of going in, and waiting
674.08 for him, at which he immediately flung down
674.09 his tools and accompanied me, in the office of
674.10 watchdog, not as a substitute for the host.
674.11    We entered together; Catherine was there,
674.12 making herself useful in preparing some vege-
674.13 tables for the approaching meal; she looked
674.14 more sulky, and less spirited than when I had
674.15 seen her first. She hardly raised her eyes to
674.16 notice me, and continued her employment with
674.17 the same disregard to common forms of polite-
674.18 ness, as before; never returning my bow and
674.19 good morning, by the slightest acknowledg-
674.20 ment.
674.21    "She does not seem so amiable," I thought,
675.01 "as Mrs. Dean would persuade me to believe.
675.02 She's a beauty, it is true; but not an angel."
675.03    Earnshaw surlily bid her remove her things
675.04 to the kitchen.
675.05    "Remove them yourself," she said; pushing
675.06 them from her, as soon as she had done; and
675.07 returning to a stool by the window, where she
675.08 began to carve figures of birds and beasts, out
675.09 of the turnip parings in her lap.
675.10    I approached her, pretending to desire a
675.11 view of the garden; and, as I fancied, adroitly
675.12 dropped Mrs. Dean's note onto her knee, un-
675.13 noticed by Hareton -- but she asked aloud --
675.14    "What is that?" And chucked it off.
675.15    "A letter from your old acquaintance, the
675.16 housekeeper at the Grange," I answered, an-
675.17 noyed at her exposing my kind deed, and fear-
675.18 ful lest it should be imagined a missive of my
675.19 own.
675.20    She would gladly have gathered it up, at
675.21 this information, but Hareton beat her; he
676.01 seized, and put it in his waistcoat, saying Mr.
676.02 Heathcliff should look at it first.
676.03    Thereat, Catherine silently turned her face
676.04 from us, and, very stealthily, drew out her
676.05 pocket-handkerchief and applied it to her
676.06 eyes; and her cousin, after struggling a
676.07 while to keep down his softer feelings, pulled
676.08 out the letter and flung it on the floor beside
676.09 her as ungraciously as he could.
676.10    Catherine caught, and perused it eagerly;
676.11 then she put a few questions to me concern-
676.12 ing the inmates, rational and irrational of her
676.13 former home; and gazing towards the hills,
676.14 murmured in soliloquy.
676.15    "I should like to be riding Minny down
676.16 there! I should like to be climbing up there
676.17 -- Oh! I'm tired -- I'm \stalled#, Hareton!"
676.18    And she leant her pretty head back against
676.19 the sill, with a half yawn and half a sigh, and
676.20 lapsed into an aspect of abstracted sadness,
676.21 neither caring, nor knowing whether we re-
676.22 marked her.
677.01    "Mrs. Heathcliff," I said, after sitting some
677.02 time mute, "you are not aware that I am an
677.03 acquaintance of yours? so intimate, that I
677.04 think it strange you won't come and speak to
677.05 me. My housekeeper never wearies of talk-
677.06 ing about and praising you; and she'll be
677.07 greatly disappointed if I return with no news
677.08 of, or from you, except that you received her
677.09 letter, and said nothing!"
677.10    She appeared to wonder at this speech and
677.11 asked,
677.12    "Does Ellen like you?"
677.13    "Yes, very well," I replied unhesitatingly.
677.14    "You must tell her," she continued, "that
677.15 I would answer her letter, but I have no
677.16 materials for writing, not even a book from
677.17 which I might tear a leaf."

677.18    "No books!" I exclaimed. "How do you
677.19 contrive to live here without them? If I may
677.20 take the liberty to inquire -- Though provided
677.21 with a large library, I'm frequently very dull
678.01 at the Grange -- take my books away, and I
678.02 should be desperate!"
678.03    "I was always reading, when I had them;"
678.04 said Catherine, "and Mr. Heathcliff never
678.05 reads; so he took it into his head to destroy
678.06 my books. I have not had a glimpse of one,
678.07 for weeks. Only once, I searched through
678.08 Joseph's store of theology; to his great irrita-
678.09 tion: and once, Hareton, I came upon a se-
678.10 cret stock in your room ... some Latin and
678.11 Greek, and some tales and poetry; all old
678.12 friends -- I brought the last here -- and you ga-
678.13 thered them, as a magpie gathers silver spoons,
678.14 for the mere love of stealing! They are of no
678.15 use to you -- or else you concealed them in the
678.16 bad spirit, that as you cannot enjoy them, no-
678.17 body else shall. Perhaps \your# envy counsel-
678.18 led Mr. Heathcliff to rob me of my treasures?
678.19 But, I've most of them written on my brain
678.20 and printed in my heart, and you cannot de-
678.21 prive me of those!"
679.01    Earnshaw blushed crimson, when his cousin
679.02 made this revelation of his private literary ac-
679.03 cumulations, and stammered an indignant de-
679.04 nial of her accusations.
679.05    "Mr. Hareton is desirous of increasing his
679.06 amount of knowledge," I said, coming to his
679.07 rescue. "He is not \envious# but \emulous# o
679.08 your attainments -- He'll be a clever scholar in
679.09 a few years!"
679.10    "And he wants \me# to sink into a dunce,
679.11 meantime," answered Catherine. "Yes, I hear
679.12 him trying to spell and read to himself, and
679.13 pretty blunders he makes! I wish you would
679.14 repeat Chevy Chase, as you did yesterday -- It
679.15 was extremely funny! I heard you ... and I
679.16 heard you turning over the dictionary, to seek
679.17 out the hard words, and then cursing, because
679.18 you couldn't read their explanations!"
679.19    The young man evidently thought it too
679.20 bad that he should be laughed at for his ig-
679.21 norance, and then laughed at for trying to
679.22 remove it. I had a similar notion, and, remembering
680.01 Mrs. Dean's anecdote of his first
680.02 attempt at enlightening the darkness in which
680.03 he had been reared, I observed,
680.04    "But, Mrs. Heathcliff, we have each had a
680.05 commencement, and each stumbled and tot-
680.06 tered on the threshold, and had our teachers
680.07 scorned, instead of aiding us, we should stum-
680.08 ble and totter yet."
680.09    "Oh!" she replied, "I don't wish to limit
680.10 his acquirements ... still, he has no right to ap-
680.11 propriate what is mine, and make it ridiculous
680.12 to me with his vile mistakes and mis-pronun-
680.13 ciations! Those books, both prose and verse,
680.14 were consecrated to me by other associations,
680.15 and I hate to have them debased and profaned
680.16 in his mouth! Besides, of all, he has selected
680.17 my favourite pieces that I love the most to re-
680.18 peat, as if out of deliberate malice!"
680.19    Hareton's chest heaved in silence a minute;
680.20 he laboured under a severe sense of mortifica-
680.21 tion and wrath, which it was no easy task to
680.22 suppress.
681.01    I rose, and from a gentlemanly idea of re-
681.02 lieving his embarrassment, took up my station
681.03 in the door-way surveying the external pros-
681.04 pect, as I stood.
681.05    He followed my example, and left the room,
681.06 but presently re-appeared, bearing half-a-dozen
681.07 volumes in his hands, which he threw into
681.08 Catherine's lap, exclaiming,
681.09    "Take them! I never want to hear, or read,
681.10 or think of them again!"
681.11    "I won't have them, now!" she answered.
681.12 "I shall connect them with you, and hate
681.13 them."
681.14    She opened one that had obviously been
681.15 often turned over, and read a portion in the
681.16 drawling tone of a beginner; then laughed,
681.17 and threw it from her.
681.18    "And listen!" she continued provokingly,
681.19 commencing a verse of an old ballad in the
681.20 same fashion.
681.21    But his self-love would endure no further
682.01 torment -- I heard, and not altogether disap-
682.02 provingly, a manual check given to her saucy
682.03 tongue -- The little wretch had done her ut-
682.04 most to hurt her cousin's sensitive though
682.05 uncultivated feelings, and a physical argument
682.06 was the only mode he had of balancing the
682.07 account and repaying its effects on the inflic-
682.08 ter.
682.09    He afterward gathered the books and
682.10 hurled them on the fire. I read in his coun-
682.11 tenance what anguish it was to offer that sa-
682.12 crifice to spleen -- I fancied that as they con-
682.13 sumed, he recalled the pleasure they had al-
682.14 ready imparted; and the triumph, and ever
682.15 increasing pleasure he had anticipated from
682.16 them -- and I fancied, I guessed the incitement
682.17 to his secret studies, also. He had been con-
682.18 tent with daily labour and rough animal en-
682.19 joyments, till Catherine crossed his path --
682.20 Shame at her scorn, and hope of her approval
682.21 were his first prompters to higher pursuits;

683.01 and instead of guarding him from one, and
683.02 winning him the other, his endeavours to raise
683.03 himself had produced just the contrary result.
683.04 "Yes, that's all the good that such a brute
683.05 as you can get from them!" cried Catherine,
683.06 sucking her damaged lip, and catching the
683.07 conflagration with indignant eyes.
683.08 "You'd \better# hold your tongue, now!" he
683.09 answered fiercely.
683.10 And his agitation precluding further speech,
683.11 he advanced hastily to the entrance, where I
683.12 made way for him to pass. But, ere he had
683.13 crossed the door-stones, Mr. Heathcliff, coming
683.14 up the causeway, encountered him and laying
683.15 hold of his shoulder, asked,
683.16 "What's to do now, my lad?"
683.17 "Naught, naught!" he said, and broke
683.18 away, to enjoy his grief and anger in solitude.
683.19 Heathcliff gazed after him, and sighed.
683.20 "It will be odd, if I thwart myself!" he
683.21 muttered, unconscious that I was behind him.
683.22 "But, when I look for his father in his face,
684.01 I find \her# every day more! How the devil
684.02 is he so like? I can hardly bear to see
684.03 him."
684.04 He bent his eyes to the ground, and walked
684.05 moodily in. There was a restless, anxious
684.06 expression in his countenance, I had never re-
684.07 marked there before, and he looked sparer in
684.08 person.
684.09 His daughter-in-law on perceiving him
684.10 through the window, immediately escaped to
684.11 the kitchen, so that I remained alone.
684.12 "I'm glad to see you out of doors again,
684.13 Mr. Lockwood," he said in reply to my greet-
684.14 ing, "from selfish motives partly. I don't think
684.15 I could readily supply your loss in this desola-
684.16 tion. I've wondered, more than once, what
684.17 brought you here."
684.18 "An idle whim, I fear sir," was my answer,
684.19 "or else an idle whim is going to spirit me
684.20 away --I shall set out for London, next week,
684.21 and I must give you warning, that I feel no
684.22 disposition to retain Thrushcross Grange, beyond
685.01 the twelvemonths I agreed to rent it.
685.02 I believe I shall not live there any more.
685.03 "Oh, indeed! you're tired of being banished
685.04 from the world, are you?" he said. "But, if
685.05 you be coming to plead off paying for a place,
685.06 you won't occupy, your journey is useless -- I
685.07 never relent in exacting my due, from any
685.08 one."
685.09 "I'm coming to plead off nothing about it!"
685.10 I exclaimed, considerably irritated. "Should
685.11 you wish it, I'll settle with you now," and I
685.12 drew my notebook from my pocket.
685.13 "No, no," he replied coolly, "you'll leave
685.14 sufficient behind, to cover your debts, if you
685.15 fail to return ... I'm not in such a hurry -- sit
685.16 down and take your dinner with us -- a guest
685.17 that is safe from repeating his visit, can gene-
685.18 rally be made welcome -- Catherine! bring the
685.19 things in -- where are you?"
685.20 Catherine re-appeared, bearing a tray of
685.21 knives and forks.
686.01 "You may get your dinner with Joseph,"
686.02 muttered Heathcliff aside, "and remain in the
686.03 kitchen till he is gone."
686.04 She obeyed his directions very punctually --
686.05 perhaps she had no temptation to transgress.
686.06 Living among clowns and misanthropists, she
686.07 probably cannot appreciate a better class of
686.08 people, when she meets them.
686.09 With Mr. Heathcliff, grim and saturnine,
686.10 on one hand, and Hareton absolutely dumb,
686.11 on the other, I made a somewhat cheerless
686.12 meal, and bid adieu early -- I would have de-
686.13 parted by the back way to get a last glimpse
686.14 of Catherine, and annoy old Joseph; but
686.15 Hareton received orders to lead up my horse,
686.16 and my host himself escorted me to the door,
686.17 so I could not fulfil my wish.
686.18 "How dreary life gets over in that
686.19 house!" I reflected, while riding down the
686.20 road. "What a realization of something more
686.21 romantic than a fairy tale it would have been
687.01 for Mrs. Linton Heathcliff, had she and I
687.02 struck up an attachment, as her good nurse
687.03 desired, and migrated together, into the stir-
687.04 ring atmosphere of the town!"
688.01 [VOL. 2 CHAPTER 18]
688.02 1802. -- This September, I was invited to de-
688.03 vastate the moors of a friend, in the North;
688.04 and, on my journey to his abode, I unexpect-
688.05 edly came within fifteen miles of Gimmerton.
688.06 The hostler, at a roadside public-house, was
688.07 holding a pail of water to refresh my horses,
688.08 when a cart of very green oats, newly reaped,
688.09 passed by, and he remarked --
688.10 "Yon's frough Gimmerton, nah! They're
688.11 allas three wick' after other folk wi' ther har-
688.12 vest."
689.01 "Gimmerton?" I repeated, my residence in
689.02 that locality had already grown dim and
689.03 dreamy. "Ah! I know! How far is it from
689.04 this?"
689.05 "Happen fourteen mile' o'er th' hills, and a
689.06 rough road," he answered.
689.07 A sudden impulse seized me to visit Thrush-
689.08 cross Grange. It was scarcely noon, and I
689.09 conceived that I might as well pass the night

689.10 under my own roof, as in an inn. Besides, I
689.11 could spare a day easily, to arrange matters
689.12 with my landlord, and thus save myself the
689.13 trouble of invading the neighbourhood again.
689.14 Having rested a while, I directed my servant
689.15 to inquire the way to the village; and, with
689.16 great fatigue to our beasts, we managed the
689.17 distance in some three hours.
689.18 I left him there, and proceeded down the
689.19 valley alone. The grey church looked greyer,
689.20 and the lonely churchyard lonelier. I distin-
689.21 guished a moor sheep cropping the short turf
689.22 on the graves. It was sweet, warm weather
690.01 -- too warm for travelling; but the heat did
690.02 not hinder me from enjoying the delightful
690.03 scenery above and below; had I seen it nearer
690.04 August, I'm sure it would have tempted me to
690.05 waste a month among its solitudes. In winter,
690.06 nothing more dreary, in summer, nothing
690.07 more divine, than those glens shut in by hills,
690.08 and those bluff, bold swells of heath.
690.09 I reached the Grange before sunset, and
690.10 knocked for admittance; but the family had re-
690.11 treated into the back premises, I judged by one
690.12 thin, blue wreath curling from the kitchen
690.13 chimney, and they did not hear.
690.14 I rode into the court. Under the porch, a
690.15 girl of nine or ten, sat knitting, and an old
690.16 woman reclined on the horse-steps, smoking a
690.17 meditative pipe.
690.18 "Is Mrs. Dean within?" I demanded of the
690.19 dame.
690.20 "Mistress Dean? Nay!" she answered,
690.21 "shoo doesn't bide here; shoo's up at th'
690.22 Heights."
691.01 "Are you the housekeeper, then?" I con-
691.02 tinued.
691.03 "Eea, Aw keep th' hause," she replied.
691.04 "Well, I'm Mr. Lockwood, the master --
691.05 Are there any rooms to lodge me in, I wonder?
691.06 I wish to stay here all night."
691.07 "T' maister!" she cried in astonishment,
691.08 "whet, whoiver knew yah wur coming? Yah
691.09 sud ha' send word! They's nowt norther dry --
691.10 nor mensful abaht t' place -- nowt there is n't!"
691.11 She threw down her pipe and bustled in,
691.12 the girl followed, and I entered too; soon per-
691.13 ceiving that her report was true, and, more-
691.14 over, that I had almost upset her wits by my
691.15 unwelcome apparition.
691.16 I bid her be composed -- I would go out for
691.17 a walk; and, meantime, she must try to pre-
691.18 pare a corner of a sitting-room for me to sup
691.19 in, and a bed-room to sleep in -- No sweeping
691.20 and dusting, only good fires and dry sheets
691.21 were necessary.
691.22 She seemed willing to do her best; though
692.01 she thrust the hearth-brush into the grates
692.02 in mistake for the poker; and mal-appropriated
692.03 several other articles of her craft; but I retired,
692.04 confiding in her energy for a resting-place
692.05 against my return.
692.06 Wuthering Heights was the goal of my pro-
692.07 posed excursion. An after-thought brought
692.08 me back, when I had quitted the court.
692.09 "All well at the Heights?" I enquired of
692.10 the woman.
692.11 "Eea, f'r owt Ee knaw!" she answered,
692.12 skurrying away with a pan of hot cinders.
692.13 I would have asked why Mrs. Dean had
692.14 deserted the Grange; but it was impossible to
692.15 delay her at such a crisis, so, I turned away
692.16 and made my exit, rambling leisurely along
692.17 with the glow of a sinking sun behind, and the
692.18 mild glory of a rising moon in front; one
692.19 fading, and the other brightening, as I quitted
692.20 the park, and climbed the stony by-road
692.21 branching off to Mr. Heathcliff's dwelling.
692.22 Before I arrived in sight of it, all that remained
693.01 of day was a beamless, amber light
693.02 along the west; but I could see every pebble
693.03 on the path, and every blade of grass by that
693.04 splendid moon.
693.05 I had neither to climb the gate, nor to
693.06 knock -- it yielded to my hand.
693.07 That is an improvement! I thought. And
693.08 I noticed another, by the air of my nostrils; a
693.09 fragrance of stocks and wall flowers, wafted on
693.10 the air, from amongst the homely fruit trees.
693.11 Both doors and lattices were open; and,
693.12 yet, as is usually the case in a coal district, a
693.13 fine, red fire illumined the chimney; the com-
693.14 fort which the eye derives from it, renders the
693.15 extra heat endurable. But the house of
693.16 Wuthering Heights is so large, that the in-
693.17 mates have plenty of space for withdrawing
693.18 out of its influence; and, accordingly, what
693.19 inmates there were had stationed themselves
693.20 not far from one of the windows. I could
693.21 both see them and hear them talk before I
693.22 entered; and, looked and listened in consequence,
694.01 being moved thereto by a mingled
694.02 sense of curiosity, and envy that grew as I
694.03 lingered.
694.04 "Con-\trary#!" said a voice, as sweet as a
694.05 silver bell -- "That for the third time, you
694.06 dunce! I'm not going to tell you again -- Re-
694.07 collect, or I pull your hair!"
694.08 "Contrary, then," answered another, in
694.09 deep, but softened tones. "And now, kiss me,
694.10 for minding so well."

694.11 "No, read it over first correctly, without a
694.12 single mistake."
694.13 The male speaker began to read -- he was a
694.14 young man, respectably dressed, and seated at
694.15 a table, having a book before him. His hand-
694.16 some features glowed with pleasure, and his
694.17 eyes kept impatiently wandering from the page
694.18 to a small white hand over his shoulder, which
694.19 recalled him by a smart slap on the cheek,
694.20 whenever its owner detected such signs of in-
694.21 attention.
694.22 Its owner stood behind; her light shining
695.01 ringlets blending, at intervals, with his brown
695.02 locks, as she bent to superintend his studies;
695.03 and her face -- it was lucky he could not see
695.04 her face, or he would never have been so steady
695.05 -- I could, and I bit my lip, in spite, at having
695.06 thrown away the chance I might have had, of
695.07 doing something besides staring at its smiting
695.08 beauty.
695.09 The task was done, not free from further
695.10 blunders; but the pupil claimed a reward and
695.11 received, at least five kisses, which, however,
695.12 he generously returned. Then, they came to
695.13 the door, and from their conversation, I judged
695.14 they were about to issue out and have a walk
695.15 on the moors. I supposed I should be con-
695.16 demned in Hareton Earnshaw's heart, if not
695.17 by his mouth, to the lowest pit in the infernal
695.18 regions if I showed my unfortunate person in
695.19 his neighbourhood then, and feeling very mean
695.20 and malignant, I skulked round to seek refuge
695.21 in the kitchen.
695.22 There was unobstructed admittance on that
696.01 side also; and, at the door, sat my old friend,
696.02 Nelly Dean, sewing and singing a song, which
696.03 was often interrupted from within, by harsh
696.04 words of scorn and intolerance, uttered in far
696.05 from musical accents.
696.06 "Aw'd rayther, by th' haulf, hev'em swear-
696.07 ing i' my lugs frough morn tuh neeght, nur
696.08 hearken yah, hahsiver!" said the tenant of the
696.09 kitchen, in answer to an unheard speech of
696.10 Nelly's. "It's a blazing shaime, ut Aw can-
696.11 nut oppen t' Blessed Book, bud yah set up
696.12 them glories tuh sattan, un' all t' flaysome
696.13 wickednesses ut iver wer born intuh t' warld!
696.14 Oh! yah're a raight nowt; un' shoo's another;
696.15 un' that poor lad 'ull be lost, atween ye. Poor
696.16 lad!" he added with a groan; "he's witched,
696.17 Aw'm sartin on't! O, Lord, judge 'em, fur
696.18 they's norther law nur justice amang wer
696.19 rullers!"
696.20 "No! or we should be sitting in flaming
696.21 fagots, I suppose," retorted the singer. "But
696.22 wisht, old man, and read your Bible, like a
697.01 christian, and never mind me. This is 'Fairy
697.02 Annie's wedding' -- a bonny tune -- it goes to
697.03 a dance."
697.04 Mrs. Dean was about to recommence, when
697.05 I advanced, and recognising me directly, she
697.06 jumped to her feet, crying --
697.07 "Why, bless you, Mr. Lockwood! How
697.08 could you think of returning this way?
697.09 All's shut up at Thrushcross Grange. You
697.10 should have given us notice!"
697.11 "I've arranged to be accommodated there,
697.12 for as long as I shall stay," I answered. "I
697.13 depart again to-morrow. And how are you
697.14 transplanted here, Mrs. Dean? tell me that."
697.15 "Zillah left, and Mr. Heathcliff wished me
697.16 to come, soon after you went to London, and
697.17 stay till you returned. But, step in, pray!
697.18 Have you walked from Gimmerton this even-
697.19 ing?"
697.20 "From the Grange," I replied; "and, while
697.21 they make me lodging room there, I want to
697.22 finish my business with your master, because
698.01 I don't think of having another opportunity
698.02 in a hurry."
698.03 "What business, sir?" said Nelly, conduct-
698.04 ing me into the house. "He's gone out, at
698.05 present, and wont return soon."
698.06 "About the rent," I answered.
698.07 "Oh! then it is with Mrs. Heathcliff you
698.08 must settle," she observed. "or rather with
698.09 me. She has not learnt to manage her affairs
698.10 yet, and I act for her; there's nobody else."
698.11 I looked surprised.
698.12 "Ah! you have not heard of Heathcliff's
698.13 death, I see!" she continued.
698.14 "Heathcliff dead?" I exclaimed, astonished.
698.15 "How long ago?"
698.16 "Three months since -- but, sit down, and
698.17 let me take your hat, and I'll tell you all about
698.18 it. Stop, you have had nothing to eat, have
698.19 you?"
698.20 "I want nothing. I have ordered supper at
698.21 home. You sit down too. I never dreamt of
698.22 his dying! Let me hear how it came to pass.
699.01 You say you don't expect them back for some
699.02 time -- the young people?"
699.03 "No -- I have to scold them every evening,
699.04 for their late rambles -- but they don't care for
699.05 me. At least, have a drink of our old ale -- it
699.06 will do you good -- you seem weary."
699.07 She hastened to fetch it, before I could re-
699.08 fuse, and I heard Joseph asking, whether "it
699.09 warn't a crying scandal that she should have
699.10 fellies at her time of life? And then, to get
699.11 them jocks out uh t' Maister's cellar! He fair

699.12 shaamed to 'bide still and see it."
699.13 She did not stay to retaliate, but re-entered,
699.14 in a minute, bearing a reaming, silver pint,
699.15 whose contents I lauded with becoming ear-
699.16 nestness. And afterwards she furnished me
699.17 with the sequel of Heathcliff's history. He
699.18 had a "queer" end, as she expressed it.
699.19 "I was summoned to Wuthering Heights,
699.20 within a fortnight of your leaving us," she
699.21 said; and I obeyed joyfully, for Catherine's
699.22 sake.
700.01 "My first interview with her grieved and
700.02 shocked me! she had altered so much since
700.03 our separation. Mr. Heathcliff did not explain
700.04 his reasons for taking a new mind about my
700.05 coming here; he only told me he wanted me,
700.06 and he was tired of seeing Catherine, I must
700.07 make the little parlour my sitting room, and
700.08 keep her with me. It was enough if he were
700.09 obliged to see her once or twice a day.
700.10 "She seemed pleased at this arrangement;
700.11 and, by degrees, I smuggled over a great num-
700.12 ber of books, and other articles, that had
700.13 formed her amusement at the Grange; and
700.14 flattered myself we should get on in tolerable
700.15 comfort.
700.16 "The delusion did not last long. Cathe-
700.17 rine, contented at first, in a brief space grew
700.18 irritable and restless. For one thing, she was
700.19 forbidden to move out of the garden, and it
700.20 fretted her sadly to be confined to its narrow
700.21 bounds, as Spring drew on -- for another, in
700.22 following the house, I was forced to quit her
701.01 frequently, and she complained of loneliness;
701.02 she preferred quarrelling with Joseph in the
701.03 kitchen, to sitting at peace in her solitude.
701.04 "I did not mind their skirmishes; but
701.05 Hareton was often obliged to seek the kit-
701.06 chen also, when the master wanted to have the
701.07 house to himself; and, though, in the begin-
701.08 ning, she either left it at his approach, or
701.09 quietly joined in my occupations, and shunned
701.10 remarking, or addressing him -- and though he
701.11 was always as sullen and silent, as possible --
701.12 after a while, she changed her behaviour, and
701.13 became incapable of letting him alone. Talk-
701.14 ing at him; commenting on his stupidity and
701.15 idleness; expressing her wonder how he could
701.16 endure the life he lived -- how he could sit a
701.17 whole evening staring into the fire, and dozing.
701.18 "'He's just like a dog, is he not, Ellen?'
701.19 she once observed, 'or a cart-horse? He does
701.20 his work, eats his food, and sleeps, eternally!
701.21 What a blank, dreary mind he must have! Do
702.01 you ever dream, Hareton? And, if you do,
702.02 what is it about? But, you can't speak to me!'
702.03 "Then she looked at him; but he would nei-
702.04 ther open his mouth, nor look again.
702.05 "'He's perhaps, dreaming now,' she con-
702.06 tinued. 'He twitched his shoulder as Juno
702.07 twitches hers. Ask him, Ellen."
702.08 "'Mr. Hareton will ask the master to send
702.09 you up stairs, if you don't behave!' I said.
702.10 He had not only twitched his shoulder, but
702.11 clenched his fist, as if tempted to use it.
702.12 "'I know why Hareton never speaks, when
702.13 I am in the kitchen,' she exclaimed, on an-
702.14 other occasion. 'He is afraid I shall laugh
702.15 at him. Ellen, what do you think? He began
702.16 to teach himself to read once; and, because I
702.17 laughed, he burned his books, and dropped it --
702.18 was he not a fool?'
702.19 "'Were not you naughty?' I said; 'answer
702.20 me that,'
702.21 "'Perhaps I was,' she went on, 'but I did
703.01 not expect him to be so silly. Hareton, if I
703.02 gave you a book, would you take it now? I'll
703.03 try!'
703.04 "She placed one she had been perusing on
703.05 his hand; he flung it off, and muttered, if she
703.06 did not give over, he would break her neck.
703.07 "'Well I shall put it here,' she said, 'in the
703.08 table drawer, and I'm going to bed.'
703.09 "Then she whispered me to watch whether
703.10 he touched it, and departed. But he would not
703.11 come near it, and so I informed her in the
703.12 morning, to her great disappointment. I saw
703.13 she was sorry for his persevering sulkiness and
703.14 indolence -- her conscience reproved her for
703.15 frightening him off improving himself -- she
703.16 had done it effectually.
703.17 But her ingenuity was at work to remedy
703.18 the injury; while I ironed, or pursued other
703.19 stationary employments I could not well do in
703.20 the parlour -- she would bring some pleasant
703.21 volume, and read it aloud to me. When Hare-
703.22 ton was there, she generally paused in an interesting
704.01 part, and left the book lying about --
704.02 that she did repeatedly; but he was as obsti-
704.03 nate as a mule, and, instead of snatching at her
704.04 bait, in wet weather he took to smoking with
704.05 Joseph, and they sat like automatons, one on
704.06 each side of the fire, the elderly happily too deaf
704.07 to understand her wicked nonsense, as he
704.08 would have called it, the younger doing his
704.09 best to seem to disregard it. On fine evenings
704.10 the latter followed his shooting expeditions,
704.11 and Catherine yawned and sighed, and teased
704.12 me to talk to her, and ran off into the court
704.13 or garden, the moment I began; and, as a last
704.14 resource, cried and said, she was tired of liv-

704.15 ing, her life was useless.
704.16 "Mr. Heathcliff, who grew more and more
704.17 disinclined to society, had almost banished
704.18 Earnshaw out of his apartment. Owing to an
704.19 accident, at the commencement of March, he
704.20 became for some days a fixture in the kitchen.
704.21 His gun burst, while out on the hills, by him-
704.22 self; a splinter cut his arm, and he lost a good
705.01 deal of blood before he could reach home.
705.02 The consequence was, that, perforce, he was
705.03 condemned to the fire-side and tranquillity,
705.04 till he made it up again.
705.05 "It suited Catherine to have him there: at
705.06 any rate, it made her hate her room up stairs,
705.07 more than ever; and she would compel me to
705.08 find out any business below, that she might accom-
705.09 pany me.
705.10 "On Easter Monday, Joseph went to Gim-
705.11 merton fair with some cattle; and, in the
705.12 afternoon, I was busy getting up linen in the
705.13 kitchen -- Earnshaw sat, morose as usual, at the
705.14 chimney corner, and my little mistress was be-
705.15 guiling an idle hour with drawing pictures on
705.16 the window panes, varying her amusement by
705.17 smothered bursts of songs, and whispered eja-
705.18 culations, and quick glances of annoyance and
705.19 impatience in the direction of her cousin, who
705.20 steadfastly smoked, and looked into the grate.
705.21 "At a notice that I could do with her no
705.22 longer, intercepting my light, she removed to
706.01 the hearthstone. I bestowed little attention on
706.02 her proceedings, but presently, I heard her
706.03 begin --
706.04 "'I've found out, Hareton, that I want --
706.05 that I'm glad -- that I should like you to be
706.06 my cousin, now, if you had not grown so cross
706.07 to me, and so rough.'
706.08 "Hareton returned no answer.
706.09 "'Hareton, Hareton, Hareton! do you
706.10 hear?' she continued.
706.11 "'Get off wi' ye!' he growled, with un-
706.12 compromising gruffness.
706.13 "'Let me take that pipe,' she said, cauti-
706.14 ously advancing her hand, and abstracting it
706.15 from his mouth.
706.16 "Before he could attempt to recover it, it
706.17 was broken, and behind the fire. He swore at
706.18 her and seized another.
706.19 "'Stop,' she cried, 'you must listen to me,
706.20 first; and I can't speak while those clouds are
706.21 floating in my face.'
707.01 "'Will you go to the devil!' he exclaimed,
707.02 ferociously, 'and let me be!'
707.03 "'No,' she persisted, 'I wont -- I can't tell
707.04 what to do to make you talk to me, and you
707.05 are determined not to understand. When I
707.06 call you stupid, I don't mean anything -- I
707.07 don't mean that I despise you. Come you shall
707.08 take notice of me, Hareton -- you are my cou-
707.09 sin, and you shall own me.'
707.10 "'I shall have naught to do wi' you, and
707.11 your mucky pride, and your damned, mock-
707.12 ing tricks!' he answered. 'I'll go to hell,
707.13 body and soul, before I look sideways after
707.14 you again! Side out of t' gait, now; this
707.15 minute!'
707.16 "Catherine frowned, and retreated to the
707.17 window-seat, chewing her lip, and endeavour-
707.18 ing, by humming an eccentric tune, to conceal
707.19 a growing tendency to sob.
707.20 "'You should be friends with your cousin,
707.21 Mr. Hareton,' I interrupted, 'since she repents
707.22 of her sauciness! it would do you a great deal
708.01 of good -- it would make you another man, to
708.02 have her for a companion.'
708.03 "'A companion?' he cried; 'when she
708.04 hates me, and does not think me fit to wipe her
708.05 shoon! Nay, if it made me a king, I'd not be
708.06 scorned for seeking her good will any more.'
708.07 "'It is not I who hate you, it is you who
708.08 hate me!' wept Cathy, no longer disguising
708.09 her trouble. 'You hate me as much as Mr.
708.10 Heathcliff does, and more.'
708.11 "'You're a damned liar,' began Earnshaw;
708.12 'why have I made him angry, by taking your
708.13 part then, a hundred times? and that, when
708.14 you sneered at, and despised me, and -- Go on
708.15 plaguing me, and I'll step in yonder, and say
708.16 you worried me out of the kitchen!'
708.17 "'I didn't know you took my part,' she an-
708.18 swered, drying her eyes; 'and I was misera-
708.19 ble and bitter at everybody; but, now I thank
708.20 you, and beg you to forgive me, what can I
708.21 do besides?'
708.22 "She returned to the hearth, and frankly
708.23 extended her hand.
709.01 "He blackened, and scowled like a thun-
709.02 der cloud, and kept his fists resolutely clenched,
709.03 and his gaze fixed on the ground.
709.04 "Catherine, by instinct, must have divined
709.05 it was obdurate perversity, and not dislike,
709.06 that prompted this dogged conduct; for, after
709.07 remaining an instant, undecided, she stooped,
709.08 and impressed on his cheek a gentle kiss.
709.09 "The little rogue thought I had not seen
709.10 her, and, drawing back, she took her former
709.11 station by the window, quite demurely.
709.12 "I shook my head reprovingly; and then
709.13 she blushed, and whispered --
709.14 "'Well! what should I have done, Ellen?
709.15 He wouldn't shake hands, and he wouldn't

709.16 look -- I must show him some way that I like
709.17 him, that I want to be friends.'
709.18 "Whether the kiss convinced Hareton, I
709.19 cannot tell; he was very careful, for some
709.20 minutes, that his face should not be seen; and
709.21 when he did raise it, he was sadly puzzled
709.22 where to turn his eyes.
710.01 "Catherine employed herself in wrapping
710.02 a handsome book neatly in white paper; and
710.03 having tied it with a bit of ribband, and ad-
710.04 dressed it to 'Mr. Hareton Earnshaw,' she de-
710.05 sired me to be her ambassadress, and convey
710.06 the present to its destined recipient.
710.07 "'And tell him, if he'll take it, I'll come
710.08 and teach him to read it right,' she said, 'and,
710.09 if he refuse it, I'll go up stairs, and never
710.10 tease him again.'
710.11 "I carried it, and repeated the message,
710.12 anxiously watched by my employer. Hareton
710.13 would not open his fingers, so I laid it on his
710.14 knee. He did not strike it off either. I re-
710.15 turned to my work: Catherine leaned her head
710.16 and arms on the table, till she heard the slight
710.17 rustle of the covering being removed, then she
710.18 stole away, and quietly seated herself beside
710.19 her cousin. He trembled, and his face glowed
710.20 --all his rudeness, and all his surly harshness
710.21 had deserted him -- he could not summon courage,
711.01 at first, to utter a syllable, in reply to her
711.02 questioning look, and her murmured petition.
711.03 "'Say you forgive me, Hareton, do! You
711.04 can make me so happy, by speaking that little
711.05 word.'
711.06 "He muttered something inaudible.
711.07 "'And you'll be my friend?' added Cathe-
711.08 rine, interrogatively.
711.09 "'Nay! you'll be ashamed of me every day
711.10 of your life,' he answered. 'And the more,
711.11 the more you know me, and I cannot bide it.'
711.12 "'So, you wont be my friend?' she said,
711.13 smiling as sweet as honey, and creeping close
711.14 up.
711.15 "I overheard no further distinguishable
711.16 talk; but on looking round again, I perceived
711.17 two such radiant countenances bent over the
711.18 page of the accepted book, that I did not
711.19 doubt the treaty had been ratified, on both
711.20 sides, and the enemies were, thenceforth, sworn
711.21 allies.
711.22 "The work they studied was full of costly
712.01 pictures; and those, and their position had
712.02 charm enough to keep them unmoved,
712.03 till Joseph came home. He, poor man,
712.04 was perfectly aghast at the spectacle of Ca-
712.05 therine seated on the same bench with Hareton
712.06 Earnshaw, leaning her hand on his shoulder;
712.07 and confounded at his favourite's endurance of
712.08 her proximity. It affected him too deeply to
712.09 allow an observation on the subject that night.
712.10 His emotion was only revealed by the im-
712.11 mense sighs he drew, as he solemnly spread his
712.12 large bible on the table, and overlaid it with
712.13 dirty bank-notes from his pocket-book, the
712.14 produce of the day's transactions. At length,
712.15 he summoned Hareton from his seat.
712.16 "'Tak' these in tuh t' maister, lad,' he said,
712.17 'un' bide theare; Aw's gang up tuh my
712.18 awn rahm. This hoile's norther mensful, nor
712.19 seemly fur us -- we mun side aht, and seearch
712.20 another!'
712.21 "'Come, Catherine,' I said, we must 'side
712.22 out,' too -- I've done my ironing, are you ready
712.23 to go?'
713.01 "'It is not eight o'clock!' she answered,
713.02 rising unwillingly, 'Hareton, I'll leave this
713.03 book upon the chimney-piece, and I'll bring
713.04 some more to-morrow.'
713.05 "'Only books ut yah leave, Aw suall tak'
713.06 intuh th' hahse,' said Joseph, 'un' it 'ull be
713.07 mitch if yah find 'em agean; soa, yah muh
713.08 plase yourseln!'
713.09 "Cathy threatened that his library should pay
713.10 for hers; and, smiling as she passed Hareton,
713.11 went singing up stairs, lighter of heart, I ven-
713.12 ture to say, than ever she had been under that
713.13 roof before; except, perhaps, during her ear-
713.14 liest visits to Linton.
713.15 "The intimacy, thus commenced, grew ra-
713.16 pidly; though it encountered temporary inter-
713.17 ruptions, Earnshaw was not to be civilized with
713.18 a wish; and my young lady was not philosopher,
713.19 and no paragon of patience; but both their
713.20 minds tending to the same point -- one loving
713.21 and desiring to esteem; and the other loving
713.22 and desiring to be esteemed -- they contrived
713.23 in the end, to reach it.
714.01 "You see, Mr. Lockwood, it was easy enough
714.02 to win Mrs. Heathcliff's heart; but now, I'm
714.03 glad you did not try -- the crown of all my
714.04 wishes will be the union of those two; I shall
714.05 envy no one on their wedding-day -- there
714.06 won't be a happier woman than myself in
714.07 England!"
715.01 [VOL. 2 CHAPTER 19]
715.02 "On the morrow of that Monday, Earnshaw
715.03 being still unable to follow his ordinary em-
715.04 ployments, and, therefore, remaining about
715.05 the house, I speedily found it would be imprac-
715.06 ticable to retain my charge beside me, as here-
715.07 tofore.
715.08 She got down stairs before me, and out into

715.09 the garden; where she had seen her cousin per-
715.10 forming some easy work; and when I went to
715.11 bid them come to breakfast, I saw she had per-
715.12 suaded him to clear a large space of ground
716.01 from currant and gooseberry bushes, and they
716.02 were busy planning together an importation of
716.03 plants from the Grange.
716.04 "I was terrified at the devastation which
716.05 had been accomplished in a brief half hour;
716.06 the black currant trees were the apple of Jo-
716.07 seph's eye, and she had just fixed her choice of
716.08 a flower bed in the midst of them!
716.09 "`There! That will be all shewn to the
716.10 master,` I exclaimed, `the minute it is disco-
716.11 vered. And what excuse have you to offer for
716.12 taking such liberties with the garden? We
716.13 shall have a fine explosion on the head of it:
716.14 see if we don't. Mr. Hareton, I wonder you
716.15 should have no more wit, than to go and make
716.16 that mess at her bidding!`
716.17 "`I'd forgotten they were Joseph's,` ans-
716.18 wered Earnshaw, rather puzzled, `but I'll tell
716.19 him I did it.`
716.20 "we always ate our meals with Mr. Heath-
716.21 cliff. I held the mistress's post in making tea
716.22 and carving; so I was indispensable at table.
717.01 Catherine usually sat by me; but to-day, she
717.02 stole nearer to Hareton, and I presently saw
717.03 she would have no more discretion in her
717.04 friendship, than she had in her hostility.
717.05 "`Now, mind you don't talk with and notice
717.06 your cousin too much,` were my whispered
717.07 instructions as we entered the room; `It will
717.08 certainly annoy Mr. Heathcliff, and he'll be
717.09 mad at you both.`
717.10 "`I'm not going to,` she answered.
717.11 "The minute after, she had sidled to him,
717.12 and was sticking primroses in his plate of
717.13 porridge.
717.14 "He dared not speak to her, there; he dared
717.15 hardly look; and yet she went on teasing, till
717.16 he was twice on the point of being provoked to
717.17 laugh; and I frowned, and then, she glanced
717.18 towards the master, whose mind was occupied
717.19 on other subjects than his company, as his
717.20 countenance evinced, and she grew serious for
717.21 an instant, scrutinizing him with deep gravity.
717.22 Afterwards she turned, and re-commenced her
718.01 nonsense; at last, Hareton uttered a smothered
718.02 laugh.
718.03 "Mr. Heathcliff started; his eye rapidly
718.04 surveyed our faces. Catherine met it with her
718.05 accustomed look of nervousness, and yet de-
718.06 fiance, which he abhorred.
718.07 "`It is well you are out of my reach;" he
718.08 exclaimed. "What fiend possesses you to
718.09 stare back at me, continually, with those infer-
718.10 nal eyes? Down with them! and don't re-
718.11 mind me of your existence again. I thought
718.12 I had cured you of laughing."
718.13 "`It was me," muttered Hareton.
718.14 "`what do you say?" demanded the master.
718.15 Hareton looked at his plate, and did not re-
718.16 peat the confession.
718.17 Mr. Heathcliff looked at him a bit, and then
718.18 silently resumed his breakfast, and his inter-
718.19 rupted musing.
718.20 we had nearly finished, and the two young
718.21 people prudently shifted wider asunder, so I
718.22 anticipated no further disturbance during that
719.01 sitting; when Joseph apppeared at the door,
719.02 revealing by his quivering lip, and furious eyes,
719.03 that the outrage committed on his precious
719.04 shrubs was detected.
719.05 He must have seen Cathy, and her cousin
719.06 about the spot, before he examined it, for
719.07 while his jaws worked like those of a cow
719.08 chewing its cud, and rendered his speech diffi-
719.09 cult to understand, he began:
719.10 "`Aw mun hev my wage, and Aw mun
719.11 goa! Aw \hed# aimed tuh dee, wheare Aw'd
719.12 sarved fur sixty year; un' Aw thowt Aw'd
719.13 lug my books up intuh t' garret, un' all my
719.14 bits uh stuff, un' they sud hev t' kitchen tuh
719.15 theirseln; fur t' sake uh quietness. It wur
719.16 hard tuh gie up my awn hearthstun, bud Aw
719.17 thowt Aw \could# do that! Bud, nah, shoo's
719.18 taan my garden frough me, un' by th' heart!
719.19 Maister, Aw cannot stand it! Yah muh bend
719.20 tuh th' yoak, an ye will -- \Aw# noan used to't
719.21 and an ow'd man doesn't sooin get used tuh
720.01 new barthens -- Aw'd rayther arn my bite, an'
720.02 my sup, wi' a hammer in th' road!"
720.03 "`Now, now, idiot!" interrupted Heathcliff,
720.04 "cut it short! what's your grievance? I'll
720.05 interfere in no quarrels between you, and
720.06 Nelly -- She may thrust you into the coal-hole
720.07 for anything I care"
720.08 "`It's noan Nelly!" answered Joseph. "Aw
720.09 sudn't shift fur Nelly -- Nasty, ill nowt as shoo
720.10 is, Thank God! \shoo# cannot stale t'sowl uh
720.11 nob'dy! Shoo we niver soa handsome, bud
720.12 whet a body mud look at her 'baht winking.
720.13 It's yon flaysome, graceless quean, ut's witched
720.14 ahr lad, wi' her bold een, un' her forrard ways
720.15 -- till Nay! It fair brusts my heart! He's
720.16 forgotten all E done for him, un made on
720.17 him, un' goan un' riven up a whole row ut t'
720.18 grandest currant trees, i' t' garden!" and here
720.19 he lamented outright, unmanned by a sense of
720.20 his bitter injuries, and Earnshaw's ingratitude

720.21 and dangerous condition.
721.01 "Is the fool drunk? asked Mr. Heathcliff.
721.02 "Hareton is it you he's finding fault with?"
721.03 "I've pulled up two or three bushes," re-
721.04 plied the young man, "but I'm going to set
721.05 'em again.
721.06 "And why have you pulled them up?" said
721.07 the master.
721.08 Catherine wisely put in her tongue.
721.09 "we wanted to plant some flowers there,"
721.10 she cried. "I'm the only person to blame, for
721.11 I wished him to do it."
721.12 "And who the devil gave \you# leave to touch
721.13 a stick about the place?" demanded her father--
721.14 in-law, much surprised. "And who ordered
721.15 \you# to obey her?" he added turning to Hare-
721.16 ton.
721.17 The latter was speechless; his cousin replied --
721.18 "You shouldn't grudge a few yards of
721.19 earth, for me to ornament, when you have
721.20 taken all my land!"
721.21 "Your land, insolent slut? you never had
722.01 any!" said Heathcliff.
722.01 "And my money," she continued, return-
722.02 ing his angry glare, and meantime, biting a
722.03 piece of crust, the remnant of her breakfast.
722.04 "Silence!" he exclaimed. "Get done, and
722.05 begone!"
722.06 "And Hareton's land, and his money," pur-
722.07 sued the reckless thing. "Hareton, and I
722.08 are friends now; and I shall tell him all about
722.09 you!"
722.10 The master seemed confounded a moment,
722.11 he grew pale, and rose up, eyeing her all the
722.12 while, with an expression of mortal hate.
722.13 "If you strike me, Hareton will strike you!`
722.14 she said, "so you may as well sit down."
722.15 "If Hareton does not turn you out of the
722.16 room, I'll strike him to Hell," thundered
722.17 Heathcliff. "Damnable witch! dare you pre-
722.18 tend to rouse him against me? Off with her!
722.19 Do you hear? Fling her into the kitchen!
722.20 I'll kill her, Ellen Dean, if you let her come
722.21 into my sight again!"
722.22 Hareton tried under his breath to persuade
722.23 her to go.
723.01 "Drag her away!" he cried savagely. "Are
723.02 you staying to talk?" And he approached to
723.03 execute his own command.
723.04 "He'll not obey you, wicked man, any
723.05 more!" said Catherine, and he'll soon detest
723.06 you, as much as I do!"
723.07 "wisht! wisht! muttered the young man
723.08 reproachfully. "I will not hear you speak so
723.09 to him -- Have done!"
723.10 "but you won't let him strike me?" she
723.11 cried.
723.12 "Come then!" he whispered earnestly.
723.13 It was too late -- Heathcliff had caught hold
723.14 of her.
723.15 "Now \you# go!" he said to Earnshaw. "Ac-
723.16 cursed witch! this time she has provoked me,
723.17 when I could not bear it; and I'll make her
723.18 repent it for ever!"
723.19 He had his hand in her hair; Hareton at-
723.20 tempted to release the locks, entreating him
723.21 not to hurt her that once. His black eyes
723.22 flashed, he seemed ready to tear Catherine in
724.01 pieces, and I was just worked up to risk
724.02 coming to the rescue, when of a sudden, his
724.03 fingers relaxed, he shifted his grasp from her
724.04 head, to her arm, and gazed intently in her
724.05 face -- Then, he drew his hand over her eyes,
724.06 stood a moment to collect himself apparently,
724.07 and turning anew to Catherine, said with as-
724.08 sumed calmness,
724.09 "You must learn to avoid putting me in a
724.10 passion, or I shall really murder you, some-
724.11 time! go with Mrs. Dean, and keep with her,
724.12 and confine your insolence to her ears. As to
724.13 Hareton Earnshaw if I see him listen to you
724.14 I'll send him seeking his bread where he can
724.15 get it! your love will make him an outcast,
724.16 and a beggar -- Nelly, take her, and leave me,
724.17 all of you! Leave me!"
724.18 I led my young lady out; she was too glad
724.19 of her escape, to resist; the other followed, and
724.20 Mr. Heathcliff had the room to himself, till
724.21 dinner.
724.22 I had counselled Catherine to get hers upstairs;
725.01 but, as soon as he perceived her vacant
725.02 seat, he sent me to call her. He spoke to
725.03 none of us, eat very little, and went out di-
725.04 rectly afterwards, intimating that he should not
725.05 return before evening.
725.06 The two new friends established themselves
725.07 in the house, during his absences, where I
725.08 heard Hareton sternly check his cousin, on her
725.09 offering a revelation of her father-in-law's con-
725.10 duct to his father.
725.11 He said he wouldn't suffer a word to be
725.12 uttered to him, in his disparagement; if he
725.13 were the devil, it didn't signify; he would
725.14 stand by him; and he'd rather she would abuse
725.15 himself, as she used to, than begin on Mr.
725.16 Heathcliff.
725.17 Catherine was waxing cross at this; but he
725.18 found means to make her hold her tongue, by
725.19 asking, how she would like \him# to speak ill of
725.20 her father? and then she comprehended that
725.21 Earnshaw took the master's reputation home

725.22 to himself: and was attached by ties stronger
726.01 than reason could break -- chains, forged by
726.02 habit, which it would be cruel to attempt to
726.03 loosen.
726.04   She showed a good heart, thenceforth, in
726.05 avoiding both complaints and expressions of anti-
726.06 pathy concerning Heathcliff; and confessed to
726.07 me her sorrow that she had endeavoured to
726.08 raise a bad spirit between him and Hareton --
726.09 indeed, I don't believe she has ever breathed
726.10 a syllable, in the latter's hearing, against her
726.11 oppressor, since.
726.12   When this slight disagreement was over,
726.13 they were thick again, and as busy as pos-
726.14 sible, in their several occupations, of pupil,
726.15 and teacher. I came in to sit with them, after
726.16 I had done my work, and I felt so soothed,
726.17 and comforted to watch them, that I did not
726.18 notice how time got on. You know, they both
726.19 appeared in a measure, my children: I had
726.20 long been proud of one, and now, I was sure,
726.21 the other would be a source of equal satisfac-
726.22 tion. His honest, warm, intelligent nature
727.01 shook off rapidly the clouds of ignorance, and
727.02 degradation in which it had been bred; and
727.03 Catherine's sincere commendations acted as a
727.04 spur to his industry. His brightening mind
727.05 brightened his features, and added spirit and
727.06 nobility to their aspect -- I could hardly fancy
727.07 it the same individual I had beheld on the day
727.08 I discovered my little lady at Wuthering
727.09 Heights, after her expedition to the Crags.
727.10   While I admired, and they laboured, dusk
727.11 drew on, and with it returned the master. He
727.12 came upon us quite unexpectedly, entering
727.13 by the front way, and had a full view of the
727.14 whole three, ere we could raise our heads to
727.15 glance at him.
727.16   Well, I reflected, there was never a plea-
727.17 santer, or more harmless sight; and it will be
727.18 a burning shame to scold them. The red fire-
727.19 light glowed on their two bonny heads, and
727.20 revealed their faces, animated with the eager
727.21 interest of children; for, though he was
727.22 twenty-three, and she eighteen, each had so
728.01 much of novelty to feel, and learn, that nei-
728.02 ther experienced, nor evinced the sentiments
728.03 of sober disenchanted maturity.
728.04   They lifted their eyes together, to encoun-
728.05 ter Mr. Heathcliff -- perhaps, you have never
728.06 remarked that their eyes are precisely similar,
728.07 and they are those of Catherine Earnshaw.
728.08 The present Catherine has no other likeness to
728.09 her, except a breadth of forehead, and a certain
728.10 arch of the nostril that makes her appear ra-
728.11 ther haughty, whether she will, or not. With
728.12 Hareton the resemblance is carried farther, it
728.13 is singular, at all times -- then it was particu-
728.14 larly striking: because his senses were alert,
728.15 and his mental faculties wakened to unwonted
728.16 activity.
728.17   I suppose this resemblance disarmed Mr.
728.18 Heathcliff: he walked to the hearth in evident
728.19 agitation; but it quickly subsided, as he looked
728.20 at the young man; or, I should say, altered its
728.21 character, for it was there yet.
728.22   He took the book from his hand, and
729.01 glanced at the open page, then returned it
729.02 without any observation; merely signing Ca-
729.03 therine away -- her companion lingered very
729.04 little behind her, and I was about to depart
729.05 also, but he bid me sit still.
729.06   "It is a poor conclusion, is it not," he ob-
729.07 served, having brooded a while on the scene he
729.08 had just witnessed. "An absurd termination
729.09 to my violent exertions? I get levers, and
729.10 mattocks to demolish the two houses, and train
729.11 myself to be capable of working like Hercules,
729.12 and when everything is ready, and in my
729.13 power, I find the will to lift a slate of either
729.14 roof has vanished! My old enemies have not
729.15 beaten me -- now would be the precise time to
729.16 revenge myself on their representatives -- I
729.17 could do it; and none could hinder me -- But
729.18 where is the use? I don't care for striking; I
729.19 can't take the trouble to raise my hand! That
729.20 sounds as if I had been labouring the whole
729.21 time, only to exhibit a fine trait of magnanimity.
730.01 It is far from being the case -- I have
730.02 lost the faculty of enjoying their destruction,
730.03 and I am too idle to destroy for nothing.
730.04   "Nelly, there is a strange change approach-
730.05 ing -- I'm in its shadow at present -- I take so
730.06 little interest in my daily life, that I hardly
730.07 remember to eat, and drink -- Those two, who
730.08 have left the room are the only objects which
730.09 retain a distinct material appearance to me;
730.10 and, that appearance causes me pain, amount-
730.11 ing to agony. About \her# I won't speak; and
730.12 I don't desire to think; but I earnestly wish
730.13 she were invisible -- her presence invokes only
730.14 maddening sensations. \He# moves me diffe-
730.15 rently; and yet if I could do it without seem-
730.16 ing insane, I'd never see him again! You'll
730.17 perhaps think me rather inclined to become
730.18 so," he added, making an effort to smile, "if
730.19 I try to describe the thousand forms of past
730.20 associations, and ideas he awakens, or embodies
730.21 -- But you'll not talk of what I tell you, and
731.01 my mind is so eternally secluded in itself, it is
731.02 tempting, at last, to turn it out to another.

731.03   "Five minutes ago, Hareton seemed a per-
731.04 sonification of my youth, not a human being --
731.05 I felt to him in such a variety of ways, that
731.06 it would have been impossible to have accosted
731.07 him rationally.
731.08   "In the first place, his startling likeness to
731.09 Catherine connected him fearfully with her --
731.10 That however which you may suppose the
731.11 most potent to arrest my imagination, is ac-
731.12 tually the last -- for what is not connected
731.13 with her to me? and what does not recall her?
731.14 I cannot look down to this floor, but her fea-
731.15 tures are shaped on the flags! In every cloud,
731.16 in every tree -- filling the air at night, and
731.17 caught by glimpses in every object, by day I
731.18 am surrounded with her image! The most
731.19 ordinary faces of men, and women -- my own
731.20 features mock me with a resemblance. The
731.21 entire world is a dreadful collection of memoranda
732.01 that she did exist, and that I have lost
732.02 her!
732.03   "Well, Hareton's aspect was the ghost of
732.04 my immortal love, of my wild endeavours to
732.05 hold my right, my degradation, my pride, my
732.06 happiness, and my anguish --
732.07 "But it is frenzy to repeat these thoughts
732.08 to you; only it will let you know, why, with
732.09 a reluctance to be always alone, his society is
732.10 no benefit, rather an aggravation of the con-
732.11 stant torment I suffer -- and it partly contri-
732.12 butes to render me regardless how he and his
732.13 cousin go on together. I can give them no
732.14 attention, any more.
732.15   "But what do you mean by a \change#, Mr.
732.16 Heathcliff?" I said, alarmed at his manner,
732.17 though he was neither in danger of losing his
732.18 senses, nor dying, according to my judgment
732.19 he was quite strong and healthy; and, as to
732.20 his reason, from childhood, he had a delight
732.21 in dwelling on dark things, and entertaining
733.01 odd fancies -- he might have had a monoma-
733.02 nia on the subject of his departed idol; but on
733.03 every other point his wits were as sound as
733.04 mine.
733.05   "I shall not know that, till it comes," he
733.06 said, "I'm only half conscious of it now."
733.07   "You have no feeing of illness, have you?"
733.08 I asked.
733.09   "No, Nelly, I have not," he answered.
733.10   "Then, you are not afraid of death?" I pur-
733.11 sued.
733.12   "Afraid?" No!" he replied. "I have nei-
733.13 ther a fear, nor a presentiment, nor a hope of
733.14 death -- why should I? with my hard con-
733.15 stitution, and temperate mode of living, and
733.16 unperilous occupations, I ought to, and proba-
733.17 bly \shall# remain above ground, till there is
733.18 scarcely a black hair on my head -- And yet I
733.19 cannot continue in this condition! -- I have to
733.20 remind myself to breathe -- almost to remind
733.21 my heart to beat! And it is like bending
733.22 back a stiff spring ... it is by compulsion, that I
734.01 do the slightest act, not prompted by one
734.02 thought; and by compulsion, that I notice
734.03 anything alive, or dead, which is not associa-
734.04 ted with one universal idea ... I have a single
734.05 wish, and my whole being, and faculties are
734.06 yearning to attain it. They have yearned
734.07 towards it so long, and so unwaveringly, that I'm
734.08 convinced it \will# be reached -- and \soon# -- be-
734.09 cause it has devoured my existence -- I am
734.10 swallowed in the anticipation of its fulfil-
734.11 ment.
734.12   "My confessions have not relieved me -- but,
734.13 they may account for some, otherwise unac-
734.14 countable phases of humour, which I show.
734.15 O, God! It is a long fight, I wish it were
734.16 over!"
734.17   He began to pace the room, muttering ter-
734.18 rible things to himself; till I was inclined to
734.19 believe, as he said Joseph did, that conscience
734.20 had turned his heart to an earthly hell -- I won-
734.21 dered greatly how it would end.
734.22   Though he seldom before had revealed this
735.01 state of mind, even by looks, it was his habit-
735.02 ual mood, I had no doubt: he asserted it him-
735.03 self -- but, not a soul, from his general bearing
735.04 would have conjectured the fact. You did
735.05 not, when you saw him, Mr. Lockwood -- and
735.06 at the period of which I speak, he was just the
735.07 same as then, only fonder of continued solitude,
735.08 and perhaps still more laconic in company.
736.01 [VOL. 2 CHAPTER 20]
736.02 FOR some days after that evening, Mr. Heath-
736.03 cliff shunned meeting us at meals; yet he
736.04 would not consent, formally, to exclude Hare-
736.05 ton and Cathy. He had an aversion to yield-
736.06 ing so completely to his feelings, chosing, ra-
736.07 ther, to absent himself -- And eating once in
736.08 twenty-four hours seemed sufficient sustenance
736.09 for him.
736.10   One night, after the family were in bed, I
736.11 heard him go down stairs, and out at the front
736.12 door: I did not hear him re-enter
737.01 and, in the morning, I found he was still
737.02 away.
737.03   We were in April then, the weather was
737.04 sweet and warm, the grass as green as showers
737.05 and sun could make it, and the two dwarf
737.06 apple trees, near the southern wall, in full
737.07 bloom.

737.08   "After breakfast, Catherine insisted on my
737.09  bringing a chair, and sitting, with my work,
737.10  under the fir trees, at the end of the house;
737.11  and she beguiled Hareton, who had perfectly
737.12  recovered from his accident, to dig and arrange
737.13  her little garden, which was shifted to that
737.14  corner by the influence of Joseph's complaints.
737.15   "I was comfortably revelling in the spring
737.16  frangrance around, and the beautiful soft blue
737.17  overhead, when my young lady, who had run
737.18  down near the gate, to procure some primrose
737.19  roots for a border, returned only half laden,
737.20  and informed us that Mr. Heathcliff was com-
737.21  ing in.
738.01   "'And he spoke to me,' she added with a
738.02  perplexed countenance.
738.03   "'What did he say?' asked Hareton.
738.04   "'He told me to begone as fast as I could,'
738.05  she answered. 'But he looked so different
738.06  from his usual look that I stopped a moment
738.07  to stare at him.'
738.08   "'How?' he enquired.
738.09   "'Why, almost bright and cheerful -- No,
738.10  almost nothing -- \very# \much# excited, and wild
738.11  and glad!' she replied.
738.12   "'Night-walking amuses him, then,' I re-
738.13  marked, affecting a careless manner. In reality,
738.14  as surprised as she was; and, anxious to ascer-
738.15  tain the truth of her statement, for to see the
738.16  master looking glad would not be an every
738.17  day spectacle, I framed an excuse to go in.
738.18   "Heathcliff stood at the open door; he was
738.19  pale, and he trembled; yet, certainly, he had a
738.20  strange joyful glitter in his eyes, that altered
738.21  the aspect of his whole face.
739.01   "'Will you have some breakfast?' I said,
739.02  'You must be hungry rambling about all night!',
739.03   "I wanted to discover where he had been;
739.04  but I did not like to ask directly.
739.05   "'No, I'm not hungry,' he answered, avert-
739.06  ing his head, and speaking rather contempt-
739.07  uously, as if he guessed I was trying to divine
739.08  the occasion of his good humour.
739.09   "I felt perplexed -- I didn't know whether
739.10  it were not a proper opportunity to offer a bit
739.11  of admonition.
739.12   "'I don't think it right to wander out of
739.13  doors,' I observed, 'instead of being in bed:
739.14  it is not wise, at any rate, this moist season.
739.15  I dare say you'll catch a bad cold, or a fever --
739.16  you have something the matter with you
739.17  now!'
739.18   "'Nothing but what I can bear,' he replied,
739.19  'and with the greatest pleasure, provided you'll
739.20  leave me alone -- get in, and don't annoy me.'
739.21   "I obeyed; and, in passing, I noticed he
739.22  breathed as fast as a cat.
740.01   "'Yes!' I reflected to myself, "we shall
740.02  have a fit of illness. I cannot conceive what
740.03  he has been doing!'
740.04   "That noon, he sat down to dinner with us,
740.05  and received a heaped up plate from my hands,
740.06  as if he intended to make amends for previous
740.07  fasting.
740.08   "'I've neither cold, not fever, Nelly,' he
740.09  remarked, in allusion to my morning's speech.
740.10  'And I'm ready to do justice to the food you
740.11  give me.'
740.12   "He took his knife and fork, and was going
740.13  to commence eating, when the inclination ap-
740.14  peared to become suddenly extinct. He laid
740.15  them on the table, looked eagerly towards the
740.16  window, then rose and went out.
740.17   "We saw him walking, to and fro, in the
740.18  garden, while we concluded our meal; and
740.19  Earnshaw said he'd go, and ask why he would
740.20  not dine; he thought we had grieved him
740.21  some way.
741.01   "'Well, is he coming?' cried Catherine,
741.02  when her cousin returned.
741.03   "'Nay,' he answered, 'but he's not angry;
741.04  he seemed rare and pleased indeed; only, I
741.05  made him impatient by speaking to him twice;
741.06  and then he bid me be off to you; he won-
741.07  dered how I could want the company of any
741.08  body else.'
741.09   "I set his plate, to keep warm, on the fen-
741.10  der: and after an hour or two, he re-entered,
741.11  when the room was clear, in no degree calmer
741.12  -- the same unnatural -- it was unnatural -- ap-
741.13  pearance of joy under his black brows; the
741.14  same bloodless hue: and his teeth visible, now
741.15  and then, in a kind of smile; his frame shiver-
741.16  ing, not as one shivers with cold or weakness,
741.17  but as a tight-stretched cord vibrates -- a strong
741.18  thrilling, rather than trembling.
741.19   "I will ask what is the matter, I thought,
741.20  or who should? And I exclaimed --
741.21   "'Have you heard any good news, Mr.
741.22  Heathcliff? You look uncommonly animated,'
742.01   "'Where should good news come from, to
742.02  me?' he said. 'I'm animated with hunger;
742.03  and, seemingly, I must not eat.'
742.04   "'Your dinner is here,' I returned; 'why
742.05  wont you get it?'
742.06   "'I don't want it now,' he muttered, has-
742.07  tily. 'I'll wait till supper. And, Nelly, once
742.08  for all, let me beg you to warn Hareton and
742.09  the other away from me. I wish to be trou-
742.10  bled by nobody -- I wish to have this place to
742.11  myself.'

742.12   "'Is there some new reason for this banish-
742.13  ment?' I inquired. 'Tell me why you are so
742.14  queer, Mr. Heathcliff? where were you last
742.15  night?' I'm not putting the question through
742.16  idle curiosity, but --'
742.17   "'You are putting the question through
742.18  very idle curiosity,' he interrupted, with a
742.19  laugh. 'Yet, I'll answer it. Last night, I
742.20  was on the threshold of hell. To-day, I am
742.21  within sight of my heaven -- I have my eyes
742.22  on it -- hardly three feet to sever me! And
743.01  now you'd better go -- You'll neither see nor
743.02  hear anything to frighten you, if you refrain
743.03  from prying.'
743.04   "Having swept the hearth, and wiped the
743.05  table, I departed more perplexed than ever.
743.06   "He did not quit the house again till that
743.07  afternoon, and no one intruded on his solitude,
743.08  till, at eight o'clock, I deemed it proper,
743.09  though unsummoned, to carry a candle, and his
743.10  supper to him.
743.11   "He was leaning against the ledge of an
743.12  open lattice, but not looking out; his face
743.13  was turned to the interior gloom. The fire
743.14  had smouldered to ashes; the room was filled
743.15  with the damp, mild air of the cloudy evening,
743.16  and so still, that not only the murmur of the
743.17  beck down Gimmerton was distinguishable, but
743.18  its ripples and its gurgling over the pebbles,
743.19  or through the large stones which it could not
743.20  cover.
743.21   "I uttered an ejaculation of discontent at
743.22  seeing the dismal grate, and commenced shutting
744.01  the casements, one after another, till I
744.02  came to his.
744.03   "'Must I close this?' I asked, in order to
744.04  rouse him, for he would not stir.
744.05   "The light flashed on his features, as I
744.06  spoke. Oh, Mr. Lockwood, I cannot express
744.07  what a terrible start I got, by the momentary
744.08  view! Those deep black eyes! That smile,
744.09  and ghastly paleness! It appeared to me, not
744.10  Mr. Heathcliff, but a goblin; and, in my ter-
744.11  ror, I let the candle bend towards the wall, and
744.12  it left me in darkness.
744.13   "'Yes, close it,' he replied in his familiar
744.14  voice. 'There, that is pure awkwardness!
744.15  Why did you hold the candle horizontally? Be
744.16  quick, and bring another.'
744.17   "I hurried out in a foolish state of dread,
744.18  and said to Joseph --
744.19   "'The master wishes you to take him a
744.20  light, and rekindle the fire.' For I dare not go
744.21  in myself again just then.
744.22   "Joseph rattled some fire into the shovel, and
745.01  went; but he brought it back, immediately,
745.02  with the supper tray in his other hand, ex-
745.03  plaining that Mr. Heathcliff was going to bed,
745.04  and he wanted nothing to eat till morning.
745.05   "We heard him mount the stairs directly;
745.06  he did not proceed to his ordinary chamber,
745.07  but turned into that with the panelled bed --
745.08  its window, as I mentioned before, is wide
745.09  enough for anybody to get through, and it
745.10  struck me, that he plotted another midnight
745.11  excursion, which he had rather we had no sus-
745.12  picion of.
745.13   "'Is he a ghoul, or a vampire?' I mused.
745.14  I had read of such hideous, incarnate demons.
745.15  And then, I set myself to reflect, how I had
745.16  tended him in infancy; and watched him grow
745.17  to youth; and followed him almost through
745.18  his whole course; and what absurd nonsense it
745.19  was to yield to that sense of horror.
745.20   "'But, where did he come from, the little
745.21  dark thing, harboured by a good man to his
745.22  bane?' muttered superstition, as I dozed into
746.01  unconsciousness. And I began, half dreaming,
746.02  to weary myself with imagining some fit paren-
746.03  tage for him; and repeatng my waking medi-
746.04  tations, I tracked his existence over again, with
746.05  grim variations; at last, picturing his death
746.06  and funeral; of which, all I can remember is,
746.07  being exceedingly vexed at having the task of
746.08  dictating an inscription for his monument, and
746.09  consulting the sexton about it; and, as he
746.10  had no surname, and we could not tell his age,
746.11  we were obliged to content ourselves with the
746.12  single word, 'Heathcliff.' That came true;
746.13  we were. If you enter the kirkyard, you'll
746.14  read on his headstone, only that, and the date
746.15  of his death.
746.16   "Dawn restored me to common sense. I
746.17  rose, and went into the garden, as soon as I
746.18  could see, to ascertain if there were any foot-
746.19  marks under his window. There were none.
746.20   "'He has stayed at home,' I thought, 'and
746.21  he'll be all right, to-day!'
746.22   "I prepared breakfast for the household, as
747.01  was my usual custom, but told Hareton, and
747.02  Catherine to get theirs, ere the master came
747.03  down, for he lay late. They preferred taking
747.04  it out of doors, under the trees, and I set a
747.05  little table to accommodate them.
747.06   "On my re-entrance, I found Mr. Heath-
747.07  cliff below. He and Joseph were conversing
747.08  about some farming business; he gave clear,
747.09  minute directions concerning the matter dis-
747.10  cussed, but he spoke rapidly, and turned his
747.11  head continually aside, and had the same ex-
747.12  cited expression, even more exaggerated.

747.13 "When Joseph quitted the room, he took
747.14 his seat in the place he generally chose, and I
747.15 put a basin of coffee before him. He drew it
747.16 nearer, and then rested his arms on the table,
747.17 and looked at the opposite wall, as I supposed,
747.18 surveying one particular portion, up and down,
747.19 with glittering, restless eyes, and with such
747.20 eager interest, that he stopped breathing, dur-
747.21 ing half a minute together.
747.22 "'Come now,' I exclaimed, pushing some
748.01 bread against his hand. 'Eat and drink that,
748.02 while it is hot. It has been waiting near an
748.03 hour.'
748.04 "He didn't notice me, and yet he smiled.
748.05 I'd rather have seen him gnash his teeth than
748.06 smile so.
748.07 "'Mr. Heathcliff! master!' I cried. 'Don't
748.08 for God's sake, stare as if you saw an unearthly
748.09 vision.'
748.10 "'Don't, for God's sake, shout so loud,' he
748.11 replied. 'Turn round, and tell me, are we by
748.12 ourselves?'
748.13 "'Of course,' was my answer, 'of course,
748.14 we are!'
748.15 "Still, I involuntarily obeyed him, as if I
748.16 were not quite sure.
748.17 "With a sweep of his hand, he cleared a
748.18 vacant space in front among the breakfast
748.19 things, and leant forward to gaze more at his
748.20 ease.
748.21 "Now, I perceived he was not looking at
748.22 the wall, for when I regarded him alone, it
749.01 seemed, exactly, that he gazed at something
749.02 within two yards distance. And, whatever it
749.03 was, it communicated, apparently, both plea-
749.04 sure and pain, in exquisite extremes, at least,
749.05 the anguished, yet raptured expression of his
749.06 countenance suggested that idea.
749.07 "The fancied object was not fixed, either;
749.08 his eyes pursued it with unwearied vigilance;
749.09 and, even in speaking to me, were never wean-
749.10 ed away.
749.11 "I vainly reminded him of his protracted
749.12 abstinence from food; if he stirred to touch
749.13 anything in compliance with my entreaties, if
749.14 he stretched his hand out to get a piece of
749.15 bread, his fingers clenched, before they reached
749.16 it, and remained on the table, forgetful of their
749.17 aim.
749.18 "I set a model of patience, trying to at-
749.19 tract his absorbed attention from its engross-
749.20 ing speculation; till he grew irritable, and got
749.21 up, asking, why I would not allow him to have
749.22 his own time in taking his meals? and saying
750.01 that, on the next occasion, I needn't wait, I
750.02 might set the things down, and go.
750.03 "Having uttered these words, he left the
750.04 house; slowly sauntered down the garden
750.05 path, and disappeared through the gate.
750.06 "The hours crept anxiously by: another
750.07 evening came. I did not retire to rest till
750.08 late, and when I did, I could not sleep. He
750.09 returned after midnight, and, instead of going
750.10 to bed, shut himself into the room beneath. I
750.11 listened, and tossed about; and, finally, dress-
750.12 ed, and descended. It was too irksome to lie
750.13 up there, harassing my brain with a hundred
750.14 idle misgivings.
750.15 "I distinguished Mr. Heathcliff's step, rest-
750.16 lessly measuring the floor; and he frequently
750.17 broke the silence, by a deep inspiration, re-
750.18 sembling a groan. He muttered detached
750.19 words, also; the only one, I could catch, was
750.20 the name of Catherine, coupled with some
750.21 wild term of endearment, or suffering; and
750.22 spoken as one would speak to a person present
751.01 -- low and earnest, and wrung from the depth
751.02 of his soul.
751.03 "I had not courage to walk straight into
751.04 the apartment; but I desired to divert him from
751.05 his reverie, and, therefore, fell foul of the
751.06 kitchen fire; stirred it, and began to scrape
751.07 the cinders. It drew him forth sooner than I
751.08 expected. He opened the door immediately,
751.09 and said--
751.10 "'Nelly, come here -- is it morning? Come
751.11 in with your light.'
751.12 "'It is striking four,' I answered; 'you
751.13 want a candle to take up stairs -- you might
751.14 have lit one at this fire.'
751.15 "'No, I don't wish to go up stairs,' he said.
751.16 'Come in, and kindle me a fire, and do anything
751.17 there is to do about the room.'
751.18 "'I must blow the coals red first, before
751.19 I can carry any,' I replied, getting a chair and
751.20 the bellows.
751.21 "He roamed to and fro, meantime, in a
752.01 state approaching distraction: his heavy sighs
752.02 succeeding each other so thick as to leave no
752.03 space for common breathing between.
752.04 "'When day breaks, I'll send for Green,'
752.05 he said; 'I wish to make some legal inquiries
752.06 of him, while I can bestow a thought on those
752.07 matters, and while I can act calmly. I have
752.08 not written my will yet, and how to leave my
752.09 property, I cannot determine! I wish I could
752.10 annihilate it from the face of the earth.'
752.11 "'I would not talk so, Mr. Heathcliff,' I
752.12 interposed. 'Let your will be, a while -- you'll
752.13 be spared to repent of your many injustices,
752.14 yet! I never expected that your nerves would

752.15 be disordered -- they are, at present, marvel-
752.16 lously so, however; and, almost entirely,
752.17 through your own fault. The way you've
752.18 passed these three last days might knock up a
752.19 Titan. Do take some food, and some repose.
752.20 You need only look at yourself, in a glass, to
752.21 see how you require both. Your cheeks are
753.01 hollow, and your eyes blood-shot, like a person
753.02 starving with hunger, and going blind with
753.03 loss of sleep.'
753.04 "'It is not my fault, that I cannot eat or
753.05 rest,' he replied. 'I assure you it is through
753.06 no settled designs. I'll do both, as soon as I
753.07 possibly can. But you might as well bid a
753.08 man struggling in the water, rest within arms--
753.09 length of the shore! I must reach it first,
753.10 and then I'll rest. Well, never mind, Mr.
753.11 Green; as to repenting of my injustices, I've
753.12 done no injustice, and I repent of nothing --
753.13 I'm too happy, and yet I'm not happy enough.
753.14 My soul's bliss kills my body, but does not
753.15 satisfy itself.'
753.16 "'Happy, master?' I cried. 'Strange hap-
753.17 piness! If you would hear me without being
753.18 angry, I might offer some advice that would
753.19 make you happier.'
753.20 "'What is that?' he asked. 'Give it.'
753.21 "'You are aware, Mr. Heathcliff,' I said,
753.22 'that from the time you were thirteen years
754.01 old, you have lived a selfish, unchristian life;
754.02 and probably hardly had a Bible in your
754.03 hands, during all the period. You must have
754.04 forgotten the contents of the book, and you
754.05 may not have space to search it now. Could
754.06 it be hurtful to send for some one -- some min-
754.07 ister of any denomination, it does not matter
754.08 which, to explain it, and show you how very
754.09 far you have erred from its precepts, and how
754.10 unfit you will be for its heaven, unless a change
754.11 takes place before you die?'
754.12 "'I'm rather obliged than angry, Nelly,'
754.13 he said, 'for you remind me of the manner that
754.14 I desire to be buried in -- It is to be carried to
754.15 the churchyard, in the evening. You, and
754.16 Hareton may, if you please accompany me --
754.17 and mind, particularly, to notice that the sex-
754.18 ton obeys my directions concerning the two
754.19 coffins! No minister need come; nor need
754.20 anything be said over me -- I tell you, I have
754.21 nearly attained my heaven; and that of others
754.22 is altogether unvalued, and uncoveted by me!'
755.01 "'And supposing you persevered in your ob-
755.02 stinate fast, and died by that means, and they
755.03 refused to bury you in the precincts of the
755.04 Kirk?' I said shocked at his godless indiffer-
755.05 ence. 'How would you like it?'
755.06 "'They wont do that,' he replied; 'if they
755.07 did, you must have me removed secretly; and
755.08 if you neglect it, you shall prove, practically,
755.09 that the dead are not annihilated!'
755.10 "As soon as he heard the other members of
755.11 the family stirring he retired to his den, and I
755.12 breathed freer -- But in the afternoon, while
755.13 Joseph and Hareton were at their work, he
755.14 came into the kitchen again, and with a wild
755.15 look, bid me come, and sit in the house -- he
755.16 wanted somebody with him.
755.17 "I declined, telling him plainly, that his
755.18 strange talk and manner, frightened me, and I
755.19 had neither the nerve, nor the will to be his
755.20 companion, alone.
755.21 "'I believe you think me a fiend!' he said,
756.01 with his dismal laugh, 'something too horrible
756.02 to live under a decent roof!'
756.03 "Then turning to Catherine, who was there,
756.04 and who drew behind me at his approach, he
756.05 added, half sneeringly.
756.06 "'Will you come, chuck? I'll not hurt you.
756.07 No! to you, I've made myself worse than the
756.08 devil. Well, there is one who wont shrink
756.09 from my company! By God! she's relentless.
756.10 Oh, damn it! It's unutterably too much for
756.11 flesh and blood to bear, even mine.'
756.12 "He solicited the society of no one more.
756.13 At dusk, he went into his chamber -- through
756.14 the whole night, and far into the morning, we
756.15 heard him groaning, and murmuring to himself.
756.16 Hareton was anxious to enter, but I bid him
756.17 fetch Mr. Kenneth, and he should go in, and
756.18 see him.
756.19 "When he came, and I requested admittance
756.20 and tried to open the door, I found it locked;
756.21 and Heathcliff bid us be damned. He was
757.01 better, and would be left alone; so the doctor
757.02 went away.
757.03 "The following evening was very wet, indeed
757.04 it poured down, till day-dawn; and, as I took
757.05 my morning walk round the house, I observed
757.06 the master's window swinging open, and the
757.07 rain driving straight in.
757.08 "He cannot be in bed, I thought, those
757.09 showers would drench him through! He must
757.10 either be up, or out. But, I'll make no more
757.11 ado, I'll go boldly, and look!'
757.12 "Having succeeded in obtaining entrance
757.13 with another key, I ran to unclose the panels,
757.14 for the chamber was vacant -- quickly pushing
757.15 them aside, I peeped in. Mr. Heathcliff was
757.16 there -- laid on his back. His eyes met mine
757.17 so keen, and fierce, I started; and then, he
757.18 seemed to smile.

757.19   I could not think him dead -- but his face,
757.20 and throat were washed with rain; the bed--
757.21 clothes dripped, and he was perfectly still.
757.22 The lattice, flapping to and fro, had grazed
758.01 one hand that rested on the sill -- no blood
758.02 trickled from the broken skin, and when I put
758.03 my fingers to it, I could doubt no more -- he
758.04 was dead and stark!
758.05   I hasped the window; I combed his black
758.06 long hair from his forehead; I tried to close
758.07 his eyes -- to extinguish, if possible, that fright-
758.08 ful, life-like gaze of exultation, before any one
758.09 else beheld it. They would not shut -- they
758.10 seemed to sneer at my attempts, and his parted
758.11 lips, and sharp, white teeth sneered too!
758.12   Taken with another fit of cowardice, I cried
758.13 out for Joseph. Joseph shuffled up, and made
758.14 a noise, but resolutely refused to meddle with
758.15 him.
758.16   "Th' divil's harried off his soul!" he cried,
758.17 "and he muh hev his carcass intuh t' bargin,
758.18 for ow't Aw care! Ech! what a wicked un
758.19 he looks girnning at death!" and the old sinner
758.20 grinned in mockery.
758.21   I thought he intended to cut a caper round
758.22 the bed; but suddenly composing himself, he
759.01 fell on his knees, and raised his hands, and re-
759.02 turned thanks that the lawful master and the
759.03 ancient stock were restored to their rights.
759.04   I felt stunned by the awful event; and my
759.05 memory unavoidably recurred to former times
759.06 with a sort of oppressive sadness. But poor
759.07 Hareton the most wronged, was the only one
759.08 that really suffered much. He sat by the
759.09 corpse all night, weeping in bitter earnest.
759.10 He pressed its hand, and kissed the sarcastic,
759.11 savage face that every one else shrank from
759.12 contemplating; and bemoaned him with that
759.13 strong grief which springs naturally from a
759.14 generous heart, though it be tough as tempered
759.15 steel.
759.16   Kenneth was perplexed to pronounce of what
759.17 disorder the master died. I concealed the
759.18 fact of his having swallowed nothing for four
759.19 days, fearing it might lead to trouble, and
759.20 then, I was persuaded he did not abstain on
759.21 purpose; it was the consequence of his strange
759.22 illness, not the cause.
760.01   We buried him, to the scandal of the whole
760.02 neighbourhood, as he had wished. Earnshaw,
760.03 and I, the sexton and six men to carry the
760.04 ffin, comprehended the whole attendance.
760.05   The six men departed when they had let it
760.06 down into the grave: we stayed to see it co-
760.07 vered. Hareton, with a streaming face, dug
760.08 green sods, and laid them over the brown
760.09 mould himself; at present it is as smooth and ver-
760.10 dant as its companion mounds -- and I hope its
760.11 tenant sleeps as soundly. But the country
760.12 folks, if you asked them, would swear on their
760.13 bible that he \walks#. There are those who
760.14 speak to having met him near the church, and
760.15 on the moor, and even within this house -- Idle
760.16 tales, you'll say, and so say I. Yet that old
760.17 man by the kitchen fire affirms he had seen two
760.18 on 'em looking out of his chamber window, on
760.19 every rainy night, since his death -- and an odd
760.20 thing happened to me about a morth ago.
760.21   I was going to the Grange one evening -- a
760.22 dark evening threatening thunder -- and, just
761.01 at the turn of the Heights, I encountered a
761.02 little boy with a sheep, and two lambs before
761.03 him, he was crying terribly, and I supposed
761.04 the lambs were skittish, and would not be
761.05 guided.
761.06   "'What is the matter, my little man?' I
761.07 asked.
761.08   "'They's Heathcliff, and a woman, yonder,
761.09 under t' Nab,' he blubbered, 'un' Aw darnut
761.10 pass 'em.'
761.11   "I saw nothing; but neither the sheep nor
761.12 he would go on, so I bid him take the road
761.13 lower down.
761.14   "He probably raised the phantoms from
761.15 thinking, as he traversed the moors alone, on
761.16 the nonsense he had heard his parents and
761.17 companions repeat -- yet still, I don't like being
761.18 out in the dark, now -- and I don't like being
761.19 left by myself in this grim house -- I cannot
761.20 help it, I shall be glad when they leave it, and
761.21 shift to the Grange!"
762.01   "They are going to the Grange then?" I
762.02 said.
762.03   "Yes," answered Mrs. Dean, "as soon as
762.04 they are married; and that will be on New
762.05 Year's day."
762.06   "And who will live here then?"
762.07   "Why, Joseph will take care of the house,
762.08 and, perhaps, a lad to keep him company.
762.09 They will live in the kitchen, and the rest
762.10 will be shut up."
762.11   "For the use of such ghosts as choose to in-
762.12 habit it," I observed.
762.13   "No, Mr. Lockwood," said Nelly, shaking
762.14 her head. "I believe the dead are at peace,
762.15 but it is not right to speak of them with
762.16 levity."
762.17   At that moment the garden gate swung to;
762.18 the ramblers were returning.
762.19   "\They# are afraid of nothing," I grumbled,
762.20 watching their approach through the window.

762.21   "Together they would brave satan and all his
762.22 legions."
763.01   As they stepped onto the door-stones, and
763.02 halted to take a last look at the moon, or,
763.03 more correctly, at each other, by her light, I
763.04 felt irresistibly impelled to escape them again;
763.05 and, pressing a remembrance into the hand of
763.06 Mrs. Dean, and disregarding her expostula-
763.07 tions at my rudeness, I vanished through the
763.08 kitchen, as they opened the house-door, and
763.09 so, should have confirmed Joseph in his opinion
763.10 of his fellow-servant's gay indiscretions, had
763.11 he not, fortunately, recognised me for a re-
763.12 spectable character, by the sweet ring of a
763.13 sovereign at his feet.
763.14   My walk home was lengthened by a diver-
763.15 sion in the direction of the kirk. When be-
763.16 neath its walls, I perceived decay had made
763.17 progress, even in seven months -- many a win-
763.18 dow showed black gaps deprived of glass; and
763.19 states jutted off, here and there, beyond the
763.20 right line of the roof, to be gradually worked
763.21 off in coming autumn storms.
763.22   I sought, and soon discovered, the three
764.01 head-stones on the slope next the moor -- the
764.02 middle one, grey, and half buried in heath --
764.03 Edgar Linton's only harmonized by the turf,
764.04 and moss creeping up its foot -- Heathcliff's
764.05 still bare.
764.06   I lingered round them, under that benign
764.07 sky; watched the moths fluttering among the
764.08 heath, and hare-bells; listened to the soft wind
764.09 breathing through the grass; and wondered
764.10 how any one could ever imagine unquiet slum-
764.11 bers, for the sleepers in that quiet earth.
764.12 [THE END.]